Introduc

Welcome to the 2010 edition of the *Time Out London Eating & Drinking Guide*, the most authoritative and comprehensive guide to good restaurants, gastropubs, cafés, bars and pubs in the capital. The book in your hands is the best-selling London restaurant guide – a fact we put down to the reliability and breadth of our reviews, and the high standards we set for our critics and the venues they cover. It's the only guide for which anonymous critics visit every establishment included every year, and pay for their meal and drinks just like a regular customer (Time Out then reimburses their expenses). We do not tell the restaurants we are coming, nor do we reveal who we are after the meal. Restaurants can exert no pressure on us as to the content of their reviews and do not pay to be included in the guide. Our editors select all the establishments featured in the guide.

We want our readers to know just what the experience of eating at each restaurant might be like for them and take pains to ensure that our reviewers remain totally objective on your behalf. Our insistence on undercover reporting means that our experience is much more likely to reflect *your* experience. Well-known critics often receive preferential treatment: photos of them are pinned up in many restaurant kitchens to ensure that they do not go unrecognised.

Time Out reviewers have a great passion for food, and for finding the best places to eat and drink in London. Many also have extraordinary expertise in specialist areas. Several are trained cooks or former chefs, others are well-established food and/or wine authors, and some are simply dedicated enthusiasts who have lived in foreign countries and learned much about that region's cuisine. We have pâtissiers visiting pâtisseries and cafés, Mandarin and Cantonese speakers surveying Chinese restaurants, a former chef and fishmonger working on the Fish chapter, and our Malaysian and Singaporean eateries are covered by Malaysian and Singaporean expatriates.

For the weekly *Time Out London* magazine alone, our reviewers visit around 200 new places every year. Their better discoveries are then included in this guide. Reviewers also check other new openings, as well as revisiting places included in the previous edition. As a result, at least 2,000 anonymous visits were made in the creation of this guide. We also take in recommendations and feedback from readers and from users of the Time Out website (www.timeout.com/restaurants). Then we eliminate the also-rans to create the annual list of London's best eateries and drinking spots that this guide represents. We hope you find it useful, and that it helps you get more enjoyment from eating out in the capital.

EDITION 27

timeout.com/restaurants

Restaurants

Cheap Eats

Drinking

Eating & Drinking 2010
Contents

Maps & Indexes

Features

100% INDEPENDENT

The reviews in the **Time Out Eating & Drinking Guide** are based on the experiences of Time Out restaurant reviewers. All restaurants, bars, gastropubs and cafés are visited anonymously, and Time Out pays the bill. No payment of any kind has secured or influenced a review.

About the guide

LISTED BY AREA

The restaurants in this guide are listed by cuisine type: British, Chinese, Indian, Middle Eastern etc. Then, within each of chapter, they are listed by geographical area: ten main areas (in this example, Central), then by neighbourhood (City). If you are not sure where to look for a restaurant, there are two indexes at the back of the guide to help: an **A-Z Index** (starting on p401) listing restaurants by name, and an **Area Index** (starting on p384), where you can see all the places we list in a specific neighbourhood.

STARS

A red star ★ means that a restaurant is, of its type, very good indeed. A green star ★ identifies budget-conscious eateries – expect to pay an average of £20 (for a three-course meal or its equivalent, *not* including drinks or service).

AWARD NOMINEES

Winners and runners-up in Time Out's Eating & Drinking Awards 2009. For more information on the awards, *see p18*.

OPENING HOURS

Times given are for *last orders* rather than closing times (except in cafés and bars).

MAP REFERENCE

All restaurants that appear on our street maps (starting on p344) are given a reference to the map and grid square where they can be found.

Central
City

★ ★ **Skint** (*100*) **NEW**
2009 RUNNER-UP BEST CHEAP EATS
501 Cheapside, EC2Q 4JJ (9876 4321).
Bank tube/DLR. **Lunch served** noon-3pm, **dinner served** 6-11pm daily. **Main courses** £3-£13. **Set meal** (6-8pm Mon-Sat) £12 2 courses, £14 3 courses. **Cover** £1.99. **Credit** AmEx, DC, MC, V.
Foosball champ turned chef-patron Dwayne McDonald has single-handedly reinvigorated City lunches with this canteen for bereft hedgies. The menu, listed on the back of an old envelope, offers an economical collection of gruels, boiled meats and potato dishes, but the careful construction and presentation of long-lost haute cuisine days have not been forgotten. A tasting platter featured three textures of pease porridge – hot, cold and cured in a pot for nine days, giving the yellow paste an aromatic, cheese-like crust. Turnip velouté garnished with milk skin and own-made 'turkey twizzler' was good enough to cause a bull market. Shirtless waiters in red braces and trews bring tap water and tumblers of Albanian house wine; for those in need of something stronger (windows are barred to stop anyone jumping out) the lengthy cocktail list includes the Kwik Save (cold Nescafé with a shot of dry gin) and Declining Shares (a fragrant mix of Diamond White cider, crushed ice, cucumber and 'wild' mint from out the back). Sadly, service can be brusque and, when we queried the high cover charge, the manager, dressed in an old raincoat, replied: 'You try pulling up a chair in the middle of Tesco and asking the shelf stackers to bring you a free glass of water.'
Babies and children welcome: high chairs; abacuses; old boxes. Disabled: toilet. Tables outdoors (10, gutter). **Map 1 A1**.

NEW ENTRIES

The **NEW** symbol means new to this edition of the *Eating & Drinking Guide*. In most cases, these are brand-new establishments; in some other instances we've included an existing restaurant for the first time.

TIME OUT HOT 100

The (*100*) symbol means the venue is among what we consider to be London's top 100 iconic eating and drinking experiences. For details of the complete 100, *see p20*.

PRICES

We have listed the cheapest and most expensive main courses available in each restaurant. In the case of many oriental restaurants, prices may seem lower – but remember that you often need to order several such dishes to have a full meal.

COVER CHARGE

An old-fashioned fixed charge may be imposed by the restaurateur to cover the cost of rolls and butter, crudités, cleaning table linen and similar extras.

SERVICES

These are listed below the review.

Babies and children We've tried to reflect the degree of welcome extended to babies and children in restaurants. If you find no mention of either, take it that the restaurant is unsuitable.

Disabled: toilet means the restaurant has a specially adapted toilet, which implies that customers with walking disabilities or wheelchairs can get into the restaurant. However, we recommend phoning to double-check.

Vegetarian menu Most restaurants claim to have a vegetarian dish on the menu. We've highlighted those that have made a more concerted effort to attract and cater for vegetarian (and vegan) diners.

Anonymous, unbiased reviews

The reviews in the *Eating & Drinking Guide* are based on the experiences of Time Out restaurant reviewers. Restaurants, pubs, bars and cafés are always visited anonymously, and Time Out pays the bill. No payment or PR invitation of any kind has secured or influenced a review. The editors select which places are listed in this guide, and are not influenced in any way by the wishes of the restaurants themselves. Restaurants cannot volunteer or pay to be listed; we list only those we consider to be worthy of inclusion. Advertising and sponsorship has no effect whatsoever on the editorial content of the *Eating & Drinking Guide*. An advertiser may receive a bad review, or no review at all.

ABOUT THE GUIDE

So what do you think?

Every year we post a questionnaire on the Time Out website to find out what Londoners really think about dining and drinking in the capital. What's good, what's bad, what needs improvement? More than 1,300 people responded to the 2009 survey, and these were the most noteworthy results.

How much do you spend per person when eating out?

Under £20	28.69%
£20-£29	42.08%
£30-£39	20.54%
£40-£59	7.23%
Over £60	1.38%

68.15%
have used **discount vouchers** in restaurants in the last 12 months

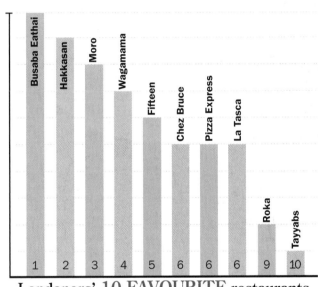

Busaba Eathai — 1
Hakkasan — 2
Moro — 3
Wagamama — 4
Fifteen — 5
Chez Bruce — 6
Pizza Express — 6
La Tasca — 6
Roka — 9
Tayyabs — 10

Londoners' 10 FAVOURITE restaurants

London's most Overrated restaurants

1 The Ivy
2 'anything by Gordon Ramsay'
3 Nobu
4 Oxo Tower Restaurant, Bar & Brasserie

Gordon Ramsay Holdings — **2**

Alan Yau — **1**

D&D London — **3**

London's favourite restaurateurs

▶ So what do
you think?

👉 **What's your favourite type of restaurant?**

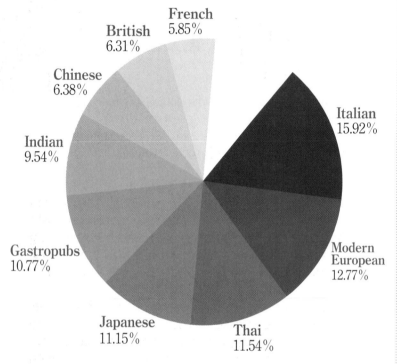

French 5.85%
British 6.31%
Chinese 6.38%
Indian 9.54%
Gastropubs 10.77%
Japanese 11.15%
Thai 11.54%
Modern European 12.77%
Italian 15.92%

Pizza Express

is where most readers have used **discount vouchers**

80.46% think the **variety of cuisines** on offer is the most exciting thing about eating out in London

75.46% spend less than £5 on weekday lunches

How often do you eat out?

More than three times a month	**50.46%**
More than twice a week	**26.46%**
Once a month	**16%**
Only on special occasions	**4.85%**
Every day	**2.15%**

The most annoying things about eating out in London

Expensive **bottled waters** 7.54%

Too expensive 38.46%

Service charge **9.69%**

Bad service 17.31%

Mediocre food 10.69%

Having to **book ahead** 6.62%

Overrated celebrity chefs 5.77%

Already a huge success in Oxford, Bath, Kingston and Brighton, Jamie Oliver has opened his first London-based Jamie's Italian in Canary Wharf. Inspired by his passion for Italy, Jamie's Italian offers what Italians are most proud of - fantastic rustic dishes using recipes that have been tried, tested and loved. We've created a contemporary, informal restaurant environment which is energetic, vibrant and live!

Canary Wharf is a great location for us as the "neighbourhood" is quite unique. We've combined a kitchen full of the best chefs with cutting edge technology and a talented front of house team that really personifies the word "hospitality". The action takes place in a stunning 200 cover dining room with another 40 seats on our outside terrace.

We believe that the key to the success of Jamie's Italian is its versatility: the menu is authentic and affordable and the restaurant is designed to make everyone feel at home, no matter how much you spend or how long you stay.

For menus, opening times and information, check out our website:
www.jamiesitalian.com

jamie's
ITALIAN

Churchill Place
Canary Wharf E14 5RB
T 020 3002 5252

Great nosh for less dosh

Time Out critics offer 20 tips to help you dine out in style without breaking the bank

We've been charting the capital's restaurant scene for nearly 30 years and there is one thing we know for sure about the economic downturn: Londoners are not going to spend the entire recession eating at home. And nor do they have to. There are plenty of ways to enjoy dining out without maxing out your credit card. Here our critics round up their very best tips for eating well on a budget.

1 Find out what discounts are available before you go

Restaurants want your custom now more than ever because they want to stay in business, and to tempt you through their doors they are offering plenty of special deals. These are easy to find on the internet. Many chain operators (burgers, pizza and so on) offer vouchers on their websites that you simply print out and take to the restaurant with you; others like you to sign up for email news of discounts sent to your in-box every few weeks.

Yet two-for-ones and 40%-off food bill offers are by no means restricted to the big high-street companies. Visit www.timeout.com/london/restaurants, click on the word 'Offers' below the masthead and you will find an impressive list of special deals available at independent eateries, ranging from informal Indian, American and Middle Eastern establishments to some of Britain's most admired restaurants. At the time of writing, one of our favourite Modern European restaurants, Patterson's, was offering 40% off food bills, as was Chino Latino, a red-star restaurant in our Oriental chapter. Offers change from week to week, so it's worth checking regularly to see what's available.

You can take this a step further by joining Taste London, which gets you a 50% discount on bills at more than 800 restaurants in the capital. See page 28 for the special offer to readers of the *Time Out Eating & Drinking Guide*.

2 Choose wisely

Even at top-flight restaurants you can make substantial savings by choosing dishes based on the least expensive ingredients. These change seasonally but also with dining trends: pork belly, for example, used to be cheap but once chefs made it fashionable, pork fillet became a comparative bargain. Lobster, dover sole, langoustines, good cuts of beef and, of course, foie gras and truffles are always costly and the resulting dish doesn't necessarily taste better; offal, eggs, lentils and pasta should be cheap.

Let's take a menu from Sketch: The Lecture Room (a famously pricey haute cuisine establishment) as an example. Choose langoustine dressed five ways to start, beef with peppered butter as a main, and follow with Pierre Gagnaire's Grand Dessert (a procession of five bite-sized desserts) and the meal would cost £134 for one person, not including drinks or service. On the other hand, you could have Gagnaire's Greens starter (six ways with seasonal greens served with mozzarella ice-cream), cod or chicken as a main course, and the peach-themed dessert, and three courses just as carefully conceived and cooked would cost £58 – less than half as much.

3 Pay a little more

London has plenty of mediocre eateries (chains and restaurants in tourist hotspots especially) that may seem value-oriented, but, when the bill arrives with drinks and service included, you realise you are paying more than you thought. And for another fiver or so per person you could have eaten somewhere really terrific. Don't get us wrong: we love reliable chain restaurants, but think it best to avoid places that are both mediocre and expensive with it.

4 Say 'Tap water's fine, thanks' – because it is.

5 Look for emerging wines and unknown territories

A restaurant shouldn't have any bad wines on its list. That's the point of a wine list: regardless of its size, they (should) have selected a variety of bottles to suit the food served and the different moods and occasions their customers are likely to enjoy. Now more than ever it is time to ditch the famous wine names (chablis, burgundy, chianti, barolo and so on) in favour of the unfamiliar. When looking through an Italian wine list, opt for lesser-known regions such as Puglia, Calabria and the Marche: they may not yet have the cachet of Tuscan wines, but that's exactly why they offer such tremendous value. Similarly, you can be confident exploring wines from Argentina, Chile and South Africa if bottles from Australia, California and New Zealand seem too pricey.

6 If you mush go posh, go for lunch

Set lunch menus are the savvy way to experience haute cuisine and other high-end dining without breaking yet another bank. True, there are some places where the set lunch seems like a mean compromise on the à la carte, but plenty offer genuine value and decent choice. We love the lunch menu at Maze, because you can choose four, five or six dishes from a wide-ranging list of 13.

Other great options are Hibiscus, where a glass of wine is included with the set lunch, and Tom Aikens, which serves a fabulous array of petits fours. Even on Park Lane you can dine like royalty for just £25 by booking at the Dorchester Grill: you get three courses plus an amuse bouche. In Browns Hotel, the Albermarle's daily-changing set menu is excellent value too, the three choices at each course including the same well-sourced British ingredients as the rest of the menu.

7 Think about the things you won't be paying for

Eating out in London can be very affordable if you are willing to forgo famous names and luxurious settings. There's no designer interior at Moroccan Tagine, an exotic little café on Golbourne Road, but it still has bags of character, great cooking and the dark chocolate pudding is only £2.50. Patogh, a cramped Iranian grill on Crawford Place, doesn't take credit cards and the decor is humble, but multi-starred restaurants would envy its sesame-studded taftoun bread and saffron-marinated organic chicken.

8 Meet for breakfast

Author Somerset Maugham famously said that to eat well in England one should have breakfast three times a day, but the morning meal is still underused for romantic, social and business occasions. Whether you order a full english, omelette Arnold Bennet or granola and pancakes, you have to work (and drink) pretty hard to spend more than £20 a head at plenty of top establishments. For breakfast we particularly like Tom's Kitchen, the Providores & Tapa Room, Canteen, the Botanist, Smiths of Smithfield and pub the Fox & Anchor, where a pint of Guinness with your fry-up is almost mandatory.

9 Share starters and puds – who really needs to eat three or four full dishes anyway?

10 Ring-fence it

It's so easy, especially when taking yourself or a loved one out for a special meal, to think 'the set menu is inexpensive, so let's have a glass of champagne'. That's a glass of champagne each, of course, so you've just added another £15 or so to the net cost of your bill, and that will bump up the service charge a bit more too. If not champagne, then the spendthrift voice inside your head might tell you it's a good idea to order something more impressive than the house wine, or to have coffee, pudding wines and digestifs afterwards.

Much better is to settle these issues in advance by booking at one of the superb restaurants offering an all-inclusive menu. Most famous, perhaps, is Le Gavroche's set lunch, which features three courses, half a bottle of wine, mineral water and coffee for £48 per person. Nearby Galvin at Windows has a similar deal for £45 per person – and you get a great view.

A look through the offers on Time Out's website will reveal plenty of temporary deals of a similar nature. Recently, our critics booked for Thai restaurant Nahm's special offer of a bottle of classy pinot gris with dinner for £55 per head – normally the set meal alone would cost that.

11 Eat African or Vietnamese

Or Turkish, Korean, Caribbean or Malaysian. These are the cuisines in which our reviewers find it easiest to eat really well for under £20 a head. You won't feel as though you're missing out on fine dining when you are exploring the equally exciting flavours and textures of foreign menus. Have you ever tried the tangy, sourdough flavour of injera bread, the Ethiopian staple? Or a bowl of springy noodles, served cold and smothered with chilli sauce, as found in Korea? What about Vietnam's cá kho to, fish cooked in caramel? Now is the time to try. Your taste buds will thank you, and so will your wallet.

查查月亮 Cha Cha Moon
Chinese noodle bar
www.chachamoon.com

2nd floor, Whiteleys
151 Queensway
London W2 4YN
+44 (0)20 7792 0088
Takeaway available

15-21 Ganton Street
London W1F 9BN
+44 (0)20 7297 9800
Outside seating
Takeaway available
Breakfast served
Mon–Fri 8am–11.30am
Sat–Sun 9am–11.30am

Opening Hours
Mon–Thur 12pm–11pm
Fri–Sat 12pm–11.30pm
Sunday 12pm–10.30pm

12 Dine earlier

Restaurants love customers who don't want a table at 8pm and many actively try to tempt people with bargain menus for early diners. In the West End these tend to be called pre-theatre menus, but you don't have to have theatre tickets to take advantage of them. Our favourite this year was at L'Atelier de Joël Robuchon, a restaurant many Londoners would usually find cost-prohibitive. Here between 5.30pm and 6.30pm you can eat the same standard of cooking as the premium-priced à la carte (salmon with spiced honey and curry polenta, say, or vegetable-stuffed black-leg chicken) for just £19 for two courses and £25 for three.

It's worth noting, too, that early bird discounts are by no means restricted to ritzy restaurants. Leicester Square's Tokyo Diner, for example, offers £1 off food served between 3pm and 6pm, and, on our last visit, Olley's, Herne Hill's much loved chippie, was advertising cod and chips for £7 between 5pm and 6.30pm. Look after the pennies and the pounds will take care of themselves, as the old saying goes.

13
Opt for dim sum, tapas or mese when going out with friends – leisurely grazing can make you feel full while also eating less.

14 Beware hidden charges

Cover charges may seem like a rip-off, but there is a transparency to them that's perfectly reasonable. You might expect a charge of £1-£1.50 per person to cover the cost of the bread, butter, oil, olives, nuts and so on that are put on the table and would be considered 'free' in other establishments. The lack of a cover charge is just an illusion, because the restaurants simply incorporate the costs of the 'freebies' in their dish prices. However, charging separately for bread and olives has become prevalent with the growth of bar menus and gastropubs. It's not in itself a bad thing – after all, if you don't want to eat bread or olives, why should you pay for them? The problem is the surprise you may get come bill time if you've ordered them unawares: maybe £2 for the bread and £3.50 for the olives. Fortunately, the web can help you reccie a restaurant's menu online before you go.

15 Meet in the pub first

You can cut down on the cost of aperitifs and bottles of wine in a restaurant if you have a cheap drink in a pub beforehand, then just enjoy a glass of wine with your meal.

16 Order carafes, not bottles – but beware

Many restaurants have used the trend of offering wines by the large glass and carafe as an opportunity to help wine-lovers sample fine wines without shouldering the cost of a whole bottle. Ordering a glass of white with the starter and a glass of red with the main course often makes sense, and if your companion does the same but chooses different wines you could taste four different wines with dinner – great. Enjoying wines by the glass and carafe is a great way to ease down your consumption too. But the costs can easily add up to more than a bottle of house wine. Beware of this at fine-dining and hotel restaurants in particular, when the number of inexpensive wines offered is still disappointingly brief.

17 Choose a BYO restaurant

We list around 30 in this guide. Mark-ups on wine in restaurants tend to be three times what you would pay in a shop, so this is a great way to save money. Some restaurants charge a token corkage fee (you are, after all, using their glasses and ice-buckets), but many don't even bother with that. London's BYO establishments range from Turkish and Middle Eastern grills to Indian curry houses, vegetarian eateries and smartly informal restaurants such as Rochelle Canteen. And BYO certainly doesn't mean food quality is compromised: among our top-rated red star places are Tre Viet and 19 Numara Bos Cirrik.

18
Have dessert, cheese and coffee at home – you can enjoy the same quality more cheaply by shopping in a top delicatessen.

19 Check you haven't paid service already

We all wish restaurants wouldn't do it, but it happens: the service charge is included on the bill, then, when the credit card slip or machine is produced, you're asked if you would like to pay a tip or gratuity. *Caveat emptor* as they say in the classics – buyer beware. It's your responsibility to make sure you are not paying service twice.

20 Be guided

The *Time Out Eating & Drinking Guide*'s very reason for existing is to point you towards London's best places to eat and drink. We constantly refine our selection to reflect those unfortunate times when businesses take a turn for the worse. Sometimes we drop places not because they are bad, but because we have decided they no longer represent good value for money – that's quite different from cheapness. And occasionally we keep disappointing places in the guide because they are well known and we'd like to warn you what to expect if you visit. Look on the our website and you will also find the opinions of many other Time Out readers, and can add your own views on each restaurant, café, pub and bar – all of which helps you make the best choices about where to eat.

The year that was

Jenni Muir looks back over a year of moving and shaking in London's eating and drinking scene.

Time Out has been reporting on London's best and best-value eating and drinking for nearly 30 years. Every week our expert critics digest and assess everything from ice-cream parlours and caffs to fine gastronomy and a veritable planet of ethnic cuisines. Since the publication of our last *Eating & Drinking Guide* 12 months ago, we've seen plenty of new developments that are worth attention. Here are some of the most notable.

2008

AUGUST

Angela Hartnett of the Gordon Ramsay group is busy launching not one, but two high-profile restaurants, plus a bar and delicatessen. **Murano**, a glamorous yet understated Italian spot in Mayfair, and boutique hotel the **York & Albany** near Camden, with attached food store Nonna's, are well received by critics – which must have come as a relief given how well the Connaught had been doing with Hartnett's replacement, French chef Hélène Darroze.

Indeed, the Connaught is on something of a roll with its refurbishment programme. Having already wowed critics with the cosy Coburg (which narrowly lost our 2008 Best Bar award to local favourite the Loft), the hotel opens another bar within a matter of months. Called the **Connaught** and designed by David Collins, it immediately pulls in a young,

Princi

sexy crowd (something the hotel was not renowned for) with its superior spirits and exciting, expertly made cocktails.

Down in Battersea, the capital sees the opening of its first wine bar to specialise in organic and biodynamically produced wines. **Artisan & Vine** has the drinking side of the business well sorted, offering more than 30 varieties by glass, carafe, bottle and for take-home sale, but takes a while to get the food offer up to the standard we expect.

On the Highgate/Kentish Town borders, gastropub the **Bull & Last** quietly reopens as… a gastropub, but this time a superior version. Complete with a fine choice of real ales and gourmet renditions of scotch eggs and sausage rolls (plus some of the best chips in town), it steadily attracts a local following that, by October, is to become effusive press and result in an avalanche of customers from across the capital. Securing a table is still something of a challenge.

SEPTEMBER

Back in November 2007 contract caterer Searcy's had an immediate hit on its hands when the Champagne Bar opened as part of the £800 million restoration of St Pancras station, and the queues were only just beginning to die down the following September when the company opens **St Pancras Grand**, a romantic and luxurious British brasserie. The menu of smoked fish, les rosbif and comfort puddings is just the sort of thing you'd want French visitors to encounter the second they step off Eurostar.

With Thai food consistently being voted high among *Time Out* readers' favourite cuisines, it was a pleasure to welcome the arrival of an inexpensive Thai café just off Brick Lane. The authenticity and quality of **Rosa's** menu is impressive, and its cool pink and wood decor (complete with photo of Elvis Presley meeting King Bhumipol and Queen Sirikit of Thailand) just right for its location. Meanwhile. **Chaat** (the name means 'snack food') opens in Shoreditch to offer Londoners a taste of Bangladeshi home-style cooking.

This month also sees the start of what is to become a major theme of the year's dining scene: popular Spanish restaurants opening more branches. **Tierra Brindisa**, an offshoot of Borough Market's perennially popular Tapas Brindisa, opens in Soho. Before too long, **Casa Brindisa** also appears in South Kensington.

OCTOBER

Highbury Park welcomes **Garufa** serving Argentinian food. This sibling to Alberto Abbate's Battersea grill Santa María del Sur does not aim to be a steakhouse, offering dishes of salmon and veal as well as breakfasts of choripan (Argentina's sausage sarnie) and mate tea, but in our view the meat is still the main reason to visit.

Meat lovers also delight in the opening of the **Harwood Arms** gastropub, from a team comprising TV chef and game specialist Mike Robinson of Berkshire's Pot Kiln, Brett Graham from French restaurant the Ledbury, and publican Edwin Vaux. The venison (often shot by Robinson himself) is particularly good, so too the bramley apple doughnuts.

Up in Chalk Farm, Chinese restaurant **Yum Cha** opens, specialising in dim sum snacks produced by expert chefs from Hong Kong. We aren't quite so impressed by **Min Jiang**, the new Chinese spot in Kensington's Royal Garden Hotel, finding the service of its wood-fired peking duck, served in the traditional multi-course manner, too meagre. Still, the views from this classy tenth-floor restaurant alone make it worth a visit.

NOVEMBER

Alan Yau does it again with **Princi**, his joint venture with Italian baker Rocco Princi. The stylish yet egalitarian Wardour Street bakery-cafeteria thrums with customers from day one, everyone struggling to choose between the wide range of cakes, tarts, sandwiches, salads and hot dishes colourfully displayed behind the counters.

In South Kensington, another great idea for informal eating: **Madsen** is a smart café-restaurant specialising in Danish cooking. It particularly appeals at lunchtime when the menu focuses on smørrebrød (open sandwiches) – perfect with one of the fabulous Danish beers.

The Kings Place development at King's Cross takes a step closer to full-functioning this month with the opening of **Rotunda Bar & Restaurant**. Beef is a speciality on the British menu – and the restaurant has its own purpose-built hanging facility – but prices are on the high side for the standard of cooking and we reckon the real draw is the lovely canalside views.

Already a hit in Bath and Oxford, **Jamie's Italian** – the trattoria chain conceived by Jamie Oliver and Gennaro Contraldo – opens in Kingston with plans to steadily work its way into the heart of the capital. A match for Carluccio's? We're not completely convinced, but Kingstonians welcome it enthusiastically. Renowned Mumbai restaurant **Trishna**, which specialises in seafood dishes, opens in Marylebone. We think the London decor lacks the excitement of the Indian original, but the cooking is sound.

In fact, expansion turns out to be a key theme this month, as the Martin Brothers launch another gastro-boozer, the **Hat & Tun** on Hatton Wall, and Mayfair Italian restaurant **Semplice** opens a bar and trattoria a few doors along from the restaurant. At the Connaught, Hélène Darroze's high-end bistro-style restaurant, **Espelette**, fails to set our pulses racing (though it's a great spot for afternoon tea) and old favourite **Kettner's** finally dumps its champagne pizzeria pitch in favour of a French menu and feminine interior from designer Ilse Crawford.

But perhaps the most excitement is caused by **Double Club**, a temporary Congolese and western restaurant, bar, disco and all-round cultural event in a converted warehouse near Angel tube. Mourad Mazouz, founder of Momo and Sketch, is involved as operating partner, and the menu is a juxtaposition of Congolese dishes (goat stew, yam leaves with ground peanuts, saltfish with onion, tomato and chilli)

with French-based Modern European fare. While it undoubtedly adds glamour to the capital, it is destined to close in July 2009.

DECEMBER

With the lease shortly to expire on Richard Corrigan's Soho restaurant Lindsay House, the ebullient Irish chef finds a new home at the side of the Grosvenor House Hotel. **Corrigan's Mayfair** offers the same blend of traditional Irish dishes and haute cuisine themes in a luxe, spacious setting and in the initial excitement it's hard to snare a booking. **Terroirs** near Charing Cross sends wine buffs into a frenzy, offering an intriguing and sometimes challenging selection of 'natural' wines and marrying them to rustic Mediterranean cooking. We love the champagne-style French perry, duck scratchings, chorizo with Basque-style piperade and informal setting.

Not far away, **Bocca di Lupo** opens on the Soho side of Piccadilly Circus. Chef Jacob Kennedy previously worked at Moro and serves a menu of Italian regional cooking in small (or large) dishes for sharing. Great idea, but the enthusiastic reception from critics results in a clamour for tables and this is one eaterie where enjoyment relies very much on where you are seated. As far as we're concerned, if we can't sit at the marble counter by the kitchen, we don't want to be there.

Eating at a restaurant's bar can, in any case, be great fun and another instant hit is **J Sheekey's Oyster Bar**, an extension of the much-loved fish restaurant. British comfort cuisine is the focus at Golden Square's **Bob Bob Ricard**, but while the menu's a great read, and the all-day dining policy appeals, it's David Collins' romantic interior that lingers in the memory.

Goodbye

We bid farewell to those restaurants that have changed hands or shut since the last edition of the *Time Out Eating & Drinking Guide*.

Aaya
Gary Yau's Japanese was all design, no trousers.

Ambassade de l'Ile
Sinking island, not floating islands.

Brackenbury
Beaten by the Bush.

Brasserie St Quentin
The beau monde now have Brompton Bar & Grill.

Le Bodeguita del Medio
Cuban history.

Chinese Experience
Chinese inconsequence.

Flâneur
Strolled off into the sunset.

Greyhound
Off, but not racing.

Iznik Kaftan
Not enough Turkish delight in Chelsea.

Haiku
17 syllables too many.

Lindsay House
No longer home to Richard Corrigan.

Munchkin Lane
Followed the yellow brick road.

Pick More Daisies
Now they have plenty of time to do just that.

Snows on the Green
Not in the pink.

Spiga
No power to the pizzeria.

Tapas y Vino
Adios y buena suerte.

Ubon
Nobu spelled backwards went backwards.

Yakitoria
Sunk in Paddington Basin.

In Crouch End, **St James** is a bold attempt to bring fine dining to a local audience. We liked the food and the chic white restaurant, but the front bar and lounge looked worryingly like a lap-dancing club – good news then, to hear that they're planning to rework that part of the building.

2009

JANUARY

The return of Sir Terence Conran. Having sold his stake in what was Conran Restaurants (the group now known as D&D London), Terence and wife Vicki collaborated with Conran's former operations director Peter Prescott on Shoreditch hotel the Boundary Project. Its British caff and deli, **Albion**, includes the design witticisms expected from the founder of Habitat: stools made from tractor seats, brown betty teapots with hand-knitted tea cosies. Also in the hotel is a posher French restaurant, **Boundary**, with chef Ian Wood bringing his charcuterie trolley from Islington's Almeida and dispensing plenty of rotisserie-cooked meats.

Seafood is flavour of the month down in Croydon, where Malcolm John opens **Fish & Grill**, serving locally sourced and sustainably caught fish along with Angus beef and exemplary chips. Our first visit finds the terrific food and decor marred by ungracious service.

Another Spanish restaurant spawns: this time Northcote Road's charming **Lola Rojo**, which specialises in *nueva cocina*, opens a branch in Fulham. The new restaurant has the same menu as the original but much more space, creating quite a different dining experience.

Also this month we visit **Callooh Callay** in Shoreditch, named after Lewis Carroll's nonsense poem. Its neo-Victorian decor features a Narnia-style oak wardrobe (sorry for mixing the literary references there), which opens the way to a laid-back lounge, mirrored bar and loos tiled in old cassettes. Westminster's acclaimed Indian restaurant Cinnamon Club opens **Cinnamon Kitchen** in a converted City warehouse, while back in Westminster Claudio Pulze opens Italian restaurant **Osteria dell'Angolo**.

FEBRUARY

The time has come to chart the growing number of rodizios in the capital. These informal Brazilian barbecue grills serve beef, pork, chicken and offal plus salad buffet in an all-you-can-eat format. The high-profile opening that prompts our survey is **Comida** on South Molton Street, but on the whole we prefer Pimlico's **Rodizio Preto**.

Brazil is also the theme for Chelsea's **Sushiñho**, a cocktail bar and restaurant inspired by Sao Paolo's Japanese community. Or is it just a good opportunity to satisfy the demand for sushi at the same time as serving popular cocktails of cachaça and sake? If that doesn't appeal, you could always pop up to **Gilmour's**, the new British restaurant on Park Walk, owned by Christopher Gilmour of long-running American restaurant Christopher's.

It seems west London is on something of a roll. **Daylesford Organic** opens a huge outlet on Westbourne Grove; the decor is more inviting than the Pimlico flagship, and it has more dining options too, including a trendy raw bar that's bound to be a hit with local fashionistas. The **Queen Adelaide** opens bang-opposite last year's Best New Gastropub winner the Princess Victoria. Part of the Realpubs group, the Queen Adelaide is typically decked in floral wallpaper and chandeliers, but the cooking is decent and there is a great choice of real ales. Also in Shepherd's Bush is smart Polish restaurant **Tatra**, serving vodka shots and modern dishes of buckwheat and leniwe, plus classics such as gulasz and pierogi.

Meanwhile, we welcome the opening of two inexpensive Malaysian restaurants: **Rasa Sayang**, which brings the cuisine of the Straits to Chinatown, and **Sedap**, a Clerkenwell restaurant from the chefs who earned such a good reputation at Notting Hill's Nyonya. Aficionados consider their char kway teow (fried flat noodles) the best in the capital.

MARCH

The credit crunch is in full swing, so what better time to open a new take on the British caff. Roasts with yorkshire puddings, cod cheeks with green pea mash, spotted dick and custard are all on the menu at the **Brill** and with two courses costing £13.50, the prices are very appealing. So too is the location: after all, there aren't many bright culinary spots on the Caledonian Road.

Finsbury Park isn't known for the excellence of its restaurants either, so tiny Korean-Japanese spot **Dotori** is a welcome discovery. It's inexpensive too, so no wonder locals take to it with gusto. Back in Chinatown, we're raving about the bite-sized xiao chi (small eats) menu at **Ba Shan**, the third outlet from the team behind Baozi Inn and Bar Shu.

Spitalfields doesn't really need another cool place for coffee, but **Nude Espresso** earns its street space with smartly cheerful decor, friendly vibe, excellent flat whites and generously filled foccacia. Further east in Victoria Park, yet another gastropub appears, but we like the **Britannia** for its lack of pretension. If you want to eat, there's good British cooking; if you just want to drink, you can.

In the heart of the City, by the Thames, **High Timber** opens. It's a British steakhouse with meats from popular Borough Market fixture Farmer Sharp, but part-owned by the Jordan Wine Estate of South Africa. The margins on wine are high, but will the City clientele notice or care?

Down in Battersea, **Lost Angel** aims to fuse boozer, bar and restaurant and has the advantage of a terrific garden. It's only three streets away from older sister Lost Society, but tries to differentiate itself with a come-as-you-are local vibe and a 'no house music' policy. Successful? We think so.

APRIL

After a period out of the public eye, and disappointment with a proposed vegetarian restaurant on Brick Lane, ex-Delfina chef Maria Elia resurfaces at **Whitechapel Gallery Dining Room**. Always one of the more inventive of Modern European chefs, Elia makes strong use of seasonal British ingredients and rich Mediterranean spicing in the food here. Having quietly attracted queues for coffee and Lebanese wraps at its stall in the Westfield shopping centre, **Comptoir Libanais** opens a standalone deli-café on Wigmore Street with a striking interior design. We are particularly impressed by the pumpkin kibbeh and meze plates – great for refuelling while shopping.

Not far away, **Il Baretto** opens on the Marylebone site that was quality basement pizzeria Giusto. Given that Zuma and Roka owner Arjun Waney is the owner, the place is surprisingly low-key but its straightforward, authentic cooking is good.

FIRST RESTAURANT GROUP

First Restaurant Group provides distinctive venues for a variety of events including: business meetings, cocktail parties, corporate functions and social events.

HARRY MORGAN

THE EBURY

THE RUNNING HORSE

THE WATERWAY

TAMAN GANG

NOTTING HILL BRASSERIE

The Waterway
54 Formosa Street
London W9 2JU
020 7266 3557

The Ebury
11 Pimlico Road
London SW1W 8NA
020 7730 6784

The Running Horse
50 Davies Street
London W1K 5JE
020 7493 1275

Harry Morgan
31 St. Johns Wood High St.
London NW8 7NH
020 7722 1869

Harrods Food Hall
London SW1X 7XL
020 7730 1234 ext.2997

Fenwick Brent Cross
London NW4 3FN
020 8202 1999

NOTTING HILL Brasserie
92 Kensington Park Road
Notting Hill Gate
London W11 2PN
020 7229 4481

Taman gang
141 Park Lane
Mayfair, London
W1K 7AA
020 7518 3160

For information on any of our venues please contact Joanna on:
+44 (0) 207 266 6320 or email: joanna@frgroup.co.uk

www.frgroup.co.uk

MAY

In time for summer (or what there was to be of it) the folk behind café chain Benugo open **Serpentine Bar & Kitchen** in Hyde Park. Everyone loves the waterside setting, but the food doesn't do it justice. Good on them, though, for offering proper hand-pumped beers in a quintessentially English setting. More revamped gastropubs come to the fore this month: **Villiers Terrace** in Crouch End has us satisfied by the food, but perplexed by the absence of real ales. And the **Drapers Arms** surprises with lacklustre cooking – given that one of the owners, Ben Maschler, is son of *Evening Standard* restaurant critic and industry consultant Fay Maschler. We're not that impressed by **Palm** either, the American steakhouse that opens in Knightsbridge. Prices are very high, which begs the question why pay for imported grain-fed beef from the USA when British grass-fed beef is superior and cheaper?

In Farringdon, chef Bjorn van der Horst opens a double-sided venue, French restaurant **Eastside Inn Bistro** and fine-dining establishment **Eastside Inn**. Our meals in both eateries are good, but the place certainly doesn't wow all the critics. Fingers crossed they can up the consistency.

JUNE

Another popular chef resurfaces – this time Theodore Kyriakou, along with his business partner from the original outlets of Livebait and the Real Greek, Paloma Campbell. **More** is an all-day café-bar-restaurant with a globally inspired menu and we think it's terrific – but is the concept suitable for another corporate-style roll-out? Any area would love to have a branch of **Kensington Wine Rooms**, where a wide range of superior wines are kept in good nick in Enomatic machines so that they can be dispensed by the glass. Cocktail fiends, on the other hand, are excited by the opening of **69 Colebrooke Row**, the latest bar from Tony Conigliaro, formerly of Zuma, who brings a scientific approach to mixology.

JULY

It's Sir Terence again: this time opening a discreet French restaurant and bar, **Lutyens**, on Fleet Street. And while it lacks the design quirks of the Boundary Project in Shoreditch, it is nevertheless classic Conran – it has counters for charcuterie and crustacea, and a chef poached from Le Pont de la Tour.

Not far away, the **Restaurant at St Paul's** impresses with British cooking and, well, the very brilliant idea of siting a restaurant and café in Wren's masterpiece. We also welcome new places in some rather under-served settings: **Fleet River Bakery's** efforts to bring quality cakes, bread and café cooking to Lincoln's Inn Fields, and the Martin brothers King's Road gastropub the **Cadogan Arms**.

This month the capital is also introduced to the delights of real Argentinian ice-cream with the opening of **Freggo** on Swallow Street. Can they persuade us to do as the Argentinians do and spend evenings scoffing ice-cream rather than quaffing beer and cocktails? Only time will tell.

As we go to press in mid August 2009, there are still some exciting restaurant openings to look forward to (*see below* **Hello**). For all the latest restaurant and bar reviews, log on to www.timeout.com/restaurants, where our critics assess each new venue and fellow Londoners add their own feedback.

Hello

Time Out magazine's food and drink editor Guy Dimond gives us a peep at his current to-do list.

LATE SUMMER

Comptoir Libanais
26 London Street, W2 1HH; O2 Centre, 255 Finchley Road, NW3 6LU.
Two useful new branches of this vibrant and popular Lebanese deli-café from Tony Kitous.

Elgin
96 Ladbroke Grove, W11 1PY.
One of several imminent new openings from gastropub group Geronimo Inns.

AUTUMN

Aqua London
240 Regent Street, W1B 2EL.
Huge corner terraces at the top of the former Dickins & Jones department store will undoubtedly draw crowds to this double-restaurant opening from Hong Kong-based restaurant group Aqua. Kyoto will serve sushi and sumibiyaki, while Aqua Nueva will specialise in San Sebastian-style Spanish cooking.

Dean Street Townhouse & Dining Room
69-71 Dean Street, W1D 4QJ.

The Soho House formula of club, guest rooms and all-day dining seems to be working: this place will sit just around the corner from the original.

Galvin La Chapelle
St Botolph's Hall, 36 Spital Square, E1 6DY.
A wood-fired oven is planned to be at the heart of Chris and Jeff Galvin's new restaurant, café and bar in the City.

Green's Restaurant & Oyster Bar
14 Cornhill, EC3 3ND.
Simon Parker Bowles's new spot for seafood promises a spectacular banking hall setting and views over City landmarks.

Lower East Liquor Bar & Bistro
28 Westferry Circus, E14 8RR.
Inspired by the neighbourhood eateries of Manhattan, this bistro and cocktail bar on the site of an old Jamie's wine bar will boast a tree-covered riverside terrace.

Luxe
109 Commercial Street, E1 6BG.
John Torode's much-delayed Spitalfields bar-restaurant, where the menu will focus on game and poultry.

Not Bistrot 11
11 Abingdon Road, W8 6AH.
Phillip Howard of the Square is teaming up with restaurateur Rebecca Mascarenhas (Sonny's, the Phoenix) to open a new restaurant on the site that was recently her Bistrot 11.

Orange
37-39 Pimlico Road, SW1W 8NE.
The team behind the Pantechnicon Rooms takes over the site of the former Orange Brewery.

Pétrus
1 Kinnerton Street, SW1X 8EA.
A new Belgravia home for this Gordon Ramsay group reincarnation.

WINTER

RICS
12 Great George Street, SW1P 3AD.
The Royal Institute of Chartered Surveyors has invited Michel Roux Jr to open a restaurant in its Grade II-listed Parliament Square premises.

The Savoy
Strand, WC2R 0EU.
The great hotel is scheduled to reopen after a £100 million refurbishment programme with the Savoy Grill, River Room and Beaufort Bar.

Busaba Eathai

106–110 Wardour Street
Phone 020-7255 8686
London W1T 0TR

22 Store Street
Phone 020-7299 7900
London WC1E 7DF

Pre-booking available
for groups of 12+

Take away available

8–13 Bird Street
Phone 020-7518 8080
London W1U 1BU

Take away available

Time Out's 20th annual Eating & Drinking Awards 2009

Time Out has an unrivalled reputation for promoting the best of London's eating and drinking places – something of which we are very proud. It is not just those with the grandest credentials that we champion, either, but the little places that are, in their own field, worthy of note. This is the ethos behind our broad coverage of London's gastronomic delights – from weekly reviews in *Time Out* magazine to our numerous guides. And this is why our annual Eating & Drinking Awards take in not only London's restaurant élite, but also representatives from neighbourhood restaurants, gastropubs, cafés and other bargain eateries, as independently selected by a panel of Time Out judges.

The award categories, which vary each year, reflect the diverse needs and tastes of London's diners and drinkers. With a fresh crop of reviews appearing each week in *Time Out* magazine (and on our website, www.timeout.com/restaurants), the list of potential candidates can seem dauntingly long, but our panel of independent (and anonymous) reviewers have been able to whittle them down to a shortlist of 40: four nominations in each of ten categories. We ask readers of the magazine and website for their feedback, which helps inform our judges' choices.

Finally, the judges revisit every shortlisted venue as normal paying punters (we never accept PR invitations or freebies), so that a final decision can be reached.

> **This year's judges:** Jessica Cargill Thompson, Guy Dimond, Alexi Duggins, Will Fulford-Jones, Sarah Guy, Susan Low, Charmaine Mok, Jenni Muir, Cath Phillips.

And the winners are... in alphabetical order.

BEST NEW BAR

Winner
69 Colebrooke Row *See p323.*

Runners-up
Calloch Callay *See p320.*
Lost Angel *See p319.*
Portobello Star *See p318.*

BEST NEW CAFÈ

Winner
Lantana *See p289.*

Runners-up
Fleet River Bakery *See p289.*
J&A Café *See p288.*
Luca's *See p293.*

BEST NEW CHEAP EATS

Winner
Albion (British) *See p60.*

Runners-up
Princi (Brasseries) *See p46.*
Rasa Sayang (Malaysian, Indonesian & Singaporean) *See p200.*
Rosa's (Thai) *See p254.*

BEST NEW DESIGN

Winner
Bob Bob Ricard (Brasseries) *See p45.*

Runners-up
L'Anima (Italian) *See p162.*
Comptoir Libanais (Middle Eastern) *See p205.*
St Pancras Grand (Brasseries) *See p44.*

L'Anima

The Giaconda Dining Room

Giaconda Dining Room

Bob Bob Ricard

Cambio de Tercio

BEST NEW GASTROPUB

Winner
Harwood Arms *See p107.*

Runners-up
Britannia *See p113.*
Bull & Last *See p116.*
Cadogan Arms *See p107.*

BEST NEW RESTAURANT

Winner
Giaconda Dining Room (Modern European) *See p211.*

Runners-up
Ba Shan (Chinese) *See p72.*
Boundary (French) *See p98.*
Corrigan's Mayfair (British) *See p57.*

BEST NEW ITALIAN RESTAURANT

Winner
L'Anima *See p162.*

Runners-up
Il Baretto *See p165.*
Bocca di Lupo *See p169.*
Murano *See p166.*

BEST SPANISH RESTAURANT
in association with

Winner
Lola Rojo *See p246.*

Runners-up
Cambio de Tercio *See p243.*
Fino *See p239.*
Tapas Brindisa *See p247.*

BEST NEW LOCAL

Winner
Exhibition Rooms (Modern European) *See p226.*

Runners-up
Fish & Grill (Fish) *See p89.*
Garufa (The Americas) *See p41.*
St James (International) *See p161.*

BEST SPANISH WINE LIST
in association with

Winner
Cambio de Tercio *See p243.*

Runners-up
Cigala *See p239.*
Fino *See p239.*
El Pirata *See p242.*

Time Out's Hot 100

The editors of the **Time Out Eating & Drinking Guide** have picked 100 places, entirely subjectively, that we believe offer some of London's most interesting eating and drinking experiences. We're not saying these venues have the best food and drink in the capital, but we believe each adds something life-enhancing to our city. Here they are, in alphabetical order. Each review is marked with a (100) in the relevant chapter of the guide.

Adam's Café
North African p232.
Popular and good-value Tunisian restaurant that's been serving top-notch north African fare for more than 15 years.

Amaya
Indian p136.
Glamorous and groovy modern Indian grill with impeccable service.

Ambassador
Modern European p212.
Exmouth Market's all-day café has a modern British twist to its menu and a Gallic slant to its wine list.

Anchor & Hope
Gastropubs p109.
Most consider the often lengthy wait for a table a small price to pay for a meal at this pub.

Arbutus
Modern European p219.
Seasonal ingredients are served with a hint of southern European flavours at this popular Soho spot.

Assaggi
Italian p171.
Low-key Bayswater restaurant with an exquisite and carefully thought out Italian menu.

Ba Shan
Chinese p72.
Small dishes (xiao chi) from Sichuan, Henan and Shaanxi served in a tea house-style setting.

Baltic
East European p80.
Pan-east European food with light, innovative twists, served in glamorous surroundings.

Barrafina
Spanish p242.
A small, buzzy space in the heart of Soho offering stylish, authentic tapas and a good selection of sherries and Spanish wine.

Bentley's Oyster Bar & Grill
Fish p85.
Historic fish restaurant and oyster bar just off Piccadilly, updated in ebullient style by chef-patron Richard Corrigan.

Bistrotheque
French p98; Bars p320.
Bistro food, modish bar and camp cabaret make an original combination at this east London hotspot.

Blue Bar
Bars p316.
First-class cocktails in starry surroundings at the Berkeley hotel.

Breads Etcetera
Cafés p292.
Clapham's best breakfasts showcase artisanal breads toasted at the table.

Brew House
Cafés p297.
A walk on Hampstead Heath isn't complete without a stop at this popular cafeteria.

Buen Ayre
The Americas p39.
Authentic Argentinian parillada (steak-grill) on Broadway Market in Hackney.

Bull & Last
Gastropubs p116.
Superior Scotch eggs, fabulous fat chips and even home-made ice-cream: the local boozer as you want it to be, but more popular.

Busaba Eathai
Thai p249.
Beautifully designed Thai restaurants serving first-class cooking at economy prices.

Le Café Anglais
Modern European p221.
Rowley Leigh's seductive evocation of a British brasserie.

Cah Chi
Korean p197.
Friendly Korean restaurants in Raynes Park and Earlsfield serving unusually good home-style fare.

Chez Bruce
French p98.
Wandsworth Common restaurant with high-class cooking and wine list.

China Tang
Chinese p71.
All the romance and elegance of 1930s China inside the Dorchester hotel.

Clarke's
Modern European p222.
Sally Clarke takes carefully sourced ingredients and serves them simply.

Club Gascon
French p92.
The culinary traditions of south-west France inspire some of London's most inventive cooking, with foie gras a speciality.

Coach & Horses
Gastropubs p102.
Take a table in the bar for a pint of real ale and your choice of snacks from scotch eggs to herring roe and duck hearts.

Connaught Bar
Bars p317.
The Connaught hotel has two hip bars, both superb: this one attracts the livelier crowd.

Cow
Gastropubs p107.
Shellfish, especially oysters, are as much of a draw as the convivial bar at Tom Conran's popular Notting Hill pub.

Czechoslovak Restaurant
East European p80.
The city's only Czech restaurant and bar is a piece of living history serving dumplings, pancakes and potatoes.

Dukes Hotel
Bars p317.
Exquisite martinis are made tableside and with a theatrical flourish at this luxurious hotel bar.

Eyre Brothers
Global p119.
Mozambique meets the Mediterranean at this sleek restaurant and bar run by Rob and David Eyre.

Fernandez & Wells
Cafés p290.
Precision-made espresso and luxuriously filled sandwiches: the quality office escape.

Fish Club
Fish & Chips p300.
Careful to promote lesser-known varieties of fish, this modern chippie serves traditional fish and chips alongside international recipes.

Franco Manca
Pizza & Pasta p309.
Unassuming pizza parlour topping sourdough bases with first-rate ingredients.

La Fromagerie
Cafés p289.
Dine among the deli ingredients at this charming fine food store.

Le Gavroche
Hotels & Haute Cuisine p129.
Classic and modern French cuisine served with exacting service standards in Michel Roux Jr's landmark basement restaurant.

Geales
Fish p87.
Sustainable fish species are the inspiration for some terrific dishes at Gary Hollihead's revamp of an old Notting Hill chippie.

Giaconda Dining Room
Modern European p211.
Simple Aussie-run restaurant: great food, no messin'.

Golden Hind
Fish & Chips p298.
Serving fish and chips to Marylebone since World War I.

Hakkasan
Chinese p69; Bars p314.
Whether you come for drinks, dim sum or cutting-edge Chinese cooking, Hakkasan's glamorous interior never fails to thrill.

Harwood Arms
Gastropubs p107.
Fulham has no shortage of good gastropubs, but the Harwood Arms sets a new standard with its game-heavy menu and classy bar snacks.

Hawksmoor
The Americas p33; Bars p314.
Spitalfields steakhouse serving excellent cocktails and some of the best meat in the capital.

Hélène Darroze at the Connaught
Hotels & Haute Cuisine p129.
Grand panelled dining room serving specialities of France's Landes region with modern fusion touches.

Hereford Road
British p59.
Forthright British cooking and similarly bold, sparse decor at this relaxed Notting Hill restaurant.

Hibiscus
Hotels & Haute Cuisine p130.
Claude Bosi's flair has found an appreciative London audience.

Hix Oyster & Chop House
British p52.
Mark Hix's first independent project after leaving Caprice Holdings is a roll-call of local, seasonal produce.

Hummus Bros
Budget p281.
Good houmous, good bread, good vibes – what's not to like about this clever, casual concept?

Jerusalem Tavern
Pubs p324.
Superb organic beers from St Peter's Brewery in Suffolk are served in a cosily tatty pub.

LAB
Bars p318.
An encyclopedic drinks menu, all perfectly mixed by graduates of the London Academy of Bartending.

Landau
Hotels & Haute Cuisine p124.
Futuristic grand hotel dining courtesy of designer David Collins and chef Andrew Turner.

Lobby Bar
Bars p314.
Handy for Covent Garden, an excellent hotel cocktail bar with theatrical touches.

Locanda Locatelli
Italian p165.
A sexy, lounge-like dining room serving fine Italian cuisine and impressive wines.

Lola Rojo
Spanish p246.
Battersea tapas bar that introduced Northcote Road to nueva cocina.

Loungelover
Bars p322.
Booking is essential at this louche, low-lit cocktail lounge, making a night amid its camp excesses all the more of an event.

Macaron
Cafés p293.
Innovative French pâtisserie lines up with classic eclairs and ice-creams at this characterful Clapham tea room.

Mandalay
Global p118.
It may be a basic caff on the Edgware Road, but the Burmese menu is astonishing.

M Manze
Budget p283.
Gorgeous turn-of-the-20th-century tiling and traditional wooden benches make this the grandaddy of pie and mash shops.

Masa
Global p117.
Harrow is the setting for London's most flamboyant Afghan restaurant.

Maze
Hotels & Haute Cuisine p130.
Sophisticated morsels and mini main courses allow leisurely dining across a feast of flavours.

Milk & Honey
Bars p318.
Speakeasy-style Soho bar with lighting so dim you can barely read the cocktail list. Grown-up fun, however.

Momo
North African p231.
A great Maghrebi soundtrack, cool Marrakech decor and some of the best Moroccan food in London.

Moro
Spanish p239.
Enduringly popular Exmouth Market restaurant with menu stretching from Spain right along the Mediterranean.

Nahm
Thai p249.
Royal Thai cuisine served with style and grace in a glittering dining room.

National Dining Rooms
British p58.
With sensational views over Trafalgar Square, Oliver Peyton's restaurant inside the National Gallery is the ideal place to enjoy the best of British ingredients.

Nauroz
Indian p153.
Pakistani community caff that's a magnet for curry aficionados from across London.

Nobu
Japanese p183.
London, New York, Miami, Melbourne, Tokyo, Hong Kong, Cape Town, Dubai, Milan, Moscow, Athens, Waikiki…

Ottolenghi
International p161.
Salads as you've never seen them, and a stunning range of cakes.

E Pellicci
Budget p283.
Everyone's favourite greasy spoon, with a Grade-II listed art deco-style interior and homely British and Italian cooking.

Petersham Nurseries Café
Modern European p229.
The surrounding gardens inspire Skye Gyngell's inventive, flavour-packed cooking style.

Princess Victoria
Gastropubs p106.
It offers refined cooking and an expert wine list, but this grand Victorian spot hasn't forgotten it is also a pub.

The Providores & Tapa Room
International p158.
From miso rice porridge and Turkish eggs to cucumber martinis and a cheese plate, this all-day eaterie suits every occasion.

Racine
French p93.
An atmospheric slice of 1930s Paris from chef-patron Henry Harris.

Ram's
Indian p155.
Pani puri, pau bhaji and pooris to die for.

Ranoush Juice
Middle Eastern p205.
Magic meze and sensational shawarma served until 3am daily.

Rasa Samudra
Indian p136.
Colourfully authentic fish and vegetarian cookery from Kerala offered in an equally colourful setting.

Riva
Italian p172.
Classy neighbourhood Italian restaurant in Barnes serving simple yet sophisticated dishes.

The River Café
Italian p171.
It's not a café and you can't see the river, but this Hammersmith hotspot remains for many their favourite London restaurant.

Roast
British p60.
Iqbal Wahhab's handsomely porticoed meat specialist in the heart of Borough Market.

Roka
Japanese p178.
Spectacularly designed restaurant based around a central grill and great for people-watching.

S&M Café
Budget p284.
The former Alfredo's greasy spoon retains much of its vintage charm, and the modern bangers and mash menu is similarly sympathetic.

Saf
Vegetarian p273.
Raw vegan food has never been so appealing, or stylish.

Sagar
Indian p143.
A rare opportunity to taste the vegetarian specialities of Udupi in South India.

St John
British p52.
This former smokehouse near Smithfield Market has acquired an international reputation for its nose-to-tail treatment of meats.

Saké No Hana
Japanese p184.
Japanese fine dining from restaurant supremo Alan Yau.

Sakonis
Indian p157.
The original Indian vegetarian chat (snack) house, serving South Indian and Gujarati specialities.

Satay House
Malaysian p201.
Classic dishes of Malaysia served in a stylish yet relaxed setting.

Scoop
Cafés p292.
Covent Garden's superior Italian ices to eat-in, or grab and lickety split.

Sketch: The Gallery
International p158.
Hip crowd, hip decor and astonishing food from Pierre Gagnaire.

Smiths of Smithfield
Modern European p212.
Enduringly popular – and useful – bar and restaurant complex from *Masterchef* host John Torode.

Song Que
Vietnamese p274.
Authentic Vietnamese dishes at affordable prices in Shoreditch.

Sushi-Hiro
Japanese p185.
Sushi for purists – the surprise is it's served in

Ealing and is great value for money.

Sweetings
Fish p84.
Convivial old City canteen specialising in fish.

The Table
Budget p282.
A treat on Bankside, a new-wave café-cum-canteen with architect-designed interior.

Tapas Brindisa
Spanish p247.
The pioneering Spanish food importer's authentic tapas kitchen has been such a hit it's spawned two branches.

Tiroler Hut
Eating & Entertainment p341.
Decorated like a ski lodge in the Tyrol, this Austrian restaurant's accordion music and cowbell shows will make your party go with a swing – and a singalong.

Tre Viet
Vietnamese p278.
Veteran Vietnamese café that does a brisk trade every night thanks to its uncompromisingly authentic cooking.

Les Trois Garçons
French p100.
This former pub in Shoreditch is home to hippo heads, stuffed bulldogs and a collection of vintage handbags, as well as some terrific French cuisine.

Veeraswamy
Indian p139.
Sensational Indian cooking in a silky, sensual setting.

Vinoteca
Wine Bars p332.
Perennially popular Italian-style enoteca (wine shop and bar) near Smithfield Market.

Wapping Food
Modern European p228.
An old East End pumping station is the setting for contemporary art exhibitions and contemporary cooking.

White Horse
Pubs p327.
London's widest choice of ales served in a bright, airy pub near Parsons Green.

The Wolseley
Brasseries p45.
The listed interior of this former car showroom on Piccadilly is a dapper dining destination at any hour.

Where to...

Got the hunger, the people, the occasion, but not the venue? These suggestions will help you find the perfect spot to eat, drink and be merry.

Looking for something more specific? Then consult the **Subject Index** starting on page 378.

GO FOR BREAKFAST

Breakfast is offered every day unless stated otherwise. *See also* **Cafés** and **Brasseries**.

Albion British p60
Ambassador (Mon-Fri)
   Modern European p212
Automat The Americas p34
The Botanist Modern European p224
Café Strudel Global p117
Canteen British p59
The Capital Hotels & Haute Cuisine p126
Cecconi's Italian p166
Cinnamon Club (Mon-Fri) Indian p141
Le Coq d'Argent (Mon-Fri) French p90
Curve Fish p88
The Diner The Americas p37
Dorchester Grill Room British p57
Eagle Bar Diner The Americas p34
Engineer Gastropubs p113
Fifteen (Trattoria) Italian p174
Fifth Floor (Café, Mon-Sat)
   Modern European p214
Fox & Anchor Pubs p324
Garufa The Americas p41
Gastro French p98
Harry Morgan Jewish p194
Inn The Park British p57
Lansdowne Gastropubs p114
Lutyens French p91
The Mercer British p50
Modern Pantry International p158
Mulberry Street (Fri, Sat)
   Pizza & Pasta p304
Nicole's (Mon-Sat) Modern European p217
1 Lombard Street (Brasserie, Mon-Fri)
   French p91
Only Running Footman Gastropubs p104
Prism (Mon-Fri) Modern European p211
The Providores & Tapa Room
   International p158
Roast (Mon-Sat) British p60
St John Bread & Wine British p51
Sakonis (Sat, Sun) Indian p157
S&M Café Budget p284
Simpson's-in-the-Strand (Mon-Fri)
   British p58
Smiths of Smithfield
   Modern European p212

Sotheby's Café (Mon-Fri)
   Modern European p218
Tapas Brindisa (Fri, Sat) Spanish p247
The Terrace (Holborn) (Mon-Fri)
   Modern European p214
York & Albany Modern European p228

EAT/DRINK BY THE WATERSIDE

See also the Southbank Centre branches of Giraffe, Strada and Wagamama; and **Dining afloat** section on p337.

Blueprint Café Modern European p226
Curve Fish p88
Gaucho (Tower Bridge and Richmond
   branches) The Americas p37
Grapes Pubs p328
Marco Polo Italian p174
Narrow Gastropubs p113
Northbank Modern European p211
Royal China (Docklands branch)
   Chinese p77
Oxo Tower Restaurant, Bar & Brasserie
   Modern European p226
Le Pont de la Tour Modern European p227
Rotunda Bar & Restaurant British p55
Saran Rom Thai p253
Skylon Modern European p226
Stein's Budget p284
Thai Square Thai p249
Wild Cherry Vegetarian p271

ENJOY THE VIEW

Babylon Modern European p222
Blueprint Café Modern European p226
Le Coq d'Argent French p90

Galvin at Windows
   Hotels & Haute Cuisine p129
National Dining Rooms British p58
Northbank Modern European p211
Oxo Tower Restaurant, Bar & Brasserie
   Modern European p226
Ozu Japanese p187
Plateau Modern European p227
Roast British p60
Rhodes Twenty Four British p51
Skylon Modern European p226
Tamesa@oxo Brasseries p48
Thai Square Thai p249
Tate Modern Café Brasseries p49
Top Floor at Smiths British p52
Vertigo 42 Champagne Bar
   Eating & Entertainment p342

TAKE THE KIDS

See also **Cafés**, **Brasseries**, **Fish & Chips**, and **Pizza & Pasta**.

Ambassador Modern European p212
Babylon Modern European p222
The Belvedere French p97
Benihana Japanese p190
Blue Elephant Thai p253
Le Cercle French p90
Chez Kristof French p97
The Depot Brasseries p47
Engineer Gastropubs p113
fish! Fish p88
Hard Rock Café Americas p35
Harrison's Brasseries p47
Inn The Park British p57
Marco Polo Italian p174
Marine Ices Budget p284

Masala Zone Indian p152
Namo Vietnamese p277
Perry Hill Gastropubs p109
Ping Pong Chinese p73
Rainforest Café
  Eating & Entertainment p341
Rousillon French p90
S&M Café Budget p284
Tamarind Indian p139
Victoria Modern European p223
Wagamama Oriental p233

TRY UNUSUAL DISHES
See also **Global**.

Abeno Too Japanese p177
Adulis African p31
Asadal Korean p195
Baozi Inn Chinese p64
Biazo African p32
Divo East European p83
Esarn Kheaw Thai p253
Faanoos Middle Eastern p209
Hélène Darroze at The Connaught
  Hotels & Haute Cuisine p129
Hereford Road British p59
Hibiscus Hotels & Haute Cuisine p130
Hunan Chinese p64
Lola Rojo Spanish p246
Little Lamb Chinese p66
Modern Pantry International p158
Nahm Thai p249
The Providores & Tapa Room
  International p158
Red Sea African p30
Saf Vegetarian p273
Saké No Hana Japanese p184
Snazz Sichuan Chinese p69
Song Que Vietnamese p274
Tbilisi East European p80
Texture Hotels & Haute Cuisine p127
Umu Japanese p183

DO BRUNCH
See also **Cafés** and **Brasseries**.

Ambassador (Sat, Sun)
  Modern European p212
Bermondsey Kitchen (Sat, Sun)
  Modern European p226
Bord'eaux French p95
Bumpkin (Sat, Sun) Modern European p221
Christopher's (Sat, Sun)
  The Americas p33
Le Comptoir Gascon (Sat) French p92
The Farm (Sat, Sun)
  Modern European p224
Fifth Floor (Sun) Modern European p214
Joe Allen (Sat, Sun) The Americas p33
Modern Pantry International p158
Ottolenghi International p161
Penk's (Sat) Global p120
Ransome's Dock (Sat, Sun)
  Modern European p225
Roast (Sat) British p60
Sabor (Sat, Sun) The Americas p43
Sam's Brasserie & Bar
  Modern European p222

DINE ALFRESCO
See also **Park cafés** on p295.

Babylon Modern European p222
Back to Basics Fish p84
Bank Westminster International p159
Chez Kristof French p97
Clerkenwell Kitchen Cafés p287
Clissold Arms Gastropubs p116
Le Coq d'Argent French p90
Curve Fish p88
Daylesford Organic Café Cafés p291
Deep Fish p87
Dolphin Gastropubs p112
Duke of Sussex Gastropubs p104
Ealing Park Tavern Gastropubs p104
Engineer Gastropubs p113
Geales Fish p87
Greek Affair Greek p121
High Road Brasserie Brasseries p46
Hoxton Apprentice Modern European p228
Inn The Park British p57
Lemonia Greek p122
Manicomio Italian p172
Narrow Gastropubs p113
Northbank Modern European p211
El Parador Spanish p248
Paternoster Chop House British p51
Perry Hill Gastropubs p109
Rootmaster Vegetarian p273
Petersham Nurseries Café
  Modern European p229
Phoenix Bar & Grill
  Modern European p225
Plateau Modern European p227
Le Pont de la Tour Modern European p227

The River Café Italian p171
Royal China (Docklands branch)
  Chinese p77
Saran Rom Thai p253
Scott's Fish p84
Stein's Budget p284
The Terrace Modern European p214
La Trouvaille French p96

PEOPLE-WATCH
Blue Bar Bars p316
Le Café Anglais Modern European p221
Champagne Bar at St Pancras
  Wine Bars p332
Embassy Modern European p217
Eyre Brothers Global p119
Fifth Floor Modern European p214
Hix Oyster & Chop House British p52
The Ivy Modern European p214
Kensington Place
  Modern European p222
Loungelover Bars p322
Mahiki Bars p316
Mr Chow Chinese p69
Obika Italian p171
Papillon French p97
Quo Vadis British p57
St Alban Global p119
Scott's Fish p84
Sketch: The Gallery International p158
Tate Modern Café Brasseries p49
The Wolseley Brasseries p45
Zuma Japanese p180

TAKE A DATE
Almeida French p100
Amaya Indian p136
Andrew Edmunds Modern European p219
Angelus French p96
L'Anima Italian p162
Assaggi Italian p171
L'Autre Pied Modern European p216
The Bingham
  Hotels & Haute Cuisine p133
Bistroteque French p98
Bob Bob Ricard Brasseries p45
The Botanist Modern European p224
Brickhouse Eating & Entertainment p337
Le Café Anglais Modern European p221
Le Cassoulet French p101
Eyre Brothers Global p119
Fifteen Italian p174
Hakkasan Chinese p69
Harrison's Brasseries p47
Kenza Middle Eastern p204
Kettners Brasseries p45
Lamberts Modern European p225
Locanda Locatelli Italian p165
Lost Society Bars p320
Magdalen British p59
Maze Hotels & Haute Cuisine p130
Odette's Modern European p228
Osteria Emilia Italian p176
Pasha North African p230
Penk's Global p120
Plateau Modern European p227
Roka Japanese p178

Rosemary Lane French p91
St Pancras Grand Brasseries p44
Saké No Hana Japanese p184
Sardo Italian p164
J Sheekey Fish p84
Singapore Garden Malaysian, Indonesian & Singaporean p203
St James International p161
Theo Randall at the Intercontinental Italian p166
Le Trois Garçons French p100
Upstairs Modern European p225
Wapping Food Modern European p228
Wild Honey Modern European p218

EAT AT THE BAR
Anchor & Hope Gastropubs p109
Arbutus Modern European p219
Barrafina Spanish p242
Bentley's Oyster Bar & Grill Fish p85
Bocca di Lupo Italian p169
Le Caprice Modern European p219
Dehesa Spanish p242
Eyre Brothers Global p119
Maze Hotels & Haute Cuisine p130
More Brasseries p49
Moro Spanish p239
Roka Japanese p178
Salt Yard Spanish p240
J Sheekey Fish p84
Tapas Brindisa Spanish p247
Wild Honey Modern European p218
Wright Brothers Oyster & Porter House Fish p88
Zetter Brasseries p44

GRAB A MEAL BEFORE A SHOW
Almeida French p100
Anchor & Hope Gastropubs p109
Axis Modern European p212
The Botanist Modern European p224
Canteen (South Bank branch) British p59
Christopher's The Americas p33
Le Deuxieme International p158
Gaucho Piccadilly The Americas p37
Le Mercury Budget p284
Manicomio Italian p172
Noura Middle Eastern p207
Ottolenghi International p161
Veeraswamy Indian p139

BOOK A PRIVATE ROOM
Alloro Italian p165
Almeida French p100
Amaya Indian p136
Angelus, French p96
Baltic East European p81
Bam-Bou Oriental p233
Chez Bruce French p98
Fish Central Fish & Chips p298
Marquess Tavern Gastropubs p115
Mildred's Vegetarian p270
Osteria dell'Arancio Italian p172
Pasha Turkish p265
Pearl Liang Chinese p71
Phoenix Palace Chinese p69

Rasa Samudra Indian p136
The River Café Italian p171
Sketch Hotels & Haute Cuisine p131, International p158, Cafés p289
Smiths of Smithfield Modern European p212
Tom's Kitchen Brasseries p47
Via Condotti Italian p166
Zetter Brasseries p44

EAT LATE
Artesian Bars p316
Camino Spanish p240
D'Den African p32
Ed's Easy Diner The Americas p35
Fish in a Tie Budget p282
Floridita The Americas p42
Gilgamesh Oriental p236
Hoxton Grille Brasseries p49
Joe Allen The Americas p33
Kenza Middle Eastern p204
Mangal II Turkish p263
Le Mercury Budget p284
Meza Spanish p243
New Mayflower Chinese p67
Nosh Bar (Fri, Sat) Jewish p191
PJ's Grill The Americas p35
Planet Hollywood The Americas p34
Sariyer Balik Turkish p263
Vingt-Quatre Eating & Entertainment p342
The Wolseley Brasseries p45

LOVE THE LOOK
Amaya Indian p136
L'Anima Italian p162
L'Autre Pied Modern European p215
L'Atelier de Joël Robuchon Modern European p212
Baltic East European p81
Benares Indian p138
Bob Bob Ricard Brasseries p45
Le Cercle French p90
Comptoir Libanais Middle Eastern p205
China Tang Chinese p71
Cocoon Oriental p233
Dinings Japanese p180
Fifth Floor Modern European p214
Gilgamesh Oriental p236
Hakkasan Chinese p69
Jerusalem Tavern Pubs p324
Kenza Middle Eastern p204

Ladurée Cafés p296
Landau Hotels & Haute Cuisine p124
Lost Society Bars p320
Loungelover Bars p322
Modern Pantry International p158
Pearl Bar & Restaurant Hotels & Haute Cuisine p125
Pearl Liang Chinese p71
E Pellicci Budget p283
Petersham Nurseries Café Modern European p229
Rhodes W1 Hotels & Haute Cuisine p127
Roka Japanese p178
St Pancras Grand Brasseries p44
Saké No Hana Japanese p184
Saran Rom Thai p253
Shanghai Blues Chinese p69
Sketch: The Lecture Room Hotels & Haute Cuisine p131
Skylon Modern European p226
Trailer Happiness Bars p318
Les Trois Garçons French p98
Wapping Food Modern European p228
Yauatcha Chinese p73
Zuma Japanese p180

PICK UP SOME PRODUCE
Albion British p60
Breads Etc Cafés p292
Chez Kristof French p97
Clissold Arms Gastropubs p116
Le Comptoir Gascon French p92
Comptoir Libanais Middle Eastern p205
Fifth Floor Modern European p214
Fish Club Fish & Chips p300
FishWorks Fish p88
Franklins British p59
La Fromagerie Cafés p289
Ibérica Food & Culture Spanish p240
Kensington Place Modern European p222
Luca's Cafés p293
Manicomio Italian p172
Modern Pantry International p158
Olivomare Fish p84
Petersham Nurseries Modern European p229
Saki Japanese p177
St John, St John Bread & Wine British p52, p51
Taqueria The Americas p43
Tom's Kitchen Brasseries p47
Truc Vert Brasseries p45

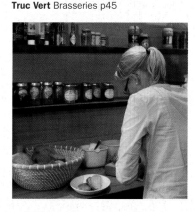

tastelondon

Enjoy 50% off at more than 800 London restaurants

Time Out has teamed up with tastelondon to bring you a fantastic one month trial – absolutely free – so that you can enjoy 50% off at more than 800 London restaurants, from popular chains such as Pizza Express and Prezzo, to establishments run by the likes of Marco Pierre White and Aldo Zilli.

Note that there's no obligation to purchase an annual tastelondon card at the end of the free period and, unlike many other free trials, you won't be asked to hand over your bank details.

Simply show your free one-month tastelondon card at any of the restaurants included in their portfolio (some need booking ahead) and receive **50% OFF** the total food bill (not drinks). You can order anything from the main à la carte selection and use your card as many times as you wish. After your free trial has run out, you will be offered the opportunity to join tastelondon at the preferential annual rate of £49.95 (RRP £69.95).

To take advantage of this great offer, visit www.timeout.com/tastelondon.

Restaurants include:

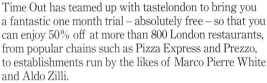

Admiralty | Almeida | Awana | Bam-Bou | Bincho Soho | Café Spice Namaste | Champor-Champor | The Farm | Gay Hussar | Haozhan | Iberica | Imli | Iznik | Malmaison | Mango Tree | Noura | One-O-One | Patterson's | Pizza Express | Prezzo | Prince Albert | Real Greek | Rivington Grill | Tentazioni | Thai Square | Villandry

Restaurants

African

Although establishments from Nigeria, Ethiopia and Eritrea still dominate, the African restaurant scene is starting to become more reflective of the diverse communities from that continent that call London home. This year we welcome **Jambo**, a Ugandan restaurant whose humble exterior belies its culinary prowess; the **Village**, a popular Somali restaurant in Hammersmith; Eritrean café **Kitfo House**; and two new Nigerian restaurants – the glamorous **Iroko** on Brixton Hill and the upmarket shebeen that is Cricklewood's **D'Den**. North African restaurants have their own chapter (see pp230-232), as do the African-influenced Caribbean venues (pp61-63). South African restaurant **Chakalaka** can be found in the Global section (pp117-120).

The bar-club-restaurant Double Club caused a flurry of excitement when it opened in November 2008, fusing Congolese food with French in an art-installation venue in Islington. It was an instant hit, but, sadly, was only a temporary venture and closed in July 2009.

almost unreasonably good value. Our selections of spring lamb served with a special pilau rice, and lamb stew with okra and onions, were two of the more conservative options. The four-page menu (a whole page of which is dedicated to 'Abyssinian' cuisine) offers innards in spiced butter, among other delicacies. Customers are a blend of young, urban expats, veiled women of various nationalities sipping on refreshing lemon milkshakes (like a creamy freshly squeezed lemonade), and single men enjoying the hearty cooking of home. Service is languid, the decor a kitsch collage of Eritrean landscapes and London skylines, and there's no drinks licence (but many non-alcoholic options). Still, at such prices these are minor grumbles. *Babies and children welcome: high chairs. Tables outdoors (2, pavement). Takeaway service. Vegetarian menu.* **Map 20 B1.**

Westbourne Park

★ ★ Mosob

339 Harrow Road, W9 3RB (7266 2012, www.mosob.co.uk). Westbourne Park tube. **Meals served** 6pm-midnight Mon-Fri; 3pm-midnight Sat, Sun. **Main courses** £7-£11. **Set meal** £12.50 per person (minimum 4), £14 per person (minimum 2). **Credit** AmEx, MC, V. Eritrean
There are plenty of reasons why Mosob is one of the best family-run restaurants in town, as its cosmopolitan clientele can attest. The genuinely warm welcome bestowed on every customer (even first-timers) makes you feel like you're visiting long lost friends. The food – traditional Eritrean home

West

Hammersmith

★ The Village NEW
95 Fulham Palace Road, W6 8JA (8741 7453). Hammersmith tube. **Meals served** 11.30am-11.30pm daily. **Main courses** £7-£8. **Set lunch** £5. **Credit** MC, V. Somali
While London boasts a number of Somali restaurants, most are known only to expats and dotted across the capital's outer suburbs. Set at the Hammersmith end of Fulham Palace Road, the Village is not only one of the most readily accessible Somali venues, but much of its Italian-influenced halal cuisine will be familiar to newcomers – even though the European staples (various meat and fish fillets, linguine and ravioli dishes) have been given a unique Somali twist. We didn't book, so had a 45-minute wait for a table, during which we made our way through a complimentary pitcher of lime cordial. The intimate basement restaurant looks none too dissimilar to an upmarket working men's club. Bowdo ari iyo soor (braised lamb shank with creamed maize) was delicious, although chicken mufo was only saved from culinary banality by the soft and delicately herbed Somali bread that accompanied it. The Village was packed with sophisticated Somalis of all ages, and service was as friendly and efficient as you'd expect in a full restaurant with only three waiting staff. Still, you'll get a good insight into Somali food and culture here. *Available for hire. Babies and children admitted. Takeaway service.* **Map 20 C5.**

Shepherd's Bush

★ Red Sea
382 Uxbridge Road, W12 7LL (8749 6888). Shepherd's Bush Market tube. **Meals served** 11am-11pm Mon-Thur, Sun; 11am-midnight Fri, Sat. **Main courses** £5-£7. **Unlicensed** no alcohol allowed. **Credit** MC, V. Pan-African
The Red Sea is one of those London secrets you almost don't want to share, lest it should shed the ramshackle appeal of its MDF tables and workman caff aesthetic for mainstream respectability. The menu offers an intriguing mix of Eritrean, Ethiopian, Somali and Yemeni cuisine, plus the odd bit of Italian (African spag bol anyone?), and the food is an eccentric delight. Here you'll find one of the broadest Horn of African choices around, at

Kitfo House

cooking, made by mum, served by son and nephew – is as good as it gets, but if you want to eat, make sure you brush up on your Eritrean knowledge. When a companion erroneously named Addis Ababa as the capital of Eritrea, we were told to name the world's 13 capitals that start and end with the same letter – then the staff would bring out the food. By the time we struggled to four, our waiter showed mercy and brought the injera, which we mopped up with richly spiced zigni (lamb stew) and hamli mis sega (green cabbage cooked with lamb, garlic and onions). Me'ss, a sweet aromatic honey wine, is the only Eritrean drink offered. Unlike other African restaurants in London, you won't find any elaborate coffee ceremonies or burning frankincense. You will, however, find a winning combination of great food and excellent service that makes Mosob well worth visiting.
Babies and children welcome: high chairs. Booking advisable. Separate room for parties, seats 22. Takeaway service. **Map 1 A4.**

South

Brixton

★ Asmara

386 Coldharbour Lane, SW9 8LF (7737 4144). Brixton tube/rail. **Dinner served** 5.30pm-midnight daily. **Main courses** £4.50-£8. **Set meals** £27 (2 people) vegetarian, £29 (2 people) meat. **Credit** MC, V. Eritrean
The 24-hour street theatre that Coldharbour Lane so ably provides feels a million miles away from Asmara's calming oasis of appetite-whetting incense and warm hellos. A small and intimate place, the restaurant features the odd traditional mosob (a woven table with low seating) alongside western dining tables, set against creamy walls bedecked with paintings of Eritrean landscapes. The food is very traditional, and we've found standards to be consistently high. We began by sampling the zelzel tibssi, in which tender pieces of spicy lamb are dipped in rich Eritrean spiced butter. This was accompanied by mounds of spongy injera – still the best in town, in our estimation. Dinner is topped off with a traditional coffee ceremony, where a waiter wafts pan-roasted coffee beans around the dining area before serving the delicious drink with warm popcorn as an accompaniment. Asmara's closing times vary depending on how busy the restaurant is, so if you get here any later than 10pm on a week night, you may find that the kitchen has closed.
Babies and children welcome: high chairs. Booking advisable. Separate room for parties, seats 35. Takeaway service. Vegetarian menu. Vegan dishes. **Map 22 E2.**

Iroko Bar & Grill NEW

226-228 Brixton Hill, SW2 1HE (07728 667820, www.irokobar.com). Brixton tube/rail/Streatham Hill rail. **Meals served** 2pm-12.30am daily. **Main courses** £6.95-£10.50. **Set meal** £10.95 2 courses incl glass of wine. **Credit** AmEx, MC, V. West African
Since opening in 2008, Iroko has brought a much-needed splash of glamour to London's African restaurant scene, with top-floor dining, a buzzy bar (with DJs) and a subterranean nightclub. The destination of choice for trendy Afropean scenesters, this purpose-built venue features large windows peering over Brixton Hill. While the view isn't quite Beverly Hills, it's elegantly complemented by interior decor of curios, wall-hangings and giant yucca plants, and outside, a fabulous black telephone box displaying photos of Iroko's fare. The well-presented menu is an extensive mix of West African classics with the odd Portuguese flourish, although the latter doesn't stretch far beyond a peri-peri chicken that required rather too much jaw-work, as did the jollof we ordered on the side. The Iroko special waakye (beans and rice served with a meat stew) was nicely seasoned, but the rice was lukewarm and hard. If only the cooking were as impressive as the decor, Iroko would be a top Double Club-esque venue for discerning, cosmopolitan Londoners. For now, it has some way to go.

Babies and children admitted. Booking advisable. Entertainment: DJs 9pm Fri-Sun. Separate room for parties, seats 100. Tables outdoors (4, pavement). Takeaway service.

Kennington

Adulis

44-46 Brixton Road, SW9 6BT (7587 0055, www.adulis.co.uk). Oval tube. **Meals served** 5pm-midnight Mon-Thur; 1pm-midnight Fri, Sun; 1pm-1.30am Sat. **Main courses** £8.45-£10.95. **Credit** MC, V. Eritrean
It might be named after an archaeological site in the Red Sea region of Eritrea, but there's nothing archaic about this place. With its contemporary, airy interior, two well-stocked bars and a nightclub/private dining space in the basement, Adulis flies the flag for modern Eritrean food and culture in London. Walls and alcoves in the two spacious dining rooms are crammed with fascinating artefacts from the mother country; diners of all hues populate the space. Start your meal with an organic Asmara beer, before moving straight to the main courses (there aren't many starters, and the mains are so big you probably won't have room anyway). The extensive menu revolves around the traditional injera (made in-house daily) and tsebhi (stew) combo, but there are other options. The ghemberi (Red Sea prawns) were succulent and delicious, served with a spicy tomato and onion sauce on a bed of rice and salad. Adulis also has an excellent range of vegetarian dishes such as shiro (spicy ground chickpeas) and azifa (spicy lentil stew). The spinach (cooked with garlic, lemon, chilli and olive oil) comes highly recommended – as does this restaurant in general.
Babies and children welcome: high chairs; nappy-changing facilities. Booking advisable. Separate room for parties, seats 150. Takeaway service. **Map 16 M13.**

Vauxhall

★ Kitfo House NEW

49 South Lambeth Road, SW8 1RH (7735 8915). Vauxhall tube/rail. **Meals served** 8.30am-11.30pm Mon-Fri; 10.30am-11pm Sat, Sun. **Main courses** £5.50-£7.95. **Credit** AmEx, MC, V. Eritrean
Named after Eritrea and Ethiopia's favourite dish of herb- and chilli-flavoured minced beef, this café produces African food in the evenings, fry-ups and Thai fare during the day. The extensive menu is made simple for novices with the inclusion of three special platters featuring several dishes served on a bubbly, tangy injera. One platter is enough for two. Choose from vegetarian or meat platters, or a mixture of the two (this last one is the largest, and also the most expensive at £20). Among the array of dishes we liked were awaze tibsi (lamb cubes marinated in hot-pepper sauce and fried in ghee), and shiro (finely ground chickpeas cooked in oil). Stay awhile to savour the coffee ceremony, where incense is wafted beneath your nose before the caffeine hits your veins. Kitfo House is a modest little place with just a few tables and some kitsch tourist art on the walls, but it clearly has aspirations. The area nearest the door has been turned into a bar; should you wish to linger, there are East African spirits amid the more usual rums, vodkas and whiskies.
Available for hire. Babies and children admitted. Disabled: toilet. Separate room for parties, seats 25. Takeaway service. Vegetarian menu. **Map 16 L13.**

South East

Peckham

805 Bar Restaurant

805 Old Kent Road, SE15 1NX (7639 0808, www.805restaurant.com). Elephant & Castle tube/rail then bus 53 bus. **Meals served** 2pm-midnight daily. **Main courses** £7-£15. **Set meal** £9-£15. **Credit** MC, V. Nigerian
It will take some doing to knock 805 off the Nigerian restaurant top spot it has occupied since opening in 2001. The Old Kent Road location may

not provide luxurious surroundings, and some venues may have more intrepid menus, but for food and atmosphere 805 is in a class of its own. Behind the inconspicuous exterior, you'll find a well-presented airy space with white walls decorated with colourful African art. Well-heeled Nigerian families and other in-the-know Londoners dine here. The restaurant boasts a simple, unchanging menu of Nigerian classics such as egusi with spinach, or efo riro – spinach stew served with meat or fish and pounded yam or eba (a staple made with gari). Full explanations come from the friendly staff. King prawns with jollof rice was spicy and plentiful, although the rice was unusually hard. Asaro was soft and tender, with a generous portion of spicy tilapia providing the perfect accompaniment in texture and taste. Service can be slow – our cocktail was ordered before the food, but came towards the end of the meal, and group orders might arrive at different times. Although not a place for a quick bite, 805 is a culinary experience to savour.
Babies and children welcome: high chairs. Disabled: toilet. Separate room for parties, seats 55. Tables outdoors (6, pavement). Takeaway service.

South Norwood

Gold Coast Bar & Restaurant

224 Portland Road, SE25 4QB (8676 1919, www.thegoldcoastbar.com). Norwood Junction rail/Woodside tramlink.
Bar **Open/snacks served** noon-midnight Mon-Thur, Sun; noon-2am Fri, Sat.
Restaurant **Dinner served** 6-10.30pm Mon-Fri. **Meals served** 1-10.30pm Sat, Sun. **Main courses** £7-£11.
Both **Credit** MC, V. Ghanaian
So popular has Gold Coast proven, owner William Quagraine has opened another restaurant in Brixton (multi-location African eateries are extremely rare in London). The upstairs dining area at the Norwood branch now only operates at weekends, but in the ground-floor gastropub, you can enjoy a full menu alongside an impressive selection of Ghanaian beers and spirits. Service lacks vitality but is very friendly. The menu features Ghanaian staples such as palm nut soup (a thick stew of okra, aubergine and dried fish served with various meat accompaniments) and hearty starch side dishes like waatse (rice and beans), jollof and banku (fermented cassava served in banana leaves). The cape malay chicken stew was a gingery and flavoursome south/west African fusion dish, spoilt only by being served lukewarm. An over-seasoned guinea fowl was tempered by a tasty tomato and onion sauce. Portions are hefty. Given the popularity of its big-screen TV with football fans, the pub probably isn't the place to go for a quiet meal, but for a lively dose of Ghanaian food and hospitality, Gold Coast hits the spot.
Available for hire. Babies and children welcome: high chairs (restaurant). Entertainment: DJs 8.30pm-2am Fri, Sat. Separate room for parties, seats 15-80. Tables outdoors (7, patio). Takeaway service. **For branch see index.**

North East

Tottenham

★ ★ Jambo NEW

127 High Cross Road, N17 9NR (8885 5738). Tottenham Hale tube/rail. **Meals served** 2-10.30pm Mon, Tue, Thur-Sun. **Main courses** £6-£9. **Set meal** £9. **Credit** MC, V. Ugandan
In the middle of a Tottenham council estate, miles from the magic wand of regeneration, lies an undiscovered culinary gem. Family-owned, with space for around 30 diners, Jambo might look like a converted day centre (albeit one with bamboo chairs and African art), but it serves top-notch Ugandan food. The name means 'hello' in Swahili and the atmosphere is warm and friendly. After an informative talk through the menu by our waitress/host, we started with the kebab: tender meat wrapped in buttery Indian-style parathas (Ugandan cuisine fuses Indian and East African

cooking) and served with tangy tomato salsa called kachumbari. For mains, the 'variety meal' of three hearty relishes (stews or vegetables) and two starch staples provides an excellent introduction to Ugandan cooking. The beef, ground-nut stew and spinach were perfectly accompanied by lumonde (fluffy Ugandan sweet potatoes) and kalo, a thick millet porridge that's as tasty as it is nutritious. We've heard the nyama choma (roast meat, in this case goat) is as good as any you'll find in Kampala. There's also an impressive selection of Ugandan beers (including Tusker lager) and soft drinks. Visit at the weekend and you can follow your meal with a night of music and dancing at the Ugandan nightclub around the corner.
Available for hire. Babies and children welcome: crayons; high chairs. Booking advisable weekends. Separate room for parties, seats 12. Takeaway service.

North
Kentish Town

Queen of Sheba
12 Fortress Road, NW5 2EU (7284 3947, www.thequeenofsheba.co.uk). Kentish Town tube/rail. **Meals served** 1-11.30pm Mon-Sat; 1-10.30pm Sun. **Main courses** £5-£10.50. **Set meal** £28 (2-3 people). **Credit** MC, V. Ethiopian
Like its namesake of biblical legend, the Queen of Sheba is one of the capital's most regal Ethiopian eateries. Diners are greeted with the smell of incense and some of the most dazzling waiting staff around – two glamozons with afros, who look like they should be doing backing vocals for Prince rather than serving up wots in north London. The walls are tastefully decorated in chocolate and hazelnut hues. Tables are tightly packed, but the mood is buzzy and the service friendly. A

cosmopolitan mix of local regulars, Ethiopian cuisine first-timers and the odd expat is attracted. After looking through the menu, which features a page each of starters, lamb, beef, chicken, vegetarian and house specials, we settled on yeb alich'a wot (tender lamb with ginger, onion and Ethiopian spiced butter) and qwant'a firfir (pieces of grilled lean beef, which tasted like dried meat, cooked in Ethiopian butter with a creamy red-pepper sauce). As tradition demands, the stews are heaped upon fresh injera to be shared in a manner that is as leisurely as the service. Ethiopian beers and coffees are on the drinks list.
Available for hire. Babies and children welcome: high chairs. Booking advisable Fri, Sat. Tables outdoors (2, patio). Takeaway service. Vegetarian menu. Vegan dishes. **Map 26 B4.**

Tufnell Park

Lalibela
137 Fortress Road, NW5 2HR (7284 0600). Tufnell Park tube/134 bus. **Dinner served** 6pm-midnight daily. **Main courses** £8.50-£9.95. **Credit** MC, V. Ethiopian
With its mix of western seating and traditional low-level wooden table arrangements, Lalibela – named after a UNESCO World Heritage site in northern Ethiopia – provides a great introduction to Ethiopian cuisine and culture in London. The restaurant is a long-standing favourite with expats and locals. Its heavily decorated walls are almost as ornate as the coffee ceremony available at the end of your meal. Although starters are listed, the size and choice of mains makes them easy to bypass. As well as traditional stews (wots) and sautéed meat and fish dishes (tibs), Lalibela also serves a number of house specialities. Tilapia marinated in rosemary and lemon and cooked with peppers, onion, garlic and tomato complemented the alicha wot (creamy split peas cooked in ginger,

onion and garlic) in texture and flavour. All dishes come with heaps of freshly made injera. If you're in a group, be prepared to share your food from one plate, the traditional Ethiopian way, as dishes are spooned directly on to the sourdough pancakes to be eaten with your hands. Service can be a little too relaxed, but the food makes up for it.
Babies and children welcome: high chairs. Booking advisable. Takeaway service. Vegetarian menu. Vegan dishes. **Map 26 B3.**

North West
Kilburn

D'Den **NEW**
47 Cricklewood Broadway, NW2 3JX (8830 5000). Kilburn tube/Cricklewood rail. **Meals served** noon-3am Mon-Thur; noon-6am Fri, Sat; 1pm-4am Sun. **Main courses** £10-£25. **No credit cards.** Nigerian
Simmering at the centre of the cultural melting pot that is Cricklewood Broadway, D'Den is a remarkably inconspicuous Nigerian restaurant. Were it not for the steady stream of well-dressed African men lighting up outside, you wouldn't even know it existed. Inside, this isn't the glitziest of establishments; tables fill a narrow space decked with chintzy Africana, giving it the feel of a slightly upmarket shebeen. Nevertheless, something keeps the punters – everyone from Joe Public to Premiership footballers and visiting dignitaries – returning for more. The food is solid Nigerian fare, and the menu is one of the most extensive around, with delicacies such as abodi (cow intestine stew) and more traditional favourites such as okra soup. There's a late licence (the place is open until 6am at weekends), and live football matches are screened, making D'Den popular with a lively expat crowd. Our asaro came with a portion of tilapia so big it could easily have fed two, while a dish of beans, rice and plantain was far tastier than its humble title suggests. This was complemented by a spicy goat stew that was crying out to be accompanied by a cold, strong Nigerian Guinness.
Available for hire. Babies and children welcome: high chairs. Booking advisable weekends. Takeaway service.

Outer London
Edgware, Middlesex

Biazo
307 Hale Lane, HA8 7AX (8958 8826, www.biazo.co.uk). Edgware tube. **Meals served** noon-11pm Tue-Fri; 1-11pm Sat; 1-10pm Sun. **Main courses** £3.50-£14.50. **Set lunch** (1-4pm Sun) £13.95 2 courses. **Credit** MC, V. Nigerian
Biazo is certainly one of the best-looking African restaurants in town, with its sharp African minimalist interior in hues of mahogany and cream. Diners are given a warm welcome from the attentive waiting staff, who are poised to guide you through their large menu of contemporary Nigerian food. Shame then that we were denied the opportunity to explore it. Despite phoning to check the restaurant was open, we weren't informed that Sundays is buffet only, and that the restaurant was closing at 5pm, not 10pm as advertised on the website. But at £13.95 for as much as you can eat, the buffet is a great way of sampling a variety of Nigerian food. Jollof and seafood rice dishes and pounded yam featured among the slim but tasty selection of stews and side dishes. The chicken and beef stews had a delicate palm-oil base and were lightly spiced. With the accompanying diced plantain, adalu (creamed beans with sweetcorn) and egusi with bitter leaf, they made for a satisfying, if slightly tepid meal. The restaurant has recently begun serving alcohol (South African wines, Kenyan and Nigerian beers) but the chilled ambience and wide range of soft drinks still makes this a great place for families. Given a little more attention to detail, Biazo could really hit the spot.
Babies and children welcome: high chairs; nappy-changing facilities. Booking advisable weekends. Disabled: toilet. Takeaway service; delivery service (over £20, within 3-mile radius).

Menu

Accra or **akara**: bean fritters.
Aloco: fried plantain with hot tomato sauce.
Asaro: yam and sweet potato porridge.
Ayeb or **iab**: fresh yoghurt cheese made from strained yoghurt.
Berbere: an Ethiopian spice mix made with many hot and aromatic spices.
Cassava, **manioc** or **yuca**: a family of coarse roots that are boiled and pounded to make bread and various other farinaceous dishes. There are bitter and sweet varieties (note that the bitter variety is poisonous until cooked).
Egusi: ground melon seeds, added to stews and soups as a thickening agent.
Froi: fish and shrimp aubergine stew.
Fufu: a stiff pudding of maize or cassava (qv) flour, or pounded yam (qv).
Gari: a solid, heavy pudding made from ground fermented cassava (qv), served with thick soups.
Ground rice: a kind of stiff rice pudding served to accompany soup.
injera, **enjera** or **enjerra**: a soft, spongy Ethiopian and Eritrean flatbread made with teff/tef (a grain originally from Ethiopia), wheat, barley, oats or cornmeal. Fermented with yeast, it should have a distinct sour tang.
Jollof rice: like a hot, spicy risotto, with tomatoes, onions and (usually) chicken.
Kanyah: a sweet snack from Sierra Leone made of rice, peanuts and sugar.
Kelewele or **do-do**: fried plantain.
Kenkey: a starchy pudding that's prepared by pounding dried maize and

water into a paste, then steaming inside plantain leaves. Usually eaten with meat, fish or vegetable stews.
Moi-moi, **moin-moin** or **moyin moyin**: steamed beancake, served with meat or fish.
Ogbono: a large seed similar to egusi (qv). Although it doesn't thicken as much, it is used in a similar way.
Pepper soup: a light, peppery soup made with either fish or meat.
Shito: a dark red-hot pepper paste from Ghana, made from dried shrimps blended with onions and tomatoes.
Suya: a spicy Nigerian meat kebab.
Teff or **tef**: an indigenous gluten-free Ethiopian grain used for making the injera flatbread (qv).
Tuo or **tuwo**: a stiff rice pudding, sometimes served as rice balls to accompany soup.
Ugali: a Swahili word for bread made from cornmeal and water.
Ugba: Nigerian soy beans; also called oil beans.
Waakye: a dish of rice and black-eyed beans mixed with meat or chicken in gravy.
Waatse: rice and black-eyed beans cooked together.
Wot or **we'ts**: a thick, dark sauce made from slowly cooked onions, garlic, butter and spices – an essential component in the aromatic stews of East Africa. **Doro wot**, a stew containing chicken and hard-boiled eggs, is a particularly common dish (qv).

The Americas

NORTH AMERICAN

Londoners' appreciation of a good sirloin seems to have been clocked by international operators. This year has seen the arrival of two upmarket New York-style steakhouses, Mayfair's **Goodman** and **Palm** in Knightsbridge (as well as a clutch of Argentinian openings – see p37). However, neither is better in our view than Brit-owned **Hawksmoor**, which continues to thrill diners in Spitalfields with meat sourced from North Yorkshire. But steak is not all we love from the US of A and in this section you will find the best of the capital's American-themed eateries, from places where you can get a burger and cheese-doused fries, to the carefully produced barbecued ribs and pulled pork of **Bodean's**. Still, as Tom Conran of ever-popular Notting Hill hangout **Lucky 7**, interviewed on p37, suggests, there is great opportunity for more authentic and more diverse North American cooking styles in London.

Central

Belgravia

Palm NEW

1 Pont Street, SW1X 9EJ (7201 0710, www.the palm.com/london). Knightsbridge or Sloane Square tube. **Lunch served** noon-2.30pm, **dinner served** 6-11pm Mon-Fri. **Meals served** noon-11pm Sat; noon-9pm Sun. **Main courses** £11.50-£49. **Set lunch** £15 2 courses. **Credit** AmEx, DC, MC, V.
High-profile Palm is basically an upmarket version of a classic US steakhouse. But while steakhouses are generally affordable and unpretentious, Palm is neither of these. Part of an American chain, this outpost is intended to evoke New York high society in the 1920s, with its caricatures of 'celebrity' customers on the walls, plus classic fixtures and fittings. Starters (lobster bisque, jumbo shrimp cocktail, mixed salad) are joined by a selection of larger salads and sandwiches – possibly the only way to eat at Palm and not spend a fortune. But of course the steak's the thing. And USDA prime beef is what it's all about. A seven-ounce filet mignon comes in at £31; a ten-ounce fillet is £39; vegetables are extra and none are cheaper than £7. For a little less, some 'British selections' are available. Does perfect cooking justify the prices? On a recent visit, our fillet, requested medium rare (very pink in the centre, very brown towards the edges) was actually cooked 'medium well'. In brief: of most appeal to wealthy but unadventurous eaters.
Babies and children welcome: booster seats; high chairs. Booking advisable. Disabled: toilet. Separate room for parties, seats 40. **Map 15 G10**.

City

Green Door Bar & Grill

33 Cornhill, EC3 V3ND (7929 1378, www.green doorsteakhouse.co.uk). Bank tube/DLR. **Meals served** 11.30am-11pm Mon-Fri. **Main courses** £9-£30. **Credit** AmEx, DC, MC, V.
This City archetype opened relatively recently in a grand old Cornhill building formerly occupied by late, lamented wine retailer Lay & Wheeler (swallowed up by Majestic in 2009 after some 150 years in operation) and, before that, a bank. Set against the recession, Green Door appears to come from a different era entirely. The centrepiece is the imposing, handsome oyster bar, straight out of the ostentatious 1980s; behind it sits the main

restaurant space, done out with dark woods (and not quite as expensively as it'd like to appear). The menu, like the decor, is stereotypical City – heavy on the meat, light on imagination – and the kitchen doesn't do much to bring it alive. A crab-cake starter was generous (three of them, battered, for £5.95), but not especially impressive; our other choice, slices of smoked duck, was stronger on flavour than texture. To follow, fillet steak, ordered and cooked medium rare, was sound; less so the rack of lamb, its pinkishness eradicated by overcooking. Flamboyant destination restaurants such as this can feel pretty forlorn when they're empty; perhaps lunchtimes are busier than the quiet evening we experienced.
Available for hire. Babies and children admitted. Booking advisable. Disabled: toilet. **Map 12 Q6**.
For branch see index.

★ Hawksmoor (100)

157 Commercial Street, E1 6BJ (7247 7392, www.thehawksmoor.com). Liverpool Street tube/rail. **Lunch served** noon-2.30pm Mon-Fri. **Dinner served** 6-11pm Mon-Sat. **Main courses** £16-£26. **Credit** AmEx, MC, V.
The raison d'être of Hawksmoor – found behind an anonymous door in a drab building on an unappealing road – is obvious from a glance at the menu. Partly from what's featured on it, of course, but also from what isn't; the sole vegetarian dish is listed, with entertaining reluctance, simply as 'vegetarian'. Hawksmoor's thing is meat: in particular, steaks, savvily sourced from the Ginger Pig and cooked by kitchen staff who know the value of great ingredients and understand that you sometimes don't need to do much to them. On our most recent visit, we judged the ribeye to be just ahead of the bone-in sirloin, but both were tremendous. Diners with big appetites should check the board for the available sizes of the shareable chateaubriand and prime rib cuts. There's more meat on the list of starters, with the Tamworth pork ribs a highlight, but you'll do just as well with a lively, summery prawn cocktail. Chocolate fudge sundae makes a suitably decadent finish. The only letdown is the dull room, handicapped by low ceilings and a lack of natural light. Otherwise, from the excellent cocktails to the note-perfect staff, this remains a terrific operation.
Babies and children welcome: high chairs. Booking advisable. Separate room for parties, seats 12. Takeaway service. **Map 6 R5**.

Clerkenwell & Farringdon

Dollar Grills & Martinis

2 Exmouth Market, EC1R 4PX (7278 0077, www.dollargrillsandmartinis.com). Farringdon tube/rail/19, 38, 341 bus.
Bar **Open** 6pm-1am Tue-Sat. **Main courses** £6.50-£11.95.
Restaurant **Lunch served** noon-5pm daily. **Dinner served** 6-11pm Mon-Sat; 6-10pm Sun. **Main courses** £9.95-£31.50. **Credit** AmEx, MC, V.
Londoners with long memories will remember this place as the Penny Black, an unvarnished working-class corner pub of the type that is disappearing all over town. This one bit the dust a few years ago; since its refurbishment, which saw the owners of Beach Blanket Babylon put a restaurant on the ground floor and a cocktail bar downstairs, it has drawn bright young Clerkenwellians in search of a little more metropolitan sophistication than they might expect at the area's earthier gastropubs. Glossing over the distracting and infuriatingly pointless addition of a plasma-screen TV on one wall, the decor – low lights, exposed brick – is holding up pretty well. And while neither the food nor the cocktails are scintillating, they're as good as they need to be, delivered efficiently by smiling staff. The highlights, by a distance, are the steaks and burgers: rich, hearty and cooked with precision by an ever-busy kitchen. Other mains are less impressive (a forgettable dish of chicken breast with peperonata, for instance); and, of the starters, all but the soup failed to live up to the expectations raised by the slightly elevated prices.
Babies and children admitted. Booking advisable weekends. Entertainment: DJs 8pm Fri, Sat. Tables outdoors (10, pavement). Takeaway service. **Map 5 N4**.

Covent Garden

Christopher's

18 Wellington Street, WC2E 7DD (7240 4222, www.christophersgrill.com). Covent Garden tube.
Bar **Open/snacks served** noon-midnight Mon-Fri; 11.30am-midnight Sat; 11.30am-10.30pm Sun.
Restaurant **Brunch served** 11.30am-3.30pm Sat, Sun. **Lunch served** noon-3pm Mon-Fri. **Dinner served** 5-11.30pm Mon-Sat; 5-10.30pm Sun. **Main courses** £14-£34. **Set brunch** £15.25 2 courses, £18 3 courses. **Set meal** (5-7pm, 10-11pm Mon-Sat) £14.50 2 courses, £17 3 courses.
Both **Credit** AmEx, DC, MC, V.
Backed by a blaze of positive publicity, Christopher's eased through the early 1990s recession, dazzling diners with its grand location and a cultured take on North American food that was both enticing and exotic. Nearly two decades later, the building remains a treat. Above the handsome ground-floor cocktail bar, a sweeping staircase leads to a crisp, clean dining room. But the cooking is almost diffident, coasting on a reputation that the restaurant no longer deserves. Our starters (salmon carpaccio, creamy pumpkin risotto) were pretty fair: nothing great, but nothing shocking either. The mains, though, were ordinary at best, with prices ranging from steep (£22 for an adequate but forgettable rump steak and a side of rather sorry chips) to very steep (£19 for a not especially fresh sea bass fillet, pan-seared and served with squid and cannellini bean ragout). The pricey wine list (virtually nothing below £20) and dear desserts (£7.25 for the likes of cheesecake and sticky toffee pudding) add further financial injury to insult. Service was fine, but with four waitresses covering a mere six occupied tables on the night of our visit, we'd have been disappointed if it had been anything but. This needs an overhaul, and soon.
Available for hire. Babies and children welcome: children's menu; high chairs. Separate room for parties, seats 40. **Map 18 F4**.

Joe Allen

13 Exeter Street, WC2E 7DT (7836 0651, www.joeallen.co.uk). Covent Garden tube. **Breakfast served** 8-11.30am Mon-Fri. **Brunch served** 11.30am-4pm Sat, Sun.

Meals served noon-12.30am Mon-Fri; 11.30am-12.30am Sat; 11.30am-11.30pm Sun. **Main courses** £8-£19.50. **Set brunch** £18.50 2 courses, £20.50 3 courses incl drink. **Set meal** (noon-3pm Mon-Fri, 5-6.45pm Mon-Sat) £15 2 courses, £17 3 courses. **Credit** AmEx, MC, V.
This dim basement room in the heart of Theatreland isn't the ideal place for a meal on a sunny summer's day, but its after-dark ambience is hard to beat. The bare-brick walls are all but obscured by posters, signed photographs and other theatrical ephemera. Actors have long favoured the place as a post-show hangout, and a few still head here after their curtains have fallen. The cannily arranged seating – the chairs along the walls are tilted towards the main floor, as if stage-side at a theatre in the round – further adds to the spectacle, in a room that comes as close as any in London to replicating the atmosphere of an old-school New York brasserie. The unsubtle comfort cooking is unlikely to win any awards, but won't disappoint if you avoid anything that sounds over-ambitious. Highlights included tender slow-roasted pork, edged with crisp crackling. Less successful was a dish of barbecue ribs, over-caked in sauce and served with a rather forlorn corn muffin. As ever, service was swift, helpful and, with both men and women clad in classic white-shirt-black-tie combos, impeccably dressed.
Babies and children welcome: booster seats; high chairs. Booking advisable. Entertainment: pianist 9pm-1am Mon-Sat. Takeaway service. **Map 18 E4**.

Sophie's Steakhouse & Bar
29-31 Wellington Street, WC2E 7DB (7836 8836, www.sophiessteakhouse.com). Covent Garden tube. **Meals served** noon-12.45am Mon-Fri; 11am-12.45am Sat; 11am-11pm Sun. **Main courses** £9.95-£34.95. **Set lunch** £12.50 2 courses. **Credit** AmEx, MC, V.
The Sophie in question is Sophie Mogford, who cut her teeth at Smollensky's and the Conran Group before joining forces with Rupert Power and setting up Sophie's seven years ago. The duo's time with their previous employers is much in evidence at the original branch in Chelsea (still open): a polite, faintly provincial and entirely professional British take on a New York steakhouse. However, their Conran-inspired showiness is really to the fore at this enormous Covent Garden offshoot, which takes the original's mock-warehouse motifs (exposed pipes, brick walls, high ceilings) and amplifies them for a brasher central London crowd. Given the new location, the food is about as good as it needs to be. The fairly priced menu is careful not to ruffle any feathers. From the list of uncomplicated and over-familiar starters (so-so calamares, tired caesar salad, dull chicken liver

pâté) to the string of tried-and-tested desserts (cheesecake, brownies, lemon meringue pie), surprises are conspicuous by their absence. So too is inspiration. The steaks are fine, as they should be, and the service is unfailingly impressive, but little else will linger long in the memory.
Babies and children welcome: children's menu; high chairs; nappy-changing facilities. Bookings not accepted. Disabled: toilet. **Map 18 E4**.
For branch see index.

Fitzrovia

Eagle Bar Diner
3-5 Rathbone Place, W1T 1HJ (7637 1418, www.eaglebardiner.com). Tottenham Court Road tube. **Open** noon-11pm Mon-Wed; noon-1am Thur, Fri; 10am-1am Sat; 11am-6pm Sun. **Main courses** £5.95-£14.50. **Credit** MC, V.
Having served its millionth burger in 2009, the Eagle Bar Diner is now very much a Fitzrovian fixture. It attracts lunching locals with time for something more interesting than a deskbound Pret, but a disinclination for the wallet-busting involved in a three-course feed at nearby Pied à Terre. The name offers a clue as to its double life. After work, the music gets louder (there are DJs several nights a week) and the room draws at least as many drinkers as eaters. But during the day, it's more of a diner, delivering ersatz American comfort cooking in surprisingly quiet and pleasingly kitsch-free surroundings. The cooking is a bit spotty, but you'll be fine if you choose with care. The breakfasts are decent, as are the burgers made with beef; the milkshakes and malts also stand out from the crowd. On the downside, the non-beef burgers – made in combinations such as lamb, beetroot and a fried egg (the Kiwi) – are less successful, and the ribs will probably just make Americans homesick for proper barbecue. Drinks include well-made cocktails and American beers; service is a little forgetful, but will get there in the end.
Babies and children welcome (until 9pm if dining): children's menu. Booking advisable weekends. Disabled: toilet. Entertainment: DJs 7.30pm Wed-Sat. Takeaway service. **Map 17 B2**.

Leicester Square

Planet Hollywood
57-60 Haymarket, SW1Y 4QX (7437 7639, www.planethollywoodlondon.com). Leicester Square tube. **Meals served** 11am-1am daily. **Main courses** £10.45-£21.95. **Credit** AmEx, DC, MC, V.
Zooming from a high-profile 1991 launch and subsequent overzealous expansion, to the American bankruptcy protection courts (twice), the Planet

Hollywood chain has led a rollercoaster existence. Indeed, it's something of a surprise to find that it's still going, much less that it moved to a new room on the Haymarket in June 2009. The old space was hardly attractive, but the cinematic ephemera and knowingly brash ambience did combine to lend it a certain kitsch quality. This new room, though, decorated but not quite designed, is blandness personified, bafflingly devoid of glamour and charisma. There's still movie memorabilia, but apparently less of it, and much of what remains is pretty low grade; it seemed appropriate that we were watched during our lunch by a life-size cut-out of George Lazenby. The food's decent at best (sparky shrimp fajitas) and poor at worst (artificial-tasting milkshakes, dry burgers), with prices reflecting a sense of prestige that's conspicuous by its absence. The chirpy young staff do their best, but they're being asked to star in a sequel with all the box-office appeal of *Arthur 2: On the Rocks*.
Babies and children welcome: children's menu; crayons; high chairs; nappy-changing facilities. Booking advisable. Disabled: toilet. Entertainment: DJs Mon-Fri dinner; all day Sat, Sun, school holidays. **Map 17 B5**.

Mayfair

Automat
33 Dover Street, W1S 4NF (7499 3033, www.automat-london.com). Green Park tube. **Breakfast served** 7-11am Mon-Fri. **Meals served** noon-midnight Mon-Fri; 11am-midnight Sat; 11am-10pm Sun. **Main courses** £13-£26. **Credit** AmEx, MC, V.
'Recession? What recession?' was the message emanating from Automat this summer, and most particularly from the financially belligerent diners who continue to flood this still-fashionable Mayfair success story. The long premises are split into three distinct spaces: an unmemorable café-type room at the front; a handsome, quiet middle section designed to resemble a railway carriage (Pullman, not Transport for London); and the main space, a brash attempt at aping New York brasserie culture (white tiles, battered wood, deafening echo). The food is American comfort cooking, rendered competently, delivered swiftly and priced ridiculously. Highlights include a suitably gloopy if slightly under-salted macaroni and cheese, and decent ribeye steak; marks off for the apple pie, which tasted as if it had been microwaved. It's all devoured by a clientele that, on our visit, was a virtual library of Mayfair stereotypes: two unnaturally blonde debutantes leaving half their salads before ordering lattes with skimmed milk; various 40-plus financiers wearing well-pressed open-neck shirts and expensive haircuts; and, in the corner, Lily Allen. Neither the restaurant nor its prices will be to everyone's taste, but Automat succeeds on its own terms.
Booking advisable. Children admitted. Disabled: toilet. Takeaway service. **Map 9 H7**.

Goodman NEW
26 Maddox Street, W1S 1HQ (7499 3776, www.goodmanrestaurants.com). Oxford Circus tube. **Meals served** noon-11pm Mon-Sat. **Main courses** £14-£65. **Set lunch** £13 2 courses, £15 3 courses. **Credit** AmEx, DC, MC, V.
'Bringing the New York steakhouse to London.' Not the most original brief, but this (Russian-owned) newcomer has a decent stab at bringing Manhattan to Mayfair: dark-wood panelling, inviting leather booths, a bar counter running the length of the restaurant, and staff so chatty and involved in your order they practically sit down to eat with you. (Our waiter gave us a five-minute wine discourse, talking through the choice of 20-odd on the red-heavy list.) If the server did up a seat, you wouldn't be happy to share the excellent steak – be it a 250g fillet, superbly rich and tender, or a less subtle 400g 'Goodman ribeye' from the US, rippled with delicious golden fat. We used the chips, thick and salty, to soak up excess juices from the meat; the classic American side dish, creamed spinach, made an excellent further accompaniment, softening the strong flavours. If a starter of rocket

The Diner. See p37.

salad with pine nuts and roasted tomatoes was forgettable, it was our fault for ordering boringly; likewise an apple tart for dessert – we wanted to concentrate on the top-quality meat for mains. Is Goodman a bit of NY in LON? Pretty close.
Babies and children welcome. Booking advisable. Disabled: toilet. Separate room for parties, seats 25. Tables outdoors (2, pavement). Takeaway service. **Map 9 J6.**

Hard Rock Café
150 Old Park Lane, W1K 1QZ (7629 0382, www.hardrock.com). Green Park or Hyde Park Corner tube. **Meals served** 11.30am-12.30am Mon-Thur, Sun; 11am-1am Fri, Sat. **Main courses** £9.95-£15.95. **Credit** AmEx, MC, V.
The music industry is collapsing, brought to its knees by arrogance, mismanagement and a profound failure to deal with 21st-century challenges. But stepping through the doors of the Hard Rock Café, you'd think the old business was in the rudest of health. You'd also think it was 1983: the walls are lined with gold records (remember records?); videos by A Flock of Seagulls and Billy Joel play without irony on myriad TV screens; and glass-fronted cabinets proudly display such consecrated treasures as a bass guitar once cradled by Felix Pappalardi of Mountain. Only the prices bring you back to the future: £13.25 for a burger and chips might not seem too bad if you're on holiday and unfamiliar with the value of sterling, but the relative absence of British accents tells its own story. The food is exactly as you might expect: garish cocktails; chicken wings coated in orange sauce of indeterminate origin; mammoth plates of nachos; and burgers, which are actually pretty good. The relentlessly enthusiastic staff aren't shy about directing you to the shop over the road, where yet more rock relics sit alongside dazzlingly expensive T-shirts and other take-home ephemera.
Available for hire. Babies and children welcome: children's menu; crayons; high chairs; nappy-changing facilities. Bookings not accepted. Disabled: toilet. Entertainment: monthly live music events, call for details. **Map 9 H8.**

Maze Grill
10-13 Grosvenor Square, W1K 6JP (7495 2211, www.gordonramsay.com/mazegrill). Bond Street tube. **Breakfast served** 7am-10.30am, **dinner served** 6-10.30pm daily. **Lunch served** noon-3pm Mon-Fri; noon-4pm Sat, Sun. **Main courses** £13.50-£28. **Set lunch** £15 2 courses, £18 3 courses. **Credit** AmEx, DC, MC, V.
Gordon Ramsay's Maze Grill is housed in a branch of the bland Marriott hotel chain, which might explain the dreary, deliberate anonymity of the decor. Without the views on to Grosvenor Square, you could be anywhere in the world. By contrast, the pricey menu is grounded in two countries: Britain, which provides several highlight ingredients, and the US, with New York steakhouses serving as an inspiration for Ramsay and executive chef Jason Atherton (though you wouldn't know it from the sterile atmosphere). The menu is headlined by steaks: five varieties, working up from the comparatively affordable Casterbridge meat to outlandishly expensive wagyu cuts. We chose the 25-day-aged Herefordshire beef; arriving with ceremony on a chunky wooden board, our bone-in ribeye cut was thick, rich and basically flawless. The Casterbridge meat provided the filling for the burger, over-salted but nonetheless decent. The kitchen excels elsewhere too, especially with the Spanish-influenced small plates: three of them make a worthy starter for two diners, with the best being a pungent 'pigs on toast'. Our main grumble was with the service, which lurched uncomfortably from over-rehearsed to faintly sniffy. Perhaps hotel guests get treated a little better.
Babies and children welcome: high chairs. Booking essential. Disabled: disabled toilet. **Map 9 G6.**

Soho

★ Bodean's
10 Poland Street, W1F 8PZ (7287 7575, www.bodeansbbq.com). Oxford Circus or Piccadilly Circus tube. **Lunch served** noon-3pm,

dinner served 5.30-11pm Mon-Fri. **Meals served** noon-11pm Sat; noon-10.30pm Sun. **Main courses** £8-£16. **Credit** AmEx, MC, V.
Although this barbecue chain now has five branches around town, the two-floor Soho original remains our favourite. The location and the clientele combine to make it feel urban rather than faintly provincial (as is the case, for instance, at the Fulham incarnation). The food is still good too; despite the showier efforts of the dismal Chicago Rib Shack in Knightsbridge, this is definitely the best barbecue in town. However, there were a few signs this year that the kitchen could use a nudge. The chicken was great and the ribs were decent, but the pulled pork, usually a standout, was noticeably soggier than on previous visits. At the Soho branch, the menu is longer in the cosy basement Rib Room, with steaks and more starters. But the best buys, the pork or beef sandwiches served with crisp fries, are only available in the plainer ground-floor 'deli', where service is speedy and American sports play on big-screen TVs. Burnt ends (tasty beef trimmings) are offered just two nights a week, but they're worth the diversion. Less so the drinks list, with the absence of worthwhile American beers both an oversight and an irritation.
Available for hire. Babies and children welcome: children's menu; high-chairs; nappy-changing facilities. Booking advisable. Tables outdoors (10, pavement). Takeaway service. **Map 17 A3.**
For branches see index.

★ Ed's Easy Diner
12 Moor Street, W1V 5LH (7434 4439, www.edseasydiner.co.uk). Leicester Square or Tottenham Court Road tube. **Meals served** noon-midnight daily. **Main courses** £4.95-£7.95. **Minimum** £4.95. **Credit** MC, V.
It's 10.30pm on a Thursday, and Elvis croons 'In the Ghetto' from Ed's chrome jukebox. In homage to the King we perch on a red vinyl bar stool and order a peanut butter shake, a 'Big Bubba' burger (with bacon and cheese) and 'Atomic' fries, which come with five dips (chilli, melted cheese, sweet onion relish, guacamole and cream cheese). Girls in cowboy hats kissing lager-boys in suits – the flotsam and jetsam of the Soho night – ebb and flow through the brightly lit little diner: a post-*Grease*, 1987 take on the 1950s. Behind the circular bar, cheery staff dole out dogs, burgers, fried chicken, chilli and even the occasional salad. It's good fun, but food is pretty average: our chips and burger were dryish, with the cheese, beef and bacon lacking much flavour other than salt; the peanut butter shake was a thick, sweet gross-out; and the meal as a whole was akin to a drunken raid on the fridge. New owner, Rankvale Hospitality, could learn much from the gourmet-burger restaurants, which have left Ed's way behind. Like a warning on our cholesterol intake, Buddy Holly chirps out 'Heartbeat' as we leave.
Babies and children welcome: children's menu. Bookings not accepted. Tables outdoors (2, pavement). Takeaway service. **Map 17 C3.**
For branch see index.

South Kensington

PJ's Grill
52 Fulham Road, SW3 6HH (7581 0025, www.pjsgrill.net). South Kensington tube. **Meals served** noon-11.45pm Mon-Fri; 10am-11.45pm Sat; 10am-11.15pm Sun. **Main courses** £10.95-£27.95. **Credit** AmEx, MC, V.
There's another PJ's in Covent Garden, which always seems to be doing decent business whenever we've walked past it. But this South Kensington spot remains the signature branch, its wide frontage beckoning diners into a woody room that's quite handsome in a slightly posh, slightly timeworn way. Kensingtonians, Chelsea-ites and other denizens of west London have been coming here for 20 years, made to feel at home by personable staff, a faintly upscale atmosphere and walls of polo ephemera (the name refers to a long-forgotten 1930s movie called Polo Joe; owner Brian Stein is a keen player). Certainly, it can't be the food that's drawing the crowds. With 18 starters, 14 mains and six salads, the lunch menu is long enough to raise suspicions

Interview
TOM CONRAN

Who are you?
Restaurateur with establishments including **Lucky 7** (*see p37*), **Tom's** (*see p291*) and the **Cow** (*see p107*).
How did you start in the catering business?
In 1983 I wanted to find a career I was passionate about, and tried to make sure it was one my father [Terence Conran] didn't already have a monopoly on. If only I knew then what was to come! I went to train in Paris as a chef.
What's the best thing about running a restaurant in London?
People in this industry are quite pleasant and respectful to one another; you feel that you are part of a genuine community. And one is never bored.
What's the worst thing?
It's a non-stop carousel – your life passes by in a blur. Also, the local authorities love to move the goalposts.
Which are your favourite London restaurants?
I like ethnic ones as it gives me an opportunity to eat food I am least likely to prepare at home or in my own establishments: **Bar Shu** (*see p73*), **Four Seasons** (*see p74*), **Lahore Kebab House** (*see p150*), **Defune** (34 George Street, W1U 7DP, 7935 8311) for sushi and **19 Numara Bos Cirrik** (*see p263*).
What's the best bargain in the capital?
Any of the above, save Defune.
What's your favourite treat?
It's 250g of oscietra caviar from Reza's Iranian shop in Kensington.
What is missing from London's restaurant scene?
A really great, authentic Kansas City barbecue restaurant wouldn't go amiss. I would also like to see more people try harder with British food.
What does the next year hold?
People like to eat less formally these days and enjoy a more fun and stimulating experience, so I would imagine that there will be an increase in the number of Latin and Mexican restaurants. And perhaps a better standard of fast food.

that the kitchen may be cutting the occasional corner; a forlorn opener of soggy pasta and bland crab, its lack of flavour part-hidden by a surfeit of chilli, did nothing to disperse them. If anything, a special of toughish pork fillet wrapped in parma ham and then absolutely suffocated by mozzarella was even less appealing. Disappointing, all told. *Babies and children welcome: high chairs. Booking advisable. Separate room for parties, seats 20-82. Tables outdoors (3, pavement).* **Map 14 E11**. **For branch see index.**

West

Westbourne Park

Lucky 7

127 Westbourne Park Road, W2 5QL (7727 6771, www.lucky7london.co.uk). Royal Oak or Westbourne Park tube. **Meals served** noon-10.30pm Mon; 10am-10.30pm Tue-Thur; 9am-11pm Fri, Sat; 9am-10.30pm Sun. **Main courses** £4.50-£15.95. **Credit** MC, V.
Tom Conran's clever take on American diner culture remains an appealing room: six green Naugahyde booths set off by a tin ceiling, rock-show posters and an array of other desirable tchotchkes in front of an open kitchen and a wall-mounted menu. In our experience, though, the food is of a variable quality, and the hipster service seems to have finally collapsed over the fine line separating agreeably casual and irritatingly insouciant. In the past, burgers here have been a strong point; breakfasts, however, are a little more hit or miss. Huevos rancheros (fried eggs, chorizo hash, flour tortillas, beans, guacamole and salsa) is hardly authentic (especially given the rather plain pico de gallo: a chopped onion and tomato assembly), but it remains a worthwhile and generous option. However, a peach melba milkshake tasted as though it was compiled solely from foodstuffs found in tins or the freezer. And charging £11 for two indifferent crab cakes is opportunistic at best. Your food will probably be delivered with wholehearted indifference by staff more interested in talking about their weekend than looking after their diners. Could do better.
Babies and children welcome: children's menu. Bookings not accepted. Separate room for parties, seats 35. Takeaway service. **Map 7 A5**.

North

Camden Town & Chalk Farm

The Diner

2 Jamestown Road, NW1 7BY (7485 5223, www.goodlifediner.com). Camden Town tube. **Meals served** 10am-11pm Mon-Thur; 10am-midnight Fri; 9am-midnight Sat; 9am-11pm Sun. **Main courses** £5-£8.50. **Credit** AmEx, MC, V.
The third venue in a four-strong chain, this is the brainchild of the folks behind the Hoxton Square Bar & Kitchen. The Diner builds on the success of its predecessors by offering fashion-conscious young Londoners a facsimile of the American diner experience. In truth, it's more of a transatlantic mistranslation than a carbon copy, but it does nonetheless avoid collapsing under the weight of decorative kitsch. The food reads more authentically than it tastes: an 'open meatloaf sandwich' was more like congealed mince on toast; and the very existence of a 'vegetarian burrito', tasty though we found it, would be anathema across the water. You're on safer ground with the basics: the burgers are fine, the breakfasts are better, and the milkshakes are both generous and winningly thick (especially if you splash out an extra 50p for the piggy addition of peanut butter). All this is dished up in a handsome and pretty capacious room lined with booths and decorated with vintage odds and sods. You can also choose to eat at one of a handful of pavement tables or, in season, on a surprising roof garden.
Babies and children welcome: high chairs; nappy-changing facilities. Booking advisable. Disabled: toilet. Tables outdoors (13 terrace; 9 pavement). Takeaway service **Map 27 C2**.
For branches see index.

LATIN AMERICAN

While London's North American restaurants seem to be in the doldrums, the cuisines of Latin America are thriving. Argentina, in particular, appears to be taking over London à la Galtieri – small independents approaching from all sides. The arrival of **Garufa** in Arsenal sees Alberto Abbate (of Battersea's **Santa María del Sur**) expanding north, while **Constancia**, Bermondsey's new parrilla (grill) is a project fronted by Sebastian Harguindey, ex-waiter at Hackney's excellent **Buen Ayre**. In the city centre, the glamorous **Gaucho** chain continues to expand, opening a new branch close to Smithfield's meat market.

This year the capital has also seen the opening of several Brazilian rodizio-style grills – rodizio being an all-you-can-eat term applied to many restaurants in Brazil from pizzerias to sushi joints, though it's most commonly associated with meat grills. Most aren't good enough to list here, but we welcome **Rodizio Preto** and **Comida**. Noteworthy too is the fact that takeaway Mexican burrito outlets are spreading round the West End and City like peyote. Our favourite, El Burrito (5 Charlotte Place, London W1T 1SF) is an offshoot of the ever-reliable Euston restaurant **Mestizo**.

Argentinian

Central

Piccadilly

★ Gaucho Piccadilly

25 Swallow Street, W1B 4QR (7734 4040, www.gauchorestaurants.co.uk). Piccadilly Circus tube. **Meals served** noon-10.30pm Mon, Sun; noon-11pm Tue-Sat. **Main courses** £12.25-£37. **Credit** AmEx, MC, V.
It's not especially satisfying to admit that a chain restaurant sources and serves some of the best steak in the capital, but ever-expanding Gaucho (a new branch was being prepared in Charlotte Street as we went to press) keeps its focus simple and smart. The dark, cowhide-wallpaper cocktail-bar setting is almost too stylish for a grill restaurant, and we've always found the service at Swallow Street too gauche, but the beef (whether you go for the delicately marbled ribeye, the aesthetically perfect fillet or the tasty sirloin) is top-notch. Cooked carefully, as they invariably are, these steaks are as tender and sliceable as butter. All the extras – morcilla (blood sausage), chorizo, fries, empanadas – are excellent too, and in fact more flavoursome than the beef. So, consider sharing a 400g steak between two and exploring the menu, as there are also humitas (corn wraps), ceviches and a delicious baby squid dish that will provide balance to all the protein and allow some space for desserts. Fabulous too are dulce de leche cheesecake, and bread and butter pudding; cheese platters go well with a glass of torrontés. In summer 2009 Gaucho opened Freggo (see p292), an ice-cream parlour, next door.
Babies and children welcome: high chairs. Booking advisable Thur-Sat. Separate rooms for parties, seating 12-80. Takeaway service. **Map 17 A5**.
For branches see index.

South West

Chelsea

El Gaucho

Chelsea Farmers' Market, 125 Sydney Street, SW3 6NR (7376 8514, www.elgaucho.co.uk). Sloane Square or South Kensington tube. **Meals served** noon-7pm daily. **Main courses** £11.90-£16.90. **Credit** AmEx, MC, V.

Although roofed, El Gaucho is a small shed of a restaurant with a ranch-like feel and fresh air rushing through an open door. You can hear, and smell, the meat sizzling, there's lively banter among the staff, and you sit on benches: cramped when it gets busy. Beef, sourced in Argentina, is buttery-soft to the knife and full of flavour. There are ribeyes, sirloins, rumps and fillets, but the churrasco (slimmer, flash-grilled and juicy) is a great lunch option. Try it 'a caballo' ('horse-style') with two fried eggs. It's delicious, the blood and yolk swirling into an oily dip ideal for the cobs of white bread. Milanesas (breaded escalopes) and lamb chops are also available, but don't compare with the steaks for tastiness or tenderness. Salads are basic – as they should be – and there are some drippingly succulent meat empanadas. The wine list features blends as well as malbec and merlot; one blend uses tannat grapes from Uruguay, which have a tannic, woody quality ideal for meaty meals. Flan (crème caramel) is best among the limited (and rather listless) desserts. On sunny days a few tables are placed outside. Come at noon to bag one.
Babies and children admitted. Tables outdoors (14, pavement). Takeaway service. **Map 14 E12**.
For branch see index.

South

Battersea

Santa María del Sur

129 Queenstown Road, SW8 3RH (7622 2088, www.santamariadelsur.co.uk). Queenstown Road rail. **Dinner served** 6.30-10.30pm Mon-Fri. **Meals served** noon-10.30pm Sat, Sun. **Main courses** £8-£19. **Credit** AmEx, MC, V.
On our last visit, this Argentinian grill was full: not bad for a Thursday in a recession, in deepest Battersea. Slightly scruffy wooden decor and T-shirted waiters make Santa Maria the laid-back local you wished was on your street. We were perplexed by a pot of odd-tasting butter, until we learned it was (intentionally) mixed with blue cheese. Instead, we covered our so-so bread with the grilled provolone cheese starter. At £4, the chorizo starter (one small spicy sausage, halved) struck us as silly. But the main event – Argentinian steaks – didn't disappoint. The fillet was big and juicy enough to sate a craving for red meat for months. Second best was sirloin, which was packed with fatty flavour but needed less time on

RESTAURANTS

Get the local experience

Over 50 of the world's top destinations available.

the grill (we asked for medium; it was a little tough). Green salad (a bowl of undressed strong rocket and baby spinach) cut through the meat and greasy cheese. The friendly staff (all Argentinian and stereotypically good-looking) were unintrusive and alert, at one point politely asking a party to quieten down. By then, we were deep into the house red (a fine Norton malbec) and were immune to a slightly shouty Sloane fiesta.

Babies and children welcome: children's portions; high chairs. Booking advisable weekends.

Clapham

La Pampa Grill

4 Northcote Road, SW11 1NT (7924 1167). Clapham Junction rail. **Dinner served** 6-11pm Mon-Thur; 6-11.30pm Fri, Sat; 6-11pm Sun. **Main courses** £8.50-£16.50. **Credit** MC, V.
Aiming at rustic allure and (sort of) urban cool, Pampa Grill manages to miss both – although soft lighting and candles make it a fair choice for a date. First-daters, however, should avoid or share the aubergine starter, which tasted mainly of garlic. Like the decor, the rest of the meal was pleasant yet unconvincing. Bread and butter appears automatically, but is charged for (£1.95). Our steak was delicious, though cooked longer than wanted and not as tender as we expected from an Argentina-themed steakhouse. Grilled chicken breast was tasty and generously portioned, unlike the accompanying vegetables. La Pampa's pièce de résistance may well be the chunks of potato it serves as chips: crackling on the outside, with a melt-in-the-mouth interior. Desserts include light and subtly lemon-flavoured pancakes, and a fresh, floppy crème caramel. A decent, extensive wine list offers moderately priced regional classics and a couple of big-budget choices. Our waiter was friendly and attentive (although we sat outside, he made sure we were looked after), but the bar-woman seemed grumpy and hostile. Tellingly, on a Thursday night there were 20-plus empty seats.
Available for hire. Babies and children admitted. Booking advisable. Tables outdoors (10, pavement). Takeaway service. **Map 21 C4**.
For branch see index.

South East

Bermondsey

Constancia NEW

52 Tanner Street, SE1 3PH (7234 0676, www.constancia.co.uk). Bermondsey tube/ London Bridge tube/rail. **Lunch served** noon-4pm Sat, Sun. **Dinner served** 6-10.30pm Tue-Sun. **Main course** £8.50-£21.50. **Mixed grill** £18, £23 per person (minimum 2). **Credit** MC, V.
Sebastian Harguindey, an emigré from another London parrilla, has taken over a Bermondsey pub and given it a cool makeover in dark wood and tones of cream and red. The menu features the usual empanadas, steaks and desserts (though, disappointingly, no sweetbreads). Chorizo is made locally, to an Argentinian recipe, and may well be the capital's best – try it in a choripán with red pepper and chimichurri sauce. The best of our steaks was the 11oz ribeye, which, like the others ranging in size from 8oz to 14oz, is from grass-reared Argentinian cattle. We liked the generous sides of chips and salad too. Constancia also offers parrillitas (small table braziers) featuring a sampling of cuts and extras, but order one and you risk your steak cooking too long while you explore the starters (grilled provolone with oregano, say, or a platter of Tuscan meats and cheeses). Reds dominate the wine list, which starts at £14.50 for a blend of sangiovese, bonarda and malbec grapes. Desserts include dulce de leche cheesecake, ice-creams, brownies and flan (crème caramel). This is no place for vegetarians, but meat-free choices include grilled portobello mushroom with pesto, or aubergine with tomato, mozzarella and parmesan.
Babies and children admitted. Booking advisable dinner Fri, Sat. Disabled: toilet. **Map 12 R9**.

Blackheath

★ Buenos Aires Café

17 Royal Parade, SE3 0TL (8318 5333, www.buenosairesltd.com). Blackheath rail. **Lunch served** noon-3pm Mon-Fri; noon-4pm Sat, Sun. **Dinner served** 6-10.30pm daily. **Main courses** £8.50-£26. **Credit** MC, V.
On a Thursday evening, Buenos Aires Café – which isn't a café at all – was lively, happy and warm. Operations were being overseen by its owner: an ex-dancer, ex-paparazzo from Argentina. Waiters dashed about discreetly, the evening sun poured in from the heath. Walls are hung with large photos of Maradona, Che Guevara and immigrants arriving in Buenos Aires in the 1900s. The place looks like the model local restaurant, and our food kept up the standard. The mollejas (sweetbreads) were golden-brown, and there was plenty for two; add a few small morcillas (black puddings) and a good Tapiz malbec and the starter experience was near-celestial. Then came a 400g sirloin and a milanesa (breaded veal cutlet). The latter is a staple of Argentina, and a good measure of a restaurant; this one was a bit oily, but tasty, tender and moist. The steak was huge and deep-red inside – though at more than £20 it ought to be. Alternatives include great pastas and slim-based pizzas, as well as puchero (a heavy but hearty stew). For dessert, the dulce de leche pancake impressed, but the bread pudding, while flavoursome, was a bit dry. All told, though, this was a sublimely pleasurable evening.
Babies and children welcome: booster seats. Booking advisable; essential Fri, Sat. Tables outdoors (4, pavement).
For branch see index.

North East

Hackney

★ Buen Ayre (100)

50 Broadway Market, E8 4QJ (7275 9900, www.buenayre.co.uk). London Fields rail/26, 48, 55, 106, 236 bus. **Lunch served** noon-3.30pm Sat, Sun. **Dinner served** 6-10.30pm daily. **Main courses** £7.50-£22. **Credit** MC, V.
Carnivores of the world unite at this buzzy little local Argentinian restaurant. A huge parrilla (charcoal grill) dominates the room; most parties at the rough-hewn tables (packed throughout our visit) eventually get their own mini-grill, complete with vast amounts of sausage, steak and sweetbreads. The less carnivorous don't starve: the provoleta (a simple plate of 'melted until crispy at the edges' smoked cheese flavoured with thyme) was a delicious accompaniment to a starter of serrano ham with palm hearts; and ordering the hongos (a vegetarian main course of portobello mushrooms stuffed with own-made 'heavy on the garlic' pesto) between two, meant that we could also share an enormous hunk of bife de lomo (fillet steak). Tender, melt-in-the-mouth meat, it arrived with butter beans, marinated pepper and a bowl of pungent chimichurri (garlic, pepper and herb sauce). Choose a malbec from an almost entirely Argentinian wine list and the two-hour dining slot will whizz by. Even an over-enthusiastic waiter whisking plates away before we'd finished couldn't spoil it. Buen appetit!
Babies and children welcome: high chairs. Booking advisable. Disabled: toilet. Tables outdoors (5, garden).

Comida. See p41.

RESTAURANTS

SPECIALS:
OSTILLAS £5.50
GRILLED PORK RIBS W
CHAYOTE RELLENOS en
N CHOW (GREEN SQUASH)
CHEESE, DIPPED IN SOUFF
CREAMS: VANILLA, MEXIC
AINABLE FISH: POLLA
SPECIAL

Taqueria. See p43.

North
Highbury

Garufa NEW
2009 RUNNER-UP BEST NEW LOCAL
104 Highbury Park, N5 2XE (7226 0070, www.garufa.co.uk). Arsenal tube. **Meals served** 10am-10.30pm daily. **Main courses** £12-£34. **Set lunch** £9.80-£12.50 1 course incl glass of wine, beer or soft drink. **Credit** AmEx, MC, V.

Smiling, relaxed staff and a cosy interior make Garufa a warm, inviting spot. Sepia-tinted photos of old Buenos Aires line bare-brick walls, and twinkly table lights shine from red glass holders on polished wooden tables. Towards the rear, diners can glimpse the chefs in the open kitchen. This is the latest venture from Alberto Abbate, who has past form with Buen Ayre (*see p39*) and Battersea's Santa Maria del Sur (*see p37*). As you'd expect, steak takes centre stage – fillet, sirloin, ribeye and rump, available in three sizes, sourced from Argentina and cooked perfectly – plus mixed grills to share, pork sausages and black pudding (richer and meatier than the Spanish version). But Garufa is more than a steakhouse; there's a surprising number of vegetarian dishes, including mains such as grilled aubergine with tomato sauce and provolone cheese, and smaller dishes like humita norteña (fried sweetcorn purée), morrón asado (smoky grilled red peppers sprinkled with garlic) and porotos a la provenzal (butter beans doused in oil, garlic and parsley). All were good, and the crispy yet fluffy chips were excellent Add breakfast dishes (served until 5pm), desserts (dulce de leche features heavily), an impressive, red-dominated, all-Argentine wine list and a soundtrack of soft tango, and the experience is complete.
Babies and children welcome: children's menu (until 5pm); high chairs; nappy-changing facilities. Booking advisable.

Brazilian
Central
Mayfair

Comida NEW
46 South Molton Street, W1K 5RX (7495 1177, www.comidabar.co.uk). Bond Street tube. **Meals served** 11am-10pm Mon-Sat; noon-9pm Sun. **Buffet** £16.90 lunch, £21.50 from 6pm. **Credit** MC, V.

On our latest visit to this rodizio grill restaurant, the salad bar seemed small, and featured roasted courgette and peppers, good pão de queijo (cheese bread), standard farofa (roasted manioc flour), and lacklustre feijão (black bean stew). But we wanted meat, so, unperturbed, we waited for the procession of skewer-wielding waiters to come over from the open grill. Disappointment ensued: a herb-filled pork sausage was tough on the outside and dry within; chicken wrapped in bacon was passable but greasy; and chicken legs could have done with longer on the grill. The sirloin steak lacked any flavour other than its garlic marinade, and the usual rodizio pièce de résistance, picanha (rump steak), was tough and veiny. Grilled pineapple was great, but not what you would expect to pay almost £20 for. Apart from the lamb, which was flavoursome and perfectly pink, and a good bottle of Chilean house red, Comida's star attraction was a good-fun, chatty waitress who epitomised Brazilian warmth. If it's done right, we're fans of the rodizio's eat-all-you-like concept, but we're not sure it works so well in London at these fairly budget prices (£16.90 at lunch, £21.50 in the evening).
Babies and children welcome: high chairs. Booking advisable dinner. Disabled: toilet. Entertainment: DJ 8pm Fri, Sat. Separate room for parties, seats 50. Tables outdoors (8, pavement). Vegetarian menu. **Map 9 H6**.

Garufa

Pimlico

Rodizio Preto NEW
72 Wilton Road, SW1V 1DE (7233 8668, www.rodiziopreto.co.uk). Victoria tube/rail. **Lunch served** noon-3pm, **dinner served** 6-11pm Mon-Fri. **Meals served** noon-11pm Sat; noon-9.30pm Sun. **Buffet** £8.95-£19.95. **Credit** AmEx, MC, V.

There's a few Brazilian all-you-can-eat restaurants in town, but Rodizio Preto is one of our favourites. The vibe is part slick São Paulo rodizio, part camp Rio lanchonete bar – the former evident in the lighting and silver crocodile-skin wallpaper; the latter in the open-front main room and the (mercifully silent) carnival DVD on the flatscreen TV. The buffet salad bar features many Brazilian classics, including deep-fried plantain, black bean feijão stew and palm heart salad, as well as salami, properly marinated olives and jalapeño peppers. Beef stew with potato was unremarkable, as were many of the green salads, but the meats (sliced off grill skewers on to your plate by roaming waiters) were mostly very good. The pork and chicken were dry, but chicken hearts weren't too rubbery; picanha rump steak was wonderfully tender, pink and dripping with juice; and nuggets of sirloin came wrapped in thick back bacon that wasn't dry or too crispy. Meals are long drawn-out affairs; our chatty waiters were in no hurry to move us on. Desserts seem an afterthought, but that's fine – if you've room, you haven't been trying hard enough.
Babies and children welcome: high chairs. Booking advisable weekends. Tables outdoors (6, pavement). **Map 15 J10**.

West
Bayswater

Rodizio Rico
111 Westbourne Grove, W2 4UW (7792 4035, www.rodiziorico.com). Bayswater tube. **Dinner served** 6pm-midnight Mon-Fri. **Meals served** noon-midnight Sat, Sun. **Buffet** £15.50 vegetarian, £22.50 meat. **Credit** MC, V.

Chilled Brazilian music, many free tables at 8pm on a Friday, and a football team of waiters

suggested that a return visit to the original Rodizio Rico might be a more laid-back affair than last year's scrum at the Islington branch. A buffet salad with unlimited meat dishes (£22.50) is what's on offer (a cheaper vegetarian buffet is also available). The cheapest red wine by the glass (an Argentinian shiraz bonarda at £4.90/175ml) was pretty mediocre. Having amassed tasty plates of crisp salad, rice, beans, some cheesy bread and bland croquettes, we awaited the waiters and their swords. These charming, chatty men always seem to proffer chicken legs, chicken hearts, sausages and the like before offering any prime beef or pork loins; they seemed to interrupt our meal every five minutes (keen to push the cheaper cuts, and move things on apace), despite the restaurant only filling up slowly. In addition, some of the best cuts of meat were over-salted and dry – overcooked on the revolving grills. The owners of this expanding chain (there's a new venue at the O₂ stadium) should slow down, be more gentle with their guests, and cut their prices.
Babies and children welcome: high chairs. Booking advisable, essential weekends. Separate room for parties, seats 55. Tables outdoors: 6, pavement. Takeaway service. Vegetarian menu. **Map 7 B6.** **For branches see index.**

North
Finchley

Casa Brasil
289 Regents Park Road, N3 3JY (8371 1999). Finchley Central tube. **Meals served** 11am-6pm Tue-Thur; 11am-9.30pm Fri, Sat; 11am-5pm Sun. **Main courses** £6.90-£12.50. **Unlicensed. Corkage** £1 per person. **No credit cards**.

Bereft of a booze licence and an electronic card reader, tucked away in Finchley, and with opening hours unsuited to a proper night out, it's a wonder that proud Casa Brasil has survived this past couple of years. Somehow, through owner Roy's warm service, cosy decor (shelves of deli items, wooden parrots, grandma tables) and general enthusiasm, the place is thriving. Starters include pão de queijo (cheese bread), assorted empanadas (such as our chicken and palm hearts) and a faggot-like meat bomb called a quibe; they're OK, but ours seemed reheated and was dry and not hugely tasty. The mains, though, were hearty, delicious and freshly cooked. We tried hake moqueca (a stew featuring coriander-enhanced white fish), and a feijoada with slabs of tender, slow-cooked pork rib, a viciously powerful chilli sauce, gritty farofa and crisp salad. Desserts were either very plain and dry (almond cake) or tropically exuberant and moist (passion-fruit mousse), but even the cake made a fine match with the perfectly prepared organic coffee. Casa Brasil is more casa than restaurant, but is a fine place for a long, slow lunch – and at £40 for a big spread for two, no one's complaining.

Babies and children welcome: high chairs. Booking advisable Fri-Sun. Tables outdoors (8, patio).

Cuban

Central
Soho

Floridita
100 Wardour Street, W1F 0TN (7314 4000, www.floriditalondon.com). Tottenham Court Road tube.
Bar Open 5.30pm-2am Tue, Wed; 5.30pm-3am Thur-Sat.

Wahaca

Restaurant **Dinner served** 5.30pm-midnight Tue, Wed; 5.30pm-1am Thur-Sat. **Main courses** £13.50-£35. **Admission** (after 9pm Fri, Sat) £15. *Both* **Credit** AmEx, DC, MC, V.
Last year, we liked this approximate remodelling of the famous Havana bar; our return trip was less appealing. The blingy decor of mirrors, cut-glass and polished black pillars creates a classy setting as you descend into the basement dining area: all dim lighting and candles. A well-stocked cocktail bar offers a delicious and exotic array of drinks. We enjoyed a free appetiser of warm dough balls shot through with tangy cheese and olives, but things then went downhill. A starter of tender confit duck with poached egg and jalapeño crème fraîche desperately lacked flavour (or discernible jalapeño). A fillet of salmon with mussels and leeks in white wine sauce featured watery fish with too crisp a skin, overly-crunchy leeks, and insipid mussels. Chargrilled rump of lamb with plantain, bacon and mint salsa was chewy and knife-resistant. After we returned the dish as inedible, the second attempt was only moderately better, and the plantain was bland. Even the noisy Cuban band looked bored. Floridita was busy for a Wednesday evening, yet for such a pricey meal (and there's an additional £6 charge for the band from 8pm) we expected more.

Booking advisable. Disabled: toilet. Dress: smart casual. Entertainment: Cuban band, DJ 8pm Tue-Sat. Separate rooms for parties, seating 52-72. **Map 17 B3**.

Mexican & Tex-Mex

Central
Covent Garden

Wahaca
66 Chandos Place, WC2N 4HG (7240 1883, www.wahaca.co.uk). Covent Garden or Leicester Square tube. **Meals served** noon-11pm Mon-Sat; noon-10.30pm Sun. **Main courses** £3.25-£9.95. **Credit** AmEx, MC, V.
Out-of-towners love Wahaca for its central location, colourful, casually fashionable decor, trendy Mexican menu and achievable prices. To top it off, they get to brag they've been to a celebrity chef's restaurant (Thomasina Miers, a former *Masterchef* winner, appears frequently on telly and in the recipe press). We're not so wowed by the cooking, but can't deny it's a fun place. Our waiter recited the menu and relentlessly suggested further items to purchase as though he'd swallowed a copy of *Think and Grow Rich*. The kitchen's aim is to marry locally sourced ingredients with Mexican-inspired recipes, some more authentic than others. Quinoa, for example, is not a Mexican grain, but appears in a hearty fuerza salad with beetroot, avocado, mint and hibiscus flowers. Greasy pork pibil taco – part of the £19.75 Wahaca selection of sharing plates for two – suffered from a surfeit of orange oil. Substantial main courses include grilled steak, chicken and fish, plus burritos and enchiladas. To drink, try the refreshing cinnamon-licked horchata: a dairy-free concoction made from ground rice and almonds. We finished on a high note with superb lemon margarita sorbet and churros y chocolate featuring wonderfully dark rich chocolate sauce.

Babies and children welcome: high chairs; nappy-changing facilities. Bookings not accepted. Disabled: toilet. **Map 18 D5**.
For branches see index.

Fitzrovia

Mestizo
103 Hampstead Road, NW1 3EL (7387 4064, www.mestizomx.com). Warren Street tube/Euston tube/rail. **Meals served** noon-11pm Mon-Sat. **Lunch served** noon-4pm, **dinner served** 5-10pm Sun. **Main courses** £9.50-£14.50. **Credit** MC, V.
On a dreary traffic-ridden street north of Euston Road, Mestizo has a well-presented interior that belies its drab location. Crimson walls, white banquettes and pristine tablecloths keep things smart, while the colourful Aztec calendar – not to mention the TV showing Mexican tourist scenes – is a reminder of what you're here for. With a choice of around 120 tequilas and a multitude of cocktails, you could simply stop by for a sip of something strong, accompanied by tacos or tamales. But it's the authentic Mexican mains that keep local office workers, as well as Latin American expats, coming back. We particularly liked the ceviche. It may be more gloopy than some are used to, but its fresh-tasting tomato sauce is perfect with the juicy prawns. All main courses come with a pot of black beans and crumbled cheese. If you're cool about trying corn fungus, the chicken with huitlacoche sauce will be an earthy joy. We also reckoned that the mole sauce (packed with prunes, nuts and smoky chillies) made an ideal partner for duck. Well worth a visit if you're in the neighbourhood.

Babies and children welcome: high chairs. Booking advisable weekends. Disabled: toilet. Separate room for parties, seats 80. Takeaway service. **Map 3 J3**.

West
Ladbroke Grove

Santo NEW
299 Portobello Road, W10 5TD (8968 4590, www.santovillage.com). Ladbroke Grove tube. **Lunch served** noon-3pm, **dinner served**

6-10pm Tue-Thur. **Meals served** noon-11pm Fri, Sat; noon-10pm Sun. **Main courses** £4.50-£15.50. **Credit** AmEx, MC, V.

Dedicated *gastrónomos* agree that London often doesn't do Mexican food proper justice, so Santo deserves plaudits for rejecting the default nachos-and-sombreros setting, and aiming for a modern approach. Situated at the sleepier end of Portobello Road, it makes the most of tasteful bare-brick walls and floorboards, high ceilings and tall windows: not a stuffed donkey in sight. On our visit, drinks were brought by friendly, efficient staff: zingy limonada (made in-house) and pomegranate margarita, served on the rocks with a sugar rim. Sadly, the food didn't match this quality. A special of fish tacos worked well; mini-fillets of sea bass were crisply battered and came with a smoky chipotle mayo. Another special disappointed, however; the unusual and potentially exciting ingredients in a salad of nopal (cactus leaf) and hibiscus were let down by uninspiring presentation, insipid tomatoes and iceberg lettuce. The chargrilled steak in our ribeye burrito tasted too much of charcoal, and was partnered by an indistinct salsa – you'll find many better versions for less than the £13.80 charged here. On weekend evenings though, Santo lets down its hair, providing cheap cocktails, finger food, salsa dancing and latin music.
Babies and children welcome: children's menu; high chairs; nappy-changing facilities. Booking advisable Fri, Sat. Entertainment: DJ 9pm Fri, Sat. Tables outdoors (4, pavement). Takeaway service; delivery service (over £12 within 2-mile radius). **Map 19 B2.**

Notting Hill

★ Taqueria

139-143 Westbourne Grove, W11 2RS (7229 4734, www.taqueria.co.uk). Notting Hill Gate tube. **Meals served** noon-11pm Mon-Thur; noon-11.30pm Fri; noon-10.30pm Sat, Sun. **Main courses** £5.50-£8.50. **Set lunch** (noon-4.30pm Mon-Fri) £6 1 course. **Credit** MC, V.

Pop-art prints of iconic Mexican revolutionary Emiliano Zapata adorn the walls of this classy cantina. The food here isn't exactly revolutionary – we're talking classic Mexican street food of tacos, tortas and tostadas – but the standard is sound. With its regal red-leather upholstery against white, with a spot of chrome, Taqueria is a cool place for grabbing an after-work drink and snack, or breaking up a day shopping on Westbourne Grove. Prices aren't bad for the area, and it's best to share a few small plates. Cutlery and napkins are casually left in pots at the table; either use hands or not, it's up to you. Choriqueso, a dreamy taco featuring a slab of grilled cheese stuffed with crumbly own-made chorizo, had us licking our fingers long after the delicate tomato salsa had been devoured. To drink, there's a good choice of fruit juices, as well as posh tequilas and Mexican beer. Taqueria's traditional Mexican hot chocolate is every bit as spicy and frothy as it should be – which also keeps us coming back for more.
Babies and children welcome: high chairs. Bookings not accepted Sat, Sun. **Map 7 A6.**

South

Clapham

Café Sol

54-56 Clapham High Street, SW4 7UL (7498 8558, www.cafesol.net). Clapham Common or Clapham North tube. **Meals served** noon-midnight Mon-Thur, Sun; noon-1am Fri, Sat. **Main courses** £5.95-£12.95. **Credit** AmEx, MC, V.

Clapham's Café Sol has toned down its zany decor in recent years and now features a large open dining hall painted in shades of brown, with colourful mosaics dotted about. The food is pure Tex-Mex and, in our experience, generally unremarkable. The higgledy-piggledy layout of the menu can be confusing. Variations of wrapped tortillas dominate, though there are also daily fish specials chalked up on the board. On our recent trip, the tortilla chips were more North American than Central; the salsa was far too watery and the queso fundido (melting cheese dip) just didn't melt enough. 'Swamp thing' (deep-fried alligator) wasn't worth the fuss either, being vaguely reminiscent of a turkey twizzler. We liked the beef chilli con carne with its combination of minced beef and chunks of stewing steak – classic comfort cooking – and the lightly spiced cajun tuna hit the spot too. The menu also contains a selection of premium tequilas and playful cocktails, plus some very retro desserts. Café Sol appears to be comfortable with itself, but we found the experience no better than average.
Babies and children welcome: high chairs. Booking advisable Fri, Sat. Disabled: toilet. Tables outdoors (6, pavement). Takeaway service. **Map 22 B1.**

East

Shoreditch

Green & Red

51 Bethnal Green Road, E1 6LA (7749 9670, www.greenred.co.uk). Liverpool Street or Old Street tube/rail/8 bus.
Bar **Open** 6.30pm-midnight Thur; 6.30pm-1am Fri, Sat.
Restaurant **Lunch served** noon-3pm Mon-Fri. **Dinner served** 6-11pm daily. **Main courses** £10.50-£16.50.
Both **Credit** AmEx, MC, V.

Green & Red boasts a bar of back-lit bottles of serious tequilas made with 100% agave. The cocktails can be over-laden with ice, but you can't go wrong with the house margarita. The ground-floor cantina is grown-up Mexican in style, with wood panelling, sophisticated lighting and pockets of heady colour and religious iconography. It is generally filled with a pre-clubbing crowd nattering over sharing platters. On our visit, a starter of elote (corn on the cob) lacked the lime-chilli zing of this Mexican market staple, and chilli con carne – one of the 'antojitos' (small dishes) – was also gutless. 'Platos fuertes' (main courses like pork belly, steak, chicken, and sea bass) come with an array of accompaniments (salsas, salads and the like); we recommend the steak. In the basement, the drinking den has more of a party vibe than the cantina, with murals of skeletons knocking back the booze, leather loungers for chilling, and the odd salsa class on the go. Prices in general reflect the high quality of the liquor. All in all, a good choice to kick off the night.
Available for hire. Babies and children welcome: high chairs. Disabled: toilet. Entertainment (bar): DJs 9pm Fri, Sat. Takeaway service. **Map 6 S4.**

North

Stoke Newington

Mercado Bar & Cantina

26-30 Stoke Newington Church Street, N16 0LU (7923 0555, www.mercado-cantina.co.uk). Stoke Newington rail/73, 476 bus. **Dinner served** 6-11pm Mon-Fri. **Meals served** noon-11pm Sat, Sun. **Main courses** £8-£14. **Credit** AmEx, MC, V.

It's impossible to miss this bright yellow-fronted restaurant with its striking façade, but the interior doesn't live up to the promise. All the Mexican clichés are here – sombreros, sunflower oil-cloths, plastic shopping bags and Catholic icons. Flashing multicoloured lights add a touch of pathos to the faded kitsch. As for the food, you won't go far wrong if you stick with staples of quesadillas, tacos, burritos and fajitas, though the meat in our steak tacos was a little on the tough side. An enchilada was served smothered in poblano mole sauce (the chocolate one), yet it lacked the depth of flavour expected from this dish. There's a wide choice of traditional mains on the menu; chicken stuffed with mushrooms and a creamy red-pepper sauce was a safe bet. The nice selection of cocktails includes some luscious non-alcoholic examples, and there are also Mexican beers and sipping tequilas to choose from. Mercado might not be worth a trip across the Chihuahuan Desert, but if you're a Stoke Newington local and crave some Mexican food, it may well satisfy.
Available for hire. Babies and children welcome: high chairs. Takeaway service.

Pan-American

North

Camden Town & Chalk Farm

Guanabana

85 Kentish Town Road, NW1 8NY (7485 1166, www.guanabanarestaurant.com). Camden Town tube. **Dinner served** 5.30-11pm Mon-Thur. **Meals served** 12.30-11pm Fri, Sat; 12.30-10pm Sun. **Main courses** £6.75-£14. **Set meal** (5.30-7pm Mon-Fri) £9.75 2 courses. **Unlicensed. Corkage** £2/bottle. **Credit** MC, V.

Guanabana claims to be pan-South American and Caribbean, but in reality has an almost pan-global outlook. Everywhere you look, there's something to drag your thoughts elsewhere: here's a Vettriano print on the wall; there's a string of apparent Christmas decorations; a pretty back terrace is filled with Middle Eastern hookahs and Japanese fans. The effect is fun and quirky, if a little distracting. Unfortunately, the kitchen seems confused too. From the equally roaming menu, we chose cream cheese-stuffed jalapeños with a Thai-style sweet chilli sauce, and spicy papa criollas (roasted potatoes) served with a tomato sauce, patatas bravas-style. Both were fine, but the main courses didn't match up. Grilled red snapper with a vibrant salsa was artfully presented, but the fish was tough, and its advertised roast plantain accompaniment absent. A traditional-looking chickpea, green mango and coconut stew with tasty rice and peas was more successful, yet didn't over-excite. Still, staff are helpful and attentive, and the decent prices, outdoor area and BYO policy make this a good party venue. Perhaps if it could reign-in its wanderlust and retain culinary focus, Guanabana could fulfil its Latin promise.
Babies and children welcome: high chairs. Booking advisable Fri, Sat. Separate room for parties, seats 30. Tables outdoors (14, garden). **Map 27 D1.**

Islington

Sabor

108 Essex Road, N1 8LX (7226 5551, www.sabor.co.uk). Angel tube/Essex Road rail/38, 73 bus. **Dinner served** 6-10pm Tue, Wed; 6-11pm Thur, Fri. **Meals served** noon-11pm Sat, Sun. **Main courses** £8-£19.50. **Set lunch** £10 2 courses, £12.50 courses. **Credit** MC, V.

If Sabor's enticing menu were a person, it would be a well-travelled backpacker a few years on from a trip to Latin America, all grown-up. Ingredients come from across the continent – a metaphorical map of the Americas. Meats and grains are served with exotic fruit salsas, avocados and yuca: all treated with a Modern European touch. The menu can seem overwhelming; each choice reflects a country. Red snapper with Nicaraguan beans, Argentinian steak, Cuban bean stew and Colombian patties are among the alluring collection. But sometimes a dish can be listed with so many flavours it's easy to forget what you've ordered before it comes. Peruvian chicken had around seven ingredients jostling for attention in the description, but it was the heady saffron mash that shone through in the end. A starter of textbook-perfect Peruvian ceviche was lush; quinoa fritters had a chewy, meaty texture reminiscent of Thai fish cakes. Cocktails are made with fancy fruits, and there's a decent choice of Latin American beers, rums, tequilas, cachaças, piscos and aguardientes. Desserts might incorporate even more intriguing exotic fruits: lulo, for instance. A classy, colourful restaurant with an out-of-the-ordinary menu.
Babies and children welcome: high chairs. Booking advisable. **Map 5 P1.**

RESTAURANTS

Brasseries

The restaurant trade seems to have finally got the message that people want to eat what they want when they want. In the past year London has welcomed the opening of several eminently user-friendly brasseries, where you can enjoy breakfast at 11am, say, or lunch at 4pm, in stylishly relaxed surroundings. A few will even rustle up something after most eateries have closed for the night. Brasseries are usually great places to take children too, many offering kids' menus that go way beyond chicken nuggets and burgers. Plenty also specialise in weekend brunches and make ideal venues for a leisurely browse through the papers, while ingesting a nourishing hangover-cure. Yet it would be wrong to think of all these establishments as simply utilitarian dining places. Our favourites, the **Wolseley**, **Tom's Kitchen**, **Joanna's** and Alan Yau's trendy new **Princi** also inject a large dose of pzazz into proceedings, as do the new-look **Kettners**, **St Pancras Grand** and **Bob Bob Ricard**, winner of our Best Design award.

Central

Belgravia

Chelsea Brasserie

7-12 Sloane Square, SW1W 8EG (7881 5999, www.sloanesquarehotel.co.uk). Sloane Square tube.
Lunch served noon-3pm Mon-Sat. **Brunch served** 11am-4pm Sun. **Dinner served** 6-10.30pm Mon-Sat. **Main courses** £13-£21.50. **Set lunch** £23.50 2 courses. **Set dinner** (6-7.30pm, 9.45-10.30pm) £18.50 2 courses, £24.50 3 courses. **Credit** MC, V.
Urbane and sophisticated, the Chelsea Brasserie fits its Sloane Square location like a hand in a glove. With bare brick walls, contemporary art, sparkling glassware and crisp, white tablecloths, this is a modern update on the classic brasserie – correct without being too formal. The menu stays true to its French roots, with starters such as foie gras and chicken liver parfait served with Calvados jelly; or asparagus with morels, almonds and herb vinaigrette. The occasional global influence creeps in; a tuna sashimi starter was delicate and perfect, with translucent slices of moist raw tuna and a drizzling of sweet, piquant soy sauce. Orientally inspired mains such as five-spice pork belly with ginger dressing sit alongside European meat and fish dishes, like our main of Elwy lamb with peas. This was another confidently executed dish, with the very best meat slow-roasted to perfection, served with tender young peas. Wild sea trout with spinach, glazed salsify and sorrel beurre blanc was also a successful combination. Puddings are traditional, full-on and not to be missed; we shared a deeply decadent, alcoholic zabaglione.
Babies and children welcome: children's menu; high chairs. Booking essential. Disabled: lift; toilet. Dress: smart casual. Separate room for parties, seats 18. Tables outdoors (4, pavement). Map 15 G10.

City

Royal Exchange Grand Café & Bar

The Royal Exchange, EC3V 3LR (7618 2480, www.danddlondon.co.uk). Bank tube/DLR.
Breakfast served 8-11am, **meals served** noon-10pm Mon-Fri. **Main courses** £6.50-£19. **Credit** AmEx, DC, MC, V.
A financial centre for over 450 years, the Royal Exchange is now a mechanism for parting City folk from their bonuses, inhabited by top-end shops and dominated by the Grand Café, which spreads expansively over two floors, alongside its formal French sister restaurant Sauterelle. The ground-floor café occupies the central courtyard of the Grade I listed building; half the pleasure of stopping here is for the views it affords of the grand galleries. A striking central bar and a bevy of pinstriped and black-aproned staff create an illusion of swish continental efficiency, but an illusion it is: service is a tad random, and it can be hard to order quickly, particularly as there aren't any menus on the tables. The menu lists rich persons' snack food: gourmet sandwiches (up to £17.50 for lobster and avocado brioche); seafood and steak, and some appealing seasonal dishes (salmon with samphire; an OK gazpacho). All this was going down well with the suited crowd on our visit, so we must assume our cloying lasagna vinci grassi was an anomaly – though we'd suggest that summer truffles are best not used in thick scales covering a cheesy crust. Still, a cocktail in the bar upstairs cheered us up.
Available for hire. Babies and children welcome (restaurant). Bookings not accepted except for breakfast. Disabled: toilet. Dress: smart casual. Separate room for parties, seats 26. Map 12 Q6.

Clerkenwell & Farringdon

Brasserie de Malmaison

Malmaison, 18-21 Charterhouse Square, EC1M 6AH (7012 3700, www.malmaison-london.com). Barbican tube/Farringdon tube/rail. **Breakfast served** 7-10am Mon-Fri; 8-10.30am Sat, Sun. **Brunch served** 11am-3pm Sun. **Lunch served** noon-2.30pm Mon-Fri. **Dinner served** 6-10pm daily. **Main courses** £12-£20. **Set meal** £15.50 2 courses, £17.50 3 courses. **Credit** AmEx, DC, MC, V.
Diners head down a winding iron staircase in the Malmaison hotel to this stylish basement brasserie: an intimate space furnished in rich colours, with subdued lighting and comfortable seating. The menu majors in French-based classics, with boeuf bourguignon and roast poussin sitting alongside a slightly more adventurous 'Homegrown & Local' section, containing the likes of fried skate cheeks with chorizo and bean stew. A Malmaison salad was fresh and plentiful: full of haricots verts, asparagus and crumbled ricotta, with fennel adding a welcome edge. Seared scallops arrived with morsels of caramelised pineapple and crisp pancetta, plus a creamy cauliflower purée; the dish worked, the sweet and salty ingredients making an effective foil for the soft scallops. A main course of halibut with grilled asparagus and sauce vierge featured a chunky piece of fish, but was rather bland. Pork fillet with puy lentils and mashed potato was better; the pork was perfectly cooked, and the lentils were paired with a thick, slightly unctuous apple and mustard gravy that was full of flavour, while the pommes purée was a lovely creamy mash. A pudding of bakewell tart was OK, if not exceptional. In all, a bit hit and miss.
Babies and children welcome: booster seats; high chairs. Booking advisable weekends. Disabled: lift; toilet. Dress: smart casual. Separate rooms for parties seating 10 & 15. Map 5 O5.

Zetter

86-88 Clerkenwell Road, EC1M 5RJ (7324 4455, www.thezetter.com). Farringdon tube/rail.
Breakfast served 7-10.30am Mon-Fri; 7.30-11am Sat, Sun. **Brunch served** 11am-3pm Sat; 11am-4pm Sun. **Lunch served** noon-2.30pm Mon-Fri. **Dinner served** 6-10.30pm Mon-Wed, Sun; 6-11pm Thur-Sat. **Main courses** £8.50-£18.50. **Credit** AmEx, MC, V.
A strong selling point for the Zetter Hotel's popular restaurant is its lovely location, backing on to peaceful St John's Square. In summer, tables are set outside. Inside, the rather dated 'modern' decor (abstract squiggle designs on white bare-brick walls, big brown cylindrical lampshades and a slick curved bar), the young professional, cocktail-swigging clientele and the energetic staff create a buzzy if slightly prosaic vibe. Quality is evident, though, both in the professional approach and the standard of food. Top-drawer bread and olive oil were followed by tasty starters of prawns (garlic-roasted with chorizo, pork belly and a sweet potato purée) and bruschetta (with buffalo mozzarella, baby artichokes, tomato and wild rocket). Lamb (rather gristly) with couscous and minted yoghurt, and lightly seared (top-quality) tuna with scallops made for satisfying mains. Pasta and risotto dishes are also offered – part of a menu that epitomises the Italianate Modern European trend of yesteryear. Zetter is a good place for post-dinner lingering, with a tempting 'afters' menu (summer berry and Frangelico trifle, an Italian-led cheeseboard) and a large range of dessert wines, liqueurs and digestifs. However, we've had some very disappointing breakfasts here.
Available for hire. Babies and children welcome: children's menu; crayons; high chairs; nappy-changing facilities. Booking advisable. Disabled: toilet. Separate rooms for parties, seating 8 & 50. Tables outdoors (14, terrace). Map 5 O4.

Euston

St Pancras Grand NEW

2009 RUNNER-UP BEST NEW DESIGN
Upper Concourse, St Pancras Station, NW1 2QP (7870 9900, www.searcys.co.uk/stpancrasgrand). King's Cross St Pancras tube/rail. **Meals served** 11am-11pm daily. **Main courses** £14-£22. **Set lunch** £18.47 2 courses **Set dinner** £25 3 courses. **Credit** AmEx, MC, V.
The revival of British cuisine has hitherto been less than evident at its gateways to the world. Now, at last, we have a station restaurant to be proud of. Running along the side of the upper gallery, from where the trains depart, St Pancras Grand convincingly evokes a grand European café, with high ceilings, globe lamps and contemporary-brasserie style. Design is from Martin Brudnizki, who did Scott's and the Ivy, and it shares their intimations of glamour. The menu offers the between-meals traveller necessities – all-day brunch, afternoon tea, oyster bar, seafood – but essentially comprises well-sourced British food served both simply (a Quickes cauliflower cheese; Trealy Farm charcuterie) and with ambition (chicken with rhubarb stuffing and pommes fondant). The stripy-aproned staff are first-rate, but did encourage us to spend on (none too generous) side dishes we didn't need; they also convinced us to upgrade to a grüner veltliner wine that didn't work with the food (although points for clocking the GV trend). The Grand is run, like the

RESTAURANTS

nearby Champagne Bar, by Searcy's. It thoroughly deserves to succeed; our only worry was that some customers seemed to interpret the romantic atmosphere too literally, and the prices are pretty high. Our place or yours, Delors? We'll take ours. .
Available for hire. Babies and children welcome: children's menu; high chairs. Booking advisable dinner & weekends. Disabled: toilet. Entertainment: jazz band 6.30-10.30pm Sun. Separate room for parties, seats 12. **Map 4 L3.**

Mayfair

Truc Vert
42 North Audley Street, W1K 6ZR (7491 9988, www.trucvert.co.uk). Bond Street tube. **Meals served** 7.30am-10pm Mon-Fri; 9am-10pm Sat; 9am-3pm Sun. **Main courses** £14.95-£17.50. **Credit** AmEx, MC, V.
The retail aspect of Truc Vert seems to have been gradually sidelined, so many visitors might not realise that the rustic jars of jam and honey on the front shelves are (a) for sale and (b) extremely good. On our lunchtime visit, this fun place was every inch the bustling brasserie, full of smartly dressed businessmen in shirt-sleeves, and glossy Vuitton-toting ladies in white jeans and gold jewellry. Staff make good recommendations – courgette fries were spot-on: soft inside, crunchy and crusty without – but the kitchen sometimes falters. Own-made gnocchi with tomato sauce (an end-of-lunch substitute for the menu's spinach and ricotta ravioli) had been badly overcooked, so the dumplings stuck unpleasantly to the roof of the mouth. Lamb neck fillet was nicely roasted and presented, but its yoghurt and mint sauce was too sweet. We finished with commendable carrot cake (frosting, but not too much) and a fudgey hot chocolate brownie with pistachio ice-cream and a sauce that looked more like spilt cold latte than coffee anglais. Wines by the glass start at £4.25; Sancerre rosé was £7.25 a glass (ouch!) but a pleasant summery drop. Samuel Smith's organic ale and lager also make excellent choices.
Available for hire. Babies and children welcome: high chairs; nappy-changing facilities. Booking advisable. Tables outdoors (12, pavement). Takeaway service. Vegetarian menu. **Map 9 G6.**

Piccadilly

★ The Wolseley (100)
160 Piccadilly, W1J 9EB (7499 6996, www.the wolseley.com). Green Park tube. **Breakfast served** 7-11.30am Mon-Fri; 8-11.30am Sat, Sun. **Lunch served** noon-3pm Mon-Fri; noon-3.30pm Sat, Sun. **Tea served** 3.30-6.30pm Mon-Fri, Sun; 3.30-5.30pm Sat. **Dinner served** 5.30pm-midnight Mon-Sat; 5.30-11pm Sun. **All-day menu served** 11.30am-midnight daily. **Main courses** £6.75-£28.75. **Set tea** £9.75-£19.75. **Cover** £2. **Credit** AmEx, DC, MC, V.
An interpretation of the grand cafés of continental Europea, the Wolseley serves breakfast, lunch, tea and dinner to a smart set of Londoners and visitors in its large opulent dining room. The building is reminiscent of fin de siècle, but in fact dates from the 1920s when it was built as a car showroom. It was then used as a banking hall, before becoming today's café-restaurant in 2003. Enormous bronze doors open up to an art deco-style dining room with vaulted ceilings and gilded Japanese wall panels. An entrance table displays a selection of the day's choices, with breakfast featuring an impressive pyramid of tourier-crafted viennoiserie. No one comes here just for the food, but breakfast at the Wolseley is a fail-safe treat. On our last visit we tried the omelette arnold bennett with flaked smoked haddock, hollandaise sauce, double cream and an eye-watering five egg yolks per person. Fried haggis with duck eggs came in a rich beef-stock sauce laced with whisky. Service is generally very good, the staff as knowledgeable as they are well-turned out. Attention to detail from beginning to end suggests the Wolseley is in no threat of losing its iconic status.
Babies and children welcome: high chairs; nappy-changing facilities. Booking advisable. Disabled: toilet. **Map 9 J7.**

Soho

Bob Bob Ricard [NEW]
2009 WINNER BEST NEW DESIGN
1 Upper James Street, W1F 9DF (3145 1000, www.bobbobricard.com). Piccadilly Circus tube. **Meals served** 7am-1am Mon-Fri; 8am-1am Sat, Sun. **Main Courses** £12-£40. **Credit** AmEx, DC, MC, V.
One thing's for sure: Bob Bob Ricard wasn't created by committee. From the exuberantly eclectic decor via the near-surreal menu, not forgetting the baffling name (derived from those of its owners), it is wilfully individualistic – and as such, divides critics and puzzles the public. We like the place a lot, as its approach shows commitment, humour and, generally, flair. Visually, everything's in your face, including the pink and turquoise uniformed staff (all well rehearsed). Loosely, the decorative scheme is Orient Express meets American diner, with the luxury of the former dominating, and nice details including a 'press for Champagne' button at each table. That the menu includes jelly, milkshake, scotch eggs and Frosties doesn't mean it should all be taken as a joke. Some of the cooking is entirely serious, despite the witty presentation. We'd advise you to steer clear of the sometimes disappointing comfort food, in favour of the likes of Cornish crab cake, cured Orkney

beef with hazelnuts and celeriac, or the miniature cakes – all exquisite. BBR has been criticised as expensive, but its prices (and many dishes) are not dissimilar to those at the Ivy or the Wolseley. The difference is, perhaps, that this new enterprise has yet to generate the buzz and status it needs to justify them.
Babies and children welcome: crayons; high chairs. Booking advisable. Disabled: toilet. Separate room for parties, seats 10. **Map 17 A4.**

Kettners
29 Romilly Street, W1D 5HP (7734 6112, www.kettners.com). Leicester Square or Piccadilly Circus tube. **Meals served** noon-midnight Mon-Sat; noon-9pm Sun. **Main courses** £9.15-£19.90. **Credit** AmEx, MC, V.
It was incongruous, but it worked: this grand building's former incarnation as a pizza house was a Soho institution. The French and European cooking it now serves is undoubtedly more fitting at a venue established by Auguste Kettner, chef to Napoleon III, in 1867, but its identity hasn't quite gelled yet. Staff (smart, unctuous and attentive) and decor (rococo Soho courtesy of Ilse Crawford, with big-windowed views of the street life) signal glamour dining, but the kitchen hasn't quite got the message. Our meals have been variable and sometimes small in portion. For the prosecution: a goat's cheese salad made almost entirely of rocket;

St Pancras Grand

a sour monkfish ceviche; a too-salty onion soup. For the defence, excellent details (chips, bread, butter, pretty serving ramekins) and some blow-away main courses: seared diver scallops were nicely caramelised yet lightly cooked; a fricassee of rabbit with pappardelle and morels almost carnal in its earthiness. Out-of-town diners predominated on a Saturday evening. If Soho-ites are to take Kettners to their heart as they did its predecessor, they may need to see more consistency from the kitchen.
Babies and children welcome: children's menu. Booking advisable Fri, Sat. Entertainment: pianist 6.30-9.30pm Mon-Sat; 6.30-8.30pm Sun. Separate rooms for parties, seating 12-85. **Map 17 C4.**

Princi NEW

2009 RUNNER-UP BEST NEW CHEAP EATS
135 Wardour Street, W1F 0UF (7478 8888, www.princi.co.uk). Leicester Square or Tottenham Court Road tube. **Meals served** 7am-midnight Mon-Sat; 9am-11pm Sun. **Main courses** £5-£8.50. **Credit** AmEx, MC, V.
Given his track record with successful oriental ventures, you might not have expected Alan Yau to team up with an Italian bakery chain. But if you had, you might have guessed it would look like this. The vast L-shaped counter is clad with rough black granite; seating is communal, at dark marble counters or long burnished-metal tables. On a Thursday evening, it was crammed with trendy Soho couples flitting between counter and seat. As well as numerous glazed, bright-red strawberry cakes, tiramisus, pastries and a moist, booze-heavy torta di pane (stuffed with pear chunks and dried fruit), there's a vast range of savoury dishes. The big rectangular slices of pizza have a springy, bready base; a margherita (only £2.50) was pungent with fresh thyme, and a caprese salad came packed with creamy balls of buffalo mozzarella and big slices of beef tomato (but no basil leaves that we could discern). To follow, a cheesy aubergine parmigiana was pleasingly firm and dense, although arancini (saffron rice balls) stuffed with mozzarella had fused into overly tart globes. You might struggle if you suffer from option-paralysis, and Princi can get hectic, but for a quick inexpensive snack, it's a solid option.
Babies and children admitted. Bookings not accepted. Disabled: toilet. Takeaway service; delivery service (over £100 within 3-mile radius). **Map 17 B3.**

Trafalgar Square

National Café

East Wing, National Gallery, Trafalgar Square, WC2N 5DN (7747 2525, www.thenational cafe.com). Charing Cross tube/rail. **Breakfast served** 8-11.30am, **lunch served** noon-5pm, **tea served** 3-5.30pm daily. **Dinner served** 5.30-11pm Mon-Sat. **Main courses** £8.50-£16.50. **Set dinner** (5.30-7pm) £14.50 2 courses, £17.50 3 courses. **Credit** MC, V.
This handsome space at the Charing Cross Road side of the National Gallery is thronged with sightseers and local workers during the day (when the self-service sandwich bar at the rear is also open), but it can make a calming retreat for dinner or drinks come the evening. Glossy black walls and high windows overlook smart little wooden tables and red seating in the brasserie area; the bar occupies the wall opposite. Breakfasts (porridge, pastries, eggs benedict, cheese on toast), afternoon tea and extravagant ice-cream sundaes (ideal for placating youngsters) are also served. As you expect from an Oliver Peyton operation, the quality of ingredients and cooking is high and the menu is a seasonal treat encompassing all tastes. There are old-school classics (burger, steak and ale pie), salads, pasta dishes, grills, a kids' menu and top-notch cheese and charcuterie boards. Staff were amenable, though could have been more attentive considering the lack of custom on our midweek visit. The main problem is pricing. Cod and chips for £13.50, macaroni cheese for £9.50, gooseberry fool for £7.50: everything costs a couple of quid more than you expect. And that, despite the enjoyable food, leaves a bad taste in the mouth.

Available for hire. Babies and children welcome: children's menu; high chairs; nappy-changing facilites. Booking advisable. Disabled: toilet. Separate room for parties, seats 30. **Map 10 K7.**

West

Chiswick

High Road Brasserie

162-166 Chiswick High Road, W4 1PR (8742 7474, www.highroadhouse.co.uk). Turnham Green tube. **Breakfast served** 7am-noon Mon-Fri; 8am-noon Sat, Sun. **Meals served** noon-11pm Mon-Thur; noon-midnight Fri. **Brunch served** noon-5pm Sat, Sun. **Dinner served** 5pm-midnight Sat; 5-10pm Sun. **Main courses** £10-£22. **Set lunch** £12 2 courses, £14 3 courses. **Credit** AmEx, MC, V.
Full of families at 4.30pm on a Sunday afternoon, High Road Brasserie is a vibrant, good-looking establishment. We love the colourful mixed Victorian-style floor tiles, the 1930s lighting and the green banquette that stretches all round one side. The brunch menu lists breakfast dishes – eggs benedict, maybe, or yoghurt with stewed fruit – as well as sandwiches (croque monsieur, salt beef and gherkin), small plates, starters (smoked salmon, asparagus with hollandaise), grills and regular main courses (some with brunch-like qualities such as smoked haddock hash with double fried egg). As with any true brasserie, you can stop here simply for a drink or coffee. Our late lunch was a mixed bag. Crispy squid with aïoli was rather pub-grubbish; the batter may have been crispy, but it was bland, and the accompanying aïoli seemed like mayonnaise with a sprinkling of paprika. Steak frites was much better: a juicy steak cooked rare as requested, made even more moist by a generous dollop of garlic butter, and served with a huge portion of matchstick chips. Such food may be unambitious, but it's enjoyable when done well, and the lively atmosphere makes this venue a good local meeting place.
Babies and children welcome: crayons; high chairs; nappy changing facilities. Booking advisable weekends & dinner. Disabled: toilet. Tables outdoors (9, pavement).

BEST BRASSERIES

Romantic liaisons
Indulge in brief encounters at **Bob Bob Ricard** (see p45), **Kettners** (see p45) and **St Pancras Grand** (see p44).

Ready for brekkie?
Start the morning like a monarch by breakfasting at **Chapters** (see p49), **High Road Brasserie** (see above), **Kettners** (see p45), **Tom's Kitchen** (see right) and the **Wolseley** (see p45).

Youth culture
Kids are especially welcome at **Banners** (see p49), the **Depot** (see right), **Giraffe** (see p48), **Hugo's** (see p49) and **Tate Modern Café: Level 2** (see p49).

For the Gaul of it
Pretend you're in Paris at **High Road Brasserie** (see above), **Newtons** (see p48) and **Truc Vert** (see p45).

Fair-weather friends
Dine al fresco at **Butcher & Grill** (see right), **Gallery Mess** (see right), **The Depot** (see right), **Giraffe** (see p48), **Hoxton Grill** (see p49), **Newtons** (see p48), **Truc Vert** (see p45) and the **Zetter** (see p44).

Late-night munchies
Eat after 11pm at **Banners** (see p49), **Bob Bob Ricard** (see p45), **Kettners** (see p45), **Princi** (see left) and the **Wolseley** (see p45).

Notting Hill

Electric Brasserie

191 Portobello Road, W11 2ED (7908 9696, www.the-electric.co.uk). Ladbroke Grove tube. **Meals served** 8am-11pm Mon-Fri; 8am-5pm, 6-11pm Sat; 8am-5pm, 6-10pm Sun. **Main courses** £10-£28. **Set lunch** (noon-4.45pm Mon-Fri) £13 2 courses, £16 3 courses. **Credit** AmEx, DC, MC, V.
There's a real brasserie buzz to this place, and with a private members' club upstairs (run by Soho House) and the Electric Cinema next door, it has become something of a landmark on the Portobello scene. Terrace tables looking on to the Portobello Road fill up quickly on sunny lunchtimes. Inside is a dimly lit area with a long wooden bar and tables alongside, which opens into a proper restaurant section at the back. Food has a retro tendency. There are much-loved steak sandwiches – dripping with melted cheese and balsamic onions – and hefty burgers, alongside a selection of tapas-style small plates and a main menu with classics like lobster, moules marinière and steak frites. Thick slices of beetroot with crumbly goat's cheese, pine nuts and a tangy dressing made a great summer starter. A fennel and garlic soup was creamy, original and had a finely tuned balance of flavours. For mains, perfectly rendered steak frites featured chunky, golden chips in a pot (ideal for sharing). Staff were pleasant and professional, but a little slow on our most recent visit.
Babies and children welcome: booster seats; children's menu; crayons; high chairs; nappy-changing facilities. Booking advisable Thur-Sun. Disabled: toilet. Separate rooms for parties, seating 14 & 60. Tables outdoors (6, terrace). Vegetarian menu. **Map 19 B3.**

Westbourne Grove

Raoul's Café

105-107 Talbot Road, W11 2AT (7229 2400, www.raoulsgourmet.com). Ladbroke Grove or Westbourne Park tube. **Meals served** 8.30am-10.15pm daily. **Main courses** £10.50-£15.50. **Credit** AmEx, MC, V.
The Notting Hill branch of Raoul's (the original is in Maida Vale) is particularly strong on brunch (available until 6pm). The full range of egg-based dishes (omelettes, frittata, eggs benedict, poached) as well as options like smoked haddock, lamb's kidneys on toast, a selection of pastries and very generous smoothies, make this an ideal hangover-soothing grazing spot at weekends. The rest of the menu is equally extensive, with seven main courses (all meat) featuring the likes of cottage pie and organic hamburgers; a range of pasta dishes; excellent sandwiches (Raoul's focaccia comes recommended: avocado, grilled aubergine, buffalo mozzarella, pesto); and daily specials. Salads are of the Mediterranean ilk – grilled halloumi with roasted vegetables, salade niçoise – with olive oil glugged over the top. The decor has a slick 1970s feel, with tan leather chairs, wooden spherical lampshades hanging from the ceiling, tones of amber and brass, and streaked dark-wood tables with single curved metal legs (plus a kitsch painting of the Queen with her eyes closed). On sunny days, the tables out front are the most coveted. Service is efficient and pleasant enough, if fairly disinterested. Patrons are west London to a tee.
Babies and children welcome: high chairs. Disabled: toilet. Separate room for parties, seats 30. Takeaway service. **Map 19 C3. For branches see index.**

South West

Barnes

The Depot

Tideway Yard, 125 Mortlake High Street, SW14 8SN (8878 9462, www.depotbrasserie.co.uk). Barnes, Barnes Bridge or Mortlake rail/209 bus. **Brunch served** 9.30am-12.30pm Sat. **Lunch served** noon-3pm Mon-Fri; 12.30-3.30pm Sat, noon-4pm Sun. **Dinner served** 6-11pm Mon-Sat; 6-10.30pm Sun. **Main courses** £9.95-£15.

Set meal (noon-3pm Mon-Fri) £12.50 2 courses, £15.50 3 courses; (Jan-Feb, Oct-Nov) £10 2 courses. **Credit** AmEx, DC, MC, V.

This riverside brasserie, once a coach house and stables, is tucked away from the road in a courtyard. It's a popular spot, and was almost full on a Tuesday night. Burnished wood floors and furniture, bold paintings and subdued lighting provide a mellow setting; diners on the Thames side of the long space get sterling sunset views. The menu is helpfully divided by theme rather than size, with veggies and salads, fish and shellfish, meat and grills, plus side dishes and puddings. The cooking is reliably good. Seasonal ingredients appear (asparagus, oysters – both excellent), and there are oriental touches (roast pork belly with steamed chinese greens and shiitake broth, say), as well as more typical brasserie classics such as softly textured and intensely flavoured corned beef hash adorned with fried eggs. Smoked haddock monte carlo (a stack of mash, fish and poached eggs, with creamy sauce) produced falling-apart flakes of fish, though the sauce was too sloppy and the dollop of intensely flavoured purée of tomatoes an unnecessary extra. Warm chocolate cake with pistachio ice-cream and raspberries was rich yet summery – desserts are a forte. A wide-ranging wine list (and separate bar area), Saturday brunch and a recently introduced morning menu add to the Depot's appeal.
Available for hire. Babies and children welcome: children's menu; crayons; high chairs; nappy-changing facilities. Booking advisable. Tables outdoors (11, courtyard).

Chelsea

Gallery Mess NEW

Saatchi Gallery, Duke of York's HQ, King's Road, SW3 4LY (7730 8135). Sloane Square tube. **Breakfast served** 9-11.30am, **meals served** 11.30am-9pm daily. **Main courses** £9.50-£12. **Credit** AmEx, MC, V.

Art is the USP at Gallery Mess: this fabulous brasserie is in the Saatchi Gallery and you can sit inside surrounded by modern art. Alternatively, there are tables outside in the grounds until 6pm, ideal for summer eating. The menu offers something for everybody, at all times of day. A simple breakfast and brunch choice (served until 11.30am) features the likes of pastries, bacon roll, smoked salmon on toast, or a superior 'Great British' breakfast; there's afternoon tea too (after 2.30pm). The lunch and dinner menu includes retro touches (prawn cocktail), plus salads (avocado and fennel), and standard dishes like a pasta of the day, chargrilled chicken breast, and excellent burgers. The daily specials are far more ambitious, including starters such as venison carpaccio with truffle dressing and parmesan, and mains like saddle of lamb with red-pepper couscous, yoghurt and jasmine sultanas. Puddings are sweet and traditional: milk chocolate sundae, rhubarb and strawberry crumble, or a glorious knickerbocker glory (a sundae glass stuffed with high-quality fruit-flavoured ices and topped with a freshly made, buttery shortbread biscuit). Staff are conscientious and attentive.
Babies and children welcome: high chairs; nappy-changing facilities. Booking advisable lunch & dinner. Disabled: toilet. Separate room for parties, seats 30. Tables outdoors (30, terrace). Takeaway service. **Map 14 F11**.

★ Tom's Kitchen

27 Cale Street, SW3 3QP (7349 0202, www.tomskitchen.co.uk). South Kensington or Sloane Square tube. **Breakfast served** 7-10am, **lunch served** noon-3pm Mon-Fri. **Brunch served** 10am-3pm Sat, Sun. **Dinner served** 6pm-11pm daily. **Main courses** £12-£29. **Credit** AmEx, MC, V.

His fish and chip shop may have floundered, but the retro-butcher chic of Tom's Kitchen has netted a loyal clientele of stylish locals, as well as quality-breakfast seekers from further afield. White tiled walls, vast expanses of marble, and a busy open kitchen ensure the venue sounds full even when it isn't (though for weekend lunches it usually is).

Gallery Mess

Portraits of artisan food producers (prestige organic suppliers include Daylesford and Rhug Estate), a couple of old columns, and mirrors made from rusty window frames soften the look, but not the noise. If you see a handsome Mr Aikens about the place it may not be Tom. Twin brother Rob, also an esteemed chef, is head of operations here. The real hot dish however is the pancake – note singular. Well over an inch thick and almost as big as the serving plate, it is categorically London's best: filled with blueberries and drizzled with maple syrup. Add a side of smoky bacon (£4) if you need some protein. The smoothie (berry, banana and yoghurt) is lush, though pricey at £5.50 – and a large orange juice is a fiver. Lunch and dinner menus make the most of the wood-smoked oven, spit-roast and grill, with roasts of chicken and lamb, steak sandwiches and burgers, plus a few terrines and pasta dishes.
Babies and children welcome: high chairs; nappy-changing facilities. Booking advisable dinner & weekends. Disabled: toilet. Separate room for parties, seats 22. **Map 14 E11**.

South
Balham

Harrison's

15-19 Bedford Hill, SW12 9EX (8675 6900, www.harrisonsbalham.co.uk). Balham tube/rail. **Lunch served** noon-3pm Mon-Fri. **Dinner served** 6-10.30pm Mon-Sat, 6-10pm Sun. **Breakfast served** 9am-noon, **brunch served** noon-4pm Sat, Sun. **Reduced menu served** 3-6pm Mon-Fri; 4-6pm Sat, Sun. **Main courses** £9.50-£17.50. **Set lunch** (Mon-Sat) £12 2 courses, £15 3 courses; (Sun) £21 3 courses. **Set dinner** £14 2 courses, £17 3 courses. **Credit** AmEx, MC, V.

Tucked into a row of urban eateries near the tube, Balham sibling of Sam Harrison's Chiswick bar-brasserie has wide appeal thanks to a buzzy atmosphere and relaxed self-assurance. Smoothly efficient service provides lunch, brunch, kids' meals, dinner menus and all-day bar food. Order a single Maldon rock oyster if you're inclined; a salad 'side' for 'something to start'; or an affogato to combine coffee and pud – and your tap water will still be poured with aplomb by friendly waiters. Bottled ketchup is provided without a blink as an adjunct to a very grown-up steak, or burger with fries, even though the tangy own-made chutney is sublime. Rick Stein's partnership is evidenced by sound seafood. A sliver of raw salmon with Japanese condiments showed off the sheer perfection of the fish on a recent visit. Meat and veg are treated with equal respect, and generously served, whether a mound of tender, free-range chicken livers, a nicely made bed of spinach, or a robust and toothsome artichoke and ricotta penne pasta assembly. A nicely constructed wine list includes several 500ml carafes and halves of excellent house champagne. Handsome decor, soft lighting and decent elbow room mute the busy brasserie clatter.
Babies and children welcome: children's menu; crayons; high chairs; nappy-changing facilities. Booking advisable Fri-Sun. Disabled: toilet. Separate rooms for parties, seating 24 & 40. Tables outdoors (8, terrace).

Battersea

Butcher & Grill

39-41 Parkgate Road, SW11 4NP (7924 3999, www.thebutcherandgrill.com). Clapham Junction rail then 170 bus/bus 19, 49, 319, 345. **Breakfast served** 8.30am-noon daily. **Lunch served** noon-3.30pm Mon-Sat; noon-4pm Sun. **Dinner served** 6-11pm Mon-Sat. **Main courses** £7.50-£25. **Set meals** £12.50 2 courses; £15 3 courses. **Credit** AmEx, MC, V.

'Um, I don't know about that,' said our waiter, when asked about an Italian red (the pricey wine list, irritatingly, doesn't mention grape varieties). The wine had sold out, anyway. Given the meaty menu, we settled for an Australian grenache: a real bruiser at 14.5%. Butcher & Grill styles itself a high-end butcher's with tables, though in fact is a high-ceilinged, capacious bar-restaurant that seems to hanker after a Chelsea location. A foie gras and chicken liver parfait starter was smooth as cheesecake, lacking the guts to match its sweet brioche. A whole salt and pepper squid fared better, its big hits of pepper and chilli offset by sweet slivers of roast pimento. A main of sage- and marjoram-marinated pork fillet came pleasingly rugby ball-shaped, with curly kale and garlic-roasted ratte potatoes; it was perfectly moist, but seemingly undercooked at one end. Calf's liver and bacon made serviceable comfort food yet, when mash and broccoli were added, cost £22.25. However, if ordering from set menus, it is possible to dine frugally here. An Australian wine evening was advertised, offering five courses and five glasses to match for £50. Let's hope the waiters are up to speed by then.
Available for hire. Babies and children welcome: children's menu; high chairs; nappy-changing facilities. Booking advisable weekends. Disabled: toilet. Tables outdoors (5, pavement; 6, terrace). Takeaway service. **Map 21 C1**.
For branch see index.

Clapham

Newtons

33-35 Abbeville Road, SW4 9LA (8673 0977, www.newtonsrestaurants.co.uk). Clapham South tube. **Lunch served** noon-4pm daily. **Dinner served** 6-11pm Mon-Sat; 6-10.30pm Sun. **Main courses** £9.50-£16. **Set lunch** (noon-4pm Mon-Sat) £8 2 courses, £10.50 3 courses; (Sun) £18.50 3 courses. **Set dinner** (Mon-Sat) £15 2 courses, £18.50 3 courses. **Credit** MC, V.

Newtons has been split in half since last time we visited. You enter via a cosy, living-room of a bar – all stripped floorboards, grand fireplaces and cream-painted brick – before taking your table in the adjacent restaurant. It's easy to see why this is a much-loved local. Our ebullient maître d' insisted we change tables to allow ourselves more space, and discreetly raised the volume of the football on our return to the bar: the kind of hospitality that makes you want to grab a striped armchair and order another bottle. The owners support fellow traders too (our bacon burger came with a tangy wedge of cheese from MacFarlane's across the road, as did the abundance of mustards and relishes), though they could have invested in a better bun. Another main of chilli and herb-crusted cod was a succulent treat, yet the meagre portion made us long for something more substantial. Fortunately, we opted for the freshly made puddings and were rewarded with an unctuous sunken chocolate soufflé boosted by mint-leaf-dotted ice-cream, and a zesty blueberry mousse topped with hazelnuts. Perhaps this isn't a destination restaurant, but once you've found Newtons, you'll find it hard to leave.

Available for hire. Babies and children welcome: crayons; high-chairs. Booking advisable weekends. Tables outdoors (8, terrace). Vegan dishes. **Map 22 A3**.

Waterloo

Giraffe

Riverside Level 1, Royal Festival Hall, SE1 8XX (7928 2004, www.giraffe.net). Embankment tube/ Waterloo tube/rail. **Meals served** 8am-10.45pm Mon-Fri; 9am-10.45pm Sat; 9am-10.15pm Sun. **Main courses** £7.95-£14.95. **Set meal** (5-7pm Mon-Fri) £7.25 2 courses. **Credit** AmEx, MC, V.

Giraffe restaurants aim to please all ages and all tastes and, to a degree, they succeed. The pleasant staff at this South Bank branch welcome lots of families during the day, while an older crowd of couples and tourists takes over in the evening. No matter which branch you find yourself in, the colour scheme is orange, world music is on the stereo and murals of happy, smiling faces adorn the walls. The menu is lengthy and incorporates flavours from every corner of the world, but the cooking is a little hit and miss. There are more than ten starters, including mixed meze with warm nan (a tasty, if small, dish to share), wok-fried edamame and Japanese tiger prawns. Substantial salads offer a healthy alternative to the array of main dishes that include some excellent burgers, noodle dishes and a disappointing vegetable burrito. Desserts are on the small side, but the warm chocolate brownie with hot chocolate sauce was lovely. On a sunny day, aim for a table on the riverside patio and order a tutti frutti life-saver or a giddy giraffe (one of *Giraffe's* decidedly cheery, but tempting, smoothies).

Babies and children welcome: children's menu; crayons; high chairs; nappy-changing facilities. Disabled: toilet. Tables outdoors (40, terrace). Takeaway service. **Map 10 M8**. **For branches see index.**

Tamesa@oxo

2nd floor, Oxo Tower Wharf, SE1 9PH (7633 0088, www.tamesaatoxo.com). Blackfriars or Waterloo tube/rail. **Lunch served** noon-3.30pm, **dinner served** 5.30-10.30pm Tue-Sat. **Main courses** £9.50-£18.50. **Set meal** (lunch, 5.30-7.30pm Tue-Sat) £12.50 2 courses, £15.50 3 courses. **Credit** AmEx, MC, V.

Far below the high-flyers on the Oxo Tower's pricey top floor sits Tamesa, which boasts the same glorious river views but lower prices. It's not cheap, mind – around £15 for a main course, albeit one made with impressively seasonal ingredients. No-nonsense furnishings (and an awful lot of yellow paint) suggest an unpretentious lunchtime joint, but Tamesa seems to hanker after higher things. There's an incongruous digestif trolley, and some fussy items on the menu. Mushrooms à la grecque with cauliflower purée and truffle contained no discernible truffle, and the purée was excess to requirements. But watermelon and feta salad was achingly fresh and exceptionally pretty. Lamb was cooked to perfection and chips were terrific. A samphire side dish was so flavourful and crunchy, and so rife with garlic, that it vanished in seconds, to the delight of the lovely staff. There aren't many places in London that offer riverside dining without the bother of booking. Were it not for our waiter's open-mouthed incomprehension when asked to replace a substandard bottle of wine, nothing would have spoiled the view.

Bob Bob Ricard. See p45.

Available for hire. Babies and children welcome: children's menu; crayons; high chairs. Booking advisable dinner & weekends. Disabled: lift; toilet. Separate room for parties, seats 24. Vegan dishes. **Map 11 N7**.

South East

Bankside

Tate Modern Café: Level 2
2nd floor, Tate Modern, Sumner Street, SE1 9TG (7401 5014, www.tate.org.uk). Southwark tube/London Bridge tube/rail. **Meals served** 10am-6pm Mon-Thur, Sat, Sun; 10am-10pm Fri. **Main courses** £10.50-£12.95 **Credit** AmEx, DC, MC, V.
A venue as awe-inspiring as Tate Modern would let itself down without a stylish eating space. Fortunately, this ground-floor café is aesthetically impressive, with huge windows, an industrial metal ceiling, square black tables and chairs, and halo-like pendant lights. Food is of a decent standard, with a fairly diverse range of dishes (and plate sizes) catering to a wide variety of appetites. The cooking is unlikely to bowl you over – but that's what the art is for. Lunch options range from pasta siciliana with salted ricotta, to smoked haddock and Shetland salmon fish cake with wilted spinach. Lighter options include a meze plate, and a dish of potted beef with mustard and toasted sourdough. In the evening, choose from a range of Spanish and English 'tapas', and a smaller selection of mains. This is also a good spot for afternoon nibbles, or coffee and cakes (bakewell tart and the like). Service was the only problem on our visit. Staff were pleasant enough, but it took a long time to get their attention. There was another long wait for our dishes, and our drinks order went forgotten.
Babies and children welcome: children's menu; high chairs; nappy-changing facilities. Disabled: toilet. **Map 11 O7**.

Blackheath

Chapters All Day Dining NEW
43-45 Montpelier Vale, SE3 0TJ (8333 2666, www.chaptersrestaurants.com). Blackheath rail. **Breakfast served** 8-11.30am Mon-Fri; 8am-noon Sat; 9am-noon Sun. **Lunch served** noon-3pm Mon-Sat; noon-4pm Sun. **Tea served** 3-6pm Mon-Sat; 4-6pm Sun. **Dinner served** 6-11pm Mon-Sat; 6-9pm Sun. **Main courses** £7.50-£22.95. **Credit** AmEx, MC, V.
What used to be Chapter Two has undergone a refurbishment and reopened as Chapters All Day Dining. The former incarnation was a fine-dining establishment, but Chapters (sister of esteemed Kent restaurant Chapter One) is more of a brasserie. Exposed brickwork, wooden flooring, banquette seating and scatter cushions create a relaxed, informal setting. The all-day dining menu spans from eggs benedict to cream teas, including delicate fish dishes and traditional roasts. You won't find any particularly adventurous dishes, but standards are high. Steaks are a speciality, and are cooked on a Josper charcoal oven that gives the meat an almost magenta appearance and a smoky barbecue flavour. We enjoyed a well-balanced pea and sweet-basil soup and an equally well-executed risotto with herbs. A main course of lemon sole with horseradish cream sauce was exceptional and very reasonably priced. Like most brasseries, Chapters accommodates children happily. We noticed (and appreciated) that diners with kids in tow had all been tactfully seated on the upper floor.
Babies and children welcome: children's menu; high chairs; nappy-changing facilities. Booking essential dinner & weekends. Disabled: lift; toilet. Tables outdoors (4, pavement).

Crystal Palace

★ Joanna's
56 Westow Hill, SE19 1RX (8670 4052, www. joannas.uk.com). Crystal Palace or Gipsy Hill rail. **Breakfast served** 10am-noon Mon-Sat. **Meals served** noon-11pm Mon-Sat; noon-10.30pm Sun. **Main courses** £9-£16. **Set meal** £9.95 2 courses; £12.95 3 courses. **Credit** AmEx, MC, V.
Offering a Wolseley-like elegance without the star-spotting, Joanna's is old-fashioned in the best sense: all bentwood chairs, etched glass and starched white tablecloths. The matter-of-fact one-page menu lists a small selection of dishes served from breakfast to supper. Staff had no problem rustling up high chairs for children (and provided kids' portions, though they're not widely advertised). Our cottage pie was picture-perfect: a pristine rectangle of golden piped cheesy mash, topping a mix of lamb and beef mince served with a rich red wine gravy and shredded savoy cabbage. Joanna's burger was equally satisfying, its bun holding up well to an abundance of produce – crisp, gratifyingly misshapen hand-cut chips too. Desserts were sinful; neither the dense dark chocolate mousse nor the sticky banoffi and toasted almond pancake was for the faint-hearted. With well-chosen beers such as Samuel Adams ales augmenting the wine list, Joanna's is a place for savouring the finer things in life. The best seats? They're at what locals call 'table 99', enclosed in its own glass snug. If there were any celebs in Crystal Palace, this would be the perfect spot to draw some discreet attention to themselves.
Babies and children welcome: booster seats; children's menu; high chairs. Booking advisable; essential weekends. Tables outdoors (3, pavement).

London Bridge & Borough

More NEW
104 Tooley Street, SE1 2TH (7403 0635, www.moretooleystreet.com). London Bridge tube/rail. **Meals served** 8am-11pm Mon-Fri; 10am-11pm Sat; 10am-4pm Sun. **Main courses** £10-£16. **Credit** AmEx, MC, V.
A new venture from chef Theodore Kyriakou and business partner Paloma Campbell, the pair who created Livebait and the Real Greek (and then sold them on, after which quality declined), More is a true all-day brasserie. Small, sleek and chic (there's lots of white, with red accents), it swings effortlessly from breakfast muesli and fruit plates to full-on lunches and dinners. The happy fluidity continues with the types of cuisine offered. Our starter of braised squid, with fennel, leeks, and gremolata in a fish and wine stock resembled a variation on bouillabaisse, and its strong saffron flavour contrasted with the delicacy of our other choice: a stack of crab meat with roasted tomatoes and peach flesh, garnished with peppery watercress. Mains consist of classics with added touches – such as seared salmon with cauliflower caponata, or marinated roast chicken with warm cannellini bean salad, spicy salami and sauce vierge – along with more unusual, fusion-style dishes. 'Surf and turf' was actually more of a laksa-like spiced broth with slivers of white fish and beef submerged in it. With jolly staff, lively customers, big-flavoured, creative food and a real feel-good factor, More deserves to do well.
Babies and children admitted. Booking advisable. Takeaway service. **Map 12 Q8**.

East

Shoreditch

Hoxton Grille
81 Great Eastern Street, EC2A 3HU (7739 9111, www.grillerestaurants.com). Old Street tube/rail/ 55, 135 bus. **Meals served** 7am-11pm daily. **Main courses** £7-£20. **Credit** AmEx, MC, V.
Part of the hip Hoxton Hotel, the Grill has recently been taken over by the Soho House group. There are 'urban eaterie' touches in abundance here – a large, dimly lit dining area, exposed piping and brickwork, open kitchen and slick leather banquettes. The food is surprisingly good, and varied. Retro classics such as prawn cocktail, and sardines on toast, were highly successful, as were tasty dishes of coq au vin, and steak and chips with béarnaise sauce. Meat-lovers will adore the mixed grill, but those looking for something a little lighter should try the sandwiches and pasta dishes. Hefty desserts include chocolate fudge brownies with bourbon ice-cream, and vanilla cheesecake. The staff are charming and well informed (our waitress recommended a great bottle of Chilean Tiera Antica merlot), but, despite the lack of custom on our Saturday night visit, service was undeniably slow. Loud music and merriment from the adjoining bar meant that the restaurant was far too noisy, hence the Grill is a great option for a night out with friends, but not so appealing for a civilised meal with your parents.
Babies and children welcome: children's menu; high chairs; nappy-changing facilities. Booking advisable weekends. Disabled: toilet. Entertainment: DJ 8pm Fri, Sat. Separate room for parties, seats 20. Tables outdoors (20, courtyard). Vegan dishes. Vegetarian menu. **Map 6 Q4**.

North

Crouch End

Banners
21 Park Road, N8 8TE (8348 2930, www.bannersrestaurant.co.uk). Finsbury Park tube/rail then W7 bus. **Meals served** 9am-11.30pm Mon-Thur; 9am-midnight Fri; 10am-4pm, 5pm-midnight Sat; 10am-4pm, 5-11pm Sun. **Main courses** £9.25-£14.75. **Set lunch** £6.95 1 course. **Credit** MC, V.
With its vintage posters, shelves of ketchup and King Curry, and a soundtrack ranging from world music to Bruce Springsteen, Banners is the place Hard Rock Café forgot to be. The menu (complete with local advertising, and a cover drawn by Louis, age 13) draws inspiration from Sri Lanka to the Caribbean, via good old Blighty. It is complemented by a list of specials, though our rather offhand waitress neglected to tell us what they were. Smoothies are popular; there's also a long list of cheapish cocktails plus decent Argentinian chardonnay by the glass. Huge plates of wild boar sausages, and curries with flatbreads, are carried swiftly through the dimly lit, cosy dining area. Eating at the bar out front is similarly cramped, and turnover is high. Jerk chicken burger didn't look appealing but tasted delicious, with beautifully tender slices of nicely spiced bird. But fried spoon bread was too oily an accompaniment for rich saltfish and ackee presented on a banana leaf. Still, we liked the ruddy-coloured, skin-on chips. Banners is not without faults, then, but it is perennially and justifiably popular.
Babies and children welcome: children's menu; crayons; high chairs; toys. Booking advisable.

North West

Queen's Park

Hugo's
21-25 Lonsdale Road, NW6 6RA (7372 1232). Queen's Park tube/rail. **Meals served** 9.30am-11pm daily. **Main courses** £11.50-£15.80. **Credit** MC, V.
This appealingly laid-back restaurant is located down a small street of workshops. Deep-red walls, dark wooden tables and large glinting mirrors create a mellow atmosphere in what is a spacious room. Hugo's attracts customers of all ages, particularly at the weekend, when local families come to tuck into classic brunch dishes, own-made cakes and sandwiches – and then happily hang around well into the afternoon. The venue was once called the Organic Café, and there is still an emphasis on organic and ethical food and drink here (our decently priced wine was Fairtrade). The small selection of starters is made up mostly of fish and seafood dishes (fried calamares with aïoli was a moreish assembly), while the range of main courses is more extensive: tasty burgers, simple pasta dishes, a delicious mediterranean fish stew, and a good version of classic smoked haddock with a poached egg, spinach and hollandaise. The service is relaxed but efficient. Jazz nights, held every Sunday (free of charge for diners), complete the chilled-out vibe.
Available for hire. Babies and children welcome: crayons; high chairs; nappy-changing facilities. Booking advisable weekends. Entertainment: musicians 8pm Wed, Thur, Sun. Tables outdoors (7, pavement). Takeaway service. **Map 1 A1**.

RESTAURANTS

British

There's still a huge gulf in style, if not in cuisine, between the old guard and the new in this chapter. Visit **Wiltons**, **Rules** and **Simpson's-in-the-Strand**, which have notched up over 600 years in business between them, and you'll discover the unyielding Englishness of the upper classes: a world of ultra-proper service, venerable wooden panelling and gentlemen's clubbiness. Game, simple fish dishes and roast meats are mainstays. Since the renaissance of British cookery, brought about by pioneers such as Gary Rhodes (of **Rhodes Twenty Four**) and Fergus Henderson (**St John**), those restaurants that produce a creative reinterpretation of the cuisine can themselves be split in two, with the likes of **Market**, **Hereford Road** and **Great Queen Street** at the more casual end, and the new **Corrigan's Mayfair** and the **Albemarle** among the more formal modern restaurants.

Seasonality has become a watchword across London's restaurants, but is pursued with vigour at many of the establishments listed here. Look no further if you're after blood oranges in February, wild garlic in April, English asparagus in May, and winter-time game. The top-end venues also reflect the British love affair with vintage wines, and many have voluminous lists to browse through – though, interestingly, St John has not a single English wine on its list. Others, notably **Roast**, also take tea seriously.

British food continues to be a modish theme for London's chefs, and there have been several new openings in the past year. **Rotunda** and **High Timber** both showcase British meat, naming the farms that supply their produce. **The Brill** and **Albion** (winner of our 2009 Best Cheap Eats award) offer a modern take on a more plebeian British cuisine. We also welcome the **Restaurant at St Paul's** – after all, what location could be more British?

gnocchi with wild mushrooms and truffles, perhaps; Gloucester Old Spot sausages and mash; rack of lamb, or fish. Prestige suppliers are name-checked (Denham Estates venison, Label Anglais chicken, Forman's smoked salmon). In summer, desserts of Kentish strawberries with shortbread and strawberry and lemon thyme soup, and apple and elderflower jelly with raspberries and vanilla ice-cream, hit just the right light note.
Available for hire. Babies and children admitted. Booking advisable. Disabled: toilet. Separate room for parties, seats 18. Tables outdoors (4, riverside). Map 11 O7.

The Mercer
34 Threadneedle Street, EC2R 8AY (7628 0001, www.themercer.co.uk). Bank tube/DLR. **Breakfast served** 7.30-10am, **lunch served** noon-3pm, **dinner served** 5.30-9.30pm Mon-Fri. **Main courses** £13-£26.50. **Credit** AmEx, DC, V.
These handsome old bank premises have been sensitively transformed into a pleasing restaurant, unfussily decorated and with kind lighting. There's a bar too, offering cocktails alongside the substantial wine list (plenty by the glass and carafe). Staff are young and friendly. On a midweek evening, the place quietly buzzed with a mixed clientele (even the odd dating couple). Starters run from ox-tongue salad with pea shoots to comfort options of hot goat's cheese and fig toasts with spiced green lentils. Mains, though, are the stand-out. From melt-in-the-mouth calf's liver (with bubble, grilled bacon and onion gravy) to slow-braised venison shank so tender it fell off the bone, to decent Mercer pie (rump steak, mushrooms, London porter ale) – British meat and game were given a fine showcase. Seared scallops with artichoke mash, leeks, and lobster dressing was good too, if rich, though a side of roast garlic potatoes wasn't garlicky. After that it's a hard choice between the classic puddings, savouries and British cheeses. We solved the dilemma with a plate of 'lovely things' (five sweet items) and sorbets – including, unusually, poached pear. Not cheap, but less pricey than many City restaurants, and definitely more relaxed.
Available for hire. Babies and children welcome: high chairs. Booking advisable lunch. Disabled: toilet. Separate room for parties, seats 40. Map 12 Q6.

Central
Belgravia

Pantechnicon Rooms
10 Motcomb Street, SW1X 8LA (7730 6074, www.thepantechnicon.com). Hyde Park Corner or Knightsbridge tube.
Bar **Meals served** noon-10pm Mon-Sat; noon-9pm Sun. **Main courses** £8.50-£15.50.
Dining Room **Lunch served** noon-3pm Mon-Fri. **Dinner served** 6-9.30pm Mon-Sat. **Main courses** £11.50-£29.50.
Both **Credit** AmEx, MC, V.
This pub and dining room is nice enough in a Belgravia-meets-gastropub way; everything is clean and polished, and natural light floods through huge period windows. But a meal in the first-floor dining room (the casual ground-floor bar also serves food) revealed a huge disparity in dish quality. Best were a finger-lickingly good chicken liver parfait with port jelly and toast; zesty goat's curd, pea shoot, rocket and walnut salad; and beautifully tender 8oz fillet steak with pommes frites (a hefty £27.50). Vanilla panna cotta with caramel strawberries was delightful too. But smoked haddock and salmon pie, topped with mash and breadcrumbs, was a dry, near-tasteless horror, while roast tomato and Norfolk asparagus risotto with lord-of-the-hundreds cheese was a salty waste of good asparagus, and fig and almond financier with port-glazed figs did not a good pudding make. Other dishes, such as a baby gem lettuce and blue cheese side, a starter of steak tartare with quail's egg and sourdough, and the

(£10) cheese plate were fine, but this was too erratic a performance for such prices. Service is well meaning and friendly, if slightly amateurish. Fellow diners are what you'd expect of SW1.
Babies and children welcome: high chairs. Booking advisable (not accepted in bar). Separate room for parties, seats 12. Tables outdoors (6, pavement). Map 9 G9.

City

High Timber NEW
8 High Timber Street, EC4V 3PA (7248 1777, www.hightimber.com). Mansion House tube. **Brunch served** 11am-3pm Sat. **Lunch served** noon-3pm Mon-Fri. **Dinner served** 6.30-10pm Mon-Sat. **Main courses** £12.50-£27. **Set lunch** (Mon-Fri) £15 2 courses. **Credit** AmEx, MC, V.
Smart, with an air of classy simplicity (slate floor, wooden tables, picture windows with amazing views of the Globe, Millennium Bridge and Tate Modern), High Timber has an equally unfussy menu, akin to that of a superior steakhouse. Starters – pan-fried foie gras with apricots and fig galette; terrine of pressed ham hock with parsley, onion marmalade and gherkins – are standard Modern European. However, it's the grill that counts here – and the Lake District beef. Sold in two weights and according to cut, it's pricey (rump and ribeye are £19/250g, £27/350g), but geared to the expense-account clientele. Quality is assured, and meat is cooked exactly as requested. Sauces (including a luxury truffle butter) cost extra, but all steaks come with braised mushrooms, onion rings and chips. There are other options too: roast

BEST BRITISH

London landmarks
Take in the sights at **Inn The Park** (see p57), **National Dining Rooms** (see p58), the **Restaurant at St Paul's** (see p51) and **Roast** (see p60).

Style it out
Get clad in your glad rags for the **Albemarle** (see p55), **Corrigan's Mayfair** (see p57), **Dorchester Grill Room** (see p57), the **Pantechnicon Rooms** (see left), **Quo Vadis** (see p57), **Rhodes Twenty Four** (see p51) and **Top Floor at Smiths** (see p52).

Fab food without flummery
When a suit doesn't suit, relish **Albion** (see p60), **Great Queen Street** (see p54), **Hereford Road** (see p59), **High Timber** (see left), **Hix Oyster & Chop House** (see p52), **Market** (see p60), **Medcalf** (see p52) and **Quality Chop House** (see p52), plus **St John** (see p52) and its **Bread & Wine** offshoot (see p51).

Keep it in the family
Multi-generational dining at **Canteen** (see p59), **Inn The Park** (see p57), **National Dining Rooms** (see p58), **Paternoster Chop House** (see p51), **Rivington Bar & Grill** (see p60), **Roast** (see p60) and **Rules** (see p54).

Paternoster Chop House

Warwick Court, Paternoster Square, EC4M 7DX (7029 9400, www.danddlondon.co.uk). St Paul's tube. **Lunch served** noon-3.30pm Mon-Fri; noon-4pm Sun. **Dinner served** 5.30-10.30pm Mon-Fri. **Main courses** £11.50-£20. **Set meal** (Mon-Fri) £19.50 2 courses, £24.50 3 courses. **Set lunch** (Sun) £20 2 courses incl tea or coffee, £25 3 courses incl tea or coffee. **Credit** AmEx, DC, MC, V.

We know from past experience that PCH can deal efficiently with City customers – business lunches and dinners are its bread and butter, with the likes of Colchester rock oysters or Berkshire pig sausages and mustard mash going down splendidly with a glass of something from the mighty drinks list (ales and ciders as well as wine). This time we went for Sunday lunch, accompanied by a toddler, and found that the place easily adapts to the needs of families and tourists at weekends. The Sunday lunch deal includes a side dish plus tea or coffee; portions are substantial. Watercress soup and chicken livers on toast were swiftly dispatched. They were good, but no match for 'beast of the day', Galloway beef, spit roasted and served with all the trimmings, including fresh horseradish and yorkshire pudding. Squeaker (young pigeon) with bread sauce and game chips was also a winning main. We finished with the retro delight of rum baba, but a lavender custard and shortbread was rather too sweet (there's always the option of British cheeses). The bright, light-filled room suits any occasion, and the open kitchen means there's always something to view.
Available for hire. Babies and children welcome: crayons (Sun); high chairs; toys (Sun). Booking advisable. Disabled: toilet. Separate room for parties, seats 13. Tables outdoors (20, courtyard). **Map 11 O6.**
For branch (Butlers Wharf Chop House) see index.

Restaurant at St Paul's NEW

St Paul's Cathedral, St Paul's Churchyard, EC4M 8AD (7248 2469, www.restaurantatstpauls.co.uk). St Paul's tube.
Café **Open/meals served** 9am-5pm Mon-Sat; 10am-4pm Sun.
Restaurant **Lunch served** noon-3pm, **tea served** 3-4.30pm daily. **Set lunch** £16 2 courses, £20 3 courses. **Set tea** £12.50-£18.
Both **Credit** MC, V.

The shop and café at St Paul's thrum with tourists, but this new restaurant (which shares an entrance with both, on the north side of the cathedral) seems more of a hit with locals. Despite being in a crypt, it's a light-filled, beautifully designed space (there's even some natural light). Well-spaced modern oak tables and chairs are laid with mismatched antique cutlery, slate mats and gorgeous white rough linen napkins. The ground floor has earthenware tiles, the mezzanine herringbone seagrass matting; walls are painted cream, woodwork sage-green. Food – by caterers Harbour & Jones (who also run the café, with chef Candice Webber at the helm – matches this promise. Pastry is a strength, as demonstrated in portobello mushroom wellington with spinach (a main), and gooseberry cobbler with pouring cream. From organic bread and green olives, via fresh-tasting asparagus and poached Gressingham duck egg, to prettily pink Trigger Farm barnsley chop with mint jelly and earthy jersey royals, we were well fed. English wine-makers (Chapel Down, Three Choirs, Carter's) figure strongly; beer and soft drinks are Brit-heavy too. Afternoon tea is worth sampling, especially if you hanker after fresh scones with clotted cream.
Babies and children welcome: high chairs. Booking advisable. Disabled: lift; toilet. **Map 11 O6.**

★ Rhodes Twenty Four

24th floor, Tower 42, Old Broad Street, EC2N 1HQ (7877 7703, www.rhodes24.co.uk). Bank tube/DLR/Liverpool Street tube/rail. **Lunch served** noon-2.15pm, **dinner served** 6-8.30pm Mon-Fri. **Main courses** £16.20-£32. **Credit** AmEx, DC, MC, V.

Riding the lift to the 24th floor, after clearing the airport-style security downstairs, we thought no meal could be worth the hassle. On the way back

High Timber

down, we decided we were wrong. Rhodes Twenty Four can make you see traditional British cooking in a new light. The long, curved, low-ceilinged room is comfortable, and the views are spectacular. But the cooking – British ideas taken apart and reassembled in exalted form – is even more spectacular. Dishes are presented with the heading of the principal ingredient: scallops, leeks, beef, and so on. Everything we ate delivered the highest quality. Starters of celeriac soup with a soft-boiled duck egg, and seared scallops with a heavenly shallot mustard sauce, were sublime. Mains were even better: the vegetarian choice (potato, onion and lincolnshire poacher cheese tart) and a steamed mutton pie. The pie was astounding: perfect suet crust, first-class meat and gravy, a trio of wonderful sauces. The wine list is chosen with care, and while much is at City prices there are excellent bottles for around £35. Service is mostly French, and very polished. The food can be very rich (we couldn't even think about pudding), so order with care. A meal costs serious money, but Rhodes Twenty Four is a top choice for a celebration. Going through a metal detector was never so rewarding.
Available for hire. Babies and children welcome: high chair. Booking essential, 2-4 wks in advance. Disabled: lift; toilet. Dress: smart casual. **Map 12 Q6.**

St John Bread & Wine

94-96 Commercial Street, E1 6LZ (7251 0848, www.stjohnbreadandwine.com). Liverpool Street tube/rail. **Breakfast served** 9-11am Mon-Fri; 10-11am Sat, Sun. **Lunch served** noon-4pm daily. **Dinner served** 5-10.30pm Mon-Fri; 6-10.30pm Sat; 6-9pm Sun. **Main courses** £12.50-£14. **Credit** AmEx, MC, V.

The glorious bread – white and brown sourdough, baked on the premises – that arrives at table minutes after you're seated, impedes full enjoyment of the menu here. Indulge too freely and you won't manage pudding. The cool, whitewashed, high-ceilinged room soon becomes convivial when full; efficient, charming staff add to the feeling of well-being, as does the ungreedily priced menu. Venison pie with deliciously bronzed pastry was the priciest item on our visit, but it served two for £28. Also generously sized was a beautifully cooked lemon sole with sea purslane. Lentils with butternut squash and goat's curd was satisfyingly rich and savoury. Smaller dishes, such as three rock oysters, or an assembly of cauliflower, leek and chickpeas, and the super-zingy green salad, also scored well. But, with the honourable exception of sticky date pudding with butterscotch sauce (dense and cloying in a good way), the desserts were below their usual splendidness. Eton mess with blood orange was a mistaken pairing; treacle tart with vanilla ice-cream wasn't rich and treacley enough, and was dry around the edges. We wished that we'd chosen cheese instead (gubbeen, ragstone, spenwood and strathdon blue). Drinks come from a manageable, mainly French wine list; or there's Meantime Pale Ale.
Babies and children welcome: high chairs. Booking advisable. **Map 12 S5.**

SHELF LIFE

Queues of patient customers every Saturday are proof that London's independent butchers easily outclass the supermarkets when it comes to first-rate organic and free-range meat and game in season.

Frank Godfrey

7 Highbury Park, N5 1QJ (7226 2425, www.fgodfrey.co.uk). Highbury & Islington tube/rail. **Open** 8am-6pm Mon-Fri; 8am-5pm Sat.

This quaint old shop is a family business founded in 1905 and today run by brothers Chris, Jeremy and Phillip Godfrey. Own-made sausages are a particular source of pride. Speciality suppliers from the south east of England include Plantation Pigs and Temple Farm (for poultry).

Ginger Pig

99 Lauriston Road, E9 7HJ (8986 6911, www.thegingerpig.co.uk). Mile End tube then 277 bus. **Open** 9am-5.30pm Tues; 9am-6.30pm Wed-Fri; 9am-6pm Sat; 9am-3pm Sun.

The Ginger Pig's North Yorkshire farm is the source of much of the meat for this burgeoning chain. There are also branches in Borough Market, Moxon Street Marylebone, and a counter in the Greeensmiths shop at Waterloo.

Jack O'Shea's

11 Montpelier Street, SW7 1EX (7581 7771, www.jackoshea.com). Knightsbridge tube. **Open** 8am-7pm Mon-Fri; 8am-5pm Sat.

Continental cuts are a speciality of this prestige butcher selling Black Angus beef from southwest Ireland, lamb from Orkney, and pork from Dorset. Chef Richard Corrigan is a customer and recommends the flank steak and offal. O'Shea also runs the meat counter in Selfridges food hall.

C Lidgate

110 Holland Park Avenue, W11 4UA (7727 8243). Holland Park tube. **Open** 7am-7pm Mon-Fri; 6.30am-6.30pm Sat.

If you can drag your eyes away from the own-made recipe dishes, delicious pies and sausages, note the organic meats from royal estates (Highgrove, Gatcombe Park) and small farms where superior breeds are fed a natural diet – all hand-selected by David Lidgate and son Danny.

M Moen & Sons

24 The Pavement, SW4 0JA (7622 1624, www.moen.co.uk). Clapham Common tube. **Open** 8.30am-6.30pm Mon-Fri; 8.30am-5pm Sat.

This gloriously old-fashioned emporium specialises in organic and free-range meats. For the aspiring chef there is an excellent choice of offal (sweetbreads, hearts, pigs' trotters), game in season, and rarities such as gulls' eggs.

Clerkenwell & Farringdon

Hix Oyster & Chop House (100)

36-37 Greenhill Rents, off Cowcross Street, EC1M 6BN (7017 1930, www.restaurants etcltd.co.uk). Farringdon tube/rail. **Lunch served** noon-3pm Mon-Fri; noon-5pm Sun (single seating at 2pm). **Dinner served** 6-11pm Mon-Sat; 6-10pm Sun. **Main courses** £10.75-£34.50. **Credit** AmEx, MC, V.

Although the name tells diners what to expect, there's more to Hix than chops and oysters – Blythburgh pork crackling with apple sauce, for example (an ideal nibble), or irresistible deep-fried sprats with caper mayonnaise, followed by roast free-range Goosnargh chicken with wild garlic sauce (for two). But oysters (there's always a choice, Helford natives for £3.20 each, say, or Colchester rocks at £1.95), chops and steaks feature prominently. Most diners have been male whenever we've dined here. We watched in admiration as one table tucked into a medley of steaks; the choice includes porterhouse (for two) and hanger steak with baked bone marrow. We can vouch for the barbecued Galloway beef ribs. Mixed beets with goat's curd and watercress is among the lighter starters. Puds are nicely retro with modern twists; you can stick to steamed treacle sponge with custard, or dare to try absinthe jelly with vanilla ice-cream. Alongside the global wine list there's a good choice of beers and ciders, including Hix Oyster Ale, brewed by Palmers of Bridport. Like St John nearby, Hix offers feasts for ten or more people. Owner Mark Hix is also director of food at the Albemarle, *see p55.*
Babies and children admitted. Booking essential. Tables outdoors (4, pavement). **Map 5 O5.**

Medcalf

38-40 Exmouth Market, EC1R 4QE (7833 3553, www.medcalfbar.co.uk). Farringdon tube/rail/ 19, 38, 341 bus. **Lunch served** noon-3pm Mon-Fri; noon-4pm Sat, Sun. **Dinner served** 6-10pm Mon-Wed; 5.30-10pm Thur; 5.30-10.30pm Fri, Sat. **Main courses** £8.50-£14.50. **Credit** MC, V.

Very much part of the new wave of British restaurants, Medcalf is a casually styled space consisting of two rooms and a small patio out back. Fairly plain, slightly battered furnishings are enlivened by modern art and some statement lighting, including a huge chandelier. A simple but pleasing menu runs from oysters, welsh rarebit and the likes of black pudding with granny smith and watercress salad, through to bavette steak with big chips, horseradish cream and leaf salad: never the tenderest steak, this one had good flavour and fine accompaniments. Other credit-crunch fare included braised neck of lamb with pearl barley and button onions, but we plumped for lemon sole with chorizo and a spring onion and new potato salad. The combination of delicate fish with strong flavours worked well, helped by fruity olive oil. For dessert, an overly sweet chocolate mousse with sugared walnuts and shortbread made us think wistfully of the British cheeses – or even orange steamed pudding and custard. There's a huge selection of drinks (draught and bottled beers, wine, cocktails): naturally enough, as Medcalf is more bar than restaurant at night. Lunch is a mellow affair, where staff have time to be attentive and you dine surrounded by creatives networking.
Babies and children welcome: high chairs. Booking advisable dinner. Disabled: toilet. Separate room for parties, seats 18. Tables outdoors (7, pavement; 5, garden). **Map 5 N4.**

Quality Chop House

92-94 Farringdon Road, EC1R 3EA (7837 5093, www.qualitychophouse.co.uk). Farringdon tube/ rail/19, 38 bus. **Lunch served** noon-3pm Mon-Fri; noon-4pm Sun. **Dinner served** 6-11pm Mon-Fri; 6-11.30pm Sat; 6-10pm Sun. **Main courses** £9.95-£19.95. **Credit** AmEx, MC, V.

This carefully revamped, late 19th-century chop house makes a charming setting for a meal – once you've adjusted the cushions on the unforgiving oak settles. For anyone desiring unfussy British food,

the menu is a treat: from salmon fish cake with sorrel sauce (a rich, filling main that's always available) to comfort food such as cumberland sausages with bubble and squeak. This time, a starter of purple sprouting broccoli with mustard sauce let the side down: fridge-cold and lacking in fresh-tasting zestiness. Smoked eel was much better, and came with sprightly horseradish cream. Mains saved the day: salt beef with celeriac salad and beetroot was a blast of flavours, while a special of grilled tuna steak with shaved fennel salad and mash was excellent (but it should have been for £18.95). Prices are generally much more wallet-friendly than this, with soup of the day at under a fiver, and puddings such as gooseberry fool or rice pudding at just over. A short wine list is similarly well priced, with white and red win de pays starting at £3.50; beer includes Nethergate's Suffolk County bitter. Staff are personable and deal efficiently with a mixed bag of diners.
Available for hire. Babies and children welcome: high chairs. Booking advisable. **Map 5 N4.**

★ St John (100)

26 St John Street, EC1M 4AY (7251 0848/4998, www.stjohnrestaurant.com). Barbican tube/ Farringdon tube/rail. **Lunch served** noon-3pm Mon-Fri; 1-3pm Sun. **Dinner served** 6-11pm Mon-Sat. **Main courses** £13.50-£22.50. **Credit** AmEx, DC, MC, V.

Another year, another stellar meal at the daddy of new-wave British restaurants. The highlight was two huge, very pink, very tender, supremely tasty slices of beef with horseradish cream, but super-rich venison liver and kidney with flavoursome lentils, and heartily good pigeon with beetroot tops, were both contenders. Peas in the pod may seem an odd pre-dinner nibble, but in this spare white dining room devoted to the best of everything British, it seems just right. Sides of well-dressed green salad and garden-fresh greens are always worth ordering. Starter of roast bone marrow with parsley salad is a menu regular, and rightly so; brown shrimp and white cabbage was a pleasingly astringent dish. On a hot night, apricot sorbet was heaven: a nice contrast to rude figs with honey ice-cream and brioche. Buttermilk pudding (like panna cotta) with summer fruits and shortbread also slipped down a treat. For a world-famous restaurant, St John is completely unstuffy: staff are approachable as well as highly competent; the French wine list won't frighten anyone (bottles are available as off-sales, as is the magnificent bread). Prices aren't low (though not excessive for the quality); a cheaper option is to have a snack or drink in the airy bar – the giant welsh rarebit makes a great stomach-liner.
Babies and children welcome: high chairs. Booking essential dinner & weekends. Disabled: toilet (bar). Separate room for parties, seats 18. **Map 5 O5.**

Top Floor at Smiths

Smiths of Smithfield, 67-77 Charterhouse Street, EC1M 6HJ (7251 7950, www.smithsof smithfield.co.uk). Barbican tube/Farringdon tube/rail. **Lunch served** noon-2.45pm Mon-Fri; 12.30-3.45pm Sun. **Dinner served** 6.30-10.45pm Mon-Sat. **Main courses** £16-£30. **Credit** AmEx, DC, MC, V.

More sober than the three storeys below, Top Floor at John Torode's Smiths is a spacious, plainly decorated room, given colour by a red back-lit bar and the crimson glow of the lift interior. Balcony seating and two huge glass walls offer attractive views of City rooftops. Steak is king here, but there's plenty else on the menu. Our best two starters were venison terrine, with a succulent piece of rare meat in the middle, and smoked eel with a warm, fluffy potato pancake. However, these were preambles to the main event. John dory with pesto and greens, and roast pork special (perfectly cooked apart from chewy crackling) were fine, but were blown out of the water by ten ounces apiece of pan-fried sirloin and grilled rump steak (£29.50 and £28.50 respectively). Choose from béarnaise sauce, parsley butter or rather tame creamed horseradish, plus a side such as huge golden chips or veg of the day – a lively dish of courgettes with

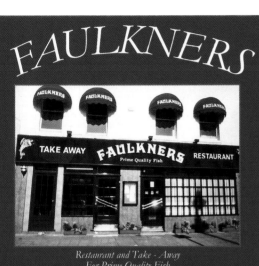

Corrigan's Mayfair. See p57.

gremolata on our visit. Pudding can be a challenge after this, but pear and brandy soufflé with pear sauce and shortbread was sublime. The wine list is a big hitter, aimed at expense account diners. Customers are overwhelmingly male, waited on by delightful, if faintly scatty, staff. You'll be landed with a big bill, but mostly it's worth it.

Babies and children welcome: crayons; high chairs; nappy-changing facilities. Booking advisable. Disabled: toilet. Separate rooms for parties, seating 6-24. Tables outdoors (8, terrace). Map 11 O5.

Covent Garden

Rules

35 Maiden Lane, WC2E 7LB (7836 5314, www.rules.co.uk). Covent Garden tube. **Meals served** noon-11.30pm Mon-Sat; noon-10.30pm Sun. **Main courses** £16.95-£22.95. **Credit** AmEx, MC, V.

London's oldest eaterie (founded 1798) has many lovable qualities. The dining room is dark, cosy, and crammed with pictures: reminiscent of a 19th-century gentlemen's club. Service is commendable, with occasional touches of an old-fashioned insouciance. And the menu is awash with traditional British food, featuring home-grown (and carefully credited) ingredients. But Rules needs to sharpen up its cooking – sometimes a little, sometimes a lot. A dressed crab was beautifully presented and spanking-fresh, but a crab bisque had too much cream and too little depth of flavour. One pie, the signature steak and kidney, was just as it should have been, apart from a slightly tired puff-pastry cap. However, a daily special of duck pie contained stringy meat in a lacklustre gravy. Side dishes were similarly humdrum, a little too close to school-dinner blandness. Our one pudding, rhubarb crumble with good custard, was a high point. The wine list doesn't offer much below £35, though the house claret, from top London wine merchant Lea & Sandeman, was excellent value at £22. In all, Rules is a place of mixed quality. Raise the cooking by just a notch or two and it would do justice to the restaurant's long history.

Babies and children welcome: high chairs. Booking advisable. Dress: smart casual. Separate rooms for parties, seating 8-18. Map 18 E5.

Holborn

Great Queen Street

32 Great Queen Street, WC2B 5AA (7242 0622). Covent Garden or Holborn tube.
Bar **Open** 5-11pm Tue-Sat.
Restaurant **Lunch served** noon-2.30pm Mon-Sat; noon-3pm Sun. **Dinner served** 6-10.30pm Mon-Sat. **Main courses** £10.80-£22. **Set lunch** (Sun) £20.50 2 courses, £25 3 courses.
Both **Credit** MC, V.

Staff at this bustling, casual eaterie are a helpful young bunch, identifiable by blue butcher's aprons. The ex-pub premises have been tarted up, but not too much – the long bar remains, and diners eat at closely packed, slightly too small tables. It's a popular spot; booking is essential, though there are seats at the bar. Drinks and snacks (cheese and desserts, nibbles such as lupin seeds) are served in the basement. To start, smoked cod's roe with carrot, beetroot and horseradish was an interesting and successful combo, while a sprightly green salad had a dressing with kick. 'Hare and noodles' was pretty much hare ragù on wide strips of pasta: deeply savoury and wonderful. Hereford top of leg with horseradish and watercress was a flavour-packed steak, yet needed plenty of mastication. Puds are taken seriously; we find the ice-cream irresistible (this time vanilla and Calvados flavours, and blood-orange sorbet: very moreish). We also like the fact wines come in glass, carafe and bottle sizes, and that there's a changing house cocktail (campari and blood orange, say). The sourdough bread is superb, and coffee first rate. Overall, GQS is close to being the ideal local in the centre of town.

Babies and children admitted. Booking essential. Disabled: toilet. Tables outdoors (4, pavement). Map 18 E3.

Albion. See p60.

King's Cross

The Brill NEW

6-8 Caledonian Road, N1 9DT (7833 7797, www.thebrill.co.uk). King's Cross tube/rail.
Breakfast served 7-11am, **lunch served** noon-5pm, **dinner served** 5-10.30pm Mon-Sat.
Main courses £12-£14. **Set meal** £13.50 2 courses, £16 3 courses. **Credit** AmEx, MC, V.
We can see this likeable new spot becoming a favourite with denizens of 21st-century King's Cross, but it's also unfussy enough and close enough to the station to accommodate travellers. The Brill occupies a corner-shop site with large windows overlooking unkempt Cally Road. Inside, brown predominates, with caff-style furniture, tan banquettes and arty London photos. Downstairs there's a cellar bar; next door, posh sandwiches and burgers are dispensed from a gleaming takeaway counter. Lunch is similarly simple, with sarnies boosted by the likes of duck salad and bacon. At night, to a background of chilled beats, a friendly eastern European waitress handed us a menu of robust British food. Prices are attractive: £4 for starters, £12 for mains, with good-value set meals too. Specials, such as our sumptuous sliced ox cheek on decent mash surrounded by delicious gluey gravy, are around £14. Not everything's perfect – a starter of parsley-flecked ham hock loaf came with insipid 'pickled' veg; crisp fried hake and chips was marred by dryish mashed peas; and lemon tart with raspberry purée and sweet cream didn't need its sour poached plums – but standards are generally high, the wine list is varied and the food enticing. The result: contentment.
Available for hire. Babies and children welcome. Booking advisable Wed-Fri. Separate room for parties, seats 22. Takeaway service; delivery service (within 3 mile radius). **Map 4 L2**.

Konstam at the Prince Albert

2 Acton Street, WC1X 9NA (7833 5040, www.konstam.co.uk). King's Cross tube/rail.
Lunch served 12.30-3pm Mon-Fri; 10.30am-4pm Sun. **Dinner served** 6.30-10.30pm Mon-Sat. **Main courses** £11.50-£17. **Credit** AmEx, MC, V.
Konstam does much with an uninspiring location and limited (ex-pub) space. The restaurant occupies one small room, with a (very) open kitchen at the back. Tables are close together, making lunch (when some tables are empty) preferable to dinner (when private conversation is difficult). The interior is deliberately unlike most gastropub conversions: notably in the Thomas Heatherwick-designed chain 'lampshades'. Food is seasonal. Chef-owner Oliver Rowe is committed to over 85% of his produce being 'grown or reared within the area covered by the London Underground network'. At lunch, everything is available as a takeaway; there are also sandwiches (pan-roast Waltham Abbey chicken with tarragon dressing) and salads (pea shoot and mixed herb; barley, shallot and allspice). Our salads were good, if a little heavy, but didn't compare to the taste sensation of mushroom and crème fraîche pierogi plus chive and spenwood-cheese dumplings, served with sour cream, breadcrumbs and brown butter. We also enjoyed starters: refreshing, summery nettle soup with shredded lettuce, and Mersea skate cheeks with apple balsamic and rhubarb compote (lovely, almost-caramelised flavour). Finish with traditional puds or English cheeses. Staff are young and friendly, and the vibe welcoming, but it's hard to feel entirely relaxed here.
Babies and children welcome: booster seat. Booking advisable. Disabled: toilet. Separate room for parties, seats 14. Tables outdoors (2, pavement). **Map 4 M3**.

Rotunda Bar & Restaurant NEW

Kings Place, N1 9AG (7014 2840). King's Cross tube/rail. **Lunch served** noon-3pm daily.
Dinner served 5-11pm Mon-Sat; 5-9pm Sun.
Main courses £10-£21.95. **Credit** AmEx, MC, V.
It's a treat to duck out of the grime and chaos of King's Cross and into this curvaceous canal-side venue. If weather permits, the riverside patio is great for sipping white wine and watching the ducks and barges cruise past; inside is more problematic. The decor is somewhat incongruous, as if, faced with all the curving space and the wall-to-wall windows, the architects just chucked about some dark wood and navy material and fled. Fortunately, the food is more successful: asparagus in season, with a pleasingly tart hollandaise; avocado and tomatoes that actually give your taste buds employment in a bacon salad starter. Main courses were variable. The Northumberland beef is apparently hung for 35 days, but our steak was distinctly chewy. The lamb was much better – soft and succulent. But though hand-cut twice-cooked chips looked hefty and expertly fried, they tasted unpleasant. In recompense, Rotunda's wine list is terrific: an immense range, with interesting choices across the price points. Beware if you indulge too freely, however: the toilets are miles away, and pretty much devoid of signage.
Babies and children welcome: high chairs; nappy-changing facilities. Booking advisable. Disabled: toilet. Separate room for parties, seats 24. Tables outdoors (50, terrace). **Map 4 L2**.

Mayfair

★ Albemarle

Brown's Hotel, 33-34 Albemarle Street, W1S 4BP (7493 6020, www.roccofortecollection.com). Green Park tube. **Lunch served** noon-3pm Mon-Sat; 12.30-3pm Sun. **Dinner served** 6-10.30pm Mon-Sat; 7-10.30pm Sun. **Main courses** £14.50-£32.50. **Set menu** £25 2 courses, £30 3 courses. **Credit** AmEx, DC, MC, V.
The combination of handsome dining room (blending period and modern furnishings), twinkly-eyed, well-drilled staff and marvellous food make the Albemarle one hotel restaurant that's a destination in itself. Diners – informally clad hotel guests and glammed-up dates and celebratory groups – seemed to be enjoying themselves as much as we were. The set meal is excellent value; the three choices at each course include the same well-sourced British ingredients as the rest of the menu. Only 'olde english' sausage with mash and onion gravy failed to shine: perfectly nice, but lacking any wow factor. Arbroath smokies, with soft-boiled quails' eggs and potatoes (from the set menu), and duck liver with pea shoots and an amazing deep-fried Braddock White duck egg were outstanding starters. Quality continued through mains of pork chop with black pudding hash, and pan-fried fillet of cod with West Mersea sea vegetables and brown shrimps, to sigh-inducing steamed treacle sponge pudding and rhubarb syllabub with shortbread. Sides are worth ordering, though cost around £4; these extras, plus unwary choices from the 400-strong wine list push up the bill. We can't fault the generosity, though; only one of us ordered coffee, but it came with enough chocolate truffles for four. At lunch, a carving trolley showcases a different beast every day. We can't wait to return.
Babies and children welcome: children's menu; crayons; high chairs. Booking advisable. Disabled: toilet (in hotel). Separate rooms for parties, seating 2-70. Vegetarian menu. **Map 9 J7**.

I ♥ STREET**SMART**
HELPING THE HOMELESS

"All it takes is one well-fed quid next time you're dining at any of the damned fine establishments taking part in this glorious campaign, and that tiny extra sum will go straight to an excellently worthwhile cause. Go on, it'll make you feel good about that expanding waistband"
Ian Rankin, author

STREET**SMART**
HELPING THE HOMELESS
Supported by

For a full list of participating restaurants and for information on how to take part visit our website:
www.streetsmart.org.uk

Deutsche Bank

★ Corrigan's Mayfair [NEW]
2009 RUNNER-UP BEST NEW RESTAURANT
28 Upper Grosvenor Street, W1K 7EH (7499 9943, www.corrigansmayfair.com). Marble Arch tube. **Lunch served** noon-3pm Mon-Fri; noon-4pm Sun. **Dinner served** 6-10.30pm Mon-Sat; 6-9.30pm Sun. **Main courses** £9-£26. **Set lunch** (Mon-Fri) £19.50 2 courses, £23.50 3 courses; both incl carafe of wine. **Set meal** (Sun) £27 3 courses. **Credit** AmEx, MC, V.
For a fine-dining establishment in a sleek setting, Corrigan's is a remarkably relaxed place. The welcome starts the moment you walk through the door, from formal yet smiling staff. Lighting is gentle, the chatter sotto voce, the decor subtle. Diners were here for both pleasure and business. Most dishes from the long menu exceeded our (high) expectations: from amuse bouche of olives rolled in goat's cheese, to the enigmatic 'chocolate, hazelnut' which turned out to be a medley of wonderful tastes (including a lovely parfait) around this theme. Best dish of all was a main of ox cheek with mushroom ravioli and garlic leaf – superb ingredients beautifully arranged – though two starters (octopus carpaccio with baby squid, chorizo and feta; and 'Cornish crab jelly melba toast') ran it close for flavour and verve of execution. A main of lamb three ways (roast, chop and liver) also saw the plate wiped clean. Not everything reached these heights; butter poached smoked haddock with lobster was rather dull. Food apart, we've minor niggles: the irritating £2 cover charge; being allotted a two-hour dining slot (on a Monday night); and service trailing off as the meal went on (at bill time, it was hard to find anyone to take the money). But a very alluring restaurant, all the same.
Babies and children welcome: high chairs. Booking essential. Disabled: toilet. Dress: smart casual. Separate rooms for parties, seating 10-30.
Map 9 G7.

★ Dorchester Grill Room
The Dorchester, W1K 1QA (7629 8888, www.thedorchester.com). Hyde Park Corner tube. **Breakfast served** 7-10.30am Mon-Fri; 8-11am Sat, Sun. **Lunch served** noon-2.30pm Mon-Fri; 12.30-3.30pm Sat, Sun. **Dinner served** 6.30-11pm Mon-Fri; 6-11pm Sat; 7-10.30pm Sun. **Main courses** £14.50-£36. **Set lunch** (Mon-Sat) £19.50 2 courses, £25 3 courses; (Sun) £35 3 courses. **Set dinner** (6.30-7.30pm) £19.50 2 courses, £25 3 courses. **Set meal** £45-£65 tasting menu. **Credit** AmEx, DC, MC, V.
The riot of tartan upholstery and lampshades, and larger-than-life-sized Scots warrior murals help remove any stuffiness from the Dorchester's imposing Grill Room. Twinkly staff and a relaxed dress code do the rest, so even though service is very correct, the atmosphere is mellow. Some prices on the menu and hefty wine list are frightening, making the set lunch a boon. For £25 you can dine like a king: after amuse bouche of asparagus velouté and foam, topped by a slice of quail's egg and dusted with truffle, starters of little balls of salmon fish cakes with tartare sauce, and whipped Somerset brie with grilled bacon, caramelised figs and trails of pea shoots nicely piqued the taste buds. Next, Angus roast beef (carved at table from a magnificent trolley), delightfully pink and tender, came with good yorkshire pudding, gravy, vegetables and crunchy roast potatoes; melt-in-the-mouth pork belly with perfect crackling, plus pork fillet, arrived with super-smooth mash. Baked vanilla cheesecake (with berry sorbet), though fine tasting, was slightly moussey in texture – but this was quickly forgotten after excellent coffee and petits fours. Brian Hughson joined the Grill as head chef in March 2009; judging by this visit, the appointment has been a roaring success.
Babies and children welcome (Sat, Sun): high chairs. Booking advisable; essential weekends. Disabled: toilet. Dress: smart casual. **Map 9 G7.**

St James's

Inn The Park
St James's Park, SW1A 2BJ (7451 9999, www.innthepark.com). St James's Park tube. **Breakfast served** 8-11am Mon-Fri; 9-11am Sat, Sun. **Lunch served** noon-3pm Mon-Fri; noon-4pm Sat, Sun. **Tea served** 3-5pm Mon-Fri; 4-5pm Sat, Sun. **Dinner served** 5-9pm daily. **Main courses** £10.50-£18.50. **Credit** AmEx, MC, V.
After several years of so-so meals at this beautifully appointed and designed café-restaurant, we weren't expecting much. We were, however, expecting hot food. A Herdwick beef burger with glazed goat's cheese and chips suffered most from being served cold, while a still-tasty lemon sole with squid came off best, but this was a lacklustre performance, especially as prices aren't cheap. Disappointment was compounded by various ingredients being unavailable. Intentionally-cold dishes – mackerel tartare, and pressed ham hock with piccalilli (starters), and British cheeses (to finish) – were by far the most successful choices, though crab salad was watery. On the plus side, staff are lovely (and on a cool evening, happy to cope with diners dithering about whether to sit inside or out), and the setting (overlooking the duck lake, with trees all around and the London Eye lit up in the distance) is wonderful. Inn the Park has to cater for all-comers, and the strain of offering everything from summer barbecues to formal sit-down three-course meals, and being open all day (breakfast includes a build-your-own option) is showing. Our recommendation? Wait for warm weather, grab a takeaway, and picnic on the grass.
Babies and children welcome: children's menu; high chairs. Booking advisable. Disabled: toilet. Tables outdoors (23, terrace). Takeaway service.
Map 10 K8.

Wiltons
55 Jermyn Street, SW1Y 6LX (7629 9955, www.wiltons.co.uk). Green Park or Piccadilly Circus tube. **Lunch served** noon-2.30pm, **dinner served** 6-10.30pm Mon-Fri. **Main courses** £15-£50. **Credit** AmEx, DC, MC, V.
If you want to glimpse a vanishing way of life (and have deep pockets), head for Wiltons. The cossetting service, the classic decor (muted colours and paintings that won't frighten the horses) and the sense of calm are perfect for anyone who finds the 21st century a bit much. It almost doesn't matter what the food's like, but it's better than you might think, and there's always the long wine list to soothe. Warm potted shrimps were a neat little mound of comfort food, and better than a generous portion of workaday kipper pâté. There's game in season, and a dish of the day from the magnificent carving trolley (salmon coulibiac on this occasion), but roast rack of lamb did us proud: four beautifully pink pieces, with gravy and gratin potatoes, plus vividly green broad beans as a side. Sea bass on wild mushrooms and bacon also passed muster. Puddings are English or cheese, but we decided against a £12 bowl of strawberries, especially as excellent coffee comes with a divine dark chocolate and a classy coffee macaroon. Seating is in snug booths or at nicely spaced tables or on bar seats. Hampers are available too. Worth a visit just for the experience.
Babies and children welcome: high chairs. Booking advisable. Disabled: lift; toilet. Dress: smart; jacket required. Separate room for parties, seats 20.
Map 17 B5.

Soho

Quo Vadis
26-29 Dean Street, W1D 3LL (7437 9585, www.quovadissoho.co.uk). Leicester Square, Piccadilly Circus or Tottenham Court Road tube. **Lunch served** noon-2.30pm, **dinner served** 5.30-10.30pm Mon-Sat. **Main courses** £12.50-£27. **Set meal** (5.30-6pm) £17.50 2 courses, £19.50 3 courses. £2 cover charge. **Credit** AmEx, DC, MC, V.
It was indisputable good news when Soho legend Quo Vadis was reinvigorated by Sam and Eddie Hart (owners of Spanish restaurants Fino and Barrafina). Beautiful linen, gleaming glassware, classic fittings and modern art, set against the backdrop of colourful stained-glass windows, makes for an attractive room. But on a busy Friday night, it was hard to relax. Tables were too close for us to ignore the complaints of neighbouring diners (about a persistent draught, about wine arriving after the food). Service was rather brusque. And

Interview
PATRICK CLAYTON-MALONE

Who are you?
Co-founder and director of **Canteen** (*see p59*).
How did you start in the catering business?
I worked as kitchen porter for a couple of terrible restaurants, then jumped head first into promoting acid house parties.
What's the best thing about running a restaurant in London?
No day is the same; it's a multi-disciplined job. Designing and building restaurants is an exciting and rewarding process – if you get it right. It's great to be able to offer people a menu you totally believe in. It's a cliché, but giving people a good time is very rewarding too. So was meeting the other caterers who inspired us to start Canteen.
What's the worst thing?
Where did the last five years go? Tendering for contracts, slippery fish...
Which are your favourite London restaurants?
York & Albany (*see p228*) is special without being snobby, with wholesome food, a brilliant front-of-house team and a great bar. **Pied à Terre** (*see p125*) is one of the most egalitarian of the haute cuisine restaurants I've been to: the food is amazing and exciting and the staff are warm and welcoming. The **Charles Lamb** (*see p114*) is a friendly free house with fabulous Meantime on tap and delicious bar snacks.
What's the best bargain in the capital?
Our pie and mash with greens and gravy; at £10.50, it's a complete dish.
What is your favourite treat?
Riding my bike on Friday night, for Italian at **L'Anima** (*see p162*).
What is missing from London's restaurant scene?
Bicycle racks and a good chicken concept.
What does the next year hold?
Good restaurants will be able to negotiate their way through a tough year; there will be a weeding out of places not offering good enough food, service or value.

RESTAURANTS

Quo Vadis. See p57.

while we were reasonably content with our food, at these prices we needed to be much more satisfied. Too many dishes from the decidedly retro menu were merely OK. A smoked salmon starter was just dull; ditto roast squab pigeon (£24). And while roast turbot was a perfectly nice piece of fish, it had an over-salted crust and cost £26. Most mains needed extra side dishes, so add £4.75 for purple sprouting broccoli or £4.50 for (very good) chunky chips, and Quo Vadis is pricing itself at haute cuisine level. The wine list is similarly wallet unfriendly, and the cover charge an irritant. There were successes – a rich, smooth fish soup; flavourful sea bass carpaccio; a large, taste-packed rump steak; and a stand-out pear sorbet – but overall, nowhere near enough bang for your beleaguered buck.
Babies and children admitted. Booking essential. Separate rooms for parties, seating 12-24.
Map 17 B3.

Strand

Simpson's-in-the-Strand

100 Strand, WC2R 0EW (7836 9112, www.simpsonsinthestrand.co.uk). Embankment tube/Charing Cross tube/rail. **Breakfast served** 7.15-10.30am Mon-Fri. **Lunch served** 12.15-2.45pm Mon-Sat; 12.15-3pm Sun. **Dinner served** 5.45-10.45pm Mon-Sat; (Grand Divan) 6-9pm Sun. **Main courses** £15.50-£32.50. **Set meal** (5.45-7pm) £24.50 2 courses, £29.50 3 courses. **Credit** AmEx, DC, MC, V.
For those over thirtysomething, the Simpson's name is forever associated with roast beef and olde-Englishe clubbiness. For anyone younger, it may just be another London restaurant. Both camps might like to visit the place, with its lovely wood panelling and reassuringly hideous carpet, as long as they have time to endure some truly glacial service. We waited nearly 40 minutes for our lunchtime pies. But the food showed that, in the kitchen at least, Simpson's is still going strong. Steak and kidney had a crisp puff-pastry crust, while fish pie (special of the day) featured feathery-light blobs of crunchy dough. The fish was a mixture of white varieties and salmon, its creamy gravy just right in consistency. At around £15, these were among the cheapest mains. The rest of the menu combines old-fashioned British with some appealing nods to France and Mod Euro; and, of course, there's the famous roast beef, wheeled ceremoniously around in its silver-domed trolley. Tradition is important at Simpson's (established 1828). Most of our fellow lunchers were business folk entertaining overseas guests, or elderly parents with their grown-up children. They could afford the wine list, which is well chosen but contains few bottles under £30.
Babies and children welcome: high chairs. Booking advisable. Disabled: toilet. Dress: smart casual; no trainers, T-shirts or sportswear. Separate rooms for parties, seating 25 and 150.
Map 18 E5.

Trafalgar Square

National Dining Rooms (100)

Sainsbury Wing, National Gallery, Trafalgar Square, WC2N 5DN (7747 2525, www.the nationaldiningrooms.co.uk). Charing Cross tube/rail.
Bakery **Meals served** 10am-5.30pm Mon-Thur, Sun; 10am-8.30pm Fri; 10am-7.30pm Sat. **Main courses** £5.90-£9.50.
Restaurant **Lunch served** noon-3.30pm daily. **Dinner served** 5-7.15pm Fri. **Main courses** £14.50-£19.25. **Set meal** £18.50 2 courses incl glass of wine, £21.50 3 courses incl glass of wine.
Both **Credit** AmEx, MC, V.
Oliver Peyton's restaurant in the Sainsbury Wing of the National Gallery offers far better food than museum diners are accustomed to: but at a price. An excellent starter of seared scallops and mash with crispy pancetta cost £13.50, and rabbit pie with spring carrots (a main) was £18.25. All of which makes the weekly set lunch (three choices in each course, plus a glass of cava) great value – especially when it's as satisfying as super-savoury leek and goat's cheese pancakes followed by a cockle-warming lamb stew. From the regular menu, a main of smoked haddock and salmon fish cakes with poached egg and hollandaise also won approval, as did sherry trifle, though this was rather light on alcohol. British cheeses are an enticing alternative. Service is pleasant, though if you want a fast lunch, opt for the bakery/café area at the back – it's not as nicely situated, but it is cheaper. The high-ceilinged interior, quite plain apart from the enormous Paula Rego mural, adds grandeur to any lunch. Especially prized are the window seats, which have views over Trafalgar Square. Fifty-plus culture junkies love the place.
Babies and children welcome: children's menu; high chairs. Booking advisable. Disabled: toilet.
Map 17 C5.

Victoria

Boisdale of Belgravia

13-15 Eccleston Street, SW1W 9LX (7730 6922, www.boisdale.co.uk). Victoria tube/rail.
Bar **Open** noon-1am Mon-Fri; 7pm-1am Sat.
Restaurant **Lunch served** noon-2.30pm Mon-Fri. **Dinner served** 7-11.15pm Mon-Sat. **Main courses** £15-£56.50. **Set meal** £18.70 2 courses.
Both **Credit** AmEx, DC, MC, V.
You'll get a very Belgravian view of the good life here: top-quality beef, plush surroundings, cigars, and wine and whisky lists that make the eyes pop. Boisdale is clearly doing something right, as the place was packed for lunch. It occupies an entire house, and offers five places to eat and drink – six if you count the private dining room – including a 'cigar terrace' that beats the smoking ban in style. The two bars are the least expensive places: either the pub-style Back bar or the clubby Macdonald bar. Both offer simpler food, with meals costing around half those of the main restaurant. Seafood and beef are the stars. We stuck with burgers (both made from great Aberdeen Angus beef and both cooked correctly to order) and a shared side of excellent thick-cut chips. Marine life features in various guises including sandwiches and small plates of salmon, herring, oysters and crab. Boisdale was buzzy yet fairly sedate during our lunch. At night, it might get more boisterous as locals let down their hair, helped by those single malts. The outstanding wine list is surprisingly affordable, with house selections starting at under £20. Jazz musicians play six nights a week.
Booking essential. Children admitted. Dress: smart casual. Entertainment: jazz 10pm Mon-Sat. Separate rooms for parties, seating 16-34.
Map 15 H10.
For branch see index.

Goring Hotel

Beeston Place, Grosvenor Gardens, SW1W 0JW (7396 9000, www.goringhotel.co.uk). Victoria tube/rail. **Breakfast served** 7-10am Mon-Fri; 7-10.30am Sat; 7.30-10.30am Sun. **Lunch served** 12.30-2.30pm Mon-Fri, Sun. **Dinner served** 6-10pm daily. **Set lunch** (Mon-Fri) £35 3 courses; (Sun) £40 3 courses. **Set dinner** £47.50 3 courses, (6-6.30pm) £32 2 courses. **Credit** AmEx, DC, MC, V.
The Goring wasn't on top form the night of our visit. Normally we can guarantee a fine feed at this family-owned hotel dining room, but this time dishes such as pigeon pithivier and braised beef with mash were so-so (almost school-dinnerish in the case of the beef), and that's not good enough given the (set) price. Twice-baked goat's cheese soufflé with spinach, cherry tomatoes and onion sauce was better, but generally the best dishes were those that the kitchen did least with, such as half a

RESTAURANTS

dozen sparklingly fresh Rossmore oysters, and the choice of British cheeses from Paxton & Whitfield from a splendid cheese trolley. Service didn't run entirely smoothly either, occasionally lapsing into a caricature of haute-cuisine attentiveness. The room alone remained as delightful as ever – a vision in soft yellow, enhanced by modern Swarovski crystal chandeliers. Fellow diners (business people, hotel residents and family groups – this is not the place for a hot date) seemed happy enough, but our advice is: go at lunchtime, when the cost of the meal will be more in line with the quality and you won't be quite so tempted by the pricey wine list.
Babies and children welcome: high chairs. Booking essential. Disabled: toilet (in hotel). Dress: smart casual. Separate rooms for parties, seating 6-40. Tables outdoors (9, terrace). **Map 15 H9.**

West
Bayswater

★ Hereford Road (100)
3 Hereford Road, W2 4AB (7727 1144, www.herefordroad.org). Bayswater tube. **Lunch served** noon-3pm Mon-Fri; noon-3.30pm Sat, Sun. **Dinner served** 6-10.30pm Mon-Sat; 6-10pm Sun. **Main courses** £9.50-£13.50. **Set lunch** (Mon-Fri) £13 2 courses, £15.50 3 courses. **Credit** AmEx, MC, V.
This old butcher's has brushed up nicely; the place has been subtly designed, and opened up with a huge circular skylight. It's on two levels, with dark wood tables and chairs, and red banquettes contrasting nicely with gleaming white tiled walls. Despite only opening in October 2007, Hereford Road has the assurance of somewhere that's been around much longer. It's an easy place in which to relax. Translucent (undyed) smoked haddock with white beans and leeks in an unctuous dressing made a sublime start; fresh and tangy green salad was happily reminiscent of one served at St John (chef Tom Pemberton used to run the kitchen at St John Bread & Wine, *see p51*). A big slab of Blythburgh pork with fabulous swede and greens saw the only dip in quality – it tasted good, but was a little dry, and the crackling was only partially successful. Slightly pink mallard with braised chicory and lentils worked a treat though. Toffee ice-cream with roast hazelnuts and shortbread was well matched with a reasonably priced glass of Calvados (£3.50). Wine is generally keenly priced, and the carafe option is laudable. A neighbourhood vibe is achieved here, despite the distraction of such excellent cooking. There was a happy buzz of chatter from a mixed crowd on this weekend lunchtime, served by friendly staff who know their business.
Babies and children welcome: high chairs. Booking advisable. Disabled: toilet. Tables outdoors (3, pavement). **Map 7 B6.**

Olympia

Popeseye Steak House
108 Blythe Road, W14 0HD (7610 4578, www.popeseye.com). Kensington (Olympia) tube/rail. **Dinner served** 7-10.30pm Mon-Sat. **Main courses** £10.95-£47.45. **No credit cards.**
When the idea of making yet another decision seems too much to bear, head for the Popeseye. The menu doesn't run to much more than steak and good red wine, but as long as you like both, you'll be happy. Steaks are rump (popeseye), sirloin and fillet, in sizes from 6oz to 30oz; 6oz costs £10.95 for rump, £13.45 for sirloin and £14.95 for fillet. All steaks are served with chips. A french-dressed mixed-leaf and tomato salad costs £3.45. And that's it – no starters, and no vegetables to distract from the matter in hand. We've never had a bad meal here, though on this occasion the chips could have been more bronzed and the fillet steak a little tastier. Both fillet and sirloin were tender and cooked just as requested (medium rare). All beef is grass-fed Aberdeen Angus from the Highlands, hung for at least two weeks. Trenchermen can tackle the likes of sticky toffee pudding, but we prefer sorbets. Decor is as down to earth as the

menu – though there's a huge, splendid new painting of a herd of cows on one whitewashed wall – and service is efficient and very friendly. A proper local, albeit a highly focused one.
Babies and children admitted. Booking advisable. **Map 20 C3.**
For branch see index.

South West
Chelsea

Gilmour's NEW
9 Park Walk, SW10 0AJ (7349 6800, www.gilmoursparkwalk.com). Fulham Broadway tube or West Brompton tube/rail. **Meals served** noon-11pm Mon-Sat; noon-10pm Sun. **Main courses** £9.50-£16.50. **Set meal** (noon-7pm Mon-Fri) £12.50 2 courses, £16.50 3 courses. **Credit** AmEx, MC, V.
This new venture by Christopher Gilmour (owner of North American bar-restaurant, Christopher's, *see p33*) aims to produce homely cooking in chic surroundings. In a smart street off Fulham Road, it certainly looks good with its immaculate white tablecloths and Paul Smith-style striped wallpaper. But our waitress twice brought the wrong menus and seemed to know little about the wine. When the right menu arrived, it betrayed a scattergun approach – a burger here, a belly of pork there, potted shrimp here, mozzarella and tomato there. Salad of smoked eel, bacon and endive was fine, but fried squid rings seemed to have been seasoned with a tablespoon of salt. Roast hake with mussels and spinach was good, yet pork belly was stringy and the accompanying mash bland. The wine list is worth celebrating. A low mark-up on bottles is capped as a 'service charge' at £3.75, which makes expensive wines the best value. But even at the cheaper end there are bargains; we shared a delightful carafe of house rosé and an excellent sub-£20 bottle of Muscadet. Nevertheless, a restaurant is judged on its cooking, and we found Gilmour's food only mediocre. A staff member admitted that customer numbers had 'fizzled' after the initial buzz.
Available for hire. Babies and children welcome: high chairs; nappy-changing facilities. Booking advisable. Disabled: toilet. Tables outdoors (2, pavement). **Map 14 D12.**

Kings Road Steakhouse & Grill NEW
386 King's Road, SW3 5UZ (7351 9997, www.kingsroadsteakhouseandgrill.com). Sloane Square tube. **Lunch served** noon-3pm Mon-Sat; noon-4pm Sun. **Dinner served** 5.30-11pm Mon-Sat; 6-10pm Sun. **Main courses** £12.50-£16.50. **Credit** AmEx, DC, MC, V.
What was Jimmy's has mutated into a King's Road version of a steakhouse. Two very plainly decorated rooms (a chandelier being the only expression of glitz amid tasteful tones and white tablecloths) are dotted with colour provided by jars of Coleman's mustard and bottles of Heinz ketchup. There's a mezzanine, but we opted for the more appealing ground floor, which has doors open to the pavement. A wallet-friendly set menu delivered generous portions of slow roasted tomato and red pepper soup, followed by plump moules marinière with triple-cooked chips, and a mousse-like vanilla cheesecake with blueberries – all good, though best of the lot was the portion of super-crunchy chips. An 8oz ribeye with peppercorn sauce (there's a choice of sauces) slipped down nicely, but was eclipsed by calves liver with crispy bacon and Pommery mustard sauce – a lovely, tender piece of offal cooked just so. Side salads (green, tomato and onion) were fresh and well dressed. Service was charming. KRSG won't win any prizes for innovation, but shouldn't produce many complaints either, particularly not with the fairly conservative local crowd.
Babies and children admitted. Booking advisable. Separate rooms for parties, seating 12-24. **Map 14 D12.**
For branch (Marco Pierre White Steakhouse & Grill) see index.

South
Waterloo

Canteen
Royal Festival Hall, Belvedere Road, SE1 8XX (0845 686 1122, www.canteen.co.uk). Embankment tube/Waterloo tube/rail. **Meals served** 8am-11pm Mon-Fri; 9am-11pm Sat, Sun. **Main courses** £8.50-£14.50. **Credit** AmEx, MC, V.
Canteen's warm globes of light shine out like beacons in the grey back-end of the Royal Festival Hall. Inside is a buzzy restaurant that looks too 1980s for comfort, but is cosy and not excessively noisy, despite the austere steel and glass. Tables are well spaced, but the best seats are the dinky stuffed-leather booths. Would that the food – an enticing read – were as good. We'd admired the piled-high plates of fish and chips flying from the kitchen, but were disappointed by crumb-coated parcels of cod, and bitty, greasy pan-bottom chips. Own-made mushy peas were lovely though. Beef stew, presented in a faux country-kitchen dish, had rich gravy with stray strands of beef and not much else. A daily roast – in our case duck legs – was much better, but had soggy skin. Puds were equally mixed: raspberry ripple bore no trace of raspberries or ripples (it was the wrong ice-cream), but rice pudding was perfect (creamy grains of rice topped with quality raspberry jam). Through it all staff were attentive and friendly, and their geniality was infectious. With food to match, Canteen would be a top choice on the South Bank.
Babies and children welcome: high chairs; nappy-changing facilities. Booking advisable. Disabled: toilet. Tables outdoors (20, terrace). **Map 10 M8.**
For branches see index.

South East
East Dulwich

Franklins
157 Lordship Lane, SE22 8HX (8299 9598, www.franklinsrestaurant.com). East Dulwich rail. **Meals served** 11am-10.30pm Mon-Fri; 10am-10.30pm Sat; noon-10pm Sun. **Main courses** £11-£18. **Credit** AmEx, MC, V.
After a slight wobble following expansion into Kennington (and subsequent contraction), Franklins is back on form, serving creative seasonal dishes to high standards. Attentive staff look after the loyal following of regulars. The menu changes daily according to availability of fresh produce, all sourced from the British Isles. The kitchen isn't afraid of less fashionable cuts of meat, rare breeds or offal. In spring you might see ox heart (an under-appreciated delicacy, here served rare and tender), razor clams, smoked ham hock, samphire, wild garlic or nettles. A meat-free dish is always available, but vegetarians are clearly not the target audience. The airy interior, with brick walls, local art, and a view into the kitchen, is a relaxing place to dine, though space can be tight and tables are quite small; the front bar is cosy with stripped wood and leather sofas. The weekday lunch menu is exceptionally good value, but bar snacks such as black pudding on toast and welsh rarebit are also available, and the weekend brunches are becoming hugely popular. Franklins sells its fish cakes, terrines and some other dishes in its neighbouring farm shop, should you still feel hungry.
Available for hire. Babies and children welcome: high chairs; nappy-changing facilities. Booking advisable. Disabled: toilet. Separate room for parties, seats 34. Tables outdoors (4, pavement). **Map 23 C4.**

London Bridge & Borough

Magdalen
152 Tooley Street, SE1 2TU (7403 1342, www.magdalenrestaurant.co.uk). London Bridge tube/rail. **Lunch served** noon-2.30pm Mon-Fri. **Dinner served** 6.30-10pm Mon-Sat. **Main courses** £13.50-£20. **Set lunch** £15.50 2 courses, £18.50 3 courses. **Credit** AmEx, MC, V.

A low-key but agreeable restaurant, Magdalen makes the most of a fairly unprepossessing location and surroundings. A small bar has a few stools drawn up to it; otherwise, there are tables covered in white cloths, and dark-plum walls decorated with a few paintings. Staff are young, friendly and efficient. But overall the place lacks oomph – and the food can't quite deliver the missing excitement. Pickled herring with a medley of potato, carrot, onion, capers, chives and crème fraîche was a surprisingly expensive starter at £8.50. Other prices were just about reasonable, yet portions aren't huge: £17.50 for a flavoursome, fatty Middle White belly with carrots, celeriac and good gravy; and £16.50 for a beautifully presented fish stew comprising gurnard, brill, salt-cod, mussels, clams, and a swirl of aïoli perched on an elegant toasted stick of bread. Poached rhubarb with shortbread and crème anglaise was the pick of the puddings; there's a tempting collection of British cheeses too. A densely typed wine list has no tasting notes, but plenty by the glass (including three sherries) and carafe. Maybe we went on a quiet night. Next time we'll go around midday; the set lunch is an absolute steal.
Babies and children admitted. Booking advisable. Disabled: toilet. Separate room for parties, seats 30. **Map 12 Q8.**

Roast (100)

The Floral Hall, Borough Market, Stoney Street, SE1 1TL (7940 1300, www.roast-restaurant. com). London Bridge tube/rail. **Breakfast served** 7-11am Mon-Fri; 8-11.30am Sat. **Lunch served** noon-3pm Mon-Wed; noon-4pm Thur-Sat; 11.30-6pm Sun. **Dinner served** 5.30-11pm Mon-Fri; 6-11pm Sat. **Main courses** £14.50-£24.50. **Set lunch** (Sun) £22 2 courses, £26 3 courses. **Credit** AmEx, MC, V.
A big airy restaurant by Borough Market, Roast gets crammed on market days. Sundays are even more family friendly, while weekdays see a businesslike clientele; staff cope with all admirably. This time we ate from the restaurant menu, but in the bar (there's a truncated, much cheaper bar menu from 3pm), which meant people-watching through floor-length windows, and very comfortable seats. Best of British sums up Roast's mission statement; many native suppliers are name-checked on the menu. Cold poached Devon sea trout with wild garlic salad cream is typical. We tucked into pan-fried chicken livers with smoked bacon and toast, then relished roast Gressingham duck breast with beetroot and capers. Pot-roast featherblade of beef with spring vegetables was gelatinously good. Tomato, onion and pea-shoot salad made a refreshing side order; potatoes roasted in beef dripping, a delicious one. Torn between Neal's Yard cheeses and desserts, we plumped for rum and pear pudding (almost a rum baba), and ice-cream – a tangy blackberry water ice and a punchy coffee ice-cream – it was the right choice. Add to this an impressive drinks list including a fine roster of teas, plus a well-regarded breakfast menu, and you have a great all-rounder. It ain't cheap (the duck cost £20, the side salad £5), but we applaud its ambition.
Available for hire. Babies and children welcome: children's menu; high chairs. Booking advisable. Disabled: lift; toilet. Dress: smart casual. **Map 11 P8.**

East

Shoreditch

★ Albion NEW

2009 WINNER BEST CHEAP EATS
2-4 Boundary Street, E2 7DD (7729 1051, www.albioncaff.co.uk). Old Street tube/rail/26, 48, 67, 149, 242 bus. **Meals served** 8am-midnight daily. **Main courses** £8-10. **Credit** AmEx, MC, V.
It's ludicrously modish for new restaurants to mine the vein of nostalgia for traditional British cuisine, but few pull it off as well as the British 'caff' that Terence Conran has opened on his return to the business. Once you've stepped past the collection of kitsch British products for sale in the entrance shop (HP sauce, Marmite, Lea & Perrins), you're faced with china platters of freshly baked cupcakes,

doorstop-thick slices of battenberg slathered heavily with jam, and chunky bourbons stuffed with fresh cream. It's all cooked in front of diners, as the contemporary dining room (which occupies a former Victorian warehouse) is arranged around the long metal counter of an open kitchen. On the menu, toad in the hole, devilled kidneys, and fish and chips sit next to an English breakfast featuring buttery scrambled eggs, juicy field mushrooms and a tall tower of stunning black pudding so oaty it was virtually haggis. A parsley-scattered stew of plump rabbit joints, prunes and root veg came in a light, sweet gravy, but the stand-out was easily the mouth-watering Aubrey Allen pork scratchings, served with a gently zingy apple sauce. Perhaps our beef-dripping chips were slightly chewy, but that's our only objection, and a very small one indeed.
Babies and children welcome: high chairs; nappy-changing facilities. Bookings not accepted. Disabled: toilet. Tables outdoors (10, pavement). Takeaway service. **Map 6 R4.**

Rivington Bar & Grill

28-30 Rivington Street, EC2A 3DZ (7729 7053, www.rivingtongrill.co.uk). Old Street tube/rail.
Bar **Open/meals served** 11am-12.30am Mon-Sat; 11am-midnight Sun.
Restaurant **Breakfast served** 8-11am, **lunch served** noon-3pm Mon-Fri. **Brunch served** 11am-4pm Sat, Sun. **Dinner served** 6-11pm Mon-Sat; 6-10pm Sun. **Main courses** £9.75-£27. **Set lunch** (Sun) £18.50 3 courses.
Both **Credit** AmEx, DC, MC, V.
Full on a Monday night, the Rivington was giving off great vibes. The whitewashed dining room looks down on an equally stripped-down bar, where food is also served. Works from local artists provide decoration. The user-friendly menu includes breakfast (brunch at weekends) and all-day bar food – bangers and mash, skate knobs with chips. Most dishes succeed, without thrilling, as in a recent meal that began with potted shrimps on toast (one of several 'on toast' options) and a pretty watercress soup with a poached egg floating in it. Tender Speyside flat-iron steak with so-so chips, and glamorgan leek and caerphilly sausages with creamed leeks were capable mains. Chocolate mousse, and a super-indulgent honeycomb ice-cream with hot toffee sauce made a fine ending. The odd dish is outstanding, such as scallops with pumpkin purée and black pudding; it was a measly portion though – we were grateful the waitress had insisted we ordered side dishes (great heritage carrots, slightly soggy broccoli). If the kitchen raised its game a little, this could be a destination restaurant, rather than a convivial local. (Drivers beware: staff are so used to seeing cars removed, they keep the number of the pound to hand.)
Babies and children welcome: crayons; high chairs. Booking advisable. Vegetarian menu. **Map 6 R4.**
For branch (Rivington Greenwich) see index.

Rochelle Canteen

Rochelle School, Arnold Circus, E2 7ES (7729 5677, www.arnoldandhenderson.com). Old Street tube/rail/26, 48, 67, 149, 242 bus. **Breakfast served** 9-11am, **lunch served** noon-3pm Mon-Fri. **Main courses** £8.50-£15. **Unlicensed. Corkage** £5. **Credit** MC, V.
What started life as a canteen for artists working in the studios at Rochelle School has become a lovely local. Run by the catering company formed by Margot Henderson and Melanie Arnold, this small light-filled space lies next to a neat lawn; big windows open wide in summer. Service is as relaxed as you like: grab a quick bite or stay for hours. A short daily-changing menu has shades of St John (*see p51*; Fergus Henderson is married to Margot) – anchovy toast, say, or a plate of spelt, red chard and berkswell cheese – but isn't as rigidly British. Meatballs and new potatoes was the dish we wanted, but it had all gone by 1.30pm (as had smoked haddock with poached egg). Juicy lamb chops with saffron courgettes almost compensated; niçoise salad with glorious roast tomatoes and vibrant yellow yolks was even better. A starter of pea, broad bean and rocket salad was summer on a plate, while tymsboro goat's cheese came with melt-in-the-mouth oatcakes – worth forgoing chocolate pot or lemon

sorbet. Coffee is good and strong. Hidden behind the old school wall, Rochelle is hard to find: press the buzzer on the metal plate outside to enter.
Available for hire, evenings only. Babies and children welcome: high chairs; nappy-changing facilities. Booking advisable Thur, Fri. Tables outdoors (12, courtyard). **Map 6 S4.**

North

Camden Town & Chalk Farm

Market

43 Parkway, NW1 7PN (7267 9700, www.market restaurant.co.uk). Camden Town tube. **Lunch served** noon-2.30pm, **dinner served** 6-10.30pm Mon-Sat. **Meals served** 1-3.30pm Sun. **Main courses** £9-£14. **Set lunch** (Mon-Fri) £10 2 courses. **Credit** AmEx, DC, MC, V.
Parkway doesn't have a reputation as a foodie destination, so hats off to Market for succeeding on this tricky thoroughfare. Behind an unassuming black frontage, the restaurant was busy for Saturday lunch, with virtually every demographic covered: groups, couples, families and lone diners all lapping up the good-value, high-quality fare. The place is unfussily but thoughtfully designed. Walls are bare brick, tables zinc-topped and tap water comes in enamel jugs. There's a compact private dining room on the first floor. From a short menu, lamb breast with celeriac remoulade was a fine contrast of flavours, the remoulade cutting through the lamb's fat. We also enjoyed a rich yet zingy salad of bell's blue cheese, trevise lettuce, blood orange and hazelnuts. A main of lemon sole with cockles and chips was a winner on all fronts (especially the chips), its super-buttery sauce made piquant by capers. Rose veal with anchovy butter, spinach and chilli was also a success. Honey and rosemary ice-cream split opinion – should this herb be used in puddings? – but a treacle-laden sponge with custard was wonderful. Brisk service comes with a smile; we wished we could linger into the afternoon. Long may Market prosper. Camden needs such places.
Babies and children welcome: high chairs. Booking advisable. Separate room for parties, seats 12. Tables outdoors (2, pavement). **Map 27 C2.**

Outer London

Kew, Surrey

Kew Grill

10B Kew Green, Surrey TW9 3BH (8948 4433, www.awtrestaurants.com). Kew Gardens tube/rail/Kew Bridge rail. **Lunch served** noon-2.30pm Tue-Fri; noon-4pm Sat. **Dinner served** 6.30-10.30pm Mon-Thur; 6.30-11pm Fri; 6-11pm Sat. **Meals served** noon-10pm Sun. **Main courses** £12.50-£45.50. **Credit** AmEx, MC, V.
Regrettably, the retro dishes here aren't accompanied by old-fashioned prices. We found the cooking lacklustre, and Kew Grill felt provincial and untouched by the creativity and passion of the best British restaurants. Take the bread: four types are offered; all are merely OK, rather than showing what the kitchen can do. The small, bare-brick room is made cosy with warm lighting and cushions. Staff are slightly too attentive (constantly asking if we were enjoying our meal). Portions are large. In descending order of enjoyment, the 6oz steak au poivre was the best dish, equalled by a crème brûlée. Specials of grilled goat's cheese with pine nuts, honey and mixed salad, followed by grilled sea bass fillets with crushed new potatoes, with brown shrimp and lemon butter were decent dishes. Cheese and bacon burger was so-so, and the chunky chips too dry (skinny chips were good). Avocado vinaigrette was overpowered by an oniony dressing, yet was nicer than spiced soft-shell crab on thai red curry sauce, which was mushy. Owner Antony Worrall Thompson has had to close some restaurants; after this meal we think we know why. A step back in time, but not in a good way.
Available for hire. Babies and children welcome: high chairs. Booking advisable Thur-Sun.

Caribbean

Recreating that island feeling is important to many of London's Caribbean restaurants. Rum cocktails, vibrant colour schemes and a laid-back vibe help transport diners to beach-side eateries or Kingston backstreets. Soho's **Jerk City**, Brixton's **Bamboula**, **Cottons** of Clerkenwell and Crystal Palace's **Island Fusion** all do a good job of conjuring up the authentic atmosphere. Food is slowly evolving, though this year we have no new restaurants to report. Some chefs concentrate on providing big portions of home-style cooking (**Savannah Jerk** in Soho, Cottons, Island Fusion and Bamboula are prime exponents) whereas others – such as Battersea's **Ace Fusion**, Camden's **Mango Room** and **Glistening Waters** of Brentford provide an increased level of sophistication in a more upmarket setting.

Central

Clerkenwell & Farringdon

★ Cottons
70 Exmouth Market, EC1R 4QP (7833 3332, www.cottons-restaurant.co.uk). Farringdon tube/rail/19, 38, 341 bus. **Lunch served** noon-4pm Mon-Fri. **Dinner served** 5.30-11pm Mon-Thur; 6.30-11pm Fri, Sat. **Meals served** noon-11pm Sun. **Main courses** £12.50-£14.50. **Credit** AmEx, MC, V.
You could easily miss Cottons' unassuming entrance, but as you leave the busy road behind, you're transported to the West Indies. The large 'Jamaica Bar' greets you, stocked high with rum bottles – 250 types. The friendly rich-voiced barman seems part of the cliché, but the warmth is genuine; from an exquisite cocktail list, he suggested strawberry daiquiri and Raas berry special: both strong yet refreshing drinks. Tender slow-roasted pork belly with a sweet ginger glaze arrived on a herby cassava cake with caramel sauce: a delicious combination of sweetness and spice. Fiery jerk beef fillets on a salad of mixed leaves, avocado, mango and roasted cashews left our tongues tingling. For mains, Cottons' mixed jerk grill had succulent chicken, kofta and jerked pork ribs (a bit short on meat); the accompanying plantain was soft and warm, the rice and peas spot on. Deep-fried tilapia stuffed with chilli and tomato paste with callaloo fell away from the bones. We had no room for dessert, but banana and pineapple cinnamon crumble beckoned temptingly.
Available for hire. Babies and children welcome: high chairs. Disabled: toilet. Entertainment: DJs 9.30pm-2am Fri, Sat. Separate room for parties, seats 65. Tables outdoors (5, patio). Takeaway service. **Map 5 N4.**

Soho

★ Jerk City
189 Wardour Street, W1F 8ZD (7287 2878). Tottenham Court Road tube. **Meals served** 10am-10.30pm Mon-Wed; 10am-11pm Thur-Sat; noon-8pm Sun. **Main courses** £6-£8.50. **Credit** MC, V.
A cold Tuesday night in Soho turned into a laid-back slice of West Indian warmth in this tiny space filled with pine tables, Afro-Caribbean art on warm-coloured walls, and lots of enthusiastic, mixed diners. Spicy smells and friendly staff – from the Rasta who takes orders at the counter, to the young women who bring the food a few minutes later – add to the authenticity, as does the menu. Rice and peas transported us back to carnival food in Trinidad, while the accompanying saltfish and ackee is perfect Jamaica (though many Jamaicans would have serious words with anyone who served such tiny portions of it). A roti (curried goat wrapped in a flatbread) was less successful: the bread thick and heavy, the sauce convincing but too sloppy for what is essentially takeaway food. Jerk chicken wings were dry and chewy and seemed to have been cooked a while beforehand, suggesting that Jerk City hits its peak at lunchtime. Come early for the genuine Caribbean experience.
Babies and children welcome: high chairs; nappy-changing facilities. Takeaway service. **Map 17 B3.**

★ Savannah Jerk
187 Wardour Street, W1F 8ZB (7437 7770). Tottenham Court Road tube. **Meals served** 11am-11pm Mon-Sat; noon-8pm Sun. **Main courses** £7-£9. **Credit** MC, V.
It's comforting to know that Caribbean chefs still believe people deserve a substantial break at lunchtime – and substantial feeding. For about £25 two people can fill up on delicious peppery, meaty dishes at this smart, spacious little restaurant. Savannah Jerk changed its name from Mr Jerk in 2009 after new owners took over, though the menu and chef remain the same. You can't judge Caribbean food without sampling the jerk sauce, and the chicken wing starter here truly inflames the taste buds. Skip wine and drink ginger beer: it's sugary, but the sharp, bubbly liquid melds with jerk sauce's own ginger, allspice and scotch bonnet peppers to eye-opening effect. Main courses also pack a peppery punch. Chicken roti was filled with an old-school bright-yellow curry sauce and moist chicken. Slow-cooked, tender curried mutton was full of luscious, dark flavours, and came in a vast portion. Coleslaw, iceberg lettuce salads and rice and peas are the only accompaniments, but the package works. Savannah Jerk also makes a decent stopover for dinner, though this isn't the sort of food you'll want before a night of dancing.
Babies and children welcome: high chairs; nappy-changing facilities. Takeaway service. **Map 17 B3.**

South

Battersea

Ace Fusion
110 St John's Hill, SW11 1SJ (7228 5584, www.acefusion.co.uk). Clapham Junction or Wandsworth Town rail. **Meals served** 5-11pm Mon-Thur; noon-11.30pm Fri; 10am-11.30pm Sat; 10am-10pm Sun. **Main courses** £6.95-£13.95. **Credit** AmEx, MC, V.
This cosy, friendly restaurant (not a common species around Clapham Junction) serves some of London's most creative Caribbean food. Ace is a bright place, with dark-wood flooring, a red-and-yellow colour scheme, big windows and a mezzanine dining area. A quick scan of its menu promises much in the way of tantalising fruit, vegetable, meat and booze concoctions: sautéed prawns in garlic butter, flamed with dark rum; West Indian houmous (a purée of sweet cannellini beans mixed with sour cream and monterey jack cheese) served with plantain wedges; breast of chicken stuffed with mango and coated in breadcrumbs. Fortunately, the food is cooked with great care, whether you order these specials or opt for classics such as jerk chicken (available mild or hot), freshly prepared coleslaw, ackee, curried goat, or baked cod. There are British options too, but you'd be mad not to sample the jollof rice, or the peppery (and not overly sweet) house sauces. One clever addition is a fruit bowl dessert containing bananas, mango and strawberries: the ideal coda to a fiery jerk dish or curry. Staff gently encourage diners to try something different – or at least another cocktail. A warm, wonderful little local.
Available for hire. Babies and children admitted. Tables outdoors (3, pavement). Separate room for parties (seats 20). Takeaway service. **Map 21 B4.**

Mango Room. See p63.

Discover the city from your back pocket

Essential for your weekend break, 25 top cities available.

POCKET SIZED from £6.99 / $11.95

Menu

Ackee: a red-skinned fruit with yellow flesh that looks and tastes like scrambled eggs when cooked; traditionally served in a Jamaican dish of salt cod, onion and peppers.
Bammy or **bammie:** pancake-shaped, deep-fried cassava bread, commonly served with fried fish.
Breadfruit: this football-sized fruit has sweet creamy flesh that's a cross between sweet potato and chestnut. Eaten as a vegetable.
Bush tea: herbal tea made from cerese (a Jamaican vine plant), mint or fennel.
Callaloo: the spinach-like leaves of either taro or malanga, often used as a base for a thick soup flavoured with pork or crab meat.
Coo-coo: a polenta-like cake of cornmeal and okra.
Cow foot: a stew made from the hoof of the cow, which is boiled with vegetables. The cartilage gives the stew a gummy or gelatinous texture.
Curried (or **curry**) **goat:** usually lamb in London; the meat is marinated and slow-cooked until tender.
Dasheen: a root vegetable with a texture similar to yam (qv).
Escoveitched (or **escovitch**) **fish:** fish fried or grilled then pickled in a tangy sauce with onions, sweet peppers and vinegar; similar to escabèche.
Festival: deep-fried, slightly sweet dumpling often served with fried fish.
Foo-foo: a Barbadian dish of pounded plantains, seasoned, rolled into balls and served hot.
Jerk: chicken or pork marinated in chilli spices, slowly roasted or barbecued.
Patty or **pattie:** a savoury pastry snack, made with turmeric-coloured short-crust pastry, usually filled with beef, saltfish or vegetables.
Peas or **beans:** black-eyed beans, black beans, green peas and red kidney beans.
Pepperpot: traditionally a stew of meat and casereep, a juice obtained from cassava; in London it's more likely to be a meat or vegetable stew with cassava.
Phoulorie: a Trinidadian snack of fried doughballs often eaten with a sweet tamarind sauce.
Plantain or **plantin:** a savoury variety of banana that is cooked like potato.
Rice and peas: rice cooked with kidney or gungo beans, pepper seasoning and coconut milk.
Roti: Indian flatbread, usually filled with curried fish, meat or vegetables.
Saltfish: salt cod, classically mixed with ackee (qv) or callaloo (qv).
Sorrel: not the herb, but a type of hibiscus with a sour-sweet flavour.
Soursop: a dark green, slightly spiny fruit; the pulp, blended with milk and sugar, is a refreshing drink.
Yam: a large tuber, with a yellow or white flesh and slightly nutty flavour.

Brixton

Bamboula
12 Acre Lane, SW2 5SG (7737 6633). Brixton tube/ rail. **Meals served** 11am-11pm Mon-Sat; 1-9pm Sun. **Main courses** £7.50-£10. **Credit** MC, V.
The green, hand-painted plaque inside declares Bamboula a 'nuff niceness eatry'. After sampling the home-style Jamaican cooking, we couldn't disagree. The green and yellow interior resembles a Montego beach shack; coupled with a gentle reggae soundtrack and friendly service, it sets the perfect scene for a Caribbean feast. All the Jamaican staples (curry goat, jerk chicken, ackee and saltfish) are offered, along with a few Bamboula specials. We tried the house lamb and the jerk lamb: both succulent chops, marinated in a spicy sauce (though the jerk lamb was much hotter) and served with a thick gravy, rice and peas, salad and freshly made coleslaw. The side dish of plantain seemed a little overripe, and the combined flavours were a bit too sweet (particularly after a slightly overpowering rum punch). Lovers of British bread and butter pudding should try the classic West Indian version served here. It's made with hard-dough bread, soaked in rum and served with rum and raisin ice-cream – and an excellent reminder of why, for hearty Caribbean food, Bamboula is hard to beat.
Babies and children admitted. Booking advisable. Tables outdoors (3, garden). Takeaway service. **Map 22 D2.**

South East
Crystal Palace

★ Island Fusion
57B Westow Hill, SE19 1TS (8761 5544, www. islandfusion.co.uk). Crystal Palace or Gypsy Hill rail. **Dinner served** 5-11pm Mon-Thur; 5-11.30pm Fri, Sat. **Meals served** 4-10pm Sun. **Main courses** £9.50-£17.50. **Set lunch** (Sun) £18 2 courses, £22 3 courses incl coffee. **Credit** MC, V.
The owners of this cleverly converted basement have a soft spot for marine life. Prawns and saltfish are prepared with love – and a spicy sauce on the side. You'll also find rarities such as barbados duck, with the bird marinated in a mild coconut-based curry sauce, and decorated with coriander and a delicious seared dumpling. Staples such as callaloo and jerk chicken are here too. A starter platter for two costs just £9 and contains grilled prawns, jerk wings, saltfish fritters and plantain and callaloo rounds, with dipping sauces. For £11 you get prawns, fish bits, squid rings and crab and lobster cakes (delicious with the spicy dip). Order either platter and your mouth will run the gauntlet of West Indian taste sensations: burning, tingling, salty, sugary, fruity, spicy. Bereft of windows, Island Fusion could have been a dingy subterranean hole, but a sort of postcard experience has been created, with the glow of firefly lamps, beach-shack bamboo decor, murals of Caribbean sunsets and the glassy sheen of well-used bottles of rum.
Babies and children welcome (until 7pm): high chairs. Booking advisable. Disabled: toilet.

East
Docklands

Caribbean Scene
ExCeL Marina, E16 1AQ (7511 2023, www.caribbeanscene.co.uk). Royal Victoria DLR. **Meals served** noon-10.30pm daily. **Main courses** £11.50-£35.50. **Credit** AmEx, MC, V.
Given its location amid Canary Wharf hotels and pretty views across the Royal Docks, this upmarket restaurant ought to be busy on a weekday afternoon when the likes of 'Grand Designs' is on at the ExCeL Centre nearby. So, we were surprised to discover there were no other diners. The friendly waitress told us the restaurant had been packed the previous night. Thin, soggy crab cakes may have been a result of the chef suffering the after-effects of his late night, but the meal improved a little with nicely presented saltfish and ackee and escovitch fish.

Both dishes illustrate how complex good Caribbean cooking can be, however the former was let down by a meagre amount of saltfish, the latter by no evidence of a hot pepper, herb and spice marinade. Staples like jerk chicken, curry goat and oxtail are served with sides of steamed rice and dumpling, fried plantain and green banana. Wooden shutters and a beach mural evoke the Caribbean, though this time the food was found wanting.
Available for hire. Babies and children welcome: children's menu; high chairs. Disabled: toilet. Entertainment: Caribbean music 7pm Sat. Separate room for parties, seats 40-60. Tables outdoors (22, patio). Takeaway service. Vegetarian menu.

North
Camden Town & Chalk Farm

Mango Room
10-12 Kentish Town Road, NW1 8NH (7482 5065, www.mangoroom.co.uk). Camden Town tube. **Meals served** noon-11pm daily. **Main courses** £10-£13. **Credit** AmEx, MC, V.
Mango Room is one of the smartest venues on this grimy corner of Camden. It was dead on a Thursday lunchtime, but the service was fast and informative, the Cubist paintings were bright and cheery, and the sun streamed in through big windows. The menu is short yet alluring. Cocktails (mojito and rum punch) were strong and nicely mixed, going well with a platter of crisp plantain and sweet-potato fritters in a sweet chilli dip. Main courses were a step up in quality, especially the chicken roti – think upmarket burrito, but with a delicate wheat wrap and oozing spices and juice; coriander, ginger, tomatoes and chillies came through clearly. Jerk chicken caesar salad featured a jerk sauce that seemed much milder and considerably more gelatinous than the norm, but it was shot through with spice. Rice and peas was as good as that classic gets: nutty in texture and smoky in aspect. Soft reggae played quietly and all was well as we sampled a shared warm fruit cake with fresh cream. Mango Room is worth repeated visits and deserves busier lunchtimes.
Babies and children welcome: high chairs. Booking advisable weekends. Separate room for parties, seats 20. Takeaway service. Vegan dishes. **Map 27 D2.**

Outer London
Brentford, Middlesex

Glistening Waters
5 Ferry Lane, Ferry Quays, Brentford, Middx TW8 0AT (8758 1616, www.glistening waters.co.uk). Brentford or Kew Bridge rail. **Meals served** 6-11.30pm Tue-Fri; 3pm-midnight Sat; 3-10.30pm Sun. **Main courses** £11.95-£50. **Credit** MC, V.
Barbados, Jamaica, Antigua… Brentford. No, it doesn't trip off the tongue, but you could do worse than dining at this cool-looking yet friendly little spot. The restaurant first appears like a glass cuboid. Inside, however, with a soundtrack of cool funk and gentle dub, and a warm, busy bar, the atmosphere soon turns West Indian. Prices are substantial. Lobster costs £45, the banana leaf mahi mahi fillets are £16.50 and even curried goat is £14.95. In recompense, the chef manages his produce and sauces with finesse, and flavours such as tamarind, capsicum and sesame oil are clearly discernible. Side dishes, called 'provisions', are especially enticing: thyme potatoes, sauté callaloo, sweet potatoes with yam and coco. Unusually, great pride is taken in presentation; dishes come artfully designed, baking hot and are paced to allow customers to chat, digest and enjoy. Portions are big too. Desserts seem a bit of an afterthought, but the sweet potato pudding with rum and raisin ice-cream is a treat for sharing. Good Jamaican coffee rounds things off magnificently.
Babies and children welcome: high chairs. Booking advisable. Tables outdoors (4, terrace).

RESTAURANTS

Chinese

It was **Yauatcha** that started the trend, and now everyone's getting in on the act. Alan Yau's modish dim sum venue opened in 2004 and, among other innovations, it served the dumplings and snacks into the night. Previously, diners could rarely find dim sum after 5pm (and rightly so, many Chinese would argue...) but chains such as **Ping Pong** and **dim t** (see p233) are thriving, not least because dim sum is ideal for sharing and traditionally inexpensive. This year we welcome **Yum Cha** in Chalk Farm, which produces some of London's best xiao long bao, and **Ba Shan**, which specialises in xiao chi (small eats). These street food snacks from Sichuan, Henan and Shaanxi include pan-fried guotie (similar to potstickers), and Chengdu-style chaoshou (large wonton-like dumplings) – a welcome change from the usual Cantonese dim sum seen in the capital, and a sign of Londoners' increasing confidence with regional Chinese cuisines. More upmarket is Kensington's elegant new **Min Jiang**, where wood-fired peking duck is presented rather theatrically in the traditional multi-course manner. So while this year has seen a couple of disappointing closures in Chinatown, there is still evidence that London's Chinese food scene is happily diversifying for the greater enjoyment of all.

Central

Belgravia

Hunan

51 Pimlico Road, SW1W 8NE (7730 5712, www.hunanlondon.com). Sloane Square tube. **Lunch served** 12.30-2pm, **dinner served** 6.30-11pm Mon-Sat. **Set meal** £38.80-£150 per person (minimum 2). **Credit** AmEx, DC, MC, V.
It can feel like the emperor's new clothes at Hunan. While the elegant, narrow room is consistently packed with Pimlico diners who trill at the novelty

of the dining concept, others come away bewildered. We welcome the 'no menu', multi-course style of dining (almost like a tasting menu), which offers freedom and surprise, but question the quality of some dishes. After giving the green light to the waiters (who take into account any dislikes or allergies), we were launched into a lengthy meal of many small dishes. It began well, with an impressive pork broth served in a tiny bamboo cup with soft minced pork, shreds of ginger and a deeply savoury consommé – almost like a deconstructed Shanghainese xiao long bao. Also excellent were dry-fried green beans in a light batter, and a meaty salmon and red snapper roll. The rest failed to impress in execution or presentation: frogs' legs with bamboo shoots were clouded in a cornflour-heavy sauce; tung po pork in a clay pot was charred and dry; spicy beef seemed straight out of a Chinatown caff. The plates keep on coming, so call a stop when ready – or the bill might shock.
Babies and children admitted. Booking essential. Vegetarian menu. **Map 15 G11.**

Chinatown

★ Baozi Inn

25 Newport Court, WC2H 7JS (7287 6877). Leicester Square tube. **Meals served** 11.30am-10pm daily. **Main courses** £6.10-£6.50.
No credit cards.
Generally speaking, the only useful purpose of a picture menu is for laughing out loud as you try to reconcile what's on your plate with what's in the picture. But at this cheap, cheerful little brother of Soho's Bar Shu (see p72) and Ba Shan, what you see really is what you get: an interesting choice of dumplings, noodles and gutsy, hearty soups from China's north and west. What should be the stars – the pork baozi dumplings – are trencherman fare, solid and bland, but luckily, there are more delicate, smaller dumplings such as plump cheng du crescent dumplings in chilli oil sauce, and pork-filled dragon wun tuns in broth. We loved the hot and sour flower beancurd in a wham-bam sauce of vinegar, chilli oil and mouth-numbing sichuan peppercorns, and a crunch-out-loud, 'three sliver

salad' of carrot, kelp and bean-thread noodles. Serious appetites should head straight for a giant bowl of sichuan spicy beef noodles or the tongue-tingling sour and hot sweet potato noodles. Baozi Inn is not the sort of place for lingering, but its woody, folksy, Mao-inspired decor has a nice tongue-in-cheek whimsy to it.
Babies and children admitted. Bookings not accepted. Takeaway service. **Map 17 C4.**

Feng Shui Inn

4-6 Gerrard Street, W1D 5PG (7734 6778, www.fengshuiinn.co.uk). Leicester Square or Piccadilly Circus tube. **Meals served** noon-11.30pm Mon-Sat; noon-10.30pm Sun. **Main courses** £6.80-£24.80. **Set lunch** (noon-4.30pm) £3.90 1 course incl tea, £5.90-£10.90 2 courses incl tea. **Set meal** £12.80-£33.80 per person (minimum 2). **Credit** AmEx, MC, V.
With its glass-topped tables, cosy burgundy interior and ceiling festooned with Chinese ornaments, Feng Shui Inn makes a fine place in which to relax and enjoy a leisurely meal – particularly during quiet midweek lunchtimes. No dim sum is served, and you won't find the accompanying paper tablecloths and bustle of neighbouring eateries either. The regular menu offers the usual Cantonese choices with a few Sichuan and Beijing favourites, executed with varying degrees of success. More interesting options are available on the double-sided Chinese-language menu. On our visit the helpful staff gave a number of knowledgeable recommendations. In general, the quality of food this time was high. Steamed sea bass and 'golden sand' lobster appear to be signature dishes; we tried 'golden sand' king prawns and found them to be dry and overcooked, despite their crisp deep-fried shells and a generous mound of garlic chips. Dried oyster and pork patties combined smoky, meaty flavours with salty preserved vegetables and crisp water-chestnuts, while a dish of layered tofu, steamed egg white and seafood pieces was well-balanced and enjoyable.
Babies and children admitted. Booking essential weekends. Entertainment: karaoke (call for details). Separate rooms for parties, seating 12, 20 and 40. Vegetarian menu. **Map 17 C4.**

Golden Dragon

28-29 Gerrard Street, W1D 6JW (7734 2763). Leicester Square or Piccadilly Circus tube. **Meals served** noon-11.30pm Mon-Thur; noon-midnight Fri, Sat; 11am-11pm Sun. **Dim sum served** noon-4.45pm Mon-Sat; 11am-4.45pm Sun. **Main courses** £6-£25. **Dim sum** £2.40-£4.30. **Set meal** £13.50-£40 per person (minimum 2). **Credit** AmEx, MC, V.
Golden Dragon's auspicious name, large façade and prominent location give it an advantage when it comes to attracting passing trade in busy Chinatown. Its reputation as a good-value destination for dim sum and other Cantonese fare was evidenced by the number of full round tables when we visited for a midweek lunch. The cooking is generally decent enough, although quality of ingredients often loses out in favour of keeping prices down. The large, spacious dining room is decorated in red and gold, with panels depicting Chinese ladies at leisure. The dim sum are generally more filling than refined. We found most meaty fillings bland, whether in steamed siu mai dumplings or beef cheung fun, while some pastry cases were overcooked and stodgy. In contrast, our har gau were full of bouncy prawns, and the taro croquettes were deep-fried perfectly to form a crisp lacy shell encasing a mushroom and pork filling. Dishes of quick-fried squid with straw mushrooms and sweetcorn, and chinese broccoli stir-fried with garlic and ginger, were generously portioned and fine. This isn't a place to be adventurous, but its classic Chinatown dishes rarely disappoint.
Babies and children welcome: high chairs. Booking advisable. Separate rooms for parties, seating 8-36. Takeaway service. **Map 17 C4.**

Haozhan

8 Gerrard Street, W1D 5PJ (7434 3838, www.haozhan.co.uk). Leicester Square or Piccadilly Circus tube. **Meals served** noon-11.30pm Mon-Thur; noon-midnight Fri, Sat; noon-10.30pm Sun.

Ba Shan. See p72.

Main courses £6-£38. **Set lunch** (Mon-Fri) £8 2 courses, £10 3 courses. **Credit** AmEx, MC, V.
Dinner starts with complimentary edamame. Hang on: Japanese soy beans in a Chinese restaurant? Yes, Haozhan is not your average Chinatown chow house. It is sleeker, darker and more modern, with a menu that extends beyond Chinatown staples to fuse Cantonese, Thai, Malaysian and Japanese influences – hence the edamame. Some dishes don't transcend the fusion remit; a confit duck salad tossed with strawberries and blueberries was a bit weird, as was the idea of serving spring rolls propped up in a whisky glass. More on the money is the Thai gai lan, a jazzy mix of chinese broccoli and minced salt-fish. Malaysian ho fun noodles with squid, egg, bamboo shoot and prawns were wok-fried over such intense heat, they bore that alluring smokiness that is the difference between good char kway teow, and bad. We also liked the easy street-food charms of san pei, a Taiwanese clay pot of chicken thigh with sweet basil, peppers and a hint of chilli. Choose carefully, and Haozhan could be your number one Chinatown option. The dining experience is already the best in the street: caring, wine-savvy and responsive.
Babies and children welcome: high chairs. Booking advisable Wed-Sat. **Map 17 C4**.

Imperial China

White Bear Yard, 25A Lisle Street, WC2H 7BA (7734 3388, www.imperial-china.co.uk). Leicester Square or Piccadilly Circus tube. **Meals served** noon-11.30pm Mon-Sat; 11.30am-10.30pm Sun. **Dim sum served** noon-5pm daily. **Main courses** £5.90-£26.50. **Dim sum** £2.30-£3.60. **Set meal** £16.50-£31.50 per person (minimum 2). **Minimum** £10. **Credit** AmEx, MC, V.
A reliable destination in Chinatown, Imperial China attracts a slightly more upmarket clientele with its clean linen tablecloths and subdued wood and cream decor. A soothing, clean broth is a good way to start a Chinese meal, and it's done well here – ask for the house soup of the day (often a slow-simmered, savoury essence of pork bones and sweet root vegetables). Whole chicken and Cantonese-style duck were better than on our last visit: the duck skin crisp and the meat of both juicy and tender, served in generous portions. We asked for the kitchen to use less oil in our stir-fried pea shoots and choi sum,

yet both arrived grease-slicked, detracting from the delicate superior consommé in which the vegetables were served. Better was a clay pot stuffed with braised shiitake mushrooms, which ticked all the boxes for flavour, texture and aroma. Service can be notably forgetful at times; our request for the air-conditioning to be turned on during a hot evening was granted after the third time. While the food may not be adventurous, Imperial China does serve solid Cantonese cooking in comfortable surroundings.
Babies and children welcome: high chairs. Booking advisable. Disabled: toilet. Entertainment: pianist 7.30pm Wed-Fri. Separate rooms for parties, seating 10-70. Tables outdoors (5, courtyard).
Map 17 C4.

Joy King Lau

3 Leicester Street, WC2H 7BL (7437 1132). Leicester Square or Piccadilly Circus tube. **Meals served** noon-11.30pm Mon-Sat; 11.30am-10.30pm Sun. **Dim sum served** noon-5pm Mon-Sat; 11am-5pm Sun. **Main courses** £6.80-£20. **Dim sum** £2.10-£4.50. **Set meal** £10-£35 per person (minimum 2). **Credit** AmEx, MC, V.
Spread over four rather small floors, this bustling Chinatown stalwart has a cosy tea-house atmosphere. The space is not much to look at and the tables are closely packed, but diners from all demographics come here to enjoy the reliably decent dim sum and the home-style rice or noodle dishes – everything very reasonably priced. We enjoyed soft cheung fun rolls spiked with spring onions and sesame seeds, and a sticky glutinous rice parcel stuffed with wind-dried sausage, pork, mushrooms and dried shrimp, wrapped in lotus leaves and steamed until fragrant. Mixed meat croquettes were a little undercooked, with a slightly bland filling, but nonetheless crisp, chewy and savoury as expected. Less successful were a trio of gluey and over-peppered chiu chow dumplings stuffed with peanuts, shredded cabbage and char siu, and some deep-fried cuttlefish cakes that were spongy and bland. Deep-fried egg custard buns were a mite dry, but otherwise made an enjoyable, sweet finish to the meal. A little more attention to culinary execution would make this dim sum destination even better value.
Babies and children welcome: high chairs. Booking advisable weekends. Takeaway service. **Map 17 C5**.

Leong's Legends

4 Macclesfield Street, W1D 6AX (7287 0288). Leicester Square or Piccadilly Circus tube. **Meals served** noon-11pm, **dim sum served** noon-5pm daily. **Main courses** £4.50-£18.50. **Dim sum** £1.90-£6. **Credit** (over £12) MC, V.
This newish Taiwanese restaurant offers flavours not present in the kitchens of its elderly neighbours. The unusual name refers to a classical Chinese novel, *The Water Margin*, which revolves around the rebel Song Jiang and his comrades (sometimes referred to as 'Liang's legends') who rise up against a corrupt government while taking refuge on Mount Liang (aka Leong). A lively Chinese crowd comes for the bitter and, to the untrained tongue, at times bland (let's call them subtle) flavours. Leong's soup dumplings (xiao long bao) – eight pork or crab dumplings with rich broth sealed inside – are among the best in Chinatown. They could easily make a meal in themselves, if ordered in quantity. An omelette with pickled radish was large (only for sharing, really, but pleasantly homely); it made a nice contrast to spicy pig's offal, which did just what the name promised, offering spicy, rich flavours. The dining room, with tables separated by wooden beams in the manner of a traditional Chinese café, bustles with rapid turnover. Service can be slow in the hectic environment.
Babies and children admitted. Bookings not accepted. Takeaway service. **Map 17 C4**.

★ Little Lamb

72 Shaftesbury Avenue, W1D 6NA (7287 8078). Piccadilly Circus tube. **Meals served** noon-10.30pm daily. **Set meal** £20 per person (minimum 2). **Credit** MC, V.
Mongolian hotpot is a communal affair, and young groups of Chinese stream into Little Lamb to cook choice titbits in bowls of bubbling stock. The restaurant is small and simply furnished, with a dark wooden bar at the rear and plain wooden tables, each with a hotplate inset. There's a similarly attired room in the basement. Choose your stock (you can have up to three, partitioned in the same bowl) and the raw ingredients to cook, from a long list of meat, seafood, mushrooms, beancurd, vegetables and noodles. The £20 set meal is a good deal, entitling diners (minimum of two) to a stock and five ingredients. We plumped for 'herbal tonic and spicy twin-flavours pot' – half tangy, half faintly medicinal – into which we chucked lamb, tea-tree mushrooms, rice cakes, wax gourd (like sliced marrow) and pea shoots. Portions are enormous: the mushrooms were chewy and ungainly; rice cakes came as slippery lozenges. The plateful of wafer-thin sliced lamb was cooked in a trice, as were the leafy pea shoots, yet as our eating-bowls were scarcely bigger than tea-cups, attempts to keep up with the cooking process resulted in scalded tongues. Good messy fun nonetheless.
Babies and children admitted. **Map 17 C4**.

Mr Kong

21 Lisle Street, WC2H 7BA (7437 7341, www.mrkongrestaurant.com). Leicester Square or Piccadilly Circus tube. **Meals served** noon-2.45am Mon-Sat; noon-1.45am Sun. **Main courses** £6.90-£26. **Set meal** £10 per person (minimum 2); £17.80-£23.50 per person (minimum 4). **Minimum** £7 after 5pm. **Credit** AmEx, DC, MC, V.
Infuriatingly inconsistent where it used to be dependable, Mr Kong continues to attract full houses, but few Chinese. The menu is gargantuan and that's part of the problem: it's not always easy to separate Cantonese wheat from Anglo-Chinese chaff. A 'chef's special' of baby squid with chilli arrived lukewarm and gaudily clad in lurid-orange, chewy batter – dreadful. It was in stark contrast to a plate of crunchy-fresh gai lan (chinese broccoli) in ginger; and an equally excellent soup of tender sliced pork, salted eggs and gai choi (mustard cabbage) in hearting-warming pork stock. Somewhere in between was a hotpot of belly pork with preserved vegetables, and a brace of razor clams with vermicelli and soy-chilli dipping sauce – both dishes a mite too dry, as was the steamed rice. Vegetarians have their own sizeable list of specials, including mock abalone, pork, shark's fin and crispy duck. The restaurant's layout

Regional cooking

A basic knowledge of the four 'schools' of Chinese cuisine is helpful when examining restaurant menus. The traditional categories (Cantonese: fresh; western China: fiery and spicy; northern China: stodgy and chilli-hot; eastern China: sweet and oily) may be over-simplistic, but they are not incorrect. Sichuan's rising profile in London has taught diners about western China's penchant for spicy, numbing flavours: from sichuan peppercorns, chillies and zesty tangerine peel, for example.

China's geographical diversity is key to explaining the contrasting approaches to food. The north's cold winters have led to a culinary repertoire that includes comforting, filling noodles, buns and breads, aided by chillies and plenty of preserved and pickled meats and vegetables, plus slow-cooked stews and soups. Beef and lamb are more common here than in the inland provinces of the west, where pork is the favoured meat. Both Sichuan and Yunnan are known for their reliance on pork, the latter famed for its air-cured ham – China's answer to parma and serrano.

Also inland is Hunan; its milder climate, fertile land and proximity to

lakes and rivers have earned it the nickname 'the land of rice and fish'. Guangdong and Hong Kong's humid, sub-tropical coastal locations lie behind its delicately flavoured seafood dishes and a concentration on simple fresh produce. Similarly, Fujianese cuisine is influenced by its 'shan sui' (mountain, water) landscape. As a result, seafood is one of its most treasured ingredients – succulent oyster omelettes and bouncy fish balls being just two of the most favoured exports. Fujianese influences are strong in Taiwanese cuisine, which favours seafood because of the island's limited arable space. Also significant are Japanese dishes, thanks to the 50-year occupation of Taiwan.

Shanghai, as one of China's most cosmopolitan areas, inevitably draws in culinary influences from far and wide; however, its eastern China signature is in the use of alcohol (particularly rice wine), as well as the 'red cooking' method (where soy sauce used in slow-cooking imparts a reddish hue to food) also favoured by the western Chinese. With such diversity, it's no wonder the country is so fiercely proud of its culinary traditions.

RESTAURANTS

Leong's Legends

has been frequently changed over its quarter-century history. There are now three small dining rooms (ground, lower-ground and first floor) where anodyne surroundings of white walls and dark-green carpets are jazzed up with yellow tablecloths and framed artefacts on the walls.

Babies and children welcome: booster seats; high chairs. Booking advisable. Separate room for parties, seats 30. Takeaway service. Vegetarian menu. **Map 17 C4**.

New Mayflower

68-70 Shaftesbury Avenue, W1D 6LY (7734 9207). Leicester Square or Piccadilly Circus tube. **Meals served** 5pm-4am daily. **Main courses** £7-£48. **Set meal** £14.50-£22 per person (minimum 2). **Minimum** £8. **Credit** MC, V.

A Chinatown stalwart, the New Mayflower is a cavernous venue, set over two floors and several rather small rooms. The red-carpeted, white-walled interior is drab and could use a little updating. Nevertheless, the kitchen is capable of producing Cantonese cuisine to a high standard, if you know what to order. Sadly, a certain proportion of diners here (tourists wafting over from Piccadilly Circus) do not, and are nudged towards the lacklustre set meals. A dish of succulent clams with a mild chilli and salty black bean sauce was the star of our meal. We also enjoyed a home-style steamed minced pork patty, studded with water-chestnuts and topped with salted egg. Emperor chicken, ordered from the menu written only in Chinese, was fine, but the accompanying ginger and spring onion sauce lacked salt. Finally, a plate of stir-fried water spinach was too oily and contained no trace of the fermented beancurd sauce we requested. The generous portions resulted in plenty of our dinner being boxed up and taken home. On our weekday visit the restaurant was packed, causing cramped seating conditions and leading to inattentive service. We've had such problems here before.

Babies and children welcome: high chairs. Booking advisable. Takeaway service. Vegetarian menu. **Map 17 B4**.

New World

1 Gerrard Place, W1D 5PA (7734 0396). Leicester Square or Piccadilly Circus tube. **Meals served** noon-11.45pm Mon-Fri; 11am-midnight Sat; 11am-11pm Sun. **Dim sum served** noon-6pm Mon-Fri; 11am-6pm Sat, Sun. **Main courses** £7.50-£10.50. **Dim sum** £2.40-£3.50. **Set meal** £10.50-£14.50 per person (minimum 2). **Minimum** (after 6pm) £5. **Credit** AmEx, DC, MC, V.

The patina on New World's aged red carpet speaks of decades spent under the wheels of parading trolleys. This immense three-storied restaurant (basement, ground and first floor) keeps to the Hong Kong tradition of doling out dim sum direct from stainless-steel vehicles, pushed by hard-working waitresses (not always fluent in English). Stop one and point to your choice. More recently, around a dozen dim sum have also been served in the evening, from a menu. We sampled a selection, along with two chef's specials. The snacks passed muster, though lacked delicacy: barbecued pork puffs veered towards stodginess, chiu chow dumplings contained abundant diced carrot, shark's fin and minced pork dumplings seemed a bit dry. The chef's specials were more appealing, though slippery sautéed aubergine with minced pork and salt-fish arrived in enough oil to grease a politician's palm. Sautéed beancurd with seafood in XO sauce was the best dish: the lightly fried tofu properly wobbly within, the sauce adding piquancy to the squid, scallops and prawns. The atmosphere is more relaxed by night, leaving time to appreciate the venerable surroundings: the capacious ground-floor decorated with red paper lanterns and huge bas-relief wall pictures.

Babies and children welcome: high chairs. Bookings not accepted Sun lunch. Takeaway service. Vegetarian menu. **Map 17 C4**.

Royal Dragon

30 Gerrard Street, W1D 6JS (7734 1388). Leicester Square or Piccadilly Circus tube. **Dinner served** 5.30pm-3am daily. **Main courses** £7.50-£23. **Set dinner** £14, £17.50, £18.50 per person (minimum 2). **Credit** AmEx, MC, V.

RESTAURANTS

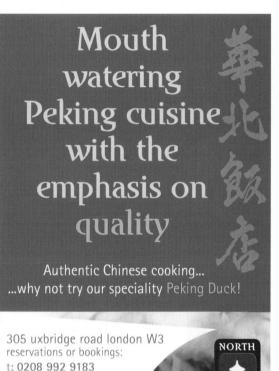

The extensive menu here offers many of the usual Chinatown favourites – deep-fried shredded beef; deep-fried squid in salt and pepper – and on the whole these are of a good standard. We were less keen on our kung po chicken, despite the tender meat, as it included cashew nuts and a sweet-sour sauce rather than the anticipated peanuts and chillies. More adventurous diners may opt for crab steamed in wine sauce: a generous portion of whole crab that's heady with the fragrance of Shaoxing wine. Pei pa duck is also delicious, comprising moist, rich meat and crisp lacquered skin. Homesick Chinese students and those in search of comfort food like to order the excellent beef brisket, either in noodle soup or on its own with rice. We loved the tender chunks of slow-cooked beef blanketed in rich, flavourful sauce. The restaurant now only serves dinner, but opens until very late to cater for young Chinese and others with a penchant for karaoke. The singing takes place in private rooms, so diners need not fear any disturbance. Furnishings are mostly dark and low key, making a change from the bright red found in neighbouring restaurants.
Babies and children welcome: high chair. Booking advisable weekends. Entertainment: karaoke (7pm daily). Separate room for parties, seats 20. **Map 17 C4**.

Euston

Snazz Sichuan
New China Club, 37 Chalton Street, NW1 1JD (7388 0808, www.newchinaclub.co.uk). Euston tube/rail. **Meals served** 11am-11pm daily. **Main courses** £7.50-£38. **Set meal** £18 per person (minimum 2). **Credit** (over £10) MC, V.
While more stylish purveyors of Sichuanese cuisine have risen to near cult status in Soho, Snazz Sichuan has continued to serve spicy and authentic dishes from China's famous western province in the quieter neighbourhood around Euston. Since the restaurant opened a few years ago, the flavours have been slightly subdued – don't be afraid to ask for lashings of chilli and mouth-numbing sichuan peppercorns. However, the ingredients, for spicy and numbing dishes, hotpots, and everything in between, continue to be uncompromisingly Sichuanese. Strange-flavoured rabbit remains a favourite, the meat drowning in a silky sauce of chilli and sesame oil. Fried pomfret was served with great fanfare in a dish weighed down by french fries, peanuts, and wonderfully crunchy lotus root. The bizarrely designed dining room, which purports to double as an art gallery, has photographs of old China and modern paintings lining the walls. Together with the chaotic but friendly service (if there's a crowd, you're in for a long meal), it is pleasingly reminiscent of lively restaurants in Beijing, so adding to the authenticity of the experience.
Babies and children welcome: high chairs. Booking advisable dinner. Separate rooms for parties, seating 15 and 50. Takeaway service. **Map 4 K3**.

Fitzrovia

Hakkasan (100)
8 Hanway Place, W1T 1HD (7907 1888, www.hakkasan.com). Tottenham Court Road tube. **Bar Open** noon-12.30am Mon-Wed; noon-1.30am Thur-Sat; noon-midnight Sun. *Restaurant* **Lunch/dim sum served** noon-3pm Mon-Fri; noon-4pm Sat, Sun. **Dinner served** 6-11pm Mon-Wed, Sun; 6pm-midnight Thur-Sat. **Main courses** £9.50-£58. **Dim sum** £3-£20. *Both* **Credit** AmEx, MC, V.
More than a year since creator Alan Yau sold this esteemed restaurant to an Abu Dhabi-based company, the changes are minimal. So it's still frustrating that you must specifically request the dim sum menu at lunchtime (though it's always offered graciously). It is hard not to be enamoured by the sultry enclave of chinoiserie that is this underground restaurant, where sleek staff glide out of the shadows carrying all manner of elegantly presented modern Chinese fare. An excellent vegetarian selection, for instance, elevates ingredients like beancurd, lily bulbs and cloud-ear fungus above their humble appearances. To dine on dim sum is a pleasure here, and the sweet scallop siu mai topped with glistening flying-fish roe is a highlight. There was also much skill displayed in the translucent rice noodle wrappers of our prawn and gai lan (chinese broccoli) cheung fun. In contrast, Hakka-style vermicelli noodles were greasy and limp, while fried rice with salted egg – that comfort food of many Chinese households – was again oily. A light touch is a skill sought by the greatest Chinese chefs; while many of Hakkasan's offerings live up to their starry status, it is worrying how some simple dishes do not.
Available for hire. Babies and children admitted. Booking essential, 6 weeks in advance. Disabled: lift; toilet. Entertainment: DJs 9pm daily. **Map 17 C2**.

Holborn

Shanghai Blues
193-197 High Holborn, WC1V 7BD (7404 1668, www.shanghaiblues.co.uk). Holborn tube. **Meals/dim sum served** noon-11.30pm daily. **Main courses** £12-£30. **Dim sum** £4-£5.30. **Set lunch** (Mon-Fri) £15 per person (minimum 2). **Credit** AmEx, MC, V.
From the moment you walk in, through the clubby dark foyer and electric-blue cocktail bar into a dining room that blends candle-lit Shanghai teahouse and hip cocktail bar, Shanghai Blues looks like a class act. Soon after we arrived, however, things went awry: wrong orders, long waits, dropped bottles, and spilt drinks. Our steamed har gau prawn dumplings never arrived. In spite of the flaky service, the food can be very good, and dishes such as steamed sea bass with Shanghai spice and chilli were beautifully cooked – and even beautifully filleted at the table without mishap. The dim sum shows more imagination than most, particularly a delicate, juicy scallop dumpling in green (spinach juice) pastry. For those prepared to go beyond the knee-jerk British order of crispy shredded duck, the barbecued pipa (banjo) duck, served with fingers of steamed white bread, is a lacquered, action-packed treat. Wines are pricey, and puds are very modish, à la warm green-tea pancakes and edgy dessert cocktails. Smooth out the service, and Shanghai Blues could be the class act it promises to be.
Babies and children welcome: high chairs. Booking advisable. Disabled: toilet. Dress: smart casual. Entertainment: jazz 7.30pm Fri, Sat. Separate rooms for parties, seating 30-90. Takeaway service. **Map 18 E2**.

Knightsbridge

★ Mr Chow
151 Knightsbridge, SW1X 7PA (7589 7347, www.mrchow.com). Knightsbridge tube. **Lunch served** 12.30-3pm Tue-Sun. **Dinner served** 7pm-midnight daily. **Main courses** £12.50-£25. **Set lunch** £23. **Set dinner** £38. **Credit** AmEx, DC, MC, V.
The decor and waiters at this long-established, high-end restaurant are western, but the food is authentically Chinese – and very good too. Fine linen and silverware, smoked mirrors and white marble floors create an elegant, though not unfriendly, feel, and many of the equally elegant customers are warmly greeted by name in Spanish or Italian accents. There's something Italian-looking too about the signature Mr Chow noodles, but the spaghetti turns out to be springy and typically northern Chinese, while the bolognese-type minced pork and yellow bean sauce tastes slightly sweet and fruity, and surprisingly moreish. Lighter starters included hot, fresh frogs' legs in a salt-and-peppery batter, and some daintily perfect pot-sticker dumplings. Mains were similarly hard to fault. Quail was golden and crispy on the outside, dark and tender within. The strangely named 'three withs' was a banquet-style dish of scallops, prawns and chicken in a reduced wine sauce that was creamy yet had enough vinegar to add a pleasant piquancy. A good place to impress someone, then, but to be greeted by name you might need to become a regular – and dining here doesn't come cheap.
Babies and children admitted. Booking advisable; essential dinner. Separate rooms for parties, seating 20-75. **Map 8 F9**.

Marylebone

Phoenix Palace
5 Glentworth Street, NW1 5PG (7486 3515, www.phoenixpalace.uk.com). Baker Street tube. **Meals served** noon-11.30pm Mon-Sat; 11am-10.30pm Sun. **Dim sum served** noon-5pm Mon-Sat; 11am-5pm Sun. **Main courses** £6.50-£25. **Set meal** £20-£48 per person (minimum 2). **Credit** AmEx, MC, V.
Corny faux-antique furnishings, carved wooden screens, red lanterns and gold dragons are reminiscent of a time when Chinese restaurants were an exotic novelty. Still, high standards prevail at Phoenix Palace in the form of crisp clean tablecloths and exceedingly helpful staff. A robust following of Chinese regulars suggests the cooking is far more authentic than the decor – which is

exactly what we found. Hakka-style salt-baked chicken was crisp skinned, with tender meat and a fragrant galangal and salt dipping sauce; a dish of tofu steamed with prawns, squid and sea cucumber typified classic Cantonese cuisine to perfection. Whole crab coated in a spicy sour sauce and served with fried peking buns was a hands-on affair, and very enjoyable despite the meat being slightly dry. We also sampled minced pork with salt-fish and water-chestnuts, which came fried and crunchy with a pleasing contrast of tastes and textures. Morning glory, stir-fried with pungent shrimp paste and garlic, was earthy and delicious. Less impressive were the har gau and peking dumplings with chilli oil, although it may be better to order such dishes during the day when the popular dim sum menu is served.
Babies and children welcome: high chairs. Booking advisable. Separate rooms for parties, seating 12-30. Takeaway service; delivery service (over £10 within 1-mile radius). Map 2 F4.

★ Royal China Club
40-42 Baker Street, NW8 6ER (7486 3898, www.royalchinagroup.co.uk). Baker Street or Marble Arch tube. **Meals/dim sum served** noon-4.30pm Mon-Thur; noon-11.30pm Fri, Sat; noon-10.30pm Sun. **Dim sum** £3-£7.50. **Main courses** £9-£35. **Credit** AmEx, MC, V.
Royal China Club is in the top set of London's luxury Chinese restaurants. Scan the room for Hong Kong pop stars as you feast on creative and luxurious dim sum that's completely Chinese in sensibility, and not in the least diluted by a fusion instinct found elsewhere in the capital. Daily specials – including roast pigeon, and the lightest of fried turnip paste with wind-dried ham on our visit – are brought around by friendly staff. Roast suckling pig featured rich, smoky meat and perfect crispy skin that made Chinatown imitators seem like bricks in comparison. Lamb dumplings in chilli oil similarly maintained a lightness that belied their hefty ingredients. Exquisitely light fish dumplings in rice noodle wrappers floated in soy milk dotted with bamboo, providing an exciting diversion from the usual dim sum snacks. Befitting the elegant dining room (which is bedecked in royal plum lacquer and gold paper surfaces), even the humble cheung fun gets top-notch treatment, with fillings of dover sole, prawn and scallop. For a sweet note, try the baked mini pumpkin pies. Be sure to peruse the separate tea menu too. Dining here is a treat well worth the expense.
Babies and children admitted. Booking advisable Sat, Sun. Disabled: toilet. Separate room for parties, seats 24. Takeaway service. Map 9 G5.

Mayfair

★ China Tang (100)
The Dorchester, 53 Park Lane, W1K 1QA (7629 9988, www.thedorchester.com). Hyde Park Corner tube. **Meals/dim sum served** 11.30am-11.45pm daily. **Main courses** £12-£48. **Dim sum** £4-£5. **Set lunch** £15. **Credit** AmEx, DC, MC, V.
The entrepreneurial David Tang has combined an art deco theme with an oriental ethic to create a beguiling underground Mayfair nether world: a decadent space with a slinky cocktail bar and private dining rooms shimmering with lacquered wood, lush art, and book-lined shelves. The sumptuous dining room is upheld by mirrored, illuminated pillars, and lined with white-clothed tables set with elegant silver and cut-glass cruets for soy sauce and chilli. Even if the food here was so-so, China Tang would still be worth a visit for the glamour – but the food is much better than that. Peking duck, ceremonially carved at the table, is among London's best, while Emperor's chicken, interleaved with yunnan ham and black mushroom, is delicately, deliciously and classically Cantonese. Water spinach (ong choi) with chilli and garlic makes a welcome change from the ubiquitous broccoli with oyster sauce, and China Tang's version of grandma's beancurd (ma po) is a fiery beauty. Only the thin metal chopsticks strike the wrong note; ask for wooden ones instead. Alas, no Kate Moss or Sir Philip Green tonight, just Prince Andrew at the next table.

Babies and children welcome: high chairs. Booking advisable. Disabled: lift; toilet. Dress: smart casual. Separate rooms for parties, seating 18-50. Map 9 G7.

Kai Mayfair
65 South Audley Street, W1K 2QU (7493 8988, www.kaimayfair.co.uk). Bond Street or Marble Arch tube. **Lunch served** noon-2.15pm Mon-Fri; 12.30-2.45pm Sat, Sun. **Dinner served** 6.30-10.45pm Mon-Sat; 6.30-10.15pm Sun. **Main courses** £16-£53. **Set lunch** £19 3 courses. **Credit** AmEx, DC, MC, V.
Kai serves posh food with Chinese characteristics to a lofty international Mayfair crowd, yet manages to defy many preconceptions. Sure, it's costly, and the attractive dining room has a slightly corporate feel, but service is friendly and some dishes sing with innovation. The epic wine list name-drops epic châteaux like *Hello!* magazine drops royal names, though many vintages are off-years and seem listed more for prestige value than to match Chinese flavours. The Malaysian chef (who trained in Changsha, capital of Hunan) has created an intriguing menu that diverges from traditional Chinese culinary logic to cater for all tastes. Instead of crispy duck, vegetarians are offered crispy aromatic beancurd, complete with pancakes, plum sauce, cucumber and spring onions, but the flavour (not bad, though too highly spiced) was more reminiscent of smoky bacon crisps. Better was the 'phoenix and rising sun': flavourful chicken with organic honshimeji mushrooms perfectly contrasted with preserved chilli, and topped with tempura mushrooms – high-quality ingredients all. However, roasted pork belly with julienned apple, mint, sesame, chilli and rice wine went too far; supposedly British pub food in a Chinese context, it was jarring rather than clever, and expensive for a small amount of food.
Babies and children welcome: high chairs. Booking advisable. Separate rooms for parties, seating 6-10. Map 9 G7.

★ Princess Garden
8-10 North Audley Street, W1K 6ZD (7493 3223, www.princessgardenofmayfair.com). Bond Street tube. **Lunch served** noon-4pm Mon-Fri; noon-4.30pm Sat, Sun. **Dinner served** 6.30-11pm Mon-Sat; 6.30-10.30pm Sun. **Dim sum served** noon-4pm daily. **Main courses** £7.50-£12. **Dim sum** £2.30-£3.80. **Set lunch** £12 per person (minimum 2). **Set dinner** £30-£85 per person (minimum 2). **Credit** AmEx, DC, MC, V.
It's wise to book before visiting this popular establishment, particularly at weekends. The atmosphere is one of calm, understated elegance, with white marble floors and huge windows providing a serene backdrop for linen-clad tables, dark wooden chairs and elegant tableware. Carved wooden screens and antique artefacts break up the large dining area, and several private rooms offer yet more intimacy. The daytime menu lists classic dim sum with modern additions, while the carte is an intriguing mix of banquet dishes like peking duck (order in advance), shark's fin and abalone, interspersed with more home-style family fare. A wide selection of vegetable preparations and appetising beancurd dishes makes Princess Garden a good spot for vegetarians. Our dim sum was among the best we've tasted in London, in particular the excellent chicken's feet in XO sauce, and cheung fun of minced cuttlefish wrapped in crisp beancurd skin, cloaked in soft steamed rice pastry and sweet soy sauce. A chef's recommendation of fragrant chicken casserole was full of aromatic fresh ginger and dried galangal; pea shoots in superior stock provided a perfect partner. Bilingual staff are courteous and very helpful with menu suggestions.
Babies and children welcome: high chairs. Booking advisable. Separate rooms for parties, seating 6-50. Takeaway service. Map 9 G6.

Paddington

Pearl Liang
8 Sheldon Square, W2 6EZ (7289 7000, www.pearlliang.co.uk). Paddington tube/rail. **Meals served** noon-11pm daily. **Main courses**

Interview
PETER LAM

Who are you?
Managing director of the **Royal China** Group (*see left* and *p77*).
How did you start in the catering business?
Restaurants have been in my family for many years. I've been working in and around them since I was in my teens.
What's the best thing about running a restaurant in London?
The cosmopolitan mix of Londoners and the fact they are willing to try foods from all over the world. As London is a powerful European city, it offers a great chance to add converts to Cantonese gastronomy. I also like the intense competition as it ensures no one can rest on their laurels.
What's the worst thing?
The complex labour laws make it hard to find quality staff with the necessary skills. Also, many crucial ingredients can only be sourced from overseas.
Which are your favourite London restaurants?
Barrafina (*see p242*) is my favourite at the moment as it has a relaxed and soothing atmosphere.
What's the best bargain in the capital?
The traditional pint is a highlight of London life. Nothing comes close to the feeling of having a cold Guinness with friends after work.
What's your favourite treat?
I like to collect and enjoy fine wines when I have the time. My personal favourite is Burgundy.
What is missing from London's restaurant scene?
Truly authentic ethnic cuisines. London needs more restaurants that serve traditional, often-overlooked Chinese cooking styles.
What does the next year hold?
Spanish cuisine will become more popular; the tapas style makes unknown foods more approachable. I also think there will be a move towards better quality ingredients, and a lot of complex menus will go back to basics.

£6.80-£28. **Set meal** £23 per person (minimum 2); £38-£68 per person (minimum 4). **Credit** AmEx, MC, V.

Set on the lower terrace of Sheldon Square, this dark, cavernous site is cleverly arranged so that bar and dining rooms feel more intimate than their dimensions. The contemporary decor riffs on pink, with oval-backed leather chairs, tea-lights, screens and a stunning picture of a plum branch snaking along one wall. Staff on our visit were welcoming, interested and attentive, asking politely if we wanted our wine glasses refilled (this got rather wearing). We've enjoyed proficient dim sum here in the past, but this time opted for dinner. The ten-page please-all menu incorporates Anglo favourites (crispy seaweed, egg fried rice, sweet and sour), Sichuan and Cantonese classics (ma po dofu, sea bass or turbot steamed with ginger and spring onion), traditional specialities of shark's fin and fish maw, and even Thai dishes. The lip-smacking savoury quality of deep-fried prawns sautéed with salted egg yolk was just right. Homely clay-pot stew of chicken, beancurd and salted fish was gloriously juicy, kept piping-hot over a flame. The menu

suggests diners consult staff on seasonal greens (all £7.20); we received mossy dao miu (pea shoots) in oyster sauce, and finished a delightful meal with exquisite chrysanthemum buns filled with custard. *Babies and children welcome: high chairs. Booking advisable. Disabled: toilet. Separate room for parties, seats 40. Takeaway service.* **Map 8 D5**.

Soho

Ba Shan NEW (100)

2009 RUNNER-UP BEST NEW RESTAURANT
24 Romilly Street, W1D 5AH (7287 3266). Leicester Square tube. **Meals served** noon-11pm Mon-Thur, Sun; noon-11.30pm Fri, Sat. **Main courses** £5.50-£7.50. **Credit** AmEx, MC, V.
The latest restaurant from the team behind Bar Shu (*see below*) and Baozi Inn (*see p64*) looks a treat, with nooks and crannies, wooden screens and splashes of colour breaking up the sleek, dark decor. The menu, based on xiao chi (small eats), is similar in concept to Cantonese dim sum, but with many unfamiliar dishes. Staff are happy to offer explanations, and the menu is clearly divided into easily understandable sections. We had to try

'strange-flavour peanuts' to start (not unlike honey roasted); better appetisers by far were zingy five-spiced beef salad with coriander and garlic, and deeply savoury cold buckwheat noodles with beancurd in a sour-hot dressing. To follow, lotus leaf buns with tender stewed pork, and prawn and water-chestnut dumplings with a spicy garlicky sauce, were moreish morsels, but our favourite dishes came from the Sichuanese home-style part of the menu. Fish-fragrant aubergines melted in the mouth; stir-fried potato slivers with chilli and sichuan pepper were deeply flavoured; and pock-marked old woman's beancurd belied its unattractive name to offer silky tofu in a rich sauce. This isn't a place to linger – the stool seating puts paid to that – but it is a fine addition to London's Chinese restaurants.
Babies and children admitted. Booking advisable. Disabled: toilet. Separate room for parties, seats 12. **Map 17 C4**.

★ Bar Shu

28 Frith Street, W1D 5LF (7287 6688, www.bar-shu.co.uk). Leicester Square or Tottenham Court Road tube. **Meals served** noon-11pm

Café society

Chinatown and surrounding areas of the West End are host to myriad tiny Chinese caffs where you can eat your fill and get change from a tenner. Laid-back and often filled with an eclectic mix of students, adventurous families and Chinese pensioners, these venues do brisk trade in one-plate meals and slurpingly good noodles.

Some excel in particular dishes. Our favourite for roast duck and other barbecued meats is **Canton**, while **Noodle Oodle** impresses with its hand-pulled Shanghainese noodles (la mian). Quintessential Hong Kong-style caffs **HK Diner** and **Café de Hong Kong** are charming places that serve the drink of choice among eastern youth: Taiwanese bubble teas (concoctions with chewy tapioca pearls that are sucked up with extra-wide straws – delightful).

Traditional Chinese desserts are often overlooked, and rarely available in Britain. At **Café TPT** the puddings range from refreshing fruity sago concoctions, to sweet and silky beancurd in syrup – both of which make it worth a visit.

★ Café de Hong Kong

47-49 Charing Cross Road, WC2H 0AN (7534 9898). Leicester Square or Piccadilly Circus tube. **Meals served** 11am-11pm Mon-Sat; 11am-10.30pm Sun. **Main courses** £5.50-£6.50. **Credit** (over £10) MC, V.
Welcoming isn't quite the right word but you'll soon feel at home in this happy, busy diner with blond wood booth-style seating and an expansive view of Newport Street from the mezzanine. Noodles are the main event – there are nearly 50 versions, not including the hawker-style soup noodles or instant noodle dishes. It took a while to find the salted fish in our plate of udon with chicken and spicy aubergine, but the combination was tender, juicy heaven. Snacks range from familiar french fries to ducks' tongues in sesame and chilli sauce. There's no shortage of soft drinks, either, including red beans with ice, and grass jelly combos.

To finish, go for the bouncy buns with richly flavoured custard cream filling. *Babies and children admitted. Bookings not accepted.* **Map 17 C4**.

★ Café TPT

21 Wardour Street, W1D 6PN (7734 7980). Leicester Square or Piccadilly Circus tube. **Meals served** noon-1am daily. **Main courses** £6.50-£22. **Set meal** £12.50-£19.50 per person (minimum 2). **Credit** MC, V.
Roast meats are displayed in the window but there is much more to the menu of this friendly utilitarian eaterie, not least around 50 seafood dishes. Pineapple ice is a revitalising, healthy take on the slushy – don't go mad with the tempting soft drinks, though, because the desserts are fabulous too. Our wooden pail of cold coconut milk with black sticky rice, sago and mango was compulsive eating, even after a filling bowl of Malaysian-style ho-fun with scrambled eggs, fish balls, pork, squid and colourful veg – one of the specials printed on sheets of paper stuck up on the walls. *Babies and children welcome: high chairs. Takeaway service. Vegetarian menu.* **Map 17 B5**.

★ Canton

11 Newport Place, WC2H 7JR (7437 6220). Leicester Square or Piccadilly Circus tube. **Meals served** noon-11.30pm Mon-Thur, Sun; noon-12.30am Fri, Sat. **Main courses** £4.50-£10. **Credit** AmEx, MC, V.
Canton keeps lunchtime turnover high, with plates typically whisked away as soon as you down chopsticks and the next diners having to make do with a napkin covering any stains left on the tablecloth. The barbecued duck and pork from the roastery at front are top-notch and inexpensive, though you'll also find good noodle dishes, stir-fries, soups and hotpots of fish, eel, pork, beef and beancurd. Rice piled simply with chicken soya (at room temperature) and Chinese cabbage is a refreshing dish that invites you to get up-close and personal with the neatly cleavered, tangily burnished bird. *Babies and children admitted. Separate room for parties, seats 22. Takeaway service.* **Map 17 C4**.

★ Hing Loon

25 Lisle Street, WC2H 7BA (7437 3602). Leicester Square or Piccadilly Circus tube. **Meals served** noon-11.30pm Mon-Thur; noon-midnight Fri, Sat; noon-11pm Sun. **Main courses** £3.70-£7.50. **Set lunch** £4.95. **Set meal** £5.95-£9.95 per person (minimum 2). **Credit** MC, V.
It's unlikely to win any design awards, but this cosy restaurant with blue velour chairs and not-quite-matching carpet is one of the friendliest pit stops in Chinatown. We can even forgive the soft rock radio soundtrack when the congee's as good as this: just £4.10 will get you a nutritious, belly-filling (melamine) bowl of fragrant jasmine rice porridge with ginger, juicy slices of pork, flecks of salted egg and finely sliced spring onions. A few pence more allows mandarin and fishermen's versions. Look to the rice dishes section of the sizeable menu for other one-plate bargains, such as rice topped with braised eel and crispy pork, squid, or barbecued pork and scrambled egg. The noodle dishes tend to be good too. *Bookings not accepted. Takeaway service.* **Map 17 C4**.

★ HK Diner

22 Wardour Street, W1D 6QQ (7434 9544). Leicester Square or Piccadilly Circus tube. **Meals served** 11am-4am daily. **Main courses** £5-£25. **Set meal** £10-£30 per person (minimum 2). **Credit** MC, V.
With a smarter decor than most Chinatown gaffs, this is the favourite of many expats. They come for comforting plates of roast duck or pork on rice, and who can blame them when the five-spice aroma wafts so enticingly from the preparation area by the door? The list of clay-pot dishes is intriguing: lamb breast (on the bone) with preserved bean curd is a hearty, homely and richly flavoured dish. House wine from Bordeaux is just £9.80 a bottle, and we enjoyed a sesame pearl drink, but Chinese tea is generally the best accompaniment to the food served here. *Babies and children welcome. Takeaway service. Vegetarian menu.* **Map 17 C4**.

RESTAURANTS

Mon-Thur, Sun; noon-11.30pm Fri, Sat. **Main courses** £8.50-£28. **Credit** AmEx, MC, V.
Fans of Sichuanese food have endured several months without their favourite spot for spicy cooking – Bar Shu has been shut for a refit since a fire destroyed the kitchen. As we went to press, the already-delayed reopening was scheduled for the middle of August 2009. We're looking forward to returning for dishes such as dongpo pork knuckle, dry-fried green beans with minced pork and preserved mustard greens, and steamed scallops with fragrant chilli sauce. Ordering is made easy by a menu featuring photographs of the dishes. Uncompromising authenticity means this is no place to take someone hoping for a mundane sweet and sour – it's the addictive numbing, and eye-streamingly hot sensation that characterises Sichuan cuisine. Also typical is the 'fish-fragrant' combination of pickled chillies, ginger, garlic and spring onion. Bar Shu's classic teahouse decor features faux-Ming Dynasty furniture, dark stone floors and decorative wood carvings; the bar, lit in neon blue, adds a modern contrast. Staff are knowledgeable and friendly. Esteemed consultant

★ Jen Café
4-8 Newport Place, WC2H 7JP (no phone). Leicester Square or Piccadilly Circus tube. **Meals served** 10.30am-9.30pm Thur-Sun. **Main courses** £4.50-£16. **No credit cards.**
We've had great meals here in the past, but on our latest visit Jen Café was resting so hard on its laurels it practically squashed them. Never much of a looker, despite its high-profile corner position, the draw has always been the dumplings made right in the front window. Yet while these arrived swiftly, their floury dough was a flabby letdown. Same problem with the determinedly unsilky noodles, although there was a deeply savoury meaty flavour to the spicy pork sauce. We consoled ourselves with a delectable lavender-coloured taro bubble drink, creamy and icy cold enough to be considered pudding.
Babies and children admitted. Takeaway service. **Map 17 C4.**

★ Noodle Oodle
25 Oxford Street, W1D 2DW (7287 5953). Tottenham Court Road tube. **Meals/dim sum served** noon-11pm Mon-Wed; noon-midnight Thur-Sat; noon-10.30pm Sun. **Main courses** £5-£11.60. **Dim sum** £2.20-£4.80. **Set meal** £9.80 3 courses. **Credit** AmEx, MC, V.
Not going down to Chinatown? This modern spot with flashing fairy lights is popular with Chinese students and a useful luncheonette for anyone appreciating the true way of the noodle – fresh, hand-pulled ones, that is. These are made in the front window in full view of passers-by and the results are gloriously soft and springy. The roast duck and other burnished titbits also on display taste great too. Our char siu was lean, juicy, sweet and porky – just as it should be. A range of steamed and fried dumplings are also available. Finish with red bean paste dumplings, mango fudge or a coconut juice with scoops of white coconut flesh in the bottom of the glass.
Babies and children admitted. Takeaway service. **Map 17 C2.**

Peter McCombie has devised an international wine list (including eight Chinese varieties) specially to match the food. Alternatively, there's Tsingtao and Tiger beers and the usual soft drinks.
Map 17 C3.

★ Cha Cha Moon
15-21 Ganton Street, W1F 9BN (7297 9800, www.chachamoon.com). Oxford Circus tube. **Meals served** 8am-11pm Mon-Fri; 9am-11.30pm Sat, Sun. **Main courses** £4.80-£7.50. **Credit** AmEx, MC, V.
Like Wagamama before it, Alan Yau's Cha Cha Moon is fast food, of mixed Asian inspiration, at low prices, served on long cafeteria-style tables in a sleek dining room. Unlike the now-ubiquitous Wag, the food here bears a close resemblance to its roots, and represents very good value for money. Yau famously spent months perfecting the broths for the soups on the largely noodle-based menu, and it has paid off – particularly in the case of taiwan beef noodle soup, which presents wheat noodles in a bowl of rich, sweet, beefy stock, with meat so tender it melts, and enough greenery to keep the health-conscious diner feeling somewhat smug. The use of authentic ingredients makes the restaurant more interesting than many other purveyors of noodles in London. Zhajiang mian, with pork, cucumber, carrot and red chilli, was invigorated with rich fermented beancurd. The fried turnip cakes are delicious, their low, rich, solid tones enlivened by the accompanying beansprouts and scrambled egg. Fresh juices provide a bright, if pricey, accompaniment. Intriguingly, this spot also serves breakfast (including thai banana porridge, and various oriental takes on egg and bacon) from 8am weekdays.
Babies and children admitted. Bookings not accepted. Disabled: toilet. Tables outdoors (6, courtyard). **Map 17 A4.**
For branch see index.

Ping Pong
45 Great Marlborough Street, W1F 7JL (7851 6969, www.pingpongdimsum.com). Oxford Circus tube. **Dim sum served** noon-midnight Mon-Sat; noon-10.30pm Sun. **Dim sum** £2.99-£3.50. **Set lunch** (noon-5pm) £11.49-£11.99. **Set meal** £9.99-£11.79; (Sun) £18.49. **Credit** AmEx, MC, V.
Catchy name, catchy concept – a chain of snazzy teahouses serving dim sum. More than a dozen Ping Pongs have bounced up around town in the past few years, and lunchtime business at this Oxford Circus branch is lively. You can see the attraction: slick service, stylish decor, swish drinks. We were given the choice of sharing a table downstairs or perching on slippery stools at a counter overlooking a two-storey glass atrium. The food slips down easily. Char siu baos were suitably robust and porky, and the chicken dumplings nicely piquant. But other dishes tended to taste sweet or bland or both, and portions were modest. The prawn in our har gau was so finely minced, and the crab in 'lucky' dumplings so well-mashed, that we couldn't distinguish between the two. Vegetable puffs and choi sum were equally soft and squidgy, and the spicy pork fillets weren't spicy at all – nor very Chinese, being more like wiener schnitzel. Doubtless everything is made in the kitchens here, but even if the whole chain was linked to a central production line the results could scarcely be further away from homemade dim sum.
Babies and children welcome: high chairs; nappy-changing facilities. Bookings not accepted for fewer than 8 people. Disabled: toilet. Takeaway service. **Map 17 A3.**
For branches see index.

★ Yauatcha
15 Broadwick Street, W1F 0DL (7494 8888, www.yauatcha.com). Leicester Square, Oxford Circus, Piccadilly Circus or Tottenham Court Road tube. **Open** 11am-11.30pm Mon-Thur; 11am-11.45pm Fri, Sat; noon-10.45pm Sun. **Dim sum served** noon-11.30pm Mon-Thur; noon-11.45pm Fri, Sat; noon-10.45pm Sun. **Dim sum** £3.50-£7. **Set tea** £24.50-£31.50. **Credit** AmEx, MC, V.
Serving dim sum day and night over two floors (ground and basement), Yauatcha happily cocks a

Gold Mine. See p74.

snook at traditionalists who believe the treats to 'touch the heart' should never be served past 5pm. The decor still looks terrific, with low green leather seating and tiny twinkling lights. Its popularity with Soho creatives shows no sign of easing. Much is made of the unusually good (and lengthy) tea list, but it's also worth checking out the cocktails and wines. In addition to several rosés, this range includes two sparkling and two chilled reds – rarities in London. The choice of dim sum dishes is extended with congee, noodles and some intriguing stir-fries. Staff (friendlier than you might expect of such a fashionable establishment) wipe down the tables frequently, and adroitly carve, unwrap and serve the plates and parcels that arrive steaming hot from the kitchen: faultless jasmine tea-smoked organic ribs, for instance, or sticky rice in lotus leaf with shrimp, chicken and tangy salted egg. The plump prawns flavoured with lychee and wrapped in a cylinder of crunchy pastry filaments are a popular order. Asparagus and mushroom cheung fun disappointed slightly – with scant asparagus at the height of the English season – but was tasty nonetheless. Desserts include chocolate and passion-fruit tiramisu.
Babies and children admitted. Booking essential for set tea. Disabled: lift; toilet. **Map 17 B3.**

Yming

35-36 Greek Street, W1D 5DL (7734 2721, www.yminglondon.com). Leicester Square, Piccadilly Circus or Tottenham Court Road tube. **Meals served** noon-11.45pm Mon-Sat. **Main courses** £5.50-£9. **Set lunch** (noon-6pm) £10. **Set meal** £16.50-£35 per person (minimum 2). **Credit** AmEx, DC, MC, V.
From the start, Yming seems to have aimed at providing something a notch up from the more casual, 'eat and leave' atmospheres of most Chinatown diners. The royal-blue and aquamarine interior is smartly dressed European-style, with white linen and wine glasses. Staff are courteous and helpful; Chinese diners are few. The menu is mainly Cantonese, with a few eclectic regional dishes added. We ordered Hakka-style duck with black fungus and lily flower, but the lilies seemed

absent when the dish arrived, and while the duck was earthy with red fermented beancurd, it was also dry and overcooked. Sichuan prawns were bouncy and fresh, yet lacked the fiery spice that characterises the region's cuisine. Likewise, double-braised pork in hotpot with preserved vegetables lacked the unctuousness that makes this dish delectable. Spicy aubergines were the most disappointing – described as fish-fragrant aubergines in Chinese, they resembled nothing of the sort and were very greasy. Yming has the style to appeal to diners looking for something smarter than the standard Chinese restaurant, but it needs to improve its substance for success.
Babies and children welcome: high chairs. Booking advisable evenings. Separate rooms for parties, seating 10-25. Takeaway service. **Map 17 C4.**

West
Acton

North China

305 Uxbridge Road, W3 9QU (8992 9183, www.northchina.co.uk). Acton Town tube/207 bus. **Lunch served** noon-2.30pm daily. **Dinner served** 6-11pm Mon-Fri, Sun; 6-11.30pm Fri, Sat. **Main courses** £5.50-£12.80. **Set meal** £14.50-£22.50 per person (minimum 2). **Credit** AmEx, MC, V.
Opened over 30 years ago, this institution serves decent Anglo-Cantonese dishes and first-rate northern Chinese cuisine, on separate menus. The excellent three-course peking duck (order in advance) is a real treat and roasted to perfection. We watched the chef separate pieces of crisp, glossy skin followed by succulent slices of meat, before presenting them to be enjoyed on own-made pancakes with North China's plum sauce. We opted out of the second course of stir-fried duck with lettuce wraps, but didn't miss the finale of deeply flavourful soup, made from duck bones, chinese cabbage and salty, aromatic yunnan ham. We also sampled starters of marinated beef shin, drunken chicken heady with Shaoxing wine, and a delicately seasoned jelly with soft shreds of pork, served with

a salad of pickled leaves and wafer-thin egg. Equally commendable was a plate of flaky fish with a sweet vinegar and wine sauce and crunchy cloud-ear mushrooms. The intimate atmosphere and friendly, knowledgeable staff make North China ideal for a romantic night out – or a dining adventure with friends. Acton Town residents are fortunate to have such a restaurant in their midst.
Babies and children welcome: high chairs. Booking advisable; essential dinner Fri, Sat. Separate room for parties, seats 36. Takeaway service; delivery service (over £20 within 2-mile radius). Vegetarian menu.

Bayswater

Four Seasons

84 Queensway, W2 3RL (7229 4320). Bayswater tube. **Meals served** noon-11pm Mon-Sat; noon-10.30pm Sun. **Main courses** £5.80-£25. **Set meal** £15.50-£20 per person (minimum 2). **Credit** MC, V.
No trip to this long-standing Queensway favourite is complete unless you order the speciality roast duck. Other roasts, including the soya chicken and crispy pork, are also worth trying. Four Seasons' Cantonese menu focuses mainly on home-style dishes and western favourites. There's plenty of choice, including more expensive seafood such as dover sole and turbot, but you won't find the more elaborate Chinese banquet delicacies such as abalone or fish maw. Our sliced roast duck was as juicy, savoury and rich as ever, while chunks of crispy roast pork were moist and well-seasoned, but lacked their usual lovely crackly skin (which was disappointingly chewy this time). We asked to see the additional 'Four Seasons Specials menu' and from it ordered a wonderfully comforting melange of egg and beancurd, steamed until silky, studded with soft shiitake mushrooms and bouncy prawns, and dressed with a light, fragrant soy-based sauce. Weekday lunches are bustling; in the evenings and at weekends be prepared to queue, even if you've booked. Service is friendly enough, but has a tendency to become inconsistent and inattentive during busy periods.
Babies and children admitted. Booking advisable. Takeaway service. **Map 7 C6.**

Gold Mine

102 Queensway, W2 3RR (7792 8331). Bayswater tube. **Meals served** noon-11.15pm daily. **Main courses** £6.80-£20. **Set meal** £14-£19 per person (minimum 2). **Credit** MC, V.
Although one of the newer additions to Queensway's dining strip, Gold Mine looks like it's been here for years. There's nothing remotely fashionable about the red and gold chairs or anodyne walls. The menu ranges from Anglo-Chinese staples (sesame prawn toast, satay, chicken mince wrapped in lettuce) to the likes of braised frogs' legs with bitter melon, and a hotpot of ducks' feet, sea cucumber and fish lips. Order roast meats, for which Gold Mine is justly famed, and you won't go wrong. The flesh and fat of the pork belly is drier here than at some specialists, but the meat has great flavour and a satisfyingly crunchy top. Char siu was lean and tangy. Other dishes didn't fare so well. Beancurd with crab sauce contained too much cornstarch, giving it a gloopy texture and plastic sheen; we left plenty of the huge portion untouched. Pak choi with juicy, crunchy stems in a mild garlic sauce was a plateful too. Best was one of the Malaysian interlopers – a glistening oyster omelette with plump bivalves tasting freshly of the sea. Friendly staff (a little too prompt at times) brought orange wedges to finish alongside the last of the lovely jasmine tea.
Babies and children welcome: high chairs. Booking advisable. Takeaway service. **Map 7 C6.**

Magic Wok

100 Queensway, W2 3RR (7792 9767). Bayswater or Queensway tube. **Meals served** noon-11pm daily. **Main courses** £6.50-£18. **Set meal** £12.50 per person (minimum 2); £25 per person (minimum 4). **Credit** AmEx, MC, V.
The first thing that hits the table at this cosy Queensway restaurant is a plate of crisp prawn

Princess Garden. See p71.

Spain. As many wineries as landscapes.

In Spain there are almost as many wineries as there are landscapes.
The diversity of viticulture in the country is reflected in more than 90
grape varieties from 65 denominations of origin. Our wines mirror our
country's infinite beauty. Soil and climatic conditions ensure variety,
personality and richness of style to please all discerning palates.

WINES
from SPAIN

www.winesfromspainuk.com

The art of dim sum

The Cantonese term 'dim sum' can be translated as 'touch the heart'. It is used to refer to the vast array of dumplings and other titbits that southern Chinese people like to eat with their tea for breakfast or at lunchtime. This eating ritual is simply known as 'yum cha', or 'drinking tea' in Hong Kong. Many of London's Chinese restaurants have a lunchtime dim sum menu, and at weekends you'll find them packed with Cantonese families. A dim sum feast is one of London's most extraordinary gastronomic bargains: how else can you lunch lavishly in one of the capital's premier restaurants for £15-£20 a head?

Dim sum are served as a series of tiny dishes, each bearing two or three dumplings, perhaps, or a small helping of steamed spare ribs or seafood. Think of it as a Chinese version of tapas, served with tea. You can order according to appetite or curiosity; a couple of moderate eaters might be satisfied with half a dozen dishes, while *Time Out's* greedy reviewers always end up with a table laden with little snacks. Some people like to fill up with a plateful of stir-fried noodles, others to complement the meal with stir-fried greens from the main course. But however wildly you order, if you stick to the dim sum menu and avoid more expensive specials that waiting staff may wave under your nose, the modesty of the bill is sure to come as a pleasant surprise. The low price of individual dishes (most cost between £1.80 and £3) makes eating dim sum the perfect opportunity to try delicacies such as chicken's feet

Two of London's Chinese restaurants serve dim sum Hong Kong-style, from circulating trollies: the cheerful **New World** (*see p67*) and the less-cheerful **Chuen Cheng Ku** (17 Wardour Street, W1D 6PJ, 7437 1398). Some of the snacks are wheeled out from the kitchen after being cooked; others gently steam as they go or are finished on the trolley to order. The trolley system has the great advantage that you see exactly what's offered, but if you go at a quiet lunchtime some of the food may be a little jaded

by the time it reaches you. Other places offer snacks à la carte, so everything should be freshly cooked.

Dim sum lunches at the weekend tend to be boisterous occasions, so they are great for children (take care, though, as adventurous toddlers and hot dumpling trolleys are not a happy combination). Strict vegetarians are likely to be very limited in their menu choices, as most snacks contain either meat or seafood – honourable exceptions include **Golden Palace** (*see p84*) which has a generous selections of vegetarian snacks.

HOW TO EAT DIM SUM

Dim sum menus are roughly divided into steamed dumplings, deep-fried dumplings, sweet dishes and so on. Try to order a selection of different types of food, with plenty of light steamed dumplings to counterbalance the heavier deep-fried snacks. If you are lunching with a large group, make sure you order multiples of everything, as most portions consist of about three dumplings.

Tea is the traditional accompaniment. Some restaurants offer a selection of teas, although they may not tell you this unless you ask. Musty bo lay (pu'er in Mandarin Chinese), grassy Dragon Well (long jing) or fragrant Iron Buddha (tie guan yin) are delicious alternatives to the jasmine blossom that is usually served by default to non-Chinese guests. Waiters should keep teapots filled throughout the meal; leave the teapot lid tilted at an angle or upside down to signal that you want a top-up. **Royal China Club** (*see p71*) and **Yauatcha** (*see p73*) have the most extensive lists of fine Chinese teas.

WHERE TO EAT DIM SUM

London's best dim sum are found at the **Royal China Club** (*see p71*), **Hakkasan** (*see p69*), **Yauatcha** (*see p73*) and **Pearl Liang** (*see p71*), all of which offer fine dumplings in glamorous settings. The typically Cantonese **Phoenix Palace** (*see p69*), **Dragon Castle** (*see p78*), and any of the **Royal China** (*see right*) group branches tend to have exciting specials. If you're eating in Chinatown, **Royal Dragon** (*see p67*) and **Imperial China**

(*see p66*) are a cut above the rest. **Yum Cha** (*see p79*) has brought good all-day dim sum to Chalk Farm and Camden Town. Outside central London, try **Shanghai** (*see p78*) in Dalston, **Peninsula** (*see p78*) in Greenwich, **Royal China** in Putney (*see p78* – it is not part of the Royal China chain), **Golden Palace** (*see p79*) in Harrow and **Mandarin Palace** (*see p79*) in Gants Hill.

Below is a guide to the basic canon of dim sum served in London:
Char siu bao: fluffy steamed bun stuffed with barbecued pork in a sweet-savoury sauce.
Char siu puff pastry or **roast pork puff:** triangular puff-pastry snack, filled with barbecued pork, scattered with sesame seeds and baked in an oven.
Cheung fun: slithery sheets of steamed rice pasta wrapped around fresh prawns, barbecued pork, deep-fried dough sticks, or other fillings, splashed with a sweet soy-based sauce. For some non-Chinese the texture is an acquired taste.
Chiu chow fun gwor: soft steamed dumpling with a wheat-starch wrapper, filled with pork, vegetables and peanuts. Chiu chow is a regional Chinese cooking style popular in Hong Kong.
Chive dumpling: steamed prawn meat and chinese chives in a translucent wrapper.
Har gau: steamed minced prawn dumpling with a translucent wheat-starch wrapper.
Nor mai gai or **steamed glutinous rice in lotus leaf:** lotus-leaf parcel enclosing moist sticky rice with chicken, mushrooms, salty duck-egg yolks and other bits and pieces, infused with the herby fragrance of the leaf.
Paper-wrapped prawns: tissue-thin rice paper enclosing prawn meat, sometimes scattered with sesame seeds, deep-fried.
Sago cream with yam: cool, sweet soup of coconut milk with sago pearls and morsels of taro.
Scallop dumpling: delicate steamed dumpling filled with scallop (sometimes prawn) and vegetables.
Shark's fin dumpling: small steamed dumpling with a wheaten wrapper pinched into a frilly cockscomb shape on top, stuffed with a mix of pork, prawn and slippery strands of shark's fin.
Siu loon bao or **xiao long bao:** Shanghai-style round dumpling with a whirled pattern on top and a juicy minced pork and soup filling.
Siu mai: little dumpling with an open top, a wheat-flour wrapper and a minced pork filling. Traditionally topped with crab coral, although minced carrot and other substitutes are common.
Taro croquette or **yam croquette:** egg-shaped, deep-fried dumpling with a frizzy, melt-in-your mouth outer layer of mashed taro, and a savoury minced pork filling.
Turnip paste: a heavy slab of creamy paste made from glutinous rice flour and white oriental radishes, studded with wind-dried pork, sausage and dried shrimps and fried to a golden brown.

crackers. The last thing is a traditional platter of cut orange segments. That's how savvy the place is, making sure to appeal to both western and Chinese diners. While you can do the good old spring roll/sweet and sour pork/crispy-fried-everything thing here, it's better by far to try the more esoteric, Chinese home-cooking dishes on the menu, such as stewed trotters and baked salty chicken. A hotpot of brisket-like lamb belly with red dates and dried beancurd skin was like a Cantonese Irish stew; gai lan (chinese broccoli) with garlic and ginger was snappingly fresh; and large, head-on prawns tossed with salt, chilli and garlic were reassuringly ungreasy. Not as good were long-life noodles with egg and crab, the noodles so soft they broke on lifting – not a good sign to the superstitious Chinese. When in doubt, stick to the roast duck, which never fails to please. It may not be the best duck on the street (that's in Gold Mine next door), but it's close.
Babies and children admitted. Booking advisable dinner. Separate room for parties, seats 30. Takeaway service. Vegetarian menu. **Map 7 C6**.

Mandarin Kitchen

14-16 Queensway, W2 3RX (7727 9012). Bayswater or Queensway tube. **Meals served** noon-11.30pm daily. **Main courses** £5.90-£28. **Set meal** £10.90 per person (minimum 2); £20 per person (minimum 4). **Credit** AmEx, MC, V.
Located near the corner of Queensway and Bayswater Road, Mandarin Kitchen attracts a mixed bag of Chinese, locals and tourists. Its market-priced lobster noodles is one of the main attractions during busy evenings and weekends. Comfy banquettes for small groups and larger round tables seating up to 12 make the restaurant a popular place for entertaining, although the decor is utilitarian rather than inspiring. A few dried seafood delicacies, such as abalone, do feature, alongside some meat dishes (both traditional and Anglo-Canto), but the menu gives more prominence to a selection of fish and shellfish in classic preparations (spring onion and ginger, black bean, and so on). The famous lobster was sweet and fresh, but slightly overcooked, presented on a bed of noodles that quickly coagulated into a solid mass due to an overabundance of cornstarch. Large chunks of ginger and spring onion made the dish look less refined than expected. Several sauces suffered from gloopiness – this let down an otherwise very good steamed aubergine stuffed with minced prawns. The ingredients are generally of a high quality and the cooking is capable, but Mandarin Kitchen seems to cater more to tourists, and is less exciting as a result.
Babies and children welcome: booster seats. Booking advisable dinner. Takeaway service. **Map 7 C7**.

★ Royal China

13 Queensway, W2 4QJ (7221 2535, www.royal chinagroup.co.uk). Bayswater or Queensway tube. **Meals served** noon-11pm Mon-Thur; noon-11.30pm Fri, Sat; 11am-10pm Sun. **Dim sum served** noon-4.45pm Mon-Sat; 11am-4.45pm Sun. **Main courses** £7.50-£50. **Dim sum** £2.30-£5. **Set meal** £30-£38 per person (minimum 2). **Credit** AmEx, MC, V.
There's a retro feel to the glamorous glossy black and gold interior of this long-standing Cantonese institution. The panels of flying geese, mirrored pillars and black lacquered waiters' stations may look a little tired, but Royal China remains a dependable option for high-quality cooking and excellent dim sum. A choice of menus caters for the wide cross-section of customers who visit, including tourists, local Chinese, and business diners entertaining clients. Staff glide discreetly among guests, ensuring that the service is smooth. We were delighted by the unctuous braised pork belly with preserved cabbage, and the steamed cod with dried yellow bean sauce from the 'chef's recommendations'. A dish of chinese broccoli in ginger juice was cooked to sparkling crisp perfection, and a version of ma po tofu with minced beef was rustic but satisfying and a touch spicy. It's difficult for such a large menu to avoid occasional duff notes, such as our deep-fried squid

Min Jiang. See p78.

stuffed with spongy, tasteless prawn mince, but the knowledgeable staff tend to be very helpful in steering diners in the right direction.
Babies and children admitted. Booking advisable (not accepted lunch Sat, Sun). Separate rooms for parties, seating 20-40. Takeaway service. Vegetarian menu. **Map 7 C7.**
For branches see index.

Kensington

Min Jiang NEW

10th floor, Royal Garden Hotel, 2-4 Kensington High Street, W8 4PT (7361 1988, www.minjiang. co.uk). High Street Kensington tube. **Lunch/ dim sum served** noon-3pm daily. **Dinner served** 6-10.30pm daily. **Main courses** £10-£48. **Dim sum** £3.60-£5.20. **Set lunch** (Mon-Fri) £19.80. **Set dinner** £48-£68 per person (minimum 2). **Credit** AmEx, MC, V.
On a summer's evening, the view from this tenth-floor hotel restaurant at the corner of Hyde Park is breathtaking. An expanse of trees and lawn, water, sky and a veritable shopping list of London landmarks are wisely offset by the dining room's muted cream and wood decor. There are bold red walls, an attractive arrangement of black-and-white photographs and blue-and-white vases, but these play to the rear. It's a delightful setting for enjoying confident Chinese cooking, elegantly served by kind waiters. Min Jiang has made wood-fired peking duck its calling card, though we've found this disappointing more than once. This time, a shared steamer of delicate dim sum quickly won us over. Most impressive was the pumpkin dumpling with mixed seafood: the tender wrapper conveying the true flavour of the gourd, not just the colour. The carte is good for dishes from northern and western China, and seafood. Aubergine with minced chicken and sichuan chilli sauce was satisfyingly slithery; fried rice with prawns, scallops and salted fish far exceeded takeaway fodder – though at £12 it should. The list of fusion-style desserts (sweet chilli and lychee panna cotta, passion-fruit curd and ice-cream with chocolate leaf) is appealing.
Babies and children welcome: high chairs; nappy-changing facilities. Booking advisable: essential Fri-Sun. Disabled: lift; toilet. Separate room for parties, seats 20. **Map 7 B8.**

South West

Putney

Royal China

3 Chelverton Road, SW15 1RN (8788 0907, www.royalchinaputney.co.uk). East Putney tube/Putney rail/14, 37, 74 bus. **Lunch served** noon-3.30pm Mon-Sat; noon-4pm Sun. **Dinner served** 6.30-11pm Mon-Sat; 6.30-10pm Sun. **Dim sum served** noon-3.30pm daily. **Main courses** £5.50-£40. **Dim sum** £2-£5. **Set meal** £26-£35 per person (minimum 2). **Credit** AmEx, DC.
Most diners are probably none-the-wiser, but this outfit isn't part of the Royal China group (and hasn't been since some time in the last century), even though its decor remains strikingly similar to restaurants in the esteemed mini chain. The smallish dimly lit dining room has black lacquered walls decorated with golden landscapes and flying geese. Customers are a mixed bag of Putney locals and Chinese families from farther afield, who fill their tables with all manner of dim sum. We've found the snacks to be hit and miss in the past, but most dishes were agreeable on this visit: deep-fried yam croquettes were crisp, with a creamy filling studded with juicy morsels of pork; chicken feet in classic black bean sauce were deeply coloured and just as flavoursome. Fried dough stick wrapped with thin sheets of rice noodles was messy in presentation, yet a good rendition; ditto the prawn cheung fun. Fried rice with dried scallop and egg whites seemed greasier than it should be, but came in a fair-sized portion. Service was friendly, if a bit pushy. Note: the only credit cards accepted are American Express and Diners Club.
Babies and children admitted. Booking advisable. Takeaway service; delivery service (over £15 within 3.5-mile radius).

South East

Elephant & Castle

★ Dragon Castle

100 Walworth Road, SE17 1JL (7277 3388, www.dragoncastle.eu). Elephant & Castle tube/rail. **Meals served** noon-11.30pm Mon-Sat; 11.30am-10.30pm Sun. **Main courses** £5.50-£25. **Set meals** £14.80-£32.80 per person (minimum 2). **Credit** AmEx, MC, V.
The shock of finding a half-decent restaurant in an area as unpromising as Elephant & Castle has moved some critics to give rapturous reports of this vast, barn-like venue. It has even been called one of the best Cantonese restaurants in the country. It isn't. It is, however, a commendable attempt to recreate an authentic Hong Kong-like dining experience, complete with carp ponds, gilt dragons and a menu that runs to duck tongues and poached eels. A starter of bouncy jellyfish strips and sliced boned pork hock was authentic, but overly cold and not thrilling; and although the stir-fried crab was well-priced and generously portioned, its ginger and garlic sauce was thick and grey with cornflour. Far better was the simple, steamed corn-fed chicken in a lightly spicy root-ginger stock, and an enormous serving of glossy, green morning glory in XO chilli sauce. Service runs from bossy-boots to nice-as-pie, but it's all pretty much on the ball. If you live in Elephant & Castle, you'll be over the moon about this place. If you don't, you might wonder why the fuss.
Babies and children welcome: high chairs. Booking advisable Fri, Sat. Disabled: toilet. Separate room for parties, seats 60. Takeaway service. Vegetarian menu.

Greenwich

★ Peninsula

Holiday Inn Express, Bugsby's Way, SE10 0GD (8858 2028, www.mychinesefood.co.uk). North Greenwich tube. **Meals served** noon-11.30pm Mon-Fri; 11am-11.30pm Sat; 11am-11pm Sun. **Dim sum served** noon-4.45pm Mon-Fri; 11am-4.45pm Sat, Sun. **Main courses** £5.50-£33. **Dim sum** £2.20-£3.80. **Set meal** £18.50 per person (minimum 2), £20.50 per person (minimum 4). **Credit** AmEx, MC, V.
The setting (a Holiday Inn in the Millennium Village) is hardly Chinatown, but the Peninsula is not only handily placed for O2 Stadium visitors, it has also become a popular alternative to the West End for Chinese diners who want a venue for yum cha – drinking tea and eating snacks and maybe reading a newspaper or two. It's not the most beautiful of restaurants, nor is the dim sum of the kind to dazzle and amaze with its inventiveness, delicacy and sheer perfection, but the atmosphere is authentically convivial and the food genuinely satisfying. The prawns in our har gau were big and juicy; the meat on the spare-ribs seemed a little fatty, it's true, but none the worse for it when paired with such a businesslike black bean sauce; and the chinese sausage and chicken on rice was a meal in itself, complete with succulent winter mushrooms. Chinese broccoli (gai lan) was also generously portioned – as well as being hot, fresh and crunchy, with lots of chopped ginger. You can even watch Chinese television here as you eat.
Babies and children welcome: high chairs; nappy-changing facilities. Booking advisable. Disabled: toilet. Separate rooms for parties, seating 40-100. Takeaway service. Vegetarian menu.

East

Docklands

China Palace

2 Western Gateway, E16 1DR (7474 0808, www.chinapalaceexcel.com). Custom House DLR. **Meals served** noon-11pm Mon-Thur; noon-11.30pm Fri, Sat; 11am-11pm Sun. **Dim sum served** noon-4.45pm daily. **Main courses** £7.80-£20. **Dim sum** £2.60-£5. **Set meal** £16.50 per person (minimum 2); £28.50 per person (minimum 4). **Credit** MC, V.

Both the setting and food here are enjoyable, without ever being quite as good as you'd hoped. The short walk from the station leads you to expect a dramatic waterfront location. And the conversion of this former grain warehouse looks classy, the old girders painted red and neatly turned into Chinese pillars. But there's no river view, and the restaurant can feel large and anonymous – perhaps not surprisingly, as it's next to a conference centre. As for the dim sum, some of ours was superb. Grilled chive dumplings stuffed with prawns and water-chestnut were crisp outside and crunchy within. Turnip cake was firm yet creamy, with tiny flakes of pork and burnt onion and a distinctive taste of turnip. The cheung fun, though, were gelatinous, and the pak choi less al dente than plain gloopy. Whelks in black bean sauce was a nice idea for the East End, but didn't quite come off. With more Chinese people once again living in Docklands, it's perhaps not surprising that you have to book here at weekends, when a more authentic atmosphere might make up for any occasional shortfall in cooking standards.
Babies and children welcome: high chairs. Booking advisable. Separate rooms for parties, seating 10-40. Tables outdoors summer only (6, pavement). Takeaway service.

Yi-Ban

London Regatta Centre, Dockside Road, E16 2QT (7473 6699, www.yi-ban.co.uk). Royal Albert DLR. **Meals served** noon-11pm Mon-Sat; 11am-10.30pm Sun. **Dim sum served** noon-5pm daily. **Main courses** £6-£25. **Dim sum** £2.20-£4. **Set meal** £18-£32 per person (minimum 2). **Credit** AmEx, MC, V.
Yi-Ban is a trek for virtually anyone who doesn't live at the Docklands ExCeL Centre, but it's still a strong draw for aficionados of dim sum and Cantonese cuisine. The backdrop, through large windows, of planes lined up at City Airport and industrial east London, adds drama to the room's decor, which takes its cue from a subdued Chinatown wedding banquet. One end of the room is dominated by a golden dragon and phoenix; the rest is divided with columns wrapped in gold lamé. But the buzz, the views and the food attract crowds. Dim sum offers slightly more variety than the typical Chinatown range, including sweet steamed bread filled with minced pork and greens, fried on one sesame-seed-covered end – a sweet-meets-savoury pleasure. Prawn with chive dumplings in rice wrappers were perfectly steamed. Large bundles filled with pork, vegetables and peanuts were a treat too. Flavours are authentic, and the kitchen doesn't shy away from pungency; a bowl of rice topped with minced pork and preserved fish pulled no punches. At 4pm, paper tablecloths and ceramic teacups make way for cloth and wine glasses, but the sparkling view continues to delight.
Babies and children welcome: booster seats; high chairs. Booking advisable. Disabled: toilet. Entertainment: jazz (8pm Fri, Sat). Takeaway service. Vegetarian menu.

North East

Dalston

★ Shanghai

41 Kingsland High Street, E8 2JS (7254 2878, www.wengwahgroup.com). Dalston Kingsland rail/38, 67, 76, 149 bus. **Meals served** noon-11pm, **dim sum served** noon-5pm daily. **Main courses** £5.50-£7.80. **Dim sum** £2.10-£4.30. **Set meal** £16.80-£18.80 per person (minimum 2). **Credit** MC, V.
A former eel and pie shop reincarnated as an art deco Chinese teahouse, Shanghai combines the best of both worlds. The ambience is comfortably down-to-earth, but also exotic enough to make you feel a pleasant tingle of anticipation as you take your seat, whether it's on the diner-style banquettes at the front or under the round green skylights in the main restaurant at the rear. Having picked your food from a choice of several menus – including a half-price dim sum list in the afternoon – you may have to stay put for a while, if our experience was typical. Still, the occasional plate of pan-fried

Shanghainese dumplings accompanied by a decent house red helped preserve our anticipatory tingle, and the main courses, when they came, didn't disappoint: the freshest sea bass steamed with ginger and spring onion; smoky aubergine and beancurd in black bean sauce; pork belly that looked garishly orange and gelatinous, but proved velvety and delicious. Tung choi (morning glory) with dried shrimp paste was a delight too: green and crunchy, with a touch of chilli.

Babies and children welcome: high chairs. Booking advisable. Disabled: toilet. Separate rooms for parties, both seating 45. Takeaway service. **Map 25 B5**.

North

Camden Town & Chalk Farm

Teachi
29-31 Parkway, NW1 7PN (7485 9933, www.teachi.co.uk). Camden Town tube. **Meals/ dim sum served** noon-11pm Mon-Sat; 11am-10.30pm Sun. **Main courses** £6.50-£11. **Dim sum** £2-£3.20. **Set lunch** £6.80 1 course. **Credit** AmEx, MC, V.

According to its website, Teachi offers Chinese food with 'a modern twist' which, judging by the menu, refers to the pan-Asian influences evident in some of dishes. Dim sum is served at all times, alongside a selection of small plates ideal for sharing, and larger dishes. Overall the cooking is fine, if not particularly exciting. Chargrilled chicken wings were crisp, salty and juicy: definitely the best dish we ordered. Dim sum had a tendency to be dry and stodgy. And although slow-cooked pork belly with yam featured tender meat and yam in a thick sauce, the dish lacked textural variation and was bland. Likewise, quick-fried beans, supposedly Sichuanese, were promisingly dry-fried first, but were then reduced to what resembled uninspiring fast food by a mildly spicy, congealing soy-based sauce. Teachi's interior is an almost-riotous blend of bright Chinese paintings on large sections of wall, dark screens and redwood tables with horseshoe-backed chairs. When we visited during a weekday lunch hour, only a few tables were occupied despite neighbouring restaurants appearing to be almost full.

Babies and children admitted. Tables outdoors (2, pavement). Takeaway service. **Map 27 C2**.

Yum Cha [NEW]
27-28 Chalk Farm Road, NW1 8AG (7482 2228, www.silks-nspiceyumcha.co.uk). Chalk Farm tube. **Meals/dim sum served** noon-11pm Mon-Thur,

Sun; noon-midnight Fri, Sat. **Main courses** £6-£9.80. **Dim sum** £2.50-£5. **Credit** AmEx, MC, V. Occupying the premises of a former Thai restaurant, this new dim sum venue has been slow to embrace its own identity. On our visit, the sign outside still had 'Silks & Spice' written above Yum Cha; inside, a reclining gold Buddha remained the centrepiece of the café-like space. Happily, the food is almost 100% Cantonese, as testified by the handful of Chinese families who were the only diners on a Sunday afternoon. Our dim sum were as good as at comparable places in Hong Kong: moderately priced, and made with all the right ingredients and techniques. Dumplings best flaunted the chef's expertise. Plump balls of chive and prawn were encased in a delicate, glutinous pastry, and the xiao long bao was the best we've had in London (the soft pork dumplings collapsed in the mouth with a generous burst of savoury broth). Other staples such as turnip cake, beef cheung fun, char siu bao and chickens' feet were respectable rather than outstanding, as was a larger dish of deep-fried salt and pepper squid (well-flavoured, but lacking the desired lightness). Service was prompt and obliging, making Yum Cha a worthy local destination.

Babies and children welcome: high chairs. Booking advisable weekends. Disabled: toilet. Separate rooms for parties, seating 5-40. Tables outdoors (2, pavement). Takeaway service. **Map 27 C1**.

Outer London

Harrow, Middlesex

Golden Palace
146-150 Station Road, Harrow, Middx HA1 2RH (8863 2333). Harrow-on-the-Hill tube/rail. **Meals served** noon-11.30pm Mon-Sat; 11am-10.30pm Sun. **Dim sum served** noon-5pm Mon-Sat; 11am-5pm Sun. **Main courses** £5.20-£8.50. **Dim sum** £2.30-£3.50. **Set meal** £15-£26.50 per person (minimum 2). **Credit** AmEx, DC, MC, V.

A large proportion of Golden Palace's menu is devoted to vegetarian dishes. Chinese menus often limit anything that isn't meat or fish to just one section, but here every course, from 'hot starters' to 'secondary dishes' and 'noodles' has a vegetarian counterpart. Apart from the high-quality cooking, almost all other aspects of this sparsely decorated restaurant – from the white walls and blue carpet and chairs, to the wood-veneer reception – made little impact. Dim sum is very popular here and the place was pleasantly full during a weekday lunch. Steamed siu mai arrived packed with whole chunks of prawn and rich, fatty pork, while beef

cheung fun, despite being quite chunky, was slippery smooth, spiked with water-chestnuts and infused with the sweet taste of dried mandarin peel. Chicken claws were soft and giving in their mild chilli sauce, and spare ribs were chewy and salty as expected, served on a bed of rice soaked with savoury sauce. Braised shiitake mushrooms with chinese broccoli and asparagus, stir-fried with garlic, contained burnt garlic nibs whose smoky flavour overpowered the whole dish; nevertheless, the green vegetables retained a perfect crunchy texture. Harrow has a gem here.

Babies and children welcome: booster seats. Booking advisable. Disabled: toilet. Separate rooms for parties, seating 60-100. Takeaway service.

Ilford, Essex

★ Mandarin Palace
559-561 Cranbrook Road, Ilford, Essex IG2 6JZ (8550 7661). Gants Hill tube. **Lunch served** noon-4pm, **dinner served** 6.30-11.30pm Mon-Sat. **Meals served** noon-11.30pm Sun. **Dim sum served** noon-4pm Mon-Sat; noon-5pm Sun. **Main courses** £7-£15. **Dim sum** £2-£3.80. **Set meal** £22.50 per person (minimum 2); £27.50 per person (minimum 4). **Credit** AmEx, MC, V.

There's an ageing glamour to the decor of this spacious and much-loved local. Decorated bamboo poles, tiger paintings, tassled lanterns, huge fans – it looks something like an old movie set, but there's nothing fake about the cooking. Pickled cabbage and peanuts were waiting on the table when we arrived for Sunday dim sum, taking advantage of the useful rear car park. Service was mostly – but not entirely, it must be said – warm and friendly. A short selection of specials included spicy ducks' feet and wings, and the main menu lists plenty of rarely seen options such as sweet grilled taro paste. Prawn and chive dumplings arrived hot, translucent and jewel-like, while succulent chicken and mushroom cheung fun had plenty of filling with a deep umami flavour. We tucked into comforting parcels of lotus rice with grated scallop, and also crunched our way through perfectly stir-fried and fragrant gai lan (chinese broccoli). Custard tarts seemed to have a thousand layers in their moist, rich pastry; custard buns were equally good. Evenings offer mostly Cantonese cuisine, with favourites from Sichuan and Beijing added to the mix. Overall, prices are very keen for this level of quality.

Babies and children welcome: high chairs. Separate room for parties, seats 50. Takeaway service; delivery service (over £20 within 2-mile radius).

For branch see index.

China Palace

East European

Few other cuisines in London can boast such a collection of eccentric, quirky restaurants as East European. Long-lived establishments such as the clubby **Gay Hussar**, the cherished café **Daquise**, and the retro-tastic **Czechoslovak Restaurant** and **Polish White Eagle Club** have devoted fans and character aplenty, but newer ventures such as the Georgian duo **Tbilisi** and **Little Georgia** also have bags of charm. What of the future? With the economy in a state of flux, and eastern European migrant workers returning to their native lands in droves, few new restaurants are opening. Two exceptions are **Tamada** of St John's Wood and **Tatra** of Shepherd's Bush – both with smart demeanours that indicate they seek to attract affluent locals from outside London's east European community. Existing restaurants too must widen their nets, and the most successful, notably the stylish **Wódka** and even more stylish **Baltic** (both run by Polish restaurateur Jan Woroniecki) appeal across the spectrum of London's diners.

Czech

North West

West Hampstead

★ Czechoslovak Restaurant (100)
74 West End Lane, NW6 2LX (7372 1193, www.czechoslovak-restaurant.co.uk). West Hampstead tube. **Dinner served** 5-10pm Tue-Fri. **Meals served** noon-10pm Sat, Sun. **Main courses** £4-£12. **No credit cards.**
Feel like cocking a snook at healthy eating? The Czechoslovak Restaurant won't disappoint with its calorie-fest of dumplings swimming in butter and trademark streaky pork. As befits this social club for Czech and Slovak émigrés, open for more than 60 years, the look is retro heaven (swirly carpets, patriotic portraits, typical pub furniture). Opt for the more formal restaurant if you want to avoid the one concession to modernity – big screens showing the latest Czech soaps. If you're partial to draught Pilsner Urquell or Budweiser Budvar, try the great drinking food: bramborák se slaninou (potato pancakes with pork), bratwurst-style sausage with mustard, or smazeny syr (fried breaded cheese). Or go the whole hog with creamy cabbage soup or scarily rich fried goose-liver to start, followed by our long-time favourite, sviåková na smetanú with knedliky (meltingly tender roast beef in vegetable and cream sauce and the famous sliced Czech dumplings). Pancakes with syrupy strawberries and cream beckon those with heroic appetites.
Babies and children welcome: high chairs. Booking advisable weekends. Disabled: toilet. Separate room for parties, seats 25. Takeaway service. Vegetarian menu. **Map 28 A3.**

Georgian

West

Kensington

Mimino
197C Kensington High Street, W8 6BA (7937 1551, www.mimino.co.uk). Kensington High Street tube. **Dinner served** 6-11pm Mon-Thur; 6pm-midnight Fri, Sat. **Main courses** £10-£15. **Credit** MC, V.

We've heard tell of occasional nights of wild dancing here, but Mimino still lacks character, despite the warmth of its traditional Georgian welcome. Evocative Georgian artworks hang on the walls, soulful Russian and Georgian ballads play in the background, and waiting staff are charming – yet though all this has improved the 'international-hotel dining room' feel of the place, something's still missing. All the trademark Georgian treats are here: golden yeasty khachapuri; excellent salads with the exotic addition of pounded walnuts and the distinctive khmeli sumeli spice mix; and bazhe, cold chicken breast in creamy walnut sauce. The generous meze plate groans with dense spinach and leek phkali (vegetable pâtés), warmly spiced aubergine, and lobio (slow-cooked herbed red beans). You'll also find the widest choice of Georgian wines this side of the Caucasus. Georgia claims to be the historical cradle of wine making, and the many centuries of experience are well demonstrated here. The pomegranate-hued, semi-sweet red wines (oaky Khvanchkara, velvety Kindzmarauli and fruity Ojaleshi) may be an acquired taste, but they're a perfect foil for the rich, spicy food. Or try a summery Mtatsminda rosé. And don't miss the mighty mineral hit of Borzhomi water.
Available for hire. Babies and children welcome: high chairs. Booking advisable weekends. Takeaway service. Vegetarian menu. **Map 7 A9.**

East

Bethnal Green

Little Georgia
87 Goldsmith's Row, E2 8QR (7739 8154). Liverpool Street tube/rail then 26, 48 bus/ Old Street tube/rail then 55 bus. **Meals served** 9am-5pm Mon; 9am-11pm Tue-Sat; 10am-11pm Sun. **Main courses** £8-£11. **Unlicensed. Corkage** no charge. **Credit** MC, V.
This small but characterful café in a quiet corner of Hackney is often buzzing, due in no small part to its homely yet ambitious Georgian food. There are tables on the pavement for when the sun shines, and the simple, tasteful decor inside is perked up with quirky touches – vintage gramophones, fairy lights and stern, old black-and-white portraits. Service on our visit could have been more animated and it sometimes lacked urgency, but the tempting aromas wafting from the tiny kitchen were enough to distract us. Georgian borscht is served hot, and is the test of any east European menu; here it is comforting yet summery, with a deep, rich stock and layers of flavour. Another starter, soothing soft cheese blini, combined well with a garlicky carrot salad and herby yoghurt. Of our mains, from the weekly changing specials board, the most successful was the kharcho, beef stew with ground walnuts; tabaka, chicken with red plum sauce, was a bit dry and tasted as if it had been reheated. Nevertheless, Little Georgia's generous no-corkage BYO policy, laid-back atmosphere and generally solid cooking are serious draws.
Babies and children welcome: high chairs. Separate room for parties, seats 25. Tables outdoors (2, pavement). Takeaway service. **Map 6 S3.**

North

Holloway

★ Tbilisi
91 Holloway Road, N7 8LT (7607 2536). Highbury & Islington tube/rail. **Dinner served** 6.30-11pm daily. **Main courses** £8.95-£9.45. **Credit** AmEx, MC, V.

Tatra. See p82.

We can't understand why Tbilisi, a quiet Georgian gem at the Highbury end of Holloway Road, isn't buzzing with happy diners. For a start, the wines are alluring; the velvety semi-sweet reds, Khvanchkara and Kindzmarauli, may not suit everyone, but, redolent of the mountainside vineyards of the sunny Caucasus, they're voluptuously rounded rather than cloyingly sweet, and perfect with rich spicy dishes. Generous starter platters feature such regional specialities as kolkheti or kakheti (intense spinach, carrot, or beetroot and pounded walnut pâtés), served with scrumptious stuffed yeasty bread: khachapuri (with cheese) or lobiani (with beans). A substantial bowl of borscht brims with veg and earthy spicing. The ubiquitous chicken tabaka is a whole spring chicken flattened and fried, served with spicy walnut or plum sauce. Or try a fragrant stew such as coriander-infused lamb chanakhi or garlic-rich tomatoey chicken chakhokhbili. Service used to be a touch cursory, but on our recent visit friendly staff were happy to explain the wine list and menu. Rich-red walls, dark-wood furniture, gleaming glassware and a soulful soundtrack of Russian and Georgian ballads give Tbilisi a stylish touch that belies its unglamorous location. A well-kept secret. *Available for hire. Babies and children welcome. Booking advisable Fri, Sat. Separate room for parties, seats 40. Takeaway service.*

North West
St John's Wood

Tamada NEW
122 Boundary Road, NW8 0RH (7372 2882, www.tamada.co.uk). Kilburn Park or St John's Wood tube/Kilburn High Road rail. **Lunch served** noon-2.30pm Sat, Sun. **Dinner served** 6-11pm Tue-Sun. **Main courses** £9-£16. **Credit** MC, V.
Tamara Lordkipanidze, political economist and former basketball player for the Republic of Georgia, owns this smartish new venue in north-west St John's Wood. Tamada's simple ground-floor dining room, not full but well attended on our visit, has pale walls and plush, peach-coloured chairs; downstairs employs more dramatic colours. The all-Georgian wine list features just nine varieties and starts at £16 a bottle, but it's worth forking out £7 extra for the soft, rich, spicy red Satrapezo. Alternatively, try the favourite Georgian soft drink, alien-green Tarxun, sweetly reminiscent of mouthwash. Service was hardly slick, but friendly. The menu contains around 15 starters, many a riff on walnuts. Badrijani was sliced aubergine layered with a paste of walnuts, onions and herbs: not pretty, but scrumptious. Main of sacivi (on-the-bone chicken in a creamy walnut sauce similar to tahini) was properly served just warm, and with a side dish of gooey maize, though more chicken would have been welcome given the £15.50 price tag. Coriander-laden lamb chaqapuli arrived in its oven-proof dish bubbling fiercely, accompanied by shoti puri (bread baked in a charcoal oven). The next table's plump khinkali (meat dumplings) looked sensational – definitely a temptation to return.
Babies and children welcome: high chair. Booking advisable Fri, Sat. Takeaway service.

Hungarian
Central
Soho

Gay Hussar
2 Greek Street, W1D 4NB (7437 0973, www.gayhussar.co.uk). Tottenham Court Road tube. **Lunch served** 12.15-2.30pm, **dinner served** 5.30-10.45pm Mon-Sat. **Main courses** £9.75-£16.95. **Set lunch** £17 2 courses, £19.50 3 courses. **Credit** AmEx, DC, MC, V.
While the Gay Hussar may not have quite the caché of old, when parliamentary careers were made and broken here over a bottle of Bull's Blood,

it still oozes character. Wood-panelled walls are crammed with caricatures of diners past; shelves are stocked with political biographies. A masterful maître d' runs proceedings; on our last visit he made short shrift of a loud American couple who arrived without a reservation, but he enjoys wry banter with guests wise enough to book ahead. The Hussar caters mainly to an older, greyer clientele, but the mix of old-school formality with a friendly twist attracts cosmopolitan younger folk too. The mixed hors d'oeuvres plate is a great way to explore Hungarian starters: tender marinated herring with sour cream; rich, coarse fish terrine with a vibrant beetroot sauce; dense duck liver pâté; and spicy salami. For mains, it's hard to resist fish dumplings in sour cream and dill sauce or, for hearty appetites, paprika-rich venison goulash, almost chocolatey in its intensity, served with tarhonya, a traditional Hungarian grain-like pasta. Desserts are enticing if artery-clogging: baked cheesecake with zesty lemon, poppy-seed strudel with vanilla ice-cream. Retro at its best.
Babies and children welcome: high chairs. Booking essential dinner. Separate rooms for parties, seating 12 and 24. **Map 17 C3**.

Pan-East European
South
Waterloo

★ Baltic (100)
74 Blackfriars Road, SE1 8HA (7928 1111, www.balticrestaurant.co.uk). Southwark tube/rail. **Lunch served** noon-3pm, **dinner served** 5.30-11.15pm Mon-Sat. **Meals served** noon-10.30pm Sun. **Main courses** £10.50-£17. **Set meal** £14.50 2 courses, £17.50 3 courses. **Credit** AmEx, MC, V.
Jan Woroniecki's stylish Baltic remains the brightest star on London's east European restaurant scene. Arrive early and enjoy being distracted by rows of gleaming bottles in the buzzing front bar area, where jazz musicians regularly play. We love the imaginative cocktails; try the super-summery watermelon martini, or the champagne with house-infused strawberry vodka. In the high-ceilinged main restaurant, you can gaze up at hundreds of glimmering shards of golden Baltic amber in the stunning chandelier, which is set against the spare white expanse and rough red-brick wall: all referencing the great Baltic port of Gdansk. The menu combines the best of east European cuisine – from Georgian-style lamb with aubergines to Romanian sour cream mamaliga (polenta) – with a light, Modern European twist. The vivid, clear Polish-style barszcz is beetroot bliss. Breaded pork escalopes and garlic mushrooms are lent light freshness with the wonderful mizeria. Subtle vodka-cured gravadlax comes with perfect potato and leek latkes: just the right crunchy-chewy combo and ideal with house-infused dill vodka. For afters, savour an almond- or vanilla-flavoured vodka with one of the enticing puds, such as sour cherry crème brûlée. Still poles apart from (and ahead of) its rivals.
Babies and children admitted. Disabled: toilet. Separate room for parties, seats 30. Tables outdoors (4, terrace). **Map 11 N8**.

West
Kensington

Wódka
12 St Alban's Grove, W8 5PN (7937 6513, www.wodka.co.uk). High Street Kensington tube. **Lunch served** noon-3pm Sat, Sun. **Dinner served** 6.30-11.15pm daily. **Main courses** £12.90-£17.50. **Set lunch** £13.50 2 courses, £17 3 courses. **Set meal** £24.50-£28 3 courses. **Credit** AmEx, MC, V.
On a residential backstreet, this comely former dairy (to Kensington Palace) has been quietly producing cut-above Polish and east European fare since 1989. Smart but assuredly laid-back, it

has an understated bohemian vibe that attracts locals and sophisticated tourists who've clocked its write-ups in the gourmet travel press. As the name suggests, vodka is a speciality: there are 25 bottles (gold, grain, rye, spelt, potato and so on), plus another 15 own-flavoured varieties (from vanilla to tarragon). The wine list is mainly French with a couple of international departures. Expected starters (zurek, barszcz, pierogi) are complemented by such treats as grilled quail with walnut sauce and pomegranate, and a couple of modish salads. Main courses include a wide range of protein centrepieces, from breaded pork escalopes (schabowy) to hare. Attention to detail in the beef and pepper goulash sets it above many competitors; served in a black Staub casserole, the rich sauce is well reduced, the potato dumplings exquisitely light, the meat melting. Things weren't so good for dessert. White chocolate cheesecake was OK, but chocolate and hazelnut torte tasted stale. Casually chic, experienced staff keep things moving nicely, helping to compensate for any glitches in the food.
Babies and children admitted: high chairs, nappy-changing facilities. Booking advisable. Separate room for parties, seats 30. Tables outdoors (3, pavement). **Map 7 C9**.

THE DISH

Blini
Buckwheat is a pretty divisive ingredient to those not born in eastern Europe or the few locales where it also has a traditional following (Japan, Brittany, hippy communes, dusty old health food shops). But like anchovies, olives and strong blue cheese, this tangy, earthy-flavoured grain is one of those foods that seems to taste better as you get older. Really. True, drinking vodka alongside improves it too, which brings us to blini, little buckwheat pancakes enjoyed as appetisers with various savoury toppings and ideally (though not compulsorily) a shot or two of vodka.

Blini look like drop-scones or pikelets but the recipe has a key difference from that which an English or Scottish granny would use: blini contain yeast. This helps them rise and gives a slightly bubbly texture to the batter. Buckwheat has no gluten, and in the absence of a raising agent the blini batter would run all over the pan, staying thin, flat and papery.

Blini can be as large as 12cm across but most served in London restaurants are only half as big – blinchiki (or mini blini). Those served at **Baltic** are top-notch and come with various toppings including mushroom and beetroot pâtés, and marinated herring. Order a selection platter if you can't decide. Sister restaurant **Wódka** adds indulgent foie gras and oscietra caviar options for its Kensington patrons. Lumpfish caviar, as served at **Trojka**, is not the posh, rare stuff and you'll find the blini taste just as good with smoked trout or aubergine purée. We like **Daquise's** stodgily high-rise blini too: grey from the flour and brown from the frypan, served simply with lean smoked salmon and soured cream.

RESTAURANTS

Polish

Central

South Kensington

Daquise

20 Thurloe Street, SW7 2LT (7589 6117).
South Kensington tube. **Meals served** noon-11pm daily. **Set lunch** (noon-3.30pm Mon-Fri) £9.50 2 courses. **Credit** MC, V.
You want classic Polish cooking? In summer there are four types of beetroot soup on the menu at this old world café. Dark-wood shutters with heart-shaped cut-outs, a fake mezzanine with turned wood railings, a wagon wheel, and food coming from a little roofed hatch – all enhance Daquise's rural vibe, yet its walls are lined with paintings of London tourist sights and, outside, the South Kensington traffic is relentless. Much of the menu is about frying. Food can arrive at table very quickly. A long list of main courses takes in the likes of lemon sole with garlic mushrooms, and almond trout with sautéed potatoes. Lovely doughy pierogi come scattered with bacon bits, the bigos is laden with cabbage, and the burnished potato pancakes are large and firm enough to double as Frisbees. We also liked the galabki, filled with mild, creamy mince. For dessert, the house pancake with orange syrup and generous mounds of vanilla ice-cream was better than another filled with cheese and raisins, rolled into a sausage and fried. Next time we'll try the Polish coffee, made with honey-flavoured vodka and whipped cream. Service was nicely unpretentious, as it should be. *Babies and children admitted. Booking advisable. Separate room for parties, seats 25.*

West

Bayswater

Antony's

54 Porchester Road, W2 6ET (7243 8743, www.antonysrestaurant.com). Royal Oak tube. **Dinner served** 6-11pm Tue-Sun. **Main courses** £10.50-£16. **Cover** 70p. **Credit** MC, V.
Antony's is a little-known treat, attracting locals, the occasional wandering tourist and a few diners from further afield wise to the fact that there are some perfectly executed Polish classics here. You'll rarely come across a better, more intensely beetrooty barszcz in London. The potato pancakes (the warm and chatty owner swears by maris piper potatoes) have just the right degree of crisp exterior to chewy interior; served with sour-cream and mushroom sauce, they're ideal old-fashioned comfort food. Bring out your inner Pole some more with meltingly tender herrings with egg, onion and sour cream. We're often tempted to choose a selection of starters with a vodka or four, in preference to the less enticing mains. On our recent visit, beef zrazy were tired and bland, and some of the international dishes have a slightly sad retro feel. In contrast, the generous array of freshly cooked accompanying vegetables (fried potatoes, tender and sweet red cabbage, and fresh young carrots) are clearly prepared with love. With its dark-wood furnishings, large gilt mirrors, starched tablecloths and charming hostess, Antony's creates a sense of Mitteleuropa in the unlikely surroundings of Royal Oak. Enjoy! *Available for hire. Babies and children welcome: high chairs. Booking advisable weekends. Separate room for parties, seats 30.* **Map 7 C5**.

Hammersmith

Knaypa

268 King Street, W6 0SP (8563 2887, www. theknaypa.co.uk). Hammersmith tube. **Lunch served** noon-3pm, **dinner served** 6-10.30pm Mon-Thur. **Meals served** noon-10.30pm Fri, Sat; noon-9.30pm Sun. **Main courses** £6.99-£16.49. **Credit** AmEx, MC, V.
In an effort to distinguish itself from west London's more folksy Polish enclaves, the Knaypa has a striking black and red decor reminiscent of a continental nightclub – not quite the place for a relaxing lunch, but fun for a lively dinner if busy. On the quiet evening of our visit, the pavement tables were popular. In addition to wines and various flavoured vodkas, there's a tempting list of beers including draught Zwyiec and delicious, not-too-sweet Redd's raspberry. Despite the extravagant interior, prices and portions are generous: more so if you take advantage of one of the many special offers. De volaille, Poland's torpedo-shaped version of chicken kiev, featured good poultry and crisp breadcrumbs, though the workaday pile of accompanying chips made the dish seem more like a builder's lunch. But we loved the tall stack of potato pancakes with homely goulash and a dollop of cooling soured cream – so too the plump pierogi with the vinegary tang of sauerkraut, and the lean, firm herring fillets to start. Dessert (a moist, crumbly square of cheesecake) was let down by an excess of over-whipped cream and a shower of icing sugar. Staff were friendly. *Available for hire. Babies and children welcome: high chairs. Booking advisable weekends. Disabled: toilet. Separate room for parties, seats 38. Tables outdoors (2, pavement). Vegetarian menu.* **Map 20 A4**.

★ Polanka

258 King Street, W6 0SP (8741 8268, www. polanka-rest.com). Ravenscourt Park tube. **Meals served** noon-9.30pm Mon-Sat; noon-7.30pm Sun. **Main courses** £4.90-£11.50. **Unlicensed. Corkage** £3 wine, £6 spirits. **Credit** MC, V.
Lively Polish ballads play in the folksy pale-wood panelled dining room hidden behind this attractive Hammersmith deli/restaurant. An eerie blonde mannequin decked in brightly embroidered costume gazes at diners. Pelts of wild boar decorate the walls. So far, so mountain-kitsch. The friendly service is utterly genuine, however; coupled with the generous portions of traditional food, it makes Polanka a place worth frequenting. Mild herrings in oil were enlivened with lashings of raw onion and pickled cucumber – perhaps not a great date dish. A gargantuan plate filled to the edges with four Frisbee-sized potato pancakes and a lake of rich pork goulash might have lacked something in aesthetics (resembling a brown reservoir garnished with a slice of orange), but it certainly made up for this in flavour. The pancakes were pleasingly crisp on the outside, firm on the inside, and contrasted with the rich stew filled with wonderfully cooked pork that melted in the mouth. A skylight brightens what would otherwise be a poky room, making it a very pleasant place to linger over a tasty piece of cake from the deli's display case. *Babies and children welcome: high chairs. Booking advisable. Separate room for parties, seats 8. Takeaway service.* **Map 20 A4**.

Shepherd's Bush

★ Patio

5 Goldhawk Road, W12 8QQ (8743 5194). Goldhawk Road tube. **Lunch served** noon-3pm Mon-Fri. **Dinner served** 6-11.30pm daily. **Main courses** £7-£10.50. **Set meal** £16.50 3 courses incl vodka shot. **Credit** AmEx, MC, V.
If you miss your Polish granny, or feel life has cheated you by denying you one, repair to Patio with haste. The olde worlde charm – ornate gold-framed mirrors, upright piano, worn red carpet – of the cosy dining room evokes a grandmother's sitting room. Caring and friendly service and hearty, authentic flavours continue the theme. Tasty brown and white bread comes with butter and smalec (a spread made of rendered pork fat dotted with bits of bacon). The extensive menu and lists of specials cover most Polish comfort food. Red borscht was the perfect starter: a wonderfully rich and vibrant broth with three meaty dumplings. We followed this with classic golabki (cabbage leaves stuffed with rice and meat and flooded with sweet tomato sauce). Enormous platters of roast potatoes, rich spiced shredded beetroot, and radish and corn in mayonnaise, were served on the side. Dessert might seem impossible after this, but is worth the effort. Fresh fruit and divine doughnut-like pieces of sponge coated in coconut (complimentary snacks while you consider afters) could well finish you off. But the brave should follow the waitress's advice, and plump for coffee, dessert or a soothing vodka. *Available for hire. Babies and children welcome: high chairs. Booking advisable Fri, Sat dinner. Separate room for parties, seats 45. Takeaway service. Vegetarian menu.* **Map 20 C2**.

Tatra

24 Goldhawk Road, W12 8DH (8749 8193). Goldhawk Road tube. **Lunch served** 11am-4pm, **dinner served** 6-11pm Mon-Fri. **Meals served** 11am-11pm Sat; 11am-10pm Sun. **Main courses** £8.50-£13.50. **Set lunch** £10.50 2 courses, £13.50 3 courses. **Credit** AmEx, MC, V.
Named after the mountain range that forms the border between Poland and Slovakia (rather than the eponymous golden lager sold here), Tatra brings a smart yet relaxed mood to a strip of Shepherd's Bush more often associated with rowdy pubs and takeaways. Bare brick walls, high-backed leather chairs, dark wood and modern art set it apart from more traditional Polish eateries; on our last visit, most customers were go-ahead young expats. We've enjoyed the goulash here in the past. This time it had a good smoky flavour, with tender cubes of meat and comforting dumplings, but the vibrant red sauce was too thin. Buckwheat 'risotto' was sensibly judicious with cream; it contained grated carrot, finely sliced green beans and crisp fresh leaves to garnish, and was rather like a hot grain salad – in a good way. The highlight, however, were the delectably soft leniwe (pasta-like dumplings shaped like slugs), which came tossed with meatily fragrant wild mushrooms and parsley. All portions were generous, and service sweet. To drink there's a tempting list of flavoured vodkas (we were brought complimentary shots of ice-cold, thick pear vodka), as well as beers and a serviceable range of wines. *Available for hire. Babies and children admitted. Booking advisable weekends. Disabled: toilet. Tables outdoors (1, pavement).* **Map 20 B2**.

South

Clapham

Café Wanda

153 Clapham High Street, SW4 7SS (7738 8760). Clapham Common tube. **Lunch served** 11am-3pm, **dinner served** 7-11pm Tue-Thur. **Meals served** 11am-11pm Fri-Sun. **Main courses** £6.25-£14.95. **Credit** MC, V.
It can be difficult to enter Café Wanda and not focus on the enticing cake display. The café is ideal for an afternoon coffee and cake while you watch Clapham pass by outside. Everything is giant here – the human-sized poppies on the wall, the portions of food, and the friendliness of staff. Wanda tries to be all things to all eaters, so the menu contains a random collection of non-Polish food: jacket potatoes, salad niçoise, lasagne. Ask for the special Polish menu to discover the true delights. The mammoth polski platter is the perfect starter for two, and indicates the kitchen's strengths: heavy traditional fare, elegantly plated. Bigos, a stew of sauerkraut and large chunks of bacon (often considered Poland's national dish), had a fabulous salty-sour kick. Potato pancake with pork goulash could have been a meal in itself. The platter was further diversified by stuffed golabki (cabbage leaves) and a range of salads. Although we didn't need them, we also ordered a plate of mixed pierogi, which were perfectly cooked and filled with rich, contrasting packages of potato and fresh cheese, mushroom and sauerkraut, and meat. If you can manage cake after all that – and it would be a waste not to – try the poppy-seed cheesecake: highly recommended. *Babies and children welcome: high chairs. Booking advisable. Entertainment: pianist 8.30-11pm Fri, Sat. Tables outdoors (2, pavement). Takeaway service. Vegetarian menu.* **Map 22 B2**.

Balham

★ Polish White Eagle Club

211 Balham High Road, SW17 7BQ (8672 1723, www.whiteeagleclub.co.uk). Tooting Bec tube/ Balham tube/rail/49, 155, 181, 319 bus.
Bar **Open** 6-11pm Mon-Thur; 6pm-2am Fri; noon-2am Sat; noon-10.30pm Sun.
Restaurant **Lunch served** noon-3pm Mon-Fri. **Dinner served** 6-10pm Mon-Thur; 6-11pm Fri. **Meals served** noon-11pm Sat; noon-10pm Sun. **Main courses** £6-95-£11.95. **Set lunch** (Mon-Sat) £7 2 courses. **Set dinner** £9.90 2 courses. **Both Credit** MC, V.

Nestled between a church and an army recruitment centre, the restaurant in the Polish White Eagle Club is an unusual spot. Wind your way through the bar of the dilapidated club and you'll reach a dark dining room that resembles a church recreation room: all metal chairs, paper tablecloths and napkins, mirrors and sponge-painted walls. Popular with elderly Poles, seemingly thrilled to be enjoying traditional food with friends, this place is, indeed, a club. Polish is the preferred language; the fact that still water rather than sparkling was brought to our table was probably due to linguistic misunderstanding. Abrupt service and aesthetics aside, this is a fun way to enjoy hearty and determinedly traditional food. Sour soup was appropriately tangy, served in a bread bowl filled with boiled eggs, kielbasa and carrots that lent a subtle sweetness. Pierogi filled with mushrooms and sauerkraut were adorned with the merest hint of butter, looking somewhat forlorn without the addition of fried onions or bacon bits. Nevertheless, for its unfussy cooking, generous portions and low prices, the White Eagle warrants a visit.
Babies and children welcome: high chairs. Booking advisable. Entertainment: musicians, dance classes (phone for details). Separate rooms for parties, seating 30-120. Takeaway service.

Russian

Central

Clerkenwell & Farringdon

Potemkin

144 Clerkenwell Road, EC1R 5DP (7278 6661, www.potemkin.co.uk). Farringdon tube/rail. **Meals served** noon-11pm Mon-Fri. **Dinner served** 6-11pm Sat. **Main courses** £12-£17. **Set dinner** £20 3 courses. **Credit** AmEx, DC, MC, V.

We've usually rated Potemkin as one of the better options on London's limited Russian dining scene, but our last visit was beset by problems. As we descended the stairs to the further formal basement restaurant, the once-glam decor with gleaming khokhloma (papier-mâché work) displayed in artfully lit alcoves looked a little tired. As the room began to fill with two large parties, it became clear that service was in difficulties. A solitary sweet, apologetic waitress tried to cope as cross, hungry punters faced interminable waits. The kitchen also seemed to be in trouble. The smoked fish plate was fine, though portions were small, especially of the delectable, wafer-thin halibut. Herring fillet was tender and the shocking-pink layered herring, beetroot, potato and mayo salad (pod shuboy) was tasty enough. Other dishes left much to be desired: borscht was watery and lukewarm; and a main of pan-fried red mullet in mustard and shallot sauce, usually a firm favourite here, oozed oil. With a choice of 100 vodkas, drowning our sorrows seemed the only sensible option. Perestroika urgently needed!
Available for hire. Booking advisable. **Map 5 N4**.

St James's

Divo

12 Waterloo Place, SW1Y 4AU (7484 1355, www.divolondon.co.uk). Piccadilly Circus tube. **Meals served** 5pm-midnight Mon-Fri; 6-11pm Sat. **Main courses** £12-£18. **Credit** AmEx, MC, V.

Having begun life as an extraordinary post-Soviet Ukrainian kitsch-fest, and earning itself some derisive reviews, Divo has been trying to turn itself around. The opulence of the premises (stunning crystal chandeliers, OTT drapes, swags and tassels galore) is juxtaposed with incongruous faux-folk fripperies. On our last visit, we were ushered to a first-floor room that had more restrained decor, but was pounded by the disco beat from the echoingly empty downstairs bar. The food is serviceable, but fails to measure up to the grandiose surroundings. We eschewed mains for a selection of classic zakuski: decent salad olivier (potatoes, chicken, peas and carrots in creamy mayonnaise); pretty layered herring salad, pink with beetroot; and a dish of smoked salmon with what purported to be blinis, yet were very ordinary English-style pancakes – all served too cold from the fridge. An insipid Ukrainian borscht was enlivened only by sharply fresh dill. Normally zakuski merit a good few vodkas, but at £8.50 a shot, frugality was the name of our game. A friendly, efficient waitress did her best to bring some cheer, but with only one other couple dining, the mood was one of glowering gloom.
Babies and children admitted. Disabled: toilet. Separate rooms for parties, seating 12-50. **Map 10 K7.**

North

Camden Town & Chalk Farm

Trojka

101 Regents Park Road, NW1 8UR (7483 3765, www.troykarestaurant.co.uk). Chalk Farm tube. **Meals served** 9am-10.30pm daily. **Main courses** £6-£9. **Set lunch** (Mon-Fri) £9.95-£11.95 2 courses. **Licensed. Corkage** £4 wine, £14 spirits. **Credit** MC, V.

After a bracing walk on Primrose Hill, or a browse in the shops, where better to while away some time than Trojka? Prices are remarkably reasonable for the chic location, helping attract a diverse crowd. The place is thronged at weekends, with people stopping by for anything from coffee and Hungarian chocolate cake to a three-course blow-out. On a recent Sunday visit, despite things being slightly frenetic and noisy (with some long waits), our waitress was friendly and attentive. Earthy Ukrainian borscht was perfectly peppery: great with chewy rye bread. Armenian salad mixed new potatoes and beetroot with avocado, feta and olives. Succulent melt-in-the-mouth herring with potato, onion and sour cream was close to zakuski heaven. Such food demands vodka or beer rather than wine – try the hard-to-find velvety Ukrainian Obolon porter, or an Estonian lager. Dark-red walls hung with gilt-framed oil-paintings (including a Chagall-esque trojka: a horse-drawn sleigh) give a bohemian Mitteleuropa feel to the dining room, enhanced some evenings by a gipsy violinist. With its laid-back, 'anything at anytime' approach, Trojka is deservedly popular.
Babies and children welcome: high chairs. Booking advisable dinner Fri, Sat. Entertainment: Russian folk music 8-10.30pm Fri, Sat. Tables outdoors (4, pavement). Takeaway service. **Map 27 A1.**

Menu

Dishes followed by (Cz) indicate a Czechoslovak dish; (G) Georgian; (H) Hungarian; (P) Polish; (R) Russian; (Uk) Ukrainian. Others have no particular affiliation.

Bigos (P): hunter's stew made with sauerkraut, various meats and sausage, mushrooms and juniper.
Blini: yeast-leavened pancake made from buckwheat flour, traditionally served smothered in butter and sour cream; **blinchiki** are mini blinis.
Borscht: beetroot soup. There are many varieties: Ukrainian borscht is thick with vegetables; the Polish version (**barszcz**) is clear. There are also white and green types. Often garnished with sour cream, boiled egg or mini dumplings.
Caviar: fish roe. Most highly prized is that of the sturgeon (**beluga, oscietra** and **sevruga**, in descending order of expense), though **keta** or salmon caviar is underrated.
Chlodnik (P): cold beetroot soup, bright pink in colour, served with sour cream.
Galabki, golabki or **golubtsy:** cabbage parcels, usually stuffed with rice or kasha (qv) and sometimes meat.
Golonka (P): pork knuckle, often cooked in beer.
Goulash or **gulasz (H):** rich beef soup.
Kasha or **kasza:** buckwheat, delicious roasted: fluffy, with a nutty flavour.
Kaszanka (P): blood sausage made with buckwheat.
Khachapuri (G): flatbread; sometimes called Georgian pizza.
Kielbasa (P): sausage; Poland had dozens of widely differing styles.
Knedliky (Cz): bread dumplings.
Kolduny (P): small meat-filled dumplings (scaled-down pierogi, qv) often served in beetroot soup.
Kotlet schabowy (P): breaded pork chops.
Koulebiaka, kulebiak or **coulebiac (R):** layered salmon or sturgeon pie with eggs, dill, rice and mushrooms.
Krupnik (P): barley soup, and the name of a honey vodka (because of the golden colour of barley).
Latke: grated potato pancakes, fried.
Makowiec or **makietki (P):** poppy seed cake.
Mizeria (P): cucumber salad; very thinly sliced and dressed with sour cream.
Nalesniki (P): cream cheese pancakes.
Paczki (P): doughnuts, often filled with plum jam.
Pierogi (P): ravioli-style dumplings. Typical fillings are sauerkraut and mushroom, curd cheese or fruit (cherries, apples).
Pirogi (large) or **pirozhki** (small) **(R):** filled pies made with yeasty dough.
Placki (P): potato pancakes.
Shashlik: Caucasian spit-roasted meat.
Shchi (R): soup made from sauerkraut.
Stroganoff (R): beef slices, served in a rich sour cream and mushroom sauce.
Uszka or **ushka (P):** small ear-shaped dumplings served in soup.
Vareniki (Uk): Ukrainian version of pierogi (qv).
Zakuski (R) or **zakaski (P):** starters, traditionally covering a whole table. The many dishes can include pickles, marinated vegetables and fish, herring, smoked eel, aspic, mushrooms, radishes with butter, salads and caviar.
Zrazy (P): beef rolls stuffed with bacon, pickled cucumber and mustard.
Zurek (P): sour rye soup.

Fish

Britain's piscivores, who view fishmongers' displays in Madrid and Paris with envy, often complain that the best of our fish goes abroad. But the process is not all one way. Some of the most outstanding dishes served in London's fish restaurants hail from overseas. Sample the Scandinavian-influenced delights at **Deep**, for instance, or the French-accented cooking at Chiswick's **Fish Hook**, the heavenly Sardinian luxuries at **Olivomare**, or the Mauritian specials at **Chez Liline**. Even long-lived establishments such as the glamorous **Scott's** and Richard Corrigan's excellent **Bentley's Oyster Bar & Grill** occasionally hop down to the Med for ideas. However, simplicity is often the key to great fish and seafood, as evidenced by the likes of South Woodford's family-friendly **Ark** and the new **Fish & Grill** in Croydon.

Stocks of several popular marine species remain dangerously low. To find out which fish and seafood are certified as sustainable, check out the Marine Stewardship Council's website (www.msc.org.uk). For budget restaurants specialising in fish and chips, see pp298-302.

Central

Belgravia

★ Olivomare

10 Lower Belgrave Street, SW1W 0LJ (7730 9022). Victoria tube/rail. **Lunch served** noon-2.30pm Mon-Sat, noon-3pm Sun. **Dinner served** 7-11pm Mon-Sat; 7-10.30pm Sun. **Main courses** £14-£26.50. **Credit** AmEx, DC, MC, V.

It's rare to see a clean-lined contemporary dining room with such quirky decor, but that's not Olivomare's only distinction: this is London's only dedicated Sardinian seafood restaurant. Owned by Mauro Sanna of Belgravian stalwart Olivo (*see p162*), it attracts a cosmopolitan, affluent crowd with a menu that sings of simple luxuries. Typical are the likes of octopus carpaccio with celery salad; or burrata cheese with bottarga, cherry tomatoes and basil – the bottarga (salted fish roe) arriving both in dusty specks and thin curls like orange zest. Big, springy slices of monkfish were smokily fresh from the chargrill, served with just-tender courgettes. There's also a good choice of pastas and risottos for starters or mains; bottarga features here again, adding savoury saltiness to a dish of own-made twisted-rope pasta (lorighttas) with clams. In addition to Sardinian specialities, the wine list includes a choice of pinot neros from Alto Adige: unadulterated pleasure for fish-eating red wine lovers. We waited longer than we'd have liked between courses, but service was affable. Saffron ice-cream and sebada with honey stood out on the otherwise generic Italian dessert list.
Babies and children admitted. Booking advisable. Disabled: toilet. Tables outdoors (4, terrace). **Map 15 H10.**
For branch (Olivetto) see index.

City

Sweetings (100)

39 Queen Victoria Street, EC4N 4SA (7248 3062). Mansion House tube. **Lunch served** 11.30am-3pm Mon-Fri. **Main courses** £12-£27.50. **Credit** AmEx, MC, V.

Even at 12.30pm on a Tuesday this no-bookings City favourite was teeming with suited customers, plenty of whom happily drank in the bar area for nearly an hour before being seated. What keeps them returning? No-nonsense British food served in a quintessentially English setting with little but ice buckets and stool seating to distinguish it from Tom Brown's school days. Diners at the communal tables at the rear can survey walls hung with old cartoons, photographs and cricket and polo mementos. Specials might include gull's eggs (£4 each), seafood cocktail, smoked salmon pâté, and lobster offered as salad or thermidor. The 'bill of fare' proffers traditional dishes from smoked eel to fish and chips. Wines of unspecified provenance are all over £20, but good with it, such as our 2007 chardonnay. Chef's fish pie contained a pleasing mix of fish and shellfish yet was heavy on mashed potato and needed some tabasco to get it going. Dover sole, of minerally flavour, is among the premium fish offered grilled, fried or steamed, on or off the bone. Bubble and squeak, thick with cabbage and pleasingly browned, was best of the sides. The white-jacketed, seen-it-all waiter handled guffawing questions about spotted dick with aplomb and kept everything moving swiftly.
Available for hire (dinner only). Babies and children admitted. Bookings not accepted. Takeaway service. **Map 11 P6.**

Fitzrovia

Back to Basics

21A Foley Street, W1W 6DS (7436 2181, www.backtobasics.uk.com). Goodge Street or Oxford Circus tube. **Lunch served** noon-3pm, **dinner served** 6-10.30pm Mon-Sat. **Main courses** £13.75-£21.75. **Credit** AmEx, DC, MC, V.

No frills is the rule at this relaxed neighbourhood bistro. On a wet Wednesday lunchtime, the small dining room was packed and the decibel level was rising. The menu ranges widely, with plenty of piscine starters (oysters, fish soup, marinated herrings, gravadlax), a couple of salads and some pasta dishes. A blackboard lists the catch of the day. Choices might include classics (fried codling with mushy peas and tartar sauce, grilled lemon sole) or more imaginative fare, but in keeping with the restaurant's name, the kitchen seems happiest with simpler preparations. Steamed mussels with garlic and herbs showcased plump bivalves in buttery juices; the accompanying bib brought a touch of theatricality to proceedings. Dressed crab was let down by a fridge-cold, joyless crustacean. To follow, the zesty crayfish salsa with our sea trout was a highlight, but a generous portion of halibut tasted tired and was overwhelmed by baby spinach. Amid the noise, service was pleasant yet distracted. Desserts like bread and butter pudding aim at comfort eating, but a greater attraction is the sensible wine list, which has admirably fair mark-ups and a decent choice by the glass.
Babies and children welcome: high chairs. Booking advisable. Disabled: toilet. Tables outdoors (10, pavement). Takeaway service. **Map 17 A1.**

Leicester Square

J Sheekey

28-34 St Martin's Court, WC2N 4AL (7240 2565, www.caprice-holdings.co.uk). Leicester Square tube. **Lunch served** noon-3pm Mon-Sat; noon-3.30pm Sun. **Dinner served** 5.30pm-midnight Mon-Sat; 6-11pm Sun. **Main courses** £13.50-£39.50. **Set lunch** (Sat, Sun) £24.75 3 courses. **Cover** £2. **Credit** AmEx, DC, MC, V.

Recession-proof Sheekey's has added a sumptuous oyster bar this year, annexing adjoining premises to extend the operation into a restaurant row all of its own. The new bar conforms to the firm's comfortably elegant style, with wooden floor and monochrome photos on the wall. The place was full on our Saturday night visit. We were squeezed into a table right by the desk – not the best seat in the house, but a good place to view the plush clientele and hear staff issuing special instructions for the service of favoured customers. (And yes, celebrities continue to attend.) Sheekey's seldom turns out a dud from a menu that runs from sparklingly simple seafood platters to dishes that are interesting without being elaborate. The cooking is competent and quality-controlled (good basic grills, classic sides); it sometimes lacks cojones (a monkfish and tiger prawn curry was insipid), but occasionally knocks your socks off (the famous fish cake, and awesome grilled cuttlefish with cockles and romero pepper). That said, and we don't mean this in a bad way, it isn't just about the food here.
Babies and children welcome: booster seats; colouring books; high chairs. Booking essential. Disabled: toilet. Vegetarian menu. Vegan dishes. **Map 18 D5.**

Mayfair

Scott's

20 Mount Street, W1K 2HE (7495 7309, www.caprice-holdings.co.uk). Bond Street or Green Park tube. **Meals served** noon-10.30pm Mon-Sat; noon-10pm Sun. **Main courses** £16.50-£39.50. **Cover** £2. **Credit** AmEx, DC, MC, V.

Owner Caprice Holdings is keen to remind us that Scott's was Ian Fleming's favourite restaurant – and it's true that 007 wouldn't look out of place among the well-groomed and monied crowd here. There's even the odd wannabe Bond girl perched at the onyx bar, peering at the works from contemporary British artists festooning the walls. Bond would be very much at home with the food too, which is rooted in Anglo-French classicism (including several savouries, from welsh rarebit to herring milts on toast). A starter of dressed crab was generously proportioned but bland, while some lovely deep-fried sprats would have benefited from more acidity in the accompanying caper mayonnaise. Sea bass came neatly butterflied, yet with citrus flavour noticeably absent from the lemon and herb butter. Puddings strayed further from the classics and suffered for it: vanilla cheesecake was deconstructed as a quenelle of cheesecake-style mousse, complete with chunks of crunchy base; a chocolate fondant showcasing Tuscan chocolate-house Amadei was better. The wine list sensibly majors in zingy, mineral whites and offers a varied choice by the glass or 500ml carafe. Scott's isn't cheap, but it exudes glamour.
Babies and children welcome: high chairs. Booking advisable. Disabled: toilet. Separate room for parties, seats 40. Tables outdoors (5, pavement). Vegetarian menu. Vegan dishes. **Map 9 G7.**

Bentley's Oyster Bar & Grill

Piccadilly

★ Bentley's Oyster Bar & Grill (100)
*11-15 Swallow Street, W1B 4DG (7734 4756,
www.bentleysoysterbarandgrill.co.uk). Piccadilly
Circus tube.*
Oyster Bar **Meals served** noon-midnight Mon-
Sat; noon-10pm Sun. **Main courses** £8.50-£24.
Restaurant **Lunch served** noon-3pm Mon-Fri.
Dinner served 6-11pm Mon-Sat; 6-10pm Sun.
Main courses £16.50-£38.
Both **Credit** AmEx, MC, V.
There's something timeless about Richard
Corrigan's restoration of this classic oyster house.
World War I was raging when Bentley's first
opened, but the suited gentlemen who flock here
today enjoy their seafood with the same gusto as
their great-grandfathers before them. Upstairs is
the more sedate grill restaurant. Spread over three
rooms and featuring a wider range of meat options
than the bar, it's a fine spot to enjoy game in season.
Things get more lively in the ground-floor oyster
bar, where you can sit either at the long marble-
topped bar or in red leather banquettes at marble
tables. The food is a synthesis of classic and
modern. There are oysters (on our visit five
varieties) and other shellfish, but we were taken
with the beautifully textured fish soup, one of the
best we've encountered, with outstanding depth of
flavour. Across the menu there are nods towards
Corrigan's Irish heritage (gorgeous soda bread
with salted butter; smoked salmon from Frank
Hedderman; West Cork beef), but also the odd
splash of Mediterranean colour (cod with
piperade). British classics abound too, including a

huge portion of deep-fried haddock and mushy
peas. Knowledgeable, friendly professionalism
characterises the front-of-house operation. The
excellent wine list, arranged by style, is easily
navigable. A grown-up treat.
*Booking essential. Disabled: toilet. Dress: smart
casual; no shorts. Separate rooms for parties,
seating 14 and 60.* **Map 17 A5**.

St James's

Green's
*36 Duke Street, SW1Y 6DF (7930 4566,
www.greens.org.uk). Green Park or Piccadilly
Circus tube.* **Lunch served** 11.30am-3pm,
dinner served 5.30-11pm Mon-Sat. **Main
courses** £15.50-£42.50. **Cover** £2. **Credit**
AmEx, DC, MC, V.
On paper, Green's is in danger of becoming a
caricature of itself. Located in St James's, it is
owned by Simon Parker Bowles, erstwhile brother-
in-law of Camilla. Old-fashioned comfort food is
served to gents in gold-buttoned blazers and their
pearls-and-twin-set wives. In fact, it's much more
appealing than this might sound. Yes, customers
tend to be well-padded, well-heeled males, mobile
phones are banned, the green-leather booths
evoke a gentlemen's club, and staff (including the
women) wear absurd waistcoats and ties. But the
atmosphere is convivial, the setting homely rather
than stuck-up, and the food can be excellent. Fish
and crustacea are the draw, although you'll also
find some meat dishes. Smoked haddock Parker
Bowles (the signature dish) featured a generous
slab of perfectly cooked fish and creamy mash
topped with a wobbly poached egg, while a huge

plate of top-quality Scottish smoked salmon and
scrambled eggs was an unadulterated delight.
Colchester rock oysters were superb examples of
the genre too. Don't expect fancy flavours or
modern attitudes, and you'll be fine. The wine list
isn't for the faint-hearted, and the whisky selection
must be one of London's longest and best.
*Babies and children admitted. Booking advisable.
Dress: smart casual. Separate room for parties,
seats 36.* **Map 9 J7**.

Soho

Zilli Fish
*36-40 Brewer Street, W1F 9TA (7734 8649,
www.zillialdo.com). Piccadilly Circus tube.* **Meals
served** noon-11.30pm Mon-Sat. **Main courses**
£9-£29.50. **Set dinner** (5-11.30pm Mon-Sat)
£19.50 2 courses, £24 3 courses. **Credit** AmEx,
MC, V.
Media types dominate this flagship of chef Aldo
Zilli's Soho mini-empire; the party next to us loudly
discussed a film deal. The restaurant is littered
with material publicising Zilli's books, television
appearances and master-classes. Decor is
otherwise a studiously neutral brown, although the
large picture windows allow for plenty of daylight
at lunchtime. Food is broadly Italian, in as much
as there's a selection of pasta dishes, although
main courses range alarmingly across the globe:
beer-battered cod sitting next to teriyaki-marinated
black cod. Our set dinner was disappointing.
Steamed mussels were entirely satisfactory, but a
crab salad with mango and avocado was
practically inedible: the mango jarringly sweet and
the avocado hard and unripe. To his credit, our

waiter noticed that we had barely touched the crab and swiftly offered a replacement in the form of a (much better) portobello mushroom stuffed with goat's cheese and sun-dried tomato. A main course of Italian sausage and tiger prawn ravioli was attractively spiced with ginger, but a portion of salmon with grilled vegetables was overcooked, and had a faintly metallic tang. To finish, a grim chocolate and vanilla cake tasted stale.

Babies and children welcome: high chairs. Booking advisable. Tables outdoors (2, patio). Takeaway service. **Map 17 B4.**
For branches (Signor Zilli, Zilli Café) see index.

South Kensington

Bibendum Oyster Bar

Michelin House, 81 Fulham Road, SW3 6RD (7589 1480, www.bibendum.co.uk). South Kensington tube. **Meals served** noon-10.30pm Mon-Sat; noon-10pm Sun. **Main courses** £8-£15. **Credit** AmEx, DC, MC, V.
There's an irony in the corpulent form of Bibendum, the Michelin man, looking down upon the stick-thin ladies lunching at this relaxed seafood café in the tiled foyer of the Michelin building. Oysters are what to order, with four varieties offered, including a seasonal treat of six native Colchester No.2s for £19.75. Elaborate plateaux de fruits de mer are available, but we were delighted with a large crab (in the shell) with a mustard-rich mayonnaise. Shellfish is also sold to take home, from the crustacea stall outside. The menu incorporates salads and lighter dishes too: gravadlax or smoked salmon perhaps, or maybe roll-mops with crème fraîche and onion salad. Non-piscivores have the likes of egg mayonnaise, or the house terrine, and there are daily-changing specials. Veal polpettone meatballs with penne was let down by oddly crispy pasta. Desserts are excellent renditions of classics, like our crème brûlée. You can also order nibbles (crostini, a charcuterie plate) to accompany drinks from the concise wine list, which offers house wines by the glass or 469ml carafe. Vinophiles might prefer to choose from the impressive (if pricey) full list from the first-floor Bibendum restaurant (*see p219*), which is also available here.
Available for hire. Babies and children welcome: high chairs. Bookings not accepted. Tables outdoors (6, terrace). **Map 14 E10.**

Poissonnerie de l'Avenue

82 Sloane Avenue, SW3 3DZ (7589 2457, www.poissonneriedelavenue.co.uk). South Kensington tube. **Lunch served** noon-3pm Mon-Sat; noon-4pm Sun. **Dinner served** 7-11.30pm Mon-Sat; 7-11pm Sun. **Main courses** £12.50-£28. **Set lunch** £14 1 course, £20 2 courses, £26 3 courses. **Cover** £2. **Credit** AmEx, DC, MC, V.
You get the sense that little has changed at Poissonnerie de l'Avenue since it opened in 1964. With its wood panelling, thick carpet and nautical prints, the place appears to be stuck in a time-warp. Many of the elderly clientele have been patrons since the beginning, but a long menu that was once a favourite of the Swinging London set (you can well imagine Mick Jagger bumping into Mary Quant here) has become a caricature. Although fish is sourced from the attached fishmonger, a starter of mackerel tartare was oily and lifeless (and came with toasted white-sliced bread). Lobster linguine was light on the crustacean and featured a huge portion of overcooked noodles. Mains were little better: a mushy salmon fish cake, and deep-fried goujons of plaice with a cherry-tomato relish that matched a ketchup-like consistency with unpleasant chunks of raw garlic. The wine list too belongs to another era (though at the higher end there are some outstanding bargains); of the 36 whites on the French-dominated, predictable list, only four move beyond chardonnay or sauvignon blanc. The waiting staff seemed uninterested, yet took home a 15% service charge.
Babies and children welcome (babies admitted lunch only). Booking advisable dinner. Dress: smart casual. Separate room for parties, seats 20. Tables outdoors (4, pavement). **Map 14 E10.**

West
Chiswick

★ Fish Hook

6-8 Elliott Road, W4 1PE (8742 0766, www.fishhook.co.uk). Turnham Green tube. **Lunch served** noon-2.30pm Mon-Fri; noon-3.30pm Sat, Sun. **Dinner served** 6-10.30pm Mon-Sat; 6-10pm Sun. **Main courses** £17-£29. **Set lunch** £12.50 2 courses, £15 3 courses. **Credit** AmEx, MC, V.
Chef-patron Michael Nadra delivers outstanding value to savvy locals with his imaginative yet sensible menus. During a relaxed Saturday lunch, the atmosphere in the dining room was convivial; the painted wood panelling and fish-themed photographs help emphasise that Fish Hook aims beyond the usual repertoire of piscine classics. At just £15 for three courses the set lunch menu is a bargain, particularly considering the generous portions. A light velouté of pea and asparagus was given texture by crunchy whitebait tempura. Black forest ham with celeriac remoulade was a more traditional combination, dominated by the smoky cure of the ham. The kitchen is at home with luxurious textures, like the rich mashed potato and crustacean-sweet bisque sauce served with a fillet of sea bream. Another main course of crisp and well-seasoned deep-fried hake playfully subverted mushy peas with its garnish of fresh peas and broad beans. Pain perdu with blueberry mousse, and a refreshing yoghurt sorbet, rounded

Ark Fish Restaurant. See p88.

things off nicely. In the evenings prices rise (although they're still good value) and more luxury ingredients come into play – so soft-shell crab, lobster, foie gras and truffles are all possibilities.
Babies and children admitted. Booking advisable.

Notting Hill

Geales (100)

2 Farmer Street, W8 7SN (7727 7528, www.geales.com). Notting Hill Gate tube. **Lunch served** noon-2.30pm Tue-Fri. **Dinner served** 6-10.30pm Mon-Fri. **Meals served** noon-10.30pm Sat; noon-9.30pm Sun. **Main courses** £8-£17. **Credit** AmEx, MC, V.
Once an upmarket chippie, Geales has been a highly regarded destination for what feels like centuries. You needn't come looking for exotic species or even fancy cooking, but you will find good classic dishes, served in simple smart premises. The interior is painted throughout in an austere, battleship grey with black trim. What colour there is comes from a sturdy oak floor. The chef's only glance beyond these shores is towards the Continent, with steamed mussels and a good, sweet-tasting, tomatoey fish soup bearing a cappuccino-like froth. Otherwise it's oysters, smoked salmon and prawn cocktail. You can enjoy a gorgeous ribeye steak, but it would be a shame not to try the fish pie: a chunky salmon, prawn and pea composition in a neat glazed trough. Likewise, the batter on five kinds of white fish was faultlessly crisp. A £2.95 charge is made for side dishes, so costs can rack up, but spinach was al dente and the chips had clearly benefited from an infernally hot fryer. Desserts, including crumble and steamed chocolate sponge pudding, confirm the fine British pedigree of the cooking. Only the intelligently arranged wine list is allowed to go globe-trotting.
Babies and children welcome: children's menu. Booking advisable Fri, Sat. Separate room for parties, seats 12. Tables outdoors (6, pavement). Takeaway service. **Map 7 A7.**

South West
Fulham

★ Deep

The Boulevard, Imperial Wharf, SW6 2UB (7736 3337, www.deeplondon.co.uk). Fulham Broadway tube then 391, C3 bus. *Bar* **Open/snacks served** 9am-3pm Mon-Fri; 10am-3pm Sun. **Snacks** £4-£11.50. *Restaurant* **Meals served** 7-11pm Wed, Thur, Sat; 5-11pm Fri. **Main courses** £14.50-£26.50. *Both* **Credit** AmEx, MC, V.
With floor-to-ceiling windows and cream upholstery, Deep is a monument to Scandinavian minimalism stranded in the heart of the soulless Imperial Wharf development. On our visit there were only four other people dining. Nonetheless, charming front-of-house staff made everyone welcome. Food is impressive, both in ambition and execution. While shellfish (oysters, mussels, lobster) is available at market price, the best food reflects the Swedish origins of owners Kerstin and Christian Sandefeldt. It's refreshing for once to leave the Med and sample fish cookery from more northerly climes. The meal started well, with lovely fennel crisp-bread and an amuse-bouche of creamy mussel soup. Presentation reflects Deep's lofty aspirations: three prosciutto-wrapped turrets of green beans were each topped with a thin escalope of sautéed monkfish. The dish of the evening, however, was a starter consisting of three little pots of cured herrings (pickled, with mustard, and in a creamy sauce) served with potato salad and a chunk of Montgomery's farmhouse cheddar. Scandinavian flavours continued with the garnish of prawns, chopped egg and horseradish with a slab of just-cooked steamed halibut; a hot-smoked trout with buttery braised lentils was prosaic by comparison. Technical skill is also evident in the puddings: witness a textbook baked alaska.
Babies and children welcome: high chairs. Booking advisable. Disabled: toilet. Dress: smart casual. Entertainment: music 7pm Fri (bar). Tables outdoors (14, terrace). **Map 21 A2.**

Richmond

FishWorks

13-19 The Square, Richmond, Surrey TW9 1EA (8948 5965, www.fishworks.co.uk). **Lunch served** noon-3pm. **dinner served** 6-10.30pm Mon-Fri. **Meals served** noon-10.30pm Sat, Sun. **Main courses** £9.50-£25. **Set lunch** £12.50 2 courses. **Credit** AmEx, MC, V.

FishWorks was bought out of administration in January 2009 and the new owners have kept only the best-performing sites. There are now just

---

SHELF LIFE

Restaurants in the **FishWorks** chain (*see above*) have a wet fish counter attached, as do **Fish Club** (*see p300*) and **Kensington Place** (*see p222*).

Steve Hatt

88-90 Essex Road, N1 8LU (7226 3963). Angel tube. **Open** 8am-5pm Tue-Thur; 7am-5pm Fri, Sat.

A family business dating back to 1895, this esteemed fishmonger is renowned for expert gutting and filleting, as well as authoritative advice on cooking. Haddock, trout, mackerel and kippers are smoked on the premises and very popular.

Golborne Fisheries

75-77 Golborne Road, W10 5NP (8960 3100). Ladbroke Grove tube. **Open** 9am-5pm Tue-Thur; 8am-6pm Fri, Sat.

A great choice for exotic lines such as fresh abalone, live eels, conch meat, clams and frogs' legs – all at keen prices.

Moxon's

17 Bute Street, SW7 3EY (7591 0050, www.moxonsfreshfish.com). South Kensington tube. **Open** 8.30am-7.30pm Tue-Fri, 8.30am-5.30pm Sat.

A third branch from the much-loved fishmongers of East Dulwich and Clapham. Salmon comes from reputable farm Loch Duart, crabs from the Isle of Wight, and plenty of good stuff from Kent, Sussex and Cornwall.

Walter Purkis & Sons

17 The Broadway, N8 8DU (8340 6281, www.purkis4fish.com). W7 bus. **Open** 8.30am-5pm Tue-Sat.

This long-established family business has a 100-year-old smokehouse where buckling, sardines, spratts and cod's roe are smoked, as well as the more common salmon, mackerel and haddock. Stock comes from all the UK's major fishing ports, from Aberdeenshire to Cornwall. There is a branch in Muswell Hill.

Sandy's

56 King Street, Twickenham, Middx TW1 3SH (8892 5788, www.sandys fish.net). Twickenham rail. **Open** 7.30am-6pm Mon-Wed, Sat; 7.30am-8pm Thur; 7.30am-7pm Fri.

Sandy's is a large store but even so attracts long queues at weekends. You'll find a huge selection of attractively displayed fish and shellfish, plus cheeses and meats, including game in season.

three branches in London, although the formula remains much the same: a small fishmonger's shop at the front, a seafood café round the back. The Richmond branch is a useful addition to the local scene, and the corporate colour scheme of blue and white gives the high-ceilinged dining room an airy, open feel. Simple preparations are great here, but on our visit the food suffered from timid seasoning in the kitchen. Crab cakes were lacking in vitality and their chilli sauce was cloyingly sweet; a seafood cocktail was bland but inoffensive. Main courses continued the theme: skate with black butter and capers was a perfectly capable rendition of a classic, but zuppa del pescatore was insipid, the broth lacking the advertised punch of saffron and garlic. The short wine list concentrates on styles best-suited to piscine flavours, sticking with whites and light reds, organised by price, most cost below £30. In all, FishWorks has a sound concept, but the pricing remains ambitious for a chain restaurant.
Available for hire. Babies and children welcome: high chairs. Booking advisable weekends. Disabled: toilet. For branches see index.

South East

London Bridge & Borough

fish!

Cathedral Street, SE1 9AL (7407 3801, www.fish diner.co.uk). London Bridge tube/rail. **Meals served** 11.30am-11pm Mon-Thur; noon-11pm Fri, Sat; noon-10.30pm Sun. **Main courses** £9.95-£26.95. **Credit** AmEx, DC, MC, V.

On weekday lunchtimes, this swanky glass pavilion overlooking Southwark Cathedral and Borough Market is full of suits and well-heeled tourists. The interior is all hard surfaces under a tall ceiling, so business secrets can be shouted aloud in safety, barely heard even by the ears for which they were intended. It's noisy, but staff are friendly, the views are pretty, and sitting at the long bar overlooking the open kitchen is fun. The restaurant prides itself on using sustainable raw ingredients from trusted suppliers like its own fishmonger, Jarvis, in Surrey. At the core of the menu is a long list of fish – organic salmon, skate, tuna, lemon sole, Icelandic cod, plaice, and more, with seasonal specials too – which you can have steamed or grilled and served with a choice of dressing. Or there's great old-fashioned fish and chips (at modern prices). The mushy peas are among the finest we've tasted. We were surprised to find mushrooms in the 'Classic Fish Pie', but were satisfied nonetheless with its rich flavour and buttery mash crust. Takeaway fish and chips can be bought from the kiosk to the side of the restaurant for half the price.
Babies and children welcome: children's menu; crayons; high chairs. Booking advisable. Disabled: toilet. Tables outdoors (27, terrace). **Map 11 P8.**

Wright Brothers Oyster & Porter House

11 Stoney Street, SE1 9AD (7403 9554, www.wrightbros.eu.com). Borough tube/London Bridge tube/rail. **Lunch served** noon-3pm Mon-Fri; noon-4pm Sat. **Dinner served** 6-10pm Mon-Sat. **Main courses** £7.30-£25.50. **Credit** AmEx, MC, V.

A visit to this showcase outlet of London's foremost oyster supplier is akin to a forage around Borough market, on whose periphery it's located: sensually stimulating, holding out the promise of perfection, but busy, brash and curiously graceless at prime times. It's a handsome enough venue, yet never deviates from the business of serving fresh seafood: all seating is on bar stools, either at wooden bar tables or a gleaming strip of steel; blackboards list menu essentials and daily specials; waiters veer between fiercely efficient and fleetingly smiling. Food sampled on a recent visit was faultless. Deep-fried oysters proved particularly impressive: a hot, crisp-crumbed batter enclosing baby-soft bivalves. Griddled scallops remained translucent at centre; sauces were spot on; and salads were young and sprightly. Prosecco and picpoul by the glass are among the

more affordable alternatives to expense-account champagne. Alternatively, savour Meantime Brewery's robust, excellent stout or porter. Tap water was served swiftly, without objection. Chance on an open french-window spot by the bar on a sunny day and you could linger a while, but be prepared for a City-boy crush. That said, lone diners who love shellfish might consider this an inconspicuous corner of heaven.
Booking advisable. Disabled: toilet. Tables outdoors (3, pavement). **Map 11 P8.**

East

Docklands

Curve

London Marriott, West India Quay, 22 Hertsmere Road, E14 4ED (7093 1000 ext 2622, www.marriotthotels.com). Canary Wharf tube/DLR/West India Quay DLR. **Breakfast served** 6.30-11am Mon-Fri; 7-11am Sat, Sun. **Lunch served** noon-2.30pm daily. **Dinner served** 5-10.30pm Mon-Sat; 5-10pm Sun. **Main courses** £10.50-£22. **Credit** AmEx, DC, MC, V.

Located on the ground floor of the Docklands' Marriott, Curve is, perhaps unsurprisingly, slightly corporate in feel, though it benefits from views over the water. The clientele is also a little staid. The menu contains plenty of seafood and fish, and a handy 'mix and match' option: choose your fish, way of cooking (grilled, pan-fried, and so on), then your sauce (coriander and chilli, garlic and mustard). A Pacific prawn starter in a tangy sauce of curry leaves and mustard seeds was excellent, but 'mix and match' haddock disappointed: three rather bland and weedy fillets that didn't marry with the flavours of the sauce. A chunky piece of salmon with a jalapeño and tomato sauce was better. Side dishes didn't impress: spinach was overcooked, and the paprika chunky chips arrived plain and unappetising. The confusing wine menu lists half-bottles before full-sized, so a seemingly reasonably priced Pouilly Fumé (£17.50) was in fact £33. The attractive location makes Curve a fair option for Docklanders and hotel guests, but don't cross town for it.
Babies and children welcome: children's menu: crayons; high chairs. Booking advisable. Disabled: toilet (in hotel). Tables outdoors (10, terrace).

North East

South Woodford

Ark Fish Restaurant

142 Hermon Hill, E18 1QH (8989 5345, www.arkfishrestaurant.com). South Woodford tube. **Lunch served** noon-2.15pm Tue-Sat. **Dinner served** 5.30-9.45pm Tue-Thur; 5.30-10.15pm Fri, Sat. **Meals served** noon-8.45pm Sun. **Main courses** £9.75-£23.50. **Credit** MC, V.

Good fish and shellfish restaurants outside central London are a rarity, but they don't come much better than South Woodford's Ark. Maybe it's the fact that the district is full of East Enders made good. Certainly, the light-filled, airy space was packed with well-to-do couples, elegant ladies-who-lunch and even lone diners on the day we visited, suggesting a broad appeal. The simplicity and freshness of the seafood are the obvious draws: from appetisers such as whelks, winkles, venus clams and oysters (or all of them – as one man was enjoying), to daily-changing specials like deep-fried rock eel and whole plaice on the bone. Smoked sprats showed a great balance of smokiness and meatiness, neither overpowering the other, and battered haddock was simply perfect. Monkfish on mash with pesto was more of a mixed bag, the mash a little bit lumpy. A small but tempting list of traditional desserts (including bread and butter pudding), is augmented by specials with a seasonal twist, such as rhubarb crumble trifle. Everything is served by attentive, efficient staff who do a fine line in unobtrusiveness.
Babies and children welcome: children's menu; high chairs. Bookings not accepted.

Wanstead

★ Applebee's
17 Cambridge Park, E11 2PU (8989 1977, www.applebeesfish.com). Wanstead tube. **Lunch served** noon-3pm Tue-Fri. **Dinner served** 6.30-10.30pm Tue-Sat. **Meals served** noon-9pm Sun. **Main courses** £13.50-£18.50. **Set lunch** £11.50 2 courses, £15.50 3 courses. **Set dinner** £21.50 3 courses. **Credit** MC, V.

Applebee's runs a high-profile fish shop and café in Borough Market, but has the good sense to recognise that its Wanstead operation is primarily a local restaurant. The menu consequently features red meat and vegetarian choices (beetroot tart, say), and popular Sunday roasts of beef, lamb and turkey. The comfortable cream and orange dining room keeps things safely contemporary, with mosaic tiling, bamboo pendant lights and cheerful artwork. A complimentary appetiser got our meal off to a swimming start: salad of spindly baby octopus legs and rocket, served in Chinese spoons. Could the kitchen maintain this standard? Crab and avocado millefeuille didn't have quite the same verve, but we had no complaints about razor clams with chorizo and broad beans. From the specials, three generous fillets of perfectly cooked brill arrived on garicky sautéed courgettes. Barramundi (a less generous portion) was slightly overwhelmed by its red onion salad, though we liked the red peppers and balsamic that sat underneath. Best pud was a golden-yellow rhubarb crème brûlée. Friendly staff, and details such as good butter, and sliced citrus fruit in the water jugs make this the sort of place most neighbourhoods would envy. *Available for hire. Babies and children welcome: high chairs. Booking advisable dinner. Dress: smart casual. Tables outdoors (6, courtyard).* **For branch see index.**

North

Camden Town & Chalk Farm

Coast Dining NEW
108 Parkway, NW1 7AN (7267 9555, www.coast dining.co.uk). Camden Town tube. **Lunch served** noon-3pm, **dinner served** 6-11pm daily. **Main courses** £8-£21. **Set meal** £16 2 courses incl glass of wine. **Credit** AmEx, DC, MC, V.

A bright spot on busy Parkway, Coast Dining's gleaming white frontage and cool, clean-lined interior brings a welcome degree of smart informality to Camden. Owner Cornishman David Upton aims to take the restaurant down the sustainable route, avoiding threatened species such as cod, for example. Two plateau de fruits de mer are offered – one with Dorset crab, the other for an extra tenner featuring a whole split lobster. Those who don't want to eat seafood will find ribeye steaks and burgers from the chargrill, marinated chicken, vegetarian risotto, soup and maybe a salad of sea vegetables with ticklemore cheese. We enjoyed starters of grilled sardines with pesto, and tiger prawns with aioli but were a little disappointed by the comparatively ordinary fish pie (this should surely be a calling card) and soggy tagliatelle with mussels. Desserts (rhubarb-apple crumble with rhubarb and custard sorbet, banana parfait with peanut caramel) aim to please. Lovely service and details such as own-made ice-creams and chutney (which accompanies the appealing cheese plate) were impressive enough to warrant a return visit. *Babies and children welcome: high chairs. Booking advisable dinner. Separate room for parties, seats 28. Tables outdoors (2, pavement). Takeaway service.* **Map 27 C2.**

Finsbury Park

Chez Liline
101 Stroud Green Road, N4 3PX (7263 6550). Finsbury Park tube/rail. **Dinner served** noon-3pm, 6.30-11pm Tue-Sun. **Main courses** £10.95-£17.75. **Set lunch** £10 2 courses. **Set dinner** £12.50 2 courses. **Credit** AmEx, MC, V.

Fish & Grill

This reliable, homely Mauritian restaurant was looking a bit forlorn on last year's visit, so it was a pleasant surprise to find a new soft wash of light over a spruced-up interior creating a much brighter and nicer space. Locals flock here for daisy-fresh fish dishes combining Mauritius's Creole, Chinese, European and Indian influences. Our starters – a perfectly seasoned moules marinières and a generous seafood salad studded with plump clams, chunky mussels and springy squid – were delicate and fine, but the mains gloried in their lengthier acquaintance with warm spices like nutmeg, chilli, saffron and cinnamon. Creole fish assiette, a white fish tower with tomatoes and onions, was sweet and tangy; brill fillets with ginger and spring onions came in a creamy, complex curry sauce. We squeezed in Jekyll and Hyde side dishes of green beans and sweet potato (the former perfectly al dente, the latter soggy), before finishing with an eggy crème brûlée from an underwhelming dessert list. The lone white wine by the glass, a rough and ready pinot grigio, was disappointing too. Nevertheless, the starters and mains had us vowing to return before the next paint job. *Available for hire. Babies and children welcome: high chairs. Booking advisable. Tables outdoors (6, pavement). Takeaway service.*

Islington

The Fish Shop
360-362 St John Street, EC1V 4NR (7837 1199, www.thefishshop.net). Angel tube/19, 38, 341 bus. **Lunch served** noon-3pm, **dinner served** 5.30-11pm Tue-Sat. **Meals served** 11am-4pm Sun. **Main courses** £11-£21. **Set meal** (noon-3pm, 5.30-7pm Tue-Sat, all Sun) £15 2 courses, £18 3 courses. **Credit** AmEx, DC, MC, V.

Within a *pas de chat* of Sadler's Wells, the Fish Shop is a stylish, three-storey wood, steel and glass shrine to the sea world. Most diners opt for the reliably good fish and chips: a daily changing fillet (haddock, pollock, ling) served with broad bean and pea mash and hand-cut chips. Nevertheless, it's worth casting your net wider: perhaps a plate of deliciously lemony marinated anchovies served with thin slivers of toast, before a starter of succulent scallops with an artichoke purée, or a salmon and lobster raviolo topped with lemongrass and chervil velouté. Despite a bit of finagling to release the gurnard en papillote on to a plate of new potatoes and french beans, it was worth the effort; the fish was perfectly steamed and infused with rosemary, lemon and orange. Firm and tasty pan-fried sea bass also held its own when matched

with a pile of chorizo mash. The set menus are a bargain (£15 two courses, £18 three). Service is attentive but not too fussy. If you're not rushing over the road for curtain-up, enjoy the candle-lit glow and order something special from the wine list, along with a plate of British cheeses. *Available for hire. Babies and children welcome: high chairs. Booking advisable dinner Fri, Sat. Disabled: toilet. Tables outdoors (7, terrace).* **Map 5 O3.**

Outer London

Croydon, Surrey

★ Fish & Grill NEW
2009 RUNNER-UP BEST NEW LOCAL
48-50 South End, Croydon, Surrey CR0 1DP (8774 4060, www.fishandgrill.co.uk). South Croydon rail/119, 466 bus. **Meals served** noon-10.30 daily. **Main courses** £10.95-£44. **Set lunch** £11.95 2 courses, £14.95 3 courses. **Credit** AmEx, MC, V.

Chef-proprietor Malcolm John is determined to improve Croydon's culinary life. First came French outfit Le Cassoulet (*see p101*), winner of the Best Local Restaurant category in the 2008 Time Out Awards; now he's opened this fish specialist on South Croydon's restaurant row. A montage of dark brown and green, with high-backed banquettes, polished wood furniture, exposed brick and smoked mirrors, it's a handsome, masculine space: casual enough for a fish supper, smart enough for a birthday celebration. Tempting starters range from a huge seafood platter to Dorset crab salad (generous too, and super-fresh), oysters, shellfish bisque, and whitebait. Top-quality, locally sourced, simply cooked fish – served whole, on the bone, with chips and tartare sauce – is the highlight of the mains, but there's plenty of other options, including meat grills. Halibut, with perfect pearly-white flakes, came with parsley-flecked mash and crayfish butter; market coconut fish stew was subtly spiced, and crammed with fish, mussels, clams and shell-on prawns. There are a few affectations (bread served in a paper bag, chips in dinky metal pots), and service was slightly distracted, but this is a sophisticated operation in keeping with the high standards of John's other enterprises (in addition to Le Cassoulet, he runs Chiswick's Le Vacherin – *see p97*). *Available for hire. Babies and children welcome: children's menu; high chairs; nappy-changing facilities. Booking advisable Fri, Sat. Disabled: toilet. Tables outdoors (3, pavement).*

French

RESTAURANTS

London's French restaurants stretch from steakhouses and neighbourhood bistros offering onion soup, coq au vin and tarte du jour to the stellar gastronomic experiences that we list in Hotels & Haute Cuisine (see pp124-133). However it's the upper end of the mid-market that has seen the most dynamism this year with the opening of Bjorn van der Horst's **Eastside Inn Bistro** in Farringdon, and the return of Terence Conran with two restaurants, **Boundary** in Shoreditch and **Lutyens** in the City.

Classic French cooking may no longer grab the culinary headlines, but several of our favourite establishments in this chapter (among them **Galvin Bistrot de Luxe**, **La Petite Maison**, **Chez Bruce**, **La Trompette**, and **Le Comptoir Gascon**) seem as popular as ever with diners. For first-class food and wine for a very special occasion, it is still hard to beat **Club Gascon**, the **Ledbury** and **Trinity** – though, with its romantic decor, Covent Garden's **Clos Maggiore** now comes close.

Central

Belgravia

★ Le Cercle

1 Wilbraham Place, SW1X 9AE (7901 9999, www.lecercle.co.uk). Sloane Square tube.
Bar Open/snacks served noon-midnight Tue-Sat.
Restaurant Lunch served noon-3pm, **dinner served** 6-11pm Tue-Sat. **Set lunch** £15 3 dishes, £19.50 4 dishes. **Set dinner** (6-7pm) £17.50 3 dishes, £21.50 4 dishes. **Tapas** £6-£16.
Both Credit Both AmEx, MC, V.
We couldn't fault any aspect of our midweek lunch at this Sloaney outpost of the Club Gascon group. The basement room is elegant and discreet – ideal for a quiet lunch. Le Cercle's USP is small portions, essentially French tapas, which at lunchtime can be ordered as a low-cost set meal. There are few better bargains in London for gastronomic razzle-dazzle. The menu changes seasonally, but our meal gives a

sense of the style of cooking: salmon carpaccio with a delicate green salad and pickled apricot dressing; ravioles barigoule (stuffed with artichokes), sturgeon served with bordelaise sauce; meltingly tender confit ox cheek, served with a pungent black-olive paste to cut the richness; and the most perfect lozenge of guinea fowl, accompanied by fondant potato and crisp bacon. Presentation is artful, but flavour is king. There are also full-size portions of many dishes, but the lightness of three small courses at lunch is an unusually attractive alternative to many places at this level, where you often have to order a full three-course meal. There's also a tasting menu with matched wines, from a wine list that's predictably fine (Gascon restaurants always get this right) and offers fair choice in the lower price range. In short: one of the best.
Available for hire. Babies and children welcome: children's menu. Booking advisable dinner & Sat, Sun. Disabled: lift; toilet. Dress: smart casual. Separate room for parties, seats 12. Vegan dishes. **Map 15 G10.**

La Poule au Pot

231 Ebury Street, SW1W 8UT (7730 7763). Sloane Square tube. **Lunch served** 12.30-2.30pm Mon-Fri; 12.30-4pm Sat, Sun. **Dinner served** 6.45-11pm Mon-Sat; 6.45-10pm Sun. **Main courses** £15.50-£21. **Set lunch** £18.75 2 courses, £22.75 3 courses. **Credit** AmEx, DC, MC, V.
Few places scream 'Chelsea' more loudly than La Poule. The place is normally packed with smart couples discussing holiday plans in plummy accents. On a sticky summer's day, the terrace (its tables attired in starched linen) made a pleasantly fresh-aired dining venue, but the romantic interior is more atmospheric. This wooden, rustic affair features cosily arranged tables, dimmed lights and candles. Wicker baskets, dried flowers and fake grapes hang from the ceiling and from bare-brick walls. But our food was underwhelming – especially considering the high prices. A starter of rocket, grated cheese and mushrooms seemed to have come pre-prepared from the fridge, with dry rocket, unexciting cheese and oily mushrooms. Asparagus was fresh and generous, yet drenched in a thick supermarket-style vinaigrette that seemed to cover several dishes. Mains weren't much better: tuna steak was overcooked, despite being requested rare; dorade with fennel was tasty enough but unmemorable. Desserts tend to be classic (tarte tatin, chocolate mousse), and there's plenty of dessert wines and digestifs. Service was pleasant if rather inefficient (with long waits

between courses, and side dishes forgotten). So, a popular spot with people who seem to have more money than discernment.
Babies and children welcome: high chairs. Booking essential. Separate room for parties, seats 16. Tables outdoors (12, terrace). **Map 15 G11.**

Roussillon

16 St Barnabas Street, SW1W 8PE (7730 5550, www.roussillon.co.uk). Sloane Square tube. **Lunch served** noon-2.30pm Mon-Fri. **Dinner served** 6.30-10.30pm Mon-Sat. **Set lunch** £35 3 courses. **Set dinner** £55 3 courses. **Set meal** £65-£75 tasting menu. **Credit** AmEx, MC, V.
Appearing deceptively like a smart neighbourhood restaurant, Roussillon isn't for those 'let's go round the corner for supper' moments. Except, this is Belgravia, so some locals (middle aged and, at the next table, discussing money) seem to be regulars. For the rest of us, it's for occasional treats – especially for vegetarians as, unexpectedly, a meat-free menu is here in all its seasonal glory (spring vegetables in tempura with herb salad, and truffle risotto, for instance). Chef Alexis Gaultier is exceptionally good with vegetables, despite his culinary influences coming from south-west France and the seasonally changing carte being strictly for carni- and piscivores. Dishes conjure with contrasting textures, as in an utterly original starter of broccoli and cauliflower turned into a nubbly sort of risotto, with ceps giving an earthy depth and Quavers-like pork scratchings, a parmesan tuile and strips of mooli providing variations on crunch. Sharp pink micro radish leaves joined peeled grapes to accessorise halibut turned pink by its accompanying beetroot. Gorgeously pink roast meat (this time English rose veal, but sometimes lamb) with a gamey confit of shredded slow-cooked shoulder and a roast kidney (plus chard stalks and Chantenay carrots) made a rewarding main course. It takes two waiters to carry the cheese tray. Wines from Languedoc Roussillon include crisp white Picpoul Coustellier.
Booking essential dinner & Fri, Sat. **Map 15 G11.**

City

Le Coq d'Argent

No.1 Poultry, EC2R 8EJ (7395 5000, www.coqdargent.co.uk). Bank tube/DLR.
Brasserie Lunch served 11.30am-3pm Mon-Fri. **Set meal** £18 2 courses, £21.50 3 courses.
Restaurant Breakfast served 7.30-10am Mon-Fri. **Lunch served** 11.30am-3pm Mon-Fri; noon-3pm Sun. **Dinner served** 6-10pm Mon-Fri; 6.30-10pm Sat. **Main courses** £17.50-£52. **Set lunch** £24 2 courses, £29 3 courses.
Both Credit AmEx, DC, MC, V.
The Coq d'Argent is an obvious recommendation for people seeking a special-occasion venue. With a private lift that whooshes you up to the top of the No.1 Poultry centre, an outdoor terrace within a secret rooftop garden and great City views both outside and in, it ticks those 'wow factor' boxes. But the food and service, while less showy, are currently standing very well on their own merits. The French cooking veers towards Modern European/British, with a light and contemporary touch. Our lunch looked good and tasted better: prettily dressed clams with onion ceviche; bright, bold-tasting heirloom tomatoes at the peak of ripeness; prawns in just the right amount of garlic butter; notably tasty chicken in a provençal salad containing too much aubergine. Only a lifeless white chocolate vacherin let the side down. The staff were deft and friendly throughout, the sommelier happy to discuss rather than declaim. The set brasserie menu is served only at lunch; at dinner, there's a slightly more expensive prix fixe along with an à la carte; seafood is prominent throughout. There are breakfast and Sunday lunch menus, and a cocktail-capable bar that opens an outdoor outpost in summer that has customers queueing at the lift doors.
Available for hire. Babies and children welcome: high chairs. Booking advisable. Disabled: lift; toilet. Entertainment: jazz 12.30-4pm Sun. Tables outdoors (34, terrace). **Map 11 P6.**

Le Cercle

Lutyens NEW

*85 Fleet Street, EC4Y 1AE (7583 8385, www.lutyens-restaurant.co.uk). Blackfriars rail. Bar **Open** noon-midnight, **meals served** noon-9pm daily. Restaurant **Breakfast served** 7.30-10.30am, **lunch served** noon-3.30pm, **dinner served** 5.30-10pm daily. **Main courses** £12.50-£33. Both **Credit** AmEx, MC, V.*

Three years after selling off Conran Restaurants, Terence Conran is back in the restaurant business, this time with his wife Vicki Conran and partner Peter Prescott. Boundary (*see p98*) was their first, Lutyens is the follow-up, located in the classically proportioned former Reuters building. Lutyens has a familiar Conranesque feel, with a buzzy bar and more formal, hushed restaurant, complete with crustacea bar. Heading up the kitchen is David Burke, once of Pont de la Tour, who produces food based mainly on classical French cooking – coquilles st jacques, escargots, foie gras and steak tartare feature among the starters. Our lobster mousse resembled a very rich custard, moulded then garnished with a creamy sauce and slivers of lobster meat and tomato. It looked, and tasted, like something from a bygone age, but was beautifully made. Traditional French mains might include buttered lobster, suckling pig with apple sauce and crackling, and roast rabbit with bacon and mustard. Our bourride (a seafood stew) came with monkish served as one intact piece virtually 'dry', the shellfish and sauce as accompaniments – this was a Languedoc version of the dish, but tamer and less garlicky. Burke also throws in the occasional reference to his Irish roots, with dishes like crubeens (salted pigs' trotters) with a celeriac rémoulade.

Babies and children admitted. Booking advisable. Disabled: lift; toilet. Separate rooms for parties, seating 6-20. **Map 11 N6**.

1 Lombard Street

*1 Lombard Street, EC3V 9AA (7929 6611, www.1lombardstreet.com). Bank tube/DLR. Bar **Open** 11am-11pm, **tapas served** 5-11pm Mon-Fri. **Tapas** £7.50-£14.50. Brasserie **Breakfast served** 7.30-11am, **meals served** 11.30am-10pm Mon-Fri. **Main courses** £16.50-£25.50. **Set meal** £19.50 2 courses. Restaurant **Lunch served** noon-3pm, **dinner served** 6-9.45pm Mon-Fri. **Main courses** £24-£34.50. **Set meal** £32 5 courses, £45 9 courses. All **Credit** All AmEx, DC, MC, V.*

City slickers should feel right at home in this neo-classical former bank opposite the Royal Exchange. Despite shrinking bonuses, they'll probably be the only ones who can afford the prices in the haute cuisine restaurant at the rear. Fortunately, the bar-brasserie is more kindly priced. It's a grand, striking space, all cream walls and marble, with a huge domed skylight above a circular bar, surrounded by high-backed stools for drinkers. Diners eat at tables and semi-circular booths; the best spots are near the bar rather than by the entrance, which is cramped and feels far from the action. The long menu ranges from lobster to bangers and mash, including a vegetarian section. Our experience was mixed. Salade niçoise showcased quality ingredients, but a main of grilled squid with thai risotto was feebly spiced, and the squid tough and chewy. Coq au vin (from a black-leg chicken) with mash was better: tender, juicy meat, richly flavoured sauce, creamy mash – but rhubarb tarte tatin was overcooked and dry. Staff weren't quite on the ball, bringing the wrong menu and muddling dishes, but were unfailingly courteous. The French-heavy wine list offers much enjoyment, but you'll need deep pockets.

Available for hire. Booking advisable. Children over 10 admitted. Disabled: toilet. Entertainment: pianist and singer 6.30pm Fri. Separate room for parties, seats 40. **Map 12 Q6**.

Rosemary Lane

*61 Royal Mint Street, E1 8LG (7481 2602, www.rosemarylane.btinternet.co.uk). Tower Hill tube/Fenchurch Street rail/Tower Gateway DLR. **Lunch served** noon-2.30pm Mon-Fri. **Dinner served** 5.30-10pm Mon-Fri; 6-10pm Sat. **Meals served** by appointment Sun. **Main courses** £13-£19. **Set meal** £15 2 courses, £18 3 courses. **Set dinner** (Sat) £30 tasting menu. **Credit** AmEx, MC, V.*

A treasured neighbourhood restaurant at the rim of the City, Rosemary Lane is set in an old pub and retains dark wood panelling, green velvet curtains and the occasional tapestry cushion for a cosily genteel atmosphere. We love the brief list of intriguing wines – our Portuguese rosé was so dark it could almost be considered a chilled red. There is also a thoughtful selection of beers from the US and Belgium. Careful staff rush dishes down a rickety old staircase to the dining room. Unfortunately the upstairs kitchen was not performing to its usual high standards on our most recent visit. Promised soy and hoi sin flavours were missing from the lime vinaigrette served with Lincolnshire smoked eel and potato salad, putting the dish in straightforward gastropub territory despite the plump, juicy fillets of uncommonly good eel. Gritty spinach spoiled an otherwise pleasant dish of halibut with lentils and mushrooms. And to finish, the acclaimed chocolate fondant was burnt, though we consoled ourselves with the lovely valencia orange ice-cream that accompanied. In all, the best dish was a simple salad of smoked chorizo, heirloom beetroots (including yellow beets), rocket and parmesan, though presentation was hardly slick. Saturday nights see guests offered a tasting menu in addition to the à la carte.

Available for hire. Babies and children admitted. Booking advisable lunch. Dress: smart casual. **Map 12 S7**.

Rosemary Lane. See p91.

Sauterelle

Royal Exchange, EC3V 3LR (7618 2483, www.danddlondon.com). Bank tube/DLR. **Lunch served** noon-2.30pm, **dinner served** 6-10pm Mon-Fri. **Main courses** £14-£35. **Set dinner** £18 2 courses, £21 3 courses. **Credit** AmEx, DC, MC, V.

This attractive restaurant, perched on the mezzanine level of the Royal Exchange, has seen several changes of chef with attendant changes in style. At present, the chef's name is Robin Gill – and we hope he stays for a long time, as our meal was the best we've eaten here. Gill likes an attractive picture on the plate, and isn't averse to exoticism (think lemon wasabi sorbet), but mostly he likes to make everything taste honestly and forthrightly of itself. Careful sourcing of raw materials was exemplified in the fabulous fresh peas and Sicilian tomatoes in a delightful risotto of spring vegetables. Flavour profiles can be delicate, as in lovely starters of heritage-potato vichyssoise, and marinated mackerel (which featured the wasabi sorbet), or robust and rustic, as in another starter of braised ham-hock salad. Pudding, poached apple with an olive oil and pistachio cake and apple sorbet, was the best dish of the meal – and that's saying a lot. Service was accomplished and attentive (perhaps occasionally a little too attentive), keeping things moving at the right pace. Wine starts at under £20, offering solid quality for well under £30. The set dinner is one of London's best bargains.
Babies and children admitted. Booking advisable. Disabled: toilet. **Map 12 Q6.**

Clerkenwell & Farringdon

Café du Marché

22 Charterhouse Square, Charterhouse Mews, EC1M 6AH (7608 1609, www.cafedumarche.co.uk). Barbican tube/Farringdon tube/rail.
Le Café **Lunch served** noon-2.30pm Mon-Fri. **Dinner served** 6-10pm Mon-Sat. **Set meal** £33.85 3 courses.
Le Grenier **Lunch served** noon-2.30pm Mon-Fri. **Dinner served** 7-10pm Mon-Sat. **Set meal** £33.85 3 courses.
Le Rendezvous **Lunch served** noon-2.30pm Mon-Fri. **Main courses** £9-£16.
All **Credit** All MC, V.
Set in a former warehouse on an idyllic alleyway off Charterhouse Square, Café du Marché is divided into three separate eateries: Le Café is the smartest and most atmospheric, with a pared-down country-meets-city aesthetic (bare brick walls, starched

white tablecloths, original wooden floors, candles), and a jazz pianist to set the sophisticated but warm tone. The romantic location is popular with couples; customers tends toward the 'lawyer with a house in the Dordogne' type. The fixed-price three-course à la carte (the only option) features a nice balance of French provincial dishes. We opted for soupe du jour (vegetable), and purple-sprouting broccoli with hollandaise for starters. Entrecôte, for a main, came with roquefort-buttered spinach and crispy new spuds, while the swordfish daily special arrived with ratatouille. Dishes were beautifully presented and near faultless – save for the rather stringy swordfish. Chocolate mousse to follow was deliciously rich and appropriately small. The wine list (almost exclusively French) provides a satisfying read for oenophiles. Professional, pleasant staff deserve the hefty ('optional') 15% service charge. Complimentary extras such as a large salad bowl with the mains and constantly refilled bread baskets reinforce the feeling of being well looked after.
Babies and children admitted. Booking advisable (not accepted Le Rendezvous). Entertainment (Le Café): jazz duo 8pm Mon-Thur; pianist 8pm Fri, Sat. Separate rooms for parties, seating 35 and 65. **Map 5 O5.**

★ Club Gascon (100)

57 West Smithfield, EC1A 9DS (7796 0600, www.clubgascon.com). Barbican tube/Farringdon tube/rail. **Lunch served** noon-2pm Mon-Fri. **Dinner served** 7-10pm Mon-Thur; 7-10.30pm Fri, Sat. **Dishes** £8-£28. **Set lunch** £18-£28 3 courses. **Set meal** £48 5 courses (£75 incl wine). **Credit** AmEx, MC, V.
From the peeled grapes and two butters – bloody mary or smoked salt flavour – nothing comes as nature intended at this cherished restaurant. Mostly it's far better. Sometimes (as with the butter) it seems like unnecessary interference. Plates are rarely round, but designed for each dish: even the intricate pre-course freebies, like the blob of escabeche with flecks of seaweed, wisps of foam and a parchment-thin crisp dusted with dried, powdered capsicum skin. This condiment appeared again on foie gras carpaccio, which was arranged like rose petals with slivers of pink artichoke leaves and tiny sweet pearls of fresh ginger. Characteristic of south-west France, whence come many of the wines, foie gras and other fowl parts such as duck hearts are a speciality. But with the likes of red saké marinated scallop, piquillos coulis and icy watermelon, scaled down to be eaten as one of several tapas-sized

dishes, expect much more than classic Gascon cooking, plus some wild (but never wayward) flavours. Desserts are often refreshingly sharp and fruit-driven, exemplified by a plate riffing on green apples: ice-cream, purée, dinky doughnut and apple snow. Petits fours come festooned on a coral-like tree. The room has a subtle lustre, partially retaining the faded charm of its former life as a tea house. Service is French and professional.
Available for hire. Booking essential. **Map 11 O5.**

Le Comptoir Gascon

61-63 Charterhouse Street, EC1M 6HJ (7608 0851, www.comptoirgascon.com). Farringdon tube/rail. **Lunch served** noon-2pm Tue-Fri. **Brunch served** 10.30am-2.30pm Sat. **Dinner served** 7-10pm Tue, Wed, Sat; 7-10.30pm Thur, Fri. **Main courses** £7.50-£13.50. **Credit** AmEx, MC, V.
The bistro offshoot of Club Gascon is a deservedly popular spot. A small, convivial brick-lined room that doubles as a deli, it offers the over-30s refuge on a street lined with raucous bars and clubs. Even more importantly, the food is great, and very nicely priced; most main courses hover around £12. 'Humble beginnings' saw three exemplary starters: piggy treats (a fine selection of cured ham and sausages), potted duck rillettes (rich but not overly fatty) and fromage blanc provençale, a bland-sounding dish that's anything but, served with crisp flatbreads. Splendid, taste-packed mains of grilled lamb with confit vegetables, beef onglet with sauce bordelaise and sautéed baby squid with 'barleysotto' and piquillos brought only praise, apart from the slightly too salty bordelaise. Sides are worth ordering, especially the mighty french fries cooked in duck fat; the juicy, lemony greens are good too. Try own-made ice-creams for pudding, or gascon mess if you like meringue that's slightly chewy. There's a short but interesting (and ever-evolving) choice of wines. Saturday brunch features a 'full French' (two fried eggs, toulouse sausage, bacon, beans and tomato) and croissants alongside regular mains. Service veers from friendly to froid, but is always efficient.
Babies and children welcome: high chairs. Booking advisable. Tables outdoors (4, pavement). **Map 11 O5.**

Eastside Inn Bistro `NEW`

40 St John Street, EC1M 4AY (7490 9240, www.esilondon.com). Farringdon tube/rail. **Lunch served** noon-2.30pm, **snacks served** 2.30-7pm, **dinner served** 7-10pm Tue-Sat. **Main courses** £13-£20. **Credit** AmEx, MC, V.

This is the more affordable side of chef-proprietor Bjorn van der Horst's twin restaurant, the other being Gastro (see p98). It's styled to look like a modern French bistro, with a rather insipid toffee-toned interior, and might pass for one if the dishes weren't priced so eyebrow-raisingly high: on our visit you could pay £3.25 for a bowl of radishes, or £11.95 for a niçoise salad starter. Instead, a baby squid à la Basquaise was a simple grill of tender tentacle and body that still retained some bite, accompanied by grilled peppers with a pleasing smoked paprika tang. Portion sizes are not for the robust of appetite – this place is for City brokers after all, not Smithfield porters. An individual bowl of cassoulet resembled a posh ready meal, with its tidy breadcrumb crust and absence of any rough edges or challenging meats. Spit-roasted 'short rib' of beef was a cut of meat that had been slow-cooked for hours before being spit-roasted just prior to serving, presumably to give depth of flavour; the accompanying baby gem salad added lightness to an otherwise heavy, wintery dish. Puds include ice-cream sundae and crème brûlée. For reliably unadventurous French cooking, the Bistro's the place. But for more show and sparkle, try Gastro, on the other side of the kitchen divide. *Babies and children admitted. Booking advisable. Separate room for parties, seats 20.* **Map 5 O5.**

Covent Garden

★ Clos Maggiore

33 King Street, WC2E 8JD (7379 9696, www. closmaggiore.com). Covent Garden or Leicester Square tube. **Lunch served** noon-3pm daily. **Dinner served** 5-11pm Mon-Sat; 5-10.30pm Sun. **Main courses** £15.50-£21.50. **Set lunch** (Mon-Fri) £19.50 3 courses or 2 courses incl half bottle of wine; (Sat, Sun) £24.50 2 courses incl half bottle of wine. **Set meal** £55 tasting menu. **Credit** AmEx, MC, V.
Is this restaurant home to London's greatest set meal? Close by Covent Garden piazza, a Georgian townhouse opens into another world – that of provincial France – which is on visitors' radar thanks to the *Wine Spectator* award-winning 2000-bin list, but is less well known to Londoners. Tables and comfortable chairs are spread between a clubby room lined with glass cabinets of digestifs and faux clipped hedges, and an enchanting sky-lit courtyard where a fire burns after dark. Though prime ingredients are British (Welsh lamb, Scotch beef, Isle of Wight crab, English rhubarb) cooking is provençal, wholeheartedly embracing shellfish, meat (a porky main-course plate fielded belly, succulent roast meat, air-dried ham in a sandwich, and black pudding) and cheese. There are, however, good vegetarian choices. Ballotines and stuffings are beautifully done, as in squid stuffed with rice and provençal vegetables on a slick of tapenade. Artichoke, sea bass, lobster and a herby finger of the roe with leeks and dill in a shellfish sauce was another outstanding starter on the faultlessly generous prix fixe, culminating in peerless crème brûlée with strawberry ice-cream. The wine list contains verticals of first-growth Bordeaux and Burgundies and Grand Crus galore, but plenty for less than £30, and wines by the glass aren't extortionate. Service is terrific; staff are numerous and the maître d' is ex-Gavroche. Fabulous. *Babies and children welcome: high chairs. Booking advisable; essential weekends, 3 wks in advance for conservatory. Separate room for parties, seats 25. Tables outdoors (6, conservatory). Vegetarian menu.* **Map 18 D4.**

Mon Plaisir

21 Monmouth Street, WC2H 9DD (7836 7243, www.monplaisir.co.uk). Covent Garden tube. **Meals served** noon-11.15pm Mon-Fri; 5.45-11.15pm Sat. **Main courses** £13.95-£22. **Set lunch** £14.50 2 courses, £16.50 3 courses. **Set meal** (5.45-7pm Mon-Sat; after 10pm Mon-Thur) £13.50 2 courses, £15.50 3 courses incl glass of wine and coffee. **Credit** AmEx, MC, V.
Family-owned Mon Plaisir trumpets its status as 'London's oldest French restaurant', but it could also claim to be the city's most quintessential – if French restaurants are based on an Edith Piaf

infused cliché. Original Ricard signs and red-and-white checked tablecloths set the scene in the original room at the front (open since the 1940s); the menus feature classic dishes (alongside more innovative creations); there's an all-French wine list and an impressive cheeseboard; and staff have such thick accents you might wonder if they're playing a role. Things are less OTT in the three other rooms, added in the 1970s and '80s, but Francophiles will still be in their element. Our meal was satisfying throughout (think small portions but rich flavours) if not especially memorable, with starters of herrings and blinis followed by coq au vin, and monkfish with herb risotto and sautéed mushrooms. Nice touches such as very fresh, crusty bread, various carafe sizes for house wine, and a friendly maître d', help explain the loyal clientele. The brasserie menu, encompassing everything from onion soup to steak frites via escargots, is better value than the carte, and worth considering for a late lunch (available 2.15-5.45pm). *Babies and children admitted: high chairs. Booking advisable. Separate room for parties, seats 25.* **Map 18 L6.**

Fitzrovia

Elena's L'Étoile

30 Charlotte Street, W1T 2NG (7636 7189, www.elenasletoile.co.uk). Goodge Street or Tottenham Court Road tube. **Lunch served** noon-2.30pm Mon-Fri. **Dinner served** 6-10.30pm Mon-Sat. **Main courses** £15.75-£20.25. **Set meal** £19 2 courses, £22 3 courses. **Credit** AmEx, DC, MC, V.
Now aged 89, Elena Salvoni, the legendary doyenne of maître d's, still makes an appearance every lunchtime, and life continues at the same mannered pace. Highly alert waiters glide about the narrow, mustard-yellow dining room (leaving little scope for dawdling over dinner). The interior remains resolutely unchanged, with its red velvet chairs, glinting silverware and sea of autographed celebrity photographs on the walls (Ella Fitzgerald, Ginger Rogers and more). The menu mostly plays it safe with upmarket comfort food: salmon and leek fish cake with mushy peas, say, or linguine with broad beans and truffle oil (the creamy richness tempered by a dash of lemon). Despite unimpeachable ingredients, a chicory, chorizo and asparagus salad, topped with a perfectly poached egg, lacked cohesion, while lamb confit needed a sharper foil than smooth, buttery mash and a cream-heavy sauce dotted with capers that were unusually lacking in flavour. However, for the classics, the kitchen rarely falters; accompanied by crisp slivers of onion and bacon and abundant mustard mash, calf's liver in a sage crust was precision-cooked, deliciously yielding and unapologetically rich. Traditional desserts (tarte tatin, crème brûlée, or sumptuously smooth two-tone chocolate mousse) round things off in calorific fashion. *Babies and children admitted. Booking advisable; essential lunch. Separate rooms for parties, seating 10, 16 and 32.* **Map 9 J5.**

Knightsbridge

Racine (100)

239 Brompton Road, SW3 2EP (7584 4477). Knightsbridge or South Kensington tube/14, 74 bus. **Lunch served** noon-3pm Mon-Fri; noon-3.30pm Sat, Sun. **Dinner served** 6-10.30pm Mon-Sat; 6-10pm Sun. **Main courses** £12.50-£20.75. **Set meal** (lunch, 6-7.30pm) £17.50 2 courses, £19.50 3 courses. **Credit** AmEx, MC, V.
Racine is usually a firm favourite of ours – from the moment we walk through the velvet curtains and take a seat on the dark leather banquettes, to the time we leave, having paid a bill that's not cheap but is good value. But this time we felt less certain. The lighting, usually subdued, was positively dim, with little to reflect off the mirrors on the side walls. Perhaps temporary scaffolding next door didn't help. More pointedly, the clientele was less varied than usual; the small groups were almost exclusively male and monied, contributing to an atmosphere that seemed old-fashioned rather than

RESTAURANTS

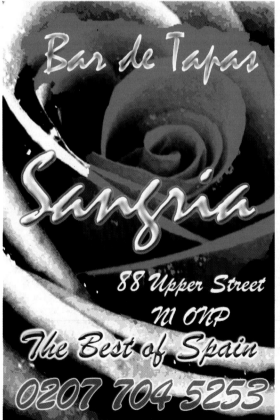

confidently retro. There was still plenty to enjoy from the menu: a garlic and saffron mousse starter with mussels stood out, delicate, yellow and spring-like; a dessert, clafoutis with morello cherries in kirsch, was pleasantly eggy. Lentils with pork (petit salé) was deeply flavoured, but the accompanying choucroute, though tangy, had us reaching for tap water to counter the salt – as did a simple confit duck leg. Our French waiter was attentive, yet slightly nervous and not quite so well informed about the menu as others have been. Surely a temporary blip?

Available for hire. Babies and children welcome: high chairs. Booking essential. Dress: smart casual. Separate room for parties, seats 18. Map 14 E10.

Marylebone

Galvin Bistrot de Luxe

66 Baker Street, W1U 7DJ (7935 4007, www.galvinrestaurants.com). Baker Street tube. **Lunch served** noon-2.30pm Mon-Sat; noon-3.30pm Sun. **Dinner served** 6-10.30pm Mon-Wed; 6-10.45pm Thur-Sat; 6-9.30pm Sun. **Main courses** £11.50-£21. **Set lunch** £15.50 3 courses. **Set dinner** (6-7pm) £17.50 3 courses. **Credit** AmEx, MC, V.

Stepping into this dark-panelled restaurant – alive with the convivial sounds of laughter and urbane conversation – is just charming. A place for business lunches it may be, as testified by the number of suits, but the absence of any stiffness makes it equally suitable for a fun meet-up with friends. The cooking is superb. We began with a simple but perfect salad of endives, roquefort, pear and roasted walnuts, and a marvellous Dorset crab lasagne dressed in beurre nantais speckled prettily with chives. A piece of sea bass was crisp-skinned and tender, served with octopus tossed into a salad with Italian parsley and capers. Equally good was the pithivier of quail and wood-pigeon: a very beautiful pastry filled with pork and game-bird, served with a soothing carrot purée and Madeira sauce. Given such fabulous food, we were bemused by the offhand service. The two of us were accidentally shown on arrival to different, distant tables, where we languished for 15 minutes before anyone realised what had happened. An honest mistake this, but it was followed by an inexplicably long wait for bread and menus, and a yawning gap between starters and mains. Out of character? We hope so.

Babies and children welcome: high chairs. Booking advisable. Disabled: toilet. Separate room for parties, seats 22. Tables outdoors (3, pavement). Map 9 G5.

Le Relais de Venise l'entrecôte

120 Marylebone Lane, W1U 2QG (7486 0878, www.relaisdevenise.com). Bond Street tube. **Lunch served** noon-2.30pm Mon-Thur; noon-2.45pm Fri; 12.30-3.30pm Sat, Sun. **Dinner served** 6-10.45pm Mon-Fri; 6.30-10.45pm Sat; 6.30-10.30pm Sun. **Set meal** £19 2 courses. **Credit** AmEx, MC, V.

How we love having decisions made for us. You can't book for this successful pastiche of a Parisian steak frites joint and there's barely any choice. Not when it comes to starters – a salad of soft lettuce leaves, scanty chopped walnuts and a sharp, mustardy vinaigrette. Plus baguette, but no butter. You're asked how you like your steak cooked. The wine list is short and there's a handful of puddings including crème brûlée, ice-creams, sorbets and lemon tart. But at 7pm on a week-night, the joint has queues outside. It's a shrewd operation. No reservations means tables are always full, and no time is wasted deliberating over a menu. Orders are scribbled on the paper table covers, and nippy, pretty French waitresses in cute black-and-white uniforms get the job done. Don't expect to linger: not that you'd want to on the hard wooden chairs. Cleverly too, staff hold back some meat and frites so you can have hot seconds. The two little lemon tarts for pudding seem generous. It's all well done (or rare if that's your choice) and thoroughly enjoyable. The meat is great, the sauce moreish, and the wine in carafes slips down all too easily, raising the bill to more than you might have bargained for.

Babies and children welcome: high chairs. Bookings not accepted. Disabled: toilet. Tables outdoors (3, pavement). Map 9 G5. For branch see index.

The Wallace

Wallace Collection, Hertford House, Manchester Square, W1U 3BN (7563 9505, www.thewallacerestaurant.com). Bond Street tube. *Café* **Meals served** 10am-4.30pm daily. *Restaurant* **Lunch served** noon-3pm Mon-Fri; noon-3.30pm Sat, Sun. **Dinner served** 5-9.30pm Fri, Sat. **Main courses** £14.50-£21.50. *Both* **Credit** AmEx, DC, MC, V.

Occupying the glass-roofed courtyard in the middle of a wonderful townhouse gallery, this spacious, gracious-looking restaurant is filled with wrought-iron chairs and potted (plastic, mind you) trees. With the café menu of croissants and omelettes replaced at midday by a serious lunch, we struggled to find much for the light of wallet or appetite. We also struggled to attract the attention of desultory staff. Nobody asked if we'd like to order wine from the France-wide list. God knows, we needed a decent drink. An uninspiring, poorly seasoned sea bass on an oily mush of peppers and capers would have been disappointing at half the price. Filo mushroom parcel was also greasy, over-browned and unappetisingly accompanied by slices of aubergine and spinach, diced cucumber, raw onion and more capers. Depressingly, the side order of spinach pretentiously served in a copper pan was the only bright spot in a lacklustre meal. Poire belle hélène was as syrupy a confection as one of the Fragonard paintings in the gallery – and with overcooked pear and synthetic-tasting chocolate sauce, less skilfully executed. A pretty sorry picture then, yet the Wallace has delighted several times in the past.

Available for hire. Babies and children welcome: children's menu; high chairs. Booking advisable. Disabled: lift; toilet. Map 9 G5.

Mayfair

Bord'eaux

Grosvenor House Hotel, 86-90 Park Lane, W1K 7TN (7399 8460, www.bord-eaux.com). Marble Arch tube. **Breakfast served** 6.30-11am Mon-Fri; 7-11am Sat, Sun. **Lunch served** noon-3pm Mon-Sat. **Brunch served** noon-3pm Sun. **Dinner served** 6-10.30pm Mon-Thur, Sun; 6-11pm Fri, Sat. **Main courses** £14-£24.50. **Set meal** £20 2 courses, £25 3 courses. **Credit** AmEx, DC, MC, V.

Look at Bord'eaux's website and you can imagine a rather plush, intimate brasserie, showcasing modern cuisine from Aquitaine and south-west France. The restaurant is installed in a giant 1920s Park Lane hotel which, we are told, has had an expensive refit since joining the Marriott group. When we arrived, however, we found the dining room was a vast, over-lit hotel space that showed little sign of a makeover in many years. It does have a leafy outlook on Hyde Park, but the mirrors-and-wood-panel decor is frankly dreary. One section was being readied for next day's breakfast. Service by the all-French staff was charmant but disconnected. To start, a fennel, pistachio, coriander, watercress and orange salad was pleasant, yet unexceptional; a main of grilled tuna with niçoise salad was similarly unmemorable. The night's menu offered only two of the advertised south-western specialities, of which andouillettes with grain-mustard sauce had, yes, a proper mix of gutsiness and fragrance. Prices, though, are high, especially for wines and extras (dinky bowl of frites, £4.50). The kitchen's wider ambitions are perhaps not helped by the fact that many hotel guests seem happiest ordering just grills or club sandwiches.

Babies and children welcome: high chairs. Booking advisable. Disabled: toilet (hotel). Separate room for parties, seats 12. Map 9 G7.

La Petite Maison

54 Brooks Mews, W1K 4EG (7495 4774, www.lpm.co.uk). Bond Street tube. **Lunch served** noon-2.15pm, **dinner served** 6-10pm daily. **Main courses** £9-£35. **Credit** AmEx, MC, V.

RESTAURANTS

Chez Kristof

Defiantly bucking the recession with ever-full lunch sittings, La Petite Maison hums loudly with the conversation of heavily tanned men and glossy haired women all dressed expensively in embellished leather and gold jewellery from nearby Bond Street. Tables are carefully styled with bottles of green olive oil, knobbly lemons and plump tomatoes on the vine. If this is all sounding too much, rest assured that the French-Mediterranean food of chef Raphael Duntoye is fabulously uncomplicated in its luxuriousness. Witness the signature dish of a whole roast black-leg chicken with foie gras: it is just that. No fancy-schmancy stuffing, sous vide techniques or architectural presentation. The chicken arrives in manageable pieces with black legs akimbo and thick slices of foie gras mingling with the caramelised pan juices. On the side, simple mixed leaf salad, haricots verts, and frites fat, golden and crunchy enough to earn the name chips. If you haven't got two or three friends to help you consume it, work a dish of green beans and foie gras into your selection of starters to share (pissaladière, maybe, plus a tuna or scallop carpaccio and some marinated peppers). Finish with crème brûlée or sorbet.

Babies and children admitted. Booking advisable. Tables outdoors (8, terrace). **Map 9 H6**.

Soho

Côte

124-126 Wardour Street, W1F 0TY (7287 9280, www.cote-restaurants.co.uk). Oxford Circus, Piccadilly Circus or Tottenham Court Road tube. **Meals served** 8am-11pm Mon-Wed; 8am-midnight Thur, Fri; 9am-midnight Sat; 9am-10.30pm Sun. **Main courses** £8.50-£17.60. **Set meal** (3-7pm Mon-Fri; noon-6pm Sat, Sun) £9.75 2 courses, £11.75 3 courses. **Credit** AmEx, MC, V.

Côte has ambitions to be the Pizza Express among bistros (or, rather, the Strada – it's the latest concept from the duo who set up that chain). From one outpost in Wimbledon a couple of years ago it currently has six sites in London and one in Guildford – so expect its signature grey and white striped awning to be coming to a high street near you soon. The Soho branch is typical: a smart, glossy affair, all polished dark wood and moody grey paintwork, with mirrors, fold-back french doors and modish light fittings, and separate bar and restaurant areas. The drinks list is as Gallic as can be: wine, champagne, beer, cider and aperitifs

are all French, with only the spirits and soft drinks hailing from elsewhere. The menu holds no surprises, with the likes of rillettes, steak tartare or moules marinières for starters, followed by assorted fish dishes, lighter options (such as tuna niçoise) or grilled meat. Many diners opt for the latter: Les Landes free-range chicken or steak (ribeye, sirloin, fillet) with a choice of sauces and a side of frites. The cooking holds no surprises either, being acceptable but uninspiring – slightly wizened mussels in a too-creamy sauce; vegetarian risotto more an assemblage of green vegetables with rice than a well-rounded dish; the sirloin tasty but a tad chewy.

Babies and children welcome: high chairs. Booking advisable. Disabled: toilet. **Map 17 B3**.
For branches see index.

La Trouvaille

12A Newburgh Street, W1F 7RR (7287 8488, www.latrouvaille.co.uk). Oxford Circus tube. **Lunch served** noon-3pm Mon-Fri. **Dinner served** 6-11pm Mon-Sat. **Set lunch** £16.50 2 courses, £20 3 courses. **Set dinner** £29.50 2 courses, £35 3 courses. **Credit** AmEx, MC, V.

Hidden in a narrow backstreet behind Carnaby Street, La Trouvaille's bijou premises are a hive of activity. The ground-floor wine bar has rickety wooden tables, candlelight and a rustic menu: croque monsieurs and duck rillettes for lunch; charcuterie and cheese platters come supper-time. The dapper first-floor dining room is much smarter (and pricier). Stripped floorboards, pale pistachio-hued walls and flower-filled window-boxes create an airy feel – though the pseudo-Philippe Starck Perspex chairs may be too much for traditional tastes, and too small for some derrières. The kitchen has a similarly playful approach; goat's cheese might be turned into a panna cotta and served with chive macaroon and green apple purée, or pan-fried foie gras teamed with roasted banana. Mains are more traditional: rack of lamb with ratatouille, say, and a delicate, piquant lavender sauce. Tender pigeon breast was equally impressive, perched on tiny, wonderfully sweet baby carrots and accompanied by beetroot and raspberry chutney. If iced parfaits and millefeuille sound too rich for dessert, the cheeseboard is a reliable standby. Paired with a pot of black truffle-infused honey, it featured a stellar pont l'évêque on our visit – but portions were on the small side.

Babies and children admitted. Booking advisable. Tables outdoors (8, pavement). **Map 17 A3**.

Strand

The Admiralty

Somerset House, WC2R 1LA (7845 4646, www.somerset-house.org.uk). Embankment or Temple tube/Charing Cross tube/rail. **Lunch served** noon-2.30pm, **dinner served** 6-9.30pm Mon-Sat. **Main courses** £12.50-£18. **Set lunch** £15.50 2 courses, £19.50 3 courses. **Credit** AmEx, DC, MC, V.

A stroll away from the Strand's traffic and through the glorious courtyard of Somerset House provides an eminently suitable approach to this calm haven of a restaurant. Lofty ceilings and pale-green walls can make the Admiralty feel a little cold at night so the restaurant is at its best by day, when sunlight streams in through the tall windows. There's no river view (unless you stand up), but in summer a separate riverside terrace is opened, with a lighter menu. The mostly French/Modern European dishes on the main menus maintain a high enjoyability-factor. To start, salmon tartare with lemon-dressed herb salad was a deliciously fresh mix; and we weren't too bothered that the mussels marinière turned out to be à la crème, as the cream sauce was beautifully smooth. Of our mains, spinach and wild mushroom risotto was a pinch bland, but still satisfying, while pork fillet wrapped in pancetta with glazed beans was exceptional, the meat ideally tender and full of flavour. Friendly, obliging service makes it easy to sit back and linger here.

Available for hire. Babies and children admitted: nappy-changing facilities. Booking advisable. Disabled: lift; toilet. Separate rooms for parties, seating 30-60. **Map 18 F4**.

West

Bayswater

Angelus

4 Bathhurst Street, W2 2SD (7402 0083, www.angelusrestaurant.co.uk). Lancaster Gate tube. **Meals served** 11am-11pm daily. **Main courses** £18-£33. **Set lunch** £36 3 courses incl half of wine. **Set dinner** £38 3 courses. **Credit** AmEx, MC, V.

A charming bit of Paris in Bayswater, Angelus is something of a hybrid. It's a flexible spot: open all day, serving both brunch and a much more elaborate fine-dining menu. We rolled up for Sunday brunch and ate three excellent dishes: a

piquant steak tartare with fat chips; well-dressed caesar salad with juicy sautéed prawns; and the house 'club' sandwich, in which ingredients that often taste of nothing (avocado, chicken breast, tomatoes) were of impeccable quality. Portions aren't huge, so we had room for puddings – and were glad we did, as they were extraordinary. Chocolate fondant with espresso foam and mascarpone ice-cream, and blueberry financier with blueberry jelly and frozen lemon curd, both showed a dazzling contrast of textures and complementary flavours. They were two of the best dishes we've eaten in any London restaurant. We winced a little at the prices, however, including those on the wine list (scant choice in the lower reaches). Tables outside are the best choice in summer, before or after a walk in the park. The dining room is understated in an art nouveau way, and there's a quirkily decorated bar at the back with its own menu.
Babies and children admitted. Booking advisable. Disabled: lift; toilet. Separate room for parties, seats 22. Tables outdoors (5, terrace). Map 8 D6.

Chiswick

La Trompette
5-7 Devonshire Road, W4 2EU (8747 1836, www.latrompette.co.uk). Turnham Green tube. **Lunch served** noon-2.30pm Mon-Sat; 12.30-3pm Sun. **Dinner served** 6.30-10.30pm Mon-Sat; 7-10pm Sun. **Set lunch** (Mon-Fri) £23.50 3 courses; (Sat) £25 3 courses; (Sun) £29.50 3 courses. **Set dinner** £37.50 3 courses, £47.50 4 courses. **Credit** AmEx, MC, V.
Little has changed at La Trompette since it opened: something worth celebrating when so much here is so right. OK, some of the lampshades at the back are singed, but otherwise the decor is standing up well, the gold and grey walls reflecting kindly on the faces of the largely (though not exclusively) middle-aged local crowd. There were birthday groups too, adding to the contented burble in the slightly crowded room, along with young professionals on dates, happy to be seated so close to each other. Food is the big draw, the standard so consistently high that it rejuvenates diners like a patented serum. A starter of quail stuffed with ham and mushrooms, inside a glazed pastry case, was a humbling delight on a sweet and sticky Madeira sauce; large ravioli, plump with crab and scallop, were light and fresh. A duck breast and richer leg confit with foie gras were balanced with grilled chicory and sharp cherries. The menu is priced so that three courses

are only slightly more expensive than two, which makes the puddings seem a bargain – particularly when they're as good as our chocolate marquise. There's a notably strong wine list too.
Babies and children welcome (lunch): high chairs. Booking essential. Disabled: toilet. Tables outdoors (7, terrace).

Le Vacherin
76-77 South Parade, W4 5LF (8742 2121, www.levacherin.co.uk). Chiswick Park tube. **Lunch served** noon-3pm Tue-Sun. **Dinner served** 6-10.30pm Mon-Thur; 6-11pm Fri, Sat; 6-10pm Sun. **Main courses** £12.50-£19. **Set lunch** (Tue-Sat) £14.95 2 courses, £16.95 3 courses; (Sun) £19.50 3 courses. **Set dinner** £19.50 3 courses. **Credit** AmEx, MC, V.
A welcome reminder of what a successful local restaurant feels like, Le Vacherin is positioned well: opposite a green and next to a pub. Inside, despite a replica feel to the decoration, the restaurant has the atmosphere of the local bistro you might hope to find on a French holiday. On our visit, there was a wide range of diners, including a group of French friends, a mother meeting her son's new partner, and an assured couple asking for 'red champagne' but settling for rosé. The food was generally good, sometimes better than that. Desserts were surprise stars: a warm fig tart with goat's cheese ice-cream looked great (the fruit sliced into bright red coins) and tasted even better. Before that, roast lamb loin was so good that a member of our party, who rarely eats meat, wanted at first to taste it, then share it, then eat it all. A courgette flower stuffed with gnocchi and mozzarella was not so impressive, and we weren't sure whether a starter of wild salmon trout was deliberately crisp and dry on the outside while very rare in the middle. Overall, though, we envied the locals.
Babies and children welcome: high chairs. Booking advisable. Separate room for parties, seats 30.

Hammersmith

Chez Kristof
111 Hammersmith Grove, W6 0NQ (8741 1177, www.chezkristof.co.uk). Goldhawk Road or Hammersmith tube.
Deli **Open** 8am-7.30pm Mon-Fri; 8.30am-7pm Sat; 9am-6pm Sun.
Restaurant **Lunch served** noon-3pm Mon-Fri; 11.30am-4pm Sat, Sun. **Dinner served** 6-11pm Mon-Sat; 6-10.30pm Sun. **Main courses** £12.50-£17.50.
Both **Credit** AmEx, MC, V.
There's an outside seating area on this corner spot, protected from the traffic by a low green hedge, and from the sun by striped awnings. The interior has a cosy, convivial feel – tables with more space around them than the norm, avoiding strictly regimented rows. A curtain of fairy lights reinforces a sense of fun. On our visit, the French and Polish waiting staff and the kitchen seemed well able to manage an almost full dining room, with good humour and some style. The food is presented theatrically, brought near the table on a round tray by one waiter then set down by another. Every course hit home, from baby squid stuffed with crumbly black pudding, to pork with fennel, roasted until it fell apart; and from a particularly tender rabbit thigh, to a creamy saffron cheesecake dotted with lemon curd. Sure, some figs, with pain perdu, were flavourless, but this was the only off-note. A broad range of diners eats here (couples and friends, twentysomethings with their grandparents), apparently enjoying themselves as much as we did. It was a pleasure to find Chez Kristof in such good form.
Babies and children welcome: children's menu; films; high chairs. Booking advisable. Disabled: toilet. Separate room for parties, seats 45. Tables outdoors (15, terrace). Map 20 B3.

Holland Park

The Belvedere
Holland House, off Abbotsbury Road, in Holland Park, W8 6LU (7602 1238, www.whitestar line.org.uk). Holland Park tube. **Lunch served**

noon-2.15pm Mon-Sat; noon-2pm, 2.30-4.30pm Sun. **Dinner served** 6-10pm Mon-Sat. **Main courses** £12-£22. **Set menu** £24.95 3 courses. **Credit** AmEx, MC, V.
An art deco beauty in the middle of one of London's most gorgeous parks? The venue alone is worth the price of entry, and that's before a morsel of food has passed the lips. Marco Pierre White still has his name on the board outside, but although he doesn't cook here on a day-to-day basis, the food is still memorable. We ordered from a three-course Sunday lunch set menu, and the appropriately rare lamb came with rich fondant potato and fresh mint sauce. The roast pork was pinned down by a wedge of proper crackling. Sticky toffee pudding consisted of an enormous dome of nutty, gooey cake that came with pod-fresh vanilla ice-cream; our other choice, pear tarte tatin, was rich and perfectly caramelised. We also loved the white tablecloths, leather chairs and smart period features, and the faultlessly friendly service from staff who are great with children. We even quite enjoyed the pianist tinkling away in the hall between the first-floor and ground-floor dining rooms. This is a great place to have a special-occasion family meal.
Available for hire. Babies and children welcome: high chairs. Booking essential. Separate room for parties, seats 20. Tables outdoors (5, terrace).

Westbourne Grove

★ The Ledbury
127 Ledbury Road, W11 2AQ (7792 9090, www.theledbury.com). Westbourne Park tube. **Lunch served** noon-2.30pm Mon-Sat; noon-3pm Sun. **Dinner served** 6.30-10.30pm Mon-Sat; 7-10pm Sun. **Set lunch** (Mon-Sat) £19.50 2 courses, £24.50 3 courses; (Sun) £40 3 courses. **Set dinner** £60 3 courses. **Credit** AmEx, MC, V.
Testament to the reputation of Brett Graham's cooking is the happy buzz during a midweek lunch in a Notting Hill residential backwater. The occupants of the next table were French, here for the impressive contemporary expression of their national cuisine. There's little trace of the chef's Australian origins. Maggie Beer's non-alcoholic rosé (as sophisticated a soft drink as ever was) came from an exceptional list with as much Austrian as New World heft. Australian-accented staff intervened very ably – to pour sauce from a little jug on to asparagus ravioli (surrounded by teeny vegetables including slices of radish the size of a child's fingernail); or to explain the exquisite petits fours – but forgot our bread. The warm apricot, hazelnut and fig loaf served with cheese from an awesome trolley made up for the earlier lack. The imaginative, meticulous dishes avoid being overwrought, and sourcing is ahead of the game. A stand-out main course featured superb skate, expertly deboned, with tiny brown shrimps, samphire and (especially cleverly) the underrated noble cauliflower in different forms: the pale inner leaves, the heart, and as a purée. A mirrored wall, black drapes and chandeliers, plus a gold and beige colour scheme, might not be le dernier cri, but the comfort and noise-level, well-spaced tables, service and food seamlessly knit together producing unruffled pleasure.
Babies and children admitted. Booking advisable; essential dinner. Disabled: toilet. Tables outdoors (9, pavement). Map 7 A5/6.

South West
South Kensington

Papillon
96 Draycott Avenue, SW3 3AD (7225 2555, www.papillonchelsea.co.uk). South Kensington tube. **Lunch served** noon-3pm Mon-Fri; noon-4pm Sat, Sun. **Dinner served** 6-11.30pm Mon-Sat; 6-10pm Sun. **Main courses** £15-£25. **Set lunch** £16.50 2 courses, £19.50 3 courses. **Credit** AmEx, MC, V.
You can wear jeans to this traditional French restaurant, but ladies might want to include high heels, statement jewellery and a designer handbag in their ensemble, for Papillon nestles among the

exclusive boutiques of Brompton Cross. With its green leather chairs, well-padded banquettes, parquet floor, arched windows and pleated half-curtains, it's as handsomely Gallic as Jean-Paul Belmondo and the menu includes all the stars of the classic French repertoire: Marseilles fish soup, sole bonne femme, steak tartare, escargots and regionally themed salads. In addition to the à la carte, a choice of inexpensive set menus was offered on our visit. A basket of gorgeous olive and fruit and nut bread got the meal off to a winning start. Similarly classy was a summer truffle risotto that came with half a fresh truffle on the side and a grater to shave it over the dish at will. For dessert, the millefeuille maison was a contemporary take on the many-layered theme, featuring two free-form discs of caramelised pastry, vanilla ice-cream, pristine fresh berries and discreetly employed white chocolate sauce. When asked about a wine to accompany, the manager didn't hesitate to suggest the cheapest on the Europe-wide list.
Babies and children welcome: high chairs. Booking advisable. Dress: smart casual. Separate room for parties, seats 18. Tables outdoors (6, pavement). **Map 14 E10.**

Wandsworth

★ Chez Bruce ⑩⓪

2 Bellevue Road, SW17 7EG (8672 0114, www.chezbruce.co.uk). Wandsworth Common rail. **Lunch served** noon-2pm Mon-Fri; noon-3pm Sat, Sun. **Dinner served** 6.30-10pm Mon-Thur; 6.30-10.30pm Fri, Sat; 7-10pm Sun. **Set lunch** (Mon-Fri) £25.50 3 courses; (Sat, Sun) £32.50 3 courses. **Set dinner** £40 3 courses. **Credit** AmEx, DC, MC, V.
There's a softer, less minimalist feel to Chez Bruce these days. Colourful artworks are grouped around the muted wall lighting; tables are angled and mellowed with candles; numerous, dapper staff tread lightly on the worn, dark floorboards to a background of merry chuntering from local bankers and celebrating young couples. It's almost cosy. Some things don't change though and the wine list remains a gorgeous (and gorgeously priced) parade through the world's best, with lovely left-field surprises, presided over by one of our favourite sommeliers. Chez Bruce is still the destination of choice for fine dining in south London – even if our most recent meal sometimes fell short. The brief menu changes slightly through the week and seasonally, with a backbone of stalwarts. We started with a sumptuously light scoop of crab salad with slivered chunks of potato, green beans and vinegary cockles; and beautifully presented mozzarella with caponata, rocket and hazelnuts. But mains were disappointing. Small, grilled slices of veal, with large parcels of pasta and an intense bolognese sauce, were tough; tomato tarte with fennel, olives and pesto was bland. Puddings – especially a sensational bowl of strawberry trifle with lemon sorbet – restored a sense of order. We'll certainly be back.
Babies and children welcome (lunch): high chairs. Booking essential. Separate room for parties, seats 14.

South

Clapham

Gastro

67 Venn Street, SW4 0BD (7627 0222). Clapham Common tube. **Breakfast served** 8am-3pm, **meals served** noon-midnight daily. **Main courses** £12.95-£16.75. **Set lunch** (noon-3pm Mon-Fri) £9.95 2 courses incl coffee. **Credit** MC, V.
If you want somewhere more French, take the Eurostar. Everything – the dark interior; the classic cuisine; the smouldering, shrugging staff – is straight out of central casting and gloriously, uninhibitedly Gallic. Such bustling brasseries used to be all over France, places to eat croissants before work, or steak frites before visiting the cinema opposite. The cooking makes no concessions: start with snails, moules, fruits de mer or a chèvre salad; follow with bavette steak, andouillette sausages, magret de canard, salade niçoise or a lobster

whisked straight from the tank. The menu enfant does indeed feature steak haché or escalope volaille; desserts bring you mont blanc and crème caramel – or maybe strong cheeses from the mesh box on the zinc bar. Spread across the two dark rooms are rickety tables (and a very large communal one), the lobsters in their tank (and their plastic brethren on the ceiling), French adverts on the walls, and a phalanx of strong liqueurs behind the bar. OK, the chips were lukewarm on our visit, and the salade verte rather gritty; but grilled entrecôte was done to a turn, and a lovely syrah house wine came in a Duralex glass. Vegetarians can, it seems, eat frites.
Babies and children admitted. Booking advisable Fri, Sat dinner. Disabled: toilet. Separate room for parties, seats 25. Tables outdoors (6, pavement). **Map 22 A2.**

★ Trinity

4 The Polygon, SW4 0JG (7622 1199, www.trinityrestaurant.co.uk). Clapham Common tube. **Lunch served** 12.30-2.30pm Tue-Sat; noon-4.30pm Sun. **Dinner served** 6.30-10.30pm Mon-Sat. **Main courses** £15-£28. **Set lunch** (Tue-Sat) £15 2 courses, £20 3 courses; (Sun) £25 2 courses, £28 3 courses; £38 tasting menu. **Credit** AmEx, MC, V.
There's a sense of energy and purpose about Trinity. The kitchen used to stick to the idea of dishes' ingredients coming in threes (hence the restaurant's name), though things are no longer so rigid and that's no loss. The cooking is still sensational. There's plenty of movement on the menu over the year, but if you can't choose (and we couldn't), then the six-course tasting menu (£38) is worth investigating. Typical dishes include a rich and earthy vichyssoise of asparagus and Jersey Royal potatoes, a lovely little quail carbonara, roast salmon with yet more Jersey Royals (and a beautiful dab of pea foam), a cottage pie made from thick chunks of braised beef and carrots, a cleansing sorbet, and – it sounds excessive, but portions are small and we all managed it – an intensely dark chocolate hotpot with ice-cream. Everything is very delicately presented. Vegetarians are well cared for if they want to go off piste; indeed, staff are genuinely helpful. It's not so big a place, but includes a curtained alcove for larger, private parties, and a small bar at the back. Tables are well spaced, and huge windows at the front, an open hatch to the kitchen and clever use of light and colour keep things breezy. We can recommend it.
Babies and children welcome: high chairs. Booking essential. Disabled: toilet. **Map 22 A1.**

Waterloo

★ RSJ

33 Coin Street, SE1 9NR (7928 4554, www.rsj. uk.com). Waterloo tube/rail. **Lunch served** noon-2pm Mon-Fri. **Dinner served** 5.30-11pm Mon-Sat. **Main courses** £12-£17. **Set meal** £15.95 2 courses, £18.95 3 courses. **Credit** AmEx, DC, MC, V.
The light, airy dining room at this little bistro exudes tranquillity. A location near the South Bank has made RSJ a favourite pre- or post-event call-in for culture-goers, but this isn't its only attraction. The wine list, entirely devoted to the Loire, is something special: a remarkable compendium of Touraines, Chinons, Bourgueils and other appellations from the region, with bottles from small vineyards often at under £25 – remarkable, given the scarcity of these wines. If you're not wine-seeker enough to plough through all the list, head for the regularly changed, user-friendly 'house selection'. The menus, changed every month and supplemented by specials, offer plenty to enjoy too. The special starter on the night we visited, pan-fried squid with chorizo, rocket and a shallot dressing, was a delicious combination of excellently fresh seafood and punchy but fragrant seasoning. From the great-value set menu, a main of pan-fried mackerel with niçoise salad stood out both for the quality of the fish and the skill in its cooking. Roast pork cutlet with apple and black pudding, sauerkraut

and red-pepper coulis was perhaps a little over-busy, yet still pleasant. Service is charming.
Babies and children admitted. Booking advisable. Separate room for parties, seats 25. **Map 11 N8.**

East

Bethnal Green

Bistrotheque ⑩⓪

23-27 Wadeson Street, E2 9DR (8983 7900, www.bistrotheque.com). Bethnal Green tube/rail/Cambridge Heath rail/55 bus. **Bar Open** 6pm-midnight Tue-Sat; 1-11pm Sun. *Restaurant* **Brunch served** 11am-4pm Sat, Sun. **Dinner served** 6.30-10.30pm Mon-Thur, Sun; 6.30-11pm Fri, Sat. **Main courses** £10-£21. **Set lunch** £21 3 courses. **Set dinner** (6.30-7.30pm Mon-Fri) £17.50 3 courses. *Both* **Credit** AmEx, MC, V.
A hip dinner, brunch and entertainment spot, Bistrotheque is renowned for four things: its gritty NYC-style warehouse-chic location; its excellent cocktail bar; its weekend brunches; and its new-skool risqué cabaret. Bar and cabaret room occupy the ground floor; brunch (11am-4pm) is served in the first-floor black-and-white restaurant (factory floors, whitewashed walls, original industrial ceiling fittings, and a piano sometimes utilised by the poptastic Xavier). It features such mouth-watering dishes as birchermüesli, pancakes with raspberries and chocolate sauce, egg florentine, or white bean, chorizo and wild rocket. Main-course dishes for dinner include fish and chips with pea purée and tartare sauce. Bellinis and bloody marys make perfect accompaniments. In our experience, food at dinner is satisfying but not outstanding. Half a dozen rock oysters made a fresh, tasty starter. Main of ribeye steak with roquefort and garlic butter was enjoyable, yet £22 seemed too high a price for the quality. Grilled lemon sole with a herb crust fared better, but wasn't memorable. Sides of chips (excellent) and green salad (fine) bump up the prices. Service was OK, but lacked energy. The early-evening weekday prix-fixe menu is good value.
Babies and children admitted: high chairs. Booking advisable. Disabled: toilet. Entertainment: cabaret (check website or phone for details); pianist noon-4pm Sun. Separate room for parties, seats 50.

Shoreditch

Boundary NEW

2009 RUNNER-UP BEST NEW RESTAURANT
2-4 Boundary Street, entrance at 9 Redchurch Street, E2 7DD (7729 1051, www.theboundary. co.uk). Liverpool Street tube/rail/8, 26, 48 bus. **Lunch served** noon-3pm Tue-Sat; noon-2pm Sun. **Dinner served** 6.30-10.30pm Mon-Sat. **Main courses** £9.25-£23.50. **Set lunch** £23.50 3 courses. **Credit** AmEx, MC, V.
After all the hoo-ha over one of the few grand openings in the recession, and the rave reviews that followed, we were nonplussed to be underwhelmed by Boundary. It's an interesting space, with plenty going on in the high-ceilinged, light-filled basement. The kitchen runs down one side, facing a splendid array of antique trays on the brick wall opposite; there's art everywhere, plus a handsome room divider between the cosy bar and the restaurant. Service was slightly strained – we were never made to feel particularly welcome. Fellow diners were couples on serious dates and business groups tucking into towers of fruits de mer. The Anglo-French menu felt far more like the Terence Conran of old than did the decor, but while some dishes were absolute stunners, some were more mundane. Of the former, a starter of charcuterie, terrines, pâtés and rillettes from the trolley was a triumph. Also good was anjou pigeon with petits pois à la française, a savoury treat with wonderfully crispy skin; and a delightfully summery elderflower and blackberry jelly with cream and a madeleine. But half a rotisserie Les Landes chicken was so bland it would have been ideal for a convalescent, and flavour was also lacking in an artichoke and shallot tart. In short, not good enough at these prices.

Available for hire. Babies and children welcome: high chairs; nappy-changing facilities. Booking essential. Disabled: toilet. Separate room for parties, seats 35. Map 6 R4.

Les Trois Garçons (100)

1 Club Row, E1 6JX (7613 1924, www.lestrois garcons.com). Liverpool Street tube/rail/8, 388 bus. **Dinner served** 7-10pm Mon-Thur; 7-10.30pm Fri, Sat. **Set dinner** (Mon-Wed) £27 2 courses, £31 3 courses; (Mon-Sat) £42.50 2 courses, £49.50 3 courses, £72 tasting menu. **Credit** AmEx, DC, MC, V.

Behind the sober façade of a converted East End pub, Les Trois Garçons is a paean to decorative excess. Crystal chandeliers hang from the ceiling, interspersed with rows of vintage handbags, while stuffed animals perch on the bar or crane from the walls, swathed in costume jewellery. It's surreal but harmonious, with mellow wood panelling and dim lighting to offset the flourishes. There's more to this place than appearances, though. Rich, classical French cuisine is tempered with modern British influences and simple but impeccably sourced ingredients. While foie gras may feature in two of the six starters, Lyme Bay crab and spenwood sheep's milk cheese also appear. To start, wonderfully delicate, own-smoked Shetland Island sea trout, with potato salad, pink grapefruit and capers, was beautifully presented and self-assured – outshining even an indulgent slab of pan-seared Landes foie gras, served with apple, foie gras caramel and slightly overpowering cherry compote. Mains proved equally accomplished: saddle of rabbit came with a liver- and kidney-stuffed roulade and rich, creamy polenta; and thick, tender slices of Herdwick lamb were matched with braised shallots, spätzle and an unctuous, star anise-spiked carrot purée. Service is impeccable, with tap water delivered graciously, along with relatively affordable recommendations from the weighty wine list. A fiercely popular venue.
Available for hire. Booking advisable. Children admitted over 12. Separate room for parties, seats 10. Map 6 S4.

North

Camden Town & Chalk Farm

L'Absinthe NEW

40 Chalcot Road, NW1 8LS (7483 4848). Chalk Farm tube. **Lunch served** noon-2.30pm Mon-Fri; noon-4pm Sat, Sun. **Dinner served** 6-10.30pm Tue-Sat; 6-9.30pm Sun. **Main courses** £8.95-£15.95. **Set lunch** (Tue-Fri) £9.50 2 courses; (Sun) £14.95 2 courses. **Credit** AmEx, MC, V.

There's so much to love about L'Absinthe, it's hard to know where to start. The welcome is genuinely warm, as if the staff were friends who'd invited you for dinner. Then there's the feel of the place: a ground floor and basement that recreate the French bistro of your dreams. Prices are eminently reasonable for such an upmarket location. Last but not least, there's the food – bistro classics little affected by fad or fashion. Our meal contained nothing that was less than very good, and some of it was wonderful. Top marks to our mains: braised lamb shank with an abundance of roasted root vegetables, and textbook saucisse de toulouse with buttery mash and a fine salad. A tiny flaw (overly sweet stock) denied perfection to an otherwise impeccable onion soup, with a layer of gruyère so thick it made the dish a meal in itself. The wine list derives from the restaurant's own wine shop, and is marked up in fixed increments: from £6 for the cheapest bottles to zero for fine wine. Prices start at around £13. A French local that others would do well to imitate.
Babies and children welcome: high chairs. Booking advisable. Tables outdoors (5, pavement). Map 27 B2.

Crouch End

Les Associés

172 Park Road, N8 8JT (8348 8944, www.les associes.co.uk). Finsbury Park tube/rail then W7 bus. **Lunch served** 1-3pm, **dinner served** 7.30-10pm Tue-Sat. **Set dinner** (Tue-Fri) £12 2 courses, £15 3 courses. **Credit** AmEx, MC, V.

This curious bistro has operated from the same Crouch End sitting room for over 20 years, and is showing its age. Not just in the decor, which could do with sprucing up, but in the cooking – essentially French, with English touches in the form of ample vegetal accompaniments (both on the plate and in a standard side dish served with main courses). Our vegetables were cooked imprecisely and, in the case of fried potatoes with a spiced coating, unappetisingly. The same imprecision marred main courses of duck, rack of lamb and black-leg chicken. The raw ingredients were fine, but dull, gloopy sauces added nothing. There were good things in our meal, especially a flavour-packed provençal fish soup and a special of roasted langoustines. But there were too many letdowns, culminating in a tired tarte au citron. The high point is the all-French wine list, especially the page of bottles imported by the restaurant and chosen with skill. The shortcomings don't seem to bother locals, who've kept this place going so long. We've eaten better here before, but would like to see more of the care that's shown on the wine list brought to bear on the food.
Available for hire. Babies and children admitted. Booking advisable. Tables outdoors (8, garden).

Hornsey

Le Bistro

36 High Street, N8 7NX (8340 2116). Turnpike Lane tube/Hornsey rail/41, W3 bus. **Brunch served** 12.30-5pm Sun. **Dinner served** 6.30-11pm Mon-Sat; 5-10pm Sun. **Main courses** £11.95-£20. **Set meal** £10.95 2 courses, £12.95 3 courses. **Credit** MC, V.

With its glimmering candlelight, black-and-white tiling and clutter of junk shop finds, this charming venue has the feel of a Left Bank bistro that hasn't changed in decades. Moth-eaten stags' heads peer across the dimly lit dining room; vintage Orangina posters adorn the walls. All that's missing is an authentic soupçon of superiority; the waiters are far friendlier than their Parisian counterparts, if considerably slower. Appealing brasserie standards are on the carte: half a dozen oysters or rouille-topped fish soup to start, say, followed by slow-roasted pork belly with braised red cabbage, or rack of lamb with lyonnaise potatoes. The smart money is on the compact set menu, though, which offers sterling value (though no vegetarian mains on our visit). A delicately dressed smoked chicken salad, and a wedge of deep-fried brie with blackcurrant coulis, were artfully assembled and generously portioned. Star main course was a tender, perfectly pink Argentinian steak with pepper sauce and crunchy, matchstick-thin frites – a steal, even taking a £3 supplement into account. Le Bistro isn't perfect (a side dish of vegetables was under-seasoned and overcooked), but easy charm and modest prices make it an ideal neighbourhood bolt-hole.
Babies and children welcome: high chairs. Booking advisable. Tables outdoors (18, garden).

Islington

★ Almeida

30 Almeida Street, N1 1AD (7354 4777, www.danddlondon.com). Angel tube/Highbury & Islington tube/rail. **Lunch served** noon-2.30pm Tue-Sat. **Dinner served** 5.30-10.30pm Mon-Sat. **Meals served** noon-3.30pm Sun. **Set lunch** £8.95 1 course. **Set dinner** £24.50 2 courses, £29.50 3 courses. **Set meal** (5.30-6.30pm daily; 9.30-10.30pm Mon-Sat) £14.50 2 courses, £17.50 3 courses. **Credit** AmEx, MC, V.

Opposite the Almeida Theatre in the chattering-class heart of Islington, this member of the group formerly known as Conran is an asset to the area and not just for the pre- and post-theatre deals. The handsome room is a cool backdrop to some good artwork and statement flowers in goldfish bowls. Tables are well spaced, the floor is partly carpeted and there's no music (allowing conversation). Add unshowy, impeccable cooking – calmly carried out in the open kitchen – and you have a pleasingly grown-up restaurant. The good-value set menu

makes ingenious use of cheaper and spare parts of top-quality ingredients, turning asparagus into an intense velvety soup, and chunks of roquefort into salad with red and white chicory (a touch too chilled), walnuts and watercress. Organic salmon was perfectly cooked, with crisp skin and a resistant centre; broad beans (peeled), proper peas and spinach planted the dish squarely in the right season. Braised fillet of lamb, a fatty cut, was cleverly cooked to gamey tenderness, and the promised Jersey Royals appeared in bubble and squeak form. The cheese trolley is an inviting prospect, but had to compete with a sublime lemony passion-fruit tart with yoghurt sorbet. Staff were willing if sometimes uncomprehending.
Babies and children welcome: children's menu; high chairs; nappy-changing facilities. Booking advisable. Disabled: toilet. Separate rooms for parties, seating 10 and 20. Tables outdoors (8, pavement). Map 5 O1.

★ Morgan M

489 Liverpool Road, N7 8NS (7609 3560, www.morganm.com). Highbury & Islington tube/rail. **Lunch served** noon-1.30pm Wed-Fri, Sun. **Dinner served** 7-9pm Tue-Sat. **Set lunch** £22.50 2 courses, £26.50 3 courses, £39-£43 tasting menu. **Set dinner** £39 3 courses, £43-£48 tasting menu. **Credit** MC, V.

Morgan Meunier's creative enterprise occupies premises that resemble a bijou living room. That's not to suggest it's in any way amateurish: quite the contrary. Tables dressed in linen are tended precisely by black-clad waiting staff. Dinner is either a three-course or tasting-menu affair, punctuated by amuse bouche and pre-dessert fripperies. The intricate dishes – foams, purées, uncanny textures and unexpected flavour combinations abound – arouse a greedy curiosity to sample as many as possible. Vegetarian highlights included a starter of luscious red-pepper sorbet and creamy avocado 'caviar' decorated with paper-thin tomato tuile. This was followed by an intensely flavoured and skilfully executed mushroom cannelloni on a bed of forest-green spinach (though so full-on was the dish, we couldn't finish it). The seafood creations – red mullet and razor clams in a saffron broth – were more subtle and highly accomplished. Frou-frou dessert plates might include a composition of cloud-like meringue straws, stewed strawberries and buttery madeleines. Our visit on a hot day was marred by overpowering and all-pervading fumes emanating from the uncovered, marble-topped cheese trolley next to us. Morgan M's formality makes it suitable for special-occasion dining.
Babies and children admitted (lunch). Booking essential. Dress: smart casual. Separate room for parties, seats 12. Vegetarian menu.

Palmers Green

Café Anjou

394 Green Lanes, N13 5PD (8886 7267, www.cafeanjou.co.uk). Wood Green tube then 329 bus/Palmers Green rail. **Lunch served** noon-3pm Tue-Sun. **Dinner served** 6.30-11pm Mon; 6.30-10.30pm Tue-Sun. **Main courses** £8.95-£12.75. **Set lunch** (noon-2pm Tue-Sat) £7.95 1 course incl glass of wine and coffee. **Set meal** (Tue-Fri, lunch Sat) £12.95 2 courses, £14.45 3 courses. **Credit** MC, V.

With its terracotta-tiled floor, faded prints of Parisian street scenes and sprays of carnations on the tables, this bistro is a sweetly old-fashioned affair – though the tinny background music (Cliff Richard, Céline Dion) could do with overhauling. From the modestly priced prix fixe menu, a bowl of cauliflower crème dubarry soup was silky-textured but woefully under-seasoned; far better were the tender pork medallions in sage and white wine sauce that followed, deftly wrapped in parma ham and accompanied by a heaped dish of celeriac and honeyed, rosemary-sprinkled carrots. An appealingly concise à la carte menu offered bistro standards (salmon roulade, beef bourguignon, duck magret with confit prunes) at fair prices – but execution, again, proved patchy. Salade de champignons et de lard comprised a vast pile of cold, sliced mushrooms and snippets of chive,

Boundary. See p98.

doused in vinegary dressing and scattered with dry, unappetising morsels of bacon. A main of sea bass à la niçoise, with sweet, juicy tomatoes and peppers and a gargantuan portion of boulangère potatoes, was much more promising, yet the fish was slightly overcooked. Service is quietly attentive. If the kitchen upped its game, this would be a pleasant spot for an inexpensive supper.
Available for hire. Babies and children welcome: high chairs. Booking essential dinner Fri, Sat. Tables outdoors (3, pavement).

North West
St John's Wood

L'Aventure
3 Blenheim Terrace, NW8 0EH (7624 6232). St John's Wood tube/139, 189 bus. **Lunch served** 12.30-2.30pm Mon-Fri. **Dinner served** 7-11pm Mon-Sat. **Set lunch** £16.50 2 courses, £19.50 3 courses incl coffee. **Set dinner** £29.50 2 courses, £37.50 3 courses. **Credit** AmEx, MC, V.
L'Aventure plays the role of civilised neighbourhood restaurant well, and is an unsurprising find in this upmarket neck of the woods. The interior is classic with a capital C: white linen tablecloths, exposed-brick and white walls, and dark-wood furniture. Menus hand-written in French and fairy lights on the front terrace add a welcoming touch. This is the sort of place where innovation isn't really expected or, indeed, wanted. Of the various dishes we sampled, the best were the simplest. Perfectly cooked scallops with shredded cabbage, flecks of smoked salmon and chives made for a tasty, generous starter, while a pea soup was deliciously creamy. For mains, sole with grapefruit, cranberry, peas and potatoes was, frankly, unsuccessful; the sourness of the fruit jarred with the delicate flavour of the fish. Pot au feu was more enjoyable, although let down by rather tough meat and overcooked vegetables. So, L'Aventure might not be worth a trip across town, but if you're around NW8, the professional service, smart but local vibe, and excellent wine list might be enough to make up for the inconsistent cooking. One last tip: avoid the conservatory area on cold evenings.
Babies and children welcome: high chairs. Booking advisable dinner. Tables outdoors (6, terrace). **Map 1 C2**.

Outer London
Croydon, Surrey

Le Cassoulet
18 Selsdon Road, Croydon, Surrey CR2 6PA (8633 1818, www.lecassoulet.co.uk). South Croydon rail. **Lunch served** noon-3pm Mon-Sat; noon-4pm Sun. **Dinner served** 6-10.3pm Mon-Thur, Sun; 6-11pm Fri, Sat. **Main courses** £12.50-£20. **Set lunch** £16.50 3 courses (Mon-Sat); £19.50 3 courses (Sun). **Set dinner** £19.50 3 courses. **Credit** AmEx, MC, V.
Chef-patron Malcolm John's first restaurant in South Croydon (the second is Fish & Grill, *see p89*) has been a hit since opening; it won our Best Local Restaurant award in 2008. Burgundy paintwork, together with red-and-gold striped banquettes, and floral wallpaper provide a smartly feminine setting; black-aproned staff zip about in a professional manner. Food – traditional French with a focus on the south-west, home of the hearty pork, duck and bean stew after which the restaurant is named – is reliably excellent. The place was humming for Sunday lunch, no doubt because of the bargain set menu: eight choices apiece for mains and starters, six for dessert, many identical to the carte and amply portioned. Dishes may be rustic in origin, but there's nothing basic about the cooking or presentation. Witness the thin discs of pressed pinky-white octopus in a starter salad, with fennel shavings, orange segments and capers. For mains, rabbit pie, presented in its own mini metal pot, was brimming with tender meat, carrots and mushrooms beneath a flaky pastry crust. Fleshy, juicy tiger prawns were simply cooked in a buttery chilli-garlic sauce. To finish, vanilla-speckled crème brûlée provided the perfect mix of cream and crunch. The all-French wine list (with half-litre carafes) is worth scrutinising.
Available for hire. Babies and children welcome: high chairs; nappy-changing facilities. Disabled: toilet.

Richmond, Surrey

Chez Lindsay
11 Hill Rise, Richmond, Surrey TW10 6UQ (8948 7473, www.chezlindsay.co.uk). Richmond tube/rail.
Crêperie **Meals served** noon-10.45pm Mon-Sat; noon-9.45pm Sun. **Main courses** £6.50-£10.75.
Restaurant **Meals served** noon-10.45pm Mon-Sat; noon-9.45pm Sun. **Main courses** £9.25-£18.75. **Set lunch** (noon-6pm Mon-Sat) £14.50 2 courses, £17.50 3 courses. **Set dinner** (after 6pm) £17.50 2 courses, £21.50 3 courses.
Both **Credit** MC, V.
An authentic tranche of France tucked at the bottom of Richmond Hill, Chez Lindsay has been specialising in traditional Breton cuisine for years. Its sunny-yellow walls and waterside perch, jutting out over the Thames, evoke memories of Brittany beach holidays; creaky wooden floorboards and proper French waiters lend rustic charm. Lindsay Wotton's menu celebrates seafood (as in a satisfying starter of moules à la st malo, doused in a creamy white wine sauce), but it's her galettes that steal the show. Cooked to order on a flat griddle, these buckwheat beauties come as starter or main with an array of fillings. Opt for the simple-but-effective (cheese, ham, spinach); the more challenging (chitterling sausage and mustard); or sweet (apple and caramel). Grands plats provide more substantial dining: a whole grilled sea bass was a whopper and great value for its size; the feuilleté de st jacques, a shell shape carved out of puff pastry and encasing scallops, leeks and cidery butter, was beautifully presented. The wine list emphasises the Loire, while sparkling ciders provide classic accompaniment to galettes. Lively and perennially popular, Chez Lindsay is a neighbourhood restaurant par excellence – and a treasured asset in chain-dominated Richmond.
Babies and children welcome: high chairs. Booking advisable. Separate room for parties, seats 38.

Twickenham, Middlesex

Brula
43 Crown Road, Twickenham, Middx TW1 3EJ (8892 0602, www.brula.co.uk). St Margaret's rail. **Lunch served** noon-3pm daily. **Dinner served** 6-10.30pm Mon-Sat. **Main courses** £10 lunch; £16-£18 dinner. **Credit** AmEx, MC, V.
This intimate neighbourhood bistro is a charmer with its unusual decor (once a Victorian butcher's shop, it retains its stained-glass windows and worn parquet flooring), friendly service and general air of bonhomie. It's smart enough for a family celebration, casual enough for a quick lunch. The menu offers French classics and Modern European dishes. A salad of Devonshire crab, prawns, baby squid and avocado made a light, fresh-tasting start to the meal: perfect for a summer's evening. Sauté of gnocchi, broccoli, chilli and anchovy went well with steamed sea bream, though our lamb main, despite being top-quality meat, was too pink (we weren't asked how we wanted it cooked). Starters are all £6.75, mains £15.75, desserts £6.50 (lunch prices are cheaper) – which makes life easier, but doesn't always seem fair. Should you pay the same price for goat's cheese tarte tatin as onglet steak? Leave room for pud (apricot clafoutis and delicate milk ice-cream was a winner) or there are cheeses from La Fromagerie. The all-French wine list is a treat, with many lesser-known varieties and regions represented (and available as off-sales in multiples of six). Brula celebrated a decade in St Margaret's in 2009; its success has spawned siblings in East Sheen and Richmond.
Babies and children admitted. Booking advisable. Separate rooms for parties, seating 8, 10 and 24. Tables outdoors (6, pavement).

Gastropubs

Now over 18 years old, the London gastropub is old enough to drive, vote and walk into a pub to buy a beer – or an inexpensive glass of red from the blackboard wine list. The capital has come to know and love gastropubs in all their forms, from small boozers that offer cut-above cooking, to those that serve great food in the bar area as well as in separate dining rooms, and others that seem to wish they were a restaurant (though, frankly, some of these seem to be struggling in the recession).

This year's new crop ranges from a game specialist (Fulham's **Harwood Arms**, winner of our Best New Gastropub award), to one making its own charcuterie (the bijou **Bull & Last** on Highgate Road), to the something-for-everybody cheer of the spacious **Britannia** near Victoria Park, and Balham's **Avalon**, which is attracting plenty of custom to its designer garden. We welcome back the **Drapers Arms**, reborn under new owners, and applaud the latest offering from Ed and Tom Martin, the **Cadogan Arms**.

Now with seven pubs, the ETM Group (the Martin brothers) is the capital's leading gastropub group in terms of quality cooking, but there are other significant players: Realpubs, Food & Fuel and the behemoth Geronimo Inns, which has 21 branches and another six scheduled to open in London as we go to press. The food and drink at such places tends to be the same, so this year we have decided to focus on one interesting pub in each group and list the best of its other outlets as branches.

Central

Bloomsbury

Norfolk Arms
28 Leigh Street, WC1H 9EP (7388 3937, www.norfolkarms.co.uk). Euston tube/rail. **Open** 11am-11pm Mon-Sat; 11am-10.30pm Sun. **Lunch served** noon-3pm, **dinner served** 6.30-10.15pm Mon-Sat. **Meals served** noon-10.15pm Sun. **Main courses** £8.50-£14.50. **Credit** AmEx, MC, V.
Intimate, white-painted antique tables and food for sharing make this popular spot appealing for those in the first flush of romance. Groups best aim for an outdoor table as inside gets steamy-hot, but staff sensibly dimmed the lights to help cool things down on the warm spring night of our visit. Charcuterie – mostly Spanish – hangs above the bar and is sliced to appear on platters for two to nibble over drinks. Our ploughman's platter had good components (baked ham, pâté, Quicke's cheddar) but the quantities seemed meagre. Baba ganoush had a wonderfully smoky flavour, and we couldn't fault the chorizo in cider or burrata cheese drizzled with balsamic vinegar and green olive oil. In addition to the sizeable tapas and bar snacks list is a menu of starters, mains and desserts that draws from Mediterranean cuisines and the British countryside; Sundays offer a roast. We found it hard to get the staff's attention – they always seemed to be on the go – but they were friendly enough. And we had to wait ages, without warning, for drinks to be delivered as the keg of IPA was being changed. The sophisticated sherry kick of the Spanish viognier (£17) from Jumilla helped compensate.
Babies and children admitted: high chairs. Booking advisable. Separate room for parties, seats 25. Tables outdoors (15, pavement). **Map 4 L3.**

Clerkenwell & Farringdon

Coach & Horses (100)
26-28 Ray Street, EC1R 3DJ (7278 8990, www.thecoachandhorses.com). Farringdon tube/rail. **Open** noon-11pm Mon-Fri; 5-11pm Sat; noon-4pm Sun. **Lunch served** noon-3pm Mon-Fri, Sun. **Dinner served** 6-10pm Mon-Sat. **Main courses** £9.50-£14. **Credit** AmEx, MC, V.
Snag a table in the bar room or the beer garden, or even out front, rather than the dark 'garden room' at the Coach & Horses. It's a proper Victorian pub, with real ales, a more than decent wine list, helpful bar staff and no-nonsense decor with wood-panelling and etched glass. Food is treated seriously, but doesn't take centre stage; diners and drinkers have equal rights here. So soak up the alcohol with bar snacks such as excellent bread (baked in-house) and olive oil, or a scotch egg with english mustard, or a ploughman's (£6 buys a pork pie, wensleydale, piccalilli, chutney, pickled onions, tomato, celery and bread). Or try something fancier from the main menu: we had high hopes for the rabbit and wild garlic pie with mash, but it wasn't quite the rich and savoury dish we desired; better was a whole plaice with purple sprouting broccoli and caperberry butter. Apple crumble with lots of custard was tooth-crumblingly sweet – the British cheese plate is a good savoury alternative. A pub with its heart in the right place.
Available for hire. Babies and children welcome: high chairs. Booking advisable. Separate room for parties, seats 30. Tables outdoors (9, garden). **Map 5 N4.**

Eagle
159 Farringdon Road, EC1R 3AL (7837 1353). Farringdon tube/rail. **Open** noon-11pm Mon; noon-5pm Sun. **Lunch served** 12.30-3pm Mon-Fri; 12.30-3.30pm Sat, Sun. **Dinner served** 6.30-10.30pm Mon-Sat. **Main courses** £5-£17. **Credit** MC, V.

From the welcome through to the quality stove-top coffee, the Eagle (often cited as London's first gastropub) shows its pedigree. Having a swift, sharp-eyed waiter rather than yo-yoing bar staff working the big windowed space points to its competence. (Be aware that table sharing is required, however: not necessarily ideal when drinkers and diners come together.) The kitchen takes up one half of the long bar, with the menu chalked up above it. As you choose, that steak grilling in front of you becomes irresistible even at £17.50, and rightly so. A big main of nearly-disintegrating sardines came with roast tomatoes, gremolata and a brilliantly saturated bed of bruschetta. Spicy crab linguine was generously meaty and glistening with natural juices. Smaller dishes are limited (taleggio, pear and toast, say, plus olives, boquerones and frittata) and there are just two sweet options: a classy rosemary cake and pastel de nata. A short wine list – five each of red and white – is available by the glass (£3.20-£4.60) or bottle (from £12.50). On draught, there are Eagle IPA, Bombardier and Addlestones. Lagers, Hoegaarden, Leffe and keenly priced cocktails complete an altogether appealing line-up.
Babies and children admitted. Bookings not accepted. Tables outdoors (4, pavement). **Map 5 N4.**

Easton
22 Easton Street, WC1X 0DS (7278 7608). Farringdon tube/rail. **Open** noon-11pm Mon-Thur; noon-1am Fri; 10am-midnight Sat; noon-10.30pm Sun. **Lunch served** 12.30-3pm Mon-Fri; noon-3.30pm Sat; 1-4pm Sun. **Dinner served** 6.30-10pm Mon-Sat; 6.30-9.30pm Sun. **Main courses** £8-£16. **Credit** MC, V.
It's not often that you'll get a table and the undivided attention of the bar staff here. Its shabby chic vibe ('vintage' wallpaper, scruffy sofas, huge plate-glass windows) attracts a young, arty, professional crowd, and decent drinks and fabulous food mean it's usually packed. On a big football night, however, it was deserted (no Sky

Eagle

Sports), but who needs company when the food is this good? Starters included perfectly soft pillows of own-made gnocchi smothered in creamy asparagus and pesto sauce, and two juicy scallops with orange coral in a wonderfully garlicky rocket salsa verde. Mains too were delectable: ox cheek in a mustard crumb was as sticky and unctuous as it should be (we made a makeshift doggy bag for what couldn't be finished). It came on a bed of endive, beetroot and subtle horseradish cream; a 'Will it be enough?' side of mash was unnecessary – but so delicious and creamy we almost took that home too. Pancetta-wrapped chicken breast, bone in, was pan-fried and served with crispy rosemary potatoes in a wonderfully flavourful gravy. The quality of the food and cooking is unquestionably high and though we've read of service gripes, our waitress was enchanting (though she did forget the wine). There was no question of dessert, but the Easton mess with strawberries was tempting. Roll on the World Cup, we say…
Available for hire. Babies and children admitted (until 9pm). Tables outdoors (4, pavement).
Map 5 N4.

Hat & Feathers
2 Clerkenwell Road, EC1M 5PQ (7490 2244, www.hatandfeathers.com). Barbican tube/Farringdon tube/rail. **Open** noon-midnight Mon-Sat. **Lunch served** noon-3pm Mon-Fri. **Dinner served** 6-9.30pm Mon-Sat. **Main courses** £13.50-£18.95. **Credit** AmEx, MC, V.
What can you get for £10 these days? The Hat and Feathers' 'beat the crunch' menu for one, with a main dish and a drink (a bottled beer or glass of wine) served for a tenner every weekday lunch and

evening until 7.30pm. This enterprising gastropub in a grand old Victorian boozer has responded to the recession with a crowd-pleasing set of offers. To meet the £10 mark, costs are obviously pared down, and our chicken burger came with just chips and lettuce (no tomato, no onion), but the Chinese five-spice marinated chicken was nicely tangy. Other options might be cumberland sausage and mash, fisherman's pie or grilled swordfish (£2 extra), and there's a range of paninis and wraps with chips and salad; should you wish to eat later in the evening, prices are still competitive. The pub's makeover has attractively combined the 1860s patterned glass and woodwork with an airier modern look, and comfortable high-backed leather dining chairs add a stylish touch. Outside, there's a sizeable terrace. The beer and wine range holds no surprises, but covers all the bases. The upstairs dining rooms, which had a broader menu, are now only available for private parties.
Available for hire. Babies and children welcome: children's menu; high chairs; nappy-changing facilities. Disabled: toilet. Separate room for parties, seats 60. Tables outdoors (50, terrace).
Map 5 O4.

Peasant
240 St John Street, EC1V 4PH (7336 7726, www.thepeasant.co.uk). Angel tube/Farringdon tube/rail/19, 38 bus.
Bar **Open** noon-11pm Mon-Sat; noon-10.30pm Sun. **Meals served** noon-10.45pm Mon-Sat; noon-9.30pm Sun. **Main courses** £8.50-£14.
Restaurant **Brunch served** noon-4pm Sun. **Dinner served** 6-11pm Tue-Sat. **Main courses** £9.50-£16.
Both **Credit** AmEx, MC, V.

This grand old pub offers food on two floors. The more sedate first-floor dining room has tablecloths and serves the likes of truffled ducks' eggs with asparagus and soldiers, followed by spring lamb rump with buttered Jersey Royals and pea and mint beignet. Downstairs, the high quality of the somewhat cheaper food comes as a surprise amid the cheerfully rowdy bar atmosphere, until you remember that the same kitchen serves both floors. Poppy-seed bread and a decent cream of cauliflower soup were swiftly followed by exemplary fish and chips with mushy peas and tartare sauce. Roast haddock with welsh rarebit crust and squeak wasn't bad – but by the end we longed for some green stuff to cut through the richness. Sharing platters are a good idea: either the vegetarian meze, or the British platter of potted salt beef, smoked salmon, horseradish and celeriac salad, pickles and cheese, and ale bread. There's a good choice of drinks, with a decent wine list and a range of beers on tap. The only problem is that later in the week the sound level makes conversation difficult.
Babies and children welcome (until 9pm): high chairs. Booking advisable. Tables outdoors (5, garden terrace; 5, pavement). **Map 5 O4**.

Marylebone

Duke of Wellington
94A Crawford Street, W1H 2HQ (7723 2790). Baker Street tube/Marylebone tube/rail. **Open** noon-11pm Mon-Sat; noon-10.30pm Sun. **Lunch served** noon-3pm Mon-Fri; noon-4pm Sat; 12.30-4pm Sun. **Dinner served** 6.30-10pm Mon-Sat; 7-9pm Sun. **Main courses** £8-£16. **Credit** AmEx, MC, V.

An interior designer has had their way here: the small, quiet first-floor dining room has walls the colour of putty, wooden school chairs and prim white tablecloths – all very subtle, apart from the ostentatious light fittings. The bar downstairs has a darker colour scheme, but also flashy ceiling lights and can get quite lively. The kitchen aims slightly higher than the gastropub norm, and mostly makes it. Starters are the likes of crab bisque, steak tartare or warm lingot goat's cheese with pickled cherries, toasted hazelnuts and mixed leaves. Local Marylebone suppliers are well used: a Ginger Pig pork chop with apple sauce, leeks and prunes was a big meaty chop just the right side of pink. Cottage pie, served with greens, lost marks for presentation (it looked like a ready meal), but was splendidly comforting. Puddings were a mixed bag: blood orange sorbet with blood orange and rosemary jelly was nicely zingy but hampered by the rosemary; more successful was a dark chocolate mousse topped with a vividly pink rose-water marshmallow. Service comes with a smile. Drinks include real ales (Black Sheep, Adnams Broadside) alongside a well-chosen wine list.
Babies and children admitted: high chairs. Separate room for parties, seats 25. Tables outdoors (6, pavement). **Map 2 F5.**

Queen's Head & Artichoke
30-32 Albany Street, NW1 4EA (7916 6206, www.theartichoke.net). Great Portland Street or Regent's Park tube. **Open** 11am-11pm Mon-Sat; noon-10.30pm Sun. **Lunch served** noon-3.30pm Mon-Fri; 12.30-4pm Sat. **Dinner served** 6.30-10.15pm Mon-Sat. **Meals served** noon-10.15pm Sun. **Main courses** £9.50-£13.50. **Credit** AmEx, MC, V.
This spot is something of a gastroboozer, achieving a fine balance between its sophisticated dining and its strong drinking culture. Restaurant-focused by day, the mains (veal rump, skate wing, spicy Italian sausages, say) are paired generally successfully with big-flavoured accompaniments, while starters emphasise shellfish and vegetables. By evening, the after-work drinkers pour in and the tapas menu comes into its own. It features anything from almonds and marinated anchovies to skewers of free-range chicken marinated in lemon, rosemary and garlic, and a classy Spanish cheeseboard served with honey. From the Mediterranean to South-east Asia via the Middle East, the meat and fish options on the main menu are strongest. On Sundays, tuck into all-day roast dinners. Dressed Dorset crab was served too cold with an end-of-service weariness to its flavour and texture. Much better was a heady coconut pavlova – crisp, chewy and soft with its butterscotch sauce and banana. The choice between candelabras and low chatter in the elegant upstairs room and wood panelling, lead windows and clamour downstairs is a nice dilemma, and the same menu is served in both. The back yard is lovely, with a soft banquette, exotic maroon and gold cushions and a red glow from the heaters come evening. Service was a little slow, but friendly enough. Expect four draught lagers, Leffe, Hoegaarden, plus Marstons and Adnams cask ales. Factor in nine wines by the glass, plenty of bottles in the £12.50-£25 range and £6.50 cocktails and you'll soon be scrutinising that lengthy tapas list.
Babies and children admitted. Separate room for parties, seats 55. Tables outdoors (6, garden; 8, pavement). **Map 3 H4.**

Mayfair

Only Running Footman
5 Charles Street, W1J 5DF (7499 2988, www.the runningfootman.biz). Green Park tube. **Open** 7.30am-midnight daily. **Meals served** 7.30am-10.30pm daily. **Main courses** £5.50-£19.50. **Credit** AmEx, MC, V.
The only running footman here was, on our recent visit, a pleasant young waitress: the rest of the staff were hanging out laddishly behind the bar and displaying no interest at all in attending to customers' needs. This lack of attention was typical of the place. Environs: handsome pub-style room with blue leather banquettes and picture window let down by scuffed tables, piped music and poor acoustics. Menu: British-inflected pub-aspirational that reads better than it tastes. A beetroot, horseradish and girolle salad lacked the last two ingredients altogether and puzzlingly included a large slice of warm goat's cheese; Cromer crab and wild fennel linguine was a good dish stuggling to escape from its oversalting. In fairness, some of the ingredients were high quality (there's an ethical sourcing policy), there are a couple of real ales on tap including Highgate Special, and the wine list is well constructed, with some intriguing bottles at the lower end. But we've rather lost confidence in the Footman after our second disappointing visit in a row.
Babies and children admitted: high chairs. Disabled: toilet. Separate rooms for parties, seating 14 and 30. Tables outdoors (4, pavement). **Map 9 H7.**
For branches (Bull, House) see index.

West

Chiswick

Duke of Sussex
75 South Parade, W4 5LF (8742 8801). Chiswick Park tube. **Open** 5-11pm Mon; noon-11pm Tue-Thur, Sun; noon-midnight Fri, Sat. **Meals served** 5-10.30pm Mon; noon-10.30pm Tue-Sat; noon-9.30pm Sun. **Main courses** £7.50-£16.50. **Credit** MC, V.
This fine old pub on the Chiswick/Acton borders has been sympathetically restored: it's hung with fine chandeliers, the carved cherubs around the magnificent skylight are artfully coloured and tables nicely spaced. The menu is half British and half Spanish, although it was rather odd to sit with plates of traditional pub grub while spicy paella wafted from the next table. Fish and chips were delightful: perfect chips and a crisp batter that had inflated, so that eating it was like prising the flakes of cod from a shell – in a good way. The tartare sauce was delicious too, but the mushy peas were flat and lifeless. Our steak was cooked exactly as requested. Attentive and helpful service was badly let down by some kitchen snafu with one of our desserts, which kept us waiting for about an hour, albeit with regular apologies. Unfortunately, the long-in-coming desserts weren't worth the wait: apple and nectarine crumble had an odd oaty topping, and sticky toffee pudding was jarringly over-sweet. Regrettably, there were few Hispanic puds the night we were there (we were looking forward to the much-lauded churros). Still, prices are reasonable: with a 375ml carafe of viognier and a bottle of Heineken the bill, without service, came to less than £25 a head.
Babies and children welcome: high chairs. Booking advisable dinner. Disabled: toilet. Separate room for parties, seats 64. Tables outdoors (34, back garden; 3, front garden).

Roebuck
122 Chiswick High Road, W4 1PU (8995 4392, www.theroebuckchiswick.co.uk). Turnham Green tube. **Open** 11am-11pm Mon-Sat; noon-10.30pm Sun. **Meals served** noon-10.30pm Mon-Sat; noon-10pm Sun. **Main courses** £8.50-£17.50. **Credit** AmEx, DC, MC, V.
Part of the growing Food & Fuel empire (currently comprising eight gastropubs and two café-bars), this spacious corner pub on restaurant-saturated Chiswick High Road combines the twin concerns of drinking and dining well. Dark polished floorboards and furniture, bare white walls and judicious lighting provide a stark but stylish setting. You can eat anywhere, but if you want table service head for the more formal dining area at the rear; there's also a section at the side for families, and a large and attractive back garden. The menu mixes gastropub stalwarts (cumberland sausages and mash) with more restaurant-like dishes (flaky roast cod with mussels and new potatoes in a delicate broth of tomato, parsley and white wine). A simple starter salad of mozzarella, broad beans, mint and rocket highlighted the use of first-rate seasonal fare, while fettucine laden with wild mushrooms was an earthy (if slightly oily) treat. Care is evident in all aspects of the enterprise, from the widely spaced tables and well-trained staff to the all-encompassing drinks selection (including a short but top-notch wine list, three real ales, cocktails and pressés). The weekday lunch is a bargain at a fiver.
Babies and children welcome: children's menu; high chairs. Disabled: toilet. Tables outdoors (20, garden; 4, pavement).
For branches (Lots Road Pub & Dining Room, Queens Pub & Dining Room) see index.

Ealing

★ Ealing Park Tavern
222 South Ealing Road, W5 4RL (8758 1879). South Ealing tube. **Open** 11am-11pm Mon-Sat; noon-10.30pm Sun. **Lunch served** noon-3pm Mon-Sat; noon-3.45pm Sun. **Dinner served** 6-11pm Mon-Sat; 6-9pm Sun. **Main courses** £11.95-£16.50. **Credit** AmEx, MC, V.
Tucked away in a corner of south Ealing, this big airy, rather spare place, with huge windows looking across to a park is doing roaring trade despite, or perhaps because of, a fairly 'fine dining' menu. It's not often you see anything but oriental restaurants featuring more than one soft-shell crab dish, but it's normal here: the garrulous maître d' (an escapee from the Ivy) told us it is because the regulars love them. So for starters we tried the assiette of soft-shell crab, black pudding beignets, buffalo mozzarella and chilled roast butternut soup, as well as tempura soft-shell crab with salt and pepper squid and pickled vegetables (that included some delicious samphire). Both were impeccably presented and cooked. Mains of roast magret of duck with celeriac marmalade, spiced polenta, sugar snap peas, and port and gooseberry jus, and roast Elwy lamb with carrot ribbons, peas and truffle crisps were again outstanding – though the truffle crisps failed to add anything to the dish. We enjoyed glasses of prosecco and red wine (the latter taking rather too long to come) from the excellent wine list, though rest assured, beer and cider drinkers are not forgotten here. Prices are reasonable given the standard of cooking.
Babies and children welcome (until 8.30pm): high chairs. Tables outdoors (20, garden).

Hammersmith

★ Carpenter's Arms
91 Black Lion Lane, W6 9BG (8741 8386). Stamford Brook tube. **Open** noon-11pm daily. **Lunch served** noon-2.30pm Mon-Fri; 12.30-3pm Sat; 12.30pm-4pm Sun. **Dinner served** 6.30-10pm Mon-Fri; 7-10pm Sat; 7.30-9.30pm Sun. **Main courses** £10.50-£17. **Credit** AmEx, DC, MC, V.
Tucked in a posh street between unprepossessing King Street and the noisy A4, the Carpenter's Arms splits the difference between a restaurant and a pub. There are scuffed floorboards, dark leather banquettes, a fireplace and a large back yard with pub-style wooden tables, but the bar is tiny and the wine list much better than the beer selection (just one draught offering: Adnams). It's flooded with light by day, twinkly and cosy at night. Diners take priority over drinkers, and most people come to eat. As they should: the food is inventive and consistently excellent. Sunday lunch in August brought an array of enticing dishes from simple (potted crab and toast) through surprising (crisp pork belly with watermelon and feta) to sublime (grilled plaice with samphire, charlotte potatoes and brown shrimps). Pea, lettuce and parmesan soup was typical of the seaonally-led approach: a light, summery broth packed with fresh-tasting vegetables. The only duff note came with a starter of scallops (four plump specimens) in a black bean and spring onion dressing that was too heavy on soy sauce. We didn't have room for gooseberry and almond tart, but vanilla ice-cream doused in 'very old sherry' made a great finish. Staff were casual, confident and charming – a description that sums up the enterprise as a whole.
Babies and children admitted: high chairs. Booking advisable. Tables outdoors (8, garden).
Map 20 A4.

Cadogan Arms

Ladbroke Grove

Fat Badger

310 Portobello Road, W10 5TA (8969 4500, www.thefatbadger.com). Ladbroke Grove or Westbourne Park tube. **Open** 11.30am-10.30pm Mon; 11.30am-11pm Tue-Thur; 11.30am-midnight Fri; 10am-midnight Sat; 10am-10.30pm Sun. **Breakfast served** 10am-noon Sat, Sun. **Lunch served** noon-3pm Mon-Fri; noon-5pm Sat, Sun. **Dinner served** 6-10pm daily. **Main courses** £11-£16.50. **Credit** AmEx, DC, MC, V.

The once buzzy Fat Badger opened a couple of years ago to a spate of rave reviews praising everything from the quirky London-themed wallpaper (designed by Timorous Beasties) to the wonderful British food. Sadly, it's not just the wallpaper that seems scuffed around the edges. Downstairs is where most of the action takes place, as a downbeat, dressed-down crowd tuck into pints of lager and the occasional plate of food to a retro blend of '80s tunes. We had to ask permission to sit in the slightly grander dining room upstairs. Staff seemed a little put out to have to turn the lights on, let alone open it on a Wednesday night – little wonder considering only two other tables were taken for the rest of the evening. The menu was brief and boring. A starter of cuttlefish with chorizo was tasty but unrefined, the cuttlefish a large chewy chunk of protein. Of the four mains, steak and chicken were the most exciting options. Ribeye, not cheap at £16.50, was chewy and fatty, served with a pile of anaemic chips and an overly tangy béarnaise sauce. Chicken breast, moist and flavoursome with creamy savoy cabbage and bacon, was better, but served lukewarm. Typical desserts include chocolate brownie and eton mess. If the Fat Badger doesn't find its mojo soon it could be in danger of becoming roadkill.
Babies and children admitted. Tables outdoors (4, terrace). **Map 19 B1.**

Olympia

Cumberland Arms

29 North End Road, W14 8SZ (7371 6806, www.thecumberlandarmspub.co.uk). West Kensington tube/Kensington (Olympia) tube/rail. **Open** noon-11pm Mon-Sat; noon-10.30pm Sun. **Lunch served** noon-3pm Mon-Fri; noon-4pm Sat. **Dinner served** 7-10pm Mon-Sat. **Meals served** 12.30-9.30pm Sun. **Main courses** £7-£15.50. **Credit** AmEx, MC, V.

Flower-filled exterior aside, there's nothing fancy about this local favourite. From the well-worn furniture to the order-at-the-bar chalkboard menu, it's all very familiar. In summer, outside is the place to be, a young after-work crowd spilling into the good-sized courtyard. Inside, with its candlelit tables and open fireplace, is more suited to cosy winter catch-ups, the homely vibe only tarnished by the undeniable whiff of bleach. The food has a homespun feel too, with portions on the massive side and a Mediterranean-inspired menu that may not be particularly inventive, but is generally appealing with a good range of seafood, steak and pasta dishes. A tender chargrilled ribeye steak surrendered easily to the knife, and the taste buds, while roast sea bream fillets with chorizo and potatoes proved a pleasant, if safe, combination. The wine list covers most parts of the world, with a particular slant toward New Zealand varieties. Desserts were straight out of the 1970s, trifle and ice-cream among them, and profiteroles with chocolate sauce were familiar, unchallenging and safe – much like the Cumberland Arms itself.
Available for hire. Babies and children welcome (until 7pm): high chairs. Tables outdoors (11, pavement).

Shepherd's Bush

Anglesea Arms

35 Wingate Road, W6 0UR (8749 1291). Goldhawk Road or Ravenscourt Park tube. **Open** 11am-11pm Mon-Sat; noon-10.30pm Sun. **Lunch served** 12.30-2.45pm Mon-Fri; 12.30-3pm Sat; 12.30-3.30pm Sun. **Dinner served** 7-10.30pm Mon-Sat; 7-10pm Sun. **Main courses** £12.50-£15.50. **Credit** MC, V.

The Anglesea Arms is the kind of corner pub that every neighbourhood wants but very rarely gets. Laid-back and friendly, it oozes character inside and out. On sunny days locals flock to the tables outdoors, facing on to the quiet streets of Brackenbury. In winter the hotspot is the comfortable old leather couch by the fire, perfect for an afternoon sprawl with the Sunday papers. There's usually a dog close by – in the less formal front bar, anyway. The sky-lit back area is all about the food. On a Monday night it buzzed with the happy din of couples, families and groups of all ages, tucking into freshly shucked oysters and various other hearty-sized plates of thoroughly good grub. Our ever-attentive waiter went out of his way to describe what a barnsley chop was,

even scrawling a diagram on his order pad to illustrate. The lamb was meltingly tender and the right shade of pink, served with sweet caramelised roast violet artichokes and potatoes. A wintry-sounding pork leg with lentils became satisfyingly spring-like with the addition of radishes and baby carrots. A classic gastropub with bags of charm.
Babies and children admitted. Tables outdoors (10, pavement). **Map 20 A3.**

★ Princess Victoria (100)

217 Uxbridge Road, W12 9DH (8749 5886, www.princessvictoria.co.uk). Shepherd's Bush tube. **Open** 11.30am-midnight Mon-Sat; 11.30am-11pm Sun. **Lunch served** noon-3pm Mon-Sat; noon-4.30pm Sun. **Dinner served** 6.30-10.30pm Mon-Sat; 6.30-9.30pm Sun. **Main courses** £10.50-£16.50. **Set lunch** (Mon-Fri) £12.50 2 courses, £15 3 courses. **Credit** MC, V.

Regal by name, regal by nature, this imposing pub on famously multicultural Uxbridge Road has done wonders for Shepherd's Bush's long-held shabby reputation. The former gin palace has been restored to its grand former glory, all wooden furniture and opulent light fittings with separate areas for drinking and dining, while the pretty walled garden is worth seeking out on sunnier days. The dining area is particularly impressive with its high sky-lit ceiling and banquet-like central table perfect for groups of up to 16. It prides itself on its wine list featuring over 300 bottles, and has a reassuring selection of ales on tap for those who want more pub and less ponce. One look at the menu and it's clear the Princess Vic takes its food seriously too. The succinct but appealing menu changes daily, serving fine British food with finesse and flair. A perfectly cooked fillet of sea bass with pea purée and runny-yolked poached egg was admirably both delicate and hearty, but that old gastropub favourite, roast pork belly, was not quite as fall-off-the-fork tender as we had hoped. Service is slick, the crowd as well turned out as the whole operation. In just over a year the Princess Victoria has established itself as the kind of grown-up eating and drinking destination many other pubs aspire to be. A weekly Saturday artisan market held outside underlines the foodie credentials – no surprise it won our 2008 Best New Gastropub Award.
Babies and children welcome: high chairs. Booking advisable. Separate room for parties, seats 60. Tables outdoors (10, garden). **Map 20 A2.**

Westbourne Grove

Cow (100)

89 Westbourne Park Road, W2 5QH (7221 0021, www.thecowlondon.co.uk). Royal Oak or Westbourne Park tube. **Open** noon-11pm Mon-Sat; noon-10.30pm Sun. **Lunch served** noon-3.30pm daily. **Dinner served** 6-10.30pm Mon-Sat; 6-10pm Sun. **Main courses** £12-£15. **Set lunch** (Sun) £24 2 courses, £26 3 courses. **Credit** MC, V.

The walls of this wee gem of a gastropub are covered in old signs proclaiming that 'Guinness is good for you', and, after a pint or two with a plate of Irish rock oysters, you're unlikely to disagree. Upstairs is a slightly stuffy room dedicated to somewhat pricey dining; downstairs is where the action unfolds. Efficient bar staff pour pint after pint of excellent Guinness, laid-back tunes and chat fill the air, and pretty Notting Hillbillies jostle for first come, first served tables around the snug but charmingly retro room. Foodwise, it's all about the seafood. A gutsy fish stew came packed with generous chunks of white fish, salmon and mussels, and the platters piled high with crab, oysters, prawns, clams, whelks and winkles are a seafood lover's dream. Less successful was the ambitious (and unusual) attempt at cooking rook. The small, chargrilled bird arrived needing a steak knife to cut through it, and looked faintly disturbing too, although the accompanying bubble and squeak almost made up for it. The wine list favours France and is suitably seafood-friendly. This isn't the place for a long leisurely meal as staff are intent on keeping tables turning, but for a buzzy casual seafood meal with a group of friends it's difficult to beat.
Available for hire. Babies and children admitted (restaurant only). Tables outdoors (2, pavement). **Map 7 A5**.

South West

Barnes

Brown Dog

28 Cross Street, SW13 0AP (8392 2200). Barnes Bridge rail. **Open** noon-11pm Mon-Sat; noon-10pm Sun. **Lunch served** noon-3pm Mon-Fri; noon-4pm Sat, Sun. **Dinner served** 7-10pm Mon-Sat; 7-9pm Sun. **Main courses** £10.50-£17. **Credit** AmEx, MC, V.

In the slumbering backstreets of Barnes lurks this rather special local. Customers can choose between a cosy public bar and a modest dining room cluttered with retro posters and decked in classic dark green and cream paint. At first glance the menu can seem a bit unexciting – starters of prawns, asparagus and scallops followed by mains of steak, fish, and bangers, among others. But the food, when it arrives, is delicious and hard to fault. Those scallops, added to thin strips of courgette, spring onion and pea shoots, made a beautifully balanced dish; bream, potatoes, peppers and tapenade radiated flavour without being too fishy. Cumberland sausage with mash, and a wonderful hot chocolate pudding proved the kitchen's comfort food credentials. Service was attentive and the mix of young and old customers created a pleasant din. The Brown Dog was runner-up for Time Out's 2007 Best Gastropub award and one senses that friendly landlord Jamie Prudhom pays attention to every detail. Superb breads come from esteemed London bakery the Flour Station. The wine list represents the best of Australia and California, alongside a good number of bottles from Burgundy and the Rhône, while two small breweries set up in the last five years provide the draught highlights – a light, golden Wandle ale brewed nearby at Sambrook's in Battersea, and the darker Grasshopper bitter from Kent. There's even a small beer garden at the back.
Available for hire. Babies and children welcome: high chairs. Tables outdoors (12, garden).

Chelsea

★ Cadogan Arms NEW

2009 RUNNER-UP BEST NEW GASTROPUB
298 King's Road, SW3 5UG (7352 6500, www.thecadoganarmschelsea.com). Sloane Square tube. **Open** 11am-11pm daily. **Lunch served** noon-3pm daily. **Dinner served** 6-10.30pm Mon-Sat; 6-9pm Sun. **Main courses** £11-£18.50. **Credit** AmEx, DC, MC, V.

In 2009 this Chelsea pub was given a major rebuild by new owners, the Martin Brothers. It now has a countrified look, complete with stuffed creatures and encased fly-fishing displays on the walls. While still a proper boozer with good real ales, towards the back is the snug and smoothly run dining area. On more than one visit we've found the dishes to be expertly cooked, and always attractively presented. This was the case on one midsummer occasion, when a vivid green pea soup arrived garnished with pancetta, double cream and microgreens. Duck breast, with the fat rendered away and neatly cut into fingers, rested on a salad of green beans, beetroot and potato, the plate adorned with more of those colourful microgreens – pretty as a picture. On a late summer visit, a perfectly cooked pan-roasted veal chop appeared with a mash rich in olive oil. Puddings tend towards the old school, such as a rum and raisin sticky toffee pudding, served with butterscotch sauce and vanilla ice-cream. The wine list offers many intriguing choices, and there's even a good cheeseboard. A 'formula' Martin Brothers gastropub, perhaps – but what a formula.
Available for hire. Babies and children welcome: children's menu; high chairs. Booking advisable. Separate room for parties, seats 60. **Map 14 E12**.
For branches (Empress of India, Gun, Prince Arthur, Well, White Swan Pub & Dining Room) see index.

Pig's Ear

35 Old Church Street, SW3 5BS (7352 2908/ www.turningearth.co.uk/thepigsear). Sloane Square tube. **Open** noon-11pm Mon-Sat; noon-10.30pm Sun. **Lunch served** 12.30-3pm, **dinner served** 7-10pm Mon-Fri. **Meals served** noon-11pm Sat, noon-10.30pm Sun. **Main courses** £10.50-£18.50. **Credit** AmEx, MC, V.

Although it lies in a smart residential area, the Pig's Ear is a very manageable stroll from the King's Road, making it an appealing choice after an afternoon's shopping. The bar teems with Chelsea totty, older chaps in corduroy and linen jackets, and tourists who've clocked the pub's myriad recommendations from travel and restaurant guides. There is a dining room upstairs by the kitchen, but it's the bar that seems the most convivial choice for eating, even though chairs and tables are dinky. A picture of the Dalai Lama above the waiters' workstation might inspire them to keep their cool, but there simply weren't enough staff on our visit and despite their best efforts and mostly good humour, getting served was a struggle. Typical starters include smoked gammon terrine, rock oysters and peppered mackerel with beetroot. Mains are rustic and hearty. Lamb leg steak was tender, perfectly cooked and well matched with fruity couscous and red wine sauce. Also good was pan-fried lemon sole spiked with capers and gremolata and served with a tangle of samphire and cherry tomatoes. Other options might be half a corn-fed chicken, half a lobster thermidor (well, this is deepest Chelsea) or, for vegetarians, creamy wild mushrooms on toast, or a plate of linguine.
Available for hire. Babies and children welcome: high chairs; nappy-changing facilities. Booking advisable (dining room). Disabled: toilet. **Map 14 E12**.

Fulham

★ Harwood Arms NEW (100)

2009 WINNER BEST NEW GASTROPUB
27 Walham Grove, SW6 1QP (7386 1847). Fulham Broadway tube. **Open** noon-11pm Mon-Fri; noon-midnight Sat; noon-10.30pm Sun. **Lunch served** noon-3pm Mon-Sat; 12.30-4pm Sun. **Dinner served** 6-9.30pm Mon-Sat; 7-9.30pm Sun. **Main courses** £13.50-£15.50. **Credit** AmEx, MC, V.

A villagey neighbourhood and an interior as English as cricket on the green could turn this delightful pub in Fulham into a parody of itself. It's true that the well-mannered waiting staff wear stripy pressed shirts, and 'A Good Old Boy' here could refer to half the locals, but it's also the name of a guest beer from the excellent selection of real ales pulled at the bar. The posh-country feel extends from the details (hessian napkins tied with raffia) to the menu, which includes plenty of game, with seasonal oddities such as pheasant eggs. It's run by a team including TV chef Mike Robinson, who already owns a hit gastropub, the Pot Kiln in Berkshire. Robinson hunts many of the deer served at both places himself. Our roe deer was tender and properly gamey, served with a little pot

of grated beetroot and horseradish for added zing. A steak of Cornish cod, topped with brown shrimps and sprigs of foraged sea purslane, also revealed the kitchen's commitment to seasonal ingredients. The precision of the cooking rarely slips: the pastry of a rhubarb pie was very slightly overcooked, but the piped meringue topping looked like gilded cathedral domes, turning this edifice into a work of art. One of London's best gastropubs, no question.
Available for hire. Babies and children welcome: children's menu; high chairs. Booking advisable dinner. **Map 13 A13**.

Putney

Prince of Wales
138 Upper Richmond Road, SW15 2SP (8788 1552, www.princeofwalesputney.co.uk). East Putney tube/Putney rail. **Open** noon-11pm Mon-Wed; noon-11.30pm Thur; noon-midnight Fri, Sat; noon-10.30pm Sun. **Lunch served** noon-3pm Mon-Fri; noon-4pm Sat, Sun. **Dinner served** 6-10pm Mon-Sat; 6-9pm Sun. **Main courses** £8-£18. **Credit** MC, V.
This Victorian corner pub manages to mix some original flavour with serious gastropub pretensions – and a distinctly weird edge. The two small bars at front offer good drinking to a backdrop of pewter mugs, stuffed animals, flagstones, brasses and pictures of Botham winning the Ashes. The dining room at back feels isolated from the bar and also manages to seem bigger than it is, thanks to a glorious Victorian

pyramidical skylight. In fact, there is just a smattering of tables among yet more stuffed rabbits, antlers, artful black and white photos and a rotisserie grill. The menu changes regularly and you'll do just as well dining in the pub as the restaurant. Fish and chips, lovely light gazpacho, platters of sesame prawn toast, own-made houmous and pot-roast poussin with caesar salad give the idea. We tried succulent slow-roast rump cap with bearnaise sauce; the triple-cooked chips were sensational. Finish with some great unpasteurised cheeses or something from the brief list of puddings: mint humbug chocolate fondant with mint choc chip ice-cream, say. Staff are very keen and you'll find the drinkers and diners a more mixed bunch that at many other Putney boozers.
Available for hire. Babies and children welcome: high chairs. Separate room for parties, seats 45. Tables outdoors (8, pavement).

Spencer Arms
237 Lower Richmond Road, SW15 1HJ (8788 0640, www.thespencerarms.co.uk). Putney Bridge tube/22, 265, 485 bus. **Open** 11am-midnight Mon-Sat; 11am-11pm Sun. **Lunch served** noon-2.30pm Mon-Fri; noon-3pm Sat. **Dinner served** 6.30-10pm Mon-Sat. **Meals served** noon-9.45pm Sun. **Main courses** £7.50-£18. **Credit** MC, V.
Finding this unassuming pub at the wrong end of the Lower Richmond Road, hard by a mini bus terminus, is not easy, but the pleasantly quirky menu makes the effort worthwhile. On our visit the rather plain interior was almost devoid of customers and seemingly uncharismatic staff

didn't enhance the atmosphere. Nevertheless, starters of black pudding with poached egg and ox tongue with capers and parsley came to the table on chic little slate slabs and were out of this world; the taste and texture of the tongue were particularly memorable. Mains of copious mussels with merguez and a side of chips, and lamb noisettes with sage stuffing in a broth with summer vegetables were no less impressive and well judged. Things were going so well, we just had to try more, so ordered a trio of fabulous Jude's ices (vanilla, chocolate chip and a peach sorbet), plus a selection of British cheeses (cheddar, stilton and an English brie). The cheese platter was generous and served with own-made apple chutney and crackers. With a carafe of Alquezar rosé, extra chips and service, our three courses came to just over £30 a head, confirming that this is a little local legend in the making.
Babies and children welcome (until 9pm): high chairs; nappy-changing facilities. Disabled: toilet. Entertainment: jazz 8pm, call for details. Tables outdoors (11, pavement).

Wimbledon

Earl Spencer
260-262 Merton Road, SW18 5JL (8870 9244, www.theearlspencer.co.uk). Southfields tube. **Open** 11am-11pm Mon-Thur; 11am-midnight Fri, Sat; noon-10.30pm Sun. **Lunch served** 12.30-2.30pm Mon-Sat; 12.30-3pm Sun. **Dinner served** 7-10pm Mon-Sat; 7-9.30pm Sun. **Main courses** £8.50-£14. **Credit** AmEx, MC, V.

Harwood Arms. See p107.

The setting may be unprepossessing, but this is a cracking gastropub. Blue and cream paintwork, stripped floorboards and worn furniture fit the mould, but it's attractively done and suits the casual, come-as-you-like vibe – as do the friendly staff and no-booking policy. Drinks, comprising well-kept real ales (Fuller's London Pride, Hook Norton Best and Sharp's Doom Bar on our visit), own-made summer specials (including a refreshing ginger, lemon and barley cordial) and a diverse wine list (from £3 a glass), are dispensed from the central bar, while customers, some eating, some in for a quick pint, spread themselves around the periphery of the light and spacious interior. The front terrace is softened by shrubs and hanging baskets, though this doesn't really succeed in masking the traffic noise. The nicely priced, daily-changing menu emphasises seasonal ingredients, and the bread is baked on the premises. All our dishes were good, from a half-pint of shell-on prawns with aïoli to mains of perfectly cooked whole grilled bream with Jersey Royal potatoes, baby leeks and succulent spinach, and a chunky, flavourful quiche of sweet potato, goat's cheese and spinach. To finish, there is always ice-cream and a tempting cheese plate.
Babies and children welcome: high chairs. Bookings not accepted. Separate room for parties, seats 70. Tables outdoors (10, patio).

South
Balham

Avalon NEW
16 Balham Hill, SW12 9EB (8675 8613, www.theavalonlondon.co.uk). Clapham South tube. **Open** noon-11pm Mon-Wed; noon-midnight Thur; noon-1am Fri, Sat; noon-10.30pm Sun. **Lunch served** noon-3.30pm Mon-Fri; noon-4pm Sat. **Dinner served** 6-10.30pm Mon-Sat. **Meals served** noon-9pm Sun. **Main courses** £9-£14.95. **Credit** AmEx, MC, V.
A huge place, the Avalon has a deep, awning-covered terrace facing a busy road, a pretty side garden, a big and beautifully landscaped rear garden (complete with barbecue station), and a spacious bar area that wouldn't look out of place in *Country Living*. Proper beers might include Timothy Taylor Landlord or Sambrook's Wandle; the wines by the glass and the bar menu also suffice. The main dining area is even grander, with white-tiled walls decorated with curious Victorian etchings and bizarre chainmail chandeliers. The menu suggests considerable ambition, but, on our visit, the more tempting dishes, such as pigeon faggots, were off. Instead, we settled for croquettes that apparently contained pigs' trotters and 'crispy' ham hock, though the texture and taste of the filling was disappointingly bland and soft. Smoked eel had better texture, though again, the flavour of the smoking process was muted. Ribeye steak was full-flavoured, but served medium, not medium-rare as requested. Prices are reasonable for what is now Balham's most appealing gastropub, but given the lavish refurb, we'd hoped for more impressive cooking.
Babies and children welcome: children's menu; crayons; high chairs; nappy-changing facilities. Booking advisable. Disabled: toilet. Separate room for parties, seats 20. Tables outdoors (22, garden; 10, pavement; 10, courtyard).

Waterloo

Anchor & Hope (100)
36 The Cut, SE1 8LP (7928 9898). Southwark or Waterloo tube/rail. **Open** 5-11pm Mon; noon-11pm Tue-Sat; noon-5pm Sun. **Lunch served** noon-2.30pm Tue-Sat; 2pm sitting Sun. **Dinner served** 6-10.30pm Mon-Sat. **Main courses** £11.80-£22. **Credit** DC, MC, V.
The most common gripes about this place concern the stubby wine glasses they insist on using and the Monday to Saturday no-booking policy. We got a table immediately, and our first glass was a delicious Seville rosé infused with orange and vodka, so no complaints so far. The obnoxiously loud diner who joined our communal table was an

irritant, but hardly the fault of the establishment. Those who do have to wait can salivate over the scrumptious seasonal menu written up on the blackboard, but choose carefully: a single gull's egg with a couple of radishes was measly for its price tag, and hollandaise sauce would have made a better accompaniment to the delicious asparagus than the melted butter (with nary a crack of black pepper). The dover sole was a handsome fish, but poaching with leek and cockles did nothing to enhance it. Arbroath smokie on the other hand was dreamy – firm-fleshed and salty enough to combine perfectly with side dishes of huge fluffy potatoes and a pile of spring greens. Neighbouring diners tucked happily into desserts of meringue and rhubarb fool and a fruit mango ice-cream while we headed to the bar for pints of Young's beer and some respite from loud boy.
Babies and children welcome: high chairs. Bookings not accepted Mon-Sat; advisable Sun. Tables outdoors (5, pavement). **Map 11 N8**.

South East
Bermondsey

Garrison
99-101 Bermondsey Street, SE1 3XB (7089 9355, www.thegarrison.co.uk). London Bridge tube/rail. **Open** 8am-11pm Mon-Fri; 9am-midnight Sat; 9am-10.30pm Sun. **Breakfast served** 8-11.30am Mon-Fri; 9-11.30am Sat, Sun. **Lunch served** noon-3.30pm Mon-Fri; 12.30-4pm Sat, Sun. **Dinner served** 6.30-10pm Mon-Sat; 6-9.30pm Sun. **Main courses** £10.30-£15.50. **Credit** AmEx, MC, V.
Down on hipper-than-you Bermondsey Street, the Garrison is one restaurant pretending to be a pub that is very sure of itself, thank you very much. A corner boozer stylishly made over with mock-William Morris wallpaper and super-cool bucket chairs, this gastropub has a high enough opinion of itself to book two sittings at dinner time – even if being told you must eat against the clock is never the most relaxing way to start your evening. This attitude makes itself felt throughout the meal, from the, er, bold starters of avocado and pea soup (unfinished) and crab with bloody mary sorbet (just as odd, but much more palatable), to the slapdash service that failed to make us feel particularly wanted. Main courses were more conventional and much more successful than openers: an excellent ribeye steak came with oversalted chips, but the crispy pork belly with split pea casserole was pretty much faultless. Fellow diners were much as you'd expect for the top end of Bermondsey Street: young, fresh-faced, well dressed and easily impressed.
Babies and children admitted (lunch Sat, Sun). Booking advisable. Disabled: toilet. Separate room for parties, seats 25. **Map 12 Q9**.

Catford

Perry Hill
78-80 Perry Hill, SE6 4EY (8699 5076, www.theperryhill.co.uk). Catford Bridge or Lower Sydenham rail. **Open** noon-11pm daily. **Lunch served** noon-3pm, dinner served 6-10pm Mon-Sat. **Meals served** noon-10pm Sun. **Main courses** £8.50-£13.50. **Credit** AmEx, MC, V.
Local boy Robbie O'Neill and his experienced team have created a welcoming venue for all comers, and all seasons. You can pop in for a pint of real ale – a modest range, but well kept and correctly served – or linger over a glass of wine from an affordable list that offers interest rather than intimidation, in the cosy bar area. Decide to dine and you can migrate to the more brightly lit, spacious restaurant, its comforting dark wood and leather leavened by contemporary touches. On a summer evening the decking-clad garden beckons irresistibly, not least to children. The menu, too, is designed to please all generations and traditionalists as much as adventurers. Chef Andrew Belew espouses the gastropub calling with correct and vigorous precision: Italian pastas benefit from the same deft execution as dishes graced with South-east Asian seasoning, while

Interview
STEPHEN WILLIAMS

Who are you?
Head chef of the **Harwood Arms** (*see p107*) in Fulham.
How did you start in the catering business?
I have always wanted to cook. After three years at Westminster College, my first cooking job was at the **Square** (*see p131*).
What's the best thing about running a restaurant in London?
London is so large and has such a diverse restaurant scene that there is space for many different styles and concepts. As a result, most diners are informed about food and happy to search out quality.
What's the worst thing?
It is a 24/7 city, so we have to be open 14 shifts a week. And the internet has made almost every diner a critic.
Which are your favourite London restaurants?
Milkbar (Noel Street branch of **Flat White**, *see p290*) for coffee and slouching. The **Anchor & Hope** (*see p109*) for the atmosphere of a lazy Sunday afternoon.
What's the best bargain in the capital?
The lunch menu at the **Ledbury** (*see p97*): something special for not very much money.
What's your favourite treat?
More than four hours of sleep! One of each cake from **Princi** (*see p46*) after a film at the Curzon Soho.
What is missing from London's restaurant scene?
After the response to our bar snacks, I'd say a scotch egg bar – all different flavours and different eggs served with British beers.
What does the next year hold?
It's certainly uncertain times, but everyone loves eating out. I think somewhere offering quality and value for money will always be busy.

traditional staples – bangers and mash, haddock and chips with mushy peas – are properly staunch, even when a mischievous twist intervenes. On our visit, chargrilled asparagus in season was smoky, crunchy perfection and beer batter tempura-light over moist and flaky fish. Seasoning tends to the barely noticeable, but is nicely offset by deeply caramelised chutneys and sauces. Service is friendly, intelligent and flexible.
Available for hire. Babies and children welcome: high chairs. Tables outdoors (24, garden).

Dulwich

Rosendale

65 Rosendale Road, SE21 8EZ (8670 0812, www.therosendale.co.uk). West Dulwich rail. **Bar Open** noon-11pm Mon-Thur, Sun; noon-midnight Fri, Sat. **Meals served** noon-10pm daily. **Main courses** £9.50-£16. *Restaurant* **Lunch served** noon-3pm Fri, Sat; noon-4pm Sun. **Dinner served** 7-10pm Mon-Sat. **Set meal** £20 2 courses, £24 3 courses. *Both* **Credit** MC, V.
The faithful local clientele – and anyone happy to detour in search of excellence – will be delighted to know that the Rosendale's doors are still open wide despite the demise of its equally esteemed cousin the Greyhound (a victim of the credit crunch). The menu still delivers its promise and the superb wine list is as extensive as ever. One compromise is the restriction of à la carte dining to weekends; 'aimed firmly at the local neighbourhood', the Rosendale seems to depend on the regular take-up of its more readily affordable options. So, snack on the extensive bar menu (everything well presented – from smoked pork collar, apple, celery and walnut salad through gammon, egg and chips, to pea and ham soup) in the light-filled front bar or bright outdoor terrace. But a visit to the dark-wood formality of the restaurant is rewarded with an assured, and refreshingly short, menu of classic plates and roast dinners on Sundays. Starters include own-smoked salmon chunks with sublime horseradish mousse and intensely flavoured pork rillettes served with pickled cabbage; mains cover Icelandic halibut and organic salmon fillets as well as confidently handled beef ribs and fillets.
Babies and children welcome: high chairs; nappy-changing facilities. Disabled: toilet. Separate rooms for parties, seating 25-100. Tables outdoors (40, garden).

East Dulwich

★ Herne Tavern

2 Forest Hill Road, SE22 0RR (8299 9521, www.theherne.net). East Dulwich or Peckham Rye rail/12, 197 bus. **Open** noon-11pm Mon-Thur; noon-1am Fri, Sat; noon-10.30pm Sun. **Lunch served** noon-2.30pm Mon-Fri; noon-3pm Sat; noon-4pm Sun. **Dinner served** 6.30-9.45pm Mon-Sat; 6.30-9.30pm Sun. **Main courses** £8.50-£12. **Credit** MC, V.
Is there a better-tasting or better-kept pint in London than the light and hoppy Hogs Back Summer Ale pulled at the Herne Tavern? No wonder this pub is as attractive to the workmen at the wood-panelled bar as it is to the families that pack out the happily shabby back garden. And the food? Starters were excellent: own-made gravadlax served mouth-meltingly tender, the salmon balanced well between sweet and salty. But the star was the scotch duck egg: the yolk half-soft, half-set; the sausage meat kicking with spicy flavour. Mains were similarly confident. Black bream was slightly over-salted, but in combination with clams and samphire, it delivered a briny bowl of big seaside flavours. Our burger patty was so rare it was virtually steak tartare; cheap meat would be exposed by such treatment, but this passed the test easily – a great wallop of high-quality mince. It hardly mattered that the french fries were nondescript; and anyway, who would want to waste pudding room on chips when the afters are this good? Dark chocolate mocha tart was, in essence, a big slab of chocolate. Less calorifically disastrous (just), the Secretts Farm strawberries and balsamic ice-cream was massively sweet,

Britannia. See p113.

though could perhaps have been more balsamic, but that's to quibble; pretty much everything was very good indeed.
Babies and children welcome: children's menu; high chairs; nappy-changing facilities. Separate room for parties, seats 60. Tables outdoors (25, garden).

Palmerston

91 Lordship Lane, SE22 8EP (8693 1629, www.thepalmerston.net). East Dulwich rail/185, 176, P13 bus. **Open** noon-11pm Mon-Thur; noon-midnight Fri, Sat; noon-10.30pm Sun. **Lunch served** noon-2.30pm Mon-Fri; noon-3pm Sat, Sun. **Dinner served** 7-10pm Mon-Sat; 7-9.30pm Sun. **Main courses** £11-£16. **Set lunch** (Mon-Fri) £11.50 2 courses, £14.50 3 courses. **Credit** MC, V.
The Palmerston is the prince of East Dulwich's Lordship Lane, a bustling thoroughfare where you can't turn around without bumping into a trendy parent pushing a Bugaboo out of an organic grocery. Faced with such clientele, many local establishments have a tendency to over-compensate, but the Palmerston plays its cards cannily, creating an environment that is welcoming to children – staff are attentive and friendly – but that equally doesn't exclude child-free customers. It also manages to retain a very publike atmosphere despite serving seriously good food. The menu, which changes between lunch and dinner, focuses on superior Modern British dishes such as pan-fried fillet of lemon sole with watercress, and rump of salt marsh lamb and grilled lamb's tongue with caper and thyme gravy. Sunday lunch is a particular treat: huge plates piled high with meat and yorkshires, with large dishes of seasonal veg on the side. Desserts are splendid and very English – eton mess was meringue heavy, just the way we like it, while rhubarb crumble with custard was comforting and classically executed.
Babies and children welcome: high chairs; nappy-changing facilities. Booking advisable dinner and weekends. Tables outdoors (6, pavement). **Map 23 C4**.

Herne Hill

Prince Regent

69 Dulwich Road, SE24 0NJ (7274 1567, www.theprinceregent.co.uk). Herne Hill rail/3, 196 bus. **Open** noon-11pm Mon-Thur; noon-midnight Fri, Sat; noon-10.30pm Sun. **Lunch served** noon-3pm Mon-Sat. **Dinner served** 7-10pm Mon-Sat; 6-9pm Sun. **Main courses** £8.85-£16. **Credit** MC, V.
Large airy pubs with an outdoor terrace (even one adjacent to a busy bus route) and plenty of room

for pushchairs are always going to be popular in this area. Indeed, at weekends the Prince Regent gets so crowded with younger customers that it hosts a family Sunday lunch (serious roasts), and also sets aside a child-free upstairs room for those seeking some peace. As a pub, it's a hit, with four guest ales, branded lagers and decent wine, while booths, books and board games clearly invite drinkers to linger. Regrettably, the food menu is limited and uninspiring, focusing on such predictable classics as burger, steak frites, sausage and mash, sea bass, fish pie, steak and ale pie (though on the day we visited they were out of pies and hadn't come up with an alternative). Surprisingly, there is no children's menu, though staff are happy to rustle up scrambled eggs, sausage and chips or any combination of that day's ingredients. Our visit was rescued by some unexpectedly good rice dishes – a tasty kedgeree, a creamy risotto – and substantial salads.
Babies and children welcome (until 7pm): high chairs; nappy-changing facilities. Booking advisable evenings, Sun lunch. Disabled: toilet. Separate room for parties, seats 50. Tables outdoors (12, terrace). **Map 22 E3**.

Peckham

Old Nun's Head

15 Nunhead Green, SE15 3QQ (7639 4007, www.oldnunshead.com). Nunhead rail/78, P12 bus. **Open** noon-midnight Mon-Thur, Sun; noon-1am Fri, Sat. **Lunch served** 12.30-2.15pm, **dinner served** 6.30-10.15pm Mon-Fri. **Meals served** noon-10.15pm Sat; noon-9pm Sun. **Main courses** £6.95-£13. **Credit** AmEx, MC, V.
Drinkers and diners are both happy at this brick and timber 1930s boozer. The former get a sterling selection of cask-conditioned ales (Harveys Sussex, Woodforde's Wherry, Hopback Summer Lightning and York Constantine on our visit), plus cocktails and an acceptable wine list. The latter get massive plates of hearty, unpretentious food at decent prices (the most expensive dish, sirloin steak, was £13; most were around £8). There's plenty of seating: at large wooden tables next to the central bar, in the back garden and in the front yard facing Nunhead Green. Carnivores get the best deal: there was just one fish and one vegetarian main (puy lentil and mushroom lasagne, served with chunky chips and salad – decent but no better than most home cooks could turn out). More ambitious were lamb chops (slightly dry) with roasted garlic and anchovies, new potatoes and a tasty salsa of red pepper, green beans and black olives. Top marks went to a starter of salmon and spring onion fish cakes: grease-free

RESTAURANTS

and fluffy yet crammed with chunks of fish. And the name? A nunnery once occupied this site; the rebellious Mother Superior was murdered during the Reformation and her head stuck on a pikestaff on the green.

Babies and children welcome (until 9pm): high chairs; nappy-changing facilities. Disabled: toilet. Entertainment: open mic, music Wed 9pm. Separate room for parties, seats 30. Tables outdoors (4, garden).

Sydenham

Dolphin

121 Sydenham Road, SE26 5HB (8778 8101, www.thedolphinsydenham.com). Sydenham rail. **Open** noon-11.30pm Mon-Thur; noon-midnight Fri, Sat; noon-11pm Sun. **Lunch served** noon-3.30pm Mon-Fri, noon-4pm Sun. **Dinner served** 6.30-10pm Mon-Fri, 5-9pm Sun. **Meals served** noon-10pm Sat. **Main courses** £9-£14.95. **Credit** MC, V.

It's worth coming here for the garden alone, a formal criss-cross of box, privet and gravel around a central water sculpture, edged by apple trees. The pub's occasional cultural event programme means you may find live theatre taking place, or a string quartet playing inside. The menu is less adventurous, however, offering pretty standard contemporary pub grub. Our starters of scotch duck egg and mackerel pâté – creamy, almost mousse-like, nudged along by sour capers – were both well executed, but there was more fun to be had with a main course of grilled sardines on toast. The dish showed a kitchen unafraid to go simple and get it right: moist fish, crispy toast and cheekily piquant salsa verde made for perfect alfresco eating. Lamb kofta wasn't quite as impressive – good meat but the flatbread was a little unhappy – and the unexceptional house white was pricey at £13.90 a bottle. However, the pub has a reasonable range of beers and lagers (Adnams, San Miguel), though it's poor on perry and cider. Desserts – a nicely paired lemon posset with shortbread biscuit, and a treacle tart with crème fraîche – were more than fine, so we left happy.

Babies and children welcome (until 8pm) high chairs; nappy-changing facilities. Tables outdoors (30, garden).

East

Bow

Morgan Arms

43 Morgan Street, E3 5AA (8980 6389, www.geronimo-inns.co.uk). Mile End tube. **Open** noon-11pm Mon-Thur, Sun; noon-midnight Fri, Sat. **Lunch served** noon-3pm Mon-Sat; noon-4pm Sun. **Dinner served** 7-10pm Mon-Sat; 6-9pm Sun. **Main courses** £9.50-£17. **Credit** AmEx, MC, V.

In a serenely well-heeled pocket of rundown Bow, the Morgan is a grown-up pub. Twinkly fairy lights and plenty of wood make it irresistibly cosy in winter, while big paintings and even bigger windows give an airy feel to summer visits. But it seems to be struggling on the food front. Perhaps that explains why it was cheerfully boisterous on a Friday night, but pleasantly quiet for a sunny Sunday lunch. The menu is gastropub staples, served in big portions, but lacking simple finesse. In a generous Sunday roast, the collar of pork was overcooked and the veg barely seasoned; a crunchy pair of salmon and smoked haddock fish cakes – packed with flavour themselves – each sat under a bland poached egg and splat of wilted spinach; a light drizzle of walnut oil hardly disguised the lack of care that had gone into a stilton, date and rocket salad. Service oscillates between dourly efficient and absentmindedly enthusiastic, but three well-kept ales or a guest bottle of Yalumba Series Y viognier will keep drinkers happy. Seating by the window feels crammed in, but there are more tables tucked into a neat walled courtyard.

Babies and children admitted (dining room). Disabled: toilet. Tables outdoors (4, pavement; 3, terrace).
For branches (Duchess of Kent, Lord Palmerston, Phoenix) see index.

Perry Hill. See p109.

RESTAURANTS

Limehouse

Narrow

44 Narrow Street, E14 8DQ (7592 7950, www.gordonramsay.com). Limehouse DLR. **Open** noon-11pm Mon-Sat; noon-10.30pm Sun. **Lunch served** noon-3pm, **dinner served** 6-10pm Mon-Fri. **Meals served** noon-10pm Sat, Sun. **Main courses** £8-£15.50. **Credit** AmEx, MC, V.

There aren't many pubs that offer to call you a taxi as you prepare to leave, but then this isn't an ordinary pub, more an informal outpost of the Gordon Ramsay empire. On our visit a raucous crowd was making the most of a sunny weekend, gorgeous river views and extensive outdoor seating and conservatory tables. It's no problem to just pop in for a drink and the beer list is excellent, including Deuchars IPA and Adnams Explorer on the handpumps, Peroni, Meantime and Leffe beers on tap, and bottled delights such as Wells & Young's Banana Bread and Double Chocolate Stout. Food ranges from OK to first rate: chicken and tarragon pie tasted good enough, but who isn't just a bit disappointed with a single-crust pie? Golden-brown battered hake with fat chips and mushy peas, on the other hand, was an apotheosis of the art. Desserts were not as well executed: 'steamed' lemon sponge arrived browned and crusted from a spell in the oven; Pimm's jelly and mint ice-cream were good, but we're not convinced they belong on a plate together, let alone with cucumber and fruit salad as well. Staff impressed with their handling of children and enthusiasm for leading a chorus of 'Happy Birthday' as a cake arrived from the kitchen.

Babies and children welcome: high chairs. Booking essential. Disabled: toilet. Separate room for parties, seats 16. Tables outdoors (36, riverside terrace).

For branch (Devonshire) see index.

Shoreditch

Princess

76-78 Paul Street, EC2A 4NE (7729 9270, www.theprincessofshoreditch.com). Old Street tube/rail. **Open** noon-11pm Mon-Fri; 3-11pm Sat; noon-10pm Sun. **Lunch served** noon-3pm, **dinner served** 6.30-10pm Mon-Fri. **Meals served** noon-6pm Sat; 6.30-10pm Sun.**Main courses** £10.50-£16.50. **Credit** AmEx, MC, V.

Someone here has a way with a blender. Two of our dishes included purées (asparagus and carrot), and both were outstanding, smooth and subtle in a way that invited you to roll them around the tongue. The asparagus purée came with just-right scallops, grilled asparagus and shiso cress as a very satisfying starter; the carrot version came with cider-braised pork belly, baby turnip, spinach, black pudding and crackling. This might sound like overkill, but the combination was delicately handled, and while the pork may have been slightly overcooked this didn't detract from a lunch that was refined and most agreeable. The full restaurant menu is usually available both in the chic little upstairs dining room (reached via an iron spiral staircase), or in the bar, with wooden tables and deep-red banquettes. A range of bar snacks is offered downstairs on weekdays (club sandwich and chips, pork pie, apple pie and more). The European and Latin American-oriented wine list has plenty to enjoy at decent prices, and Adnams Explorer, Timothy Taylor Landlord and other good beers are on tap. Service was friendlier and more attentive than one sometimes gets in Shoreditch.

Available for hire. Booking advisable. Children admitted. **Map 6 Q4.**

Royal Oak

73 Columbia Road, E2 7RG (7729 2220, www.royaloaklondon.com). Bus 26, 48, 55. **Open** 6-11pm Mon; noon-11pm Tue-Fri; 11am-11pm Sat; 11am-10.30pm Sun. **Lunch served** noon-4pm Tue-Sun. **Dinner served** 6-10pm Mon-Sat; 6-9pm Sun. **Main courses** £9-£17. **Credit** AmEx, MC, V.

A meal at the Royal Oak is very different depending on whether you take it in the main pub or the upstairs dining room. The former is a raffishly atmospheric corner room with a handsome central bar that's usually busy, often raucous and best suited to groups. The latter is at the other extreme: quiet, charming and folksy, in keeping with the vintage-clothing and homecrafts character of the neighbourhood. There's a parlour sensibility to the decor, with drop-leaf tables, a tiled fireplace and green walls prettily adorned with pictures. The food is similarly homespun and appealing – all made on the premises, pâtisserie included – but thankfully not retro: dishes might include fish and chips, spaghetti vongole, steak or tagine. It's generally very tasty, and good value, though you might experience the odd misstep – our pork belly was too dry and our rhubarb custard tart too wet. Still, service was friendly and personal and the wines nicely priced, all of which conspired to charm. It's worth noting that you can often get a table upstairs when the pub is rammed, though the flower-market crowds make it essential to book for Sunday lunch.

Babies and children welcome: high chairs. Booking advisable: dining room. Tables outdoors (3, yard). **Map 6 S3.**

William IV

7 Shepherdess Walk, N1 7QE (3119 3012, www.williamthefourth.co.uk). Old Street tube/rail/394 bus. **Open** noon-11pm Mon-Wed; noon-1am Thur-Sat; noon-10.30pm Sun. **Lunch served** noon-3pm, **dinner served** 6-10pm Mon-Fri. **Meals served** 1-10pm Sat; 1-7pm Sun. **Main courses** £8-£10. **Credit** MC, V.

Seemingly lost on the rather bleak 394 bus route between Islington and Shoreditch, the frequently heaving William IV evidently has magnetism. Downstairs, it has perfected the gastropub recipe of ragged elegance. Upstairs, the 'Geography Room' feels like a dusty small-town museum with its mounted moths and vintage maps. (The owner was originally a film set designer – and it shows.) Another strongly atmospheric upstairs room features one large round table for private dining. The menu describes its offerings as 'British boozer food', which may mean an unambitious lowering of the gastropub bar (reflected in the reasonable pricing), but nonetheless they cleared it at most attempts. Mixed mezedes simply contained dips (though fresh and tasty), while the light domed pastry top of an excellent steak and ale pie begged for childish demolition. A disappointing burger and chips was followed by a knickerbocker glory whose second-rate ice-cream rendered it pointless. There are 14 wines by the glass (from £4.95); bottles start at £13.50. Beer-lovers will find four lagers joined by Leffe, Hoegaarden and Guinness, and ales represented by Timothy Taylor Landlord, Fuller's London Pride and Black Sheep.

Babies and children admitted. Booking advisable. Disabled: toilet. Separate rooms for parties, seating 12 and 40. Tables outdoors (4, yard). **Map 5 P3.**

Victoria Park

★ Britannia NEW

2009 RUNNER-UP BEST NEW GASTROPUB

360 Victoria Park Road, E9 7BT (8533 0040, www.thebritanniapub.co.uk). Mile End tube then 277 bus/Hackney Wick rail/26 bus. **Open** 11am-midnight Mon-Thur; 11am-2am Fri, Sat; 11am-10.30pm Sun. **Meals served** 11am-10pm Mon-Sat; 11am-9pm Sun. **Main courses** £9.50-£15.50. **Credit** MC, V.

This huge 19th-century pub beside Victoria Park has a large garden (complete with busy 'garden grill' in summer), a main bar decorated with Victoriana and *Eagle*-style comic annuals that serves creditable pub fare and, tucked away at the side, a full-blown dining room furnished with retro British Ercol Windsor tables and chairs. This Britishness is celebrated on the menu too, though we were grateful for the inclusion of continental touches such as a pretty bowl of gnocchi topped with crayfish tails, peas and a well-judged saffron sauce. New-season lamb rump was perfectly pink and tender and served with a piquant salsa verde and caper dressing. Fat mackerel fillets came draped over roasted potatoes, a warm fennel salad cutting through the oiliness of the fish. Puddings included elderflower jelly with mixed berries, and treacle tart with apple sorbet. Slow service – a result of understaffing on this occasion – let the generally good standard of cooking down, but the drinks list is enlightened, with good beers (Meantime and various guest ales) and interesting, affordable wines by the glass.

Babies and children welcome: high chairs; nappy-changing facilities. Booking advisable. Disabled: toilet. Separate room for parties, seats 30. Tables outdoors (17, garden).

North

Archway

St John's

91 Junction Road, N19 5QU (7272 1587). Archway tube. **Open** 5-11pm Mon-Thur; noon-11pm Fri, Sat; noon-10.30pm Sun. **Lunch served** noon-3.30pm Fri; noon-4pm Sat, Sun. **Dinner served** 6.30-11pm Mon-Sat; 6.30-9.30pm Sun. **Main courses** £10.75-£16.50. **Credit** AmEx, MC, V.

St John's cathedral of a dining room at the back of the pub, lined with an eccentric art collection and featuring an open-plan kitchen, is something of a haven in never-really-gentrified Archway. This pub has long managed to create a seamless blend of trendy meeting spot and casual local; on weekend lunchtimes, you have to step around the pushchairs to get a seat. The mostly Spanish and French wine list is always worth reading, with off-the-beaten track labels at good prices, and beers include Adnams and 6X. In the past the cooking has often been quite ambitious, but things were unusually conventional when we last called. To start, creamy duck liver pâté with gherkins, and a goat's cheese, bean and lentil salad were both pleasant. The fairly short list of mains also stuck to gastropub standards: cumberland sausages with mash and a punchy mustard jus, and pan-fried plaice with crispy chips and mushy peas were both competent and satisfying. On weekdays St John's is a reliable standby for an after-work supper, but come the weekend booking is essential.

Babies and children welcome: high chairs. Booking essential weekends. Tables outdoors (6, patio). **Map 26 B1.**

Camden Town & Chalk Farm

Engineer

65 Gloucester Avenue, NW1 8JH (7722 0950, www.the-engineer.com). Chalk Farm tube/31, 168 bus. **Open** 9am-11pm Mon-Sat; 9am-10.30pm Sun. **Breakfast served** 9-11.30am Mon-Fri; 9am-noon Sat, Sun. **Lunch served** noon-3pm Mon-Fri; 12.30-4pm Sat, Sun. **Dinner served** 7-11pm Mon-Sat; 7-10.30pm Sun. **Main courses** £12.50-£19.50. **Credit** MC, V.

A more elegant option than the nearby Lansdowne (*see p114*), the Engineer's eating area is kept apart from the bar. On our Friday night visit the softly lit restaurant had tables to spare (in stark contrast to the busy bar area) – perhaps indicating that the skilfully prepared food comes at quite a price. Grilled ribeye steak with chips was beautifully tender – but cost £19.50. That said, the standard of cooking is excellent and dishes are thoughtfully prepared. Starters of sweet potato and goat's cheese galette, and smoked mackerel with chive pancake and horseradish were deliciously fresh; mains of roast duck breast with dauphinoise potatoes, and miso-marinated sea bass were every bit as good. The menu changes regularly, but it's a safe bet for high-quality, well-balanced dining. The modest portions may leave you with enough space for one of the fabulous deserts (the chocolate sticky toffee pudding was sublime). Upstairs offers a great venue for a private dinner party, and there's also a lovely garden for lazy summer afternoons.

Babies and children welcome: children's menu; crayons; high chairs; nappy-changing facilities. Booking advisable. Disabled: toilet. Separate rooms for parties seating 20 and 32. Tables outdoors (15, garden). **Map 27 B2.**

Lansdowne

90 Gloucester Avenue, NW1 8HX (7483 0409, www.thelansdownepub.co.uk). Chalk Farm tube/31, 168 bus. **Open** noon-11pm Mon-Fri; noon-11pm Sat; noon-10.30pm Sun. **Lunch served** noon-4pm, **dinner served** 6-10pm Mon-Fri. **Meals served** 12.30-10pm Sat; 12.30-9.30pm Sun. **Main courses** £9.50-£16.50. **Credit** MC, V.

Family-friendly yet rough around the edges, the Lansdowne attracts a remarkably down-to-earth crowd for this neck of the woods. Happily, it hasn't sacrificed its local vibe in favour of gastronomic pomp, though it has all the requisite features – food takes pride of place with a huge blackboard chalked up with the day's menu, and the decor is tasteful. The scent of Italian cooking wafting through the large space is due to the additional pizza menu that makes an appealing alternative to the more expensive fare. Choose from six or seven starters encompassing an array of salads, seafood and soups: pork belly salad was good and fresh though simple, and goat's cheese with lentils and lemony dressing was tasty. Mains could be wild mushroom goulash with fried rosemary polenta, or juicy steak and chips. Generally, the food is of a high standard, though sloppiness can creep in, but the demands of maintaining a menu that changes daily may account for that. The service is slow, but thanks to the pub's good cheer you probably won't mind hanging round a little longer than usual.
Babies and children welcome: high chairs. Booking advisable. Disabled: toilet. Tables outdoors (4, pavement). Takeaway service.
Map 27 B2.

Prince Albert

163 Royal College Street, NW1 0SG (7485 0270, www.princealbertcamden.com). Camden Town tube/Camden Road rail. **Open** noon-11pm Mon-Thur; noon-midnight Fri, Sat; noon-10.30 Sun. **Lunch served** noon-3pm, **dinner served** 6-10pm Mon-Fri. **Meals served** noon-10pm Sat, 12.30-6pm Sun. **Main courses** £8.95-£15.95. **Set meal** (noon-3pm, 6-10pm Mon-Wed; 6-10pm Thur-Sat) £9 2 courses, £10.50 3 courses. **Credit** AmEx, MC, V.

This big old place certainly plays the Camden gastropub part. The bar has a classic battered-wood look, and boho touches like bright colours and old movie posters offset the fine original glass; the great dining room, at the top of an impressively creaky staircase, is more Victorian-decadent in style, with sumptuous dark fabrics. Live jazz and other music helps keep the crowds coming at weekends, and the range of drinks is imaginative, including a choice of quality ciders. Food prices are lower than at many gastropubs nowadays – especially if you take advantage of the set menus – yet the cooking is less notable than the setting. The menu is an impressive read, but doesn't really deliver, and the dishes we tried were all pleasant but unmemorable. To start, chicken liver pâté was mildly liverish, while a goat's cheese and spinach tart had too much egg and spinach and too little cheese. Mains of smoked duck breast with marinated pear salad in red wine, and chicken parmigiano with chips were again satisfying but not much more. Service was friendly but slow, even on a quiet lunchtime.
Babies and children welcome: children's menu; high chairs; toys. Disabled: toilet. Entertainment: jazz 8pm Sat. Separate room for parties, seats 60. Tables outdoors (12, garden). Map 27 D2.

Crouch End

Villiers Terrace NEW

120 Park Road, N8 8JP (8245 6827, www.villiersterrace.com). Hornsey Rail. **Open** noon-11pm Mon, Tue; noon-midnight Wed; noon-1am Thur-Sat; noon-11pm Sun. **Meals served** noon-10.30pm daily. **Main courses** £11-£16.50. **Credit** MC, V.

Looking every inch the groovy Cotswold import, Villiers Terrace has gorgeous tall wooden shutters, a Victorian bow window, a designer garden and a decked terrace with as fine a view of a petrol station as you'll find anywhere in the capital. Inside is a visual riot that doffs its cap to the country pads of rock aristocracy: large-print floral wallpaper,

ornate settees and worn chesterfields, art deco mirrors and a bar built of neatly cut logs. The overall effect is feminine, so it's no surprise to find groups of Crouch End ladies enjoying wine and cocktails (shaken in flamboyant style by bar staff on our visit) – and scant regard given to proper ales. Fortunately, there's a steady hand in the kitchen, the menu a prudent mix of foodie favourites and familiar pub grub. Lovely fresh flaky cod with a crisp skin sat on top of a bowl of firm white beans, tomato and some rather unassertive chorizo – it went well with the second cheapest wine on the list, a blend of chardonnay and chenin blanc from Argentina (£16). Extras such as chips with aïoli and curly kale were precision-cooked, the bread basket not as opulent as the decor but featuring a good rosemary-flavoured loaf. To finish, friendly staff recommended the agreeably rich sticky toffee pudding with well-made honeycomb ice-cream.
Babies and children welcome: children's menu; high chairs; nappy-changing facilities. Bookings not accepted. Separate room for parties, seats 50. Tables outdoors (20, garden; 10, terrace).

Finsbury Park

Old Dairy NEW

1-3 Crouch Hill, N4 4AP (7263 3337, www.the olddairyn4.co.uk). Crouch Hill rail. **Open** noon-11pm Mon-Thur; noon-1am Fri, Sat; noon-10.30pm Sun. **Dinner served** 6.30-10pm Mon-Sat. **Meals served** noon-10.30pm Sun. **Main courses** £9-£15. **Credit** MC, V.

With its charming friezes of life in a Victorian dairy along the outside walls, this ornate 1890 building is Stroud Green's proudest landmark. It was turned into a pub in the late 1990s, but its food and atmosphere have rarely proved memorable. However, a takeover by the Realpubs group brought welcome new energy in 2007, especially in the kitchen. Menus intelligently mix old favourites (beer-battered cod and chips, steak sandwiches) and Modern European-style dishes; the distinctive touch comes from imagination and verve in the cooking, and, particularly, the sourcing of quality ingredients. A warm salad of avocado, spinach, hazelnuts and a poached egg made a lively opener; steak (so often a letdown in gastropubs nowadays) was a fabulous, succulent slab of ribeye, with a rich shallot and red wine butter. There were a few glitches (steak ordered rare should have been a bit redder; service, always charming, got slow as the tables filled up), but these were minor grumbles. The old building is so big there are plenty of places to choose from, whether you want a quiet corner, a smarter-looking dining area or just to sit and eat or drink in the bar.
Available for hire. Babies and children welcome: children's menu; high chairs; nappy-changing facilities; play area. Booking essential Sun. Disabled: toilet.
For branches (Bald-Faced Stag, Oxford, Queen Adelaide) see index.

Islington

Charles Lamb

16 Elia Street, N1 8DE (7837 5040, www.the charleslambpub.com). Angel tube. **Open** 4-11pm Mon, Tue; noon-11pm Wed-Sat; noon-10.30pm Sun. **Lunch served** noon-3pm Wed-Sat; noon-6pm Sun. **Dinner served** 6-9.30pm Mon-Sat. **Main courses** £8-£12. **Credit** AmEx, MC, V.

Tranquillity reigns in the streets of (now plush) Regency houses east of Upper Street in N1, and the owners of this distinctive pub have deliberately – and successfully – created something with the feel of a village local, albeit one adapted to metropolitan ways. No bookings are taken, and at weekends you need to be there early to get a table in the charming old rooms. Non-regulars could feel left out, but the able staff are usually friendly. For Sunday lunch the blackboard menu stuck mainly to the classics, with a few departures including such starters as globe artichokes with wild garlic and aïoli. After that, rare roast beef and roast duck with all the trimmings both hit all the right notes. At other times, the fare on offer might include

southern French (merguez sausages with puy lentils) and British favourites (steak, mushroom and Guinness pie), but the kitchen is inventive, and regularly changes menus in line with market availability. Special mention goes to the drinks range: the Charles Lamb has own-label house wines, sourced from Languedoc, and plenty of other fine bottles, and the beer and spirits ranges are equally superior. It's great to see a foodie pub that doesn't try to be like all the others.
Babies and children admitted. Bookings not accepted. Tables outdoors (4, pavement).
Map 5 O2.

Compass NEW

58 Penton Street, N1 9PZ (7837 3891, www.the compassn1.co.uk). Angel tube. **Lunch served** noon-3pm Thur-Sat; noon-4pm Sun. **Dinner served** 5-10pm Mon-Sat. **Main courses** £9.50-£22.50. **Credit** AmEx, MC, V.

Not another Islington gastropub, you may say, but the good news is that the new Compass is reminiscent of the Eagle (*see p102*) when it started in the early 1990s – the welcome sort of hostelry that is a pub first, but also serves good, rustic food. Most of the regularly changing hand-pumped beers are from small independent breweries; lagers include Bitburger and Amstel, and bottled options Mexico's Modello. Wines by the glass are unusually good, given the keen pricing (£4-£6 for 175ml); bottles start at £13.50 for Santa Isido Pegroes white and red from Portugal and rise to £130 for Dom Perignon. Head chef Ben Bishop, formerly at the Duke of Cambridge (*see p115*) favours fine provenance and local, seasonal ingredients. You may well find New Forest mushrooms, brown trout from the River Test, gulls' eggs from Hampshire and snails from Somerset on the menu, plus a choice of game dishes in season (roast snipe rossini, grouse with sweetbread). Appealing bar snacks include duck scotch egg with brown sauce, black pudding sausage rolls, welsh rarebit, and pints of prawns. Lunchtime may offer English radishes with rock salt, smoked herring with potato salad, rare-breed ribeye steak with watercress and stilton butter, and a broad bean and mint risotto with parmesan and poached egg – unless it's Sunday, when the focus is on roasts.
Babies and children welcome: high chairs. Booking advisable. Disabled: toilet. Separate room for parties: seats 40. Tables outdoors (5, pavement).
Map 5 N2.

Drapers Arms NEW

44 Barnsbury Street, N1 1ER (7619 0348, www.thedrapersarms.com). Highbury & Islington tube/rail. **Open** 11am-midnight Mon-Fri; 10am-midnight Sat; 10am-11pm Sun. **Lunch served** noon-3pm Mon-Fri; noon-4pm Sat, Sun. **Dinner served** 6-10.30pm Mon-Fri; 6-9.30pm Sat, Sun. **Main courses** £8.50-£15. **Credit** MC, V.

New owners Nick Gibson and Ben Maschler (son of restaurant critic Fay) have taken over this handsome Georgian-style Islington gastropub. The upstairs restaurant has been simply renovated in pale tones with painted boards and bare wooden tables, lending an airy, spacious, even slightly austere look. Karl Goward, formerly of St John, is in charge in the kitchen and is keeping the daily-changing menu firmly in the contemporary British camp, matching the no-nonsense aesthetics of the pub's refit. Starters are the likes of potted pork, toast and pickles, pickled herring with horseradish and capers, and rock oysters. Mains are from the same school of sophisticated simplicity: roast suckling pig with sage mash and quince, say, kedgeree, slip soles with samphire or a whole crab with mayonnaise. Puddings also go back to old roots, sometimes in contemporary combinations: there might be lardy cake with crème fraîche and raspberries on the menu in summer, or a more traditional strawberries with shortcake and vanilla ice-cream. We've found service to be impeccable, the team well mannered to a fault, and eager to ensure their equally well-mannered customers lack for nothing.
Babies and children welcome: high chairs; nappy-changing facilities. Booking advisable weekends. Separate room for parties, seats 50. Tables outdoors (8, garden). Map 5 N1.

Bull & Last. See p116.

Duke of Cambridge

30 St Peter's Street, N1 8JT (7359 3066, www.dukeorganic.co.uk). Angel tube. **Open** noon-11pm Mon-Sat; noon-10.30pm Sun. **Lunch served** 12.30-3pm Mon-Fri; 12.30-3.30pm Sat, Sun. **Dinner served** 6.30-10.30pm Mon-Sat; 6.30-10pm Sun. **Main courses** £11-£20. **Credit** MC, V.

Ten years on, and this light-filled corner pub may no longer be singular in its commitment to an organic menu and drinks list, but it remains near the top in terms of sheer good food. Its dishes reliably display the simple techniques and seasonal ingredients that mark out those gastropubs worthy of the name: in July 2009, for example, it was serving feta salad with grilled courgette and fillet of whiting with fennel, chard and salsa verde. Drinks too are discerning, with Freedom and Pitfield beers, an organic cocktail list and some notably palatable wines. There's always an appreciative crowd at the large wooden tables, especially for Sunday lunch. Our roast beef was tip-top – as it should have been at £17.75 – with excellent but not abundant vegetables. And there's the rub: now that high-quality ingredients are the norm at any serious gastropub, the Duke of Cambridge seems expensive. Perhaps this is because its ethical credentials go beyond the merely organic to energy use, food miles, fair prices for suppliers, and training and promoting from within. Regrettably, the servers are slightly less than eager to please.

Babies and children welcome: high chairs; nappy-changing facilities. Tables outdoors (4, pavement). **Map 5 O2**

Marquess Tavern

32 Canonbury Street, N1 2TB (7354 2975, www.themarquesstavern.co.uk). Angel tube/ Highbury & Islington tube/rail. **Open** 5-11pm Mon-Thur; 5pm-midnight Fri; noon-midnight Sat; noon-10.30pm Sun. **Lunch served** noon-5pm Sat, Sun. **Dinner served** 6-10pm Mon-Sat; 6-8pm Sun. **Main courses** £12-£17. **Credit** AmEx, MC, V.

It's always busy at this gastropub off the Essex Road. The Marquess opened in 2006 and has since maintained a loyal and buoyant customer base despite mixed reviews and rough economic times. It was jammed on our Friday night visit – a testament to the efforts of the tireless staff pumping Young's real ales from the ornate horseshoe bar, and the imagination of the kitchen team turning out Modern British dishes for customers in the dining room. Mains included an oily fillet of bream with rich mashed potato, plus a mouth-watering barnsley chop served with gamey sweetbread and mash again (though why didn't the waitress warn us about all that unlisted mash, when we ordered an additional third portion?). Starters were less successful, a plate of asparagus overcooked and mushy, the mussels portion rather mean. For dessert, the rhubarb tart was wincingly sharp but cooled by a dollop of crème fraîche. The wine list offers around eight of each colour, most available by the glass. Aesthetically, the two segments of the Marquess don't match – the drinking area all rickety tables and battered leather sofas, the dining space a bright, mirror-clad canteen with a permanent echo bouncing off its high ceiling – but the whole has enough appeal to make this a pack-'em-in local favourite. Long may it remain busy.

Babies and children welcome (until 6pm). Separate room for parties, seats 14. Tables outdoors (6, patio).

Northgate

113 Southgate Road, N1 3JS (7359 7392). Essex Road rail/21, 141 bus. **Open** 5-11pm Mon-Thur; 5pm-midnight Fri; noon-midnight Sat, Sun. **Lunch served** noon-4pm Sat, Sun. **Dinner served** 6.30-10.30pm Mon-Sat; 6.30-9.30pm Sun. **Main courses** £9.50-£15. **Credit** MC, V.

With its standard-issue battered wooden tables, stripped-down decor, leather sofas, open kitchen and chalked-up menu, the Northgate has been a fixture in the gastropub world for quite a while, but on the evidence of our last visit has grown somewhat tired. Often intricate-sounding main dishes read much better than they eventually tasted, and several of the ingredients featured – such as asparagus in late winter – showed that more attention could be paid to seasonality and sourcing. As a starter, cherry tomato, cucumber, feta, olive and rocket salad was conventional, but nicely crisp. However, in baked cod fillet wrapped in prosciutto with grilled asparagus and crab and lemon risotto, the fish was too moist, the asparagus low on flavour (we should have known) and the risotto gooey. Chargrilled ribeye with chips, mixed leaves and paprika aïoli was just plain ordinary – one of those steaks oddly without real meatiness, and frankly pricey at £17. It's a pity, because the wine and beer lists are nicely varied, the staff are welcoming, and the bar always feels convivial. *Babies and children admitted (patio, restaurant). Booking advisable weekends. Tables outdoors (15, patio).* **Map 6 Q1.**

Kentish Town

★ Bull & Last NEW (100)

2009 RUNNER-UP BEST NEW GASTROPUB
168 Highgate Road, NW5 1QS (7267 3641). Kentish Town tube/rail then 214, C1, C2, C11 bus/Gospel Oak rail. **Open** noon-11pm Mon-Thur; noon-midnight Fri, Sat; noon-10.30pm Sun. **Lunch served** noon-3pm Mon-Fri; 12.30-4pm Sat, Sun. **Dinner served** 6.30-10pm Mon-Sat; 7-9.30pm Sun. **Main courses** £12-£18.95. **Credit** MC, V.
The Bull & Last might look like an archetypal gastro boozer with its patina of wear and blackboard menu. And it always has proper real ales on draught (Hooky and Black Sheep bitters on our visit). But, like a more formal restaurant, the tables are reserved for diners: drinkers have to fight for the bar stools. Order any of the dishes and the reason for the Bull's popularity becomes clear, however: ingredients and dishes are of the highest quality – even the charcuterie is made in-house. These meats, served on a wooden platter, include slivers of duck 'prosciutto' and the intense meaty flavours of pork strands from a pig's head encapsulated in breaded, deep-fried balls. Cornichons, a (watery) remoulade and a wedge of lemon lighten up the meat-fest. Main courses also showed great prowess; slow-cooked pig cheeks, served beside a slab of boulangère potatoes, garnished by a prune, is very French and was rich with its intense, browned-meat flavours. Roast Cornish cod, served with brown shrimps and a tangle of watercress, was less heavy but no less bold. Puds might include rhubarb fool with ginger ice-cream, or toffee-banana clafoutis with banana ice-cream. Doorstep sandwiches, sensational chips and huge scotch eggs draw their own fans during the day. We've always found the service charming and accommodating. The Bull is a real pleasure if you can only get a seat.
Babies and children welcome: high chairs; nappy-changing facilities. Booking advisable. Separate room for parties, seats 70. Tables outdoors (5, pavement).

Junction Tavern

101 Fortess Road, NW5 1AG (7485 9400, www.junctiontavern.co.uk). Tufnell Park tube/ Kentish Town tube/rail. **Open** noon-11pm Mon-Sat; noon-10.30pm Sun. **Lunch served** noon-3pm Mon-Fri; noon-4pm Sat, Sun. **Dinner served** 6.30-10.30pm Mon-Sat; 6.30-9.30pm Sun. **Main courses** £10.50-£15. **Set lunch** (Sun) £15 2 courses. **Credit** MC, V.
The Junction has slid into the role of neighbourhood gastropub like an old shoe – not that there's anything beaten-up about it – but without any of the complacency that affects some of its competitors. Its three spaces (big wooden tables around the front bar, a spacious conservatory, and a leafy terrace for summer) make it ideal for long, leisurely lunches. Welcoming staff never seem overrun or flustered. Menus change frequently, with a nice eye to seasonality, and are not over-long but still offer an attractive choice of inventive, consistently enjoyable dishes. On our last visit, cold roast chicken with parma ham, capers,

croûtons and an aïoli dressing was a bright, impressively fresh summer salad, with a beguiling smokey flavour in the chicken. Classic dishes are creatively handled too: we had a fine, generous bowl of moules marinière, and beer-battered coley with mushy peas and tartare sauce was a great – even light – version of fish and chips. The wine list is very well priced and user-friendly, and this CAMRA north London pub of the year (2008) takes good care of its beer range, with regularly changing cask ales. Deuchars IPA and Addlestone's cider are fixtures on the bar, while independent Cornish breweries (St Austell, Sharp's, Skinner's, Wooden Hand) are particularly welcome guests.
Babies and children admitted (until 7pm). Booking advisable weekends. Tables outdoors (20, garden). **Map 26 B4.**

Muswell Hill

Clissold Arms

105 Fortis Green, N2 9HR (8444 4224). East Finchley tube. **Open** noon-11pm Mon-Fri; noon-midnight Sat; noon-10.30pm Sun. **Lunch served** noon-4.30pm Mon-Sat. **Dinner served** 6-10pm Mon-Sat. **Food served** noon-9pm Sun. **Main courses** £11-£18.50. **Credit** MC, V.
The Clissold Arms is famed as site of the Kinks' first gig (Ray and Dave Davies grew up in Denmark Terrace just opposite), but the only traces of this heritage are photos in the corridor by the gents. Most of the pub is a rather bright, scrubbed-oak and beige restaurant area designed to appeal to well-heeled Muswell Hill diners, with plenty of family space for weekends. Menus follow a familiar gastropub style, but with a certain full-on quality, sometimes approaching carelessness: a salad of fennel, onion, plums, cucumber and pecans had far too much fruit and too little fennel to be a balanced starter. Mains were much better: roast duck wrapped in parma ham came with a sharp lemongrass syrup and blood orange sauce, which again threatened to be over-fruity but managed to stay just short of excessive. Sirloin steak arrived with a traditional béarnaise, and at lunchtime you'll find fine sandwiches of roast pork belly, or steak and fried egg. The cask ales are well kept and the wine list is extensive, but quite pricey once you go beyond the house wines. Outside there's a leafy terrace for dining, a separate area for smokers, and, in the rear shed, the Clissold Grocer, which sells organic produce, fine deli items and coffee and croissants to commuters.
Available for hire. Babies and children welcome: children's menu; high chairs; nappy-changing facilities. Booking essential Thur-Sat dinner, Sun lunch. Disabled: toilet. Tables outdoors (15, terrace; 25, garden).

North West

Hampstead

Horseshoe

28 Heath Street, NW3 6TE (7431 7206). Hampstead tube. **Open** 10am-11pm Mon-Thur; 10am-midnight Fri, Sat; 10am-10.30pm Sun. **Lunch served** noon-3.30pm Mon-Sat; noon-4.30pm Sun. **Dinner served** 6-10pm Mon-Thur; 6.30-11pm Fri, Sat; 6.30-9.30pm Sun. **Main courses** £8-£15. **Set lunch** £7 1 course incl glass of wine. **Credit** MC, V.
This smart but laid-back, very Hampstead gastropub has a lot going for it. The layout is a nice blend of no-fuss and stylishness, intimacy and spaciousness. Staff are friendly, alert and knowledgeable. There's a microbrewery in the basement producing Australian-influenced light beers (reflecting the owners' heritage), and a carefully selected, excellent-value wine list. In the past the farm-sourced, mostly organic ingredients have sometimes been let down by a lack of refinement in the cooking, but things were much improved on our last visit. Every impressive ingredient had kept its sparkle: an artichoke, tomato, basil and ragstone cheese salad was bright and refreshing. Some of the meaty main courses sound heavy on first reading, but they're very delicately handled and well balanced. In a dish of

Blythburgh pork fillet with celery and walnuts, the meat was deliciously juicy; the natural quality of a Heveningham Hall lamb loin was allowed to shine, while offset against some beautifully flavoured white beans in marjoram pesto. Desserts, such as a fresh raspberry and lemon cheesecake, and strawberries with passion-fruit curd, are worth leaving space for too. We look forward to returning.
Babies and children welcome: high chairs. Booking advisable. Tables outdoors (2, pavement). **Map 28 B2.**

Wells

30 Well Walk, NW3 1BX (7794 3785, www.the wellshampstead.co.uk). Hampstead tube. **Open** noon-11pm Mon-Sat; noon-10.30pm Sun. **Lunch served** noon-3pm Mon-Fri; noon-4pm Sat, Sun. **Dinner served** 6-10pm Mon-Fri; 7-10pm Sat, Sun. **Main courses** £9.95-£16. **Credit** MC, V.
This lovely Georgian pub is located down a picturesque street between villagey Hampstead and the sprawling Heath. Once a straightforward local boozer, the Wells has been transformed into a smart gastropub that comfortably caters for wealthy locals (who on our Sunday night visit were there in droves). You can choose to dine in the elegantly decorated upstairs dining rooms or in the relaxed and spacious downstairs bar. The bar has cosy sofas where you can enjoy a drink (there are real ales on tap, an international wine list and cocktails), as well as tables if you want to eat. The menu has an emphasis on seasonal produce and changes regularly, but starters could be pear, goat's cheese and dandelion salad, or pan-fried scallops with pea purée and dry-cured bacon. Mains include chicken with Jersey Royal potatoes and asparagus, and barbary duck with gratin dauphinoise and braised cabbage. For something simpler, order a burger with cheese and bacon options, or ribeye with chips and watercress. We took our time savouring the cheese plate, but there are some great sweets on offer too (sticky date pudding, dark chocolate pot with clotted cream). Prices are reasonable for this area, which makes it a sound choice for a treat after a stroll on the Heath.
Babies and children welcome: children's menu; colouring books; high chairs. Disabled: toilet. Separate room for parties, seats 12. Tables outdoors (8, patio). **Map 28 C2.**

Kilburn

Salusbury

50-52 Salusbury Road, NW6 6NN (7328 3286). Queens Park tube/rail. **Open** 5-11pm Mon; noon-11pm Tue-Thur, Sun; noon-midnight Fri, Sat. **Lunch served** 12.30-3.30pm Tue-Sun. **Dinner served** 7-10.15pm Mon-Sat; 7-10pm Sun. **Main courses** £11.50-£16. **Credit** MC, V.
Packed tables on a Tuesday evening confirm that this gastropub is the destination of choice for the increasingly trendy Salusbury Road crowd. Stepping inside, it's easy to see why. Atmospheric and intimate with a cosy candlelit ambience, it's immediately apparent that this is more than just another standard gastropub experience. With a proper bar on one side and an area dedicated to dining on the other, romantic meals can stay exactly that, while social drinkers can chink glasses and chatter to their hearts' content without risk of being glared at. The decor is generic (stripped wooden tables and chairs) with a couple of flourishes to give it a lift: the dining room wall is artfully scattered with mirrors, and old Bob Marley record covers feature in the bar. Foodwise, it hits the spot too. We jealously watched fellow diners dive into a big bowl of mussels and sop up the juices with plenty of good bread. Duck ragu pasta was tender and tasty, while crab linguine was packed with fresh chunks of crab offset with a chilli kick. Service was informal and friendly, the wine list lean but reasonably priced, and the bar stocked with a good range of draught lagers. A gastropub with real character.
Available for hire. Babies and children welcome (until 7pm): high chairs. Tables outdoors (4, pavement).

Global

H ere we celebrate London's multiculturalism by detailing the restaurants that don't fit comfortably into any other chapters in this guide. Diners who actively revel in the capital's joyous ethnic diversity will find much to explore on the following pages. Ever wondered what Central Asian cooking tastes like? Head to **Kazakh Kyrgyz** in Camberwell. Want to relive that South African holiday? Make a booking at **Chakalaka**. Joining Kazakh Kyrgyz among this year's new entries is **Madsen**, a handy and smartly designed Danish café-restaurant in South Kensington. For a sophisticated night out (or business lunch) it's still hard to beat **Eyre Brothers**, where the food of Mozambique and the Iberian peninsula sit happily together. Burmese restaurant **Mandalay** also continues as one of our favourites – the food is terrific, and cheap too. So here you go: something different for the weekend.

Afghan

North

Islington

★ Afghan Kitchen

35 Islington Green, N1 8DU (7359 8019). Angel tube. **Lunch served** noon-3.30pm, **dinner served** 5.30-11pm Tue-Sat. **Main courses** £5-£6.50. **No credit cards**.
Few restaurants stick to their guns with the grim conviction of Afghan Kitchen, which has refused to begin pampering its legion of devotees (including *Guardian*-reading ethnographer-types) despite years of effusive praise from high places. The two floors boast nothing in the way of decoration save a green paint job and the occasional expansive pot plant. At peak times, customers are forced to dine elbow-to-elbow with complete strangers at a handful of shared tables after extensive waits. The menu continues to list four meat and four vegetarian dishes, offering an insight into homely Afghan dining, if little variation. We've noticed a slipping of standards lately. On a recent visit, the famous community-sized loaf of bread (sprinkled with poppy-seeds) was substituted by something resembling a nan from the local supermarket, while ghorm-e sabzi (lamb and spinach curry) was oily and contained excessively fatty meat. Lavand-e murgh (chicken in yoghurt) offered a glimpse of former glories, the meat luxuriating in the minty freshness of its sauce. But with so few dishes on the menu, it seems fair to expect a degree of reliability that has been sadly lacking of late.
Babies and children welcome: high chairs. Booking advisable Fri, Sat. Takeaway service. **Map 5 O2**.

Outer London

Harrow, Middlesex

★ Masa (100)

24-26 Headstone Drive, Harrow, Middx HA3 5QH (8861 6213). Harrow & Wealdstone tube/rail. **Meals served** 12.30-11pm daily. **Main courses** £4.50-£12. **Set meal** £19.95 (2 people); £30 (2-3 people); £49.95 (4-5 people). **Unlicensed**. **Corkage** no charge. **Credit** MC, V.
The Middle East meets the Indian subcontinent in this unsung corner of Harrow, with gratifying results. Sited on a rundown shopping parade, Masa looks incongruously smart. Within there's a certain glitziness emphasised by shiny floor tiles,

heavy wooden furniture and a sparkling chandelier. A large flatscreen TV and an open kitchen provide further entertainment. Few diners were present during our Sunday lunch, though local Afghans often eat here. The menu is attractively priced and appealing, with North Indian/Pakistani-style karahi curries sharing space with Middle Eastern kebabs and a few distinctively Afghani dishes. Sadly, a couple of the latter – ash afghani (macaroni and vegetables with meatballs) and ashak (pasta stuffed with leeks) – were unavailable, but we relished the mantoo: chewy pasta parcels overflowing with spicy minced lamb topped with yoghurty quroot sauce. Flatbread, challow rice (lightly spiced with cardamom and cumin) and the juicy seared kebabs (lamb, chicken wings, chicken tikka) were Middle Eastern-perfect too. Drink dogh (yoghurt with

cucumber and dried mint) or bring your own alcohol. A great place for a culinary adventure. *Babies and children welcome: high chairs. Disabled: toilet. Takeaway service; delivery service (over £12 within 3-mile radius).*

Austrian/German

South West

Barnes

Café Strudel

429 Upper Richmond Road West, SW14 7PJ (8487 9800, www.cafestrudel.co.uk). Mortlake rail/33, 337, 493 bus. **Open** 10am-10.30pm Tue-Sat; 10am-4pm Sun. **Lunch served** noon-4pm Tue-Sun. **Dinner served** 6.30-10.30pm Tue-Sat. **Main courses** £12.50-£17.50. **Credit** MC, V.
The traditional Viennese kaffeehaus is a place for quiet contemplation, the perusal of literature and newspapers, and the enjoyment of food and drink. While Orly Kritzman's Austrian brasserie might not beat its grand Viennese counterparts, the decor – globe lighting, elaborately framed mirrors, bentwood chairs – offers a slice of tranquillity. A table is laid with the day's newspapers, while an antique dresser holds all manner of Austrian sweet treats. Hearty portions are the norm; our 'small' plate of button spätzle (mini dumplings) in an aromatic tomato and basil sauce was a generous, comforting dish, the dumplings light yet with a bit of chew. Beef goulash served with potatoes cooked with caraway seeds is another classic. Other iconic dishes of the Wiener Küche, including schnitzel, are available for dinner and at weekends. There's also a fine selection of Austrian wines. In the afternoon, while away the day enjoying the classical music and sampling the cakes and pastries (apfelstrudel, sachertorte, and various streusels and cheesecakes): ideal when paired with a Viennese coffee (sourced from the esteemed Julius Meinl company), properly served on a silver tray with a small glass of water. *Babies and children welcome: crayons; high chairs; nappy-changing facilities. Tables outdoors (4, pavement). Takeaway service.*

Kazakh Kyrgyz. See p119.

Belgian

North West

Camden Town & Chalk Farm

Belgo Noord

72 Chalk Farm Road, NW1 8AN (7267 0718, www.belgo-restaurants.com). Chalk Farm tube.
Lunch served noon-5pm daily. **Dinner served** 5-11pm Mon-Thur; 5-11.30pm Fri, Sat; 5-10.30pm Sun. **Main courses** £8.95-£15.95. **Set lunch** £6.50 1 course. **Credit** AmEx, MC, V.

Beer, mussels and chips made this chain famous and continue to be Belgo's strengths. Many and varied dishes are produced using rope-grown mussels (the marinière was tasty), and the long list of continental beers is even more appealing. The choice of brews runs to more than 70, from blonde to amber to fruit and Trappist – there are even some specially selected for the 'connoisseur'. If beer and mussels aren't your thing, consult the menu for a decent array of hearty alternatives. The sausage with stoemp mash, beer-basted rotisserie chicken or Hoegaarden beer-battered haddock and frites reflect the prominent Belgian theme (as do the staff dressed in Trappist monks' habits). Finish your meal with a belgian waffle, a chocolate-flavoured cheesecake or a crème brûlée. However, this comfort food is served in less-than-cosy surroundings. The decor is cool and industrial, with curved walls, exposed pipes and an open kitchen. Early diners may wish to take advantage of 'Beat the Clock'; between 5pm and 6.30pm, you pay the price of the time you place your order (so £6 at 6pm): a bargain.
Available for hire. Babies and children welcome: children's menu; crayons; high chairs; nappy-changing facilites. Booking advisable dinner; essential weekends. Disabled (phone ahead): toilet. Tables outdoors (4, pavement).
Map 27 B1.
For branches (Belgo Centraal, Bierodrome) see index.

Burmese

Central

Edgware Road

★ ★ **Mandalay** (100)

444 Edgware Road, W2 1EG (7258 3696, www.mandalayway.com). Edgware Road tube.
Lunch served noon-2.30pm, **dinner served** 6-10.30pm Mon-Sat. **Main courses** £4.40-£7.90. **Set lunch** £3.90 1 course, £5.90 3 courses. **Credit** AmEx, MC, V.

Success hasn't gone to Mandalay's head. London's only Burmese restaurant first won a Time Out award in 1996, and – hurrah! – has hardly changed since. Behind a drab frontage is a welcoming little room (only 28 covers) with red hearth-like tiled flooring and basic furniture. Plastic flowers, gold plastic tablecloths and Burmese pictures provide decoration. Diners (crowds of students and former-student types, some of Burmese ancestry) are served by patient staff happy to describe the food of their homeland. The menu is long and appealing, with plenty of dishes rarely found in London. Burmese cuisine has Chinese, Indian and South-east Asian influences, so at Mandalay you can get both curries and stir-fries: lemongrass, cumin and dried shrimps too. Mixed fritters (containing various vegetables, onions, beansprouts and prawns) make a fine opening, clothed in crisp batter and served with three dips (mild chilli, tamarind and soy sauce). Order the moreish papaya and cucumber salad as a foil. Main courses are equally enticing. Try the coconut and chicken noodles, which come in a rich, laksa-style sauce; or the tender, tangy lamb pickle curry. The

Chakalaka. See p120.

typically Burmese balachaung (chewy dried shrimps in oil) acts as a piquant relish. We loved everything – including the tiddly bill.
Available for hire Mon-Fri. Babies and children admitted. Booking essential dinner. Takeaway service. **Map 2 D4**.

Central Asian

South East
Camberwell

★ Kazakh Kyrgyz NEW
Pasha Hotel, 158 Camberwell Road, SE5 0EE (7277 2228). Bus 12, 35, 40, 42, 45, 68, 171, 176, 148, 468. **Dinner served** 6-11pm daily. **Main courses** £7-£15. **Set dinner** £16.50 3 courses incl tea or coffee. **Credit** MC, V.
Kazakh Kyrgyz might not showcase Central Asian food at its very best, but eating here is quite an experience, nonethess. The restaurant lies in the otherwise discreet Pasha boutique hotel and is accessed via a footbridge over an indoor pond. Mongolian, Turkic, Dungan (Chinese Muslim) and Slavic people, young and old, come to chat at long, low tables and enjoy the camaraderie fostered by the restaurant's Facebook group, belly-dancing classes, parties and special-occasion menus. Seating ranges from benches to colourful bean-bags on the exotic carpet. Kazakhstan and Kyrgyzstan were both on the Silk Road and consequently both their cuisines incorporate influences from Russia, Turkey and China. Pickled herring may seem to sit oddly alongside starters of meze and funchoza (a cold Chinese noodle salad), but the variety is actually rather exciting, and prices are low. It's the Central Asian specialities – plov (rice dishes), flatbreads, kebabs, stir-fries, lagman (wheat noodles) and plump, moist hoshani (steamed, fried meat dumplings) – that shine. Finish your meal with warm pistachio and cinnamon-flecked baklava, or chak-chak (squares of puffed rice with nuts and honey). Wines are as inexpensive as the cooking (well under £20 a bottle). Come on a Friday night and you'll get entertainment from musicians and a belly dancer too.
Babies and children admitted. Booking advisable Fri, Sat. Disabled: toilet. Entertainment: belly-dancing 6pm Fri.

Mediterranean

Central
Piccadilly

St Alban
4-12 Regent Street, SW1Y 4PE (7499 8558, www.stalban.net). Piccadilly Circus tube. **Lunch served** noon-3pm, **dinner served** 5.30-11pm daily. **Main courses** £8.75-£30. **Credit** AmEx, DC, MC, V.
St Alban's USP is its large retro-chic, multicoloured interior, with jewel coloured banquettes, murals by Michael Craig-Martin and artwork by Damien Hirst. Such surroundings engender a sense of occasion, and the oversized juicy olives, own-made breads and superb olive oil brought to the table further raise expectations. Most of the menu consists of modish dishes from France, Spain and Italy, along with pizzas from the wood-burning oven. The food has garnered much praise, but on a recent visit we felt that the olives and bread were the highlight. A starter of tortellini was dense, rich and creamy, but otherwise lacked flavour. Piquant Cornish mackerel came with a tangy salsa, yet the addition of diced, carved carrots seemed amateurish. Carrots were a better match for a main of pork belly that featured tender, wonderfully moist meat. We just wished the waiter had told us we'd be doubling up on carrots. Paella is never a delicate dish, but St Alban's version was so strongly spiced, heavy on chorizo and – above all

– salty, it was a little overwhelming. Perhaps the kitchen was having an off-night; certainly the staff were consummate professionals and the operation ran like clockwork.
Babies and children welcome: crayons; high chairs; nappy-changing facilities. Booking advisable. Disabled: toilet. **Map 10 K7**.

South Kensington

Brompton Quarter Café
223-225 Brompton Road, SW3 2EJ (7225 2107). Knightsbridge or South Kensington tube. **Meals served** 7am-10.30pm Mon-Fri; 8am-10.30pm Sat, Sun. **Main courses** £9.75-£24.95. **Credit** AmEx, MC, V.
You could be in New York or Sydney – the high-ceilinged, light-filled room that is Brompton Quarter Café is more often than not swarming with a chichi Knightsbridge crowd, relishing the fresh cocktails (margaritas, mojitos, strawberry juleps) and vibrant Mediterranean salads and nibbles. One side of the room is flanked by a large blackboard, artistically painted with exotic flowers, displaying the specials of the day: sumac-marinated steak with grilled artichokes, say. A sharing menu features small bowls of Mediterranean-style salads, such as moutabal with sesame oil and lemon juice, or tabouleh with parsley, tomato and bulgar wheat. Our 'Tunisian' salad with roasted chunks of aubergine, coriander and chilli lacked much zing, while a 'spicy' vegetable and chickpea soup was curiously bland. Better was a meaty slab of juicy grilled swordfish served with a summery tomato and basil bruschetta and thin spears of asparagus (which were quickly added by our solicitous yet forgetful waiter, after we'd noticed their absence). Chips were golden and fat, but were served with a selection of uninteresting condiments (bog-standard ketchup, for example). You get the feeling here that you're paying over the odds for poshed-up café fare – but this is Knightsbridge, after all.
Available for hire. Babies and children welcome: high chairs; nappy-changing facilities. Disabled: lift; toilet. Separate room for parties, seats 60. Takeaway service. **Map 14 E10**.

South
Balham

★ Fat Delicatessen
7 Chestnut Grove, SW12 8JA (8675 6174, www.fatdelicatessen.co.uk). Balham tube/rail. **Meals served** 8am-8pm Mon-Wed; 8am-10pm Thur, Fri; 9am-10pm Sat; 11am-6pm Sun. **Main courses** £4-£8. **Credit** MC, V.
A welcome retreat from Balham High Road, Fat Delicatessen is a cool, casual deli-cum-café that provides an ideal perch for a light snack or tapas lunch. The low white ceilings and wooden beams evoke the feel of a continental bar. Empty tins of smoked paprika and wooden crates engraved with the name of that most well known of jamón producers, Joselito, are scattered throughout the room. Chillers hold packs of charcuterie, fresh lemons and garlic mayonnaise. Shelves are packed with jars of caperberries, artichokes and roasted red peppers. We've heard of lapses in standards, but quality was high on our most recent visit. The tapas menu is simple, with categories such as 'bread', 'cheese', 'meats' and 'vegetables'. Crisp crostinis loaded with ricotta-stuffed mozzarella offered a tantalising hint of truffle oil among the creaminess, while a mixed charcuterie board held a fine array of chorizo, salami and serrano ham. Terracotta dishes of hot green padrón peppers, and spicy golden patatas bravas were excellent. An intense chorizo-flavoured mash with garlicky snails may have been salty, but was enjoyable nonetheless. There's a relaxed vibe here, thanks to unintrusive yet helpful service and a clientele of *Guardian* readers and young families.
Available for hire. Babies and children welcome: high chairs. Booking advisable dinner Thur-Sat. Disabled: toilet. Takeaway service.

South East
Crystal Palace

Mediterranea
21 Westow Street, SE19 3RY (8771 7327, www.mediterranealondon.com). Crystal Palace or Gypsy Hill rail. **Lunch served** 12.30-2.30pm Tue-Sun. **Dinner served** 6.30-9.30pm Mon; 6.30-10.30pm Tue-Sun. **Main courses** £7.90-£14.50. **Set lunch** (Tue-Sat) £4.90 1 course incl drink, £6.90 2 courses incl drink. **Credit** MC, V.
With its unassuming, local-café look, Mediterranea risks being ignored among the flashier eating places in this lively, independent little town centre. Don't walk on by, however, because within its portals you can feast off a colourful collection of dishes from a variety of Mediterranean destinations: Sardinia to the Lebanon, with various nods to Turkey, Spain and Greece along the way. We were particularly impressed by crunchy Sardinian bread with sea salt and rosemary, served alongside a tangy starter of sun-dried tomatoes and olives; a softer, Lebanese bread also went down well, grilled and wrapped round a hearty, brightly marinated filling of lamb mince and pine nuts. The recommended daily special proved a good-value choice – a large, juicy sea bream on a multicoloured stew of tomatoes, courgettes, fennel and onion. A risotto with tender asparagus and parmesan was richly rewarding too. Slightly full, we ordered the orange-topped crème brûlée and the baked cheesecake out of pure greed, and we weren't sorry when we'd licked our plates clean. Chatty, smiley service is another bonus here.
Babies and children welcome: high chairs. Booking advisable Fri-Sun.

Gipsy Hill

Numidie
48 Westow Hill, SE19 1RX (8766 6166, www.numidie.co.uk). Gipsy Hill rail. **Dinner served** 6-10.30pm Tue-Sat. **Meals served** noon-10.30pm Sun. **Main courses** £9.50-£15. **Set meal** (Tue-Thur, Sun) £12 2 courses, £14 3 courses. **Credit** MC, V.
Local denizens are spoiled by Westow Hill's parade of neighbourhood bistros and cafés. Numidie is one such option, boasting a concise menu of what it describes as French-Algerian cooking. The cool interior comprises a hotchpotch of wooden tables and mismatched chairs, offset by slightly garish chandeliers and brightly painted walls. Our waitress could have been more au fait with the menu, but was charming nonetheless. The set meals are a bargain, at two courses for £12 and three for £14 – and you choose your courses from the carte. Baby squid stuffed with crabmeat was the highlight of our meal, the slightly smoky flavours from the grill playing off the sweetness of the crab and accompanying pan-fried spinach. Also excellent was a mound of grilled fresh anchovies, served with a gloriously rich smoked paprika mayonnaise: not with the advertised salsa and aïoli, but we forgave the substitution. Chicken and green-olive tagine in a fresh tomato sauce, with perfectly buttery couscous on the side, was a plain but generous serving, though the chicken-leg meat had been slow-cooked to near mushiness. Desserts are agreeably French (chocolate tart with crème anglaise, crème brûlée), but it's unlikely you'll have room.
Babies and children welcome: booster seats; high chairs; nappy-changing facilities. Booking advisable Fri, Sat. Vegetarian menu.

East
Shoreditch

★ Eyre Brothers (100)
70 Leonard Street, EC2A 4QX (7613 5346, www.eyrebrothers.co.uk). Old Street tube/rail. **Lunch served** noon-2.45pm Mon-Fri. **Dinner served** 6.30-10.45pm Mon-Fri; 7-11pm Sat. **Main courses** £15-£25. **Credit** AmEx, DC, MC, V.
This long, attractive room – all dark wood, with a bar lining one side – is extremely popular with

City gents. It's easy to see why. Robert and David Eyre have taken the food of the Iberian peninsula into their heart and soul, and reproduce it in a form that's true to its rustic roots yet sophisticated enough to compete with top-level French or Italian cooking. Mozambique (where they grew up) and London are further influences. There are two ways to eat here. We chose a stool at the bar, where you can order either from the main menu or from a short list of tapas/petiscos. The tapas were sensational: a masterfully cooked fritura mixta (mixed fry) of fish, heavenly pîparras (lightly pickled green chillies) and olives so addictive you could eat them all day. At the tables sat business people and casual lunchers tucking into enormous plates of hearty fare. On the main menu meat is king, with ample garnishes and big flavours. The wine list, nearly all Iberian, enables you to drink very well for £20-£25; there's plenty by the glass too. Tables are particularly hard to secure from Friday lunchtime through to Saturday dinner. With food this good, that's hardly surprising.

Available for hire. Babies and children admitted. Booking advisable Thur-Sat. Disabled: toilet. **Map 6 Q4.**

North West
Queen's Park

Penk's
79 Salusbury Road, NW6 6NH (7604 4484, www.penks.com). Queen's Park tube/rail. **Brunch served** 10am-3pm Sat, Sun. **Lunch served** noon-3pm Mon-Fri. **Dinner served** 6-11pm Mon-Sat. **Meals served** 10am-10.30pm Sun. **Main courses** £11-£17. **Set meal** (noon-3pm, 6-7.30pm) £13.50 2 courses. **Credit** MC, V.
With its smart red awning, large windows (that fold back in summer), and leafy potted plants marking the entrance, Penk's is an attractive prospect even from a distance. Up close it doesn't disappoint. The limited space has been thoughtfully arranged for maximum effect: the dining room is tastefully decorated with bright-white and warm-red walls; bottles of wine are placed artfully on shelves; lots of small tables are covered with white tablecloths; there's banquette seating; and a small bar area at the entrance serves aperitifs. The classic bistro menu changes weekly, but might include a delicious goat's cheese tartlet with crumbly all-butter pastry, or an equally appealing warm salad of confit of duck. Main courses could be fish cakes with creamy white wine sauce, or wonderfully tender lamb shank. We enjoyed side

dishes of mash and wilted spinach too. For afters, there's an array of classic desserts. Unsurprisingly, Penk's is popular with the local groomed and moneied crowd, but with service that is both slick and friendly, the atmosphere is completely without stuffiness or pretension.
Available for hire. Babies and children admitted (lunch). Booking advisable. Separate room for parties, seats 25. **Map 1 A2.**

Scandinavian

Central
Marylebone

Garbo's
42 Crawford Street, W1H 1JW (7262 6582). Baker Street or Edgware Road tube/Marylebone tube/rail. **Lunch served** noon-3pm Mon-Fri, Sun. **Dinner served** 6-11pm Mon-Sat. **Main courses** £8.50-£17.95. **Set lunch** (Mon-Fri) £10.95 2 courses, £11.95 3 courses; £13.95 smörgåsbord. **Set buffet lunch** (Sun) £14.95. **Cover** £1 (à la carte only). **Credit** AmEx, MC, V.
With its blue awning and folk-art window decorations, Garbo's – named after actress Greta – promises a taste of traditional Swedish home life rather than movie star sophistication. Even IKEA's Scandi-modern design seems a foreign country here, so no surprise that most customers on our visit were elderly expats. A cheeky stuffed moose with viking helmet oversees proceedings in the small, elongated dining room, exuding more confidence than the shy but sweet staff. Sunday lunch kicks off with a small smörgåsbord. Dishes on the mini buffet range from the sublime (gorgeous plump herring several ways, fresh potato salad flecked with parsley) to the ridiculous (crabstick, sliced cheese, cucumber, and green and yellow peppers tossed together – were they cleaning out the fridge?). The bread basket (sliced baguette, soft seeded bread and a few rye crispbreads) gave little evidence of the glories of Swedish bakery. To follow, there's the likes of kåldolmar (cabbage rolls with meatball-like pork and beef filling and gravy) and decently rendered wiener schnitzel, both with uninspiring boiled veg of the type you'd expect at old Aunt Helga's. Finnish and Swedish lagers and cider provide a pleasant diversion from the simple wine list.
Babies and children welcome: high chairs. Booking advisable. Separate room for parties, seats 35. **Map 8 F5.**

South Kensington

Madsen **NEW**
20 Old Brompton Road, SW7 3DL (7225 2772, www.madsenrestaurant.com). South Kensington tube. **Open** noon-10pm Mon, Sun; noon-11pm Tue-Thur; noon-midnight Fri, Sat. **Lunch served** noon-4pm Mon-Sat; noon-3.30pm Sun. **Dinner served** 6-9.30pm Mon, Sun; 6-10pm Tue-Thur; 6-11pm Fri, Sat. **Main courses** £11.50-£17.50. **Set lunch** £9.95 2 courses. **Set dinner** £19.95 3 courses. **Credit** MC, V.
Madsen is everything you want in a South Ken eaterie: a stylish, informal, unsloaney, mwah-mwah-free zone serving fresh, comely food and well-made coffee all day. Yet when it tries too hard to be a restaurant, things can go awry. Lunchtime smørrebrød looked picture-perfect with sprigs of the freshest dill and chervil, but the succession of artfully arranged plates that arrived made things confused and pretentious. We had to shift a lit candle – at 2pm in summer! – to make room for the large Scandi-trendy side plate of rye bread and curry salad that came with a herring platter. This and hamburgerryg (sliced smoked pork with mayo, new potatoes and asparagus on rye) arrived far too slowly given both are based on deli ingredients. Dinner sees Danish traditions such as fiskefrikadeller (fish cakes) and koldskål (cold buttermilk soup-pudding with rusks and, at Madsen, citrus fruits) offered alongside mains of meat and veg. The European wine list starts at £4 a glass, but we recommend the superb Ærø beers. Staff are gracious and it's nice to linger in such an airy, chic setting (with plywood chairs of course, and PH5 lamps by Poul Henningsen). If the lunchtime operation were simplified, we reckon the place would be packed.
Available for hire. Babies and children welcome: children's menu; crayons; high chairs; nappy-changing facilities. Booking advisable dinner. Separate room for parties, seats 14. Tables outdoors (4, terrace). Takeaway service. **Map 14 D10.**

South African

South West
Putney

Chakalaka
136 Upper Richmond Road, SW15 2SP (8789 5696, www.chakalakarestaurant.co.uk). East Putney tube. **Dinner served** 6-10.45pm Mon-Fri. **Meals served** noon-10.45pm Sat, Sun. **Main courses** £9.95-£17.95. **Set meal** (dinner Mon-Fri; lunch Sat; lunch & dinner Sun) £15 2 courses. **Credit** AmEx, MC, V.
If meat is your thing, head straight for this stretch of Putney, where a game-park full of exotic flesh awaits you. Billed as 'one of the few truly authentic South African joints in London', Chakalaka has meat flown in three times a week from Namibia. And very tasty it is too. We started with the signature dish of boerewors and chakalaka: a hearty South African farmer's sausage served with spicy tomato and onion salsa and a delightful splodge of sweetcorn mealie pap. This was followed by surprisingly tender chargrilled ostrich steak and a kudu steak wrapped in bacon, which despite requiring slightly more enthusiastic jaw movements, was equally good. We were rather disappointed by the temporary absence of crocodile, but the very American 25oz steak-challenge (diners who finish their giant rump steaks in less than 25 minutes get a free T-shirt) provides a suitably testosterone-addled replacement. Amarula crème brûlée was a guilty pleasure. A varied selection of South African wines is available. Friendly waiting staff and a sunny decor of tribal prints help create a buzzy atmosphere, which, with the great food, makes for a memorable experience.
Babies and children welcome: high chairs; nappy-changing facilities. Booking advisable. Separate room for parties, seats 60.
For branch see index.

Madsen

Greek

London's Hellenic dining scene has been through various phases in the past three decades. First came the local tavernas. These were usually Greek-Cypriot establishments, often based in areas where members of that community decided to settle (most notably Camden). Some tavernas then aimed to appeal to a wider clientele by recreating a holiday atmosphere, complete with dancing and plate-smashing – though few such establishments paid sufficient attention to the food. Then came Theodore Kyriakou, who co-created Hoxton's original Real Greek restaurant, leading the cuisine off in new modern directions. The Real Greek has since become a chain, with the consequent dilution of ideas, and at present London Greek dining is in the doldrums. However, there are still some laudable restaurants in this section: **George's Fish & Souvlaki Bar** is a refreshing new find in South Woodford; the area around Parliament Hill Fields has welcomed **Carob Tree**; **Daphne** continues to serve high-quality seafood in Camden; but this year's favourite is **Lemonia**, a popular neighbourhood eaterie in Primrose Hill, with consistently first-rate food.

West
Bayswater

Aphrodite Taverna
15 Hereford Road, W2 4AB (7229 2206, www.aphroditerestaurant.co.uk). Bayswater, Notting Hill Gate or Queensway tube. **Meals served** noon-midnight Mon-Sat. **Main courses** £9.50-£23.50. **Set mezédes** £18 vegetarian, £21 meat, £29.50 fish per person (minimum 2). **Cover** £1. **Credit** AmEx, MC, V.
'Atmospheric' doesn't do justice to this warm little Greekerie. Not a place for intimate diners à deux, Aphrodite is packed (perhaps too) tightly most nights, the hectic decor somehow transcending kitsch. Roxanna (on kissing terms with half her clientele) and her crew greeted us warmly. Platters of olives, chillies, radishes and bean salad arrived immediately with pitta. We ordered three starters to share: gorgeous houmous that really tasted of chickpeas, grilled halloumi on a thick slice of tomato, and stunning fried calamares in broad ribbons and hoops (served al dente without a hint of rubberiness, and with a superb full flavour). Main courses were generous. Lamb kléftiko, redolent of an array of herbs, was accompanied by delicious gently roasted potatoes. A mixed kebab of chicken and lamb had been cooked just so: the chicken moist and the lamb tasty, all generously sprinkled with green herbs and finely chopped onion. Sadly, the accompanying chips were limp. An unbidden plate of turkish delight on cocktail sticks with our bill was a nice touch. Glasses of house red, white and retsina (each £4) were excellent.
Available for hire. Babies and children welcome: high chairs. Booking advisable dinner. Tables outdoors (12, terrace). Takeaway service. **Map 7 B6.**

Notting Hill

Greek Affair
1 Hillgate Street, W8 7SP (7792 5226, www.greekaffair.co.uk). Notting Hill Gate tube. **Lunch served** noon-3pm Tue-Sun. **Dinner served** 6-11pm daily. **Main courses** £8.50-£12.90. **Credit** MC, V.
Just by the Coronet cinema lies this unusual little place. The main ground-floor dining room (there's also a basement and first floor) feels like a cosy seaside tea shop, with several wooden tables for two – and one whopping dining table that would seat a large party, but seems awkward for the average restaurant grouping. Smiling service came promptly from a charming Japanese woman. We ordered various mezédes to start. The houmous was a sensation: neither the oil, garlic nor the tahini predominated. Prasokeftédes (leek rissoles), gigantes and dolmádes were all similarly delicious, with delicately balanced fresh flavours. To follow, arni fournou (roast lamb leg) was meltingly tender and brimming with flavour, while a grilled and lemony sea bass on mash had been wonderfully spiced to give an earthiness without masking the fish's fresh flavour. We can readily believe the restaurant's claim that its ingredients are mostly organic and imported from Greece. All this with a glass of retsina and a glass each of red and white house wines and one bottle of sparkling water came to £60 with service.
Babies and children welcome: high chairs. Booking advisable. Tables outdoors (10, roof garden). Takeaway service. Vegetarian menu. **Map 19 C5.**

South West
Earl's Court

★ As Greek As It Gets
233 Earl's Court Road, SW5 9AH (7244 7777/ www.asgreekasitgets.co.uk). Earl's Court tube. **Dinner served** 5-11pm Mon-Thur. **Meals served** noon-11pm Fri-Sun. **Main courses** £7.50-£14.90. **Credit** MC, V.
With its modishly un-Greek interior, this place is unusually named. The first floor is metro smart, but with inexplicable banks of TVs all showing the same thing along one side of the main dining room. Downstairs (where the owner seems to hang out) is cold and a little intimidating, but upstairs, away from the screens, there's a nice relaxed atmosphere. A tasty starter of courgette fritters were not at all as imagined, but batter-free slices of the seemingly sautéed vegetable strewn with shreds of halloumi. Calamares was nicely cooked if rather bland. Main courses were intriguingly different, so we decided to choose a couple of stews: lamb with lemon was quite fabulous, and arrived with a large pat of good fresh mash. Almost as appealing was beef with

honey, accompanied by a similar pat of fava bean purée. An extra portion of fries was a real treat, nicely salted and scattered with fresh oregano. Several wines, including retsina, are available by the glass, and there's also a varied selection of beers.
Available for hire. Babies and children welcome: high chairs. Booking advisable weekends. Entertainment: live music 9pm Fri. Tables outdoors (2, pavement). Takeaway service.

East
Spitalfields

The Real Greek
6 Horner Square, E1 6EW (7375 1364, www.therealgreek.com). Liverpool Street tube/rail. **Meals served** noon-11pm Mon-Sat; noon-8pm Sun. **Main courses** £4.95-£6.25. **Set mezédes** £18.50 vegetarian, £22 fish, £25 meat (minimum 2). **Credit** AmEx, MC, V.
There's no escaping the fact that TRG is a chain. Now eight branches strong, its latest outposts are in Shepherd's Bush's Westfield shopping centre and at Spitalfields Market. All continue to draw punters for reliable food in glossy surrounds. The Spitalfields venue sports attractive raised banquettes in inky leather, rust-coloured ceramic plates, rustic touches (baskets for lampshades) and a long, reconstituted-granite bar ideal for City lunches. Sundays see shoppers replace local workers in the outside seating area. As well as souvláki, served in mainland Greek style – wrapped in pitta and paper – the meze picks from the islands and beyond. Santorinian fava dip was smooth, bland but surprisingly moreish; tabouleh was bulgar wheat-heavy with barely detectable herbage. The pittas, grill-blackened and glistening with olive oil, are finger-licking. Thyme-sprinkled lamb cutlets were lean; greasy whitebait came with unremarkable lemon mayo; fresh, batter-less, pleasantly chewy calamares was the tastiest dish. The dance-lite music is fit for purpose, if the aim is rapid customer turnover. TRG is fine for a quick, dependable refill but not somewhere to linger.
Available for hire. Babies and children welcome: children's menu; high chairs; nappy-changing facilities. Booking advisable weekends. Disabled: toilet. Tables outdoors (15, pavement). Takeaway service. **Map 12 R5.**
For branches see index.

North East
South Woodford

George's Fish & Souvlaki Bar NEW
164 George Lane, E18 1AY (8989 3970, www.georgesfishbar.co.uk). South Woodford tube. **Lunch served** noon-2.30pm, **dinner served** 5-10.30pm Tue-Sat. **Meals served** noon-6pm Sun. **Main courses** £9.50-£15.50. **Set lunch** £7 2 courses. **Set mezédes** £20. **Credit** MC, V.
Don't be fooled by the takeaway price-boards and metal deep-fat fryers. Behind the chip shop exterior lies a cosy taverna with an eye fixed firmly on modern presentation. Candles light the dark-wooden varnished tables, and a selection of cold starters arrives artfully laid out on a big triangular plate. The menu's an odd mix of chippy fare and Cypriot home-cooking, with side orders of pickled egg and mushy peas sitting next to keftédes and kléfitko, and several main courses coming with huge helpings of chunky fish-shop chips. As the notice in the entrance points out, these are certified by Keith Chegwin as a 'perfect portion'. A flagstone-sized serving of moussaká was topped with thick, creamy béchamel. Stuffed vine leaves were produced in typical Cypriot style: coated in tomato and filled with minced meat rather than rice. Leave room for dessert lest you miss the delicate rosewater scent of the stunning galatoboureko (custard baked in filo pastry). Service is attentive and skilled.
Available for hire. Babies and children welcome: children's menu; high chairs. Booking advisable Thur-Sun. Tables outdoors (8, patio). Takeaway service.

George's Fish & Souvlaki Bar. See p121.

North
Camden Town & Chalk Farm

Andy's Taverna
81-81A Bayham Street, NW1 0AG (7485 9718, www.andystaverna.com). Camden Town or Mornington Crescent tube. **Lunch served** noon-2.30pm, **dinner served** 6pm-midnight Mon-Fri. **Meals served** noon-midnight Sat, Sun. **Main courses** £8.95-£14. **Set mezédes** £13.95 per person (minimum 2). **Credit** AmEx, MC, V.
A homely little taverna just off the main Camden drag, Andy's caters to those looking for an easy-going meal in welcoming, unfussy surroundings. Diners range from groups of overseas students to couples who are clearly regulars. Everyone is well looked-after by the congenial owner. The low-ceilinged space is simply decorated in typically Greek blue and white, the walls adorned with touristy island photos and snaps of the owner smiling alongside various customers. The food, unfortunately, could do with a little more work. Green olives with a bitter tinge and too-salty pickles brought with the menu were improved upon by satisfying starters of tzatziki made with thick, creamy yoghurt and served with puffy, oven-warm, sesame-sprinkled bread. The vegetarian platter appeared to be good value, and included toothsome grilled halloumi, but had little else to recommend it – the spanakópitta and moussaká were too greasy, the pepper had been stuffed with bland rice and scant veg. Meat dishes are somewhat better: the souvláki tender yet lacking that essential chargrilled flavour; the perennially popular kléftiko cooked, rather unusually, with tomatoes. Be sure to order a malty, refreshing Keo beer, which beats insipid lagers every time.
Available for hire. Babies and children welcome: high chairs. Booking advisable weekends. Tables outdoors (6, garden). Takeaway service. **Map 27 D2.**

Daphne
83 Bayham Street, NW1 0AG (7267 7322). Camden Town or Mornington Crescent tube. **Lunch served** noon-2.30pm, **dinner served** 6-11.30pm Mon-Sat. **Main courses** £9-£14.50. **Set lunch** £7.75 2 courses, £9.25 3 courses. **Set mezédes** £16.50 meat or vegetarian, £20.50 fish per person (minimum 2). **Credit** MC, V.

Looking rather unprepossessing and cramped from the front, Daphne is a pleasant surprise within. Though narrow, it is much more spacious than at first appears, as the kitchens are on the second floor. Rather like the façade, the menu initially looked lacklustre and predictable, but when the specials blackboard came to our table, we had to revise our opinion. From a wealth of seafood dishes we chose kavourosaláta (crab salad) and baby scallops to start, both of which were first-rate. For mains we plumped for an inviting fish combination platter (including king scallops, huge prawns, monkfish and salmon), with some rather overcooked green beans, and the seldom-seen option of grilled sweetbreads, with a greek salad. Beans apart, everything was perfectly cooked and full of flavour, although the sizeable platter of sweetbreads could have done with some sort of sharp accompaniment, like grilled tomatoes (we wished there were some mushrooms or even a bit of bacon). Service too was almost perfect: intelligent, polite and informative without being obsequious. The evening was so pleasant, we stayed for desserts (figs in cream and baklavá) with some bracing fresh mint tea.
Available for hire. Babies and children welcome: high chairs. Booking advisable weekends. Disabled: toilet. Tables outdoors (24, roof terrace; 2, pavement). **Map 27 D2.**

★ Lemonia
89 Regent's Park Road, NW1 8UY (7586 7454). Chalk Farm tube. **Lunch served** noon-3pm Mon-Fri; noon-3.30pm Sun. **Dinner served** 6-11.30pm Mon-Sat. **Main courses** £9-£15. **Set lunch** (Mon-Fri) £9 2 courses, £10.50 3 courses. **Set mezédes** £18.50 per person (minimum 2). **Credit** MC, V.
One of the most popular Greek-Cypriot establishments in town, Lemonia is usually heaving with convivial chattering customers. A well-placed skylight and plants on every surface create a light, airy atmosphere. At weekends, families with kids still muddy-kneed from football practice share the space with cosy groups of well-heeled friends, emphasising the unpretentious, local-restaurant feel. Small plates of crunchy radishes and excellent, garlicky tsakistés keep punters placated while they wait for tables. Staff remain affable and composed, coping like seasoned pros with the bustle. When chips arrived instead of the requested roast potatoes, the waiter immediately brought the correct order in addition

to the chips. A communal horiátiki to start featured fantastic feta and the unconventional addition of red and orange peppers, which lent it an unexpected but not unpleasant sweetness. Both pork and lamb souvláki were infused with a heavenly chargrilled flavour (the aroma of which wafts temptingly out of the restaurant). Portions are large, whether for vegetable moussaká layered with juicy aubergines and velvety béchamel, or for the beautifully tender kléftiko, not quite melting off the bone but close enough. Little cups of strong, swampy coffee and complimentary, icing sugar-dusted cubes of rosy loukoúmi provide the perfect end to a merry-making meal.
Babies and children admitted. Booking advisable. Separate room for parties, seats 40. Tables outdoors (6, pavement). **Map 27 A1.**

Limani
154 Regent's Park Road, NW1 8XN (7483 4492). Chalk Farm tube. **Lunch served** noon-3pm Sat. **Dinner served** 6-11.30pm Tue-Sat; 3.30-10.30pm Sun. **Main courses** £8.75-£16.50. **Set mezédes** £16 meat or vegetarian, £18 fish per person (minimum 2). **Credit** MC, V.
Expect groups of young, chichi Primrose Hill types on girly nights out, middle-aged couples and a smattering of lone-dining Greek regulars at this little sister to Lemonia (*see above*). Decor varies depending on where you sit. A low ceiling, dark wooden beams and nautical paintings of Greek-Cypriot vessels lend the entrance an almost ship-like feel, but hanging green vines in the wooden-floored mezzanine offer more of a tree-house ambience. Service is friendly, and with a wine-list half comprised of Hellenic varieties (although none is available by the glass), plus ouzo, retsina and tsipouro available, there's plenty of chance to get into the (ahem) Greek spirit. An enjoyably smoky melitzanosaláta and a pine-nut studded tabouleh were highlights of a menu that seemed largely to consist of meagre portions of disappointing cooking. Lowlights included grey, mushy keftédes; too-salty tzatziki; rubbery calamares; and an attempt to bolster the cold mezédes with a cheap-tasting tuna mayo. Diners in search of impressive Greek-Cypriot cuisine might be better off elsewhere, but the genial atmosphere makes Limani a decent venue for an evening out.
Babies and children admitted. Booking advisable; essential weekends. Separate rooms for parties, seating 24-60. Tables outdoors (4, pavement). **Map 27 A1.**

Kentish Town

Carob Tree NEW

*15 Highgate Road, NW5 1QX (7267 9880).
Gospel Oak rail/C2, C11, 214 bus.* **Lunch served**
noon-3pm, **dinner served** 6-10.30pm Tue-Fri.
Meals served noon-10.30pm Sat; noon-9pm Sun.
Main courses £2.95-£11.95. **Credit** MC, V.
In previous guises, this site (opposite the
Parliament Hill entrance to Hampstead Heath) has
housed the Duke of St Albans pub and the
Platinum Bar. It has now been transformed into a
casually chic 'Mediterranean kitchen' with stylish
lighting, moody red walls and chefs working in
view of customers. A blackboard above the
counter highlights the day's fresh fish for cooking
on the chargrill, but in contrast to the modish
decor, the printed menu is largely based on familiar
Cypriot dishes. Meze include cured meats, scallops
with chilli and bacon, koubes (bulgar wheat
parcels filled with spiced pork), roast aubergine
and tomato dip, roast peppers marinated in lemon
and oil, and some very good spanakópitta. Five
dishes between two people is the recommendation
from the friendly staff. Of the mains, pork keftédes
and lamb souvláki were impressive. Beef steaks
(sirloin, T-bone) are 28-day hung Aberdeen Angus;
you can also have grilled veal chop or calf's liver.
On the wine list we were pleased to find an organic
assyrtiko (Greece's best white grape) blend by
Sillogi in Paros – or there's Keo lager. An outdoor
table is prized in good weather.
*Babies and children welcome: high chairs.
Booking advisable. Disabled: toilet. Tables
outdoors (10, garden). Vegetarian menu.*

Wood Green

Vrisaki

*73 Myddleton Road, N22 8LZ (8889 8760).
Bounds Green or Wood Green tube.* **Lunch
served** noon-4pm, **dinner served** 6-11.30pm
Mon-Sat. **Meals served** noon-9pm Sun. **Main
courses** £10-£18. **Set mezédes** £18 per person
(minimum 2). **Credit** AmEx, MC, V.
Portions served in Greek-Cypriot restaurants are
generally vast, but Vrisaki takes it to gargantuan
extremes. Course one of the three-course set meze
menu for two features no less than 20 dishes,
ranging from standards like tahini-heavy houmous
through to less frequently found offerings such as
bamies (sliced okra in tomato sauce) – along with
the occasional bizarre inclusion (asparagus spears
in syrupy orange sauce, anyone?). A fat, crisply
grilled bream and an outstanding cinnamon-
redolent sheftaliá were the highlights of our meat
and fish courses. Despite verging on the bland at
times, the food attracts the area's Greek diners in
droves. Animated Hellenic chatter, combined with
the red/green plastic plants trailing from the ceiling,
the main dining room's softly lit dark wooden
interior, and the waistcoat-clad waiters' tendency
to pepper conversation with Greek ('endaxi' means
'OK'), give this lively eaterie the feel of a taverna
garden. The photo-board of celeb visitors includes
two snaps of Greek-Cypriot and Blue singer
Antony Costa. Presumably the portions explain
Costa's 'healthier' look in the second shot.
*Available for hire. Babies and children welcome:
high chairs. Booking advisable: essential weekends.
Takeaway service.*

North West

Belsize Park

Retsina

*48-50 Belsize Lane, NW3 5AR (7431 5855,
www.retsina-london.com). Belsize Park or Swiss
Cottage tube.* **Lunch served** noon-3pm Tue-Sun.
Dinner served 6-11pm daily. **Main courses** £9-
£22.50. **Set mezédes** £18.50 meat, £22.50 fish per
person (minimum 2). **Cover** £1. **Credit** MC, V.
This calm spot is nicely decorated in cool white
and natural wood; service is pleasant and the menu
extensive and exciting. We chose to share the hot
and cold meze at £7.50 per person, which was
lovely and seemingly generous – taramosaláta,
tahini, houmous, delicious tzatziki, singingly fresh
tabouleh, halloumi, loukánika, crab (actually crab
stick) salad and pantzarosaláta (dressed beetroot).
It came at a cost, however, as we'd been served two
portions rather than one to share. Main courses,
alas, weren't quite to the same standard. Calf's liver
arrived with grilled tomatoes and chips, plus a
great thick slice of almost raw onion. The liver was
generous and well-cooked, but had none of the
fresh herbs so prevalent in the meze. Mixed soúvla
(chicken and lamb grill) came with more tzatziki
and tabouleh, but neither meat had been graced
with any flavouring, and the lamb was dry and
tasteless. It seemed as if there were two different
cooks in the kitchen.
*Babies and children welcome: high chairs. Booking
advisable. Separate room for parties, seats 50.
Tables outdoors (5, pavement). Takeaway service.*
Map 28 B3.

Menu

Dishes followed by (G) indicate a
specifically Greek dish; those marked
(GC) indicate a Greek-Cypriot speciality;
those without an initial have no particular
regional affiliation. Spellings often vary.

Afélia (GC): pork cubes stewed in wine,
coriander and other herbs.
Avgolémono (G): a sauce made of
lemon, egg yolks and chicken stock.
Also a soup made with rice, chicken
stock, lemon and whole eggs.
Dolmádes (G) or **koupépia (GC):** young
vine leaves stuffed with rice, spices and
(usually) minced meat.
Fasólia plakí or **pilaki:** white beans in
a tomato, oregano, bay, parsley and
garlic sauce.
Garídes: prawns (usually king prawns
in the UK), fried or grilled.
Gígantes or **gígandes:** white butter
beans baked in tomato sauce;
pronounced 'yígandes'.
Halloumi (GC) or **hallúmi:** a cheese
traditionally made from sheep or goat's
milk, but increasingly from cow's milk.
Best served fried or grilled.
Horiátiki: Greek 'peasant' salad of
tomato, cucumber, onion, feta and
sometimes green pepper, dressed with
ladolémono (oil and lemon).
Hórta: salad of cooked wild greens.
Houmous, hoúmmous or **húmmus (GC):**
a dip of puréed chickpeas, sesame seed
paste, lemon juice and garlic, garnished
with paprika. Originally an Arabic dish.
Htipiti or **khtipiti:** tangy purée of matured
cheeses, flavoured with red peppers.
Kalamári, kalamarákia or **calamares:**
small squid, usually sliced into rings,
battered and fried.

Kataïfi or **katayfi:** syrup-soaked
'shredded-wheat' rolls.
Keftédes or **keftedákia (G):** herby
meatballs made with minced pork or
lamb (rarely beef), egg, breadcrumbs
and possibly grated potato.
Kléftiko (GC): slow-roasted lamb on the
bone (often shoulder), flavoured with
oregano and other herbs.
Kopanistí (G): a cheese dip with a
tanginess that traditionally comes from
natural fermentation, but is often
boosted with chilli.
Koukiá: broad beans.
Loukánika or **lukánika:** spicy coarse-
ground sausages, usually pork and
heavily herbed.
Loukoumádes: tiny, spongy dough
fritters, dipped in honey.
Loukoúmi or **lukúmi:** 'turkish delight'
made with syrup, rosewater and pectin,
often studded with nuts.
Loúntza (GC): smoked pork loin.
Marídes: picarel, often mistranslated as
(or substituted by) 'whitebait' – small
fish best coated in flour and flash-fried.
Melitzanosaláta: grilled aubergine purée.
Meze (plural **mezédes,** pronounced
'mezédhes'): a selection of either hot or
cold appetisers and main dishes.
Moussaká(s) (G): a baked dish of mince
(usually lamb), aubergine and potato
slices, topped with béchamel sauce.
Papoutsáki: aubergine 'shoes', slices
stuffed with mince, topped with sauce,
usually béchamel-like.
Pourgoúri or **bourgoúri (GC):** a pilaf of
cracked wheat, often prepared with stock,
onions, crumbled vermicelli and spices.
Saganáki (G): fried cheese, usually
kefalotyri; also refers to anything

(mussels, spinach) served in a
cheese-based red sauce.
Sheftaliá (GC): little pig-gut skins
stuffed with minced pork and lamb,
onion, parsley, breadcrumbs and
spices, then grilled.
Soutzoukákia or **soutzoúki (G):** baked
meat rissoles, often topped with a
tomato-based sauce.
Soúvla: large cuts of lamb or pork,
slow-roasted on a rotary spit.
Souvláki: chunks of meat quick-grilled on
a skewer (known in London takeaways
as kebab or shish kebab).
Spanakópitta: small turnovers stuffed
with spinach, dill and often feta or some
other crumbly tart cheese.
Stifádo: a rich meat stew (often beef or
rabbit) with onions, red wine, tomatoes,
cinnamon and bay.
Taboúlleh: generic Middle Eastern
starter of pourgoúri (qv), chopped
parsley, cucumber chunks, tomatoes
and spring onions.
Taramá, properly **taramosaláta:** fish roe
pâté, originally made of dried, salted
grey mullet roe, but now more often
smoked cod roe, plus olive oil, lemon
juice and breadcrumbs.
Tavás (GC): lamb, onion, tomato
and cumin, cooked in earthenware
casseroles.
Tsakistés (GC): split green olives
marinated in lemon, garlic, coriander
seeds and other optional flavourings.
Tyrópitta (G): similar to spanakópitta
(qv) but usually without spinach and with
more feta.
Tzatzíki, dzadzíki (G) or **talatoúra (GC):**
a dip of shredded cucumber, yoghurt,
garlic, lemon juice and mint.

Hotels & Haute Cuisine

After a flurry of exciting openings, 2009 has been a year of consolidation in the haute cuisine sector. French newcomer Ambassade de l'Ile closed in August after just a year of trading, but we welcome the return of Bjorn van der Horst at **Eastside Inn** in Farringdon, and the bold efforts of Shay Cooper to establish fine dining in the glamorous surrounds of the **Bingham** boutique hotel in Richmond. The industry's main talking point is a forthcoming venture, however: Heston Blumenthal will open a restaurant in the Mandarin Oriental Hyde Park in autumn 2010. Given the media profile of Britain's grand poobah of molecular gastronomy, it should attract wide custom even if the economy has not improved by then. Elsewhere, we'd be lying if we said all these high-end restaurants were packed at every sitting, but at some (**Maze**, **Hibiscus**) it's still reassuringly difficult to nail a table.

For the grandeur of hotel dining without the cost of a menu gastronomique, why not treat someone to a proper afternoon tea? An increasing number of top-flight chefs are getting involved in the tea service and introducing marvellous desserts and pastries of the standard you would expect at dinner.

Central

City

Addendum
Apex City of London Hotel, 1 Seething Lane, EC3N 4AX (7977 9500, www.addendum restaurant.co.uk). Tower Hill tube. **Lunch served** noon-2.30pm, **dinner served** 6-9.30pm Mon-Fri. **Main courses** £15-£20. **Credit** AmEx, DC, MC, V.
When Apex Hotels, which is based mainly in Scotland, opened this offshoot in London, Tom Illic was brought in to head the restaurant. However, Illic left to open his own place shortly afterwards, and the original aspirations were considerably downscaled. The formal dining area at the rear of the restaurant is now only used for breakfast by the residents. So we're left with a gastro-bar on the mezzanine floor and this glossy brasserie. Dining takes place in a light-washed space with floor-to-ceiling windows. The sociable atmosphere can be a draw, especially in warm weather when tables stretch on to the pavement. The design is modern, with oak panelling and granite flooring brightened by cream leather and splashes of colourful artwork. Food is straightforward and somewhat lacking in ambition, evidenced by chicken caesar salad as well as burger and fries. A few twists on familiar classics do appear, however, such as chocolate fondant served with Ovaltine ice-cream. Prices are fair, although there's no longer a fixed-priced lunch. We enjoyed the wild boar scotch egg, its runny yolk a good match for the mustard mayonnaise. Such dishes – perfect for a quick lunch – underscore the restaurant's drive towards simplicity. Main courses cover a similar gamut of expertise. Roast loin of rabbit wrapped with pancetta and stuffed with black olives came with braised leeks and a fried polenta cake; the flavours were a little evanescent, the impact fizzing out too quickly. Frozen pistachio parfait with black cherry sorbet made a vividly coloured and pleasant end to the meal. Service was keen and friendly. The wine list, starting at £18, has an obvious French accent and spans a wide price spectrum, with plenty of choice by the glass and half-bottle. *Babies and children welcome: high chairs. Disabled: lift; toilet (in hotel). Separate rooms for parties, seating 10-50.* **Map 12 R7.**

Bonds
Threadneedles, 5 Threadneedle Street, EC2R 8AY (7657 8088, www.theetongroup.com). Bank tube/DLR. **Lunch served** noon-2.30pm, **dinner served** 6-10pm Mon-Fri. **Main courses** £12.95-£19.95. **Set lunch** £15.50 3 courses. **Set dinner** £17.50 3 courses. **Credit** AmEx, DC, MC, V.
Part of a boutique hotel, converted from a former Victorian bank, the interior of this vast dining room is one of stately elegance, with lofty ceilings and columns. Furnishing, on the other hand, is contemporary, accented by burgundy coloured chairs, brown leather banquettes and dark wood. At lunchtimes the room fills with spirited conversation, but dinner is a more muted affair. Prices have been lowered since our previous visit and set-price options for both lunch (£15.50) and dinner (£17.50) are offered alongside the carte. Barry Tonks leads the kitchen and his cooking is right on the money: a refreshing take on modern European cookery punctuated with clever twists and picture-perfect presentations. Seasonality and careful sourcing are priorities and slow cooking continues to be the favoured technique for meat, though you will also find plenty of fish, vegetable and cheese dishes. We started with an exemplary country-style terrine served with fruit chutney and toasted sourdough bread. Breast of duck, served rare with caramelised endive and date purée, allowed the original flavours to shine and typified the elegance of the cooking. Proportion was an issue here, however, with the vegetable serving double the size of the duck breast. Desserts, like the rest of menu, are keyed to the seasons. The French classic, îles flottantes, was given a new lease of life by with crushed raspberries and pink praline, and straightforward rice pudding was made special with alphonso mango and coconut sorbet. If only the service could keep up: we found it frustratingly patchy, seemingly just going through the motions. The wine list is a good one: well organised and varied in price, with two-dozen wines by the glass, and some noteworthy bottles, such as Cheval Blanc 1990, ageing gracefully for when the big bonuses return (if you really want to know, it costs £1,450). *Available for hire. Booking advisable. Disabled: lift; toilet. Dress: smart casual. Separate rooms for parties, seating 8, 14 and 16.* **Map 12 Q6.**

Clerkenwell & Farringdon

Eastside Inn Restaurant
40 St John Street, EC1M 4AY (7490 9230, www.esilondon.com). Farringdon tube/rail. **Lunch served** noon-2.30pm, **dinner served** 7-10pm Mon-Fri. **Set lunch** £25 2 courses, £35 3 courses. **Set meal** £55 3 courses, £70 tasting menu. **Credit** AmEx, MC, V.
This is the fancier side of Bjorn van der Horst's twin restaurant (the other side being French venue Bistro, *see p92*). It opened eight months behind schedule in mid 2009, and has made a few concessions to the economic slowdown. Set menus, including lunch, give a few choices at each course. The wine list is mainly French, and heavily populated with expensive Burgundy and Bordeaux. Luxury ingredients abound; the best of the appetisers was a generous slab of foie gras. Of the starters, densely flavoured braised veal sweetbreads were good, so too Van der Horst's signature dish of foie gras covered with a delicate foam of coffee and amaretto flavours. Less impressive was a steamed slice of eel, with the bones still in; this was bland and mushy, and the accompanying fresh peas added colour but little else to the dish. A main course aged ribeye of beef had perfectly tender slivers of rare flesh, served with a 'ratte mash' rich in butter. Although it was pleasant enough, we had expected more fireworks and risk-taking from this renowned chef, who won plaudits while at the Greenhouse, then a more muted response at the now-closed La Noisette. We were rewarded for our wait when the desserts arrived: two hollow spheres resembling Christmas tree ornaments, one edible gold-plated orb holding a milk sorbet, the other a meringue with fruit and a sorbet inside which disintegrated as the waiter flambéed it. This Swiss-born chef of Dutch-Spanish parentage, who learned his craft in New York, seems unsure if he's out to create a Eurocracy of dishes, or to shock and awe; and in attempting to do both, has created a slightly clumsy detente that could rival a UN resolution. *Babies and children admitted. Booking advisable. Separate room for parties, seats 20.* **Map 5 O5.**

Fitzrovia

Landau (100)
The Langham, 1C Portland Place, W1B 1JA (7965 0165, www.thelandau.com). Oxford Circus tube. **Breakfast served** 7-10.30am Mon-Fri; 7-noon Sat, Sun. **Lunch served** 12.30-2.30pm, **tea served** 3-5pm Mon-Fri. **Dinner served** 5.30-11pm Mon-Sat. **Main courses** £19-£30. **Set lunch** £21.50 2 courses, £28.50 3 courses. **Set dinner** £57.50 5 courses, £65 6 courses, £72.50 tasting menu. **Credit** AmEx, DC, MC, V.
A visit to the Landau brings an immediate sense of occasion thanks to the sweeping stone staircase that allows customers to enter the restaurant without negotiating the hotel lobby. Inside, dark green brickwork and brightly lit wine racks provide an intimate route to the light, high-ceilinged dining room decorated with bespoke antique brass chandeliers, pastel paisley leather, wood pannelling and majestic photographs of trees. Whatever aspects of molecular gastronomy chef Andrew Turner takes delight in, this is still a hotel dining room, so weary (wealthy) travellers might console themselves with pea soup, grilled dover sole, and lemon tart with vanilla ice-cream. Meals begin with a generous bread basket packed with rolls of varying shapes and favours, and pane carasau smeared with fresh pesto. There was an Asian kick to the pear chutney accompanying pressed Landes foie gras with microcress and cubes

of truffle-flavoured marshmallow from the à la carte menu. A light salad of apple and fennel brought zingy freshness to a main course of Scottish halibut on curried mussels and tender strips of red and yellow peppers. Desserts allow the kitchen to unleash its creativity and we were delighted with a large sphere of blueberry chocolate encasing blueberry mousse and an inky liquid centre, set on a bed of compote and served with a side plate of blueberry madeleines. The petits fours, presented on a black slate tile, are gorgeous: among them white chocolate and lime fudge, and black and white sesame chocolates. Staff asked constantly if the meal was OK. The room was hardly bustling, but the atmosphere is ever-lovely and there are wonderful views over Nash's All Souls Church and Broadcasting House to enjoy if people-watching opportunities are scant.
Babies and children welcome: children's menu; high chairs. Booking advisable; essential weekends. Disabled: toilet. Dress: smart casual. Separate room for parties, seats 16. **Map 9 H5**.

★ Pied à Terre
34 Charlotte Street, W1T 2NH (7636 1178, www.pied-a-terre.co.uk). Goodge Street or Tottenham Court Road tube. **Lunch served** 12.15-2.30pm Mon-Fri. **Dinner served** 6.15-10.45pm Mon-Sat. **Set lunch** £24.50 2 courses. **Set dinner** £54.50 2 courses, £67.50 3 courses. **Set meal** £85 tasting menu (£143 incl wine). **Credit** AmEx, MC, V.
Chef Shane Osborn's dazzling dishes capture classic flavours in a stylish, modern way. This innovative approach to fresh British ingredients makes for a winning combination at Pied à Terre, long loved by locals and celebrated by critics. An arty shattered-glass wall forms the backdrop to the front dining room, where you'll bounce a bit with your neighbours on a shared leather couch lining the perimeter. A gorgeous charger showcasing a single large purple gerber daisy set on a square platinum-lined plate offers a prelude to the simple yet stunning creations to come. The menu degustation and thoughtful international wine pairings (including a Brazilian vintage) piqued our palate and curiosity. A flight of amuse bouche bites began with bright beetroot gnocchi, balanced with creamy ricotta cheese and the sweet texture of candied walnut. A swig of gazpacho foam followed, hiding treasured morsels of mozzarella and olives beneath its frothy bubbles. At times we've found the service here unwelcoming and slow, but our Asian-Australian sommelier was extremely educated and effortlessly guided us through the eight-course adventure that followed. Seared foie gras was elevated by the delectable marriage of an orange and cardamom reduction. Jaw-droppingly good best end of lamb was buttery smooth, slow cooked by the sous vide technique. For dessert, sophisticated stout ice-cream schmoozed smoothly with luxuriously rich warm chocolate tart. Just when we couldn't possibly eat anything more, a show-stopping tiered rack of architecturally arranged petits fours arrived. Chewy walnut fudge, delicate crisp tuiles, dark chocolates, and flavourful apple pâté de fruit demanded to be devoured, and greedily was. In food-coma bliss, we gazed at our bill and deemed our pied à terre indeed worthy of its down-payment.
Babies and children admitted. Booking advisable; essential weekends. Dress: smart casual. Separate room for parties, seats 12. Vegetarian menu. **Map 17 B1**.

Holborn

Pearl Bar & Restaurant
Chancery Court Hotel, 252 High Holborn, WC1V 7EN (7829 7000, www.pearl-restaurant.com). Holborn tube.
Bar **Open** 11am-11pm Mon-Fri; 6-11pm Sat. *Restaurant* **Lunch served** noon-2.30pm Mon-Fri. **Dinner served** 6-10pm Mon-Sat. **Set lunch** £26 2 courses, £29 3 courses. **Set dinner** £52 3 courses, £60 tasting menu (£105 incl wine). *Both* **Credit** AmEx, DC, MC, V.
Lunchtime sees the occasional shopping bag of a well-heeled tourist but mostly it's laptops on the tables, pads and pens under the chairs and jaded businessmen asking for a plate of fruit instead of

Marcus Wareing at the Berkeley. See p126.

RESTAURANTS

COOKING CLASSES

Whether you need to learn the basics or want to explore and expand your culinary creativity, these cookery schools will have something to suit. **Books for Cooks** (*see p291*) also offers demonstration classes and hands-on workshops.

L'Atelier des Chefs

19 Wigmore Street, W1U 1PH (7499 6580, www.atelierdeschefs.co.uk). Bond Street tube.
Quick, one-off classes are the speciality of this slick operation. The exciting programme includes lunch-hour courses, sessions where students learn to make a three-course menu, and focused themes such as pasta, sushi and desserts.

Cookery School at Little Portland Street

15B Little Portland Street, W1W 8BW (7631 4590, www.cookeryschool.co.uk). Oxford Circus tube.
Specialist subjects at this well-organised school range from understanding meat and fish to making pies and perfect cupcakes. Expect to don an apron and get your hands dirty.

Divertimenti

227-229 Brompton Road, SW3 2EP (7581 8065, www.divertimenti.co.uk). South Kensington or Knightsbridge tube.
Evening sessions attract a wide range of guest chefs keen to promote their latest book or restaurant. Multi-week 'Cooking with Confidence' courses for absolute beginners are also available.

Eat Drink Talk

190 St John Street, EC1V 4JY (7689 6693, www.eatdrinktalk.co.uk). Barbican tube/Farringdon tube/rail.
Jennifer Klinec's friendly sessions are taught to a maximum of ten students. Beginners should opt for knife skills or 'Help! I Can't Cook Anything!', which focuses on very easy yet glamorous dishes.

Hampstead Cuisine School

The Artisan House, 70 Fortune Green Road, NW6 1DS (0844 884 2788, www.hampsteadcuisineschool.co.uk). West Hampstead tube/rail.
Charismatic teacher Chico Francesco will bring out your experimental side. The programme includes full-day courses and evening workshops, with subjects including cooking for blokes and a wide range of foreign cuisines.

The Kitchen

275 New Kings Road, SW6 4RD (7736 8067, www.visitthekitchen.com). Parsons Green tube.
Learn to cook while making your own ready meals for a week of hassle-free eating. Sessions are led by chef Thierry Laborde, who has worked in many top restaurants. Guest presenters feature in masterclasses such as Japanese vegetarian cooking, knife skills and chocolate.

dessert at Jun Tanaka's prettily pearl-themed restaurant in the Renaissance Chancery Court Hotel. The old building, entered through a heavy wooden revolving door, is magnificent, with an ornate plaster ceiling, columns so fat you could not put your arms around them, and marble-lined walls carefully chosen to show off the stone's intricate patterns. Those tourists must love the opportunity to dine in such a chic, grand establishment with a procession of red double decker buses gliding past outside. The wine list focuses the reader's mind on the sommelier's choices (generally over £10 for a £175ml glass), but there are also cheaper options with brands familiar from the posher supermarkets some pages on. An amuse bouche of sweet, silky gazpacho with watermelon, goat cheese balls and pine nuts seemed a poor choice given we'd chosen heritage tomato salad with goat cheese as a starter, but we shouldn't have worried: the dishes were sufficiently different not to detract from the meal. Similarly summery was the roast chicken main, with tender juicy strips of meat and fancy-trim portions on the bone, served with glazed macaroni, girolles, pea purée and a pretty mess of fresh peas, broad beans and pea shoots. Strawberry trifle arrived in a tall thin kilner jar to show off its delectable layers, with a Chinese-style spoon of sorbet on the side. We were less convinced by the passionfruit bombe alaska: it included good chewy meringue and ice-cream, but didn't go well with its coffee jelly accompaniment.
Babies and children welcome (restaurant): high chairs. Booking advisable. Disabled: toilet. Entertainment: pianist 7.30pm Wed-Sat. **Map 18 F2.**

Knightsbridge

★ Boxwood Café

The Berkeley, Wilton Place, SW1X 7RL (7235 1010, www.gordonramsay.com). Hyde Park Corner or Knightsbridge tube. **Lunch served** noon-3pm Mon-Fri; noon-4pm Sat, Sun. **Dinner served** 6pm-12.45am Mon-Fri; 6-10.45pm Sat, Sun. **Main courses** £10.50-£28. **Set lunch** (Mon-Fri, Sun) £23 2 courses, £28 3 courses (both incl half bottle of wine); (Sat) £25 3 courses. **Set meal** £55 tasting menu. **Credit** AmEx, MC, V.
Although we've been ambivalent about this Gordon Ramsay Group restaurant in the past, our most recent visit showed that the Boxwood Café kitchen can really perform. A meal from the three-course lunch menu, with half a bottle of wine included in the price, was nearly flawless. The surroundings here are attractive and quietly elegant, and every element of both food and service did them full justice. The unflappable staff deserve special praise for their smooth handling of a couple of misunderstandings that arose during the meal. Our lunch featured generous portions, with big flavours the dominating themes. Especially notable were a ham hock terrine served with piccalilli and grilled ciabatta, and a lovely warm salad of smoked haddock, endive, potato and poached egg. If money is no object, order from the carte, which is long and full of promise for both omnivores and vegetarians. Wine includes plenty of three- and four-digit splendours, but there's enough under £30 to accommodate those on a budget; £35 is the more reasonable target, and sensible for such wonderful cooking. The only flat note was a woeful peanut butter ice-cream accompanying a delicious cherry tart. Otherwise, we lunched like royalty here – but at commoners' prices: that set lunch is one of London's mega-bargain meals. Outstanding.
Babies and children welcome: children's menu; high chairs. Booking essential. Disabled: toilet (in hotel). Dress: smart casual. Separate room for parties, seats 16. **Map 9 G9.**

The Capital

22-24 Basil Street, SW3 1AT (7589 5171/7591 1202, www.capitalhotel.co.uk). Knightsbridge tube. **Lunch served** noon-2.30pm daily. **Dinner served** 6.45-11pm Mon-Sat; 6.45-10.30pm Sun. **Set lunch** £27.50 2 courses, £33 3 courses. **Set dinner** £55 2 courses, £63 3 courses. **Credit** AmEx, DC, MC, V.
On the ground floor of a discreet luxury hotel, the Capital's dining room has just 12 tables, making it

one of the smallest of London's fine-dining restaurants. The interior by Nina Campbell – with woodwork by David Linley – reflects the upper echelon of British design and provides a tranquil modern setting, with light-wood panelling, elegant chandeliers, cerise coloured chairs and ostrich-leather banquettes. On our lunchtime visit, most diners seemed to be from overseas. Service was gracious. The carte showcases the spectrum of the kitchen's abilities, from modern French classics (crab lasagne with langoustine cappuccino, say) to creative variations such as roast lobster with chilli and coconut broth. Happily, the lunch menu isn't eclipsed by the carte, providing more than a glimpse of craftsmanship. To start, marvellous rissoles of pig's head were made special with the addition of aïoli and a jelly with a hint of balsamic. Next came a superb ensemble – scallops, sensitively cooked, atop braised cabbage, cleverly contrasted with a cromesqui of calf's foot. East-West flavour combinations came to fore with a risotto featuring tiger prawn and a whisper of coconut. A seemingly simple breast of duck à l'orange was given a seductive undertone of ginger, counterbalanced by the bitter edge of caramelised endive and completed with terrific pommes pailles. You can also sample some of the finest cheeses in town, supplied by stellar affineur Bernard Antony. Desserts are picture-perfect; exotic fruit arrived on a base of meringue with white chocolate foam and an exemplary mango sorbet. Coffee is Colombia's best and petits fours are from the top drawer. The lengthy wine list is impressive but spoilt by elevated prices (starting at £35 a bottle).
Booking essential. Dress: smart casual. Separate rooms for parties, seating 10, 14 and 24. **Map 8 F9.**

Marcus Wareing at the Berkeley

The Berkeley, Wilton Place, SW1X 7RL (7235 1200, www.the-berkeley.co.uk). Hyde Park Corner or Knightsbridge tube. **Lunch served** noon-2.30pm Mon-Sat. **Dinner served** 6-10.45pm Mon-Sat. **Set lunch** £35 3 courses. **Set dinner** £75 3 courses. **Set meal** £90 tasting menu. **Credit** AmEx, DC, MC, V.
Having jettisoned past links with Gordon Ramsay, Marcus Wareing is now his own man – although you need eagle eyes to notice any difference. The dining room emits the same allure, with warm claret-coloured wall coverings and elegant lamps. The carte features much complexity – such as ballotine of tuna with spicy pineapple, mooli, cardamom and mint – requiring a deft hand to ensure flavours don't go astray. The most significant change is to the wine list, which (though still regal) is relatively more affordable. The Italian manager seemed chuffed to see us, yet newer staff were rather anodyne. We felt rushed at the start. Lunch kicked off with a somewhat under-seasoned glazed quail, served with pan-fried foie gras and caesar salad with alsace bacon. Warm terrine of suckling pig arrived with barbecued white beans and a beignet filled with snails and garlic – but the meat was too fatty, and the flavourings too rich and sweet. Main courses fared better, especially a game and black pudding torte, made with bread pastry and served with glazed winter vegetables and a classy truffled Madeira sauce. Pan-fried sea bass with broccoli, soused Chantenay carrots and creamy dauphinoise potato purée demonstrated the kitchen can also handle delicate flavours. Interludes bridging the courses are striking, such as sweetcorn velouté with tarragon foam, and a fanciful pre-dessert of passion-fruit jelly with lychee and vodka sorbet. Desserts shouldn't be missed, including a popular baked egg custard tart. Bananas, neatly charred, came paired with an exceptional bitter-chocolate ganache; for extra magic, Wareing added a toasted marshmallow ice-cream. A bon bon trolley guarantees a memorable finish. The formidable charms of this restaurant win over most diners; a meal here is like a reinvigorating spa treatment for your palate.
Babies and children welcome: high chairs. Booking essential. Dress: smart; jacket preferred. Separate rooms for parties, seating 8 and 16. Vegetarian menu. **Map 9 G9.**

Galvin at Windows. See p129.

★ One-0-One

101 William Street, SW1X 7RN (7290 7101, www.oneoonerestaurant.com). Knightsbridge tube. **Lunch served** noon-2.30pm Mon-Fri; 12.30-2.30pm Sat, Sun. **Dinner served** 7-10.30pm daily. **Main courses** £22-£29. **Set lunch** £19 3 courses. **Set dinner** £38 3 courses, £68 6 courses. **Credit** AmEx, DC, MC, V.

One-0-One occupies a nicely understated room that could be a yacht club, were it planted by the ocean. You hardly realise it's part of a hotel. It offers a full carte or a selection of small plates. We ate small, from the low-priced 'business lunch' menu. These three courses proved chef Pascal Proyart's ability to combine visual flair with intense, precisely judged flavour balances. Technical mastery met playful experimentation both in the fish dishes (for which One-0-One is best known) and in meaty food and puddings. Three of the star dishes may convey a sense of the weird and wonderful cuisine: roasted peppered beef carpaccio, pickled mushrooms, wild rocket and summer-truffle salad; slow-poached Arctic cod with onzen quail's egg, watercress velouté, hazelnut and brioche croûtons; and a deconstructed lemon meringue tart with summer raspberries and four-fruit sorbet. Service was formally precise but engaging; we exchanged happy banter with a waiter who clearly loved our evident pleasure in the food. The wine list bulges with beautiful bottles, but there's really nothing you'd be delighted to drink under £40. If a little more choice were added between £30 and £40, you'd have a nigh-on perfect restaurant. When you're feeling rich, ordering à la carte with suitable wines should produce a really memorable meal. *Available for hire. Babies and children welcome: high chairs. Booking advisable Thur-Sun. Disabled: toilet. Dress: smart casual. Separate room for parties, seats 10.* **Map 8 F9.**

Marble Arch

Rhodes W1

The Cumberland, Great Cumberland Place, W1H 7AL (7616 5930, www.rhodesw1.com). Marble Arch tube. **Lunch served** noon-2.15pm Tue-Fri. **Dinner served** 7-10.15pm Tue-Sat. **Set lunch** £19.95 2 courses, £23.95 3 courses. **Set dinner** £55 2 courses, £65 3 courses, £75 7 courses, £85 8 courses. **Credit** AmEx, MC, V.

Perhaps the most beautiful chandeliers in any London restaurant grace Rhodes W1. They're like inverted fountains of light, and they make you constantly look up at the ceiling while you're eating. There's plenty to look at on the plates as well, some of it exceptional. This is Gary Rhodes' Modern European fine-dining restaurant, aiming at the same gastro-artistry as his British enterprise, Rhodes 24. Sometimes it succeeds brilliantly, with unusual presentations of classic ideas, as in a fine rabbit terrine served with pineapple pickle, and a beautiful fillet of halibut poised atop wonderful spiced lentils. Other things, including honey panna cotta with fresh mango, didn't quite reach those heights (though entirely satisfactory, this was lacking a little of the excitement found in our best dishes). Service was flawless: friendly and precise at the same time. The wine list isn't huge, but it is very good, and offers sufficient quality around £30 to suit even relatively modest budgets. Rhodes W1 had a change of chef after its much-feted launch in 2008, and it's possible he hadn't fully settled down when we ate here. The place holds much promise, even if many diners will have to confine their visit to that well-priced lunch. *Available for hire. Booking advisable. Disabled: toilet. Dress: smart casual. Separate room for parties, seats 8.* **Map 9 G6.**

Marylebone

★ Texture

34 Portman Street, W1H 7BY (7224 0028, www.texture-restaurant.co.uk). Marble Arch tube. *Bar* **Open/snacks served** noon-midnight Tue-Sat. *Restaurant* **Lunch served** noon-2.30pm, **dinner served** 6.30-11pm Tue-Sat. **Main courses** £19.50-£27.50. **Set lunch** £18.50 2 courses. **Set meal** £59 tasting menu. *Both* **Credit** AmEx, MC, V.

Texture's period dining room (complete with corniced ceiling) may be grand, but the design is contemporary. We took drinks at the cool-looking bar before slipping into soft caramel leather chairs to peruse the menu and the vividly coloured paintings. The trio of chefs preparing dishes behind a glass wine cabinet add to the anticipation. From the start, our experience was memorable and fun. A quirky array of crisps made from potato, bread and parmesan was rounded off by crisp cod skin, accompanied by wasabi cream and barley yoghurt. Breads were excellent. The first course – asparagus with parmesan snow, olive bread, pea shoots and hazelnuts – was an exuberance of contrasting textures. Then, slow-cooked Lancashire pork belly, Asian in conception, arrived with a spring roll of the meat, and pickled turnips, the tart note cutting through the supple meat. Executive chef and co-owner Agnar Sverrisson hails from Iceland and his style reveals imaginative sequences; you're rewarded by some pure and startling flavours. Dessert was ravishing: raspberries served with a subtle lemon verbena and yoghurt ice-cream. There were surprises throughout the meal; 'tea' of cold pea cream with fresh peas and asparagus, topped with mint granita, was a fizzy success. Acting as a palate cleanser, smooth Icelandic skyr (yoghurt-like soft cheese) was married to a grassy sorrel granita and served on a bowl of dry ice. At the end, we were treated to a tiny lollipop of meringue imbued with a hint of Fisherman's Friend, among textbook petits fours. Staff can be reserved, and seemed lacking a little in experience. Co-owner Xavier Rousset oversees an international wine list, full of intrigue, with a spectrum of prices to encourage experimentation. Lovers of Madeira, champagne and sweet wines will be especially pleased. Texture is one of London's most interesting culinary adventures right now. *Available for hire. Babies and children admitted. Disabled: toilet. Separate room for parties, seats 16. Vegetarian menu.* **Map 9 G6.**

Mayfair

Alain Ducasse at the Dorchester

The Dorchester, 53 Park Lane, W1K 1QA (7629 8866, www.alainducasse-dorchester.com). Hyde Park Corner tube. **Lunch served** noon-2pm Tue-Fri. **Dinner served** 6.30-10pm Tue-Sat. **Set lunch** £39.50 2 courses, £45 3 courses (both incl 2 glasses of wine, mineral water, coffee). **Set dinner** £75 3 courses, £95 4 courses. **Set meal** £115 tasting menu. **Credit** AmEx, DC, MC, V.

Not welcomed with open arms by the British press, Alain Ducasse's restaurant at the Dorchester continues to frustrate by steadily maintaining its course and collecting stars and other accolades. There's nothing wrong with this place; it just feels irrelevant to London, and overpriced. Patrick Jouin's design for the over-large room sensibly includes break-out areas for more intimate dining, plus a rather pretentious crystal-lit curtain that looks disconcertingly like an alien shower cubicle.

Hotel teas

For visitors to the capital, afternoon tea is the quintessential English occasion, yet many Londoners are understandably wary of the prices charged in top hotels. Confusion arises perhaps because some don't realise that a proper hotel tea is an event, however genteel, and a sizeable meal, rather than the cuppa and scones you might have more often in a tea room or park café. Furthermore, competition and therefore quality is on the rise, and you can expect some very indulgent, extravagantly served treats. At the **Connaught**, for example, afternoon tea is overseen by top-flight chef Hélène Darroze and includes some beautiful puddings. The **Berkeley**'s Prêt-a-Portea takes things a step further, producing cakes and confections inspired by the latest catwalk collections – an ideal way to wind up a day's shopping in Knightsbridge. Tea (as in the drink) enthusiasts should head to the **Lanesborough** for its range of rare varieties and an expert sommelier to serve them. The grandeur of the establishment also has a role to play and the **Ritz**'s Palm Court is solidly booked with good reason. The central glass atrium covering the **Landmark**'s Winter Garden (complete with real palm trees) also makes a spectacular setting

in which to enjoy the sandwiches, scones and pastries, and for those who particularly love chocolate, or follow a gluten-free diet, there are special tea menus. For a fabulous oriental fusion afternoon tea, we recommend **Yauatcha**'s ground-floor pâtisserie (*see p290*).

The Bentley
27-33 Harrington Gardens, SW7 4JX (7244 5555, www.thebentley-hotel.com). Gloucester Road tube. **Tea served** 3-6pm. **Set tea** £21, £30 incl glass of champagne. **Credit** AmEx, DC, MC, V. *Babies and children welcome: children's menu; high chairs. Booking advisable. Disabled: toilet.* **Map 13 C10.**

The Berkeley
Wilton Place, SW1X 7RL (7235 6000, www.the-berkeley.co.uk). Knightsbridge tube. **Tea served** 1-6pm daily. **Set tea** £35, £43-£49 incl glass of champagne. **Credit** AmEx, DC, MC, V. *Babies and children welcome: children's menu; high chairs. Booking essential. Disabled: toilet. Dress: smart casual.* **Map 9 G9.**

The Capital
22-24 Basil Street, SW3 1AT (7589 5171/ 7591 1202, www.capitalhotel.co.uk). Knightsbridge tube. **Tea served** 3-5.30pm daily. **Set tea** £18.50, £29 incl glass of champagne. **Credit** AmEx, DC, MC, V. *Booking essential. Dress: smart casual.* **Map 8 F9.**

Claridge's
55 Brook Street, W1K 4HA (7409 6307, www.claridges.co.uk). Bond Street tube. **Tea served** 3-5.30pm daily. **Set tea** £33, £40 incl glass of champagne. **Cover** (if not taking set tea) £3.50. **Credit** AmEx, DC, MC, V. *Babies and children welcome: high chairs. Booking essential. Disabled: toilet. Dress: smart casual. Entertainment: musicians 3-9.30pm daily.* **Map 9 H6.**

The Connaught
16 Carlos Place, W1K 2AL (7499 7070, www.theconnaught.com). Bond Street or Green Park tube. **Tea served** 3-5.30pm daily. **Set tea** £28, £38 incl glass of champagne. **Credit** AmEx, DC, MC, V. *Babies and children welcome: high chairs; nappy-changing facilities. Booking advisable. Disabled: toilet. Dress: smart casual.* **Map 9 H7.**

The Dorchester
53 Park Lane, W1K 1QA (7629 8888, www.thedorchester.com). Hyde Park Corner tube. **Tea served** 2.30pm, 4.45pm daily. **Set tea** £33.50, £42.50 incl glass of champagne. **Credit** AmEx, DC, MC, V. *Babies and children welcome: children's menu; high chairs. Booking essential. Disabled: toilet. Dress: smart casual.* **Map 9 G7.**

The Haymarket
1 Suffolk Place, SW1Y 4BP (7470 4000, www.firmdale.com). Piccadilly Circus tube. **Tea served** 2-6pm daily. **Set tea** £17, £19.50-£25 incl glass of champagne. **Credit** AmEx, MC, V. *Babies and children welcome: high chairs. Booking advisable. Disabled: toilet.* **Map 17 C5.**

The Landmark
222 Marylebone Road, NW1 6JQ (7631 8000, www.landmarklondon.co.uk). Marylebone tube/rail. **Tea served** 3-6pm daily. **Set tea** £30, £35-38 incl glass of champagne. **Credit** AmEx, MC, V. *Babies and children welcome: high chairs. Booking advisable. Disabled: toilet.* **Map 2 F4.**

The Lanesborough
1 Lanesborough Place, Hyde Park Corner, SW1X 7TA (7259 5599, www.lanesborough. com). Hyde Park Corner tube. **Tea served** 4-6pm daily. **Set tea** £31, £39 incl glass of champagne. **Credit** AmEx, DC, MC, V. *Babies and children welcome: children's menu; high chairs; nappy-changing facilities. Booking essential. Disabled: toilet. Dress: smart casual.* **Map 9 G8.**

The Ritz
150 Piccadilly, W1J 9BR (7493 8181, www.theritzhotel.co.uk). Green Park tube. **Tea served** (reserved sittings) 11.30am, 1.30pm, 3.30pm, 5.30pm, 7.30pm daily. **Set tea** £37. **Credit** AmEx, MC, V. *Babies and children welcome: children's menu; high chairs. Booking essential. Dress: jacket and tie; no jeans or trainers. Entertainment: pianist daily.* **Map 9 J7.**

Soho Hotel
4 Richmond Mews, W1D 3DH (7559 3007, www.firmdale.com). Tottenham Court Road tube. **Tea served** noon-6pm daily. **Set tea** £15-£18.50, £20.50-£25 incl glass of champagne. **Credit** AmEx, DC, MC, V. *Babies and children welcome: children's menu; high chairs. Booking advisable Fri, Sat. Disabled: toilet. Dress: smart casual.* **Map 17 B3.**

Green feature walls underline the link to the park opposite but not as well as the terrace, where guests can eat in warm weather. Executive chef is Auvergne-born Jocelyn Herland, who has risen through the ranks at several of Ducasse's Parisian restaurants. The seasonally changing menus range from the Lunch Hour, of two courses with two glasses of wine, mineral water and coffee for £39.50, to a £115 tasting menu. Our meal got off to an excellent start with plump, sweet and juicy Scottish langoustine cooked just so. Then we revelled in the sweet and savoury saltiness of foie gras ravioli, chestnuts and butternut squash with rich buttery sauce. Two tender nuts of Limousin veal followed with seasonal root vegetables, truffles and cabbage. Girl from Ipanema (with pineapple and coconut cream) is one of the few tarted-up versions of crème brûlée we've tasted that really works a treat. The wine list is naturally heavy on French regions but also looks further afield; bottles start at £25. Meals finish with a trolley of young, fresh herbs in pots (pineapple sage, chocolate mint, lemon verbena) offered as tisanes – a very French and fitting digestif.
Booking advisable. Children admitted. Disabled: toilet (in hotel). Dress: smart. Separate rooms for parties, seating 10-24. **Map 9 G7**.

Galvin at Windows

28th floor, The London Hilton, 22 Park Lane, W1K 1BE (7208 4021, www.galvinatwindows.com). Green Park or Hyde Park Corner tube.
Lunch served noon-3pm Mon-Fri; 11.45am-3pm Sun. **Dinner served** 6-11pm Mon-Fri; 5-11pm Sat. **Set lunch** £29 3 courses (£45 incl half bottle of wine, mineral water, coffee). **Set dinner** £58 3 courses. **Set meal** £75 tasting menu. **Credit** AmEx, DC, MC, V.
Sited on the 28th floor of the Hilton, Windows has one of gastronomic London's most sumptuous views. Decor is sophisticated: glossy dark-wood flooring contrasting with pale-cream walls and crisp white napery. Cooking is good too, making this a great choice for romantic trysts and impressing guests. Buoyed by the success of Galvin Bistrot de Luxe, brothers Chris and Jeff Galvin have triumphed with this venture, eschewing bistro classics in favour of modern, fine-dining French creations. Set menu deals offer outstanding value, and although the wine list is pricey, it does boast excellent regional French bins. We ordered from the set menu and were largely impressed by head chef André Garrett's culinary confidence. Sea-fresh Cornish crab meat – surrounded by smoked salmon from Loch Duart, and moistened with the refreshing tang of lemon dressing – was notable for its clean flavours. We loved this simple yet refined starter. Adapting the classic combo of asparagus and hollandaise, Garrett gave his buttery sauce a lovely grapefruit twist, which worked a treat with the perfectly blanched spears. A main course of braised halibut fillet was delectably succulent, its sauce a carefully honed blend of cooking juices from the fish, cut with citrussy notes and hints of lemon oil. However, slow-cooked pork belly, although meltingly tender, was overwhelmed by a huge helping of chewy puy lentils. Desserts missed the grade too: the infusion of green tea, liquorice and vanilla in our trio of crème brûlées was way too strong; and shaped chocolate ganache was a tad too rich, and the malted milk ice-cream accompaniment needed more maltiness. Service is spot on: attentive, friendly and informal. Despite our occasional gripes, we reckon Windows is worth visiting for its lively atmosphere, decent cooking – and fabulous views.
Available for hire. Babies and children welcome: high chairs. Booking advisable. Disabled: lift; toilet (in hotel). Dress: smart casual. Separate room for parties, seats 30. **Map 9 G8**.

★ Le Gavroche (100)

43 Upper Brook Street, W1K 7QR (7408 0881, www.le-gavroche.co.uk). Marble Arch tube. **Lunch served** noon-2pm Mon-Fri. **Dinner served** 6.30-11pm Mon-Sat. **Main courses** £27-£60. **Set lunch** £48 3 courses incl half bottle of wine, mineral water, coffee. **Set dinner** £95 tasting menu (£150 incl wine). **Credit** AmEx, DC, MC, V.
Booked up weeks in advance, Le Gavroche is a culinary icon, famous for its uncompromisingly French haute cuisine. Founded by the Roux brothers over 40 years ago, this basement establishment is overseen by Michel Roux Jr and head chef Rachel Humphrey. Furnishings are conservative and luxurious: shades of bottle green, old-fashioned lamps, formal floral arrangements, and a smattering of understated modern art. Prices are top-drawer, but the animated chatter of the contented clientele says something about the restaurant's worth. The door-stopper of a wine list is as extensive as it gets, offering bottles ranging from the relatively affordable to the stratospheric. Set lunches are easier on the pocket – and worth every penny. During our weekday lunchtime visit, every table was filled with a mix of loyal regulars, business types, and young professionals. Service is almost intuitive: unobtrusive yet attentive, warm and friendly. Don't be fazed by the all-French menu; there are no written translations, but the team will pitch in and explain the nuances of each dish. Gratin of delicately smoked haddock, served with a poached egg and accompanied by buttery, lemony hollandaise, was finished with streaks of sweet green-pea purée: a visual feast and a marvellous match of sublime flavours. Lamb noisettes, notable for their juicy tenderness, were served with full-flavoured chopped black olives, glistening in a robust jus of meaty goodness. Mediterranean sunshine flavours triumphed in a second main course of lightly fried fillet of john dory, served with garlicky ratatouille and a shallow moat of scrumptious, cream-enriched red-pepper sauce. Desserts continued the theme of excellence – a selection of freshly churned ice-creams, memorable for their silky texture and distinctive flavours. If old-fashioned charm, classic French cooking, and superlative service are your weakness, give in to temptation here.
Available for hire. Babies and children admitted. Booking essential. Dress: jacket; no jeans or trainers. **Map 9 G7**.

★ Gordon Ramsay at Claridge's

Claridge's, 55 Brook Street, W1K 4HR (7499 0099, www.gordonramsay.com). Bond Street tube.
Lunch served noon-2.45pm Mon-Fri; noon-3pm Sun. **Dinner served** 5.45-11pm Mon-Sat; 6-11pm Sun. **Set lunch** £30 3 courses. **Set dinner** £70 3 courses, £80 6 courses. **Credit** AmEx, DC, MC, V.
Paying homage to the art deco heritage of Claridge's, GR balances glamour and vintage sparkle with a relaxed and inviting atmosphere. Sweeping drapes, an abundance of fresh flowers, and plenty of space add to the special-occasion feel. Top marks to the accomplished service team, who lend warmth, wit and bonhomie to the theatrical setting. The weighty wine list can be overwhelming – best ask for guidance from the sommelier, who will also match wines by the glass. The kitchen produces food with confidence and flair, for an audience of tourists, celebratory families, business folk, and romancing couples. Salad of plump chicken livers, juicy and pink in the centre, played well with crisp-fried smoky bacon strips, and a soft-boiled quail's egg; we even mopped up the tangy dressing with an obliging slice of caramelised onion bread. The star act was our second starter: a delectable melange of warm linguine, tossed in creamy velouté sauce with crab meat and crayfish morsels, finished with a flurry of chopped red chillies. Fish is a highlight. Sea trout fillets, golden and glistening, were cooked to perfection, making a happy marriage with lightly smoked mussels warmed through in a creamy haricot bean cassoulet. Delicate Cornish lemon sole fillets, perched on a bed of neatly arranged blanched asparagus, were enriched with lemon butter sauce – a simple, yet tasty main course. Desserts made a fitting finale to a fabulous meal. Hot chocolate sponge yielded to uncover a centre of warm molten sauce: a delicious contrast to the chill of ice-cream infused with fresh mint. Chocolate parfait also got the thumbs-up for its creamy texture and hazelnut praline coating. A consistent high-performer in the Ramsay empire.
Babies and children welcome: high chairs. Booking essential. Disabled: toilet. Dress: smart; jacket preferred; no jeans or trainers. Separate rooms for parties, seating 6, 10, 12 and 24. **Map 9 H6**.

★ Greenhouse

27A Hay's Mews, W1J 5NY (7499 3331, www.greenhouserestaurant.co.uk). Green Park tube. **Lunch served** noon-2.30pm Mon-Fri. **Dinner served** 6.45-11pm Mon-Sat. **Set lunch** £25 2 courses, £29 3 courses. **Set meal** £65 3 courses, £65-£80 tasting menu. **Credit** AmEx, DC, MC, V.
This secluded, serenely modern Mayfair restaurant produced a meal that was close to perfection: seamless, smiling, unobtrusive service; and gastronomic bedazzlement. We couldn't stop gasping. Chef Antonin Bonnet understands complementary contrasts – in flavour, texture and presentation – as well as any chef in London. Our four dishes from the fortnightly-changing lunch menu astonished in every way: visual, gustatory and (though we hate to apply the word to cooking) intellectual. Starters: mangetout salad with parmesan cream, pine nuts and basil; and spider crab parfait with cucumber relish and wood sorrel. The parfait was particularly distinguished, and technically dazzling. Mains: roast duck breast stuffed with veal sweetbreads and served with purées of carrot, potato and beetroot; and gnocchi, so light in texture they were nearly liquid, sauced with crunchy courgettes, minuscule girolle mushrooms, seared calamares and courgette leaves fried in tempura batter. These descriptions don't begin to convey the precision of the cooking, which incorporates all sorts of trendy innovations (foams, jellies and the like), but renders everything in unforgettably flavoursome assemblies. The wine list, like the kitchen, aims for the very highest level: over 100 pages with precious little under £30; millionaires' terrain. But you shouldn't come here looking to save money. You should come looking for the meal of a lifetime. If everything's working the way it was on our lunch, you'll get it.
Babies and children admitted. Booking essential. Dress: smart casual. Separate room for parties, seats 10. Vegetarian menu. **Map 9 H7**.

★ Hélène Darroze at the Connaught (100)

The Connaught, Carlos Place, W1K 2AL (3147 7200, www.the-connaught.co.uk). Bond Street tube. **Lunch served** noon-2.30pm Tue-Fri. **Dinner served** 6.30-10.15pm Tue-Sat. **Brunch served** 11am-3pm Sat. **Set lunch** £29 2 courses, £32 3 courses. **Set dinner** £75 3 courses, £85 7 courses. **Set brunch** £29 3 courses; £34 incl glass of champagne. **Credit** AmEx, MC, V.
Parisian designer India Mahdavi has worked a treat on the Connaught's grand old dining room, mixing geometric and floral fabrics with the expanse of wood panelling. Tables are spacious and seats extremely comfortable, all the better for cossetting from the phalanx of black-waistcoated staff. A long table displaying breads, huge pats of butter and mouthwatering cheeses from maitre fromager Bernard Antony quickly sets the tone, and before long you'll see the scarlet red meat slicer wheeled around the room to shave air-cured ham for canapes: it's an appropriate real food message because Hélène Darroze's cuisine is refreshingly judicious with the molecular gastronomy faffing that blights many haute cuisine establishments. Yes there's the occasional dollop of foam, but much is readily-identifiable food cooked with care and creativity. Canapés and amuse bouches may include such familiar fare as vichyssoise, or a tiny coffee cup of polenta favoured with ewes' milk cheese and espelette pepper. The duck foie gras from Landes – two dense slabs of liver, one confit, the other coated in mild spices – is so good it barely needs its accompanying rhubarb and strawberry chutney. Plump ravioli stuffed with aubergine and anchovies worked well with juice and pips of heritage tomatoes, but the layer of clear tomato jelly across the bottom of the dish detracted from the overall effect. Three generous fillets of john dory were steamed with jasmine fumet and scattered with crumbs of ginger and lime, lending

a faint oriental scent to the fish. Milk-fed lamb was deliciously crusted with piquillo peppers and served with tiny chipolatas flavoured with espelette pepper – a dish let down slightly by the crunchiness of the accompanying coco beans. Since our last visit the choice of wines by the glass has been expanded and now features classic grape varieties from old and new worlds.

Babies and children welcome: high chairs. Booking essential. Disabled: toilet. Dress: smart; no jeans or trainers. **Map 9 H7**.

★ Hibiscus (100)

29 Maddox Street, W1S 2PA (7629 2999, www.hibiscusrestaurant.co.uk). Oxford Circus tube. **Lunch served** noon-2.30pm Tue-Fri. **Dinner served** 6.30-10pm Tue-Fri; 6-10pm Sat. **Set lunch** £25 3 courses; £70 6 courses. **Set dinner** £65 3 courses, £80 tasting menu. **Credit** AmEx, MC, V.

The pale oak panelling used in this simple Mayfair dining room is a knowing wink to the original Hibiscus restaurant in Ludlow, a decor that owners Claude and Claire Bosi in fact inherited from the previous tenant. Tables are arranged around a large central workstation topped with an extravagant floral display dominated by lillies and gladioli; overhead is a fabulously non-ostentatious chandelier. The crowd is well-heeled and rather businesslike, even when their intentions are social. On our visit, most stuck with the set lunch, which essentially offers two choices for each course, plus another dish per course requiring a supplement (£6 more for a duck egg and lobster starter, say, and £10 extra for roast beef). The moussaka of Elwy Valley mutton with feta and anchovy jus has become something of a signature. We opted for the pollack, which came with a highly scented carrot and cardamon purée that made sense only when tasted with the pile of buttery young carrots piled on top. Gherkin and olive sauce and another of red pepper ensured this dish was all about tang. For dessert, almonds added a layer of nutrition that often seems lacking in clafoutis. Staff were careful to remind us that the exquisitely flavoured cherries retained their stones in the traditional manner and the lot was served with unusually rich toasted pistachio ice-cream. The non-arrival of the hibiscus and pineapple amuse served with such grandeur at other tables, and of the petits fours (because we didn't want coffee?, but they were meant to be included in the price), made us feel rather unloved, but a slip with the booking was quickly handled and, in other respects, service was charming.

Babies and children welcome: high chairs. Booking essential. Disabled: toilet. Separate room for parties: seats 18. Vegetarian menu. **Map 9 J6**.

★ Maze (100)

13-15 Grosvenor Square, W1K 6JP (7107 0000, www.gordonramsay.com). Bond Street tube. **Lunch served** noon-2.30pm, **dinner served** 6-10.30pm daily. **Main courses** £15-£29.50. **Set lunch** £28.50 4 courses, £35.50 5 courses, £42.50 6 courses. **Credit** AmEx, DC, MC, V.

Jason Atherton's Maze restaurant continues to shine a little brighter than the other starry establishments in the Gordon Ramsay firmament. The sleek, handsome room with curved wood veneer and cream leather seating is cheerfully light-filled and offers pleasing leafy views over Grosvenor Square. The set lunch menu is brilliant: from a list of around 13 dishes you can select any four, five or six courses as desired (yes, choosing three desserts is very tempting). Lighter savoury fare such as heritage tomato gazpacho with compressed cucumber and pepper purée is listed first, heavier dishes later, including our roasted barbary duck served with English cherries and roast parsley root (also known as hamburg parsley – an under-utilised vegetable in this country though common in Scandinavia). The duck was straightforward, almost homely, so too confit shoulder of lamb with pea purée, but you can expect plenty of creativity too. Typical is the prawn cocktail, with delightfully translucent shellfish, a foam version of the classic marie rose sauce, and impressively savoury-tasting lettuce granita on top. 'Warm Scottish breakfast' paired

Maze

cured salmon with quail egg, a tiny slice of bacon and creamy soft smoked haddock risotto. For dessert we chose a tongue-in-cheek Arctic roll – just like the original but made with premium ingredients – and a serious contender for the title of London's best rice pudding, made with clotted cream for extra richness, and topped with pecan ice-cream and maple syrup. Friendly, aproned waiters were keen to please, yet maintained a dignified professionalism – spot on, really. A tour of the capacious and surprisingly subdued kitchen, where the chef's table is a popular setting for special meals, may be offered before leaving. *Babies and children admitted. Booking essential. Dress: smart casual; no trainers. Separate rooms for parties, seating 15 and 36.* **Map 9 G6.**

Sketch: The Lecture Room

9 Conduit Street, W1S 2XZ (7659 4500, www.sketch.uk.com). Oxford Circus tube. **Lunch served** noon-2.30pm Tue-Fri. **Dinner served** 7-10.30pm Tue-Sat. **Main courses** £28-£55. **Set lunch** £30 2 courses, £35 3 courses. **Set meal** £65-£90 tasting menu. **Credit** AmEx, DC, MC, V.
The property that houses Sketch was originally a townhouse, so it seems appropriate that guests to the formal dining room are given such a personal welcome from staff. The red velvet rope guarding the path upstairs adds to the exclusive, members-only vibe – something the celebrity patrons are presumably used to (we spied the new Dr Who and a couple of ex-footballers) – yet all you need to do to get inside this 'exclusive' enclave is ring and make a booking. Pierre Gagnaire was in attendance the week of our visit, so the kitchen was on especially fine form. But while everything may be note-perfect here, the style of cooking is not for everybody. So many little recipes for this and that go together to comprise one dish, and so much creativity is lavished on each ingredient, that the effect can be like a long, slow rollercoaster ride. Our tasting menus took a full three hours to complete – amazing and thought provoking, yes, masterful certainly, but the fact is you have to be in the mood for this sort of cooking. Even ordering a glass of champagne as an aperitif is turned into an experience with the offer of a tasting flight of three champagnes made with varying degrees of sugar. Still, who'd have thought artichokes went so well with mustard sauce, or fresh apricots with girolle mushrooms, or raw scallops with almond milk? Even when it comes to meat and fish dishes, its clear that Gagnaire is inspired by vegetables, fruits and herbs, and there is a tasting menu specifically for vegetarians. A 'gourmet rapide' lunch has been introduced (three courses for £35 including coffee and petits fours) but don't expect things to be simplified: its starter is a combination of four combination dishes, and the dessert is in fact three desserts.
Available for hire. Babies and children welcome: high chairs. Booking advisable. Dress: smart casual. Separate rooms for parties, seating 12 & up. **Map 9 J6.**

The Square

6-10 Bruton Street, W1J 6PU (7495 7100, www.squarerestaurant.com). Bond Street or Green Park tube. **Lunch served** noon-2.45pm Mon-Fri. **Dinner served** 6.30-10.pm Mon-Fri; 6.30-10.30pm Sat; 6.30-9.30pm Sun. **Set lunch** £30 2 courses, £35 3 courses. **Set dinner** £60 2 courses, £75 3 courses. **Set meal** £95 tasting menu (£150 incl wine). **Credit** AmEx, DC, MC, V.
This restaurant opened right in the eye of the last recession and its enduring success can be put down to the dream team of Nigel Platts-Martin and chef Philip Howard, who understand the essential criteria for running a sophisticated restaurant. The tasteful interior shimmers with excitement, its swish club atmosphere accented by polished parquet flooring, pearlised walls and abstract art. Howard's cooking has clarity of flavour yet constantly surprises. As a preamble, delicate asparagus bavarois and Jersey Royal foam with an egg yolk tucked between was out of the top drawer. Consommé of duck topped with sweetcorn foam was accompanied by a mini foie gras club

sandwich and a dollop of burnt orange purée. Rump of lamb worked well with borlotti beans, girolles and courgettes, kicked into life by a garlicky undertone. We enjoyed a fine selection of cheeses, and the taste sensations did not let up with dessert: a splendid gooseberry and almond tart was married to elderflower ice-cream. However, there is a tendency to overindulge on a theme; last year it was beignet, and now it is foam with everything. Disappointment too, when a bowl of rather ordinary cherries arrived with coffee – the explanation was that petits fours were considered 'too heavy' in summer. After this grumble a plate of dark chocolate truffles miraculously appeared. Staff were punctilious, although our waiter forgot to announce the main courses, then got the name of the dessert wrong. The wine list, built with care and passion over a number of years, weighs in at 80 pages, with prices from £18. There are some majestic Burgundies on offer, including an astonishingly good collection from Coche-Dury. It's unusual, too, to see German and Austrian wines so well represented.
Available for hire. Babies and children admitted. Booking advisable. Disabled: toilet. Dress: smart; no jeans or trainers. Separate room for parties, seats 18. **Map 9 H7.**

Piccadilly

The Ritz

150 Piccadilly, W1J 9BR (7493 8181, www.theritzhotel.co.uk). Green Park tube. *Bar* **Open** 11.30am-midnight Mon-Sat; noon-10.30pm Sun.
Restaurant **Breakfast served** 7-10am Mon-Sat; 8-10am Sun. **Lunch served** 12.30-2.30pm daily. **Tea served** (reserved sittings) 11.30am, 1.30pm, 3.30pm, 5.30pm, 7.30pm daily. **Dinner served** 5.30-10.30pm Mon-Sat; 7-10pm Sun. **Main courses** £25-£40. **Set lunch** £37 3 courses. **Set tea** £37. **Set dinner** £45 4 courses; (Mon-Thur, Sun) £65 4 courses; (Fri, Sat) £85 4 courses. *Both* **Credit** AmEx, MC, V.
Sighing with opulence, the interior of this spacious dining hall was apparently inspired by the Palace of Versailles. Decor is indeed an indulgence of sparkling chandeliers, majestic pillars, gilded walls, frescoes and Louis XIV antiques. The resident pianist is happy to play 'Happy Birthday' for those so privileged. Monied tourists and a clientele who live by exacting old-school standards find their way here. Menus are a tribute to traditional French cooking and resolutely British roasts and grills. Prices are eye-wateringly steep, both for the extensive wine list and the à la carte dishes. We opted for the more affordable, daily-changing set menu. Vegetarians be warned: on our visit, there were no meat- or fish-free main courses on this menu. Our meal was good in parts, but marred by lows. A salad of blanched asparagus, crowned with sage foam, was let down by overcooked spears, insipid froth, and an unremarkable onion purée base. Neither were we convinced by the proliferation of haddock-infused foam, over ravioli filled with salty cod brandade. Things improved with a deliciously tender duck breast, cooked to perfect pinkness, making a marvellous match with the sweet tanginess of slow-cooked red cabbage. In contrast, the seared beef rump was undistinguished in flavour and lost points for its garnish of chewy bacon strips. Desserts revived our spirits: the quivering height of a warm pear soufflé was impressive, the dish delivering deliciously fruity flavour, tastefully complemented by Armagnac ice-cream; and a millefeuille was delectable for its rich chocolatey cream, praline crunchiness, and wafer-thin wisps of crisp puff pastry. The wine list is lengthy, offering a small, but well-chosen selection by the glass. Unfortunately, service didn't make the grade, being tardy and exhibiting little warmth.
Babies and children welcome: children's menu; high chairs. Booking advisable restaurant; essential afternoon tea. Dress: jacket and tie; no jeans or trainers. Entertainment: dinner dance Fri, Sat (restaurant); pianist daily. Separate rooms for parties, seating 16-60. Tables outdoors (8, terrace). **Map 9 J7.**

South Kensington

★ Tom Aikens

43 Elystan Street, SW3 3NT (7584 2003, www.tomaikens.co.uk). South Kensington tube. **Lunch served** noon-2.30pm, **dinner served** 6.45-10.45pm Mon-Fri. **Set lunch** £29 3 courses. **Set meal** £65 3 courses, £80 tasting menu. **Credit** AmEx, MC, V.
Once an enfant terrible and now something of a stalwart on the fine dining circuit, Tom Aikens' eponymous restaurant remains a good-looking room with chocolatey pinstripe carpet, dark chairs and wooden screens offset with white walls and linens. The set lunch is a proper bargain, with plenty of complimentary add-ons that allow the seriously hungry to enjoy their fill (the bread selection is huge). At the height of summer, our dishes arrived decked with flowers as well as

---

THE DISH

Foam

Foam is usually associated with the bathroom cabinet, not the kitchen cupboard, yet for many chefs producing haute cuisine it has become as conventional as salt and pepper. What's the big deal? Foams are a light way of adding extra flavour to a dish without the heavy textures and calories of egg and butter sauces.

The simplest way to make foam is to blend milk with a flavouring (fresh basil, say), heat it up, then whisk it with a hand blender or cappuccino frother until bubbly – unlike a lot of molecular gastronomy affectations, this one can easily be done at home. However, these foams eventually dissipate, just like the froth on your morning coffee, so chefs began looking for ways to keep them looking good until the last spoonful of the dish. Gelatine, agar, and lecithin granules are all commonly used in foams these days, as are soda siphons to force air into the mixture. The results have a thicker texture than frothy milk, but aren't as rich as mousse as they don't contain eggs.

For sheer intensity of flavour, it's hard to beat the loose froth served over **Maze**'s version of bouillabaisse, which has all the shellfish, tomato and saffron richness of the traditional recipe, but leaves you ready to enjoy the next dish on the tasting menu. Among other favourites are **Tom Aikens'** lemongrass foam served with beetroot, lobster and tarragon oil – a great example of skill in combining seemingly disparate ingredients – and the light peanut bubbles **Hélène Darroze** uses to cover her amuse bouche of foie gras. But perhaps the most unusual example is found at **Sketch: The Lecture Room**, where Pierre Gagnaire's sweet lemon wurtz, which tastes rather like uncooked meringue, tops a terrine of roquefort cheese.

Still, you can have too much of a good thing, and with anything this fashionable in the world of gastronomy you have to wonder how long before the foam bubble bursts.

RESTAURANTS

herbs. If we have a criticism, it's of serving the food in roomy glass and pottery bowls, forcing diners to eat with elbows cocked, as though doing the funky chicken. For starters, shaved slices of avocado were curled over large chunks of juicy Dorset crabmeat. There followed a wide thin slice of salmon over sliced Jersey Royals and teensy dill gnocchi, the lot topped with lightly pickled threads and ribbons of cucumber and plenty of fresh dill. The à la carte offers as many fish options as meat and poultry, and flags up esteemed sources such as Ark chickens and Rhug Estate. Wine prices are on the high side even for this location, though some enthusiasts may appreciate the opportunity to have a glass of Gewürztraminer Vignoble d'E Domaine Ostertag for £14. But any complaint on this front is quickly forgiven when the petits fours arrive: a spectacular display of warm madeleines, fruity pots, flavoured chocolates, crisp caramelised sugar tuilles and intriguing flavoured creams. Impeccable service is genuinely welcoming. Fellow diners could range from young couples in jeans to tables of businessmen in celebratory mode.
Booking essential. Children admitted. Disabled: toilet. Dress: smart. Separate room for parties, seats 10. **Map 14 E11.**

St James's

L'Oranger

5 St James's Street, SW1A 1EF (7839 3774, www.loranger.co.uk). Green Park tube. **Lunch served** noon-2.30pm Mon-Fri. **Dinner served** 6.30-10.30pm Mon-Sat. **Main courses** £26-£31. **Set lunch** £25 2 courses, £29 3 courses.

Set dinner £49 3 courses, £75 tasting menu.
Credit AmEx, DC, MC, V.
A period frontage greets arrivals on swanky St James's Street. Inside, everything is shipshape. Aged oak panels, luxurious upholstery and a conservatory make L'Oranger a pretty restaurant. The room is warm and tranquil, and in summer you can dine in the delightful belle époque courtyard. The menu arrives in a gold cover, with dishes described in fanciful terms such as 'caramelia' – toffee mousse, salted butter toffee and chocolate sorbet. Service is courteous in the main, but it's hard to forgive an amuse bouche of leek and cauliflower velouté (a little stodgy) appearing at the same time as our first courses, and forgetfulness over the cutlery. When we queried this we were blanked by a sulky waiter. From the lunch menu, we started with a delicate ravioli of artichoke, which proved a blithe companion for pan-fried artichoke core, jazzed up with a black truffle sauce. The kitchen can fluff its lines, though, and this ravioli dish was under-seasoned. Flirtation with the Mediterranean continued with beignet of cod, which proved a snappy match for sautéed green beans and earthy mousserons mushrooms, stirred into life by a tangy cherry-tomato coulis, with pesto adding a final flourish. Desserts can be whimsical; a mandarin orange and earl grey 'babakuba' style, turned out to be square-shaped rum baba, served with a classy Valrhona Xocomeli chocolate ganache, and topped with sweet spices. With coffee, mini-chocolate fondant was a sure-fire winner. The cooking, from chef Laurent Michel, is hardly trend-setting, but it possesses a sunny Provençal appeal. Combinations

of ingredients are usually agreeable, yet can lack pronounced flavours. However, this doesn't entirely detract from the pleasure of the surroundings. Wines are expensive, and focused on Burgundy and Bordeaux, with the New World appearing as an afterthought.
Babies and children admitted. Booking essential. Dress: smart casual; no trainers. Separate rooms for parties, seating 15 and 36. Tables outdoors (6, courtyard). **Map 9 J8.**

South West

Chelsea

Aubergine

11 Park Walk, SW10 0AJ (7352 3449, www.auberginerestaurant.co.uk). Bus 14, 345, 414. **Lunch served** noon-2.15pm Mon-Fri. **Dinner served** 7-11pm Mon-Sat. **Set lunch** £29 3 courses (£34 incl half bottle of wine). **Set dinner** £64 3 courses, £85 tasting menu (£145 incl wine). **Credit** AmEx, DC, MC, V.
Aubergines are everywhere. From the moulded door handles, bespoke plates, and the silverware: each piece is intricately laden with the ovoid. However, they are surprisingly absent from the menu. Upon our arrival, front of house skilfully swooped us up and tucked us in a cushy corner flanked with towering fragrant lilies in the front room. Although this was cosy and comfortable, the main dining room seemed the better bet, with its starry skylight and shielded view of the swinging kitchen door. The classically French menu gourmand was deemed most appropriate in

Tom Aikens. See p131.

such a luxurious setting (velvet chairs, starched linen and bone china); only the silver-haired clientele seemed more polished than the silverware. We embarked on four hours of decadence with a refreshing carpaccio of scallops, sliced with surgical precision and gently kissed with lemon vinaigrette. Luscious plump morels stuffed with savoury chicken mousse then brought smiles of satisfaction to our lips. A beautifully moist and flaky sea bass followed, complemented by a vivid creamy basil mash. The indulgent cheese trolley harboured a number of interesting specimens on board; langres doused in champagne proved as ambrosial as it sounds. Service was usually efficient, yet confused and rushed at times: staff presenting dishes backwards and spilling wine when pouring without apology or clean up. *Available for hire. Booking advisable; essential weekends. Children admitted. Dress: smart casual.* **Map 14 D12**.

★ Gordon Ramsay

68 Royal Hospital Road, SW3 4HP (7352 4441, www.gordonramsay.com). Sloane Square tube. **Lunch served** noon-2.15pm, **dinner served** 6.30-10.45pm Mon-Fri. **Set lunch** £45 3 courses. **Set meal** £90 3 courses, £120 tasting menu. **Credit** AmEx, DC, MC, V.
Gordon Ramsay's troubles have become a constant source of amusement for the press, which may partly explain why it was easier to secure a reservation at his flagship restaurant this year. The demand for a credit card and threat of penalties for no-shows can make visits here feel more like a corporate than a culinary venture, however we

were greeted with Gaelic charm by the exceptional staff. The room is understated, dressed in coffee-cream; despite elegant Murano wall lights, it exudes little drama. The menu is divided into a fixed-price lunch, carte, prestige, and a vegetarian choice. Signature dishes such as the ravioli of lobster and langoustine have been around since Ramsay's Aubergine days. The kitchen, spearheaded by Mark Askew and Clare Smyth, revolves around premium ingredients; the mantra is technical excellence and consistency. Tomato consommé, poured over a poached langoustine served with baby spring vegetables and Osetra caviar, made a ravishing opening. Another sublime consommé, this time made from shellfish, helped elevate a 'paella style' saffron risotto paired with clams, mussels and langoustine, with spicy chorizo providing the final Spanish inflection. Equally splendid: confit of slow-cooked suckling pig arrived with caramelised endive, apple and grelot onions, finished off with a superb Madeira jus. Cheese is excellent too. Flawless rum baba, delicately cut in half at the table before vanilla cream was scooped on to it, arrived with in-season gariguette strawberries and a perfumed lemon balm. Cooking is delicate, punctuated by subtle flavours and lightness. Coffee was accompanied by smoke-effect – dry ice used to introduce delectable strawberry ice-cream coated with white chocolate, tantalising the palate before melting away. The 35-page wine list starts at £22 a bottle and rises rapidly, including a notable collection of Hermitage. This restaurant remains an essential gastronomic pit-stop, although the repertoire can leave you wishing for more adventure and spontaneity. *Available for hire. Booking essential. Children admitted. Dress: smart; jacket preferred; no jeans or trainers.* **Map 14 F12**.

Outer London
Richmond, Surrey

The Bingham `NEW`

61-63 Petersham Road, Richmond, Surrey TW10 6UT (8940 0902, www.thebingham.co.uk). Richmond tube/rail. **Breakfast served** 7-10am Mon-Fri; 8-10am Sat, Sun. **Lunch served** noon-2.30pm Mon-Sat; 12.30-4.30pm Sun. **Dinner served** 7-10pm Mon-Sat. **Set meals** £39 3 courses, £55 tasting menu. **Credit** AmEx, DC, MC, V.
This boutique hotel by the Thames in Richmond is a wonderful destination for a romantic getaway, with a leafy terrace and seductive, high-ceilinged cocktail bar. However, chef Shay Cooper's dining room is steadily acquiring its own fine reputation. Decked in serene cream tones with the natural world themes of Clarissa Hulse fabrics, glittering chandeliers and dainty art deco-inspired chairs, the mood is one of exclusivity and privacy. The menu is based on good British ingredients (veal cheeks, salt marsh mutton, Label Anglais chicken, organic spelt and salmon), but Cooper adds plenty of elegant modern touches with spices and swooshes of sauces. Standout dishes from our tasting menu included roast foie gras with pineapple relish, espresso syrup and coffee crumbs, and brilliant white brill fillet lacquered with a red wine glaze and served with samphire and squid shredded to such tender fineness that it was almost like pasta. Nor will we forget the fine slices of venison saddle with raw pickled cauliflower and pickled mushrooms providing a crunchy, tangy contrast to sweet, silky cauliflower purée. To finish, mostly French cheeses with own-made quince compote, and an intense chocolate and peanut mousse with yoghurt jelly and banana sorbet. Elegantly dressed service was professional and correct throughout. The wine list is truly international, including unusual bottles from Brazil, Luxemburg, Georgia and Lebanon, with 16 available by the glass or carafe. There are 19 fizzes, too, including English pinot brut and prosecco – a selection no doubt targeted at those romantic weekends.
Babies and children welcome: high chairs; nappy-changing facilities. Booking advisable Thur-Sun. Disabled: toilet. Separate room for parties, seats 90. Tables outdoors (6, balcony).

Interview
TOM AIKENS

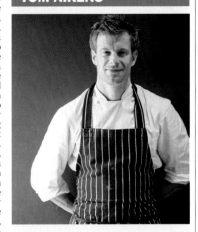

Who are you?
Executive chef-patron of Tom Group restaurants and judge on BBC3 TV's *Young Talent of the Year* show.
How did you start in the catering business?
I studied at Norwich City College Hotel School and completed the Advanced Catering Diploma in 1989.
What's the best thing about running a restaurant in London?
The chance to be creative every day with dishes and menus, and then being able to watch it all perfectly executed.
What's the worst thing?
Staying on trend and trying to keep ahead of the game, as the restaurant world and consumer tastes change very quickly. It can be hard to switch off, but to be honest, it's the adrenaline I love!
Which are your favourite London restaurants?
The Wolseley (*see p45*) has great atmosphere, fantastic food to suit everyone and, above all, it serves until 11.30pm so I can go there after service for a midnight feast. Also **Moshi Moshi Sushi** (*see p177*) follows the fundamental principles of Japanese culinary tradition, serving fantastic sushi that is sustainably sourced, which is very important to me.
What's the best bargain in the capital?
The set lunch menu at Tom Aikens of course – three courses for £29!
What's your favourite treat?
White truffles, though I can't say I eat them on a regular basis.
What is missing from London's restaurant scene?
A restaurant that just does grilled food: everything – meat, fish, veg etc – cooked on an open fire.
What does the next year hold?
There will be lots of good deals kicking around, enabling people to try places they once avoided. And I think healthy eating will become more popular.

Indian

The best of London's Indian restaurants have a justified reputation as among the finest in the world. London easily trumps New York, say – and some would argue that London's top restaurants even hold their own against many in India. What is certain is that the profusion, diversity and quality of South Asian food in our city is the world's best outside the subcontinent. The years of economic boom saw a blossoming of Indian fine dining – overturning customers' previously held prejudice that they shouldn't pay top whack for such cooking. Grinding and blending spices is both a labour-intensive and highly skilful process, and kitchen staff practised in the art deserve due recompense. As part of this flowering of top-end dining, Modern Indian cuisine has developed. This marries the highlights of modern western cooking – especially the attention to presentation, and the counterbalance of textures – with exquisite flavours combinations, honed by generations of cooks across the Indian subcontinent. The top practitioners of this cuisine – **Chutney Mary**, **Cinnamon Club**, **Moti Mahal**, **Painted Heron**, **Red Fort**, **Veeraswamy** and **Zaika** – rank among London's very best restaurants.

Though we've called this section 'Indian', it includes restaurants specialising in most cuisines of the Indian subcontinent: Pakistani, Sri Lankan, and even the disapora cooking of Indians in East Africa, in addition to the regions of the modern state of India. We're still hoping to see a decent restaurant serving the real food of Nepal; we've waited a long time – perhaps a newly arrived Gurkha will take up the challenge. This year we welcome several additions to the section, notably **Cinnamon Kitchen** and Mumbai seafood restaurant **Trishna London**.

Central

City

Cinnamon Kitchen NEW
9 Devonshire Square, EC2M 4YL (7626 5000, www.cinnamonkitchen.co.uk). Liverpool Street tube/rail.
Bar **Open** 11am-midnight Mon-Fri; 6pm-midnight Sat.
Restaurant **Breakfast served** 7-9am, **lunch served** noon-3pm Mon-Fri. **Dinner served** 6-10.30pm Mon-Sat. **Main courses** £12-£32. **Set lunch** £15 2 courses, £18 3 courses.
Both **Credit** AmEx, DC, MC, V. Modern Indian
There's something almost karmic about the location of this new sibling to the Cinnamon Club (*see p141*), occupying as it does a former warehouse of the East India Company. And it occupies it stylishly, with walls in soft pewter hues inset with lustrous mother-of-pearl patterns. The juxtaposition of exposed air-con ducts with intricate filigree light-shades works unexpectedly well under the lofty ceilings – as does the long tandoori-grill bar where chefs cook to order. Most dishes emerging from the conventional kitchen are clever, not contrived. An intensely coloured but subtly spiced creamy sweetcorn soup was perfectly paired with corn on the cob kebabs. Hot fruit kebabs were a joy: juicy sweetness coated with a tangy, hot chat-style masala, with apple, pineapple, starfruit and pear delivering a burst of sugar and spice. Fat red chillies stuffed with delicately seasoned hyderabadi lamb mince completed a triumphant trio of starters. Mains

didn't hit such high notes, but were still good. Tender roasted black-leg chicken with a crust of pungent fenugreek leaves worked well; and pleasingly plump prawns with bengali kedgeree were both comforting and lively, as was a side order of masala-spiked mash. The menu might be fairly short, but the queue lining up for a taste of it was decidedly long.
Babies and children welcome: high chairs. Booking advisable; essential Thur, Fri. Disabled: lift; toilet. Separate room for parties, seats 12. Tables outdoors (15, terrace). **Map 12 R6.**

Covent Garden

★ Moti Mahal
45 Great Queen Street, WC2B 5AA (7240 9329, www.motimahal-uk.com). Covent Garden or Holborn tube. **Lunch served** noon-3pm Mon-Sat. **Dinner served** 5.30-11.30pm Mon-Sat; 5.30-10.45pm Sun. **Main courses** £8-£16. **Set lunch** £13-£15. **Set meal** £33-£45. **Credit** AmEx, DC, MC, V. Modern Indian
The London rep of an upmarket Indian chain, Moti Mahal is dressed to impress – as is the food. Large windows look towards Freemasons Hall on the ground floor, where chefs perform behind a curved glass partition, lighting is subdued, background jazz plays, and tables are clothed in expensive white linen. Rounded banquettes in the basement are ideal for cosy chats. The Modern Indian food is excellent. Presentation is top notch and careful attention is given to flavour and texture: witness a starter of seafood-packed 'tikki' cakes boosted by ginger and chilli, topped with thick raita and

surrounded by lentil 'stew' enhanced with crunchy morsels of fresh green beans. Next came a tender lamb curry with a goan sausage (aka chouriço) sliced length-ways in a gorgeously intense tomato-based sauce, served with a spiced potato and peas stir-fry. We finished with an apricot and cinnamon kulfi on a stick, with a dainty pot of apricot rice pudding. Other innovative dishes include roasted partridge with crab-eye bean stew and partridge spring roll. Our delight was tempered by the service: the set menu wasn't produced until we asked, and staff needed reminding to bring tap water – we got the impression wealthy diners and business-accounters (who comprise most of the custom) had few such problems.
Available for hire. Babies and children welcome: high chairs. Booking advisable dinner. Dress: smart casual. Vegetarian menu. **Map 18 E3.**

Sitaaray
167 Drury Lane, WC2B 5PG (7269 6422, www.sitaaray.com). Covent Garden or Holborn tube. **Lunch served** noon-3pm, **dinner served** 5.30-11pm Mon-Sat. **Set lunch** £14.50 2 courses. **Set dinner** (5.30-7pm) £14.50-£16.50 2 courses, £22.95 buffet. **Credit** AmEx, MC, V. Pan-Indian
Maroon walls festooned with posters and photographs from blockbuster films lend a glamorous flourish to this Bollywood-themed restaurant. If flatscreen TVs aren't to your taste, head upstairs to the cosy first-floor alcoves for a more restrained vibe. The fixed-price, all-you-can-eat menu is excellent value and provides a selection of meat grills and kebabs from the North West Frontier, plus curries and dahl. Expect at least a dozen dishes. Highlights included smoky paneer cubes, cloaked in a thin lime-ginger crust, yielding to soft cheese below. The velvety texture of pounded griddle-cooked lamb patties – seasoned with freshly ground cardamom, leafy coriander and green chillies – delivered an impressive tease of flavours. Not all kebabs were winners: chicken tikka was marred by overcooking and saltiness. Sweetcorn and mustard green patties were too dense and stodgy. Back on track, superb makhani dahl, simmered with cream and butter, elevated black lentils to star status. On our evening visit, service was a tad perfunctory. Despite the occasional glitches, Sitaaray puts on a decent

BEST INDIAN

Best fine dining
Chutney Mary (*see p144*), Cinnamon Club (*see p141*), Moti Mahal (*see p134*), Painted Heron (*see p144*), Rasa Samudra (*see p136*), Red Fort (*see p141*), Veeraswamy (*see p139*) and Zaika (*see p143*).

That's sealife
Sample the pick of the ocean at Rasa Samudra (*see p136*), Shilpa (*see p143*) and Trishna London (*see p138*).

Low price, high quality
Authentic flavours for a bargain at Dosa n Chutny (*see p149*), Five Hot Chillies (*see p155*), Lahore Kebab House (*see p150*), Masala Zone (*see p152*) and Ram's (*see p155*).

Doing the subcontinental
Dine Sri Lankan at Apollo Banana Leaf (*see p149*), Punjabi at Brilliant (*see p155*), Five Hot Chillies (*see p155*) and Asian Tandoori Centre (Roxy) (*see p155*), Bangladeshi at Chaat (*see p149*), Keralite at Rasa Samudra (*see p136*), and Pakistani at Lahore Kebab House (*see p150*) and Salloos (*see p138*).

Meat-free menus
Dosa n Chutny (*see p149*), Ram's (*see p155*) and Sagar (*see p143*).

Tamarind. See p139.

spread, and attracts a mix of young Asian professionals and office groups from the lcoal area. *Babies and children admitted. Booking advisable dinner. Disabled: toilet. Takeaway service.* **Map 18 E3**.

Fitzrovia

★ Rasa Samudra ⑩

5 Charlotte Street, W1T 1RE (7637 0222, www.rasarestaurants.com). Goodge Street tube. **Lunch served** noon-3pm Mon-Sat. **Dinner served** 6-10.30pm Mon-Wed, Sun; 6-10.45pm Thur-Sat. **Main courses** £6.25-£12.95. **Set meal** £22.50 vegetarian, £30 seafood. **Credit** AmEx, MC, V. South Indian

For novices, and even for many hungry regulars, the seafood feast is the thing to order at Rasa's flagship Keralite fish restaurant. You can tailor the feast to include your choice of dishes, but it invariably starts with the trademark crispy snacks that are accompanied by seven own-made chutneys (our favourites: lemon, shrimps, garlic). Though the old Charlotte Street townhouse has had its frontage painted in Rasa's trademark shocking pink, inside its structure remains a higgledy-piggledy collection of little rooms. These have been decorated with drapes, bright colours and plentiful carved wooden artefacts. Lighting is subdued; staff are serene and prompt; only the lack of space tempers the romance. A tangle of crab,

perhaps slightly overcooked, was the centrepiece of our feast for four, which also comprised a large tilapia fillet in a creamy sauce, and a hugely enjoyable kingfish curry, tangy with fish tamarind. Vegetable accompaniments included the nutty stir-fry cabbage thoran, made famous at Rasa's original (and bargain-priced) vegetarian branch in Stoke Newington. Perhaps next time we'll choose the moru kachiathu (sweet mangoes and green bananas cooked in yoghurt) to give extra zest to our feast. A worthy showcase for Keralite cuisine, Rasa Samudra remains firmly in the top bracket of London's Indian restaurants.
Babies and children welcome: high chairs. Booking advisable. Separate rooms for parties, seating 12-25. Takeaway service. Vegan dishes. Vegetarian menu. **Map 9 J5**.
For branches (Rasa Express, Rasa Maricham, Rasa Travancore, Rasa W1, Rasa Mudra) see index.

Knightsbridge

Amaya ⑩

19 Motcomb Street, 15 Halkin Arcade, SW1X 8JT (7823 1166, www.amaya.biz). Knightsbridge tube. **Lunch served** 12.30-2.15pm Mon-Sat; 12.45-2.45pm Sun. **Dinner served** 6.30-11.30pm Mon-Sat; 6.30-10.30pm Sun. **Main courses** £8.50-£25. **Set lunch** £22-£25. **Set dinner** £38.50 tasting menu. **Credit** AmEx, DC, MC, V. Modern Indian

Slinky by night, when its black leather seating, modish chandeliers and soundtrack of cool beats attract smooching couples, Amaya is light and breezy by day, thanks to a large, if unattractive, skylight. The best seats, taken by well-groomed business people and dollar-rich US tourists on our visit, overlook the strikingly designed open kitchen. Here, black-aproned chefs display consummate skill at the tawa griddle, the tandoor oven and at the house-speciality charcoal grill. Others construct salads from the immaculate display of fruit, veg and herbs. Our set lunch platter began with a refreshing assembly of apple, mixed leaves and fennel, made zesty by a fruity dressing. Next came a geometric plate containing three chargrilled morsels: chicken in a delicious herby coating, a delicate seer fish tikka, and a 'chilli and rose petal' chicken tikka whose exterior needed more searing. The accompanying vegetable biriani featured overcooked asparagus, though we'd no complaints about the (albeit tiny) red pepper stuffed with cream cheese, sweet-potato chat, beetroot raita or spinach and fig tikka. The carte contains such delicacies as oysters chargrilled and served with coconut and ginger moilee. Service was capable if a trifle stern. Part of the Masala World group, Amaya is undoubtedly stylish, but the kitchen seems to need a buzzing dining room to perform at its best.
Babies and children admitted until 8pm. Booking advisable. Disabled: toilet. Dress: smart casual. Separate room for parties, seats 14. **Map 9 G9**.

Pan-Indian menu

Spellings of Indian dishes vary widely; dishes such as gosht may appear in several versions on different menus as the word is transliterated from (in this case) Hindi. There are umpteen languages and several scripts in the Indian subcontinent, the most commonly seen on London menus being Punjabi, Hindi, Bengali and Gujarati. For the sake of consistency, however, we have tried to adhere to uniform spellings. The following are common throughout the subcontinent.

Aloo: potato.
Ayre: a white fish much used in Bengali cuisine.
Baingan: aubergine.
Balti: West Midlands cooking term for karahi cooking (qv, North Indian menu), which became all the rage a decade ago. Unfortunately, many inferior curry houses now apply the name to dishes that bear little resemblance to real karahi-cooked dishes.
Bateira, batera or **bater**: quail.
Bengali: Bengal, before Partition in 1947, was a large province covering Calcutta (now in India's West Bengal) and modern-day Bangladesh. 'Bengali' and 'Bangladeshi' cooking is quite different, and the term 'Bengali' is often misused in London's Indian restaurants.
Bhajee: vegetables cooked with spices, usually 'dry' rather than sauced.
Bhajia or **bhaji**: vegetables dipped in chickpea-flour batter and deep-fried; also called pakoras.
Bhatura: deep-fried doughy discs.
Bhindi: okra.
Brinjal: aubergine.
Bulchao or **balchao**: a Goan vinegary pickle made with small dried prawns (with shells) and lots of garlic.
Chana or **channa**: chickpeas.
Chapati: a flat wholewheat griddle bread.

Chat or **chaat**: various savoury snacks featuring combinations of pooris (qv), diced onion and potato, chickpeas, crumbled samosas and pakoras, chutneys and spices.
Dahi: yoghurt.
Dahl or **dal**: a lentil curry similar to thick lentil soup. Countless regional variations exist.
Dhansak: a Parsi (qv) casserole of meat, lentils and vegetables, with a mix of hot and tangy flavours.
Dhaniya: coriander.
Ghee: clarified butter used for frying.
Gobi: cauliflower.
Gosht, josh or **ghosh**: meat, usually lamb.
Gram flour: chickpea flour.
Kachori: crisp pastry rounds with spiced mung dahl or pea filling.
Lassi: a yoghurt drink, ordered with salt or sugar, sometimes with fruit. Ideal to quench a fiery palate.
Machi or **machli**: fish.
Masala or **masaladar**: mixed spices.
Methi: fenugreek, either dried (seeds) or fresh (green leaves).
Murgh or **murg**: chicken.
Mutter, muter or **mattar**: peas.
Nan or **naan**: teardrop-shaped flatbread cooked in a tandoor (qv, North Indian menu).
Palak or **paalak**: spinach; also called saag.
Paan or **pan**: betel leaf stuffed with chopped 'betel nuts', coconut and spices such as fennel seeds, and folded into a triangle. Available sweet or salty, and eaten at the end of a meal as a digestive.
Paneer or **panir**: Indian cheese, a bit like tofu in texture and taste.
Paratha: a large griddle-fried bread that is sometimes stuffed (with spicy mashed potato or minced lamb, for instance).
Parsi or **Parsee**: a religious minority

based in Mumbai, but originally from Persia, renowned for its cooking.
Pilau, pillau or **pullao**: flavoured rice cooked with meat or vegetables. In most British Indian restaurants, pilau rice is simply rice flavoured and coloured with turmeric or (rarely) saffron.
Poori or **puri**: a disc of deep-fried wholewheat bread; the frying makes it puff up like an air-filled cushion.
Popadom, poppadom, papadum or **papad**: large thin wafers made with lentil paste, and flavoured with pepper, garlic or chilli. Eaten in the UK with pickles and relishes as a starter while waiting for the meal to arrive.
Raita: a yoghurt mix, usually with cucumber.
Roti: a round, sometimes unleavened, bread, thicker than a chapati and cooked in a tandoor or griddle. Roomali roti is a very thin, soft disc of roti.
Saag or **sag**: spinach; also called palak.
Tamarind: the pods of this East African tree, grown in India, are made into a paste that imparts a sour, fruity taste – popular in some regional cuisines, including Gujarati and South Indian.
Thali: literally 'metal plate'. A large plate with rice, bread, metal containers of dahl and vegetable curries, pickles and yoghurt.
Vadai or **wada**: a spicy vegetable or lentil fritter; dahi wada are lentil fritters soaked in yoghurt, topped with tamarind and date chutneys.
Vindaloo: originally, a hot and spicy pork curry from Goa that should authentically be soured with vinegar and cooked with garlic. In London restaurants, the term is usually misused to signify simply very hot dishes.
Xacuti: a Goan dish made with lamb or chicken pieces, coconut and a complex mix of roasted then ground spices.

RESTAURANTS

Trishna London

Haandi

7 Cheval Place, SW7 1EW (7823 7373, www.haandi-restaurants.com). Knightsbridge tube. **Lunch served** noon-3pm daily. **Dinner served** 5.30-11pm Mon-Thur, Sun; 5.30-11.30pm Fri, Sat. **Main courses** £6-£16. **Set lunch** £8-£12 incl soft drink. **Credit** AmEx, MC, V. East African Punjabi

Part of a restaurant chain with branches across Africa, Haandi serves homely Punjabi dishes to a diverse clientele of tourists, shoppers and smart business types. Its striking, glassed-in kitchen provides a theatrical centrepiece for diners to watch chefs tossing rotis and wielding laden skewers. Potted palms, a beige colour scheme, and cane seating arrangements set a smart, if dated, look. The tandoori food here is notable for its full-flavoured, spicy marination. Tilapia chunks, cooked to smoky perfection, were succulent and infused with lime-drenched flavour and tart chat masala (mango powder blended with toasted aromatic spices). Dhaba chicken curry was outstanding – russet-hued onion masala, spiked with whole spices, ginger and chillies, and cooked on the bone for added flavour. Lentils and pulses are deliciously earthy and perfectly balanced. Our smooth-textured tarka dahl, underpinned by the caramel-like character of fried onions and ginger, was memorable for its simplicity. Other vegetarian dishes, however, didn't quite make the grade, marred by underwhelming spice blends. Service, which veers towards indifference, isn't in the same league as the cooking.
Available for hire. Babies and children admitted. Booking advisable. Separate room for parties, seats 30. Takeaway service; delivery service (within 2-mile radius). Map 14 E9.
For branch see index.

Salloos

62-64 Kinnerton Street, SW1X 8ER (7235 4444). Hyde Park Corner or Knightsbridge tube. **Lunch served** noon-2.15pm, **dinner served** 7-11pm Mon-Sat. **Main courses** £13.50-£16.50. **Credit** AmEx, DC, MC, V. Pakistani

Salloos is discreet inside and out – so neatly tucked away on the corner of a Knightsbridge sidestreet that it's easy to miss; and so quietly elegant inside that it's instantly soothing. The first-floor space is light and bright, despite the windows being prettily obscured by latticework. Vibrant artwork lends a note of liveliness to the decor, and some pretty vibrant spicing does the same for the cuisine. Salloos has been serving Pakistani food to Londoners for more than three decades, reproducing the forthright flavours of the country faithfully. The much-lauded signature lamb chops lived up to their reputation. Tiny and tender, they were a perfect, if extremely pricey, prelude to the more intensely flavoured mains. A traditional frontier dish of chicken karahi, and a gurda (kidney) masala, were both suitably assertive. The chicken held its own personality in a sauce of fresh tomatoes deepened with ginger and a generous scattering of coriander, but the finely diced kidneys were slightly smothered by the sweetness of the onions with which they were stir-fried. Still, the smoky popadoms, nans, rice and service were all absolutely correct.
Booking advisable. Children over 5 admitted. Takeaway service. **Map 9 G9.**

Marylebone

Trishna London NEW

15-17 Blandford Street, W1U 3DG (7935 5624, www.trishnalondon.com). Bond Street tube. **Lunch served** noon-2.45pm Mon-Sat; noon-3pm Sun. **Dinner served** 6-10.45pm Mon-Sat; 6.30-10.30pm Sun. **Main courses** £6-£17.50. **Set lunch** £19.50 3 courses plus side dish; £25 3 dishes, side dish and carafe wine. **Credit** AmEx, MC, V. South Indian

Looking very much the chic London restaurant, Trishna London is a smarter venue than its Mumbai namesake and attracts business diners. The interior consists of two narrow dining areas, furnished with Scandinavian furniture, exposed brickwork and dark-wood flooring. Chef Ravi Deulkar, formerly of Rasoi Vineet Bhatia, heads up the kitchen, producing a tapas-style menu that pays tribute to coastal cooking styles – especially those of western India. Butterflied king prawns, slathered with mustardy masala, cut through with fresh dill, were cooked to smoky perfection over glowing coals: an innovative twist on regular grills. If it wasn't for over-salting, grilled bream fillets, cloaked in a mint, coriander and ginger masala would have been equally popular for their freshness and texture. Vegetarian dishes aren't overlooked. Squishy baby aubergines, simmered in a sweet peanut masala sharpened with tamarind, were quickly mopped up with nans. Our main gripe was with the consistent over-salting, which let down an otherwise satisfying meal. Trishna also holds back on cooking with fiery chillies and robust masalas; we wish the chef would be less restrained with the spice box. Staff should be better acquainted with their menu too.
Available for hire. Babies and children welcome: high chairs. Booking advisable evenings. Separate room for parties, seats 12. Tables outdoors (3, patio). Vegetarian menu. **Map 9 G5.**

Mayfair

Benares

12A Berkeley Square House, Berkeley Square, W1J 6BS (7629 8886, www.benaresrestaurant. com). Green Park tube. **Lunch served** noon-2.30pm daily. **Dinner served** 5.30-10.30pm Mon-Sat; 6-10pm Sun. **Main courses** £19.50-£45. **Set meal** (lunch, 5.30-6.30pm) £24.95 2 courses, £29.95 3 courses. **Credit** AmEx, DC, MC, V. Modern Indian

Of all the prime exponents of Modern Indian cuisine, Atul Kochar has perhaps moved furthest from tradition. His set meal in particular reads like an Italian menu. An amuse bouche of fennel-infused watermelon and a starter of battered squid with rocket, parmesan crisp and a dribble of tart mango sauce underlined this, though execution and presentation were excellent. Benares is above all a Mayfair restaurant: liked by the wealthy, who enjoy being escorted to the slinky first-floor bar for a cocktail before being seated in the adjacent, sizeable, black and white restaurant. Presumably they're not bothered about the high prices either – or the slick staff, practised at hard-selling wines (from a formidable list) and side dishes. A set menu main of tandoori guinea fowl had wonderful chargrilled flavours, but the meat was dry, and the supposed marination in pesto wasn't evident. A la carte tandoori rabbit (three chunks) was tough, though a main of sea bass fillet was pan-fried to juicy, crisp exactitude, served with mash containing nutty split peas and a mild coconut, tamarind and tomato sauce. Pity about the small portion. Some of our

★ Veeraswamy (100)

Mezzanine Floor, Victory House, 99-101 Regent Street, W1B 4RS (7734 1401, www.veeraswamy.com). Piccadilly Circus tube. **Lunch served** noon-2.30pm Mon-Fri; 12.30-2.45pm Sat, Sun. **Dinner served** 5.30-10.45pm Mon-Sat; 6-10.15pm Sun. **Main courses** £14-£29.50. **Set meal** (lunch, 5.30-6.30pm Mon-Sat) £32; (lunch Sun) £22. **Set dinner** £42. **Credit** AmEx, DC, MC, V. Pan-Indian

Veeraswamy might be London's oldest surviving Indian restaurant (est 1926), but you'd not know it. The look under its current owners is metropolitan-bazaar, with coloured glass lanterns, chandeliers and carved screens. The views across Regent Street from the first-floor dining room are a treat. Smooth service heralds a menu of faultlessly executed heritage dishes from north to south India, as you'd expect from the people behind Chutney Mary (*see p144*) and Amaya (*see p136*). Nihari is a poor-man's breakfast dish of lamb slow-cooked on the bone in Pakistan and north India; this version has a refined gravy with complex spicing fit for a Lucknowi nawab, with even the lamb shank on the bone prettily arranged. South Indian dishes also have the right flavours and aromas, such as pollichathu, a simple marinate-then-barbecue technique from Kerala; here, sea bass is used to substitute the firm meat of the Indian karimeen fish, wrapped in banana leaf. Birianis are a strong suit, with two styles to choose from, served in dainty Staub casserole dishes. For culinary details, we can't fault Veeraswamy; even the spices are hand-ground daily to make fresh masalas. However, such standards don't come cheap: you'll not see much change out of £50 per head at dinner, with even a (small) glass of Cobra beer costing £4.40.

Babies and children admitted until 8pm. Booking advisable weekends. Disabled: lift; toilet. Dress: smart casual. Separate room for parties, seats 36. **Map 17 J7.**

St James's

Quilon

41 Buckingham Gate, SW1E 6AF (7821 1899, www.thequilonrestaurant.com). St James's Park tube. **Lunch served** noon-2.30pm Mon-Fri; 12.30-3.30pm Sun. **Dinner served** 6-11pm Mon-Sat; 6-10.30pm Sun. **Main courses** £9-£23. **Set lunch** £20 3 courses. **Credit** AmEx, MC, V. South Indian

Owned by the Taj Group of Hotels, Quilon (located within the St James's Court Hotel) looks more like a bland business lounge than a fine-dining destination. Kitsch murals and an L-shaped dining area aren't much help either. Cooking, however, is distinctive and showcases the diversity of regional South Indian food. On our latest visit, almost every dish was a treat. Masala dosai – a golden rice and lentil pancake filled with crushed potatoes – was delectable for its crisp texture, and made a marvellous match with tamarind lentils. Fried tilapia fillets coated with ground lentils were cooked to perfection, but let down by heavy-handed coriander spicing – the only glitch in an otherwise tasty meal. Portuguese-inspired chicken morsels from Goa were served with sticky-cooked onions sharpened with vinegar and red chillies: delectable for their relish-like quality. Pale, lemon-hued mango curry was top notch too, its whipped yoghurt sauce simmered with ground coconut and fried curry leaves: a triumph of sweet and tangy flavours. Although evening meals cost a pretty penny, lunchtime set menus are fantastic value and worth every pound. Nevertheless, a restaurant of this stature deserves a more polished performance from its service team.

Babies and children welcome: high chairs. Booking advisable. Takeaway service. Vegetarian menu. **Map 15 J9.**

Soho

★ Chowki

2-3 Denman Street, W1D 7HA (7439 1330, www.chowki.com). Piccadilly Circus tube. **Meals served** noon-11.30pm Mon-Sat; noon-10.30pm

Sun. **Main courses** £9.95-£15. **Set meals** (vegetarian) £17.95 3 courses, (non-vegetarian) £19.95 3 courses. **Credit** AmEx, DC, MC, V. Pan-Indian

A low-budget venue close to Piccadilly Circus, Chowki makes a big deal of its regional Indian cooking promotions, and we've had excellent meals here in the past. On our most recent visit, however, we needed culinary detective work to differentiate some dishes from everyday curry-house staples. We were presented with no less than four menus, some with conflicting information. 'You need to order a vegetarian main course with this one,' our waiter said scornfully, before realising his mistake and then wandering off without an apology. The dishes we tried were all perfectly acceptable, yet only a few were better than average. Yam curry was the highlight, a coconutty dish bursting with fresh spice flavours; but dhaba lamb curry was chewy, not slow-cooked for long enough. At least the nan breads, crisp but dripping with hot ghee, were tip-top. At the far end of our shared table, the manager was having his staff lunch when two school-age, self-styled 'charity workers' strolled in shaking their collection buckets at customers. Instead of chasing them out, the manager carried on eating.

Babies and children welcome: high chairs. Booking advisable. Separate room for parties, seats 40. Takeaway service. Vegan dishes. Vegetarian menu. **Map 17 K7.**
For branch (Mela) see index.

Imli

167-169 Wardour Street, W1F 8WR (7287 4243, www.imli.co.uk). Oxford Circus or Tottenham Court Road tube. **Meals served** noon-11pm Mon-Sat; noon-10pm Sun. **Tapas** £3.95-£7.95. **Set lunch** £6.25-£9.95 2-3 dishes. **Credit** AmEx, MC, V. Pan-Indian

best dishes were traditional: a side of sag paneer (trilling with peppercorns and star anise), buttery nan. Puddings (rose-petal infused panna cotta, say) and petits fours are in the Italianate mould too.
Available for hire. Babies and children welcome: high chairs. Booking advisable. Disabled: toilet. Dress: smart casual. Separate rooms for parties, seating 14, 22 and 30. Takeaway service. **Map 9 H7.**

Tamarind

20-22 Queen Street, W1J 5PR (7629 3561, www.tamarindrestaurant.com). Green Park tube. **Lunch served** noon-2.45pm Mon-Fri, Sun. **Dinner served** 5.30-11pm Mon-Sat; 6-10.45pm Sun. **Main courses** £12.95-£24.75. **Set lunch** £14.95 2 courses, £18.95 3 courses. **Set dinner** (5.30-6.45pm, 10.30-11pm) £25 3 courses. **Credit** AmEx, DC, MC, V. Pan-Indian

Tamarind's set menu deals initially look appealing, but we're not convinced cooking lives up to expectations. If you have deep pockets and are searching for a luxurious venue, this basement restaurant will impress. Speckled mirrors, muted lighting, and big bold flower arrangements add to the glamour. On our visit, the restaurant buzzed with the conversation of affluent business types. A first course of ground-chicken griddle cakes was aromatic and benefited from a distinctive flavouring of fried onions, pounded mace, and leafy coriander. A vegetarian dish, sago-crusted potato cakes, was overwhelmed by the starchy, raw taste of a binding ingredient. Tandoori choices lifted our spirits, with crunchy, smoky broccoli florets, sweetened with honey and contrasted with the astringent bite of nigella seeds. However, curries were, at best, canteen-like; a mixed vegetable offering was simmered in an undistinguished tomato masala. Service was unpredictable; the waiter couldn't identify our poshed-up chicken tikka masala, and only after prodding with a fork did he suggest it might contain fowl. The bill was unceremoniously plonked on the table. We took the message and left. We've had much better meals in the past at this former star of London's Indian restaurant scene.
Babies and children welcome: children's menu; high chairs. Booking advisable weekends. Takeaway service. Vegetarian menu. Vegan dishes. **Map 9 H7.**

THE DISH

Biriani

The ultimate party number, a biriani is a melange of slow-cooked spiced meat layered with basmati rice. The South Indian varieties, like those from Hyderabad, are richly spiced, regal affairs and a complete meal in themselves. Anything more than yoghurt and a crisp salad accompaniment would be greeted with tears – visit **Moti Mahal** (*see p134*) for a marvellous lamb rendition cooked in a sealed pot.

Further north, in Lucknow and in Pakistan, cooks prefer more delicate interpretations and lighter pulaos. Rice for meat pulao is simmered in yakhani (cardamom and ginger stock) – but in biriani, it is par-boiled and layered with meat before the cooking is completed. Head to **Red Fort** (*see p141*) for a northern-style biriani made with lamb cloaked in sweet cardamom and mace. The biriani at **Amaya** (*see p136*) is prized for its tangy yogurt masala and fragrant grains. For an interesting variation, check out the chicken lamprais at **Sekara** (*see p141*) – not strictly a biriani, and influenced by the Dutch colonial presence, the bold cardamom and clove notes make for a fiery Sri Lankan flavour. The real test of a biriani is to toss a ladleful of cooked rice on the floor – if all the grains separate out, you're on to a winner. Best not to try this in a restaurant, though.

Discover India!

CHOWKI
TASTE INDIA!

Join Chowki, the acclaimed modern Indian restaurant, in a journey through the subcontinent and explore regional dishes that are bursting with flavour and subtle spices.

Discover new regions of India each quarter with our unique, seasonally changing, menus.

PRIVATE ROOMS AVAILABLE FOR PARTIES AND EVENTS.

2-3 Denman Street
London, W1D 7HA
020 7439 1330

info@chowki.com

www.chowki.com

Mela
The Joy Of Indian Dining

"Mela has earned an enviable reputation for delivering authentic dishes at fair prices"
Time Out Eating and Drinking Guide

Celebrate the full flavour of Indian cuisine at Mela, the award winning vibrant restaurant where serious dishes meet sensible prices.

PRIVATE PARTY/EVENT ROOMS AVAILABLE, PLEASE CONTACT US FOR FURTHER DETAILS
(we can cater to your requirements and budgets)

152-156 Shaftesbury Avenue,
London WC2H 8HL
020 7836 8635
info@melarestaurant.co.uk

1 Linkfield Street, Redhill,
Surrey RH1 1HQ
01737 766 154
redhill@melagroup.net

www.melarestaurant.co.uk

Last year we were thrilled with the fantastic value and adventurous cooking at Imli ('tamarind' in Hindi, and run by the team behind Mayfair's exalted Tamarind, *see p139*). This year some sloppiness seemed evident, but there's still much to like. The long thin premises are a riot of designer statements, from a mosaic tiled wall near the plate-glass windows, to the blown-up food-market photos at the more spacious rear. There's room for parties in the basement. Functional furniture, breezy staff (including one irritatingly flamboyant waiter), and a young, exuberant crowd, position Imli as a speedy good-time joint. The menu emphasises this, with drinks including lassi cocktails and food styled as 'Indian tapas'. Three dishes supposedly equal a two-course meal, though portions vary. Malabar seafood stew was almost main-course sized, featuring overcooked fish, chewy squid and perfect prawns in a sauce dominated by desiccated coconut. In contrast, 'assorted flavours' (nan with three curry dips) made a great snack for £2.95. Traditional dishes surpassed the Modern Indian forays, with decent dahl and a savoury aubergine masala preferable to stuffed paneer with too-sweet mango and basil chutney, and a chicken satay salad with dry meat and drab leaves.
Babies and children welcome: children's menu; high chairs. Booking advisable Thur-Sat. Disabled: toilet. Separate room for parties, seats 45. Takeaway service; delivery service (over £20 within half-mile radius). **Map 17 J6.**

★ Red Fort
77 Dean Street, W1D 3SH (7437 2115, www.redfort.co.uk). Leicester Square or Tottenham Court Road tube.
Bar Open 5pm-1am Tue-Sat.
Restaurant **Lunch served** noon-2.15pm Mon-Fri. **Dinner served** 5.45-11.15pm daily. **Main courses** £15-£29. **Set lunch** £12 2 courses. **Set meal** (5.45-7pm) £16 2 courses incl tea or coffee.
Both **Credit** AmEx, MC, V. North Indian
Since opening in 1981, Red Fort has seen its ups and downs. But following a stylish and expensive refurb in 2001, and the recruitment of a star chef from India (no longer here), the restaurant once again took the crown of the best Indian in Soho. Several years on, the interior looks as tastefully opulent as ever, with subtle references to Mughal art and architecture in the low-lit dining room. The food also pays homage to the sophisticated cooking of the Mughal courts, exemplified by dishes such as dumpukht biriani, which takes several hours and expensive spices to prepare; the chunks of lamb were tender, the spicing and flavours in the rice complex. The menu still contains recognisably Lucknowi and Hyderabadi dishes (the northern and southern centres of the Mughal court), but is also inventive, incorporating oddities such as stone bass: a deep-sea fish with firm white flesh that went well with a southern-style lemony sauce, mustard seed and curry leaf garnish. Cherry tomatoes creep into a roasted aubergine dish (with a peanut, sesame and tamarind sauce), but otherwise the rendition tastes like the real thing – a creamy Hyderabadi recipe with the rich texture provided by almonds and peanuts, not dairy. Cooking of this standard in such a smart setting doesn't come cheap, but we think it's worth it.
Babies and children admitted. Booking advisable. Dress: smart casual. Entertainment (bar): DJs 8pm Fri, Sat. Vegan dishes. Vegetarian menu. **Map 17 K6.**

Victoria

★ Sekara
3 Lower Grosvenor Place, SW1W 0EJ (7834 0722, www.sekara.co.uk). Victoria tube/rail.
Lunch served noon-3pm daily. **Dinner served** 6-10pm Mon-Sat. **Main courses** £9.95-£15.95. **Set lunch** (Mon-Fri) £4.50-£7.95 1 course; (Sun) £12 buffet. **Credit** MC, V. Sri Lankan
The traffic may roar outside, but serenity reigns within this popular and well-established little Sinhalese restaurant. Tranquillity is fostered as much by the kindly service (which can be slow) as

by the dark-red and white colour scheme, and oil paintings of Sri Lankan people and landscapes. The menu has been streamlined and most common-or-garden curry-house dishes removed. This leaves a selection of Sri Lankan set meals (kothu roti stir-fries, string hopper assemblies, birianis and lamprais) plus 'devilled' dishes, vegetables, and sambol relishes. Starters are a routine choice of rissoles and patties that seem little better than pre-packaged varieties. It's probably better to head straight for main courses. Our chicken lamprais consisted of a mound of rice served on a banana leaf and accompanied by on-the-bone chicken curry (creamy with coconut milk, mildly spiced with own-made curry powder), and side dishes of aubergine curry (lovely sweet-sour and caramelised flavours) and chilli-hot seeni (onion) sambol. Less pleasing were devilled prawns that had little spicing (more resembling a sizzling stir-fry of onions, peppers and tomatoes) and a bony little portion of seer fish curry. Traditional wattalapam (a coconut custard) is among the desserts.
Available for hire. Babies and children admitted. Booking advisable. Separate room for parties, seats 25. Takeaway service. Vegetarian menu. **Map 15 H9.**

Westminster

★ Cinnamon Club
The Old Westminster Library, 30-32 Great Smith Street, SW1P 3BU (7222 2555, www.cinnamonclub.com). St James's Park or Westminster tube.
Breakfast served 7.30-9.30am Mon-Fri. **Lunch served** noon-2.30pm, **dinner served** 6-10.45pm Mon-Sat. **Main courses** £11-£29. **Set meal** £20 2 courses, £24 3 courses. **Credit** AmEx, DC, MC, V. Modern Indian
Aiming to create a complete Modern Indian fine-dining experience, Cinnamon Club provides cocktails, fine wines, tasting menus, breakfasts (Indian, Anglo-Indian, British), pre-starters, private dining rooms and all attendant flummery. Members of the English plutocracy duly fill the tables, weighed down by suits and expense accounts. Once a Victorian library, the impressive dining room is a big wood-lined space with vast light fittings and a book-lined gallery. Executive chef Vivek Singh devises innovative dishes that are expertly presented by head chef Hari Nagaraj. Even the well-priced set meal veers from the norm, perhaps starting with skate wing delicately encased in spicy batter on hollandaise, followed by

North Indian menu

Under the blanket term 'North Indian', we have included dishes originating in the Punjab (the region separating India and Pakistan), Kashmir and all points down to Hyderabad. Southall has some of London's best Punjabi restaurants, where breads cooked in the tandoor oven are often preferred to rice, marinated meat kebabs are popular, and dahls are thick and buttery.

Bhuna gosht: a dry, spicy dish of lamb.
Biriani or **biryani:** a royal Moghul (qv) version of pilau rice, in which meat or vegetables are cooked together with basmati rice, spices and saffron. It's difficult to find an authentic biriani in London restaurants.
Dopiaza or **do pyaza:** cooked with onions.
Dum: a Kashmiri cooking technique where food is simmered in a casserole (typically a clay pot sealed with dough), allowing spices to permeate.
Gurda: kidneys.
Haandi: an earthenware or metal cooking pot, with handles on either side and a lid.
Jalfrezi: chicken or vegetable dishes cooked with fresh green chillies – a popular cooking style in Mumbai.
Jhingri, jhinga or **chingri:** prawns.
Kaleji or **kalezi:** liver.
Karahi or **karai:** a small iron or metal wok-like cooking dish. Similar to the 'balti' dish made famous in Birmingham.
Kheema or **keema:** minced lamb, as in kheema nan (stuffed nan).
Kofta: meatballs or vegetable dumplings.
Korma: braised in yoghurt and/or cream and nuts. Often mild, but rich.
Magaz: brain.
Makhani: cooked with butter (makhan) and sometimes tomatoes, as in murgh makhani.
Massalam: marinated, then casseroled chicken dish, originating in Muslim areas.

Moghul, Mogul or **Moglai:** from the Moghul period of Indian history, used in the culinary sense to describe typical North Indian Muslim dishes.
Nihari or **nehari:** there are many recipes on the subcontinent for this long-simmered meat stew, using goat, beef, mutton or sometimes chicken. Hyderabadi nihari is flavoured with sandalwood powder and rose petals. North Indian nihari uses nutmeg, cloves, dried ginger and tomato. In London, however, the dish is made with lamb shank (served on the bone).
Pasanda: thin fillets of lamb cut from the leg and flattened with a mallet. In British curry houses, the term usually applies to a creamy sauce virtually identical to a korma (qv).
Paya: lamb's feet, usually served on the bone as paya curry (long-cooked and with copious gravy); seldom found outside Southall.
Punjabi: Since Partition, the Punjab has been two adjoining states, one in India, one in Pakistan. Lahore is the main town on the Pakistani side, which is predominantly Muslim; Amritsar on the Indian side is the Sikh capital. Punjabi dishes tend to be thick stews or cooked in a tandoor (qv).
Roghan gosht or **rogan josh:** lamb cooked in spicy sauce, a Kashmiri speciality.
Seekh kebab: ground lamb, skewered and grilled.
Tak-a-tak: a cooking method – ingredients (usually meat or vegetables) are chopped and flipped as they cook on a griddle.
Tandoor: clay oven originating in north-west India in which food is cooked without oil.
Tarka: spices and flavourings are cooked separately, then added to dahl at a final stage.
Tikka: meat, fish or paneer cut into cubes, then marinated in spicy yoghurt and baked in a tandoor (qv).

RESTAURANTS

sliced slow-braised lamb shoulder in a tomato-based sauce topped with onions and peppers. Despite an imbalance in the main course, which came with roast potato when steamed rice would have better countered the rich sauce, this was expertly rendered, imaginative cooking, grounded in the Indian idiom. We especially recommend two curried side dishes of bouncy sweetbreads with minced heart, and the sweet, tangy nutty ensemble of rajasthani sangri beans with fenugreek and raisins. Service, though smart and attentive, was uninformed. We were told the lamb came with 'rice, or, um, mash'. Never mind: the drinks list contains Aspall's cider, the tangy acidity of which aptly complements the food.

Babies and children welcome: high chairs. Booking essential. Disabled: lift; toilet. Separate rooms for parties, seating 30-60. **Map 16 K9.**

West

Hammersmith

Sagar ⑩⑩

157 King Street, W6 9JT (8741 8563).
Hammersmith tube. **Lunch served** noon-3pm Mon-Fri. **Dinner served** 5.30-10.45pm Mon-Thur. **Meals served** noon-11.30pm Fri, Sat; noon-10.45pm Sun. **Main courses** £4.25-£13. **Thalis** £12.25-£14.95. **Credit** AmEx, MC, V. South Indian vegetarian

This original restaurant of a four-strong group serves well-priced vegetarian meals to aficionados of authentic South Indian cooking. Furnished in blond wood, the walls are enlivened with attractive brass statues, bestowing restrained elegance to the room. Staple dishes are themed around variations on ground rice and lentils. On our visit, the idlis (steamed rice cakes) were light and fluffy, and the sambar was deliciously tart with tamarind and peppery curry leaves. Only the herby coconut chutney accompaniment lacked its customary green-chilli punch. Dosais (crisp, ground rice and lentil pancakes) are top quality. Our paper dosai arrived with a theatrical flourish in the shape of a wizard's hat, and was served with a delectable heap of crushed potato masala pepped up with crisp-fried lentils and mustard seeds. In previous years, the pan-Indian options have been excellent, but on this occasion, the indifferent spicing in the chickpea curry was disappointing. Pani poori also fell short of expectation: the pastry globes betraying a whiff of oiliness, and the tamarind water lacking robust chilli hits. Still, service remains on the ball and helpful, and the South Indian choices are excellent.

Babies and children welcome: high chair. Booking advisable. Takeaway service. Vegetarian menu. Vegan dishes. **Map 20 B4.**
For branches see index.

Shilpa

206 King Street, W6 0RA (8741 3127, www.shilparestaurant.co.uk). Hammersmith tube.
Lunch served noon-3pm daily. **Dinner served** 6-11pm Mon-Wed, Sun; 6pm-midnight Thur-Sat. **Main courses** £2.95-£10.50. **Set lunch** £4.99 (vegetarian), £5.99 (non-vegetarian). **Credit** MC, V. South Indian

Don't be put-off by the no-frills decor, Shilpa quietly goes about its business of putting speciality Keralite cooking on tables at surprisingly low prices. It's a functional space; two flatscreen TVs hog most of the attention, while faded touristy posters provide the only other distraction. The kitchen emphasises fish and seafood, although vegetarian and meat options are also executed with precision. An outstanding Keralite fish curry, crammed with chunks of tender kingfish fillets, owed its delicious tartness to an infusion of cocum (fish tamarind), which contrasted with the creaminess of coconut milk. Lamb pepper masala was a surprise success, memorable for tender morsels of boneless lamb, fried in a pounded cashew-nut and onion masala, seasoned with cracked black peppercorns. A crunchy stir-fried thoran of finely diced green beans and carrots, tossed with grated coconut and toasted dried red chillies, provided a lovely foil to the richness of the curries. Only the sweet mango pachadi – a whipped yoghurt and coconut curry

simmered with mangoes, mustard seeds and curry leaves – was marred by cloyingly sweet fruit. Service is on the ball and friendly.

Babies and children admitted. Booking advisable. Takeaway service; delivery service (over £15 within 3-mile radius). Vegetarian menu. **Map 20 B4.**

Kensington

★ Zaika

1 Kensington High Street, W8 5NP (7795 6533, www.zaika-restaurant.co.uk). High Street Kensington tube. **Lunch served** noon-2.45pm Tue-Sun. **Dinner served** 6.30-10.45pm Mon-Sat; 6.30-9.45pm Sun. **Main courses** £15-£19.50. **Set lunch** £20 2 courses incl glass of wine

and coffee, £25 3 courses incl glass of wine and coffee. **Set meal** £58 tasting menu. **Credit** AmEx, DC, MC, V. Modern Indian

The fragrance of fresh lilies greets visitors to Zaika's impressive, high-ceilinged premises. This former bank has been transformed into something almost ecclesiastical, with carved stone mullions, Hindu sculptures and wood-panelled walls. A spacious bar fronts the operation. Smart staff ran our lunch with admirable alacrity, their only slip was in not providing the three-course 'credit crunch' menu until asked. This £20 meal is a stupendous bargain, delivering some of London's best Modern Indian cuisine, created by chef-patron Sanjay Dwivedi. From an appetite-honing pre-starter of chicken and yoghurt soup paired with a

Cinnamon Kitchen. See p134.

RESTAURANTS

succulent cube of fried chicken, to a sublime dessert of rich chocolate praline, fruit sorbet and (unadvertised) strawberries and melons, the food was a triumph. In between came a perfectly balanced first course of octopus in tomato and fennel-seed sauce, over a mini-nan peppered with nigella seeds and beneath some delicately deep-fried squid; and a main course of freshest fried cod on mash topped with fragile florets of battered cauliflower, matched with a vibrant turmeric and yoghurt sauce. Presentation was supreme, and when combined with a voluminous wine list and à la carte enticements – masala duck breast with black lentil sauce, celeriac and parsnip mash, crispy okra and wild mushroom nan – show a restaurant at its peak.

Available for hire. Babies and children welcome: high chair. Booking advisable; essential weekends. Vegetarian menu. **Map 7 C8.**

South West

Barnes

★ Mango & Silk

199 Upper Richmond Road West, SW14 8QT (8876 6220, www.mangoandsilk.co.uk). Mortlake rail/33, 337, 493 bus. **Lunch served** noon-3pm Sun (by reservation only Sat). **Dinner served**

6-10pm Tue-Thur, Sun; 6-10.30pm Fri, Sat. **Main courses** £7.95-£10.50. **Set buffet** (Sun) £12.95. **Credit** AmEx, MC, V. Pan-Indian

Udit Sarkhel was head chef at the Bombay Brasserie in the 1980s before setting up his own place in Earlsfield, called Sarkhel's. Now he works at this self-effacing neighbourhood restaurant in Sheen, which has a much simpler menu. However, Sarkhel's training and discipline show through, and the pan-Indian menu is far better than the humble setting might suggest. The day's specials are chalked on a blackboard. On our visit these included lamb nihari (lamb in a spicy gravy): a Delhi cab-driver's favourite, but this version was much more refined, with a whole lamb shank in a red-hued, subtly spiced sauce. Bombay bhel was also an exemplary version of this cold snack, with a dense, sour-sweet sauce cloaking the crisp bhel. There's attention to detail in everything, from the masala chai in a teapot to the lassi, which had a slight hint of the kala namak (black salt) spice, giving it an oddly appealing sulphurous undercurrent. Owner Radhika Jerath keeps the front of house running smoothly, but on occasion we also spotted Mr Sarkhel pop out from the kitchen to greet guests.

Babies and children welcome: booster seats; crayons; nappy-changing facilities. Booking advisable. Disabled: toilet. Tables outdoors (2, decking). Takeaway service.

Chelsea

★ Chutney Mary

535 King's Road, SW10 0SZ (7351 3113, www.chutneymary.com). Fulham Broadway tube/11, 22 bus. **Lunch served** 12.30-2.45pm Sat, Sun. **Dinner served** 6.30-11.15pm Mon-Sat; 6.30-10.15pm Sun. **Main courses** £14.50-£26. **Set lunch** £22 3 courses. **Credit** AmEx, DC, MC, V. Pan-Indian

A pioneer of Anglo-Indian and regional Indian food in London when it opened in 1990, Chutney Mary remains on top form. A refurb a few years back has left it a more romantic place, best at night when oil lamps and candles glint off mirrored walls and mosaics to sparkly effect. As well as the main lower-ground, split-level dining room there's a party room on the ground floor (along with the reception) and a leafy conservatory. Intelligent, well-presented staff keep things running smoothly. The expertly prepared food is grounded in tradition but given a modern edge with light sauces and innovative accompaniments (strawberry chutney with chicken tikka, say). A dryish piece of chicken in the otherwise exemplary kebab platter (gorgeously juicy king prawn boosted by lemon thyme) was the only component that was less than excellent in a memorable meal. The £22 'overcome the crunch' menu (Mon-Thur) was a notable bargain, producing delicate rings of squid, 'Goa style' in an enticing tomato-based sauce followed by succulent baked sea bream with a ginger and black pepper crust, then a luscious bread and butter pud (more an orange-flavoured egg custard) with orange and chilli sorbet – Anglo-Indian puddings are another highlight here, as is the well-matched wine list. In all, reliably first-rate.

Babies and children welcome (under 10, until 8.30pm): booster seats. Booking advisable; essential Thur-Sat. Dress: smart casual. Separate room for parties, seats 34. **Map 13 C13.**

★ Painted Heron

112 Cheyne Walk, SW10 0DJ (7351 5232, www.thepaintedheron.com). Sloane Square tube/11, 19, 22, 319 bus. **Lunch served** noon-2.30pm Mon-Fri. **Dinner served** 6-10.30pm Mon-Sat; 6-9.30pm Sun. **Main courses** £13-£18. **Set meal** £32. **Thalis** £15. **Credit** AmEx, MC, V. Modern Indian

Painted Heron follows few of the conventions of Indian restaurants. It looks more like a smart Modern European venue with its airy interior and well-spaced tables; the Cheyne Walk location ensures lots of plummy voices. The dishes also seem to have been modelled on Modern European presentation, with plenty of drizzles, leaf garnishes and tapas-style platters. A dosai-like wrap encased a cashew nut and pea filling, and was cut into quill-shaped segments served with baby leaves of red chard. Yet the flavours are pukka, especially with the classic dishes; we almost swooned at the perfection of butter chicken. The dun-coloured pilau rice was great too: fragrant with cardamom, cloves and cinnamon. What distinguishes Painted Heron, though, are the more offbeat dishes, such as duck tikka with mint chutney, or the juicy tiger prawns in a lime pickle marinade. Even a dish as ubiquitous as kulfi is exemplary, served as a lollipop but with a texture like butter. Our only caveats are that the standard of cooking, restaurant and location are reflected in the bill; and that the set-price menu is served in such generous portions that either doggy bags or food waste is inevitable.

Babies and children admitted. Booking advisable weekends. Separate room for parties, seats 35. Tables outdoors (5, garden). Vegetarian menu. Vegan dishes. **Map 14 D13.**

Rasoi Vineet Bhatia

10 Lincoln Street, SW3 2TS (7225 1881, www.rasoirestaurant.co.uk). Sloane Square tube. **Lunch served** noon-2.30pm Mon-Fri. **Dinner served** 6-11pm Mon-Sat. **Set meal** £45 2 courses, £55 3 courses, £75 tasting menu. **Credit** AmEx, DC, MC, V. Modern Indian

---

South Indian menu

Much South Indian food consists of rice, lentil- and semolina-based dishes (semolina being small grains of crushed wheat). Fish features strongly in non-vegetarian restaurants, and coconut, mustard seeds, curry leaves and red chillies are widely used as flavourings.

If you want to try South Indian snacks like dosas, idlis or uppama, it's best to visit restaurants at lunchtime, which is when these dishes are traditionally eaten, and they're more likely to be cooked fresh to order. In the evening, we recommend you try the thalis and rice- and curry-based meals, including South Indian vegetable stir-fries like thorans and pachadis. For the tastiest Tamil food, try **Dosa n Chutny** (*see p149*) in Tooting. **Satya** (*see p157*) in Uxbridge offers some of the liveliest and most colourful Keralite specialities. **Sagar** (*see p143*) in Hammersmith is best for Udupi vegetarian cooking from Karnataka.

Adai: fermented rice and lentil pancakes, with a nuttier flavour than dosais (qv).
Avial: a mixed vegetable curry from Kerala with a coconut and yoghurt sauce. Literally, 'mixture' in Malayalam (the language of Kerala).
Bonda: spiced mashed potatoes, dipped in chickpea-flour batter and deep-fried.
Dosai or **dosa:** thin, shallow-fried pancake, often sculpted into interesting shapes; the very thin ones are called **paper dosai.** Most dosais are made with fermented rice and lentil batter, but variants include **rava dosai,** made with 'cream of wheat' semolina.
Masala dosais come with a spicy potato filling. All variations are traditionally served with sambar (qv) and coconut chutney.
Gobi 65: cauliflower marinated in spices, then dipped in chickpea-flour batter and

deep-fried. It is usually lurid pink due to the addition of food colouring.
Idli: steamed sponges of ground rice and lentil batter. Eaten with sambar (qv) and coconut chutney.
Kadala: black chickpea curry.
Kalan: a thin curry made from yoghurt, coconut and mangoes.
Kancheepuram idli: idli (qv) flavoured with whole black peppercorns and other spices.
Kappa: cassava root traditionally served with kadala (qv).
Kootu: mild vegetable curry in a creamy coconut and yoghurt sauce.
Kozhi varutha: usually consists of pieces of chicken served in a medium-hot curry sauce based on garlic and coconut; it is very rich.
Moilee: Keralite fish curry.
Pachadi: spicy vegetable side dish cooked with yoghurt.
Rasam: consommé made with lentils; it tastes both peppery-hot and tamarind-sour, but there are many regional variations.
Sambar or **sambhar:** a variation on dahl made with a specific hot blend of spices, plus coconut, tamarind and vegetables – particularly drumsticks (a pod-like vegetable, like a longer, woodier version of okra; you strip out the edible interior with your teeth).
Thoran: vegetables stir-fried with mustard seeds, curry leaves, chillies and fresh grated coconut.
Uppama: a popular breakfast dish in which onions, spices and, occasionally, vegetables are cooked with semolina using a risotto-like technique.
Uthappam: a spicy, crisp pancake/pizza made with lentil- and rice-flour batter, usually topped with tomato, onions and chillies.
Vellappam: a bowl-shaped, crumpet-like rice pancake (same as appam or hoppers, qv, Sri Lankan menu).

Ring the bell of Rasoi's well-appointed townhouse and smart staff (ours was French) will show you through a grotto-like bar to a sumptuously furnished front room with space for scarcely 12 diners, or to another slightly roomier dining area behind the bar. Sit on tapestry armchairs (avoiding the bolt-upright leather banquettes if possible) and peruse the menus. The grandiose wine list, together with gourmand and tasting menus, speak of luxurious fine dining, and Rasoi has its Michelin star and (in Vineet Bhatia) celebrity chef duly in place. Modern Indian is Bhatia's métier, but we found the lunchtime tasting menu (£36) veered between the exhilarating and the mundane. Courses flowed freely, from chutneys and popadoms via a routine vadai pre-starter, to an espresso-cup appetiser of tomato and lentil soup. Next came the highlight: two perfectly grilled scallops, their creaminess balanced by a tangy roast-potato chat and chilli oil. In contrast, the ensuing seekh kebabs lacked the requisite freshly seared flavour. And though juicy chunks of chicken tikka were paired with outstanding saffron rice, their tomato sauce bore too striking a resemblance to Campbell's condensed soup. The finale of a dryish squat 'chocomosa' (samosa filled with white and dark chocolate) made few amends. Perhaps it would be better to sample the carte, which contains such attractions as grilled pepper duck breast with potato khichdi and foie gras brûlée. *Booking essential (£45 deposit per person for groups over 5). Dress: smart casual. Separate rooms for parties, seating 8-12. Vegetarian menu.* **Map 14 F11.**

Putney

Ma Goa

242-244 Upper Richmond Road, SW15 6TG (8780 1767, www.ma-goa.com). East Putney tube/Putney rail/74, 337 bus. **Lunch served** noon-2.30pm Tue-Fri; 1-3.30pm Sun. **Dinner served** 6.30-11pm Mon-Sat; 6-10pm Sun. **Main courses** £7.50-£12. **Set dinner** (6.30-8pm) £10 2 courses. **Set buffet** (Sun lunch) £10. **Credit** AmEx, DC, MC, V. Goan
A glass frontage and neutral tones lend an airy feel to this well-liked family-run venue. Although Ma Goa's menu offers ubiquitous pan-Indian favourites, we suggest ordering dishes that celebrate Goa's Portuguese heritage. Cooking is homely, if a bit inconsistent, and the service is friendly and attentive. Pork vindaloo, with its tender morsels of boneless meat, was based around a robust masala of pounded red chillies, toasted coriander seeds and garlic, cut through with the spikiness of palm vinegar – a top-class rendition. Venison samosas looked promising, but failed to exhibit any hoped-for Goan spicing and lacked depth of flavour. Things improved with the shrimp balchao, served with sanna (a spongy rice and coconut cake), though the saucy tomato and onion masala could have done with an extra hit of pickling spices. However, the vegetarian thali was a disaster: an expensive and unimaginative assortment of bitter dahl, bland chickpeas, greasy bhajia, boring potato masala, and under-seasoned spinach paste. Despite the unevenness of the cooking, Ma Goa remains popular with Putney residents and local office workers.

Available for hire. Babies and children welcome: children's menu; high chairs. Booking advisable; essential weekends. Dress: smart casual. Takeaway service; delivery service (over £15 within 3-mile radius).

South

Tooting

Tooting has been a destination for cheap South Indian meals since Sree Krishna (192-194 Tooting High Street, SW17 0SF, 8672 4250) opened back in 1973. The area has an unusual diversity of 'Indian' restaurants: from East African Asian to Sri Lankan and Pakistani. Standards tend to be high, but rarely outstanding; old stalwarts such as Kastoori (188 Upper Tooting Road, SW17 7EJ, 8767 7027) appear to be surviving on past glories, while Tanzanian Punjabi restaurant Masaledar (121 Upper Tooting Road, SW17 7TJ, 8767 7676) still cooks great dishes, but now prioritises takeaway orders over restaurant service.

Of the two newest South Indian/Sri Lankan Tamil restaurants in the area, Sarashwathy Bhavans (70 Tooting High Street, SW17 0RN, 8682 4242) is refreshingly low-priced and serves good food, but we've found that the service and ambience of **Dosa n Chutny** (*see p149*) make it slightly better of the two.

RESTAURANTS

Gujarati menu

Most Gujarati restaurants are located in north-west London, mainly in Wembley, Sudbury, Kingsbury, Kenton, Harrow, Rayners Lane and Hendon, and they tend to be no-frills, family-run eateries.

Unlike North Indian food, Gujarati dishes are not normally cooked in a base sauce of onions, garlic, tomatoes and spices. Instead they're tempered; whole spices such as cumin, red chillies, mustard seeds, ajwain (carom) seeds, asafoetida powder and curry leaves are sizzled in hot oil for a few seconds. The tempering is added at the start or the end of cooking, depending on the dish. Commonplace items like grains, beans and flours – transformed into various shapes by boiling, steaming and frying – are the basis of many dishes. Coriander, coconut, yoghurt, jaggery (cane sugar), tamarind, sesame seeds, chickpea flour and cocum (a sun-dried, sour, plum-like fruit) are also widely used.

Each region has its own cooking style. Kathiyawad, a humid area in western Gujarat, and Kutch, a desert in the north-west, have spawned styles that are less reliant on fresh produce. Kathiyawadi food is rich with dairy products and grains such as dark millet, and is pepped up with chilli powder. Kutchis make liberal use of chickpea flour (as do Kathiyawadis) and their staple diet is based on khichadi. In central Gujarat towns such as Baroda and Ahmedabad, grains are widely used; they appear in snacks that are the backbone of menus in London's Gujarati restaurants.

The gourmet heartland, however, is Surat – one of the few regions with heavy rainfall and lush vegetation. Surat boasts an abundance of green vegetables like papadi (a type of broad bean) and ponk (fresh green millet). A must-try Surti speciality is undhiyu. Surti food uses 'green masala' (fresh coriander, coconut, green chillies and ginger), as opposed to the 'red masala' (red chilli powder, crushed coriander, cumin and turmeric) more commonly used in western and central regions.

The standard of Gujarati food available in restaurants has improved in recent years. Authentic Surti food is now available at **Ram's** (*see p155*; and **Sakonis** (*see p157*) offers good Kenyan-Gujarati versions of Mumbai street snacks. The best time to visit Gujarati restaurants is for Sunday lunch, which is when you'll find little-seen regional specialities on the menu – but you will almost certainly need to book.

Bhakarvadi: pastry spirals stuffed with whole spices and, occasionally, potatoes.
Bhel poori: a snack originating from street stalls in Mumbai, which contains crisp, deep-fried pooris, puffed rice, sev (qv), chopped onion, tomato, potato and more, plus chutneys (chilli, mint and tamarind).
Dhokla: a steamed savoury gram-flour cake.
Farsan: Gujarati snacks.
Ganthia: Gujarati name for crisply fried savoury confections made from chickpea flour; they come in all shapes.
Ghughara: sweet or savoury pasties.
Kadhi: yoghurt and chickpea flour curry, often cooked with dumplings or vegetables.
Khandvi: tight rolls of 'pasta' sheets (made from gram flour and curds) tempered with sesame and mustard seeds.
Khichadi or **khichdi:** rice and lentils mixed with ghee and spices.
Mithi roti: round griddle-cooked bread stuffed with a cardamom-and-saffron-flavoured lentil paste. Also called puran poli.
Mogo: deep-fried cassava, often served as chips together with a sweet and sour tamarind chutney. An East African Asian dish.
Pani poori: bite-sized pooris that are filled with sprouted beans, chickpeas, potato, onion, chutneys, sev (qv) and a thin, spiced watery sauce.
Patra: a savoury snack made of the arvi leaf (colocasia) stuffed with spiced chickpea-flour batter, steamed, then cut into slices in the style of a swiss roll. The slices are then shallow-fried with sesame and mustard seeds.
Pau bhajee: a robustly spiced dish of mashed potatoes and vegetables, served with a shallow-fried white bread roll.
Puran poli: see mithi roti.
Ragda pattice or **ragada patties:** mashed potato patties covered with a chickpea or dried-pea sauce, topped with onions, sev (qv) and spicy chutney.
Sev: deep-fried chickpea-flour vermicelli.
Thepla: savoury flatbread.
Tindora: ivy gourd, a vegetable resembling baby gherkins.
Undhiyu: a casserole of purple yam, sweet potatoes, ordinary potatoes, green beans, Indian broad beans, other vegetables and fenugreek-leaf dumplings cooked with fresh coconut, coriander and green chilli. A speciality of Surat.

Tayyabs. See p150.

RESTAURANTS

Although Tooting and Colliers Wood have a mixed Asian community, with a majority of Sri Lankan Tamils (some estimates put the community at 30,000), the growth in the Muslim population has been pronounced over the past few years. New halal butchers and cafés are appearing all the time in the stretch between Tooting Bec and Broadway, and the area now has a couple of sizeable mosques, a couple of madrasahs (religious colleges) as well as a few small Islamic bookshops. Of the halal restaurants, we rate the Tooting branch of the karahi joint, Mirch Masala (213 Upper Tooting Road, SW17 7TG, 8672 7500) as the best, with a varied selection of hearty, warming Punjabi dishes that you can also find at the Norbury original. There are good 'pure vegetarian' Indian sweet and snack shops in the same stretch too, notably Pooja (168-170 Upper Tooting Road, SW17 7ER, 8672 4523) and Shiv Darshan (169 Upper Tooting Road, SW17 7TJ, 8682 5173).

★ Apollo Banana Leaf
190 Tooting High Street, SW17 0SF (8696 1423). Tooting Broadway tube. **Lunch served** noon-3pm, **dinner served** 6-10.30pm Mon-Thur. **Meals served** noon-10.30pm Fri-Sun. **Main courses** £3.50-£6.25. **Unlicensed. Corkage** no charge. **Credit** MC, V. Sri Lankan
Although not as well-known locally as the neighbouring (and very good) Sree Krishna, ABL is worthy of attention. First, prices are incredibly low. Second, it's BYO, which makes the bill even lower. And thirdly, we don't detect any economies made in the standard of the cooking. It's true that the heat of many dishes has been toned down for non-Tamil diners, but this isn't always a bad thing when even the medium-heat dishes (marked by a two-chilli symbol) are enough to have us reaching for a cooling lassi. While the many South Indian dishes here are good, the Sri Lankan food is very good. Vegetable string-hopper fry looks like a biriani, but comprises grain-sized cuts of browned vermicelli stir-fried with curry leaves, mixed veg and chilli: not for the faint of palate. Crab masala is also challenging; the slithery sauce over the shell makes using your fingers inevitable. Tender squid fry is a simpler dish we can recommend, and the devilled mutton isn't ragingly hot. Service is relaxed. Decor won't win any prizes, but the prices are so low it's churlish to expect everything to be perfect.
Babies and children welcome: high chairs. Booking advisable weekends. Takeaway service.

★ Dosa n Chutny
68 Tooting High Street, SW17 0RN (8767 9200, www.dosa-chutny.com). Tooting Broadway tube. **Meals served** 10.30am-10.30pm daily. **Dosai** £1.95-£4.25. **Set lunch** (takeaway only) £3.95-£4.95. **Unlicensed. Corkage** no charge. **Credit** MC, V. South Indian
Rarely have we seen such a perfect dosai: crisp on the outside, moist and rice-fragrant on the inside, a perfect oval bent over in the shape of a curling leaf. The accompanying sambar (spicy lentil dip) is rich and sweet, in the Chennai style, the coconut chutneys fresh (though only in two variants: red or green). Most of these meals cost under £3. It's true that this South Indian and Sri Lankan café might not have the most alluring of interiors – it is lit like a Tamil truck-stop, with furniture the colour of Sunny Delight – but at least you get to see movies on the flatscreen TV by way of diversion. On our visit, we watched a portly hero wiggle his moustache through enough song-and-dance routines to have us begging for some masala chai as a fortification. Although the vegetarian choice is exemplary, the non-veg options are OK too: mutton and chicken, mostly. But we suggest sticking to the meat-free meals, as this is Dosa n Chutny's forte; the classic breakfast and snack dishes are beautifully rendered.
Babies and children welcome: high chairs. Takeaway service.

Chaat

Radha Krishna Bhavan
86 Tooting High Street, SW17 0RN (8682 0969, www.radhakrishnabhavan.co.uk). Tooting Broadway tube. **Dinner served** 6-11pm Mon-Thur, Sun; 6pm-midnight Fri, Sat. **Main courses** £4.50-£7.95. **Minimum** £5. **Credit** MC, V. South Indian
Radha Krishna Bhavan was a spin-off from the nearby Sree Krishna a decade or so ago, and beats its older cousin on two scores: the handy location near Tooting Broadway tube; and the fantastically kitsch interior, which outdoes most Bollywood sets. Walls are papered with sunsets and beaches; a life-size statue of a Keralite kathakali dancer stands in one corner. There are also, of course, smaller effigies of the Hindu blue boy Krishna and his consort Radha, keeping a watchful eye over this bhavan (house). Although the menu attempts to cover most tastes in high-street Indian food, we suggest you avoid the usual meaty curries and seek out the Keralite specialities. The vellappams (large saucer-shaped crumpets), thorans (vegetable stir-fries), and lemon rice are revelations, and the South Indian breakfast snacks – dosais, idlis and vadai – are also good. We still find RKB inconsistent though. Sometimes the food is faultless, but on our last visit, the vellappams were unevenly cooked and one of the thorans didn't seem as fresh as it should be. Despite this, we never regret eating here; the service is smiling, and the bill, although not the cheapest in Tooting, is comfortingly low.
Babies and children admitted. Booking advisable Fri, Sat. Takeaway service; delivery service (over £20 within 3-mile radius). Vegetarian menu.
For branch (Sree Krishna Inn) see index.

East

Whitechapel is a predominantly Bangladeshi neighbourhood, though you'll look hard for much evidence of this on the menus at the northern, 'trendy' end of Brick Lane. Yet many low-budget caffs in Whitechapel do serve Bangladeshi specialities alongside the more usual pan-Indian dishes – either advertised in Bengali script only, or not written down but available if you ask.

Among our favourites are Ruchi (303 Whitechapel Road, E1 1BY, 7247 6666), which looks like a generic fast-food joint selling fried chicken and formula curries, but the dining room is concealed upstairs at the back. Sabuj Bangla (102 Brick Lane, E1 6RL, 7247 6222) also gets the flavours right, but it's a basic, absolutely no-frills venue with a point-and-order display cabinet containing unlabelled dishes. If you're looking for a more conventional approach to good and cheap 'Indian' food, try the Pakistani-run **Tayyabs** or **Lahore Kebab House** (for both, *see p150*). If you're too lazy to go that far, **Chaat** (*see below*) is a new-wave Bangladeshi caff aimed squarely at non-Bangladeshis.

You may be surprised that this guide doesn't carry reviews of any Brick Lane Indian restaurants. The reason is simple: we have tried many, year after year, but in recent times none has been of a sufficient standard to be included.

Despite this, Brick Lane touts still make claims to be recommended by *Time Out*. In 2006, Tower Hamlets Council introduced a by-law that banned restaurateurs from touting for customers. It waned for a while, but on our recent visits to Brick Lane, it had returned to previous levels. The salesman's patter might offer a free bottle of wine, two-for-one pricing, or other special deals. The clincher, for many, seems to be 'recommended by *Time Out*'. Maybe the restaurant was – five, ten, or more years ago. Ask to see proof, as we did. The only evidence they could summon up was favourable reviews that were several years old, some with the dates conveniently removed. A review that is old is, of course, no recommendation at all.

Shoreditch

Chaat NEW
36 Redchurch Street, E2 7DP (7739 9595, www.chaatlondon.co.uk). Liverpool Street tube/rail then 8, 388 bus. **Meals served** 6-11pm Mon-Sat. **Main courses** £5-£6.95. **Credit** AmEx, MC, V. Bangladeshi

RESTAURANTS

Chaat has a lot going for it. It's located in the hippest street in ultra-fashionable Shoreditch; it has a charming, engaging young female owner, Shanaz Khan; and unusually, it serves home-style Bangladeshi dishes, not the Anglo-Moghul cooking found in most Brick Lane curry houses. This is simple fare: comfort food for British diners of Bangladeshi parentage. The menu's aimed squarely at Shoreditch trendies, with five multiple-choice columns listing dishes in English translation. Keema was the pick of the main courses, the lamb mince pleasingly spiced with cardamom, cloves and cinnamon. Niramish, a Bengali vegetarian dish, lacked delicacy in flavour or texture. A shredded lentil and cabbage dish also lacked finesse, though we appreciated the 'panch phoran' Bengali spicing. Dishes can suffer when they aim for the broadest appeal; a starter of paneer roti wrap, 'rolled in crisp salad and a hot 'n' herby mayo', might have been the creation of a sandwich-chain focus group (looking good, but tasting bland). Not so the own-made dip using naga morich, the world's hottest chilli on the Scoville scale, which fortunately has been diluted to make it palatable, and provides the right kick for milder dishes.
Available for hire. Babies and children admitted. Booking advisable weekends. Tables outdoors (2, pavement). Vegetarian menu. **Map 6 S4.**

Whitechapel

Café Spice Namaste
16 Prescot Street, E1 8AZ (7488 9242, www. cafespice.co.uk). Aldgate East or Tower Hill tube/ Tower Gateway DLR. **Lunch served** noon-3pm Mon-Fri. **Dinner served** 6.15-10.30pm Mon-Fri; 6.30-10.30pm Sat. **Main courses** £12.50-£18.55. **Set meal** £30 3 courses, £40 4 courses, £60 tasting menu. **Credit** AmEx, DC, MC, V. Pan-Indian
The interior of this lofty Victorian building is a mix-and-mismatch of Mediterranean colours and swathes of Indian fabric – looped over big, beautiful arched windows that should have been left well alone. However, there's nothing haphazard about the finely judged cooking. Chef-patron Cyrus

Todiwala is famous for his Parsi specialities and of these, a finely balanced starter of akuri was sensationally good: the creaminess of the scrambled eggs holding back the heat of the chillies just enough. The restaurant takes obvious pride in sourcing high-quality ingredients, and regularly features game on the menu. Specials included a dish of pheasant kofte (meatballs) which, instead of being light and melting, were dense and slightly dry. Still, the rich, cardamom-infused sauce in which they were simmered provided ample consolation. Creamy coconut curry of plump fresh king prawns was a treat: mild at first bite, but building to a pleasant hit of heat. Service was considerate and well-informed. This, together with the joyfully inventive yet careful cooking, makes for a pleasant evening, regardless of your taste in interior design.
Babies and children welcome: high chairs. Booking advisable. Disabled: toilet. Tables outdoors (8, garden). Takeaway service; delivery service (within 2-mile radius). **Map 12 S7.**

★ ★ Lahore Kebab House
2 Umberston Street, E1 1PY (7488 2551, www.lahore-kebabhouse.com). Aldgate East or Whitechapel tube. **Meals served** noon-midnight daily. **Main courses** £5.50-£9.50. **Unlicensed. Corkage** no charge. **Credit** MC, V. Pakistani
The unprepossessing interior might seem at odds with this restaurant's almost legendary status – it's little more than a big space lined with tiles and Formica-topped tables. The anodyne room is relieved by a couple of TVs blaring out Bollywood hits, and the sight, through large windows, of chefs at work in a steamy kitchen. At weekends they turn out some notable specials, including paya, an unctuous dish based on lamb trotters, but usually the menu is almost as basic as the surroundings. British Asian locals and curry addicts from across London congregate here for punchy Punjabi fare at its best. On weekend evenings, queues often form outside, many punters holding bottles from the off-licence opposite. Starters are the stars: lamb samosas were crisp, with a hint of ginger; smooth, succulent

seekh kebabs had been laced with chilli and coriander; tandoori chicken wings were tender, salty, tangy and so good we could have ordered many more. To follow, methi gosht – lamb (almost mutton in this case) in a sauce of fenugreek leaves – was rich and fragrant, just right for mopping up with a good soft nan dusted with cumin seeds and a hint of charcoal. All this cost less than £15. With food so good, and so cheap, the decor is irrelevant.
Babies and children welcome: high chairs. Disabled: toilet. Takeaway service; delivery service (by taxi).

★ Tayyabs
83 Fieldgate Street, E1 1JU (7247 9543, www.tayyabs.co.uk). Aldgate East or Whitechapel tube. **Meals served** noon-11.30pm daily. **Main courses** £6-£10. **Unlicensed. Corkage** no charge. **Credit** AmEx, MC, V. Pakistani
Behind the green frontage of a former pub, Tayyabs is a bright, modern Pakistani café that bucks up this down-at-heel backstreet. Droves of City suits are attracted for lunch, along with a few multinational locals and students. The upbeat mood is accentuated by Bollywood beats, a crimson, ochre and mustard colour scheme, spotlights and the bustle from an open-view, stainless-steel kitchen at the rear. Black-garbed waiters are plentiful, and geared to hurrying things along. It was a pity about the food on our visit. Seared tandooris, flash-fried karahis and puffy breads – Tayyabs' stock-in-trade – should all benefit from the quick throughput, but a masala fish starter, served in meaty chunks sizzling on an iron plate, was more notable for its hefty portion than its flavour, hinting at inadequate marination. To follow, sag gosht (available in small or large portions) had more oil than spinach, and a karela dahl, featuring strips of near-burnt bitter gourd, had a dried-out demeanour. Perhaps increased effort is made for dinner (we had a good meal here last year), when a more relaxed clientele has time for discernment.
Babies and children welcome: high chairs. Booking advisable. Separate room for parties, seats 35. Tables outdoors (8, garden). Takeaway service.

Sri Lankan menu

Sri Lanka has three main groups: Sinhalese, Tamil and Muslim. Although there are variations in the cooking styles of each community and every region, rice and curry form the basis of most meals, and curries are usually hot and spicy. The cuisine has evolved by absorbing South Indian, Portuguese, Dutch, Malaysian, Arabic and Chinese flavours over the years. Aromatic herbs and spices like cinnamon, cloves, curry leaves, nutmeg, and fresh coriander are combined with South-east Asian ingredients such as lemongrass, pandan leaves, sesame oil, dried fish and rice noodles. Fresh coconut, onions, green chillies and lime juice (or vinegar) are also used liberally, and there are around two dozen types of rice – from short-grained white varieties to several long-grained, burgundy-hued kinds.

Curries come in three main varieties: white (cooked in coconut milk), yellow (with turmeric and mild curry powder) and black (with roasted curry powder, normally used with meat). Hoppers (saucer-shaped pancakes) are generally eaten for breakfast with kithul palm syrup and buffalo-milk yoghurt, while string hoppers (steamed, rice-flour noodles formed into flat discs) usually accompany fiery curries and sambols (relishes).

Sri Lankan cafés in Tooting, Southall, Wembley and Harrow are becoming increasingly popular.

Ambul thiyal: sour fish curry cooked dry with spices.
Appam or appa: *see* Hoppers.
Badun: black. 'Black' curries are fried; they're dry and usually very hot.
Devilled: meat, seafood or vegetable dishes fried with onions in a sweetish sauce; usually served as starters.
Godamba roti: flaky, thin Sri Lankan bread, sometimes wrapped around egg or potato.
Hoppers: confusingly, hoppers come in two forms, either as saucer-shaped, rice-flour pancakes (try the sweet and delectable milk hopper) or as string hoppers (qv). Hoppers are also known as appam.
Idiappa: see string hoppers.
Katta sambol: onion, lemon and chilli relish; fearsomely hot.
Kiri: white. 'White' curries are based on coconut milk and are usually mild.
Kiri hodi: coconut milk curry with onions and turmeric; a soothing gravy.
Kuttu roti, kottu or kothu roti: strips of thin bread (resembling pasta), mixed with mutton, chicken, prawns or veg to form a 'bread biriani'; very filling.

Lamprais or lumprice: a biriani-style dish where meat and rice are cooked together, often by baking in banana leaves.
Lunnu miris: a relish of ground onion, chilli and maldives fish (qv).
Maldives fish: small, dried fish with a very intense flavour; an ingredient used in sambols (qv).
Pittu: rice flour and coconut steamed in bamboo to make a 'log'; an alternative to rice.
Pol: coconut.
Pol kiri: see kiri hodi.
Pol sambol: a mix of coconut, chilli, onions, maldives fish (qv) and lemon juice.
Sambols: strongly flavoured relishes, often served hot; they are usually chilli-hot too.
Seeni sambol: sweet and spicy, caramelised onion relish.
Sothy or sothi: another name for kiri hodi.
String hoppers: fine rice-flour noodles formed into flat discs. Usually served steamed (in which case they're dry, making them ideal partners for the gravy-like kiri hodi, qv).
Vellappam: appam (qv) served with vegetable curry.
Wattalappan or vattilapan: a version of crème caramel made with kithul palm syrup.

North

Camden Town & Chalk Farm

★ Masala Zone

25 Parkway, NW1 7PG (7267 4422, www.masala zone.com). Camden Town tube. **Lunch served** 12.30-3pm, **dinner served** 5.30-11pm Mon-Fri. **Meals served** 12.30-11pm Sat; 12.30-10.30pm Sun. **Main courses** £6.85-£12.95. **Thalis** £7.80-£12.95. **Credit** MC, V. Pan-Indian

The Masala Zone chain appears to maintain high standards across its five branches. They're all quirkily decorated, and this Camden one – handy for the Jazz Café – has walls festooned with kitsch Indian advertising art. Reservations aren't taken, and table turnover is swift. The menus are a good reflection of the variety of regional fast-food stall and café dishes found in India. Some new dishes have recently been added, such as the Mumbai street snack called keema pau (spicy lamb mince with a Portuguese-style bread bun) and other dishes dropped (like the khandvi, which we found lacklustre on a previous visit). Perennial favourites include the Sindhi chickpea curry, the Gujarati undhiyo (yam and plantain curry), and the starter of moist shami kebabs. Vegetarians are well-catered for, and snacks such as the sour-sweet bhel (a crunchy salad of crisp sev and diced veg) are a must-try, even if you're an omnivore. All the dishes are made with unusual care and attention to detail; the sweets are own-made, and the caramel kulfi is particularly toothsome. You don't often find real Indian food like this in central London, at so fair a price.
Babies and children welcome: children's menu; high chairs. Bookings for fewer than 10 people not accepted. Separate room for parties, seats 30. Takeaway service. **For branches see index**.

North West

Swiss Cottage

Atma

106C Finchley Road, NW3 5JJ (7431 9487, www.atmarestaurants.com). Finchley Road or Swiss Cottage tube. **Lunch served** noon-3pm, **dinner served** 6-11pm Tue-Sun. **Main courses** £7.95-£11.30. **Credit** MC, V. Modern Indian

Located on an uninspiring stretch of the Finchley Road, Atma produces pan-Indian dishes with a South Indian slant. Over the past three years, its style of cooking has evolved (or been reined in) from wacky, new-wave flavour combinations to down-to-earth dishes such as tandoori grills and familiar curries. On our week-night visit, we were the only diners – a shame, as the candles and maroon colour scheme lent welcoming warmth to the dining room, and the waiters were happy to please. The signature salad provided a tasty tease of flavours and contrasting textures (leaves tossed with coconut slivers and shredded beetroot, embellished with juicy pomegranate kernels, toasted cashew nuts and crisp gram-flour munchies, anointed with a refreshing lime and peppery mustard dressing). Main courses didn't inspire. The rough-hewn flavours of our lamb biriani showed none of the typical characteristics of this world-renowned, aromatic rice dish. Equally disappointing, chettinad chicken had more in common with chicken tikka masala dressed up with ground coconut. Tarka dahl scented with toasted cumin seeds, made some amends.
Babies and children welcome: high chair. Booking advisable weekends. Takeaway service. **Map 28 B3**.

Eriki

4-6 Northways Parade, NW3 5EN (7722 0606, www.eriki.co.uk). Swiss Cottage tube. **Lunch served** noon-2.30pm Mon-Fri, Sun. **Dinner served** 6-10.30pm daily. **Main courses** £7.95-£11.95. **Set lunch** £12.95 2 courses. **Credit** AmEx, MC, V. Pan-Indian

A trusted destination for proper Indian cooking, Eriki is unsurprisingly popular with British Asians

Masala Zone

and old India hands. It's a spacious venue, furnished with chunky wooden furniture, framed fabric hangings, and warm maroon hues – as stylish as it is warmly inviting. Although the menu is predominantly North Indian, its nods to regional cuisine deliver tasty and authentic results. A starter of mini masala dosai, filled with mustardy crushed potatoes, worked well with a dollop of pounded coconut chutney: shame there wasn't any sambar to accompany this classic dish. Butterflied, crumbed and fried amritsari prawns were delectable for their robust garlicky flavour. Main courses were just as winsome. Murgh makhani palak, the Punjabi inspiration for chicken tikka masala, was fabulous; seared chicken morsels, succulent and smoky, were complemented by a moat of delectable buttery tomato masala. Equally enjoyable, kashmiri roghan gosht boasted meltingly tender meat. The distinctive curry, scented with cardamom, was emboldened by a caramelised onion base. Only the peri peri sea bass sizzler disappointed. Its tomatoey sauce, spiked with chilli and sweet cinnamon, was let down by saltiness. Service is exemplary: attentive, knowledgeable and friendly.
Available for hire. Babies and children admitted. Booking advisable. Takeaway service; delivery service (6-9.45pm, over £20 within 4-mile radius). Vegetarian menu.

Nauroz

Outer London
Eastcote, Middlesex

★ Nauroz (100)
219 Field End Road, Eastcote, Middx HA5 1QZ (8868 0900). Eastcote tube. **Meals served** noon-midnight Tue-Sun. **Main courses** £3.50-£9. **Licensed**. **Corkage** no charge. **No credit cards**. Pakistani

Behind a semi-frosted plate-glass frontage on a run-of-the-mill 1930s shopping parade, Nauroz is a sparklingly clean Pakistani café with friendly staff and a flair for spicing. Last year we lauded the meat dishes, though this time chana chat (chickpeas and potato cubes in creamy yoghurt) outshone a mixed grill of chicken and salty lamb tikka, and seekh kebabs that lacked the requisite freshly seared tang. Likewise, a main dish of tawa keema was a one-paced, if flavourful, mush of mince (showing no sign of being heated on a 'tawa' stone) when compared to a superb butter bean methi that bellowed the praises of fresh fenugreek. Smashing too was a tasty bowl of tinda (like marrow chunks), a moist, flavour-packed chicken biriani, and a spaghetti-strewn stew of tender lamb malai. Best of all were the nans. You can BYO here, though there's wine, draught Cobra and spirits available. Mid Saturday afternoon, we dined alone, yet Nauroz is deservedly popular at peak times – as evidenced by the immense vat of sauce being prepared (using a blender the size, and sound, of a pneumatic drill) in the shiny stainless-steel kitchen at the rear.
Babies and children welcome: high chairs. Booking advisable Fri, Sat. Takeaway service; delivery service (over £15 within 3-mile radius). Vegetarian menu.

Harrow, Middlesex

Mumbai Junction
231 Watford Road, Harrow, Middx HA1 3TU (8904 2255, www.mumbaijunction.co.uk). Northwick Park tube/Sudbury Hill Harrow rail. **Lunch served** noon-2,45pm, **dinner served** 6-10.45pm daily. **Main courses** £3.95-£9.95. **Credit** (over £10) MC, V. North Indian

A refurbished former boozer, Mumbai Junction retains the furnishings of a traditional pub, save for the plethora of flatscreen TVs: a nod to its aspirations as a sports bar. This spacious, informal restaurant is a popular choice with young families, who come here for unpretentious, well-priced, mainly North Indian cooking. The menu offers a range of snacks as well as full meals – and the portions are huge. In addition to the usual array of curries, you'll find a substantial selection of smoky tandoori bites and bar nibbles,

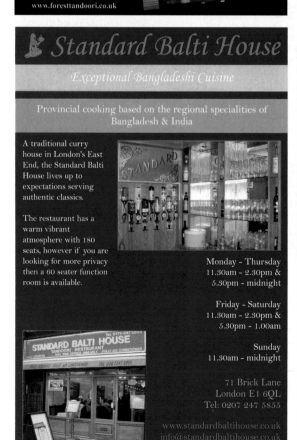

including Indian-style Chinese dishes. Our meal turned out to be one of hits and misses. Although piping hot, vegetable bhajias were marred by dense, spongy gram-flour batter. Main courses had more in their favour. Fried garlicky minced lamb with green peas boasted a lively green-chilli and tomato kick. On the other hand, paneer makhani was a disappointment, with a soupy tomato sauce and chewy cubes of paneer. Service was slow on our visit. Cooking techniques and service need to be spruced up if this restaurant is to attract lasting local custom.
Babies and children welcome: high chairs. Booking advisable weekends. Separate room for parties, seats 80. Takeaway service; delivery service (over £15 within 3-mile radius). Vegetarian menu.

★ Ram's (100)

203 Kenton Road, Harrow, Middx HA3 0HD (8907 2022). Kenton tube/rail. **Lunch served** noon-3pm, **dinner served** 6-11pm daily. **Main courses** £4-£5. Thalis £4.99-£8.99. **Set meal** £22 (unlimited food and soft drinks). **Credit** AmEx, MC, V. Gujarati vegetarian
The alluring specialities of the Surti district of Gujarat beckon from Ram's long menu, but for a weekday lunch, we had our arms strongly twisted (by the otherwise accommodating and congenial staff) to choose the £4.99 buffet. On our insistence, an extra starter of banana methi bhajia was produced, but these small spongy blobs had been overcooked to aridity. Bad news over. The half dozen or so dishes in the buffet ranged from the good (sambar) to the terrific. Best was vengan na bhartu (aka baingan bharta), a glorious mush of aubergine and onion, tangy with tomatoes, spiced with strips of fresh fenugreek. Not far behind was the richly flavoured chana masala (boosted by curry leaves), the garlicky coriander relish, and our chosen drink of refreshing lime soda. Behind its plate-glass windows, Ram's is a pleasingly functional café, with long lines of slate-black, easy-wipe tables, tiled flooring and stainless-steel utensils. Framed pictures of Hindu deities, decorated with gaudy paper chains, add subcontinental zest. Next time, we'll come in the evening or, better still, at the weekend when such delights as surti undhiyu and bhagat muthiya (chana dahl dumplings with potatoes in methi gravy) are served.
Available for hire. Babies and children welcome: high chairs. Booking advisable weekends. Disabled: toilet. Takeaway service.

Southall, Middlesex

As 'authentic' as markets in North India, the shops and stalls on Southall's Broadway and surrounding roads bring the flavours of Punjabi street life to Middlesex. There's little you can't pick up here – from crisp samosas and smoky kebabs, to sequinned salwar suits, glittering gold jewellery, and swathes of brightly hued silk. Visit Kwality Foods (47-61 South Road, UB1 1SQ, 8917 9188) for its vibrant display of exotic vegetables, fragrant seasonal mangoes, and aisles crammed with pickles.

Southall is best enjoyed at the weekend when its thoroughfares are jammed with noisy vendors and bargain hunters haggling over prices. Arrive just after 10am when shops open for business and you'll be greeted by the soothing melodic refrain of devotional music. Decibel levels increase as the morning progresses, the earthy tones of Punjabi vernacular a backdrop to noisy traffic and bhangra beats.

Join the jostling crowds around pavement kiosks as they tuck into creamy kulfis and hot jalebis (crisp-fried whirls of batter) coated in sticky, rose-scented syrup. Sample alfresco sweet treats at Moti Mahal (94 The Broadway, UB1 1QF, 8571 9443), but don't confuse this venue with the identically named ('pearl palace'), but unrelated

restaurant in Covent Garden (*see p134*). For fudge-like blocks of barfi, and patisa (wispy, honeycomb-like squares of sweetened gram flour fried in ghee), Ambala (107 The Broadway, UB1 1LN, 8843 9049) offers consistently good quality. If milky puds are your weakness, head for Royal Sweets (92 The Broadway, UB1 1QF, 8570 0832), which has excellent ras malai (curd-like dumplings simmered in sweetened spiced milk).

Southall's Punjabi community – which hails from the Sikh heartlands on the Indian side of the border, as well as from Pakistan and East Africa – has improved its financial lot in recent years. Flashy cars, glitzy shop fronts and redecorated restaurants are a testament to the newly acquired wealth. Cooking, however, remains homely and true to its rustic subcontinental roots.

For hearty feasts, make for the **New Asian Tandoori Centre** (*see p155*). It's well worth the brisk walk away from Broadway and down South Street. Our current favourite meal here (available at weekends) is kadhi and rice (toasted gram-flour curry spiked with tart yoghurt, ginger flecks and fried curry leaves). If you're looking for low-fat spins on crunchy snacks, curries and buttery breads, there's not much to choose from, although **Brilliant** (*see p155*) makes some attempt to address healthy cooking.

Most Southall cafés have pan (pronounced 'parn') on the menu. These tasty mouth-fresheners are served at the end of a meal and are made by wrapping astringent betel nut leaves around a usually sweetish filling of dates, cardamom, coconut and a sliver of betel nut.

If you're driving, take the car to the main car park behind The Broadway's Himalaya Centre to be assured of a place. Better still, take the train or bus; shops are close by and there's plenty to see on the way. Although standards of cooking at the multifarious caffs might vary, the street life of Southall is incomparable.

★ Brilliant

72-76 Western Road, Southall, Middx UB2 5DZ (8574 1928, www.brilliantrestaurant.com). Southall rail. **Lunch served** noon-3pm Tue-Fri. **Dinner served** 6-11.30pm Tue-Sun. **Main courses** £4.50-£14. **Credit** AmEx, DC, MC, V. East African Punjabi
A photo of a curly locked Prince Charles visiting Brilliant in the 1970s attests to the longevity of this Kenyan Asian stalwart, yet the interior had a complete overhaul a couple of years back, rejuvenating the enterprise to astounding effect. High spirited groups – some British Asian, some not, some mixed – filled the place on a Wednesday night, waited on by smart, alert staff in black garb. The surroundings are glitzy but classy, with a multi-hued water wall, flatscreen TVs blurting out Bollywood beats, wooden flooring and cocktails served from a burnished copper bar. There's plenty more space on the first floor. Food is of a very high standard. The menu is Punjabi by way of Kenya, so fish pakora consists of delicate chunks of tilapia clothed in a soft, spicy gram-flour batter: delectable, especially when combined with the choice of six chutneys provided. Many dishes are designed for group dining (an entire butter chicken, a bowl of masaladar lamb). Our palak lamb was merely good when compared to the addictive aloo chollay (the salty chickpeas balanced by the tang of mango powder in the masala) and perfect kesari rice (generously strewn with saffron). A lustrous star of Southall.
Babies and children welcome: high chairs. Booking advisable weekends. Separate room for parties, seats 120. Takeaway service. Vegetarian menu.

Desi Tadka

148 Uxbridge Road, Hayes, Middx UB4 0JH (8569 0202, www.desitadka.co.uk). Bus 207, 427. **Meals served** 10am-11pm daily. **Main courses** £6.50-£9.50. **Credit** MC, V. Punjabi
Life-sized models of be-turbanned gents outside Desi Tadka's hint at the exhilarating spectacle within. Set on a drab parade by the A4020, this is a deceptively large, attractive restaurant. A stainless-steel kitchen with takeaway counter is to the fore. Engaging waiters, clad in cerise robes and glittering waistcoats, lead you to the rear dining room where expensive wooden flooring and furniture is juxtaposed with yellow brick walls, dangling lanterns, and a bhangra soundtrack. Half way through our Sunday night meal, the music was cranked up to distortion and two waiters burst into dazzling, synchronised bhangra dance moves, earning applause from the assembled Sikh families and young Punjabis. Food is straightforward Punjabi, with breads and tandooris the best (and most popular) choices. Tandoori machi was terrific: glisteningly fresh chunks of expertly marinated cod, scorched on the chargrill and served with sizzling onions. Butter nan and bhatura were faultless too, and not far behind were bhindi bhajee, tarka dahl and lamb taka tak (here served in tender chunks in a lentil and fenugreek-based sauce). A dry chicken biriani and chewy bhel poori indicated these weren't the kitchen's strengths, but we left smiling – with a beat to our step.
Babies and children welcome: high chairs. Booking advisable. Disabled: toilet. Takeaway service.

★ New Asian Tandoori Centre (Roxy)

114-118 The Green, Southall, Middx UB2 4BQ (8574 2597). Southall rail. **Meals served** 8am-11pm Mon-Thur; 8am-midnight Fri-Sun. **Main courses** £5-£7. **Credit** MC, V. Punjabi
Authentic street food doesn't get better than this. Over the past three decades, this canteen has earned an enviable reputation for recreating a taste of the Punjab for its loyal fan club of nostalgic expatriates, British Asian families, and aficionados of North Indian cooking. A recent refurbishment has spruced up the interior, but the menu remains resolutely traditional. The pani poori ranks as one of the best in London: puffed globes of wafer-thin semolina pastry filled with diced potatoes, chickpeas and minted tamarind water – an explosion of tongue-tingling flavour. Keep an eye out for weekend specials: spicy buttery spinach served with cornmeal flatbreads, and kadhi (whipped yoghurt curry studded with gram-flour dumplings). Chickpea masala, simmered with a garlic-ginger spice-blend and sharpened with tart pomegranate powder, is best mopped up with bhaturas (deep-fried yeasted bread). Other acclaimed Punjabi staples include chats (yoghurt- or tamarind-drenched crunchy snacks), meat curries, and green-pea and paneer curry. Over the years, we've worked our way through most of the menu; only the biriani doesn't quite match expectation. Fresh pickles and pitchers of salted lassi endorse the 100% Punjabi experience.
Babies and children welcome: high chairs. Disabled: toilet. Separate room for parties. Takeaway service. Vegetarian menu.

Sudbury, Middlesex

★ Five Hot Chillies

875 Harrow Road, Sudbury, Middx HA0 2RH (8908 5900). Sudbury Town or Sudbury Hill tube. **Meals served** noon-midnight daily. **Main courses** £4-£10. **Unlicensed. Corkage** no charge. **Credit** MC, V. Punjabi
A no-fuss Punjabi corner café, Five Hot Chillies puts all its efforts into the food. Even during a sparsely attended Sunday lunch, the fish tikka arrived from the open stainless-steel kitchen freshly seared, and the mixed bhajias (big chillies, onions, potato patties) had seemingly leapt straight from the pan, so crisp and light was the batter. Less satisfying was some overcooked rounds of patra. There's a huge choice of mains (arranged in non-veg and veg sections, and here called 'steamers') with the array of vegetarian

RESTAURANTS

dishes especially notable. Karahi methi chana featured soft chickpeas and abundant fenugreek leaves in a copious gravy. Karahi corn on the cob came in half-inch slices bathed in a tomato-based sauce. Good too was the karahi tinda gosht the flavour of the lamb marrying well with the juicy marrow-like tinda. There's also plenty of unusual breads and rice to try. We relished the pungent garlic nan and onion kulcha. A request for mild dishes brought forth curries that might have been called medium elsewhere, but despite its name, not everything at Five Hot Chillies is a scorcher. Staff were friendly and prompt.

Babies and children welcome: high chairs. Booking advisable. Takeaway service. Vegetarian menu.

Uxbridge, Middlesex

Satya

33 Rockingham Road, Uxbridge, Middx UB8 2TZ (01895 274250). Uxbridge tube. **Lunch served** noon-3pm, **dinner served** 6-11pm daily. **Main courses** £5.50-£9.50. **Set buffet** (noon-3pm Mon-Fri) £6.50. **Credit** AmEx, MC, V. South Indian

Bright and cheerful looking, stylishly softened with coloured cushions, Indian artefacts and white napery, this well-placed South Indian local is a popular choice for families and other Uxbridge residents. Satya does Kerala proud with its fried fish dishes, coconut-based curries and rice-based snacks. An impressive pomfret-fry – served whole and steeped in a piquant paste of ginger, turmeric, curry leaves and lime juice – was deliciously juicy and notable for its boldly spiced crust, yielding to delicate flesh below. Dosais (rice and lentil pancakes) are listed as starters on the menu, but arrive in main-course portions; we recommend sharing. Filled with spicy mashed potato, our dosai was accompanied by delectable sambar (lentils simmered with tamarind, aubergine and drumstick pieces). Keralite lamb curry was top drawer too: meltingly tender meat, simmered in onion sauce, scented with toasted coriander seeds and ginger. Only the vegetable pilao was a letdown, with its pronounced flavour of floral essence. Service is slow, if well meaning, but the standard of cooking outshines that of many pricey venues in central London.

Babies and children welcome: high chairs. Booking advisable. Disabled: toilet. Separate room for parties, seats 10. Takeaway service.

Wembley, Middlesex

Karahi King

213 East Lane, Wembley, Middx HA0 3NG (8904 2760). North Wembley tube/245 bus. **Meals served** 11.30am-midnight daily. **Main courses** £4-£12. **Unlicensed**. **Corkage** no charge. **Credit** AmEx, MC, V. Punjabi

A kerfuffle of school children pushed their way into Karahi King, lining up at the counter, eager for their takeaway lunch of kebab-filled nan bread. It would seem this well-worn local favourite is keen on fostering its future clientele. An environmental health inspection of the premises appeared to be under way during our visit, but staff need have few worries there; this is a spick and span operation with easy-wipe tables, new blond-wood chairs and a well-run open kitchen. Here, atop furious gas burners, rest KK's raison d'être: capacious wok-like karahi pans, ready to accommodate any number of ingredients and masala mixes. A karahi methi chicken was wonderfully tangy with fresh leafy fenugreek, while a starter of masala fish consisted of two flaky chunks of well-marinated cod clothed in a light, spicy batter. A notch down in class was some sloppy tarka dahl topped with powdered masala, and a keema nan of almost omelette-like consistency. But jeera rice, nutty with freshly toasted cumin, was a fine dish, and overall the meal was a pleasure to eat. Staff were prompt, but they get more of a workout at weekends and for dinner.

Babies and children welcome: high chairs. Separate room for parties, seats 60. Takeaway service. Vegetarian menu.

★ Sakonis (100)

129 Ealing Road, Wembley, Middx HA0 4BP (8903 9601). Alperton tube/183 bus. **Breakfast served** 9-11am Sat, Sun. **Meals served** noon-10pm daily. **Main courses** £2-£7. **Set buffet** (breakfast) £3.99; (noon-4pm Mon-Fri, noon-5pm Sat, Sun) £7.99; (6-9.30pm) £10.99. **Credit** MC, V. Gujarati vegetarian

Famed for reasonably priced vegetarian street food, this Wembley café is the better known of the two surviving Sakoni branches – the other is in Harrow. It's a functional operation; the tiled walls, easy-wipe tables, and melamine tableware are as authentic as you'd find in the caffs of South Asia. At weekends, expect a serpentine queue for tables. The buffet, at the rear of the restaurant past the takeaway counter, is the biggest draw for families. They come for crunchy snacks drizzled with tamarind chutney, South Indian pancakes, Indianised chinese noodles, curries, and dahls. Ordering from the standard menu, we polished off a plate of piping-hot onion bhajias, notable for crisp gram-flour batter flecked with chopped coriander. A huge helping of bhel poori delivered a scrumptious mélange of crisp rice and gram-flour crunchies, tossed with diced onions, tamarind sauce and tangy coriander chutney. We suggest ordering snacks, rather than the less impressive main courses (an exception being the excellent crisp dosais filled with potato masala). Vegetarian biriani was an underwhelming combination of plain boiled rice tossed with green bean curry. If palate cleansers made from betel leaves filled with coconut and dates are your thing – try one here.

Babies and children welcome. Takeaway service. Vegetarian menu.
For branch see index.

Sweets menu

Even though there isn't a tradition of serving puddings at everyday meals in South Asia, there is much ceremony associated with distributing sweetmeats at auspicious events – especially weddings and religious festivals. Many of these delicacies are rarely found in the West: shahi tukra (nursery-like bread and butter pudding); nimesh (rose-scented creamy froth, scooped into clay pots); and misti dhoi (jaggery-flavoured set yoghurt from Bengal).

Desserts served at many Indian restaurants in London include the likes of gulab jamun, cardamom-scented rice pudding, creamy kulfi, and soft, syrup-drenched cheese dumplings. In the home, family meals don't often include a dessert; you're more likely to be treated to a platter of seasonal fruit. Even in Britain, thousands of miles away from mango groves, the onset of India's mango season in May is a date for the calendar. To appreciate this lush fruit at its best, look for boxes of alphonso mangoes in Asian stores.

Winter warmers also have their place, including comforting, fudge-like carrot halwa, a Punjabi favourite and popular street snack. In Punjabi villages, a communal cauldron is often simmered for hours on end, sending out wafts of aromatic cardamom and caramelised carrots as the halwa cooks down into an indulgent treat. Winter is also the season for weddings, where other halwas, made with wholewheat flour, semolina, lentils and pumpkin, might be served. Most 'sweets' take a long time to make, which is why people prefer to visit sweetmeat shops, the best known of which is **Ambala**'s flagship store near Euston station (112 Drummond Street, NW1 2HN, 7387 3521). Here, an impressive array of eye candy for the seriously sweet-toothed includes soft cheese-based dumplings immersed in rose-scented syrup, cashew-nut fudgy blocks, toasted gram-flour balls, and marzipan-like rolls. Expect floral flavours, shed-loads of sugar and a good whack of calorie-laden ghee (clarified butter). It's hard to believe that with all the varieties offered, specialist sweet-makers (known as halwais) cook with so few ingredients; milk products, dried fruit, sugar and ghee are the key constituents.

Barfi: sweetmeat usually made with reduced milk, and flavoured with nuts, fruit, sweet spices or coconut.

Bibenca or **bibinca**: soft, layered cake from Goa made with eggs, coconut milk and jaggery.

Falooda or **faluda**: thick milky drink (originally from the Middle East), resembling a cross between a milkshake and a sundae. It's flavoured with either rose syrup or saffron, and also contains agar-agar, vermicelli, nuts and ice-cream. Very popular with Gujarati families, faloodas make perfect partners to deep-fried snacks.

Gajar halwa: grated carrots, cooked in sweetened cardamom milk until soft, then fried in ghee until almost caramelised; usually served warm.

Gulab jamun: brown dumplings (made from dried milk and flour), deep-fried and drenched in rose-flavoured sugar syrup, best served warm. A traditional Bengali sweet, now ubiquitous in Indian restaurants.

Halwa: a fudge-like sweet, made with semolina, wholewheat flour or ground pulses cooked with syrup or reduced milk, and flavoured with nuts, saffron or sweet spices.

Jalebis: spirals of batter, deep-fried and dipped in syrup, best eaten warm.

Kheer: milky rice pudding, flavoured with cardamom and nuts. Popular throughout India (there are many regional variations).

Kulfi: ice-cream made from reduced milk, flavoured with nuts, saffron or fruit.

Payasam: a South Indian pudding made of reduced coconut or cow's milk with sago, nuts and cardamom. Semiya payasam is made with added vermicelli.

Rasgullas: soft paneer cheese balls, simmered and dipped in rose-scented syrup, served cold.

Ras malai: soft paneer cheese patties in sweet and thickened milk, served cold.

Shrikhand: hung (concentrated) sweet yoghurt with saffron, nuts and cardamom, sometimes with fruit added. A traditional Gujarati favourite, eaten with pooris.

International

In the 1990s, culinary London was like a small child in a roomful of new toys. Chefs in this most multicultural of cities discovered the global larder of ingredients at their disposal – and also found there was a rapidly expanding band of adventurous diners eager to experiment. Some filled their menus with crowd-pleasing dishes from the world's great cuisines, so a thai green chicken curry might be listed alongside roghan gosht or even spanish omelette. The birth of the London gastropub soon followed. Other more experimental souls began combining international ingredients on the same plate. The results were often an alarming hodgepodge, but the successful dishes gave rise to the new eclectic cuisines we call Modern European, Oriental and Modern Indian. Today, most international restaurants are a mite more conservative, sticking to recipes that have become modern classics, but the pioneers continue to experiment. Top among these is Peter Gordon at the **Providores & Tapa Room** and Anna Hansen at the **Modern Pantry**, both of whom throw a measure of Antipodean bravura into the mix.

Central
Clerkenwell & Farringdon

★ The Modern Pantry
47-48 St John's Square, EC1V 4JJ (7250 0833, www.themodernpantry.co.uk). Farringdon tube/rail.
Café **Meals served** 8am-11pm Mon-Fri; 9am-11pm Sat; 10am-10pm Sun. **Main courses** £12.50-£17.
Restaurant **Lunch served** noon-3pm Tue-Fri. **Dinner served** 6-10.30pm Tue-Sat. **Main courses** £12.50-£20.
Both **Credit** AmEx, MC, V.
A culinary three-parter spilling across two floors of neighbouring Georgian townhouses, the Modern Pantry feels savvy and of the moment. Both pantry (takeaway) and café (informal) are at street-level; upstairs there are adjoining dining rooms (still informal). With an enthused clientele in the first flush of foodie-ism, the venue is fashionable without being achingly so, and the service is spot-on. Anna Hansen's menu is a genre-bending fusion of fine ingredients in the style of Peter Gordon (of Providores, *see right*). The influence of New Zealand and Australia, where she has worked, shines through in the likes of poached tamarillo with manuka honey. The café menu includes such inviting options as spicy swiss chard and fennel soup, or sugar-cured prawn omelette. Dishes in the dining rooms are more involved, as you'd expect, featuring a successful celeriac, wild mushroom and leek gratin, served with grilled spring onions, sumac dressing and a deep-fried egg, as well as meaty fare such as roast lamb chump marinated in cumin and preserved lemon, with chickpea and turmeric chips. The weekend brunch is special, offering enviable choice, but it's popular, so book.
Available for hire. Babies and children welcome: high chairs. Disabled: toilet. Separate room for parties, seats 30. Tables outdoors (9, square). Takeaway service. Map 5 O4.

Covent Garden

Le Deuxième
65A Long Acre, WC2E 9JD (7379 0033, www.ledeuxieme.com). Covent Garden tube.
Lunch served noon-3pm, **dinner served** 5pm-midnight Mon-Fri. **Meals served** noon-midnight Sat; noon-11pm Sun. **Main courses** £14.50-£18.50. **Set meal** (noon-3pm, 5-7pm, 10pm-midnight Mon-Fri; noon-midnight Sat; noon-11pm Sun) £13.50 2 courses, £16.50 3 courses. **Credit** AmEx, MC, V.
For theatregoers this understated restaurant is a bona fide West End hit. Playing nightly to an appreciative audience, waistcoated staff nimbly navigate the tables (which bear starched-linen tablecloths) under the careful orchestration of the immaculate maître d'. The pace is fast but never rushed; the approach formal, but never brusque. That said, the gloss of French savoir faire stops short of the menu, which has merely a whisper of Gallic flourish in the shape of escargots bourguignon or pan-fried foie gras with toasted brioche. Chef Simon Conboy regales diners with the kind of classics that have become 'British' favourites, be that pork belly with mustard mash, chargrilled ribeye of Scottish beef, or green thai prawn curry. It's proficient cooking with decent ingredients at a fair price (especially if you look to the two- and three-course set menus). Braised ox cheeks were richly dense yet tender, while rump of lamb was cooked just so, medium rare. The boom and bust rhythms of pre- and post-theatre diners mean that Le Deuxième isn't a relaxed destination, but should you pass by mid-performance, about 8pm, you might just walk in and get a table.
Available for hire. Babies and children admitted. Booking advisable. Map 18 E3.

Marylebone

★ The Providores & Tapa Room (100)
109 Marylebone High Street, W1U 4RX (7935 6175, www.theprovidores.co.uk). Baker Street or Bond Street tube.
The Providores **Lunch served** noon-2.45pm Mon-Fri. **Brunch served** noon-2.45pm Sat, Sun. **Dinner served** 6-10.30pm Mon-Sat; 6-10pm Sun. **Main courses** (lunch) £18-£26. Set meal (dinner) £29 2 courses, £42 3 courses, £52 4 courses, £60 5 courses. **Cover** (brunch) £1.50.
Tapa Room **Breakfast/brunch served** 9-11.30am Mon-Fri; 10am-3pm Sat, Sun. **Meals served** noon-10.30pm Mon-Fri; 4-10.30pm Sat; 4-10pm Sun. **Tapas** £2-£14.40.
Both **Credit** AmEx, MC, V.

Upstairs, the serene Providores restaurant is the calming counterpoint to the street-level Tapa Room. If the cream dining area is as polished and even-featured as a matinée idol, the menu is more a character actor. Chef-proprietor New Zealander Peter Gordon has long harmonised ingredients that would form a mishmash in lesser hands. His latest menu reins-in the complexity a little, presenting diners with starter-sized dishes, flexibly priced at courses per person (rather than per table). Yet given 'permission' to indulge, in truth you rarely want to scoff all the candy in the store. Dividing the menu into soups, vegetarian, fish and meat dishes, and desserts, should have made choosing easier – but each dish is extraordinary. On reflection, the plantain coconut fritter was slightly lost under the baba ganoush, but the glossy pea shoots and pomegranate made it look divine. Roast Norwegian cod with tomato chilli jam and miso beurre blanc stood out, and even linguists would have forgiven the menu promising 'arancini' on experiencing the wasabi tingle of the single arancino that arrived. You eat so well here, there's scant reason to complain. Nevertheless, service didn't always come with a smile, which irked, especially as a service charge is automatically added to the bill.
Babies and children welcome: high chairs. Booking advisable Providores; bookings not accepted Tapa Room. Disabled: toilet. Tables outdoors (2, pavement). Map 9 G5.

Mayfair

Sketch: The Gallery (100)
9 Conduit Street, W1S 2XG (7659 4500, www.sketch.uk.com). Oxford Circus tube.
Dinner served 7-10.30pm Mon-Wed; 7-11pm Thur-Sat. **Main courses** £12-£32. **Credit** AmEx, MC, V.
A garden swing chair festooned with woollen pom-poms resides opposite the cloakroom, but no sitting is allowed – which seems so very Sketch. Eccentric, delightful and pretentious, the operation includes three eateries, of which the Gallery (art gallery by day, restaurant by night) is in the middle in terms of formality. The high walls, in soul-searching black, are employed for light projections: Tim Fothergill's *Chaos* was in fact a soothing succession of butterflies, inspired by the science of the butterfly effect. Yet if a seemingly insignificant movement, such as the flutter of many waiters (offering bread at £5 a basket), were to alter history, we weren't aware of it. Executive chef Pierre Gagnaire's eclectic food was better than the grammatically confounding menu (inviting you to 'eat music drink art') might suggest. Lobster bisque was elegant and flavoursome, and pumpkin soup with smoked bacon and salsify was creamy and unguent, if over-salted. Mains include ravioli and risotto alongside the more experimental – stone bass, with grapefruit marmalade and turnips cooked in Campari, was bold, bitter-sweet, and not entirely successful. Portions were larger than on previous visits. The 'Sketch etcetera…' menu has a handful of more purse-friendly options.
Available for hire. Booking essential. Entertainment: DJs 11pm-2am Thur-Sat. Separate rooms for parties, seating 50. Map 9 J6.

Soho

Refuel
The Soho Hotel, 4 Richmond Mews, W1D 3DH (7559 3007, www.refuelsoho.com). Tottenham Court Road tube. **Meals served** 7am-midnight Mon-Sat; 8am-11pm Sun. **Main courses** £14-£35. **Set meal** (5-7pm Mon-Sat) £12.95 2 courses, £19.95 3 courses. **Set meal** £12.95 2 courses, £14.95 3 courses. **Credit** AmEx, MC, V.
Open to all-comers, but set discreetly back from the street in a secluded mews, the elegant Refuel at the even more elegant Soho Hotel is like a private members' club, though a mite more egalitarian. At one time the bar adjoining the dining room was overrun by excitable media show-offs, but –

fortunately for diners – its pulling power seems to have waned. Now the casual chic of the restaurant proper is more of a lure, a fact possibly attributable to the modestly priced set menu and dishes that, while uneventful, are at least reliable. Starters of chorizo and fennel frittata, and smoked bacon and caramelised onion quiche, were satisfying; mains of poached salmon with crushed potatoes, and steamed hake with squash and wild mushrooms, were decent, if unimaginatively presented and fairly small. Refuel, apparently so named because a car park was once located on this spot, seems intent on steering a safe course – all the more pleasing, then, when a friendly waiter rounded off our dinner by inviting us to choose from a surprise tray of complimentary bite-sized cones of sorbet.
Available for hire. Babies and children welcome: children's menu; high chairs. Booking advisable Fri, Sat. Disabled: toilet. Dress: smart casual. Separate room for parties, seats 12. Vegetarian menu. Vegan dishes. **Map 17 B3**.

Westminster

Bank Westminster
45 Buckingham Gate, SW1E 6BS (7379 9797, www.bankrestaurants.com). St James's Park tube. **Meals served** noon-11pm Mon-Fri; 5.30-11pm Sat. **Main courses** £10.50-£30. **Credit** AmEx, MC, V.
Perhaps it was because the political class had gone into hiding, but American accents seemed most prominent among the lunching suits the day we visited this smart brasserie – one of several separately managed dining options in the Crowne Plaza St James hotel. Visually, it's a stunner. Beyond a revolving door and a sleek wood and blue-glass corridor, you emerge into a light-filled, semi-circular modern conservatory facing the grand Edwardian courtyard garden. Staff are attentive to the point of touchy-feely. Bank also stands out, from the plush anonymity of the hotel restaurant, for the liveliness of its food. Menus reflect the international-hotel setting by offering something for most tastes, from Brit and American favourites like fish and chips, caesar salad and steaks, through mushroom risotto to tandoori-baked sea bass. Thankfully, there was no sense of routine cooking in our delicately handled king prawns in tempura, served with a chilli and lime jam that was spicy without being crude. Crispy duck with chinese greens and sesame and honey dressing also had plenty of subtle, satisfying flavours. Prices are reasonable (both for food and the nicely varied wine list), considering you're in an upmarket Westminster hotel.
Available for hire. Babies and children welcome: high chairs. Booking advisable. Disabled: toilet. Separate room for parties, seats 40. Tables outdoors. **Map 15 9J**.

West
Kensington

Abingdon
54 Abingdon Road, W8 6AP (7937 3339, www.theabingdonrestaurant.com). High Street Kensington tube. **Lunch served** 12.30-2.30pm Mon-Fri; 12.30-3pm Sat, Sun. **Dinner served** 6.30-10.30pm Mon; 6.30-11pm Tue-Sat; 7-10.30pm Sun. **Main courses** £12.50-£22. **Set lunch** (Mon-Fri) £15.95 2 courses. **Credit** AmEx, MC, V.
A sign in the gents announces that the management won't tolerate drug-taking on the premises. That must be the only negative message at the Abingdon, a restaurant where staff instantly make you feel at home. This charming local serves the quiet area where genteel Kensington shades into Earl's Court. On a sunny Thursday a diverse bunch of customers mingled in the comfy bar and more formal dining area. Prices suit the affluent district, but aren't gouging; the compact wine list lets you drink pleasurably for under £30. What disappoints is the inconsistent and sometimes over-complicated cooking. Redundant reductions (sticky sauces), artfully drizzled and annoyingly

sweet, marred our two starters: baked camembert with caramelised chicory, and seared scallops with broad bean purée and pickled fennel. The principal ingredients were well cooked in both cases, but hated the reductions (one of balsamic vinegar, the other of sorrel) and didn't much like their vegetable companions. Main courses – the likes of baked sri lankan marinated chicken breast with puy lentil and red bean dal, and coriander sauce; or teriyaki tuna with watercress and water-chestnuts, and wasabi butter – are similarly ambitious. Regulars clearly love the Abingdon, but greater simplicity in the kitchen is needed.
Available for hire. Babies and children welcome: high chairs. Booking advisable. Tables outdoors (4, pavement). Vegetarian menu. **Map 13 A9**.

South East
London Bridge & Borough

Champor-Champor
62-64 Weston Street, SE1 3QJ (7403 4600, www.champor-champor.com). London Bridge tube/ rail. **Lunch served** by appointment. **Dinner served** 6-10pm Mon-Sat. **Set meal** £25 2 courses, £29.50 3 courses. **Credit** AmEx, MC, V.

An unprepossessing exterior makes this distinctive dining room seem like a hidden gem, stepping in, as you do, from the grey grit of London Bridge to a heady eastern experience of embroidered place settings, tribal artefacts and fragrant incense. The effect could seem contrived, but in fact is entirely charming, thanks to the polite service and convivial atmosphere. Chef Adu Amran Hassan's menu nourishes its Malay roots with a variety of Asian cuisines ('champor-champor' means 'mix and match') and is, for the most part, hearty and highly spiced in the manner of Malay kampong (village) cooking. Vegetarians are creatively catered for with the likes of steamed sweetcorn and red curry 'custard' to start, and smoky roast aubergine teriyaki with celeriac and harissa mash to follow. Everything is pleasantly presented – even fish balls and silken tofu in an okra broth came arranged just so, in a porcelain bowl. Beer lovers will want to dip into the less familiar brews from Mongolia and Vietnam. If you're particularly taken by the east-meets-east dishes, come and recreate your favourites at the Saturday afternoon cooking class.
Available for hire. Babies and children welcome: high chairs. Booking essential. Separate room for parties, seats 8. **Map 12 Q9**.

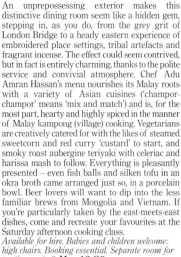

The Modern Pantry.

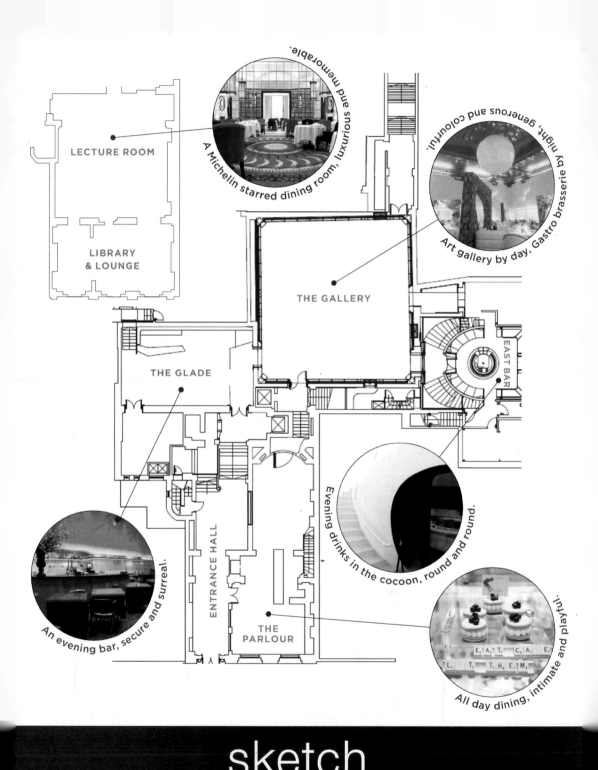

LECTURE ROOM

A Michelin starred dining room, luxurious and memorable.

LIBRARY & LOUNGE

Art gallery by day, Gastro brasserie by night, generous and colourful.

THE GALLERY

THE GLADE

EAST BAR

Evening drinks in the cocoon, round and round.

An evening bar, secure and surreal.

ENTRANCE HALL

THE PARLOUR

E A T   C A   E

L   T   T H E M

All day dining, intimate and playful.

sketch

sketch, a mosaic of experience, served full of warmth with a dash of intrigue on the side.

North East
Wanstead

Hadley House
*27 High Street, E11 2AA (8989 8855).
Snaresbrook or Wanstead tube.* **Breakfast served** 10-11.30am Sat, Sun. **Lunch served** noon-3pm, **dinner served** 6-10pm daily. **Main courses** £11-£15. **Set lunch** (Mon-Sat) £14.50 2 courses, £19.95 3 courses. **Set dinner** (Tue-Thur) £14.50 2 courses; £19.95 incl wine. **Credit** MC, V.

Hadley House is a dream of a local restaurant: inexpensive, friendly and with great talent in the kitchen. The menus are exceptionally flexible, encompassing a carte and set meals. Any of the options let you eat three courses for around £14.50-£19.95 at lunch and dinner. And you'll eat extremely well. A vegetable soup featured perfectly cooked asparagus, broccoli and carrots in a sweet, olive oil-scented broth. Chicken livers on toasted brioche, served with reduced pan juices and a hint of sherry, were cooked with split-second exactitude. Spanish omelette was crisp outside, properly gooey within. Best was a large skate wing with brown butter and capers (from the set lunch), which few Parisian brasseries could better. There's a Sunday roast too, and grills in the evening. Minor complaints: there could have been more of the soup; and the skate should have been served with its excellent vegetables on the side, not underneath. The short, craftily selected wine list starts at under £15. Service was warm and solicitous, not the polished professionalism of the West End but local people serving their neighbours with genuine friendliness. The high-ceilinged dining room is attractive and spacious; a seat outside, in warm weather, is bliss.
Available for hire. Babies and children welcome (lunch, Sun): high chairs. Booking advisable. Tables outdoors (7, patio).

North
Crouch End

★ St James NEW
2009 RUNNER-UP BEST LOCAL RESTAURANT
4 Topsfield Parade, N8 8PR (8348 8348, www.stjamesn8.co.uk). Bus W7. **Meals served** noon-11pm Mon-Wed; noon-1am Thur-Sat; noon-10.30pm. **Main courses** £12.95-£19.95. **Set lunch** £4.95 1 course. **Set dinner** £12 2 courses. **Credit** MC, V.

There's something of a heavenly aura to the dining room at this Crouch End newcomer. With unadorned white walls, white tablecloths and lampshades, a long white banquette along one wall and a mirror covering another, you almost expect an angel, rather than a waitress, to appear at your side to take your order. The dining room is at the rear of the venue (it was formerly Florians); at the front is a bar. Its first incarnation was in stark contrast to the restaurant, all black marble, mirrors and blue neon lighting, but it will have transformed into a more soothing space by the time this guide is published, serving breakfast and brunch as well as booze. The food menu won't change, however: a mix of British, French, Mediterranean and oriental dishes, offered à la carte and as a fixed price 'market menu'. The latter is a bargain, with generous portions and an ambitious, creative approach to the food – that doesn't always pay off. A starter of grilled halloumi with strawberries, parma ham and leaves was, frankly, odd; simpler, and much better, was a dish of crispy-coated, soft-centred whitebait. To follow, seared calf's liver atop a crusty potato cake married well with green beans flecked with bacon bits. 'Chilli tempura cod' featured nuggets of lovely, flaky fish, but the batter wasn't notably tempura-like, and there was no hint of the promised chilli. The brief wine list is approachable, and service deft and friendly.

Available for hire. Babies and children welcome: high chairs. Booking advisable weekends. Entertainment: DJs/bands 9pm Wed-Sat. Tables outdoors (3, garden).

Islington

Ottolenghi (100)
287 Upper Street, N1 2TZ (7288 1454, www.ottolenghi.co.uk). Angel tube/Highbury & Islington tube/rail. **Meals served** 8am-11pm Mon-Sat; 9am-7pm Sun. **Main courses** £8-£10. **Credit** AmEx, MC, V.

Founder Yotam Ottolenghi is a self-confessed cake geek, which explains a lot. Piles of extravagant pastries are displayed in the window, and are clearly taken extremely seriously. Even to look at these platefuls of temptation – from big, blowsy meringues to tidy white chocolate cheesecake tarts – can feel ruinous to your waistline. But there's life beyond dessert. For a start, the cooked breakfasts are among the best in town. Counter salads, which double as eat-in starters or takeaways, are a vibrant riot of fresh ingredients. Spiced steamed aubergine in tomato sauce with coriander, lemon and almonds was a tiny bonfire of flavour. However, the real surprise for readers of Ottolenghi's 'New Vegetarian' column in the *Guardian* will be the meat and fish dishes from the kitchen: dainty, starter-sized (the menu suggests three per person, but a robust appetite requires at least four) and very good. Fried calamares was accompanied by a lively mint salad and lime dressing; crispy rice-coated king prawns were counterpointed with miso mayo. Service was much improved from our last visit. The colourful food stands out in the white deli-style space, where a long communal table dominates. Tables à deux line either side.
Babies and children welcome: high chairs. Booking advisable evenings; not accepted lunch. Tables outdoors (2, pavement). Takeaway service.
Map 5 O1.
For branches see index.

RESTAURANTS

Italian

London's love affair with Italian cooking shows no sign of ending. In this edition we are adding an astonishing seven new restaurants in what was already one of our largest chapters. They range in style from Jamie Oliver's no-bookings, come-as-you-are trattoria chain, **Jamie's Italian**, to the fine dining of Angela Hartnett's **Murano**, where foam is as likely to appear as a garnish as parmesan cheese. It wasn't, however, a celebrity chef who took our Best New Italian Restaurant award, though you might want to keep an eye on the talented Francesco Mazzei of **L'Anima**. He focuses on the big-flavoured dishes of southern Italy and the islands – cuisines that, on the whole, are already executed with great flair in the capital by stalwarts such as **Olivo** and **Sardo**. Looking further afield, **Theo Randall at the Intercontinental**, the **River Café**, **Locanda Locatelli** and **Via Condotti** also happily continue to rank among our favourite Italian eateries in London.

Central

Belgravia

Il Convivio
143 Ebury Street, SW1W 9QN (7730 4099, www.etruscagroup.co.uk). Sloane Square tube/ Victoria tube/rail. **Lunch served** noon-2.45pm, **dinner served** 7-10.45pm Mon-Sat. **Main courses** £16.50-£26. **Set lunch** £17.50 2 courses, £21.50 3 courses. **Credit** AmEx, MC, V.
Tucked away in a quiet Belgravia street, this comfortably upmarket Italian restaurant may not set new culinary standards, but it still wins plaudits for elegantly presented classic dishes with a modern twist. The attention to detail is outstanding (including the offer of amuses bouches and freebies between courses) and worthy of haute cuisine restaurants. Most of the wine list may be beyond the reach of diners lacking a bulbous expense account (unless they're celebrating a special occasion), but ordering by the glass is taken seriously here, with staff bringing the bottle to the table to check and taste. Even a simple starter of buffalo mozzarella and tomatoes arrives beautifully presented, and the pasta dishes are elegant and imaginative, such as black spaghetti with lobster. Take note, though, that main courses come with little accompaniment, and the addition of side dishes will push the bill even higher. While regulars may not flinch, the final bill can easily reach levels that can only be justified at the very best establishments.
Available for hire. Babies and children admitted. Booking advisable dinner. Separate room for parties, seats 14. **Map 15 G10.**
For branch (Caravaggio) see index.

Olivo
21 Eccleston Street, SW1W 9LX (7730 2505). Sloane Square tube/Victoria tube/rail. **Lunch served** noon-2.30pm Mon-Fri. **Dinner served** 7-11pm Mon-Sat; 7-10.30pm Sun. **Main courses** £14.50-£19. **Set lunch** £19.50 2 courses, £22.50 3 courses. **Credit** AmEx, DC, MC, V.
This buzzy atmospheric little Sardinian restaurant is the lynchpin of a Belgravia chain that also includes a pizza joint, a seafood restaurant and a deli, all within a few blocks. The hand-painted gold and azure walls with a classic motif along the divide are initially a bit of a surprise but do manage to make one feel transported to the Med. Service was slick and enthusiastically friendly; the menu filled with must-haves. Starters included a wonderfully tasty buffalo mozzarella with grated bottarga and an outstanding crab linguine. Main course of grilled quail with prunes in balsamic sauce was superb, while grilled lemon sole with saffron was good but unexceptional. An interesting all-Italian wine list included an excellent Gavi di Gavi at a very reasonable price (£24.75). The dessert menu features some intriguing novelties, like poached pear in syrup with mascarpone cream and crushed amaretti, and sebada, traditional Sardinian cheese fritters served with honey. With three courses and a slightly more modest wine, expect to pay just over £50 a head with service, although at lunch there are good-value set menus.
Babies and children admitted. Booking advisable. **Map 15 H10.**

City

★ L'Anima
2009 WINNER BEST NEW ITALIAN RESTAURANT
2009 RUNNER-UP BEST NEW DESIGN
1 Snowden Street, EC2A 2DQ (7422 7000, www.lanima.co.uk). Liverpool Street tube/rail. *Bar* **Open/meals served** 9am-midnight Mon-Fri; 5.30-11pm Sat. *Restaurant* **Lunch served** 11.45am-3pm Mon-Fri. **Dinner served** 5.30-10.30pm Mon-Fri; 5.30-11pm Sat. *Both* **Main courses** £8.50-£28.50. **Set lunch** £23.50 2 courses, 26.50 3 courses. **Credit** AmEx, DC, MC, V.
Designed by architect Claudio Silvestrin, this classy operation features floor-to-ceiling windows, milky limestone floors, an onyx bar, square-shouldered white leather furniture, and monochrome settings – even the fresh-cut roses are white. Action in Francesco Mazzei's busy kitchen can be glimpsed through strips of glazing and a curved passageway leads round to the impressive wine cellar where guests can dine surrounded by fine Italian vintages. L'Anima (which means 'soul' in Italian) focuses on the cuisines of southern Italy and a corner of the menu helpfully offers definitions of speciality ingredients such as n'duja (spicy, spreadable salami) and stracci (an irregular pasta shape). Bread was served formally with a spoon and fork by the single slice – we could have done with some more alongside our starter of soft, creamy burrata cheese and wood-roast aubergine mash. Fresher-tasting mussels would have improved our fish stew with fregola, but its assertive sauce of dill, tomato and garlic worked brilliantly with the sea bass, prawns and clams. The kitchen is proud of its high-tech Josper charcoal oven; from this came dessert of apricots spiked with lavender – the effect was very herbal, but the big juicy fruit pieces, boozy sauce and ice-cream were luscious. We felt a little stranded at points during our meal and dishes didn't come quite as quickly as desirable at lunch. Overall, though, the concepts here are bold, and the execution slick.
Babies and children welcome: high chairs. Booking advisable. Disabled: toilet. Separate rooms for parties, seating 6-14. **Map 6 R5.**

Refettorio
Crowne Plaza Hotel, 19 New Bridge Street, EC4V 6DB (7438 8052, www.refettorio.com). Blackfriars rail. **Lunch served** noon-2.30pm Mon-Fri. **Dinner served** 6-10.30pm Mon-Thur; 6-10pm Fri, Sat. **Main courses** £11.50-£22. **Credit** AmEx, MC, V.
A real City slicker, this restaurant is housed (along with a hotel) behind the Grade II-listed façade of a grand old stationery warehouse. At lunchtime it's busy with a business clientele; evenings are quieter but attract a smattering of well-to-do hotel guests looking for simple Italian cooking and an early night. The warmly glossy wood interior, with savvy mix of refectory-style central table, booths and tables for two is inviting, so too the lengthy menu, which offers 15 starters and pasta dishes, and around ten mains. The latter tend towards the classic: calf's liver with spinach and balsamic, or roast lamb with peperonata. Fresh pasta is made in-house and is used in dishes such as salt cod ravioli and pennette with pork ragu. Our conchiglie (shell-shaped pasta) with mashed green pea sauce was given a salty lift with chunks of pancetta. Tiramisu with liquorice ice-cream sounded exciting but the parfait that arrived lacked substance. Much better was the coppa classica (vanilla, chocolate and choc-chip ice-creams topped with morello cherries), though the portion was not as bodacious as we remember from previous visits. The wine list features over 100 Italian bins. Keep an eye out for seasonal specials such as a white truffle menu.
Babies and children welcome: high chairs. Booking advisable. Disabled: lift; toilet. Separate room for parties, seats 30. **Map 11 O6.**

Terra Nostra
27 Old Bailey, EC4M 7HS (3201 0077, www.terranostrafood.co.uk). St Paul's tube. **Lunch served** noon-3pm Mon-Fri. **Dinner served** 6-10pm Mon-Fri, occasional Sat. **Main courses** £8.90-£16.90. **Credit** AmEx, MC, V.
Gutsy cooking with a Sardinian accent helps make this small Italian restaurant popular with City workers at lunchtime, when it's usually packed. The warm, rustic decor and smiling, friendly Italian staff proffering olives and pane carasau (the crisp Sardinian flatbread) create a holiday-like Mediterranean feel. Although several classic dishes – the likes of meat lasagne – have popped up on the menu, it's best to follow the lead of the many Italian regulars and opt for Sardinian dishes and wines, which are among the mainstays of Terra Nostra. The starter of calamari ripieni (baby squid filled with a dense sauce of squid meat, tomatoes and herbs) has been around since the restaurant's opening, and is deservedly popular. Another must-try is the traditional aromatic sausage, grilled over charcoal and presented in a coil. Malloreddus, the maggot-shaped Sardinian pasta, and spaghetti with bottarga (dried grey mullet roe) remain two of the best pasta options. The dessert list is less appealing, forsaking the numerous, delightful Sardinian pastries for a safer selection that includes the usual panna cotta, tiramisu and ice-cream.
Babies and children admitted. Disabled: toilet. Tables outdoors (10, pavement). **Map 11 O6.**

Covent Garden

Carluccio's Caffè
2A Garrick Street, WC2E 9BH (7836 0990, www.carluccios.com). Covent Garden tube. **Meals served** 8am-11.30pm Mon-Fri; 9am-11.30pm Sat;

Fratelli la Bufala

If you have been brought up and taught correctly, the benefits will always shine through. There's no better example of this than Mimo Rimoli, owner of South End Green's popular Fratelli la Bufala. Born in Pozzuoli, Naples (birthplace of Sofia Loren), the Italian was destined to make his mark in the restaurant world. While Mimo was growing into the man he is today, his family restaurant business was continuing to grow.

For 4 consecutive years now the restaurant has been nominated for the Archant Food and Drink Awards - this year 2009 having won the Italian category for the North of London. Nominations and shortlists have been received from The Evening Standard London Restaurant Awards.

Fratelli la Bufala is a brand that showcases the gastronomic heritage of Naples, using bufalo meat and mozzarella cheese. The bufalo meat is healthy, low in fat and beautifully tender. Whilst the acclaimed Fratelli la Bufala were springing up all over Italy, the rest of the world was taking notice. Mimo decided he would be the first to bring the family business to England.

Showing the same passion he has had for art and motorcycles, Mimo threw himself into creating a menu that showcased what Fratelli la Bufala was all about.

Lip-smacking bufalo fillets, sausages, mozzarella and authentic pizzas, all cooked in a traditional rural Italian way, with the emaphasis on quality and freshness. The weekly blackboard specials are innovative and creative offering free range cuts of meats - home made fresh pasta and freshly caught seasonal fish.

We now have a daily fish special with a list of seasonal fish dishes which are proving to be extremely popular. Choose from fresh sea bass and sea bream baked in the wood oven, king prawns, scallops and seared tuna or halibut steaks. Our fish menu sells quickly so booking is essential at the weekends and evenings. Famous in Italy for its family and group welcome the restaurant is now able to offer children's portions and cater for larger groups and outside functions.

Northwest London has some fantastic restaurants and it is places like Fratelli la Bufala that bring something different.

'Best Italian'

food & drink awards
ARCHANT LONDON

45a South End Road, NW3
www.fratellilabufala.com

020 7435 7814

9am-10.30pm Sun. **Main courses** £6.95-£13.95. **Set meal** (Mon-Fri) £9.95 2 courses, £12.95 3 courses. **Credit** AmEx, DC, MC, V.

Carluccio's products line the walls of its flagship Covent Garden branch. When we arrive ten minutes early for our booking, we're practically told off and sent to wait in the deli. After we're pointed to our table, a waiter dashes over to inform us there's a waiting list. Fortunately, things improve after these two false starts. The busy, noisy ambience here is lightened by bright and breezy furnishings: slate-blue booths, turquoise tiles and titchy tables for two. This is a speedy-turnover zone and no place for lingering. But that's fine, as the casual atmosphere is paired with on-the-ball service and food that's surprisingly good for a chain of such ubiquity (the empire extends to Dublin and Dubai). A ramekin of smooth chicken liver pâté was followed by spicy sausage penne – both simple dishes whose uncomplicated flavours made them easy to devour. A salad of pillowy mozzarella with a mix of oven-dried and fresh tomatoes, beefed up with fine focaccia, made a fresh, satisfying light meal. Fireworks are few, but Carluccio's delivers decent quality for its price bracket.
Babies and children welcome: children's menu; crayons; high chairs; nappy-changing facilities. Booking advisable pre-theatre. Disabled: toilet. Separate room for parties, seats 80. Takeaway service. **Map 18 D4.**
For branches see index.

Orso
27 Wellington Street, WC2E 7DB (7240 5269, www.orsorestaurant.co.uk). Covent Garden tube. **Meals served** noon-midnight daily. **Main courses** £8.50-£17. **Set meal** (5-6.45pm Mon-Sat) £16 2 courses, £18 3 courses incl coffee. **Credit** AmEx, MC, V.

Slick, suited and booted service gives a first impression of formality at Orso. However, this is countered by folksy hand-painted crockery and the ebullient chatter of the well-dressed continentals who fill the tables in this basement venue. The enduring popularity of the place slightly baffles us, as the food, though undoubtedly appetising and nicely presented, hardly merited a standing ovation on our visit, and some dishes were priced somewhat above their station. We resented paying £17 for some grilled calf's liver with broccoli and balsamic vinegar, and our £10.50 goat's cheese and grilled vegetable ravioli, though delicious and punchy with roast garlic, gone too soon – we wanted more. Of the starters, warm baby artichokes with roast tomato and mint were a little bland and weirdly textured, but the grilled sardine fillets with salsa rossa scored highly with their crisply grilled finish. Glasses of Puglian Salento

---

BEST ITALIAN

Vino italiano
Sample the best regional wines at **Alloro** (*see p165*), **Il Convivio** (*see p162*), **Enoteca Turi** (*see p172*), **Locanda Locatelli** (*see p165*), **Osteria dell'Arancio** (*see p172*), **Philpott's Mezzaluna** (*see p176*), **Ristorante Semplice** (*see p166*), **Riva** (*see p172*), the **River Café** (*see p171*) and **Zafferano** (*see p164*).

Alfresco dining
It's great outdoors at **La Collina** (*see p175*), **Manicomio** (*see p172*), **Marco Polo** (*see p174*), **Osteria dell'Arancio** (*see p172*), the **River Café** (*see p171*) and **Vineria** (*see p176*).

Meet the family
Children are welcome at **Carluccio's Caffè** (*see p162*), **La Famiglia** (*see p172*), **Jamie's Italian** (*see p176*), **Manicomio** (*see p172*), **Marco Polo** (*see p174*), **Philpott's Mezzaluna** (*see p176*) and **La Trattoria** (*see p174*).

---

negroamaro and Umbrian cabernet sauvignon (£8.50 and £7 respectively) were unremarkable, and we were left cogitating over whether to order pudding – although we fell for the blood-orange cake with vanilla sauce in a big way.
Babies and children welcome: booster seats. Booking advisable. **Map 18 E4.**

Fitzrovia

Latium
21 Berners Street, W1T 3LP (7323 9123, www.latiumrestaurant.com). Goodge Street, Oxford Circus or Tottenham Court Road tube. **Lunch served** noon-3pm Mon-Fri. **Dinner served** 6.30-10.30pm Mon-Fri; 6.30-11pm Sat. **Main courses** £12.50-£16. **Set lunch** £15.50 2 courses, £19.50 3 courses. **Set meal** £26.50 2 courses, £29.50 3 courses. **Credit** AmEx, MC, V.

Sited in a faceless Fitzrovia street opposite the glum façade of the Sanderson, this smart and inviting restaurant, with dark leather banquettes, mosaic walls and abstract art is a pleasant surprise. A well-heeled mixed clientele largely comprised those who worked nearby and the place was all but empty by the time we left at 10.30pm. An interesting menu betrayed a chef trying to move Italian food forward. A lavish platter of nibbles kept us happy while we scanned the menu. First courses of fiore de zucchini ripieno with Devon crab and broad bean sauce and pappardelle with wild boar ragout were both excellent. Mains of slow-cooked pork belly with savoy cabbage and balsamic vinegar, and fillets of red mullet wrapped with basil and lardo de colonnato, with sun-dried tomatoes and buffalo mozzarella sauce were superb, and the latter exquisitely presented. Rum baba with marsala sabayon and pistachio ice-cream, and white chocolate bavaroise with raspberry coulis and pistachio biscuit rounded off a memorable meal, but there was yet more delight in the chocolate petits fours that came with coffee.
Babies and children welcome: high chairs. Booking advisable weekend. **Map 17 A2.**

★ Sardo
45 Grafton Way, W1T 5DQ (7387 2521, www.sardo-restaurant.com). Warren Street tube. **Lunch served** noon-3pm Mon-Fri. **Dinner served** 6-11pm Mon-Sat. **Main courses** £8.90-£18. **Credit** AmEx, MC, V.

Sardo is a gem – step over its portals and you could be in Cagliari. The cues are all very subtle: the understatedness of the cosy interior, the precise tone of the deep-coloured walls, the simple, almost rustic furnishings, the quiet warmth of the welcome and unobtrusive attentiveness of the service, but above all, the freshness and quality of the inventive Sardinian food. Although tempted by the rarely-seen mosciame di tonno (sun-dried tuna fillet in thin slices) we opted for a simple and delicious tartara di tonno and an ambrosial broccoli and mussel soup to start. Main courses of grilled swordfish with rocket and tomatoes and a perfectly chillied crab linguine were both markedly fresh and brimming with flavour to match the bottle of full-flavoured almondy Vernaccia Karmis, a snip at £26. Not to have a pudding in such a comfortable environment would have been madness, and the brilliant panna cotta with fresh raspberries and the simplest but tastiest tortino de mele (apple tart) with cinnamon ice cream were the perfect finishing notes to a truly memorable meal. For two with service, reckon on spending just over £100, which for decent Italian restaurants is fairly standard – but Sardo itself is far from standard.
Babies and children admitted. Booking advisable. Separate room for parties, seats 36. Tables outdoors (4, patio). **Map 3 J4.**
For branch see index.

Knightsbridge

San Lorenzo
22 Beauchamp Place, SW3 1NH (7584 1074). Knightsbridge tube. **Lunch served** 12.30-3pm, **dinner served** 7-11pm Mon-Sat. **Main courses** £15.50-£28.50. **Cover** £2.50. **Credit** AmEx, MC, V.

Famed as a celeb hangout and favourite of Princess Diana, San Lorenzo tries to create an air of upmarket intimacy with its basement setting and mix of eclectic artwork, yet somehow remains safe and square. Food is trad Italian, with a tendency – on our most recent visit – to arrive in huge portions with slightly disconcerting haste. A starter of tuna carpaccio was a large plateful, swathed in rocket and diced tomatoes, and drowning in olive oil dressing, with the result that we couldn't discern any tuna flavour. Calamari fritti was similarly oversized, and rubbery: OK for a beach café, but not a dish for which you'd expect to pay £14.50. Things improved with a main course of rabbit, which had good depth of flavour and came in a rich jus; a big pool of buttery polenta was less appetising. Halibut alla griglia was an old-fashioned-looking assembly of fish, laid out alongside asparagus, a single white potato covered in dark-green bits of herb, and large sticks of plain boiled carrots; the fish was a little overcooked and lacking in flavour. Inflated prices added to our dissatisfaction; the halibut was £25.50. San Lorenzo does engender a slight sense of occasion, and staff were professional, but food was at best indifferent.
Available for hire. Babies and children welcome: high chairs. Booking advisable. Separate rooms for parties, seating 20-40. **Map 14 F9.**
For branch see index.

Zafferano
15 Lowndes Street, SW1X 9EY (7235 5800, www.zafferanorestaurant.com). Knightsbridge tube. **Lunch served** noon-2.30pm Mon-Fri; 12.30-3pm Sat, Sun. **Dinner served** 7-11pm Mon-Sat; 7-10.30pm Sun. **Main courses** £17-£29.50. **Set lunch** £29.50 2 courses, £34.50 3 courses, £39.50 3 courses. **Set dinner** £34.50 2 courses, £44.50 3 courses, £54.50 4 courses. **Credit** AmEx, DC, MC, V.

International modern in decor – pale walls, some in exposed brick, banquettes against smart wooden tables, and extravagant floral displays – this acclaimed restaurant can still produce the standard of food that made it famous back when Giorgio Locatelli was in the kitchen. It's a pity the stuffy Knightsbridge patrons can suck the life out of the place. The menu is also slightly dull. Starters included chilled tomato soup with tuna tartare and a langoustine risotto. We had a delicious buffalo mozzarella on grilled aubergine (though tomato would have been much nicer) and tagliolini with crab, courgettes and sweet chilli, which was surprisingly lacking in flavour. Main courses included roast sea bass with pesto and artichokes and ribeye with mushrooms. Roast Gressingham duck with honey and balsamic onions was superb, as was our calf's liver, although the latter seemed a rather mean portion. Worse was to come, however. To accompany the rest of our bottle of delicious Morellino di Scansano (£34.50), we shared a selezione di formaggi (with a £5 supplement it cost £15): it consisted of one almost wafer-thin slice of each of four cheeses, barely enough for one.
Babies and children welcome: high chairs. Booking essential. Dress: smart casual. Separate room for parties, seats 20. **Map 15 G9.**

Marble Arch

★ Trenta
30 Connaught Street, W2 2AF (7262 9623). Marble Arch tube. **Lunch served** 12.30-2.30pm Tue-Fri. **Dinner served** 6.30-10.30pm Mon-Sat. **Main courses** £5.90-£13.50. **Set lunch** £17.50 2 courses. **Credit** AmEx, MC, V.

This small, quietly inviting restaurant sits opposite the policed mews behind Tony and Cherie Blair's townhouse. On a summer evening the whole front window opens up, while pale walls and large mirrors accent the airiness. Pizzette bits, tasty olives and a nice selection of breads, delivered promptly and with charm, quickly made us feel welcome. From a well-judged selection of Italian and other wines we chose a trebbiano: delicious with starters of asparagus salad on a bed of lightly fried egg and a spaghetti vongole that would have been perfect had the abundant clams in their shells been properly

RESTAURANTS

Il Baretto

seasoned before cooking. These were followed by triangoli filled with porcini and white truffle in a meaty porcini broth, which was nice enough but could have benefited from a last-minute sprinkling of truffle oil, and a magnifico, meltingly textured lamb shank brimming with flavour. For dessert, crème brûlée with frutti de bosca was delightfully perfumed; mascarpone tart with ice cream was very good too. An appealing interlude during the meal was watching a quartet of local twenty-somethings arriving with plates in hand and trooping out with them piled with steaming food. Our bill (a model of clarity) was £79 for two without service.
Babies and children admitted. Booking essential Fri, Sat; advisable Mon-Thur. Separate room for parties, seats 12. **Map 8 E/F6**.

Marylebone

Il Baretto `NEW`

2009 RUNNER-UP BEST NEW ITALIAN RESTAURANT
43 Blandford Street, W1U 7HF (7486 7340, www.ilbaretto.co.uk). Baker Street tube. **Lunch served** noon-3pm, **dinner served** 6.30-11pm Mon-Sat. **Main courses** £10-£28. **Credit** AmEx, MC, V.
There is little to mark this neighbourhood trattoria as a restaurant from Arjun Waney, owner of slick Japanese establishments Zuma and Roka. The decor is subdued – black and white photographs, a bit of leather, a bit of pinstripe – though it's much smarter than the average local. At street level is a small reception area (the welcome was almost nonexistent, despite our booking), which leads down to a huge basement restaurant. At lunchtime the room wasn't packed but still had a lively atmosphere. The menu of classic Italian dishes is divided into bites to share, grill, oven and pasta dishes. Show-stopping scallops were so huge they needed carving and had just the right amount of lemony, buttery breadcrumbs. Also perfectly cooked was a generous piece of tuna, served with tomato and rocket. Toothsome gnocchi

with chives and cream of Sardinian cheese was just the right side of stodgy. From the predictable dessert list, we chose flourless chocolate cake, whose nod to modernity was being served on end: the sponge was exceptionally light yet deeply flavoured. When the rosé we ordered was unavailable, staff impressed by offering a more expensive Veneto wine at the same price, yet they also persuaded us to order an unnecessary side dish for the main courses.
Babies and children welcome: high chairs. Booking essential. Separate room for parties, seats 20. Tables outdoors (2, pavement). **Map 9 G5**.

Caffè Caldesi

118 Marylebone Lane, W1U 2QF (7935 1144, www.caldesi.com). Bond Street tube.
Bar **Open** noon-11pm Mon-Sat. **Lunch served** noon-3pm, dinner served 6-10.30pm Mon-Fri. **Meals served** noon-10.30pm Sat. **Main courses** £9-£16.
Restaurant **Lunch served** noon-3pm Mon-Fri. **Dinner served** 6-10.30pm Mon-Sat. **Main courses** £11.50-£21.
Both **Credit** AmEx, MC, V.
There are three strands to Giancarlo and Katie Caldesi's London operation: an informal bar-caffè on the ground floor, a smarter restaurant upstairs, and a cookery school in the mews round the back – and that's without the cooking holidays in Giancarlo's native Tuscany. Downstairs is the most lively: a warmly lit space filled with the clatter of cutlery. Antipasti platters, pasta dishes and a limited selection of meat main courses are served here. Several of these plates recur on the menu of the starched, professionally staffed first-floor restaurant, which attracts an older, more buttoned-up class of customer. The kitchen's output is pretty hard to fault, especially when it turns out confident dishes like raw sea bass, with a brininess tempered by refreshing orange and fennel slivers. More muscular flavours are just as well-executed, such as a rich calf's liver with the yielding texture of butter, draped languidly over a mound of spinach. Pasta dishes bear the melt-in-the-mouth, home-

style hallmark, so they can shine without much more adornment than a smattering of fresh fungi and cherry tomatoes. Capital dining then, even if the atmosphere is a little restrained upstairs.
Babies and children welcome: high chairs. Booking advisable (restaurant). Disabled: toilet (bar). Tables outdoors (6, pavement). **Map 9 G5**.

★ Locanda Locatelli `100`

8 Seymour Street, W1H 7JZ (7935 9088, www.locandalocatelli.com). Marble Arch tube. **Lunch served** noon-3pm Mon-Fri; noon-3.30pm Sat, Sun. **Dinner served** 6.45-11pm Mon-Thur; 6.45-11.30pm Fri, Sat; 6.45-10.15pm Sun. **Main courses** £24-£29.50. **Credit** AmEx, MC, V.
The decadent, almost louche 1970s atmosphere, the softly lit dining room and the almost pampering service may be a draw. But it's the spectacular cooking and astounding attention to detail that keep the booking lines busy here, and the dining room packed every day. The bread basket is so artfully presented that it often sends diners into raptured exclamations. Starters may include a wintry Lombardy dish of pork meatballs, called mondeghili, with savoy cabbage and saffron rice, or a more liberal interplay of flavours with pan-fried scallops, celeriac purée and saffron vinaigrette. Pasta is one of Locatelli's strengths, as shown by a simple dish of ricotta and spinach parcels with butter sage sauce: an Italian classic executed to perfection with the best ingredients available. Desserts are sublime, especially zingy eton mess made with Amalfi lemon cream and sorbet. The wine list matches the impressive menu, both in quality and cost, but there are several wines available by the glass, if the wallet can't stretch to the most prestigious options. Although it's easy to feel like lingering after such an outstanding meal, don't expect to be allowed to soak in the loungey atmosphere and indulge in people-watching; the two-hour time-slot policy is subtly enforced by the impeccably trained staff. And that's our only gripe about Locanda Locatelli.
Babies and children welcome: high chairs. Booking essential. Disabled: toilet. Dress: smart casual. **Map 9 G6**.

2 Veneti

10 Wigmore Street, W1U 2RD (7637 0789, www.2veneti.com). Bond Street or Oxford Circus tube. **Lunch served** noon-3pm Mon-Fri. **Dinner served** 6-10.30pm Mon-Sat. **Set meals** £16 1 course, £25 2 courses, £29 3 courses, £33 4 courses. **Credit** AmEx, MC, V.
The rustic brick walls and prints of Palladian villas give the game away; the food of Venice and its surrounding countryside is the forte here. But while 2 Veneti is popular with local office workers and other regulars, it is unlikely to attract homesick Venetians if the cooking remains as disappointingly uneven as it was on our visit. The kitchen can yield treats such as grilled polenta slabs topped with octopus in tomato sauce, and baccalà mantecato (cod purée) – just like the cicchetti (tapas-like snacks) found in Venetian wine bars. But at the same time it can also deliver a dismally chewy, woolly fritto misto. This selection of battered fried fish is one of the mainstays of Venetian cuisine and it's a shame a restaurant that prides itself on its origins should offer such a substandard version. We consoled ourselves with good battered deep-fried courgette sticks, another cicchetti staple, accompanying them with refreshingly dry prosecco. The textbook tiramisu here is not to be missed; along with the astounding selection of grappa and Veneto wines, and the friendly service, it helped lessen the disappointment of unfulfilled promises.
Available for hire. Babies and children admitted. Booking advisable. Tables outdoors (4, pavement). **Map 9 H5**.

Mayfair

Alloro

19-20 Dover Street, W1S 4LU (7495 4768, www.alloro-restaurant.co.uk). Green Park tube.
Bar **Open** noon-10pm Mon-Fri; 7-10pm Sat.
Lunch served noon-2.30pm Mon-Fri. **Dinner served** 7-10.30pm Mon-Sat. **Main courses** £12-£16.

Restaurant **Lunch served** noon-2.30pm Mon-Fri. **Dinner served** 7-10.30pm Mon-Sat. **Set lunch** £27 2 courses, £32 3 courses. **Set dinner** £29.50 2 courses, £35 3 courses, £39 4 courses. *Both* **Credit** AmEx, DC, MC, V.

This modish Italian gets things right, from the polished but friendly service, to the crisp, spare, modern surroundings – as well as where it counts most, on the plate. Alloro's menu changes frequently to showcase seasonal produce. On our spring visit, chicory had supporting roles in a starter of maltagliata (silky little pieces of hand-cut own-made pasta) served with mildly bitter trevisano leaves, tiny broad beans and cherry tomatoes, and in a main course of pan-fried cuttlefish. In the latter, three plump, very tender cephalopods, served on a dramatic square glass plate, were topped with chicory hearts, a mild anchovy dressing and a dusting of dried, crushed tomato skin. Equally accomplished was a starter of gnocchi with pesto (light-as-air potato dumplings bathed in an emerald-green sauce with al dente green beans adding crunch), and a main of sea bream with sautéed swiss chard and an earthy-tasting smooth chickpea velouté. The kitchen has a welcome lightness of touch, but at times this translates as timidity in the flavouring. The all-Italian wine list is strong on the white wines of Friuli and reds of Tuscany (including a whole page of expensive 'SuperTuscans'), but there's little below £35 per bottle.
Available for hire. Babies and children admitted. Booking advisable. Separate room for parties, seats 16. **Map 9 J7**.

Cecconi's

5-5A Burlington Gardens, W1S 3EP (7434 1500, www.cecconis.co.uk). Bond Street tube. *Bar/restaurant* **Breakfast served** 7am-noon Mon-Fri; 8am-noon Sat, Sun. **Meals served** noon-11.30pm Mon-Fri. **Brunch served** noon-5pm Sat, Sun. **Dinner served** 5-11.30pm Sat; 5-10.30pm Sun. **Main courses** £12-£28. **Credit** AmEx, MC, V.

Part of the Soho House group, and decorated in a stunning combination of green leather and black and white marble, Cecconi's flexible all-day dining offers something for everyone with the cash or credit rating to enjoy it. Mornings are as buzzing as the cocktail hour as people take advantage of one of the few quiet corners near Regent and Bond Streets for a coffee. Action is centred round a large square bar: take a seat here for coffee or drinks and nibbles, or book (well in advance) for one of the rear tables for dinner. Wines start at £18 for a cheerful bottle of trebbiano. The cicchetti (tapas-

like dishes of Venice) can make an appealingly light accompaniment, but while we applaud this stab at bringing one of the lesser-known aspects of Italian cuisine to London, none of those offered on our visit was particularly Venetian. Citrussy tasting meatballs with tomato sauce were fine; there was nothing special about chicken liver crostini topped with capers; best were courgette flowers stuffed with creamy cheese. From an intriguing carpaccio list, we chose lamb with rocket and pecorino, yet the dish that arrived lacked the anticipated wow-factor: perhaps its flavours were deadened by chilling. Opt for the generous plates of pasta, however, and you won't go far wrong.
Babies and children welcome: high chairs. Booking essential. Disabled: toilet. Dress: smart casual. Tables outdoors (10, terrace). **Map 9 J7**.

Murano NEW

2009 RUNNER-UP BEST NEW ITALIAN RESTAURANT

20-22 Queen Street, W1J 5PR (7592 1222, www.gordonramsay.com/murano). Green Park tube. **Lunch served** noon-2.30pm, **dinner served** 6.30-10.15pm Mon-Sat. **Set lunch** £25 2 courses. **Set meal** £55 3 courses, £75 tasting menu. **Credit** AmEx, DC, MC, V.

This handsomely formal room in pearly tones of cream, white and grey has fitted seamlessly into the Mayfair dining scene. Part of the Gordon Ramsay stable, the kitchen is overseen by Angela Hartnett. Things start well. Nibbles include a plate of fine charcuterie with lovely breads and a dish of Planeta olive oil from Sicily. Roast sea scallops, served with gnocchi, apple and cucumber chutney and iberico ham, were beautifully cooked. Tortelli, presented with a flourish of a white china dome, were filled with a terrific balance of light, creamy Sairass ricotta cheese and bitter chard leaves. Sweet things are the weak point, though. A predessert of myriad mini ice-cream scoops includes some flavours that are more curious than delicious. The haute cuisine styling of the rhubarb pudding, incorporating terrine, foam, sliced rhubarb and cream-filled cylinders made us long for something simpler; the regimented presentation of the chocolate mousse was better, but it was partnered with dry, disappointing sachertorte. And the little basket of fresh cherries that came with petits fours was appreciated more than the cheesy pesto flavour of the basil chocolates. On the plus side, staff are impressively aware of guests' needs and were prompt with every aspect of the meal. For those without an eye on the budget, the wine list is fun, with treats such as lagrein sold by the glass.

Babies and children welcome: high chairs. Booking essential; Fri, Sat dinner one month ahead. Disabled: toilet. Dress: smart casual. Separate room for parties, seats 12. **Map 9 H7**.

Ristorante Semplice

9-10 Blenheim Street, W1S 1LJ (7495 1509, www.ristorantesemplice.com). Bond Street tube. **Lunch served** noon-2.30pm Mon-Fri. **Dinner served** 7-10.30pm Mon-Sat. **Main courses** £18-£26.50. **Set lunch** £16 2 courses incl coffee, £22 3 courses incl glass of wine & coffee. **Credit** AmEx, MC, V.

In restaurant parlance, 'Mayfair Italian' often means overwrought, expensive food. Not so at Semplice, where, as the name suggests, simplicity wins out. The clean lines and polished surfaces of the restaurant are echoed in the dishes, served on plain white crockery. Quality of the ingredients, many of which are imported from Italy, is high. In late May, a gazpacho made with ripe San Marino tomatoes, with a few tender young peas and a drizzle of top-class olive oil, tasted of summer to come. A main of thyme-scented rabbit, the shoulder, rack and leg served three different ways, with glazed carrots and an earthy artichoke sauce, was the star dish. Grilled squid couldn't have been more tender, but the accompanying grated carrot was an odd choice for such a Mediterranean dish. Light, tender black squid-ink gnocchi topped with sautéed cuttlefish was artfully presented, with a dramatic chiaroscuro effect. Service is prompt and professional and the wine list has a great selection of Italian regional wines to suit various budgets. Three doors away is the less formal, less pricy Bar Trattoria Semplice, which has a similar approach to provenance and cooking, at rather more 'diffusion range' prices.
Babies and children admitted. Booking advisable. Disabled: toilet. Tables outdoors (4, pavement). **Map 9 H6**.

★ Theo Randall at the Intercontinental

1 Hamilton Place, Park Lane, W1J 7QY (7409 3131, www.theorandall.com). Hyde Park Corner tube. **Lunch served** noon-3pm Mon-Fri. **Dinner served** 5.45-11pm Mon-Sat. **Main courses** £24-£34. **Set lunch** £21 2 courses, £25 3 courses. **Credit** AmEx, DC, MC, V.

For someone who claims to hate formality and pretence, Theo Randall (former executive chef of the River Café, *see p171*) has chosen a strange place to open his own restaurant – a cavernous space on the ground floor of a Park Lane hotel. Modern art, brightly coloured glass and waiters' shirts, arctic mint chairs and creamy pompom flowers can't quite detract from the grace of the room and ceremony of service that the location demands. Yet the food can be wonderfully simple, and the set lunch is good value, offering such delights as organic egg frittata with chanterelles, ricotta and herbs. Meals begin with toasted focaccia and a chargrilled slice of bread with olive oil and seasoned tomatoes smeared over it. Ravioli erbette with sage was a good balance of creamy ricotta and delicate pasta parcels. A robust, smokily chargrilled organic steak topped with zingy verdant parsley and chilli paste was well worth its £4 supplement and came partnered with a succulent tangle of red pepper, courgette, aubergine and basil. For dessert, roast rhubarb with richly eggy vanilla ice-cream won out over soft chocolate cake or strawberry sorbet. We finished with tiny crisp biscotti, chocolate truffles and well-made Musetti macchiato served in decorative cups. The international wine list includes a strawberry-scented rioja rosé by the glass as well as Italian staples like Soave and Montepulciano.
Babies and children welcome: high chairs. Booking advisable. Disabled: lift; toilet. Dress: smart casual. Separate room for parties, seats 24. **Map 9 G8**.

★ Via Condotti

23 Conduit Street, W1S 2XS (7493 7050, www.viacondotti.co.uk). Oxford Circus tube. **Lunch served** noon-3pm Mon-Fri; 12.30-3pm Sat. **Dinner served** 5.45-10.30pm Mon-Sat. **Main courses** £16-£20. **Set meal** (lunch, 5.45-7pm) £14.50 2 courses, £18.50 3 courses; £27.50 3 courses. **Credit** AmEx, MC, V.

Murano

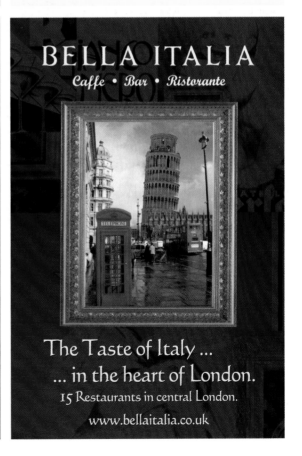

Make the most of London life

Named after the boutique-lined Roman street, and opposite Vivienne Westwood's store in an equivalent Mayfair location, Via Condotti is nevertheless a refreshingly unflashy restaurant. An understated interior of honey-coloured wood and 1930s posters set a tone of classic elegance rather than bling. Superb service extended to anticipating tap water refills. Food was near faultless, from the outstanding bread – carta di musica and focaccia, brown and white – through to the white and dark chocolate truffles that accompany espresso and make desserts almost superfluous. Only cavil: oversalted green beans. Although not a huge challenge to get right, artichoke salad with rocket, lamb's lettuce and pecorino was perfect. Poached egg on a purée of cannellini beans with a crisp pancetta hat on top was comfort at its classiest; the broached yolk made golden streaks in the smooth earthy bean base with pancetta providing contrasting salty crunch. Tagliolini with crab, chilli and the tiniest flecks of finely chopped parsley was made satisfyingly complete with cherry tomatoes. Three generous slices of calf's' liver on extremely creamy white polenta was gorgeous. The concise, but by no means pedestrian, pudding selection includes tiramisu and white chocolate mousse with lavender and caramelised orange zests. Simply excellent.

Babies and children admitted. Booking advisable. Separate rooms for parties, seating 18-35. Map 9 J6.

St James's

Franco's
61 Jermyn Street, SW1Y 6LX (7499 2211, www.francoslondon.com). Green Park tube. **Breakfast served** 7.30-11am, **lunch served** noon-2.30pm Mon-Sat. **Dinner served** 2.30-11pm Mon-Thur; 5.30pm-midnight Fri, Sat. **Main courses** £15-£26. **Set lunch** £20 courses, £25 3 courses, £30 4 courses. **Credit** AmEx, MC, V.
Franco's attracts an untrashy Euro crowd including businessmen, well-groomed young women who like the convenience of all-day dining and the odd film director. Inviting pavement tables, which bring a classy continental feel to traditionally English Jermyn Street, are most popular; there is also a relaxing café-bar and a more formal Italian restaurant next door. In the café-bar, where a long maroon banquette provides seating at a series of round dark wood tables, is a huge silver Taittinger champagne bucket, a glass dome protecting morning pastries, a little nude art, and copies of the *International Herald Tribune* and *Financial Times*. Staff hit the right balance of friendliness and correctness – happy to chat about the latest Jackie Collins novel, concerned how we wanted the house salad dressed, and whether the coffee should come before, with or after dessert. Fennel, green beans, tomato, red onion and pomegranate brought crunch and colour to the salad leaves. Lasagne, a popular order, arrived piping-hot in a square white ceramic baking dish – comforting layers of quality pasta, rich meat and creamy cheese. To finish, ginger panna cotta had an exquisite fusion flavour but even with its accompanying strand of pristine redcurrants seemed a meagre portion – perhaps not a problem in this part of town.
Available for hire. Babies and children welcome: booster seats; high chairs. Booking advisable Fri, Sat lunch. Disabled: toilet. Separate room for parties, seats 60. Tables outdoors (4, pavement). Vegetarian menu. Vegan dishes. Map 9 J7.

Luciano
72-73 St James's Street, SW1A 1PH (7408 1440, www.lucianorestaurant.co.uk). Green Park tube. **Lunch served** noon-3pm Mon-Fri; noon-2.30pm Sat. **Dinner served** 6-11pm Mon-Sat. **Main courses** £16.50-£28.95. **Set meal** £51 3 courses, £57 4 courses. **Credit** AmEx, MC, V.
The Italian job from Marco – half-Italian Yorkshireman and devillish overlord of TV's *Hell's Kitchen* – is bang in the middle of hedge fund country. The spacious, handsome art deco bar and restaurant look good but the timeless dignity is

Bocca di Lupo

spoiled (as a woman's appetite may be) by the work of Bob Carlos Clarke, photographer of MPW's glory days, of dominatrixes, overflowing bras and other soft pornish images not of the gastro variety. Location and taste in 'art' may explain why most diners are male. The cooking is classical Italian but not of the less-is-more persuasion; portions and presentation are anglicised and man-sized. In Italy such lavish slices of saltimbocca and correspondingly huge sage leaves probably wouldn't come draped over pommes purée. A zucchini fritti side order was unnecessary but still irresistible. Vitello tonnato, tender slices of veal and lots of them, in a not especially fishy sauce, had green beans and yellow endive thrown in. While the cooking's a shade the wrong side of maximum flavour, it is still satisfying and generously served. After being ignored at the bar, service turned matey in the restaurant. 'How's your wine?' the waiter popped up to ask.
Babies and children admitted. Booking advisable. Disabled: toilet. Map 9 J8.

Soho

Bocca di Lupo NEW
2009 RUNNER-UP BEST NEW ITALIAN RESTAURANT
12 Archer Street, W1D 7BB (7734 2223, www.boccadilupo.com). Piccadilly Circus tube. **Lunch served** 12.30-3pm, **dinner served** 5.30-11pm Mon-Sat. **Main courses** £8.50-£22. **Credit** AmEx, MC, V.
We've had mixed experiences at this bustling informal Italian. It's undoubtedly a welcome addition to Soho, with its lively open kitchen and tapas-style menu of regional specialities, drawing groups of friends, work colleagues and dating couples down this otherwise seedy street. A seat at the kitchen-side counter is something to prize, a fun setting in which to enjoy Jacob Kennedy's well-researched dishes and original creations (which are marked as such on the menu). Unfortunately, the cramped rear dining area has terrible acoustics, forcing everyone to shout when the room is full. Select one small dish from several different categories of the menu (raw and cured, fried, pastas and risottos, soups and stews, roasts, and so on) and you should enjoy a fairly balanced meal; for those who prefer not to share, large portions of each dish are also offered. We loved the truffle scent and crunchy texture of the radish and celeriac salad, but it was low on the promised pecorino cheese. Ewes' milk ricotta gnudi (large ball-shaped dumplings similar to gnocchi) were divinely light; squid with gremolata and deep-fried artichokes also could not be faulted. The long list of desserts is tempting, however our lumpen almond granita

was entirely the wrong texture and barely saved by its accompanying bitter chocolate sorbet.
Babies and children welcome: high chairs. Booking advisable. Disabled: toilet. Separate room for parties, seats 35. Map 17 B4.

Vasco & Piero's Pavilion
15 Poland Street, W1F 8QE (7437 8774, www.vascosfood.com). Oxford Circus or Tottenham Court Road tube. **Lunch served** noon-3pm Mon-Fri. **Dinner served** 5.30-10.30pm Mon-Sat. **Main courses** £9.50-£20. **Set lunch** £15 2 courses. **Set dinner** £26.50 2 courses, £31.50 3 courses; (5.30-7pm) £19.50 2 courses. **Credit** AmEx, MC, V.
This Soho stalwart has served up unfussy Umbrian dishes since 1971 (and in this location since 1989). It is convenient for pre-theatre fill-ups, but don't expect much privacy; the cramped tables are so closely packed, a meal here approaches communal dining. Like a reliable old uncle with no aspirations to modernity, the Pavilion seems content with its decidedly untrendy, old-school decor and workmanlike service. The menu changes twice a day. If you choose badly – as we did with a swordfish that was unevenly cooked and pink in places – it can seem overpriced. Dinner has a minimum spend of £26.50 for two courses, and the meat- or fish-based mains often need a side dish, which further raises the cost. The lunch menu is more flexible. Simple, unfussy dishes could include lamb steak with rosemary and cannellini beans, or grilled salmon on lentils. Plump, spinach-and ricotta-stuffed tortelloni was clearly made in-house, but was far from memorable, despite the addition of fragrant sage. Desserts are all-round crowd-pleasers such as chocolate fudge cake and straightforward panna cotta. In short, this is a trad Italian that could be a comforting fall-back were it less cramped and clamorous.
Booking advisable. Children admitted. Separate room for parties, seats 36. Map 17 A3.

South Kensington

Daphne's
112 Draycott Avenue, SW3 3AE (7589 4257, www.daphnes-restaurant.co.uk). South Kensington tube. **Lunch served** noon-3pm, **dinner served** 5.30-11.30pm Mon-Fri. **Meals served** noon-11.30pm Sat; noon-10.30pm Sun. **Main courses** £12.75-£26.50. **Set meal** (until 7pm) £16.50 2 courses, £18.50 3 courses. **Credit** AmEx, DC, MC, V.
Daphne's always makes visitors feel special, however busy it is – and usually it's very busy. Service is swift and immaculate, the décor grandly traditional, comforting and warm, with well spaced and dressed tables. The food is generally

RESTAURANTS

Daphne's. See p169.

good and the menu a nice mix of familiar and new. Mushroom risotto, for example. used girolles rather than porcini and tartare of veal (ethically raised) with shallots, capers and grilled focaccia was a joy. Main courses of calf's liver with pancetta and onions, and grilled cuttlefish with Calabrian sausage and garlic were just as they should be: the liver perfectly pink and the cuttlefish tender and smoky. The excellent side dishes are hard to refuse: zucchine fritte, say, olive oil mash or a bowl of green beans sprinkled with pecorino. To drink we ordered a 300ml carafe of fine Castel Firmian Mezzacorona chardonnay (£18). Desserts tend to be well-executed standards: a Jersey cream panna cotta with strawberries, and raspberries with zabaglione. With wine and service, three courses for two came to almost exactly £50 a head, but Daphne's also offers good-value set meals at lunch and dinner until 7pm (extended to all evening in July and August).

Babies and children welcome: high chairs. Booking advisable. Separate room for parties, seats 40. **Map 14 E10**.

Trafalgar Square

Obika

7 Northumberland Avenue, WC2N 5BY (3002 7400, www.obika.co.uk). Leicester Square tube. **Breakfast served** 7am-11am; **meals served** noon-11pm daily. **Main courses** £9-£16. **Credit** AmEx, DC, MC, V.

There were more staff than customers on our weekday lunchtime visit to Obika, a branch of the ritzy Italian mozzarella bar chain that stretches from Milan to Madison Avenue. This is a shame, as the venue is a useful, if pricey, addition to the district. Campania's famous buffalo-milk cheese being the speciality, the firm tries to get poncey about the types offered; pontina is stronger than paestum, but only the smoked variety has an assertive flavour. Unalluring blackboard specials seemed too similar to the regular menu, which offers pasta, antipasti and salads, as well as the cheese-plus-accompaniment blueprint. We opted for stracciatella di burrata (a very creamy, mild-tasting cheese), and caponata (Sicily's beloved sweet-sour vegetable casserole-cum-salad). The cheese arrived in two endive leaves shaped into a boat and accompanied by pane carasau bread, a few wrinkly black olives and a token salad. The latter was marred by bruised and browning baby spinach (unforgivable given salad ingredients form the crux of both menu and decor), but the caponata was delicious. The bread basket was a treat too. Praline semifreddo with deepest-dark chocolate sauce, and an extra-short smoky-tasting espresso finished the meal on a high.

Babies and children welcome: high chair. Booking advisable. Disabled: toilet. Takeaway service. Vegetarian menu. **Map 9 G6**. **For branch see index.**

Westminster

Osteria dell'Angolo NEW

47 Marsham Street, SW1P 3DR (3268 1077, www.osteriadellangolo.co.uk). St James's Park tube/88 bus. *Bar* **Open/snacks served** noon-11pm Mon-Fri; 6-11pm Sat. *Restaurant* **Lunch served** noon-2.30pm Mon-Fri. **Dinner served** 6.30-10.30pm Mon-Sat. **Main courses** £14.50-£26. **Set meal** £45 tasting menu. *Both* **Credit** AmEx, MC, V.

A welcome edition to Westminster's dining options, Osteria dell'Angolo is the newest opening from Claudio Pulze, who has been involved with some of London's most esteemed Italian restaurants. A limestone tile path leads from the entrance, past the bar, to the main dining area. A few Tuscan landscapes add colour, as does an open kitchen at back, but the decor is largely anodyne, which perhaps suits the lunch meetings likely to take place here. In contrast, the food tries too hard to be interesting. Deep-fried medallions of lamb on a raft of chopped aubergine and mint was very good, the red wine-flavoured bruschetta a reasonable partner, but the addition of dollops of horseradish

cream overpowered the sweet meat and resulted in too many competing flavours. Desserts continued the theme: truffle-like balls of honey rice mousse lacked sweetness and had a gelatinous coating that did nothing to enhance the flavour. Better was ice-cream coated in chocolate and nuts, served swimming in a bowl of grapefruit foam sprinkled with olive oil. Service is correct and friendly though we waited so long to be approached after dessert that we had to go and ask them for the bill.

Babies and children welcome: high chairs. Booking advisable. Disabled: toilet. Separate room for parties, seats 19. Tables outdoors (3, pavement). **Map 16 K10**.

Quirinale

North Court, 1 Great Peter Street, SW1P 3LL (7222 7080, www.quirinale.co.uk). St James's Park or Westminster tube. **Lunch served** noon-2.30pm Mon-Fri. **Dinner served** 6-10.30pm Mon-Sat. **Main courses** £12.50-£19. **Set meal** (lunch, 6-7.30pm) £19 2 courses, £22 3 courses. **Credit** AmEx, DC, MC, V.

Set in the vaultingly high basement of a Westminster house, this place obviously does well at lunch, packed with politicos and journos. In the evening, however, it feels more like the chic antechamber to a 1930s Ealing Studios evocation of heaven. An almost pathetically welcoming maître d' gushed us to our huge choice of table. He seemed the only person in the place with any command of English, or Italian. Ordering was a bit of a performance, with the young waiter walking off silently to the maître d' whenever posed with a question. The menu was brief but interesting, and our starters of crab gazpacho and bigoli with duck ragout came relatively swiftly and were excellent. A main course of pork saltimbocca was rather odd, with no evidence of any wrapping of ham. Guinea fowl stuffed with ricotta was tasty, but the stuffing added nothing to the dish. A rather fine licorice tiramisu and a substantial three-cheese Italian cheeseboard finished the meal on a high note. On arrival, one table of six had been making enough noise for the whole room, but when they left the silence felt awkward – underlining that lunch is the better time to visit if you're looking for a buzz.

Babies and children admitted. Booking advisable lunch. **Map 16 L10**.

West

Bayswater

★ Assaggi (100)

1st floor, 39 Chepstow Place, W2 4TS (7792 5501). Bayswater, Queensway or Notting Hill Gate tube. **Lunch served** 12.30-2.30pm Mon-Fri; 1-2.30pm Sat. **Dinner served** 7.30-11pm Mon-Sat. **Main courses** £18-£24. **Credit** MC, V.

This Notting Hill icon, a favourite of AA Gill and Michael Winner, fills the first floor of a Georgian terraced house above the Chepstow pub. The dining room is the 'first floor front', with tall French windows, a mere dozen wooden tables and a wooden floor, so it is clamorous when full – as it always is. Assaggi does seem, however, to be resting on its allori. The effusive greeting and uncompromising menu, both entirely in Italian, that once gave an exciting sense of place, now come across as affected and theatrical; the once brilliant Sardinian-inspired food tricksy and tired. A starter of perfectly seared scallops (rather measly) was swamped by an ill-judged, over-seasoned radicchio purée. Seppie con piselli was ho-hum, the cuttlefish slightly overcooked. The much-acclaimed fritto misto of seafood, sporting a single prawn as its non-fish element, although impeccably cooked, was again slightly mean, bulked out by being piled on a mound of shoestring potatoes that had been either overcooked or reheated so were tough. With service, expect to pay about £50 a head for two courses. Challenged to find fault with Assaggi, Winner was reported to have said: 'Not enough ice in the Coke, darling' – and our tepid sparkling water is a lingering memory of the meal.

Babies and children welcome: booster seats. Booking essential. **Map 7 B6**.

Hammersmith

★ The River Café (100)

Thames Wharf, Rainville Road, W6 9HA (7386 4200, www.rivercafe.co.uk). Hammersmith tube. **Lunch served** 12.30-5pm daily. **Dinner served** 7-11pm Mon-Sat. **Main courses** £12.50-£30. **Credit** AmEx, DC, MC, V.

Jam-packed even late on a Monday night, the River Café's popularity shows no sign of waning. Last year's refit has not transformed the winning formula, but there's now a bar near the entrance and the wood-fired oven has been made into a focal point – appropriate, given its output forms the crux of the menu's main courses: Dorset blue lobster with dried chilli and wild oregano, and whole dover sole flavoured with capers, lemon and summer savoury are typical. Bistecca fiorentina is a thick, smoky-tasting Aberdeen Angus steak chargrilled first then finished in the oven, served on our visit with a thick dollop of salsa verde and plump, rose-coloured fresh borlotti. Start, maybe, with the famous chargrilled squid with chilli and rocket, or mozzarella marinated in crème fraîche and herbs and served with olive bruschetta. A cheese room has been added, allowing a greater range of cheeses to be offered for those who like a savoury finish – such as an ewes' milk cheese plate, plus five artisan varieties from Sardinia and such regions as Veneto, Piemonte and Lombardy. Alternatively, valpolicella gives a grown-up edge to summer pudding, while for big kids there are big bowls of ice-cream (burnt caramel, straciatella). The wine list, and staff, are friendlier and more relaxed than those in many upmarket restaurants.

Babies and children welcome: high chairs. Booking essential. Disabled: toilet. Separate room for parties, seats 18. Tables outdoors (15, terrace). **Map 20 C5**.

Holland Park

Edera

148 Holland Park Avenue, W11 4UE (7221 6090). Holland Park tube. **Meals served** noon-11pm Mon-Fri; noon-10pm Sun. **Main courses** £15-£24. **Credit** AmEx, MC, V.

Bright, minimally styled Edera provides a haven from the busy traffic of Holland Park Avenue. Well-off locals come here for simple yet elegantly presented Italian fare with a Sardinian bent. Prices seem to have been tailored to the upmarket neighbourhood, with several prestigious bins on the wine list reaching the £600 mark, and a truffle degustation menu set at £100 a head. But choose from the specials menu, and the remarkable selection of wines by the glass, and the expense can be contained. Sea bream ravioli with creamy artichoke sauce came with a generous sprinkling of black truffle shavings; at £12 it was better value than simpler pasta dishes on the menu, which are similarly priced. The dessert selection spans the usual tiramisu and sorbets to a quirky concoction of hazelnut ice-cream and black truffle, which will set you back £20. If they're available, we recommend trying the exquisite sebadas: Sardinian cheese-filled puff-pastry parcels drizzled with honey. Service is attentive, but can be a bit sullen at times. Although Edera's pavement tables are very tempting in fine weather, they're only a few steps away from heavy, noisy traffic and exhaust fumes.

Available for hire. Babies and children admitted. Booking advisable. Separate room for parties, seats 24. Tables outdoors (4, pavement). **Map 19 B5**.

Kensington

Timo

343 Kensington High Street, W8 6NW (7603 3888, www.timorestaurant.net). High Street Kensington tube. **Lunch served** noon-2.30pm, **dinner served** 7-11pm Mon-Sat. **Main courses** £14.90-£21.95. **Set meal** (lunch, 7-8pm) £13.90 2 courses, £17.90 3 courses. **Credit** AmEx, MC, V.

Timo remains a popular lunchtime spot for locals and office workers, no doubt thanks to its set meals. These start at £13.90 for two courses and include a scrumptious bread basket. Soothing

RESTAURANTS

piped music, courtesy of Classic FM, also has an appeal. The menu is compact and offers the usual stalwarts of classic Italian cuisine, but this doesn't necessarily exclude more intriguing dishes. We opted for a spring-inspired lemon and courgette risotto, which had a perfect texture and a delicate, yet zingy flavour. It was a pity that it arrived on a large, glass plate, instead of in a more traditional bowl, which would have kept the rice warm for longer. The dessert list seems fairly limited and uninspiring, except for a selection of Italian cheeses served with own-made walnut bread, which attracts a £3 surcharge. Surcharges are common and can easily bump up the final bill here. We also thought £3.50 for an espresso a bit steep for a neighbourhood restaurant, even given that the neighbourhood is Kensington. Service remains friendly and solicitous, and the ambience is serene and classy.
Available for hire. Babies and children admitted. Booking advisable. Separate room for parties, seats 18. **Map 13 A9.**

Ladbroke Grove

Essenza

210 Kensington Park Road, W11 1NR (7792 1066, www.essenza.co.uk). Ladbroke Grove tube. **Meals served** noon-11.30pm daily. **Main courses** £15.50-£19.80. **Set lunch** (Mon-Fri) £13 2 courses. **Credit** AmEx, MC, V.
Opposite its sibling Italian restaurant Mediterraneo, just off the Portobello Road, tiny Essenza feels like it's glaring balefully at its brash big sister. But an intimate setting and understated modern decor are part of its charm. In the evening sun, we took a table just inside the restaurant, where a breeze and open french windows let us people-watch in the best Italian style. Service was the right side of leisurely to allow this, and staff were friendly and efficient. So, with everything nicely set up, would the food deliver? It did, but intermittently. Veal in lemon sauce, and squid in a tomato sauce, were robust and generous, and benefited from a side order of light, crispy battered courgettes. A bowl of plump, orange mussels was perfect. But why put bland tomatoes, rubbery mozzarella and a measly limp basil leaf in a classic salad where the ingredients are everything? And why have five veal dishes on a small à la carte menu? Still, the fish selection is strong, and desserts – the likes of panna cotta and affogato – are pleasingly authentic. A decent wine list and excellent espresso convinced us that Essenza has nothing to feel small about.
Babies and children welcome: children's menu; high chairs. Booking essential Fri, Sat. Tables outdoors (2, pavement). **Map 19 B3.**
For branches (Mediterraneo, Osteria Basilico) see index.

Olympia

Cibo

3 Russell Gardens, W14 8EZ (7371 6271/2085, www.ciborestaurant.co.uk). Sloane Square tube, then 22 bus. **Lunch served** noon-2.30pm Mon-Fri, Sun. **Dinner served** 7-11pm Mon-Sat. **Main courses** £10.50-£23.50. **Set lunch** (Mon-Fri) £17.50 2 courses; (Sun) £19.50 2 courses, £24.50 3 courses. **Credit** AmEx, MC, V.
Don't be fooled by the truly terrible 3-D 'art' featuring buxom women on the walls, and the cartoonish giant earthenware platters on the tables. This delightful Italian restaurant offers some seriously good food, most of it fish- and shellfish-based, expertly cooked, well-presented, and professionally served by smiling staff. What impresses most is the quality of the ingredients: a mozzarella starter was melt-in-the-mouth creamy; clams were small but intense in flavour, lending spaghetti frutti di mare a truly evocative taste of southern Italy. There's a pleasing selection of pastas here, along with fish dishes and a handful of meat main courses to appease omnivores. Top of the range is a mixed seafood grill boasting half a lobster, various other shellfish, squid and octopus – all of it tender and succulent enough to leave an exquisite juice, ideal

for mopping up with the restaurant's bread, which came piled high. Desserts were as colourful and much better looking than the art, and house wine at £14.50 was highly drinkable. Coffee, served with pretty petits fours, left us feeling we'd been to Italy and back in two short hours.
Babies and children welcome: high chairs. Booking advisable dinner. Separate rooms for parties, seating 12-16. Tables outdoors (4, pavement).

South West

Barnes

Riva (100)

169 Church Road, SW13 9HR (8748 0434). Barnes or Barnes Bridge rail/33, 209, 283 bus. **Lunch served** 12.15-2.15pm Mon-Fri, Sun. **Dinner served** 7-10.30pm Mon-Sat; 7-9pm Sun. **Main courses** £13-£24. **Credit** AmEx, MC, V.
This much-loved restaurant attracts crowds of plummy locals and is often full, even midweek. It can't be the decor, which is bland to the point of anonymity and dimly lit, though a mirror along one wall helps enlarge the small room, and flowers add colour. It's partly the service – deft, informative and attentive (especially to regulars) – but it's mainly the food, which is generally excellent. The menu changes little, offering classic dishes and specialities from owner Andrea Riva's home of Lombardy, plus daily specials (starter, fish, meat, pasta). Keeping it simple pays dividends; we've yet to meet anyone who isn't wowed by the grilled baby squid, served in their own juices with a big pile of flash-fried wild herbs. Similarly, crab ravioli was a fuss-free delight: perfectly al dente parcels of pasta stuffed with the freshest crab meat, in a creamy, delicate sunflower-yellow sauce. More complicated was roast best end of lamb with roast potatoes, peperonata and pecorino; the meat was fantastically tender but overpowered by its mustard-mint sauce. The all-Italian wine list and lengthy dessert menu (ice-creams and sorbets feature heavily) round off an experience that can be short on atmosphere but is usually high on culinary pleasure.
Babies and children welcome: high chairs. Booking essential dinner. Tables outdoors (3, pavement).

Chelsea

Manicomio

85 Duke of York Square, SW3 4LY (7730 3366, www.manicomio.co.uk). Sloane Square tube. *Deli* **Open** 8am-7pm Mon-Fri; 10am-7pm Sat; 10am-6pm Sun.
Restaurant **Lunch served** noon-3pm Mon-Fri; noon-5pm Sat, Sun. **Dinner served** 6.30-10.30pm Mon-Sat; 6.30-10pm Sun. **Main courses** £16.50-£22.50.
Both **Credit** AmEx, MC, V.
From spring to autumn, well-heeled locals in the know seem to book Manicomio's solid alfresco tables overlooking the Duke of York Square shopping precinct, leaving the main dining room to late-comers. The extensive terrace, not to mention the numerous patio heaters, helps create the impression of being on holiday in Italy, just a stone's throw from the manic King's Road traffic. The menu comprises several 'safe' modern Italian dishes that make liberal use of Mediterranean ingredients such as capers, olives and fresh herbs. The own-made pastas are a popular option, their appeal often surpassing that of the more aspirational, yet less remarkable, main courses. We were won over by silky pappardelle with creamy yet gutsy artichoke sauce, but less so by a much blander dish of monkfish with courgettes, rosemary and chilli. If it's available, chocoholics shouldn't miss the hot chocolate fondant served with pistachio ice-cream. Service can be confused at times, and the staff quite aloof. The deli-cum-café next door offers simpler fare as well as a selection of Italian ingredients for sale. A new branch has opened in the City.
Babies and children welcome: booster seats. Booking advisable. Separate room for parties, seats 30. Tables outdoors (30, terrace). **Map 14 F11.**
For branch see index.

Osteria dell'Arancio

383 King's Road, SW10 0LP (7349 8111, www.osteriadellarancio.co.uk). Sloane Square tube, then 22 bus. **Lunch served** noon-3pm Tue-Sun. **Dinner served** 6.30-11pm Mon-Sat. **Main courses** £13.50-£16.50. **Credit** AmEx, DC, MC, V.
A gloriously boho restaurant on the World's End edge of Chelsea, with mismatched wooden, painted tables, art on the walls, old crockery and coloured glassware, Osteria dell'Arancio is serious but not sombre about its food. The cooking is simple, bright and bold, rustic yet contemporary. Starters shone on a recent visit: grilled squid was softly charred perfection, drizzled with best oil and a sharp, tiny drop of balsamic, and served with a courgette flower stuffed with ricotta. Scallops were just as good, served with orange slices and an orangey jus that perfectly matched the delicate flavours. We ate on the roadside front terrace, which was very pleasant on a warm summer evening. For mains, a veal chop with rosemary and olives was cooked to perfection and full of herby flavour. Turbot was the only dish that seemed a little lacking; perhaps the quiet taste of the fish was slightly overwhelmed by its strongly herbed tomato and olive sauce. A dish of roasted potato slices transformed it – making a great foil for the sauce – but had to be ordered separately. We couldn't resist chocolate soufflé, and it lived up to expectations, oozing chocolate and served with vanilla-specked ice-cream – fantastic.
Babies and children welcome: high chairs; nappy-changing facilities. Booking advisable. Disabled: toilet. Separate room for parties, seats 35. Tables outdoors (12, terrace). **Map 14 D12.**

Fulham

La Famiglia

7 Langton Street, SW10 0JL (7351 0761/7352 6095, www.lafamiglia.co.uk). Sloane Square tube then 11, 22 bus/31 bus. **Lunch served** noon-3pm, **dinner served** 7-11.30pm daily. **Main courses** £8.50-£26. **Cover** £1.85. **Minimum** £18.50 dinner. **Credit** AmEx, MC, V.
Walking into this World's End institution is like entering a time warp. You get the feeling that very little has changed in decades. La Famiglia is owned by Alvaro Maccioni, who has been overseeing the white-tiled dining room (its walls hung with family portraits) since the mid 1970s. Scrupulously polite, white-jacketed waiters, breadsticks wrapped in plastic, and a dessert trolley laden with profiteroles and fruit salad are anachronistic in today's trend-centred London restaurant scene. Much of the Tuscan-influenced menu seems little-changed too. This is one of the few places in London to serve the classic bistecca alla fiorentina, a massive T-bone steak for two, made here from organic Chianina beef, cooked over charcoal and served 'rare only'. The weekly specials list is where to look for seasonal dishes such as deep-fried baby artichokes, tender-hearted in their crisp batter. A starter of puréed chickpeas with tuna, red onion and salad leaves was simplicity itself, but breast of duck, served rare with a sauce made of vin santo (a dessert wine that's a speciality of Tuscany), was too sweet for our taste. As you'd expect given the posh postcode, the prices aren't cheap, but the solicitous service and friendly atmosphere ensure continued loyal custom.
Available for hire. Babies and children welcome: high chairs. Booking advisable dinner & Sun. Separate room for parties, seats 20. Tables outdoors (30, garden). **Map 13 C13.**

Putney

Enoteca Turi

28 Putney High Street, SW15 1SQ (8785 4449, www.enotecaturi.com). Putney Bridge tube/Putney rail/14, 74, 220, 270 bus. **Lunch served** noon-2.30pm, **dinner served** 7-11pm Mon-Sat. **Main courses** £10.50-£20.50. **Set lunch** £15.50 3 courses. **Set dinner** (Mon-Thur) £25.50 3 courses. **Credit** AmEx, DC, MC, V.

Fanatical About Fish

PESCATORI CHARLOTTE STREET
57 CHARLOTTE STREET, LONDON W1
T: 020 7580 3289 F: 020 7580 0539

OPENING TIMES:
LUNCH: MONDAY TO FRIDAY 12.00PM - 3.00PM
DINNER: MONDAY TO SATURDAY 6.00PM - 11.00PM

PESCATORI DOVER STREET
11 DOVER STREET, MAYFAIR, LONDON W1
T: 020 7493 2652 F: 020 7499 3180

OPENING TIMES:
LUNCH: MONDAY TO FRIDAY 12.00PM - 3.00PM
DINNER: MONDAY TO SATURDAY 6.00PM - 11.00PM

ZUPPA • ANTIPASTI • PASTA • RISOTTI • PESCE • CROSTACE
PIATTA FREDDI • CARNI • DOLCI • GELATI • FORMAGGI • CAFF

It's easy to walk straight past Enoteca Turi; its unimposing frontage gets lost among the hurlyburly at the river end of Putney High Street. But it would be a shame to miss it, as it offers a consistently high-quality dining (and drinking) experience. Set up and run for many years by Giuseppe Turi, it's a polished operation that pitches itself just right for its well-to-do local clientele. The long space, all earthy Tuscan tones, crisp white tablecloths, pale floorboards and soft lighting, is divided into three, providing a sense of intimacy wherever you're seated. Courteous, well trained and knowledgeable staff add to the feeling that you're in capable hands. Oenophiles have nothing but praise for the mammoth Italian wine list, one of the best in the capital, with plenty of choice at all price points. But novices don't need to feel daunted; wine pairings are suggested for each dish on the menu. The hearty regional cooking impresses. A main of tender rabbit (roasted and braised, off the bone) was a particular highlight, the gamey meat well matched with the powerful flavours of turnip tops, broccoli, sun-dried tomato and taggiasche olives. Broccoli also turned up in a lip-smacking starter of own-made orecchiette with garlic and chilli. Creamy, vanilla-speckled panna cotta – with just the right amount of wobble – provided a soothing finish.

Babies and children welcome: high chairs. Booking advisable. Disabled: toilet. Separate room for parties, seats 18.

Marco Polo

6-7 Riverside Quarter, SW18 1LP (8874 7007, www.marcopolo.uk.net). East Putney tube. **Meals served** noon-11pm Mon-Thur; noon-11.30pm Fri, Sat; noon-10.30pm Sun. **Main courses** £7.50-£21.50. **Set lunch** £9.95 1 course, £11.95 2 courses. **Credit** MC, V.

This is very much a place to lunch on a summer's day. Part of a new development off the Putney Bridge Road, it has extensive multi-level outdoor terraces with smart canopies, pretty planting and views across the river. Local friends and online comments had led us to rein in expectations as to service and quality of food, but we were pleasantly surprised by both. Despite a huge party arriving to fill a long table near ours, we had nothing but the most attentive friendly service throughout. Our starters were a totally delicious calamari fritti and a carpaccio cipriani, the latter very attractively plated, with a tent of parmesan shavings keeping the tasty beef slices cool. Spaghetti granchio (with crab) was pretty good but, although perfectly pleasant, the saltimbocca alla romana was distinctly odd, not tasting much like veal and with no evidence of sage or parma ham. Crespelle marco polo (crisp pancakes filled with mascarpone, chocolate, crushed amaretti and Tia Maria) and a quite perfect crème brûlée, together with the last glass of our Rovereto Gavi (£27), finished our Thameside reverie on a high note. Keep an eye out for attractive discounts offered online.

Babies and children welcome: children's menu; high chairs. Booking advisable. Separate room for parties, seats 60. Tables outdoors (60, terrace).

South
Clapham

La Trattoria

36A Old Town, SW4 0LB (7627 1166, www.moolirestaurant.com). Clapham Common tube. **Meals served** 11am-4pm Tue-Fri; 10am-4pm Sat, Sun. **Dinner served** 6.30-11pm daily. **Main courses** £12.95-£14.50. **Set lunch** £10 2 courses. **Credit** AmEx, MC, V.

What used to be Mooli now calls itself La Trattoria, but it's all the same to most diners. This is an accommodating local with delightful staff, pavement seating and a front that opens up to catch the breezes on summer evenings. With its banquettes and cushions, cocktails and mood music, it's a relaxing, all-day venue that covers many bases, offering startlingly un-European brunches as well as reassuringly Italian dinner staples. Our choices from a short, seafood-heavy Sicilian-influenced menu included a prettily presented pomodoro di mare (a tomato stuffed with sautéed courgettes and shrimps, wearing a king prawn as a hat), and a less nicely arranged but splendid crostini with minced mushrooms and cherry tomatoes. Impeccable thinly sliced lamb's liver with creamy mash and pancetta earned much praise too. Our other main, a highly cheesed risotto of disturbing pallor, appeared as an unappetising splat on a plate; it would have benefited from some modicum of colour or garnish. Appetites returned for an oozingly delicious cioccolata fondente for pudding. A fine trat, despite the splat.

Babies and children welcome: children's menu; high chairs. Booking advisable. Tables outdoors (5, pavement). **Map 22 A1.**

South East
Tower Bridge

Tentazioni

2 Mill Street, SE1 2BD (7237 1100, www.tentazioni.co.uk). Bermondsey tube/London Bridge tube/rail. **Lunch served** noon-2.45pm Mon-Fri. **Dinner served** 6.30-10.45pm Mon-Sat. **Main courses** £12.25-£20.50. **Set lunch** £11.95 2 courses incl drink, £15 3 courses incl drink & coffee. **Set dinner** £41.50 tasting menu (£63 incl wine). **Credit** AmEx, MC, V.

Despite its door being hidden in a Bermondsey alleyway, Tentazioni has gathered a following of faithful regulars, who ensure its strikingly decorated dining room is often fully booked at weekends. It's easy to see why: the menu offers bold dishes that veer from tradition with quirky combinations, rarely missing the mark, while the ambience feels almost decadent, aided by a red and plum colour scheme and charming, almost pampering service. The delicate, marine flavour of black tagliolini with crab meat was heightened by tangy saffron sauce; and guinea fowl-filled ravioli, prepared with flour made from chickpeas rather than the more usual wheat, was a gutsy starter. On the other hand, beef fillet with blue buffalo cheese was one of the kitchen's rare misses (having mismatched, over-the-top flavours, despite the otherwise perfect execution and the prime meat cut). A light, crumbly millefeuille pastry with zabaglione and strawberries was just one of the highlights of the dessert menu. Vegetarians are also well catered for, with suitable dishes clearly highlighted on the menu.

Available for hire. Babies and children admitted. Booking advisable Fri, Sat dinner. Separate room for parties, seats 24. **Map 12 S9.**

East
Shoreditch

★ Fifteen

15 Westland Place, N1 7LP (0871 330 1515, www.fifteen.net). Old Street tube/rail.
Trattoria **Breakfast served** 7.30am-11am Mon-Sat; 8-11am Sun. **Lunch served** noon-3pm Mon-Sat; noon-3.30pm Sun. **Dinner served** 6-10pm Mon-Sat; 6-10.30pm Sun. **Main courses** £14-£21.
Restaurant **Lunch served** noon-3pm daily. **Dinner served** 6.30-9.30pm Mon-Thur, Sun; 6-9.30pm Fri, Sat. **Main courses** £17.50-£23. **Set lunch** (Mon-Fri) £22.50 2 courses, £25 3 courses. **Set dinner** £60 tasting menu. *Both* **Credit** AmEx, MC, V.

The popularity of Jamie Oliver's first-born – and, lest we forget, charitable – restaurant has shown no signs of abating since its genesis in 2002. This remains a destination for youthful diners, who don't hold back on photo-snapping inside and outside the inconspicuous venue. Consequently, there's a distinctly casual feel to the joint, with jeans in evidence both in the designer-rustic trattoria and the more expensive basement restaurant (splashed with trademark fuchsia colouring). Dining downstairs offers a hip sense of occasion, especially when sampling a succession of show-off creations on the tasting menu. Seasonality is a strong consideration, as is considered sourcing, from Italy and across Britain. The advent of Jersey Royals in May might prompt the showcasing of asparagus and even ale from the isle. The menu is somewhat mongrel, then, but

Osteria dell'Angolo. See p171.

most agreeable, and enthusiastically promoted by an international crew of waiting staff. Lesser-known dishes are all the more alluring for it. Piadina, a chickpea-flour pancake filled with goat's cheese, was kept fresh (rather than overpowering) by spinach and that asparagus, and sprinkled with a dainty topping of diced olives and seasonal leaves. Perfect spring fare, though the punchy flavours of toothsome pork belly served on pistachio- and anchovy-spiked lentils were just as pleasing. Charitable enterprises are rarely so pulled-together.
Babies and children welcome: high chairs. Booking essential restaurant. Disabled: toilet (trattoria). **Map 6 Q3.**

Lena NEW

66 Great Eastern Street, EC2A 3JT (7739 5714, www.lenarestaurant.com). Old Street tube/rail. **Bar Open** noon-midnight Mon-Sat; 5.30-10.30pm Sun. *Restaurant/bar* **Lunch served** noon-3pm Mon-Sat. **Dinner served** 6-11pm Mon-Sat; 6-10.30pm Sun. **Main courses** £12-£21. **Set meal** (Mon-Thur) £19.95 3 courses.
Both **Credit** AmEx, MC, V.
Lena sets out to deliver a contemporary take on trattoria cooking. It starts with the look: white leather sofas, pea-green banquette seating, curvy white plastic chairs, white drapes, grey-green walls. It looks rather ethereal, and special. On a recent visit the food was exceptional. We particularly liked the contrast between the delicate and the robust. A starter of sea bream carpaccio exemplified the former; translucent slices of bream with paper-thin slivers of fennel was a fairy-light combination. Warm salad of steamed octopus, potatoes and roast red peppers was altogether different: gorgeous soft squidgy octopus, potatoes and peppers a good foil, in a lemony dressing – full of robust flavour. To follow, tagliolini alle vongole (clams in white wine sauce with garlic and chilli) was a classic dish in which the flavour-bar had been raised several notches. Calf's liver was lightly cooked on the chargrill (giving a great texture), served with fennel and roast tomatoes – more strong, successful tastes. Puddings are a highlight. Dark chocolate truffle torte was dense, almost hard, but it was the sorbet that blew us away – sweet, but with a delicate kick, hinting of tinned mandarins (in a good way). Add friendly, informal but knowledgeable service and you have a great restaurant experience.
Babies and children welcome: high chairs. Booking advisable. Entertainment: jazz 9pm Fri, Sat. Tables outdoors (6, pavement). **Map 6 R4.**

North

Archway

★ 500 Restaurant

782 Holloway Road, N19 3JH (7272 3406, www.500restaurant.co.uk). Archway tube/ Upper Holloway rail. **Lunch served** noon-3pm Tue-Sat. **Dinner served** 5.30-10pm Tue-Sun. **Main courses** £7.40-£13.50. **Credit** MC, V.
When was the last time the bill was less than you expected? Named after the Fiat Cinquecento, not its address, the equally dinky No.782 puts the 'low' in the Holloway Road in the best possible way. The kitchen's as keen as mostarda di frutta, and so are prices, starting with Italian wines for less than £4 a glass; nibble the crunchy deep-fried ravioli filled with cheese and mint while sipping a glass of Sardinian vermentino. From the kitchen come enticing smells of dishes, often southern Italian, cooked to order before arriving piping hot. That sweet, sharp aroma is the caponata, an aubergine-rich relish with a celery crunch accompanying a stunning, pink-inside veal chop smothered in oregano and rosemary. Gnocchi is a speciality; the feather-light little pillows often come with a slightly spicy sausage, tomato and fennel sauce. Classic desserts like tiramisu or panna cotta are definitive versions: the latter with a crunchy topping of chopped pistachios and intense strawberry sauce. The chef and manager

co-owners have good Italian restaurant pedigrees, yet service gives the impression of a friends- or family-run affair. At the end of the evening the faint whiff of bleach as the chefs scrubbed down was a reassuring sign of a hard-working kitchen with a lot of poke for its size.
Babies and children admitted. Booking essential dinner. **Map 26 C1.**

Camden Town & Chalk Farm

Caponata NEW

3-7 Delancey Street, NW1 7NL (7383 7808, www.caponatacamden.co.uk). Camden Town tube. *Osteria/bar* **Meals served** 9.30am-11pm Mon-Sat; 10am-10.30pm Sun. **Main courses** £7-£13. **Set meal** £11 2 courses, £15 3 courses. *Restaurant* **Dinner served** 6-11pm Tue-Sat. **Main courses** £14-£18.
Both **Credit** AmEx, MC, V.
Part of the Forge music venue, which showcases jazz-oriented music in premises next door, Caponata consists of a first-floor restaurant, plus an osteria and bar on the ground floor. They are attractive Scandinavian-style spaces: a two-storey interior wall has been planted with ferns and creepers to create a stunning, green living wall; another wall of wooden planks is a partition that can be folded back for concerts. As well as serving up mainly Sicilian flavours in good-value set meals (caponata and bruschetta, say, for starters, perhaps followed by squid ink tagliatelle or risotto), the Osteria also hosts occasional concerts. The upstairs restaurant is a little more formal. Here, starters might include Sicilian tuma cheese with pears, red chard and rocket or baby squid filled with pecorino cheese, pine nuts and parsley in a tomato sauce. Pastas with a Sicilian slant might include oven-baked anelletti with sardines, with pine nuts, fennel and a saffron sauce, while mains could be the likes of grilled swordfish or rack of lamb with olive tapenade and rosemary potatoes. Puddings include some unusual combinations, such as Sicilian lemon tart with a prickly pear sorbet, and a pistachio panna cotta with a jasmine coulis.
Babies and children welcome: children's menu (brasserie); crayons; high chairs; nappy-changing facilities. Booking adivisible. Disabled: lift; toilet. Separate rooms for parties, seating 30-50. Tables outdoors (5, pavement). Takeaway service. **Map 3 H/J 1.**

La Collina

17 Princess Road, NW1 8JR (7483 0192). Camden Town or Chalk Farm tube. **Lunch served** noon-3pm Sat, Sun. **Dinner served** 6.30-11pm daily. **Main courses** £10-£15. **Credit** AmEx, MC, V.
The folks on Primrose Hill love La Collina. Blow-ins are greeted as warmly as regulars and, with a massive plate of green olives ready on the table, the cheesy-as-Dolcelatte sound of 'That's Amore' seemed forgiveable. Especially as there were smooching lovers, a lone diner, an elderly couple, family groups and friends (whose request to merge tables was willingly granted) among the customers in the plain ground floor room hung with local artists' work. Spot-on starters – melt in the mouth marinated raw tuna with fennel, tomatoes, thyme and capers and tender, sweet and smoky grilled squid – were swiftly brought up via a spiral staircase from the kitchen below where there are less sought-after tables and a lovely garden. Dishes are attributed to different regions of Italy, but the emphasis is more to the north and on fish. Mezzelune nere – half moon black pasta parcels filled with sweet briney crab with a vibrant, herby tomato sauce – confirmed that seafood is a forte. Despite another lively tomato sauce with olives and capers the firm white flesh of a farmed, slow-cooked rabbit was flavourless. Occasional disappointing dishes apart, La Collina has some great attributes: friendly staff, a good heart and generosity of spirit.
Babies and children admitted. Booking advisable. Separate room for parties, seats 16. Tables outdoors (14, garden). **Map 27 B2.**

Interview
ANDREW AND NINAI ZARACH

Who are you?
Owners of **Manicomio** (*see p172*) restaurants and delicatessens in Duke of York Square and on Gutter Lane near St Paul's Cathedral.
How did you start in the catering business?
We started our business basically with a bottle of olive oil, which was pressed on the farm we used to own in Tuscany; that created the birth of our distribution business Machiavelli. We have specialised in importing true artisan products and distributing to shops, stores and London restaurants. Seven years later, we were given the opportunity by Cadogan Estates to take over the site in Duke of York Square.
What's the best thing about running a restaurant in London?
Having the satisfaction of seeing fabulous food going out on a plate, and the positive customer feedback and interaction with staff.
What's the worst thing?
Eating and tasting too much!
Which are your favourite London restaurants?
Locanda Locatelli (*see p165*) for great Italian food and wonderful service. **Salloos** (*see p138*) simply has the most delicious 'Indian' food in all London. **Yauatcha** (*see p73*) for consistently excellent Chinese food in beautiful surroundings.
What's the best bargain in the capital?
Free tap water in restaurants.
What's your favourite treat?
Going to the opera in Covent Garden.
What is missing from London's restaurant scene?
Good-quality but reasonably priced places to eat that are also cool for teenagers.
What does the next year hold?
We will all sharpen up our act even more and it will make us stay on our toes. There will be many more restaurants opening due to the large availability of good sites at better rent.

Islington

Metrogusto

13 Theberton Street, N1 0QY (7226 9400, www.metrogusto.co.uk). Angel tube. **Brunch/ lunch served** 10am-5pm Fri-Sun. **Dinner served** 6.30-10.30pm Mon-Thur; 6.30-11pm Fri, Sat; 6-10pm Sun. **Main courses** £11.50-£18.50. **Set meal** (lunch, 6-9pm Mon-Fri, Sun) £14.50 2 courses, £18.50 3 courses. **Credit** AmEx, MC, V.
Modern Italian restaurants tend towards understated chic, but not this off-Upper Street oddball. Decorated with rather in-your-face fantastical figurative paintings it's best described as eccentric. 'Life is too short to drink the wrong wine,' quipped the witty, intellectual-looking maître d' and the quirky Italy-wide list has many opportunities for drinking the right one. Cooking is described as progressive Italian but rarely is progress swift or smooth, and here too we've found food can take its time and be a little hit or miss. Outstanding focaccia shows the kitchen's flair. They got away with the foamy sauce on gloriously seasonal jerusalem artichoke ravioli with broad bean sauce, and sea bream nicely grilled with crisp salty skin on a bed of black olives and tomatoes didn't disappoint. But calf's liver and a tagliatelle with wild boar and rosemary ragú lacked oomph, and a side order of chickpea frites were a bit greasy. Though chocolate fondant with unusually lovely rosemary ice cream and coffee sauce worked beautifully, not all dishes had what it takes to lift this likeable and distinctive local restaurant from above average to consistently great.
Babies and children welcome: high chairs. Booking advisable. Separate room for parties, seats 38. Tables outdoors (4, pavement). **Map 5 O1**.

Kentish Town

Pane Vino

323 Kentish Town Road, NW5 2TJ (7267 3879). Kentish Town tube/rail. **Lunch served** noon-3pm Mon-Sat; 1-4pm Sun. **Dinner served** 6.30-11pm Mon-Sat. **Main courses** £10.80-£19.90. **Credit** MC, V.
It would be easy to overlook this southern Italian gem – a pretty front-parlour dining room with domestic-looking kitchen at the back – on unlovely Kentish Town Road. Sometimes nothing tastes better tfhan a combination of flavours as basic as salt, oil and rosemary, and here crisp Sardinian pane carasau anointed with this trinity, formed the base for an exceptional antipasto sardo, a selection of meaty, fishy and veggie goodies – highly recommended. Caponata, the characteristically Sicilian sweet and sour celery and aubergine salad, made a perfect a foil for the grassiest, milkiest mozzarella. Squeezing out between the tightly packed tables is even more difficult after pastas, which raise peasant food to the most pleasurable heights. Gnocchi dough stuffed with ragu, in a mushroom and sage sauce, was glorious stodge; linguine with parsley and bottarga (dried mullet roe) a simple success. Specials such as roast rabbit or pollack with spinach would suit an evening dedicated to the full works, but this charming trattoria is versatile enough for a family outing for the vast, thin, aromatic pizzas or a credit-crunch lunch. Great home-style cooking seems guaranteed. Smiley, swift service is unfortunately not.
Babies and children admitted. Booking advisable. Tables outdoors (3, pavement). Takeaway service. **Map 26 B5**.

North West
Belsize Park

Osteria Emilia

85 Fleet Road, NW3 2QY (7433 3317). Belsize Park tube/Hampstead Heath rail. **Lunch served** noon-2pm, **dinner served** 6.30-10pm Tue-Sat. **Main courses** £9-£19. **Credit** AmEx, MC, V.
Osteria Emilia's owners, Renate and Raffaele Giacobazzi, have a good reputation locally for their well-established delicatessen further along Fleet Road. Their first restaurant is discreetly tucked into a ruddy brown new-build property with dining tables spread over two floors. Upstairs, a skylight, white shiplap ceiling and painted white brickwork make the limited space seem generous and relaxed. Starters include the likes of bresaola, grilled polenta with various toppings, and specials such as pea soup with mint and olive oil; pasta dishes might be tagliatelle with courgettes and prawns, or spaghetti with bottarga. A simple dome of lemony venus black rice (purple once cooked) came with perfectly done squid, prawns, clams and gorgeous scallops. Roast duck was as good as it gets – tender, pink, juicy and with crispy skin – but partnered with a chestnut disc with all the lightness of an ice-hockey puck. Chocolate cake was drier than ideal – thank heavens for the good ice-cream served alongside – but we couldn't fault the correctly wobbly vanilla panna cotta. It came with delicious cherries poached in lambrusco, giving the meal a grown-up finish that wasn't too sweet. Service can be slow, but is well-meaning, and you can't argue with house wines of Umbrian tribbiano and Veneto merlot for £12.50 a bottle.
Babies and children welcome: booster seats. Booking advisable. Disabled: toilet. Separate room for parties, seats 30. **Map 28 C3**.

Golders Green

Philpott's Mezzaluna

424 Finchley Road, NW2 2HY (7794 0452). Golders Green tube. **Lunch served** noon-2.30pm Tue-Fri; noon-3pm Sun. **Dinner served** 7-11pm Tue-Sun. **Set lunch** £12 1 course, £17 2 courses, £20 3 courses, £25 4 courses. **Set dinner** £19.50 1 course, £23 2 courses, £28 3 courses, £33 4 courses. **Credit** MC, V.
With its odd, Andy Warhol-inspired portraits of Italian-American celebrities, Philpott's Mezzaluna has been a north London stalwart for many years. Its well-priced meals attract local families, who are also fond of the charmingly old-fashioned, friendly atmosphere (complete with pink tea roses on the tables and thick tablecloths). But on our visit we couldn't help noticing that culinary standards had slipped, with generous portions failing to make up for underwhelming food. A visually appealing dish of green ravioli turned out to be undercooked and insipid pasta, filled with stewed asparagus and spinach. A main course of roast duck and lentils had more kick, with crispy skin and buttery flesh, but was let down by a mound of plain steamed cavolo nero (which would have benefited from being sautéed or jazzed up with a more imaginative seasoning). On the other hand, the wine list is long and impressive and offers several good-value options, including half bottles. Service remains friendly, even though the staff's attentiveness diminished once the dining room got buzzing. Avoid the outside tables, unless you fancy choking on the exhaust fumes from the heavy traffic chugging along Finchley Road.
Available for hire. Babies and children welcome: high chairs. Booking advisable dinner Sat. Tables outdoors (3, terrace).

St John's Wood

Vineria

1 Blenheim Terrace, NW8 0EH (7328 5014, www.vineria.it). St John's Wood tube. **Lunch served** noon-2.30pm Tue-Sun. **Dinner served** 6.30-10.30pm Tue-Sat; 6.30-10pm Sun. **Main courses** £16.50-£21. **Credit** AmEx, MC, V.
Osteria Stecca last year underwent a change of name with the departure of chef-proprietor Stefano Stecca, being reborn as Vineria, the London outpost of a group of identically named restaurants near Venice. However, the classy feel, the bright white tablecloths and airy conservatory have remained constant, along with a menu offering elegantly executed classic dishes from northern and southern Italy, spiced up with modern takes on tradition and a keen eye on detail (witness the scrumptious bread basket). Starters may include sparkling fresh scallops, simply pan-fried, or soft polenta topped with grilled, almost caramelised radicchio (a dish typical of the countryside near Venice). A main course of crispy cod with potato purée, enlivened by a wild-mushroom sauce, won us over, as did a perfect dish of pumpkin-filled ravioli. The wine list seems to be carefully chosen, but very few bottles are priced below £20, and those available by the glass are few. Just tucked away from Abbey Road, Vineria, with its impeccable yet friendly service, seems a favoured spot for well-heeled local Italian expats, who make sure to book the large front terrace in summer.
Babies and children welcome: high chairs. Booking advisable. Tables outdoors (6, terrace). **Map 1 C2**.

Outer London
Kingston, Surrey

Jamie's Italian NEW

19-23 High Street, Kingston, Surrey KT1 1LL (8912 0110, www.jamieoliver.com/italian/ kingston). Kingston rail. **Meals served** noon-11pm Mon-Sat; noon-10.30pm Sun. **Main courses** £9.95-£15.95. **Credit** AmEx, MC, V.
Everyone loves Jamie O, or so you'd believe if you stumbled off the deserted streets of Kingston and into the action-packed environs of Jamie's Italian at 10pm on a rainy Tuesday. The no-booking policy (for fewer than eight people) means there's always a queue (apart from at opening time and 4-5pm according to the barman), as high-spirited families, couples and groups of mates clamber to try the Jamie take on rustic, relaxed Italian cuisine. We were warned of a 40-minute wait; it was 20, and two good cocktails at the slick-but-sticky bar made it whizz by. There are signs of the man himself everywhere – his mug adorning T-shirts, cookbooks, and, er, mugs, on sale in the entrance, along with the promise of 'proper posh' chips on the menu. Antipasti plates made tasty starters to share – melt-in-the-mouth crispy squid and fat polenta wedges were given zing with a sprinkle of fried herbs. Pasta is a speciality, and a big bowl of sausage pappardelle was comforting if not memorable. Food, fittings and atmosphere are all bang on brand: good value, friendly and fuss-free, with an irrepressible energy, but there's no denying it all feels formulaic. With more branches soon to open, this slick take on a traditional trattoria seems destined to become the next high-street honey.
Babies and children welcome: children's menu; crayons; high chairs; nappy-changing facilities. Bookings not accepted for fewer than 8 people. Disabled: toilet.
For branch see index.

Twickenham, Middlesex

A Cena

418 Richmond Road, Twickenham, Middx TW1 2EB (8288 0108). Richmond tube/rail. **Lunch served** noon-3pm Tue-Sun. **Dinner served** 7-10.30pm Mon-Sat. **Main courses** £13.75-£19. **Set lunch** (Sun) £25 3 courses. **Credit** AmEx, MC, V.
A Cena ('to dinner') is a well-loved local favourite serving impeccable Italian food in chic but low-key surroundings. Candles twinkle from white-clothed tables in the small but spare dining room. Service is charming. The menu covers the whole of Italy, north to south, yet each dish remains true to its regional roots. A starter of own-made capocollo (Calabrian air-dried pork collar) was soft and tender, with buttery fat. It was accompanied by grated carrot with just enough vinegar to give a punchy counterpoint to the rich meat. Tuscan-style braised rabbit bruschetta with nutmeg, peas and parmesan was equally accomplished, and we couldn't fault our lemon, basil and mascarpone risotto. A thick tranche of perfectly cooked salmon got the Sicilian treatment with sweet-and-sour stemperata sauce that was crunchy with celery and spiked with capers and just the right blend of sugar and vinegar. The wine list has some excellent producers from the length of the country; the weekly specials, served by the third-of-a-bottle carafe, are good value. A Cena is justifiably popular so booking is recommended.
Available for hire. Babies and children welcome: booster seats. Booking advisable.

Japanese

Like the latest hi-tech gadget, Japanese cuisine was rare and extremely expensive in London 20 years ago, with just a handful of practitioners charging exorbitant amounts for what would now be viewed as pretty standard sushi. Fast forward to 2010 and Japanese food is being packaged for the mass market. The capital's diet-conscious lunchers have an array of supermarkets, as well as fast-food stores selling the rice-based snacks – not to mention the specialist sushi bars and the kaiten (conveyor belt) operations. Yet though you can now buy sushi at pretty low prices, the quality hasn't soared. Indeed, the number of top sushi suppliers – the likes of **Chisou**, **Moshi Moshi Sushi**, **Sushi-Hiro**, **Sushi-Say** and **Umu** – hasn't grown by anything like the amount of the more run-of-the-mill operations. Still, it's hard to complain when London has a batch of Europe's best Japanese restaurants: forward-looking **Dinings**, the world-famous **Nobu**, Alan Yau's **Saké No Hana**, and glittering siblings **Roka** and **Zuma**. The variety and number of Japanese restaurants in our city also allows specialists like grill-virtuosos **Kushi-Tei** and **Tosa** to thrive. For our pick of the low-priced sushi and noodle bars, *see p182* **Quick bites**.

Central

City

Miyako

ANdAZ, Liverpool Street, EC2M 7QN (7618 7100, www.london.liverpoolstreet.andaz.com). Liverpool Street tube/rail. **Lunch served** noon-2.30pm, **dinner served** 6-10.30pm Mon-Fri. **Main courses** £3-£23. **Set lunch** £11-£25. **Credit** AmEx, DC, MC, V.

The ANdAZ Hotel – a young, trendy arm of the Hyatt group, occupying a Victorian red-brick edifice dating from 1884 – has various dining and drinking options, including Miyako. Despite its EC2 location, the only evidence of an economic downturn at this minimalist, bento box-sized Japanese is the half-empty dining room (in better times, it would have been crammed with City workers), as little else shows sympathy for tightening budgets. Yet although prices are high, we reckoned the quality of sushi and sashimi was only a notch above that of high street chains. Spicy tuna maki was short on spice, rice and tuna; and we consumed the tempura hand-roll in two bites, with no audible crunch. The grilled mackerel bento box (these are available to take away too) offered more satisfaction with its nicely charred chunks of plump fish, refreshing soba noodles and fresh salmon sashimi. But whatever pleasure that this set meal offered was quickly wiped out when we received the bill, which charged us £2 each for some unremarkable green tea. We left still feeling hungry.
Babies and children welcome: high chairs; nappy-changing facilities. Booking advisable. Disabled: lift; toilet. Takeaway service. **Map 12 R6.**

★ Moshi Moshi Sushi

24 Upper Level, Liverpool Street Station, EC2M 7QH (7247 3227, www.moshimoshi.co.uk). Liverpool Street tube/rail. **Meals served** 11.30am-10pm Mon-Fri. **Dishes** £1.80-£3.70. **Main courses** £8-£13. **Credit** MC, V.

Why, when somewhere as good as Moshi Moshi exists, is there so much bad conveyor-belt sushi in London? Perhaps location is to blame. You're unlikely to come across this place by chance, stuck as it is on the upper concourse of Liverpool Street station, behind an M&S food store. But local office workers have discovered it – on typical lunchtimes, almost every table is occupied, and the counter is near-full. In an unobtrusive way, this is a beautifully conceived space, with soaring curves in the ceiling, views over platform one, and an oversized calligraphic fish painting on washi paper at the point where the conveyor belt disappears. The nigiri is certainly made by hand, not machine. Salmon and sea-bass sashimi was of fine quality, and miso soup deeply flavoured. Top picks included eel-cucumber handrolls and una-ju (eel with sweet teriyaki sauce, served on rice in a lacquer box). The choice of hot dishes is wide; tempura and chicken oyako (grilled, and served on rice with omelette and vegetables) have both been reliable on previous visits. Staff are friendly and helpful. Moshi offers good-value food and deserves to have more than its current two branches.
Babies and children admitted. Disabled: toilet. Takeaway service; delivery service (within 4-mile radius). **Map 12 R5.**
For branch see index.

Clerkenwell & Farringdon

Saki

4 West Smithfield, EC1A 9JX (7489 7033, www.saki-food.com). Barbican tube/Farringdon tube/rail.
Bar **Open** noon-11pm Mon-Wed; noon-midnight Thur; Fri; 6pm-midnight Sat.
Deli **Open** 10am-7pm Mon-Fri.
Restaurant **Lunch served** 11.45am-2.30pm, **dinner served** 6-10.30pm Mon-Sat. **Set lunch** £10.90 4 courses. **Set dinner** £28.50 3 courses, £45 5 courses, £60 7 courses.
All **Credit** AmEx, MC, V.
We've had excellent meals at Saki in the past and always look forward to visiting. It's a chic alternative to Smithfield's blokey meat-celebrating restaurants: a black-and-red basement dining room with bar-style seating set around a central square garden of white pebbles and stalagmite candles. To the other side of the central stairway is a smart cocktail bar and the famous blow-dry loos; upstairs is a grocery-takeaway that looks more like a trendy jeweller's. On our lunchtime

---

visit, when diners are offered various set menus, the clientele was entirely female. Overcooked rice let down the sushi rolls, though they had good flavours; best was a tempura maki with crab and avocado, the delicacy of the batter ensuring the whole wasn't too rich. The flesh of salmon teriyaki was dry yet the skin was unappetisingly flabby rather than crisp. Miso soup was lukewarm, and its tofu cubes cold. We liked the cherry blossom and toasty soy bean ice-creams, but green tea tiramisu was dry, leathery and left unfinished. The menus are appealingly unusual and the friendly staff efficient, but the kitchen needs to rediscover some finesse and increase its accuracy to achieve its ambitions.
Babies and children admitted. Booking advisable. Disabled: lift; toilet. Separate room for parties, seats 12. Takeaway service. Vegetarian menu. Vegan dishes. **Map 11 O5.**

Covent Garden

Abeno Too

17-18 Great Newport Street, WC2H 7JE (7379 1160, www.abeno.co.uk). Leicester Square tube. **Meals served** noon-11pm Mon-Sat; noon-10.30pm Sun. **Main courses** £9-£24. **Set lunch** £8.80-£19.80. **Credit** MC, V.
The tables and counter at Abeno Too are all fitted with hot-plates for cooking the okonomiyaki (Japanese pancakes) that are the speciality of this small chain. Before you sit down, lift the top of the bench seating and store your coat and bags inside – you don't want to spoil the serenely uncluttered decor. Staff cook the pancakes to order, right in front of you: hearty, comforting stuff, chock-full of

BEST JAPANESE

Meet the specialists
Head to **Abeno Too** (*see above*) for okonomiyaki, **Benihana** (*see p190*) for teppanyaki, **Bincho** (*see p184*) for yakitori, **Kushi-Tei** (*see p187*) for kushiyaki and **Sushi-Hiro** (*see p185*) for sushi.

At the sharp end
For cutting-edge creativity, sample the offerings at **Chisou** (*see p183*), **Dinings** (*see p180*), **Nobu** (*see p183*), **Saki** (*see left*), **So Japanese** (*see p184*) and **Tsunami** (*see p187*).

Child's play
Take the youngsters to **Benihana** (*see p190*), **Chisou** (*see p183*), **Eat Tokyo** (*see p190*), **Japan Centre** (*see p182*), **Jin Kichi** (*see p190*), **Satsuma** (*see p182*), **Wow Simply Japanese** (*see p187*) and **Yo! Sushi** (*see p183*).

Non-stop food action
Watch your sushi sail by on conveyer belts at **Kulu Kulu** (*see p182*), **Yo! Sushi** (*see p183*) and **Moshi Moshi Sushi** (*see left*).

Classy and sassy
Enjoy Japanese-tinged glamour at **Nobu** (*see p183*), **Roka** (*see p178*), **Tsunami** (*see p187*), **Saké No Hana** (*see p184*), **Umu** (*see p183*) and **Zuma** (*see p180*).

View to a thrill
For parkside greenery, visit **Nobu** (*see p183*); for riverside scenery, head for **Ozu** (*see p187*).

RESTAURANTS

vegetables, seafood, pork and other titbits. If okonomiyaki doesn't suit your mood, choose from katsu curries, sashimi, salads, rice and noodle dishes and teppanyaki. The ingredients are often organic and menus highlight seasonal specials – in spring, maybe bacon-wrapped asparagus with egg and rice cooked on the hot-plate. Our om-soba was a stomach-filling sensation: top-quality, wheaty-tasting noodles tossed with pork, squid and prawns, served wrapped in omelette and decorated with a tangy and creamy combination of sauces. Saké and shochu are available with such mixers as cola, apple juice and lemonade, but we like the smoky-tasting mugi-cha: refreshing chilled barley tea. Staff are lovely, chatting to customers as they cook for them and happily explaining menu and garnish options.
Babies and children welcome: high chairs. Bookings not accepted. Disabled: toilet. Takeaway service. **Map 18 K6.**
For branch see index.

Fitzrovia

★ Roka (100)

37 Charlotte Street, W1T 1RR (7580 6464, www.rokarestaurant.com). Goodge Street or Tottenham Court Road tube. **Lunch served** noon-2.30pm Mon-Fri; 12.30-4pm Sat, Sun. **Dinner served** 5.30-11.30pm Mon-Sat; 5.30-10.30pm Sun. **Main courses** £10.60-£22.60. **Set meal** £50-£75 tasting menu. **Credit** AmEx, DC, MC, V.

Any doubts that the owners of Zuma would find it hard to repeat and sustain their success can now be laid to rest. Roka is so busy that even in recession-hit 2009, it took us three attempts to secure a reservation. Part of the recipe for success is in the presentation. On the huge wooden counter (visible to Charlotte Street passers-by through floor-to-ceiling picture windows) we spied earthenware bowls piled high with invitingly crisp and fresh vegetables. Even for a lunch starting at 2pm, the place was still heaving. The food is outstandingly good. Testing the core menu of robatayaki – skewered vegetables, fish and meat cooked on a charcoal grill in front of diners – we sampled nine perfectly grilled kinoko mushrooms with a garlicky sauce, followed by a stack of thick grilled asparagus skilfully cut on the bias, and a dish of tebasaki: humble chicken wings, crisply grilled and exquisitely flavoured. A mixed sashimi appetiser included particularly good turbot and sea bass, but the highlight was a starter of mi-cuit foie gras, rolled in seaweed like maki and served with alcoholic pickled plums and millimetre-thick slices of absolutely black toasted nori bread – weird, but memorable. Apart from the over-burdened phones when you're booking, service is unexpectedly good for such a busy place.
Babies and children welcome: high chairs. Booking advisable. Tables outdoors (9, terrace). **Map 17 B1.**

Soho Japan

52 Wells Street, W1T 3PR (7323 4661, www.sohojapan.co.uk). Oxford Circus tube. **Lunch served** noon-2.30pm Mon-Fri. **Dinner served** 6-10.30pm Mon-Sat. **Main courses** £6.50-£14 lunch; £10-£22 dinner. **Set lunch** £6-£14. **Set dinner** £9-£33. **Credit** AmEx, MC, V.

A map of Burgundy greets diners at the entrance, and chopstick rests are made of halved wine corks. The sepia and oxblood-toned wood-panelled walls and scuffed wooden floor may put you in mind of a Parisian café, but the food is 100% Japanese. Soho Japan is popular with international students; staff, mostly young Japanese-speakers, pick up on the casual, friendly-trendy vibe. Diners select sushi and sashimi by ticking boxes on a small piece of paper. Our spicy cod's roe nigiri (petals of spicy red roe overlapping the crisp nori wrapper) looked delicate but packed an umami-rich and spicy kick. Pickled radish 'inside-out' maki were crunchy and sour, wrapped in a rice blanket and speckled with sesame seeds. Well-made steamed and fried gyoza were pleasingly plump, the lean meat flecked with spring onion. From the grill, 'chicken balls' was actually one large minced chicken burger (nicely

Abeno Too. See p177.

light in texture) halved and served on bamboo skewers – good drinking fodder, if not a taste sensation. Drinks-wise, there's a decent selection of European wines and Japanese sakés, as well as shochu and shochu-based cocktails, although abstemious types might prefer the well-presented Japanese teas.
Babies and children admitted. Booking advisable. Tables outdoors (3, pavement). Takeaway service. **Map 17 A2.**

Holborn

★ Aki

182 Gray's Inn Road, WC1X 8EW (7837 9281, www.akidemae.com). Chancery Lane tube. **Lunch served** noon-2.30pm Mon-Fri. **Dinner served** 6-11pm Mon-Fri; 6-10.30pm Sat. **Main courses** £6-£12. **Set lunch** £5.60-£19. **Set dinner** £22-£46.50. **Credit** AmEx, MC, V.

This small, homely izakaya describes itself not as a bar, but a Japanese bistro. Unlike its rowdier cousins, Aki offers saké and sakana (accompanying snacks) in relaxed, familial surroundings – prioritising good food and warm service over modern decor. Diners have a handful of small, simple tables, or can perch on the cushion-covered tree trunks that serve as stools by the tiny sushi bar. Either way, they're able to feast on an appealingly diverse selection of fresh raw fish and comforting hot dishes, made from ingredients sourced from Billingsgate market and nearby Smithfield. Unagi sushi, with its buttery texture and sweet, sticky glaze, is a house favourite, landing on the tables of almost every customer. Tuna yamakake – thick-cut maguro sashimi nestled in a dollop of grated mountain yam – was a joyous blend of cool, slippery and gooey. Yellowtail sushi was respectably fresh, while tenmusu maki proved to be a balanced pairing of hot, crispy prawn tempura with warm sticky rice. Shimeji mushrooms sautéed in butter were surprisingly flavourful: at once musky and smoky. The only disappointment was a grilled mackerel fillet: neither crisp nor tender. Aki is an ideal neighbourhood haunt for impromptu weeknight meals (though booking is advisable).
Babies and children admitted. Booking advisable. Separate room for parties, seats 30. Takeaway service. **Map 4 M4.**

Matsuri

71 High Holborn, WC1V 6EA (7430 1970, www.matsuri-restaurant.com). Chancery Lane or Holborn tube. **Lunch served** noon-2.30pm, **dinner served** 6-10pm Mon-Sat. **Main courses** £8.50-£30 lunch; £18-£36.50 dinner. **Set lunch** £25. **Set dinner** £35-£79. **Credit** AmEx, DC, MC, V.

Matsuri has a handsomeness to it – big, bold sweeping architecture with floor-to-ceiling windows, dark wood furniture, and the clang of metal against metal in the teppanyaki room. By contrast, the service is sweet and demure. The interior is split into the main dining room, teppanyaki space and sushi bar, and the kitchen offers various dishes suited to each. A summer set menu featured a delicate appetiser of sweetly savoury hijiki seaweed salad, followed by a glistening row of scallop 'carpaccio' topped with tobiko and shredded myoga (Japanese ginger). An à la carte selection of Chinese-style prawn and shiitake soup dumplings, served with spicy mayonnaise, was a cleansing, virtuous dish with subtle but satisfying flavour. Less successful was a plate of squid tempura – heavily salted and with heavy batter. The set main of black cod in ginger sauce defied the rest of the meal with its inelegant presentation, but the fish itself was silky and flaky. We relished the desserts. A curious sakura (cherry blossom) ice-cream had crystallised blossoms and a slight sea-salty tang. Yuzu sorbet was equally accomplished, if rather parsimonious. There are good points to the menu, certainly, but we found it an up and down experience.
Babies and children admitted. Booking advisable. Disabled: toilet. Separate room for parties, seats 10. **Map 10 M5.**
For branch see index.

find it, slurp it, love it!

delicious noodles rice dishes
freshly squeezed juices
salads sake wine asian beers
for locations visit wagamama.com

wagamama

positive eating + positive living

Chisou. See p183.

Knightsbridge

★ Zuma

5 Raphael Street, SW7 1DL (7584 1010,
www.zumarestaurant.com). Knightsbridge tube.
Bar **Open** noon-11pm Mon-Fri; 12.30-11pm Sat;
noon-11pm Sun.
Restaurant **Lunch served** noon-2.15pm Mon-
Thur; noon-2.45pm Fri; 12.30-3.15 Sat, Sun.
Dinner served 6-10.45 pm Mon-Sat; 6-10.15pm
Sun. **Main courses** £14.80-£70.
Both **Credit** AmEx, DC, MC, V.
Zuma has established itself as a must-go
destination for every rich visitor to London, and
accordingly it's hard to bag a table here. The
restaurant design has good bones: even after a few
visits, the stylishly displayed bottles, the skilful
lighting, and the slickly presented sushi and robata
bars still impress. The clientele includes movers
and shakers from business, and dressy denizens of
Knightsbridge – by mid-evening, the bar is
deafening. Food quality seems as high as ever; it
was hard to find fault with a fine nine-piece sushi
set, a tempura of seven kinds of mixed vegetables,
and basics like ohitashi (sesame spinach) and
tebasaki (chicken wings) from the robata grill. Two
things stand out here: the quality of raw
ingredients, like the fresh tofu; and the imaginative
flavour combinations, such as ginger, lime and
coriander on the tataki (seared raw beef), or the
yuzu, truffle oil and salmon roe that accompanied
a dish of sea-bass sashimi. Zuma shouldn't rest on
its laurels (the tables are getting a little worn, for
instance, and need to be replaced), but at present
this remains a slick, professional operation that
deserves its success and its growing family of
clones in Hong Kong, Istanbul and Dubai.
Babies and children welcome: high chairs. Booking
essential. Disabled: toilet. Separate rooms for
parties, seating 12 and 14. **Map 8 F9**.

Marylebone

★ Dinings

22 Harcourt Street, W1H 4HH (7723 0666).
Marylebone tube/rail. **Lunch served** noon-
2.30pm Mon-Fri. **Dinner served** 6-10.30pm
Mon-Sat. **Main courses** £6.50-£22. **Set lunch**
£10-£15. **Credit** AmEx, MC, V.
Like a minimalist jewel box, all concrete and wood
surfaces, this sushi bar and fusion restaurant
thrives in an area more associated with Middle
Eastern and Swedish food. Set in a Georgian
townhouse, Dinings attracts a sophisticated foodie
crowd to its slip of a ground-floor sushi bar and
more spacious, but still bijou, basement tables.
Staff – friendly, keen, easygoing – are adept at
getting customers to upgrade from the keenly
priced donburi set lunches, but once you've seen
the specials board, you'll probably want to hang
the expense anyway. Japanese tapas (their term)
may seem nonsensical in a cuisine associated with
little dishes, but Dinings' food is for sharing and a
comparison with Spain's nueva cocina is
appropriate. We relished the sweet fragrance of
chargrilled vegetable salad with truffle dressing,
and the fiery pickled kick of creamy jalapeño
dressing covering perfectly ripe avocado and
prawns. Lightly smoked foie gras pieces came with
strips of roast cabbage in buttery, winey pan
juices, while wagyu beef yakiniku had a winning
peppery back-note. Desserts were less impressive
but the only duff note in our meal was jasmine
panna cotta, an overly strong infusion giving it an
apothecary quality. Bargain hunters should
confidently opt for the richly honeyed chenin
blanc, the cheapest wine. Alternatively, specialist
Japanese teas are elegantly presented in groovy
black side-handled pots.
Babies and children admitted. Booking advisable.
Separate room for parties, seats 18. Takeaway
service. Vegetarian menu. **Map 8 F5**.

Tomoe NEW

62 Marylebone Lane, W1U 2PB (7486 2004,
www.tomoe-london.co.uk). Bond Street tube.
Lunch served noon-2.15pm Tue-Sat. **Dinner**
served 6-10.30pm daily. **Dishes** £2.50-£12.90.
Set lunch £7.90-£12.90. **Credit** AmEx, MC, V.

RESTAURANTS

Quick bites

Japan Centre

Whether you're on the town or need a reviving break from the office or a day of shopping, London's Japanese canteens, diners and takeaways are a fast, healthy and inexpensive choice.

Centrepoint Sushi (Hana)
20-21 St Giles High Street, WC2H 8LN (7240 6147). Tottenham Court Road tube. **Lunch served** noon-3pm, **dinner served** 6-11pm Mon-Sat. **Main courses** £8-£17. **Set lunch** £8-£14.50. **Credit** MC, V.
Although discreetly tucked above a Korean-Japanese grocery, Hana was full-to-bursting on our visit. We soon discovered why. The be-scarfed chef behind the counter produces a spectacular procession of made-to-order sushi served on wooden boards and pretty white-and-blue pottery. Solo diners and couples can sit at the bar, groups at the spacious banquettes and booths. Grilled eel nigiri was deliciously warm and succulent. In fact the only duff note was the icing sugar used to decorate a tuna salad with creamy dressing.
Babies and children admitted. Booking advisable. Takeaway service. Vegetarian menu. **Map 17 C2**.

Feng Sushi
1 Adelaide Road, NW3 3QE (7483 2929, www.fengsushi.co.uk). Chalk Farm tube. **Lunch served** 11.30am-3.30pm Mon-Fri. **Dinner served** 6-10pm Mon-Fri. **Meals served** 11.30am-10pm Sat, Sun. **Main courses** £7-£18. **Set meal** £11.75 bento box. **Credit** MC, V.
Feng Sushi may have had some of its thunder stolen by the rival takeaway and delivery service of Itsu (*see p234*), but it's worth remembering that Silla Bjerrum's company has long advocated the use of local and sustainable seafood for sushi – and that it offers an appealing range of cooked dishes. On our visit, cuttlefish from Hastings and exquisitely fresh Cornish grey mullet were being offered as tempura, the latter with a wholesome spelt batter and zingy fennel salad. Tofu comes from Clean Bean, which manufactures on Brick Lane. A choice of chilli or miso

dressings adds finger-licking goodness to edamame, and fruity vinegar drinks make a refreshing change from tea.
Babies and children admitted. Disabled: toilet. Tables outdoors (2, pavement). Takeaway service; delivery service (over £10 within 3-mile radius). **Map 27 B1**. **For branches see index**.

Japan Centre (Toku)
212 Piccadilly, W1J 9HG (7255 8255, www.japancentre.com). Piccadilly Circus tube. **Meals served** noon-9pm Mon-Sat; noon-9pm Sun. **Main courses** £5-£14. **Set meal** £9.60-£15. **Credit** MC, V.
A welcoming Japanese canteen with all the bustle of a hit brasserie, Toku has a vast menu. However, turnover of food and tables is high, and fish and seafood are super-fresh. Hence this is an ideal place to try something like sliced raw tuna lightly dressed with sesame sauce and served over hot rice; cut-above miso soup with fried tofu comes on the side. Soba noodles, curled in a hot broth with tofu skin, was a huge yet wholesome meal-in-a-bowl. The shop next door sells takeaway sushi and is worth a browse for ingredients and homewares.
Babies and children welcome: high chairs. Booking advisable Thur-Sat. **Map 17 B5**.

Kulu Kulu
51-53 Shelton Street, WC2H 9HE (7240 5687). Covent Garden tube. **Lunch served** noon-2.30pm Mon-Fri; noon-3.30pm Sat. **Dinner served** 5-10pm Mon-Sat. **Dishes** £1.50-£3.60. **Credit** MC, V.
Handy for singles or couples, this long-established conveyor-belt sushi joint is keenly priced. Quality is good enough, though we found the thick fatty stripes in the raw salmon off-putting, the nasu (aubergine) miso oily, and the sushi rice too sticky. Still, the japanese potato salad is delicious doused with soy sauce (and easy to eat with chopsticks), the tempura is elegant and the fresh spinach rolls drum-tight under their cloak of sesame dressing. Serve yourself green tea from the urns if the blue-aproned floor-staff don't get to you in time.
Babies and children admitted. Bookings not accepted. Takeaway service. **Map 18 D3**.

Ramen Seto
19 Kingly Street, W1B 5PY (7434 0309). Oxford Circus tube. **Meals served** noon-9.30pm Mon, Tue; noon-10pm Wed-Sat; 1-8pm Sun. **Main courses** £5.70-£8. **Set meal** £6-£9.60. **Credit** MC, V.
Food arrives fast and hot, which helps explain the multicultural crowd of family shoppers and local media workers frequenting this homely café. What the cooking lacks in quality and appearance is made up for in generosity. We had to adopt the authentic stooped position to consume a heaping plate of gomoku udon – noodles (overcooked) with pork, prawns, fish balls, veg and thick bland sauce. Better were the crisp, bubbly vegetable tempura. There's a basic list of canned drinks and hot saké.
Babies and children welcome: high chairs. Booking advisable weekends. Takeaway service. **Map 17 J6**.

Satsuma
56 Wardour Street, W1D 4JG (7437 8338, www.osatsuma.com). Piccadilly Circus tube. **Meals served** noon-11pm Mon, Tue; noon-11.30pm Wed, Thur; noon-midnight Fri, Sat; noon-10.30pm Sun. **Main courses** £6.50-£19.80. **Credit** AmEx, DC, MC, V.
Split over two levels, Satsuma has a clean-lined design of wooden communal benches, bright orange walls and stone tiles that looks almost as good as when the place first opened. Dishes range from wok-fried tumbles served on large white plates to artfully presented constructs. Keep an eye out for lunchtime special deals. Workmanlike yakisoba with pork came with garish strips of pickled ginger and an overload of beansprouts, yet a large seafood salad was fresh, pretty and colourful. Finish with ice-creams of sesame and green tea, served unadorned to showcase the wondrous flavours.
Babies and children welcome: high chairs. Bookings not accepted. Disabled: toilet. Takeaway service. **Map 17 K6**.

Taro
10 Old Compton Street, W1D 4TF (7439 2275). Leicester Square or Tottenham Court Road tube. **Lunch served** noon-2.50pm Mon-Fri; 12.30-3.15pm Sat, Sun. **Dinner served** 5.30-10.30pm Mon-Sat; 5.30-9.30pm Sun. **Main courses** £5.90-£8.90. **Set meal** £8.80-£14. **Credit** MC, V.
Recognisable by its square-faced logo, sushi and noodle bar Taro has two outlets at the cheaper end of the canteen spectrum. The spacious basement eaterie on Old Compton Street features chunky pinewood furniture and attracts a young, cosmopolitan crowd of students, office workers and theatregoers. Service is cheerful and prompt enough and the atmosphere lively. The menu offers a greatest-hits collection of traditional Japanese cooking: teriyaki, tonkatsu, katsu, yakisoba and udon, plus sushi and sashimi. The wine list is short but there's Kirin, Asahi and a few sakés.
Babies and children welcome: high chairs. Booking advisable. Takeaway service. **Map 17 C3**. **For branch see index**.

RESTAURANTS

Tokyo Diner

2 Newport Place, WC2H 7JP (7287 8777, www.tokyodiner.com). Leicester Square tube. **Meals served** noon-midnight daily. **Main courses** £6.60-£13.20. **Set lunch** (noon-6pm Mon-Fri) £4.90-£9.70. **Credit** MC, V.

There's a great generosity of spirit here: rice crackers and tea are brought unbidden, bigger portions of rice are free on request, food is £1 cheaper between 3pm and 6pm and the menu expressly advises no tips. Donburis, bentos, sushi, soup noodles and other set-meal deals are on the extensive list. Grilled eel came with a sprightly salad and soba topped with mangetout, seaweed and spring onions. The small cushioned chairs are comfortable for a pitstop, though you might not think the same of the Japanese MOR rock. *Babies and children welcome. Bookings not accepted Fri, Sat. Takeaway service.* **Map 17 K7**. **For branches see index.**

Tsuru

4 Canvey Street, SE1 9AN (7928 2228, www.tsuru-sushi.co.uk). Southwark tube or London Bridge tube/rail. **Meals served** 11am-9pm Mon-Fri. **Main courses** £4.95-£12.95. **Credit** MC, V.

Much of the business is in takeaways for nearby office workers, but katsu specialist Tsuru has smart tall wooden stools with matching benches for those who want to eat-in. Cold items (japanese potato salad, spinach with oritashi sauce) are chosen from the chill cabinet that holds sushi boxes to-go, and orders for hot food (curry, teriyaki bento) are taken at the bar, so you can wind up eating half your meal from plastic containers and half from pottery plates. In the evenings you might find a saké tasting or new-music showcase. *Available for hire. Babies and children admitted. Disabled: toilet. Tables outdoors (5, pavement). Takeaway service.* **Map 11 O8**.

Yo! Sushi

52 Poland Street, W1F 7NQ (7287 0443, www.yosushi.com). Oxford Circus tube. **Meals served** noon-11pm Mon-Sat; noon-10.30pm Sun. **Dishes** £7.50-£10. **Credit** AmEx, DC, MC, V.

It's worth checking to see what discount vouchers are available before visiting this chain; many customers were taking advantage of a 40%-off offer during our visit. Yo! was founded by Simon Woodroffe (who now just takes a 1% royalty on sales). The core menu of sushi served via conveyor belt has steadily expanded to include a wide range of tempura, gyoza, katsu and hot rice dishes. It's good to see chefs cooking instead of just shaping and sprinkling. But it was no surprise that when they attempted to hand an over-full bowl of steaming-hot soup noodles all the way across the work bench, conveyor belt and counter – it spilt. *Babies and children welcome: high chairs. Disabled: toilet. Takeaway service. Vegetarian menu.* **Map 17 A3**. **For branches see index.**

Much recommended by word-of-blog, Tomoe is a bit of a scruff in a bit of a toff district. Its appearance would improve if staff stopped Blu-Tacking lunch menus and specials across the exterior of an otherwise neat expanse of glass frontage – untidy, unlaminated sheets of paper that then have to be taken down at the end of each shift. Aside from some cute but unframed calligraphy under newish spotlights, the restaurant's look appears to be inherited rather than designed. Chrome-and-rattan S-shaped chairs, dark tables, tinted-mirror walls and a black carpet create a slightly gloomy feel, but this is countered by the relaxed mix of couples, friends and families who dine here, and the smiling young Japanese waitresses who serve up authentic Japanese staples. The only surprise we've encountered is tori karaage presented as one large piece of deep-fried chicken, sliced tonkatsu-style. Sushi, sashimi, noodles, katsu, karaage, tempura – they're all here: just neither bad nor especially good. Still, this air of not trying too hard certainly seems to put customers at their ease. *Babies and children welcome: high chairs. Booking advisable Fri, Sat. Takeaway service.* **Map 9 G5**.

Mayfair

★ Chisou

4 Princes Street, W1B 2LE (7629 3931, www.chisou.co.uk). Oxford Circus tube. **Lunch served** noon-2.30pm, **dinner served** 6-10.15pm Mon-Sat. **Main courses** £12-£23.50. **Set lunch** £12.50-£18.50. **Credit** AmEx, MC, V.

Chisou looks quiet from the outside, but once through the small vestibule this modestly fashionable restaurant hums with activity. To the rear is a fun sushi bar where charming chefs prepare exquisite inside-out rolls of tempura prawn and soft-shell crab, terrific rolled omelette, and turbot sashimi with ponzu dip. Plentiful friendly waitresses keep things moving at the generously proportioned blond-wood tables, some of which are partially shielded by screens. We loved the clean flavours of salted belly pork (finely sliced and grilled with whole mild green peppers on bamboo skewers), and the nourishing purity of ume cha (rice in a light hot broth with tiny pieces of pickled plum). Spinach roll was a classy rendition, served very cold with long strips of bonito. There were moments when Chisou missed the opportunity to shine, however. Agedashidofu arrived piping hot, but the accompanying broth of soy, mirin and dashi lacked oomph. Black sesame ice-cream was dry and woolly: much better was the creamy wasabi flavour that left a subtle lingering burn at the back of the throat – both are bought-in, according to staff. There's a serious saké and shochu list, which the knowledgeable owner can guide you through. Next door is Chisou's more informal noodle and donburi bar. *Babies and children welcome: high chairs. Booking essential. Separate rooms for parties. Tables outdoors (2, terrace). Takeaway service.* **Map 9 J6**.

Nobu (100)

1st floor, The Metropolitan, 19 Old Park Lane, W1K 1LB (7447 4747, www.noburestaurants.com). Hyde Park Corner tube. **Lunch served** noon-2.15pm Mon-Fri; 12.30-2.30pm Sat, Sun. **Dinner served** 6-10.15pm Mon-Thur; 6-11pm Fri, Sat; 6-9.30pm Sun. **Dishes** £3.50-£29.50. **Set lunch** £28.50 bento box; £50, £60. **Set dinner** £70, £90. **Credit** AmEx, DC, MC, V.

Nobu seemed to be in the limelight for all the wrong reasons at the time of our most recent visit, when it was the target of a spirited environmental campaign to get over-fished bluefin tuna off the menus of posh restaurants. The glitterati may have been boycotting this celeb-magnet perched on the edge of Hyde Park, but during our lunchtime meal, in the depths of recession, well-to-do punters were happily packing the polished tables and tucking in. Our 'in and out' bento box was a roll-call of Nobu's greatest fishy hits: crisp rock-shrimp tempura with spiky ponzu dressing, a small piece of black cod with miso, seared tuna sashimi with Matsuhisa dressing, salmon maki and a few fingers of nigiri sushi, with a collection

of salted spicy vegetables on sushi rice and decent miso soup on the side. The menu hasn't evolved, but the cooking is as good as we remember it, and service seemed more attentive than on previous, pre-recession visits. The wine list caters well for those who wish to consume conspicuously and those who fancy a good match with their piscine feast. There's still a 'wow factor' to dining here, and steep prices (including an 'optional' 15% service charge) reflect this. *Babies and children welcome: high chairs. Booking essential. Disabled: lift; toilet. Dress: smart casual. Separate rooms for parties.* **Map 9 H8**. **For branch see index.**

Umu

14-16 Bruton Place, W1J 6LX (7499 8881, www.umurestaurant.com). Bond Street or Green Park tube. **Lunch served** noon-2.30pm Mon-Fri. **Dinner served** 6-11pm Mon-Sat. **Main courses** £13-£57. **Set lunch** £21-£95. **Set dinner** £65-£135. **Credit** AmEx, DC, MC, V.

With a location a couple of streets from Berkeley Square and a classy, mysterious entrance, Umu is clearly aimed at a jet-set clientele. Yet despite the sums lavished on its orange-and-brown interior, the atmosphere isn't so much glamorous as simply understated and expensive. It's the food, rather than anything else, that justifies Umu's prices. Sitting at the bar, we found that even a basic tempura assortment from the set lunch menu showed what the kitchen and sushi chefs were made of. Beautifully cut salmon and seared yellowtail sashimi came with a green salad of perfectly fresh, lightly dressed, delicate little leaves. In the bento box, vegetable and shrimp tempura was perfectly flavoured and crisp, with matcha salt to add to the usual soy-daikon-ginger dip. Alongside came perfect turnip, aubergine and cucumber pickles, top-quality white rice, and a delicate yuzu-scented soup of fine somen with nameko mushrooms, coriander and fu (folded wheat gluten). The final surprise was a small white chocolate feuillantine pastry, clearly the work of a master pâtissier, which we accompanied with earthy-tasting genmai tea. Service was swift, precise and correct. But the highlight of the meal was watching a sushi chef of rare talent wielding his knives. *Babies and children welcome: high chairs. Booking advisable dinner. Dress: smart casual. Separate room for parties, seats 10-12.* **Map 9 H7**.

Piccadilly

Yoshino

3 Piccadilly Place, W1J 0DB (7287 6622, www.yoshino.net). Piccadilly Circus tube. **Meals served** noon-9pm Mon-Sat. **Dishes** £2.80-£5.80. **Set meal** £5.80-£19.80 bento box. **Credit** AmEx, MC, V.

Hidden in a small sidestreet off Piccadilly's main drag, Yoshino isn't a place you would stumble upon accidentally. It was once the exclusive haunt of moneyed businessmen, but luckily now caters for a more general clientele. Prices have come down and the atmosphere (especially in the ground-floor sushi bar) is far less intimidating. Our midweek lunchtime visit found the bar a busy island of activity; half the room was dedicated to sushi box takeaways, bought mainly by office workers. The bento boxes here are the best bargain. Our £9.80 set menu proffered a generous slab of grilled mackerel, ten thick slices of medium fatty tuna (not always offered, depending on quantities ordered that day), miso soup, rice, various small salads (spinach with sesame, marinated cucumber with crab meat) and simmered dishes (sweet potato, cabbage roll) – exquisitely presented in lacquered boxes. The sashimi itself was worth the price, served with delicate shiso cress; the mackerel, however, was full of tiny pin bones and could have had a crisper skin. There isn't much atmosphere and the decor is minimal (head upstairs to the restaurant for a better perch), but for value-for-money Japanese food, this is a good choice in W1. *Babies and children admitted. Booking advisable. Takeaway service.* **Map 17 A5**.

Sushi-Hiro

St James's

Saké No Hana (100)
23 St James's Street, SW1A 1HA (7925 8988).
Green Park tube. **Lunch served** noon-2.30pm
Mon-Sat. **Dinner served** 6-11pm Mon-Thur;
6-11.30pm Fri, Sat. **Dishes** £4-£40. **Set lunch**
£25 bento box. **Credit** AmEx, MC, V.
Ringlets of shaved carrot, translucent slivers of
leaf-shaped daikon, delicately poised lances of
chive – food presentation at Alan Yau's upmarket
venture is unmistakably high end, as are the smart
staff's quirk-riddled black uniforms and architect
Kengo Kuma's cool tatami and cedar design.
Swathes of straw matting, with sunken footwells,
cover much of the airy dining space on the first
floor of the Grade II-listed Economist building.
Narrow tilted screens mitigate any glare that might
come through the exceptionally tall windows
running around most of the edifice. There are
western-style tables too. The same wood tones
carry through to the ground-floor sushi bar. The
food menu has been shortened since Saké No Hana
opened in 2007, but the saké and shochu lists
remain substantial. Sashimi and sushi account for
much of the list, while pricier cooked dishes such
as miso Chilean sea bass in houba leaf, or grilled
tuna with avocado and okra, make menu-perusing
more interesting. Happily, we discovered that even
though it's no longer on the menu, you can still
order tempura piece by piece; when available, the
courgette flowers are superb. We're not sure
whether the static escalators are a cost-cutting
measure, but the dimly lit lift required to reach the
bamboo-lined basement toilets was in working
order when we visited.
*Available for hire. Babies and children admitted.
Booking advisable. Disabled: lift; toilet. Separate
room for parties, seats 10.* **Map 9 J8.**

Soho

★ Bincho
16 Old Compton Street, W1D 4TL (7287 9111,
www.bincho.co.uk). Leicester Square tube. **Lunch
served** noon-3pm, **dinner served** 5-11.30pm
Mon-Fri. **Meals served** 12.30-11.30pm Sat;
1.30-10.30pm Sun. **Dishes** £1.50-£2.50. **Set
lunch** £6.50. **Set dinner** £10-£25. **Credit**
AmEx, MC, V.
The vibe at this yakitori specialist might be termed
rustic-chic. A rough-hewn wood counter and
smouldering charcoal grills at the front of the
restaurant provide a down-to-earth contrast to the
slick matt-black walls, dim lighting and dark
tables-for-two that line the way to a bar at the rear.

The menu has a few ultra-traditional dishes
unusual for a Japanese menu in London: motsu
nikomi (simmered entrails) and yuba (soy-milk
skin). But the 'Seven Samurai' special (skewered
chicken and onion, chicken wings, salmon, pork
belly, eringi mushroom, shishito peppers and a
sizeable prawn) for £10 is a good entry-level order
and helps keep the bill down. If you're splashing
out, however, exotic temptations include white
tuna with moro miso, and rib of beef with fried
garlic and lotus root. As well as the usual beer and
saké options, cocktails such as Ichigo Plum
(strawberry juice and umeshu) for the sweet-
toothed or Shiso Sparkle (shochu and prosecco
topped with a shiso leaf) for those of a more sour
disposition are worth a whirl. East meets West in
desserts, for example yuzu panna cotta, or baked
chocolate with mirin ice-cream.
*Available for hire. Babies and children welcome:
high chairs. Booking advisable. Disabled: toilet.
Separate room for parties, seats 18. Tables
outdoors (2, pavement). Takeaway service.*
Map 17 C3.

Donzoko
15 Kingly Street, W1B 5PS (7734 1974).
Oxford Circus or Piccadilly Circus tube. **Lunch
served** noon-2.30pm Mon-Fri. **Dinner served**
6-10.15pm Mon-Sat. **Main courses** £6.50-£28.
Set lunch £6.50-£30. **Credit** AmEx, DC,
MC, V.
You almost need a touch of nostalgia (a hankering
for a boisterous, saké-swilling session at a Tokyo
pub) to appreciate this noisy izakaya hidden in a
backstreet of Oxford Circus. The reception is
gruff, the mismatched furnishings are outdated,
the tables are cramped, the cooking is far from
refined – but Donzoko feels like the real thing,
which may be why so many Japanophiles love it.
The epic menu is another giveaway: fermented soy
beans, barbecued chicken gizzards, grilled fish
heads, as well as the usual sushi, sashimi, and
tempura. Yet though the range of edibles is
impressive, on our visit few scored high marks for
taste, execution or presentation. Agedashidofu was
bland; likewise the spicy tuna maki. Deep-fried
marinated beef tasted heavy and oily after a few
bites, and ika natto was a pale, sticky mince. Fresh,
plump scallop sashimi and garlicky, gooey, miso-
marinated aubergine were the exceptions. Still, no
one seemed to mind the haphazard food; it's not
the point. The long list of sakés, including a low-
priced but perfectly drinkable example brewed in
the United States, kept everyone jolly.
*Babies and children admitted. Booking
advisable. Disabled: toilet. Takeaway service.*
Map 17 A4.

So Japanese
3-4 Warwick Street, W1B 5LS (7292 0760,
www.sorestaurant.com). Piccadilly Circus tube.
Lunch served noon-3pm Mon-Fri. **Dinner
served** 5-10.30pm Mon-Thur; 6-11pm Fri. **Meals
served** noon-11pm Sat. **Main courses** £12-£30.
Set lunch £6.95-£16. **Set dinner** £30-£70.
Credit AmEx, MC, V.
The name suggests that it's superlatively Japanese,
but French influences creep into many of the
dishes at this sophisticated Soho eaterie. Foie gras
makes an appearance, as does tapenade served
with seared tuna, and duck confit. We stuck to
classic Japanese dishes such as soft-shell crab
tempura and grilled aubergine with miso. Both
were excellent renditions, the tempura light and
crisp, and the aubergine meltingly soft. The
ground-floor sushi bar turns out excellent sushi.
From a list of seasonal specials, yellowtail sashimi
was of high quality, while a spicy california roll
tasted as good as it looked in its speckled red jacket
of tobiko roe and drizzle of spicy red sauce. Our
hijiki and edamame salad, however, was
overdressed, with limp (unadvertised) rocket
leaves. Saké is taken seriously here; bottles glow in
glass presentation cases and sparkle behind the
sushi bar. If you're intrigued, a flight of four sakés,
each from a different prefecture, presented on a
wooden tray (£8.50), is a good introduction to the
styles available. Or you can opt for wine from the
mainly French and Italian list. There's also a list of
Japanese teas imported from Kyoto.
*Available for hire. Babies and children admitted.
Separate room for parties, seats 4. Takeaway
service.* **Map 17 A5.**

Westminster

Atami
37 Monck Street, SW1P 2BL (7222 2218,
www.atamirestaurant.co.uk). St James's Park tube.
Lunch served noon-2.30pm Mon-Fri. **Dinner
served** 5.30-10.30pm Mon-Sat. **Main courses**
£12.50-£21.50. **Set lunch** £8.50-£18. **Credit**
AmEx, MC, V.
Atami's seductive *Wallpaper**-esque design – all
dim lighting and low-slung, pan-Asian influences
– attracts Westminster's political crowd and, in the
evenings, the odd trysting couple seeking the dark
corners, away from the sweeping glass walls. The
menu is a mix of traditional Japanese dishes,
newfangled fusion ideas, and a few meaty grills
(ribeye steak, marinated lamb chop) that are
seemingly there to satisfy meat-and-two-veg types
unfamiliar with the Japanese menu. We steered a
course for traditional Japanese and weren't

disappointed in our tender, delicate yellowtail maki or tempura onion and sweet potato (although the tempura batter was slightly on the thick side). A more modish dish of deep-fried soft-shell crab and spinach wrapped up, nigiri-style, in a thin slice of cucumber and served with a citrus sauce studded with green peppercorns, was an unexpected delight: simultaneously hot, crisp, cool and sharp. 'New-style' sea bass sashimi wasn't served au naturel, as is traditional 'old style', but instead drizzled with a vibrant, fresh-tasting shiso vinaigrette of which Nobu (see p183) would have been proud. Prices reflect Westminster expense accounts and service can be dozy, but the standard of cooking generally warrants the wallet damage. *Babies and children welcome: high chairs. Disabled: toilet. Takeaway service. Vegetarian menu.* **Map 16 K10**.

West

Ealing

★ ★ Sushi-Hiro (100)

1 Station Parade, W5 3LD (8896 3175). Ealing Common tube. **Lunch served** 11am-1.30pm, **dinner served** 4.30-9pm Tue-Sun. **Dishes** 60p-£2.40. **Set meal** £8-£18. **No credit cards**. First impressions may not be the most auspicious – diners are greeted by an innocuous glass frontage with a display of plastic sushi and a sign stating 'Cash Only'. Once beyond the portals, things look up. There are a few other dishes on the menu (such as white miso soup with clams and edamame), but the customers in the tiny, brightly lit dining room are here for the pure piscine pleasures of unadulterated raw fish. Sashimi and sushi are the heroes, and are among the best in the capital. Our chef's selection of sashimi included sparklingly fresh, silver-skinned mackerel, ruby-red tuna and a scattering of small freshwater prawns. Highlights of the à la carte nigiri selection were melt-in-the-mouth fatty tuna, and sea urchin that released a rush of umami and ozone on the palate. The selection of maki includes the likes of shiso and pickled plum, and traditional fat futomaki made with a smear of pink fish paste. Add a glass of Asahi beer or chilled saké and you're in sushi heaven by way of Ealing Common. Be sure to book and don't forget to take cash. *Babies and children welcome: high chairs. Booking advisable Fri, Sat. Takeaway service.*

Hammersmith

★ Tosa

332 King Street, W6 0RR (8748 0002). Ravenscourt Park or Stamford Brook tube. **Lunch served** 12.30-2.30pm, **dinner served** 6-11pm daily. **Main courses** £5.30-£12. **Set lunch** £10. **Set meal** £25 3 courses. **Credit** MC, V. This popular spot has spawned a second branch in East Finchley, offering north-west Londoners the same grill thrills that have pulled in crowds to this Hammersmith original. Smoky aromas from the robata grill at the front pervade the two small dining rooms; resisting the skewers of meat and fish that are cooked over the hot coals is futile. Our top picks were little pinwheels of pork with shiso leaf, and chicken skin burnished to crisp perfection, but we were less wowed by skewered squares of tofu, singed dry from the heat. Small dishes typical of casual Japanese izakayas, such as maguro natto (small chunks of raw tuna with fermented soya beans) and sakana nanbasu – served here as fried pieces of fish, pork and konbu (kelp) with onion in a vinegar sauce – are well-rendered. Our maki roll of tempura soft-shell crab was crunchily good. A decent grade of saké is served traditionally, in a square cedar cup overflowing on to a saucer beneath. Service is friendly and happy to advise. Tosa is great for Japanese-food neophytes or for those hankering after a real taste of Japan, with prices that are equally easy to swallow. *Babies and children admitted. Booking advisable. Tables outdoors (3, outdoors). Takeaway service.* **Map 20 A4**. **For branch see index**.

Saki. See p177.

South West

Putney

Chosan

292 Upper Richmond Road, SW15 6TH (8788 9626). East Putney tube. **Lunch served** noon-2.30pm, **dinner served** 6.30-10.30pm daily. **Main courses** £3.30-£25. **Set lunch** £7.90-£13.90. **Set dinner** £18.90-£20.90; £19.90-£24.90 bento box. **Credit** MC, V.

With its charmingly eclectic decor, Chosan is one of London's more homely Japanese restaurants. Worn throws are draped over couches that line the room; wooden plaques with the names of various fish printed on them are displayed over the sushi counter; and framed photographs of nature (including Mount Fuji and some squirrels) dot the walls. Goldfish swim in a fish tank. It's a genuine mom-and-pop place, and service is appropriately welcoming and humble. Set menus are a draw; an intense, savoury red miso soup with cubes of tofu began our meal excellently. Sounds of the kitchen waft into the room. The mama-san scuttled off soon after taking our order to prepare small bowls of agedashidofu – slightly greasy, but the tofu was melt-in-the-mouth. Comfort food predominates among the main courses; crisp chicken katsu was perfectly fried and juicy within, and the quality of the katsu-don (pork cutlets on rice with softly cooked egg) belied its slightly messy presentation. Fatty tuna on rice wasn't available, so we plumped for the special of hamachi (yellowtail), the generous portion of which allowed us to overlook the varying thickness of the sliced fish.
Babies and children admitted. Separate room for parties, seats 30. Takeaway service.

Wimbledon

★ Kushi-Tei

264 The Broadway, SW19 1SB (8543 1188, www.kushi-tei.com). Wimbledon tube/rail. **Meals served** 6-11.30pm daily. **Dishes** 75p-£8.65. **Set meal** £9.95-£26.95. **Credit** MC, V.

Like any great kushiyaki-ya (restaurants specialising in grilled skewers), Kushi-Tei has a relaxed, jovial vibe. The enticing aroma of the charcoal grill mingling with sweet soy welcomes diners as they pass through the doors and cross the small room filled with closely packed tables. Most customers are Japanese: a mixture of young couples and large families. The menu focuses on grilled skewers; there's a long list of yakitori, along with other traditional offerings. Our £9.95 set meal of six chicken skewers included an excellent tsukune (minced chicken balls), and crisp chicken wings grilled with coarse salt. Accompanying maki rolls weren't comparable, with slightly overcooked rice and chewy nori wrappings. It's not a bad idea to supplement the set menus with more selections from the grill, such as golden-brown chicken skin (the fat completely rendered for a paper-thin crunch), juicy chicken rolled with aromatic shiso leaves, squelchy shiitake mushrooms, or sweet asparagus rolled in bacon. Appetisers also hit the spot, with shiokara (fermented raw squid pepped up with a dash of yuzu juice) being the highlight. The young Japanese waitresses are perfectly accommodating, though increasingly inattentive by the end of a busy dinner service. Even so, Kushi-Tei is worth crossing town for.
Babies and children welcome: high chairs. Booking advisable weekends.

South

Clapham

Tsunami

5-7 Voltaire Road, SW4 6DQ (7978 1610, www.tsunamirestaurant.co.uk). Clapham North tube. **Lunch served** 12.30-4pm Sat, Sun. **Dinner served** 6-10.30pm Mon-Thur; 6-11pm Fri, Sun; 5.30-11pm Sat. **Main courses** £7.70-£17.90. **Set lunch** (Sat, Sun) £10.50. **Credit** MC, V.

Tsunami does sleek orientalism in spades, with serene white walls and sultry dim lighting,

blushing orchids, dark wood and leather banquettes. The clubby atmosphere is enhanced by young, chic staff and equally hip customers – though the odd family also comes to dig into the modern Japanese dishes. The menu is an exciting read; influences skitter from East to West, with dishes such as yellowtail sashimi with jalapeño peppers, or prawns wrapped in kadaifi pastry. However, our Korean-style lamb cutlets marinated in gochujang (a chilli paste) were a letdown, the paste overwhelming and sloppy. Grilled scallops (too thinly sliced) came with a creamy masago sauce where the highly prized fish eggs were drowned in an unappetisingly rich and gloopy cream sauce. 'Sunkissed' salmon sashimi with hot olive oil and ponzu was as fresh and zesty as we'd hoped it would be, while yellowtail tartare with wasabi tobiko and raw quail's egg was a punchy combination of flavours – all served in a martini glass. Sadly, our main of Aberdeen Angus beef fillet with sea urchin and foie gras butter was less than the sum of its parts (though the beef was perfectly rare as requested).
Babies and children welcome: high chairs. Booking advisable; essential weekends. Takeaway service. **Map 22 B1**.

Waterloo

Ozu

County Hall, SE1 7PB (7928 7766, www.ozu london.com). Embankment tube/Charing Cross or Waterloo tube/rail. **Lunch served** noon-3pm, **dinner served** 6.30-9.30pm daily. **Main courses** £9-£12. **Set meal** £22-£35. **Credit** MC, V.

Perhaps it's a sign of the recessionary times. Ozu, housed in the grand Thames-side County Hall building, used to serve high-end Japanese food, but, following a change of ownership, it has swapped kaiseki for izakaya-style dining. The new look is low-key, with sombre brown wood and a central island surrounded by stools, some tables and a long curving sushi bar. Diners have a prime view of the Houses of Parliament. We visited soon after the reopening and were among only a handful of customers, mostly tourists. The sushi bar was sushi-less because, the waiter explained, the fish 'wasn't good today', so we contented ourselves with cooked dishes from a fairly pedestrian menu. Rice cake and aubergine agedashi was an interpretation of agedashidofu: aubergine accompanied by chewy deep-fried rice cakes, served in a well-rendered dashi and soy broth. A dish of thin slices of pork, grilled and served with 'yuzu pepper', grated lime and green chilli, was simple but imaginative. Less successful was a traditional ten don, tempura prawns and vegetables served on rice. Service was well-informed and professional, but had to battle with music that veered wildly from classical to Elvis.
Babies and children welcome: high chairs. Booking advisable. Disabled: toilet (in County Hall). Vegetarian menu. **Map 10 M9**.

North

Camden Town & Chalk Farm

★ Asakusa

265 Eversholt Street, NW1 1BA (7388 8533/ 8399). Camden Town or Mornington Crescent tube. **Dinner served** 6-11.30pm Mon-Fri; 6-11pm Sat. **Main courses** £5.50-£13. **Set dinner** £5.60-£10.80. **Credit** MC, V.

Those who regularly squeeze themselves into this cramped, shabbily decorated restaurant are often loath to recommend it: they already have difficulty getting a table. But too late – word has got out, forcing staff to turn away the parade of hopefuls showing up nightly without a booking. Why do they all come? Behind the grimy red carpet, ugly stucco walls and tacky Japanese kitsch is a genuine restaurant that serves authentic, quality food in generous portions at bargain prices. The range of edibles (including specials posted on the wall in Japanese, but absent from the English menu) is

staggering. Some highlights: sublimely fresh uni sushi and scallop sashimi; light, crisp squid tempura and soft, chewy sautéed baby squid; creamy monkfish liver (a tad over-steamed) that rivalled foie gras in texture and taste; and a sweet and sticky grilled black cod that slid apart with the slightest prodding. Drinks are equally inexpensive; on promotion was a 'saké taster' offering three small glasses, in varying degrees of strength, for around £7. Given the number of customers (including those ordering takeaways) and the variety of dishes being served, staff were pleasingly efficient.
Babies and children admitted. Booking advisable Thur-Sat. Takeaway service. Vegetarian menu. **Map 27 D3**.

Crouch End

Wow Simply Japanese

18 Crouch End Hill, N8 8AA (8340 4539). Finsbury Park tube/rail then W3, W7 bus/Crouch Hill rail. **Lunch served** noon-2.30pm Wed-Sat. **Dinner served** 6-10.30pm Mon-Sat; 6-10pm Sun. **Main courses** £7.80-£35. **Set lunch** £5.90-£8.80. **Credit** MC, V.

Is style (or at least, presentability) winning over substance here? The food lacks any wow factor yet regularly draws healthy crowds, while better-

RESTAURANTS

Tosa. See p185.

tasting sushi down the road (at Sushi Café Maco, *see below*) fails to pull in as many punters. Maybe it's the well-proportioned room. It could be the sashimi display-cabinet embedded in the back wall, playfully posing as a fish tank. Possibly it's because this was the first Japanese restaurant in N8 (established 2006). Certainly the location, on Crouch End Hill rather than Tottenham Lane, helps. As does attentive service. Whatever the reasons, Wow feels like a destination as well as a place to eat. It does offer a wider choice of dishes, and the specials blackboard is worth perusing for intriguing diversions such as tofu with asparagus and crab meat, or avocado tempura. However, quality is erratic. Said tempura batter seems to be a strong point. In contrast, though, our gyoza – steamed yet not seared – tended towards sogginess, and the agedashidofu's good tsuyu was thwarted by stodgy beancurd. But, it would seem, a 'destination' is always worth going to.
Babies and children welcome: high chairs.
Booking advisable. Takeaway service.

Hornsey

★ Sushi Café Maco NEW

50 Topsfield Parade, N8 8PT (8340 7773).
Finsbury Park tube/rail then W3, W7 bus/
Crouch Hill rail. **Lunch served** noon-3pm,
dinner served 6-11pm Tue-Sun. **Main courses**
£6-£12.50. **Set lunch** £8.50. **Set dinner** £18.
Credit MC, V.
The café formerly known as Matsu is quite a purist affair. Apart from the odd hot component (yakitori, tempura or katsu) included in good-value lunch deals and a four-course dinner set, sushi rules the roost here. Special mention, however, must go to the excellent chicken-and-chive gyoza. Even sashimi barely gets a look-in: there's just the one stand-alone option of salmon; otherwise it only crops up in a couple of sushi assortments. Just as well, then, that the back-to-front-Kangol-flatcapped itamae (sushi chef) knows what he's doing. Maki hold together nicely, while nigiri are slender and elegantly tapered. Fillings and toppings don't break out of the standard repertoire, but they do exceed expectations for a modest-looking enterprise that's often (undeservedly) quiet. The simplicity of Maco's menu is matched by the pared-down, almost industrial look that was achieved by removing Matsu's false ceiling and coating the old cream interior with matt white. We like the helpful service, and we love the doll's-house-sized food replicas in the window.
Babies and children admitted. Booking
advisable weekends. Takeaway service.
Vegetarian menu.

Islington

Sa Sa Sushi

422 St John Street, EC1V 4NJ (7837 1155,
www.sasasushi.co.uk). Angel tube. **Lunch**
served noon-2.30pm Mon-Sat. **Dinner served**
5.30-10pm Mon-Thur; 5.30-11pm Fri, Sat.
Main courses £3.50-£18. **Sushi** £1.20-£2.50.
Set dinner £22.50-£27.50. **Credit** AmEx,
MC, V.
Perhaps because it's on the wrong side of Angel tube to capitalise on the roaming herds of Upper Street, Sa Sa has a low profile. However, it serves high-grade sushi, care of the chefs manning the curved counter front of house. Nigiri come nicely proportioned, with gracefully attenuated slivers of fish atop rice at the right temperature. Maki, such as feather-light soft-shell spider crab with avocado and tobiko (flying-fish roe), are expertly packed and sliced into slimmer than usual discs, making for more manageable mouthfuls. Cooked dishes don't always attain the same standards (gyoza with tough fillings aren't unknown, for instance). Garlic fried rice is increasingly common on Japanese menus, and the Sa Sa version stands out for being moreishly infused with dashi (fish stock); it's also big enough for two. There's only fruit or ice-cream for dessert, but several varieties of both. Cream walls and furniture in shades of beige and tan might not excite, but create a calm, welcoming

Menu

For further reference, Richard Hosking's *A Dictionary of Japanese Food: Ingredients & Culture* (Tuttle) is recommended.

Agedashidofu: tofu (qv) coated with katakuriko (potato starch), deep-fried, sprinkled with dried fish and served in a broth based on shoyu (qv), with grated ginger and daikon (qv).

Amaebi: sweet shrimps.

Anago: saltwater conger eel.

Bento: a meal served in a compartmentalised box.

Chawan mushi: savoury egg custard served in a tea tumbler (chawan).

Chutoro: medium fatty tuna from the upper belly.

Daikon: a long, white radish (aka mooli), often grated or cut into fine strips.

Dashi: the basic stock for Japanese soups and simmered dishes. It's often made from flakes of dried bonito (a type of tuna) and konbu (kelp).

Dobin mushi: a variety of morsels (prawn, fish, chicken, shiitake, ginkgo nuts) in a gently flavoured dashi-based soup, steamed (mushi) and served in a clay teapot (dobin).

Donburi: a bowl of boiled rice with various toppings, such as beef, chicken or egg.

Dorayaki: mini pancakes sandwiched around azuki bean paste.

Edamame: fresh soy beans boiled in their pods and sprinkled with salt.

Gari: pickled ginger, usually pink and thinly sliced; served with sushi to cleanse the palate between courses.

Gyoza: soft rice pastry cases stuffed with minced pork and herbs; northern Chinese in origin, cooked by a combination of frying and steaming.

Hamachi: young yellowtail or Japanese amberjack fish, commonly used for sashimi (qv) and also very good grilled.

Hashi: chopsticks.

Hiyashi chuka: Chinese-style ramen (qv noodles) served cold (hiyashi) in tsuyu (qv) with a mixed topping that usually includes shredded ham, chicken, cucumber, egg and sweetcorn.

Ikura: salmon roe.

Izakaya: 'a place where there is saké'; an after-work drinking den frequented by Japanese businessmen, usually serving a wide range of reasonably priced food.

Kaiseki ryori: a multi-course meal of Japanese haute cuisine.

Kaiten-zushi: conveyor-belt sushi.

Karaage: deep-fried.

Katsu: breaded and deep-fried meat, hence **tonkatsu** (pork katsu) and **katsu curry** (tonkatsu or chicken katsu with mild vegetable curry).

Kushiage: skewered morsels battered then deep-fried.

Maki: the word means 'roll' and this is a style of sushi (qv) where the rice and filling are rolled inside a sheet of nori (qv).

Mirin: a sweetened rice spirit used in many Japanese sauces and dressings.

Miso: a thick paste of fermented soy beans, used in miso soup and some dressings. Miso comes in a wide variety of styles, ranging from 'white' to 'red', slightly sweet to very salty and earthy, crunchy or smooth.

Miso shiru: classic miso soup, most often containing tofu and wakame (qv).

Nabemono: a class of dishes cooked at the table and served directly from the earthenware pot or metal pan.

Natto: fermented soy beans of stringy, mucous consistency.

Nimono: food simmered in a stock, often presented 'dry'.

Noodles: second only to rice as Japan's favourite staple. Served hot or cold, dry or in soup, and sometimes fried. There are many types, but the most common are **ramen** (Chinese-style egg noodles), **udon** (thick white wheat-flour noodles), **soba** (buckwheat noodles), and **somen** (thin white wheat-flour noodles, usually served cold as a summer dish – hiyashi somen – with a chilled dipping broth).

Nori: sheets of dried seaweed.

Okonomiyaki: the Japanese equivalent of filled pancakes or a Spanish omelette, whereby various ingredients are added to a batter mix and cooked on a hotplate, usually in front of diners.

Ponzu: usually short for ponzu joyu, a mixture of the juice of a Japanese citrus fruit (ponzu) and soy sauce. Used as a dip, especially with seafood and chicken or fish nabemono (qv).

Robatayaki: a kind of grilled food, generally cooked in front of customers, who make their selection from a large counter display.

Saké: rice wine, around 15% alcohol. Usually served hot, but may be chilled.

Sashimi: raw sliced fish.

Shabu shabu: a pan of stock is heated at the table and plates of thinly sliced raw beef and vegetables are cooked in it piece by piece ('shabu-shabu' is onomatopoeic for the sound of washing a cloth in water). The broth is then portioned out and drunk.

Shiso: perilla or beefsteak plant. A nettle-like leaf of the mint family that is often served with sashimi (qv).

Shochu: Japan's colourless answer to vodka is distilled from raw materials such as wheat, rice and potatoes.

Shoyu: Japanese soy sauce.

Sukiyaki: pieces of thinly sliced beef and vegetables are simmered in a sweet shoyu-based sauce at the table on a portable stove. Then they are taken out and dipped in raw egg (which semi-cooks on the hot food) to cool them for eating.

Sunomono: seafood or vegetables marinated (but not pickled) in rice vinegar.

Sushi: a combination of raw fish, shellfish or vegetables with rice – usually with a touch of wasabi (qv). Vinegar mixed with sugar and salt is added to the rice, which is then cooled before use. There are different sushi formats: **nigiri** (lozenge-shaped), **hosomaki** (thin-rolled), **futomaki** (thick-rolled), **temaki** (hand-rolled), **gunkan maki** (nigiri with a nori wrap), **chirashi** (scattered on top of a bowl of rice), and **uramaki** or **ISO maki** (more recently coined terms for inside-out rolls).

Tare: a general term for shoyu-based cooking marinades, typically on yakitori (qv) and unagi (qv).

Tataki: meat or fish quickly seared, then marinated in vinegar, sliced thinly, and seasoned with ginger.

Tatami: a heavy straw mat – traditional Japanese flooring. A tatami room in a restaurant is usually a private room where you remove your shoes and sit on the floor to eat.

Tea: black tea is fermented, while green tea (**ocha**) is heat-treated by steam to prevent the leaves fermenting. **Matcha** is powdered green tea, and has a high caffeine content. **Bancha** is the coarsest grade of green tea, which has been roasted; it contains the stems or twigs of the plant as well as the leaves, and is usually served free of charge with a meal. **Hojicha** is lightly roasted bancha. **Mugicha** is roast barley tea, served iced in summer.

Tempura: fish, shellfish or vegetables dipped in a light batter and deep-fried. Served with tsuyu (qv) to which you add finely grated daikon (qv) and fresh ginger.

Teppanyaki: 'grilled on an iron plate. In modern Japanese restaurants, a chef standing at a hotplate (teppan) is surrounded by several diners. Slivers of beef, fish and vegetables are cooked with a dazzling display of knifework and deposited on your plate.

Teriyaki: cooking method by which meat or fish – often marinated in shoyu (qv) and rice wine – is grilled and served in a tare (qv) made of a thick reduction of shoyu (qv), saké (qv), sugar and spice.

Tofu: soy beancurd used fresh in simmered or grilled dishes, or deep-fried (agedashidofu), or eaten cold (hiyayakko).

Tokkuri: saké flask – usually ceramic, but sometimes made of bamboo.

Tonkatsu: see above katsu.

Tsuyu: a general term for shoyu/mirin-based dips, served both warm and cold with various dishes ranging from tempura (qv) to cold noodles.

Umami: the nearest word in English is tastiness. After sweet, sour, salty and bitter, umami is considered the fifth primary taste in Japan, but not all food scientists in the West accept its existence as a basic flavour.

Unagi: freshwater eel.

Uni: sea urchin roe.

Wakame: a type of young seaweed most commonly used in miso (qv) soup and kaiso (seaweed) salad.

Wasabi: a fiery green paste made from the root of an aquatic plant that belongs to the same family as horseradish. It is eaten in minute quantities (tucked inside sushi, qv), or diluted into shoyu (qv) for dipping sashimi (qv).

Yakimono: literally 'grilled things'.

Yakitori: grilled chicken (breast, wings, liver, gizzard, heart) served on skewers.

Zarusoba: soba noodles served cold, usually on a bamboo draining mat, with a dipping broth.

Zensai: appetisers.

ambience. Chefs greet every new customer, and staff generally pay plenty of attention, though specific requests, such as which dishes should come first, aren't always followed through.
Babies and children welcome: high chairs. Booking advisable. Disabled: toilet. Takeaway service; delivery service (over £15 within 2-mile radius). Map 5 N3.

North West

Golders Green

Café Japan

626 Finchley Road, NW11 7RR (8455 6854). Golders Green tube/13, 82 bus. **Lunch served** noon-2pm Wed-Sun. **Dinner served** 6-10pm Wed-Sat; 6-9.30pm Sun. **Main courses** £8-£9. **Set lunch** £8.50. **Set dinner** £12-£17. **Credit** MC, V.

A tiny, bustling place with pale walls that have seen better days, this noisy sushi joint hardly sets the scene for intimate meals. But the din doesn't detract from enjoyment of the food, which is well above average. The menu is heavy on raw fish, and while this didn't seem exquisitely fresh, it was still good – served in generous portions at reasonable prices. Uni and flying-fish roe sushi were particularly outstanding. A house special of ame maki (a creation served here since 1996) turned out to be warm, inside-out rolls filled with tender yellowtail grilled to a pleasing sweetness and dressed with a spicy sauce that gradually intensified on the palate. The limited selection of tempura was light and delicate, and only a touch too oily. Bizarrely, despite a sign outside promoting the place as a yakitory venue, the menu had no sign of any skewered delights. A starter of fried chicken arrived as several lacklustre pieces of fried meat served with wilted, dressed lettuce. The café has the buzz of an izakaya, yet merriment isn't fuelled by the choice of saké: there were only three types offered, including the generic 'hot'. Service throughout was impressive.
Babies and children admitted. Booking advisable. Takeaway service. Vegetarian menu.

★ Eat Tokyo

14 North End Road, NW11 7PH (8209 0079). Golders Green tube. **Lunch served** 11.30am-3pm, **dinner served** 5.30-11pm daily. **Main courses** £2.50-£10 lunch; £7-£18 dinner. **Set lunch** £4.80-£13. **Set dinner** £7-£25. **Credit** MC, V.

A grubby awning still says 'Truva Turkish brasserie'. Pink, upholstered, high-backed chairs and sizeable round tables speak of a possible former life as a Chinese restaurant. But the book-length menu is unequivocally Japanese, offering countless permutations of the standards interspersed with many a full-colour snapshot. Sushi/sashimi sets range from five slices of salmon for £7 to a wooden boatload of assorted nigiri and maki just under the £20 mark. We've had some disappointments – dull agedashidofu, mushy gyoza filling – but we are invariably consoled by decent noodles, good fish and a kind bill. The low prices, along with no-frills choices (such as ultra-plain, topping-free udon in broth) and helpful photos on the menu, also make this a child-friendly place to have lunch. Hesitant but accommodating staff help too. However, anyone with a baby, be warned: there's only one high chair for the entire restaurant. In recompense, the wall-hung monitor that screens CGI seasonal leaves and blossoms (together with insipid relaxation music) might usefully be employed to mesmerise toddlers.
Babies and children welcome: high chair. Booking advisable. Takeaway service.

Hampstead

★ Jin Kichi

73 Heath Street, NW3 6UG (7794 6158, www.jinkichi.com). Hampstead tube. **Lunch served** 12.30-2pm Sat, Sun. **Dinner served** 6-11pm Tue-Sat; 6-10pm Sun. **Main courses** £4.90-£14.80. **Set lunch** £8.80-£15.90. **Credit** AmEx, MC, V.

This isn't a glamorous restaurant: it's the kind of place that in Japan would be a good local you'd visit for a well-priced, dependable meal. But on the winding road up to the top of Hampstead, good food isn't always easy to find. Hence Jin Kichi stays crowded even though the owners haven't updated the red tiled floors, the zebra-print lampshades and the scuffed pale-green walls for a while. Nevertheless, it's the welcome and the yakitory, rather than the glamour, that should bring you here. The grilled food, cooked over charcoal right at the front on the ground floor, ranges broadly over the yakitory repertoire, including dishes rarely found in London. So along with the standard chicken-leek combination, there's tsukune (minced chicken balls), skin and liver; and to jolt you out of basics like grilled onions and mushrooms, there's bacon-wrapped asparagus and duck sticks. Sashimi was disappointing, however; although the fish was fresh and tasted fine, salmon came in curiously sliced chunks rather than prime cuts. The mostly young Japanese team are prompt and eager to please. Not a bargain meal, but you're likely to leave happy.
Babies and children welcome: high chairs. Booking advisable. Takeaway service. Map 28 B2.

Swiss Cottage

Benihana

100 Avenue Road, NW3 3HF (7586 9508, www.benihana.co.uk). Swiss Cottage tube. **Lunch served** noon-3pm daily. **Dinner served** 5.30-10.30pm Mon-Sat; 5-10pm Sun. **Set lunch** £11-£19. **Set dinner** £18-£48. **Credit** AmEx, MC, V.

The appeal of the Benihana chain lies in its 'food as event' concept. All hot dishes are prepared on a teppan: a large hot-plate at centre stage on each table. On Sunday lunchtimes particularly, when hoards of families arrive, cooking becomes theatre. First, there's an explosion of fire as the teppan is cleaned. Our chef started with an onion, which soon became a volcano and then a steam train. The rice was a beating heart, the chicken a caterpillar. Salt and pepper pots did somersaults around our heads before landing on top of the chef's hat. 'Watch this butterfly,' he said, while catapulting butter on to the grill. Butter. Fly. Geddit? It's a natty way of charging a lot for what is essentially a pretty unremarkable stir-fry. The sushi is distinctly average too. As for puddings, green tea ice-cream was overpowering and tasted of bitter stewed leaves; wasabi ice-cream was even more unpleasant (proof that just because something can be done, it doesn't mean it should). Still, service is impeccably friendly and helpful, and you won't leave feeling like you've had a bad time – though you might think you've paid too much for such food.
Babies and children welcome: high chairs. Booking advisable; essential weekends. Entertainment: clown lunch Sun. Tables outdoors (4, garden). Takeaway service. Map 28 B4.
For branches see index.

Wakaba

122A Finchley Road, NW3 5HT (7443 5609). Finchley Road tube. **Lunch served** noon-2.30pm, **dinner served** 6.30-11pm Mon-Sat. **Main courses** £4.50-£19.80. **Set lunch** £7.30 (buffet). **Set dinner** £22.50-£34. **Credit** AmEx, DC, MC, V.

On a Swiss Cottage shopping parade, where drivers are likely to get ticketed before they so much as turn off their engines, Wakaba's location seems an unlikely place for a Japanese restaurant to survive. Our most recent visit was disappointing. In the natural light of lunchtime, the minimalist dining room was showing its age, and the welcome was lacklustre. Staff did not seem keen to offer sushi à la carte as described on the table menu, so we stuck to a fixed-price buffet lunch where, self-evidently, few dishes were freshly prepared. The result was a meal that was more school-canteen than fine dining. Chicken wings sat gloopily in viscous teriyaki sauce, while tempura

was greasy and lacking in flavour. Cold salmon and cold fried agedashidofu were surprisingly tasty, and sushi rolls were of acceptable temperature and texture. Service was no more or less than what you'd expect in a buffet setting. In short, this is a good place for the ravenous to eat Japanese food on a budget, but not perhaps worth a lengthy excursion.
Available for hire. Babies and children admitted. Booking advisable Fri, Sat. Takeaway service. Map 28 B3.

Willesden

Sushi-Say

33B Walm Lane, NW2 5SH (8459 2971). Willesden Green tube. **Lunch served** noon-3.30pm Sat, Sun. **Dinner served** 6.30-10pm Tue-Fri; 6.30-10.30pm Sat; 6-9.30pm Sun. **Main courses** £6.60-£13.20. **Set dinner** £22-£37. **Credit** MC, V.

Since a refurb a few years ago moved it from a neighbourhood eatery into the destination category, Sushi-Say has become busier and more glamorous. Crowds of West Hampstead professional couples and groups of friends make their way past the mock-gruff owner behind the sushi counter, to his warmly smiling wife, who oversees the blond-wooden tables at the back. Bookings are becoming necessary. Such punters are attracted by the good, solid Japanese food – perhaps not exciting, but reliably and imaginatively cooked. Everything we tried was as it should be. Of the starters, standouts were agedashidofu, with crisply fried beancurd creamy in the middle; and a dish of simply boiled pumpkin, served in chunks in a sweet-salty broth. Choose your sushi and sashimi by looking at what's freshest in the counter fridges; chu-toro and bream were particularly good, but sweet raw shrimp the best of all. The menu is long, yet all the dishes are generally well-executed, perhaps because many are Japanese standbys that work best when prepared in advance. Friendly and informative service adds to the appeal of this good-value venue.
Babies and children welcome: high chairs. Booking advisable. Separate room for parties, seats 8. Takeaway service. Vegetarian menu.

Outer London

Richmond, Surrey

Matsuba

10 Red Lion Street, Richmond, Surrey TW9 1RW (8605 3513). Richmond tube/rail. **Lunch served** noon-3pm Mon-Sat; noon-4pm Sun. **Dinner served** 6-11pm Mon-Sat; 6-10pm Sun. **Main courses** £10-£30. **Set lunch** £10-£20. **Set dinner** £40-£45. **Credit** AmEx, MC, V.

Korean-run Matsuba is as pretty as a box of luxury chocolates – all dark wood and subtle light panels running along the length of the room, with vintage Japanese parasols and smartly turned-out waiters with quiet dispositions. It's an attractive option for locals (mostly non-oriental, affluent couples and families), not least because of the decent wine list. The menu is a melange of Japanese and Korean dishes, with a strong section on sashimi and sushi; itamae chefs can be seen working in deep concentration in the small sushi bar. Gems include dobin mushi, a clear soup traditionally served in a small clay teapot, with a small piece of lime to add a sour note. It wasn't as intensely flavoured as it should be, but commendable nonetheless. Scallops seared in butter were nutty, creamy and sweet, served in a seashell. Korean maeung tang (a spicy seafood broth) lacked the expected rich umami flavour, but had an exciting chilli kick and plenty of firm, flaky white fish and mussels. There are no real duds here, though we experienced a long wait between starters and mains. Judging by the number of people turned away at the door on the night we visited, it's worth booking.
Babies and children admitted. Booking advisable. Takeaway service. Vegetarian menu.

Jewish

There's Jewish food and then there's kosher food. All but two of the restaurants below are kosher (the exceptions being Nosh Bar and Harry Morgan), that is they are supervised to ensure compliance with the laws of kashrut. In brief this means that meat from a pig and all shellfish are forbidden; cows, sheep and poultry must be killed in accordance with strict rules; and no dairy products are served with, or for some hours after, meat.

The cuisine that has been developed by Jewish communities splits roughly into two. Ashkenazi cooking has eastern European influences, hence borscht, pickled vegetables and dumplings are commonly found on restaurant menus; **Blooms** is perhaps London's most famous exponent of this food. Sephardi cuisine came from Jews in the Mediterranean and Middle East, so at restaurants such as **Solly's** and **Dizengoff**, meze-style dishes like houmous are served.

Despite the financial climate, many establishments are thriving. Some have closed – Armando, Mattancherry (109 Golders Green Road, NW11 8HR) and Entrecote (102 Golders Green Road, NW11 8HB) – though at the time of writing the last two are scheduled to reopen under new management. Fernando's, the kosher pub (56 The Burroughs, NW4 2DX, 8203 5313), has had a makeover to turn the interior into a Moroccan tent, but sadly didn't merit an entry here. There are three newcomers: **Adam's**, a meat treat for the family; Soho's **Nosh Bar**, a revival of an old salt-beef café; and **Kanteen**, the first kosher dairy café in Brent Cross Shopping Centre. Leading the field in cooking are **Bevis Marks** and **Eighty-Six Bistro Bar**. Both serve inventive dishes, with a changing menu that includes meats rarely available in kosher restaurants elsewhere in London.

In recent years there has been an increasing demand among London's Jewish diners for a greater variety of kosher food. Thus you can now sample kashrut-compliant sushi at Sino-Japanese **Met Su Yan**, Iranian-style fare at **Olive**, or even eat like a kosher gaucho at **La Fiesta**.

Central

City

★ Bevis Marks Restaurant
4 Heneage Lane, EC3A 5DQ (7283 2220, www.bevismarkstherestaurant.com). Aldgate tube/Liverpool Street tube/rail. **Lunch served** noon-2.15pm Mon-Fri. **Dinner served** 5.30-8.30pm Mon-Thur. **Main courses** £14.95-£23.95. **Credit** AmEx, MC, V.
Still the most stylish of the London Jewish venues and the only one to have mastered parev desserts, Bevis Marks is where to take friends for a kosher meal served with elegance. The restaurant is set above a courtyard, with views of stunning brass chandeliers in the adjoining 18th-century synagogue. Dark wood and white linen create an equally impressive space inside. The chef has changed recently, though the menu doesn't change often enough. Nevertheless, you can expect a twist on the usual chopped liver or salt beef: the first served with fig compote, the second with a Thai dressing. Foie gras and celeriac was disappointing, arriving too chilled so the taste was overwhelmingly fatty. Seared tuna with mango salsa would be a better bet. On our visit, just before a festival, main courses were limited, so we weren't able to try steak and ale pie or lamb chops with thyme jus. Fish lovers might enjoy baked sea bass or herb-crusted salmon with sorrel sauce. Rib-eye steak comes with oversized chips, duck confit with pak choi and orange coulis. In general, cooking could be more consistent. Desserts meet expectations, though the chocolate pudding and ice-cream are better than the slightly heavy almond tart.
Available for hire. Babies and children admitted. Booking advisable lunch. Disabled: toilet. Kosher supervised (Sephardi). Tables outdoors (3, courtyard). Takeaway service. **Map 12 R6.**

Marylebone

Reubens
79 Baker Street, W1U 6RG (7486 0035, www.reubensrestaurant.co.uk). Baker Street tube. **Meals served/open** 11.30am-4pm, 5.30-10pm Mon-Thur; 11.30am-3pm Fri; 11.30am-10pm Sun. **Main courses** £9-£29. **Minimum** £10. **Credit** MC, V.
The only kosher eaterie in the West End, Reubens offers a wide choice at prices no higher than those in the suburbs. The menu is a mixture of ambitious and traditional. The basement restaurant is full of business people at lunchtime ordering grilled sole or tuna, and a more social crowd in the evenings who are tempted by beef wellington or magret of duck. Diners who want to play safe avoid the sauces and go for steaks or lamb chops, though few people seem to order vegetables apart from potatoes. The ground-floor cafeteria is stark with cold blue walls and granite tables, but food is brought promptly, so shoppers stop by after a jostle on Oxford Street. The chef's plate of chicken soup with the lightest knaidlach is a better pick-me-up than a stiff drink. Salt beef comes steaming with a juicy layer of fat, making the slices tender and flavourful. Chicken wings are marinated in garlic chilli jam. From past experience, we've found it best to avoid the parev desserts – apple strudel, lockshen pudding or cake – but with the size of the main courses, you'll leave happily stuffed.
Babies and children welcome: high chairs. Booking advisable (restaurant). Kosher supervised (Sephardi). Tables outdoors (3, pavement). Takeaway service. **Map 3 G5.**

Soho

Nosh Bar [NEW]
39 Great Windmill Street, W1D 7LX (7734 5638). Piccadilly Circus tube. **Meals served** noon-midnight Mon-Thur; noon-2am Fri, Sat. **Main courses** £3.50-£4.95. **Unlicensed. Credit** MC, V. Not kosher
You can't miss the bright red and white sign opposite the Windmill Theatre, where lies this recent revival of a one-time Soho success story. In tribute to the theatrical, celebrity and arty types who flocked here in the years after World War II, the walls of the Nosh Bar are lined with black and white photographs of characters such as Andy Williams, Muhammad Ali and Jack Dempsey (boxing stars trained at a nearby gym in the old days). A small pitstop-cum-takeaway, it was always supposed to be cramped – that was part of the fun. Today's version has a retro black-and-white checked floor, with a few black diner-style stools to sit on while enjoying classic Jewish nosh. This is displayed in black bowls in a glass serving cabinet, which is at the heart of the room. There ae soups (clear chicken, chicken lockshen with noodles, bean and barley), hot salt-beef sandwiches (£4.95: quite a bargain in central London), and a choice of filled bagels (smoked salmon with cream cheese, tuna and sweetcorn, chicken escalope, beef salami). Gherkins are 60p each. To finish, there's cheesecake.
Babies and children admitted. Takeaway service. **Map 17 B4.**

North

Finchley

Olive Restaurant
224 Regent's Park Road, N3 3HP (8343 3188, www.olivekosherrestaurant.co.uk). Finchley Central tube. **Meals served** 10am-11pm Mon-Thur, Sun; 10am-5pm Fri. **Main courses** £10-£18. **Set meal** £12.95-£17.95 3 courses. **Credit** AmEx, MC, V.
A ten-minute drive from the more bustling kosher restaurant scene, Olive is a calm, white haven with fresh flowers on linen tablecloths. The Iranian owner and staff are pleasant and helpful, though we've rarely found them overstretched. Persian Jewish cuisine is one of the most refined. Here it's wise to go for the specialities – a variety of stews (khoreshts) – rather than the more run-of-the-mill kebabs. Rice is the star of the show, especially shirin polo with sweet orange zest, saffron and pistachios. Several starters feature baby aubergines, while an abundance of herbs and the sourness of dried lime suffuse many of the main courses. Fesenjan is billed as a thick pomegranate and walnut sauce with chicken pieces. It's exactly that (more sauce than meat), but the flavour of the tart fruit and smooth nut-brown sauce is a winner. For dessert, there's Iranian rice pudding, or baklava that's chewier than the usual Middle

Eastern variety, but mint tea is a better way to end the meal and complement the complex flavours. *Available for hire. Babies and children welcome: children's menu; high chairs. Booking advisable. Disabled: toilet. Kosher supervised (Beth Din). Tables outdoors (3, pavement). Takeaway service.*

North West
Brent Cross

★ The Kanteen NEW
Brent Cross Shopping Centre, NW4 3FD (8203 7377, www.thekanteen.com). Brent Cross tube. **Meals served** 9am-8pm Mon-Thur; 9am-6pm Fri; 11am-6pm Sun. **Main courses** £8-£15. **Credit** MC, V.

The first kosher-supervised eatery in Brent Cross Shopping Centre has been eagerly received. Tables are packed (even outside) with shoppers needing a break from trying on shoes. You walk in past a bakery – who can resist the challah and golden bridge rolls? The menu is jokily written to appeal to children and encompasses dishes that cover the long opening hours, from all-day breakfast, through pasta, pizzas, salads and sandwiches. The appetisers are generous: smoked salmon wrapped around palm hearts, portobello mushrooms or aubergines with cheese. Thai noodles could have had more vegetables, and the pasta sauce could have been more intense, but families with children will appreciate this kind of food: the choice that lets one person have haddock and chips while another tucks into american pancakes with syrup. At less busy times it would make sense to stop off for an Israeli breakfast or a cream tea. Also worth a try is the food you wouldn't usually cook at home: fried egg and chips, deep-fried cigars and vegetarian kibbe. Service is slow, but this allows time to work up an appetite for one of the ice-cream desserts: perhaps pink paradise (soft ice-cream with strawberries). *Babies and children welcome: children's menu; high chairs. Bookings not accepted. Disabled: toilet. Takeaway service.*

Golders Green

Bloom's
130 Golders Green Road, NW11 8HB (8455 1338). Golders Green tube. **Lunch served** noon-3pm Fri. **Meals served** noon-10.30pm Mon-Thur, Sun. **Main courses** £15-£25. **Credit** MC, V.

Though its Edgware branch has closed, this long-lived landmark is still turning out traditional Ashkenazi food, with portion-sizes and menu unchanged. A bowl of barley soup followed by a helping of tongue and chips will leave you replete until the following day. It's possible to choose beef curry or spaghetti bolognese, but look around the tables (with their stylish new crockery and cutlery), and you'll see plates of chicken schnitzel, liver and onions and the not-cheap, but well-stuffed sandwiches. It's what the punters expect. They come back time and again for meat that is more than well done, and salt beef that sadly has no fat and consequently seems to lack the flavour once found here. Chips and latkes are chunky and crisp. Chopped liver with rye bread is a standard rendition, though the egg and onion has morphed into something unfamiliar with added mayonnaise. Roast duck and beef both suffered from seemingly being cooked long before serving – and the attempt at parev custard in a pudding is best avoided. Staff deal helpfully with families, and children happily munch through lockshen soup and sausages. Those with higher expectations may be less content. *Babies and children welcome: children's menu; high chairs. Kosher supervised (Beth Din). Takeaway service.*

Dizengoff
118 Golders Green Road, NW11 8HB (8458 7003, www.dizengoffkosherrestaurant.co.uk). Golders Green tube. **Meals served** 11am-midnight Mon-Thur, Sun; 11am-1hr before sabbath Fri; 1hr after sabbath-midnight Sat. **Main courses** £12-£18. **Credit** AmEx, MC, V.

A refurbishment has left Dizengoff with green tables and comfortable chairs. The pictures on the walls have changed too: on one side you can now view skyscrapers and the Tel Aviv shoreline; on the other, old stone houses in Jerusalem. But the Israeli grills remain consistently good. Though there's a well-priced lunch menu (with little choice), it's best to select from the carte and go for the lamb: tender cubes in a kebab, or braised shank casserole with potatoes and carrots in cumin-flavoured gravy. Chips and rice are cooked just right, and the accompanying side salad is pleasantly lemony. Starters include soups, houmous, falafel (also good for a light meal) and one Ashkenazi dish: chopped liver, served here with minced egg to make it lighter and less meaty. Vine leaves, tabouleh and beef cigars are more in line with the Sephardi style, and kibbe comes with a crisp bulgar shell and savoury meat filling. There's chicken, of course: grilled or fried in schnitzels, and a choice of steaks from the display at the front. Service is passable, though warm puffy pitta bread arrived when the starters were nearly finished. Never mind: go for the grills and enjoy. *Babies and children welcome: children's menu; high chairs. Booking essential weekends. Kosher supervised (Sephardi). Tables outdoors (3, pavement). Takeaway service.*

La Fiesta
235 Golders Green Road, NW11 9ES (8458 0444, www.lafiestauk.com). Brent Cross tube. **Meals served** noon-11pm Mon-Thur, Sun. **Main courses** £8.75-£26.50. **Set lunch** £15.50 3 courses. **Credit** MC, V.

At the back of what looks like a caff with a grill is a hidden kosher Argentinian restaurant. Near the entrance are plastic tables where people wait for takeaways. The meat on display is appealing: an appetising selection of steaks, asado ribs and kebabs ready to be barbecued over hot coals. The menu is for carnivores – La Fiesta is no place for vegetarians. The main dining area has a warm, Argentinian feel. There are wheels and saddles and pictures of gauchos on the walls. Tables are rustic; lights and music pleasantly low. Staff bring complimentary bread and a large salad. The extra-hungry might want to start with empanadas or soup (we prefer the tomato and roasted pepper to the chicken). Anticipation begins with the arrival of glowing coals and the accompaniments to the meat: mustard, ketchup and a herby chimichurri sauce. Our lamb cutlets and entrecôte steak were well cooked and full of flavour. Even the smallest steak (250g) seems generous. Chips or garlicky potato salteña (like an empanada) and a chargrilled vegetable brochette complete the simple grill experience. Linger over a glass of French or Israeli merlot rather than trying the dessert crêpes, which come with faux cream or ice-cream. *Babies and children welcome: children's menu; high chairs. Booking advisable. Kosher supervised (Beth Din). Takeaway service.*

Met Su Yan
134 Golders Green Road, NW11 8HB (8458 8088, www.metsuyan.co.uk). Golders Green tube. **Lunch served** noon-2.30pm, **dinner served** 6-11pm Mon-Thur, Sun. **Main courses** £12.95-£15.95. **Set lunch** £12.95 2 courses. **Set meal** £25 3 courses, £30 4 courses. **Credit** AmEx, MC, V.

The Chinese-sounding name actually means 'excellent' in Hebrew. It certainly applies to Met Su Yan's service, the stylish crockery and to the most calming and elegant decor in bustling Golders Green. There are two food styles: Chinese and Japanese. The sushi menu is written with explanations, suggesting it's for kosher diners with little experience of sashimi or nigiri. The wide choice includes vegetarian maki. It looked good, but we opted for the Chinese set meal (half price at lunchtime). Starters are a strong point: imperial hors d'oeuvres was a crisp selection of spring rolls (a bit sparse on filling), seaweed and sesame chicken toasts. Spicy peanut and dipping sauces added flavour to skewers of chicken satay and barbecued lamb ribs. Main courses were less

successful. Instead of choosing duck breast with fresh mango slices or 'crying tiger' (ribeye steak with Thai sauce), we ordered stir-fried chicken with chinese veg, and sizzling lamb in black bean sauce (which arrived with an appetising crackle). Rice and noodles were fine, but like the meats, unexceptional. A fresh fruit salad could have been juicier, but the sesame-topped toffee banana was a wow: bitingly hot and crisp. What's the Chinese/Hebrew for variable? *Babies and children welcome: high chairs. Booking advisable. Kosher supervised (Federation). Takeaway service; delivery service (over £30 within 2-mile radius).*

Novellino
103 Golders Green Road, NW11 8EN (8458 7273). Golders Green tube. **Meals served** 8.30am-11.30pm Mon-Thur, Sun; 8.30am-4pm Fri. **Main courses** £9-£18. **Credit** MC, V.

This popular dairy restaurant stays busy, especially at lunchtime, while three nearby eateries have closed. Service in the large dining area is cheerful, if occasionally slow, and the menu is appealing: fresh-looking salads, own-made pasta and a wide choice of fish. But somehow Novellino has lost its zing. Don't miss out on the basket of crusty breads, with superb walnut loaf and country white (which you must ask for). Asparagus soup was smooth but bland, and fresh tuna in a salade niçoise lacked flavour. In contrast, a leek and camembert tart was as good as you might get in a French restaurant, and own-made spinach or mushroom ravioli was up to former standards. Vegetarians have a good choice, with aubergine parmigiana and baked butternut squash standing out. Fish is a forte too. The portions of tuna, sea bass and fish cakes challenge the biggest appetites, though a salmon salad came with surprisingly thin slices. Order a glass of freshly squeezed orange juice while contemplating a dessert. With more than 20 puddings to choose from it's hard to decide between the cheesecakes, chocolate fondants and 'tendance': peach nectar with champagne mousse and almond biscuit. *Babies and children welcome: children's menu; high chairs. Booking advisable. Disabled: toilet. Kosher supervised (Beth Din). Tables outdoors (5, pavement). Takeaway service.*

Solly's
146-150 Golders Green Road, NW11 8HE (ground floor & takeaway 8455 2121/first floor 8455 0004). Golders Green tube. **Ground floor Lunch served** 11.30am-5pm Fri. **Meals served** 11.30am-11pm Mon-Thur, Sun. **Winter** 1hr after sabbath-1am Sat. **Main courses** £10-£15. **Set dinner** £26 3 courses. **No credit cards.**

Since a fire closed Solly's first-floor restaurant last year, owner Linda is happy to be running a smaller venue downstairs. Bright Israeli staff cope attentively with a large crowd, who sometimes queue for tables in the packed dining room. The menu doesn't change; the kitchen specialises in Sephardi starters and charcoal grills. Sadly, one of the principal attractions of the old 'Exclusive' space upstairs – puffy pitta bread made in front of you – is no more. What staff call Iraqi pitta is too crisp and thin for our taste, but the houmous is still the creamiest in Golders Green. The choice of aubergine dishes, cigars, kibbe and vine leaves will remind many customers of their Sephardi roots. Grilled meat came with a nondescript salad but was accompanied by brilliant rice with vermicelli. Mixed grill consisted of four huge skewers (enough for two); lamb kebabs with tomato dipping sauce were slightly overspiced. Conservative eaters might prefer a simple grill with hot sauce on the side, rather than the other way round, but the menu covers most options: from lamb chops with chips to merguez sausages and tandoori chicken. Prepare for a big plate and plenty of bustle, and imagine you're in Tel Aviv. *Babies and children welcome: high chairs. Disabled: toilet. Kosher supervised (Beth Din). Takeaway service.*

RESTAURANTS

Adam's

Hendon

★ Adam's NEW

2 Sentinel Square, NW4 2EL (8202 2327). Hendon Central tube. **Meals served** noon-midnight Mon-Thur, Sun. **Lunch served** *Summer* noon-5pm Fri. *Winter* noon-2pm Fri. **Dinner served** *Winter* 10pm-2am Sat. **Main courses** £3.80-£14. **No credit cards**.

Imagine a standard kebab house in an area that could do with improvement. Then think of appetising, Middle Eastern street food. This is the combination you get at Adam's: newly opened and attracting a young crowd in the evenings. Blown-up photos of houmous with chickpeas, and a map of Israel, give a good idea of what to expect: great-value food in the style of a Tel Aviv shwarma bar. Behind the counter is a long charcoal grill. The meats – steak, burgers or lamb shishlik skewers – are served with salads in either pitta, laffa or baguettes. Our breads could have been warmer. Also, the staff seemed not to have mastered what rare means. Chicken comes spicy (tandoori) or as schnitzel; the menu explains that the more tender thighs are used, rather than the drier breast. What makes Adam's

different is the extra dishes: slow-cooked brown eggs, aubergines, fattoush, tabouleh, and seven kinds of houmous. With plastic-topped tables, this isn't a place for lingering, so you might not stay for dessert (a range of parev cakes), but if ordering food to take away, you could include some baklava. *Available for hire. Babies and children welcome: children's menu; high chairs. Disabled: toilet. Kosher supervised (Beth Din). Tables outdoors (6, pavement). Takeaway service. Vegetarian menu.*

★ Eighty-Six Bistro Bar

86 Brent Street, NW4 2ES (8202 5575). Hendon Central tube. **Lunch served** noon-3pm Sun. **Dinner served** 5.30-11pm Mon-Thur, Sun. **Main courses** £12.95-£26. **Credit** MC, V.

You could easily walk past the dark entrance to this venue, but look up and you'll see a cheeky mural of a balcony scene starring Frank Sinatra and Charlie Chaplin. Inside, there's crisp white linen, a board with changing specials, and photos on the walls continuing the film theme. The welcome and service are warm. Think of 'bistro' and 'inexpensive local French eaterie' comes to mind. Well, Eighty-Six certainly delivers on the cuisine, but it's one of London's priciest kosher restaurants. Is it worth it?

Rack of lamb came deliciously rare on a perfectly reduced sauce with roasted tomatoes and garlic. Frites and a stack of Mediterranean vegetables completed the experience. Veal milanese – a large crumb-coated chop – was equally good, as were the starters: duck and cashew-nut salad in a slightly too sweet but savoury sauce; and herb-crusted tongue, which was meltingly soft inside a crisp exterior. Other choices include sea bass, upmarket burgers, and steak with foie gras. You'll probably be too full to finish with a fruit pie, crumble or sorbet. *Babies and children welcome: high chairs. Booking advisable. Kosher supervised (Federation). Takeaway service.*

Kavanna

60 Vivian Avenue, NW4 3XH (8202 9449, www.kavanna.co.uk). Hendon Central tube. **Dinner served** 5.30-11pm Mon-Thur, Sun. **Main courses** £9.50-£15.50. **Set meal** £20 per person (minimum 4), £22 per person (minimum 2). **Credit** MC, V.

Kavanna concentrates the mind on what's important in an Indian meal. Chandeliers and damask tablecloths, in typical Indian-restaurant style, set the mood. The long menu of curry-house starters, curries, birianis, baltis and tandoori delicacies is wide ranging in terms of heat quotient and ingredients. We started with non-dairy lamb tikka and tandoori chicken: small but succulent portions, not dyed red but golden and grilled. The onion bhaji tasted as it should, but not being spherical seemed to affect its texture. Sag bhaji was a fresh dry spinach curry perfectly cooked. Chicken badam pasanda matched its description, mild and creamy: not for the spicy palate, and you wouldn't know that soy yoghurt was used instead of the real thing. The lamb bhuna (also offered as a chicken dish) came in a rich sauce. The biggest letdown was the basmati rice; perhaps it hadn't been cooked freshly for us. Yet this didn't detract significantly from our meal, as the coconut, almond peshwari nan served as a delicious counterpoint to the meat. If ultra-kosher Indian is what you're after, Kavanna is a good choice.

Available for hire. Babies and children welcome: children's menu: high chairs. Booking advisable. Kosher supervised (Beth Din and Sephardi). Takeaway service; delivery service (over £35, within 2-mile radius). Vegetarian menu.

St John's Wood

Harry Morgan

31 St John's Wood High Street, NW8 7NH (7722 1869, www.harryms.co.uk). St John's Wood tube. **Breakfast served** 9-10am daily. **Meals served** 11.30am-10pm Mon-Fri; noon-10pm Sat, Sun. **Main courses** £9.95-£12.95. **Credit** AmEx, MC, V. Not kosher

At lunchtime, shoppers from St John's Wood's trendy boutiques stop here for a salad or coffee and cheesecake, but in the evenings it's mostly the heimische soups and meats that emerge (slowly) from the kitchen. Service can be very laid-back, with young staff who don't seem to understand the Jewish concept of hospitality: 'keep offering more'. Harry Morgan caters to those who like the idea of Jewish food, without the restrictions, so it might serve cheese blintzes and cappuccinos after chicken soup and worsht and eggs. Not what grandma would have done – but then she wouldn't have offered a lime poached salmon caesar salad, with fish perfectly moist and pink. The regular salt beef is still a favourite (the lean version has less flavour). Order rye bread or a bowl of chips to go with it. For hearty eaters, there's chunky bean and barley soup or chicken soup, though we've found the knaidlach to be hit and miss. Falafel too can be a bit leaden, but the presentation of the food is appealing. On our visit there were no blintzes or apple strudel, and the lockshen pudding could have been sweeter, but the cheesecake was a winner.

Babies and children welcome: high chairs. Booking advisable over 6 people. Tables outdoors (5, pavement). Takeaway service. **Map 2 E2.**
For branches see index.

Outer London

Edgware, Middlesex

★ **Aviv**

87-89 High Street, HA8 7DB (8952 2484, www.avivrestaurant.com). Edgware tube. **Lunch served** noon-2.30pm, **dinner served** 5.30-10.30pm Mon-Thur, Sun. **Main courses** £10.95-£16.95. **Set lunch** (noon-2.30pm Mon-Thur) £9.95 2 courses. **Set meal** £16.95-£20.95 3 courses. **Credit** AmEx, MC, V.

Lucky people who live in Edgware: their 'local' is still turning out great-value Israeli food, served by cheery and competent staff. Aviv offers two set menus, with a choice of 24 starters alone. The slightly more expensive list includes the likes off duck pancakes and a thick, juicy rib steak. Repeat visits and packed tables prove that the owners have got the formula just right: a combination of generous quantities of food and consistent cooking. Crisp-shell kibbe or soft, fatty lamb ribs make great winter starters. A cold mixed hors d'oeuvres includes five smooth tastes – chopped liver, egg salad, houmous, avocado and aubergine, with mushrooms and spicy tomatoes adding bite. Main courses come brimming with chips, roast potatoes or rice and a salad (or rather less appealing stir-fried vegetables). Those with a sweet tooth might go for chicken in barbecue sauce. Duck and schnitzel didn't look so promising, and though dover sole and salmon are offered, you rarely see fish brought to a table at Aviv. Go for the charcoal grills: succulent servings of beef or lamb large enough for the biggest appetites. After this, fresh fruit salad or mint tea might be more appealing than sticky toffee pudding or tarte tatin.

Babies and children welcome: children's menu; high chairs. Booking advisable. Kosher supervised (Federation). Tables outdoors (5, patio). Takeaway service.

Menu

There are two main strands of cooking: Ashkenazi from Russia and eastern Europe; and Sephardi, originating in Spain and Portugal. After the Inquisition, Sephardi Jews settled throughout the Mediterranean, in Iraq and further east. London used to contain mainly Ashkenazi restaurants, but now Hendon and Golders Green are full of Sephardi bakeries and cafés, specialising in the Middle Eastern food you might find in Jerusalem. You can still get traditional chicken soup and knaidlach or fried latkes, but these are never as good as you'll find in the home. Nor will you find the succulent, slow-cooked Sabbath dishes that are made in many homes every Friday. The Israeli-type restaurants are strong on grilled meats and offer a range of fried or vegetable starters.

Since most kosher restaurants serve meat (and therefore can't serve dairy products), desserts are not a strong point. Rather than non-dairy ice-cream, it's better to choose baklava or chocolate pudding. Though, by the time you've got through the generous portions served in most places, you may not have room for anything more than a glass of mint or lemon tea.

Bagels or **beigels**: heavy, ring-shaped rolls. The dough is first boiled then glazed and baked. The classic filling is smoked salmon and cream cheese.
Baklava: filo pastry layered with almonds or pistachios and soaked in scented syrup.
Blintzes: pancakes, most commonly filled with cream cheese, but also with sweet or savoury fillings.
Borekas: triangles of filo pastry with savoury fillings like cheese or spinach.
Borscht: a classic beetroot soup served either hot or cold, often with sour cream.
Challah or **cholla**: egg-rich, slightly sweet plaited bread for the Sabbath.
Chicken soup: a clear, golden broth made from chicken and vegetables.
Cholent: a hearty, long-simmered bean, vegetable and (sometimes) meat stew, traditionally served for the sabbath.
Chopped liver: chicken or calf's liver fried with onions, finely chopped and mixed with hard-boiled egg and chicken fat. Served cold, often with extra egg and onions.
Chrane or **chrain**: a pungent sauce made from grated horseradish and beetroot, served with cold fish.
Cigars: rolls of filo pastry with a sweet or savoury filling.
Falafel: spicy, deep-fried balls of ground chickpeas, served with houmous and tahina (sesame paste).
Gefilte fish: white fish minced with onions and seasoning, made into balls and poached or fried; served cold. The sweetened version is Polish.
Houmous: chickpeas puréed with sesame paste, lemon juice, garlic and oil, served cold.
Kataifi or **konafa**: shredded filo pastry wrapped around a nut or cheese filling, soaked in syrup.
Kibbe, **kuba**, **kooba**, **kubbeh** or **kobeiba**: oval patties, handmade from a shell of crushed wheat (bulgar) filled with minced meat, pine nuts and spices. Shaping and filling the shells before frying is the skill.
Knaidlach or **kneidlach**: dumplings made from matzo (qv) meal and eggs, poached until they float 'like clouds' in chicken soup. Also called matzo balls.
Kreplach: pockets of noodle dough filled with meat and served in soup, or with sweet fillings and eaten with sour cream.
Laffa: large puffy pitta bread used to enclose falafel or shwarma (qv).
Latkes: grated potato mixed with egg and fried into crisp pancakes.
Lockshen: egg noodles boiled and served in soup. When cold, they can be mixed with egg, sugar and cinnamon and baked into a pudding.
Matzo or **matzah**: flat squares of unleavened bread. When ground into meal, it is used to make a crisp coating for fish or schnitzel.
Parev or **parve**: a term describing food that is neither meat nor dairy.
Rugelach: crescent-shaped biscuits made from a rich, cream cheese pastry, filled with nuts, jam or chocolate. Popular in Israel and the US.
Salt beef: pickled brisket, with a layer of fat, poached and served in slices.
Schnitzel: thin slices of chicken, turkey or veal, dipped in egg and matzo meal and fried.
Shwarma: layers of lamb or turkey, cooked on a spit, served with pitta.
Strudel: wafer-thin pastry wrapped around an apple or soft cheese filling.
Tabouleh: cracked wheat (bulgar) mixed with ample amounts of fresh herbs, tomato and lemon juice, served as a starter or salad.
Viennas: boiled frankfurter sausages, served with chips and salt beef.
Worsht: beef salami, sliced thinly to eat raw, but usually cut in thick pieces and fried when served with eggs or chips.

Korean

Until recently, few outside London's Korean and Japanese communities frequented its Korean restaurants – so a meal for novices was an enticing adventure. It still is, though more non-Koreans are coming to appreciate this intriguing cuisine. The UK's Korean population has reached around 40,000, allowing many and varied dining establishments to survive. Several of these are located in central London, especially Soho, but even more are in the south-western suburb of New Malden where at least 20,000 Koreans now live. New this year is **Soju Korean Kitchen**, offering an extensive and inexpensive menu in Soho, and not so far away, **Naru** on the Bloomsbury/Covent Garden borders. They join some of our favourite Korean restaurants in central London: **Myung Ga**, with its great selection of traditional and barbecued dishes, and the rather stylish **Ran** and **Jin**. Another newcomer is Korean-Japanese hybrid **Dotori**, whose popularity in Finsbury Park suggests that the cuisine is set to spread across town. In New Malden, our pick of the bunch is **Jee Cee Neh**, which has first-rate panch'an, the often-pickled side dishes that are typical of the cuisine. Typical too, in our experience, is the very friendly welcome given by staff.

Central

Chinatown

★ Corean Chilli

51 Charing Cross Road, WC2H 0NE (7734 6737). Leicester Square tube. **Meals served** noon-midnight daily. **Main courses** £6.50-£15. **Set lunch** £5-£6. **Credit** (over £10) MC, V.
Spice up your life by hopping into this crowded canteen overlooking Charing Cross Road and enjoy some proper hot Korean cuisine. Smiling waiters (who sometimes get confused), bench seats and a trendy student clientele busy ordering from bargain lunch menus make for a young casual vibe. Kimchi was fresh and fiery with hints of ginger. The heat was turned up further with ojingeo teoppap: tasty tender squid stir-fried with vegetables, all slathered in red-hot chilli oil. The spiciness continued with tteokpokki ramen, offering mouth-watering bites of chewy soft rice cake coated in an addictive red pepper sauce. In an attempt to choose a milder dish, we ordered bibimbap, but were presented with a do-it-yourself hot sauce squeezy bottle to season it. A few enthusiastic squirts later, the delicious bibimbap, laden with an impressive variety of flavourful veg, matched the rest of our dinner's bright-red colour scheme. Dampen the fire by accompanying your food with one of the own-made varieties of soju – the Yakult soju is particularly scrumptious and pleasingly effective. Note: food and drinks can be served in the karaoke rooms in the basement.
Babies and children welcome: high chairs. Booking advisable dinner Fri, Sat. Separate room for parties, seats 15. **Map 17 C4.**

Covent Garden

Naru NEW

230 Shaftesbury Avenue, WC2H 8EG (7379 7962, www.narurestaurant.com). Tottenham Court Road tube. **Lunch served** noon-3pm, **dinner served** 5.30-11pm Mon-Sat. **Main courses** £8-£13. **Credit** MC, V.
This area isn't short of Korean restaurants, but we like newcomer Naru (the word means ferry or ferry crossing) for its civilised atmosphere and the loving care put into food and service. The simple decor includes colourful rice-paper lanterns and calligraphy scrolls, and there are no table-top barbecues to make the room smoky. Most of Korea's famed dishes (including kalbi, japch'ae and p'ajeon) figure on the menu, yet the kitchen aims to modernise. Presentation is classy, with delicate garnishes such as baby greens and micro herbs; at times the cooking is superb. Fabulous dak jjim – a soup-stew of shredded chicken, glass noodles, Korean radish and other vegetables in red-hot spicy broth – didn't skimp on ingredients and was properly spiced to work up a sweat. Decadent bibimbap featured flying-fish roe as well as a glossy egg yolk, flavourful ground beef and a variety of vegetables. Du bu seon (steamed tofu flecked with vegetables and drizzled with a sweet sauce) was elegant and soothing. Drinks include wine and Korean beer. Desserts are intriguing: a Korean take on tiramisu made with sweet potato, red beans and cream; pear steeped in honey; and deep-fried banana with sweet beans.
Available for hire. Babies and children admitted. Booking advisable Thur, Fri. Tables outdoors (2, pavement). Takeaway service. **Map 18 D2.**

Holborn

★ Asadal

227 High Holborn, WC1V 7DA (7430 9006, www.asadal.co.uk). Holborn tube. **Lunch served** noon-3pm Mon-Sat. **Dinner served** 6-11pm Mon-Sat; 6-10.30pm Sun. **Main courses** £6-£20. **Set lunch** £8.50-£15.80. **Set dinner** £17.50-£30. **Credit** AmEx, MC, V.
This dimly lit basement restaurant is so close to Holborn tube you half expect to hear trains rumbling past instead of the contented murmuring of customers. Stairs lead to a central open-plan corridor, lined with screens and fake hedges, from which the dining areas and private rooms extend. A wall of wooden blocks adds a chic element to the decor; elsewhere is open brickwork and ornamental masks. Asadal's choice of wines by the glass is limited, but there's also Korean Hite beer. Apart from being repeatedly pressed to order drinks quickly, service on our visit was spot-on: encouraging and keen to discuss Korean cooking. Seafood pancake starter was a bit greasy and scant on seafood, but nice enough; mixed namul were workaday. Things improved substantially with the barbecue. From around 15 choices ranging from mixed vegetables to ox tongue, we opted for mildly spicy marinated pork, and beef sirloin with sesame and garlic. The thin slices of meats were cooked with care and grace in the table-top. They were great fun to eat wrapped in lettuce with full-flavoured bean paste, though more leaves would have been welcome (especially given the £2.50 charge). Finish with cinnamon soju punch, fruit or ice-cream, and you'll probably leave vowing to make Asadal a regular haunt.
Babies and children welcome: high chairs. Booking advisable. Disabled: toilet. Separate rooms for parties, seating 6 and 12. Takeaway service. **Map 18 E2.**

Leicester Square

★ Jindalle

6 Panton Street, SW1Y 4DL (7930 8881). Piccadilly Circus tube. **Meals served** noon-11pm daily. **Main courses** £7.90-£17.90. **Set lunch** £4.95-£7.95. **Set dinner** (5-9pm) £8.90. **Credit** AmEx, MC, V.

Palace. See p199.

Just off Haymarket, Jindalle is an affordable and tasty option for pre-theatre dining. Chrome funnel-shaped ducts, black leather chairs and an exposed brick wall give the place a modern industrial feel, and though it's beginning to look a bit rundown, we don't mind: the food is as good as ever. Barbecue is the house speciality, with an exhaustive selection of beef, pork, chicken, seafood and even duck offered. It's no surprise the restaurant is packed with couples and large groups in the mood to eat meat on the cheap. The bulgogi set menu was surprisingly generous in size and accompaniments, coming with soup, a side dish and boiled own-made pork dumplings. Our waitress rushed around, but skilfully grilled our order. Kimchi tofu, a dish of stir-fried and stewed pickled cabbage and pork belly served alongside steamed tofu, left us salivating for more. Haemul pa jun was delicately fried, light in texture and chock-full of mussels and squid. Grilled mackerel seemed more deep-fried than grilled, but was deliciously moist and nicely seasoned. English wasn't the waiters' strong point, but their efficiency and smiles made us smile too. *Babies and children welcome: high chairs. Booking advisable.* **Map 17 C5**.

Mayfair

Kaya
42 Albemarle Street, W1S 4JH (7499 0622/ 0633, www.kayarestaurant.co.uk). Green Park tube. **Lunch served** noon-3pm, **dinner served** 6-11pm Mon-Sat. **Main courses** £9-£20. **Set lunch** £10-£15. **Credit** AmEx, MC, V.

Named after an ancient kingdom, Kaya is modelled on a Korean palace, and furnished in the bold bright colours of Korean art, architecture and artefacts. Beautiful waitresses clad in hanboks glide through the tranquil interior, executing seamless service. The restaurant is a temple to the finer side of Korean cuisine; its exquisite offerings include an eight-course traditional meal, a royal set menu, and two intimate screened private dining rooms. Candles and classical music help diners (couples and an after-work Mayfair crowd) relax while sipping glasses of wine. Chapch'ae – vegetables and savoury marinated beef tossed with buckwheat noodles – tickled our noses with its enticing aroma of toasted sesame oil. Dwenjang jigae arrived bubbling in an earthenware pot packed with chunks of vegetables and tofu in a soybean broth. Hoedeopbab shouldn't be missed either: a mountain of delicately seasoned raw fish, julienned veg and fish roe, accompanied by fluffy white rice and mixed with a sweet hot sauce. Quality shines through, justifying the higher prices. *Babies and children admitted. Booking advisable. Disabled: toilet. Separate rooms for parties, seating 8 and 12.* **Map 9 J7**.

Soho

★ Jin
16 Bateman Street, W1D 3AH (7734 0908). Leicester Square or Tottenham Court Road tube. **Lunch served** noon-3pm, **dinner served** 6-10.30pm Mon-Sat. **Main courses** £8-£15. **Set lunch** £7.50-£10. **Set dinner** £30-£35. **Credit** AmEx, MC, V.

With sleek granite tables, modern lighting and a shiny clean interior, Jin is a little grander than its Korean neighbours in Soho, yet remains an intimate venue. Staff, wearing black uniforms, push the service to another level. A mixed clientele of young and old, couples and groups come to barbecue beef on their table-tops and enjoy several other authentic dishes, but the Chinese-Korean food steals the show. Tangsuyuk, a signature dish of juicy pork strips battered and fried to a golden brown, topped with a thick sweet sauce scattered with fresh orange and pineapple pieces, was the best we've tasted in London. We also slurped down jajamyung, a hearty bowl of chewy noodles in a black bean sauce that conjured up fond memories of Seoul. Samgaetang – a traditional soup of whole baby chicken stuffed with medicinal ginseng, jujubes (red dates), sweet rice and garlic – was utterly divine. Boiled for hours, the silky, fragrant broth hits all the right comfort buttons. We loved the dish so much we asked for a doggy bag to take the leftovers home; the friendly waiter smiled and gladly obliged. *Available for hire. Babies and children admitted. Booking advisable weekends. Disabled: toilet. Separate room for parties, seats 10. Takeaway service.* **Map 17 C3**.

★ Myung Ga
1 Kingly Street, W1B 5PA (7734 8220, www.myungga.co.uk). Oxford Circus or Piccadilly Circus tube. **Lunch served** noon-3pm Mon-Sat. **Dinner served** 5.30-10.30pm Mon-Sat; 4.30-10.30pm Sun. **Set lunch** £11-£13.50. **Set dinner** £25-£35. **Credit** AmEx, MC, V.

Dotori

RESTAURANTS

More stylish than the exterior suggests – larger too – Myung Ga is a delight to enter thanks to the warmth of the enthusiastic welcome and the fragrant aromas of the table-top barbecues. Behind the logo-etched glass partitions, your fellow diners are likely to include theatregoers and media workers, as well as Korean and Japanese regulars. Smooth blond-wood surfaces and similarly coloured calligraphy wallpaper keep the mood calm, though things can get lively: especially when staff are cooking at the tables. Barbecue options range from popular marinated beef, pork and chicken, to squid, prawns and sliced ox tongue, but the list entitled 'traditional Korean specialities' rewards exploration. Steaming chapch'ae with succulent, savoury cellophane noodles prompted a 'let's make that at home, honey' moment. Starters include rarely seen kaeranjjim (egg steamed in a hotpot), the expected pancakes and assortments of fried dishes to share. We loved the panch'an – a wide selection of vegetable side dishes including spicy cucumber, classic cabbage kimchi, seaweed salad, seasoned beansprouts, and pickled and shredded radishes – that enhanced the virtue and variety of the meal for just a tenner. Shot glasses of smooth soju brewed from barley and sweet potato went down a treat too.
Babies and children welcome: high chairs. Booking advisable. Separate room for parties, seats 12. Takeaway service. **Map 17 A4**.

★ Nara
9 D'Arblay Street, W1F 8DR (7287 2224). Oxford Circus or Tottenham Court Road tube. **Lunch served** noon-3.30pm Mon-Sat. **Dinner served** 5.30-11pm daily. **Main courses** £6.50-£30. **Set lunch** £6.50. **Set dinner** £7.50. **Credit** AmEx, MC, V.
Hugely popular, this bustling Soho restaurant caters to a young hip crowd taking advantage of bargain set menus. Korean pop music lends a jovial tone, and a purple backlit wall adds colour to the otherwise monochrome and somewhat cluttered interior. We excitedly ordered pa jun, as it uncommonly listed oysters as a filling. A golden pancake arrived, but it proved disappointingly sparse on filling and seemingly without any oyster. Confused, we flagged down a waitress, who answered with a blank giggle. We reminded her again about our drinks, which finally arrived mid-meal. A generous portion of overripe kimchi followed, with a plate of mixed namul including the delectable yet elusive ko sari (menu description: 'bracken stalks cooked and prepared only as the Korean can do it'). Ojingeo pokkeum was a hit: fresh squid stir-fried in a spicy sauce tossed with vegetables. All around us, hotpots for two-to-three people simmered on table-tops and teemed with vegetables and stewing meats. Haemultang, a bubbling seafood potpourri, was tasty enough, but full of shells and bones. Complimentary fresh fruit arrived for dessert, yet failed to make up for the previous lack of attention.
Babies and children admitted. Takeaway service. **Map 17 B3**.

★ Ran
58-59 Great Marlborough Street, W1F 7JY (7434 1650, www.ranrestaurant.com). Oxford Circus tube. **Lunch served** noon-3pm Mon-Sat. **Dinner served** 6-11pm daily. **Main courses** £5.90-£12. **Set lunch** £7-£10. **Set dinner** £23-£69. **Credit** AmEx, MC, V.
A designer makeover complete with space-age pendant barbecue system and dark charcoal walls has turned ever-upmarket Ran into a hotspot for trendy young Koreans. They come to share pots of jeongol: one of the restaurant's specialities, of which there are six varieties on the menu. A friendly spiky-haired manager in T-shirt, jacket and square-edged glasses led us past the small front bar area to a large table with high-backed grey suede chairs. We were happy to find good South African chenin blanc was among the cheaper wines on the list; for a more authentic experience, order soju or cinnamon and persimmon punch. An outstanding Korean flatbread starter was chunky with squid and vegetables and had a delightfully crusty brown batter. We missed the advertised 'fiercely spiced' flavour lacking in the sauce for deep-fried chicken – the result being more like Chinese sweet and sour – but couldn't deny the quality of ingredients or cooking. Seafood noodles (one of a few Japanese-influenced dishes), recommended by the waitress, featured succulent, chewy udon, tender curled squid and fresh-tasting mussels. In all, a great evening in smart, hospitable surrounds – try it.
Babies and children welcome: high chairs. Booking advisable. Separate rooms for parties, seating 12 and 30. Takeaway service. **Map 17 A3**.

★ Soju Korean Kitchen NEW
32 Great Windmill Street, W1D 7LR (7434 3262). Piccadilly Circus tube. **Meals served** noon-11pm daily. **Main courses** £4.90-£18. **Set lunch** £6.50. **Set meal** £8.90-£9.90. **Credit** AmEx, MC, V.
Soju, Korea's signature rice liqueur, is a casual social drink to be shared among friends. Similarly, Soju Korean Kitchen offers diners an informal, inexpensive and friendly option for Korean cuisine. Simple, clean furnishings, including tables fitted with grills, encourage family-style eating and table-top cooking. Traditional dishes such as kalbi and bulgogi, together with street-food favourites (tteokpokki) and Korean-Chinese dishes (tang su yuk: deep-fried pork or beef strips in a sweet and sour sauce) are incorporated into a satisfying and extensive menu. Crisp and well-seasoned namul made a tasty beginning to our meal, served alongside fresh kimchi that exhibited more of a pickled tartness than the usual pungent spiciness. Sizzling in a stone bowl, the tolsot bibimbap was packed full of vegetables and was gleefully mixed table-side by our smiling waitress. Soon doo boo jigae (silken tofu casserole with seafood) was flavourful, but had us hunting for the bits of shellfish hidden within. Service was the highlight, provided by warm and welcoming staff who gladly gave detailed explanations of dishes to the curious Korean food novices seated next to us.
Babies and children admitted. Booking advisable weekends. Separate room for parties, seats 30. Takeaway service. **Map 17 B4**.

South West
Raynes Park

Cah Chi (100)
34 Durham Road, SW20 0TW (8947 1081, www.cahchi.com). Raynes Park rail/57, 131 bus. **Lunch served** noon-3pm, **dinner served** 5-11pm Tue-Fri. **Meals served** noon-10.30pm Sat, Sun. **Main courses** £6-£14. **Set dinner** £18 3 courses. **Corkage** £2. **Credit** MC, V.
Cah Chi means 'together' and this little restaurant makes you feel like you've been invited for dinner at a Korean friend's house – where there's a loving mother, hungry fussy babies, and children's drawings tacked proudly to the walls. The place feels casual and comforting, and the food is traditional home cooking all the way. A few dishes of namul and kimchi are served free with your meal: a generous practice customary to most Korean restaurants outside central London. We greatly appreciated the authentic variety of namul (a nice change from the usual beansprouts, radish and spinach). Out came an array of small dishes, notably pickled seaweed and cucumber, creamy potato salad, sweet syrupy soy beans, marinated mushrooms and seasoned Korean radish. Our order of kun mandu (juicy pork and vegetable dumplings fried to a golden brown) was eagerly devoured. Soon doo boo jigae (beancurd stew) was a little watery, but bettered by the full flavour of twaeji gogi (spicy barbecued pork). Tolsot bibimbap arrived sizzling and savoury, and was mixed with red bean rice. Our cups were constantly filled with warm porich'a and the matronly owner warmed our hearts when she lovingly commanded us to travel home safely. We'll be back soon.
Babies and children welcome: high chairs. Booking essential. Separate room for parties, seats 18. Takeaway service.
For branch see index.

RESTAURANTS

THE DISH

Tolsot bibimbap
If you like fried rice, you'll love its healthier Korean cousin, tolsot bibimbap. A mound of white rice with various goodies arranged colourfully, if not artfully, on top, it arrives at the table sizzling in a super-hot stone bowl (that's the tolsot, or dolsot), the inside of which is brushed with sesame oil before the other ingredients are added. The longer the rice stays in the bowl, the more it develops a sesame-flavoured crust that's so scrummy, some people reckon it's the whole point of the dish. On top could be all manner of things from beef and cucumber to bracken fern and a raw egg yolk, but once it's all stirred up with a scoop of Korea's favourite gochujang chilli paste, and the hot bowl resolutely continues its fiery mission, the result is as toasty and cheering as a cold morning spent under a duvet with a mug of tea.

Minced beef is the usual protein component of bibimbap (literally 'mixed rice') but London has far more interesting variations to offer. At **Myung Ga** we love the juicy crunchiness of the fish roe bibimbap (the waitress said it was her favourite too). **Dotori's** tolsots, including prawn and chicken, come with a choice of sauces for mixing and staff can advise which is best for your preferred version. **Ran** and **Asadal** both offer bibimbap piled with raw beef fillet, but the meat is sliced so finely that the searing heat of the stone bowl cooks it in a flash. An interesting trick at Asadal: they add a splash of the accompanying miso soup to the bowl when mixing it up, to give everything a blast of steam and extra moistness.

North
Finsbury Park

Dotori NEW
3 Stroud Green Road, N4 2DQ (7263 3562). Finsbury Park tube/rail. **Lunch served** noon-3pm, **dinner served** 5-11pm Tue-Sun. **Main courses** £4.50-£32. **Set lunch** £6.50 2 courses. **Set meal** £12-£25. **Credit** MC, V.
Finsbury Park has quickly embraced this homely Korean and Japanese restaurant, making booking essential. A couple of masks and a yellow-lit wall of bamboo sticks provide a modicum of decoration to the cramped but cosy dining room. A sushi chef works diligently behind a tiny bar producing good-looking plates of sushi. Staff, dressed like extras from *You Only Live Twice*, are keen to instruct in the correct method of consumption. The menu proffers two pages of Korean dishes followed by two of Japanese; we focused on the former. Japch'ae arrived steaming hot with a wonderful smoky flavour to its delicate strips of beef. Mung bean pancake was slightly too dry and mealy, but saved by its accompanying dish of savoury sauce and beautifully tender egg-battered butterfly prawns. Even the crabstick that also came with it was pleasant; our (very) near neighbour was keen to know the name of the dish so he could order it

next time. Delicious red tofu and seafood casserole arrived fiercely bubbling – but it was a long wait. While everything is freshly prepared, and the amateur enthusiasm to Dotori is charming, two hours is too long for a simple meal such as ours. *Available for hire. Babies and children welcome: nappy-changing facilities. Booking advisable dinner. Takeaway service. Vegetarian menu.*

North West

Golders Green

Kimchee

887 Finchley Road, NW11 8RR (8455 1035). Golders Green tube. **Lunch served** noon-3pm Tue-Fri; noon-4pm Sat, Sun. **Dinner served** 6-11pm Tue-Sun. **Main courses** £5.90-£8.50. **Set lunch** £5.90-£6.90. **Credit** MC, V.
Smiling black-clad waitresses came promptly to greet us on a Saturday lunchtime visit to this deservedly busy restaurant. Cosy Kimchee is styled like a yeogwan (Korean inn): all dark wood with black detailing, gleaming metal cutlery and mustard-coloured wallpaper illustrated with village scenes. It's not old-fashioned, however, and we were impressed by the clever communication system that tells waitresses which diners' food is ready by displaying the table number above the door. Few guests used the table-top barbecues on our visit, and certainly the menu holds many other delights, from soups to bibim naengmyun (cold noodles in a fiery sauce). Butter-soft fresh lettuce flecked with chilli was quickly brought to the table, along with sesame-seasoned beansprouts and kimchee to nibble. Salty, crunchy deep-fried oysters were unfeasibly large, adding a sense of

decadence to an otherwise nutritious spread of hea pa ri neang che (squid, jellyfish and crabstick salad with luminous mustard sauce) and kimchee pancake. Well-flavoured stock and silky discs of rice cake lifted mandu kuk (rice cake soup with dumplings) above its simple ingredients. Hot, sweet plum tea makes a refreshing alternative to barley tea, wine, soju or OB beer.
Babies and children welcome: high chairs. Booking essential Fri-Sun. Takeaway service.

Outer London

New Malden, Surrey

Hankook

Ground floor, Falcon House, 257 Burlington Road, New Malden, Surrey KT3 4NE (8942 1188). Motspur Park rail. **Lunch served** noon-3pm Mon, Tue, Thur, Fri. **Dinner served** 6-11pm Mon-Fri. **Meals served** noon-11pm Sat, Sun. **Main courses** £6.50-£50. **Credit** MC, V.
There's a lot going for Hankook – it just isn't apparent at first glance. The restaurant is situated far away from the cluster of Korean eateries on New Malden High Street and the busier end of Burlington Road. Its premises, flanked by some desolate-looking industrial firms, have a supremely modest façade. Hence, little passing trade is attracted by day, though at night things get busier with local families. In contrast to outside, the interior looks great – the traditional banquet rooms, with their sliding paper screens, low tables and cushioned seats, are ideal for gatherings; and live seafood (crab, lobster, eel) occupy tanks at the back of the restaurant. On our

late lunchtime visit, staff were busy making mandu (dumplings) for the evening. We tried these pan-fried and were wooed by the flavoursome pork fillings. Jogaetang (cockles in a clear vegetable broth) could have done with a stronger taste of the sea, but denjang chigae (bean paste stew) had a superb kick from added chilli and a richness from the roe-filled shrimps within. Hankook is a fine local, but perhaps not worth a long trip.
Babies and children welcome: high chairs. Booking essential dinner Fri, Sat.

★ ★ Jee Cee Neh

74 Burlington Road, New Malden, Surrey KT3 4NU (8942 0682). New Malden rail. **Lunch served** noon-3pm, **dinner served** 6-11pm daily. **Main courses** £7-£13. **Credit** (over £20) MC, V.
It may be difficult for non-Koreans to find Jee Cee Neh – the restaurant is located on a quiet residential street, and the sign is written only in Hangul (Korean phonetic script). Inside, the room is long and smartly furnished, with wooden partitions splitting the space in half (bicycle-shaped bells are available for diners hidden from view to press for service). This extremely hospitable eaterie is frequently full of a mixture of businessmen (out for a drink and some spicy food), and families with young children sharing the massive jeongol (hotpot stews, the most popular item on our visit). The various panch'an (shredded radish, cabbage kimchi, seasoned potatoes and sweet, spicy courgettes) were all fresh-tasting and clearly own-made. Seafood stew, served in a large hotpot bubbling at the table over a gas burner, was generous in its offerings – a whole half octopus (which the waitress dutifully snipped into more manageable pieces after it was cooked), fat prawns

Menu

Chilli appears at every opportunity on Korean menus. Other common ingredients include soy sauce (different to both the Chinese and Japanese varieties), sesame oil, sugar, sesame seeds, garlic, ginger and various fermented soy bean pastes. Until the late 1970s eating meat was a luxury in Korea, so the quality of vegetarian dishes is high.

Given the spicy nature and overall flavour of Korean food, drinks such as chilled lager or vodka-like soju/shoju are the best matches. A wonderful non-alcoholic alternative that's always available, although not always listed on the menu, is barley tea (porich'a). Often served free of charge, it has a light dry taste that works perfectly with the food. Korean restaurants don't usually offer desserts (some serve orange or some watermelon with the bill). Spellings on menus vary hugely; we have given the most common.

Bibimbap or **pibimbap**: rice, vegetables and meat with a raw/fried egg dropped on top, often served on a hot stone.
Bindaedok, bindaedoek or **pindaetteok**: a mung bean pancake.
Bokum: a stir-fried dish, usually including chilli.
Bulgogi or **pulgogi**: thin slices of beef marinated in pear sap (or a similar sweet dressing) and barbecued at the table; often eaten rolled in a lettuce leaf with shredded spring onion and fermented bean paste.
Chang, jang or **denjang**: various fermented soy bean pastes.

Chapch'ae or **chap chee**: mixed vegetables and beef cooked with transparent vermicelli or noodles.
Cheon, jeon or **jon**: meaning 'something flat'; this can range from a pancake containing vegetables, meat or seafood, to thinly sliced vegetables, beancurd or other ingredients, in a light batter.
Cheyuk: pork.
Chigae or **jigae**: a hot stew containing fermented bean paste and chillies.
Gim or **kim**: dried seaweed, toasted and seasoned with salt and sesame oil.
Gu shul pan: a traditional lacquered tray with nine compartments containing individual appetisers.
Hobak chun or **hobak jun**: sliced marrow in a light egg batter.
Japch'ae or **jap chee**: alternative spellings for chapch'ae (qv).
Jjim: fish or meat stewed for a long time in soy sauce, sugar and garlic.
Jeongol or **chungol**: casserole.
Kalbi, galbi or **kalbee**: beef spare ribs, marinated and barbecued.
Kimchi, kim chee or **kimch'i**: fermented pickled vegetables, usually chinese cabbage, white radishes, cucumber or greens, served in a small bowl with a spicy chilli sauce.
Kkaktugi or **kkakttugi**: pickled radish.
Koch'ujang: a hot, red bean paste.
Kook, gook, kuk or **guk**: soup. Koreans have an enormous variety of soups, from consommé-like liquid to meaty broths of noodles, dumplings, meat or fish.
Ko sari na mool or **gosari namul**: cooked bracken stalks with sesame seeds.
Mandu kuk or **man doo kook**: clear soup with steamed meat dumplings.

Naengmyun: cold noodle dishes, usually featuring thin, elastic buckwheat noodles.
Namul or **na mool**: vegetable side dishes.
Ojingeo: squid.
P'ajeon or **pa jun**: flour pancake with spring onions and (usually) seafood.
Panch'an: side dishes; they usually include pickled vegetables, but possibly also tofu, fish, seaweed or beans.
Pap, bap, bab or **pahb**: cooked rice.
Pokkeum or **pokkm**: stir-fry; for example, **cheyuk pokkeum** (pork), **ojingeo pokkeum** (squid).
Porich'a: barley tea.
Shinseollo, shinsonro, shinsulro or **sin sollo**: 'royal casserole'; a meat soup with seaweed, seafood, eggs and vegetables, all cooked at the table.
Soju or **shoju**: a strong Korean vodka, often drunk as an aperitif.
Teoppap or **toppap**: 'on top of rice'; for example, **ojingeo teoppap** is squid served on rice.
Toenjang: seasoned (usually with chilli) soy bean paste.
Tolsot bibimbap: tolsot is a sizzling hot stone bowl that makes the bibimbap (qv) a little crunchy on the sides.
Tteokpokki: bars of compressed rice (tteok is a rice cake) fried on a hotplate with veg and sausages, in a chilli sauce.
Twaeji gogi: pork.
T'wigim, twigim or **tuigim**: fish, prawns or vegetables dipped in batter and deep-fried until golden brown.
Yach'ae: vegetables.
Yuk hwe, yukhoe or **yukhwoe**: shredded raw beef, strips of pear and egg yolk, served chilled.
Yukkaejang: spicy beef soup.

Cah Chi. See p197.

and small prawns, clams, mussels and chunks of meaty white fish – and could easily have fed three. Gloriously crisp-bottomed mandu dumplings were pan-fried and equally impressive, with a juicy pork, vegetable and vermicelli noodle filling and al dente skins. First class.
Available for hire. Babies and children welcome: high chairs. Disabled: toilet. Separate room for parties, seats 20. Takeaway service.

Palace

183-185 High Street, New Malden, Surrey KT3 4BH (8949 3737). New Malden rail. **Meals served** noon-11pm Mon-Sat. **Main courses** £6-£25. **Credit** MC, V.
Despite its regal name, this charming eaterie is rather home-style. With just a dozen or so tables, the place fills up quickly even midweek. Scores of diners huddle together and slurp up the larger-than-life jeongol stews. The manager is quite a character, with a sleeve full of recommendations. Don't order too much, as each portion left us in awe – a 'small' cod hotpot could have easily fed two, while the large version was shared by an entire table. Our fish was well timed, with juicy flakes of cod soaking up the rich kimchi-flavoured stew. A Korean-Chinese dish of ja jang myun (listed in both languages as a special on the wall, but not on the menu) was excellent, with springy noodles and a well-balanced sauce made from chunjang (a black soy-bean paste), pork and a crunchy shredded cucumber garnish. Beef rib soup was a stunner too, with a rich, almost milky broth that indicated hours of simmering. The restaurant might not be a palace in terms of decor – furniture is simple, specials are hand-written on A4 paper – but the quality of food and the accommodating service make it a right royal treat.
Babies and children welcome: high chairs. Booking essential Fri-Sun. Takeaway service.

Sorabol

180 High Street, New Malden, Surrey KT3 4ES (8942 2334, www.sorabol.co.uk). New Malden rail. **Lunch served** noon-3pm, **dinner served** 6-11pm Mon-Fri. **Meals served** noon-11pm Sat. **Main courses** £6-£9.50. **Set meal** £18 4 courses. **Credit** MC, V.
On our weekday visit, Sorabol was as quiet as could be – a contrast to its usually bustling atmosphere at weekends, when tables are packed with Korean families (especially during Saturday lunch). The menu makes a wonderful read, with plenty of interesting dishes: marinated raw crab, Korean-style blood sausage. We found the kitchen to be efficient enough, but the food was less than satisfying on several counts. The highlight was a starter of

'soufflé' pancake: a fluffier version of the Korean p'ajeon, filled with chopped green beans and accompanied by a vinegar and soy dipping sauce. Yuk hwe, raw beef served with a raw egg yolk and sliced Korean pears, sounded good on paper but didn't deliver; the shredded beef was still frozen in parts, rendering it inedible. 'Anchang beef' was a big improvement, freshly seared on the barbecue at the table. However, the meal dipped again with tteok mandu kuk (rice cakes with dumplings in beef soup), which was overloaded with glutinous rice cakes, making the soup too thick and gloopy. Disappointing compared to our previous visits.
Babies and children welcome: high chairs. Booking advisable Fri, Sat. Disabled: toilet. Takeaway service.

Su La

79-81 Kingston Road, New Malden, Surrey KT3 3PB (8336 0121). New Malden rail. **Lunch served** noon-3pm, **dinner served** 6-11pm Mon-Fri. **Meals served** noon-11pm Sat. **Main courses** £7.50-£11. **Set lunch** £5-£7. **Set dinner** £12.50 per person (minimum 2). **Credit** MC, V.
One of the more sophisticated Korean restaurants in New Malden, Su-La is spacious and smartly done up with private rooms and low wooden tables – most of which were filled on our visit by rowdy Korean businessmen. There are no beers here, only teas and soju. Prices are higher than you'll find locally, but the food quality is generally good. Barbecued pork neck was smoky and tender, served with crisp lettuce, mild chillies and peppery slices of garlic, to be dipped in a hot bean paste: a wonderful explosion of flavours. A greaseless kimchi p'ajeon was thin, crisp and immensely satisfying. Cod roe chigae, chock-full of sea-flavoured, meaty roe sacks, was better than the kimchi chigae, the latter being unpleasantly thick and tasting more of tomato than spicy kimchi. The theme continued with the raw skate naengmyun, which though being texturally pleasing (the fish's crunchy wing cartilage offering plenty of bite) was a touch too sweet. While we appreciated the sleek decor and sober service, we missed the friendliness of the smaller caffs down the road.
Available for hire. Babies and children welcome: high chairs. Booking advisable Fri, Sat. Separate rooms for parties, seating 4-40. Takeaway service.

★ Yami

69 High Street, New Malden, Surrey KT3 4BT (8949 0096). New Malden rail. **Lunch served** noon-3pm, **dinner served** 6-11pm Mon-Sat. **Set lunch** £5. **Main courses** £6-£11. **Credit** MC, V.

One of the smaller café-style eateries on the High Street, Yami is nevertheless light-filled and comfortable. The cosy little nooks, created by wooden partitions between tables, are popular with the young clientele – who come in groups and pairs, pulling up seats and knocking back soju to counteract the fiery cooking. Service is equally young and chirpy; our waitress was all smiles all night, offering concise recommendations for the uninitiated. A plate of well-seasoned, almost smoky chicken gizzards was a textural delight, the gizzards fresh and pleasingly crunchy. Soo doo boo chigae, a spicy soft tofu stew with egg, was perfectly done: soft tofu curds melting in the mouth, with the bold, deeply savoury stew as a backdrop, and the richness of just-set egg yolk bringing the two together. Our next dish was less successful; slices of pork belly marinated in spicy chilli paste, consisted mainly of chewy fat and an overly sweet marinade. Still, people clearly return here, no doubt in part due to the sweet and welcoming staff.
Babies and children welcome: high chairs. Booking advisable dinner. Disabled: toilet. Separate rooms for parties, seating 8 and 10. Takeaway service.

You-Me

96 Burlington Road, New Malden, Surrey KT3 4NT (8715 1079). New Malden rail. **Meals served** noon-11pm daily. **Main courses** £4.90-£20. **Set meal** £17.90-£19.90. **Credit** MC, V.
There's an air of the curiosity shop about this small family-run café – it must be the quaint pink tablecloths, the haphazard service (charming, nonetheless, and multilingual in Korean, Chinese and Japanese) and the slightly cramped interior. Heavy leather-bound menus found their way to our table soon after we were seated: useful tomes, filled with colour pictures of every dish. Pictures do lie, however: we were pleasantly surprised by the generous serving of cold chewy glass noodles with mixed shredded vegetables, wood-ear fungus and prawns. Likewise, a plate of chapch'ae was a heaped portion, served alongside rice. The dishes satisfied in volume, but the cold noodles needed a substantial squeeze of mustard sauce to pep it up, while the chapch'ae was slightly too greasy. Oxtail meat soup had its faults too, with rather bland thin stock and dry meat. We might have done better to order the Korean-Chinese dishes that seemed to dominate the menu, and the tables of other diners, such as ja jang myun (noodles topped with a sauce of soy-bean paste, diced meat and vegetables) or the steamed dumplings, to accompany the pots of complimentary barley tea.
Babies and children welcome: high chairs. Separate room for parties, seats 10. Takeaway service.

Malaysian, Indonesian & Singaporean

With three new openings in the middle of a recession, London's Malaysian, Indonesian & Singaporean dining scene is in a relatively healthy state. Of the newcomers – Dalston's **Puji Puji**, Chinatown's **Rasa Sayang** and Clerkenwell's **Sedap** – we rate the latter most highly, especially for its superb char kway teow fried noodles. Otherwise, the well-established **Singapore Garden** in Swiss Cottage remains our top choice, serving high-quality dishes from the region in a smart setting. **Awana** continues to promote a highly stylised version of the cuisine in glamorous, South Kensington surroundings. If you are looking for more authentic flavours, Paddington's **Satay House** also scores highly, as does Bayswater's currently back-in-form **Kiasu** and **Jom Makan** on Pall Mall. Nevertheless, the cuisine of Malaysia, Singapore and Indonesia is an amalgam of cooking styles, so it's unwise to become too exercised about authenticity. Let's hope this flavoursome food – still under-represented in London – develops in new directions in our city.

Central
Chinatown

★ Rasa Sayang NEW
5 Macclesfield Street, W1D 6AY (7734 1382). Leicester Square or Piccadilly Circus tube. **Meals served** noon-11pm daily. **Main courses** £6.90-£18.80. **Credit** AmEx, MC, V.
Rasa Sayang is all about contrasts. The quietness of the brightly lit basement dining room is so far removed from the noisy, busy collection of close-set tables in the utilitarian ground floor that it could be a different restaurant. The menu too is divided in two sections – the 'heat zone' and 'Straits culinary favourites' – while the clientele is split between Chinatown regulars and a walk-in crowd of tourists. The kitchen studiously avoids oriental cuisine's clichés. Shrimp crackers are brown, with an almost wholemeal texture, and the satay sauce served with the prawn, chilli and anchovy fried rice of nasi goreng was sweet and clear, its peanut content sprinkled on top rather than blended in. A crisp roti (flatbread) was soft enough to pull apart like cotton wool, and a fish curry arrived studded with fennel seeds. Pan-fried carrot cake was an oddly gelatinous confection. The cooking can be workmanlike, but dessert is a must. The deliciously melting caramelised palm sugar crystals at the centre of the ondeh-ondeh rice cakes justify a visit on their own. No two ways about that.
Babies and children admitted. Booking advisable. Separate room for parties, seats 30. Takeaway service. **Map 17 C4.**

City

54
54 Farringdon Road, EC1R 3BL (7336 0603, www.54farringdon.com). Farringdon tube/rail. **Lunch served** noon-3pm Thur, Fri.
Dinner served 6-10.45pm Mon-Sat. **Main courses** £9.50-£15. **Set lunch** £14.95 2 courses. **Credit** AmEx, MC, V.
The cool soundtrack and colourful fairy lights can put you in a party mood here. The dining room at 54 is small but not cramped, and the modish dark-wood furniture and lattice screens are used to good effect. Chinese silks and fresh orchids on the tables contrast well with the bare floorboards. The atmosphere is easy-going, helped by jovial service. Staples such as satay and beef rendang frequently emerge from the open kitchen, but the menu makes unexpected detours into British food, such as roast pork belly and mash, or rhubarb and custard tart. Worth a punt are the 'rice'n'easy' dishes (such as Hainan chicken rice) that provide carbs and protein on a single plate. The popular street snack, curry puffs, filled with diced potato and wrapped in a crumbly pastry case, contained a sneaky note of fiery chilli. We also enjoyed a rare treat, roti jala – a lacy crêpe here served with spicy potato curry. Ikan asam pedas featured fresh, fleshy red snapper that was a perfect match for the delicious sour and spicy curry sauce. Tropical fruit trifle was the only duff note of the meal. The diverse wine list is worth checking out too.
Available for hire. Babies and children welcome: high chairs. Booking essential Fri, Sat. Disabled: toilet. Separate room for parties, seats 30. Tables outdoors (2, pavement). **Map 5 N5.**

Clerkenwell & Farringdon

Sedap NEW
102 Old Street, EC1V 9AY (7490 0200, www.sedap.co.uk). Old Street tube/rail. **Lunch served** 11.30am-3pm Mon-Fri. **Dinner served** 5-11pm daily. **Main courses** £5.70-£7.30. **Set lunch** £5.65-£6.50 2 courses. **Credit** MC, V.
This simple contemporary dining room with pale-green walls, black furniture and a few Malaysian objets is a welcome addition to dining options near Old Street. Sedap's Malaysian owners, Yeoh

Teng Chye and Mary Yeoh, were formerly at Nyonya in Notting Hill and their char kway teow (fried flat noodles) remains one of London's best. The menu is fairly extensive and reflects the range of Malay and Chinese flavours that typifies Straits cuisine. The fried bread, roti prata, is here served with tender, coconut-flavoured chicken or lamb curry. Deep-fried mackerel is a clever local substitution for ikan bilis in the nasi goreng. Vegetable kerabu (salad), with its lime dressing and tapering strips of cucumber, comes prettily arranged on square white dishes. We liked the blachan chicken, in which bite-sized pieces of the bird are fried in light batter flavoured with shrimp paste, and the smoky-tasting aubergine sambal. Multicoloured kueh (sweet steamed coconut cakes) are rarely seen in London, so make a point of trying them. Office workers note: the lunch special at £5.65 offers a choice of starters plus any beef, chicken or vegetable dish with steamed rice, fried rice or noodles.
Available for hire. Babies and children admitted. Booking advisable dinner. Separate room for parties, seats 14. Takeaway service; delivery service (over £10 within 1-mile radius). **Map 5 P4.**

Soho

★ New Fook Lam Moon
10 Gerrard Street, W1D 5PW (7734 7615, www.newfooklammoon.com). Leicester Square tube. **Meals served** noon-11.30pm Mon-Sat; noon-10.30pm Sun. **Main courses** £6.90-£11. **Set meal** £11.50-£27 per person (minimum 2). **Credit** AmEx, MC, V.
On the surface, New Fook Lam Moon looks like many other Chinatown restaurants, but above the cramped front room (with its window display of roast meats) is a larger first-floor dining area. Investigate further and you'll find a small list of Malaysian-Chinese specialities tucked into the menu of Cantonese dishes. Bak kut teh, a pork rib soup often eaten for breakfast, was pleasantly light and sweet with herbal undertones that didn't overwhelm the dish. Traditional fried dough sticks for dunking into the soup were a nice touch, if a little stale, while the addition of beancurd and intestines introduced some variety, if not authenticity. Malaysian-style chilli crab provided a handsome pay-off for getting down and dirty with our hands: fresh, sweet crab meat in a thick sambal sauce redolent of dried shrimp, its richness countered by a sprinkling of spring onion. Stewed belly pork was tender and flavourful, due to its generous layer of fat, but was marred by an overly gelatinous sauce. Still, this nicely rounded off a meal that was satisfying both as stomach-filler and heart-warmer – or eye-opener, depending on your viewpoint. Staff are more amiable than the norm hereabouts.
Babies and children welcome: high chairs. Booking advisable. Takeaway service. **Map 17 C4.**

South Kensington

Awana
85 Sloane Avenue, SW3 3DX (7584 8880, www.awana.co.uk). South Kensington tube. **Lunch served** noon-3pm daily. **Dinner served** 6-11pm Mon-Fri, Sun; 6-11.30pm Sat. **Main courses** £12-£25. **Set lunch** £12.50 2 courses, £15 3 courses. **Set dinner** £40 tasting menu. **Credit** AmEx, DC, MC, V.
Plush Awana is light years away from any hawker centre. Instead, guests join the chic crowd in their Jimmy Choos (a framed article about the designer appears on the wall) at the bar for cocktails before slipping into the dining room with its red leather chairs, buffed teak, silk panels and attention-grabbing satay bar. Service is friendly but not always on the ball. The menu tends to meander, containing a myriad options and lofty prices, but the satay is superb; we adored the juicy organic chicken and plump scallops. Sup asam pedas was a respectable version of sour and spicy seafood soup, yet too similar to Thai tom yum. However, aromatic sambal ayam (stir-fried corn-fed chicken with spicy shrimp paste) brought us back to

Malaysia. Sambal was used again to impart flavour to tasty char kway teow, but we thought £18 a lot to pay for stir-fried flat rice noodles with mixed seafood. We were thrilled to find durian ice-cream on the dessert list and burped happily all the way home (an unfortunate side-effect of this fruit, renowned for its gale-force pungency).

Available for hire. Babies and children welcome: high chairs. Booking essential Thur; advisable Fri, Sat. Takeaway service. **Map 14 E10**.

Trafalgar Square

Jom Makan

5-7 Pall Mall East, SW1Y 5BA (7925 2402, www.jommakan.co.uk). Charing Cross tube/rail. **Meals served** noon-11pm Mon-Sat; noon-10pm Sun. **Main courses** £6.50-£8.50. **Credit** MC, V.

Malay for 'let's go eat', Jom Makan is a fast, fuss-free dining option well-suited to groups and for casual impromptu meals. Malaysian dishes are served efficiently in a large canteen-like room that's modern and airy but otherwise nondescript. Many dishes on the menu – satay, roti canai, nasi goreng – are common in Straits restaurants, but some, such as nasi ayam percik (grilled chicken with spicy coconut sauce) and mee bandung (spicy noodle soup), are more unusual. We enjoyed the mee goreng, chock-full of prawns and chicken, with yellow noodles that had spent just enough time in the wok to absorb the flavours of kecap and chilli while retaining their springiness. Nasi lemak was a textbook example of coconut rice with moist, fragrant beef rendang, and squid in a sticky, sweet sambal that didn't compromise on spiciness. Side dishes and desserts fared less well, with telur dadar (omelette) being rather overwhelmed by raw onion and chilli, and a lurid-green sago gula melaka containing little of the palm sugar that epitomises this dessert. Portions are adequate and prices modest. A good pre-theatre or post-museum choice.

Booking advisable weekends. Disabled: toilet. Separate room for parties, seats 40. Vegetarian menu. **Map 10 K7**.

West

Bayswater

★ Kiasu

48 Queensway, W2 3RY (7727 8810). Bayswater or Queensway tube. **Meals served** noon-11pm daily. **Main courses** £5.90-£7.60. **Credit** (minimum £10) MC, V.

Kiasu has had its ups and downs in terms of quality, but lately seems to be on the ascendant again. The casual, modern decor can put a smile on your face with its quirky touches – such as wall murals featuring variations on phrases containing 'kia', the Hokkien word for 'scared' (kiasu means 'scared to lose'). Smiles continued with the arrival of a stellar char kway teow (wok-fried flat noodles), which managed to keep a fine balance between sweet and salty, moist and al dente. Hidden crisp nuggets of fat were a delight, imbuing the dish with flavour and texture. Chye tow kway (white radish cake) bore similar flavours of dark soy and chilli, enlivened by a generous smattering of chinese chives. Bak chor mee, a minced meat noodle dish seldom seen in London, hit close to home with the correct mix of vinegar and soy, but was let down by too much sauce and insignificantly fragrant chilli. Matters were redeemed by a chendol dessert that had just enough palm sugar to counter the rich coconut milk. As a former winner of Time Out's Best Cheap Eats award, we hope Kiasu will maintain its consistency and continue to be a strong contender in the Malaysian food scene.

Babies and children welcome: high chairs. Booking advisable dinner. Separate room for parties, seats 50. Takeaway service. **Map 7 C6**.

Paddington

Satay House ⓘ⁰⁰

13 Sale Place, W2 1PX (7723 6763, www.satay-house.co.uk). Edgware Road tube/Paddington tube/rail. **Lunch served** noon-3pm, **dinner served** 6-11pm daily. **Main courses** £5-£18.50. **Set meal** £15.50-£26.50 per person (minimum 2). **Credit** AmEx, MC, V.

The aromas wafting from the kitchen that greet your arrival here are unmistakably from the Malay peninsula. That's hardly surprising, as Satay House has been satisfying homesick expats since 1973. Dining takes place on two floors (ground and basement) and business is brisk. Staff can be distant, making little attempt to connect with diners. The interior is modern, the clean lines softened by hibiscus motifs, red leather seats and oak tables. This is a good place to try murtabak: a delicious rolled crêpe filled with spice-scented minced lamb then quickly shallow-fried. Don't expect dainty flavours; dishes can be oily too. Our sambal telor was a belter – soft-boiled eggs quickly fried to impart a crusty edge and laced with hot shrimp paste. In contrast, sotong goreng kicap (squid slathered with sweet

soy sauce) was surprisingly bland, and mee goreng, a hearty plate of fried yellow noodles with beef and shrimps, was let down by overcooked meat. Ais kacang, a street-stall favourite of red beans, jelly and creamed sweetcorn topped with shaved ice and evaporated milk, will help soothe taste buds at the meal's end.

Babies and children welcome: high chairs. Booking advisable. Separate room for parties, seats 35. Takeaway service. Vegetarian menu. **Map 8 E5**.

Westbourne Grove

★ C&R Restaurant

52 Westbourne Grove, W2 5SH (7221 7979). **Meals served** noon-11pm daily. **Main courses** £6-£15. **Set meal** (vegetarian) £16, (meat) £19 per person (minimum 2). **Credit** MC, V.

C&R clearly aspires to be different from its casual sister café in Soho. The overall impression is of a slightly updated Chinese restaurant, with white tablecloths, banquettes lining one side of the room, and abstract art (including a slightly odd piece featuring a naked reclining woman). The menu incorporates both Malaysian and Chinese standards, with the occasional Thai dish thrown too. Perhaps too much diversification has resulted in fair rather than excellent standards. Indian mee goreng tasted overwhelmingly of tomato sauce, and featured limp instant noodles instead of yellow mee (a variation that is common in Malaysia but wasn't mentioned on the menu). Butter king prawns with red chilli and curry leaf had a better flavour, retaining most of the fragrance and salty-sweet butter richness of this dish (though the texture suffered from the prawns being de-shelled). Similarly pleasant was the nasi lemak, boosted by its coconut-scented rice and fresh jam-like sambal studded with onions. We ended our meal with a chendol that satisfied rather than delighted – perhaps an apt description for C&R as a whole.

Babies and children welcome: high chairs. Takeaway service. **Map 7 B6**.
For branch (C&R Café) see index.

North

Canonbury

Puji Puji ⓝⒺⓦ

122 Balls Pond Road, N1 4AE (7923 2112, www.pujipujirestaurant.com). Canonbury or Dalston Kingsland rail/30, 38, 277 bus. **Lunch served** noon-3pm, **dinner served** 6-11pm

Sedap

RESTAURANTS

Mon-Thur. **Meals served** noon-11.30pm Fri, Sat; noon-11pm Sun. **Main courses** £3.50-£7. **Set lunch** £3.50-£5 2 courses. **Unlicensed**. **Corkage** no charge. **No credit cards**.

Puji Puji made its name at the now-defunct Oriental City complex in Colindale. Its new location is a rather unlikely setting for a Malaysian restaurant; the redwood tree trunks, and decking for alfresco dining, are clearly visible from busy Balls Pond Road. Inside, the sparely decorated room, with brown tiled flooring and cut-price furnishings, is overshadowed by a hardwood satay bar. Batik fabrics and a crimson wall and lampshades inject much-needed colour. From the wide-ranging menu, we started with chicken satay, which was overcooked and dry, although the peanut sauce was well made. The same sauce helped to boost a tohu sumbat (beancurd loosely stuffed with sliced raw carrots and beansprouts). Flaky roti canai was much better, but the flavour of the beef rendang was muffled and somewhat anglicised. That most pungent fruit, durian, arrived as an exaggeratedly sweet and wan mousse, and the teh tarik ('stretched tea') was too watery for our taste. Service is well intentioned

yet rather slow. 'Puji' means 'praise' in Malay, but there's possibly too much self-praise here. Note that this is a cash-only venue, with a BYO policy. *Available for hire. Babies and children admitted (until 7pm). Booking advisable. Disabled: toilet. Tables outdoors (3, patio). Takeaway service. Vegan dishes. Map 25 A5.*

North West
Swiss Cottage

★ Singapore Garden
83A Fairfax Road, NW6 4DY (7624 8233, www.singaporegarden.co.uk). Swiss Cottage tube. **Lunch served** noon-3pm Mon-Sat; noon-4pm Sun. **Dinner served** 6-11pm Mon-Thur, Sun; 6-11.30pm Fri, Sat. **Main courses** £7.50-£29. **Set meal** £28-£38.50 per person (minimum 2). **Minimum charge** £15 per person. **Credit** AmEx, MC, V.

Many Malaysian expats rate long-established Singapore Garden for the quality and authenticity of its cooking, but Swiss Cottagers tend to treat it like a ritzy Chinese local and takeaway. It's

certainly a smart setting, with gracious staff in colourful, elegant costumes, and vast windows that slide back in summer, giving plenty of light and leafy street views. The main menu is huge, but best order from the Singaporean and Malaysian section, or the printed card of seasonal specials. Scented towels, crab picks and crackers preceded the arrival of black pepper and butter crab, scorching hot from the pan. Tangy and fiery, the white flesh was succulent, the brown meat sweet and custardy. Moist, verdant pea shoots were stir-fried with soft whole cloves of purple-tinged garlic and proved a virtuous partner for savoury braised noodles scattered with roast pork. There's a choice of four house wines (the Chilean sauvignon blanc is very decent), but prices rise sharply thereafter, making the many cocktails such as lychee-flavoured Suzie Wong more appealing. Tables for two along the gold velvet banquette are too close together, but the mood is animated when the restaurant is full, as it was on our Sunday night visit. *Babies and children admitted. Booking advisable. Takeaway service; delivery service (within 1-mile radius). Map 28 A4.*

Menu

Here are some common terms and dishes. Spellings can vary.
Acar: assorted pickled vegetables such as carrots, beans and onions, often spiced with turmeric and pepper.
Ayam: chicken.
Bergedel: a spiced potato cake.
Blachan, belacan or **blacan:** dried fermented shrimp paste; it adds a piquant fishy taste to dishes.
Char kway teow or **char kwai teow:** a stir-fry of rice noodles with meat and/or seafood with dark soy sauce and beansprouts. A Hakka Chinese-derived speciality of Singapore.
Chilli crab: fresh crab, stir-fried in a sweet, mild chilli sauce.
Daging: meat.
Ebi: shrimps.
Gado gado: a salad of blanched vegetables with a peanut-based sauce.
Galangal: also called yellow ginger, Laos root or blue ginger, this spice gives a distinctive flavour to many South-east Asian dishes.
Goreng: wok-fried.
Hainanese chicken rice: poached chicken served with rice cooked in chicken stock, a bowl of light chicken broth and a chilli-ginger dipping sauce.
Ho jien: oyster omelette, flavoured with garlic and chilli.
Ikan: fish.
Ikan bilis or **ikan teri:** tiny whitebait-like fish, often fried and made into a dry sambal (qv) with peanuts.
Kambing: actually goat, but in practice lamb is the usual substitute.
Kangkong or **kangkung:** water convolvulus, often called water spinach or swamp cabbage – an aquatic plant often steamed and used in salads with a spicy sauce.
Kecap manis: sweet dark soy sauce.
Kelapa: coconut.
Kemiri: waxy-textured candlenuts, used to enrich Indonesian and Malaysian curry pastes.
Keropok or **kerupuk:** prawn crackers.
Laksa: a noodle dish with either coconut milk or (as with penang laksa) tamarind as the stock base.

Lemang: sticky Indonesian rice that is cooked in bamboo segments.
Lengkuas or **lenkuas:** Malaysian name for galangal (qv).
Lumpia: deep-fried spring rolls filled with meat or vegetables.
Masak lemak: anything cooked in a rich, red spice paste with coconut milk.
Mee: noodles.
Mee goreng: fried egg noodles with meat, prawns and vegetables.
Mee hoon: rice vermicelli noodles.
Murtabak: an Indian-Malaysian pancake fried on a griddle and served with a savoury filling.
Nasi ayam: rice cooked in chicken broth, served with roast or steamed chicken and a light soup.
Nasi goreng: fried rice with shrimp paste, garlic, onions, chillies and soy sauce.
Nasi lemak: coconut rice on a plate with a selection of curries and fish dishes topped with ikan bilis (qv).
Nonya or **Nyonya:** the name referring to both the women and the dishes of the Straits Chinese community.
Otak otak: a Nonya (qv) speciality made from eggs, fish and coconut milk.
Pandan leaves: a variety of the screwpine plant; used to add colour and fragrance to both savoury and sweet dishes.
Panggang: grilled or barbecued.
Peranakan: refers to the descendants of Chinese settlers who first came to Malacca (now Melaka), a seaport on the Malaysian west coast, in the 17th century. It is generally applied to those born of Sino-Malay extraction who adopted Malay customs, costume and cuisine, the community being known as 'Straits Chinese'. The cuisine is also known as Nonya (qv).
Petai: a pungent, flat green bean used in Malaysian cooking.
Poh pia or **popiah:** spring rolls. Nonya or Penang popiah are not deep-fried and consist of egg or rice paper wrappers filled with a vegetable and prawn medley.
Rempah: generic term for the fresh curry pastes used in Malaysian cookery.
Rendang: meat cooked in coconut milk, a 'dry' curry.

Rojak: raw fruit and vegetables in a sweet spicy sauce.
Roti canai: a South Indian/Malaysian breakfast dish of fried unleavened bread served with a dip of either chicken curry or dal.
Sambal: there are several types of sambal, often made of fiery chilli sauce, onions and coconut oil; it can be served as a side dish or used as a relish. The suffix 'sambal' means 'cooked with chilli'.
Satay: there are two types – terkan (minced and moulded to the skewer) and chochok ('shish', more common in London). Beef or chicken are the traditional choices, though prawn is now often available too. Satay is served with a rich spicy sauce made from onions, lemongrass, galangal (qv), and chillies in tamarind sauce; it is sweetened and thickened with ground peanuts.
Sayur: vegetables.
Soto ayam: a classic spicy chicken soup, often with noodles.
Sotong: squid.
Tauhu goreng: deep-fried beancurd and beansprouts tossed in a spicy peanut sauce, served cold.
Udang: prawns.

DESSERTS
Ais or **es:** ice; a prefix for the multitude of desserts made with combinations of fruit salad, agar jelly cubes, palm syrup, condensed milk and crushed ice.
Ais (or es) kacang: shaved ice and syrup mixed with jellies, red beans and sweetcorn.
Bubur pulut hitam: black glutinous rice served in coconut milk and palm sugar.
Cendol or **chendol:** mung bean flour pasta, coloured and perfumed with essence of pandan leaf (qv) and served in a chilled coconut milk and palm sugar syrup.
Gula melaka: palm sugar, an important ingredient with a distinctive caramel flavour added to a sago and coconut-milk pudding of the same name.
Kueh or **kuih:** literally, 'cakes', but used as a general term for many desserts.
Pisang goreng: banana fritters.

RESTAURANTS

Middle Eastern

The Lebanon is generally believed to be the cradle of Arabian cuisine, and restaurants specialising in the food of that country still dominate this section. The turbulent political history of the region may be the major cause of this, but Beirut's loss is London's gain – especially in the case of our favourite Lebanese restaurants, **Fairuz** and **Noura**. New arrivals **Comptoir Libanais** (which plans to have four branches by the end of 2009) and Soho's tiny **Yalla Yalla**, a stylish yet casual café-takeaway, suggest that Lebanese food is becoming popular across London.

Other Middle Eastern countries are represented here too, including Syria (**Abu Zaad**), Egypt (**Ali Baba**) and Iraq (the excellent **Mesopotamia**). Iranian cooking is notably different from that of all other countries in the region, often incorporating sauces made from fruit and ground walnuts. **Sufi**, a modest west London enterprise, is currently our top pick for Iranian food, closely followed by the prim and proper **Mahdi** and a brace of newcomers: Willesden's **Parsian** and Chalk Farm's **Tandis**.

Central

City

Kenza

10 Devonshire Square, EC2M 4YP (7929 5533, www.kenza-restaurant.com). Liverpool Street tube/rail.
Lounge **Open** noon-2.30am Mon-Wed; noon-3.30am Thur, Fri; 6pm-3.30am Sat.
Restaurant **Meals served** noon-10pm Mon-Wed; noon-11.30pm Thur, Fri; 6-11.30pm Sat. **Main courses** £13-£22. **Set lunch** £10.95 (Mon-Fri) 2 courses. **Set meal** £28 3 courses.
Both **Credit** AmEx, MC, V. Lebanese & Moroccan
This cavernous underground restaurant – all rich hues, carved wood and metal screens, reached by a winding staircase – is a bit groovier than its location, in an office complex off Liverpool Street, would suggest. It's a pity, then, that the food doesn't always match the decor. While perusing the menu, diners are presented with high-quality olives, a wide and fresh range of raw vegetables to dunk in minty cucumber and yoghurt dip, and excellent pickles: all complimentary. Tiger prawn falafel made an interesting departure from the norm, with minced prawns providing a pleasant lightness. Tiny Moroccan sausages were tart. Best stick to the carte, as our lunch specials (£10.95 for two courses) were dull. Starters in both vegetarian and meat meals relied heavily on pastry that tasted reheated, and thus was soggy when it should be crisp. Houmous was bland too. The wine list has a number of Lebanese options, yet is largely unexciting. The restaurant's name means 'treasure' in Arabic, but despite its looks, the venue has all the soul and originality of a Dubai nightclub. Belly dancers feature at night, when cocktails also come into play. *Booking advisable. Disabled: toilet. Entertainment: belly dancer. Separate rooms for parties, seating 15 and 50. Takeaway service.* **Map 12 R6**.

Edgware Road

Maroush Gardens

1-3 Connaught Street, W2 2DH (7262 0222, www.maroush.com). Marble Arch tube. **Meals served** noon-11.30pm daily. **Main courses** £11.95-£16. **Set lunch** £16 per person (lunch box). **Set meze** £45 per person (minimum 2). **Credit** MC, V. Lebanese
Maroush Gardens does its upmost to distance itself from the informal Lebanese kebab houses of the Edgware Road. Its marble-topped, hotel-style reception leads to a grand room divided by dark wooden pillars and palm trees. An ornate fountain funnels into a pool of koi carp. Walls are hung with oversized paintings and engraved mirrors, ceilings set with a constellation of spot lighting, and the tables clothed in crisp white linen. Service, from besuited waiters, was both fawning and awkwardly haughty – which might have been forgivable were the food outstanding. A starter of fuul was a cheerful, chunky concoction, but kibbeh were startlingly bland, and had a lacklustre consistency; only fried chicken livers in a fragrant citrus sauce hit the mark. Mains were similarly underwhelming. Courgettes, vine leaves and aubergine stuffed with minced lamb lacked bright flavours, but the biggest disappointment was shish taouk: £15 for a few chunks of clearly overcooked chicken presented with a single potato and two cherry tomatoes. We've had better meals here in the past, enjoying the houmous and tabouleh, but next time we'll visit Maroush's original Edgware Road branch, where music and belly dancing leaven the atmosphere. *Babies and children welcome: high chairs. Booking advisable.* **Map 8 F6**.
For branches see index.

★ Patogh

8 Crawford Place, W1H 5NE (7262 4015). Edgware Road tube. **Meals served** 12.30-11pm daily. **Main courses** £6-£12. **Unlicensed. Corkage** no charge. **No credit cards.** Iranian
Iranians either relish or refuse to have anything to do with Patogh, a kebab joint more akin to one of Tehran's cluttered cafés than its cosmopolitan restaurants. Walls the colour of cold coffee peel and crack; shared tables leave little room for intimacy; and decoration is limited to a handful of Persian paintings, a pair of red lanterns, and a string of coloured light bulbs such as grace the galvanised tea huts at the base of the Alborz mountains. Luxuries are rare (tap water at this BYO venue arrived in a scuffed plastic measuring jug), but few places serve Iranian street food with such an eye for detail. A starter of masto musir

Comptoir Libanais

was whipped to a pleasing thickness, and made the ideal accompaniment to fresh bread peppered with sesame and poppy seeds. Both chicken and minced lamb kebabs were artfully seasoned and cooked just so: charred on the outside, juicy within. A heaped portion of rice was served traditionally, with butter melting at its centre. Those seeking subtle Iranian stews and soups should look elsewhere, but for an authentic taste of downtown Tehran, Patogh can't be beaten.
Booking advisable weekends. Disabled: toilet. Takeaway service. **Map 8 E5.**

★ Ranoush Juice (100)
43 Edgware Road, W2 2JE (7723 5929, www.maroush.com). Marble Arch tube. **Meals served** 8am-3am daily. **Main courses** £3-£10. **No credit cards.** Lebanese

Speedy service is what it's all about at Ranoush, which is primarily the takeaway outlet of the Maroush restaurant chain. Mammoth fridges temptingly display fresh fruit ready to be juiced: ideal for a vitamin-packed pick-me-up at any time of day, or in the early hours of the morning. Shawarma skewers rotate their loads of lamb or chicken, ready to be rolled in flatbread and served as takeaways. A few stools line the mirrored wall opposite the counter, and a couple of tables are placed outside for diners who don't mind the thunder of the Edgware Road. Order and pay at the till, then watch as gherkins and tomatoes are sliced at lightning speed further along the serving counter. The fast food here includes plenty of healthy options ready to be scooped into generous foil containers – loubieh b'zeit (green bean casserole), lemony tabouleh and smoky, silken baba ganoush. For afters, there are bargain £1 trays of tooth-aching baklava. A great budget option, but make no mistake: Ranoush is a place where you grab and go, rather than luxuriate in the flavours of the Levant.
Babies and children admitted. Bookings not accepted. Takeaway service. **Map 8 F6.**
For branches (Beirut Express, Maroush Ranoush) see index.

Marylebone

★ Ali Baba
32 Ivor Place, NW1 6DA (7723 7474). Baker Street tube/Marylebone tube/rail. **Meals served** noon-midnight daily. **Main courses** £7-£10. **Unlicensed. Corkage** no charge. **No credit cards.** Egyptian

It's hard to imagine a reception more frosty than the one we received on our visit to Ali Baba. The materfamilias led us to our table as though we'd come to repossess her television, then took our order with uninterested grimness. For many, such service is all part of the quirky charm of this backstreet Egyptian eaterie. The rear dining room is decorated with little more than a hat rack, a plain mirror and a handful of framed paintings. Combined with the air of proprietary misery, it helps create an experience akin to dining at the house of disapproving Middle Eastern in-laws. Thankfully, the food on our visit was decent, partially redeeming matters. We were particularly pleased with a sizeable starter of fuul, beaten to a creamy paste and a pleasure to mop up with warm flatbread. A main of fried trout in tomato and pepper sauce was also eminently enjoyable, served with the head and tail attached and the flesh virtually falling off the bone. It made the perfect accompaniment to a mound of aromatically spiced rice. Cheap it may be, cheerful it certainly is not, but there's nowhere quite like Ali Baba.
Babies and children welcome: high chairs. Booking advisable. Takeaway service; delivery service. **Map 2 F4.**

★ Comptoir Libanais NEW
2009 RUNNER-UP BEST NEW DESIGN
65 Wigmore Street, W1U 1PZ (7935 1110, www.lecomptoir.co.uk). Bond Street tube. **Meals served** 8am-8pm daily. **Main courses** £5.95-£6.50. **No credit cards.** Lebanese

Part canteen, part delicatessen, Comptoir Libanais takes its design cues from owner Tony Kitous's

memory bank. Cutlery is stored in recycled harissa cans, the communal bar features an ancient Islamic motif, but it's the colourful murals that dominate the space: one of giant Arabic Chiclets packets, the other inspired by a poster of 1960s film star Sirine Jamal al Dien. The place is open all day, so you can pick up a wrap (falafel, say, or chicken kofta) for lunch, pop by for mint tea and a rosewater macaron in the afternoon, or linger over an informal dinner of moussaka or tagine with organic couscous or rice. Breads (baked in-house) and sweets are a key draw. Hot man'oucha flatbreads come with toppings such as za'atar (a mix of herbs and spices) and halloumi, while the sizeable cakes and pastries menu features such temptations as honey and pistachio eclairs, pistachio and almond loaves, and strawberry and white-chocolate muffins – as well as the more usual baklava. Juice combos, intriguing flavours of lemonade, and smoothies made with organic fat-free frozen yoghurt make this a great pitstop for all ages, especially during a West End shopping trip. Branches include a useful one at Shepherd Bush's Westfield shopping centre.
Available for hire. Babies and children welcome: children's menu. Bookings not accepted. Tables outdoors (3, pavement). Takeaway service. **Map 9 H6.**
For branches see index.

★ Fairuz
3 Blandford Street, W1U 3DA (7486 8108/8182, www.fairuz.uk.com). Baker Street or Bond Street tube. **Meals served** noon-11.30pm Mon-Sat; noon-11pm Sun. **Main courses** £12.95-£19.95. **Set meze** £19.95. **Set meal** £26.95 3 courses. **Cover** £1.50. **Credit** AmEx, MC, V. Lebanese

The combination of Lebanese food, neighbourhood-taverna surroundings (small space, rough-hewn white walls, outside terrace) and West End location has proved enduringly popular for Fairuz. The closely packed rustic wooden tables were nearly all occupied on a recent Sunday evening, and the place was buzzing. In fact, from where we were sitting, near the waiters' serving area, things were a little too frenetic. But our slight discomfort was forgotten as soon as the food arrived. We were treated to a collection of brilliantly executed mezes: smooth, silky houmous; fresh, zingy fuul moukala (green broad beans with olive oil, lemon and coriander); and tabouleh (a finely chopped mound of herby green goodness) too. Makdous (pickled mini aubergines stuffed with walnuts and pomegranate seeds) had a good balance of flavours, with mild pickling that allowed the dish to retain some subtlety; it featured a great contrast between soft aubergine, dry walnut and tart pomegranate. Only chicken livers were out of kilter; the dish should be lemony, but these tasted overwhelmingly of balsamic vinegar. The staff were pleasant and professional. Fairuz certainly has the feel-good factor.
Babies and children welcome: high chairs. Booking advisable dinner. Separate room for parties, seats 25. Takeaway service; delivery service (within 5-mile radius). **Map 9 G5.**

Levant
Jason Court, 76 Wigmore Street, W1U 2SJ (7224 1111, www.levant.co.uk). Bond Street tube. Bar **Open** noon-12.30am Mon-Wed, Sun; noon-2.30am Thur-Sat. *Restaurant* **Meals served** noon-11.30pm daily. **Main courses** £12.50-£26. **Set lunch** (noon-5.30pm Mon-Fri) £12.50 2 courses. **Set dinner** (Wed-Sat) £28-£50 3 courses; £50 kharuf feast. *Both* **Credit** AmEx, DC, MC, V. Lebanese

Down a crooked alleyway off Marylebone High Street we discovered people sitting on the floor – not ne'er-do-wells, but rather smart folk smoking nargiles outside Levant. Once inside this opulent den of a restaurant, you'll find the welcome is genuinely warm, as is the decor and the general mood. It would be a fun venue for a date (a single rose leaf sits on each napkin), but is perhaps no place for proposals: the cacophonous entrance of the belly dancer may wreck the moment. The light-hearted atmosphere (think Middle Eastern theme-park at times) doesn't extend to the cooking, which is seriously good. Falafel were expertly deep fried:

Interview
TONY KITOUS

Who are you?
Owner of the Levant Group, which runs **Comptoir Libanais** (*see left*), **Kenza** (*see far left*), **Levant** (*see left*) and **Pasha** (*see p230*).

How did you start in the catering business?
By accident, when I first came to London at the age of 18 and ended up working in restaurants. I opened my first restaurant when I was 22.

What's the best thing about running a restaurant in London?
The fun, the people you meet, the opportunity to serve and satisfy the hungry and thirsty.

What's the worst thing?
The chaos – there's always someone or something that doesn't turn up on time.

Which are your favourite London restaurants?
I like **Zuma** (*see p180*), **Hakkasan** (*see p69*) and **Al Waha** (*see p208*) – cosmopolitan places with interesting food. I also eat in Southall for Indian, north London for Turkish food and often go to Edgware Road for a quick Lebanese meal.

What's the best bargain in the capital?
There are special promotions everywhere at the moment, so you can try out new restaurants or cuisines quite cheaply.

What's your favourite treat?
Spending Sunday at home with my brothers and mother, having a whole roasted lamb with couscous – we don't do it often enough.

What is missing from London's restaurant scene?
Real diversity in terms of ethnic dining, and more choice in the value-for-money sector under £15 per person.

What does the next year hold?
It's going to be very challenging for the restaurant owners, but it's going to benefit diners. We'll be seeing more and more value-for-money eateries just like New York.

RESTAURANTS

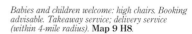

a light sheen on their sandpaper outer surface, cumin coming quietly through. Houmous topped with a dollop of fried chicken liver and pomegranate sauce was rich and delicious, the plump pomegranate seeds popping nicely. We followed this with lamb tagine heavy with delectable wedges of meat. Service was thoughtful and perfectly timed throughout. The wine list is extensive, with 14 available by the glass (£4.75-£8.50) and four dessert wines – in case the syrup-drenched baklava and fruit, served on a cake stand, aren't sweet enough.
Booking advisable. Entertainment: belly dancer 9pm Mon-Wed, Sun; 8.30pm, 11pm Thur-Sat. Separate room for parties, seats 10-14. Takeaway service. **Map 9 G6**.

Mayfair

Al Hamra
31-33 Shepherd Market, W1J 7PT (7493 1954, www.alhamrarestaurant.co.uk). Green Park or Hyde Park Corner tube. **Meals served** noon-11.30pm daily. **Main courses** £14-£22.50. **Cover** £2.50. **Minimum** £20. **Credit** AmEx, DC, MC, V. Lebanese
Londoners whose experience of Lebanese food begins and ends with the occasional shawarma on the Edgware Road may recoil at Al Hamra's cosmopolitan leanings. The small, square space is characterised by kitsch ruched curtains, an abundance of intrusive pot plants, and white linen tables so tightly packed as to negate conventionally romantic meals. Throw in some smart-suited waiters and the experience can feel a little like dining on a miniature cruise ship. The venue seems as beloved of Mayfair suits as minted Middle Easterners, but there are reassuring touches of authenticity: the miniature pastries popular during Eid and kept behind a glass counter; the heated political discussion in Arabic wafting out of the kitchen; and, of course, the food, although our last visit featured as many hits as misses. Starters were first-rate. Chilli-infused houmous beyruti made a creamy accompaniment to warm, wonderfully airy flatbread, though we were most impressed with kibbeh nayeh, a tartare of seasoned minced raw lamb mixed with bulgur wheat. Mains were less successful. Badenjan mahshi (baked aubergine stuffed with lamb) was under-seasoned and sat in a watery tomato sauce, while shish taouk was overcooked – a sin given Al Hamra's high prices and ultra-formal service.
Available for hire. Babies and children welcome: high chairs. Booking advisable dinner. Tables outdoors (8, terrace). Takeaway service; delivery service. **Map 9 H8**.

Al Sultan
51-52 Hertford Street, W1J 7ST (7408 1155/1166, www.alsultan.co.uk). Green Park or Hyde Park Corner tube. **Meals served** noon-11pm daily. **Main courses** £13.50-£20. **Cover** £2. **Minimum** £20. **Credit** AmEx, DC, MC, V. Lebanese
Inside, Al Sultan is traditional and restrained, its slightly worn carpet and pistachio-coloured paintwork smartened up with starched white linen tablecloths. In warm weather, a handful of outdoor tables lining a quiet Mayfair mews offer a pleasant place to rest from shopping at chi-chi Shepherd's Market. A Saturday lunchtime visit saw us share space with only two other tables: a group of talkative, older Arabic men and a young family. Despite this, the waiters seemed to forget we were there, needing prompting to take our order and collect plates – even after we'd been in situ for a considerable time in both instances. The food was generally good, if lacking in fireworks. Fattoush was tartly citrous, sprinkled with ample sumac, fresh sprigs of mint and tiny shards of crisp pitta. Theatrically puffed up Lebanese pittas also accompanied soft, salty slabs of grilled halloumi sprinkled with nigella seeds. To follow, tender chicken shish kebab made a light main course. Churlish though it may be to complain, a free baklava to end the meal was dry and lacking in syrup. In all, this is a competent but uninspiring restaurant for sampling Middle Eastern cooking.

Available for hire. Babies and children welcome: high chairs. Booking advisable dinner. Tables outdoors (4, pavement). Takeaway service; delivery service (over £35 within 4-mile radius). Vegetarian menu. **Map 9 H8**.

Piccadilly

Fakhreldine
85 Piccadilly, W1J 7NB (7493 3424, www.fakhreldine.co.uk). Green Park tube. **Meals served** noon-midnight Mon-Sat; noon-11pm Sun. **Main courses** £13-£23. **Set lunch** £14 2 courses. **Credit** AmEx, DC, MC, V. Lebanese
Fakhreldine benefits from two knockout features – its design aesthetics, and a stunning view over Green Park. Huge picture windows make the most of the verdant vista, which is in stark contrast to the interior design: a mirrored, angular, first-floor space exuding sleek style. That's not to say it's uncomfortable; in fact, the brassy, glossy bar and the lounge area with velvety sofa are fine places to sip a cocktail or eminently quaffable Lebanese wine. Under new management since the beginning of 2009, the elegant restaurant offers such dishes as five-spice lamb, fragrant with cinnamon and cumin and falling off the bone (which is filled with the treat of meaty marrow). Fattoush included limp lettuce, but grilled halloumi served with thyme leaves was a deeply satisfying meze, as was mujadara – lentils mashed with rice. Prices are in accordance with the Mayfair neighbourhood. Service is professional, if a little slow at times. Alluring arrangements of ruby-hued roses and candle-filled lanterns on marble steps lead down to Fakhreldine's new addition – the street-level 1001 Nights. This smaller space is geared towards casual dining, featuring the spectacle of meze and shawarma being prepared in an open kitchen.

Babies and children welcome: high chairs. Booking advisable. Takeaway service; delivery service (within 4-mile radius). **Map 9 H8**.

St James's

★ Noura
122 Jermyn Street, SW1Y 4UJ (7839 2020, www.noura.co.uk). Green Park or Piccadilly Circus tube. **Meals served** noon-midnight daily. **Main courses** £14-£22. **Set lunch** £19.50 2 courses. **Set meal** (5-7pm) £14 3 courses. **Credit** AmEx, DC, MC, V. Lebanese
Sleek and chic, the restaurants of the small Noura chain serve some of the best Lebanese food in town. They also abjure the traditional furnishings and solemn atmosphere that was once all too common in London. The look is of sumptuous fabrics on a backdrop of white paint and rendered walls. The ambience is refined yet relaxed. Noura doesn't deviate from what Lebanon does best, offering a traditional roster of hot and cold mezes, with main courses majoring in grills. Outstanding among our meatless meze choices was a dense, smoky, garlicky houmous, which made a fine contrast with the lemony tang of batinjan el-rahib. Equally appealing was a zingy, herby tabouleh, and crisp falafels. Strangely, the restaurant was out of fuul medames. No problem – the kitchen whipped up an authentic, homely version where the beans were left whole, allowing us to mash them up a bit ourselves and really taste the quality of the oil: fantastic. A Lebanese Château Ksara blanc de blancs made a delicate accompaniment. Service has been updated too; staff were warm yet professional. Noura fully deserves its success.
Available for hire. Babies and children welcome: high chairs. Disabled: toilet. Dress: smart casual. Separate room for parties, seats 40. **Map 17 B5**. **For branches see index.**

Patogh. See p204.

RESTAURANTS

Soho

Yalla Yalla NEW

1 Green's Court, W1F 0HA (7287 7663, www.yalla-yalla.co.uk). Piccadilly Circus tube. **Meals served** 8am-11pm Mon-Fri; 10am-11pm Sat; 10am-10pm Sun. **Main courses** £6.50-£10.50. **Set lunch** £5.50 2 courses. **Set meal** £7.50 2 courses. **Credit** MC, V. Lebanese
Just off Brewer Street, Yalla Yalla is a cheerful little spot decked in black, yellow and white, with only around ten tables. Character is added by cushions made from traditional scarf fabric, colourful family photographs and stencilling on the walls. Co-owner Jad Youssef worked as a chef in Beirut before working in upmarket London establishments such as Fakhreldine and Kenza. Beiruti street food – freshly made dishes to eat on the go, such as pitta wraps, falafel and kibbeh – are cooked daily and are available to eat-in or take away. Yalla Yalla is an excellent choice for workday lunches ('yalla' means 'hurry up' or 'let's go', and the dinky stools don't encourage you to linger). Hot dishes include sautéed chicken livers with pomegranate molasses, and slow-cooked stew of lamb shoulder with red pepper and butternut squash, served with spiced carrots and basmati rice. Skewers of lamb, chicken and prawns are cooked on a wood-burning grill for an authentic smoky flavour. As with many Lebanese restaurants, pickled turnips and chillies are complimentary. To drink there are fresh juices, orange blossom-scented lemonade and mint tea, and also Lebanese wines and beer.
Babies and children welcome: high chairs. Booking advisable dinner. Tables outdoors (2, pavement). Takeaway service. **Map 17 B4**.

West

Acton

★ Lazeez NEW

253 Acton High Street, W3 9BY (8752 0078). Acton Town tube. **Meals served** 11am-midnight Tue-Sun. **Main courses** £7-£9.75. **Credit** MC, V. Lebanese
It was with some trepidation that we returned to Lazeez, six months after its opening. Our culinary first encounter had been so beatific that we'd been banging on about it ever since. Would this nondescript café live up to expectations? Mercifully, yes. Little has changed aesthetically; the place remains sanitary to the point of sterility, the harsh lighting emphasising the sparseness of the decor (a few mirrors and a large flatscreen TV). This, along with the clutter of black plastic tables and the gleaming grill, produce the look of a glorified kebab shop. But what Lazeez lacks in warmth, it makes up for in its welcome; we relished the cheerful banter of the chef who managed to flit between customers and kitchen, taking and preparing orders without missing a beat. The meze dishes were excellent: chicken livers flavourful, if a little less pink than we'd have liked; chunks of spicy sujuk sausages pleasingly charred; and slices of comforting lazeez arayes (a Lebanese quesadilla stuffed with minced lamb). Best of all was the plated shish taouk: three skewers of some of the tastiest and most tender chicken kebab we've eaten anywhere in the capital. Well worth a visit.
Available for hire. Babies and children admitted. Booking advisable. Takeaway service; delivery service (over £15 within 3-mile radius). Vegetarian menu.

Bayswater

★ Al Waha

75 Westbourne Grove, W2 4UL (7229 0806, www.alwaharestaurant.com). Bayswater or Queensway tube. **Meals served** noon-11.30pm daily. **Main courses** £10.50-£13.50. **Set lunch** £12.50. **Set dinner** £21 per person (minimum 2) 3 courses, £25 per person (minimum 2) 4 courses. **Cover** £1.50. **Minimum** £13.50 (dinner). **Credit** MC, V. Lebanese
Al Waha offers the slickness and smartness of London's upmarket Lebanese restaurants, with none of the snootiness that often lets them down.

Parsian. See p210.

Tables clothed in crisp linen are packed together in a small, two-tiered room fringed with plants (including several hanging from pots set into walls that are elsewhere decorated with framed canvases of calligraphic quotations in Arabic). Black-shirted waiters flit between tables, brisk when busy but seldom brusque. The food is uniformly excellent. Staple starters on our last visit were polished to near perfection: refreshing fattoush featured a mouth-watering citrus and garlic dressing and chips of toasted Lebanese bread; houmous kawarmah was a great contrast of smooth houmous with fried lamb slivers and pine nuts. Mains were also superb. A mixed grill combined tender lahem meshwi (fillet lamb), kafta halabiyeh (seasoned minced lamb) and shish taouk (marinated chicken with garlic sauce), though it was a daily special of kharoof mahshi that most mesmerised us: an artfully constructed dome of herb-and spice-infused rice studded with peas, pistachios and pieces of lamb shank. We can't wait to return.
Babies and children welcome (until 7pm). Booking advisable; essential dinner. Tables outdoors (4, patio). Takeaway service; delivery service (over £20 within 3-mile radius). **Map 7 B6**.

Fresco

25 Westbourne Grove, W2 4UA (7221 2355, www.frescojuices.co.uk). Bayswater or Royal Oak tube. **Meals served** 8am-11pm daily. **Main courses** £5.95-£7.95. **Set meze** £11.95. **Credit** MC, V. Lebanese
Indefatigably bright and cheery, with yellow walls and rustic wooden tables, Fresco is an ever-popular café and takeaway. It continues to deliver a healthy formula of Lebanese meze dishes on plates or in pitta sandwiches, grills, western sandwiches on ciabatta, and its signature juices. The latter come in big, generous glassfuls: hard-core 'energisers' (with ingredients like broccoli and beets), fruity milkshakes, and mixed juices (including our silky apple, banana and raspberry juice). They're squeezed on demand, which means the noise of the juicer is pretty constant, but it's worth it for the freshness. A good range of basic meze dishes is displayed behind the counter. For £4.50 you can have a plateful of any three – compare that to the posh restaurants at a fiver a dish. Quality is high too, though not consistently equal to Fresco's pricier counterparts. Batata hara was warmly spiced, if a little soggy and oily; falafel came in a generous and workmanlike portion, though the shell could have been crisper. Sabanak (spinach with olive oil, garlic and lemon) was perfect: bright

green, super-fresh and full of flavour. Fresco isn't somewhere you'd linger, but for a snack and a big dose of vitamins, it's hard to beat.
Babies and children welcome: high chairs. Takeaway service. Vegetarian menu. **Map 7 B6**. **For branches see index**.

Hammersmith

★ Mahdi

217 King Street, W6 9JT (8563 7007). Hammersmith or Ravenscourt Park tube. **Meals served** noon-11pm daily. **Main courses** £5-£12. **Set lunch** (noon-6pm Mon-Fri) £4.50-£5.90 1 course. **Unlicensed** no alcohol allowed. **Credit** MC, V. Iranian
Most of London's Iranian restaurants compensate for a lack of luxury with a warm welcome and atmospheric intimacy. Mahdi, by contrast, continues to operate as though under the watchful eyes of the Ayatollahs, its staff unduly serious and seldom breaking a smile. There's something formal about the decor too, from the chandeliers and sculpted ceiling to the framed Persian paintings set into brick arches. You might even spot a stuffed peacock in one corner. On our last visit, the place was crammed to capacity as it was Iranian New Year, but the food never dipped below brilliant. Starters include kookoo sabzi (a sliced herb omelette), and baked aubergine stuffed with rice and topped with barberries. Both lubia polo (a one-pot dish of lamb and green beans with rice) and a juicy lamb fillet kebab with rice were well seasoned, perfectly cooked and so large of portion that we had to ask for plastic tubs to take home the leftovers. Service was even more abrupt and inattentive than usual, but this is something most local Iranians consider a small price to pay for food of this quality and quantity.
Booking advisable. Disabled: toilet. Takeaway service. **Map 20 B4**. **For branch see index**.

Kensington

Randa

23 Kensington Church Street, W8 4LF (7937 5363, www.maroush.com). High Street Kensington tube. **Meals served** noon-midnight daily. **Main courses** £11.95-£16. **Set lunch** £16 2 courses. **Set dinner** £45 per person (minimum 2) 3 courses. **Credit** MC, V. Lebanese
An outpost of the Maroush chain, Randa aims for a sleek, sophisticated look to attract a Kensington clientele, ditching the white tablecloths for smart

greens) was a masterclass in the stew-maker's art: hearty of portion, packed with chunks of meat and lent a subtle bitterness by dried limes.
Babies and children admitted. Takeaway service. **Map 13 A10.**

Shepherd's Bush

★ Abu Zaad

29 Uxbridge Road, W12 8LH (8749 5107, www.abuzaad.co.uk). Shepherd's Bush Market tube. **Meals served** 11am-11pm daily. **Main courses** £5-£14. **Credit** AmEx, MC, V. Syrian
If only all fast food were like this. You'll part with just £2.50 for a healthy moutabal at this London rarity: a Syrian caff. The dish made a cool contrast to the brighter flavours of an attractive and refreshing tabouleh (only £3). A generous portion of spicy grilled sausages (makanek) was a steal at £2.50. Delicious too were cheese sambousek (deep-fried pastries stuffed with cheese) and kibbeh shamieh (deep-fried lamb meatballs mixed with cracked wheat and minced onion). You'll need plenty of bread to accompany these simple but hearty starters, and to dip in the mild houmous. Main courses (largely meat with rice on the side) have more of a cafeteria feel to them; in our experience their flavours have been rather bland. The atmosphere reflects Abu Zaad's fast, takeaway orientation. Ask for a table in the back room, where murals of Damascus and decorative pots lend character to the otherwise functional tiled space. A fine place to eat well on the cheap.
Babies and children welcome: high chairs. Booking advisable weekends. Separate room for parties, seats 30. Takeaway service. **Map 20 B2.**

★ ★ Sufi

70 Askew Road, W12 9BJ (8834 4888, www.sufirestaurant.com). Hammersmith tube then 266 bus. **Meals served** noon-11pm daily. **Main courses** £6-£12. **Set lunch** (noon-5pm Mon-Thur) £8 2 courses, £9.50 3 courses. **Credit** MC, V. Iranian
Ask Iranians to name their favourite restaurant and many will tell you they simply don't have one; eating out is widely regarded as a poor substitute for the dining room of a friend or family member. Yet that's exactly the atmosphere you'll find at Sufi, an unassuming eaterie on a scuffed stretch of Askew Road that's as homely as any of London's Iranian restaurants. Traditional decoration abounds: from shisha pipes lining a high shelf and strings of red lights hanging over a turquoise clay oven, to wall-mounted Persian instruments, many of which can be heard in nostalgic songs on the stereo. It's the perfect soundtrack for an authentic feast. Few things taste of Iran like ash-e reshteh (a creamy noodle and mung bean soup with whey); Sufi is one of the few places in the capital that we've found it. Mains were also top notch – joojeh chicken kebab artfully marinated and meltingly tender; fesenjan (chicken with a pomegranate-juice and ground-walnut sauce) a perfect balance of rich and bitter – and service was spot on. Nailed to one wall is a framed collage of happy customers. We expect to see our faces up there soon.
Babies and children welcome: children's menu; high chairs. Separate room for parties, seats 40. Takeaway service. **Map 20 A2.**

South West

East Sheen

★ Faanoos

481 Upper Richmond Road West, SW14 7PU (8878 5738). Mortlake rail/33, 337, 493 bus. **Meals served** noon-11pm daily. **Main courses** £4.95-£8.95. **Credit** MC, V. Iranian
Amid the bathroom fitters and carpet showrooms of the traffic-troubled A205, Faanoos is an unexpected oasis of Iranian authenticity. In the past it has wowed us with a hearty welcome and superb home-style cooking, but our most recent visit was less memorable, soured by a sulky waiter who reacted to our request to move tables as though he'd been asked to relocate the restaurant. Nor was the food a patch on previous visits.

Starters were hit and miss; the requisite spikiness of masto musir was marred by a gloopy consistency more akin to mayonnaise, but pleasingly piquant and crunchy torshi (vegetable pickles) won us round. Mains were better: minced lamb koobideh kebab was well seasoned, if a little dried out by over-enthusiastic grilling; marinated chicken joojeh kebab was close to perfection, butter soft and bursting with citrus and saffron marinade; and a helping of zeresht (dried barberries) added zing to fluffy, saffron-tinted rice. Despite hiccups, Faanoos remains the real deal atmospherically, its straw-matted walls hung with cheap carpets and typically kitsch Persian paintings. The small, conversational space is never more appealing than when the lights go down and the candles come out.
Babies and children welcome: high chairs. Booking advisable. Dress: smart casual. Tables outdoors (2, pavement). Takeaway service.

South East
London Bridge & Borough

Hiba

Maya House, 134-138 Borough High Street, SE1 1LB (7357 9633). Borough tube. **Meals served** noon-11pm Mon-Thur; noon-midnight Fri, Sat. **Main courses** £9.75-£13. **Set meal** £39.75 2 courses (minimum 2), £79.75 3 courses incl wine (minimum 4). **Credit** AmEx, MC, V. Lebanese
Hidden behind an unprepossessing façade, Hiba has a buzzing, welcoming atmosphere. The stylish decoration is 1970s-tinged, featuring dark wood set against splashes of funky orange, and bathed in warm, low lighting that makes everyone look fabulous. Diners – from young cosmopolitans to besuited over-50s – were still arriving at 10.30pm on a Friday. Efficient, black-clad staff dart between closely spaced tables delivering dishes that, in our case, were mostly terrific. Muhamara, a crushed nut paste, was gently spiced but dry and cement-like; mint was too dominant in a tabouleh that was annoyingly fleshed out with whole lettuce leaves. However, batinjan el-rahib (a dip of grilled aubergine and tomato) was fantastically fresh and flavourful, as was houmous beiruty, heavy on silken tahini and shot through with sparky slivers of chilli. Farrouj meshwi (boneless 'baby' chicken) was simply prepared, with lightly charred skin and tender flesh; such was the quality of the meat, it needed nothing more than garlicky mayonnaise on the side. Add complimentary plates of ambrosial baklava and refreshing fruit (melon, grapes, pineapple, kiwi) and customers leave sated and happy. An ideal venue for spending a lively evening with friends, trying scores of meze.
Available for hire. Babies and children welcome (until 7pm). Disabled: toilet. Tables outdoors (4, pavement). Takeaway service. **Map 11 P8.**

North
Camden Town & Chalk Farm

Le Mignon

98 Arlington Road, NW1 7HD (7387 0600). Camden Town tube. **Lunch served** noon-3pm, **dinner served** 6pm-midnight daily. **Main courses** £9.50-£18.50. **Credit** MC, V. Lebanese
Le Mignon is part of a little cluster of businesses on residential roads near Camden High Street. Small dimensions and faded furnishings give it the look of an unremarkable local restaurant, and an understated welcome and quiet atmosphere reinforced this impression. Sadly, the food cemented it. Fattoush was flavoursome, yet managed to be a little dry. Moutabal had an intense smokiness that rivalled the heavy tahini flavour of the houmous and the vinegariness of the makdous (preserved and stuffed baby aubergines) – in each case, they were a little overbearing. The pleasingly open-textured kafta khashkhash (minced lamb with parsley, garlic and spices, grilled on skewers) came with a 'tomato sauce' that seemed identical to the 'chef's sauce' which accompanied farrouge

wooden tables. A curvy steel staircase leads to an upper storey. When it comes to food, the menu is the same as that of other Maroush restaurants, including the list of 'specialities': raw meat dishes. We stuck to basics, and most of our dishes were Lebanese food at its best. Particular praise goes to a fuul medames; the fava beans came with chickpeas and diced tomato and were infused with a gorgeous lemony flavour. Batinjan el-rahib (aubergine with onion and tomatoes) also had a superb lemony zing, and fattoush was fresh and crunchy. Thick-cut slices of halloumi were a great contrast of textures: crisply grilled on top, soft underneath. Only tabouleh was disappointing, with scant bits of raw-tasting bulgar lending it a gritty texture. In contrast, mixed grill was huge, with kofta, lamb chunks and chicken beautifully cooked and flavoursome. Service was friendly, if a bit distracted; we'd come for an early dinner so there weren't many customers, but staff seemed preoccupied preparing for the evening ahead.
Booking advisable. Separate room for parties, seats 40. Takeaway service; delivery service (over £25 within 1-mile radius). **Map 7 B8.**

Olympia

★ Mohsen

152 Warwick Road, W14 8PS (7602 9888). Earl's Court tube/Kensington (Olympia) tube/rail. **Meals served** noon-midnight daily. **Main courses** £12-£15. **Unlicensed. Corkage** no charge. **No credit cards.** Iranian
London's Iranian restaurants seldom deal in surprises; what marks out the best is a consistency in cooking the basics, and a homely atmosphere. For this reason we've been returning to Mohsen year after year, relishing the warmth with which we're greeted at the door and taking comfort in the never-changing plastic menus and decor of dog-eared travel posters. In one corner, a young man stands over the clay oven, rolling mounds of dough and walking baskets of fresh bread to tables. At the rear is a spacious room decorated with pot plants and garden furniture. The food is usually excellent, though the occasional duff dish does appear. A starter of fragrant sabzi greens was traditionally paired with walnuts, fat radishes and chunks of goat's cheese, but another of lamb's tongue tasted reheated. Koobideh minced lamb kebab was salty, but barg lamb-fillet kebab melted in the mouth, with fluffy saffron rice and grill-blackened tomatoes the ideal accompaniments. Ghorm-e sabzi (lamb and kidney-bean stew with

meshwi (charcoal grilled chicken). It was tasty, yet reminded us of tinned tomatoes. Fruity Château Kefraya 2004 Lebanese wine is a good bet at £18, and Almaza beer (also from Lebanon) made a zingy change from the norm. Altogether, though, the experience was rather flat, and we found ourselves casting eager glances across the road at the lively Crown & Goose.
Available for hire. Babies and children welcome (daytime). Booking advisable. Tables outdoors (4, pavement). Takeaway service. **Map 27 D3**.

Tandis NEW

73 Haverstock Hill, NW3 4SL (7586 8079).
Chalk Farm tube. **Meals served** noon-11.30pm Mon-Thur, Sun; noon-midnight Fri, Sat. **Main courses** £7.50-£12.90. **Credit** AmEx, MC, V.
Iranian
Classic Iranian dishes at Tandis are served in strikingly modern surroundings that were largely inherited from the bar previously occupying this site. So you can sink into a huge black leather banquette or go through to the stylish and well-lit room at the back. Traditional Persian dishes include panir sabzi (whole twigs of fresh herbs – lots of mint – with a square of feta cheese, and walnuts in this case), yoghurt dishes (masto musir is yoghurt mixed with shallots), and richer meze dishes such as salad olivieh (chicken, potatoes, eggs, gherkins and peas with mayonnaise and olive oil). As usual with Iranian cooking, mains are the stars: from subtly marinated, butter-tender lamb or chicken kebabs (served in classic style with lovely saffron-infused rice and grilled tomato), to the richly flavoured fruity stews that form so much of the Persian menu. The latter include diced lamb and split peas cooked with sun-dried lemons (khoresht-e gheymeh) and dried plum in a sweet and sour vegetable sauce (khoresht-e aloo esfenaaj). Persian sweets, or faloodeh (sorbet with the consistency of granita) make a great finale.

Babies and children welcome: high chairs. Booking advisable Fri, Sat. Separate rooms for parties, seating 14-30. Tables outdoors (5, terrace). Takeaway service. **Map 28 C4**.

North West
Willesden

★ Parsian NEW

228 High Road, NW10 2NX (8830 0772).
Dollis Hill or Willesden Green tube. **Meals served** noon-midnight daily. **Main courses** £5-£9. **Credit** MC, V. Iranian
It has taken little more than a year since opening for Parsian to establish itself among our favourite Persian restaurants. Authenticity is key: custom on our last visit was entirely Iranian, something we attribute to a menu that complements the ubiquitous chicken and lamb kebabs with plentiful well-prepared stews and a list of colourful starters. From the latter we opted for kookoo sabzi (a fluffy, delicately flavoured herb omelette) and a bowl of steaming ash-e reshteh (a smoky bean and noodle soup). Even the bread – properly perforated wheels of the rustic taftoon – was more evocative than most. Mains were also excellent: a hearty khoresht-e gheymeh (lamb and split-pea stew), lent a subtle citric bite by the addition of dried limes, and vegetarian khoresht-e bademjan (aubergine stew), both served with rice. Best of all is the sassy atmosphere: decoration is limited to a handful of framed fantasist paintings (the Persian equivalents of unicorns and rainbows), but staff are so friendly and the vibe so welcoming that you'll want to linger over tea, even if you've no room for the traditional desserts.
Babies and children welcome: high chairs. Tables outdoors (2, pavement). Takeaway service; delivery service (over £20 within 2-mile radius).

Outer London
Wembley, Middlesex

★ Mesopotamia

115 Wembley Park Drive, Wembley, Middx, HA9 8HG (8453 5555, www.mesopotamia.ltd.uk).
Wembley Park tube. **Lunch served** noon-2.30pm Thur, Fri. **Dinner served** 6pm-midnight Mon-Sat. **Main courses** £8-£15.50. **Set meze** £23. **Credit** AmEx, DC, MC, V. Iraqi
Coalition forces failed to win Iraqi hearts and minds, despite an eight-year campaign; Mesopotamia won ours over dinner. The intoxicating interior of this family-owned restaurant defies its inauspicious location on a strip studded with takeaways. White stone walls are embellished with raised icons of Babylonian beasts and decorative sabres; ornate black thrones face tables set with crisp white linen; and a billowing cloth pinned to the ceiling gives the impression of dining in a grand Bedouin tent. Here and there are ancient proverbs painted in lilting Aramaic script. We particularly agreed with 'Bread strengthens the heart', using ours to mop up starters of tamar waya laban (a house variation on the rich Iraqi walnut, date and yoghurt dip), and a halloumi salad that passed the squeak test with flying colours. Mains were even better. Malfuf bademjan featured minced lamb rolled in grilled slices of aubergine and cooked in a tomato sauce, while fesenjan was a less bitter take on the Iranian chicken stew cooked with pomegranate juice and ground walnuts; both came with plentiful fluffy rice feathered with vermicelli. Best of all was the service, so helpful and homely that we left feeling like one of the family.
Available for hire. Babies and children welcome: children's menu; high chairs. Booking advisable. Takeaway service. Vegetarian menu.

Menu

See also the menu boxes in **North African** and **Turkish**. Note that spellings can vary. For more information, consult *The Legendary Cuisine of Persia*, by Margaret Shaida, *Lebanese Cuisine* by Anissa Helou (both Grub Street), and *Flavours of the Levant* by Nadeh Saleh (Metro).

MEZE

Baba ganoush: Egyptian name for moutabal (qv).
Basturma: smoked beef.
Batata hara: potatoes fried with peppers and chilli.
Batinjan or **bazenjan el-rahib:** aubergine mashed with olive oil, garlic and tomato.
Falafel: a mixture of spicy chickpeas or broad beans ground, rolled into balls and deep fried.
Fatayer: a soft pastry, filled with cheese, onions, spinach and pine kernels.
Fattoush: fresh vegetable salad containing shards of toasted pitta bread and sumac (qv).
Fuul or **fuul medames:** brown broad beans that are mashed and seasoned with olive oil, lemon juice and garlic.
Kalaj: halloumi cheese on pastry.
Kibbeh: highly seasoned mix of minced lamb, cracked wheat and onion, deep-fried in balls. For meze it is often served raw (**kibbeh nayeh**) like steak tartare.
Labneh: Middle Eastern cream cheese made from yoghurt.
Moujadara: lentils, rice and caramelised onions mixed together.

Moutabal: a purée of chargrilled aubergines mixed with sesame sauce, garlic and lemon juice.
Muhamara: dip of crushed mixed nuts with red peppers, spices and pomegranate molasses.
Sambousek: small pastries filled with mince, onion and pine kernels.
Shankleesh: aged yogurt cheese flavoured with thyme.
Sujuk: spicy Lebanese sausages.
Sumac: an astringent and fruity-tasting spice made from dried sumac seeds.
Tabouleh: a salad of chopped parsley, tomatoes, crushed wheat, onions, olive oil and lemon juice.
Torshi: pickled vegetables.
Warak einab: rice-stuffed vine leaves.

MAINS

Shawarma: meat (usually lamb) marinated then grilled on a spit and sliced kebab-style.
Shish kebab: cubes of marinated lamb grilled on a skewer, often with tomatoes, onions and sweet peppers.
Shish taouk: like shish kebab, but with chicken rather than lamb.

DESSERTS

Baklava: filo pastry interleaved with pistachio nuts, almonds or walnuts, and covered in syrup.
Konafa or **kadayif:** cake made from shredded pastry dough, filled with syrup and nuts, or cream.
Ma'amoul: pastries filled with nuts or dates.

Muhallabia or **mohalabia:** a milky ground-rice pudding with almonds and pistachios, flavoured with rosewater or orange blossom.
Om ali: bread pudding, often made with filo pastry, also includes nuts and raisins.

IRANIAN DISHES

Ash-e reshteh: a soup with noodles, spinach, pulses and dried herbs.
Ghorm-e sabzi: lamb with greens, kidney beans and dried limes.
Halim bademjan: mashed chargrilled aubergine with onions and walnuts.
Joojeh or **jujeh:** chicken marinated in saffron, lemon and onion.
Kashk, qurut, quroot: a salty whey.
Kashk-e bademjan: baked aubergines mixed with herbs and whey.
Khoresht-e fesenjan or **fesenjoon:** chicken cooked in ground walnut and pomegranate sauce.
Kuku-ye sabzi: finely chopped fresh herbs with eggs, baked in the oven.
Masto khiar: yoghurt mixed with finely chopped cucumber and mint.
Masto musir: shallot-flavoured yoghurt.
Mirza ghasemi: crushed baked aubergines, tomatoes, garlic and herbs mixed with egg.
Sabzi: a plate of fresh herb leaves (usually mint and dill) often served with a cube of feta.
Salad olivieh: like a russian salad, includes chopped potatoes, chicken, eggs, peas, gherkins, olive oil and mayonnaise.

Modern European

If you thought you had to travel into the West End for good Modern European cooking, this year's clutch of new restaurants could not prove you more wrong. Yes, **Giaconda Dining Room**, winner of our Best New Restaurant award, is in the thick of it, just off Charing Cross Road, but north Londoners have the **York & Albany** to enjoy, the **Whitechapel Gallery** is home to Maria Elia's new kitchen, and the **Exhibition Rooms** is bringing first-rate cooking to the burghers of Crystal Palace. As the largest chapter in this guide, Modern European establishments are arguably Londoners' favourite places to dine, perhaps because the menus tend to have something for everybody: fish and chips and steaks sit happily alongside foie gras, pasta, concoctions of white beans and chorizo or puy lentils and mushrooms, or maybe a dish inspired by Middle Eastern, American, Japanese or South-east Asian cuisines. The cooking style is contemporary, yet without the laboured preparations and follies (or at least not quite as many) that you might expect in a haute cuisine restaurant. So whether you're looking for a place to take the family, meet for business, or nurture a fledgling romance, you'll find something suitably delicious here.

Central
Bloomsbury

★ Giaconda Dining Room (100)
2009 WINNER BEST NEW RESTAURANT
9 Denmark Street, WC2H 8LS (7240 3334, www.giacondadining.com). Tottenham Court Road tube. **Lunch served** noon-2.15pm, **dinner served** 6-9.15pm Mon-Fri. **Main courses** £9.50-£13.50. **Cover** £1. **Credit** AmEx, MC, V.
There's so much to like about the Giaconda, it's hard to know where to start. Yes, the decor is nothing to write home about, and the place is a bit cramped; the kitchen is amazingly small, but from it comes the kind of food that most people want to eat most of the time: what Australians Paul (the chef) and Tracey Merrony describe as French-ish with a bit of Spain and Italy. There's more than one fish of the day (we were pleased to coincide with turbot served on lentils, parsley and bread salad), and the same goes for grills (fillet steak or pork chop on our visit). More challenging dishes might include braised tripe with smoked paprika, chorizo and rigatoni. First courses are similarly appealing. The zip of cervelle de canut (fromage blanc with herbs and walnut oil, plus green salad and toast) contrasted nicely with the rich smooth perfection of chicken liver and juniper mousse with fig and prune compote; boned and crisped pig's trotters with egg mayonnaise was a hearty feast. On a warm night we loved apple sorbet, and iced nougat with raspberries, but there's also fruit crumble, fruit of the day (pineapple) or a single chocolate truffle. The wine list has plenty of choice yet isn't so long that you can't read every bottle.
Babies and children admitted. Booking advisable. Tables outdoors (2, pavement). **Map 17 C3**.

City

The Don
The Courtyard, 20 St Swithin's Lane, EC4N 8AD (7626 2606, www.thedonrestaurant.com). Bank tube/DLR.
Bistro **Lunch served** noon-3pm, **dinner served** 6-10pm Mon-Fri. **Main courses** £8.95-£14.95.
Restaurant **Lunch served** noon-2.30pm, **dinner served** 6-10pm Mon-Fri. **Main courses** £12.95-£25.50.
Both **Credit** AmEx, DC, MC, V.
The Don is aimed squarely at monied, wine-savvy City diners. Located in a cobbled courtyard in a building owned by the Sandeman port house, the restaurant has a gentlemen's club atmosphere. Polished cutlery gleams from white-clothed tables; 'trophy' bottles from prestigious wine producers are displayed. The wine list is pretty serious, with an emphasis on classic French regions, ports and sherries, with a good New Zealand selection too. Mark-ups are fair and on Friday nights bottles costing £50-plus are half price. Dining in the basement bistro feels like eating in a Gallic wine cellar. The airier ground floor has a French vibe too, with francophone staff and Anglo-French cooking. Some liberté is taken with dish descriptions: 'salt-cod brandade on a Shetland salmon tartare' was a mere quenelle of salt-cod atop a generous portion of raw salmon dressed with finely chopped tomato. Likewise, a main course of 'saddle of rabbit' was a single tender piece of rabbit enclosed in a rabbit forcemeat and formed into a sausage served on (slightly undercooked) lentils. Ingredient quality is good, but there's a tendency to over-complicate. Tender, perfectly cooked New Zealand venison came with a well-judged red wine and juniper sauce and braised cabbage; the accompanying 'fig and walnut tatin' was unnecessary. Service is smart and professional.
Booking essential. Dress: smart casual. Separate room for parties, seats 24. **Map 12 Q7**.

Northbank
One Paul's Walk, EC4V 3QH (7329 9299, www.northbankrestaurant.com). St Paul's tube/ Blackfriars tube/rail. **Lunch served** noon-3pm Mon-Sat; 11am-5pm Sun. **Dinner served** 6-10.30pm daily. **Main courses** £12.50-£22.50. **Set meal** (lunch, 6-7pm) £10 2 courses. **Credit** AmEx, MC, V.
Northbank has a marvellous location: by the Thames, at the foot of the Millennium Bridge, with views across to Tate Modern (but not the river, thanks to the embankment wall). It's a two-fold operation, with a bar at one end next to the large

outdoor terrace – both fill with City drinkers come the evening – and a corridor-like restaurant at the other. This is smart and masculine in feel, if slightly soulless, with brown leather booths along one side, cloth-covered tables next to plate-glass windows on the other, and striking bare-bulb chandeliers. We liked the Timorous Beasties wallpaper lining the booths: pastoral toile de jouy at first glance, contemporary London vignettes (tramps, a mugging, the Gherkin) on closer inspection. The menu is short and straightforward, with a focus on West Country ingredients (home of both head chef Peter Woods and owner Christian Butler). Our dishes were mixed: an indifferent spring risotto starter with too much rocket; a main of tender, good-quality lamb; a so-so rice pudding hiding a fat dollop of strawberry jam. The casually dressed waiter was slightly too casual in attitude. When we queried the contents of a dish, he said he was only concerned about what happened outside the kitchen.
Babies and children welcome: high chairs. Booking essential lunch (Mon-Fri). Disabled: toilet. Tables outdoors (11, terrace). **Map 11 O7**.

Prism
147 Leadenhall Street, EC3V 4QT (7256 3875, www.harveynichols.com). Monument tube/Bank tube/DLR.
Bar **Open** 11am-11pm, **lunch served** 11.30am-3pm Mon-Fri. **Main courses** £10-£14.
Restaurant **Breakfast served** 8-10am, **lunch served** noon-3pm, **dinner served** 6-10pm Mon-Fri. **Main courses** £18-£30.
Both **Credit** AmEx, DC, MC, V.
Harvey Nichols' City operation is a swish restaurant and bar in a converted bank that has retained many of its handsome original features. The main dining room has a very high ceiling, requiring an enormously tall and impressive flower display to match; even the grand piano in the centre of the room is dwarfed. It's all very white and cream, offset by red leather seating. Waiting staff are smartly turned out, and whisk about with an air of efficiency that proved surface deep at a recent breakfast outing. We had to keep asking for

BEST MODERN EUROPEAN

Down to business
Butter-up your clients at **Arbutus** (see p219), **Axis** (see p212), **Bibendum** (see p219), **Orrery** (see p215), **Oxo Tower Restaurant, Bar & Brasserie** (see p226), **Plateau** (see p227) and **Prism** (see above).

Art for art's sake
Consume some culture along with your meal at **Delfina** (see p226), **Rex Whistler Restaurant at Tate Britain** (see p218) and **Wapping Food** (see p228).

Morning glory
Meet for breakfast at the **Ambassador** (see p212), the **Botanist** (see p224), **Nicole's** (see p217), **Smith's of Smithfield** (see p212), **Sotheby's** (see p218), the **Victoria** (see p223) and **York & Albany** (see p228).

Take in the view
Victuals come with a vista at **Blueprint Café** (see p226), **Northbank** (see left), **Oxo Tower Restaurant, Bar & Brasserie** (see p226), **Plateau** (see p227), **Pont de la Tour** (see p227) and **Skylon** (see p226).

Got the bottle?
Top venues for wine include **Bibendum** (see p219), the **Don** (see left), **Launceston Place** (see p222), **Orrery** (see p215) and **Ransome's Dock** (see p225).

RESTAURANTS

Prism. See p211.

things (such as toast) and though we requested scrambled eggs we got two poached instead. And at these prices – £4.50 for a freshly squeezed orange juice, £9 for (admittedly delicious) bacon, avocado, egg and tomato on toasted sourdough – the customer shouldn't have to work for it. As ever, prices don't really matter if you have an expense account, but should you falter at £20 for spring vegetable risotto with white truffle paste (dinner menu) or £25 for seared calf's liver with swede purée, crispy shallots and creamed spinach (lunch), then there are better bargains to be had elsewhere. Drinks are taken seriously here, with cocktails to the fore – there are even cocktail masterclasses offered in the basement Vault bar.
Babies and children welcome: high chairs. Booking advisable. Disabled: toilet. Separate rooms for parties, seating 23 and 45. Vegetarian menu. **Map 12 Q6.**

Clerkenwell & Farringdon

Ambassador (100)

55 Exmouth Market, EC1R 4QL (7837 0009, www.theambassadorcafe.co.uk). Farringdon tube/ rail/19, 38, 341 bus. **Breakfast/lunch served** 9am-3pm Mon-Fri; 11am-3.30pm Sat, Sun. **Dinner served** 6-11pm Mon-Sat; 6-10pm Sun. **Main courses** £9.50-£17. **Set meal** (noon-3pm, 6-11pm Mon-Fri) £12.50 2 courses, £16 3 courses. **Credit** AmEx, MC, V.
Boz Scaggs' 'Dirty Lowdown' and staff responding 'It's that sort of morning, is it?' to an order for a jug of bloody mary immediately put us in the laid-back funkster mood suited for a meal at this easy-going all-day local, which spills through french windows on to the pavement. A blackboard by the dark-wood bar promotes superior snacks: cheeses (sainte-maure, barkham blue, pont l'évêque), olives (black votos, green manzanillas), chorizo (artisan), pistachios (salted). Grab a brasserie chair or a place on the red banquettes for rustic fare such as game terrine with cumberland sauce, smoked haddock and saffron risotto, and roast Middle White pork with creamed savoy cabbage. Lunchtimes see the inclusion of bacon sandwiches and crayfish omelettes. The mainly European wine list includes around 20 'Ambassador's Choice' and seasonal recommendations. The brunch menu offers eggs meurette (with bacon, mushrooms and red wine sauce) as a pleasing alternative to eggs benedict, though we were impressed by the quality of thick-cut ham and orange-yolked eggs in the latter. Regrettably, our waffles (served with excellent bacon and apple compote) were just pancakes with aspirations, lacking crispness or the indentations necessary for pooling maple syrup.

Babies and children welcome: children's menu; crayons; high chairs; toys. Booking advisable. Tables outdoors (10, pavement). **Map 5 N4.**

Clerkenwell Dining Room

69-73 St John Street, EC1M 4AN (7253 9000, www.theclerkenwell.com). Barbican tube/ Farringdon tube/rail. **Lunch served** noon-2.30pm Mon-Fri. **Dinner served** 6-11pm Mon-Fri; 6-10.30pm Sat. **Main courses** £15-£22. **Credit** AmEx, DC, MC, V.
Standing outside CDR on a dull Tuesday evening, we feel like Gordon Ramsay faced with his latest Kitchen Nightmare. The austere, manly interior looks empty, cold and uninviting, the art on the walls is horrible, and when we ask for the cocktail/aperitifs list a puzzled waitress brings us the dessert wine and digestifs list. As the restaurant starts to fill – a family here, work colleagues there, couples dotted around – it begins to feel a more human, but there's still an air of despondency. Onion soup and seared scallops with aubergine and spicy pakora warmed us up a little, though both were uninspired. Mains were a mixed blessing; chicken with leek and mushroom cannelloni was dense, heavy and unpleasant, but a bass fillet was better, a crunchy base topped with deliciously moist fish. Dessert was a triumph, a chocolate marquis with white chocolate ice-cream and cherries whose combination of flavours and textures worked together in the heavenly way a great dessert should. A terrific selection of wines available as carafes is a definite plus, but the minuses here would have Gordon nonplussed.
Available for hire. Babies and children welcome: high chairs. Booking advisable. Separate room for parties, seats 45. **Map 5 O4.**

Smiths of Smithfield (100)

67-77 Charterhouse Street, EC1M 6HJ (7251 7950, www.smithsofsmithfield.co.uk). Barbican tube/Farringdon tube/rail.
Café-Bar **Open** 7am-11pm Mon-Wed; 7am-11.30pm Sat; 9.30am-10.30pm Sun. **Meals served** 7am-4.45pm Mon-Fri, 10am-4.45pm Sat; 9.30am-4.45pm Sun. **Main courses** £4-£7.50.
Wine Rooms **Dinner served** 6-10.45pm Mon-Sat; 5pm-9.30pm Sun. **Main courses** £10-£28.
Dining Room **Lunch served** noon-2.45pm Mon-Fri. **Dinner served** 6-10.45pm Mon-Sat. **Main courses** £11-£12.50.
All **Credit** AmEx, DC, MC, V.
Nearly everything is big at John Torode's food and drink fortress: the ground-floor bar (a fun spot for breakfast) with its leather sofas, the third-floor main dining room – even the smarter Top Floor space (*see p52*) seats 70. Only the second-floor Wine Rooms, with a snacky menu, are medium in

size. The now very familiar post-industrial decor of bare brick and exposed pipes accentuates the old-warehouse style (and the noise level, so shouting is the norm). The crowds keep coming, but on our last visit the dining room had the feel of a pretty anonymous corporate operation, a bit like a TGI Friday's for the business classes (except that TGI staff have to make eye contact with punters). Gravadlax with radish and green apple salad was dry; 'lucky squid' with chilli jam would have pleased lovers of vindaloo, but the crude slap-it-on approach to chilli wasted the high-quality squid. Smiths' beef burger with cheese and bacon was rather ordinary. Only the classic Jewish-style hot salt beef, with pickles and a lovely parsnip purée, had the kind of zing we'd expect from a restaurant overseen by a chef of this stature.
Babies and children welcome (restaurant): high chairs. Disabled: toilet. Entertainment (ground floor): DJs 7pm Thur-Sat; jazz 4.30pm Sun. Separate rooms for parties, seating 12 and 24. Tables outdoors (4, pavement; 6, terrace). **Map 11 O5.**

Covent Garden

★ L'Atelier de Joël Robuchon

13-15 West Street, WC2H 9NE (7010 8600, www.joel-robuchon.com). Leicester Square tube.
Bar **Open** 2.30pm-2am Mon-Sat; 2.30pm-10.30pm Sun.
Restaurant **Lunch served** noon-2.30pm, **dinner served** 5.30-10.30pm daily. **Main courses** £15-£55. **Set lunch** £19 2 courses. **Set dinner** (5.30-6.30pm) £19 2 courses, £25 3 courses. **Set meal** £105 tasting menu, £145 incl wine.
Both **Credit** AmEx, MC, V.
Joël Robuchon has a clutch of classy restaurants around the globe. The ground-floor dining room here shares the characteristic red and black colour scheme and Japanese-inspired design. Diners sit at high stools around a central area, rather like sitting at a sushi bar, but food is Mod Euro and beautifully presented. Multi-course tasting menus (including a nine-course vegetarian meal) are the best way to experience the kitchen's skills, but the less costly pre-theatre menu gives a similar bang for fewer bucks. The simple names of dishes, such as 'l'oeuf frit' or 'le lapin' belie the complex cooking. The former, a whole soft-boiled egg encased in crisp crumbs with a 'salad' of raisins and pine nuts in a sweet and sour sauce, had a Moorish air, while saddle of rabbit stuffed with Agen prunes was a well-rendered French classic. There was a deft hand too with Colchester razor clams served with meltingly soft slow-cooked leeks, topped with a perfect circle of pesto-like herb sauce, which gave the dish a touch of glamour as well as additional flavour. The upstairs dining room has black and white decor and conventional seating; it now serves the same menu as the ground floor. A meal at L'Atelier isn't cheap, but there's a real sense of glamour, occasion and creativity.
Available for hire. Babies and children admitted. Booking essential. Disabled: toilet. Dress: smart casual. Vegetarian menu. **Map 17 C3.**

Axis

One Aldwych, 1 Aldwych, WC2B 4BZ (7300 0300, www.onealdwych.com). Covent Garden or Embankment tube/Charing Cross tube/rail. **Lunch served** noon-2.30pm Mon-Fri. **Dinner served** 5.30-10.30pm Mon-Fri; 5.30-11.30pm Sat. **Main courses** £15.50-£23. **Set meal** £16.75 2 courses, £19.75 3 courses. **Credit** AmEx, DC, MC, V.
Since its last redesign, there's a slight 'James Bond villain's lair' look to this restaurant, beneath the grand but chic One Aldwych hotel. From the separate entrance, you walk down an impressive stone-walled spiral staircase and along a little tunnel to enter the drum-like basement space. Everything is carefully styled – the curve of the walls, the colour scheme, the curious row of what look like steel bamboo poles – but the effect is mellow rather than brash. It's soothingly calm (even traffic noise scarcely enters) and popular for business lunchers not in need of extra buzz. Service cannot be faulted. When a bowl of spinach was just a few minutes late, it was immediately taken off the bill. Menus are a fairly familiar Mod Euro mix, with

Sarastro **Restaurant**
"The Show After The Show"

A sumptuous treasure trove hidden within a Grade II listed Victorian townhouse, Sarastro is perfectly located in the heart of London's Theatreland. A wide selection of delicious Mediterranean dishes are served with theatrical flair and passion against the elaborate backdrop of golden drapes and decorative frescoed walls.

Every Sunday matinee and Sunday and Monday evenings there are live performances from up and coming stars of the Royal and National Opera houses and from all over the world. Sarastro is perfect for red carpet parties and celebrations and ideal for pre- and post- theatre dining with a menu available at £14.50. Also available for lunch Monday - Saturday. A private function room is available for corporate and red carpet occasions (for up to 300 guests).

126 Drury Lane, London WC2 | Tel: 020 7836 0101 Fax: 020 7379 4666
www.sarastro-restaurant.com | E: reservations@sarastro-restaurant.com

a particularly pleasing choice of salads, such as our refreshing combination of endive, Cornish blue cheese and walnuts with honey dressing. Seconds divide into 'light mains' such as seared tuna, and slightly heftier dishes like our finely cooked, full-flavoured duck confit with colcannon, lentils and plums in a port jus. Along with other West End establishments, Axis has become more accessible of late, with good-value set-price menus.
Available for hire. Babies and children welcome: high chairs. Booking advisable. Disabled: toilet. Vegetarian menu. **Map 18 F4**.

The Ivy

1 West Street, WC2H 9NQ (7836 4751, www.the-ivy.co.uk). Leicester Square tube. **Lunch served** noon-3pm Mon-Sat; noon-3.30pm Sun. **Dinner served** 5.30pm-midnight Mon-Sat; 5.30-11pm Sun. **Main courses** £9.25-£25.50. **Cover** £2. **Credit** AmEx, DC, MC, V.
The location might be prime theatreland territory, but there's nothing overtly song-and-dance about this Covent Garden landmark. Everything about the place whispers classic: the art deco room in greens and creams that hints at a members' club; the comfortable menu; the calm, faultless service. For all its enduring popularity with celebrities and the music industry – and there are often paparazzi hovering outside – the Ivy isn't the sort of place to go and be seen; it's the kind of restaurant folk visit to enjoy their time off. The long menu is curiously old-school British, with globe-trotting recipes picked up along the way, yet it manages to succeed: an entrée of steak tartare was worth the platitudes piled upon it, the bang bang chicken had a lovely kick to its satay sauce. Delicate lamb's sweetbreads were creamy; crispy soft-shell crab was buttery and lifted with a chilli jam; and a side dish of parmesan-fried courgettes was as addictive as our waitress warned. Dessert? Sticky toffee pudding, of course. If you wanted to cause a riot, you could start by trying to change the Ivy.
Babies and children admitted: high chairs. Booking essential, 4-6 weeks in advance. Separate room for parties, seats 60. Vegetarian menu. Vegan dishes. **Map 18 D4**.

Euston

Number Twelve

12 Upper Woburn Place, WC1H 0HX (7693 5425, www.numbertwelverestaurant.co.uk). Euston tube/rail. **Lunch served** noon-3pm Tue-Fri. **Dinner served** 5.30-10.15pm Tue-Sat. **Main courses** £12-£18. **Set meal** (lunch; 5.30-7pm) £12.50 2 courses, £16.50 3 courses. **Credit** AmEx, MC, V.
Not much can be done to make the dining room of a modern conference hotel feel like a family-run Italian. Get lost on the way to the loos and you might end up facing a flip chart. But for clandestine dining you couldn't do better than this over-designed restaurant down the road from Euston Station. Tinkly lounge music sets the tone, lunch looks like a good deal, and staff are eager to please. From the selection of ever-so slightly doughy breads – glazed rolls, focaccia and knobbly grissini – the kitchen shows it's trying hard. Dishes don't always manage to pull together the components and deliver the expected earthiness. 'Wood-roasted beetroot' with goat's cheese was sliced petal-thin and lost under a heap of micro leaves. White polenta with wild garlic and mushrooms wasn't as bosky as we'd hoped. Grey mullet with black olive tapenade and chilli-ed green beans packed more punch. The appearance of a sunken-looking baked apple with pecorino, halved raspberries and toasted bread roll for dessert was a downer, yet things ended on a high with the petits fours accompanying impeccable espresso.
Babies and children admitted. Booking essential. Disabled: lift; toilet. Separate rooms for parties, seating 20-120. **Map 4 K3**.

Fitzrovia

Villandry

170 Great Portland Street, W1W 5QB (7631 3131, www.villandry.com). Great Portland Street tube.
Bar **Open** 8am-11pm Mon-Fri; 9am-11pm Sat.
Breakfast served 8-11.30am, **meals served** noon-10pm Mon-Sat. **Main courses** £11.50-£22.50.
Restaurant **Lunch served** noon-3pm Mon-Sat; 11.30am-4pm Sun. **Dinner served** 6-10.30pm Mon-Sat. **Main courses** £12.50-£22.50.
Both **Credit** AmEx, MC, V.
The once-landmark food hall seemed depleted of enticing produce on our visit, concentrating on cookies and gifts. Café tables have encroached on the deli space; the daylight-filled restaurant with white cloths, cream walls and copper lights, remains as handsome as ever. The menu of Anglo-brasserie greatest hits – smoked salmon and avocado, charcuterie, oysters, risotto, steak, eton mess and sticky toffee pudding – has become a template for expansion. Now the cheaper Villandry Kitchen, opened in Holborn in summer 2009, makes the original look pricey. And Villandry isn't exactly a concept to roll out, more a restaurant with good looks, a reputation and a useful West End location. Jazzy music and the babble of professionals give it a lively vibe, but our starters didn't set the world alight. Especially as the candle under the copper pan of anchovy sauce (the threatened little fish so scanty in portion that stocks should recover soon), accompanying endless greenhouse-pepper crudités, had gone out. A globe artichoke with thin, vinegary hazelnut dressing had four whole nuts with it. True, scallops with pancetta and creamed leeks was gratifyingly well done. And asparagus and truffled pecorino risotto was only a touch overcooked to puddingy sweetness, but made dessert resistible.
Available for hire. Babies and children welcome: children's menu; high chairs. Booking advisable. Tables outdoors (13, pavement). Takeaway service. **Map 3 H5**.
For branch (Villandry Kitchen) see index.

Gloucester Road

L'Etranger

36 Gloucester Road, SW7 4QT (7584 1118, www.etranger.co.uk). Gloucester Road tube. **Lunch served** noon-3pm Mon-Fri. **Brunch served** noon-3pm Sun. **Dinner served** 6-11pm Mon-Sat; 6-10pm Sun. **Main courses** £16.40-£49. **Set meal** (lunch, 6-6.45pm Mon-Fri) £16.50 2 courses, £19.50 3 courses. **Credit** AmEx, MC, V.
Gold and platinum credit cards can get a real work out at this bijoux, fusion-ish, romantic corner restaurant. There is a separate caviar list, with five different varieties to choose from; no less than 25 different vintages of Dom Perignon, foie gras sushi, and grade-9 wagyu fillet Rossini for a mere £55. Yet L'Etranger doesn't have to be out of bounds to those with more mortgage than millions. A sweetly conceived, bargain-priced set lunch and early dinner menu neatly showcases the talents of executive chef Jérôme Tauvron and head chef Kingshuk Dey. The line-up of small- to medium-sized dishes runs from a warm salad of poached black leg chicken with sesame dressing cutely served in a lettuce cup, to a nice tumble of tempura fish chunks and baby corn in a bamboo steamer, and a lush mush of wagyu burger with a creamy cheesy fondue sauce. Old hands tend to go à la carte for signature dishes such as caramelised black cod with miso, and honey-glazed duck breast with braised shank and kumquats. Either way, it is difficult not to be impressed by the inventive presentation of what is clearly first-rate produce.
Available for hire. Babies and children welcome: high chairs. Booking advisable. Separate room for parties, seats 20. Vegetarian menu. **Map 13 C9**.

Holborn

The Terrace

Lincoln's Inn Fields, WC2A 3LJ (7430 1234, www.theterrace.info). Holborn tube. **Breakfast served** 8-11am, **lunch served** noon-3pm, **dinner served** 5.30-8pm Mon-Fri. **Main courses** £10.50-£17.95. **Set lunch** £16.95 2 courses, £18.95 3 courses. **Credit** AmEx, MC, V.
It may look like a simple park café from the outside, but Patrick Williams' Terrace is much smarter than that. Inside has a vaguely Scandinavian feel with ice-blue tables, cream banquettes and pine wood; to the rear is an alfresco terrace with umbrellas to provide shade on days when the sun is strong. It was populated on our visit by lawyers enjoying long lunches as well as groups of friends and families. The Modern European menu has added spice in the form of Caribbean dishes: jerk chicken with sautéed potatoes was superb, generously portioned and excellent value given the approachable price of the set lunch. Perfectly grilled sea bass came on a succulent bed of roast aubergine salad with a welcome chilli kick. Crème brûlée for pudding continued the high standard. Last orders for dinner are at 8pm, but that's not a problem for those working or shopping nearby. Breakfasts – organic eggs and smoked bacon layered with American-style pancakes, or a Caribbean fry-up including sweet potato, plantain and spicy baked beans – are also appealing. Our only complaints are with the long waits for food and staff who veered from friendly to impudent.
Available for hire. Babies and children welcome: high chairs. Booking advisable. Disabled: toilet. Tables outdoors (15, terrace). **Map 10 M6**.

King's Cross

Acorn House

69 Swinton Street, WC1X 9NT (7812 1842, www.acornhouserestaurant.com). King's Cross tube/rail. **Lunch served** noon-3pm Mon-Fri. **Dinner served** 6-10pm Mon-Fri; 5.30-10pm Sat. **Main courses** £12.50-£21. **Credit** AmEx, MC, V.
Owned by the Shoreditch Trust, Acorn House and its sibling Water House in Dalston aim to produce good, seasonal food in the most environmentally responsible manner while also training novice chefs and regenerating the local community. That long to-do list partly explains why prices punch above their weight, but this is a very pleasant eaterie in an area that has been lacking them. The kitchen's meat cookery consistently impresses: this time, a crispy-topped square slab of twice-cooked pork belly with baked apples. Vegetarians are offered such interesting fare as chickpea farinata with mushrooms, chard and goats' cheese, plus a couple of pasta and gnocchi dishes. Mushroom ravioli with thyme pannagrattato (seasoned breadcrumbs) and truffle oil was lovely but a mean portion for £13.50. For dessert, peppered flourless chocolate cake was overwhelmed by the ginger ice-cream it came with (things worked better with the bay leaf ice-cream served with bakewell pudding). Lunchtime sees a choice of five salads, which you can order as one, two, or a mixture for £3-£11.50. The wine list opens at £16.50 for Italian red and whites, but beer is an appealing alternative, with three brews from Chapel Down in East Sussex and a Fairtrade ale from Kent. Service was more adept than on previous visits.
Available for hire. Babies and children welcome: high chairs, nappy-changing facilities. Booking advisable weekends. Disabled: lift; toilet. Takeaway service. **Map 4 M3**.
For branch (Water House) see index.

Knightsbridge

Fifth Floor

Harvey Nichols, Knightsbridge, SW1X 7RJ (7235 5250, www.harveynichols.com). Knightsbridge tube.
Café **Breakfast served** 8am-noon, **lunch served** noon-3.30pm, **dinner served** 6-10.30pm Mon-Sat. **Brunch served** 11am-5pm Sun. **Tea served** 3.30-6pm Mon-Sat; 3.30-5pm Sun. **Main courses** £9.50-£15.
Restaurant **Brunch served** noon-4pm Sat, Sun. **Lunch served** noon-3pm Mon-Fri. **Dinner served** 6-11pm Mon-Sat. **Set lunch** £19.50-£24.50 3 courses. **Set dinner** £34.50 2 courses, £39.50 3 courses.
Both **Credit** AmEx, DC, MC, V.
Dining in the cool, futuristic oval room at the top of self-anointed 'international luxury lifestyle store' Harvey Nichols holds a certain cachet that you wouldn't usually associate with eating in a department store. Indeed, the surroundings, set apart from the bustle of the fifth-floor food market, are as stylish as you'd hope, complete with statement floral centrepiece and views down to the street. Yet what surprised us on this visit was the service, and we're not talking about its efficiency. Swedish-born Jonas Karlsson's menu

The Terrace

is accomplished. Red snapper was astonishingly fresh, with added pep thanks to a zippy orange and fennel salad. Wood-pigeon was succulent and rare; and the pea velouté that encircled halibut on lentils was a sublimely rich shade of green. The wine list stretches to 750 choices. However, the 'buts' on our visit were many, almost amusingly so. Staff had no record of our reservation. The electronic system lost our food order. We were presented with a 'Happy Anniversary' plate of truffles apropos nothing. Front-of-house bordered on the farcical, so thank goodness the kitchen got it absolutely right.
Babies and children welcome: children's menu; high chairs; nappy-changing facilities. Disabled: lift; toilet. Tables outdoors (15, café terrace). **Map 8 F9**.

Marylebone

L'Autre Pied

5-7 Blandford Street, W1U 3DB (7486 9696, www.lautrepied.co.uk). Baker Street tube. **Lunch served** noon-2.45pm Mon-Sat; noon-3pm Sun. **Dinner served** 6-10.30pm Mon-Sat; 6.30-9.30pm Sun. **Main courses** £19.95-£22.95. **Set lunch** £19.95 3 courses. **Set dinner** (6-7pm Mon-Fri) £26.95 3 courses. **Credit** AmEx, MC, V.
Just because this is the downsized younger sibling of Pied à Terre, don't go thinking it's a bistro version. True, the price differential between the two is considerable. But for a less eye-watering outlay, a meal in the handsome rooms decorated with a modern take on chinoiserie still offers complex and nuanced cooking. An enticing

selection of wines is available by the glass and 460ml carafes. With a light touch and subtle use of herbs, chef Marcus Eaves doesn't, however, stint on the dairy, as demonstrated by an indulgent basil-infused buttery sauce with spring vegetables on swathes of silky-textured pasta; and by a deeply savoury, intensely creamy mushroom and leek risotto. This wasn't just risotto; it was served in a copper pan along with a plate decorated with a slick of shallot purée, dots of watercress purée, two baby leeks and micro leaves – a fiddly contrast to the sublime rice, but a sign of the restaurant's ambition. Rolled breast of lamb (a fatty cut rendered tender; on the à la carte it would be saddle) was accompanied by indecently buttery carrots. The small bare wooden tables are swept of crumbs by very young staff. Despite the trappings of somewhere that takes food very seriously, L'Autre Pied is accessible and relaxing – and the kitchen didn't put a foot wrong.
Babies and children welcome: high chairs. Booking advisable. Separate room for parties, seats 18. Tables outdoors (3, pavement). **Map 9 G5**.

Orrery

55 Marylebone High Street, W1U 5RB (7616 8000, www.danddlondon.com). Baker Street tube.
Bar **Open** 11am-11pm daily.
Restaurant **Lunch served** noon-2.30pm, **dinner served** 6.30-10.30pm daily. **Main courses** £35-£50. **Set meal** £42 2 courses, £48 3 courses. **Set lunch** £25 3 courses, £40 3 courses incl wine. **Set dinner** £55 tasting menu (£95 incl wine).
Both **Credit** AmEx, MC, V.

This elegant sliver of a room, open to the views through large windows and a full-length skylight, has consistently maintained high standards throughout a succession of chefs. The current maestro, Igor Tymchyshyn, is every bit as accomplished as his predecessors. There were astonishing touches of technical skill in our meal, but wizardry never masked high-impact flavours. The daily-changing menu offers a two- or three-course carte and a shorter three-course lunch menu, and our set lunch delivered the goods in most respects. Most savoury courses are complex and artful in presentation, as exemplified brilliantly in a starter of smoked salmon roulade with a cloud-like smoked trout mousse, and a main of ethereal sauté halibut à la provençale with garnishes including a pungent tapenade and a gorgeous sauté of diced aubergine. Desserts – blackberry soufflé with sour cream sorbet, and perfect strawberries with an almond sable – were simpler but no less impressive. The outstanding wine list finds good producers in Europe and the New World, and service couldn't have been better. We had just one disappointing dish, a delicious main course of gnocchi with black truffle sauce that needed something extra for contrast of texture. And the filter coffee was pretty mediocre. These lapses lower Orrery's ranking, but this is a fantastic restaurant nonetheless. You can buy dishes to take home in the grocery downstairs.
Babies and children welcome: high chairs. Booking essential. Disabled: toilet. Tables outdoors (9, bar roof terrace). Vegetarian menu. **Map 3 G4**.

Mayfair

Embassy

29 Old Burlington Street, W1S 3AN (7851 0956, www.embassylondon.com). Green Park or Piccadilly Circus tube. **Lunch served** noon-3pm Tue-Fri. **Dinner served** 6-11.30pm Tue-Sat. **Main courses** £15-£25. **Credit** AmEx, MC, V.
Embassy is a fairly bling kind of experience, but it has pretty high-quality cooking and friendly service. The USP is the black cavernous, pseudo-infernal, bohemian-chic interior. That means fake-faded mirrors and cream-coloured, glass-studded banquette seating to which we were directed by a glammed-up maître d'. And all the while, rotating lights in the subterranean discotheque beyond augured the dizzy pleasure of Mayfair's deracinated playboys and playgirls. Fortunately, Garry Hollihead's cooking avoids trendy club affectations in favour of proven combinations. Light crudités were followed by a good choice of quality starters, including an excellent rosemary-encrusted beef carpaccio. Main courses too were both classic and imaginative: a fine rump of Welsh lamb, or chicken accompanied by couscous mixed with lemon, raisins, herbs and sauce vierge. Coconut panna cotta with pineapple sorbet sounded an interesting dessert, but we were already satisfied. There's a sensible and enticing wine list to go with the assured food. Embassy's prices are very considerate for Mayfair too, and you may well find a bargain offer for meals and cocktails on the internet.
Available for hire. Babies and children admitted. Booking advisable. Dress: smart casual. Tables outdoors (6, terrace). **Map 9 J7**.

Langan's Brasserie

Stratton Street, W1J 8LB (7491 8822, www.langansrestaurants.co.uk). Green Park tube. **Meals served** 12.15-11pm Mon-Thur; 12.15-11.30pm Fri-Sat. **Main courses** £13.50-£18.50. **Cover** £1.50. **Credit** AmEx, MC, V.
As a London institution, Langan's offers some unchanging virtues. There's the grand dining room itself, with its raffish art collection and the Dorian Gray-picture of the founders still on the menu: a 1970s Michael Caine at the centre. Being attended to by the ultra-professional, slightly eccentric waiters (the senior ones resembling characters in a Graham Greene novel) is always a pleasure. Langan's has long been a favourite of gents-who-lunch. Maybe it's the economic crisis, but these were thin on the ground on the afternoon we visited, leaving staff with little to do: purring along like a Ferrari being used for the school run. London institutions often like to sit on their laurels, but thankfully there wasn't much evidence of this here. A signature seafood salad featured flavoursome prawns, octopus, cockles and more, assembled with generosity and seasoned with vibrantly fresh herbs. The day's special, succulent pan-fried beef with red wine sauce, was cooked absolutely right. It went perfectly with the punchy but suave, suitably traditional house red. Prices aren't low – especially as all vegetables cost extra, and there's a cheeky 'cover charge' – but at least you get some panache for your pounds.
Babies and children admitted: high chairs. Booking advisable; essential dinner. Entertainment: jazz 10.30pm Thur-Sat. Separate room for parties, seats 80. **Map 9 H7**.
For branches (Langan's Bistro, Langan's Coq d'Or Bar & Grill, Langan's Odin's) see index.

Nicole's

158 New Bond Street, W1S 2UB (7499 8408, www.nicolefarhi.com). Bond Street or Green Park tube.
Bar **Open** 10am-6pm Mon-Sat. **Meals served** 11.30am-5.30pm Mon-Sat. **Main courses** £9-£14.95.
Restaurant **Breakfast served** 8.30am-noon Mon-Sat. **Lunch served** noon-3.30pm Mon-Fri; noon-4pm Sat. **Tea served** 3.30-6pm Mon-Sat. **Main courses** £19-£25. **Cover** (noon-4pm Mon-Sat) £1.
Both **Credit** AmEx, DC, MC, V.
At the foot of sweeping stairs, the restaurant below Nicole Farhi's Bond Street outlet is sleek, light and airy. A long chrome bar overlooks an oak floor of linen-topped tables serviced by suited staff. On the back wall, there's a playwrighting hall of fame, with black and white photos of famous dramatists (Harold Pinter, Alan Bennett, and the boss's husband, David Hare, among others). Prices are a match for New Bond Street. The global wine list may include New Zealand riesling, but it's mostly £5-£8 for a single glass. Gazpacho with crab and avocado was a typically alluring appetiser, yet starters are mostly £9-£10. Fish options included a piquant, Indian-spiced swordfish with chickpea and rice salad, and an immaculately grilled halibut with chips, peas and tartare sauce. But at £20 and £22 respectively they really did have to be good. However, the quality of cooking is likely to tempt you into a £7.50 dessert, and we didn't regret a yellow-ochre crème fraîche cheesecake with toffee bananas. A cover charge of £1 is tight, and service at 15% is presumptuous, but if you're bothered by spending more than £80 on a light lunch for two, you're in the wrong place.
Available for hire. Babies and children admitted. Booking advisable. **Map 9 H7**.

★ Patterson's

4 Mill Street, W1S 2AX (7499 1308, www.pattersonsrestaurant.co.uk). Bond Street or Oxford Circus tube. **Lunch served** noon-3pm Mon-Fri. **Dinner served** 6-11pm Mon-Fri; 5-11pm Sat. **Main courses** £20. **Set lunch** £23 3 courses, £27 3 courses. **Credit** AmEx, MC, V.

This immaculate little gem has been run by the Patterson family since 2003. Mrs Patterson oversees front-of-house with enthusiasm and professionalism; her husband and son run the kitchen, turning out consistently excellent cooking. Mr Patterson hails from Eyemouth, the source of the restaurant's langoustines, lobsters and crabs (fish and seafood shouldn't be missed here). Diver-caught seared scallops from North Uist looked dramatic sitting on a dark pool of squid-ink risotto, but the taste was even more sensational, with a profound, umami richness from reduced squid ink and parmesan. Hot and cold smoked trout and salmon (from Shetland), with a tian of cucumber, a potato blini and a quail's egg, was styled like a semi-deconstructed Japanese maki roll. It looked so good we weren't sure whether to frame it and hang it, or eat it. The flavour was superb. Meat is of a similarly superior quality. Medium-rare loin of lamb came with a sweetbread, a plump cep mushroom, a tarte fine with shallot jam, an intensely flavoured cauliflower purée topped with toasted almonds and a squiggle of thyme-flavoured 'persillade'. This assured, complex cooking is pulled off with phenomenal skill, in an environment that seems miles away from the chill humourlessness of many haute-cuisine establishments. If you haven't discovered Patterson's yet, get your skates on.
Babies and children welcome: high chairs. Booking essential. Separate room for parties, seats 20. **Map 9 H/J6**.

Patterson's

Bumpkin. See p221.

RESTAURANTS

Sotheby's Café

Sotheby's, 34-35 New Bond Street, W1S 2RT (7293 5077). Bond Street or Oxford Circus tube. **Breakfast served** 9.30-11.30am, **lunch served** noon-3pm, **tea served** 3-4.45pm Mon-Fri. **Main courses** £14-£17.50. **Set tea** £6.25. **Credit** AmEx, DC, MC, V.

Yes, Sotheby's the auction house. So, good art and good wine are essential – and this smartly informal café doesn't disappoint, with iconic black and white photographs and a short, regularly changing wine list by Serena Sutcliffe MW. The restaurant is attached to Sotheby's grand foyer and its brown leather banquettes and dark blue chairs produce a mood like you'd find in a small club. Staff are remarkably friendly. Portions were askew for our starter salads; rare roast beef with Asian vegetables and tataki dressing was lovely, but tiny compared to grilled squid with fennel and tomatoey chilli jam. Guinea fowl pot-au-feu featured precisely cut veg that lent the winter roots an elegance more usually associated with spring varieties; tarragon dumplings were not the lightest, though, and the broth could have been stronger. Lobster club sandwich tasted good, yet its lack of meaty shellfish chunks disappointed. Dessert saw the kitchen's return to form: exquisite marmalade brioche pudding with correctly set, flavourful custard, beautifully presented with a jug of cream. As we left, tiers of goodies were being set out for afternoon tea. Sotheby's also has a brief but appealing breakfast menu.
Babies and children admitted. Booking advisable. Disabled: toilet. **Map 9 H6**.

Wild Honey

12 St George Street, W1S 2FB (7758 9160, www.wildhoneyrestaurant.co.uk). Bond Street or Oxford Circus tube. **Lunch served** noon-2.30pm Mon-Sat; noon-3pm Sun. **Dinner served** 6-11pm Mon-Wed; 6-11.30pm Fri, Sat; 6-10.30pm Sun. **Main courses** £17.50-£19.50. **Set lunch** £18.95 3 courses. **Set dinner** (6-7pm) £21.95 3 courses. **Credit** AmEx, MC, V.

What a difference six hours can make. At weekend lunchtimes, Wild Honey, sister of Arbutus (*see p219*), is calm, composed and in possession of an exceptionally good-value set menu. This is the best time to relax unfettered amid the oak panelling. In contrast, evenings are encumbered with the time limitations of two sittings and the space limitations of tables penned too close together. Dishes aren't always what you'd expect from the menu; 'ravioli' of veal saw slivers of meat enveloping warm butternut-squash mash, entirely pasta free. However, the composition is thoughtful, each main

using two to four key ingredients, often with an English bent. Grilled sea bass had a delicate anise flavour and came with a ramekin of well-seasoned boulangère potatoes. Line-caught cod was let down by an accompaniment of chorizo and chickpeas that was too oily. Service was variable: one waiter was oddly tactile, tapping an arm to remove a plate, but front-desk and the maître d' were impeccable. Previous visits have been better, yet Wild Honey still packs them in. It also seizes its sales opportunities: recommending the more expensive wines (the 250ml carafes are a life-saver) and advertising chef Anthony Demetre's cookbook.
Babies and children admitted. Booking essential. **Map 9 H6**.

Piccadilly

Criterion

224 Piccadilly, W1J 9HP (7930 0488, www. criterionrestaurant.com). Piccadilly Circus tube. **Lunch served** noon-2.30pm Mon-Sat. **Dinner served** 5.30-11.30pm Mon-Sat. **Main courses** £12.50-£28.50. **Set meal** (lunch, 5.30-7pm Mon-Sat) £18 2 courses, £23 3 courses. **Credit** AmEx, MC, V.

This grand, gorgeous restaurant was opened in 1874 and has since weathered various dining trends: from 1920s luncheon clubs to Marco Pierre White. Beautifully renovated, it's now the London flagship of a company called VINS Holdings, run by Russian-born Irakli Sopromadze. To judge by the Criterion, VINS has big ambitions. The mainly Mod Euro menu and elaborate presentation go beyond the simple brasserie style that the prominent location and Grade II-listed interior might suggest. Chef Matthew Foxon makes pasta, ricotta, sorbet and ice-cream on the premises; he churns butter; smokes fish; bakes bread; and flies seafood in from Cornwall. Beef tartare with quails' eggs and salty caramel was a gamble at £12.50 with its popcorn overtones, but its textures and tastes paid off handsomely. Sublime grilled squid and an assemblage of five pork dishes, from crispy crackling to a grown-up sausage roll, were also winners. Prices are quite high, especially at lunch (there's a single à la carte), and the menu's sections confused (why sushi and sashimi?), but it's good to see a chef given his head and a management that does not shy away from culinary character in a landmark venue. The room was half-full at lunchtime, but capable, characterful staff ensured it didn't lack atmosphere.
Babies and children welcome: high chairs. Booking advisable. Dress: smart casual. Separate room for parties, seats 70. **Map 17 B5**.

Pimlico

Rex Whistler Restaurant at Tate Britain

Tate Britain, Millbank, SW1P 4RG (7887 8825, www.tate.org.uk). Pimlico tube/87 bus. **Breakfast served** 10-11.30am Sat, Sun. **Lunch served** 11.30am-3pm, **tea served** 3.15-5pm daily. **Main courses** £15.55-£19.45. **Set lunch** £15.95 2 courses, £19.95 3 courses. **Credit** AmEx, DC, MC, V.

This place is famous for two things: the enchanting mural by Rex Whistler; and its wine list, which for decades has attracted oenophiles like bears to a honey jar. Our lunch showed it's worth visiting for other reasons as well. One: the tables outside, in a small square facing the Embankment, which are glorious on a sunny day. Two: the service, which was efficient and heart-warmingly friendly. And three: the food, which is simple but executed with consistent skill and confidence. The low-priced set lunch offered all we needed. Starters were a brilliantly tasty leek and potato soup and a meaty terrine of confit duck served with raspberry preserve. Mains were own-made garganelli pasta with peas and broad beans, and an airy smoked haddock fish cake on buttered leeks. The peas were too crunchy, but otherwise we didn't have a single complaint about the food. Chips cooked in dripping were indescribably good. It's a shame not to drink here: the wine list – nearly 50 pages, marked-up modestly, helpfully annotated, ample offerings by the glass and half-bottle – is among London's best. For a weekend art-fest with on-site lunch before or after, there's no better place in town.
Babies and children welcome: high chairs. Booking advisable. Disabled: toilet. Tables outdoors (8, terrace). **Map 16 L11**.

St James's

The Avenue

7-9 St James's Street, SW1A 1EE (7321 2111, www.theavenue-restaurant.co.uk). Green Park tube. *Restaurant* **Lunch served** noon-3pm Mon-Fri. **Dinner served** 5.45-11pm Mon-Sat. **Main courses** £10.50-19. **Set meal** £19.50 2 courses, £22.50 3 courses.
Bar **Open** noon-11pm Mon-Fri; 5.45-11pm Sat. *Both* **Credit** AmEx, DC, MC, V.

Gleaming white, modish and extravagantly spacious, the Avenue exudes an air of affluent well-being. The front bar is popular with young business people for an after-work cocktail. We were ushered to the rear restaurant area, where we settled down to some enjoyable starters. A simple

asparagus with brown shrimp and (hardly discernible) chopped egg was made wonderful by a gorgeous herby vinaigrette. Mixed shellfish cocktail was a fun riff on prawn cocktail, with crayfish, mussels and two giant prawns, plus – of course – rose-marie sauce; it was fine, but perhaps the seafood wasn't leaping with freshness. We loved the chicken breast, though, which came in a thin but properly reduced, full-flavoured broth, with broad beans, wilted lettuce and bacon – a simple-looking dish with great depth. A very fresh and tender fillet of bream with jerusalem artichokes, roast tomatoes and herb purée was equally good. Chocolate pot with tiny specks of praline crunch was similarly unshowy yet special; we were grabbed by the rich mocha flavour. Fine food, then, but service was clunky throughout. We were given wrong menus, left alone too long, and had to wait for drinks. Staff weren't unfriendly, yet didn't have the slickness you'd expect.
Babies and children welcome: high chairs. Booking advisable. Disabled: toilet. **Map 9 J8.**

Le Caprice
Arlington House, Arlington Street, SW1A 1RJ (7629 2239, www.caprice-holdings.co.uk). Green Park tube. **Lunch served** noon-3pm, **dinner served** 5.30pm-midnight Mon-Sat. **Meals served** noon-11pm Sun. **Main courses** £14-£25. **Set dinner** (5.30-6.45pm; after 10.15pm) £15.75 2 courses, £19.75 3 courses. **Cover** £2. **Credit** AmEx, DC, MC, V.
There's something unashamedly 1980s about Le Caprice, decked out in its epoch-defining black and white colour scheme, bentwood chairs and arrangements of sunflowers. The bowler-hatted doorman makes diners feel like insiders rather than interlopers when they pass through the hallowed portals, through which countless celebs trailed in the restaurant's heyday. The menu is a mix of mostly unchallenging (but well-rendered) French and Italian-inspired dishes, with a few Asian ideas thrown in. Summery pea soup, served chilled and scattered with a few pink borage flowers, was silky-smooth. Seared scallops with wild garlic mousseline were tender and cooked to a turn, while pork belly, served with garlicky mash and carrots, was crisp-skinned outside and voluptuously tender within. Baked chocolate pudding, dark and melting at its heart, was as rich as the well-heeled diners. This is not the place to come if you're on a budget, but the professional service and old-world ambience – complete with tinkling ivories from a pianist – make dining here something of an event, even if the two-hour dining slots are strictly enforced.

Babies and children welcome: high chairs. Booking essential, 2 weeks in advance. Entertainment: pianist 6.30pm-midnight Mon-Sat; 7-11pm Sun. Vegetarian menu. **Map 9 J8.**

Quaglino's
16 Bury Street, SW1Y 6AJ (7930 6767, www.danddlondon.co.uk). Green Park tube. *Bar* **Open** 11.30am-1am Mon-Thur; 11.30am-3am Fri, Sat. *Restaurant* **Lunch served** noon-3pm daily. **Dinner served** 5.30-10.30pm Mon-Thur; 5.30pm-midnight Fri, Sat. **Main courses** £12.50-£26.50. **Set meal** (Mon-Thur) £10 2 courses, £15 3 courses. *Both* **Credit** AmEx, DC, MC, V.
Quaglino's was a hit in the early 1990s and, like grunge, now seems dated. People once queued for a chance to steal the branded Q-shaped ashtrays from this one-time celebrity hangout, but the glory days are over. The vast double-height dining room resembles a food court at an American shopping mall, with a dull blue glow cast over a display of fruits de mer and bold floral arrangements. The menu succeeds where it is simple: quality smoked salmon served with a dollop of crème fraîche and a few capers was good. Yet when the kitchen (just visible from the dining room) is moved to be creative, trouble can ensue. Competently cooked sea bream shouldn't have been paired with a medley of sautéed apples and currants that would have been far more at home with roast pork. An overcooked bulb of pak choi plopped into the middle of the beurre blanc added to the mess. The venue retains hints of its glamorous past: there's still a piano in the bar, servers are courteous, the wine list offers reasonable variety. These days, however, even the food in the neighbouring clubs might be more innovative and certainly tastier.
Babies and children welcome: children's menu; high chairs. Booking advisable. Disabled: toilet. Entertainment: musicians 7-11pm, DJ 11pm-2am daily. Separate rooms for parties, seating 20 and 44. **Map 9 J7.**

Soho

Andrew Edmunds
46 Lexington Street, W1F 0LW (7437 5708). Leicester Square, Oxford Circus or Piccadilly Circus tube. **Lunch served** 12.30-3pm Mon-Fri; 1-3pm Sat; 1-3.30pm Sun. **Dinner served** 6-10.45pm Mon-Sat; 6-10.30pm Sun. **Main courses** £10-£17. **Credit** MC, V.
Andrew Edmunds seems to be a love-it-or-hate-it place. Its many fans think the tiny tables, rickety chairs and low ceilings (in the front room, basement or conservatory of an old townhouse) make it irresistibly romantic and intimate: one of Soho's nearest equivalents to a dusty old Parisian bistro. Others just find it cramped, and anyone with long legs may get bruised knees. Tales are also heard of occasions when the difficult act performed by the staff as they dash up and down the narrow staircases has broken down, which devotees presumably forgive. Whether you take to it or not may also determine your response to the food. Some dishes are elaborate, and feature such rarities as gulls' eggs. However, all those we tried this time were let down by mundane ingredients. Our mains – cod fillet with mash, clams, broad beans and salsa verde; and lamb chops with bulgar wheat, wild rice, pomegranate seeds and pecan salad – both sounded interesting, but needed better basic ingredients and more finesse in the cooking. An imaginative wine list is a plus, but nowadays you can get better food for less in many other venues, though maybe without that particular Soho buzz.
Babies and children admitted. Booking essential. Tables outdoors (2, pavement). **Map 17 A4.**

Arbutus (100)
63-64 Frith Street, W1D 3JW (7734 4545, www.arbutusrestaurant.co.uk). Tottenham Court Road tube. **Lunch served** noon-2.30pm Mon-Sat; noon-3pm Sun. **Dinner served** 5-11pm Mon-Sat; 5.30-10.30pm Sun. **Main courses** £14-£19.95. **Set lunch** £15.50 3 courses. **Set dinner** (5-7pm) £17.50 3 courses. **Credit** AmEx, MC, V.

Providing very fine cooking at very fair prices isn't an easy trick to pull off. But chef Anthony Demetre and his business partner Will Smith's excellent restaurant makes it look easy. A sense of balance and proportion pervades, and there is nothing superfluous, but no stinting on what matters either; the effect is quietly impressive. Although it's not cheap to eat à la carte, the set lunch and early dinner are famously good value. Bare tables are softened with rush mats; service doesn't falter. To keep prices keen, the kitchen is seasonal, thrifty and ingenious, using cheaper cuts such as bavette of beef, and squid and mackerel (combined into a 'burger' in a trademark starter). The restaurant pioneered 250ml carafes – not extortionately marked up – for sampling the wines from a well-edited, not endless list. So it's a carafe of macabeo with a beautifully juicy, herby mullet with gorgeous gnocchi, spinach and clams, and one of Rioja with tender rabbit, boned and caramelised on top with chickpeas, merguez and red peppers stewed together sweetly. A heavenly floating island often crops up on the set menu, though other characteristically delicate but rewarding desserts might be roast peach with lemon thyme and salted caramel ice-cream.
Babies and children welcome: high chairs. Booking advisable. **Map 17 B3.**

South Kensington

Bibendum
Michelin House, 81 Fulham Road, SW3 6RD (7581 5817, www.bibendum.co.uk). South Kensington tube. **Lunch served** noon-2.30pm Mon-Fri; 12.30-3pm Sat, Sun. **Dinner served** 7-11pm Mon-Sat; 7-10.30pm Sun. **Main courses** £16-£25. **Set lunch** (Mon-Fri) £25 2 courses, £29.50 3 courses. **Set dinner** (Sun) £29.50 3 courses. **Credit** AmEx, DC, MC, V.
After eating at Bibendum, you can be forgiven for thinking that the '80s never really went away. More than two decades after Sir Terence Conran, Simon Hopkinson and Lord (Paul) Hamlyn took over the former Michelin tyre headquarters and hailed a new age in British dining, very little has changed. The impressive stained glass windows, wrap-around chairs and sculptural waiters station are all still firmly in place. Meanwhile, the quietly rich and the noisily celebrated still pop in and order what they have always ordered – the fish and chips, the Bibendum terrine, the roast chicken, and the pithiviers au chocolat. Most of it is still as good as it ever was, due to the conscientious consistency of head chef/director Matthew Harris, who has been in the kitchen ever since the doors opened. If steak au poivre, garlicky snails, mushroom duxelles, and beurre blanc sauces make you not just nostalgic but hungry, then this is most definitely the place for you. If you can afford it, that is – the bill is the one thing that has steadfastly kept pace with modern times.
Babies and children welcome: high chairs. Booking essential; 1 wk in advance for dinner. Bookings not accepted for parties of more than 10. **Map 14 E10.**

Brompton Bar & Grill
243 Brompton Road, SW3 2EP (7589 8005, www.bromptonbarandgrill.com). Knightsbridge or South Kensington tube. **Lunch served** noon-3pm Mon-Fri. **Lunch served** noon-3pm Mon-Fri; noon-3.30pm Sat, Sun. **Dinner served** 6-10.30pm Mon-Sat; 6-10pm Sun. **Main courses** £12-£22. **Credit** AmEx, MC, V.
BB&G 'embraces the concept of what the market desires in menus, ambience, style and value,' says the website. Indeed. Despite modern appearances, this market rejects contemporary notions of healthy eating, and the pavement outside is thronged with Marlboro smokers. Indoors, a patrician clientele squashes into a room covered in an eclectic collection of pictures, for hot and plentiful food that's much better than you might expect for a Knightsbridge kind of caff. Staff cope well. There's a core menu of whitebait, grilled ribeye, calf's liver, cheeseburger, grilled tuna and chicken; there are security blankets of dauphinoise potatoes and scrambled duck egg with mushrooms;

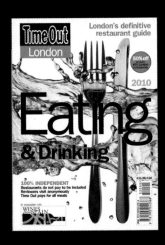

and fashionable revivals like crispy pig tails. It's sophisticated comfort food, sometimes messing with ingredients to no advantage. Hot, crisp, deep-fried quails' eggs, like mini sausage-less scotch eggs (plus a trendy salad of peas, pea-shoots and micro leaves), with grain mustard-spiked mayo, was a fattier and less pretty starter than simply boiled quails' eggs. A vast bowl of fish stew, as rich, oily and ruddy-hued as our neighbour, was packed with big chunks of fish, mussels and clams, and topped with saffrony rouille on toast. Pudding selection is a little perfunctory, but by then we'd had enough. If you're looking for hearty alternatives to Knightsbridge's salads and sushi, this is the place.
Babies and children welcome; high chairs. Booking advisable weekends. Entertainment: jazz 10pm Thur. Separate room for parties, seats 30. **Map 14 E10**.

Bumpkin
102 Old Brompton Road, SW7 3RD (7341 0802, www.bumpkinuk.com). Gloucester Road or South Kensington tube. **Lunch served** noon-3pm Mon-Fri. **Brunch served** 10am-3.30pm Sat; 11am-4pm Sun. **Dinner served** 6-10.30pm daily. **Main courses** £10-£18.50. **Set lunch** (Mon-Fri) £12 2 courses. **Credit** AmEx, MC, V.
This new branch, which opened in October 2008, shows signs of being as successful as the popular Notting Hill original. Spread over one floor with a bar area in front of the dining room, the setting is country-chic (with distressed wooden furniture and mismatched chairs). However, it's clear the look came from a design studio rather than second-hand shops. Wooden crates, sheaves of wheat and miscellaneous sacks nestling under the butcher's-block waiter station are a little twee, but the overall effect is as cosy as a country kitchen, and Bumpkin has a welcoming, convivial feel. The daily-changing menu is seasonal and modern, with many ingredients sourced in the UK. Starters of charcuterie and pan-fried Scottish mackerel with mixed leaves and citrus dressing were good, but overshadowed by a wonderfully comforting plate of macaroni and cheese, and an excellent bite ribeye steak with chips and béarnaise sauce. The only letdown was a bland grilled squash, broccoli and pumpkin-seed salad. A generous portion of sticky date pudding with butterscotch sauce and vanilla ice-cream provided a satisfyingly sweet finish. Bumpkin has a decent cocktail list and mixes great bloody marys, making this a tempting choice for weekend brunch.
Babies and children welcome: children's menu; crayons; high chairs; nappy-changing facilities. Booking advisable. Disabled: toilet. Separate room for parties, seats 36. Tables outdoors (6, pavement). **Map 14 D11**.
For branch see index.

Westminster

The Atrium
4 Millbank, SW1P 3JA (7233 0032, www.atrium restaurant.com). Westminster tube. **Lunch served** noon-3pm, **dinner served** 6-9.45pm Mon-Fri. **Main courses** £9.95-£19.75. **Set meal** £17.95 2 courses. **Credit** AmEx, DC, MC, V.
In terms of self-promotion, the Atrium is as reticent as can be. From outside the 4 Millbank building, you'd be hard-pushed even to tell that a restaurant lies within. Once inside, you descend a sweeping staircase to arrive at the central 'terrace', a surprisingly bright, sunken area situated some way beneath a conservatory-style roof. It's like dining in a rather pleasing modern hotel lobby. The place is quiet most evenings, busier at lunchtimes, thanks to the thrusting politicos who talk shop and pore over *The House* parliamentary mag. The menu has been improved since our last visit, now focusing on the Modern British dishes it does best. There's still a couple of pasta options (rigatoni with porcini cream and oyster mushrooms; squid ink linguini with mussels and prawns), but for the most part it's the likes of braised lamb shank with celeriac mash, or Gloucester Old Spot pork chop with black pudding. Tasty but short of remarkable, the food

Lamberts. See p225.

is on a par with gastropub grub, albeit at a bit of a price hike. Still, set menus and offers currently abound, so check before you book.
Available for hire. Babies and children admitted. Booking advisable lunch. Disabled: lift; toilet. Separate rooms for parties, seating 12 and 30. **Map 16 L10**.

West
Bayswater

Le Café Anglais (100)
8 Porchester Gardens, W2 4DB (7221 1415, www.lecafeanglais.co.uk). Bayswater tube. **Lunch served** noon-3.30pm Mon-Fri, Sun. **Brunch served** 11am-3.30pm Sat. **Dinner served** 6.30-11pm Mon-Thur; 6.30-11.30pm Fri, Sat; 6.30-10.15pm Sun. **Main courses** £8-£27.50. **Set lunch** (Mon-Fri) £16.50 2 courses, £19.50 3 courses. **Cover** £1.50. **Credit** AmEx, MC, V.
Despite its location at the Whiteleys shopping centre, Le Café Anglais does its best to recreate a glamorous Parisian bistro. With its pale colours, large windows, banquette seating and curving lines, this spacious restaurant recalls an art deco ocean liner. The food, under renowned chef-proprietor Rowley Leigh, makes waves too. Among the starters, fish courses, mains, cheeses and desserts on the traditional large-format carte are hors d'oeuvres (£3.50 or £4.50 each, including an unmissable signature dish of parmesan custard with anchovy toast) and daily roasts, such as roast kid, suckling pig and venison. Our dishes were mostly very good. Gnocchi romana, made with plenty of parmesan and served with an early-summer stew of artichokes, broad beans and peas and bathed in quality olive oil, was deliciously indulgent. From the daily set dinner menu, simply roasted john dory, served with saffron mash and (more) broad beans was well judged. Rabbit rillettes served fridge-cold, and an over-primped lemon meringue pie with grainy meringue were the only bum notes in our meal, served by smoothly professional staff. The wine list champions trad French regions with a few curve-balls thrown in, such as an excellent pinot noir from Austria's Burgenland for £5.25 a glass.
Available for hire. Babies and children welcome: high chairs. Booking advisable dinner. Disabled: toilet. Separate room for parties, seats 26. **Map 7 C6**.

Island Restaurant & Bar
Royal Lancaster Hotel, Lancaster Terrace, W2 2TY (7551 6070, www.islandrestaurant.co.uk). Lancaster Gate tube. **Bar Open** noon-11pm Mon-Sat; noon-10pm Sun. *Restaurant* **Breakfast served** 6.45-11am daily. **Meals served** noon-11pm Mon-Sat; noon-10pm Sun. **Main courses** £11.25-£30. **Set meal** (noon-5pm) £10 1 course incl glass of wine.
Both **Credit** AmEx, MC, V.
Being located between two busy main roads isn't ideal, but Island has the calm of an oasis, providing you don't sit by the window watching the traffic pass. The interior is decked out in shades of wood veneer and silver, with purple banquettes and cushioned seating. A view of chefs at work in the kitchen offers some entertainment, but otherwise there's little memorable about the surroundings. Service can be slow at times. If you're in the area, this would be a good option for decently prepared food, particularly at lunchtime when a set menu is offered alongside the rather pricey carte. Grills, pastas and other please-all dishes are available. Beef carpaccio was seared before being thinly sliced and dressed with balsamic vinegar, truffle oil and rocket. The portion was small for the price but delicious. Mains of beef burger with trimmings and battered pollack were good. Both dishes came with crunchy thick-cut chips, but were let down by relish and tartare sauces that tasted bland and shop-bought. For pudding, baked alaska was a bit heavy on meringue but otherwise sweet, hot, cold and lovely.
Available for hire. Babies and children welcome: children's menu; high chairs. Booking advisable. Disabled: toilet. **Map 8 D6**.

RESTAURANTS

Chiswick

Sam's Brasserie & Bar

11 Barley Mow Passage, W4 4PH (8987 0555, www.samsbrasserie.co.uk). Chiswick Park or Turnham Green tube.
Bar **Open** 9am-midnight Mon-Wed, Sun; 9am-12.30am Thur-Sat. **Meals served** 9am-10.30pm Mon-Sat; 9am-10pm Sun. **Main courses** £5-£10.50.
Restaurant **Brunch served** 9am-4pm Sat, Sun. **Lunch served** noon-3pm Mon-Fri; 9am-4pm Sat, Sun. **Dinner served** 6.30-10.30pm Mon-Sat; 6.30-10pm Sun. **Main courses** £9.50-£17.50. **Set lunch** (Mon-Fri) £12 2 courses, £15 3 courses; (Sun) £21 3 courses. **Set dinner** (Mon-Thur, Sun; 6.30-7.30pm Fri, Sat) £15 2 courses, £18 3 courses. *Both* **Credit** AmEx, MC, V.
Sam's won our Best Local Restaurant award in 2007, and the buzzy brasserie continues to function like a second home for many locals. The Sam in question is Harrison, former general manager of Rick Stein's Padstow empire (Stein backs both Sam's and its younger sibling, Harrison's; *see p47*). The look is industrial chic – befitting a restaurant built into the shell of a former paper factory. A mix of tables and benches leads the eye to the open kitchen, and there's a cracking little bar out front (good cocktails). Drop in for brunch (family-friendly), bring your laptop by day (free wi-fi) or dine from the crowd-pleasing menu (well-sourced produce). Cooking is competent if not knockout. Of eight starters, deep-fried squid lacked punch; smoked salmon with pea blinis was a little fussy (the fish wrapped up like a rose); Sam's terrine fared best. Mains are of a high standard – both ribeye and roast cod with chorizo were cooked just-so; lamb with boulangère potatoes, spring greens and salsa verde was a treat. Set menus are good value and the wine list (featuring Stein shiraz and chardonnay) is a corker. But it's the service that clinches it: smiley and quietly efficient. Sam's treats punters like old friends.
Babies and children welcome: children's menu; high chairs; toys. Booking advisable Thur-Sat. Disabled: toilet.

Kensington

Babylon

7th floor, The Roof Gardens, 99 Kensington High Street, W8 5SA (7368 3993, www.roofgardens.com). High Street Kensington tube.
Lunch served noon-2.30pm daily. **Dinner served** 7-10.30pm Mon-Sat. **Main courses** £18.50-£24. **Set lunch** (Mon-Sat) £16.50 2 courses, £19.50 3 courses; (Sun) £22 2 courses, £25 3 courses. **Credit** AmEx, DC, MC, V.
Just as Babylon's hanging gardens were one of the seven wonders of the ancient world, Kensington's rooftop gardens are among London's most glorious follies. One hundred feet above the high street lurks 1.5 acres of themed parkland, complete with four flamingos and an air fleet of resident ducks, one of whom lands in a stream in full view of our window table. In such a setting, Richard Branson's bright and breezy brasserie doesn't have to go out of its way to pull in the crowds. And nor does it. The greeting was chilly; service was perfunctory and remote; and the food, while perfectly competent, did not deliver the quality or quantity that the steepish prices might suggest. A pressed mosaic of Devon Rose chicken, liver and aubergine terrine was gorgeous to look at, but served fridge-cold with a vapid garlic and parsley dressing, while a nicely simple mixed seafood grill was let down by mushy langoustine. A starter of barbecue asparagus had the flavour of the grill, but just four spears seemed mean, leaving it to a roast fillet of cod with gruyère and parsley crust and flaky ham hock – and the gardens – to save the night.
Babies and children welcome: children's menu; entertainer (Sun); high chairs. Booking advisable. Disabled: lift; toilet. Entertainment: musicians dinner Thur. Separate room for parties, seats 12. Tables outdoors (15, balcony). **Map 7 B9.**

Clarke's (100)

124 Kensington Church Street, W8 4BH (7221 9225, www.sallyclarke.com). Notting Hill Gate tube. **Lunch served** 12.30-2pm Mon-Fri; noon-2pm Sat; 12.30-2.30pm Sun. **Dinner served** 6.30-10pm Mon-Sat. **Main courses** (lunch) £15-£17. **Set dinner** £39.50 3 courses incl coffee. **Credit** AmEx, DC, MC, V.
Chef-proprietor Sally Clarke has been espousing the 'seasonal and local' ethic since the mid 1980s, when she returned from the West Coast of the US imbued with the spirit of the organic, local-food movement that was taking root at restaurants such as Chez Panisse. Clarke's approach to cooking is a souvenir that has stood her in good stead. The food at this stylishly low-key restaurant shows influences from western Europe, executed with a deft hand. Our set dinner menu is a case in point: starter of Cornish mackerel tartare with coriander and lime, served with a crisp, thin chickpea-flour pancake typical of Liguria in Italy; followed by a main course featuring Berkshire lamb with tiny white Spanish beans and an oven-baked tomato sprinkled with crisp breadcrumbs, reminiscent of the Med. Roast chicken might seem a dull thing to order in a restaurant, but the crisp skin, moist flesh and perfect gravy served here will change your mind. Service is poised and professional. The wine list has some very good bottles, with California wines (including a selection from iconic producer Ridge) particularly well-chosen. And don't miss the breads, for which the deli next door (& Clarke's) is justly famed.
Available for hire. Babies and children welcome: high chairs. Booking advisable. Separate room for parties, seats 50. **Map 7 B7.**

Kensington Place

201-209 Kensington Church Street, W8 7LX (7727 3184, www.kensingtonplace-restaurant.co.uk). Notting Hill Gate tube. **Lunch served** noon-3pm Mon-Fri; noon-3.30pm Sat, Sun. **Dinner served** 6.30-10.30pm Mon-Thur; 6.30-11pm Fri, Sat; 6.30-10pm Sun. **Main courses** £14-£25. **Set meal** £19.50 3 courses. **Credit** AmEx, MC, V.
With its floor-to-ceiling windows and big, airy dining room, there's more than a touch of the fishbowl about this place – rather appropriate, given the attached fishmonger's. Kensington Place is part of the coterie of London restaurants that are called iconic. The upmarket Mod Euro menu has a French influence, with many nods to the seasonal. Starters of glazed lamb sweetbreads were lifted by a smear of bright pea purée and al dente baby spring vegetables; a solitary, delicious grilled sardine sat on smoked aubergine purée and borlotti beans. Mains were equally noteworthy: lamb osso bucco came with rich ratatouille with an oregano crust, while pan-seared salmon was accompanied by avocado, buttery succotash (a corn and lima bean stew) and corn ice-cream. We shared a dessert of passion-fruit curd, fighting with spoons over the coconut sorbet and fresh mango. The kitchen's success was diminished by mistakes in service. A waiter stood by our table, main courses in hand, while we finished our starters. Floor staff paid little attention to customers. We finally ordered fresh drinks after standing and waving at the chatting waiters. Food of this quality deserves much better attention.
Babies and children welcome: high chairs. Booking advisable; essential weekends. Disabled: toilet. Separate room for parties; seats 45. **Map 7 B7.**

Launceston Place

1A Launceston Place, W8 5RL (7937 6912, www.danddlondon.com). Gloucester Road or High Street Kensington tube. **Lunch served** noon-2.30pm Tue-Sat; noon-3pm Sun. **Dinner served** 6-10.30pm daily. **Set lunch** £18 3 courses; (Sun) £24 3 courses. **Set dinner** £42 3 courses, £52 tasting menu. **Credit** AmEx, MC, V.
With its warren of rooms painted a sumptuous chocolatey brown, the Kensington stalwart has shaken off the 1990s chichi to become moody, glamorous and a gastronomic force. Ex-Pétrus chef Tristan Welch offers a very British take on haute cuisine, sometimes trying too hard. The holey potato crisps tied together with ribbon, and a creamy banoffi pre-dessert that spoilt our appetite for an equally creamy eton mess pud, were daft and distracting. But the sublime cauliflower soup heady with truffle and frothy with crème fraîche justified its existence as a pre-starter. Staff seem ubiquitous; just as well as we needed help opening a scallop shell sealed with pastry to get at the fragrant steamed scallop, potato and leeks inside. The sommelier was excellent, putting great effort, enthusiasm, sensuality even, into guiding us to just one appropriate (albeit pricey) glass each from the long wine list. Another outstanding starter was a duck egg sporting a fringe of shaved black truffle. Generous to a fault, main courses (nothing for vegetarians on the set lunch) of pork T-bone and braised beef shows the kitchen is confident with bold flavours; adding leaves and seeds to the braised fennel was a nice touch. Very English fragrant puddings feature lavender, lemon curd, and raspberry-ripple ice-cream. An upper-crust restaurant that's now a destination for those from further afield.
Available for hire. Babies and children welcome: high chairs. Booking advisable. Disabled: toilet. Separate room for parties, seats 10. **Map 7 C9.**

Notting Hill

Notting Hill Brasserie

92 Kensington Park Road, W11 2PN (7229 4481, www.nottinghillbrasserie.com). Notting Hill Gate tube. **Lunch served** noon-3pm Wed-Sun. **Dinner served** 7-11pm Mon-Sat; 7-10.30pm Sun. **Main courses** £19.50-£25.50. **Set lunch** (Wed-Sat) £17.50 2 courses, £22.50 3 courses; (Sun) £25 2 courses, £30 3 courses. **Credit** AmEx, MC, V.
There's a sense of stepping back in time as you walk down the covered cobblestone lane and into the muted beige and bleached-wood interior of this outpost of First Restaurant Group. The room is divided into cosy sections and has a colonial feel created by natural materials, faded paisley upholstered chairs and African art on the walls. A grand piano in the bar takes centre stage for nightly jazz evenings. Classic European cuisine forms the basis of the menu, and while prices are high, portions of the elegantly prepared comfort food are generous and well-executed. Our starter of foie gras and chicken liver pâté with green beans and quail egg was heady with Madeira and rich enough for two to share. Baked fillet of cod came nestled in a pillow of mash and blanketed with chive velouté. Sautéed chicken was crisp skinned, moist and tender, served with earthy wild mushrooms and celeriac purée on buttery savoy cabbage. The only letdown was a dessert of wonderfully fragrant yellow peach sorbet, disappointingly partnered with a tart raspberry sauce and sticks of meringue with the texture of freeze-dried foam. Nevertheless, we left feeling warm hearted and well looked after.
Babies and children welcome: high chairs; supervised crèche (Sun lunch). Booking advisable. Entertainment: jazz/blues musicians (Sun lunch, 7pm daily). Separate rooms for parties, seating 12 and 32. **Map 7 A6.**

South West

Barnes

Sonny's

94 Church Road, SW13 0DQ (8748 0393, www.sonnys.co.uk). Barnes or Barnes Bridge rail/33, 209, 283 bus.
Café **Open** 10.30am-5pm Mon, Tue; 10.30am-5.30pm Wed; 10.30am-6pm Thur-Sat. **Lunch served** noon-4pm Mon-Sat. **Main courses** £4.50-£10.25.
Restaurant **Lunch served** 12.30-2.30pm Mon-Sat; 12.30-3pm Sun. **Dinner served** 7-10.30pm Mon-Thur; 7-11pm Fri, Sat. **Main courses** £10.25-£19.95. **Set lunch** (Mon-Sat) £13.50 2 courses, £15.50 3 courses; (Sun) £18.50 2 courses, £22.50 3 courses. **Set dinner** (Mon-Thur) £15.50 2 courses, £18.50 3 courses. *Both* **Credit** AmEx, MC, V.
Sonny's is a Barnes institution. It was at the forefront of the new wave of Modern European restaurants almost 25 years ago and is still going strong. From a recent refurb it has emerged looking somewhat more sombre and businesslike, with a bar

Skylon. See p226.

(with its own menu of snacks) at the front and a rather austere dining room at the back. The cooking seems to show less of the bold experimentation that marked it out in the past, and there's a greater emphasis on Modern British cooking these days. Our slow-cooked pig's cheeks were braised to melting succulence in a full-flavoured red wine sauce. From the set dinner menu (£18.50 for three courses), a thick-cut fillet of salmon was cooked à point and served with summery broad beans, shallots and pancetta. A rich, unctuous – and filling – soup of courgette and avocado, served chilled, was superb. The only dish that disappointed was a starter of Shetland mussels with chorizo and parsley, lacking in flavour. As with the other restaurant owned by Rebecca Mascarenhas (Phoenix, *see p225*), the wine list is eclectic and imaginative, with good choice by the glass.
Available for hire. Babies and children welcome: children's menu; high chairs. Booking advisable (restaurant). Separate room for parties, seats 20.

Victoria

10 West Temple Sheen, SW14 7RT (8876 4238, www.thevictoria.net). Mortlake rail. **Breakfast served** 8.30-11am Mon-Fri; 8.30am-noon Sat. **Lunch served** noon-2.30pm, **dinner served** 6-10pm Mon, Tue, Thur, Fri. **Meals served** noon-10pm Wed; noon-10.30pm Sat; noon-9.30pm Sun. **Main courses** £9.50-£16.50. **Credit** MC, V.
The Victoria's location, on the edge of Richmond Park, is enviable; this building was a popular spot for local park-life long before chef Paul Merrett and his business partner took it over in 2008. The site comes into its own in summer, when the large garden (popular with families – there's a kids' play area) is host to weekend barbecues. There's also a good-looking conservatory dining room and a pubbier room at the front. Merrett has 'previous': before appearing on programmes such as the BBC's *Economy Gastronomy*, he earned Michelin stars at such creditable restaurants as the Greenhouse (*see p129*) and Interlude, gaining a reputation for mixing British and Asian flavours. Nonetheless, we found our starter salad of green papaya and cucumber with chilli and mint, served with onion bhajias, far too timidly spiced. Chicken and chorizo casserole with potato and aubergine also lacked punch, but the kitchen was on better form with a true-Brit Sunday lunch of roast Middle White pork with crunchy potatoes and apple sauce. Sourcing is taken seriously, and cooking oil is recycled into bio-fuel. The wine list has some imaginative choices from Olly Smith, who appears regularly on *Saturday Kitchen*.
Babies and children welcome: high chairs. Booking advisable weekends. Tables outdoors (12, garden).

Chelsea

Bluebird

350 King's Road, SW3 5UU (7559 1000, www.bluebirdchelsea.com). Sloane Square tube then 11, 19, 22, 49, 319 bus. **Brunch served** noon-3.30pm Sat, Sun. **Lunch served** 12.30-2.30pm Mon-Fri. **Dinner served** 6-10.30pm Mon-Sat; 6-9.30pm Sun. **Main courses** £13.50-£25. **Set meal** £15.50 2 courses £18.50 3 courses. **Credit** AmEx, DC, MC, V.
It's all about choice and versatility at Bluebird, the vast art-deco Chelsea landmark that's bar and bakery, café and restaurant. In the first-floor dining room, the sassily styled red and chrome interior features a glittering bar with a smatter of inviting sofas and armchairs. On a busy Saturday lunch, the chameleon-like space neatly managed to be all-things to all-people: from twentysomethings on stools at the bar to toddlers in high chairs. The Mod Euro menu is equally flexible – a please-all read, offering eggs benedict and burgers at one end of the scale, scallops and strawberry savarin at the other. Much is made of British ingredients, notably those from Secretts Farm in Surrey, which supplies the bulk of the produce. A spring visit started with first-of-the-year asparagus, perfectly cooked with a good hollandaise, and leeks vinaigrette with eggs mimosa, plated up in a pretty little stack. Less successful was a risotto of spring vegetables, overwhelmed by saffron, although steamed New

RESTAURANTS

Whitechapel Gallery Dining Room. See p228.

Forest trout with sauce verte and lemon oil worked well. For dessert, a glazed lemon tart was beyond reproach. Service was bouncy. Honorary mention goes to the set menu – good value at £18.50 for three courses.

Available for hire. Babies and children welcome: high chairs; nappy-changing facilities. Disabled: lift; toilet. Dress: smart casual. Separate rooms for parties, seating 30 and 60. Tables outdoors (25, courtyard). **Map 14 D12.**

The Botanist

7 Sloane Square, SW1W 8EE (7730 0077, www.thebotanistonsloanesquare.com). Sloane Square tube. **Breakfast served** 8-11.30am Mon-Fri; 9-11.30am Sat, Sun. **Lunch served** noon-3.30pm Mon-Fri; noon-4pm Sat, Sun. **Tea served** 3.30-6pm, **dinner served** 6-10.30pm daily. **Main courses** £14-£19. **Set lunch** £19 2 courses, £23 3 courses. **Credit** AmEx, MC, V.

Named in honour of botanist Sir Hans Sloane, this corner of Sloane Square is cultivated by owners with gastropub form. The all-day bar and adjacent restaurant, decorated with Sloane's fine botanical illustrations reproduced on glass, is a far more evolved species of the pub genus, attracting Peter Jones shoppers for well-conceived lunches, skilfully made and pitched above brasserie prices. Though foie gras and chicken liver parfait with pickled cherries, micro leaves and a fat slice of brioche was sublime, seasonal salad didn't give much for the money. And a clear gazpacho was almost the definition of designer diet food. Linked to gazpacho by the tang of vinegar and droplets of olive oil on its surface, the clear liquid, produced by filtering raw (in this case, yellow) tomatoes, was spooned on to slices of radish, cucumber, diced tomato and micro basil leaves. Plenty of room was left for puddings, and just as well as they're a trump card – fruity, pretty, inventive and not senselessly rich. A terrine with layers each of crème fraîche and fruit-studded blueberry and raspberry matched with champagne sorbet, and a gooseberry and frangipane tart with elderflower ice-cream and meringue were delightful. At night, the cocktails kick in and the bar gets noisier.

Babies and children welcome: high chairs. Booking advisable. Disabled: toilet. Tables outdoors (4, pavement). **Map 15 G10.**

Fulham

The Farm

18 Farm Lane, SW6 1PP (7381 3331, www.thefarmfulham.co.uk). Fulham Broadway tube/ 11, 14, 211 bus. *Bar* **Open** noon-11pm Mon-Thur, Sun; noon-midnight Fri, Sat. **Meals served** noon-10pm daily. *Restaurant* **Meals served** noon-9.30pm daily. *Both* **Main courses** £9.95-£19. **Set lunch** (Sun) £19.95 4 courses plus aperitif. **Credit** AmEx, MC, V.

Lucky Fulham-ites – they're not short of good pub-dining rooms. The Farm, not far from rival Harwood Arms (*see p107*), does a good imitation of a pub at the front, but with a sleek dining room at the back, done up in a vaguely oriental style. The menu's succinct and seasonal; asparagus and samphire abounded on our June visit. A starter of asparagus with poached egg and hollandaise sauce was a bit tepid, and our other starter, a salad of artichokes, avocado, tomato and mozzarella, was a slightly ho-hum take on a classic Italian tricolore. The kitchen hit its stride with the mains; an Angus ribeye, dry-aged for 28 days, was a gorgeous, tender piece of meat, cooked perfectly medium-rare and served with butch chunky chips and peppercorn sauce. Cornish cod was of equally high quality and cooked to a turn, served with creamy mash, a healthy pile of samphire and a rich butter-caper sauce. We practically licked our plates clean. Gooey, rich chocolate fondant with strawberries and ice-cream made a fitting end. The Sunday set menu is particularly good value and there's a decent by-the-glass wine selection. Service is smiling and unrushed.

Babies and children welcome: high chairs. Booking advisable. Disabled: toilet. Tables outdoors (5, pavement; 4, terrace). **Map 13 A13.**

Parsons Green

The Establishment

45-47 Parsons Green Lane, SW6 4HH (7384 2418, www.theestablishment.com). Parsons Green tube. **Lunch served** noon-4pm, **dinner served** 6.30-10.30pm daily. **Main courses** £11-£20. **Set lunch** (Tue-Fri) £12 2 courses, £15 3 courses. **Credit** AmEx, MC, V.

A glance at the wine list is the first indication that this bar and restaurant is doing things differently. Wine flights are offered, together with a decent number of well-priced, well-chosen wines available by the glass. A changing selection of fine wines kept in tip-top condition in an enomatic system lets customers sample without having to buy the whole bottle. Brown and beige retro wallpaper, faux-leather swivel armchairs and button-back banquettes provide a calm atmosphere by day, and a neutral background for musicians and cocktails by night. Weekend brunches are very popular; there's a small outdoor area for enjoying the sunshine. The kitchen produces dishes with plenty of locally sourced ingredients, competently cooked. We ordered white onion soup with cheese on toast, hanger steak with chips and béarnaise sauce, and bouillabaisse-style fish stew with saffron mayonnaise. Passion-fruit slice with buttermilk sorbet finished off a set lunch that was great value and thoroughly enjoyable. A daily changing evening menu makes the Establishment ideal for locals who want a regular haunt.
Babies and children welcome: high chairs. Disabled: toilet. Separate room for parties, seats 25. Tables outdoors (7, courtyard). **For branch see index.**

Putney

Phoenix Bar & Grill

162-164 Lower Richmond Road, SW15 1LY (8780 3131, www.sonnys.co.uk). Putney Bridge tube/22, 265 bus. **Lunch served** 12.30-2.30pm Mon-Sat; 12.30-3pm Sun. **Dinner served** 7-11pm Mon-Sat; 7-10pm Sun. **Main courses** £9.50-£18. **Set lunch** (Mon-Fri) £13.50 2 courses, £15.50 3 courses; (Sun) £17.50 2 courses, £19.50 3 courses. **Set dinner** £15.50 2 courses, £17.50 3 courses. **Credit** AmEx, MC, V.

The big draw at the Phoenix is its large front terrace, hidden from the sight (if not the sounds) of Lower Richmond Road by bamboo screens strung with fairy lights, and protected from the sun by huge umbrellas. Patio heaters keep it toasty in colder months. The spacious interior is attractive too, with white walls hung with modern art and a mix of blond-wood furniture and leather club chairs. The Italian-themed food doesn't quite live up to the setting. Slices of citrus fruit were a tangy addition to a starter salad of pan-fried tiger prawns, but the dish was overwhelmed by uninspiring greenery. A generous hunk of sea bass with mussels and clams in tomato broth was marred by overcooked fish. Better was roast salmon, the flesh kept moist by a casing of pistachio nuts. Own-made pasta (including signature dish, vincisgrassi maceratesi, a rich lasagne based on an 18th-century recipe) adds variety. Desserts are large; mango and passion-fruit sorbets were intensely flavoured, but mango pavlova had too much (good) meringue and not enough cream. Lively staff and a nicely priced wine list keep everything running smoothly.
Babies and children welcome: children's menu; crayons; high chairs. Booking essential summer; advisable winter. Disabled: toilet. Tables outdoors (15, terrace).

South

Balham

★ Lamberts

2 Station Parade, Balham High Road, SW12 9AZ (8675 2233, www.lambertsrestaurant.com). Balham tube/rail. **Lunch served** noon-3pm Sat. **Dinner served** 7-10.30pm Mon-Sat. **Meals served** noon-5pm Sun. **Main courses** £14-£18. **Set meal** (Tue-Thur) £20 2 courses, £24 3 courses. **Credit** MC, V.

There's nothing about this calm, understated place that's trying too hard, but it can claim with some justification to have become one of south London's finest restaurants. The cooking, on our most recent visit, was exceptional. Soft, perfectly fresh breads with a little bowl of rapeseed oil are whisked to the table. To start, we tried a gorgeous melee of white fish and mussels in a strong, dark broth, as well as young May asparagus with an exquisite asparagus mayonnaise. Despite this, a main of seared scallops with saffron and fennel broth was probably the highlight; our feisty rump steak with béarnaise sauce was outshone by the accompanying fluffy chips. A melting treacle tart was the best from a short list of puddings. All this takes place in a long, unassuming room, with mustard-yellow walls, a few big blobs of art, dark-wood diner-style tables, plush seating, cascades of gladioli and a parade of young, glamorous staff. Glasses of vintage Chapel Down, a carafe of house red and coffees still kept the bill comfortably under £100 for two. Not surprisingly, Lamberts has a buzz brought on by diners who know they're on to a good thing.
Available for hire. Babies and children welcome: children's menu (weekends); high chairs. Booking advisable; essential weekends.

Battersea

★ Ransome's Dock

35-37 Parkgate Road, SW11 4NP (7223 1611, www.ransomesdock.co.uk/restaurant). Battersea Park rail/19, 49, 319, 345 bus. **Brunch served** noon-5pm Sat; noon-3.30pm Sun. **Meals served** noon-11pm Mon-Fri. **Dinner served** 6-11pm Sat. **Main courses** £11.50-£21.50. **Set meal** (noon-7.30pm Mon-Fri) £15.50 2 courses. **Credit** AmEx, DC, MC, V.

Everything in the intimate, nautically themed dining room of Ransome's Dock is carefully chosen: from the yacht prints to the peculiar, particular shade of blue paint on the walls. Owners Martin and Vanessa Lam know what they like, and, fortunately, they have excellent taste. Martin exercises his taste over the epic wine list too, which has type so dense it looks like an issue of *Private Eye* and offers an incredible range. Aperitifs of Madeira and sherry, served with spicy parmesan biscuits, were the ideal accompaniment to a perusal of the serious menu, which changes daily. The basic carte and long list of specials offer something for nearly everyone (though choice for vegetarians can be meagre). The kitchen produces intriguing flavour contrasts in dishes that are usually brilliantly executed. A stunning starter of grilled quail was an explosion of tastes: the savoury bird made sweet by dates and oranges, fresh by frisée, and lightened with a surprising accent of mint. A seasonal main course of perfectly cooked lamb cutlets was accompanied by new potatoes, peas and broad beans, and a daring mint and wine jelly – divine. Service is knowledgeable and confident; the team at this Battersea classic know that they're selling the real thing.
Babies and children welcome: high chairs. Booking advisable. Disabled: toilet. Tables outdoors (10, terrace). **Map 21 C1.**

Tom Ilic

123 Queenstown Road, SW8 3RH (7622 0555, www.tomilic.com). Battersea Park or Queenstown Road rail. **Lunch served** noon-2.30pm Wed-Sat; noon-3.30pm Sun. **Dinner served** 6-10.30pm Tue-Sat. **Main courses** £11.50-£15.50. **Set lunch** £12.50 2 courses, £14.95 3 courses; (Sun) £16.50 2 courses, £18.95 3 courses. **Set meal** £16.95 2 courses, £21.50 3 courses incl glass of wine and coffee. **Credit** AmEx, MC, V.

The Ilic logo has a cheery porker on it, giving a strong pointer on what to order – and indeed, a pressed ham hock terrine with piccalilli was terrific, almost sweet and meltingly good, but given nip by the pickle. Another starter, salad of Cornish crab atop avocado in chilled gazpacho, tasted great but lost points for the bits of shell we had to circumnavigate. Standards were maintained by baked sea bass fillet with crushed new potatoes and samphire, and saddle of rabbit wrapped in serrano ham with asparagus, wild mushrooms and roast langoustine. Peach and raspberry gratin with lavender ice-cream was a pleasant end to a lunch that represented amazing value for money – three high-quality courses for £14.95. There's a choice of more than ten wines by the glass, while a less than perfect macchiato was the only duff note of the meal. Service was welcoming and efficient, and this and the excellence of the food almost allow you to forget the dreariness of the location and the '80s-style decor (lots of terracotta colours, abstract paintings and mirrors). An ambitious local and one that deserves to thrive.
Babies and children welcome: high chairs. Booking advisable weekends.

Brixton

Upstairs

89B Acre Lane, entrance on Branksome Road, SW2 5TN (7733 8855, www.upstairslondon.com). Clapham Common tube/Brixton tube/rail. **Dinner served** 6.30-9.30pm Tue-Thur; 6.30-10.30pm Fri, Sat. **Set dinner** £22 2 courses, £26 3 courses. **Credit** MC, V.

A visit to this intimate evening restaurant is like being invited into a private gastronomic dining club. As its name suggests, Upstairs is not visible at street level, but hidden above a coffee shop; entry is via a side door and a buzzer. The interior, a converted flat, has kept its domestic scale, with a small lounge bar on the first floor and the tiny dining room on the second. Once you're seated, it's a joy to be waited on by people who are both knowledgeable and passionate about the food and drink they're serving. The ever-changing menu is slight (there are three choices per course – one fish, one meat, one veg, with the option of a tasting menu), covers are few, and the team is so small that the owners sometimes serve tables. Food, cooked by an English chef with French training and experience in top-rated kitchens, is inspired by both nations and finished with a flourish – a fresh chilled pea soup brought to life by spots of garlic oil, say; tender guinea fowl accompanied by a rich sauce; a choice between a dark crème brûlée or a white chocolate and strawberry trifle. Upstairs is far too good to be stuck in the no-man's land between Brixton and Clapham Common.
Babies and children welcome: high chairs. Booking advisable weekends. **Map 22 C2.**

Clapham

Fouronine

409 Clapham Road, SW9 8BT (7737 0722, www.fouronine.co.uk). Clapham North tube. **Lunch served** 12.30-4pm Sun. **Dinner served** 6-10.30pm daily. **Main courses** £16-£18. **Credit** AmEx, MC, V.

Fouronine has the feel of a speakeasy. You need to press a buzzer and give your name before gaining access, via a fire escape, on to a small landing-cum-garden. Perhaps this routine makes the place feel more dramatic and clandestine than it really is, but it's lovely nonetheless, with a bare-brick aesthetic made edgy by urban-themed screen-prints on the walls, and comfortable by the plush banquette seating. The menu is small and changes frequently. We chose from half a dozen starters and mains. Italian and French influences predominate, with some further-flung flavours thrown into the mix, as in a main course of black bream with tapenade and imam bayildi, a Turkish aubergine dish. There's a tendency to put several flavours into each dish, as in a starter of sautéed potato gnocchi with peas, broad beans, feta and cooked radish, but the combinations work. Cooking is equally assured for classics such as French-style country salad with mustard leaves, shredded duck and pancetta, topped with a perfectly cooked egg that oozed its yolk into the dressing. Desserts might include poached Yorkshire rhubarb with blood-orange sorbet, or Neal's Yard cheeses for savoury-lovers. Service is professional and the pace unrushed, as you'd hope in such intimate surroundings.

RESTAURANTS

Available for hire. Babies and children welcome: high chairs; nappy-changing facilities. Booking advisable. Separate room for parties, seats 16. **Map 22 C1**.

Waterloo

★ Oxo Tower Restaurant, Bar & Brasserie

8th floor, Oxo Tower Wharf, Barge House Street, SE1 9PH (7803 3888, www.harveynichols.com). Blackfriars or Waterloo tube/rail. *Bar* **Open** 11am-11pm Mon-Wed; 11am-11.30pm Thur-Sat; noon-10.30pm Sun. *Brasserie* **Lunch served** noon-3.15pm Mon-Sat; noon-3.45pm Sun. **Dinner served** 5.30-11pm Mon-Sat; 6-10.15pm Sun. **Main courses** £13-£27. **Set meal** (lunch Mon-Sat; 5.30-6pm Mon-Fri, after 10pm daily) £21.50 2 courses, £24.50 3 courses. *Restaurant* **Lunch served** noon-2.30pm Mon-Sat; noon-3pm Sun. **Dinner served** 6-11pm Mon-Sat; 6.30-10pm Sun. **Main courses** £22-£35. **Set lunch** £33 3 courses. *All* **Credit** AmEx, DC, MC, V.

The view from the top of the Oxo Tower could be one of London's finest, and becomes mesmeric as the sun goes down and the city lights go up. Everything in the layout is quite rightly designed to make the most of it: inside and on the long terrace. Setting isn't the only draw, for Harvey Nichols' management provides a classy experience all round. Both halves of the eighth floor share the view: the restaurant is quieter and more spacious; the brasserie more functional, but still stylish, even if the alignment of its tables-for-two can suggest a speed-dating session. The brasserie menu isn't much simpler (or much cheaper) than the restaurant's; both feature intricate dishes of the kind that can read better than they taste, but here are carried off with real flair. Grilled merguez sausage with pomegranate and almond couscous had an ideal balance of spiciness and delicacy; and in marinated squid with chorizo and peppers, every ingredient was first-rate. Roast pork loin chop with honeyed parsnips was a delicious variant on a trad standard, while seared scallops with creamed leeks, truffle oil, pancetta and yet more ingredients, was pure delight, leaving us beaming at the river with a contented glaze in the eye. Service, given how busy things get, was exemplary.
Available for hire. Babies and children welcome: children's menu; high chairs. Booking advisable. Disabled: lift; toilet. Entertainment (brasserie): jazz (lunch, Sat, Sun; 7.30pm daily). Tables outdoors (50, brasserie terrace; 40, restaurant terrace). Vegetarian menu. Vegan dishes. **Map 11 N7**.

Skylon

Royal Festival Hall, Belvedere Road, SE1 8XX (7654 7800, www.danddlondon.com). Waterloo tube/rail. *Bar* **Open/snacks served** noon-1am daily. *Brasserie* **Meals served** noon-10.45 daily. **Main courses** £11-£22.50. **Set dinner** (5.30-6.30pm, after 10pm) £17.50 2 courses, £21.50 3 courses. *Restaurant* **Lunch served** noon-2.30pm Mon-Sat; noon-3.30pm Sun. **Dinner served** 5.30pm-10.30pm daily. **Set meal** £37.50 2 courses, £42.50 3 courses. **Set dinner** (5.30-6.30pm, after 10pm) £24.50 2 courses, £29.50 3 courses. *All* **Credit** AmEx, MC, V.

A large space within the Festival Hall, with picture-window views over the Thames, Skylon is a smart, handsome venue where there's a happy sense of occasion and a pleasant buzz. A sophisticated Modern European menu is served in the restaurant, while the grill has more brasserie-like food and is also home to a lively bar area. We began a recent meal here with gravadlax, which, disappointingly, was more like smoked salmon with some gravadlax-style sauce on the side – an insipid start. French bean and frisée salad with feta was better, a flavourful salad with nice chunks of cheese and a tasty dressing. Good cooking was evident in the mains too: caramelised shoulder of lamb with red onion and couscous was a hearty portion of very tender meat, the little pile of couscous by its side

densely spiced, the onions sweet. Fish of the day, halibut, was served on top of a julienne of mixed veg – it was a little bland and ordinary. In all, the meal was OK, if a bit production-line, but the food didn't match the surroundings.
Babies and children welcome: children's menu; high chairs. Booking advisable. Disabled: lift; toilet. **Map 10 M8**.

South East

Crystal Palace

★ Exhibition Rooms NEW
2009 WINNER BEST NEW LOCAL
69-71 Westow Hill, SE19 1TX (8761 1175, www.theexhibitionrooms.com). Crystal Palace rail. **Lunch served** noon-4pm, **dinner served** 6-10.30pm. **Meals served** 9.30am-10.30pm Sat, Sun. **Main courses** £9.50-£17. **Set lunch** £10 2 courses. **Set dinner** (6-7pm) £12 2 courses, £15 3 courses. **Credit** AmEx, MC, V.

The name plays homage to the famous Victorian showcase that gave Crystal Palace its raison d'être. So does the decor, with its metal and mirrored arches, potted plants in stone urns, chandeliers and assorted antiquated furniture. Combined with soothing pale-green paintwork, it resembles a graceful salon. For a change of atmosphere, head downstairs where there's a boudoir-like bar and intimate, high-walled garden. Staff are informed and courteous, the wine list accessible and fairly priced. And the food is excellent. Dishes range from superior renditions of pub standards (beer-battered haddock, burger with all the trimmings – both served with fluffy fat chips) to more complex creations that a smart central-London restaurant would be proud to serve. Take Barbary duck breast (generous slices of tender, pinkish meat) artfully arranged on a potato fondant cake and curls of hispi cabbage, and surrounded by orange segments and a pool of rich, star-anise-tinged jus. Or plump seared scallops (again, no skimping on the portion) with a pile of herby salad, a scattering of peas and broad beans and a delicious, buttery chilli-flecked sauce. Details stand out, such as the little jelly cubes (lime, shellfish) served with a starter of fresh Cornish crab atop celeriac rémoulade. Crystal Palace has a new showcase to brag about.
Babies and children welcome: children's menu; high chairs. Booking advisable; essential weekends. Disabled: toilet. Tables outdoors (9, courtyard).

Greenwich

Inside
19 Greenwich South Street, SE10 8NW (8265 5060, www.insiderestaurant.co.uk). Greenwich rail/DLR. **Lunch served** noon-2.30pm Tue-Fri; noon-3pm Sun. **Dinner served** 6.30-11pm Tue-Sat. **Main courses** £10.95-£16. **Set lunch** £11.95 2 courses, £15.95 3 courses. **Set dinner** (6.30-8pm) £16.95 2 courses, £20.95 3 courses. **Credit** AmEx, MC, V.

There are too few neighbourhood restaurants in south-east London that tantalise you anew with fresh flavours, however often or seldom you dine there – especially when it's an eaterie as pleasant and well priced as this one (the set lunch menus are particularly good value). With proficient, unobtrusive service and crisp, contemporary interior, Inside serves the whole community: from celebrating family groups to dinners à deux. The food, lovingly and often locally sourced, aims pretty high and only occasionally misses. On a recent visit, goat's cheese soufflé was superb: tangy, creamy and fluffy. A starter of mussels tasted rather bland, 'not enough of the sea', but may have suffered in comparison to the soufflé. Roast Welsh leg of lamb was cooked to pink-centred perfection and served with a divine rosemary gravy, though a white bean and chorizo cassoulet accompanying a roast cod fillet wasn't as rich or flavoursome as expected. Desserts have been known to convert the resolutely pudding-averse; the white chocolate cheesecake may be unadulterated stodge, but is subtle and heavenly – yet better without its passion-fruit coulis. The inside is infinitely superior to the surrounding

vendors of mediocre gastromush, and its local foodie audience is justifiably grateful.
Babies and children admitted. Booking advisable. Disabled: toilet.

London Bridge & Borough

Bermondsey Kitchen
194 Bermondsey Street, SE1 3TQ (7407 5719, www.bermondseykitchen.co.uk). Borough tube/London Bridge tube/rail. **Brunch served** 9.30am-3.30pm Sat, Sun. **Lunch served** noon-3pm Mon-Fri. **Dinner served** 6.30-10.30pm Mon-Sat. **Main courses** £10.25-£16. **Credit** AmEx, DC, MC, V.

Bermondsey Kitchen is a low-nonsense kind of place. A recessed plate-glass front creates a goldfish-bowl view of an L-shaped, pared down canteen: shades of beige, straight lines and a bric-a-brac of tables and chairs. The open-plan kitchen not only delivers informality but also the drama of wooshing flames thrown from the hissing pans. Otherwise, the cooking is fair but undistinguished. The idea is to serve simple, classic flavours – and you certainly get that in a refreshing beetroot, chicory, walnut and berry starter, as you do with mussels steamed with paprika and fennel. But under-seasoning meant chicken and Israeli couscous didn't rise above the ordinary. Our other choice, an unremarkable ribeye steak with chips, may have been carefully sourced, but it was not carefully sauced with wild mushrooms; we didn't reckon it justified a £19 tag. And you can surely get more flavour out of a vanilla and muscat rice pudding served with rhubarb compote. In the Kitchen's favour, service is cheerfully considerate and the wine list offers an imaginative selection by the glass. A fair bet for brunches and lunch deals.
Available for hire. Babies and children welcome: high chairs. Booking advisable. Disabled: toilet. Tables outdoors (1, patio). **Map 12 Q9**.

Delfina
50 Bermondsey Street, SE1 3UD (7357 0244, www.thedelfina.co.uk). London Bridge tube/rail. **Lunch served** noon-3pm Mon-Fri. **Dinner served** 7-10pm Fri. **Main courses** £9-£16. **Credit** AmEx, DC, MC, V.

This long-serving Mod Euro outpost (founded 1994) occupies the ground floor of the Delfina Studio Trust, and its artistic connections are apparent in the paintings on the wall. These add colour to the bright white of the decor, and make the large space – originally a factory – lovely in daytime. Even without the visual appeal, Delfina would be worth visiting. Our summer lunch was a sensation from beginning to end; the only thing lacking was privacy in which to lick the plates. The fortnightly-changing, well-priced menu celebrates the seasons in its use of both fruit and vegetables. Asparagus featured in a wonderful salad with poached duck egg and hollandaise. Deep-fried courgette flowers were stuffed with creamy brandade. New-season leeks made a splendid soup with potatoes. Strawberries came three ways – soup, sorbet, parfait – in a light but thrilling dessert. Our one main course, succulently braised belly of pork with beetroot, new-season turnips, baby fennel, and spring vegetables, continued the artful deployment of seasonal produce. All was cooked precisely, all ingredients of the highest quality. Service was smiling and attentive, and the short, imaginatively assembled wine list has plenty under and around £20. Our meal was a complete pleasure, even if we couldn't lick our plates.
Available for hire. Babies and children admitted: high chairs. Booking advisable. Disabled: toilet. Tables outdoors (8, pavement). **Map 12 Q9**.

Tower Bridge

Blueprint Café
Design Museum, 28 Shad Thames, SE1 2YD (7378 7031, www.danddlondon.com). Tower Hill tube/Tower Gateway DLR/London Bridge tube/rail/47, 78 bus. **Lunch served** noon-2.45pm Mon-Sat; noon-3.45pm Sun. **Dinner served** 6-10.45pm Mon-Sat. **Set lunch** £15 2 courses, £20 3 courses. **Set dinner** £20 2 courses, £25 3 courses. **Credit** AmEx, DC, MC, V.

Glasshouse. See p229.

It is hard to top the Blueprint as a location for a leisurely lunch or a late summer dinner: bright and white, overlooking the river and Tower Bridge, with huge glass windows that are slid back in clement weather for an inside-outside experience. Being on top of the Design Museum means that place settings and other details are all supremely tasteful, and a witty touch is provided by the pair of binoculars placed on each table – either to watch the river traffic, or to spy on goings-on in the warehouse flats opposite. Jeremy Lee's food goes all-out to be seasonal, though perhaps not always imaginatively. On our visit, asparagus appeared in several dishes, when less obvious ingredients could have been celebrated instead. Although the menu reads very promisingly, dishes aren't always what they sound (no one mentioned the crispy pancake around the asparagus, good though it was), and the execution can be variable. Our meal consisted of some highs (a firm, fresh skate, followed by sensational gooseberry trifle and spot-on crème brûlée) and some lows (fatty pork cassoulet heavy on the mustard, sloppy rillettes and burnt toast). More consistency would be welcome here.
Available for hire. Babies and children welcome: high chairs. Booking advisable dinner. Disabled: lift; toilet (in museum). Tables outdoors (4, terrace). **Map 12 S9**.

Le Pont de la Tour

Butlers Wharf Building, 36D Shad Thames, SE1 2YE (7403 8403, www.danddlondon.com). Tower Hill tube/Tower Gateway DLR/London Bridge tube/rail/47, 78 bus.

Bar & grill **Meals served** noon-3pm Mon-Fri; noon-4pm Sat, Sun. **Dinner served** 6-10pm Mon-Sat; 6-10.30pm Sun. **Main courses** £11.50-£22. **Set lunch** £15 2 courses, £18 3 courses.
Restaurant **Lunch served** noon-3pm Mon-Sat; noon-4pm Sun. **Dinner served** 6-11pm daily. **Main courses** £16.50-£35. **Set lunch** £25 2 courses, £29.50 3 courses.
Both **Credit** AmEx, DC, MC, V.
Particularly on a summer's day, it's worth visiting Le Pont for the location alone, especially if you can bag a table on the riverside terrace, with its magnificent views of Tower Bridge. Inside, the decor is cool and businesslike without being too formal. Service was a mixed bag. We waited what seemed like an age to be greeted and seated, and although some of the staff were charming, one unsmiling waiter met our request for tap water (and treated us generally) with a marked froideur. The food wavered between pretty good and mediocre. Fine bread, a rather lovely scallop and whiting mousseline in a sauce infused with chilli and ginger, and Middle White pork with girolles in a tarragon cream, were the high notes. Ham hock and foie gras ballotine was marred by oversalting, while a piece of sea bream was overcooked and as underseasoned as the salad on which it lay. A final crème brûlée was beautifully textured, yet topped with more gritty sugar than caramel. In general, we'd recommend this place for a sense of occasion, but serious foodies might look elsewhere.
Babies and children welcome: high chairs. Booking advisable. Entertainment: (bar & grill) pianist 7pm Tue-Sun. Separate room for parties, seats 20. Tables outdoors (22, terrace). **Map 12 S8**.

East

Docklands

Plateau

Canada Place, Canada Square, E14 5ER (7715 7100, www.danddlondon.com). Canary Wharf tube/DLR.

Bar & grill **Meals served** noon-11pm Mon-Sat. **Main courses** £10-£19.50.
Restaurant **Lunch served** noon-3pm Mon-Fri. **Dinner served** 6-10.30pm Mon-Sat. **Set meal** £29.50 2 courses, £35 3 courses.
Both **Credit** AmEx, DC, MC, V.
You ascend to Plateau via a lift outside Waitrose, within the Canada Place shopping mall. The fourth-floor reception area is classier and leads to a bar-grill (serving hearty fish pie and the like). Beyond that, the capacious restaurant feels like a steel and glass conservatory overlooked by more steel and glass in the shape of skyscrapers around Canada Square. The venue is owned by D&D London (the former Conran empire). Decor is tasteful, in shades of grey (or is that stone?). White moulded-plastic chairs are arranged around marble-topped tables. It's hard not to be picky when the menu is pitched at £35 for three courses – excluding side dishes at £4. The food can be interesting, with scallops and prawn roulade tasting (agreeably) like cooked sushi, but pea soup needed to be more special. Blackface lamb is a fine breed, yet needs hanging to avoid being chewy as it was here. It was surpassed by a crackling-skinned roast chicken. You can blow a grand on a

bottle of claret here, but sommeliers know their stuff and help you choose excellent wines at around £7 a glass. Service is good natured, but although Plateau is pleasant, but it can be a cold and very expensive place.
Babies and children welcome: high chairs; nappy-changing facilities. Booking advisable. Disabled: toilet. Dress: smart casual. Separate rooms for parties, seating 15 and 24. Tables outdoors (17, terrace). Vegetarian menu. **Map 24 B2**.

Shoreditch

Hoxton Apprentice
16 Hoxton Square, N1 6NT (7739 6022, www.hoxtonapprentice.com). Old Street tube/rail. **Bar Open** noon-11pm Mon-Sat; noon-10pm Sun. **Restaurant Lunch served** noon-3pm daily. **Dinner served** 6-11pm Mon-Sat; 6-10pm Sun. **Main courses** £9.90-£16.75. **Set lunch** (Mon-Fri) £5 1 course.
Both **Credit** AmEx, MC, V.
The Apprentice's main draw is its location, with a front terrace looking right on to Hoxton Square. It's a great place to hang out and have weekend brunch. Inside, the premises are attractive too, with dark walls, dark wood and a gastropub feel. The place is run by the Training for Life charity, teaching catering skills to the long-term unemployed. A straightforward Modern European menu is supplemented at brunch by some egg dishes and a 'Hoxton fry-up'. Instead, we opted for a starter of fish cakes, with a good texture and flavour, accompanied by a generous bowl of herby, lemony crème fraîche. A main of steak with peppercorn sauce and hand-cut chips was also large, cooked rare as requested, the few chips golden. Other choices – some only available in the evening – might include navarin of lamb with baby vegetables and spiced rice, and pan-fried sea bream with spinach, mussels, clams and nantaise sauce. Our food was competently cooked, though service was slightly problematic. The place was almost empty, yet staff were desultory and often disappeared. We were also asked the same questions by two different waitresses. Perhaps things improve when the place is fuller.
Babies and children welcome: children's menu; high chairs. Disabled: toilet. Separate room for parties, seats 40. Tables outdoors (9, pavement). **Map 6 R3**.

Wapping

Wapping Food (100)
Wapping Hydraulic Power Station, Wapping Wall, E1W 3ST (7680 2080, www.thewappingproject. com). Wapping tube/Shadwell DLR. **Brunch served** 10am-12.30pm Sat, Sun. **Lunch served** noon-3.30pm Mon-Fri; 1-4pm Sat, Sun. **Dinner served** 6.30-11pm Mon-Fri; 7-11pm Sat. **Main courses** £11-£22. **Credit** AmEx, MC, V.
Cooking wins out in this enterprise, which is part-Victorian pumping-station museum and part modern art gallery. The handsome, clattery interior with cast-iron fittings was full of bland corporate art on the night of our visit, but this was soon eclipsed by the fabulous all-Australian wine list, which eschews that country's mass-produced plonk. There's even a list of fine and rare wines awaiting the next City bonus. Even better, wine by the glass matches practically every dish, so that an interesting tempranillo went well with lamb sweetbreads – an exceptionally sticky delight with artichokes and Marsala sauce – and a minerally riesling offset a simple smoked mackerel pâté. Quality cooking persisted with Brecon lamb on a bed of sprouting broccoli next to a dollop of harissa-like tomato relish. Roast pork and a crispy turret of baked polenta, spring greens and pear chutney was entirely satisfying too. Desserts aren't predictable either and a cloud of rhubarb and blood-orange pavlova was a surprising success – and we soberly resisted the temptation of matching it with the intriguing dessert wines.
Babies and children welcome: high chairs. Booking essential (Wed-Sun). Disabled: toilet. Entertainment: performances and exhibitions; phone for details. Tables outdoors (20, garden).

Whitechapel

Whitechapel Gallery Dining Room NEW
Whitechapel Gallery, 77-82 Whitechapel High Street, E1 7QX (7522 7888, www.whitechapel gallery.org/dine). Aldgate East tube. **Lunch served** noon-3pm Tue-Sun. **Dinner served** 6.30-9.30pm Tue-Sat. **Main courses** £13.50-£18.75. **Set lunch** £15 2 courses, £20 3 courses. **Credit** AmEx, MC, V.
The Whitechapel Gallery Dining Room is a good-looking place, with wood detailing, mirrored wall panels and heavy light fixtures. A space perhaps better suited to 20 to 30 covers has squeezed in 40 seats, so it's not a good choice for private conversation. Chef Maria Elia combines rich spicing and strong Mediterranean influences with local and seasonal British ingredients; she also has an interest in meat-free cooking. Thus pan-fried scallops are paired with date and black pudding and roast apple purée for a starter, and mains include inventive dishes such as 'textures of Heritage tomatoes', consisting of tomato kethedes, tomato, almond and feta baklava, spiced tomato and fig soup and tomato jelly. Other mains give skilful treatment to traditional ingredients: char-grilled ribeye is served with radicchio, artichoke, Jersey Royals, horseradish crème fraîche and crispy capers; slow roasted spiced pork belly comes with shaved fennel, cherry tomato salad and watercress. Puddings do a good job of mixing traditional sweet ingredients: English strawberries, say, with cream, jelly and meringue, or treacle tart with apple confit. Prices are on the high side (the ribeye is £18.75, for example), but Elia's ability shines beyond in the vibrancy of her cooking. Add in friendly and professional staff, and the Whitechapel has a lot to recommend it.
Babies and children welcome: high chairs; nappy-changing facilities. Booking advisable. Disabled: toilet. Separate room for parties, seats 12. **Map 12 S9**.

North

Camden Town & Chalk Farm

Odette's
130 Regent's Park Road, NW1 8XL (7586 8569, www.odettesprimrosehill.com). Chalk Farm tube/ 31, 168, 274 bus. **Lunch served** noon-2.30pm Tue-Fri; noon-3pm Sat; noon-3.30pm Sun. **Dinner served** 6.30-10.30pm Tue-Sat. **Main courses** £11.50-£25. **Set lunch** £12 2 courses, £16 3 courses; (Sun) £20 2 courses, £25 3 courses. **Set dinner** (6-7pm Tue-Thur) £12 2 courses, £16 3 courses. **Credit** AmEx, MC, V.
A celebratory midsummer dinner here was marred by slipshod service. Wobbly from the start (we had a long wait to order), it gave a sense of absent management. When asked how we'd enjoyed our mains, we commented that one dish – an assiette of pork featuring tiny morsels of roasted belly, a braise of cheek or possibly shoulder, and a deep-fried ball of black pudding – had arrived lukewarm. The waiter said it would be deducted from the bill. But it wasn't deducted, which made the gesture look hollow. Wine was sloshed into our glasses too. Some of our food was great, even when improbable combinations of ingredients were attempted. A starter pairing seared scallops with braised chicken wings and jerusalem artichokes was lovely; peppered wood-pigeon with sweetcorn panna cotta, bayonne ham and trompette mushrooms was even better. Desserts (orange chocolate fondant, and cinnamon crème brûlée with apples) were the meal's high point. But nothing could compensate for the gracelessness of the service. The wine list is chosen with flair, though little effort is made under £30. We learned after our meal that Bryn Williams, the talented head chef, was away that day. We hope things turn better when he's there.
Babies and children welcome: high chairs. Booking advisable. Separate room for parties, seats 25. Tables outdoors (5, garden). **Map 27 A2**.

York & Albany NEW
127-129 Parkway, NW1 7PS (7388 3344, www.gordonramsay.com). Camden Town tube. **Breakfast served** 7-10.30am Mon-Fri; 7-11.15am Sat, Sun. **Lunch served** noon-2.30pm Mon-Sat; noon-4pm Sun. **Dinner served** 6-10.30pm Mon-Sat; 7-9.30pm Sun. **Main courses** £15-£20. **Set meal** (noon-2.30pm, 6-7pm Mon-Sat) £20 3 courses; (Sun) £25 3 courses. **Credit** AmEx, MC, V.
This boutique hotel is part of the Gordon Ramsay group and overseen by exec-chef Angela Hartnett. The classy bar, which serves wood-fired oven pizzas and terrific cocktails, is appealingly relaxed. To the rear is a proper dining room with muted striped wallpaper, vintage skylight and glass doors to the courtyard – a genial setting in which to enjoy cooking of carefully sourced ingredients such as Sloke Farm pork, Casterbridge beef, Island of Gigha halibut, and cheese from La Fromagerie. The set lunch (also available early evening) offers a good choice of four dishes per course; Sunday's menu offers five and naturally includes a roast. The à la carte shows a fondness for fish, although most popular on our visit was the côte de boeuf for two with truffled chips. Portions of protein can seem slightly mean, as with our two mains, but come with generous padding: witness roast Devon plaice fillet with consoling girolle and sweetcorn risotto, elegantly topped with buttery runner beans. Our main complaint concerns over-salting. Chocolate soufflé pancake, designed for sharing, was a devilishly good finish, if not pretty in presentation. Regrettably, senior staff were so busy sucking up to one couple who had ordered a meal with wines to match each course, we were ignored for long stretches, and had trouble paying the bill.
Babies and children welcome: high chairs; nappy-changing facilities. Booking essential. Disabled: toilet. Separate room for parties, seats 40. Tables outdoors (6, pavement). **Map 3 H1:**

Islington

Frederick's
Camden Passage, N1 8EG (7359 2888, www. fredericks.co.uk). Angel tube. **Lunch served** noon-2.30pm, **dinner served** 5.45-10.30pm Mon-Sat. **Main courses** £12-£22. **Set meal** (lunch, 5.45-7pm) £14 2 courses, £17 3 courses. **Credit** MC, V.
Family-run Frederick's has always represented City-money glitz that's not quite in the bonkers-bonuses bracket. Lawyers seem to like it. Champagne's the drink for suits relaxing in the bar at the front. The restaurant behind leads to a spectacular vaulted conservatory filled with trees and striking geometric prints. And beyond that, even more of a secluded find, is a lovely garden. Spiritually and gastronomically, Frederick's has something of the 1980s wine bar about it, starting with the perfectly fresh but rather dated granary baguette and Nina Simone soundtrack. Food doesn't impress nearly as much as the setting. The kitchen seems very keen on fruit. There were cherries with the tough dry duck confit and watercress starter; raspberries with a main course of succulent pigeon with a thick, salty reduced sauce and cherry tomatoes; and blackcurrants in the hollandaise accompanying slightly overcooked sea bass. Cardboard-like biscotti let down the otherwise exemplary raspberry crème brûlée. Though the cooking lacks sparkle and staff could have done more to charm, tables are well spaced and Frederick's is a very pleasant place for a sunny alfresco lunch or a pre-theatre meal.
Babies and children welcome: children's menu; high chairs. Booking advisable weekends. Separate rooms for parties, seating 16 and 30. Tables outdoors (12, garden). **Map 5 O2.**

North West

West Hampstead

Green Room
182 Broadhurst Gardens, NW6 3AY (7372 8188, www.thegreenroomnw6.com). West Hampstead tube/rail. **Dinner served** 6.30-10.30pm daily. **Main courses** £11-£17. **Set dinner** (Mon-Thur, Sun) £15 2 courses, £19.50 3 courses. **Credit** MC, V.

When a place serves completely distinctive, own-baked bread – and then, when you show how much you like it by wolfing it down, you're immediately asked if you'd like some more – we're won over. Friendly hospitality is one of the characteristics of this model little bistro, run by an Anglo-French couple. The interior isn't actually green; instead, the decor is a rather chic mix of silver flock wallpaper on one side, all white on another, plus some adventurous artworks. Another feature is great value. Not many venues charge only £15 for two courses of imaginative cooking, such as nicely crisp calamares with aïoli, followed by a moist, finely flavoured pan-fried chicken stuffed with apricots, pine nuts and sultanas, served with spinach, roast sweet potatoes and rosemary jus. Everything has a properly fresh feel, and many items are evidently own-made. Go on to a third course in sunny months and you might be able to try a lovely summer fruits crème brûlée. The set menus offer a varied choice, but there's also a sizeable à la carte menu, and a wine list that's been assembled with care and attention. *Babies and children welcome: high chairs. Booking advisable; essential Fri, Sat. Separate room for parties, seats 16. Takeaway service.* **Map 28 3A**.

Walnut

280 West End Lane, NW6 1LJ (7794 7772, www.walnutwalnut.com). West Hampstead tube/rail. **Dinner served** 6.30-11pm Tue-Sun. **Lunch served** by arrangement. **Main courses** £9.50-£16. **Credit** AmEx, DC, MC, V.
Cheery greetings from chefs working at their mezzanine-level open kitchen are received by all who enter this quality local. Chef-patron Aidan Doyle was promoting sustainable ingredients and kitchen habits long before it became fashionable. He walks the walk with a menu incorporating organic food and wine where possible, non-threatened fish species, and local artisan suppliers; he also recycles waste oil for bio-diesel and uses plant-based cleaning products. Start, perhaps, with Scottish rope-grown mussels with white wine, garlic, cream and parsley, or pigeon breast stuffed with apricot and pine nuts. Four flavours of mash are offered to accompany main courses – made with British potatoes, of course; we also opted for a dish of sautéed samphire, which was fresh and tasty, although too many stems were on the woody side. Grilled line-caught sea bass from Grimsby worked a treat with its coriander and chilli salsa. Meat lovers could have wild boar sausages, Oxfordshire ribeye or roast barbary duck, and there were two main courses for vegetarians. Finish with Fairtrade coffees and a pud of rhubarb crumble or dark chocolate tart. The organic house wine at £11.95 a bottle is difficult to refuse. *Available for hire. Babies and children welcome: high chairs; nappy-changing facilities. Booking advisable weekends. Tables outdoors (4, pavement).* **Map 28 A2**.

Outer London

Kew, Surrey

★ Glasshouse

14 Station Parade, Kew, Surrey TW9 3PZ (8940 6777, www.glasshouserestaurant.co.uk). Kew Gardens tube/rail. **Lunch served** noon-2.30pm Mon-Sat; 12.30-2.45pm Sun. **Dinner served** 6.30-10.30pm Mon-Sat; 7-10pm Sun. **Set lunch** (Mon-Fri) £23.50 3 courses; (Sat) £25 3 courses; (Sun) £29.50 3 courses. **Set dinner** £32 2 courses, £37.50 3 courses; (Mon-Fri) £50 tasting menu. **Credit** AmEx, MC, V.
The Glasshouse might not grab the headlines or the plaudits of some of Nigel Platts-Martin's more high-profile restaurants (Chez Bruce, for one). Yet for the past ten years, chef Anthony Boyd has been sending out some of the most cleverly conceived and beautifully presented food in London. Despite the name and proximity to Kew Gardens, there is little in the way of botanic frippery. Only a scattering of paintings and a long sweeping, textural wall could take your attention from the main attraction, the food. From a seasonally driven menu, Boyd does magical things with pink slivers of wood pigeon breast lurking among crisp bacon and frisee, topped with a gorgeously crunchy deep-fried truffled egg. And can there be more compatible platefellows than juicy chunks of lamb rump, saffron couscous, piquillo peppers and crisp, crunchy falafels? Even the safer dishes, such as a simple breast of chicken with mousserons, peas and broad beans or a fresh pea soup with shredded bits of ham hock are still deeply satisfying. In summer, finish with a strawberry sorbet with strawberries and meringue that is like eton mess without the cream-laced guilt. *Available for hire. Babies and children welcome: children's menu; high chairs. Booking advisable dinner, Sun lunch.*

Kingston, Surrey

Rocksons Restaurant

17 High Street, Kingston, Surrey KT1 4DA (8977 0402, www.rocksonsrestaurant.co.uk). Kingston rail. **Dinner served** 5.30pm-10.30pm Mon-Thur; 5.30pm-11pm Fri. **Meals served** 10am-11pm Sat; 10am-3.30pm Sun. **Main courses** £9.50-£15.50. **Set dinner** £14.95 2 courses, £17.95 3 courses. **Credit** MC, V.
Small and unassuming, tucked away on the main road to Kingston Bridge, Rocksons isn't going to win any style awards, but a good few of its many customers undoubtedly believe that the no-frills, café-like decor is part of its charm. Service is smiley, if a little slow. The food, when it arrives, is a treat. Blinis, topped with oak-smoked Scottish salmon and mascarpone, were light and fluffy; fat little seared scallops arrived crowned with crisp serrano ham and served with mango salsa. The more-than-generous mains (especially the roasts) offer plenty of bang for your buck. Glazed confit of Berkshire pork belly with borlotti beans, sautéed greens, spiced onion and apple chutney was a lovely big plate of food; herb- and mustard-crusted rack of lamb served with caramelised onions, sauté potatoes, fine green beans and mint jus batted well above average. This is honest homely cooking from a decent neighbourhood restaurant – so, while there's nothing too ambitious here, Rocksons gets a big thumbs-up from Kingston residents, weary of the surrounding chains. *Babies and children welcome: children's menu; high chairs. Disabled: toilet.*

Richmond, Surrey

Petersham Nurseries Café (100)

Church Lane, off Petersham Road, Richmond, Surrey TW10 7AG (8605 3627, www.petersham nurseries.com). Richmond tube/rail then 30min walk or 65 bus. **Lunch served** 12.30-3pm Wed-Sun. **Main courses** £14-£29. **Set lunch** (Wed-Fri) £22.50 2 courses, £27.50 3 courses. **Credit** AmEx, MC, V.
Few London dining rooms can match this one: a magical glasshouse alive with palm trees and scented jasmine, the mismatched tables ornamented with terracotta pots of sage and lavender. Old Indian pictures and the odd oriental carpet on the walls lend the place an echo of the Raj, and when you cross the room your feet crunch on gravel. At weekends you must order à la carte, expensively; the weekday set menu is cheaper, and good value. Skye Gyngell's food is generous, somehow heartfelt, and beautiful to behold. We began with a pretty tumble of figs, heritage tomatoes (colourful but lacking in taste), parma ham and dates; a delicious mix of fine mozzarella and lazy roasted peppers with salmoriglio (a Sicilian relish of garlic, lemon and marjoram); and some smooth cod's roe paste served with a dollop of crème fraîche and shaved fennel. Mains included a sumptuous slow-cooked lamb with soft courgettes and peppery rocket, and pan-fried red mullet with spiced borlotti beans. Puds were lovely too: zesty lemon curd with strawberries, and a fragrant slice of almond tart. After we'd eaten, we pottered around the plants in the nurseries outside, then walked back to Richmond across the fields. An altogether delightful experience. *Babies and children welcome: high chairs; nappy-changing facilities. Booking essential, two weeks in advance. Disabled: toilet. Tables outdoors (15, garden).*

Interview
SKYE GYNGELL

Who are you?
Head chef at **Petersham Nurseries Café** (*see left*), columnist for the *Independent on Sunday*, and author of books including *A Year in My Kitchen* and *My Favourite Ingredients* (Quadrille).
How did you start in the catering business?
I took a part-time job in a wonderful deli in Sydney while I was waiting to go to law school. I fell in love with cooking and my life changed course. I then went to Paris for two years, where I worked and studied before coming to London.
What's the best thing about running a restaurant in London?
London is such a fabulous city – it's where I want to be.
What's the worst thing?
The long hours. Costs are high and people are always looking for the next new thing. Good staff are also difficult to find, especially front of house staff.
Which are your favourite London restaurants?
Yauatcha (*see p290*), **Barrafina** (*see p242*), **Tapas Brindisa** (*see p247*), Italian restaurant **Ida** (167 Fifth Avenue, W10 4DT, 8969 9853), and **Sagar** (*see p143*).
What's the best bargain in the capital?
Brick Lane Beigel Bake (159 Brick Lane, E1 6SB), or Middle Eastern shop Damas Gate (81 Uxbridge Road, W12 8NR), where in May they sell 12 alphonso mangos for £4 a box.
What's your favourite treat?
An early night and a box set!
What is missing from London's restaurant scene?
Great breakfast venues are very sparse on the ground. I love a late breakfast on the weekends. I'm not just talking about eggs, sausages and baked beans, but home-made bread and jams, birchermuesli, fresh juices and scrambled eggs on sourdough.
What does the next year hold?
I think good restaurants will stay in business and the average ones will struggle. It is also important to respect everyone's financial situation and provide value for money.

RESTAURANTS

North African

They may no longer have the fashionable following of a few years ago, but London's select band of Maghrebi restaurants continue to offer an enticing variety of dining experiences. You want chic? **Momo** still cuts the modish mustard, with sexy **Pasha** not far behind – and both serve up some of London's best North African cuisine. Restaurants such as **Occo** and **Sidi Maarouf** also make great party venues, but if good, inexpensive cooking means more to you than flashy surroundings, head for Tunisian specialist **Adam's Café**.

Central

Edgware Road

Sidi Maarouf
56-58 Edgware Road, W2 2JE (7724 0525, www.maroush.com). Marble Arch tube. **Meals served** noon-12.30am Mon-Sat; noon-midnight Sun. **Main courses** £14-£18. **Set meal** £30-£35 4 courses. **Credit** AmEx, DC, MC, V.
An offshoot of Marouf Abouzaki's Maroush restaurant empire, Sidi Maarouf combines the (sometimes starchy) efficiency of Lebanese service with smart Moroccan decor and a mainly Moroccan menu. The dining room boasts a golden silk-tented ceiling, Berber-style rugs and dark studded furniture. Those uninitiated in the ways of Middle Eastern restaurants may find the cheesy singer at his electric organ rather incongruous, but on a busy Friday night, the addition of a darbouka drummer and an accomplished belly dancer made for a great evening. From the extensive kemia (Moroccan meze) list, we can vouch for the light crispy briouats (the lemon-ginger-chicken combination and punchy pimento and prawn are our favourites), good zaalouk, and a robust taktouka (roast tomato and pepper purée). We also relished a top-notch couscous darna (with juicy chargrilled chicken brochettes, lamb shoulder, rough-textured merguez and a light vegetable broth gently spiced with ginger). To finish, mint tea arrived with complimentary fresh, flaky honeyed pastries. On a warm evening, wind down with an apple-scented shisha outside and dream of the Mediterranean. *Available for hire. Babies and children admitted. Booking advisable. Entertainment: belly dancer 9.30pm, 10.30pm Thur-Sat. Tables outdoors (6, pavement).* **Map 8 F6**.

Gloucester Road

★ Pasha
1 Gloucester Road, SW7 4PP (7589 7969, www.pasha-restaurant.co.uk). Gloucester Road tube/49 bus. **Meals served** noon-11pm Mon-Wed, Sun; noon-midnight Thur-Sat. **Main courses** £13-£26. **Credit** AmEx, DC, MC, V.
Pasha's Algerian-born owner has got things just right in combining a contemporary take on classic Middle Eastern and Moroccan dishes with sumptuously decor. Push open the heavy wooden door and enter a sensual Arabian Nights world. Swishing beaded lampshades throw a golden glow over geometric tiles, intricate wrought ironwork, red and pink silks, and starched tablecloths strewn with rose petals. A soulful Arabic soundtrack (occasionally a touch too loud) adds to the seductive feel, making this an ideal venue for a date or a party. Things get steamy when a bevy of buxom belly dancers weave their way around the tables. But it's not all show: there's great stuff happening in the kitchen. Pasha offers a huge choice of meze dishes: from succulent baby squid in a subtly sweet chilli

Momo

RESTAURANTS

and coconut sauce, to crisp-shelled pumpkin kibbeh (cracked wheat balls) stuffed with a scrumptious mix of walnuts, pomegranate molasses and onion, and minty-fresh fattoush (a herby salad with crisp flatbread sprinkled with citrusy sumac). Mains are equally appealing; try the moist mixed chargrill of spicy chicken and lamb, or couscous darna (braised shoulder of lamb, chicken and merguez) with separate bowls of vegetable broth, sultanas, chickpeas and harissa. The cocktails are great too.
Available for hire. Babies and children welcome: high chairs. Booking advisable. Entertainment: belly dancers. Separate room for parties, seats 20. Tables outdoors (2, pavement). Takeaway service. **Map 7 C9.**

Leicester Square

★ Saharaween
3 Panton Street, SW1Y 4DL (7930 2777). Leicester Square or Piccadilly Circus tube. **Meals served** noon-midnight daily. **Main courses** £8-£14. **Set lunch** £8.95 3 courses. **Set dinner** £14.95 3 courses incl glass of wine. **Credit** MC, V.
Saharaween's makeover hasn't really shaken off that *Road to Morocco* look, but at least the cheap faux-Roman columns are gone. Coffee-table books on Moroccan culture and design now provide a context for the usual bric-a-brac and rickety dark-wood tables. The excellent golden fluffy Moroccan bread is just like you'd see coming out of communal ovens in Marrakech – always an exciting find, as most London Moroccan restaurants palm off punters with pitta or Turkish bread. Here it's the real deal, sprinkled with fragrant rosemary, or garlic, and is ideal to scoop up mezze dishes such as juicy tomato and pepper, or smoky aubergine purée. Mains were poor in comparison: chicken couscous suffered from too much smen (a herbed and spiced butter) and came with a thick salty gravy rather than fragrant broth. The cheesy bread balls in the rarely seen tagine sfiria had collapsed into another salty gravy, which totally over-powered the preserved lemons and coriander. Saharaween offers a cosy bolt hole just around the corner from frenetic Leicester Square, with friendly service and reasonable prices. All it needs is a little more care in the kitchen.
Babies and children admitted. Separate room for parties, seats 40. Takeaway service; delivery service. **Map 17 B5.**

Marylebone

Occo
58 Crawford Street, W1H 4NA (7724 4991, www.occo.co.uk). Edgware Road tube. **Lunch served** noon-3pm Mon-Fri. **Dinner served** 6.30-11pm Mon-Fri; 6.30-10pm Sat. **Meals served** noon-11.30 pm Sun. **Main courses** £9.95-£13.95. **Set lunch** £8 1 course. **Credit** AmEx, MC, V.
Occo's stylish decor (a modern take on traditional Moroccan crafts) looked a touch worn on our last visit. We arrived well after the popular two-for-one happy hour, but a boisterous young crowd round the bar was more intent on drinking than sampling the Moroccan and Mod Euro fusion menu. The premises contain an intriguing warren of rooms on various levels. A tête-à-tête is best suited to the conservatory: a quiet space, but rather low on atmosphere. The cosy red boudoir room is often colonised by parties. Fresh ingredients and subtle spicing characterise the cooking, and the food made our taste buds sing, but service, though friendly, was haphazard. After an excessive wait, a cod and king prawn brochette (with sweet-potato mash and rich fig and almond-blossom chutney) arrived minus prawns. To be fair, the owner quickly made amends, providing drinks on the house and deducting the dish from our bill. Our other choices – tender calamares in feather-light batter with fragrant fennel and garlic aïoli, and chermoula-marinated sea bream with minty broad-bean and yoghurt zaalouk – ticked all the right boxes. With a sprucing up of decor and service, Occo would be a winner.
Babies and children admitted. Booking advisable: weekends. Disabled: toilet. Separate rooms for parties, seating 20, 25 and 50. Tables outdoors (6, pavement). **Map 8 F5.**

Original Tagines
7A Dorset Street, W1U 6QN (7935 1545). Baker Street tube. **Meals served** noon-midnight Mon-Sat. **Dinner served** 6.30-11pm Fri, Sun. **Main courses** £10.50-£13. **Set lunch** £10.50 2 courses. **Credit** MC, V.
Original Tagines has all the qualities of a good, friendly local. On our last visit, a boisterous table of New Zealander twentysomethings made firm friends with kids from the neighbouring Asian family party – it feels quite natural to strike up conversation with fellow diners here. In summer, doors open on to a small terrace. Inside, though tables are quite close, there's still an airy, contemporary vibe enhanced by fine gilt calligraphy on warm-yellow walls, and mosaic and wrought-iron furniture. Start with spicy merguez, tender broad beans in a cumin-rich herbed tomato sauce, or a rich garlicky zaalouk mopped up with griddled Moroccan flatbread. Our main courses came in fairly small portions but were competently executed. Couscous is fluffily light. Prawn tagine in a robust saffron-infused tomato sauce with peanuts and raisins was very flavoursome, though we longed for some vegetables to temper the richness. Chicken, olive and lemon tagine was heavy on potatoes and needed more reduction to concentrate the flavours, but was tasty nonetheless. You may well have room for a creamy rice pudding with fragrant orange flower-water.
Available for hire. Babies and children welcome: high chairs. Booking advisable. Tables outdoors (5, pavement). Takeaway service. **Map 3 G5.**

Mayfair

★ Momo (100)
25 Heddon Street, W1B 4BH (7434 4040, www.momoresto.com). Piccadilly Circus tube. **Lunch served** noon-2.30pm Mon-Sat. **Dinner served** 6.30-11.30pm Mon-Sat; 6.30-11pm Sun. **Main courses** £13-£15. **Set lunch** £15 2 courses, £19 3 courses. **Credit** AmEx, DC, MC, V.
Momo is still London's most glamorous Moroccan restaurant. You'll find a funky atmosphere here and some great cooking, but service can be patchy or downright abrupt. It's a fun venue, with a signature Maghrebi soundtrack, though the music is loud; don't expect intimate conversations. The tables are very close too. The menu offers a mix of time-honoured Moroccan dishes (like zaalouk, prawn or seafood pastilla and the extremely well-executed tagines) with contemporary recipes using traditional ingredients or treatments (such as juicy king prawns in a feather-light tempura-type batter on a bed of lemony avocado and tomato). Lamb tagine was spot-on with its sweet reduction of prunes, pears and almonds. Don't miss the sublime couscous – you'll find nothing better this side of the Channel. Tender, sliced chicken breast comes with silky fine couscous plus a fragrant, lightly spiced coriander-infused broth, vegetables cooked to just the right tenderness, and a pot of harissa (served separately, should you want more kick). So, the food is first rate, but a little more comfort in the dining room wouldn't go amiss.
Available for hire. Babies and children admitted. Booking advisable weekends. Disabled: toilet. Tables outdoors (14, terrace). Vegetarian menu. **Map 17 A4.**
For branch (Mô Tea Room) see index.

West

Bayswater

Couscous Café
7 Porchester Gardens, W2 4DB (7727 6597). Bayswater tube. **Meals served** noon-11.30pm daily. **Main courses** £9.95-£15.95. **Licensed**. **Corkage** no charge. **Credit** AmEx, MC, V.
A few steps down from the pavement and a rickety old door make a suitably clandestine entrance to this rather romantic den of weavings, ornate lanterns, hand-painted tagines and outdoor furniture. The menu spans Moroccan cuisine from harira soup and mechouia to berber pancakes and mint tea. As you

Interview
MOURAD MAZOUZ

Who are you?
A restaurateur with involvement in **Momo** (see left), **Sketch** (see p131, p158 and p289) and **Club Gascon** (see p92) in London, plus 404, Andy Wahloo and Derrière in Paris.

How did you start in the catering business?
By mistake. I was travelling and, at the age of 26, I decided to open a small restaurant in Paris. I was going to sell it quickly in order to carry on travelling, but instead I became consumed by the melée of the restaurant business.

What's the best thing about running a restaurant in London?
Running a restaurant is the same in every country. The thing I appreciate most is that you have to have the ability to express your generosity. You must be able to deal with everything, including food, employees, administration, accounts and maintenance. You must also be able to think creatively about decor, lighting and fabrics.

What's the worst thing?
Whether people like your restaurant or not, they will never tell you to your face what they really think – they only write letters.

Which are your favourite London restaurants?
I like a lot of places, depending on the day, my mood and the company.

What's the best bargain in the capital?
Busaba Eathai (see p249).

What's your favourite treat?
A dessert from Pierre Gagnaire.

What is missing from London's restaurant scene?
Restaurants that are innovative with cuisine, that are forward-thinking rather than reproducing what exists already.

What does the next year hold?
At the moment, the restaurant industry is like the fashion industry. Certain restaurants are popular because they are on trend, not because of the quality of the food or their creativity. For about eight years, it was all about Japanese or Asian restaurants; now we've moved on to pseudo-organic restaurants.

RESTAURANTS

Original Tagines. See p231.

would hope of a place bearing this name, the couscous is among London's fluffiest, though we found the bread (made in-house) so-so. Tagine djej bel mechmach with chicken, apricots, almonds and sesame seeds arrived bubbling violently; it didn't look attractive, but the fowl, cooked on the bone, had a wonderful succulence and flavour. Mouthwatering meatball tagine was lifted by a coriander-laden tomato sauce and egg baked at its centre. Pastilla bel hout – a deliciously crisp parcel of seafood, olives, vermicelli and chermoula – made a welcome change to classic poultry pastilla. The choice of milk and juice combos is terrific; we loved the complex tastes of Couscous Café's rich signature special, with milk, almonds, dates, banana, pear, mint, honey and orange-blossom water. Service wasn't stretched on our visit, which perhaps allowed staff to be sweetly attentive.
Babies and children admitted. Tables outdoors (1, patio). Takeaway service. **Map 7 C6.**

Ladbroke Grove

★ Moroccan Tagine
95 Golborne Road, W10 5NL (8968 8055). Ladbroke Grove or Westbourne Park tube/23 bus. **Meals served** 11am-11pm daily. **Main courses** £7.90-£8.50. **Unlicensed** no alcohol allowed. **No credit cards.**
A hand-scrawled sign saying 'cash only' is never a great welcome, but otherwise this little restaurant is warm and friendly. A few outdoor tables are colourfully striped, those inside feature mosaic tiling. Further decoration includes impressive framed travel photographs, rose-print wallpaper, pinewood panelling, lanterns and an overhead trellis. The mismatched seating isn't comfortable, and the plates are chipped, but this adds to the holiday atmosphere. Briouats were unavailable, so we shared a pleasing coriander-flecked dish of zaalouk. Next, the cheerful waiter in traditional costume brought brightly painted tagines of lamb with prune and egg, and fish with preserved lemon and olives. The latter featured salmon steak in a tomato and herb sauce imbued with a salty citrus tang. On the side: couscous with plump golden sultanas. Desserts completely won us over. A cinnamon-flavoured chocolate pot slicked with honey was dark and dense (good enough to grace many grander establishments) yet cost only £2.50. Mixed Moroccan sweets consisted of almonds, walnuts, dough and pastry combined in various ways – perfectly accompanied by sweet mint tea.
Babies and children welcome: high chairs. Booking advisable. Tables outdoors (4, pavement). Takeaway service. **Map 19 B1.**

Shepherd's Bush

★ Adam's Café (100)
77 Askew Road, W12 9AH (8743 0572). Hammersmith tube then 266 bus. **Dinner served** 7-11pm Mon-Sat. **Set dinner** £11.50 1 course incl mint tea or coffee, £14.50 2 courses, £16.95 3 courses. **Licensed**. **Corkage** (wine only) £3. **Credit** AmEx, MC, V.
Run by a Tunisian-British couple for over 15 years, Adam's serves Tunisian dishes rarely found elsewhere in London. The menu also offers standard North African food with an emphasis on high-quality fish and seafood at low prices. Order your meal and before you know it complimentary cumin-infused lamb meatballs, bread, olives and a dish of fiery harissa appear. Harissa, together with tabil (a spice blend including coriander and caraway), is the hallmark of Tunisian cooking; it's hotter than its North African cousins; taste it again in the vibrant chorba soup. Don't miss the classic Tunisian starter, brik au thon, an impressively light, crispy golden fan of ouarka pastry stuffed with tuna, herbs and runny egg. Moroccan chicken tagine with preserved lemon and olives had a well-reduced cinnamon, ginger and coriander sauce, but the highlight was a large, whole, super-fresh chargrilled sea bass served with french fries and another Tunisian speciality, ojja (scrambled eggs and tomato with harissa). Adam's is a gem of a local bistro, with a friendly family vibe that's welcoming to all: from small children to their great-grandparents. You're bound to go home happy.
Available for hire. Babies and children admitted. Booking advisable weekends. Separate room for parties, seats 24. Vegetarian menu. **Map 20 A1.**

North
Islington

Maghreb
189 Upper Street, N1 1RQ (7226 2305, www.maghrebrestaurant.co.uk). Highbury & Islington tube/rail. **Meals served** 6-11.30pm Mon-Thur; 5-11.30pm Fri, Sat; noon-11pm Sun. **Main courses** £8.95-£14.95. **Set dinner** £11.95 2 courses, £15.95 3 courses. **Credit** AmEx, MC, V.
Mohamed Faraji's restaurant has a soulful vibe missing from most of its Upper Street rivals. At the rear is a small bar where customers can enjoy a drink and some olives. This is a smart-ish, colourful establishment that works as well for a casual date as for groups of friends or colleagues. Service was keen but became slower as the restaurant filled. The Moroccan house wines are fun to try; once our Siroua Rouge (£11.95), made from the red carignan grape, had a chance to breathe it was very drinkable. Starters range from classics (harira, merguez, houmous) to dishes taking inspiration from French cuisine, such as goat's cheese pastilla, and pan-fried king scallops with spinach, chilli and ginger. For mains we stuck to simple, well-executed kebabs of chicken and lamb, though there are plenty of tagines (rabbit, fish, duck, artichoke and broad bean, and more), traditional couscous, and the likes of sea bass chermoula with new potatoes, mushrooms and spinach. Desserts are worth trying – a pleasingly scented rice pudding, lacy baghrir pancake with honey and almonds, and chocolate and pistachio terrine among them.
Available for hire. Babies and children welcome: high chairs. Booking advisable. Separate rooms for parties, seating 38 and 40. Takeaway service. **Map 5 O1.**

Menu

North African food has similarities with other cuisines; see the menu boxes in **Middle Eastern** and **Turkish**.
Brik: minced lamb or tuna and a raw egg bound together in paper-thin pastry, then fried.
Briouats, briouettes or **briwat:** little envelopes of deep-fried, paper-thin ouarka (qv) pastry; can have a savoury filling of ground meat, rice or cheese, or be served as a sweet, flavoured with almond paste, nuts or honey.
Chermoula: a dry marinade of fragrant herbs and spices.
Chicken kedra: chicken stewed in a stock of onions, lemon juice and spices (ginger, cinnamon), sometimes with raisins and chickpeas.
Couscous: granules of processed durum wheat. The name is also given to a dish where the slow-cooked grains are topped with a meat or vegetable stew; couscous royale usually involves lamb, chicken and merguez (qv).

Djeja: chicken.
Harira: thick lamb, lentil and chickpea soup.
Harissa: very hot chilli pepper paste flavoured with garlic and spices.
Maakouda: spicy potato fried in breadcrumbs.
Merguez: spicy, paprika-rich lamb sausages.
Ouarka: filo-like pastry.
Pastilla, bastilla or **b'stilla:** an ouarka (qv) envelope with a traditional filling of pigeon, almonds, spices and egg, baked then dusted with cinnamon and powdered sugar. In the UK chicken is often substituted for pigeon.
Tagine or **tajine:** a shallow earthenware dish with a conical lid; it gives its name to a slow-simmered stew of meat (usually lamb or chicken) and vegetables, often cooked with olives, preserved lemon, almonds or prunes.
Zaalouk or **zalouk:** a cold spicy aubergine, tomato and garlic dip.

Oriental

Borders get broken down in London restaurants. Blessed with adventurous diners keen to experiment with new flavours – who are also generally free of nationalistic desires to keep cuisines 'traditional' – the city's restaurateurs can fuse to their heart's content. Oriental cuisine emerged here during the 1990s, hastened by the tremendous success of **Wagamama**, which opened its first branch in 1992 in Bloomsbury. Dishes from Malaysia to Japan might appear on the same menu; a blend of culinary ideas from across Asia might share the same plate. The result can be a mishmash, but when it's done well, as at **Chino Latino** (which operates from the unpromising surroundings of a business hotel), it takes food in exciting new directions. The Oriental cooking style continues to develop, incorporating ingredients and techniques from far and wide. New this year is **Sushinho**, which combines Japanese cuisine with Brazilian. What's next?

Central

City

Wagamama

1 Ropemaker Street, EC2Y 9AW (7588 2688, www.wagamama.com). Moorgate tube/rail. **Meals served** 11.30am-10pm Mon-Fri. **Main courses** £6.35-£11. **Credit** AmEx, DC, MC, V.
This London-born, pan-Asian noodle chain has expanded to 15 other countries, thanks to its simple formula of providing consistent quality food, big portions and lightning service, at reasonable prices. The menu contains carbs for every craving. Udon, soba or rice noodles might arrive in a ramen broth or a coconut-based soup; or they can be stir-fried in a wok or griddled on a teppan. Rice dishes are inspired by the gamut of Asian regions and come heaped with a dizzying combination of ingredients that diners can modify. Amai udon – stuffed with egg, fried beancurd, prawns, onions, leeks and beansprouts – was a satisfying combo of sweet, sour and salty flavours, and gummy and crunchy textures. Another happy choice was ebi raisukaree: a mound of sticky rice and perfectly cooked tiger prawns surrounded by a moat of flavourful coconut and lime curry sauce. From the specials menu, chilli fried squid was soggy and spongy. Still, any disappointment was tempered by service that was so speedily efficient we barely noticed the discomfort of the canteen-style wooden benches. *Babies and children welcome: children's menu; high chairs. Bookings not accepted for fewer than 6 people. Disabled: toilet. Takeaway service. Vegan dishes.* **Map 12 Q5.**
For branches see index.

Fitzrovia

Bam-Bou

1 Percy Street, W1T 1DB (7323 9130, www.bam-bou.co.uk). Goodge Street or Tottenham Court Road tube.
Bar **Open** 6pm-1am Mon-Sat.
Restaurant **Lunch served** noon-3pm Mon-Fri.
Dinner served 6-11pm Mon-Sat. **Main courses** £9.50-£14.50.
Both **Credit** AmEx, MC, V.
Set in a smart, four-storey Georgian townhouse furnished like an Indochinese colonial manor, this South-east Asian favourite always has an appealing buzz. Tables in the cosy, low-lit dining rooms allow ample opportunity to eavesdrop on the smart media crowd. The menu, while brief, offers a tempting selection of oriental dishes. Bo la lot didn't disappoint; char-grilled wild-pepper leaves encased the most fragrant and juicy minced beef. Grilled lollipops of minced prawn on sugar cane were less exciting; the sugar cane imparted little sweetness to the under-seasoned seafood. For mains, a beef and potato thai curry was authentic yet prosaic: chunks of tender meat and potatoes swimming in a simple, rich sauce with no creative enhancements. Star of the meal was the grilled bream. Served whole, but with bones expertly removed, it was charred to crispy perfection, the topping of flavour-packed chilli jam and mango proving a delectable foil to the soft white flesh. Service was relaxed and efficient. *Babies and children admitted. Booking advisable. Separate rooms for parties, seating 8-20. Tables outdoors (4, terrace).* **Map 10 K5.**

Crazy Bear

26-28 Whitfield Street, W1T 2RG (7631 0088, www.crazybeargroup.co.uk). Goodge Street or Tottenham Court Road tube.
Bar **Open/dim sum served** noon-10.45pm Mon-Fri, Sun; 6-10.45pm Sat.
Restaurant **Meals/dim sum served** noon-10.45pm Mon-Fri, Sun; 6-10.45pm Sat. **Dim sum** £2.50-£6.50. **Main courses** £10-£28. **Set meal** £30-£40 tasting menu.
Both **Credit** AmEx, DC, MC, V.
Crazy Bear is undeniably a glamorous, good-looking and inviting set-up, but not really built for comfort. Intimate round tables for two are set at leather banquettes that aren't shaped to match them, and with low, art deco-style lamps immovably placed at centre, the trendy young couples who come here wind up squeezing on to half a table and passing dishes around the lamp. To say nothing of the potential for sore backs – soon you'll be wanting to rip that shimmery padded ostrich leather off the walls and use it as cushions. Other things pall quickly too, like the attentive waitress who we began to find a nag in the drinks department, and the exotic-sounding dishes that on arrival don't seem to match their premium prices. Still, we enjoyed a crock of brothy pot-roast ox cheek spiked with star anise, spring onions and pickled lettuce. Spicy minced chicken salad (like Thai larb) had too many leathery mint leaves, not enough limey zing; sriracha-style thai hot chilli sauce saved an omelette of prawns and shallots from tasting too greasy. Crazy Bear may cut a dash, but it doesn't always cut the mustard. *Babies and children admitted. Booking advisable. Vegetarian menu. Vegan dishes.* **Map 4 K5.**

Piccadilly

Cocoon

65 Regent Street, W1B 4EA (7494 7609, www.cocoon-restaurants.com). Piccadilly Circus tube. **Lunch served** noon-3pm Mon-Fri. **Dinner served** 5.30-11.30pm Mon-Sat. **Main courses** £11.50-£65. **Set lunch** (noon-3pm Mon-Fri) £15 bento box. **Set dinner** (5.30-11.30pm Mon-Thur; 5.30-7pm Fri, Sat) £25 3 courses. **Credit** AmEx, DC, MC, V.
A nightclub masquerading as a restaurant, Cocoon features overworked design that completely ignores the architecture and great semi-circular windows overlooking the Quadrant. Then there's the muzak – and rather brusque service. The menu is an interesting blend of East and West, but maintains a three-course mode. We plumped for the £25 set meal, which with a not-quite-cold-enough glass of Vermentino di Sardegna, a fruit punch and bottle of sparkling water, resulted in a bill of £73 for two with service. The drinks list has few wines by the glass or reasonably priced bottles, consisting mostly of champagnes and cocktails. First courses of sushi and sashimi were very poor; the sashimi didn't seem ultra-fresh. In contrast, main courses were excellent: faultless chargrilled chicken green curry with aubergine, pumpkin and coconut cream; and moist, pink lamb rump rolled in wasabi and grilled (pity, though, about its meagre accompaniment of chopped-up al dente asparagus). Rice served in tiny bowls was cold and claggy. Mini desserts of assorted sorbets and crème brûlées were momentarily tasty, but served with such huge spoons they were hard to eat. With its 'girly night out' clientele Cocoon seems to think it can serve second-rate food. *Babies and children welcome: high chairs. Booking advisable, essential Fri, Sat. Disabled: toilet. Entertainment: DJs 11pm Thur-Sat. Separate room for parties, seats 14. Dress: smart.* **Map 17 A5.**

Pimlico

dim t

56-62 Wilton Road, SW1V 1DE (7834 0507, www.dimt.co.uk). Victoria tube/rail. **Meals served** noon-11pm Mon-Sat; noon-10.30pm Sun. **Dim sum** £3.05. **Main courses** £6.80-£9.40. **Credit** AmEx, MC, V.
Despite the name, this pan-Asian chain is not quite a dim sum eaterie. While it offers the ubiquitous steamed dumplings and a range of Chinese teas, the menu also extends to trite, tried-and-true staples such as pad thai noodles and teriyaki salmon. The concept is very much Asian food for beginners, but that's not necessarily a bad thing. The dim sum, for example, is steamed to order, and made with ingredients that are tasty enough to convert first-timers, though their similarity to each other will annoy more seasoned diners. Almost all the dumplings we tried (prawn and chive; spicy beef; chicken, coriander and cashews; and mushroom and wasabi) were bulked out by bits of undercooked chopped carrots and water-chestnuts. These may lend a healthy crunch, but they also dilute other flavours. On a sunny, Sunday lunchtime (usually the most popular time for eating dim sum), the modern dark-wood interior of this branch was almost empty; a few diners occupied tables on the terrace outside. Service, given the paltry workload involved, was slow and forgetful. *Babies and children welcome: children's menu; high chairs; nappy-changing facilities. Booking advisable. Disabled: toilet. Takeaway service.* **Map 15 J10.**
For branches see index.

West

Ladbroke Grove

★ E&O

14 Blenheim Crescent, W11 1NN (7229 5454, www.rickerrestaurants.com). Ladbroke Grove or Notting Hill Gate tube.

Bar **Open** noon-midnight Mon-Sat; 12.30-11pm Sun. **Dim sum served** noon-10.30pm Mon-Sat; noon-10pm Sun.
Restaurant **Lunch served** noon-3pm Mon-Fri; noon-4pm Sat; 12.30-4pm Sun. **Dinner served** 6-11pm Mon-Sat; 6-10.30pm Sun. **Dim sum** £3.50-£7. **Main courses** £10.50-£23.
Both **Credit** AmEx, DC, MC, V.
Though something of a Notting Hill stalwart these days, E&O retains its trendy vibe. You'll still find a lively bar, timeless contemporary decor and a glamorous gaggle of loyal diners, most of whom look familiar if not famous. Cocktails are a point of pride and feature sound combinations of tropical fruits, herbs and spices. From the wine list, Bonny Doon riesling is a good versatile choice whether you go for the menu's Thai, Malaysian, Chinese or Japanese options – or decide to mix them. Pumpkin and miso gyoza were fried to chewy, toasty deliciousness on one side. Neatly trimmed Korean lamb chops were juicy and mildly spicy, served with a disc of kimchi and creamy chilli sauce designed to soothe rather than sear. The only duff note of the meal was chocolate and honeycomb mochi, which lacked the bold dark flavour hoped for, or any satisfying hit of honey. Much better was a generous plate of mango sashimi: finely sliced fruit topped with delicate grapefruit segments and perfectly

sandy lychee granita. Our waiter was friendly and hardworking; he handled a table-side accident with grace and charm, ensuring we'll happily return.
Babies and children welcome: children's menu; crayons; high chairs. Booking essential. Separate room for parties, seats 18. Tables outdoors (5, pavement). Map 19 B3.

South West
Chelsea

Itsu
118 Draycott Avenue, SW3 3AE (7590 2400, www.itsu.com). South Kensington tube. **Meals served** noon-11pm Mon-Sat; noon-10pm Sun. **Main courses** £4.50-£10.50. **Set meals** £3.95-£9.95 bento box. **Credit** AmEx, MC, V.
There's a distinct feeling of stepping into the future as you enter this upmarket kaiten-zushi bar. Some tables for four and six are set at right angles to the conveyor-belt so that groups can dine together. Charming waitresses cruise around taking orders for drinks and hot dishes. Upstairs is a darkly intimate bar, where you can wait until your pager (provided at reception) beeps that a feeding place is free. We took up residence in a lavishly cushioned anteroom at the top of the stairs, but scurried back

to the bar stools when it was invaded by a clamour of Knightsbridge 'valley girls'. Tuna sashimi, salmon 'new style' and duck crystal rolls from passing bowls (priced by means of discreet coloured rims) were all superb. To follow, beautifully flavoured grilled chicken teriyaki, served with a liquorice-like sauce, yummy tiger prawn tempura with a chilli sauce, and perfect crispy squid in spicy batter, all accompanied by a rather mean bowl of rice (at £1.50). We finished by grabbing a couple of vegetable bowls from the conveyor: edamame and tenderstem broccoli with sesame seeds.
Babies and children welcome: booster seats. Bookings not accepted. Takeaway service; delivery service (over £20 within 3-mile radius). Map 14 E10.
For branches see index.

Sushinho NEW
312-314 King's Road, SW3 5UH (7349 7496, www.sushinho.com). South Kensington tube then 49, 319 bus or Sloane Square tube then 11, 19, 22 bus.
Bar **Open** 6pm-midnight daily.
Restaurant **Lunch served** noon-3pm Mon-Fri; noon-3.30pm Sat. **Dinner served** 6-10.30pm daily. **Main courses** £16-£20. **Set menu** £35 tasting menu.
Both **Credit** AmEx, MC, V.

Great Eastern Dining Room

Brazilian-Japanese cuisine may seem like a random relationship, but São Paulo has the largest Japanese population outside Japan. At Sushinho, oriental design (sleek dark wood, bamboo walls) combined with exposed brick, textured canvas, and palm trees, set the stage for sushi to samba. We looked to our waiter for guidance. He seemed, however, only trained to push mundane fillers (edamame, miso soup) and didn't seem to have detailed menu knowledge. Trendy young couples around us were taking advantage of the Monday-night half-price sushi platters, but we wanted to go full fusion and so ordered the house specials. Sweet-potato gyoza (delicious crisp dumplings stuffed with creamy mash topped with truffles) were promptly polished off. Slow-cooked pork belly, nestled in feijoada-style black bean purée and spiced with chilli mango, looked beautiful, yet tasted muted and arrived lukewarm. Aubergine shigiyaki scored highly on the weirdness scale: a pot of aubergine and fried-tofu slivers stewed in tomato sauce and topped with melted mozzarella. But, after the first few suspicious bites, we found it strangely addictive. So, a hit and miss menu, but with plenty to fascinate.
Booking advisable. Children admitted. Disabled: toilet. Separate room for parties, seating 12. Takeaway service. **Map 14 D12**.

South
Vauxhall

★ Chino Latino
Riverbank Park Plaza Hotel, 18 Albert Embankment, SE1 7TJ (7769 2500, www.chino latino.co.uk). Vauxhall tube/rail. **Lunch served** noon-2.30pm Mon-Fri. **Dinner served** 6-10.30pm Mon-Sat; 6-10pm Sun. **Main courses** £15-£26. **Set menu** £40 tasting menu. **Credit** AmEx, MC, V.
It's not often that theme restaurants in hotel chains work well, but the Chino Latinos in the Park Plaza Hotels in Nottingham, Leeds and London's Albert Embankment seem brilliant exceptions. They have had the wit to hire ex-Nobu chef Jimmy Nakamura to pull off a vibrant pan-Asian menu. The ultra-chic interior, in dark tones with accent maroons and reds, is calming yet exciting, the tables nicely separated and the service attentive. Certainly our meal was at times up there with Nobu and Hakkasan. Diners are encouraged to share, so we began with some 'small plates' of vegetable tempura, mushroom spring rolls, seared carpaccio of marbled beef with crispy garlic and yuzu vinaigrette, and crispy soft-shell crab. Encouraged by the superlative quality, we ordered seared foie gras and duck breast slices with nashi pear poached in plum wine, and the pan-fried Chilean sea bass – both were stunning. The house dessert platter (a magnificent sharing plate of fruit, ice-creams, sorbets, chocolate fondant and crème brûlée) ended the meal on the highest note. With two glasses of prosecco, one of pinot grigio and a bottle of sparkling water, the bill of £132 for two with service seemed reasonable for such a feast.
Available for hire. Babies and children welcome. Booking advisable. Disabled: toilet. Tables outdoors (4, terrace). **Map 16 L11**.

South East
Gipsy Hill

Mangosteen
246 Gipsy Road, SE27 9RB (8670 0333). Gipsy Hill rail/322 bus. **Lunch served** noon-3pm Fri-Sun. **Dinner served** 6-11pm Mon-Sat; 6-10pm Sun. **Main courses** £8.50-£12. **Set lunch** £6.95 2 courses. **Set dinner** (Mon-Thur) £10 2 courses. **Credit** MC, V.
Winsomely decorated with dark-wood furniture and spice-coloured silk scatter cushions, the Mangosteen aims to be more than just a run-of-the-mill suburban pan-Asian restaurant. Sadly, its intentions aren't quite matched by the delivery. Starters – thai fish cakes and banh xeo crispy pancake rolls filled with chicken, tiger prawns, beansprouts and squid – arrived fried to within an inch of their lives, accompanied by sauces strong on sugar or chilli but otherwise low on flavour. Mains helped redeem matters. Mangosteen salad flavoured with chilli,

garlic and lemongrass was fresh and tangy, and a tender pile of vietnamese roast duck wrapped in steamed lettuce got the thumbs-up. The pudding selection is positively flamboyant. Tarts, both chocolate and vanilla, and lime and ginger, arrived on designer platters, covered with icing sugar and artful drizzles of chocolate sauce, though overall they failed to live up to their promise. This could be a fun, buzzing place on a summer's evening with the tables spilling on to the terrace, but facilities, decor and food standards could do with refreshment.
Babies and children welcome: high chairs. Booking advisable weekends. Tables outdoors (5, terrace). Takeaway service.

Herne Hill

Lombok
17 Half Moon Lane, SE24 9JU (7733 7131). Herne Hill rail/37 bus. **Dinner served** 6-10.30pm Tue-Sun. **Main courses** £6-£8. **Credit** MC, V.
A crisp, colonial-style interior and briskly efficient staff give you the feeling of being in safe hands at this Thai-owned establishment – and the food more than bears it out. A well-chosen selection of Thai, Vietnamese and Malaysian dishes keeps customers happy, as do starters like vietnamese lettuce wraps, packed to bursting with fresh prawns. A classic chicken satay starter was also admirably fresh and tender. The more unusual thai yellow curry, gaeng karee, was a bit disappointing, as was a massaman beef curry, whose peanut-rich sauce seemed a trifle bland. On the other hand, spicy seafood curry packed intense and delicate flavours into its creamy sauce. Desserts are better than average in range and flavour, with baked bananas or Thai-style custard cooked with palm sugar. The wine list may be unambitious, but prices are keen. Though a little too densely packed for romantic dinners (it's only open in the evenings), Lombok scores on all other counts, its staff coping effortlessly with lively family groups or celebrating grown-ups. Syrupy Thai pop music makes a perfect, piquant accompaniment.
Babies and children admitted. Booking essential weekends. Takeaway service. **Map 23 A5**.

East
Shoreditch

Great Eastern Dining Room
54-56 Great Eastern Street, EC2A 3QR (7613 4545, www.greateasterndining.co.uk). Old Street tube/rail/55, 135 bus.
Below 54 Bar **Open/meals served** 7.30pm-1am Fri, Sat. **Main courses** £9-£15.
Ground-floor bar **Open/dim sum served** noon-midnight Mon-Fri; 6pm-midnight Sat. **Dim sum** £5-£6.50.
Restaurant **Lunch served** noon-3pm Mon-Fri. **Dinner served** 6-10.45pm Mon-Sat. **Main courses** £9-£17.50.
All **Credit** AmEx, DC, MC, V.
Stepping into Will Ricker's slick, assured bar-restaurant from traffic-snarled Great Eastern Street is a relief. The dining room is decked with retro furniture and wall hangings, calming dark wood and simple, modernist chandeliers. Diners can eat here or in the relaxed bar lounge. The friendly bar staff created a virgin cocktail of the day – 'let's call it Summer's Day, yes?' – full of sweet berries and sour lime flavours. Black cod siu mai wasn't available, despite the early lunch hour. We were offered a replacement prawn dim sum, a dish we couldn't fault: the dumplings as light as the perfectly cooked prawns. Aubergine and lychee green curry was as good as it gets, with silky chunks of aubergine and whole lychees, barely drizzled with chive oil. Again, one of our puddings (ice-cream) wasn't available and was replaced with vanilla panna cotta and fresh passion-fruit, this time a disappointment as the passion-fruit struggled to cut through the creamy vanilla bean dessert. While the Dining Room no longer makes the supercool list of what to do in Shoreditch, it's all the better for it; keep this gem under your hat.
Available for hire. Babies and children admitted. Booking advisable; essential Fri, Sat. Entertainment: DJs 8.30pm Fri, Sat. **Map 6 R4**.

Interview
WILL RICKER

Who are you?
Owner of Ricker Restaurants, which has six venues including **E&O** (*see left*) and **Great Eastern Dining Room** (*see p236*). *The Eastern & Oriental Cookbook* is published in autumn 2009.
How did you start in the catering business?
I was working for a restaurateur who didn't have a clue but was successful, so I figured…
What's the best thing about running a restaurant in London?
Seeing familiar faces coming time and time again.
What's the worst thing?
There's no downtime.
Which are your favourite London restaurants?
I like Greek restaurant Halepi (18 Leinster Terrace, W2 3ET, 7262 1070) – it's inexpensive, in-and-out service, you know what you're getting and it's tasty. **Scott's** (*see p84*) has an excellent menu, a handsome room with good art, and every table is a good table. And for comfort food with a great ambience, I go to the **Pig's Ear** (*see p107*).
What's the best bargain in the capital?
My £15 set lunch menu at all my restaurants.
What's your favourite treat?
Cakes from **Ottolenghi** (*see p161*).
What is missing from London's restaurant scene?
London could do with relaxing some of the council restrictions on outside eating. Let us enjoy the summer!
What does the next year hold?
There will be some good opportunities for new restaurants as premises hit the market at more realistic prices.

RESTAURANTS

North East

Stoke Newington

★ Itto

226 Stoke Newington High Street, N16 7HU (7275 8827). Stoke Newington rail/67, 73, 76, 149, 243 bus. **Meals served** noon-11pm daily. **Main courses** £4.20-£6.20. **Credit** AmEx, MC, V.

The pair of oriental beckoning cats on a shelf, who greet customers with a smile and a wave, are one of the few giveaways as to this local eaterie's cuisine. You certainly wouldn't pick it from the otherwise nondescript and coldly modern interior – wooden floor, plain walls, bare wooden tables. Still, the sweet and friendly service warms the place up. The overly long menu trips across Japan, Thailand, China and Vietnam, picking up mostly obvious choices along the way. It's ideal if, say, you fancy a Thai and your partner has a yen for Japanese. The chilli squid was decent enough, but the batter was too thick for such a delicate meat. Vietnamese peanut salad was much better: sweet and sour and crunchy. Skewers of yakitori chicken were full of tare (Japanese barbecue sauce) flavour. Main courses of soup noodles would easily have been enough for us: the chicken pho was intense and smooth, and the bowl of spring duck and roast pork noodle soup (real comfort food, with moist meat and flavoursome stock) defeated us. Disappointingly, given the reasonable price of the menu as a whole, the portion of edamame was rather small for its hefty £3.50 price tag. *Babies and children welcome: high chairs. Takeaway service; delivery service (over £10 within 2-mile radius).* **Map 25 C1**.

North

Camden Town & Chalk Farm

Gilgamesh

Stables Market, NW1 8AH (7482 5757, www.gilgameshbar.com). Chalk Farm tube. *Bar* **Open/snacks served** 6pm-2.30am Mon-Thur; noon-2.30am Fri-Sun. *Restaurant* **Lunch served** noon-3pm, **dinner served** 6pm-midnight daily. **Dim sum** £4-£6. **Main courses** £10-£24.80. *Both* **Credit** AmEx, MC, V.

It's hard for a restaurant as cavernous as Gilgamesh to look anything other than deserted midweek. The few diners on our visit were crammed awkwardly next to each other in the centre of the room, absurdly requiring us to move chairs to allow others to visit the loo. The menu is eclectic pan-Asian, yet we reckon you can get the component cuisines better elsewhere – for the same price. The Thai-influenced dishes weren't as good as at Busaba; the dim sum was merely average. Banana and prawn dumplings were surprisingly light, and a glass of black rice risotto with truffles was delicious. There was no shortage of staff, yet service was slow and, at times, slapdash. A waiter carefully placed one dish down with his right hand, while pouring copious quantities of dip all over the table from the plate in his left hand. It took 20 minutes to get the bill, and longer again to pay for it. Still, the visit wasn't without a highlight; the cocktails in the bar were superb. Kutu gin martini had a kick of chilli through the pink grapefruit, as did the Caipirinha of Fire (tempered somewhat by fresh raspberries and lime). *Babies and children welcome: high chairs. Booking essential. Disabled: lift; toilet. Dress: smart casual. Vegetarian menu.* **Map 27 C1**.

Islington

★ Banana Tree Canteen

412-416 St John Street, EC1V 4NJ (7278 7565). Angel tube. **Meals served** noon-11pm Mon-Sat; noon-10.30pm Sun. **Main courses** £5.25-£8.95. **Set meal** (noon-5pm) £4.95-£6.45. **Credit** AmEx, MC, V.

This steadily expanding Wagamama-style chain offers superb-value Thai, Malaysian, Indonesian and Vietnamese food in a modishly spartan, semi-communal environment. The varied menu offers very good set-price deals for stir-fries that you can make up yourself, and for set meals in which you choose your preferred main course to accompany rice, glass-noodle salad, prawn crackers and thai-style corn fritters. Warned about long queues, we went early in the evening and found one whole side of the large room all but empty. As a result, service was prompt and attentive. Starters of pork and prawn dumplings and lamb and lettuce wrap were both very tasty. We were sorely tempted by the singapore laksa but went instead for blackened chilli pork, and ginger chicken with mushrooms, the latter accompanied by a good bowl of jasmine rice. Both were nicely flavoured and satisfying. With two beers and some fizzy water, our meal for two came to an equally satisfying £42, including service. In an area lacking good budget options, Banana Tree Canteen is welcome. Local office workers should check out the express lunch menu. *Babies and children welcome: children's menu; high chairs; nappy-changing facilities. Disabled: toilet. Takeaway service.* **Map 5 N3**. **For branches (Banana Leaf Canteen, Street Hawker) see index**.

Outer London

Barnet, Hertfordshire

★ Emchai

78 High Street, Barnet, Herts EN5 5SN (8364 9993). High Barnet tube. **Lunch served** noon-2.30pm daily. **Dinner served** 6-11pm Mon-Thur; 6pm-midnight Fri, Sat; 5-10pm Sun. **Main courses** £4.20-£7.90. **Set meal** £15-£18.50 per person (minimum 2). **Credit** AmEx, MC, V.

The brisk, no-nonsense efficiency of Emchai's staff belies the friendliness of this relaxed local magnet. Prawn crackers and herby dipping sauce arrive immediately to nibble on, while you peruse the menu of stir-fries, noodles and a wide variety of starters. The concise drinks list offers seven wines of each colour (the chenin blanc is good value), plus two Asian beers and freshly squeezed juices. Dishes stretch from Thailand to Japan and include some modern creations (venison with black-pepper sauce is recommended); authenticity isn't laboured. Most diners seem to order aromatic crispy duck, which staff fork through with astonishing speed. A long gap between starters and mains had us worried. Surprisingly, when pak choi in garlic sauce finally arrived it was so underdone the plant might still have been growing. But we loved golden squid stir-fried with chilli and curry leaves, and the juicy-crispy soft-shelled crab. Huge, well-spaced tables and smart woven-leather chairs make it easy to relax and enjoy a meal with friends or en (trendy) famille. The vibe is always fun, but at twilight a window seat beneath the towers of Barnet's church opposite is almost idyllic, despite the traffic. *Available for hire. Babies and children welcome: high chairs. Booking advisable weekends. Disabled: toilet. Takeaway service.*

Crazy Bear. See p233.

Portuguese

With one notable exception, London's Portuguese restaurants aim to recreate the flavours, the aromas and the sounds of their homeland. Distinctive ingredients – bacalhau (salt-cod, served every which way), chouriço sausage, sardines – are rarely absent from menus, and most wine lists have a varied choice of bottles from Portugal's much-underrated vineyards. Perhaps the principal exponent of this style is **O Fado**, where you'll also find musicians performing the typical sad folk songs of the country. At many venues, TV screens dominate proceedings on a Sunday afternoon, when they are invariably tuned to Portuguese football. For the headiest atmosphere come the World Cup, head for one of the several bar-restaurants in south London's Little Portugal area around Stockwell and Vauxhall. Ah yes, that exception to the rule we mentioned: it's **Portal** in Farringdon, where typical Portuguese ingredients are raised to a more exalted level for the delectation of City diners.

Central
Clerkenwell & Farringdon

★ **Portal**

88 St John Street, EC1M 4EH (7253 6950, www.portalrestaurant.com). Barbican tube/ Farringdon tube/rail. **Lunch served** noon-3pm Mon-Fri. **Dinner served** 6-10.15pm Mon-Sat. **Main courses** £12-£22. **Credit** AmEx, MC, V.

Its urbane take on Portugal's regional cuisine has made Portal a major addition to London's dining scene. By marrying Modern European flavours and showy techniques with staple Portuguese ingredients, the kitchen gives diners something entirely new. The restaurant is located in expense-account territory, so prices are predictably steep, but glamorous decor helps cushion the blow. A smart bar area opens up to a large glass-sided dining room, which produces the feel of eating alfresco (without the accompanying English chill). Dishes can take a while to come and ours were modestly portioned, with mains not much bigger than the petiscos served at the bar. Never mind: the food is memorable. The house special of braised bisaro (a cross-breed of wild boar and black pig) is marinated for ten days, slow-cooked for 12 hours, and tastes heavenly. Roast bacalhau stuffed with black-pig ham had a wonderfully deep flavour. A vegan stew of lentils with chestnut and boletus mushrooms was less complex yet still praiseworthy. Beautifully presented desserts include a twist on the Portuguese custard tart. Notable too is the immense wine list: on show in a walk-in wine cellar that doubles as a private dining room. *Babies and children welcome: high chairs. Booking advisable. Disabled: toilet. Separate room for parties, seats 14. Tables outdoors (5, patio).* **Map 5 O4**.

Knightsbridge

★ **O Fado**

50 Beauchamp Place, SW3 1NY (7589 3002). Knightsbridge or South Kensington tube. **Lunch served** noon-3pm, **dinner served** 6.30pm-11pm Mon-Sat. **Main courses** £13.95-£17.95. **Set lunch** £14.95 2 courses incl drink & coffee. **Credit** AmEx, MC, V.

London's oldest Portuguese restaurant inhabits a snug basement beneath the designer pavements of Knightsbridge, its interior decked with artefacts and murals of Portuguese landmarks. Nightly performances of beautifully melancholic fado music take place here. The extensive menu highlights classic regional food, and several dishes have a small map beside them showing their district of origin. If you're overwhelmed by choice, call on the informative staff; on our visit, they even related the history behind some of the dishes. We skipped starters, taking advantage of the complimentary rustic bread and olives. A plate of elegantly presented grilled prawns came with a deliciously piquant piri-piri sauce and well-seasoned vegetables. Chanfana, traditionally a goat stew, is here made with lamb, but arrived suitably tender and generously flavoured with garlic. As is the Portuguese norm, O Fado's desserts revolve around sugar and eggs. We rounded off with a creamy, gooey Madeira island honey cake, and a sweet rice pudding topped with cinnamon. The set lunch menus are good value. *Babies and children welcome. Booking advisable; essential dinner weekends. Entertainment: guitarists 8pm Mon-Sat. Separate room for parties, seats 35.* **Map 14 F9**.

South West
Wandsworth

The Algarve

314 Trinity Road, SW18 3RG (8875 0313, www.thealgarverestaurant.co.uk). Earlsfield or Wandsworth Common rail. **Meals served** 10am-11pm Tue-Fri; noon-midnight Sat, Sun. **Main courses** £9-£15.50. **Credit** AmEx, MC, V.

The Algarve region is hardly renowned for setting culinary pulses racing. However, stray from the tourist track and you'll discover beautifully prepared fish and seafood laced with spices that hark back to the Moorish occupation. A blue and white tiled mural on the wall of the restaurant illustrates this lesser-known side of the Algarve. The menu is short, but the dozen or so choices showcase southern Portuguese classics, including Alentejo-style pork with clams, and cataplanas (stews served in clam-shaped enclosed copper dishes). For a starter we extended our complimentary bread and olives with a round azeitão – a fabulously stinky sheep's milk cheese that's made just outside Lisbon. Next up was a fairly priced seafood platter of lobster tail, king prawns, green-lipped mussels and clams, with a side of piri-piri sauce. Although both courses were memorable, the high point of the evening was an own-made chocolate mousse containing almond essence: so delicious we thanked the chef in person. *Babies and children welcome: high chairs. Booking advisable. Disabled: toilet. Tables outdoors (3, pavement). Takeaway service.*

South
Brixton

The Gallery

256A Brixton Hill, SW2 1HF (8671 8311). Brixton tube/rail/45, 109, 118, 250 bus. **Dinner served** 7-10pm Thur-Sun. **Main courses** £7.50-£15. **Cover** £1. **Credit** MC, V.

Don't be put off by the takeaway chicken shop-front; a secure door at the back leads to a charming dining room, with mezzanine seating overlooking a mural-lined courtyard. The restaurant opens only for dinner Thursday to Sunday, and true to its Portuguese roots, doesn't get buzzing until 9pm. Authenticity is maintained with high-quality bread and olives arriving the moment you sit down (for a £1 cover charge). The menu favours meat, although an entire section is devoted to bacalhau dishes. We split a garlicky chouriço sausage starter, served aflame. A main of pork Alentejo-style came richly marinated, teamed with clams, cubes of fried potato and a scattering of coriander. As the Goan-style chicken curry was unavailable, we tried the chargrilled chicken (cooked out front

PASTELARIA

Funchal Bakery

141-143 Stockwell Road, SW9 9TV (7733 3134). Stockwell tube. **Open** 7am-7pm daily.

Named after the city on the island of Madeira, this friendly bakery-deli-café is a favourite with local mums as well as expats. The bolo con arroz, dome-topped cakes made with rice in the batter, are several nourishing notches above what you'll find in many London coffee shops. The custard tarts are superb too. Grab some great-value Gallo olive oil and Funchal honey on your way out.

Café Oporto

62A Golborne Road, W10 5PS (8968 8839). Ladbroke Grove or Westbourne Park tube/23, 52 bus. **Open** 8am-7pm Mon-Sat; 8am-5pm Sun.

It's not just Oporto football fans who favour this Golborne Road stalwart; we find it a more relaxing spot than its opposite number Lisboa (*see below*), and Oporto has more seating. Try the savoury pastries filled with salt-cod, chicken or cheese.

Lisboa Pâtisserie

57 Golborne Road, W10 5NR (8968 5242). Ladbroke Grove or Westbourne Park tube/23, 52 bus. **Open** 7.30am-7.30pm daily.

Excellent bica (Portuguese espresso) and custard tarts guarantee queues of Portobello market-goers down the street every Saturday morning. For something different, try the thin almond biscuits or one of the little cakes made with coconut. Freshly made sandwiches and special-occasion cakes are sold here too.

in the takeaway section). A whole, half or quarter chicken is served to your own spice specification, and ours was lip-smackingly good. The Gallery's all-Portuguese wine list is extensive, featuring some wonderful vinho tinto from the Alentejo. Desserts are bought in, except for a sickly-sweet wobbly molotov with caramel sauce.
Babies and children welcome: high chairs. Booking advisable. Takeaway service. **Map 22 D3**.

Stockwell

Bar Estrela

111-115 South Lambeth Road, SW8 1UZ (7793 1051). Stockwell tube/Vauxhall tube/rail. **Meals served** 8am-11pm daily. **Main courses** £7-£13. **Tapas** £2.70-£5.90. **Credit** AmEx, MC, V.
This lively bar-restaurant is a favoured meeting spot for local Portuguese football fans. Two mounted televisions – frequently tuned to the beautiful game – are constant dining companions. Although all eyes are on the entertainment, food is a key attraction: think simply cooked, regional Portuguese meat and fish dishes, alongside a couple of predictable Spanish and Italian favourites. A starter of Estrela-style clams arrived in classic fashion: served in a wine-based shell-sucking sauce, and scattered with coriander.

Wayward portion control means that many main dishes are large enough for two, and staff seem quite used to customers sharing. We split a simply grilled sea bass, which came with rather sad, under-seasoned vegetables and the traditional carb-combo of chips and rice. Considering the beer-drinking crowd, the wine list is impressive, and we enjoyed the popular vinho verde (a light, sparkling white Minho wine), which is sold by the glass as well as the bottle. Sunnier days see the french windows open and the pavement fill with extra tables – perfect for people watching.
Babies and children welcome: high chairs. Booking advisable Thur-Sat. Tables outdoors (10, pavement). Takeaway service. **Map 16 L13**.

Grelha D'Ouro

151 South Lambeth Road, SW8 1XN (7735 9764). Stockwell tube/Vauxhall tube/rail. **Meals served** 7am-11pm daily. **Main courses** £8.50-£14.50. **Credit** MC, V.
A home from home to the local Portuguese, Grelha D'Ouro has become even more welcoming since a recent refurbishment. It's just like a living room, with the furniture facing a television that provides a steady stream of footie and homeland soaps. Daytime sees men sinking bowls of steamed clams and Sagres beer, while young families snack on tosta mista (toasted ham and cheese sandwiches) and petiscos. We chose stewed chicken gizzards, substantial pastéis de bacalhau (salt-cod fish cakes) and plump olives. The gizzards, cooked in a rich tomato sauce, were incredibly moreish, despite their thoroughly unattractive appearance; the pastéis de bacalhau were so nicely balanced we bought an extra four to bolster office packed lunches. Coffee and the sugary pastéis de nata (custard tarts) were also of a delectably high standard. Evenings and weekends see customers take over the basement games room and back room dining area. Stop by on a Sunday afternoon to see parties of four generations of Portuguese families sharing pots of soupy seafood rice and slow-cooked feijoada.
Babies and children welcome: high chairs. Booking advisable weekends. Separate room for parties, seats 60. Vegetarian menu. **Map 16 L13**.

O Moinho

355A Wandsworth Road, SW8 2JH (7498 6333, www.moinho.co.uk). Stockwell tube/Wandsworth Road rail/77, 77A bus. **Meals served** 10am-11pm daily. **Main courses** £5.50-£17.40. **Credit** MC, V.
Moinho is Portuguese for mill, and windmill motifs feature heavily in the interior of this smart family-run restaurant. Alongside are a few signed FC Porto shirts; the restaurant's website shows various Portuguese football players eating here. On our visit almost all the customers were Portuguese, predominantly noisy laughing families. The menu is evenly split between meat, fish and seafood, and includes regional pork dishes from Minho and Alentejo, as well as the country-wide favourite, arroz de marisco (a soupy seafood rice). We kicked off with Minho-born caldo verde (sliced cabbage and potato soup served with chouriço), which was hearty enough to be a meal in itself. Grilled tuna fillet arrived cooked through (as is traditional), though lathered in a lemon and garlic sauce to ward off any dryness. Diners with bigger appetites should sample the own-made desserts, especially the creamy coffee bolo de bolacha (biscuit cake). For traditional food and authentic charm, O Moinho is a sure bet.
Babies and children admitted. Booking advisable. Tables outdoors (5, pavement). Takeaway service.

Vauxhall

Casa Madeira

46A-46C Albert Embankment, SE11 5AW (7820 1117, www.madeiralondon.co.uk). Vauxhall tube/rail. **Meals served** 11am-11.30pm daily. **Main courses** £6.95-£15.95. **Tapas** £3-£5. **Credit** (over £5) AmEx, MC, V.
The Madeira empire spans the converted arches of Albert Embankment, incorporating a delicatessen, internet café, bar and grill, and restaurant. The company also owns a handful of cafés across London, as well as a wholesale bakery and pâtisserie that keeps all the eateries stocked with fresh breads, cakes and pastries. Casa Madeira is no exception, with chunks of beautiful bread arriving at the table before you order. Its location, near a station and opposite a central thoroughfare, attracts a mixed bag of customers, including office workers, families and lone rangers. Uniformed waiters, starched tablecloths, fresh flowers and low lighting create a sophisticated air, while a dancefloor in the centre of the room reveals the potential for high-spirited occasions. The menu mirrors the island's love of the ocean, with plenty of fresh sea bass, tuna and seafood. There's also a range of pizzas, hamburgers and omelettes, but customers largely ignored these on our visit. We tried black scabbard, a simple and superb fish (a Madeiran favourite), lightly fried and seasoned with parsley. Desserts are both bought-in and own-made, so check before you order. We struck gold with pudim de maracuja (passion-fruit pudding), a tropical Madeiran classic.
Babies and children admitted. Booking advisable weekends. Tables outdoors (10, pavement). Takeaway service. **Map 16 L11**.
For branches (Bar Madeira, Café 89, Madeira Café, Pico Bar & Grill) see index.

Menu

If you think the cooking of Portugal is just a poor man's version of Spanish cuisine, you haven't eaten enough Portuguese food. It's true that many of Portugal's dishes share the Spanish love for chorizo-style sausages (chouriço), dry cured ham (presunto) and salt cod (bacalhau), but the Portuguese have developed a cooking style that has a character, a culture and a cachet all its own. Take the famous arroz (rice) dishes that appear on practically every Portuguese menu. While they are often compared to paella, they are, in fact, far soupier, with the rice used almost as a thickening agent.

Portuguese cooking is in essence a peasant cuisine: the food of farmers and fishermen. Pork, sausages and charcuterie figure prominently, as does fresh fish, seafood and olive oil. There's a strong tradition of charcoal-grilled fish and meats. The hearty bean stews from the north and the thick bready soups (açordas) are worth trying, as is the coastal speciality of caldeirada, Portugal's answer to bouillabaisse. Garlic, lemon juice, wine and wine vinegar are much used in marinades, with favoured spices being piri-piri (hot peppers, often used to flavour oil in which chicken is basted) and, for the cakes, cinnamon – the latter showing the culinary influence of Portugal's colonial past.

To finish, there is always a lush arroz doce (rice pudding), a wobbly pudim flan (crème caramel) or the world's most loved custard tart, the deliciously scorched pastel de nata.

Açorda: bread stew, using bread that's soaked in stock, then cooked with olive oil, garlic, coriander and an egg. Often combined with shellfish or bacalhau (qv).
Amêijoas à bulhão pato: clams with olive oil, garlic, coriander and lemon.

Arroz de marisco: soupy seafood rice.
Arroz de tamboril: soupy rice with monkfish.
Arroz doce: rice pudding.
Bacalhau: salt cod; soaked before cooking, then boiled, grilled, stewed or baked, and served in myriad variations – Portugal's national dish.
Bifana: pork steak, marinated in garlic, fried and served in a bread roll.
Caldeirada: fish stew, made with potatoes, tomatoes and onions.
Caldo verde: classic green soup of finely sliced spring cabbage in a potato stock, served with a slice of chouriço.
Canela: cinnamon; a favourite spice, used in sweet and savoury dishes.
Caracois: budded snails.
Carne de porco alentejana: an Alentejo dish of fried pork, clams and potato.
Cataplana: a copper cooking pan with a curved, rounded bottom and lid; it gives its name to several southern Portuguese lightly simmered seafood dishes.
Chouriço assado: a paprika-flavoured smoked pork sausage cooked on a terracotta dish over burning alcohol.
Cozido à portuguesa: the traditional Sunday lunch – various meats plus three types of sausage, cabbage, carrots, potatoes and sometimes white beans, all boiled together.
Dobrada: tripe stew.
Feijoada: bean stew, cooked with pork and sausages.
Molotov: a fluffy white pudding made from egg whites combined with caramelised sugar, often with custard.
Pastel de bacalhau (plural **pasteis**): salt-cod fish cake.
Pastel de nata: a rich egg custard tart made with crisp, thin, filo pastry.
Piri-piri or **peri-peri**: Angolan hot red pepper.
Pudim flan: crème caramel.
Queijo: cheese.
Sardinhas assadas: fresh sardines, roasted or char-grilled.

RESTAURANTS

Spanish

It was in the 1980s that the first wave of Spanish snack joints opened in London in great numbers, but in the main these bars provided a stereotypical view of Iberian cuisine, with limited menus headed by patatas bravas, tortilla and chorizo, to be accompanied by jugs of sangría. Today, the focus is firmly on high-quality ingredients and adventurous cooking, with top venues such as **Lola Rojo** (winner of our Best Spanish Restaurant award), **Barrafina**, **Dehesa**, **El Parador**, **Salt Yard** and **Tapas Brindisa** proving hugely popular – the latter opening new operations in Soho and South Ken (despite closing its Exmouth Market shop). Regional cuisine is also much easier to find, with **Fino** and Lola Rojo offering Catalan specials, **Pinchito Tapas** and **Mesón Bilbao** championing the wider Basque country, and newcomer **Ibérica Food & Culture** providing an Asturian accent.

New openings this year also include a brace of tapas bars: Tufnell Park's snug **del Parc** and Westbourne Grove's sleek **El Pirata Detapas**. Londoners' increasing appetite for Spanish cuisine is also evidenced by tapas featuring strongly on the menus of gastropubs such as the Norfolk Arms (see p102) and the Queen's Head & Artichoke (see p104).

There is much more to Spanish food than tapas, of course, and the capital has four of the classiest exponents of the cuisine in Fino, **Cambio de Tercio** (winner of our award for Best Spanish Wine List), **Laxeiro** and the Moorish **Moro**.

Central

Bloomsbury

Cigala
2009 RUNNER-UP BEST SPANISH WINE LIST
54 Lamb's Conduit Street, WC1N 3LW (7405 1717, www.cigala.co.uk). Holborn or Russell Square tube.
Bar **Open/tapas served** 5.30-10.45pm Mon-Sat. **Tapas** £2-£16.
Restaurant **Meals served** noon-10.45pm Mon-Fri; 12.30-10.45pm Sat; 12.30-9.45pm Sun. **Main courses** £11-£18. **Set lunch** (noon-3pm Mon-Fri) £15 2 courses, £18 3 courses.
Both **Credit** AmEx, DC, MC, V.
Set in a pedestrianised street lined with boutiques, Cigala has a Scandinavian design that's served it well for many years, drawing a sophisticated crowd. On warm Saturday nights the few outdoor tables are quickly snapped up, sometimes by folk just wanting wine and some bread and olives. Chef-patron Jake Hodges' flexible menus offer nearly 30 tapas as well as big-flavoured rice dishes for sharing. Kick off with a cocktail such as agua de sevilla (vodka, cava and seville orange juice) or sangría; alternatively there are several wines by the glass or carafe. Our sweet, spicy morcilla arrived with cut surface blackened from the grill, which only enhanced its flavour; served with migas (seasoned breadcrumbs) and a bubbly fried egg, it was as indulgent as a mid-evening breakfast – so too salt-cod-flecked scrambled eggs with olives and chips. Lighter palates will prefer the accurately cooked parrillada de marisco served with leaves (and a slightly too acidic dressing). Santiago tart lacked succulence, exhibiting the worthiness common in vegetarian caffs. Better was chilled rice pudding: simple, milky, lifted by zingy orange zest and cinnamon. The personable service declined dramatically as things got busier; by the time dessert arrived were ready to go.
Available for hire (Bar). Babies and children welcome: high chairs. Booking advisable. Tables outdoors (11, pavement). **Map 4 M4.**

Clerkenwell & Farringdon

★ Moro (100)
34-36 Exmouth Market, EC1R 4QE (7833 8336, www.moro.co.uk). Farringdon tube/rail/19, 38, 341 bus.
Bar **Open/tapas served** 12.30-10.30pm Mon-Sat. **Tapas** £3.50-£14.50.
Restaurant **Lunch served** 12.30-2.30pm, **dinner served** 7-10.30pm Mon-Sat. **Main courses** £14.50-£20.
Both **Credit** AmEx, DC, MC, V.
A meal that excites the senses is a rarity, but Moro can achieve this. For a restaurant with a big reputation, its decor is unpretentious: the centrepiece being a view of the kitchen's capacious wood-fired oven where the magic happens. You can enjoy tapas at the bar or sit down for a more leisurely wander through the Moorish menu, with inspiration from Egypt to Portugal, Spain to the Lebanon. Creamy artichokes on crisp chargrilled bread with cubes of chorizo made a great start to our meal. Grilled lamb was beautifully lean and complemented by a sweet pumpkin pilaf flecked with pine nuts and whisps of fried onion. Roast mackerel was no less a triumph, and a side dish of Egyptian koshary (packed with lentils, pasta and rice) confirmed that accompaniments are no afterthought here. The menu changes frequently, but the citrus yoghurt cake is a regular and makes a refreshing end to a meal. Moro's drinks list is a point of pride; almost all the vast selection of wine, sherries, cava and cocktails comes from the Iberian peninsula. The atmosphere is relaxed in the evening, with folk clad in jeans and jumpers sitting comfortably among dressed-up diners.

Available for hire. Babies and children welcome: high chairs. Booking essential. Disabled: toilet. Tables outdoors (6, pavement). **Map 5 N4.**

Fitzrovia

★ Fino
2009 RUNNER-UP BEST SPANISH RESTAURANT
2009 RUNNER-UP BEST SPANISH WINE LIST
33 Charlotte Street, entrance on Rathbone Street, W1T 1RR (7813 8010, www.finorestaurant.com). Goodge Street or Tottenham Court Road tube.
Lunch served noon-2.30pm Mon-Fri. **Dinner served** 6-10.30pm Mon-Sat. **Tapas** £4-£15.50.
Credit AmEx, MC, V.
Owners Sam and Eddie Hart preside over three London restaurants: the British-leaning Quo Vadis (see p57) and two of the capital's finest Spanish eateries, Barrafina (see p242) and this one. Fino plays the elder statesman, with well-spaced tables, plush seating (even plusher following a refurb) and a posh atmosphere – although you can also dine at the rather glam bar. As the name suggests, there's an excellent range of sherries, plus modern Spanish wines that suit the chic cooking. Many dishes, such as pan con tamate, and calçots with romesco sauce, can trace their roots to Catalonia, but the menu cherry-picks from across Spain. Calçots (think of a cross between leeks and spring onions) are feted in Catalonia. These beacons of spring were beautifully silky, the barbecue-blackened stems set off by a crunchy, tangy, gutsy romesco sauce. Octopus with capers, served with a dusting of paprika, was equally simple and well-judged. Morcilla with fried quails' eggs arrived in a stack, the two morcilla cylinders surrounded by a moat of chopped piquillo peppers and topped with a crisp fried quail's egg. The only letdown was our milk-fed lamb cutlets, which showed remarkable toughness given their tender age. A classic Galician santiago tart – moist and Moorish with its scents of almonds and orange – made a fitting end.

BEST SPANISH

Good day sunshine
Plenty of tables to eat outdoors at **Camino** (see p240), **Cigala** (see left), **El Faro** (see p247), **Goya** (see p242), **Lola Rojo** (see p246), **Mar i Terra** (see p246), **Number 22** (see p246) and **El Parador** (see p248).

Nueva cocina
Surf the new wave of Spanish cooking at **Cambio de Tercio** (see p243), **El Faro** (see p247), **Ibérica Food & Culture** (see p240) and **Lola Rojo** (see p246).

Spanish owned and run
Savour the authenticity at **Cambio de Tercio** (see p243), **Café Garcia** (see p245), **Ibérica Food & Culture** (see p240), **Lola Rojo** (see p246), **El Pirata** (see p242) and **Rebato's** (see p246).

Ingredients for success
Enjoy first-rate Iberian produce at **Camino** (see p240), **Dehesa** (see p242), **Fino** (see above) **Ibérica Food & Culture** (see p240) and **Tapas Brindisa** (see p247).

Tip-top tapas
Share sublime snacks at **Barrafina** (see p242), **Ibérica Food & Culture** (see p240), **Orford Saloon** (see p248), **El Parador** (see p248), **Tapas Brindisa** (see p247) and **Tendido Cero** (see p242).

Bars for the buzz
Sink the sangría with the lively crowds at **Camino** (see p240), **Mar i Terra** (see p246), **Meza** (see p242), **Olé** (see p245) and **Pinchito Tapas** (see p246).

Cigala. See p239.

Available for hire. Babies and children welcome: high chairs. Booking advisable. Disabled: lift; toilet. **Map 9 J5.**

Ibérica Food & Culture NEW

165 Great Portland Street, W1W 5PS (7636 8650, www.ibericalondon.com). Great Portland Street tube.
Bar **Open/tapas served** 11.30am-11pm Tue-Sat; noon-4pm Sun. **Tapas** £3.90-£19.70.
Restaurant **Lunch served** 12.30-3pm Tue-Fri. **Dinner served** 6.30-10.30pm Tue-Sat. **Main courses** £7-£19.
Both **Credit** MC, V.
The ground floor of this spacious newcomer is part Spanish grocery, part wine shop and part tapas bar, with a fine-dining restaurant upstairs. We were tempted by the long sweeping bar, but grabbed a table in the deli, which felt rather like dining in a food shop on the Continent. The tapas menu roams Spain's gastronomic regions, with plenty of cheese and charcuterie (which, like the wines on the all-Spanish list, can be purchased to take home). Head chef is Madrid-born Santiago Guerrero; executive chef is Nacho Manzano, who runs an esteemed restaurant in Asturias. Bean-based stews, such as fabada, are a staple of that region; Ibérica's textbook fabada is based on large, creamy-textured white beans, cooked with morcilla and pork belly. A home-style dish of eggs with sautéed panadera potatoes, served with a fried egg and topped with silky, salty jamón, was equally authentic. On a recent visit, the cooking was variable. 'Seared' rabbit was tough, and fried squid with aïoli flaccid. Service, though willing, can be scatty; a waiter smilingly poured water into a glass of wine (which was, smilingly, replaced). Choose carefully, though, and you'll get a taste of real Spanish cooking.
Available for hire. Babies and children admitted. Booking advisable. Disabled: toilet. Separate room for parties, seats 25. Takeaway service. **Map 3 H5.**

★ Salt Yard

54 Goode Street, W1T 4NA (7637 0657, www.saltyard.co.uk). Goode Street tube.
Bar **Open** noon-11pm Mon-Fri; 5-11pm Sat.
Restaurant **Tapas served** noon-3pm, 6-11pm Mon-Fri; 5-11pm Sat. **Tapas** £2.75-£8.50.
Both **Credit** AmEx, DC, MC, V.
Dark, sleek, calm and classy, Salt Yard offers a retreat from brash Goode Street. Its artful menu of Iberian and Italian standards is aimed at diners in search of a slow lunch or lightish dinner. The bellota ham isn't cheap (£12.80 as a starter for two) but it's sourced from Castro y Gonzalez, one of Salamanca's most acclaimed charcutiers. Sweating, almost see-through and edged with strips of buttery fat, it's the real thing. The patatas bravas here are in fact crunchy golden chips for dipping in two sauces: a mildly peppery romesco, and a smooth, punchy aïoli. Fried parsnips with rosemary and truffle honey were sweet and extremely moreish. Most surprising was a plate of crispy squid with arroz negro, chilli and fresh basil; the rice was almost jellified and had soaked up the fishy essence of the squid: so pungent the basil didn't get a look in. The waiters stagger the order, so food is always hot and eagerly awaited. Any faults? Well, the house wines are a mite drab, and the wine list quickly rises into the £25 bracket. Also, the dessert menu is packed with praline and goo, when fresh fruit might better wrap up a salty lunch. Then again, the house ice-cream is delicious. One of London's top venues for fuss-free tapas.
Available for hire. Babies and children welcome (restaurant only). Booking essential. Tables outdoors (3, pavement). **Map 9 J5.**

King's Cross

Camino

3 Varnishers Yard, Regents Quarter, N1 9FD (7841 7331, www.camino.uk.com). King's Cross tube/rail.
Bar **Open/tapas served** noon-midnight Mon-Wed; noon-1am Thur-Sat. **Tapas** £3-£7.75.
Restaurant **Breakfast served** 8-11.30am, **lunch served** noon-3pm, **dinner served**

Eating in Cantabria
A chef called nature

Cantabria
Infinita
www.turismodecantabria.com

In the north of Spain, the region of Cantabria is a "gourmet" experience for all the senses. Explore the stately towns and villages, the breathtaking, secluded beaches and stunning countryside, and discover the beautiful architecture and wonderful places to stay…

Cantabria is a little corner of the planet, where the natural surroundings have shaped a unique gastronomic menu. The cuisine in Cantabria reveals the many delights and flavours of the locally grown regional ingredients.

The harvest of the sea

The turbulent waters of the Cantabrian Sea have produced the finest flavoured fish such as hake and bass, intensely-flavoured fish such as sardines, anchovies and Northern tuna fish, and of course the exquisite shellfish and seafood - clams, crabs, lobsters, prawns, barnacles, squids - cannot be forgotten.

The flavour of the green pastures

The gently rolling Cantabrian meadows, always green and lush, have fed the Tudanca cattle and the succulent beef is a must for all meat-lovers. The shady forests and high mountains conceal top quality game: all types of deer and wild boar.

The fruit of the valley

In the orchards and warm valleys of Cantabria, fruit, vegetables and legumes are abundant. These are added to pork to create incredible stews with unforgettable flavours.

From the best milk comes the most exquisite desserts

In every village and in every valley in Cantabria, it is possible to taste specialist cheeses and desserts, which owe their flavour and quality to the marvellous milk from the area.

Simple, sensible recipes that do not disguise the flavour

Mountain stew, hake in green sauce, tuna fish "marmitako", squid and onion stew, clam casserole, braised meat served on wooden platters, cheese cake and more…

Cantabria has a rich gastronomy where the natural quality of the products is the most important ingredient, cooked with passion and using traditional methods and recipes.

ESPAÑA

www.spain.info/uk

6.30-11pm Mon-Fri. **Meals served** 9am-4pm, 7-11pm Sat; 11am-4pm Sun. **Main courses** £10.50-£23.
Both **Credit** AmEx, MC, V.
Camino indicates what's to come in the shiny, glass-and-steel world of the new King's Cross. Set in the Regents Quarter development, its cavernous premises comprise a sleek bar and restaurant; outside, drinkers spill into the courtyard, sipping iced Cruzcampo and nibbling plump, golden-crumbed croquetas. The tapas list is dotted with regional specialities; for the indecisive, generous sharing plates promise 'un poco de todo' – a bit of everything. The full menu must be sampled in the restaurant, whose stripped-down, self-consciously modern aesthetic (brick walls, modish leather seating) is softened by muted candlelight and the hum of conversation. The menu mixes classical Iberian fare (shoulder of Jabugo black pig, gazpacho andaluz) with Modern Euro forays, like a hefty, chargrilled pork cutlet served with succulent butternut squash dumplings and a touch of blue cheese and sage. Velvet-black arroz negro, topped with aïoli, was less successful: slightly undercooked and distinctly light on squid. Service was amenable but amateurish, with no change of plates between courses, a long wait for the bill, and a waitress who cheerfully admitted ignorance of the wine list – a shame, as the selection of regional wines ventures far beyond the usual Riojas and tempranillos.
Available for hire. Babies and children welcome: high chairs; nappy-changing facilities. Booking advisable. Disabled: toilet. Tables outdoors (5, garden). **Map 4 L3**.

Cambio de Tercio

Mayfair

El Pirata

5-6 Down Street, W1J 7AQ (7491 3810, www.elpirata.co.uk). Green Park or Hyde Park Corner tube. **Meals served** noon-11.30pm Mon-Fri. **Dinner served** 6-11.30pm Sat. **Main courses** £10.50-£16. **Tapas** £3.95-£9. **Set lunch** (noon-3pm) £9.95 2 dishes incl glass of wine. **Set meal** £14.95-£19.50 per person (minimum 2). **Credit** AmEx, MC, V.
It seems odd to praise a Mayfair restaurant for its unflashy authenticity, but that's exactly what the friendly Pirate provides. We were initially disappointed to be taken downstairs from the light, contemporary ground floor (with its elegant bar and packed tables), but once eyes adjust to the gloom, the cellar-like basement is ideal for an intimate dinner; there are also cavernous booths for larger groups. The menu is splendid – not too big, but with a variety of tempting-sounding tapas and main courses. Plates of cheese, ham and chorizo were pleasing without being exceptional. Both arroz negro and a dish of lentils and chickpeas infused with chorizo were hearty, while a slice of tortilla was nicely moist in the middle. A good-value house red from Navarra confirmed our belief we were in safe hands. But it was the solomillo (fillet steak) that stole the show. It didn't need the slices of manchego or rocket garnish, but once unencumbered was revealed to be an outstanding slab of succulent,

rare meat with a hint of charcoal flavour. El Pirata conjures up the true spirit of Spain, and the charming service and pleasant surroundings make for a great night out.
Babies and children admitted. Booking advisable dinner. Separate room for parties, seats 65. Tables outdoors (4, pavement). Takeaway service. **Map 9 H8**.

Pimlico

Goya

34 Lupus Street, SW1V 3EB (7976 5309, www.goyarestaurant.co.uk). Pimlico tube. **Meals served** noon-11.30pm daily. **Main courses** £10.90-£16.95. **Tapas** £1.80-£6.85. **Credit** AmEx, MC, V.
If you're after a bit of Spanish sunshine, Goya will certainly provide it. A colourful paint scheme of oranges and yellows, coupled with a warm welcome from staff, produce an immediately positive experience and no doubt contribute to the restaurant's popularity. The food is pretty good too: flavoursome and hearty in the manner of solid rustic cooking rather than sophisticated fare. We ordered a selection of tapas, but the dishes arrived in surprisingly generous portions. Five proved a little ambitious for two people, but every dish – including meatballs in rich tomato sauce, and tender chicken pieces atop saffron rice – was flavoursome and satisfying. Calamares, the true test of a Spanish kitchen, were crisp and well-seasoned with garlicky aïoli. Goya's tapas offer good value, whereas its main courses seem a little pricey. Furthermore, the carte comprises a few interlopers like chicken stroganoff and apple strudel, which we can only imagine are there to keep large groups happy. Such parties can easily be accommodated in the restaurant basement, which is furnished in a more traditional Spanish style and has plenty of space for a meal with colleagues or friends.
Available for hire. Babies and children welcome: high chairs; nappy-changing facilities. Booking advisable. Disabled: toilet. Tables outdoors (10, pavement). Takeaway service. **Map 15 J11**.

Soho

★ Barrafina (100)

54 Frith Street, W1D 4SL (7440 1463, www.barrafina.co.uk). Leicester Square or Tottenham Court Road tube. **Tapas served** noon-3pm, 5-11pm Mon-Sat; 1-3.30pm, 5.30-10pm Sun. **Tapas** £1.90-£16.50. **Credit** AmEx, MC, V.
It would be quite easy not to like this bar-restaurant. It's small, often rammed with an after-work crowd, and the open kitchen is right under your nose. Yet, on every other count, it works. Go for a late lunch early in the week and you'll probably get a couple of stools in three minutes (solos will be seated even faster). The cook-waiters (they double up) are engaging, helpful and efficient, and water is topped up without any need to ask. Food is fresh, hot and prepared with care. Sardines were crisp on the outside and meaty if a bit skinny; grilled quail was moist and tender; and tortilla with ham and spinach was tested by three members of staff before serving, to ensure it was firm but with a juicy, moist heart. A £4 glass of Etim 2007 garnacha is a perfect dry, mineral wine to accompany these oily bites. The small rhubarb dessert – a delicate, deconstructed crumble – with spicy orange sauce was all we had room for. If you don't think the experience at Barrafina is very Spanish, it's probably because you've spent time in too many grubby 'hams hanging from the ceiling' joints on holiday in Seville.
Babies and children welcome: high chairs. Bookings not accepted. Tables outdoors (4, pavement). **Map 17 C3**.

★ Dehesa

25 Ganton Street, W1F 9BP (7494 4170). Oxford Circus tube. **Tapas served** noon-11pm Mon-Sat; noon-5pm Sun. **Tapas** £3.50-£7.25. **Credit** AmEx, MC, V.
Good news: this informal yet sophisticated Spanish-Italian tapas bar, named after the woodland home of the Ibérico pig, now takes

bookings. We had no trouble nabbing a table on the off-chance early evening, but the split room and outdoor tables soon filled up. With a pub and other eateries opposite, eating alfresco is just as buzzy as inside, but you may be subjected to unwanted approaches from passers-by. The wine list champions Spain and Italy's indigenous grape varieties; good weather calls for fruity rosé Chiaretto from Lombardy, or the unusual Txakoli di Getaria from the Basque Country. The black-footed pig appears in nutty-flavoured ham and other charcuterie, but local sourcing comes to the fore in tapas such as confit Old Spot pork belly with cannellini beans, and Gressingham duck breast with PX sherry dressing, spring onions and pomegranate. Grilled squid with chickpeas, chorizo and mint was comfort cooking at its most vibrant. From the Italian tradition we loved the tender slow-roasted lamb with wild garlic risotto and salsa verde. Staff are bright, well-informed and efficient. At close of play, delectable lemon and rosemary cake knocked the thin chocolate option for six, though both werer accompanied by superb ice-creams. Dehesa's Sunday brunch appeals and, yes, includes everybody's favourite: churros with hot chocolate.
Babies and children admitted. Booking advisable dinner. Separate room for parties, seats 12. Tables outdoors (8, pavement). **Map 17 A4.**

Meza

100 Wardour Street, W1F 0TN (7314 4002, www.danddlondon.com). Leicester Square or Piccadilly Circus tube. **Meals served** 4.30pm-1am Mon-Sat. **Main courses** £6.75-£17.50. **Tapas** £3.50-£10. **Credit** AmEx, MC, V.
Part late-opening lounge bar, part restaurant, Meza is sleek and sprawling. Doormen staff the entrance, shared with Cuban bar-restaurant Floridita; inside lies a sea of low-slung seating with a long, curving bar. To the rear, the restaurant is subtly lit and elegantly monochrome, separated from the bar by screens – which do nothing to block out the relentless, house-heavy playlist. It's a disconcerting mix, as is the menu, which jumps from predominantly Spanish tapas and sharing platters to an arbitrary, pub grub-style assortment of 'big plates' (burgers, vegetable lasagne, lamb shank). For the most part, the tapas list sticks to classics, with varying success: lamb meatballs and bacalao (salt-cod fritters) arrived cold, while smoked ham croquetas, made with mash instead of béchamel, were synthetic-tasting. Better were lightly battered salt and pepper squid, decent chorizo and punchy patatas bravas. Chunky strips of mahon cheese, served with runny, floral-tasting honey, made a pleasing departure from the norm. Not the place for an intimate dinner, Meza is nevertheless perfectly geared towards cocktail-fuelled carousing, with snacks to soak up the alcohol; a bewildering array of special offers makes it a good bet for groups.
Babies and children welcome: high chairs. Booking advisable weekends. Disabled: lift; toilet. Separate room for parties, seats 38. **Map 17 B3.**

South Kensington

★ Cambio de Tercio

2009 RUNNER-UP BEST SPANISH RESTAURANT
2009 WINNER BEST SPANISH WINE LIST
163 Old Brompton Road, SW5 0LJ (7244 8970, www.cambiodetercio.co.uk). Gloucester Road or South Kensington tube. **Lunch served** noon-3pm daily. **Dinner served** 7-11.30pm Mon-Sat; 7-11pm Sun. **Main courses** £13.90-£15.50. **Credit** AmEx, DC, MC, V.
Cambio de Tercio is not for fans of package-holiday Spain, but rather for plains drifters, boutique-hotel travellers and monied Hispanophiles. Pared down, discreet, smart and decorated not with bulls' heads or hanging hams, but quirky, colourful artworks, it attracts sophisticates and – thanks to the location – Latino ambassadors with their familias. Both the wine and food menus are intended to thrill and tempt customers back for more. The cooking verges on the extraordinary: patatas bravas were rich and spicy, sardines were few but superb, and the

spinach-and-ham tortilla was moist and salted to perfection. The cured ham and the bread are as good as you'd find in Madrid. Grilled quail aïoli was our one fancy choice, but it was a foamy, rather pretentious affair and disappointed. Pudding consisted of a delicious rhubarb creation, whose acidic character went well with a glass of Etim dessert wine. In all, this was a sublime meal. We dined late on a Saturday afternoon and the atmosphere was ultra-tranquil (background music was forgettable electro-tango), yet this had no negative effect. Waiting staff were knowledgeable, friendly and discreet. Opposite is the same owner's Tendido Cero (*see below*), which is cheaper.
Available for hire. Babies and children admitted. Booking advisable dinner. Separate room for parties, seats 20. Tables outdoors (3, pavement). **Map 13 C11.**

Tendido Cero

174 Old Brompton Road, SW5 0BA (7370 3685, www.cambiodetercio.co.uk). Gloucester Road or South Kensington tube. **Tapas served** noon-3pm; 6.30-11pm daily. **Tapas** £4-£14. **Credit** AmEx, MC, V.
The food at Tendido Cero is generally excellent: an intriguing, modern take on tapas. We started with boquerones that weren't overwhelmed by vinegar (as is so often the way), and moreish pan con tomate. Delicious lamb stew with toasted almonds was followed by equally impressive squid bathed in thick, sludgy ink. The only disappointments were an inauthentically fluffy tortilla de patata and an oily dish of chicken in paprika. The wine list, displayed rather pretentiously in a thick leather folder, lacked choice at the cheaper end, but it was the service on our visit that undermined an otherwise impressive dining experience. No one offered drinks or brought bread when we sat down, and it took three attempts to get water from the elegant but ineffectual waiters. It's a shame, as the setting is smart and vibrant and the place buzzes late into the night, its well-heeled young clientele letting their hair down with mucho gusto. So much so that a disapproving woman at the next table commented to her husband: 'I think snogging in a restaurant is a bit off'.
Available for hire. Babies and children admitted. Booking advisable dinner Wed-Sat. Tables outdoors (5, pavement). **Map 13 C11**.
For branch see index.

West

Bayswater

El Pirata Detapas [NEW]

115 Westbourne Grove, W2 4UP (7727 5000, www.elpiratadetapas.co.uk). Bayswater tube. **Lunch served** noon-3pm, **dinner served** 6-11pm Mon-Fri. **Meals served** noon-11pm Sat, Sun. **Tapas** £1.50-£8. **Set tapas** £20 7 dishes **Credit** AmEx, MC, V.
Younger sister to Mayfair's El Pirata (*see p242*), this is an altogether sleeker, more ambitious affair. Behind a soberly striped awning, the dining room is crisply businesslike, with dark wood tables, leather banquettes and discreet modern art – softened by glowing pendant lights. The menu runs from traditional tapas to elaborate nueva cocina offerings such as octopus carpaccio with clementine caviar, capers and paprika; the head chef's CV includes stints at Maze and El Bulli. Serving crisp endive leaves to scoop up an airy but intense mousse of valdéon cheese sprinkled with ground walnuts, was inspired and deliciously simple. Juicy, lightly seared scallops were beautifully offset by slivers of artichoke heart and Iberian pancetta. Other concoctions felt slightly too fussy: for instance a tiny, deliciously salty wood-pigeon breast paired with fig purée and chopped nuts with apricot. Best to intersperse your order with simpler options: cheeses with quince jelly; or plump, silky-centred croquetas studded with serrano ham. Desserts follow the same gently subversive lines: confit strawberries with cheese foam for the daring; cold, creamy rice pudding sprinkled with caramelised rice puffs, for less brave souls. Alas, our signature 'two textures'

Interview
ROBERTO MATA

Who are you?
General manager of **El Pirata Detapas** (*see left*).
How did you start in the catering business?
I was never good at school so left my studies at the age of 16 and went to work for a five-star hotel in Madrid. It was the most amazing and overwhelming experience – I was hooked!
What's the best thing about running a restaurant in London?
You get to meet the most interesting and amazing characters. Londoners' expectations are very high and this makes you raise your game, improve and innovate.
What's the worst thing?
Finding and keeping great staff has been always the hardest thing.
Which are your favourite London restaurants?
I worked in South-east Asia for a while and fell in love with that part of the world, which is probably why I am a great fan of **Gilgamesh** (*see p236*). **Gordon's** wine bar (*see p334*) is like going back in time, it's a great London classic.
What's the best bargain in the capital?
The prixe fixe lunch menu at **Galvin Bistrot De Luxe** (*see p95*) – the quality of ingredients is fantastic and there's always a great choice of dishes.
What's your favourite treat?
Having a cappuccino at 3am at **Bar Italia** in Soho.
What is missing from London's restaurant scene?
When I am in Spain I love to go 'de tapas' – to streets filled with bars and restaurants where you can have a glass of wine or sherry and try a few tapas before moving on to the next one. I'd also like to see more independent restaurants and fewer chains.
What does the next year hold?
We have already seen a new wave of modern Spanish restaurants opening and I think that trend is set to continue – the idea of sharing at an affordable price seems to be hitting the spot.

RESTAURANTS

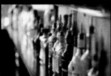

crema catalana arrived as a swirl of foamy sweetness, missing its crucial caramel layer – an oversight the kitchen should have spotted.
Available for hire. Babies and children welcome: high chairs. Booking advisable. Separate room for parties, seats 35. Takeaway service. Vegetarian menu. **Map 7 B6.**

Hammersmith

Los Molinos

127 Shepherd's Bush Road, W6 7LP (7603 2229, www.losmolinosuk.com). Hammersmith tube. **Lunch served** noon-3pm Mon-Fri. **Dinner served** 6-10.45pm Mon-Sat. **Tapas** £3.70-£6.50. **Credit** AmEx, DC, MC, V.
The small, attractive room housing simple wooden tables laid with red and white checked napkins is the best thing about this tapas bar – along with the fact it serves bottled Mahou beer, a Madrid institution far superior to better-known Spanish brews. Unfortunately, the food and wine on a recent visit didn't match the high standards set by our meal last year. The patatas bravas seemed soggy, the chorizo bland, and paella featured rather tired-looking rice. Bread didn't arrive automatically, the waitress confessed that she wasn't allowed to give us tap water in a jug, and the half bottle of red wine we ordered was disappointing. Los Molinos doesn't attempt sophisticated cooking, and yet this time even its standard tapas lacked sparkle – quite unlike our experiences here in the past. The restaurant couldn't be described as cheap either, with tiny dishes costing £5 or more. All this might go some way towards explaining the dearth of customers of late. Finally, on two recent visits the same CD was playing – surely it's time the manager gave those overworked members of the Buena Vista Social Club a night off?
Babies and children welcome: high chairs. Booking advisable dinner Fri, Sat. Separate room for parties, seats 50. **Map 20 C3.**

Kensington

L Restaurant & Bar

2 Abingdon Road, W8 6AF (7795 6969, www.l-restaurant.co.uk). High Street Kensington tube. **Lunch served** noon-2.30pm Tue-Sat. **Dinner served** 6-10.30pm Mon-Sat. **Meals/tapas served** noon-10pm Sun. **Main courses** £9.50-£17.50. **Tapas** £3.25-£4.95. **Credit** AmEx, MC, V.
We've always enjoyed eating at this contemporary Iberian restaurant, but our recent experience was disappointing. The long, narrow, cathedral-like space, bathed in light on summer evenings, is as we remember it, but the food wasn't. We chose from both the tapas and à la carte menus. Poor-quality bread was the harbinger of a lacklustre meal that reached its nadir with a tapas of tortilla and piquillo pepper, overcooked to sponginess, as if it had been microwaved. Bacalao fritters had a good crunch, but were cold at the centre. At £3.75, a tapa of one tiny piece of mackerel cooked a la plancha with a splodge of dull romesco sauce seemed poor value. Culinary adventurousness has always marked out the kitchen here, so we were looking forward to a tapa of baby scallops and prawns with leeks and 'manchego crumble'. The dish, though well-conceived, was spoiled by under-cooked leeks. A main course zarzuela (what should have been gutsy Catalan fish and shellfish stew) lacked the expected verve and passion. We received a rather polite, bisque-like version, albeit with nice meaty chunks of monkfish, prawns and mussels. Our waitress was clearly new to the trade and service lacked polish.
Babies and children admitted. Booking advisable. Separate room for parties. Tables outdoors (2, pavement). **Map 13 A9.**

Ladbroke Grove

Café Garcia

246 Portobello Road, W11 1LL (7221 6119, www.cafegarcia.co.uk). Ladbroke Grove tube. **Tapas served** 9am-5pm daily. **Tapas** £1.50-£5. **Credit** AmEx, MC, V.

It's a simple set-up at this low-key Spanish café: queue at the glass-fronted counter, point to what you want, wait while it's heated up and plated, then squeeze on to a table (not easy on frenetic Saturday lunchtimes). The food is equally fuss-free, with staff dispensing ladles of rich cocido madrileño stew, slabs of empanada and robust chorizo in red wine. The quality can be hit and miss; bland, dry albóndigas (meatballs) left us unimpressed, while ratatouille-like pisto manchego (served without an egg) was superb, along with beautifully light triangles of tortilla. Despite the lunchtime crowds, there's no sense of rush; along the mirrored counter at the front, lone diners pick at paella and sip cervezas over the café's well-thumbed copies of *El País* and *El Mundo*. Tables at the rear are a sociable mix of chattering Spanish students, weary shoppers and well-heeled locals. Sweets range from thin, crunchy olive oil and aniseed biscuits to slices of dense, almondy torta de santiago and some extravagant cream-filled confections. The best seller, though, is the unctuous hot chocolate – best consumed at a contemplative pace, with ample supplies of sweet, doughy churros.
Babies and children admitted. Disabled: toilet. Takeaway service. **Map 19 B2.**

Maida Vale

Mesón Bilbao

33 Malvern Road, NW6 5PS (7328 1744). Maida Vale tube. **Lunch served** noon-3pm Mon-Fri. **Dinner served** 6-11pm Mon-Thur; 7-11.30pm Fri; 6-11.30pm Sat. **Main courses** £9.95-£12.95. **Tapas** £3.50-£6.95. **Set meal** £12.95 2 courses incl coffee. **Credit** MC, V.
Set in an awkward location midway between Kilburn and Maida Vale, Mesón Bilbao can be disconcertingly quiet of an evening – though its old-fashioned, candlelit dining room with tables squeezed around the bar is cosy enough to make solitary diners feel at ease. True to the restaurant's Basque name, its menu is particularly strong on seafood. Couples can share merluza (hake) for two instead of the ubiquitous paella, while the tapas list includes eels and an outstanding rendition of chipirones en su tinta (squid in its own ink), with tender chunks of squid half-submerged in rich, velvet-black ink and onion sauce. Sadly, the other tapas we sampled failed to live up to the squid's dark splendour: patatas bravas, made with boiled rather than fried potatoes, were lacklustre; chorizo busturia (juicy, generous slices of chorizo sandwiched between thin slices of fried aubergine) was slightly burnt. Still, unobtrusive but friendly service and a modestly priced wine list compensate for the odd lapse. The two-course set menu offers superb value for money; you can dine on jamón serrano then sea bream for a mere £12.95, with a coffee thrown in for good measure.
Babies and children welcome: high chairs. Booking advisable dinner Fri, Sat. Tables outdoors (2, pavement). **Map 1 A3.**

South West

Putney

Olé

240 Upper Richmond Road, SW15 6TG (8788 8009, www.olerestaurants.com). East Putney tube/Putney rail. **Bar & restaurant Open/meals served** noon-11pm Mon-Thur; noon-11.30pm Fri, Sat; noon-10pm Sun. **Tapas** £3-£6.50. *Restaurant* **Main courses** £11.95-£15.50. **Set lunch** (noon-6pm) £9.95 2 courses. **Set menu** (Sun) paella. *Both* **Credit** AmEx, MC, V.
Quiet on our weekday visit, this local tapas joint has an attractive light-filled mezzanine, an extensive menu and welcoming service. The ground floor contains counter seating and a few small round tables where you can knock back tipples accompanied by tapas. Upstairs you can do the same, or opt for more substantial Spanish main courses such as grilled meats and fish, or paella

served in large cast-iron pans. We loved the small, perky padrón peppers; the meaty chorizo cooked in white wine; and the melt-in-the-mouth serrano ham. Pulpo a la gallega consisted of tender, meaty octopus and firm slices of potatoes. Our croquetas promised chicken and serrano ham nestled in the creamy filling, but these were indiscernible. Seafood paella was fantastic value, with a generous amount of robust prawns, mussels, fish and clams enrobed in the saffron-rich rice. Service was unobtrusive yet highly efficient, with empty tapas plates whisked away from the table to leave us more room. The wine list is exclusively Spanish, but with only one fino and one manzanilla available, the sherry selection could be improved.
Available for hire. Babies and children welcome: high chairs. Booking advisable weekends. Disabled: toilet.

THE DISH

Albóndigas

All the world loves meatballs – even vegetarians. After all, what are falafels, vadais and potato koftas if not ball-shaped plant foods wishing they were flesh? Killing an animal for food has always been an expensive investment, so making good use of the tough and scrappy bits of meat from a carcass has been a concern for every society, from Inuit and nomadic Berbers to modern food industry's MRM (mechanically recovered meat) merchants.

In Spain, meatballs, known as albóndigas, have generally been considered food of the urban poor. They are often made with a combination of meats (beef, veal, lamb, pork) – whatever the cook can get. Bread can comprise a larger or smaller proportion of the mixture, depending on how much meat is available.

Tomato sauce is the typical accompaniment (albóndigas en salsa), as seen at **Orford Saloon**, **Cigala** and more, though in Andalucía you're as likely to find meatballs served with saffron and almond sauce – one of many Arab influences on the region's cuisine. At **Pinchito Tapas** the albóndigas come with green olives. **El Faro** sometimes swathes them in rich, meaty-tasting mushroom sauce, while at gastropub the **Queen's Head & Artichoke** we've enjoyed them cold with a mustard sauce rather like foamy mayonnaise.

It's all good rustic stuff, but the albóndigas served at upmarket **Fino** challenge the idea that meatballs are humble. Chef Nieves Barragan uses hand-chopped premium beef fillet instead of minced scraps and offcuts, which allows the albóndigas to be served medium-rare. And, because fillet is a lean cut, the meatballs are wrapped in caul before cooking. This lacey membrane of fat, which encases the animals' internal organs, renders or melts away during cooking, basting the meatballs and adding flavour and juiciness. All proving that everybody (not just the urban poor) loves meatballs.

South

Clapham

★ Lola Rojo (100)

2009 WINNER BEST SPANISH RESTAURANT

78 Northcote Road, SW11 6QL (7350 2262, www.lolarojo.net). Clapham Junction rail. **Lunch served** noon-3pm, **dinner served** 6-10.30pm Mon-Thur. **Meals served** noon-10.30pm Fri, Sat; noon-5pm Sun. **Main courses** £7.50-£11. **Credit** AmEx, DC, MC, V.

This tapas specialist goes from strength to strength, sprouting a new branch in Fulham with the same modern red and white decor. The original restaurant seems to get better and better. It's difficult to choose from the sizeable, highly appealing list of hot and cold tapas and rice dishes (the latter shouldn't be missed). There's a Catalan influence in food such as the spinach, pine nut and raisin omelette, and the romesco sauce that accompanies several dishes (for instance the tiny boiled artichokes served with pan-fried slices of serrano ham). The kitchen's also in touch with the cocina nueva/molecular gastronomy movement, as evidenced by the odd 'foam' or lighter-than-air, cloud-like fluff served with our serrano ham-wrapped sardines (it melted on the tongue, leaving just a whisper of olive essence). Slips aren't unknown, as with confit of suckling pig, served with a ruffle of sweet-potato crisps but a too-sweet apple and vanilla sauce. Despite experimentation of this kind, this isn't show-off cooking; it's highly accomplished and true to its Mediterranean roots, based on high-quality, carefully sourced Spanish ingredients. The all-Spanish wine list is equally adventurous and well-sourced, with top new-wave producers. Service is charming, even when the pace among the tiny tables gets hectic.

Babies and children admitted. Booking advisable Thur-Sat. Separate room for parties, seats 15. Tables outdoors (16, terrace). Takeaway service. **Map 21 C5.** **For branch see index.**

Vauxhall

Rebato's

169 South Lambeth Road, SW8 1XW (7735 6388, www.rebatos.com). Stockwell tube. **Tapas bar Open** 5.30-10.45pm Mon-Fri; 7-11pm Sat. **Tapas** £15.95 3 courses. *Restaurant* **Lunch served** noon-2.30pm Mon-Fri. **Dinner served** 7-10.45pm Mon-Sat. **Set meal** £19.95 3 courses. *Both* **Credit** AmEx, MC, V.

Whether it's taverna-style tapas you fancy, or a leisurely meal in surroundings that evoke a typical Spanish restaurant, Rebato's can deliver. The cosy bar area is popular with both Spaniards and locals. Bull-fighting posters, regional maps and a big leg of serrano set the perfect scene for enjoying a traditional tapas selection. In the restaurant, overhead windows, floor tiling and plenty of greenery create a Mediterranean-courtyard feel at lunchtime and a laid-back space for evening dining. The menu provides plenty of choice and is well-executed. Fresh fish specials might include lemon sole, lightly fried in flour; ours was a great specimen. Paella facil or 'easy paella' was perfect for the lazy diner: no shells to wrestle with and clean hands at the end. You can choose three courses from the carte at a set price. Starter, main and dessert proved rather ambitious for lunch, but even if you decide to skip a course, you'll still get good value. Tapas deals are also available. In an area that contains mostly Portuguese restaurants, Rebato's remains a beacon of Spanish charm.

Available for hire. Babies and children admitted. Booking essential. Takeaway service. **Map 16 L13.**

Waterloo

Mar i Terra

14 Gambia Street, SE1 0XH (7928 7628, www.mar iterra.co.uk). Southwark tube/Waterloo tube/rail. **Tapas served** noon-3pm, 6-11pm Mon-Fri; 5-11pm Sat. **Tapas** £3.50-£7.95. **Credit** AmEx, MC, V.

A cosy restaurant, hidden in a street just off Blackfriars Road, Mar i Terra remains popular due to decent cooking and a friendly, laid-back atmosphere. The worn wooden floors and scattered tables create an informal atmosphere that works as well for lunch or dinner. Our charming waiter was endearingly enthusiastic about the fresh fish specials. Unlike many mid-range Spanish restaurants in London, Mar i Terra doesn't attempt a long and over-ambitious menu. Instead, it offers a tempting selection of typical Spanish dishes and a drinks list that includes native beers, wines, sherries and sangria. All the food we sampled was well-cooked and made to order. A tapa of grilled sardines sprinkled with crunchy rock salt had all the freshness of beach-side cooking in a Spanish town. Equally pleasing were the delicate baby squid in a light tomato sauce, with plenty of wine and parsley. The croquetas and finely sliced chorizo in cider completed a spread that was plenty for two. An inexpensive venue with authentic Spanish food that rarely disappoints.

Available for hire. Babies and children welcome: high chairs. Separate room for parties, seats 50. Tables outdoors (15, garden). **Map 11 O8.** **For branch see index.**

South East

Herne Hill

Number 22

22 Half Moon Lane, SE24 9HU (7095 9922, www.number-22.com). Herne Hill rail/3, 37, 68 bus. **Tapas served** 5-11pm Mon-Fri; noon-3pm, 5-10.30pm Sat; noon-9.30pm Sun. **Tapas** £3-£8. **Credit** MC, V.

The roaring fire was a welcome sight when we visited on a wintry evening. Number 22 continues to be a popular choice for locals of SE24 and surrounding areas. It's a simply decorated, modern eaterie with warm turquoise walls, flickering oil

burners and walnut furnishings. The menu is an encouraging one-pager that makes the most of seasonal ingredients. The chef has clearly thought about each dish, and this is reflected in the tempting flavour combinations and attractive presentation. Simple shards of manchego, heaped with cubes of sweet membrillo (quince paste) on crunchy toast, were indicative of the high-quality ingredients used. Peppery cooked mackerel, tortilla and a creamy chickpea and chorizo stew also hit the mark. For dessert, pear sorbet doused in cava offered a refreshing end to an enjoyable weekday-evening bite. The intimate atmosphere makes Number 22 an ideal choice for couples and small groups. Large parties can be accommodated too, as long as they're prepared to have a set menu. To drink, you'll find a selection of cocktails, Spanish beer on tap, sherries and wine, but enjoy these at the table as the bar area is very small. *Available for hire. Babies and children admitted. Tables outdoors (16, patio).* **Map 23 A5**.

London Bridge & Borough

★ Tapas Brindisa (100)

2009 RUNNER-UP BEST SPANISH RESTAURANT
18-20 Southwark Street, SE1 1TJ (7357 8880, www.brindisa.com). London Bridge tube/rail. **Breakfast served** 9-11am Fri, Sat. **Lunch served** noon-3pm Mon-Thur; noon-4pm Fri, Sat. **Dinner served** 5.30-11pm Mon-Sat. **Tapas** £3-£12. **Credit** AmEx, MC, V.
Long has Brindisa held sway over Borough Market, dispensing piping-hot chorizo rolls from its stall and luring Londoners into its Floral Hall deli, there to invest in sumptuous Spanish imports. A converted warehouse on the corner of the market houses the flagship restaurant – still thronged, in spite of the firm opening offshoots in Soho and South Kensington. It's a resolutely low-key affair, with no bookings and spartan surrounds (concrete flooring, menus doubling as paper place-mats). The focus is firmly on the food. Impeccable ingredients are the cornerstone of the menu, from plates of charcuterie to modish combinations such as cured León beef with pomegranate and frisée salad. Despite the unrelenting pace, the kitchen rarely falters, delivering a succession of precision-cooked tapas: perfectly grilled lamb cutlets, teamed with a leafy mint and parsley salad and garlicky aïoli, say, or deep-fried, pungent monte enebro goat's cheese, slathered with orange-blossom honey. Prices may be high, but there's no scrimping on ingredients: even onion soup is served with slivers of manchego and laced with truffle oil. Although waiting times can be substantial and there's little elbow room at the bar, most punters are content to pass the time with a sherry and a dish of huge, orange-stuffed Gordal olives, doused in fragrant olive oil. *Babies and children admitted. Bookings not accepted. Disabled: toilet. Tables outdoors (4, pavement).* **Map 11 P8**.
For branches (Casa Brindisa, Tierra Brindisa) see index.

East

Docklands

El Faro

3 Turnberry Quay, Pepper Street, E14 9RD (7987 5511, www.el-faro.co.uk). Crossharbour DLR. **Meals served** noon-3.30pm, 5-11pm Mon-Sat; noon-3pm Sun. **Main courses** £14-£17.50. **Tapas** £3.50-£14.50. **Credit** AmEx, MC, V.
Arched windows with generous water views are a key draw to this smart but informal Docklands outfit, away from the business of Canary Wharf. In good weather a table on the terrace would be a sound investment. Language can be a barrier – a waiter insisted we wait in line for the manager, to ask where the toilet was – but otherwise service was prompt (from staff clad in black logoed shirts and aprons). The kitchen aspires to artistic presentation, yet most dishes would look more appetising if rustic. Sea urchin and spring onion revuelto, for example, was shaped into three discs and served on a white plate that did nothing to enhance its pallid appearance; fortunately the fresh ozone flavour

Tapas Brindisa

compensated. Grilled vegetable salad was a pretty pile of succulent textures, served with creamy, piquant romesco sauce. Unusually grain-heavy morcilla was topped with sweet crisps made of dried apple – a little pretentious, but a successful combination. Desserts (santiago tart, fragrant rice pudding) were accomplished, but the bread wasn't worth its £2.50 charge. Other tables enjoyed good-looking roast lamb and pans of paella. An extensive Spanish wine list (including sherries and cava), plus draught Cruzcampo, cocktails and Spanish-style punches ensure there's a tipple for every mood. *Babies and children welcome: high chairs. Booking advisable. Disabled: toilet. Separate room for parties, seats 70. Tables outdoors (16, terrace).* **Map 24 B3**.

Shoreditch

★ Laxeiro

93 Columbia Road, E2 7RG (7729 1147, www.laxeiro.co.uk). Liverpool Street tube/rail then 26, 48 bus/Old Street tube/rail then 55 bus. **Lunch served** noon-3pm, **dinner served** 7-11pm Tue-Sat. **Meals served** 9am-4pm Sun. **Main courses** £3.50-£8.95. **Credit** AmEx, MC, V.
Tables are in short supply in Laxeiro's tiny, terracotta-painted dining room – and once folk are settled in with a bottle of Rioja, they're in no hurry to leave. It pays to book for dinner, and only the foolhardy would brave Sunday lunchtime, when the flower market is in full swing. Prices seem high, but these are raciones, not tapas: four dishes between two is plenty, even for the greedy. Although the famed cochillo (suckling pig) has gone from the menu, there's solace to be found in dense, flavoursome slabs of barbecued presa ibérica (shoulder of acorn-fed pork), and juicy, spring onion-sprinkled chorizo with baby squid. Vegetarian dishes are treated with equal care: asparagus in sweet Malaga wine, say, or warm broad beans topped with slowly melting shavings of semi-curado manchego cheese. Best of all was barbecued black bream, perfectly cooked and crisp-skinned with salt. Despite the quality of

cooking, there's no standing on ceremony here. The resident cat, Gilbert, snoozes on a bar stool, indifferent to the rising decibel levels. Service is friendly and forthright; when it came to our bill, the waitress was less than impressed to learn that the lady, not the gentleman, intended to pay – and told us so in no uncertain terms. *Babies and children welcome: high chairs. Booking advisable; not accepted Sun. Tables outdoors (3, pavement). Takeaway service.* **Map 6 S3**.

Pinchito Tapas

32 Featherstone Street, EC1Y 8QX (7490 0121, www.pinchito.co.uk). Old Street tube/rail. **Breakfast served** 10.30am-noon daily. **Tapas served** 10am-11pm Mon-Fri; 5-11pm Sat. **Tapas** £2-£10. **Credit** AmEx, MC, V.
The look may be 100% pure Shoreditch (bare floorboards, stripped-back brickwork, battered, vintage-chic chairs), but this low-lit tapas bar has substance as well as style. Like its acclaimed sister in Brighton, it's a convivial spot. At the bar, charming staff dispense draught Cruzcampo, cocktails and glasses of chilled sherry, along with the odd free shot for those perched at the bar. Punters eye up the pinxos: bite-sized Basque snacks, precariously piled with hunks of tortilla, octopus and manchego. For more substantial sustenance, the concise main menu runs from leisurely breakfasts of chocolate con churros and Spanish-slanted fry-ups, to classic, no-nonsense tapas (patatas bravas, padrón peppers, boquerones). Scrawled on a blackboard, ten or so tapas del dia offer more eclectic flavours, ranging from the deep-fried delights of rotos con chorizo (fried egg and chorizo, stacked with skinny chips) to tender chunks of pork belly with mango purée. Though a couple of dishes lacked bite (a watery lentil stew, and bland sardines escabeche), others had real panache; beautifully light cod fritters, drizzled with honey and spiked with garlic, were a tantalising taster of the kitchen's capabilities. *Available for hire. Babies and children admitted. Booking advisable Thur, Fri. Takeaway service.* **Map 6 Q4**.

RESTAURANTS

North East

Walthamstow

Orford Saloon

32 Orford Road, E17 9NJ (8503 6542).
Walthamstow Central tube/rail. **Tapas served**
6-10.30pm Tue-Fri; noon-3pm, 6-10.30pm Sat;
noon-5pm, 6-9.30pm Sun. **Tapas** £3.95-£14.50.
Set meal £10.50 per person (minimum 2) paella.
Credit MC, V.
A social lynchpin of picturesque Walthamstow
village, this appealingly relaxed spot has striped
cushions lining wrought-iron chairs, terracotta-
toned flooring, blue-and-white tiling, and a couple
of stunning contemporary paintings. On the wine
list there's little need to look further than the
cheapest red – smooth 2006 Tierra Seca
tempranillo-merlot blend from La Mancha –
though on an evening as steamy as a Sevillian
summer, rosé was a favourite choice at the small
bar. Tempting menu stalwarts are supplemented
with often-simple specials, such as deep-fried
mixed seafood (the batter was far too salty), or
turmeric-coloured white beans with nuggets of
morcilla. Creamed spinach with pine nuts was rich
and delectable. Seafood paella featured good fresh
shellfish and dark rice with intense flavours of
well-reduced stock; with tapas to start, it could
easily have fed three or four, so we were
disappointed to be too full for churros with
chocolate. Self-aware, mostly Spanish staff were
keen to prevent linguistic misunderstandings, and

handled an unfortunate kitchen cock-up with
professionalism. A steady stream of loyal locals
brings a convivial air to evenings here; some
reserve the tables by the front windows, but we
found these cramped.
Babies and children admitted. Booking advisable.
Disabled: toilet.

North

Archway

del Parc ![NEW]

167 Junction Road, N19 5PZ (7281 5684,
www.delparc.co.uk). Archway or Tufnell Park tube.
Lunch served 1-3pm Sun. **Dinner served** 7-
10pm Wed-Sat. **Tapas** £5.25-£7.65. **Credit** MC, V.
As intimate as it gets, this tiny Tufnell tapas
shack is run by a staff of two: waiter Alan and
chef Steve, two repatriated expats who learned
to love Spanish and North African cuisine while
living in Ibiza. (The name was originally Café del
Parc, after Café del Mar.) No glowsticks or
thumping techno here, however: decor is quiet
and understated, a dozen small tables in a
whitewashed room hung with white drapes,
planned around an open kitchen. From this
central spot, generously portioned tapas (from a
three-sheet clipboard menu) are whizzed out in
the order they're ready. Fish options include wind-
dried tuna, gorgeously moist sardinillas with
buttered toast, and giant prawns in a sweet garlic
and wine sauce. Meat might be chicken and
chorizo in a tangy lemon jus, or skewered lamb

with pomegranate. Not everything hit the mark
on our visit (tomato and mint fritters were mushy
and bhaji-like), but the standard was reliably
high. Service was unstintingly friendly too. The
wine choice is small but sturdy, featuring earthy
tempranillo wines at the top and bottom end of
the reds list – fitting for a neighbourhood
restaurant as down to earth as this.
Booking advisable; essential weekend. Children
admitted. Tables outdoors (5, pavement).

Camden Town & Chalk Farm

★ El Parador

245 Eversholt Street, NW1 1BA (7387 2789,
www.elparadorlondon.com). Mornington Crescent
tube. **Tapas served** noon-3pm, 6-11pm Mon-
Thur; noon-3pm, 6-11.30pm Fri; 6-11.30pm Sat;
6.30-9.30pm Sun. **Tapas** £4-£7.50. **Credit** MC, V.
El Parador's dated interior and paper tablecloths
may not promise great things, but the menu
certainly does – and what's more, it delivers. The
40-strong list of tapas (to say nothing of the
specials scrawled on a blackboard) is best
considered at leisure over a dish of romanesco de
almendras y pipas tostadas: a sweet, crunchy blend
of tomatoes, crushed almonds, sunflower and
pumpkin seeds, spiked with chilli and garlic and
served with fragrant wedges of rosemary bread.
The rest of the menu is equally inventive: slow
roast pork belly with fennel seeds and garlic, say;
or roasted beetroot with spinach, white beans,
horseradish cream and smoked paprika. More
conventional dishes are cooked with equal self
assurance. Both the smoky-tasting pan-fried
chipirones (baby squid), and the thickly sliced
chorizo (sautéed with brandy and paired with
slivers of chargrilled red pepper), were deliciously
plump and tender. Service is as charming as it is
attentive; as we dithered over the compact but
carefully assembled wine list, our waiter poured out
enormous 'tasters' of the reds under discussion. For
afters, own-made flan de naranja had a deliciously
bittersweet edge, while cheesecake of the day was
a coconut and white chocolate concoction, studded
with chunks of dark chocolate – dense, delicious,
but alas, too rich to finish.
Babies and children admitted. Bookings accepted
for 3 or more only. Separate room for parties,
seats 30. Tables outdoors (12, garden). **Map 27 D3**.

Crouch End

La Bota

31 Broadway Parade, N8 9DB (8340 3082,
www.labota.co.uk). Finsbury Park tube/rail then
91, W7 bus. **Lunch served** noon-2.30pm Mon-
Fri; noon-3pm Sat. **Dinner served** 6-11pm
Mon-Thur; 6-11.30pm Fri, Sat. **Meals served**
noon-11pm Sun. **Main courses** £7.50-£12.75.
Tapas £2.65-£4.50. **Credit** MC, V.
There are no surprises in store at this unassuming
neighbourhood restaurant, culinary or otherwise.
Traditional tapas dominate the menu, guitar-
plucking Gypsy Kings-style songs play on rotation,
and the sunny-yellow walls are adorned with
tasteful prints from modern masters (an all-Spanish
line-up, naturally). On our last visit, even the
illegibly scribbled specials board bore a whiff of
déjà vu – most dishes seemed like slightly tweaked
renditions of those on the lengthy main menu. As
a dependable local eaterie, though, La Bota is a
success. Service is efficient and obliging, delivering
a quick succession of competently cooked classics:
rabbit and celery casserole; a filling, meaty fabada
(white beans with pork, morcilla and chorizo);
sliced aubergine with manchego and creamy white
sauce; and tender-tentacled baby squid, cooked
with red pepper, chilli, tomato and wine. Not every
dish was stellar (sautéed spinach with chickpeas,
garlic and onions was unpleasantly watery), but the
inexpensive wine list (containing plenty of bottles
under £15) soothed over any jarring notes. Judging
by the turnover of tables and contented hum of
conversation, the formula suits locals perfectly; we
can't see things changing round here any time soon.
Babies and children welcome: high chairs. Booking
advisable dinner Fri, Sat. Takeaway service.

El Faro. See p247.

Thai

Given that London's Thai population is relatively small, the city's collection of Thai restaurants is impressive both in scope and number. Sadly, the vast bulk of venues offer a dumbed-down version of the cuisine, where more expensive authentic ingredients are substituted (garden peas commonly replacing pea aubergines) and fiery flavours are translated into sickly-sweet sauces. Such establishments pepper London's high streets and the rooms above pubs. We've ignored them here, instead concentrating on quality. Top of the Thai tree is **Nahm** where Australian David Thompson creates inspired dishes based on his profound knowledge of the cuisine. However, you don't need to pay hotel prices to get superb Thai cooking. We also give red-star ratings to the moderately priced **Chaopraya Eat-Thai** and Alan Yau's tremendously popular **Busaba Eathai** chain. Also worth noting: stylish newcomer **Rosa's** of Brick Lane made the finals of our Cheap Eats award.

Central

Belgravia

Mango Tree
46 Grosvenor Place, SW1X 7EQ (7823 1888, www.mangotree.org.uk). Victoria tube/rail. **Lunch served** noon-3pm Mon-Sat. **Dinner served** 6-11pm Mon-Wed; 6-11.30pm Thur-Sat. **Meals served** noon-10.30pm Sun. **Main courses** £12.50-£26. **Set lunch** £17 2 courses, £20 3 courses. **Credit** AmEx, DC, MC, V.
The vast dining hall at Mango Tree has high ceilings, a long banquette and evenly distributed tables. The effect, when combined with the simple dark-wood decor and Asian-inspired tableware, is reminiscent of a resort restaurant in South-east Asia (albeit a slightly tired looking example). Popular with workers from nearby offices, the restaurant and cocktail bar are often noisy and bustling at night. However, the menu is enormous and over-ambitious – and the cooking suffers because of it. On our visit 'lobster special' and 'special new' menus were available alongside the already extensive carte. The result was an incoherent mix of successes and failures. Green papaya salad was easily the best dish, refreshingly spicy with clean flavours, if a bit too sweet. Pork and coriander-stuffed squid and braised beef in penang curry from the 'special new' menu were very disappointing, featuring syrupy sweet, poorly balanced sauces and dry meat. Stick to what the restaurant does best: simple dishes with fresh ingredients, such as seared tuna with dried chilli and lemongrass, or stir-fried beef fillet with ginger, garlic and spicy soy sauce. Staff are sweet, but service can get haphazard when things are busy.
Babies and children welcome: high chairs. Booking advisable. Disabled: toilet. Dress: smart casual. Takeaway service. **Map 15 H9.**

★ Nahm (100)
The Halkin, Halkin Street, SW1X 7DJ (7333 1234, www.nahm.como.bz). Hyde Park Corner tube. **Lunch served** noon-2.30pm Mon-Fri. **Dinner served** 7-10.45pm Mon-Sat; 7-9.45pm Sun. **Main courses** £11-£16.50. **Set lunch** £30 3 courses. **Set dinner** £55 3 courses. **Credit** AmEx, DC, MC, V.
This elegant hotel dining room in gold and bronze tones feels opulent yet unfussy and is ideal for a special date. Tables for two look out over an enviable, well-manicured garden, and the opportunity to share rare dishes of startling flavour combinations makes for a memorable evening. Salad of chicken with crisp samphire, banana flower and nutty palourdes clams was exactly what you hope would come from David Thompson's kitchen: an inspired composition of tasty ingredients. Even so, it was outclassed by the sheer quality of smoky beef stir-fried with oyster sauce, onions and basil. The only minor duff note in our meal was still nice: a bland noodle salad with half a prawn on top, delicate egg basket garnish, and scant sweet and sour sauce. Plenty of steamed rice supplied in large bowls lends a sense of generosity not so prevalent in many Thai restaurants, but at these prices, you're right to expect a feast. Our special set dinner package booked via the internet included an excellent bottle of Alsatian pinot gris that matched the food perfectly. For dessert: another plate of intrigues, including crisp set tiles of pandan-flavoured agar, ethereal coconut cream, a mound of delicate tapioca pearls and tiny sweet-potato fritters. Service was kind, though we had trouble getting attention at bill time.
Available for hire. Babies and children welcome: high chairs; nappy-changing facilities (hotel). Booking advisable. Disabled: toilet. Dress: smart casual. Separate room for parties, seats 30. **Map 9 G9.**

Covent Garden

Thai Square
166 Shaftesbury Avenue, WC2H 8JB (7836 7600). Covent Garden or Tottenham Court Road tube. **Lunch served** noon-3pm daily. **Dinner served** 5.30-11pm Mon-Thur; 5.30pm-midnight Fri, Sat; 5.30-10.30pm Sun. **Set lunch** £8.95 3 courses. **Set meal** £17.95-£23.95 4 courses. **Main courses** £6.50-£22. **Credit** AmEx, MC, V.
The spacious Shaftesbury Avenue dining room is a pleasant outpost of this popular and dependable chain. Get a seat by the window and watch the world go by as you make your way through the extensive menu. Popular Thai dishes are the mainstay, along with a few Chinese-influenced guest-stars seemingly included to appease the tourist traffic. In another nod to the wide audience it attracts, Thai Square serves more vegetarian-friendly choices than many competitors. We headed directly to the purely Thai dishes – and they didn't disappoint. Duck salad with mint, roasted ground rice, chillies, fish sauce and lime was brilliantly spicy, and the meat was perfectly cooked. We also enjoyed a delightfully light and airy monkfish green curry, which was dotted with pea aubergines, bamboo shoots and liquorice-tasting thai basil: the flavours delicate enough to allow the fresh fish to shine. A papaya salad with cashews was overpowered by elderly green beans and giant sticks of very mature carrots, which detracted from the sour papaya. Reasonably priced three-course lunch menus make Thai Square a good spot for a midday meeting.
Babies and children welcome: high chairs. Booking advisable Fri, Sat. Disabled: toilet. Takeaway service. **Map 18 D3.**
For branches see index.

Marylebone

★ Busaba Eathai (100)
8-13 Bird Street, W1U 1BU (7518 8080). Bond Street tube. **Meals served** noon-11pm Mon-Thur; noon-11.30pm Fri, Sat; noon-10pm Sun. **Main courses** £5.50-£10.90. **Credit** AmEx, MC, V.
Has anyone told Alan Yau that the Thai generally don't eat with chopsticks? We can't help feeling that their routine supply on Busaba's communal tables (forks and spoons appear when food arrives) spreads ignorance. But there's no doubt this quality chain attracts an international crowd; customers on our visit included Indian families, Italian babes and Essex builders. The spacious Bird Street and smaller, quieter Store Street branches are, we feel, superior to the Wardour Street original, although the latter has undergone refurbishment. Busaba's iconic metres of smooth, shiny wood are brightened at Bird Street with floating gerberas and tea lights, wafting incense, and an expansive view of white tiles. The menu is tweaked occasionally (we long for the return of mooli omelette), but perennial favourites include Thai-style calamares; prawn pomelo with proper betel leaves; morning glory with yellow bean, garlic and chilli; and the cashew and coconut cookies that are included with the tisanes. Smoky grilled aubergine arrived pretty as a picture topped with toasted coconut, chilli and fresh mint. Fresh chillies and green peppercorns added heat to a light stir-fry of seasoned cod fillet (at £9.70 among the pricier main courses). A jasmine smoothie was expectedly fragrant and surprisingly crunchy, thanks to blended passion-fruit seeds. We've received complaints about service here, but in our experience it's usually friendly and swift.
Babies and children admitted. Bookings not accepted. Disabled: toilet. Takeaway service. **Map 9 G6.**
For branches see index.

★ Chaopraya Eat-Thai
22 St Christopher's Place, W1U 1NP (7486 0777, www.eatthai.net). Bond Street tube. **Meals served** noon-11pm daily. **Main courses** £10.50-£23.95. **Set lunch** £12.95 bento box. **Set dinner** £25-£35 per person (minimum 2-6) 3-4 courses. **Credit** AmEx, MC, V.
Gold and silver panels, gilded mirrors, and bold wallpaper of red roses lend a sense of opulence to the intimate, serene ground-floor dining room of this cosseting spot. A staircase at the end leads down to a much larger, if low-ceilinged, basement area with kitchen, waiting staff and customers happily humming. The menu is short on vegetable side dishes, but has three main courses suitable for vegetarians. Chefs will also happily make tofu pad thai on request. A stir-fry of juicy tenderised pork chunks with green peppercorns, kaffir lime leaves, basil and chilli was delightfully simple yet harmonious, and a flourish of bright-white coconut cream finished a luxurious red curry of roast duck, fresh grapes and tropical fruits. Monsoon Valley red wine (a blend of Thailand's indigenous pokdum grape and shiraz) was, as the wine list suggested, the perfect accompaniment. Unusually good too was thai pancake with young coconut ice-cream, but there were a couple of letdowns. Chaopraya cakes of crab and taro (highlighted as a special recipe) were firm and drab, while banana and sticky toffee pudding was too much like banana cake with caramel sauce.

After a slow start (with gracious apologies) service was charming and efficient, the black-clad staff weaving their way expertly through the busy, tightly packed space.

Available for hire. Babies and children welcome: high chairs. Takeaway service. Vegetarian menu. **Map 9 G6.**

Mayfair

★ Patara

3&7 Maddox Street, W1S 2QB (7499 6008, www.pataralondon.com). Oxford Circus tube. **Lunch served** noon-2.30pm, **dinner served** 5.30-10.30pm Mon-Fri. **Meals served** noon-10.30pm Sat, Sun. **Main courses** £6.75-£19.95. **Set lunch** £11.95-£14.95 2 courses. **Credit** AmEx, DC, MC, V.

Patara is a chain in the same way that Harvey Nichols is a chain – it's a reliable purveyor of top-quality fare. Outposts are popping up in smart capitals around the world. The sleek wood-lined, anonymous restaurant could be anywhere; it's all subtle lighting, perfect service and pretty table settings. In contrast, the food is creative and distinctive (as well as being expertly presented), with exotic meats a highlight; unusually for a Thai venue, knives are provided to tackle such meats. An amuse bouche of watermelon squares with a pile of sugared fish flakes was minimalist yet bold, nicely awakening the palate. Elegant starters like Thai green aubergines stuffed with warm crab (accented with liquorice-scented thai basil and dotted with sharp minced shallots and fish roe) epitomise the balance and restraint shown by the kitchen. Slow-braised beef in coconut reduction was exquisite; the flavourful meat melted in the mouth and was perfectly matched with the sweet coconut. Rather than traditional kaffir lime leaves, lime peel was diced and scattered on top, lending a modern boldness. Patara does a brisk trade in business lunches, and has fairly-priced deals costing under £15 for two courses. A treat.

Available for hire, up to 45 . Babies and children admitted. Booking advisable. Takeaway service. Vegetarian menu. **Map 9 J6.** **For branches see index.**

West

Bayswater

Nipa

Royal Lancaster Hotel, Lancaster Terrace, W2 2TY (7262 6737, www.niparestaurant.co.uk). Lancaster Gate tube. **Bar Open** 8am-11pm daily. *Restaurant* **Lunch served** noon-2pm Mon-Fri. **Dinner served** 6.30-10.30pm Mon-Sat. **Main courses** £7.85-£14. **Set meal** £27-£32 4 courses. **Credit** AmEx, DC, MC, V.

Nipa provides the type of anonymous quality and luxury beloved of frequent business travellers. To reach the first-floor dining room, you must navigate the lobby and bar of the Royal Lancaster Hotel, an uninspired 1960s concrete skyscraper. But the intimacy of the wood-panelled dining room, with a spectacular floor-to-ceiling window overlooking Hyde Park, will soon make you forget you're in a hotel. The menu holds few surprises, but the quality is high. A thai omelette with basil and chilli was brought alive with the sparky accent of salty pickled turnips, which also lent a chewy texture. Beef red curry was rich and flavourful, yet didn't merit the menu's three-chilli heat warning. Spicy prawn salad, however, showed the kitchen had no fear of proper heat; chillies competed with lemongrass and shredded green mango to dominate an impressive appetite-whetter. Deep-fried fish with shredded chicken and shiitake mushrooms combined with a sweet rich sauce to create an unusual, satisfying wintry dish. In contrast, crispy soft-shell crab with mango salad was a letdown, the delicate crab flavour obscured by heavy batter, and we failed to find any mango. Service was impeccable – kind, interested, efficient.

Available for hire. Babies and children welcome: high chairs; nappy-changing facilities (in hotel). Booking essential Fri, Sat. Disabled: toilet (in hotel). Dress: smart casual. Vegetarian menu. **Map 8 D6.**

Tawana

3 Westbourne Grove, W2 4UA (7229 3785, www.tawana.co.uk). Bayswater tube. **Lunch served** noon-3pm, **dinner served** 6-11pm Mon-Sat. **Meals served** noon-10pm Sun. **Main courses** £5.75-£19.95. **Set meal** £15.95 2 courses. **Minimum** £10 per person (food only). **Credit** MC, V.

Watch the world march by from the large front window of this pleasant, friendly restaurant in Westbourne Grove. Plants, carved wood and bamboo chairs lend a light, bright feeling to the somewhat scruffy dining room. Tawana has a loyal Thai following, which bodes well for the food. A pork broth soup with pieces of tofu and minced pork meatballs was a tasty and simple affair – the sort of homely thing you'd like your mother to make if you were ill. However, not everything here is as comforting. A fish curry was disappointing: the fish ('sole', said the server) was so heavily battered and fried that it was robbed of any flavour; the dish arrived drowning in a spicy red-curry sauce filled with pea aubergines, red peppers, coconut shoots (tasting like a softer version of bamboo shoots), basil and fresh peppercorns. The waste of the fine fish left us wishing we'd chosen one of the meat-free options from the extensive vegetarian menu. Still, Tawana hits the right notes more often than not, and the welcoming service and authentic ingredients will keep us coming back.

Babies and children admitted. Booking advisable. Separate room for parties, seats 50. Takeaway service; delivery service (over £10 within W2). Vegetarian menu. **Map 7 B6.**

Mantanah. See p254.

Shepherd's Bush

★ Esarn Kheaw

314 Uxbridge Road, W12 7LJ (8743 8930, www.esarnkheaw.com). Shepherd's Bush Market tube/207, 260, 283 bus. **Lunch served** noon-3pm Mon-Fri. **Dinner served** 6-11pm daily. **Main courses** £7.95-£10.95. **Credit** MC, V.

Esarn Kheaw won't win any beauty contests, but its food is divine. The dark dining room – mint-green walls complete with beams, and flamboyant chandeliers laden with plastic hanging flowers – is an odd, cave-like space. The earthy 'off' flavours of north-eastern Thailand are the speciality here. They're rarely found in London, but luckily, this much-acclaimed restaurant (which has been trading since the early 1990s) compromises for no one. Try the own-made cured pork sausages, for instance; they have a pungent earthiness something like French andouillettes, but also a bold sourness that is ideally offset by the accompanying peanuts and fresh ginger slices. A spicy fish dip with fresh vegetables was another example of north-eastern gold. The warm, murky fish-based sauce packs a punch, exuding a fragrant 'off' flavour that makes a perfect foil to the sweet raw vegetables (including carrots and cucumbers) served alongside. Crispy fried pomfret was superbly cooked too, and liberally sprinkled with fresh thai basil. One warning: avoid non-Thai dishes. As a relic from another time, this very friendly restaurant still serves instant coffee.
Babies and children welcome: high chairs. Booking advisable. Takeaway service. **Map 20 B1**.

South West
Fulham

Blue Elephant

4-6 Fulham Broadway, SW6 1AA (7385 6595, www.blueelephant.com). Fulham Broadway tube. **Lunch served** noon-2.30pm Mon-Sat; noon, 2.30pm Sun. **Dinner served** 6.30-11.30pm Mon-Sat; 6.30-10.30pm Sun. **Main courses** £11.90-£28. **Set buffet** (lunch Sun) £25. **Credit** AmEx, DC, MC, V.

Part of an international chain, Blue Elephant likes to style itself as the Thai establishment for everyone, but it is particularly popular with well-off families, groups and those new to the cuisine. It's not difficult to see why: smiling staff in traditional costume welcome visitors into a dining room disguised as an exotic tropical garden, complete with lily ponds, walkways and waterfalls. The extensive menu, including all the mainstays of Thai cuisine as well as lesser-known dishes, offers several set options that can help moderate your spend – the carte can be expensive. There are even discounts when Chelsea FC is playing at home. The food is visually striking and beautifully presented, adorned with delicately carved vegetables. At times, however, it can be bland, as the attempt to please as many people as possible sometimes tempers the authentic Thai fieriness. Nua nam tok (grilled beef salad) featured buttery, high-quality fillet, but the accompanying sauce only offered a hint of the lip-tingling fire of 'mouse dropping' chillies, the smallest and hottest in Thai cuisine. Some may find the food too westernised and the jungle vibe too gimmicky, but Blue Elephant provides a pleasant introduction to Thai cooking.
Babies and children welcome: crayons; high chairs; nappy-changing facilities. Booking advisable Sun lunch. Disabled: toilet. Entertainment: face painting Sun lunch. Takeaway service. **Map 13 B13**.

Saran Rom

Waterside Tower, The Boulevard, Imperial Wharf, Townmead Road, SW6 2UB (7751 3111, www.saranrom.com). Fulham Broadway tube then 391, C3 bus. **Lunch served** noon-3pm, **dinner served** 6-11pm Tue-Thur. **Main courses** £13-£19. **Set dinner** £35 per person (minimum 2) 3 courses. **Credit** AmEx, MC, V.

It took an optimistic mind to plant Saran Rom in the midst of Imperial Wharf, a fairly soulless modern development overlooking the Thames. This fancier offshoot of the Blue Elephant chain takes its design cue from the 19th-century Bangkok palace of the same name. The nicely laid-out and stylish multi-level dining room (all reproduction teak furniture and bold silks) has views of the river, and the kitchen produces well-prepared and attractively presented (if pricey) food. Saran Rom's version of the classic tom yam soup was a balanced medley of all that is key to Thai cuisine; lemongrass flavours the prawn broth, along with galangal, coriander and mushrooms, while two enormous and beautifully cooked prawns take centre stage. These were served with heads and tails on (aesthetics is important here), but were awkward to eat. A generous portion of tofu pad thai was bland; regional dishes – like a southern massaman dish of braised lamb in a spicy broth – are far more pleasing. The outdoor terrace is the perfect place to enjoy a glass of wine with such an elegant meal.
Babies and children welcome: high chairs. Disabled: lift; toilet. Separate rooms for parties, seating 8, 25, 35 and 110. Tables outdoors (28, riverside patio). Takeaway service. Vegetarian menu. **Map 21 A2**.

Parsons Green

Sukho

855 Fulham Road, SW6 5HJ (7371 7600). Parsons Green tube. **Lunch served** noon-3pm, **dinner served** 6.30-11pm daily. **Main courses** £9.95-£16.95. **Set lunch** £7.95 1 course, £10.95 2 courses. **Credit** AmEx, MC, V.

The scent of lemongrass wafts pleasantly through the intimate dining room of Fulham's star Thai venue. Everything at Sukho is discreet, delicate and charming – from the potted plants on the table, to the beautiful carved wooden wall screen and the formal bow with which you're greeted. Luckily, the food follows suit, with the extensive menu offering intriguing and subtle takes on Thai classics. A medley of dumplings provides a perfect opportunity to explore different flavours. The exquisite gemstone-coloured rice noodle packages are folded to look like flowers; they encase a joyful range of flavours, jumping from fish to prawn to meat, enlivened with chillies, peanuts and sweet or sour tangs. Crisp tempura of tofu and daikon was a novel preparation of ingredients that could have been plain, but was brightened by a sweet chilli sauce. The classics are excellent here, though they tend to be sweet rather than sour or truly hot. Morning glory stir-fried with chilli was fresh and flavourful, with high-quality ingredients. Rice

noodles stir-fried with beansprouts and egg offered a nice subtle note. Desserts are well worth a look too. Low lighting, discreet service and well-presented food make Sukho ideal for a date.
Babies and children admitted. Booking advisable. Takeaway service. Vegetarian menu.
For branch (Suk Saran) see index.

South East
Blackheath

Laicram

1 Blackheath Grove, SE3 0DD (8852 4710). Blackheath rail. **Lunch served** noon-2.30pm, **dinner served** 6-11pm Tue-Sun. **Main courses** £5-£14. **Credit** MC, V.

Laicram is the sort of relaxed, reliable and utterly unpretentious restaurant that every neighbourhood should have. To the tune of Thai pop ballads, you dine from a fairly standard menu that's accented with a few specials from the north-east of the country. Sure, the surroundings aren't glamorous. The decor is all 1970s suburban: dropped ceiling, dark carpet, stuccoed walls (all of which are showing their age), plus the additional Thai twists of portraits of the Thai royal family and carved wooden screens. But look beyond these various stylistic cobwebs to the food, and you won't be disappointed. Tom kha gai, the classic rich coconut milk broth with slices of chicken, was a perfectly balanced version: tangy from lemon, spicy from chilli, and sharp from generous slices of galangal. Fish cakes knocked the socks off standard London versions, offering real fishiness that made an ideal contrast to a honeyed cucumber relish. A north-eastern-style grilled chicken lacked crisp skin, but was nicely seasoned and cooked. Only some stir-fried prawns with chilli and onions were unremarkable. Friendly service and an authentic menu make Laicram popular and dependable.
Available for hire. Babies and children admitted. Booking essential Fri, Sat. Takeaway service. Vegetarian menu.

New Cross

★ Thailand

15 Lewisham Way, SE14 6PP (8691 4040). New Cross or New Cross Gate tube/rail. **Lunch served** 11am-2.30pm Mon-Fri. **Dinner served** 5-11.30pm daily. **Main courses** £3.95-£10. **Set meal** (lunch, 5-7pm) £3.95 2 courses. **Credit** MC, V.

Decor that's about as dismal as the endless traffic outside shouldn't distract you from the high-quality food within Thailand. Faux-stone tiles, a mock-tiki bar awning in the corner and dull paintings

Rosa's. See p254.

We've tried to give the most useful Thai food terms here, including variant spellings. However, these are no more than English transliterations of the original Thai script, and so are subject to considerable variation. Word divisions vary as well: thus, kwaitiew, kwai teo and guey teow are all acceptable spellings for noodles.

Thailand abandoned chopsticks in the 19th century in favour of chunky steel spoons and forks. Using your fingers is usually fine, and essential if you order satay sticks or spare ribs.

USEFUL TERMS

Khantoke: originally a north-eastern banquet conducted around a low table while seated on traditional triangular cushions – some restaurants have khantoke seating.
Khing: with ginger.
Op or **ob:** baked.
Pad, pat or **phad:** stir-fried.
Pet or **ped:** hot (spicy).
Prik: chilli.
Tod, tort, tord or **taud:** deep-fried.
Tom: boiled.

STARTERS

Khanom jeep or **ka nom geeb:** dim sum. Little dumplings of minced pork, bamboo shoots and water chestnuts, wrapped in an egg and rice (wun tun) pastry, then steamed.
Khanom pang na koong: prawn sesame toast.
Kratong thong: tiny crispy batter cups ('top hats') filled with mixed vegetables and/or minced meat.
Miang: savoury appetisers with a variety of constituents (mince, ginger, peanuts, roasted coconut, for instance), wrapped in betel leaves.
Popia or **porpia:** spring rolls.
Tod mun pla or **tauk manpla:** small fried fish cakes (should be lightly rubbery in consistency) with virtually no 'fishy' smell or taste.

SOUPS

Poh tak or **tom yam potag:** hot and sour mixed seafood soup.
Tom kha gai or **gai tom kar:** hot and sour chicken soup with coconut milk.
Tom yam or **tom yum:** a hot and sour soup, smelling of lemongrass. **Tom yam koong** is with prawns; **tom yam gai** with chicken; **tom yam hed** with mushrooms.

RICE

Khao, kow or **khow:** rice.
Khao nao: sticky rice.
Khao pat: fried rice.
Khao suay: steamed rice.
Pat khai: egg-fried rice.

SALADS

Laab or **larb:** minced and cooked meat incorporating lime juice and other ingredients like ground rice and herbs.
Som tam: a popular cold salad of grated green papaya.
Yam or **yum:** refers to any tossed salad, hot or cold, but it is often hot and sour, flavoured with lemon and chilli. This type of yam is originally from the north-east of Thailand, where the Laotian influence is greatest.
Yam nua: hot and sour beef salad.
Yam talay: hot and sour seafood salad (served cold).

NOODLES

Generally speaking, noodles are eaten in greater quantities in the north of Thailand. There are many types of **kwaitiew** or **guey teow** noodles. Common ones include **sen mee:** rice vermicelli; **sen yai** (river rice noodles): a broad, flat, rice noodle; **sen lek:** a medium flat noodle, used to make pad Thai; **ba mee:** egg noodles; and **woon sen** (cellophane noodle): transparent vermicelli made from soy beans or other pulses. These are often prepared as stir-fries.

The names of the numerous noodle dishes depend on the combination of other ingredients. Common dishes are:
Khao soi: chicken curry soup with egg noodles; a Burmese/Thai dish, referred to as the national dish of Burma.
Mee krob or **mee grob:** sweet crispy fried vermicelli.
Pad si-ewe or **cee eaw:** noodles fried with mixed meat in soy sauce.
Pad Thai: stir-fried noodles with shrimps (or chicken and pork), beansprouts and salted turnips, garnished with ground peanuts.

CURRIES

Thai curries differ quite markedly from the Indian varieties. Thais cook them for a shorter time, and use thinner sauces. Flavours and ingredients are different too. There are several common types of curry paste; these are used to name the curry, with the principal ingredients listed thereafter.
Gaeng, kaeng or **gang:** the generic name for curry. Yellow curry is the mildest; green curry (**gaeng keaw wan** or **kiew warn**) is medium hot and uses green chillies; red curry (**gaeng pet**) is similar, but uses red chillies.
Jungle curry: often the hottest of the curries, made with red curry paste, bamboo shoots and just about anything else to hand, but no coconut cream.
Massaman or **mussaman:** also known as Muslim curry, because it originates from the area along the border with Malaysia where many Thais are Muslims. For this reason, pork is never used. It's a rich but mild concoction, with coconut, potato and some peanuts.
Penang, panaeng or **panang:** a dry, aromatic curry made with 'Penang' curry paste, coconut cream and holy basil.

FISH & SEAFOOD

Hoi: shellfish.
Hor mok talay or **haw mog talay:** steamed egg mousse with seafood.
Koong, goong or **kung:** prawns.
Maw: dried fish belly.

suggest that this is yet another dreary Thai takeaway – but the menu holds treasures. The Thai options include well-prepared classic stir-fries and curries; for more of an adventure, go for the Laotian specials, which offer real treats. The dramatically named angry lamb featured stir-fried meat swimming in a delicious sauce that was thick, sweet and fiery, topped with fresh basil. A duck curry offered the ultimate opportunity for sweet indulgence: perfectly tender thick slices of the bird in lashings of smooth coconut milk enlivened with tomatoes, pineapple and lychees. An otherwise classic pla kung (prawn salad with mint, coriander and spring onions) was let down by slightly undercooked prawns. While Thailand is often quiet, and may not be the ideal place in which to linger over a romantic meal, the bold and varied flavours make it an excellent spot to enjoy an interesting dinner.
Babies and children admitted. Booking essential Fri, Sat. Takeaway service; delivery service (over £10 within 3-mile radius). Vegetarian menu.

South Norwood

★ Mantanah

2 Orton Building, Portland Road, SE25 4UD (8771 1148). Norwood Junction rail. **Lunch served** noon-3pm daily. **Dinner served** 6-11pm Tue-Sun. **Main courses** £6.95-£13.95. **Set dinner** £18 per person (minimum 2) 3 courses, £25 per person (minimum 2) 4 courses. **Set buffet** (lunch Sun) £7.95. **Credit** MC, V.
Mantanah looks like a predictable neighbourhood Thai – the sort of place where you might resort to grabbing a takeaway. The tired yellow and beige paint, dilapidated mobiles suspended from the ceiling, and homemade posters offering a Sunday buffet lunch don't bode well. But don't judge this book by its cover, for the kitchen prepares authentic dishes from a broad range of regional Thai culinary traditions. The friendly staff are happy to guide diners through the extensive menu, some of which is organised geographically. Mantanah's version of fish cakes, the popular Thai street snack of fish and prawn in red curry, will make you renounce your local pub's rubbery imitation. On our visit, the kitchen was out of crab, but the vegetarian substitute 'treasure bags' (white sweet potato and other vegetables in a deep-fried rice paper sack) were deliciously subtle and perfectly matched with pickled cucumber. A light dish of shredded chicken and banana blossom with thai five-spice was an earthy departure from most Thai flavours offered in London. Also from northern Thailand came a divine pork curry dotted with peanuts, pickled garlic, luscious morsels of belly pork, and pork fat so soft it melted.
Available for hire. Babies and children admitted. Booking advisable. Takeaway service. Vegetarian menu.

East
Brick Lane

★ Rosa's NEW

2009 RUNNER-UP BEST NEW CHEAP EATS
12 Hanbury Street, E1 6QR (7247 1093, www.rosaslondon.com). Liverpool Street tube/rail. **Meals served** 11am-10.30pm Mon-Thur, Sun; 11am-11pm Fri, Sat. **Main courses** £5.95-£13.50. **Set lunch** £5.50-£11.50 1 course. **Credit** AmEx, MC, V.
The bamboo panelling of Rosa's small first-floor dining room resembles Busaba's (*see p249*) updating of Thai restaurants, but the room is let down by student bedsit touches like pink-painted walls and small red wooden stools for seats. However, the dimly lit interior and modish black-wood decor of the candle-studded ground floor is lovely. Trendy Spitalfields diners come here; those who haven't booked are squeezed on to the end of other parties' tables. Aside from a few chargrilled dishes, the menu is predominantly made up of stir-fries and curries, ranked from 'mild use of spices' to 'damn hot' – although the pleasing fieriness of a green chicken curry, ringing with

RESTAURANTS

sweet basil, belied its mid-range spice grading. Stunning chargrilled rack of lamb was near charcoal at the edges, yet succulently rare in the centre, but the few blanched cauliflower florets that came with it were cold. A starter of chicken wrapped in pandan leaves seemed overly dry, though this had been cooked with more success on our previous visits. Rosa's needs to improve its consistency, but on a good night it can give Busaba a run for its money.
Available for hire. Babies and children admitted. Booking advisable Fri, Sat. Takeaway service. Vegetarian menu. **Map 12 S5**.

North
Archway

Charuwan
110 Junction Road, N19 5LB (7263 1410). Archway or Tufnell Park tube. **Lunch served** noon-3pm Mon-Fri. **Dinner served** 6-11pm daily. **Main courses** £4.95-£8.95. **Set dinner** £18-£20 per person (minimum 2) 3 courses. **Credit** MC, V.
If you thought this unassuming little restaurant was a run-of-the-mill local, think again. Regulars include some of the country's most respected haute cuisine chefs and a national newspaper's restaurant columnist – all of whom were there on an otherwise quiet Sunday night. You may not be in Chiang Mai, but with Lanna pavilion-style decor, decent, authentic cooking and gracious staff in traditional dress, guests certainly feel removed from Archway. Choosing drinks is made easy with a South African chenin blanc house wine at £12.75. Starters are fairly predictable (fish cakes, spring rolls, satay, mixed platter), as are soups (tom yam, tom kha, poh tak), but chef's specialities include some surprises. Snow prawns – king prawns stuffed with chicken mince and covered with a billowing duvet of egg white – looked like

Thailand's savoury response to lemon meringue pie, yet tasted far better than it sounds. We liked the look of moo sa doong (warm salad of grilled pork with chilli, shallots and lime juice), and enjoyed the clarity of flavours in a dish of fresh white fish steamed with preserved plum and ginger. Simple pad si-ewe (wide rice noodles stir-fried with beef and vegetables) were comforting, if slightly too soft.
Booking advisable. Children admitted. Takeaway service. Vegetarian menu. **Map 26 B2**.

Islington

Isarn
119 Upper Street, N1 1QP (7424 5153). Angel tube/Highbury & Islington tube/rail. **Lunch served** noon-3pm, **dinner served** 6-11pm Mon-Fri. **Meals served** noon-11pm Sat; noon-10.30pm Sun. **Main courses** £6.50-£14.50. **Set lunch** £6.95 bento box. **Credit** AmEx, MC, V.
Slinky, contemporary decor, with dark wood and oversized lampshades, gives Isarn a polished, expensive image, but the menu is surprisingly wallet-friendly. Set lunches, which come in a bento box, are good value, and include a selection of spring rolls or fish cakes, curry, rice and fruit. Don't expect authentic Thai fieriness or superb cooking, but do sample some of the more unusual dishes, along with stalwarts like curries and pad thai – all stylishly presented. Among the starters, betel leaf wraps with crispy duck and pomelo are a must-try, as are the traditional Thai desserts, which rarely appear on restaurant menus. Delicate coconut-cream pudding with taro and lotus seed comes wrapped in a hand-shaped pandan leaf case. Less sweet western choices include an enjoyable dense lemon cheesecake topped with strawberry ice-cream. Isarn's narrow dining room is often packed with twenty- and thirtysomethings, probably due to its prime location on Upper Street

and the reasonable prices – which also help excuse the otherwise average food. Still, this remains a cut above several local establishments. In summer, try to get a table in the small rear courtyard.
Available for hire. Babies and children admitted. Tables outdoors (6, garden). Takeaway service. **Map 5 O1**.

North West
Kensal

★ Tong Kanom Thai
833 Harrow Road, NW10 5NH (8964 5373). Kensal Rise tube. **Lunch served** noon-3pm Mon-Fri. **Dinner served** 6-10pm Mon-Sat. **Main courses** £4.20-£6.50. **Unlicensed. Corkage** no charge. **Credit** AmEx, MC, V.
The tiny dining room of this friendly, café-like local is packed with knick-knacks and feels so cosy that it's easy to forget the heavy traffic outside. As well as being extremely good value, the food is mostly authentic and flavoursome, with very few slip-ups. We were looking forward to sampling the gaeng pa (jungle curry), but were disappointed by the dry and tough texture of the meat and the lack of complex flavours that make the dish one of the highlights of Thai cuisine. Popular fare such as stir-fried chicken with fresh holy basil was more successful, along with a suitably hot yam nua (grilled beef salad). To finish, expect the likes of sticky rice with mango. With no dishes priced above £7 and no alcohol licence, Tong Kanom Thai does a brisk trade as a takeaway joint, but it also attracts a mix of locals and diners from nearby neighbourhoods, who seem keen on splurging at the off-licence next door. On our visit we spotted some Veuve Cliquot champagne at the next table.
Babies and children admitted. Takeaway service; delivery service (over £10 within 1-mile radius). Vegetarian menu.

RESTAURANTS

Turkish

London's Turkish establishments are for the most part simple grill restaurants that meat lovers will adore. With just a few exceptions (the **Tas** chain springs to mind), the capital has yet to be offered the wealth of vegetable- and grain-based dishes that are served in Turkey; neither has it been treated to the varied dairy foods that go with them. Recent years have seen the opening of more upmarket restaurants (**Pomegranate** in Richmond, and the City branches of **Haz** and **Kazan**), but still the tried-and-tested formula of meat, bread or rice and salad, plus a few vegetable dishes, prevails. When it's done well, as at **19 Numara Bos Cirrik**, **Mangal Ocakbaşı** and **Petek**, it is delightful – healthy too. Yet the success of **Moro** (*see p239*) and its cookbooks show that Londoners are keen to explore the intriguing ingredients and flavour combinations of the near east. We'd like to see more Turkish eateries embracing the country's diversity of dishes and promoting its traditional regional cuisines – much in the way that Indian and Chinese restaurateurs have done with much success.

Central

Bloomsbury

Tas

22 Bloomsbury Street, WC1B 3QJ (7637 4555). Holborn or Tottenham Court Road tube. **Meals served** noon-11.30pm daily. **Main courses** £6.95-£12.95. **Set meze** £8.65-£18.65 per person (minimum 2). **Credit** AmEx, MC, V.

Tas's lengthy menus do more than most to emphasise that Anatolian cuisine is one of the richest and most varied in the world. Almost 40 starters are offered at this cheerfully busy eaterie near the British Museum – from a soup of mussels, celery, coriander and ginger, to deep-fried salmon with sour rose sauce – making diners feel almost guilty ordering houmous, dolma or börek, regardless of how delicious they are. Kalamar were coated in feather-light batter, though the squid was not perfectly tender or improved by its pasty bitter walnut sauce. Pırasalı, a vegetarian main course of lentils, chickpeas, leeks and tomato, was reminiscent of the bland store-cupboard stews you might knock up in a bedsit, even with its red couscous and yoghurt accompaniments. However, chicken şiş and simple feta cheese salad were much more satisfying; we also liked the delicious dips, piquant olives and seeded breads. There's an extensive array of fish and rice dishes, pasta and casseroles in addition to the expected grills, making Tas a good choice for parties of friends and colleagues – all will find something they're happy to order, and staff are adept at dealing with groups. *Babies and children welcome: high chairs. Booking advisable Fri, Sat. Disabled: toilet. Separate room for parties, seats 80. Tables outdoors (14, pavement).* **Map 18 D1.** **For branches see index.**

City

Haz

9 Cutler Street, E1 7DJ (7929 7923, www.haz restaurant.co.uk). Aldgate tube or Liverpool Street tube/rail. **Meals served** 11.30am-11.30pm daily. **Main courses** £7-£13. **Set meal** £9.25 2 courses, £18.95 3 courses incl coffee. **Set meze** £6.45. **Credit** AmEx, MC, V.

There's something of the Tas chain about this place, and it's not just in the name. Both enterprises aim to bring a little Zone-1 formality to a cuisine that, at least in London, is usually served on paper tablecloths in the rather more insalubrious likes of Dalston and Harringay. And, up to a point, both succeed. The Cutler Street branch is the smartest of the three Haz restaurants in the City, and may even be the smartest Turkish spot in the capital. Blessed with high ceilings, picture windows and white tablecloths, it's a handsome room, albeit in an uncomplicated and not especially memorable way. You could say the same about the food: Turkish staples delivered without flourish. The menu is pretty lengthy, with standard starters – houmous, cacik, surprisingly airy falafel – supplemented by a few salads, a handful of soups and some more unusual dishes. Mains encompass casseroles and a large array of fish and seafood, from plain-as-day grilled salmon to steamed monkfish, but most diners seem to head directly for the traditional meat kebabs. It's all fine if you're passing, but perhaps not worth a special trip. *Available for hire. Babies and children welcome: high chairs. Booking advisable Mon-Fri. Takeaway service.* **Map 12 R6. For branches see index.**

Fitzrovia

Istanbul Meze

100 Cleveland Street, W1T 6NS (7387 0785, www.istanbulmeze.co.uk). Great Portland Street or Warren Street tube. **Meals served** noon-11pm Mon-Thur; noon-midnight Fri, Sat. **Dinner served** 5-11pm Sun. **Main courses** £7-£12. **Set lunch** £8.90 2 courses incl coffee. **Set dinner** £11.90 2 courses. **Set meze** £20. **Credit** AmEx, MC, V.

Hidden away on an uninteresting street at the wrong end of Fitzrovia, Istanbul Meze doesn't look promising. Surprise: it's a likeable spot, with a reliable if unspectacular kitchen and keen, helpful staff. The starters are worthwhile. Falafel is agreeably tender and subtle, thanks to the use of a preponderance of broad beans. The houmous, also seemingly made on site, is created to a similarly winning recipe; sturdier options include sucuk (spicy beef sausage) that carries a pleasing tang. The main courses are less characterful but pretty well-executed. Cooked over a charcoal grill at the back of the room, the familiar meaty grills – try the Istanbul special, a jumble of chicken şiş and lamb köfte over an aubergine paste, served with yoghurt and rice to one side – are

supplemented by a few more unexpected seafood dishes (a kebab made with swordfish and king prawns, for instance). It's all delivered promptly by efficient waiters in a simple but attractive room brightened by a string of coloured lamps (unusually, there's also a bar in the basement). Worth considering. *Babies and children admitted. Booking essential weekends. Tables outdoors (3, pavement). Takeaway service. Vegetarian menu.* **Map 3 J4.**

Özer

5 Langham Place, W1B 3DG (7323 0505, www.sofra.co.uk). Oxford Circus tube. *Bar* **Open** noon-11pm daily. *Restaurant* **Meals served** noon-midnight daily. **Main courses** £8.95-£23.95. **Set meals** (noon-6pm) £12.95; (6pm-midnight) £14.95. *Both* **Credit** AmEx, MC, V.

Chef-patron Hüseyin Özer founded the Sofra group and is something of an ambassador for Turkish cuisine, yet this smart bar-restaurant is an east-meets-west affair. The huge menu stretches from fish and chips to a Hakkasan-recipe salad; the variety and lack of Turkish names may be helpful to the many tourists dining here, but is confusing for those wanting to explore Turkish cuisine. Still, as newcomers are told, the kitchen will replace any dish you don't like. There's a cocktail lounge at the front, but we recommend the soft, easy-drinking Yakut red wine (£13.95 a bottle). The sesame-studded pide is nicely hot, brought swiftly to mop up the tahini dip sitting on each table. Scrambled eggs with feta (pastırma or spicy sausage are alternatives) were creamy, so too verdant baby broad beans with yoghurt and coriander. Skewer of juicy, just-right grilled monkfish was simple, but a highlight of our spread. Shame that desserts disappointed: stuffed apricots were chewy and the filling lacked the expected luxurious quality; kazandibi (caramelised milk pudding) was better, but we couldn't taste the tahini promised in the accompanying ice-cream. The welcome and service were much warmer than on previous visits, and the staff were notably good with children. *Available for hire. Babies and children welcome: high chairs. Booking advisable. Disabled: toilet. Tables outdoors (5, pavement). Takeaway service.* **Map 9 H5.**

Marylebone

★ Ishtar

10-12 Crawford Street, W1U 6AZ (7224 2446, www.ishtarrestaurant.com). Baker Street tube. **Meals served** noon-11pm Mon-Thur, Sun; noon-11.30pm Fri, Sat. **Main courses** £7.95-£15.95. **Set lunch** (noon-6pm) £8.95. **Set meal** £20-£25. **Set meze** £6.50. **Credit** MC, V.

Plenty of restaurateurs would be happy to have Ishtar's ground-floor space with its stunning copper-lined open kitchen, elegant carved doors and split-level dining, but the premises extend down to a huge basement area with many more tables and conspiratorial booths set under arches. Although quiet on the evening of our visit, this is a popular place for parties and attracts an upmarket after-work crowd. The list of starters sticks to well-known favourites, but our ıspanak tarator was a cut above the classic, thanks to the almost indulgent freshness of ingredients – all the better served in a large, sinuous bowl. Main course of çupra buğulama (sea bream and vegetables lightly braised in a clay pot) tasted as if it had been cooked in a village by the Mediterranean. İskender kuzu featured huge chunks of succulent lamb, juicy cubes of pide, and tomato sauce reduced to rich, deep fruitiness. Desserts didn't have the same wow-factor when it came to flavour or presentation, but we enjoyed a perky turkish coffee crème brûlée. Next time we'll try the intriguing kestaneli tavuk – grilled chicken with braised chestnuts, dates and vegetables. *Babies and children welcome: high chairs. Booking advisable Thur-Sat. Entertainment: musicians Thur-Sat; belly dancer Fri, Sat. Separate room for parties, seats 120. Tables outdoors (6, pavement). Takeaway service. Vegetarian menu.* **Map 2 F5.**

Mayfair

Sofra

18 Shepherd Street, W1J 7JG (7493 3320, www.sofra.co.uk). Green Park tube. **Meals served** 8.30am-11pm daily. **Main courses** £10.95-£24.95. **Set meze** £12.95 lunch; £14.95 dinner. **Credit** AmEx, MC, V.

Hüseyin Özer's chain has built a decent following, partly due to Özer's knack of opening in areas that kack reliable, casual and reasonably priced eateries. Awash in unremarkable brasseries and sandwich bars, Mayfair's Shepherd Market is one such locale, which is partly why this branch of Sofra is always humming with custom. The formula here is the same as it is elsewhere in the chain: slightly cramped seating, speedy service, a lengthy and by no means exclusively Turkish menu (steaks and fish and chips are both included), and prices that are fair if hardly rock-bottom. The grazing menu, advertised as a 'healthy meal', offers an 11-strong sample of familiar favourites: some tasty (mücver, lamb köfte), some less appetising (falafel is particularly dreary). Otherwise, you may be better off favouring adventure over simplicity; hünkar beğendi (lamb stew served with aubergine) is a more appealing bet than the rather flat kebabs. And it's definitely worth saving room for the milk pudding. You won't find the charisma or the earthiness of north-east London's best Turkish restaurants, but Sofra is a trustworthy option.

Babies and children welcome: high chairs. Booking advisable. Separate rooms for parties, seating 14-40. Tables outdoors (5, pavement). Takeaway service. **Map 9 H8**.
For branches see index.

Pimlico

Kazan

93-94 Wilton Road, SW1V 1DW (7233 7100, www.kazan-restaurant.com). Victoria tube/rail. **Meals served** noon-11pm daily. **Main courses** £11.95-£15.95. **Set meal** (noon-6.30pm) £9.99-£14.95 2 courses. **Credit** MC, V.

Kazan now has a sister restaurant in the City, but this branch, located in the restaurant row of Wilton Road near Victoria, is the original. It's a stylish, decidedly upmarket affair, done up in earthy tones with colourful glass lanterns and hookah pipes. Prices are higher than you'd usually find in north and north-east London venues, of course, but the cooking's good and the surroundings spruce. Food is mainly from the Anatolian and Aegean regions. There's a broad choice of hot and cold meze (including many vegetarian dishes), of which we took full advantage, causing our small table to practically groan under the weight. Own-made tarama, served with plenty of bread, was well flavoured; kabak köftesi (courgette and white cheese fritters) were hot, succulent and spiked with dill. A main course of izmir köfte, a meatball dish from the Aegean coast, was a hearty portion of plump little meatballs scented with ground cumin and served in a tomato sauce. Classic desserts include the likes of apricots stuffed with kaymak (Turkish clotted cream), and the Ottoman-era dish su muhallebisi (a milk pudding flavoured with rosewater) – next time. Service is friendly and professional.

Babies and children welcome: high chairs. Booking advisable Fri, Sat. Disabled: toilet. Separate rooms for parties, seating 30 and 50. Tables outdoors (3, pavement). Takeaway service. **Map 15 J11**.
For branch see index.

West

Notting Hill

Manzara

24 Pembridge Road, W11 3HL (7727 3062). Notting Hill Gate tube. **Meals served** 8am-1am Mon-Wed; 8am-3am Thur-Sat; 9am-midnight Sun. **Main courses** £6.75-£9.95. **Set meal** £13.95 2 courses incl drink. **Credit** MC, V.

Tucked behind Manzara's front takeaway counter, there's a small, bright dining room with a few white-clothed tables. The menu doesn't extend far beyond grill-house staples such as lamb and chicken kebabs, plus standby starters of tarama, houmous and grilled hellim – the latter of which comes hot and smoke-scented from the ocakbaşı. There are also a few non-Turkish dishes, such as fish and chips and an organic beefburger. If you're watching the pennies, the set-menu deal, which includes a choice of starter, main and a drink (a glass of wine or a soft drink), is where to look. Our chicken kebab featured high-quality, mildly spicy meat, served with a perky green salad and rather dull rice. İskender, which combined chargrilled mince patties and whole lamb chunks, was overwhelmed by a fresh tomato sauce, but zinged up with properly tart yoghurt on to which melted spiced butter had been drizzled. Most impressive was a boat-shaped pide, the soft, fluffy bread topped with mozzarella, spinach, tomato sauce, a small mountain of feta and some black olives – an impressive veggie-friendly feast. Service is well-intentioned but can be slow.

Babies and children welcome: high chairs. Booking advisable. Tables outdoors (2, pavement). Takeaway service. **Map 7 A7**.

Tas

RESTAURANTS

West Kensington

★ Best Mangal

104 North End Road, W14 9EX (7610 1050, www.bestmangal.com). West Kensington tube. **Meals served** noon-midnight Mon-Thur; noon-1am Fri, Sat. **Main courses** £8.50-£18. **Credit** MC, V.

Best Mangal and Best Mangal II are sister restaurants on the same strip of road. Both have busy takeaways at the front and easygoing restaurants at the back. Best Mangal is a bit smaller and perhaps even friendlier than Mangal II. On a warm spring evening, it can have the scent and sense of a Mediterranean holiday. There's a broad-ranging menu of hot and cold meze and various skewered and barbecued meats, plus a few yoghurt-sauced dishes, and salads. Our mixed hot meze was indeed mixed, in terms of quality. Fried lamb's liver and the garlicky stuffed mushrooms both received the thumbs up, but too many items – kalamar, börek, hellim – were fried and greasy. Mains, from the ockabaşı, were better. Patlıcan kebab (thick slices of aubergine interspersed with spicy minced lamb patties) had a bewitchingly smoky aroma and

flavour. Yoğhurtlu şiş, the grilled meat taken off the skewer and served in a dish topped with lashings of tomato sauce and a hearty dollop of yoghurt, tasted authentically Turkish. With side dishes of tomato-flavoured rice, excellent saç and pide bread and good olives, you're unlikely to leave hungry. A deservedly popular duo.
Babies and children welcome: high chairs. Booking advisable. Takeaway service. Vegetarian menu. **For branch see index.**

South West

Earlsfield

Kazans

607-609 Garratt Lane, SW18 4SU (8739 0055, www.kazans.com). Earlsfield rail/44, 77, 270 bus. **Meals served** noon-11pm daily. **Main courses** £7.50-£14.95. **Set meal** (noon-8pm) £10 2 courses. **Credit** AmEx, MC, V.

This friendly, family-run restaurant has been gaining a loyal following in Earlsfield since opening in 2004 (Kazans is not to be confused with the Kazan chain, *see p259*). The smoky smell of barbecued meat pervades the large, simply decorated dining room, the walls of which are hung with old black and white family photos. As well as the expected grills, the menu lists a decent selection of cold and hot meze, a few fish dishes and a daily special chalked on a blackboard. Most dishes are classics, ranging from imam bayıldı to incik, although there is some 'international' food such as salmon fillet with lemon and dill. Patlıcan salata was properly smoky-flavoured aubergine: soft in texture, generously proportioned and enlivened with lemon and a tingle of minced raw garlic. Lamb şiş was lean but well-flavoured and stylishly presented with an upturned ramekin of bulgur wheat and a grilled green pepper. There's a decent wine list too, as well as beers such as Leffe and Freedom Organic served at the bar (where you can nip in just for a drink if you choose).
Available for hire. Babies and children welcome: high chairs; nappy changing facilities. Booking advisable weekends. Disabled: toilet. Entertainment: belly dancers (phone for details). Separate rooms for parties, seating 30 and 50. Tables outdoors (4, decking). Takeaway service.

South

Waterloo

Troia

3F Belvedere Road, SE1 7GQ (7633 9309). Waterloo tube/rail. **Meals served** noon-midnight Mon-Sat; noon-10.30pm Sun. **Main courses** £8.25-£12.95. **Set lunch** £8.75 2 courses. **Set meze** £9.95 per person (minimum 2). **Credit** AmEx, MC, V.

Troia's small, dimly lit interior is made intimate with a profusion of coloured-glass chandeliers. The place appears far more roomy than it is, thanks to two massive mirrors. It's close to the London Eye and while there are several other restaurants nearby, Troia holds its own nicely. Despite the name (Ancient Troy is in the west of modern Turkey), the owners are Kurdish but the dishes are mostly similar to those of other London Turkish restaurants, including a wide selection of meze. Of these, kalamar tava (fried squid with walnut sauce, served on rocket leaves with lemon wedges) was hot and fresh from the fryer, the squid complemented by the crunchy walnut sauce. Broad beans served with yoghurt were boosted by bright-red kırmızı biber (chilli flakes). A main course of çoban kavurma (lamb stew with tomatoes and peppers) was served with a spicy red-pepper sauce, but let down by too much salt and rather dull pitta. In contrast, classic adana kebab was well-executed, with juicy minced lamb. A cheery, chatty waiter kept our bread basket topped up unbidden. We were also impressed by the olives and cacik served when we first sat down.
Babies and children welcome: children's menu; high chairs. Booking advisable. Disabled: toilet. Tables outdoors (14, pavement). Takeaway service. Vegetarian menu. **Map 10 M9.**

South East

Dulwich

★ Hisar

51 Lordship Lane, SE22 8EP (8299 2948). East Dulwich rail. **Meals served** 5pm-midnight daily. **Main courses** £4.95-£10. **Set meze** £14.95 per person (minimum 2). **Credit** MC, V.

Lordship Lane is East Dulwich's dining and drinking destination and Hisar is an established favourite. There's a takeaway to one side as well as a substantial, brown-toned restaurant. Here, a large ockabaşı holds pride of place, wafting fragrant smoke and sending forth an endless stream of kebabs (billed as 'Bar-B-Que Pit Specials'), as well as assorted grilled fish dishes. Dull pitta bread and ho-hum olives didn't whet our appetites, but a starter of patlıcan salata, the grilled aubergine accompanied by red capsicum and dill, held promise. Alti ezmeli (chunks of grilled lamb served in a tomato sauce with red and green peppers and herb butter) was rich, well-executed and satisfying. The 'Hisar special' of tender-stewed lamb, wrapped in a parcel of soft aubergine, would bring a smile to the face of any carnivore. There are plenty of vegetarian dishes too, such as börek, stuffed vine leaves and meat-free stews, but most people come here (and Hisar is highly popular) for the family-friendly atmosphere, the hearty portions, reasonable prices and grilled meats galore.
Available for hire. Babies and children welcome: high chairs. Disabled: toilet. Separate room for parties, seats 10. Tables outdoors (4, terrace). Takeaway service. Vegetarian menu. **Map 23 E4.**

Lewisham

★ Meze Mangal

245 Lewisham Way, SE4 1XF (8694 8099, www.meze-mangal.co.uk). St John's rail/Lewisham rail/DLR. **Meals served** noon-2am Mon-Thur; noon-3am Fri, Sat; noon-1am Sun. **Main courses** £7.50-£16. **Set meze** £12.50 (minimum 2); £17.50 (minimum 4). **Credit** MC, V.

Suggesting that Meze Mangal doesn't look like much from the outside is a pretty generous understatement. Happily, the rather decrepit exterior of this informal Lewisham favourite gives way to a pair of slightly more pleasant rooms – one at ground level and the other in the basement – and to a team of staff who don't miss a beat in delivering good-quality Turkish cooking to a clientele drawn largely from the neighbourhood. The focus of the traditional menu is split between grills and pide, and you can't go wrong with either. In particular, the lamb şiş was excellent: high-quality meat, nicely seasoned and then grilled to a succulent finish. Pide are cooked to a gentle crisp in a capacious brick oven; the sebzeli peynirli pide, including cheese and spinach, is probably the best vegetarian choice on the entire menu (which, as you might expect, is otherwise heavy on the meat). Skip the starters in order to save room for a nice, creamy and made-on-site sütlaç. Every table was booked on the Saturday we visited, with plenty of Turks among the diners. It's easy to see why.
Babies and children welcome: high chairs. Booking advisable; essential weekends. Takeaway service. Vegetarian menu.

East

Docklands

Shahi Mez

571 Manchester Road, E14 3NZ (7005 0421, www.mezrestaurant.com). South Quay DLR. **Meals served** noon-10.30pm Mon-Fri, Sun; noon-11pm Sat. **Main courses** £8.95-£12.45. **Set lunch** £7.95 2 courses. **Set meal** £11.95 2 courses. **Set meze** (noon-3pm) £9.45 per person (minimum 2). **Credit** MC, V.

The location of this restaurant looks a little unlikely on an A-Z, and doesn't make much more sense when you get there. Shahi Mez is housed in a capacious corner building between Docklands' commercial towers and some of the area's modern

---

TimeOut

timeout.com/travel
Get the local experience

Dream deli counter at Franchi, in the Prati district, **Rome**

© Gianluca Moggi

Gallipoli Again. See p265.

housing, but isn't exactly part of either district. Passing trade, one imagines, is not a huge source of revenue. The restaurant rethought and expanded its offerings in 2009, adding an Indian chef to the kitchen staff, some Indian dishes to the menu and the word 'Shahi' to its name. But the Turkish staples remain, and they're generally well cooked. The plate of mixed meze offered some agreeable tarama and impressive falafel, among other items. Of the grills, the iskender kebab came with a nice tomatoey tang, but grilled sea bass was less impressive, something not helped by the wildly overcooked potatoes and asparagus; best to stick with the meat. Still, this is a nice room, crisp and airy, and staff do an efficient job of keeping everyone happy.

Babies and children welcome: high chairs. Booking advisable Fri, Sat. Disabled: toilet. Separate room for parties, seats 100. Takeaway service. Vegetarian menu. **Map 24 C3.**

Whitechapel

★ Maedah Grill

42 Fieldgate Street, E1 1ES (7377 0649, www.maedahgrill.net). Aldgate East tube. **Meals served** noon-11pm daily. **Main courses** £5.95-£16.95. **Set meal** £15-£20 3 courses. **Unlicensed** no alcohol allowed. **Credit** AmEx, MC, V.

Fieldgate Street is famous around these parts for the presence of Tayyabs, an outlandishly busy Pakistani eaterie that always seems to have a queue of 20-plus people trailing out its front door. But it's not the only restaurant on this scruffy, interesting road. Parked rather unexpectedly in the middle of what is largely Asian terrain is the Maedah Grill, a roomy Turkish establishment. Compared to other restaurants of a similar bent in east and north-east London, this is a slick-looking place, all shiny furniture and ersatz-futuristic menu typography. Unfortunately, it is let down by the kitchen, which in our experience delivers pretty indifferent renditions of Turkish staples. The list of mains is split roughly down the middle between grills and pide; from the former list, our chicken beyti was generous though rather wan. Muska böreği also lacked verve. Redemption of sorts arrived with a beautifully creamy sütlaç, but only after an extended wait for one of the bustling yet not overly attentive waiters. Customers are a rich racial mix, with plenty of kids in evidence on our recent evening visit.

Babies and children welcome: high chairs. Booking essential Fri, Sat. Disabled: toilet. Separate rooms for parties, seating 6-20. Takeaway service.

North East

Between Dalston Kingsland station and Stoke Newington Church Street, you are in the Turkish and Kurdish heart of Hackney. The food available on this strip is more authentic and varied than anywhere else in London. Restaurants, cafés, takeaways, pâtisseries and grocers are constantly appearing and disappearing around a few more permanent landmarks. There's a continual race to provide different services and dishes. As well as the restaurants reviewed in full below, the following would each merit their own write-up if they were anywhere else in London: **Aziziye** (117-119 Stoke Newington Road), an alcohol-free eaterie beneath the tiled mosque; **Café Z Bar** (58 Stoke Newington Road); **Dem** (18 Stoke Newington High Street); **Dervish Bistro** (15 Stoke Newington Church Street); **Evin** (115 Kingsland High Street); **Hasan** (14 Stoke Newington Road); **Istanbul Iskembecisi** (9 Stoke Newington Road); **Sölen** (84 Stoke Newington High Street); **Şhomine** (131 Kingsland High Street); **Tava** (17 Stoke Newington Road); and **Testi** (36 Stoke Newington High Street).

Dalston

★ Mangal II

4 Stoke Newington Road, N16 8BH (7254 7888, www.mangal2.com). Dalston Kingsland rail/76, 149, 243 bus. **Meals served** 3pm-1am Mon-Thur; 2pm-1am Fri, Sat; 2pm-midnight Sun. **Main courses** £8.45-£15.99. **Credit** MC, V.

The sister restaurant to Mangal on nearby Arcola Street has achieved a measure of fame as the preferred dinner destination of Gilbert & George. They can be found almost every night at the window table to the right of the door (and, fabulously, on the publicity shots that adorn the restaurant's website). However, the food is more than good enough to conquer any novelty value afforded by the duo's omnipresence. The menu offers few surprises, and doesn't need to: the basics are delivered with great care and unexpected finesse. Starters run from the prosaic (dolma, houmous) to the more interesting (try the leeks and carrots in olive oil, or the comparatively gentle izgara sogan: grilled onion salad), but it's really all about the grills: tender and generous, served with sparkling salads and terrifyingly moreish bread. Meaty treats, among them lamb chops and tangy beytis, are complemented by a couple of fishy options, which looked lovely coming off the grill during our visit. Service is from attentive waiters in an environment that's a little smarter than the local average. Prices are slightly higher than the competition, but that's hardly a grumble: by anywhere else's standards, this is excellent value.
Babies and children welcome: high chairs. Booking advisable weekends. Takeaway service. **Map 25 C4.**

★ ★ Mangal Ocakbasi

10 Arcola Street, E8 2DJ (7275 8981, www.mangal1.com). Dalston Kingsland rail/67, 76, 149, 243 bus. **Meals served** noon-midnight daily. **Main courses** £8-£12. **Unlicensed. Corkage** no charge. **No credit cards.**

It's an age-old quandary. If success leads to expansion, how can the quality be maintained? Dalston's original Mangal started as little more than a few tables behind the charcoal trough. So many Londoners were lured east by some of the best kebabs this side of the Bosphorus, the café was obliged to take over the back room. With the most recent annexation of the next-door shop, the space wasn't the only thing to increase. The noise level, reverberating off a tiled floor in the bare, harshly lit room, seems to have risen. Prices too. Mangal has gained a printed menu, more meze, lahmacun pizzas, and desserts. Has it lost its sizzle? Grills quickly dispel misgivings. Juicily perfect kebabs hang over the edge of plates also heaped with the benchmark salad, chopped exquisitely fine and sprinkled with zesty sumac. Lamb chops are as sweet and tender as can be. And mixed meze has all the favourites done as well as you'll find them anywhere. So, though it has evolved into a destination restaurant with higher prices and more professional, serious staff, losing a bit of soul in the process, Mangal still gives great grill. You can bring your own booze too.
Babies and children admitted. Booking advisable. Takeaway service. **Map 25 C4.**

★ ★ 19 Numara Bos Cirrik I

34 Stoke Newington Road, N16 7XJ (7249 0400). Dalston Kingsland rail/76, 149, 243 bus. **Meals served** noon-midnight daily. **Main courses** £7.50-£10.50. **Credit** MC, V.

The recent expansion of the outlandishly popular Mangal on nearby Arcola Street has had the unexpected but welcome benefit of easing the crowds at this plain little place around the corner. No.19 lacks the reputation of its competitor, but is more than a match for it in the grilled meats department. You'd do well to skip the starters: for one thing, they're not especially interesting; and for another, the efficient staff will supplement your generous main courses with free bread and three salads, including a beautiful plate of grilled onions served with a rich pomegranate and turnip sauce (izgara sogan). Ignore some of the

menu's more fanciful diversions and head straight for the grilled meats (vegetarians, incidentally, might as well stay home). The immense mixed grill offers a sampling of more or less everything; those with less cavernous stomachs would do well with the tangy chicken or lamb beyti, the often-sensational lamb spare ribs, or one of the handful of kebabs served with rice and ringed by yoghurt. There are several restaurants with this name in north-east London, but this is comfortably the best of them.
Available for hire. Babies and children admitted. Booking advisable. Separate room for parties, seats 40. Takeaway service. **Map 25 C4.**
For branches see index.

Newington Green

Sariyer Balik

56 Green Lanes, N16 9NH (7275 7681). Canonbury rail/73, 141, 236, 341 bus. **Meals served** 5pm-1am daily. **Main courses** £6.50-£10. **No credit cards.**

If you thought marine kitsch was peculiar to English restaurants, come to Green Lanes for proof that few fish specialists can resist letting rip with the piscine theme. Shells and dried fish dangle from fishing nets that festoon Sariyer Balik's cosy street-level restaurant (there's more space downstairs). But under guidance from a twinkling half-Turkish, half-Italian patron, the kitchen steers clear of gimmicks. Hot starters included slightly soggy though tender vodka-marinated kalamar, mussels in batter, and delicious buttery prawns cooked with spring onions and tomato. The bread, essential for juice-mopping, is well up to standard. Cold starters – one resembling russian salad – were overwhelmingly heavy on the yoghurt. The owner told us which fish were freshest, and the ensuing mackerel, sea bass and bream tasted as if they'd been grilled on the beach. Maybe, though, the menu should be a handwritten selection of what's best, and not a routine list including what can't be recommended. A crunchy salad (carrot, red cabbage, mooli) was all that was needed to make the also-unordered syrup-soaked sponges surplus to requirements, and turkish coffee essential as a digestif. All wines are Turkish and if our choice was typical, very drinkable.
Babies and children welcome: high chairs. Booking advisable. Separate rooms for parties, seating 30 and 40 . Takeaway service. **Map 25 A3.**

North

Finchley

The Ottomans

118 Ballards Lane, N3 2DN (8349 9968, www.theottomans.co.uk). Finchley Central tube. **Meals served** noon-11pm daily. **Main courses** £5.90-£12.50. **Set lunch** (noon-4pm) £6.95 2 courses. **Set dinner** £15.90 3 courses incl coffee. **Set meze** £3.50 per person (minimum 2). **Credit** MC, V.

The Ottomans gets plenty of competition in this busy part of Finchley, but we reckon it has the edge for both food and decor. The dining room looks almost romantic when lit for dinner, and during the day is spacious yet cosy, with brown walls, mirrors, smart chairs and well-spaced tables. A mural of boating scenes and a collection of ornate lights underline the Turkish heritage. Service from black-clad staff is gracious. Lunchtime sees a bit of takeaway trade, and most appealingly, special meal deals. We opted for a £6.95 spread of seven meze and main courses. All the dishes sang with freshness, but smoky patlıcan esme (aubergine dip with yoghurt and green peppers), cacik, and crisp, parsley-flavoured falafel were especially good. Mains, garnished with dried dill, were also appealing: tangy and smoky chicken şiş with vibrant salad and light-textured rice, and juicy inegol köfte made with minced lamb, cheese and herbs. Refreshing Efes beer was the only accompaniment needed, though a few wines and raki are available. Among the advertised sweets are kadayıf (shredded pastry baked in syrup), fırında sütlaç (oven-baked rice pudding), and kayısı tatlısı (yoghurt-stuffed apricots).
Babies and children welcome: high chairs. Booking advisable weekends. Takeaway service. Vegetarian menu.

Finsbury Park

★ Petek

94-96 Stroud Green Road, N4 3EN (7619 3933). Finsbury Park tube/rail. **Meals served** noon-midnight daily. **Main courses** £6.45-£14.85. **Set meal** £8.85 2 courses. **Set meze** £6.45-£9.85 per person (minimum 2). **Credit** AmEx, MC, V.

Quick off the draw with the complimentary olives and spicy tomato dip, followed by bread that's soft

Maedah Grill

RESTAURANTS

and fluffy inside with a warm crisp exterior, Petek got off to a flying start. The pace was maintained to the last sip of fresh leaf mint tea and a reasonable bill. Thoughtful staff advised us to order before the rush, allowed a change of table, and attended to details like the well-iced tap water. Specials are recited at breakneck speed, as if by a racecourse bookie giving the odds. There are no risky punts, even if some dishes such as salmon with pear and chilli (one of several interesting fish options) sound like daring bets. Fat, crisp and minty falafel made up for what the houmous lacked in excitement. Very tender lean chunks of lamb stewed with courgettes and red peppers made a great güveç, while tantuni (lamb braised with thyme, here served with buttery rice and a salad of lollo rosso and spinach leaves) was memorable. Food came quickly, but then we were left to savour it without interruption (except from the eventually unnoticed banging music). Coloured glass lamps dangle from the ceiling like earrings, casting an attractive glow over the understandably devoted clientele.
Babies and children welcome: high chairs. Booking advisable. Tables outdoors (3, pavement). Takeaway service.

★ Yildiz
163 Blackstock Road, N4 2JS (7354 3899, www.yildizocakbasi.co.uk). Arsenal tube. **Meals served** 11am-midnight daily. **Main courses** £7.50-£12.50. **Set lunch** £8.50 2 courses incl soft drink. **Credit** MC, V.
Eastern Turkey can be chilly in winter, and a little more warmth wouldn't have gone amiss at this Finsbury Park Anatolian outpost. The guest-house dining room decor has a sombre authenticity. Customers huddled in jackets and coats at the restaurant's shiny dark-brown pub-like tables gazed enviously at the Turkish men gathered around the barbecue at the front. Everyone's here for the grills hot off the glowing coals. These are the real no-nonsense deal, with testicles, kidneys, liver and chicken wings as well as adana, şiş and the usual kebab collection. There's a children's version of köfte; adult appetites have their work cut out doing justice to the mixed grill or quails. The main courses came with rice and a salad of tough tomatoes, cucumber, onions and parsley. Onions grilled in pomegranate juice with lashings of chilli and parsley are detour-worthy, but the mixed meze – the usual suspects, very salty and reminiscent of the industrial tubs that are frequently dished out to tourists – is only passable.
Babies and children welcome: high chairs. Takeaway service.

Haringey

With some 20 cafés and restaurants along the strip, Harringay Green Lanes offers the most intense concentration of Turkish food in London. It also features a wide range of Turkish grocers, pâtisseries, greengrocers and butchers. The restaurants may lack the variety of the cluster round Dalston and Stoke Newington in Hackney, but many of the ocakbaşı grill cafés are well worth a visit. Few are licensed for alcohol, but most will let you bring your own. The menu rarely strays from the standard grills, guveç and pide (both bread and pizza), but the food is high quality, fresh and very cheap.

The following are some of the better choices: **Flame** (551 Green Lanes); **Diyarbakir** (69 Grand Parade); **Gaziantep** (52 Grand Parade); **Gökyüzü** (27 Grand Parade); **Harran** (399 Green Lanes); **Mangal** (443 Green Lanes); **Tara** (6 Grand Parade), which has a more Middle Eastern feel; and **Yayla** (429 Green Lanes).

★ Antepliler
46 Grand Parade, Green Lanes, N4 1AG (8802 5588). Manor House tube/29 bus. **Meals served** noon-11.30pm daily. **Main courses** £6-£9.50. **Credit** MC, V.

Set on one of London's more diverse commercial streets, this enterprise has proven so successful that it now stretches to three separate operations in the space of four store-fronts: a low-key café frequented almost exclusively by Turkish men; a pâtisserie offering baklava, house-made ice-cream (try the creamy turkish delight variety) and other sugary goodness; and this larger-than-it-looks restaurant, always humming with custom from a wide variety of diners. The menu covers all the Turkish basics, mostly with success. Starters include a richly flavoured, slightly fatty kelle paca (lamb soup); tempting lahmacun, the standard dips and other, unabashedly basic goodies: sahanda sucuklu yumurta, for instance (eggs and turkish sausage baked in a weighty oven dish). The restaurant is famed for its pide pizzas, and ours was decent enough: not too doughy and generously topped. But you're better off with the speciality tava stews (at least if you can spare the 30-45 minutes the kitchen takes to cook them) or the grilled meats: the chicken is fine, but the lamb şiş and lamb beyti are better bets. Prices are low and service is excellent.
Babies and children welcome: high chairs. Takeaway service.

★ Selale
2 Salisbury Promenade, Green Lanes, N8 0RX (8800 1636). Turnpike Lane tube/Harringay Green Lanes rail/29, 141 bus. **Open** 6am-2am daily. **Main courses** £5.50-£9.50. **No credit cards.**
The word means waterfall in Turkish, hence the images of running water (including an incongruous Native American scene) and the real fountain trickling away inside the caff-like premises. Outside are pavement tables. A lit-up menu above the counter at the front gives the impression of a takeaway. The lighting and tangerine-coloured walls don't encourage lingering at the rear tables either, although the speed of service doesn't make eating in a fast-food option. Starters, including the strikingly pink tarama and unmemorable houmous, weren't much to write home about, despite the decorative squiggles of balsamic. Main courses range from stews kept hot at the front, through grills, to various pide. Lahmacun would have been a better bet than a mixed pide with lamb and cheese, which wasn't a match for the identically priced large kebab (fairly chewy şiş) or the pair of pink-hued red-pepper-speckled beyti on rice. Spicy-hot, finely chopped tomato salad and smoky bread were the highlights. Tea comes in pretty glasses, wine in two colours – red or white.
Babies and children welcome: high chairs. Tables outdoors (4, pavement). Takeaway service.

Highbury

Iznik
19 Highbury Park, N5 1QJ (7354 5697, www.iznik.co.uk). Highbury & Islington tube/rail/4, 19, 236 bus. **Meals served** 10.30am-11pm daily. **Main courses** £9.75-£12.95. **Credit** MC, V.
Though its interior is prettily lamp lit and bristling with artefacts, İznik has pink-painted brick walls, bare boards and wooden chairs that amplify the sound of music and voices. But after we'd expressed concerns about the volume, the apparently brisk waitress nodded in the direction of a large cheerful party (enjoying the good value in a monied neighbourhood) and assured us they were about to leave. Then the music was turned down unasked. Such consideration for customers only partly accounts for İznik's loyal, though not generally Turkish, following. Further explanation is provided by tip-top cacik, mücver cooked with a light touch, stand-out houmous and a variation made with fava beans – all from a satisfyingly compact selection of meze invariably prepared with delicacy. Baked main courses, like the aubergine stuffed with nicely seasoned lamb, make a welcome change from robust grills, though yoğhurtlu lamb (grilled meat swathed in tomato and yoghurt sauce) combines the best of both persuasions. Even iceberg lettuce salad is given a lift with sumac berries. Save space for glorious desserts such as sun-dried organic apricots fried in crème fraîche with almonds and cream – less life-threatening than they sound.

Available for hire. Babies and children welcome: high chairs. Booking advisable; essential weekends. Takeaway service.

Islington

Bavo
105-107 Southgate Road, N1 3JS (7226 0334, www.bavo-restaurant.co.uk). Essex Road rail/21, 76, 141, 271 bus. **Meals served** noon-11pm daily. **Main courses** £9.50-£16.50. **Set meal** £18 per person (minimum 2) 4 courses. **Credit** MC, V.
In a residential backwater on the cusp of Islington and Hackney, Bavo glosses over borders; it styles itself a Mediterranean restaurant although is predominantly Turkish. Which means you'll get good value, gracious and friendly service, and a menu designed to keep the locals happy rather than convince them they're in another country. Anyway, which country? There's moussaka; parma ham-wrapped monkfish with tomato, basil, broccoli, and new potatoes; and lemon cheesecake. Tame though the Turkish cooking is, it's well-executed. Highlights of the mixed meze included notably crisp squid rings, fine and flaky börek sigara, and aubergine that was commendably lacking in oiliness. Although offal-free, a mixed grill of tender lamb and chicken, lamb chops, köfte and quail provided plenty for two to share. The bread cuts the mustard too. With its pistachio-green walls, silver-framed mirrors and modish furniture, Bavo makes a reliably pleasing neighbourhood venue, just as suited to a family outing as dinner à deux. Or a harder-to-classify occasion like the episode of *Peep Show* in which Mark at his most sycophantic met Jeremy's misguided mother and her appalling military boyfriend here.
Available for hire. Babies and children welcome: high chairs. Booking essential weekends. Disabled: toilet. Tables outdoors (4, pavement). Takeaway service. **Map 6 Q1.**

Gallipoli Again
120 Upper Street, N1 1QP (7226 8099, www.cafegallipoli.com). Angel tube. **Meals served** noon-11pm Mon-Thur; 10.30am-midnight Fri, Sat; 10.30am-11pm daily. **Main courses** £6.95-£10.95. **Set lunch** £12.95 3 courses. **Set dinner** £15.95 3 courses incl coffee. **Set meze** £8.95 lunch, £10.95 dinner. **Credit** MC, V.
Come on Saturday night to witness this place in full swing, behind the enticing window display of dolmas and baklava. There's a queue for tables. Cynics might put the attraction down to the reasonable prices and infectious party atmosphere. Packed to the rafters, the long, narrow terracotta-painted restaurant has a rosy glow and a throbbing beat, occasionally interrupted by an electronic rendition of 'Happy Birthday'. OK, one of the day's specials was lasagne, but another was chicken begendi in coriander sauce with smoked aubergine and garlic, and there are bowls of olives ready and waiting on the tables. Falafels were commendably crisp; köfte tender; and broad beans in yoghurt, parsley and red pepper pleasing. Houmous was above average too. On the debit side, börek were stodgy, and the kitchen didn't bother to barbecue the bread. The special kebab is a meat feast that's unnecessary after several meze, but plenty for two. Staff in silver monogrammed black shirts show grace under extreme pressure and the atmosphere is great. You might not get comfort – it's a squash – or consistently tip-top cooking, but Gallipoli Again's popularity seems justified.
Babies and children welcome: high chairs. Booking advisable. Tables outdoors (8, garden; 2 pavement). Takeaway service. **Map 5 O1.**
For branches (Gallipoli Bazaar, Gallipoli Café Bistro) see index.

★ Pasha
301 Upper Street, N1 2TU (7226 1454, www.pasharestaurant.co.uk). Angel tube/Highbury & Islington tube/rail. **Meals served** 11am-11.30pm Mon-Sat; 11am-11pm Sun. **Main courses** £7.95-£14.95. **Set meal** £16.95 2 courses, £19.95 3 courses. **Credit** AmEx, MC, V.

RESTAURANTS

19 Numara Bos Cirrik I. See p263.

All very Upper Street, rubbing shoulders with furniture and fashion stores, Pasha is a soigné spot a world away from a smoky backstreet ocakbaşı. As you'd expect from somewhere making such an effort to look smart (with beige faux-leather chairs, satiny olive banquettes and orange and fuchsia cushions against trendy wallpaper and chandeliers), the cooking somewhat plays down the ethnicity. There's rocket rather than lettuce with the kebabs, and red pepper salsa and mashed potato with the köfte. Mixed meze comprised excellent börek and springy green falafel, with the kısır in dainty dollops more as decoration. The main characteristic of the skewers of chicken and lamb was tenderness. While cooking is polished, with the rough-edged flavours and spices toned down, presentation is beautiful. Making even more of a pitch as an ideal destination for a date, Pasha puts on a decent dessert show, though some of these sound more tempting than they turn out. Rice pudding with rosewater was blancmangey and the accompanying black cherry compote just four ruby blobs. Fresh mint tea, charming service and sparkling table settings add to Pasha's credentials, though.
Available for hire. Babies and children admitted. Booking advisable. Tables outdoors (2, pavement). Takeaway service. **Map 5 O1**.

Sedir
4 Theberton Street, N1 0QX (7226 5489, www.sedirrestaurant.co.uk). Angel tube/Highbury & Islington tube/rail. **Meals served** 11.30am-11.30pm Mon-Thur, Sun; 11.30am-midnight Fri, Sat. **Main courses** £7.50-£12.95. **Set meal** £18.95 per person (minimum 2) 3 courses. **Credit** AmEx, MC, V.

You'll find Sedir in a row of cheek-by-jowl restaurants of various nationalities just off Upper Street. During the day and on summer evenings, one of the attractions is sun-trap outdoor tables. Indoors, the decor plays up the sultry with ox-blood coloured walls hung with copies of Victorian orientalist paintings, taking hammams and harems as an excuse to depict lightly-clad bathing beauties – the soft porn of its day. Cooking is less opulent than the surroundings (if not the prices) might suggest. Meze was a mixed success: tarama was that all-too-frequent, unappetisingly artificial shade of pink, houmous nothing special and the kısır tasted oddly of coconut. Cacik was satisfyingly thick, however, and good mücver came with a rewarding oak leaf lettuce salad. Fried peppers with yoghurt needed seasoning. All this was a tight fit on our tiny table. For those with enough appetite to move on to mains, the usual roster of grills is available, some with a nod to the west, so chicken schnitzel comes with chips, grilled seafood with mashed potato. Service is attentive.
Babies and children welcome: children's menu; high chairs. Booking essential dinner. Separate room for parties, seats 50. Tables outdoors (6, pavement). Takeaway service. Vegetarian menu. **Map 5 O1**.

Muswell Hill

Bakko
172-174 Muswell Hill Broadway, N10 3SA (8883 1111, www.bakko.co.uk). Highgate tube then 43, 134 bus. **Meals served** 11.30am-10.30pm daily. **Main courses** £8.90-£16.90. **Set lunch** (Mon-Fri) £8.90 3 courses. **Set meal** £16.90. **Credit** MC, V.

Despite its kilims and east Turkish artefacts, Bakko has a modern demeanour that attracts a lively crowd of family groups, friends and couples. It's a family-run spot, with smiling staff and reliable cooking. The menu makes the most of the charcoal grill; salmon, trout, bream and sea bass, all with new potatoes, are offered in addition to the usual chicken and lamb combos. While there are no surprises on the list of cold and hot meze, inventive twists on Turkish cuisine, such as chicken cooked with soy sauce, onions and mushrooms, do feature. A sweet trolley with tiramisu, cheesecake and the like sits seductively by the door – perhaps a factor in so many diners saving room for dessert. Rice flirted with overcooking, and shaping the grains into round pats didn't enhance presentation of our main courses. Incik with vegetables and tomato sauce was filling and terrific value. Fat chunks of chargrilled chicken with chilli-flecked marinade were deliciously tender too. The house wine is French, though the list features a Turkish red as well as raki and Efes beer. Efficient service went rather astray come payment time, but the bill showed class, presented in a carved wooden box.
Babies and children welcome: high chairs. Booking essential weekends. Takeaway service. Vegetarian menu.

North West

Belsize Park

Beyoglu
72 Belsize Lane, NW3 5BJ (7435 7733). Belsize Park tube. **Lunch served** 11am-3pm, **dinner served** 6-11pm Mon-Fri. **Meals served** 11am-11pm Sat, Sun. **Main courses** £8-£12.50. **Set meze** £12.50 per person (minimum 2). **Credit** MC, V.

This neighbourhood grill and meze bar in Belsize Village is a friendly spot where locals casually stop by each other's tables to chat, and large groups book birthday lunches. The long, thin ground floor has high-backed leather chairs; a line of glass lanterns is almost the only thing that distinguishes the place as Turkish. Downstairs, though, where a screen barely hides the kitchen from the cosy dining area, colourful woven fabrics, tassels and cushions add a luxurious harem element to meals. Among the more unusual dishes is arnavut ciğeri (lamb's liver dusted with flour and spices then sautéed) and, from the appealing vegetarian selection, kabak (a cheese-topped dish of courgettes, mushrooms, peppers and tomato, served with rice). We loved the kizartma yoğhurtlu (fried Mediterranean veg with tomato sauce and yoghurt), and greedily scooped up all the creamy juices. Equally pleasurable was havuç tarator, a thick yoghurt and carrot dip, served with hot puffy bread. Adana kebab was especially juicy, a large salad, red cabbage, grilled pepper and tomato completing a virtuous main course. Çankaya dry white from Turkey kicks off the short wine list at £14.90. Complimentary cubes of toothsome rahat locum finish meals on a sweet note.
Available for hire. Babies and children welcome: high chairs. Booking advisable. Separate room for parties, seats 25. Tables outdoors (2, pavement). Takeaway service. **Map 28 B3**.

Zara
11 South End Road, NW3 2PT (7794 5498). Belsize Park tube/Hampstead Heath rail. **Meals served** noon-11.30pm daily. **Main courses** £9-£15. **Credit** MC, V.

A few sweeps of red paint, patterned tiles and framed prints of Turkish scenes help disguise the Artex walls of this cosy and easygoing Heath-side favourite. On our arrival, staff were immediately friendly, recommending Kavaklidere's Yakut Turkish red wine: pleasingly smooth and full-bodied. The pide was over-baked and slightly burnt, but tasted fine with sautéed vegetables doused in yoghurt and halep sauce. Imam bayıldı was correctly lush, and mercimek köfte (cold torpedoes of red lentils and bulgur wheat) zingy and refreshing. The Zara special – grilled rounds of marinated lamb, with rice and salad – was tender and herbily fragrant, however chicken güveç, piping hot in its terracotta dish, was bland despite its moist nuggets of chicken. We found ourselves eyeing the next table's fat square of moussaka enviously. Sweets include Swiss ice-creams and desserts, plus some authentic offerings such as sütlaç (the top rather too burnt, though the rice had a good flavour) and a very pleasing armut tatlısı (cinnamon-poached pear covered with chocolate sauce and cream). Ups and downs, then, but we cleaned our plates and left feeling as stuffed as aubergines; our neighbours sensibly arranged for leftovers to be put in takeaway boxes.

Available for hire. Babies and children welcome: high chairs. Booking essential weekends. Tables outdoors (4, pavement). Takeaway service. Vegetarian menu. Map 28 C3.

Outer London
Richmond, Surrey

Pomegranate
94 Kew Road, Richmond, Surrey, TW9 2PQ (8940 0033). Richmond tube/rail. **Meals served** noon-midnight daily. **Main courses** £8-£14.50. **Credit** MC, V.
Looking for Turkish delight at the 'wrong' end of Richmond requires some effort, but Pomegranate could be the refuge you've been looking for. take a seat at one of the tables outside for shisha-smokers and you can smell the garlicky aromas . The menu covers the full gamut of Turkish restaurant dishes, with mixed grills, all kinds of kebabs, grilled quail, stews and salads. Falafel and kalamar starters were both pleasingly light, and the house houmous was nutty, oily and heavily spiced. Chicken beyti was delicious: hot, thin fine flatbread wrapped around cumin-scented, mildly spicy chicken pieces, with rice, tomato sauce and yoghurt neatly arranged around them. A second main of lamb ezme came with side dishes of salad, olives, pomegranate and chilli onion, but the dish itself was a rather gloopy stew – tasty but heavy on tomato. Two waiters attended us with efficiency and friendliness, and promptly brought some pitta bread to help us mop up the ezme. We chose hot fruit and mint teas instead of booze, but there are also trad drinks such as yoghurt-based ayran and salgam (a veg and garlic drink), plus a decent wine list. Come evening some of the kebabs are in the £14-£15 bracket, which is steep compared to other establishments.
Babies and children admitted. Booking advisable dinner. Tables outdoors (20, garden).

Menu

It's useful to know that in Turkish 'ç' and 'ş' are pronounced 'ch' and 'sh'. So şiş is correct Turkish, shish is English and sis is common on menus. Menu spelling is rarely consistent, so expect wild variations on everything given here. See also the menu boxes in **Middle Eastern** and **North African**.

COOKING EQUIPMENT
Mangal: brazier.
Ocakbaşı: an open grill under an extractor hood. A metal dome is put over the charcoal for making paper-thin bread.

SOUPS
İşkembe: finely chopped tripe soup, an infallible hangover cure.
Mercimek çorbar: red lentil soup.
Yayla: yoghurt and rice soup (usually) with a chicken stock base.

MEZE DISHES
Arnavut ciğeri: 'albanian liver' – cubed or sliced lamb's liver, fried then baked.
Barbunya: spicy kidney bean stew.
Börek or **böreği**: fried or baked filo pastry parcels with a savoury filling, usually cheese, spinach or meat. Commonest are **muska** or **peynirli** (cheese) and **sigara** ('cigarette', so long and thin).
Cacik: diced cucumber with garlic in yoghurt.
Çoban salatası: 'shepherd's' salad of finely diced tomatoes, cucumbers, onions, perhaps green peppers and parsley, sometimes with a little feta cheese.
Dolma: stuffed vegetables (usually with rice and pine kernels).
Enginar: artichokes, usually with vegetables in olive oil.
Haydari: yoghurt, infused with garlic and mixed with finely chopped mint leaves.
Hellim: Cypriot halloumi cheese.
Houmous: creamy paste of chickpeas, crushed sesame seeds, oil, garlic and lemon juice.
Houmous kavurma: houmous topped with strips of lamb and pine nuts.
İmam bayıldı: literally 'the imam fainted'; aubergine stuffed with onions, tomatoes and garlic in olive oil.
Ispanak: spinach.
Kalamar: fried squid.
Karides: prawns.
Kısır: usually a mix of chopped parsley, tomatoes, onions, crushed wheat, olive oil and lemon juice.
Kızartma: lightly fried vegetables.
Köy ekmeği: literally 'village bread'; another term for saç (qv).
Lahmacun: 'pizza' of minced lamb on thin pide (qv).
Midye tava: mussels in batter, in a garlic sauce.
Mücver: courgette and feta fritters.
Patlıcan: aubergine, variously served.
Patlıcan esme: grilled aubergine puréed with garlic and olive oil.
Pide: a term encompassing many varieties of Turkish flatbread. It also refers to Turkish pizzas (heavier and more filling than lahmacun, qv).
Pilaki: usually haricot beans in olive oil, but the name refers to the method of cooking not the content.
Piyaz: white bean salad with onions.
Saç: paper-thin, chewy bread prepared on a metal dome (also called saç) over a charcoal grill.
Sucuk: spicy sausage, usually beef.
Tarama: cod's roe paste.
Tarator: a bread, garlic and walnut mixture; **havuç tarator** adds carrot; **ıspanak tarator** adds spinach.
Yaprak dolması: stuffed vine leaves.
Zeytin: olive.

MAIN COURSES
Alabalik: trout.
Balik: fish.
Güveç: stew, which is traditionally cooked in an earthenware pot.
Hünkar beğendi: cubes of lamb, braised with onions and tomatoes, served on an aubergine and cheese purée.
İçli köfte: balls of cracked bulgar wheat filled with spicy mince.
İncik: knuckle of lamb, slow-roasted in its own juices. Also called kléftico.
Karni yarik: aubergine stuffed with minced lamb and vegetables.
Kléftico: *see* İncik.
Mitite köfte: chilli meatballs.
Sote: meat (usually), sautéed in tomato, onion and pepper (and sometimes wine).
Uskumru: mackerel.

KEBABS
Usually made with grilled lamb (those labelled **tavuk** or **piliç** are chicken), served with bread or rice and salad.
Common varieties include:
Adana: spicy mince.
Beyti: usually spicy mince and garlic, but sometimes best-end fillet.
Bıldırcın: quail.
Böbrek: kidneys.
Çöp şiş: small cubes of lamb.
Döner: slices of marinated lamb (sometimes mince) packed tightly with pieces of fat on a vertical rotisserie.
Halep: usually döner (qv) served over bread with a buttery tomato sauce.
İskender: a combination of döner (qv), tomato sauce, yoghurt and melted butter on bread.
Kaburga: spare ribs.
Kanat: chicken wings.
Köfte: mince mixed with spices, eggs and onions.
Külbastı: char-grilled fillet.
Lokma: 'mouthful' (beware, there's a dessert that has a similar name!) – boned fillet of lamb.
Patlıcan: mince and sliced aubergine.
Pirzola: lamb chops.
Şeftali: seasoned mince, wrapped in caul fat.
Şiş: cubes of marinated lamb.
Uykuluk: sweetbread.
Yoğhurtlu: meat over bread and yoghurt.

DESSERTS
Armut tatlısı: baked pears.
Ayva tatlısı: quince in syrup.
Baklava: filo pastry interleaved with minced pistachio nuts, almonds or walnuts, and covered in sugary syrup.
Kadayıf: cake made from shredded pastry dough, filled with syrup and nuts or cream.
Kazandibi: milk pudding, traditionally with very finely chopped chicken breast.
Kemel pasha: small round cakes soaked in honey.
Keşkül: milk pudding with almonds and coconut, topped with pistachios.
Lokum: turkish delight.
Sütlaç: rice pudding.

DRINKS
Ayran: refreshing drink made with yoghurt.
Çay: tea.
Kahve (aka Turkish coffee): a tiny cup half full of sediment, half full of strong, rich, bitter coffee. Offered without sugar, medium or sweet.
Rakı: a spirit with an aniseed flavour.

Vegetarian

London remains one of the world's top destinations for flesh-free dining. OK, so the city might not have an abundance of self-proclaimed vegetarian restaurants – and, yes, too many of its chefs continue to put just one 'vegetarian option' on their menus – but there is choice aplenty if you look for it. Lovers of food from the subcontinent should consult our Indian section (pp134-157), where several of the South Indian and Gujarati restaurants entirely avoid the use of meat. Middle Eastern restaurants (pp204-209) will also have much that is meat-less among their meze. Below we list specifically vegetarian venues ranging from well-established hippyish eateries such as **Blah Blah Blah**, **Food for Thought** and our current favourite, **Mildred's**, via more modern takes on the genre like the new **Tibits**, through to such renowned gastronomic temples as the **Gate** and **Vanilla Black**, and the stylish raw vegan joint that is **Saf**. Vegetarians looking for an elegant haute cuisine experience may enjoy **Pied à Terre**, or French fine dining establishments **Morgan M** and **Roussillon**.

revelation. A crudité plate of walnut sticks, baby carrots and parsley dip was less impressive; the dip wasn't the concentrated flavour bomb that you might think, but a herbed cream cheese. Other imaginative options include sweetcorn crème brûlée, and poached duck egg served with Duckett's caerphilly pudding: the latter indicating the restaurant's commitment to showcasing artisan produce. All our dishes showed great technical skill, and an artful hand with haute cuisine presentation. Vanilla Black's location, hidden down an alley in the legal quarter around Chancery Lane, perhaps accounts for its formal feel, which verges on the stuffy. The plain decor of neutral tones is brightened by carefully placed art deco mirrors. Diners on our visit were a mix of older, wealthy patrons, a young couple out for a dressed-up meal, and a group of female friends who looked slightly bemused at the elaborate dishes. Staff are exceedingly professional, making this a good choice for a business lunch or a special-occasion dinner.
Babies and children admitted. Booking advisable. Disabled: toilet. **Map 11 N6**.

Covent Garden

★ Food for Thought
31 Neal Street, WC2H 9PR (7836 9072). Covent Garden tube. **Meals served** noon-8.30pm Mon-Sat. **Lunch served** noon-5pm Sun. **Main courses** £4.70-£7.80. **Minimum** (noon-3pm, 6-7.30pm Mon-Sat) £3.50. **Unlicensed**. **Corkage** no charge. **No credit cards**.

Central
City

★ The Place Below
St Mary-le-Bow, EC2V 6AU (7329 0789, www.theplacebelow.co.uk). St Paul's tube/Bank tube/DLR. **Breakfast served** 7.30-11am, **lunch served** 11.30am-2.15pm, **snacks served** 2.30-3pm Mon-Fri. **Main courses** £6.20-£7.75. **Unlicensed**. **Corkage** no charge. **Credit** MC, V.
Tucked into the crypt beneath the Wren-designed St Mary-le-Bow church, this daytime-only café has served homely breakfasts, lunches and teas to City folk for decades. Customers queue for dishes to eat in or take away, in an anteroom set with a few small wooden tables and a coffee bar; the main dining room has communal white-clothed tables against thick stone walls and large pillars. Both spaces can get uncomfortably crowded at lunchtime, and the clattery, canteen-like atmosphere can make conversation difficult. Expect a menu of salads, soups, sandwiches, hot dishes and puds (a couple of choices of each), including dairy-free options, and a clientele that mixes local office workers, grannies, students and tourists. Food comes in big portions and is healthy if old-fashioned at best, flavourless at worst, so choose carefully; dishes often run out. Thai red curry featured brown rice topped with undercooked chunks of potato, carrots and water-chestnuts, with a scattering of raw peanuts and no discernible oriental flavours; much tastier was a large wedge of quiche (mediterranean vegetable and halloumi) with salad and roast potatoes. Plum and apple crumble with thick cream or yoghurt provided a comforting finale.
Available for hire. Babies and children welcome: high chairs. Tables outdoors (20, churchyard). Takeaway service. Vegan dishes. **Map 11 P6**.

★ Vanilla Black
17-18 Tooks Court, off Cursitor Street, EC4A 1LB (7242 2622, www.vanillablack.co.uk). Chancery Lane tube. **Lunch served** noon-2.30pm, **dinner served** 6-10pm Mon-Fri. **Set lunch** £18 2 courses, £23 3 courses. **Set meal** £24 2 courses, £30 3 courses. **Credit** AmEx, MC, V.
VB's USP is modern gourmet cooking, executed to a highly refined standard. A starter of 'deconstructed dahl' – a fan of puréed potatoes, drizzled with chilli oil and gingerly laid with stripes of delicately spiced puy lentils – was a

Rootmaster. See p273.

Taking the stairs to this old basement café is like a steady descent to the 1970s. A small, ramshackle glass-topped counter is lined with pottery bowls, wholemeal breads and hearty salads; pine furniture is squeezed along one white-washed wall – there's even floor-cushion seating tucked in a rear alcove. Sharing tables is the norm, though plenty of customers (grandmothers with their grandchildren, office workers, students and creatives) get up and move when a new one becomes free. Of its type, the food is excellent, with big, well-considered flavours and spirited freshness. Vietnamese stew was heavy on baby corn, but featured deliciously succulent shiitake mushrooms and a subtle star anise undertone. Strawberry scone was all wholesome sweetness that needed no butter or jam. Prices are very persuasive too. Our problem is with the service, or lack of it. Told we'd have to wait a minute for a hot dish, we waited more than ten, and staff were so absorbed in discussing their own affairs – loudly – they didn't even notice when the flowers on a table right in front of the counter were knocked over, spilling water across the table and on to the floor. *Babies and children admitted. Bookings not accepted. Takeaway service; delivery service. Vegan dishes.* **Map 18 D3**.

★ World Food Café

1st floor, 14 Neal's Yard, WC2H 9DP (7379 0298, www.worldfoodcafenealsyard.co.uk). Covent Garden tube. **Meals served** 11.30am-4.30pm Mon-Fri; 11.30am-5pm Sat. **Main courses** £4.95-£7.95. **Minimum** (lunch) £6. **Unlicensed** no alcohol allowed. **Credit** (over £10) MC, V.
Leaflets for theta healing, shamanic creativity retreats and 'five rhythms moving meditation' set the tone at this colourful café overlooking Neal's Yard. Many customers look like they've been coming here since the 1960s, so it's a surprise to discover the place didn't open until 1991. World Food Café attracts a wide-ranging hippyish crowd, with hearty recipes gleaned from the owners' travels – learn more from the lavish cookbooks on display. Order your food at the till near the door and take a perch at the horseshoe-shaped central counter, or at one of the wide pine tables by the windows. Indian and Mexican combo plates make a pleasing alternative to the inevitable houmous and falafel. West African-style stew featured succulent chunks of sweet potato in peanut and vegetable sauce, spread over a voluminous bed of brown rice and topped with tangy raw beetroot, carrot, spinach and coriander, plus sliced fresh banana. Banana lassi was a let-down, lacking fruity flavour or creamy sweetness; the predominant taste was of raw cardamom. Next time we'll order a pud instead: french chocolate cake, say, or apple crumble. *Babies and children welcome: high chairs. Takeaway service. Vegan dishes.* **Map 18 D3**.

Euston

★ Greens & Beans

131 Drummond Street, NW1 2HL (7380 0857, www.greensandbeans.biz). Euston Square tube/ Euston tube/rail. **Meals served** 9am-4pm Mon-Fri. **Main courses** £5.50-£9.95. **Set lunch** (noon-3.30pm) £6.95 buffet. **Credit** MC, V.
Under the wing of the Dru yoga and meditation organisation, this friendly spot has a loyal following of local office staff and health fiends, though the retail range (and floor space) has been cut back since opening. At ground level is a small buffet of six daily-changing dishes for takeaway – Mexican-style black beans, say, plus a tofu stir-fry, quiche, cauliflower cheese and organic potato wedges. Take a seat for a wider choice of vibrant, nutritious fare including pizzas, pastas and nut roast. Crespelle is the speciality, and these are very good: packed with bouncy spinach leaves and creamy ricotta, and daubed with tomato sauce and oozy mozzarella. A decent salad, scattered with sprouted pulses, is included. To drink there's organic fruit and veg juices freshly squeezed, and smoothies (pricey, in part due to nutraceuticals such as omega oils, lecithin and acidophilus). With its fresh flowers, trendy cushions, neat plywood chairs and white walls, the basement café certainly has the better ambience, though at quiet times staff

can become too easy-going; they didn't even try to sell us dessert or coffee. If we hadn't gone upstairs to pay, we might have been left there until closing. *Babies and children admitted. Separate room for parties, seats 24. Tables outdoors (1, terrace). Takeaway service. Vegan dishes.* **Map 3 J3**.

Marylebone

Eat & Two Veg

50 Marylebone High Street, W1U 5HN (7258 8595, www.eatandtwoveg.com). Baker Street tube. **Meals served** 9am-11pm Mon-Sat; 10am-10pm Sun. **Main courses** £8.75-£10.75. **Credit** AmEx, MC, V.
This large site could easily have been a soulless barn, but a skylight at the back, wood tones, open-plan kitchen and booth seating add warmth to the rather corporate diner-style interior. Eat & Two Veg is no Frosty Palace, but the fresh apple and passion-fruit juice (a surprisingly good combo) had us slurping through the straw like teenagers with milkshakes. The menu of soy-based dishes such as schnitzel, sausages and stews seems aimed at vegetarians who didn't want to give up meat. Prices are quite steep too (£11.50 for tofu green curry, £9.95 for the all-day breakfast). Still, there's plenty to like. There was a distinct chargrilled flavour to the moist burger, which also benefited from nutty-tasting sesame seeds on its wholemeal bun, and a gingery onion relish. Accompanying coleslaw was a high-quality mix, if heavy on mayonnaise, but the fries were dry. Chocolate cake – rich, buttery and dense – was big enough to share. The menu says everything is guaranteed GM-free, which must be a challenge when dealing with soy products in today's food industry. *Babies and children welcome: high chairs; nappy-changing facilities. Booking advisable. Disabled: toilet. Tables outdoors (2, pavement). Takeaway service. Vegan dishes.* **Map 3 G4**.

Mayfair

Tibits NEW

12-14 Heddon Street, W1B 4DA (7758 4110, www.tibits.ch). Oxford Circus tube. **Meals served** 9am-10.30pm Mon-Wed; 9am-midnight Thur-Sat; 10am-10.30pm Sun. **Buffet** £2 per 100g. **Credit** MC, V.
Touchy-feely Designers Guild fabrics in raspberry and lime contrast with a black-painted ceiling and smart wicker chairs at this modern take on the buffet restaurant. Despite all the prettiness, there were as many alpha males in situ on our lunchtime visit as women. Part of a small but impressive Swiss chain, Tibits may be vegetarian but it's not puritanical. There are organic Freedom lagers on tap, a handful of red and white wines and several cocktails. Coffees too. Fill your plate from the salads and hot dishes in the central 'boat' and take it to the counter for weighing; prices change per 100g according to whether you're here for breakfast, lunch or dinner. Food ranges from plain iceberg and cucumber slices to guacamole and creamy tofu curries. Have faith: the more unusual combinations, such as sweetly fragrant white cabbage with saffron and caraway, tend to work. Our brownie was excellent, with a thick, moist centre and appetising chunks of walnut. Staff do a great job of making you feel welcome and explaining the system – because it's all a bit Swiss. *Babies and children welcome: crayons; high chairs; nappy-changing facilities. Disabled: toilet. Separate room for parties, seats 50. Tables outdoors (5, piazza). Takeaway service. Vegan dishes.* **Map 17 A4**.

Soho

★ Beatroot

92 Berwick Street, W1F 0QD (7437 8591, www.beatroot.org.uk). Oxford Circus, Piccadilly Circus or Tottenham Court Road tube. **Meals served** 9.15am-9pm Mon-Sat. **Main courses** £3.90-£5.90. **No credit cards.**
Step into Beatroot from the bustling open-air fruit and vegetable market on Berwick Street and you'll see a counter full of fresh vegetarian food every

bit as colourful as the produce being hawked outside. This café has been offering healthy, value-for-money meals to Soho types since 1997. Choose from ten piping-hot dishes and an array of salads; the friendly staff cheerfully cram as much as they can into one of three – small, medium, large – containers. The mostly vegan fare often includes a wonderfully creamy moussaka and light-as-air quiche. Broccoli salad was bursting with al dente goodness. The canapé-sized sausage rolls (made with a flavoursome soy mince) were a sweet touch on top. Salads? It could be forever summer here, with crunchy red cabbage coleslaw flavoured with dill, carrot salad with roasted pumpkin seeds, or raw beetroot and sesame salad drizzled with tangy cider vinegar. We gave the juice and smoothie bar a workout too; the breakfast smoothie (full of bananas, oats, dates, milk and strawberries) put a spring in our step. A handy place to know. *Babies and children admitted. Tables outdoors (5, pavement). Takeaway service. Vegan dishes.* **Map 17 B3**.

★ Mildred's

45 Lexington Street, W1F 9AN (7494 1634, www.mildreds.co.uk). Oxford Circus or Piccadilly Circus tube. **Meals served** noon-11pm Mon-Sat. **Main courses** £6.50-£8.75. **Credit** AmEx, MC, V.
Mildred's is a lovely looking place. A couple of small tables mark the pavement out front, and there's a buzzy, sunlit dining room through the back, but we opted for the window-box breakfast tables – all the better to watch Soho pass by. Highly covetable retro 1950s lime tiles, skylights and beech everywhere successfully brighten what might otherwise be a dark spot. The young staff were friendly and attentive, pausing only to change the background music (Joni Mitchell to indie fare and back again) and check on our wine levels. The wine list offers plenty of organic and (mercifully) by-the-glass options. As for food, the daily specials board was too tempting to ignore. Our starters? Feta-stuffed pepper was crispy and decent enough, but pumpkin ravioli with creamy porcini sauce was outstanding. To follow, detox salad with raw tofu would easily have fed two – all seeds, nuts and good things – while the similarly massive Asian stir-fry with tofu marinated in teriyaki sauce was utterly delicious. After the meal, a confirmed carnivore declared he was suitably impressed. *Babies and children welcome: high chairs. Bookings not accepted. Separate room for parties, seats 24. Tables outdoors (2, pavement). Takeaway service. Vegan dishes.* **Map 17 A4**.

West

Hammersmith

★ The Gate

51 Queen Caroline Street, W6 9QL (8748 6932, www.thegate.tv). Hammersmith tube. **Lunch served** noon-2.45pm Mon-Fri. **Dinner served** 6-10.45pm Mon-Sat. **Main courses** £10.50-£13.70. **Credit** AmEx, MC, V.
Now in its 20th year, west London's most prominent vegetarian restaurant continues to impress with its innovative dishes and atmospheric, high-ceilinged dining room. The mood is casual and usually pleasantly noisy, with the clatter of cutlery and the chatter of bourgeois meat-avoiders. There's a plant theme to the decor, which includes a mighty bonsai and a massive tree stencil covering an entire wall. Dishes can often feature a bewildering number of flavours from around the world – not necessarily a bad thing. Halloumi tikka kebabs (a trendy starter that appears on the menu of at least three London veggie restaurants at the time of writing) are here presented with herby couscous dotted with sweet, crunchy pomegranate seeds. Thai green curry was a subtle version of the classic, accompanied by sharp ginger salsa and too-soft basmati. Aubergine charlotte (smoky strips of aubergine wrapped around a filling of wild mushroom and mild goat's cheese custard) was the strongest dish of the evening. Desserts are equally tempting, spanning lavender-infused crème brûlée to a subtle pineapple and chilli crumble surrounded by delicate crème

The Gate

anglaise. Deservedly busy, the Gate is suitable for lively lunches and candlelit dinners, whether with friends or a date.
Available for hire. Babies and children welcome: high chairs. Booking essential. Tables outdoors (15, courtyard). Vegan dishes. **Map 20 B4**.

Shepherd's Bush

Blah Blah Blah

78 Goldhawk Road, W12 8HA (8746 1337, www.gonumber.com/2524). Goldhawk Road tube/ 94 bus. **Lunch served** 12.30-2.30pm Mon-Sat. **Dinner served** 6.30-10.30pm Mon-Thur; 6.30-10.45pm Fri, Sat. **Main courses** £9.95. **Unlicensed**. **Corkage** £1.45 per person. **No credit cards**.
The menu and ambience span the globe at this hippyish joint. The warm, cosy decor is a mishmash of ethnic influences. Industrial spotlights, an enormous Buddha portrait, burgundy and white striped walls, and ruby fairy lights draped over a palm plant create a low-lit, Mexican fiesta vibe. Food includes sweetcorn tostada stacks (layers of corn and black beans between crisp tortillas), which have been a popular fixture here for years. The Indian subcontinent is represented by wonderfully succulent tikka and yoghurt-marinated halloumi and vegetable skewers. Europe gets a look-in with a potato and mushroom stack served in a pool of umami-rich, slightly sharp porcini gravy, which was let down by overcooked runner beans and carrot roundels. On our visit, service was a little brusque; the waiter took his time finishing a phone call before seating us. Small, intimate and old-school, down to its world music soundtrack, BBB is ideal for a low-key night out. Note that it's BYO, and cash or cheques only.
Available for hire. Babies and children admitted. Booking advisable. Separate room for parties, seats 35. Takeaway service. Vegan dishes. **Map 20 B2**.

West Kensington

222 Veggie Vegan

222 North End Road, W14 9NU (7381 2322, www.222veggievegan.com). West Kensington tube/West Brompton tube/rail/28, 391 bus. **Lunch served** noon-3.30pm, **dinner served** 5.30-10.30pm daily. **Main courses** £7.50-£10.50. **Set lunch** £7.50 buffet. **Credit** MC, V.
When value is as important as quality, it's hard to beat this West Kensington eatery. Step inside from the busy high street, and the soothing blond wood floors and tables and simple white walls whisper 'relax'. The all-you-can-eat lunchtime buffet is still a gem. It's difficult not to help yourself to a bit of everything, thanks to the range of hot and cold dishes on display. Chickpea curry was creamy and full of coriander; red cabbage and broccoli salad was a crunchy classic. Yes, an avocado and bean mix skimped on the avocado, but it was surprisingly moreish all the same, and the stir-fried vegetables were perfectly cooked and dripping with soy sauce and ginger flavours. There's a very short organic drinks list, including lager, fresh juices and smoothies, plus a selection of bottled juices. Dinners are from an à la carte menu – all salads, pastas and stir-fries – but it's for the generous lunchtime buffet that 222 gets so much love.
Available for hire. Babies and children welcome: high chairs. Booking advisable. Takeaway service. Vegan dishes. **Map 13 A12**.

East

Bethnal Green

★ Wild Cherry

241-245 Globe Road, E2 0JD (8980 6678, www.wildcherrycafe.com). Bethnal Green tube/rail/ 8 bus. **Meals served** 10.30am-7pm Mon-Fri; 10.30am-4pm Sat. **Main courses** £4-£5.99. **Unlicensed**. **Corkage** £1. **Credit** MC, V.
What sort of place is Wild Cherry? Well, it's run by members of the London Buddhist Centre, and has a noticeboard full of adverts for rooms to let in non-smoking flats, and alternative therapists offering their services. The tranquil garden is the prime summer spot – all pretty whitewashed walls,

What's your YAHOO! made of?

From your best friends to the West End, add whatever you love to your new Yahoo! homepage.

yahoo.co.uk

Tibits. See p270.

prayer flags and Buddhas smiling from every ledge, with tables filling the L-shaped sun trap. Inside, the daily changing menu is written on a blackboard. All-day breakfasts are popular on Saturdays (expect to wait for a table). For our weekday meal, fluffy quiche came full of chunky courgette and yellow peppers, lifted by light pastry around the edges. Salads included couscous, bright leafy greens, and a delicious shredded carrot, parsley and orange mix full of crunchy seeds and celery: sunshine on a plate. Other choices might include onion soup, jacket potatoes, and a red cabbage and apple casserole. It takes a strong diner to walk past the own-made cakes. Hummingbird cake was moist, full of apple and crushed pineapple and topped with creamy cheese icing. Alongside the herbal teas and Pukka teabags, the coffee machine dispenses smooth caffeine fixes.
Available for hire. Babies and children welcome: high chairs; nappy-changing facilities. Tables outdoors (9, garden). Takeaway service. Vegan dishes.

Brick Lane

Rootmaster
Old Truman Brewery car park, off Dray Walk, E1 6QL (07912 389314, www.root-master.co.uk). Aldgate East tube/Liverpool Street tube/rail. **Meals served** 11am-11pm Mon-Sat; 11am-10.30pm Sun. **Main courses** £5-£14. **Credit** MC, V.
This red double-decker Routemaster bus was on active service for nearly 40 years. Retired in 2004, it was converted into a popular, quirky café serving organic vegan cooking. The kitchen takes up the ground-floor deck, with takeaways served from a window. The original steep steps take you to the brilliantly converted upstairs dining area, where the floor is of red lino and the walls and ceiling are painted bright white. Banquette seating and bright, graphic cushions mean the largest table can accommodate nine; the remaining few tables seat two or four. A soundtrack of summery psychedelic guitars, pretty flowers and properly set tables complete the look. Service is laid-back and friendly (although getting our bill took a two-pronged attack). With all this, it's a shame our food was mediocre. Menus traverse the globe: Mexican bean wraps, Indian curries and a creamy, flavoursome picante tofu that was overwhelmed by a mountain of brown rice and sorely in need of greenery. Better to get a few plates to share – the meze platters and pizzas looked appealing – order from the well-considered wine list, and soak up the atmosphere.
Available for hire. Babies and children admitted. Tables outdoors (30, courtyard). Takeaway. service. **Map 6 S5.**

Shoreditch

★ Saf (100)
152-154 Curtain Road, EC2A 3AT (7613 0007, www.safrestaurant.co.uk). Old Street tube/rail/55, 243 bus. **Lunch served** noon-3.30pm, **dinner served** 6.30-11pm Mon-Sat. **Main courses** £9-£14.50. **Credit** AmEx, MC, V.
With its trendy, New York vibe, Saf has charmed London's hip and beautiful people. We overheard the waiters saying they had done 230 covers on the Saturday night we visited – and it showed, as our 10pm table (the only slot available) wasn't ready on arrival. The barman proceeded to make amends by plying us with serious cocktails. The smart, super-stylish venue, with designer glassware and zany lightshades moulded from dried ramen noodles, is an ideal place for an impressive first date. The deal here is raw vegan food without the earnestness: a revitalising and expertly executed experience. Only a third of dishes are cooked above 48°C. Pan-Asian and European influences are apparent; pad thai was perfectly raw, an artistic creation of julienned 'noodles' of courgettes, carrots, freaky enoki mushrooms and a tongue-tingling sauce both creamy and smoky, combining chipotle chillies and almonds. Swiss chard rolls (a salad rolled in leaves) was uninspiring. In contrast, desserts were heavenly: scoops of pretty pink peppercorn and cinnamon-infused chocolate ice-creams. Saf is out on its own when it comes to creativity and quality.
Available for hire. Babies and children welcome: high chairs; nappy-changing facilities. Booking advisable weekends. Disabled: toilet. Tables outdoors (10, courtyard). Vegan dishes. **Map 6 R4.**

North
Camden Town & Chalk Farm

Manna
4 Erskine Road, NW3 3AJ (7722 8028, www.manna-veg.com). Chalk Farm tube/31, 168 bus. **Lunch served** noon-3pm Sat, Sun. **Dinner served** 6.30-10.30pm Tue-Sun. **Main courses** £10-£13. **Credit** MC, V.
Going strong after upwards of 40 years, Manna appears to have settled into 2008's more mature makeover. Earthy tones of dark and light-coloured wood are made contemporary with beige wallpaper and branch-shaped lighting fixtures. The dining space consists of a tiny, street-facing conservatory and a cosy, curtained snug at the back for more

intimate encounters. The menu picks and chooses from around the world. Caribbean-influenced sweet-potato galette (perched atop a sludge of toothsome, jerk-seasoned black beans) featured good okra but fried plantains with a texture like cardboard. The ever-popular chef's salad (a deli-counter array of beetroot, avocado, balsamic-marinated onions, pumpkin seeds and protein from a selection of halloumi, feta or crispy tofu) was fine, but this sort of assemblage is nothing to write home about. Desserts display some creative ideas: lemon and cinnamon tart with blueberry coulis and limoncello-spiked clotted cream, for instance. Staff are casually competent. Recent innovations include a Sunday roast, and a buffet evening on the last Tuesday of the month (except December).
Babies and children welcome: high chairs. Booking essential weekends. Tables outdoors (2, pavement; 2, conservatory). Takeaway service. Vegan dishes. **Map 27 A1.**

Outer London
Kingston, Surrey

Riverside Vegetaria
64 High Street, Kingston, Surrey KT1 1HN (8546 0609, www.rsvegplus.com). Kingston rail. **Meals served** noon-11pm Mon-Sat; noon-10.30pm Sun. **Main courses** £7.95-£8.95. **Credit** MC, V.
Step through Riverside Vegetaria's entrance, and you step back in time. To an era of hearty hotpots and comfort casseroles, and a decor of brickwork, fake arches, wooden chairs with colourful seat cushions and posters of Indian guru Sai Baba. This venerable outpost of meat-free cooking celebrated its 20th year in 2009. The riverside terrace appeals; it's small and crammed, but any closer to the water and you'd be swimming. The lengthy menu tours the globe, from India (masala dosai) and Sri Lanka (string hoppers), via Indonesia (gado-gado), the Middle East (falafel, houmous) and the Caribbean (spicy Jamaican stew). Two-thirds of the dishes are vegan and wheat-and gluten-free, and many of the wines are organic and vegan. Portions are huge; red lentil and avocado kedgeree (delicately perfumed with cardamom) came with a large pile of salad plus a sliced avocado and a side dish of potato and tomato curry (rather bland). Stuffed avocado was drowned in a salad of tomatoes, beans, olives and mushrooms. Service was off-hand, but that seemed in keeping with the laid-back vibe.
Babies and children welcome: high chairs. Booking advisable weekends. Separate room for parties, seats 25. Tables outdoors (7, riverside terrace). Takeaway service. Vegan dishes.

RESTAURANTS

Vietnamese

Though London has a newer and smaller population of Vietnamese than that of Paris, the cuisine fast found favour within the city's wider public. Serendipity has certainly played a part in this progression. Many of London's Vietnamese came to settle east of the centre, especially in Shoreditch and Hackney. By the mid 1990s, the first dining establishments catering to this group opened. These were basic cafés and canteens geared to providing inexpensive, but authentic, meals to members of the local community. By chance, at around the same time, London's hippest bars and clubs started springing up in Shoreditch and Hoxton. It wasn't long before trendsters discovered the fresh, clean flavours of Vietnamese cuisine, finding a bowl of pho noodle soup an ideal primer for a night's clubbing. Now ambitious chain **Pho** is providing its fortifying fodder for shopping trips too, with branches in Fitzrovia and Westfield Shepherd's Bush.

East London remains the top district for Vietnamese cooking and is where you'll find our three favourite restaurants: the excellent **Song Que** on the Kingsland Road, Shoreditch; **Mien Tay**, just a short walk up the same stretch of road; and Hackney's **Green Papaya**. Though we've no brand new openings to report this year, **Café East** of Deptford has new premises, and moved a mite upmarket in the process, which makes its restaurant at Surrey Quays Leisure Park a welcome addition to south London's dining scene.

Central
Clerkenwell & Farringdon

Pho
86 St John Street, EC1M 4EH (7253 7624, www.phocafe.co.uk). Barbican tube/Farringdon tube/rail. **Lunch served** noon-3pm Mon-Fri. **Dinner served** 6-10pm Mon-Thur, 6-10.30pm Fri, Sat. **Main courses** £6.50-£8.95. **Credit** MC, V.
The manifesto can't be faulted – Pho brings pho to the masses, with branches in Fitzrovia and the Westfield shopping centre joining this original Farringdon café. With a clean red-and-white colour scheme, simple lines and modern lighting, the place looks like an IKEA showroom. However, we've rarely found the food to be an accurate representation of Vietnamese cuisine. For a start, the pho is disappointing. Our pho tai chin (with sliced beef fillet steak and beef brisket) was bland, and the rice noodles tough and undercooked. For many pho aficionados, the heart of the dish – the broth – can save it, but our limp-flavoured stock failed to speak of long hours of simmering in a pan with beef bones and spices. Arriving with a parsimonious serving of herbs (ordinary coriander, Vietnamese basil and, incongruously, mint), beansprouts, chilli and lemon, the dish was a pale imitation of the real thing. A prawn and green papaya salad had been cloaked in sweet chilli sauce, and lacked any real punch or vitality. We enjoyed a freshly made juice of coconut, apple and pineapple, though it could have been served colder. Otherwise there was little to like about this. Cynics may suspect that Pho favours style over substance; our visits have only confirmed this.
Babies and children welcome: booster seats. Takeaway service. **Map 5 O4.**
For branches see index.

West
Hammersmith

★ Saigon Saigon
313-317 King Street, W6 9NH (0870 220 1398, www.saigon-saigon.co.uk). Ravenscourt Park or Stamford Brook tube.
Bar **Open/snacks served** 6pm-midnight Fri, Sat. *Restaurant* **Lunch served** 12.30-2.30pm Mon; noon-2.30pm Tue-Sat; 12.30-3.30pm Sun. **Dinner served** 6-10pm Mon, Sun; 6-11pm Tue-Thur; 6-11.30pm Fri, Sat. **Main courses** £5.50-£13.95. **Credit** MC, V.
Intimate and romantic are words you might not ordinarily associate with a moderately priced Vietnamese restaurant in London. Nevertheless, Saigon Saigon breaks the mould with dark wood furniture, low lighting and evocative touches such as paraffin table lamps and bamboo place-mats. Dishes from a wide spectrum vary in familiarity as well as quality. Deep-fried frogs' legs (dui ech chien bo) were delicately crisp and fragrant with butter, while the smoky-sweetness of chargrilled quail (chim cut nuong) was enhanced by a tangy lime dipping sauce. Our waiter's recommendation of plump king prawns in an aromatic satay sauce of crushed chilli and lemongrass was well received, but he missed the mark with a duck dish whose dry texture wasn't concealed by a flatly sweet red soy bean sauce. Steamed sea bass was let down by over-cooking. Thankfully, this was not the case with stewed caramel pork steeped in a thin but tasty sauce that managed to balance the strong flavours of fish sauce, star anise, palm sugar and pepper. Iced Vietnamese drip coffee was properly strong and sweet, and could well encourage lingering after a meal that's likely to satisfy if not astound.
Available for hire (bar). Babies and children welcome: high chairs. Booking advisable. Tables outdoors (4, pavement). **Map 20 A4.**

East
Shoreditch

Cây Tre
301 Old Street, EC1V 9LA (7729 8662). Old Street tube/rail/55, 243 bus. **Lunch served** noon-3pm Mon-Sat. **Dinner served** 5.30-11pm Mon-Thur; 5.30-11.30pm Fri, Sat. **Meals served** noon-10.30pm Sun. **Main courses** £4.50-£22.50. **Set dinner** £19 per person (minimum 2) 2 courses. **Credit** AmEx, MC, V.
With dim lighting, undulating black-and-white line drawings (featuring oriental and Buddhist motifs), and a smattering of rainbow-coloured light bulbs, Cây Tre does the hipster look in spades. On most nights the room gets full-to-bursting with young Hoxtonites. Fans and novices of Vietnamese food flock here; the menu is clearly written and, conveniently for imbibers, there are recommended wine pairings for most dishes. Those looking for table-side theatrics won't be disappointed. Order the signature cha ca la vong, a classic Hanoi dish, and it will be cooked in front of you in a sizzling metal pan. An abundance of fresh dill and fragrant yellow turmeric make this dish a winner; eat it with cold vermicelli noodles, crushed peanuts and the accompanying pungent shrimp paste. A perfectly crisp banh xeo was delicately curled around the edges, stuffed with prawns and chicken, and served with fresh herbs. It prompted a neighbour to enquire about the dish for his next visit. The friendly atmosphere is only tempered by the quick turnover of diners; you'll be taken care of during your meal, but with the constant queues, be prepared to make a swift exit afterwards.
Babies and children admitted. Booking advisable. **Map 6 4R.**

★ ★ Mien Tay
122 Kingsland Road, E2 8DP (7729 3074). Liverpool Street tube/rail then 67, 149, 242 bus/ Old Street tube/rail then 243 bus. **Lunch served** noon-3pm, **dinner served** 5-11pm Mon-Sat. **Meals served** 11am-11pm Sun. **Main courses** £4-£7. **Unlicensed. Corkage** no charge. **Credit** MC, V.
A sweet success story, this family-run restaurant has made a solid impression on diners who've already sampled most options on Kingsland Road's 'pho mile'. Mien Tay specialises in the lighter, more delicate cookery of southern Vietnam, and exudes a soft and quiet charm. The room is simple but not austere, while service is warm and helpful. Diners (mostly young couples or groups of locals) seem to be treated like honoured guests in a family home. More importantly, the food offers the same home-style comforts. An unofficial signature dish, chargrilled quail with honey and garlic, was perfectly timed, the meat succulent and imbued with a light smokiness. We also relished the prawn and green papaya salad (bursting with fresh mint and coriander), and the roll-your-own minced beef rice paper rolls (served with crunchy lettuce, herbs, and carrot and daikon pickles). The spiced minced beef was quite dry, but remedied by sweet nuoc cham dressing for dipping. Stems of morning glory, stir-fried in garlic and chilli, were astonishingly green and full of juicy crunch. Bun thit nuong (chargrilled pork atop cold vermicelli noodles) was top grade, with good charring on the meat. A haven of consistently good Vietnamese cooking.
Babies and children welcome: high chair. Takeaway service. **Map 6 R3.**

★ ★ Song Que (100)
134 Kingsland Road, E2 8DY (7613 3222). Liverpool Street tube/rail then 67, 149, 242 bus/ Old Street tube/rail then 243 bus. **Lunch served** noon-3pm, **dinner served** 5.30-11pm Mon-Sat. **Meals served** 12.30-11pm Sun. **Main courses** £4.50-£6.20. **Credit** MC, V.
The run-down decor, utilitarian furniture and canteen-style dining won't win any awards, but they've crept into the consciousness of Song Que's loyal customers, and the place has all the makings of a classic. Though far from unfriendly, staff are efficient too; you may be given a time limit on your

Saigon Saigon

table during busy weekend evenings. The food is excellent, and has remained remarkably consistent over the years. First comes the pho. The broth here is surely one of London's best: hitting all the spice notes, with a smooth, meaty undertone and a balance between richness and clarity. But the kitchen does many other things well. Bo luc lac, a dish of stir-fried cubed steak, is appropriately smoky and juicy, served with an excellent muoi tieu chanh (dipping sauce of lime juice, salt and pepper). Bo la lot (minced beef grilled in betel leaves) is a dish that always impresses, thanks to flawless execution that renders the beef moist and full of flavour. One dud note this time was the lotus root salad: a limp version that lacked the appropriate crunch and zing. So, yes, there are some weaknesses – but they don't pop up often.
Map 6 R3.

★ Tay Do Café
65 Kingsland Road, E2 8AG (7729 7223). Liverpool Street tube/rail then 67, 149, 242 bus/ Old Street tube/rail then 243 bus. **Lunch served** 11.30am-3pm, **dinner served** 5-11.30pm daily. **Main courses** £4-£12. **Set lunch** £4.30 2 courses. **Unlicensed**. **Corkage** £1 per person. **Credit** (over £10) MC, V.
Tay Do's vast dining room is often full, perhaps because this is the first available Vietnamese restaurant at the southern tip of Kingsland Road. The BYO policy undoubtedly helps too. Service is impersonal and brusque, but not unfriendly. The tome of a menu contains nearly 300 dishes (divided by ingredient: fish, poultry, vegetables, tofu…). It's easy to order badly. Few of our dishes matched the menu's promise; best was a starter of steamed pork-stuffed squid, which was generous with the well-seasoned, minced pork stuffing, and came with an excellent dipping sauce of lemon juice, salt and white pepper. Shredded pork skin and herb rolls included the appropriately rubbery skin, but was bland and seemed to lack the required freshness. Rarely found in London, southern-style hu tieu soup is here made with tapioca noodles; yet while the south of Vietnam may be known for its sweeter, cleaner flavours, this broth was unappetisingly sweet. Better was chargrilled goat on cold vermicelli, with a nice smoky aroma that compensated for the slightly overcooked meat. Dining here seems to be a hit and miss experience. While there's great variety, we'd rather choose from a smaller menu of consistently good dishes.
Babies and children welcome: high chair. Takeaway service. **Map 6 R3**.
For branch (Tay Do Restaurant) see index.

Victoria Park

★ Namo
178 Victoria Park Road, E9 7HD (8533 0639, www.namo.co.uk). Mile End tube then 277 bus. **Lunch served** noon-3.30pm Fri-Sun. **Dinner served** 5.30-11pm Tue-Sun. **Main courses** £6.90-£8.90. **Credit** MC, V.
Sister to Huong-Viet (*see right*), Namo is a bright, clean little café. Dark wood, bamboo, and paper lanterns make for modern simple surroundings. In summer, you can dine in the quiet back patio under the peaceful gaze of a large Buddha. Goi cuon was deliciously fresh and packed a pungent punch of zesty herbs and sweet prawns. Next, we slurped from a bowl teeming with rice noodles and beef (bun hue) stewed in a spicy broth that lacked depth of flavour. Bun xa (noodle stir-fry with chicken, beansprouts and herbs) hit the spot with its piquant tang and bright crisp textures. We poked suspiciously at a pot of ca kho, with its mackerel morsels stewed in dark ginger sauce, but found it full of delicious nutty caramelised flavours. Another surprise was our solo waiter, who at one point either left the premises or perhaps decided to hide. Eventually, we had to help ourselves from the server's station to more napkins; other diners followed suit to get cutlery. We ended on a sweet note, relaxing with a tall glass of Vietnamese iced tea. A smiling finish topped by a friendly bill.
Babies and children welcome: children's menu; crayons; high chairs. Booking essential weekends. Tables outdoors (4, patio). Takeaway service.

Khoai Café. See p278.

South East
Deptford

Café East NEW
Surrey Quays Leisure Park, SE16 7LH (7252 1212). Canada Water tube. **Lunch served** 11am-3pm, **dinner served** 5.30-10.30pm Mon-Fri. **Meals served** 11am-10.30pm Sat, Sun. **Main courses** £6.50-£7.50. **Unlicensed** no alcohol allowed. **No credit cards**.
Its former location – on the corner of a residential street in Deptford – was where you might expect to find a greasy spoon. Nevertheless, Café East had built up a loyal following. In early 2009 it moved to a large, airy building on the outer reaches of the Surrey Quays Leisure Park. The room is simple and clean and has the feeling of an efficient canteen. The kitchen prides itself on serving a few dishes well. There are only a dozen or so choices, including noodle soups, curries and traditional side dishes. The broth of the pho tai was superlative, with concentrated flavour; it arrived with generous handfuls of fresh, verdant herbs. Our only caveat concerns the slightly tough beef. Banh cuon, while a smaller portion than we've had here before, was another highlight: the rice noodle wrappings delightfully springy. A fresh glass of coconut juice, complete with chunks of soft white coconut flesh, was a fitting match for the robust flavours of the food. The move hasn't seemed to harm business; the room was packed with diners of all ages. Where good food goes, crowds follow.
Babies and children welcome: high chairs. Bookings not accepted. Disabled: toilet. Tables outdoors (5, pavement). Takeaway service.

North East
Dalston

★ Huong-Viet
An Viet House, 12-14 Englefield Road, N1 4LS (7249 0877). Dalston Kingsland rail/67, 149, 236, 242, 243 bus. **Lunch served** noon-3.30pm, **dinner served** 5.30-11pm Mon-Sat. **Main courses** £5.50-£6.50. **Set lunch** (Mon-Fri) £7 2 courses. **Credit** (over £12) MC, V.
Long celebrated for its cheap, cheerful cuisine, this community centre has a fervent following of locals. Elbow your way through a mobbed waiting area to the dimly lit, noisy cafeteria. Plastic table covers, folding chairs and paper napkins are set up for no-frills dining. Our surly waiter shouted around while taking our order, then abruptly ditched us midway through. He returned to chuck a plate of dark oily spring rolls in our direction, along with some fried spare ribs. We questioned the ribs, as we hadn't ordered them, but he shrugged and promptly bolted. They appeared on the bill – adding insult to injury, as they were soggy and full of bone fragments. Things improved with the com tam bao: tender slices of pork alongside a cool bed of vermicelli topped with fresh herbs. Five-spiced lamb was a bit greasy, but chock-full of crisp vegetables. Banh xeo didn't disappoint with its melange of sautéed prawns, pork, vibrant vegetables, and herbs tossed in a pancake. We successfully wooed our waiter back for the bill; it was lean enough to ensure our return, despite the shortcomings.
Babies and children welcome: high chairs. Booking advisable weekend. Separate rooms for parties, both seating 30. Takeaway service.

Hackney

★ ★ Green Papaya
191 Mare Street, E8 3QE (8985 5486). Bus 48, 55, 253, 277, D6. **Dinner served** 5-11pm Tue-Sun. **Main courses** £5-£8. **Credit** MC, V.
We've always been impressed by the continuous push to provide new and interesting dishes and ingredients at this welcoming eaterie. Vietnamese olives, meaty-tasting smoked tofu and, now, wing beans all feature on the carte – explained with great enthusiasm by the manager. Diners perch on plain wooden chairs and eat at wooden tables (the decor is more café-style than restaurant). Even midweek there was a constant flow of custom, as eclectic as

Menu

Although most Vietnamese restaurants in London offer a range of Chinese dishes, it's best to ignore these and head for the Vietnamese specialities. These contain fresh, piquant seasonings and raw vegetables that create entirely different flavours from Chinese cuisine. Vietnamese cookery makes abundant use of fresh, fragrant herbs such as mint and sweet basil; it also utilises refreshing, sweet-sour dipping sauces known generically as nuoc cham. Look out for spices such as chilli, ginger and lemongrass, and crisp root vegetables pickled in sweetened vinegar.

Some dishes are assembled at the table in a way that is distinctively Vietnamese. Order a steaming bowl of pho (rice noodles and beef or chicken in an aromatic broth) and you'll be invited to add raw herbs, chilli and citrus juice as you eat. Crisp pancakes and grilled meats are served with herb sprigs, lettuce leaf wraps and piquant dipping sauces. Toss cold rice vermicelli with salad leaves, herbs and hot meat or seafood fresh from the grill. All these dishes offer an intriguing mix of tastes, temperatures and textures.

Aside from the pronounced Chinese influence on Vietnamese culinary culture, there are hints of the French colonial era (in sweet iced coffee, for example, and the use of beef), along with echoes of neighbouring South-east Asian cuisines. Within Vietnamese cooking itself there are several regional styles; the mix of immigrants in London means you can sample some of the styles here. The food of Hanoi and the north is known for its street snacks and plain, no-nonsense flavours and presentation. The former imperial capital Hue and its surrounding region are famed for a royal cuisine and robustly spicy soups; look out for Hue noodle soups (bun bo hue) on some menus. The food of the south and the former Saigon (now Ho Chi Minh City) is more elegant and colourful, and makes much greater use of fresh herbs (many of these unique to Vietnam), vegetables and fruit.

Below are some specialities and culinary terms; spellings can vary.

Banh cuon: pancake-like steamed rolls of translucent fresh rice pasta, sometimes stuffed with minced pork or shrimp (reminiscent in style of Chinese cheung fun, a dim sum speciality).
Banh pho: flat rice noodles used in soups and stir-fries, usually with beef.
Banh xeo: a large pancake made from a batter of rice flour and coconut milk, coloured bright yellow with turmeric and traditionally filled with prawns, pork, beansprouts and onion. To eat it, tear the pancake apart with your chopsticks, roll the pieces with sprigs of herbs in a lettuce leaf, and dip in nuoc cham (qv).

Bun: rice vermicelli, served in soups and stir-fries. They are also eaten cold, with raw salad vegetables and herbs, with a nuoc cham (qv) sauce poured over, and a topping such as grilled beef or pork – all of which are tossed together at the table.
Cha ca: North Vietnamese dish of fish served sizzling in an iron pan with lashings of dill.
Cha gio: deep-fried spring rolls. Unlike their Chinese counterparts, the wrappers are made from rice paper rather than sheets of wheat pastry, and pucker up deliciously after cooking.
Chao tom: grilled minced prawn on a baton of sugar cane.
Goi: salad; there are many types in Vietnam, but they often contain raw, crunchy vegetables and herbs, perhaps accompanied by chicken or prawns, with a sharp, perky dressing.
Goi cuon (literally 'rolled salad', often translated as 'fresh rolls' or 'salad rolls'): cool, soft, rice-paper rolls usually containing prawns, pork, fresh herbs and rice vermicelli, served with a thick sauce similar to satay sauce but made from hoi sin mixed with peanut butter, scattered with roasted peanuts.
Nem: north Vietnamese name for cha gio (qv).
Nom: north Vietnamese name for goi (qv).
Nuoc cham: the generic name for a wide range of dipping sauces, based on a paste of fresh chillies, sugar and garlic that is diluted with water, lime juice and the ubiquitous fish sauce, nuoc mam (qv).
Nuoc mam: a brown or pale liquid derived from fish that have been salted and left to ferment. It's the essential Vietnamese seasoning, used in dips and as a cooking ingredient.
Pho: the most famous and best-loved of all Vietnamese dishes, a soup of rice noodles and beef or chicken in a rich, clear broth flavoured with aromatics. It is served with a dish of fresh beansprouts, red chilli and herbs, and a squeeze of lime; these are added to the soup at the table.

Though now regarded as quintessentially Vietnamese, pho seems to have developed as late as the 19th century in northern Vietnam, and may owe its origins to French or Chinese influences. Some restaurants, such as **Song Que** (see p294), offer many versions of this delicious, substantial dish.
Rau thom: aromatic herbs, which might include Asian basil (rau que), mint (rau hung), red or purple perilla (rau tia to), lemony Vietnamese balm (rau kinh gioi) or saw-leaf herb (ngo gai).
Tuong: a general term for a thick sauce. One common tuong is a dipping sauce based on fermented soy beans, with hints of sweet and sour, often garnished with crushed roasted peanuts.

the menu. Shredded banana-flower salad doesn't disappoint, with its strong salty-sour notes and fresh coriander; cubes of fried tofu, cooked simply with chilli, salt and pepper, were milky-soft within; stir-fried hanoi beef was less spectacular, until eaten in combination with the aromatic perilla leaves lying underneath the meat. The day's special, wing beans, served with chilli and a pungent shrimp paste, delivered on all levels – texture, flavour, aroma. We also enjoyed the chicken pho: a comforting bowl of crystal-clear yet meaty broth. To our delight, the kitchen has started making desserts; the durian custard tart was an intriguing creation, but fridge-cold and with slightly soggy pastry. Once puddings are mastered, Green Papaya will be near perfect.
Babies and children welcome: high chairs. Booking advisable. Takeaway service.

★ Tre Viet (100)
251 Mare Street, E8 3NS (8533 7390). Hackney Central rail/26, 48, 55, 253, 277, D6 bus. **Meals served** noon-11pm Mon-Thur, Sun; noon-11.30pm Fri, Sat. **Main courses** £4.70-£13. **Credit** MC, V.
Tre Viet looks like many of its Hackney counterparts – a basic, slightly cramped interior jazzed up with a smattering of Vietnamese mementoes. However, it's distinguished by a very long menu, encompassing unusual recipes and ingredients. Even dishes that sound familiar on the English-language menu can look different on the plate. Seafood spring rolls were appetisingly thin, crisp pancakes stuffed with a springy seafood paste. Rare goat salad (de tai chanh) rewards adventurous diners with a flavour punch of ginger, lemongrass and chilli. Stir-fried eel (luon xao sa ot) was delicately crisp and scented with galangal, although the flavour of the eel was unfortunately masked by the non-traditional flour coating. Chargrilled monkfish (cha ca la vong) was the least authentic dish we tried: the kitchen had run out of dill. Sea bream and taro sour soup was equally nondescript, with none of the fragrance and tanginess usually associated with this dish. Our meal started strongly, but faltered as it went on, turning what could have been a noteworthy experience into one that was simply different.
Booking advisable weekend. Disabled: toilet. Separate room for parties, seats 30. Takeaway service.
For branch (Lang Nuong) see index.

North
Finchley

★ Khoai Café
362 Ballards Lane, N12 0EE (8445 2039). Woodside Park tube/82, 134 bus. **Lunch served** noon-3.30pm, **dinner served** 5.30-11.30pm Tue-Sun. **Main courses** £5-£9.95. **Set lunch** £5.45 1 course, £7.45 2 courses. **Credit** MC, V.
Khoai Café has all the hallmarks of a worthy local: a sufficiently diverse, but not intimidating menu; friendly staff; and wallet-friendly dishes. Fried spring rolls were our only disappointment, and even then suffered from lack of authenticity rather than flavour, with too many mushrooms tipping the dish over the Chinese border. Grilled minced beef in betel leaves (bo la lot) and 'shaking beef' (bo luc lac) were both adequate, the former fragrant with lemongrass and the latter featuring tender cubes of beef marinated with garlic and fish sauce. Noodle soups were immensely satisfying: pho bo (slippery rice noodles bathed in a clear, sweet beef broth); and a refreshingly spicy and tangy bun hue with 'special topping' (incorporating beef, chicken, tofu and prawns). The standout dish however was cha ca la vong: moist chunks of grilled white fish that were delicate in texture yet deeply imbued with the garlic, chilli and fish sauce. These flavours were echoed in the accompanying nuoc cham dipping sauce, and perked up with dill and spring onions. Flavours overall were fresh and clean, an impression reinforced by the café's bright interior. This corner of Finchley is short on good restaurants, let alone ones producing exciting food in an appealing setting, so Khoai Café is very welcome here.
Available for hire. Babies and children welcome: high chairs. Takeaway service.
For branch see index.

Cheap Eats

Budget

When it comes to the crunch, where can you eat during the recession without breaking yet another bank? Well, here's a good place to start. We've tried to choose venues in London's otherwise pricey districts where you can have a decent meal for less than £20 a head without slumming it. In this section too you'll also find London's native cuisine, as served at traditional pie and mash shops.

There are many other opportunities to tuck into a bargain in our city, notably at budget restaurants serving the food of a particular country. For these, see the relevant chapter in the guide (Chinese, Global, Indian, Japanese, Korean, Thai, Turkish and so on), where you'll find low-priced eateries marked with a ★. And for a range of over 500 restaurants across the metropolis where you can eat for £20 per person or less, bag a copy of Time Out's *Cheap Eats in London* guide.

Central

City

Grazing
19-21 Great Tower Street, EC3R 5AR (7283 2932, www.grazingfood.com). Monument or Tower Hill tube/Fenchurch Street rail. **Meals served** 7am-4pm Mon-Fri. **Main courses** £3.95-£6.95. **Credit** MC, V.
There's a lot of meat behind the counter at this City grazing ground. It feels more carvery than sandwich bar, though not in a Harvester way. White-tiled and modern, with a large window at one end, Grazing has plenty of natural light, giving it the feel of an upmarket pie and mash shop. There's a lot of waffle on the menu (not the butter and syrup kind), the bacon sandwich is 'arguably the best… in the world', and the pork in the ham roll, bred and cured on a Dorset farm, is then 'lovingly transported to us here in London'. Does the food live up to the blurb? More or less. Sirloin steak sandwich had pink, tender meat, cooked perfectly, though the portion seemed quite meagre. Toad-in-the-hole was more generous, and equalled the quality of a half-decent gastropub. On a sunny Wednesday lunchtime there was a steady trade of City workers, mostly ordering takeaways. Lighter salad and sandwich options are available too, in case you're not up to a weekday yorkshire pudding topped with roast meat, sage and onion stuffing, and gravy.
Babies and children admitted. Tables outdoors (2, pavement). Takeaway service. **Map 12 R7.**

Leon
3 Crispin Place, E1 6DW (7247 4369, www.leon restaurants.co.uk). Liverpool Street tube/rail. **Meals served** 8am-10pm Mon, Tue; 8am-10.30pm Wed-Fri; 9am-10pm Sat; 10am-8pm Sun. **Main courses** £5.20-£6.80. **Credit** MC, V.
With eight outlets in London (and counting) and a high-profile cookbook, Leon is fast becoming a fixture on the capital's fast-food scene. We welcome it; the company's commitment to animal welfare, sustainability and healthy but tasty food is admirable, and the simple culinary creations usually work well. This branch is perhaps the coolest (and is certainly one of the largest). Industrial ceiling fittings, glass walls and mismatched 1950s furniture (battered leather sofas, lamps with retro patterns) are juxtaposed with metal tables and chairs and wooden picnic tables in the front terrace area. Lunchtimes are busy. The hot dishes we sampled were both satisfying and fresh: grilled halloumi combined perfectly with a sweet chilli relish, while aïoli chicken was both light and creamy. A brown rice and fresh coleslaw accompaniment (the same for all hot dishes) was wholesome and flavourful. Other excellent bets include the 'better brownie' (extremely moist) and smoothies. Breakfast baps, organic porridge, various wraps (mexican salsa, chilli chicken), superfood salads, and fruit- and spice-filled tea-time treats like cranberry and pecan flapjacks provide sustaining and delicious snacks or meals. A welcome addition to the Spitalfields food court.
Babies and children welcome: high chairs. Disabled: toilet. Tables outdoors (30, marketplace). Takeaway service. **Map 12 R5.**
For branches see index.

Passage Café
12 Jerusalem Passage, EC1V 4JP (3217 0090, www.thepassagecafe.com). Farringdon tube/rail. **Meals served** 11am-11pm Mon-Fri. **Dinner served** 5-11pm Sat. **Main courses** £10. **Credit** AmEx, MC, V.
This teeny, useful bistro transports savvy Farringdon folk to provincial France with its Ricard and Lautrec posters, Peugeot pepper grinders and amenable list of crêpes. A mix of wood, white and Sainsbury-orange tones gives the café a sweet 1970s utilitarian vibe that's nicely offset with smart, sassy service. Mains (coq au vin, say, or sea bass with saffron and sultana sauce) are but a tenner, and light meals considerably less. Crêpes tend to the classic – florentine, savoyarde, normande – but the earthy tang of traditional buckwheat flour can shock the uninitiated. Our espagnole crêpe, filled with potato, chorizo and coriander, arrived as a glistening folded parcel on a white rectangular plate. Vegetarians are welcomed with the likes of endive and walnut tarte tatin and risotto of goat's cheese, tomato and confit onions. The small kitchen certainly has an experimental side, as shown in a dessert of banana, beetroot and pomegranate salad. Drinks include three farm ciders, a neat choice of wines, coffee, tea and fruit juices. A sandwich-board outside advertises takeaway specials to local office workers – £5 for a hot steak baguette sure makes the chains near the station look a poor second.
Babies and children admitted. Tables outdoors (2, pavement). Takeaway service. **Map 5 O4.**

Square Pie
105C Commercial Street, E1 6BG (7375 0327, www.squarepie.com). Liverpool Street tube/rail. **Meals served** 10.30am-4.30pm Mon-Sat; 9am-5.30pm Sun. **Main courses** £3.50-£6.99. **Credit** MC, V.
Spitalfields Market seems the natural home for this small chain, serving simple, British grub to office workers, stall-holders and tourists. Branches now reach as far west as Westfield shopping centre, but this is where it all began, and where Square Pie returned when its new shop opened last year. Pies (and there's little else) are available in two sizes, on their own, or with a substantial mash made with the potato skins left on, and a choice of baked beans or peas. Classic steak and kidney was good value, filling, meaty, and properly crusty on the outside: pukka. There are vegetarian pies (spinach and feta, wild mushroom) and a pie of the month (thai green chicken curry on our visit). Desserts – more pie (apple and banoffi), cake (chocolate and carrot) – weren't available when we ate here; other branches may be better stocked. The friendly counter staff had never heard of a flat white (strong, creamy coffee), although it appeared on the menu above our heads. They had a try (bless) and came up with an americano. There's seating outside, under the market roof, or you can take your pie away (they're all served in cardboard boxes).
Babies and children welcome: high chairs. Tables outdoors (10, marketplace). Takeaway service.
For branches see index.

Clerkenwell & Farringdon

Little Bay
171 Farringdon Road, EC1R 3AL (7278 1234, www.little-bay.co.uk). Farringdon tube/rail. **Meals served** noon-midnight Mon-Sat; noon-11pm Sun. **Main courses** £7.45. **Credit** MC, V.
Little Bay is a great little chain to know about. Each restaurant is individually decorated in fabulously over-the-top style. This Farringdon branch (one of four in London) has been decked out in gold paint and deep reds, with the odd comic touch (take a look at the light-fitting on your way to the basement dining area). It's a bit DIY – someone had fun making the lampshades – but with the lights dimmed, the effect is cosy and warm (especially if you manage to bag one of the diner-style booths at the back). The menu offers a good range of simple dishes to suit most tastes. Starters include moreish garlic mushrooms with red pepper houmous, and salmon with horseradish cream and beetroot. Main courses vary from a very tasty spring vegetable lasagne with parmesan cream and rocket salad, to grilled lamb steak with balsamic vegetables and mint. In addition there are a few burgers and a choice of four classic desserts (including vanilla cheesecake and tiramisu). All this comes at a pleasing price: mains cost £7.45, starters and desserts £3.25, and if you eat between noon and 7pm, you'll find even lower prices.
Babies and children admitted. Booking advisable. Disabled: toilet. Separate room for parties, seats 120. **Map 5 N4.**
For branches see index.

Covent Garden

★ Canela
33 Earlham Street, WC2H 9LS (7240 6926, www.canelacafe.com). Covent Garden tube. **Meals served** 9.30am-10pm Mon-Wed; 9.30am-11pm Thur-Sat; 10am-8pm Sun. **Main courses** £5.90-£9.50. **Credit** MC, V.
Just a stone's throw from Covent Garden piazza, Canela is a well-priced Portuguese/Brazilian-inspired café. Bright windows and cheery staff make it a pleasant place for a pitstop coffee or a bite to eat after a shopping spree. Food ranges from sandwiches and salads to feijoada (black bean and pork stew with rice). The daily specials are good value; on our last visit they sold out fast. We plumped for a huge piece of chorizo tart (a bit stodgy and bland, with little of the spicy sausage). Better was a large slice of moist vegetable and goat's cheese rocambole (a Portuguese pastry), served with own-made crisps and salad. A grilled chicken and rice on the next table looked better still. A couple of pão de queijos (cheese breads) made nice starters to share and were as tangy and

chewy as any you'd find in Rio. We were delighted to see Guaraná Antarctica on the menu (a green soft drink wildly popular in Brazil). Desserts are extremely sweet, ranging from brigadeiros (chocolate balls) to pastéis de nata (custard tarts). In summer, two tables out front provide some of the best people-watching opportunities in town.
Babies and children admitted. Tables outdoors (4, pavement). Takeaway service.
Map 18 D3.
For branch see index.

Fitzrovia

Nando's
57-59 Goodge Street, W1T 1TH (7637 0708, www.nandos.co.uk). Tottenham Court Road tube. **Meals served** 11.30am-11pm Mon-Thur; 11.30am-11.30pm Fri, Sat; 11.30am-10.30pm Sun. **Main courses** £5.80-£10.60. **Credit** MC, V.
The appeal of this Portuguese-inspired chain lies, like that of most restaurant franchises, in its simplicity, lack of ceremony and keen prices. Though Nando's isn't quite a fast-food chain – with proper wooden tables and chairs, and a menu centred on freshly grilled chicken – the concept is not a million miles away (meal deals, bottomless refills on drinks, and a super-casual vibe). Chicken served with spicy peri peri sauce of varying degrees of fierceness is the mainstay, and is worth sticking to. Grilled halves and quarters are crisp skinned and juicy inside, while side dishes (flavoursome corn on the cob; thick-cut, slightly school-canteen chips) make for a filling, decent-value meal. Vegetarian dishes (halloumi and roast portobello mushroom wraps, say, or bean burgers) are served too, and fairly tasty. Staff on our last visit were chirpy and efficient. Overall, for a quick, straightforward meal (especially if you've got kids), Nando's smacks the Burger Kings of this world clear out of the water.
Babies and children welcome: children's menu; crayons; high chairs; nappy-changing facilities. Disabled: toilet. Tables outdoors (1, pavement). Takeaway service.
For branches see index.

Ooze
62 Goodge Street, W1T 4NE (7436 9444, www.ooze.biz). Goodge Street tube. **Meals served** noon-11pm Mon-Sat. **Main courses** £6.95-£14.95. **Credit** AmEx, MC, V.
This risotto and pasta specialist has gone from strength to strength since opening two years ago, and remains especially popular with lunching office workers. The interior is slick, airy and relaxed; pillar-box red and white walls are lined with mirrors, blown-up monochrome prints and displays of San Pellegrino and Acqua Panna bottles. A colourful back-wall mural of Italian landmarks, and wooden school chairs, lend a fun, arty element. Food is high-quality and well-priced. A reassuringly short lunch menu lists four risottos (salmon affumicato, toscano, funghi selvatici, and primavera) and three pasta dishes (spaghetti allo scoglio, spaghetti alla bolognese, trofie al pesto), plus a daily special of each. All cost around £8. An excellent new addition is the lunchtime antipasti/salad table; staff will load a small or large plate (£3.50 and £5.50 respectively) with your selections. Desserts (£5) are classic creamy Italian: a good tiramisu, panna cotta and sbriciolata (Italian crumble). Pleasant, efficient and down-to-earth service is the icing on the cake (tap water was brought gracefully, and we were asked if we'd like our leftovers wrapped up to take away). The evening menu features a selection of secondi, such as sirloin steak or salmon fillet.
Babies and children welcome: high chairs. Tables outdoors (3, pavement). Takeaway service.
Map 17 A1.

Leicester Square

Gaby's
30 Charing Cross Road, WC2H 0DE (7836 4233). Leicester Square tube. **Meals served** 9am-midnight Mon-Sat; 11-10pm Sun. **Main courses** £5-£9. **No credit cards.**

You'd be forgiven for overlooking Gaby's, a stone's throw from the tourist mecca of Leicester Square, but forget the unassuming façade and you'll see why this New York-style deli is popular. A counter at the front holds a selection of salads, vegetable fritters and stews. At the back are small plastic tables beneath walls plastered with theatre flyers. Standards are variable. On our last visit we ordered a smoked salmon bagel that arrived toasted, with a generous amount of tasty fish, though we wished the accompanying salad consisted of the treats from the front counter rather than a dull coleslaw and potato salad we received. A large falafel and salad in pitta was better, the chickpea balls crunchy and warm and covered in a vast amount of proper houmous. For dessert, a slice of lime cheesecake was nearly luminous on top, but weighty and rich, with a lovely sticky base. Fresh orange juice was a plus, as was decent coffee. Gaby's is an unpretentious café and a good place to know about, especially as a pre- or post-show eaterie.
Babies and children admitted. Disabled: toilet. Takeaway service. **Map 18 D5.**

Soho

★ Hummus Bros (100)
88 Wardour Street, W1F 0TH (7734 1311, www.hbros.co.uk). Oxford Circus or Tottenham Court Road tube. **Meals served** noon-10pm Mon-Wed, Sun; noon-11pm Thur-Sat. **Main courses** £2.80-£5.80. **Credit** AmEx, MC, V.
Take a seat, a perch, or take away at this inspired concept canteen specialising in bowls of houmous topped with all manner of goodies: from cumin-spiced chickpeas to slow-cooked beef. A regular portion, served with two pittas, doesn't look huge but is way plenty – this is rich, filling stuff. Specials might be houmous with italian sausage casserole (it worked, as the quirkier items typically do), or falafel salad with yoghurt, coriander and tomatoes. The usual canned soft drinks are available, but Hummus Bros takes care to offer its own lemonade with mint and ginger, hot spiced apple juice, and Monmouth cappuccino. 'How to eat' paper place mats, a chickpea-counting contest and T-shirts

Vincent Rooms. See p282.

beseeching 'Give peas a chance' hint at compulsory fun, but the smart red-and-wood decor and the sheer quality of food and drink put HB light years ahead of Happy Meals. The joint was pleasantly uncrowded mid-afternoon, when David Bowie pumping out of the sound system provided reason enough to stay for dessert (wonderful milk-based malabi drizzled with date syrup – highly recommended) and some mint tea.
Babies and children admitted. Bookings not accepted. Takeaway service. Vegan dishes.
Map 17 B3.
For branch see index.

★ Just Falafs
155 Wardour Street, W1F 8WG (7734 1914, www.justfalafs.com). Oxford Circus or Tottenham Court Road tube. **Meals served** 11am-4pm Mon, Tue, Sat; 11am-8pm Wed, Thur; 11am-9pm Fri. **Main courses** £4.75-£7. **Credit** AmEx, MC, V.
It's not just falafs at this easygoing Soho pitstop serving superior wraps. Since first opening on a quiet corner of Covent Garden piazza, the menu has segued from Simon Davies and Chris Skinner's original 'this-way-and-that, falafel-plus-stuff' concept, to a merry mix including free-range chicken, lamb meatball, and tuna wrap fillings, plus salads and stews. The fragrant chorizo, pork and chickpea stew lives up to the 'totally delicious' claim, served with a cooling yoghurt and cucumber topping that's unusual but not unpleasant, and grilled khobez bread. Apart from wraps, vegetarians have the possibility of tomatoey dahl, or a 'dips 'n' bits' selection, including the terrific spicy aubergine sauce, and signature roast butternut, sweet potato and feta sauce, served with falafels, pickles and flatbread. Want something sweet? There's baklava or, in the upright chiller cabinet, tubs of dense, cream-laden rice pudding topped with verdant pistachios. You'll also find the usual range of espresso-style coffees, bought-in yoghurty things, plus some own-made multi-fruit concoctions thickened with banana and ice. The queue to order at the counter can be a bit ramshackle, but staff efficiently brought our meal over to the table.
Takeaway service. **Map 17 B3.**
For branch see index.

Mother Mash
26 Ganton Street, W1F 7QZ (7494 9644, www.mothermash.co.uk). Oxford Circus tube. **Meals served** 8.30am-10pm Mon-Fri; noon-10pm Sat; noon-5pm Sun. **Main courses** £6.95-£7.95. **Credit** AmEx, MC, V.
This light, bright dining room with white tiled walls and marble table-tops makes a pleasingly cool, clean space in which to tuck into steamy piles of comfort food. Tall wooden booths comfortably seat four, with one table at the back for larger groups. The menu is laid out in three steps. Step One: choose your mash. This isn't as easy as it seems; the list includes horseradish, colcannon, champ and classic – and do you want it mashed or bashed? Step Two: choose your pie. There's lamb and rosemary, Aberdeen Angus steak, or maybe you'd prefer sausages. Step Three: the all-important gravy. The selection includes liquor, vegetarian, and mushroom and bacon. Despite all the choice, a meal here is undoubtedly about the mash. It's perfect: buttery and whipped until fluffy. Sadly, our stingily filled pie paled in comparison; and the gravy was over-abundant. Sausages were pretty ordinary too. The sweet pies are much better; apple and rhubarb pie, from the daily specials, was lovely, and came with a scoop of vivid yellow vanilla ice-cream. Chirpy staff and an appealing list of beers and wine make Mother Mash a worthy place to begin a night on the town.
Babies and children admitted. Tables outdoors (2, pavement). Takeaway service.
Map 17 A4.

Stockpot
18 Old Compton Street, W1D 4TN (7287 1066). Leicester Square or Tottenham Court Road tube. **Meals served** 9am-11.30pm Mon, Tue; 9am-midnight Wed-Sat; noon-11.30pm Sun. **Main courses** £4.20-£7.95. **Set meal** £5.85-£6.50 2 courses. **No credit cards.**

The Stockpot has been around for decades, and little seems to have changed since its opening. The café continues to attract people of all ages and walks of life, who come for homey, hearty dishes in generous portions and at great prices. The decor is undoubtedly dated, yet this only adds to the charm. The Old Compton Street branch is light and airy, with large windows that fold right back. There's banquette seating at the rear and smaller tables for two at the front (offering the perfect vantage point from which to watch the Soho goings-on outside). In the basement is another, rather gloomy dining room. The menu includes old-school English grub (liver and bacon, gammon and pineapple), but the pasta dishes are perhaps a safer bet – and there's a good choice of them (cream and mushroom pasta was simple and tasty). You'll also find a decent selection of big salads. Desserts continue to conjure up memories of school: golden syrup sponge, and apple pie served with a good dollop of custard. Service can be a little too quick, but it's usually friendly.
Available for hire. Babies and children admitted. Tables outdoors (2, pavement). Takeaway service.
Map 17 C3.
For branches see index.

Westminster

★ Vincent Rooms
Westminster Kingsway College, SW1P 2PD (7802 8391, www.westking.ac.uk). St James's Park tube/Victoria tube/rail. **Lunch served** noon-1pm Mon-Fri. **Dinner served** 6-7pm Tue, Thur. Closed June-Sep. **Main courses** £6-£10.50. **Set meal** *Escoffier Room* £24 3 courses incl coffee. **Credit** MC, V.
Few London restaurants offer such a high standard of cooking for the bargain price of £24 for three courses including canapés, petits fours and tea or coffee. What's the catch? Most of the waiters and chefs are learning their trade at Westminster Kingsway College's school of hospitality and culinary arts, which numbers Jamie Oliver, Antony Worrall Thompson and Ainsley Harriott among its graduates. Consequently, the brasserie and posher Escoffier Room (which admittedly feel rather institutional when it comes to decor) are open only during term-time, at hours that suit the college rather than the customers. The à la carte menu of the fine-dining room comes complete with French terminology and tricksy flavour combinations, such as crab bisque served with eel, carrot and ginger tortellini and watercress cream, or poached turbot with cep gnocchi, mussel fricassee and red wine and hibiscus emulsion. We spied on-trend seasonal ingredients including pollack, brown shrimp, veal cheeks and sweetbreads, plus curly kale, underlining that the college is not stuck in the days of Escoffier (who, let's face it, didn't keep it simple, despite his claims). The wine list isn't extensive but, with all bottles except champers under £20, it suits the savvy, wallet-friendly pitch of the place.
Babies and children welcome: high chairs. Booking advisable. Disabled: toilet. Separate room for parties, seats 30. **Map 15 J10.**

South

Battersea

Fish in a Tie
105 Falcon Road, SW11 2PF (7924 1913). Clapham Junction rail. **Lunch served** noon-3pm, **dinner served** 6pm-midnight Mon-Sat. **Meals served** noon-11pm Sun. **Main courses** £8.45-£13.50. **Set lunch** (Mon-Fri) £5 2 courses. **Credit** MC, V.
There's something distinctly odd about stepping off noisy Falcon Road into a Miss Havisham world of twinkling chandeliers and red candles melting into old liqueur bottles. Fish in a Tie offers an ultra-cheap 'credit crunch' lunch (two courses for a fiver on our visit), but even choosing à la carte you'll struggle to spend more than £20 for two. A sharing plate of calamares was plentiful, dressed in crisp breadcrumbs and not too chewy. For mains, there's a wide range of specials, though

vegetarians aren't spoiled for choice (perhaps the two types of sauce on the spinach and feta parcel is the kitchen's way of making amends). Hunter's pie was a forager's feast, with pheasant, wild boar and berries tucked under a hearty layer of suet pastry. Both main courses were whopping and came with the same selection of veg: sautéed potatoes, green beans and shredded cabbage. Dessert was the only disappointment. What should have been soft meringue cake tasted like squirty cream on wet sponge. Never mind: amazed by the meagre bill, we left plotting a group gathering here; it's a place that encourages long evenings of conversation by candlelight.
Babies and children welcome: high chairs. Booking advisable. Separate rooms for parties, seating 25 and 40. **Map 21 C3.**

Galapagos Bistro-Café
169 Battersea High Street, SW11 3JS (8488 4989, www.galapagosfoods.com). Clapham Junction rail. **Meals served** 9.30am-9.30pm Tue-Sat. **Main courses** £5-£9.50. **Set meal** £10.95 2 courses, £12.95 3 courses. **Credit** AmEx, MC, V.
The stalls outside might do a brisk trade in budget king-size buns, but in-the-know Battersea market traders choose this diddy deli-diner to satisfy their morning pastry urges. It's a charming living room-sized space, piled high with Ecuadorian art (lizards, parrots, sculptures carved from coal), imported teas and coffees, and own-made pots of pickles and preserves. We pulled up a bay-window cushion to tuck into plump olives, freshly baked bread and chorizo sausage as a starter. Vegetable lasagne arrived in a comfort-food sized portion with a piquant side salad; on this occasion, it came with aubergine and courgettes, but for picnics in the park Galapagos can rustle up four flavours including asparagus and mushroom. A hearty Tuscan casserole was let down only by its chunks of chicken being a little on the scrawny side. Puds are good too; we rate the cheesecake in particular. Service is charming and prices are low, with the daily-changing set meals a steal.
Available for hire. Booking advisable. Tables outdoors (2, pavement). Takeaway service.

South East

Bankside

★ The Table (100)
83 Southwark Street, SE1 0HX (7401 2760, www.thetablecafe.com). Southwark tube/London Bridge tube/rail. **Meals served** 7.30am-5pm Mon-Fri; 9am-5pm Sat, Sun. **Main courses** £5-£10. **Credit** AmEx, MC, V.
Bankside isn't short of culinary hotspots, but this lively independent outfit is among our favourites. Table is set on the ground floor of an architectural practice, with decor that's almost inevitably monastic. Communal tables are piled with white canisters of cutlery and napkins. A blackboard highlights eco-credentials (only glass bottles are used, and British pork); bowls of flaky sea salt underline the kitchen's connoisseurship. Hot dishes are proper restaurant calibre – pan-fried sea bream with chorizo and white beans, say, or chargrilled chicken curry with peas and rice. Expect a choice of quiches sold by the wedge, luxury sandwiches and a counter of serve-yourself salads sold by weight. Panzanella frugally made use of leftover focaccia, and featured big wet cubes of punchy-tasting marinated bread. Sauce cheekily labelled 'aubergine and yoghurt surprise' was delicious, so too potato salad with red onion and herbs, and lemony courgettes with olives. A mixture of rice, sweetcorn and cucumber was a bit so-what, yet combined with the other salads and rocket leaves made a delightful lunch on a hot day. The coffee's good, and there's own-made lemonade plus varietal apple juices in the chill cabinet. At weekends the brunch menu contains the likes of sweetcorn fritters, pancakes with bacon, maple syrup and caramelised banana, plus various combinations of egg and bread.
Babies and children admitted. Disabled: toilet. Tables outdoors (8, terrace). Takeaway service.
Map 11 O8.

East

Bethnal Green

★ E Pellicci (100)

*332 Bethnal Green Road, E2 0AG (7739 4873).
Bethnal Green tube/rail/8 bus.* **Meals served**
7am-4pm Mon-Sat. **Main courses** £5-£6.
Unlicensed. Corkage no charge. **No credit
cards.**

Still going strong, despite the death of legend
Nevio Pellicci in 2008, E Pellicci is an East End
institution and a gem of a caff. This hive of
humanity, a family business to the core, has been
trading since 1900. It's an aesthetic delight too; the
primrose-yellow Vitrolite exterior is a local
landmark, and the 1940s art deco wood-panelled
interior was awarded Grade II-listed status in 2005.

Nevio Pellicci Junior – as likeable, wisecracking
and warm a character as his late father – is now at
the helm, addressing customers in the famously
cheery Italo-Cockney way. The caff has gained
legions of fans over the decades, from salt-of-the-
earth locals to magazine editors, and such notables
as Gilbert & George, various *EastEnders* actors
and, a while ago, the Krays. The cross-cultural
menu features dozens of sandwiches, rolls and
ciabattas (hot'n'spicy chicken, ham off the bone);
breakfasts (standard, vegetarian, mixed grill); own-
made lunches like steak pie and lasagne; and
classic desserts of the bread pudding ilk. All
emerge from the art deco hatch that separates the
café from the kitchen, manned by mamma Maria
for over 40 years. Prices remain firmly rooted in
the old East End: a cup of tea with a generous
round of thick-cut crusty toast comes to £1.30.
Babies and children admitted. Takeaway service.

Brick Lane

Story Deli

*Old Truman Brewery, E1 6QL (7247 3137).
Aldgate East tube/Liverpool Street tube/rail.*
Meals served noon-10.30pm daily. **Main
courses** £8-£12. **Credit** AmEx, MC, V.

With its outdoor tables on Dray Walk and its huge
picture windows, Story Deli is great for people-
watching. Fans of the same-owned Story vintage
homewares shop on nearby Wilkes Street won't be
disappointed by the interior here; gilt mirrors,
reinforced cardboard pod stools and retro objets
perfectly suit this industrial-chic space, with its
high-ceilings, white brick walls and mismatched
long wooden tables. Coffee and sweet things are
worth ordering (especially the delicate shortbread),
but pizzas are the mainstay – the supremely thin

Pie and mash shops

At one time there was a pie and mash
shop at every street market in London,
lining the stomachs of costermongers
and shoppers alike. It is the low-cost,
working-class food that preceded
McDonald's and KFC – yet pie and mash
shops seem in terminal decline, a trend
that started with the working-class
diaspora of the 1960s.

Still, few London restaurants can
match the city's remaining pie and mash
shops for simple authenticity. Their menu
has altered little since the mid 19th
century: a wedge of glutinous mashed
potatoes, pies (minced beef and gravy in
a watertight crust), liquor (loosely based
on parsley sauce) and eels (jellied and
cold, or warm and stewed) – though
with the high prices of eels, more shops
are now sticking to plain pie and mash.
However, it's often the shops' remarkably
beautiful design that gives punters an
exceptional dining experience: in the
lettering of their facades, usually pitched
somewhere between clean-cut art deco
and twirly art nouveau; the austere
hygiene of their tiled interiors, complete
with moulded ceramic dadoes, backless
wooden benches and marble-topped
tables; and the spare functionality of
their steel counters and cash registers.

From the very beginning, the business
was largely dominated by three families
– the Cookes, the Kellys and the Manzes
– and the decor of some of their first
establishments still delights the eye.
The **Cookes** came first, apparently. Their
oldest existing shop (opening in 1900)
is at Broadway Market near London
Fields, Hackney. The family's magnificent
Kingsland High Street shop, which
opened in 1910, was Grade II listed in
1991, the first of its kind in the capital
to receive that official seal of approval;
it's now a Chinese restaurant, **Shanghai**
(*see p78*), but you can still view its
lavishly decorated frontage and interior.

The first of the **Manze's** shops is still
the best-looking, on Tower Bridge Road.
Opened in 1902, though the building
itself is ten years older, it features high-
backed benches below long mirrors set
into plain white-tiled walls relieved
by flower-pattern tiles. And a signed
photograph of satisfied customers Posh

and Becks. The **Kelly** shops are on two
famous East End streets, Bethnal Green
Road and Roman Road, where they're
well patronised by market traders and
shoppers. The oldest existing branch,
at 284 Bethnal Green Road, opened in
1937. In Tooting, **Harrington's** shop is
one of the oldest, dating from the early
20th century. **Clark's** took over a 1930s
Manze operation in Exmouth Market in
the late '50s, keeping the original shop-
front (though in the '70s the signwriter
apparently misspelt their name). All are
worth a look, as well as a meal, which
would still be cheap at twice the price.

WJ Arment

*7 & 9 Westmoreland Road, SE17 2AX
(7703 4974). Elephant & Castle tube/
rail/12, 35, 40, 45, 68A, 171, 176,
468 bus.* **Open** 10.30am-5pm Tue, Wed;
10.30am-4.30pm Thur; 10.30am-5.30pm
Fri; 10.30-6pm Sat. **No credit cards.**

Castle's

*229 Royal College Street, NW1 9LT (7485
2196). Camden Town tube/Camden Road
rail.* **Open** 10.30am-3.30pm Tue-Fri;
10.30am-4pm Sat. **No credit cards.**

Clark's

*46 Exmouth Market, EC1R 4QE (7837
1974). Farringdon tube/rail/19, 38, 341
bus.* **Open** 10.30am-4pm Mon-Thur;
10.30am-5pm Fri, Sat. **No credit cards.**
Map 5 N4.

Cockneys Pie & Mash

*314 Portobello Road, W10 5RU (8960
9409). Ladbroke Grove tube.* **Open**
11.30am-5.30pm Tue-Thur, Sat; 11.30am-
6pm Fri. **No credit cards.**

F Cooke

*150 Hoxton Street, N1 6SH (7729 7718).
Liverpool Street or Old Street tube/rail/
48, 55, 149, 242, 243 bus.* **Open** 10am-
7pm Mon-Thur; 9.30am-8pm Fri, Sat.
No credit cards. Map 6 R2.

F Cooke

*9 Broadway Market, E8 4PH (7254 6458).
Liverpool Street tube/rail then 26, 48 or
55 bus/London Fields rail.* **Open** 10am-
7pm Mon-Thur; 10am-8pm Fri, Sat.
No credit cards.

AJ Goddard

*203 Deptford High Street, SE8 3NT
(8692 3601). Deptford rail/Deptford
Bridge DLR/1, 47 bus.* **Open** 9.30am-3pm
Mon-Fri; 9am-3pm Sat. **No credit cards.**

Harrington's

*3 Selkirk Road, SW17 0ER (8672 1877).
Tooting Broadway tube.* **Open** 11am-9pm
Tue, Thur, Fri; 11am-2pm Wed; 11am-
7.30pm Sat. **No credit cards.**

G Kelly

*600 Roman Road, E3 2RW (8983 3552,
www.gkellypieandmash.co.uk). Mile End or
Bow Road tube/Bow Church DLR/8, 339
bus.* **Open** 10am-2.30pm Thur, Fri; 10am-
5pm Sat. **No credit cards.**

G Kelly

*414 Bethnal Green Road, E2 0DJ (7739
3603). Bethnal Green tube/rail/8 bus.*
Open 10am-3pm Mon-Thur; 10am-6.30pm
Fri; 9.30am-4.30pm Sat. **No credit cards.**

S&R Kelly

*284 Bethnal Green Road, E2 0AG (7739
8676). Bethnal Green tube/rail/8 bus.*
Open 9am-2.30pm Mon-Thur; 9am-5.30pm
Fri; 10am-3.30pm Sat. **No credit cards.**
Map 6 S4.

Manze's

*204 Deptford High Street, SE8 3PR (8692
2375). Deptford rail/Deptford Bridge DLR/
1, 47 bus.* **Open** 9.30am-1.30pm Mon,
Thur; 9.30am-3pm Tue, Wed, Fri, Sat.
No credit cards.

L Manze

*76 Walthamstow High Street, E17 7LD
(8520 2855). Walthamstow Central
tube/rail.* **Open** 10am-4pm Mon-Wed;
10am-5pm Thur-Sat. **No credit cards.**

L Manze

*74 Chapel Market, N1 9ER (7837 5270).
Angel tube.* **Open** 11am-5pm Tue-Sat.
No credit cards.

M Manze (100)

*87 Tower Bridge Road, SE1 4TW (7407
2985, www.manze.co.uk). Bus 1, 42, 188.*
Open 11am-2pm Mon; 10.30am-2pm
Tue-Thur; 10am-2.15pm Fri; 10am-2.45pm
Sat. **No credit cards.**

M Manze

*105 Peckham High Street, SE15 5RS
(7277 6181, www.manze.co.uk). Peckham
Rye rail.* **Open** 11am-2pm Mon; 10.30am-
2pm Tue-Thur; 10am-2.15pm Fri; 10am-
2.45pm Sat. **No credit cards.**

M Manze

*226 High Street, Sutton, Surrey SM1 1NT
(8286 8787, www.manze.co.uk). Sutton
rail.* **Open** 10.30am-3pm Mon; 11am-5pm
Tue-Fri; 10.30-5pm Sat. **No credit cards.**

and crispy wood-fired oven variety. Toppings, chalked on the blackboard, are deliciously fresh and light, featuring organic herbs, quality cheeses and olive oil. Help yourself to cutlery from the boxes on the tables, and soak up the chilled vibe (or catch up on emails; ask for the Wi-Fi code). Pizzas arrive on square wooden chopping boards. A chanterelle pizza (mushrooms, pine nuts, ricotta, parmesan) was divine, and large enough for two diners of modest appetite. Story is also ideal for a late-afternoon glass of vino. Our only grumbles? Service can be unbearably slow and dismissive, and there's no toilet. Sundays are inevitably hectic.
Babies and children welcome: high chairs; toys. Tables outdoors (5, pavement). Takeaway service. **Map 6 S5.**

Shoreditch

Macondo NEW
Unit 2b, 8-9 Hoxton Square, N1 6NU (7729 1119, www.macondo.co.uk). Old Street tube/rail. **Meals served** 9am-midnight daily. **Main courses** £5.95-£7.95. **Credit** MC, V.
One of two Macondos (the other is on Islington's equally modish Camden Passage), this is what London has long been crying out for: a café-bar straight out of Barcelona's Raval district. That means pseudo-trendy art on the walls, subdued lighting, a neat terrace and a deeply casual attitude to dining. In fact the place is so relaxed you're just as likely to eat your dinner off your lap on one of the nicely battered sofas as you are to sit at a table on the terrace (where you can do a spot of Hoxton Square scenester-watching). The menu wobbles comfortably around Latin America and Spain. Guacamole tasted fresh and zingy, and a smoked ham and butter bean salad made a nice, light dinner. Sincronizadas (pan-fried maize tortillas with ham, cheese and avocado) were comforting if a little thin on flavour. Macondon's cocktail list keeps with the Latin American theme, focusing on proper margaritas and caipirinhas, and starring a perfectly balanced Pisco Sour. There is also an interesting selection of Spanish and South American wines, good coffee and fresh juices. The staff need to cheer up a bit.
Available for hire. Babies and children admitted. Booking advisable weekends. Takeaway service. **Map 6 R3.**
For branch see index.

North East

Hackney

LMNT
316 Queensbridge Road, E8 3NH (7249 6727, www.lmnt.co.uk). Dalston Kingsland rail/236 bus. **Meals served** noon-11pm Mon-Sat; noon-10.30pm Sun. **Main courses** £7.95-£9.95. **Credit** MC, V.
First-timers to LMNT should be prepared to spend time examining the eccentric decor. A huge gold Egyptian pharaoh greets you upon entering, while ceiling drapes in bright orange and blue complement the colourful hieroglyphs and Mediterranean landscape paintings on the walls. Those in the know reserve a table in the gigantic urn or opera box. The venue may seem outlandish to newcomers, yet things haven't changed much here in the past few years. If anything, dishes have become better value. LMNT has always been cheap, but it now boasts better-quality produce. Fish cakes with cucumber and fennel salsa, and a wild boar sausage made enjoyable starters. To follow, salmon was cooked just so, and served with a black bean and avocado salsa that paired perfectly with the fish (its tangy freshness counteracting the salmon's oiliness). Belly pork with spinach pesto was terrific (the meat comes from Smithfields market). The wine too is good value, with several options available by the glass. Service was attentive throughout our meal. If you think the restaurant's interior is unusual, check out the toilets: outré indeed.
Babies and children admitted. Entertainment: opera 8pm Sun. Tables outdoors (3, garden). **Map 25 C5.**

Stoke Newington

Blue Legume
101 Stoke Newington Church Street, N16 0UD (7923 1303). Stoke Newington rail/73, 393, 476 bus. **Meals served** 9.30am-11pm Mon-Sat; 9.30am-6.30pm Sun. **Main courses** £4.95-£8.95. **Credit** (Mon-Fri) MC, V.
The main change to this Stokey stalwart over the years has been the introduction of meat dishes to the once veggie-dominated menu. Vegetarian food (nut roasts, chickpea and tahini burgers) is now mainly found in the glass counter at the front. Lunch specials include the likes of wild-mushroom omelette, steak sandwich, grilled salmon and a variety of pasta dishes, plus salads (tricolore, salad niçoise) and various panini (halloumi and spicy sausage, perhaps). One thing that hasn't changed is the popularity of the breakfasts, served until 4pm. Eggs benedict, organic honey waffles, welsh rarebit and themed set breakfasts go down well with the locals, who compete for the mosaic-topped tables in the boho-meets-Mediterranean interior (there's more seating out front, or in the rear conservatory). On our visit, the place was chocker with a mix of young mothers, freelance literary types and students. A long list of smoothies, ice-creams, fruit juices and hot drinks (with a huge choice of herbal teas), plus a fridge full of (visually unappealing) cakes fill the menu. We've heard complaints of slow service, but have generally found it obliging.
Babies and children welcome: high chairs. Booking advisable dinner. Tables outdoors (5, pavement). Takeaway service. **Map 25 B1.**

North
Camden Town & Chalk Farm

Marine Ices
8 Haverstock Hill, NW3 2BL (7482 9003, www.marineices.co.uk). Chalk Farm tube. **Lunch served** noon-3pm, **dinner served** 6-11pm Tue-Fri. **Meals served** noon-11pm Sat; noon-10pm Sun. **Main courses** £6.10-£13.60. **Credit** MC, V.
Family-run, popular, and seemingly little changed since opening in 1928, Marine Ices continues to be a great place to bring children or mates for a takeaway ice-cream, or a lively and good-value Italian meal. The retro ice-cream parlour, with a slightly unusual aquatic theme, is a fun place to be. Service is no frills but friendly, and the food simple. House specials can be tempting (own-made neapolitan fennel sausage with red wine, tomato and lentil sauce, for instance), as can the meat and seafood options. Still, we think the pizzas are the best option – huge, generously topped, and with crisp bases that spill over the edge of your plate. Pasta dishes are available too, with diners expected to choose their pasta shape and then the sauce. It's hard to resist the ice-cream when you see the line of people queuing outside for a scoop of their favourite. Yield to temptation: they're worth every calorie. There's a great selection, from toffee crunch to maple walnut, along with a choice of divine fruit sorbets such as mango or melon.
Babies and children welcome: high chairs. Booking advisable weekends. Takeaway service. **Map 27 B1.**

Islington

Le Mercury
140A Upper Street, N1 1QY (7354 4088, www.lemercury.co.uk). Angel tube/Highbury & Islington tube/rail. **Meals served** noon-1am Mon-Sat; noon-11.30pm Sun. **Main courses** £6.45. **Credit** AmEx, MC, V.
Le Mercury is a winner for those on a shoestring. The food is French bistro-style, but there are a few unusual combinations thrown in. All starters cost £3.95: not bad for a choice of eight dishes, including crayfish and lobster ravioli, and foie gras and duck ballotine with dates. Mains are great value too: £6.45 each and ranging from slow-roast honeyed belly of pork with celeriac and apple

confit, to sea bass with crushed new potatoes and mint. Desserts include classic crème brûlée and more unusual glazed pineapple with coconut sorbet. The cooking isn't perfect – fish cakes with shellfish sauce were distinctly average – but given the prices, it's hard to complain. The atmosphere is also a big part of the appeal; the room is candlelit and lively, full of groups of friends and dating couples. Service, though slightly brusque, is fine too. Le Mercury is deservedly popular, but remember to check if there's a table free in the first-floor dining room after you've peered through the downstairs window and assumed it's full.
Babies and children admitted. Booking advisable weekends. Separate room for parties, seats 50. **Map 5 O1.**

S&M Café (100)
4-6 Essex Road, N1 8LN (7359 5361, www.sandmcafe.co.uk). Angel tube. **Meals served** 7.30am-11pm daily. **Main courses** £5.25-£9.95. **Credit** AmEx, MC, V.
S&M Cafés present the acceptable face of chain dining. While traditionalists will balk at the funky menus and Super Furry Animals on the stereo, they'll be reassured that – in this branch – original Italianate caff trappings have been preserved, from steel-edged laminated tables to a magnificent art deco façade complete with Vitrolite sign. And, let's be honest, the food at S&M's six branches is superior to what used to be offered in the greasy spoons they have colonised. A starter of smoked haddock fish cake came with a zesty side salad. Black pudding fritters were a guilty pleasure. A gamekeeper's combo offered one pheasant sausage (dry, uninspiring), and one wild boar banger (moist, robust) that pointed *Beano*-style out of a pile of rich, cheesy mash surrounded by peppery gravy. S&M now offers pie and mash too; our chicken and leek number came fully enclosed in moist shortcrust, its flavour bolstered by big chunks of bacon. With a bottle of London Pride – dandelion and burdock for the young 'uns – this was the best of British at half the price of a gastropub.
Available for hire. Babies and children welcome: children's menu; high chairs; nappy-changing facilities. Booking advisable. Tables outdoors (5, pavement). Takeaway service. **Map 5 O1.**
For branches see index.

Outer London
Richmond, Surrey

Stein's
55 Richmond Towpath, Richmond, Surrey TW10 6UX (8948 8189, www.stein-s.com). Richmond tube/rail then 20 mins walk or 65 bus. **Meals served** *Summer* noon-10pm Mon-Fri; 10am-10pm Sat, Sun. *Winter* noon-10pm Sat, Sun. Times vary depending on weather, call to check. **Main courses** £7.90-£14.90.**Set lunch** (noon-4pm Mon-Fri) £5.99 1 course incl soft drink. **Credit** MC, V.
Stein's planted its flag on this genteel stretch of the Thames five years ago, bringing the Rhineland to Richmond. Food – sausages, mainly – is cooked in a chic shack (owner Reinhard is an architect) where you place your order. It's only then (on proof of purchase of food) that you can buy the frothing steins of German lager that give this summer-only beer garden its name. Confusion reigns, especially when you must weave back through the queue to deliver your drinks and pick up your two types of mustard. A plump curry wurst with tangy sultana-dotted sauce and bratkartoffeln (sautéed potatoes), plus dark Erdinger Dunkel weissbier, help compensate. Sauerkraut, scooped from the barrel, makes a wonderful accompaniment, and even our vegetarian companion was happy with a bowl of kaesespaetzle (gnocchi-like pasta with cheese and onion). With above-average prices for fairly basic fare served on plastic plates, Stein's won't be for everyone. But on a summer Sunday, as passing boats make the willows ripple, it can make you feel on holiday in your own city.
Babies and children welcome: crayons; high chairs; nappy-changing facilities; play area. Bookings not accepted. Disabled. Tables outdoors (28, towpath). Takeaway service.

Burger Bars

Breaking any perceived link with fast-food chains, London's gourmet burger restaurants have come of age over the past few years and well deserve their own section of this guide. Juicy thick burgers made with prime meat cooked to order are a world away from the factory-made junk food that's available on every high street. And the best of these establishments – the likes of **Ground** and **Gourmet Burger Kitchen** – also pay careful attention to side dishes and sauces. This year we welcome four new venues: Mile End's **Greedy Cow**, the **Carnaby Burger Co** near Oxford Circus, **Cheeky Pete's** in the City, and burgeoning small chain **Byron**.

Central
Bloomsbury

Ultimate Burger
34 New Oxford Street, WC1A 1AP (7436 6641, www.ultimateburger.co.uk). Tottenham Court Road tube. **Meals served** noon-11pm Mon-Sat; noon-10pm Sun. **Main courses** £5.55-£7.25. **Credit** AmEx, MC, V.
At first glance there isn't much to differentiate Ultimate from London's other posh burger chains. Food consists of the standard upmarket take on burgers, though with limited success. A huge bacon cheeseburger came with a big dollop of sweet barbecue sauce, which made it seem no less junky than its Burger King counterpart. It was tasty, though, and had the patty not been so dry (we weren't asked how we wanted it cooked), we might have been tempted to return for this guilty pleasure. A chicken burger also disappointed: the cranberry sauce too sweet, the chicken breast too dry and the brie so tasteless and melted that we initially wondered whether it had been left out. Chips were better (fluffy inside, crunchy outside), though the portion was meagre. A dull side salad of cucumber and lettuce was lifted by a sharp dressing. The space is bright and airy, and staff are pleasant, but this place needs to try harder to live up to its name.
Babies and children welcome: high chairs. Disabled: toilet. Takeaway service. **Map 18 D2.**
For branches see index.

Fitzrovia

Hamburger+
64 Tottenham Court Road, W1C 2ET (7636 0011, www.hamburgerunion.com). Goodge Street or Tottenham Court Road tube. **Meals served** 11.30am-10.30pm Mon-Sat; 11.30am-8pm Sun. **Main courses** £5-£8. **Credit** AmEx, MC, V.
Formerly Hamburger Union, this is one of the better of the second-division deluxe burger joints. There are half a dozen branches in London, well located in tourist hotspots, but they are just as often frequented by locals in need of a quick snack. Menus are now presented Wimpey-style in a laminate format. The decent range of burgers includes a reasonable number of vegetarian choices, but the selection is nothing like the wildly original menu of, say, Gourmet Burger Kitchen. As is often the case these days, most burgers come slathered in red onion, but the beef is hefty and cooked to order. There are also chicken and chorizo burgers, fries (ours were over-salted) and pretty good shakes. The look is an approximation of a diner, but with all the warmth carefully siphoned out, removing any desire customers might have to linger.
Babies and children welcome: high chairs. Takeaway service. **Map 10 K5.**
For branches see index.

Soho

Carnaby Burger Co `NEW`
14-16 Foubert's Place, W1 7PH (7287 6983, www.burgerco.co.uk). Oxford Circus tube. **Open** noon-9.30pm Mon, Tue; noon-10.45pm Wed-Sat; noon-6.30pm Sun. **Main courses** £5.55-£17.95. **Credit** AmEx, MC, V.
Despite the capacious dimensions of the CBC's green-walled dining room, most customers cram on to the pavement in warm weather to absorb the vibe that filters over from Carnaby Street. Staff were slow to respond to our arrival (they were busy with outside tables), but we soon got a friendly nod from chefs in the open-plan kitchen, who tried to catch their attention. Our meal kicked off with a pleasing bottle of French syrah rosé. Chicken wings daubed with heady barbecue sauce and garnished with celery followed: a succulent hit in a patchy evening. The amiable waitress was keen for us to specify how we wanted our burgers cooked, yet two requests for medium arrived well-done and medium-rare. A bowl of lacklustre fries topped with beef chilli and crème fraîche failed to make a harmonious whole. Onion rings were much better. Desserts are supposedly handmade, but by whom, we wonder? Both an Oreo cheesecake and a chocolate brownie were soulless and would have looked at home in Starbucks.
Babies and children welcome: children's menu; high chairs; nappy-changing facilities. Disabled: toilet. Tables outdoors (9, terrace). Takeaway service. **Map 9 J6.**

West
Chiswick

★ Ground
217-221 Chiswick High Road, W4 2DW (8747 9113, www.groundrestaurants.com). Turnham Green tube. **Meals served** noon-10pm Mon, Tue; noon-10.30pm Wed, Thur; noon-11pm Fri; 11am-11pm Sat; 11am-10pm Sun. **Main courses** £5.75-£8.35. **Credit** AmEx, MC, V.
Ground's open kitchen and main dining room are in the modern sky-lit front section of the premises, an interesting conversion of an old building. In good weather, tables spill on to the pavement. Still a one-off, this classy joint rarely puts a foot wrong. Specials, whether burgers or beers (Tusker from Kenya and Australian fave Victoria Bitter on our visit), are worth a look – so too the side dishes, though the beer-battered onion rings and courgette fries are much better than the shoestring chips. Blue cheese burger was exactly what it should be,

Ultimate Burger

CHEAP EATS

with a whacking great slice of gorgonzola atop the meat and caramelised onions providing a sweet dimension. A New York Deli number included creamy coleslaw as well as barbecue sauce, bacon and cheddar. Lamb, chicken, salmon and a choice of vegetarian dishes are offered in addition to the staple 7oz grass-fed Aberdeen Angus patties. There are also salads and, for low-carb fiends, a burger with extra salad instead of a sesame seed bun. Cheesecake and ice-cream account for most of the short list of puddings – perhaps better to opt for one of the luxurious shakes (at £3.80 they should be), which come malted for an extra 25p.
Babies and children welcome: children's menu; high chairs; nappy-changing facilities. Disabled: toilet. Separate room for parties, seats 52. Tables outdoors (8, pavement). Takeaway service.

Kensington

Byron NEW

222 Kensington High Street, W8 7RG (7361 1717, www.byronhamburgers.com). High Street Kensington tube. **Meals served** noon-11pm Mon-Thur; noon-11.30pm Fri; 11am-11.30pm Sat; 11am-10.30pm Sun. **Main courses** £5.50-£8.25. **Credit** AmEx, MC, V.
Byron's belief that hamburgers shouldn't be 'swamped by a mass of exotic, posh or gourmet ingredients' will have some punters applauding and others finding the menu, well, rather dull. Sure, there's a choice of cheddar, blue, gruyère or monterey jack for your cheeseburger, and the signature burger adds bacon and 'Byron sauce' (essentially thousand island dressing smartened up with capers and peppers), but for more interesting combinations you'll have to pimp your classic from a limited selection of extras (£1 each). Vegetarians are simply offered portobello mushroom with goat's cheese, red peppers and spinach. Both our nicely plump beef burgers were meant to be cooked medium, yet one dripped bloody juice. Skin-on hand-cut chips and onion rings with herb-flecked bubbly-crisp batter made great accompaniments (skip the dreary french fries). We loved the milkshakes served in proper icy-cold metal beakers, and the straight-talking wine list (divided into good, better, great and best categories). Staff keep things moving swiftly.
Babies and children welcome: children's menu; high chairs; nappy-changing facilities. Bookings not accepted Sat, Sun lunch. Disabled: toilet. Tables outdoors (4, pavement). Takeaway service. **Map 7 A9.**
For branches see index.

Shepherd's Bush

★ Gourmet Burger Kitchen

Upper Southern Terrace, Westfield Shopping Centre, W12 7GB (8600 9005, www.gbkinfo.com). Wood Lane tube. **Meals served** noon-11pm Mon-Fri; 11am-11pm Sat; 11am-10pm Sun. **Main courses** £5.96-£9.95. **Credit** AmEx, MC, V.
It took mental arithmetic to figure out which of the various GBK discount vouchers that we'd printed from the web would provide the greatest saving – but these days it's madness to turn up without one. This Westfield shopping-centre branch is not, as you might think, a mega-version of the suburban outlets, but a modestly sized restaurant able to keep things on the same friendly level. GBK's milkshakes are reliable, though if you're in the mood for booze, it's worth forking out the extra 10p a glass for lush New Zealand Stoneleigh rosé over the pink pinot grigio, or opting for Laverstoke Park Farm's excellent organic ale (500ml £4.95). New Zealand-born chef Peter Gordon was consultant on the grand tour of a menu, but it was a grill chef at GBK West Hampstead who devised our lip-tingling habanero beef burger featuring mozzarella: one of eight new offerings when we visited. Fries – golden and crisp without, fluffy within – are terrific, but don't ignore the 'slaw, which comes mayo-free, adding a delicious-nutritious quality to what is one of London's great guilty pleasures.
Babies and children welcome: high chairs; nappy-changing facilities. Bookings not accepted. Disabled: toilet. Tables outdoors (20, terrace). Takeaway service. Vegetarian menu. **Map 20 C1.**
For branches see index.

East

Mile End

Greedy Cow NEW

2 Grove Road, E3 5AX (8980 7011, www.greedy cow.com). Mile End tube. **Meals served** noon-11pm daily. **Main courses** £7.95-£10.95. **Credit** MC, V.
This relatively new addition to Mile End limited range of eateries is proving popular with students. On our Sunday afternoon visit, the half-dozen couples – who nestled next to the fairy lights, bare brick walls and imposing black-and-white wallpaper – didn't look much beyond 20 years of age. Burgers form a large part of an international menu, which otherwise offers such choices as 'eastern spice'-marinated lamb chops, and salmon with spicy lime and soy dressing. The focus is on building your own burger by adding a range of toppings and sauces to a fish, chicken, beef, lamb or veg patty. From the standard options, a mexican burger came piled high with jalapeño peppers, guacamole and salsa. Jerk chicken burger contained a disappointingly thin fillet that looked like it had been malleted into an escalope, but the pineapple salsa garnish was pleasingly tangy. Both dishes came artfully presented next to a construction of chicory, tomato and rocket splashed with dijon dressing, but chips and potato wedges tasted as if they'd come out of a plastic bag. Overall, the Greedy Cow could do with paying as much attention to ingredient quality as it does to presentation.
Babies and children welcome: high chairs; nappy-changing facilities. Booking advisable weekends. Disabled: toilet. Separate room for parties, seats 25. Takeaway service.

Spitalfields

Cheeky Pete's NEW

1A Bell Lane, E1 7LA (7377 0665, www.cheeky petes.com). Aldgate East tube/ Liverpool Street tube/rail. **Lunch served** 11am-3pm, **dinner served** 6-11pm Mon-Fri. **Main courses** £5-£10.50. **Credit** MC, V.
Crazy name, crazy place. Cheeky Pete's can be found in a tiny basement off Petticoat Lane, where the liberal use of mirrors is meant to create the illusion of space. It actually creates the very real prospect of having to stare down your own throat while man-handling a monstrous burger. The USP here is building your own burgers. Arrive at the counter and you're handed a form containing a range of options: type of burger (falafel, beef, chicken), choice of cheese, toppings, sauces and side dishes. Tick the ones you fancy (you get five toppings free and pay for any more on top) and the kitchen does the rest. It's fun and quick, and could lead to a terrific game of dare where you construct the least-appetising burgers imaginable for your friends. The burgers are hefty and sides are generous, but a blaring TV had us eating and leaving as quickly as digestion would allow – which is probably exactly what was intended.
Babies and children welcome: children's menu; high chairs; nappy-changing facilities. Disabled: toilet. Takeaway service. **Map 12 R6.**

North

Camden Town & Chalk Farm

Haché

24 Inverness Street, NW1 7HJ (7485 9100, www.hacheburgers.com). Camden Town tube. **Open** noon-10.30pm Mon-Sat; noon-10pm Sun. **Main courses** £6.95-£12.95. **Credit** AmEx, MC, V.
Haché's dark, woody interior features ceiling beams, and mirrored panels that give the impression of a skylight. Slightly incongruously, the walls are decorated with Edward Hopper prints of lonely people in diners. There's a wide choice of burgers on the menu, ranging from duck and venison to a welcome vegetarian selection. We ordered steak au naturel and lamb au naturel (with sides of frites, potato wedges and a green salad), figuring that a

gourmet burger bar should be able to produce top-notch basic burgers. Haché duly excelled, raising the humble patty to restaurant standards: portions were large and the meat first-rate. The lamb was accompanied by mint sauce, redcurrant jelly and garlic yoghurt, but also on the table were the more-traditional extras of mustard and ketchup. Our one niggle was with the attitude of the staff, who seemed uninterested and dismissive.
Babies and children welcome: high chairs. Booking advisable weekends. Takeaway service. Vegetarian menu. Vegan dishes. **Map 27 C2.**
For branch see index.

Kentish Town

Grand Union

53-79 Highgate Road, NW5 1TL (7485 1837, www.gugroup.co.uk). Kentish Town tube/rail. **Meals served** noon-3pm, 5-9pm Mon-Sat; 1-8pm Sun. **Main courses** £4.99-£25. **Credit** AmEx, MC, V.
Scan its dimly lit interior, and you'll figure that Grand Union is more a .style bar than a burger restaurant. The decor incorporates kitsch floral wallpaper, Moroccan-style rugs, a bird cage and green plant-fronds poking from big, black pots. Still, the burgers are thick patties in tall, densely seeded buns, served skewered with a steak knife (although we weren't asked how we wanted the meat cooked). The sharpness of an enjoyably vinegary mint sauce combined nicely with the chargrilled tang of a lamb burger. Better still, the chips are among the finest: inside as fluffy as a little potato cloud, but with an impressively thick, crisp golden coating that belies their single frying. However, ours left a slightly disconcerting oil-slick in the bowl. The menu also lists french fries (ours were disappointingly flimsy) and 'breadless burgers'. Beware the odd misleading description: the chips aren't 'London's best (as rated in *Time Out* Magazine)', they were rated eighth best. And nice as it was, our GU earth burger probably wasn't the 'world's hottest burger'. Still, with those chips, we'll forgive them.
Available for hire. Babies and children welcome (before 9pm); high chairs. Booking advisable weekends. Disabled: toilet. Separate room for parties, seats 75. Tables outdoors (15, pavement). Takeaway service. **Map 26 A4.**
For branches see index.

North West

Swiss Cottage

Fine Burger Company

O2 Centre, NW3 6LU (7433 0700, www.fine burger.co.uk). Finchley Road tube/Finchley Road & Frognal tube/rail. **Meals served** noon-11pm Mon-Sat; noon-10pm Sun. **Main courses** £5.75-£7.90. **Credit** AmEx, MC, V.
The FBC's tomato-shaped ketchup dispensers are of white rubber, with a silver plastic nozzle. Its plastic chairs curve modishly, and stylish red and white light globes hang above its dining area. Yep, this shopping-centre eaterie has cool-diner decor off pat. Less pleasing are the pushy slogans of wall-mounted photos bearing legends like 'why not try a meal combination?' And there's no avoiding the background echo of the shopping centre. Don't be fooled by adventurous-sounding burger options like thai chicken satay; jerk chicken with avocado and pineapple salsa; or grilled chorizo with wild rocket, aïoli and piquillo pepper. This cooking is with its heart very much set in previous decades. A blue cheese dip tasted more like mayonnaise; chunky chips 'with skin left on' had a motorway-services blandness; and despite onion rings being 'chilli and cracked black pepper' tempura-battered, they were greasy and flavourless. Things improved tremendously with an outstanding rich and chunky malty peanut butter and banana milkshake. Service was prompt and polite too, but was obviously not enough for the two separate customers we saw angrily asking for refunds. So-so.
Babies and children welcome: children's menu; high chairs; nappy-changing facilities. Booking advisable weekends. Takeaway service.
Map 28 B3.
For branches see index.

Cafés

Londoners used to be so envious of continental café culture: the long hours on sunny European piazzas, indulging in a glass of wine, perfect pastries or top-notch coffee. But the fretting is over: apart from the sunshine, we have everything here. The past couple of decades have seen a tremendous broadening in the range of cafés across the city, and below we don't even include the greasy spoon caffs (the best of which can be found in the **Budget** section, starting on p280). As well as traditional British tea rooms, our favourite of which is **Orange Pekoe** in Barnes, you can now find cafés specialising in the comestibles of the world's cake hot-spots: Soho's **Nordic Bakery** and Marylebone's **Scandinavian Kitchen** for northern European delicacies; Farringdon's **Kipferl** and East Dulwich's new **Luca's Bakery & Café** for Austrian treats; **Cake Boy** of Battersea and Clapham's **Macaron** for French pâtisserie; South Ken's **Hummingbird Bakery** for US-style cupcakes – even favourite Aussie cakes can be enjoyed along with your flat white at Fitzrovia's **Lantana**, winner of our Best New Café award. We've also listed the best of the park cafés and the new breed of café – the likes of **Clerkenwell Kitchen** and Marylebone's **La Fromagerie** – where first-rate ingredients are the draw and main courses are on par with those served in good restaurants.

CAFÉS, PÂTISSERIES & TEA ROOMS

Central

Bloomsbury

★ Bea's of Bloomsbury
44 Theobalds Road, WC1X 8NW (7242 8330, www.beasofbloomsbury.com). Chancery Lane or Holborn tube. **Meals served** 8am-7pm Mon-Fri; 10am-6pm Sat; noon-6pm Sun (by appointment). **Main courses** £3-£7.50. **Credit** AmEx, MC, V.
Ladylike chairs with matching wallpaper in teal and brown bring something of the boudoir to this little Bloomsbury haven. At the rear, a sky-lit open kitchen shows bakers producing the goodies displayed seductively at the front. Ingredient quality is important at Bea's, which flags up its Valrhona chocolate, Born & Bread organic sourdough, and Square Mile coffee. Environmental efforts are reflected in the use of induction cooking methods and a rejection of air-freighted goods. Drop by early morning and you can pick up ham, cheddar and chive scones, or a feta, olive and sun-dried tomato muffin, if the toast, yoghurt and granola or sweet muffins don't take your fancy. Pizza, pasta salads, sandwiches and soup are served for lunch (or are available as takeaways). Our sweetcorn and crab chowder didn't sing of spring, but was creamily rich, with good chunks of shellfish and potato; the accompanying bread was dry on one side, but that's forgivable at the end of a busy lunchtime. Gateaux tend to be too rich and sweet, making portions heavy-going; fruity, wholesome banana cake didn't benefit from being layered with hazelnut praline cream. Sunday afternoon teas (booking essential) start at around a fiver for two scones with tea, while the unlimited spread is £13 per person.
Available for hire. Babies and children admitted. Booking advisable. Tables outdoors (2, pavement). Map 4 M4.

City

Taylor Street Baristas [NEW]
1A New Street, EC2M 4TP (7929 2207, www.taylor-st.com). Liverpool Street tube/rail. **Open** 7am-5pm Mon-Fri; 10am-4pm Sun. **Main courses** £4-£5.50. **No credit cards.**
Bravely positioned opposite Starbucks, and, more conveniently, just a teabag's-throw from Liverpool Street station, this charcoal-fronted coffee shop is the City outpost of a company that first gained renown running the coffee counter in the Source food store in central Richmond. If you don't notice the accents, the jar of anzac biscuits by the espresso machine is another clue: the gang is mostly Antipodean. Fairtrade icon Union Hand-Roasted supplies the coffee beans, which are ground to order, natch. There are a few stools by the bar, but the emphasis is on takeaway (though many people drink their fix outside on the pedestrianised street). A kitchen upstairs supplies the food – a long list of charcuterie, cheese and chicken sandwiches, plus salads and cakes. Greek salad served from the bowl in the counter wasn't exactly straight from Santorini, and a bit light on feta, but was packed with crunchy cos lettuce and green olives and had a great balance of tastes. Banana bread was well flavoured but a little dry. In addition to all the expected coffees, chai latte and a rich, frothy hot chocolate, Taylor Street Baristas has a sizeable list of health-oriented smoothies, with claims such as detox and brain booster attached.
Babies and children welcome. Takeaway service; delivery service. Vegan dishes. Map 12 R6.

Clerkenwell & Farringdon

★ Clerkenwell Kitchen
27-31 Clerkenwell Close, EC1R 0AT (7101 9959, www.theclerkenwellkitchen.co.uk). Angel tube/ Farringdon tube/rail. **Meals served** 8am-5pm Mon-Wed, Fri; 8am-11pm Thur. **Main courses** £4.50-£14. **Credit** MC, V.
Restaurant-calibre food in a stylishly informal café setting – what's not to like about Clerkenwell

Kitchen? Tucked away in an office development for creative professions (which surrounds the attractive decked terrace at the rear), it has a ready supply of enthusiastic customers who pop in for coffees, takeaway sandwiches, lunch meetings and quiet moments with the Wi-Fi. From noon, high-quality meals of fresh, often local, produce are served. On our visit, rare roast beef salad with pink fir potatoes and tarragon sauce featured meat from Ashlyn's organic farm in Essex; the pollack in the fish cakes was smoked on the premises; and a wild rabbit and spring-mushroom pie glorified the season. Cheesy, toasty, new-potato and rocket frittata was accompanied by crisp, classically dressed leaves and a beetroot salad with fresh marjoram that really made it sing. Being picky? That perfectly eggy pear and almond tart, astutely served with a blob of crème fraîche, needed a fork as well as a spoon to eat, and the range of cakes could be wider – but you can hardly call these faults. Enjoy the rich pickings with a glass of wine (lovely French rosé well worth £4), bottled Adnams or Meantime beers, Chegworth Valley juices and/or well-made Union Hand-Roasted coffee.
Babies and children welcome: high chairs. Disabled: toilet. Tables outdoors (8, courtyard). Takeaway service. Map 5 N4.

Dose Espresso [NEW]
69 Long Lane, EC1A 9EJ (7600 0382, www.dose-espresso.com). Barbican tube/ Farringdon tube/rail. **Open** 7am-5pm Mon-Fri; 9am-4pm Sat. **Main courses** £2.50-£3.50. **No credit cards.**
Dose cheerfully welcomes a steady stream of Smithfield workers and residents, some dropping by several times throughout the day. You can hang around a bit – there are a few low tables and pouffes to perch on – but even with a few

newspapers supplied, it's not really a place to linger. Coloured lettering on a blackboard details a range of beverages, from piccolo to long black and Belgian hot chocolate. Sourcing is taken seriously – the guest coffee on our visit was Balmaadi Estate from Tamil Nadu – though the regular blend, made on a La Marzocco machine, is from Square Mile. Even the Bedfordshire farm that supplies the milk is specified. Food quality is high for a place of these dimensions, partly because the owners know when to buy-in from good suppliers (Bea's of Bloomsbury among them). Salads made on the premises have a Mediterranean flavour. The sandwiches are also produced on-site, using Born & Bread products. We loved the combination of pastrami, mature cheddar, gherkin, watercress, tomato and horseradish on a crusty, seeded baguette. Spelt and white chocolate are not really natural partners, but the earthiness of the muffin we ordered was tempered somewhat by the inclusion of raspberries.

Available for hire. Babies and children admitted. Takeaway service. **Map 11 O5**.

J&A Cafe `NEW`

2009 RUNNER-UP BEST NEW CAFÉ

4 Sutton Lane, EC1M 5PU (7490 2992). Barbican tube/Farringdon tube/rail. **Open** 8am-6pm Mon, Tue; 8am-9.30pm Wed-Fri; 10am-4pm Sat. **Main courses** £3.50-£8. **Credit** MC, V.

You have to shimmy through a narrow alleyway to get here, before emerging into a tiny walkway lined with colourful tables and chairs. Sisters Johann and Aoise Ledwidge have transformed this former Victorian diamond-cutting workshop into a lovely, secluded café: as suited to contemplative readers/ artists/writers as to bunches of gossiping gals or clusters of networking creatives. A handsome communal table with long benches invites cross-party chin-wagging. Nicely spaced tables of four line the edges of the exposed-brick room. Flooded with natural light and far removed from traffic and passers-by, it's the sort of café where you feel you could linger for hours. Cakes and coffees are the highlight – a seriously moist apple cake came slicked with a creamy maple-syrup frosting; then

there was a brooding dark-chocolate and morello-cherry number – both ideal with decent cups of Atkinson & Co brews. We appreciate the home-style cooking (courgette and almond soup, irish stew, sweet-potato tart), but on our latest visit the evening menu lacked the finesse displayed in the café's early days. A chewy steak and salad (with dijon vinaigrette and a baguette) was barely seasoned and needed a good searing. Organic smoked salmon on soda bread featured good ingredients, but lacked zing. Portions were rather parsimonious for dinner.

Available for hire. Babies and children admitted. Disabled: toilet. Takeaway service. Vegetarian menu. **Map 5 O4**.

Kipferl

70 Long Lane, EC1A 9EJ (7796 2229, www.kipferl.co.uk). Barbican tube/Farringdon tube/rail. **Meals served** 8am-5pm Mon-Fri; 9am-5pm Sat. **Main courses** £3-£6.50. **Credit** MC, V.

Five small tables for two or three people is about all that can be squeezed into this bijou Austrian deli-café. Hearty soups offered daily include potato, cheese and onion, and borscht, with or without debreziner sausage. These sausages (like wiener and käsekrainer) are also available hot with bread, mustard and sauerkraut (or salad). We opted for a crunchy, salt-crusted bretzel, with smoked salmon and fresh herbs flavouring some brightly acidic quark cheese. In spring and summer you might expect baked pasta torte with spinach, tomato and pumpkin seeds, and a wider range of salads. Everything is available to take away. The solid cakes would make a hausfrau proud – linzer torte, Jewish apple cake, sachertorte, poppy-seed and walnut – and the coffee is correctly brought on metal trays with a glass of water. You don't have to ask for milk to be served hot either. Indeed, despite the proliferation of specialist coffee shops nearby, Kipferl still attracts its own devotees for office takeaway brews. Connoisseurs of luxury chocolate also appreciate the mozartkugeln and Zotter bars by the till. Look to the shelves for first-rate sauerkraut and an interesting selection of Austrian wines.

Babies and children admitted. Takeaway service. **Map 11 O5**. **For branch see index**.

Euston

Peyton & Byrne

Wellcome Collection, 183 Euston Road, NW1 2BE (7611 2138, www.peytonandbyrne.com). Euston Square tube/Euston tube/rail. **Open** 10am-6pm Tue-Wed, Fri, Sat; 10am-10pm Thur; 11am-6pm Sun. **Main courses** £3.50-£9.50. **Credit** MC, V.

'We don't have anything on the board up there.' What – this afternoon, today or forever? 'Forever: you have to look at the menu by the trays'. Silly us for thinking the gargantuan logoed menu above the counter was at all relevant. Silly us too for not realising that a bacon sandwich was going to require a knife and fork, which we had to return to the counter to collect ourselves. Oliver Peyton's group of restaurants and cafés has experienced mixed fortunes over the years, and staff training clearly has some way to go here, but we like the vibe of this popular spot in the foyer of the Wellcome Collection. The decor is cheerfully sleek; the café is a great choice for meeting friends or working on your laptop; and the food that is available is often good. The main-course bacon sarnie featured super English bacon (stripy and smoky from the charcoal grill) and a pleasingly fiery guacamole. To this day we fantasise about the succulent, sticky centre of the outsize fig roll, its brown shortcrust pastry gallantly saluting mum's baking – Peyton's inspiration for this burgeoning chain. P&B seems to be taking over Euston Road; as well as this outlet, it has branches in the British Library and St Pancras station (to show the French what English baking is all about).

Babies and children admitted. Disabled: lift; toilet. Takeaway service. **Map 4 K4**. **For branches see index**.

Lantana

Fitzrovia

★ Lantana NEW

2009 WINNER BEST NEW CAFÉ

13 Charlotte Place, W1T 1SN (7637 3347, www.lantanacafe.co.uk). Goodge Street tube.
Meals served 8am-6pm Mon-Wed; 8am-9pm Thur, Fri; 10am-6pm Sat. **Main courses** £4.50-£10. **Credit** MC, V.

This cheerful Aussie-style café (owner Shelagh Ryan is from Down Under) has become a firm Fitzrovian favourite. It's open for breakfast through to lunch and sometimes dinner, and aims to match the food at the best Sydney-side cafés. Breakfasts arrive with aplomb – sweetcorn fritters with either crispy bacon or smoked salmon, both served with lime aïoli and plenty of rocket and grilled toms; or a full-on english for the more conventional. Lunches are commendable, with the same flair applied to a frequently changing array of interesting and colourful salads that wouldn't look out of place at Ottolenghi (*see p161*). Ambitious tarts combine big flavours and textures, while hot dishes include the likes of lemongrass, ginger and coriander chicken skewers (succulent) with satay sauce; or moroccan lamb tagine with pomegranate-studded couscous. Sweets keep up the pace, with excellent friands (small almond cakes popular in the Antipodes), banana bread and hummingbird cake (a spice cake with pineapple, bananas and nuts, originating from the American South). A combination of Monmouth coffee beans and a La Marzocco espresso machine ensures that the coffee is flawless. Our only criticism is that Lantana is a tiny space, and fills up quickly – but it's a good-looking room with quirky charm, and a seat is always worth a wait.
Babies and children admitted. Tables outdoors (2, pavement). Takeaway service. **Map 17 B1**.

Holborn

Fleet River Bakery NEW

2009 RUNNER-UP BEST NEW CAFÉ

71 Lincoln's Inn Fields, WC2A 3JF (7691 1457, www.fleetriverbakery.com). Holborn tube. **Open** 7.30am-6pm Mon-Fri; 10am-4pm Sat. **Main courses** £6.50-£8. **Credit** AmEx, DC, MC, V.
This rustic café is a warren of rooms filled with homely wooden furniture and red leather stools, mellow rockabilly tunes and a mix of lawyers and LSE students. Enter from the door off Lincoln's Inn Fields and this might not be apparent – the room consists of a tiny coffee island and a main bar heaving with baskets of sandwiches (bread, fresh as a daisy, is made on the premises), sprightly salads and inviting cakes. Nearly everything runs out by early afternoon: including, on our visit, the spicy butternut squash soup with sourdough bread, and the ham and stilton or cherry tomato and feta quiches. What remained wasn't bad, but seemed unexciting. A rice and lentil salad with plenty of sun-dried tomatoes had remarkable flavour despite its bland appearance. More promising dishes include the steaks and burgers offered at Friday lunchtimes on a South African braai-style barbecue, and the sweets (fresh strawberries with cute meringues the size of table-tennis balls, ginger and walnut cake, banana cake); accompany them with Monmouth coffee. Fleet River Bakery is perhaps slightly too 'been there, done that' for our liking, but it's preferable to the soulless chains that dominate Holborn.
Babies and children admitted. Disabled: toilet. Takeaway service. **Map 18 F2**.

Marylebone

★ La Fromagerie (100)

2-6 Moxon Street, W1U 4EW (7935 0341, www.lafromagerie.co.uk). Baker Street or Bond Street tube. **Open** 8am-7.30pm Mon-Fri; 9am-7pm Sat; 10am-6pm Sun. **Main courses** £6-£12.40. **Credit** AmEx, MC, V.
There aren't many cafés in London where Herefordshire snails cooked in garlic butter make the menu, but La Fromagerie has always ploughed it's own, very stylish, culinary furrow. A pleasing extension into the former organic shop next door has seamlessly created more space for diners, staff and products. A wooden perch here among the elegantly folksy objets, with views of Moxon Street through bottles of Ruinart and Moët, is as covetable as the fashionable clothes in the store opposite. The menus are a little confusing, the basic list supplemented by a separate breakfast offer (own-made baked beans, granola with posh French yoghurt) and a 'kitchen menu' from 12.30pm (note there's a minimum spend at lunchtime, but it's easy to hit). Gravadlax (cured in-house) is served with petit suisse (two soft little cylinders slightly more sour-tasting than cream cheese), plus caperberries, crunchy Poilâne toast and an interesting selection of lightly dressed leaves. Neighbouring Ginger Pig supplies the raised pie that features (with Montgomery cheddar) on La Fromagerie's ploughman's. We've been slightly disappointed by cakes here in the past, but carrot cake thickly layered with rich, moussey lemon and vanilla cream cheese was sensory heaven and dietary hell – alone a good reason to return.
Available for hire (dinner). Babies and children admitted. Takeaway service. **Map 3 G3**.
For branch see index.

Scandinavian Kitchen

61 Great Titchfield Street, W1W 7PP (7580 7161, www.scandikitchen.co.uk). Oxford Circus tube. **Meals served** 8am-7pm Mon-Fri; 10am-6pm Sat. **Main courses** £4.95-£7.50. **Set lunch** £4.95-£7.95. **Credit** AmEx, MC, V.
Scandinavian Kitchen, with its pillar-box red frontage, is a quirky, stylish and relaxed retreat from nearby Oxford Street. A popular café with office workers, it also enjoys brisk trade as a Nordic grocery-deli selling everything from cured salmon to rye crispbreads. Staff are consistently cheerful, occasionally jollying the day along with impromptu sing-songs from behind the counter. They also put on a delectable spread of open sandwiches, big salads and wraps – all freshly made with quality produce. Favourite sandwiches include swedish meatballs with a dab of beetroot salad, a selection of pickled herrings on rye bread (in three spicy marinades), lemony gravadlax, and rare roast beef with horseradish. Capacious bowls of piping hot soup (recipes change daily) provide good insulation against cold weather. Don't forget to save space for sweets. We recommend the darkly seductive chocolate cake slathered with whipped cream: a great match with a mug of the excellent coffee. Order at the counter and take your tray to a table; if you're alone and fancy some thinking time, there's no better place.
Babies and children welcome: high chairs. Tables outdoors (4, pavement). Takeaway service; delivery service (over £35). **Map 9 J5**.

Sketch: The Parlour

9 Conduit Street, W1S 2XJ (0870 777 4488, www.sketch.uk.com). Oxford Circus tube. **Open** 8am-9pm Mon-Fri; 10am-9pm Sat. **Tea served** 3-6.30pm Mon-Sat. **Main courses** £4-£8.50. **Set tea** £9.50-£24; £3 incl glass of champagne. **Credit** AmEx, MC, V.
We love the Parlour's tongue-in-cheek sexiness. Sketch's phone number is 'handwritten' on the paper napkins, as though the waiter was trying to pick you up; saucy nudes illustrate the tapestry-covered chairs and pouffes, and the chandelier appears to be covered with old pairs of red fishnet tights. There's more: menus and bills are tucked into old novels, and there's a picture of the Mona Lisa with the Total petrol logo slapped over her face. At launch, the room had a girlier vibe and the focus was on the pastry counter. Now, a bottle-filled bar takes centre stage, club music plays in the background and the flaxen-haired beauties frequenting the place are likely to be accompanied by edgily besuited gents. No matter what you're wearing, you'll probably feel some of the glamour rubbing off. Staff are welcoming, smiley and friendly. French superchef Pierre Gagnaire oversees the menu, which includes simple hearty dishes such as macaroni cheese, as well as quirky

Interview
LAURA HEARN AND EMMA MILES

Who are you?
Owners and chefs at the **Clerkenwell Kitchen** (*see p287*).
How did you start in the catering business?
Both of us are self-taught and became involved with food because we loved it more than anything else.
What's the best thing about running a restaurant in London?
Being able to cook what we want. Building relationships with our suppliers. Fantastic produce. Lovely customers who really appreciate what we are trying to do. A great community of people working with food.
What's the worst thing?
It's very hard work and seems almost impossible to make any money. Also, always going out after work smelling of food, and continual burns up your arms.
Which are your favourite London restaurants?
There are loads. **La Fromagerie** (*see left*) for quality of produce, **Hix Oyster & Chop House** (*see p52*) for brilliant English comfort food. **Maison Bertaux** (*see p290*) is one of a kind. **Konstam at the Prince Albert** (*see p55*) has a great interior and fantastic seasonal local food. The **Charles Lamb** (*see p114*). We could go on and on.
What is your favourite treat?
All those things that are extremely unsustainable: anchovies, native oysters, truffles, Brouilly, Calvados and Gauloise, perfect roast chicken and a clear chicken broth.
What is missing from London's restaurant scene?
Good local restaurants, cooking seasonally, using local suppliers and offering value for money.
What does the next year hold?
More collaboration between restaurants regarding suppliers. This could reduce food miles, and create a market for these great suppliers who aren't quite set up enough to deliver into London.

CHEAP EATS

high-concept dishes that salute the haute cuisine served upstairs. Witness the club sandwich with red and green bread and a layer of stencilled jelly on top; it's mostly air-dried ham with tiny flecks of grapefruit – and delicious.
Babies and children welcome: high chairs. Separate rooms for parties, seating 45-200. Takeaway service. **Map 9 J6.**

St James's

5th View
5th floor, Waterstone's, 203-206 Piccadilly, W1J 9HA (7851 2468, www.5thview.co.uk). Piccadilly Circus tube. **Lunch served** noon-3pm Mon-Fri; noon-4pm Sat, Sun. **Tapas served** 5-9pm Mon-Sat. **Main courses** £9.50-£12.95. **Tapas** £3.50-£6.95. **Credit** AmEx, MC, V.
Perched on top of Europe's largest bookshop, this bright and spacious café boasts sweeping views over rooftops, and a well-stocked bar. Among the regular seating arrangements, you'll find reading tables – a popular feature among bibliophiles. The 5th Floor is as much a place to meet up with friends as it is to relish a good book. There's a smart tapas-like slant to evening snacks, while the simple lunch menu finds favour with shoppers who take their pick from sharing platters of antipasti and meze, a daily-changing soup, sandwiches and chips, plus poshed-up salads. Our chargrilled chicken sandwich was average, but no more: the chicken breast let down by blandness, undistinguished tomato sauce, and a forest of rocket leaves. Equally dispiriting were the fat chips, which although crisp on the outside, yielded to powdery potato within. Freshly squeezed juices and cocktails, from an impressive line-up, make more inspired choices. Tea time fare includes pricey wedges of victoria sponge, scones and pastry tarts; on our visit, they looked a bit drab. Service needs to be quicker off the mark too.
Babies and children (under-5s) welcome: high chairs. Disabled: lift; toilet. Separate room for parties, seats 60. **Map 17 A5.**

Soho

★ Fernandez & Wells ⑩⓪
73 Beak Street, W1F 9RS (7287 8124, www.fernandezandwells.com). Oxford Circus or Piccadilly Circus tube. **Open** 7.30am-6pm Mon-Fri; 9am-6pm Sat; 10am-6pm Sun. **Main courses** £3.50-£6. **Credit** (over £5) MC, V.
The new branch on St Anne's Court should help ease the strain of devoted fans on this much-loved, trendily utilitarian spot. The coffees are all made triple ristretto using 33g coffee, as the sign behind the counter points out, which no doubt reassures a lot of customers who have no idea what it means. They're here for the generally superior beverages, urban cool and excellent snacks. Plenty of nearby office workers drop by for impromptu meetings, which means the place can be very busy, even at 3.30pm. The quality of ingredients is first rate; esteemed bakery the Flour Station provides the chelsea buns, eccles cakes and english muffins. Ultra-fresh savouries displayed on the counter include the likes of iberico chorizo and manchego baguette; rolls filled with black pudding, pancetta and egg mayonnaise; and focaccias with roast aubergine, feta and rocket, or roast pork and apple sauce. We chose an empanada with golden yellow pastry, filled with chicken, egg, peas and olives, served with piquant chilli sauce on the side – sensational. And with everything tasting so good and nutritious, why not have a cake? You can choose from the likes of clementine, lemon drizzle, ginger and carrot.
Babies and children admitted. Takeaway service. **Map 17 A4.**
For branches see index.

Flat White
17 Berwick Street, W1F 0PT (7734 0370, www.flat-white.co.uk). Leicester Square, Oxford Circus or Tottenham Court Road tube. **Open** 8am-7pm Mon-Fri; 9am-6pm Sat-Sun. **Main courses** £3-£6.50. **No credit cards.**
Flat White's shabby chic, which could have been airlifted from any town on the central New South Wales coast, fits perfectly into Berwick Street. A 'hihowyagoin' and 'nahwurries' from a tanned, sandy-haired barista sets the tone for a relaxed pit-stop (you'd better relax, because nothing's gonna happen quickly). The photos of old Australian miners' cottages here will either seem ironic or make you homesick depending on your country of origin. Coffee comes from Square Mile (it shifted from Monmouth a while back) and can be bought in take-home bags of beans or ground coffee for £7. At the end of the counter is a tap and glasses, so you can help yourself to water. The menu – white letters on a black punchboard – offers birchermüesli, toast and scrambled eggs, tuna melts and toasted banana bread. Pide (turkish bread) filled with roast butternut squash and rocket made a fabulous lunch, followed by a chewy-crisp white chocolate and cranberry cookie served on vintage crockery by a guy with a Poirot moustache, shaved head and large-check shirt. The iced chocolate is terrific and not too sweet, with big scoops of ice-cream and chocolate sauce authentically drizzled round the glass.
Babies and children admitted. Takeaway service. **Map 17 B3.**

Maison Bertaux
28 Greek Street, W1D 5DQ (7437 6007). Leicester Square, Piccadilly Circus or Tottenham Court Road tube. **Open** 8.30am-11pm Mon-Sat; 8.30am-7.30pm Sun. **Main courses** £1.50-£4.50. **No credit cards.**
'Déshabillé' is one description. 'Bohemian' another. 'Disorganised and rather cavalier about it', is also accurate, in our experience, but Maison Bertaux's many loyal fans are a testament to its charms. Under the vintage blue-and-white awning, the window is filled with a tempting array of classic French pâtisserie and viennoiserie (eclairs, super almond croissants), though if you want something savoury, pickings aren't quite as rich – ham and cheese croissant, a mustardy rarebit-style pastry, and broccoli quiche (better than it looks, with a good cheesy flavour). The humble first-floor tea room features a mix of old office, bentwood and plywood chairs, flowers tied with purple and red tulle, and minor television celebrities in consultation with their life coaches. Portions are generous. Our gateau st honoré was a big, blowsy affair with chocolate mousse and cream. Lemon tart was temptingly deep-filled, but the pastry was not as crisp as it should be. The coffee is only as good as it need be, but if you're concerned about that, head for another establishment.
Babies and children admitted. Tables outdoors (7, pavement). Takeaway service. **Map 17 C4.**

★ Nordic Bakery
14 Golden Square, W1F 9JG (3230 1077, www.nordicbakery.com). Piccadilly Circus tube. **Meals served** 8am-8pm Mon-Fri; 9am-7pm Sat; 11am-6pm Sun. **Main courses** £1.50-£4. **Credit** MC, V.
The sign on Golden Square ('Dark rye breads, cinnamon buns, coffee') reads like a mission statement. Inside, Nordic Bakery's dark-blue paint, pine wood and high ceiling evoke an Arctic forest beneath the midnight sun. Well, almost. We like it here. The denim-aproned service team dispenses taupe mugs of cappuccino and filter coffee with a curious mix of undisguised boredom and genuine care. The coffee's good stuff indeed, but it's the fine Fenno-Scandinavian food and cool chic of the decor that make this place addictive. Karelian pies with their papery pastry and subtly spiced potato (or rice) filling are a steal at £1.50 – say yes to the egg butter. We also like the thin, round soft rye rolls holding salmon tartare with chives and red onion. Cakes (orange and poppy-seed, ginger) and oatmeal bickies are displayed on the counter; look in the front window for more options. Retail ambitions have been reined-in since opening, but bread and pastries are still sold to take home, plus the likes of organic Swedish jams, wild bilberry juice and julkaffe (dark roast 'Christmas' coffee). Aisles are spaced well enough to park a baby buggy or two, but please don't.
Babies and children admitted. Takeaway service. **Map 17 A4.**

Sacred
13 Ganton Street, W1F 9BL (7734 1415, www.sacredcafe.co.uk). Oxford Circus tube. **Open** 7.30am-8pm Mon-Fri; 10am-8pm Sat; 9.30am-7pm Sun. **Main courses** £5-£5.50. **No credit cards.**
Since making the shortlist for Time Out's Best Coffee Bar award a few years ago, Sacred has grown to include five outlets ranging from simple kiosks to a bolthole at Westfield shopping centre. At the original Ganton Street outlet, a small counter on the ground floor holds the likes of organic carrot cake, caramelised pecan brownies, filled baguettes and bowls of gnocchi, while a blackboard advertises soup of the day. Take your drink and a seat – the food will be brought to you. The incense-scented basement area is fairly spacious, with a mix of bench seating, sofas, old chairs and pouffes. Your fellow drinkers might include hip young freelances working the Wi-Fi, and hairdressers discussing how to cut each other's hair (the not-quite-ambient music tends to drown any raised voices). New York-style cheesecake came in a very thin slice with fresh kiwi, pineapple and strawberries on the side. It was decent enough, but not really worth the calories. Powdery, slightly overspiced chai latte (a pricey £3.75) was a pleasant change from London's syrup-based versions, which are often too sweet. Proper tea from a Sri Lankan estate is served in high-camp vintage pots.
Available for hire. Babies and children admitted. Tables outdoors (6, pavement). Takeaway service. **Map 17 A4.**
For branches see index.

★ Yauatcha
15 Broadwick Street, W1F 0DL (7494 8888). Leicester Square, Oxford Circus, Piccadilly Circus or Tottenham Court Road tube. **Open** 11am-11.30pm Mon-Thur; 11am-11.45pm Fri, Sat; noon-10.45pm Sun. **Dim sum served** noon-11.30pm Mon-Thur; noon-11.45pm Fri, Sat; noon-10.45pm Sun. **Dim sum** £3.50-£7. **Set tea** £24.50-£31.50. **Credit** AmEx, MC, V.
The ground-floor pâtisserie of Alan Yau's much-loved dim sum destination has arguably been sidelined over the years, as demand for tables in the basement restaurant became overwhelming. However, we reckon the quality of goodies coming from Stéphane Sucheta's pastry kitchen has improved outasight. If you're looking for a place for a birthday treat or other special-occasion tea, this is our top pick – and prices compare very favourably with the famous hotels. The buzz of Nathan Barleys chowing down on cheung fun and char siu bao nearby can add to the fun, even if you're sticking with puds and fruity mocktails. However, order the set tea and you'll get mini-portions of three dim sum with pickles and punchy sauces to kick off the afternoon in fine savoury style. There follows a sumptuous range of puds and pastries with flavours of assam, yuzu, rose and lychee – and enough gold leaf to gild a lily. The huge, tender scones (green tea, coconut) are sensational and arrive piping hot, their warmth protected with proper napkins. Such is the sugar rush, most people seem to need the fine chocs and sweeties that finish the set tea to be put in a doggie bag. You could, of course, just have a cake and a cup of tea.
Babies and children admitted. Booking essential for set tea. Disabled: lift; toilet. **Map 17 B3.**

South Kensington

Hummingbird Bakery
47 Old Brompton Road, SW7 3JP (7584 0055, www.hummingbirdbakery.com). South Kensington tube. **Open** 10.30am-7pm daily. **Main courses** £1.55-£2.50. **Credit** MC, V.
Red velvet ropes and red velvet cupcakes greet customers at this posh South Ken bakery. After braving the crowds of yummy mummies with youngsters on a sugar high, settle down among shades of pink and brown in the small café, or bag one of the coveted outdoor tables. US-style sweets are the order of the day, with cupcakes being the clear claim to fame. These moist spongy cakes

Breads Etcetera. See p292.

slathered with a dollop of super-sweet butter-cream satisfyingly nip any sugar cravings. Their pastel shades of pink, green, blue, and yellow icing topped with colourful sprinkles make delicious eye-candy too. Classic red velvet had won the popularity contest on our visit, with every table eagerly stuffing down this rouge-dyed chocolate cake. Our massive slice of homey carrot cake layered with cream-cheese frosting was nicely spiced with cinnamon and nutmeg, but a savoury muffin speckled with spinach, mushrooms, ham and cheese was dry and uninspiring. Go early to avoid the frustrating queues and patchy service or, better yet, take a cake for the road.
Babies and children admitted. Tables outdoors (4, pavement). Takeaway service; delivery service (1-6pm Mon-Fri, over £12.95, within zones 1 & 2). **Map 14 D10**.
For branch see index.

West
Ladbroke Grove

Books for Cooks
4 Blenheim Crescent, W11 1NN (7221 1992, www.booksforcooks.com). Ladbroke Grove tube. **Open** 10am-6pm, **lunch served** noon-1.30pm Tue-Sat. **Set lunch** £5 2 courses, £7 3 courses. **Credit** MC, V.
Go early or you'll be disappointed – enthusiasts start lining up before 11.40am to ensure a seat at noon. The word has long been out on the tiny test kitchen tucked in the back of Notting Hill's famed cookbook shop. This quaint bright café culls daily inspiration from any of the hundreds of books lining the shelves. The erudite denouement takes the form of a fresh and homely three-course set menu that amply feeds the soul for a bargain £7. We queued and prayed the food wouldn't run out before we were seated; patience was rewarded with a cosy table for two nuzzled next to the open kitchen. Seated there, we toured Morocco starting with a deep fragrant bowl of red lentil soup accented with hints of orange, and a baladi salad (cucumbers, peppers, tomatoes, onions) paired with nicely spiced bean dip. An individual crock of Moroccan lamb and filo pie with harissa yoghurt followed, and proved just as pleasing as our starters. A choice of rustic cakes ended the meal on a sweet note. On Tuesdays there's a vegetarian menu.
Bookings not accepted. Disabled: toilet. **Map 19 B3**.

Westbourne Grove

Daylesford Organic
208-210 Westbourne Grove, W11 2RH (7313 8050, www.daylesfordorganic.com). Ladbroke Grove or Notting Hill Gate tube. **Open** 8am-11pm Mon-Sat; 11am-5pm Sun. **Main courses** £9.95-£13.95. **Credit** AmEx, MC, V.
Pretty things often cost a pretty penny, and everything here is indeed quite pretty. Pretty pictures of perfect produce deck the walls, and pretty people flank the tables of this rustic-styled food hall-cum-café. Daylesford has a museum-like, look-but-don't-touch quality, with pristine polished fruits and vegetables precariously stacked in pyramids. Its calming atmosphere strives towards a 'back to the farm' simplicity, yet the overt decadence somewhat derails the dogma. To dine, you have your pick of three venues, each on a different floor. The basement raw bar dishes out detox fare like carrot and ginger soup and marinated mushrooms. Head for the first floor to find the bread bar, which serves more filling sustenance like pizza and rotisserie food. We opted for the ground-floor larder, for its popularity and views of Westbourne Grove. Tap water arrived in an attractive carafe with fresh cucumber. Mushroom soup fell short of expectations: a bland, languid experience not enhanced by a side of burnt toast. Delicious bread and butter pudding, however, saved the day and was demolished with relish. The pretty high prices reflect those of a restaurant rather than a café – but, hey, Daylesford is pretty good.
Babies and children welcome: children's menu; crayons; high chairs; nappy-changing facilities. Booking advisable dinner. Disabled: toilet. Separate room for parties, seats 30. Tables outdoors (6, pavement). Takeaway service. Vegetarian menu. **Map 7 A6**.
For branches see index.

Tom's Deli
226 Westbourne Grove, W11 2RH (7221 8818, www.tomsdelilondon.co.uk). Notting Hill Gate tube. **Open** 8am-6.30pm Mon-Sat; 9am-6.30pm Sun. **Main courses** £7.95-£11.95. **Credit** MC, V.
Walk down Westbourne Grove and join the throngs amassing in this bric-a-brac filled diner and deli. Ladies-who-lunch account for the weekday crowd, along with others simply craving the all-day breakfasts. Posh nosh is the name of the game: upmarket toasties, club sandwiches, tarts and casseroles. Colourful retro sweets and

homely cakes are displayed by the entrance. A disco ball, hanging above, sets a fun, casual vibe. In the mood for a boozy brunch, we bought a bottle of fizz in the basement deli and relaxed in one of the few coveted booths upstairs. Butternut squash soup was joyfully slurped up: a silky and filling intro. Lamb casserole hit the spot too, with tons of vegetables in play. We popped back down to the main floor to pick a pudding. Our cake de choix was a fluffy lemon meringue pie – the only variety made in-house. We eagerly dived in, but found the meringue a gooey, sticky mess and the lemon curd a bit too dense. Note: on sunny days, the outside tables on the back balcony are where to head.
Babies and children welcome: high chairs. Tables outdoors (6, garden; 2, terrace). Takeaway service. **Map 7 A6**.

South West
Barnes

★ Orange Pekoe
3 White Hart Lane, SW13 0PX (8876 6070, www.orangepekoeteas.com). Barnes Bridge rail/209 bus. **Meals served** 7.30am-5.30pm Mon-Fri; 9am-5.30pm Sat, Sun. **Main courses** £4.50-£8. **Credit** AmEx, DC, MC, V.
Tea lovers come hither and hail Orange Pekoe! This cosy little shop in Barnes epitomises the traditional British tea room. Situated on a quiet roundabout near the river, it has deservedly earned a diverse loyal following. Large windows decorated with hand-painted flowers add a whimsical charm and make an appropriate prelude to the delights found inside. A wall full of large black canisters filled with numerous varieties of speciality tea welcomed us. An educated, passionate server expertly guided us through the custom blends. She offered a whiff of the shop's signature afternoon blend, a delicate mix of darjeeling and ceylon; the floral aroma accented with a spiced earthiness had us sold immediately. An extensive choice of sweet and savoury snacks and lunch platters, written on a long blackboard, helps to whet the palate. In the end, though, it seemed fitting to order tea and scones. We settled in one of three jewel-box rooms, furnished with worn wooden tables laid with lacy table coverings. Our warm scone was served with fresh Cornish clotted cream and sweet strawberry jam. Every bite transported us back to grandma's house; we can't wait to visit again.
Babies and children welcome: crayons; high chairs; nappy-changing facilities. Tables outdoors (5, pavement). Takeaway service.

South

Battersea

Cake Boy
Kingfisher House, Battersea Reach, Juniper Drive, SW18 1TX (7978 5555, www.cake-boy.com). Wandsworth Town rail. **Open** 8am-6pm Mon-Fri; 9am-6pm Sat. **Main courses** £4.20-£4.80. **Credit** MC, V.
Hidden in the sterile glass and steel complex of Battersea Reach, Cake Boy offers comfort and colour in an otherwise stark setting. Here, French pastry chef Eric Lanlard, best known for his special-occasion cakes, entices the sweet-toothed with smaller bites of his creations. One side of Cake Boy boasts a modern open kitchen with white counters, pink stools, and bright blue walls where monthly cooking classes are held. The other side is a lush lounge with pink and orange armchairs, black wallpaper adorned with pink roses, and a back wall lit with twinkling lights. Although tempted to order a savoury tart or sandwich, we were distracted by the beautiful array of sweets on cutesy cake stands. Coffee eclair looked gorgeous, decorated with chocolate coffee beans, but didn't live up to its presentation and was disappointingly soggy. Satisfyingly rustic apricot and pistachio tart, however, was baked to a tasty golden brown. We perched at a counter overlooking the courtyard where another couple quietly enjoyed the afternoon in style with pastries and wine. Service was brisk, but efficient.
Available for hire. Babies and children admitted. Disabled: toilet. Tables outdoors (10, terrace). Takeaway service. **Map 21 A3**.

Crumpet
66 Northcote Road, SW11 6QL (7924 1117, www.crumpet.biz). Clapham Junction rail. **Open** 8.30am-6pm Mon-Sat; 9.30am-6pm Sun. **Main courses** £4.20-£7.50. **Credit** AmEx, MC, V.
Slap bang in the middle of south London's famous buggy territory, this café is intimate with the desires of its well-heeled clientele and their offspring. The owners, who have lived nearby for many years, have thought of everything – from the well-stocked play corner and bookshelf, to the vast children's menu. There's a large space to park buggies, and even the bathroom features free nappies and a child-size loo. Lunches for adults suffer from zealous portion control, but what there was of our quiche and salad leaves was gratifyingly tasty. Crumpet's real passion is proper teas, with scones, imaginative sandwiches and cakes baked by local mums, plus its own blends of tea from a small specialist based in Blackfriars. Cheese and ham come from deli Hamish Johnston and Hennessy's the butcher's, both just along the street. Naturally, provisions are organic and free-range where possible, including soft drinks from Luscombe Farm in Devon. Childless customers tend to take their cappuccinos and sauvignon blanc at the tables in the front of the serving section and kitchen, which make a good sound barrier from the families at the back.
Babies and children welcome: children's menu; high chairs; nappy-changing facilities; play area. Disabled: toilet. Tables outdoors (2, pavement). Takeaway service. **Map 21 C5**.

Clapham

Breads Etcetera (100)
127 Clapham High Street, SW4 7SS (07717 642812). Clapham Common or Clapham North tube. **Open** 10am-10pm Tue-Sat; 10am-4pm Sun. **Main courses** £3.50-£7.75. **No credit cards.**
The first thing you notice at this café and artisan bakery is the bittersweet smell of flour; the second is the shiny white Dualit toasters on the tables. These are provided for 'DIY toast' ('Cut it, toast it, spread it, eat it… then do it again'), all emphasising that bread is the main attraction. Following a management restructure, the organic sourdoughs are now baked on the premises, but the daily brunch menu and choice of sandwiches (made from wholemeal, white, six-seed, olive and herb, or

CHEAP EATS

walnut varieties) remain the same. The decor of brick walls, wooden floorboards and ornately framed mirrors is also unchanged, evoking the feel of a Victorian greasy spoon in modern Clapham. Young, savvy locals fill the place at weekends. A New York salt beef sandwich on toasted dark rye bread with tangy gherkins couldn't be faulted. Cowboy's Breaky, with a fried egg inside a slice of sourdough toast, spicy baked beans and bacon, was full of flavour, without being full of grease, but the portion was modest. Coffee is a big plus, from the Monmouth Coffee Company. A new evening menu offers soups and stews: with plenty of freshly baked bread to soak them up, no doubt.
Babies and children welcome (high chairs).
Tables outdoors (2, pavement). Takeaway service.
Map 22 B2.

Macaron (100)

22 The Pavement, SW4 0HY (7498 2636).
Clapham Common tube. **Meals served** 7.30am-7pm Mon-Fri; 9am-7pm Sat, Sun. **Main courses** £2.95-£4.10. **No credit cards**.
Look for the huge ice-cream-cone sculptures outside this bucolic-looking French café and pâtisserie, nestled on a corner of Clapham Common. Go early to snatch a perfectly baked baguette or any of the other excellent breads. Own-made ice-cream draws in the families, and happy children dawdle around in wide-eyed anticipation. Huge windows coax in the sunlight, while the brightly painted blue ceiling (complete with fluffy clouds) captures the sunbeams inside. Light lunches and sweets arrive on charmingly worn mismatched bone china. A large wooden communal table adds a touch of cosy conviviality. Brightly coloured macaroons with jammy fillings in tempting flavours like blueberry, banana, chocolate and green tea make a pleasing accompaniment to one of the many fragrant teas available. A plumpish round croissant was adorable, and beautifully light and crisp. We also happily devoured plum tart: a thin sweet crust spread with almond cream and graced with green plums. The afternoon was capped with a soothing pot of earl grey, kindly topped up with hot water by the smiling waitress.
Babies and children admitted. Tables outdoors (3, pavement). Takeaway service.
Map 22 A2.

South East
Deptford

Deptford Project

121-123 Deptford High Street, SE8 4NS (07545 593279, www.thedeptfordproject.com).
Deptford rail/Deptford Bridge DLR. **Meals served** 9am-6pm Mon-Sat; 11am-4pm Sun.
Main courses £3.50-£4.75. **No credit cards**.
Providing civilised snacks in London's finest high street, this train carriage-cum-café by Deptford station decks its sandwiches with avocado and rocket, and its surfaces with rail-themed rock references. Being in Deptford, it's boho, cheap and improbably well meaning. The food comprises bruschettas of sundry toppings (smashed cannellini beans and spinach on our visit); sandwiches, from the humble fried egg to the stand-out salmon with rocket; and full breakfasts at weekends. The impecunious or drastically hungover might choose toast with Marmite, Nutella or jam. Cakes include notable, hand-crafted muffins and brownies, and nut-free options set atop an enticing salad counter. Behind this flit hospitable, mainly nose-pierced staff. Park yourself on a stool, or grab a spot on the terrace, where you'll find exotic foliage, a park bench, a deck-chair and a garden shed/shrine to Elvis. This is the ElvisShoesToilet, where you may mirror-pose as the King while adjusting your undies. Behind the carriage, posters proclaim Deptford's claims to fame: once frequented by Christopher Marlowe (hooray!) and Dire Straits (boo!), and the source of the Jolly Roger pirate flag (three cheers!).
Babies and children welcome: high chairs; nappy-changing facilities. Disabled: toilet. Tables outdoors (7, terrace). Takeaway service.

East Dulwich

Blue Mountain Café

18 North Cross Road, SE22 9EU (8299 6953, www.bluemo.co.uk). *East Dulwich rail.* **Open** 9am-6pm Mon, Tue; 9am-10pm Wed-Sat; 10am-6pm Sun. **Main courses** £4.50-£8. **Credit** AmEx, DC, MC, V.
An East Dulwich institution that predates the Bugaboo pushchairs and loft conversions, Blue Mountain has long been drawing the crowds with its quality all-day breakfasts and calorific cakes. The perennial best seller is the Full Monty: herby butcher's sausage, bacon, beans, portobello mushroom, grilled tomato, chunky toast, choice of eggs, and a cup of tea. Unfortunately, our poached eggs were solid and contained a lump of shell, the bacon was leathery and the tomatoes dried out – all down to an overstretched kitchen no doubt. More interesting, and better value, are the lunchtime specials. On our visit these included pan-fried haddock with capers and sun-dried tomatoes; and stuffed pepper with aubergine, chickpeas in Moroccan sauce and couscous. Jerk chicken (served with plantain) is also highly recommended. The funky mosaic patio (made by local artists from multicoloured broken crockery) is a sunny spot to observe the relative bustle of North Cross Road and its market. Packed with families and freelancers during the day, Blue Mountain is also open some evenings, hosting occasional laid-back music nights on Saturdays.
Babies and children welcome: children's menu; high chairs; nappy-changing facilites; toys. Disabled: toilets. Separate room for parties, seats 10. Tables outdoors (5, garden; 5, terrace).
Map 23 C4.
For branch see index.

Luca's [NEW]

2009 RUNNER-UP BEST NEW CAFÉ
145 Lordship Lane, SE22 8HX (8613 6161, www.lucasbakery.com). *East Dulwich rail.* **Open** 8.30am-5.30pm Mon-Sat; 9am-5pm Sun. **Main courses** £3.50-£6.50. **Credit** (over £10) MC, V.
The popular bread stall previously camped outside Moxon's fishmonger's has acquired its own premises, and with it a heavy Austrian accent. The counter is piled with treats: cinnamon buns bigger than your fist, apfel strudel, brezels, schweineohren ('pigs ears' aka palmiers), cheese straws, tea loaves, muffins, cookies, brownies... Behind the glass are glistening sachertorten, baked cheesecakes, and sausage rolls with apricots. Regulars still queue for the serious bread – dark, heavy rye, sourdough, bauernbrot, satisfyingly chewy baguette. There's plenty of space to linger over strong coffee, cream tea or weekend brunch at the relaxed communal tables, in the shady garden or on the sunny patio out front. Almost everything is available to take out, including own-made granola, Kentish jams, and Somerset milk and butter direct from the farm. As far as we were concerned, all that was needed was a few more staff to cut the exasperatingly long waits – we understand this is being sorted out.
Babies and children admitted. Tables outdoors (12, garden). Takeaway service. **Map 23 B4**.

Peckham

Petitou

63 Choumert Road, SE15 4AR (7639 2613).
Peckham Rye rail. **Open** 9am-5.30pm Mon-Sat; 10am-5.30pm Sun. **Main courses** £3.50-£4.80. **Credit** AmEx, MC, V.
A charming café at the leafier end of Peckham, Petitou is just around the corner from the boutiques and art bookshops of Bellenden Road. Fundamentally wholesome food, overlaid with a degree of nostalgia, is what you get. Lunches (£6.75 each) are along the lines of salads, quiches and a light fish pâté, freshly made and sourced locally. All-day breakfasts encompass childhood favourites such as scrambled egg, muesli with honey, english muffins, peanut butter, marmalade, and (love 'em or hate 'em) cheesy Marmite crumpets. Cakes are comfortingly homely, juices are freshly squeezed, herbal teas plentiful, milk can

be made from soya or rice if requested, and almost everything is prefixed with 'organic'. Though the café attracts an arty crowd alongside bourgeois buggy wielders, there's nothing pretentious here – furniture is a junk shop potpourri, with an old-fashioned coat stand and mismatched wooden chairs. Walls and surfaces are covered with community notices and posters for local events, while the radio softly hums Classic FM. Petitou's laid-back atmosphere, airy interior and shady front patio make it the sort of place where you could easily lose an afternoon.
Babies and children welcome: high chairs. Disabled: toilet. Tables outdoors (4, pavement).
Map 23 C3.

East
Docklands

Mudchute Kitchen

Mudchute Park & Farm, E14 3HP (7515 5901, www.mudchutekitchen.org). *Mudchute DLR.* **Open** 9am-5pm Tue-Sun. **Main courses** £3.50-£8.50. **Credit** MC, V.
Locals are understandably drawn to what passes for rural on the Isle of Dogs. Mudchute Kitchen lies in the middle of Mudchute City Farm; its courtyard is also the riding school's stable block. Inside, the wax tablecloths, toys and local anecdotal history on the walls give the spacious hut a homely air; there's free Wi-Fi too. The fresh, seasonal menu isn't extensive – usually a pasta dish, a meat dish and a soup, as well as the all-day breakfast – but everything's own-made. There's a recently installed bread oven, which means most meals come with a hearty and delectable slice, fresh from a warm loaf and loaded with butter. This is a community hub, not a fine-dining establishment, but all the same, service at the counter is a bit casual (we had to call into the kitchen to order). The disappointingly small bowl of lentil soup was under-seasoned, the fried egg was overcooked, and we weren't sure about Mudchute's version of baked beans (with butter beans) – but the baked goods more than made up for these shortcomings. Cakes (especially the carrot cake) are superb. Accompany it with strong coffee before heading off to inspect the animals.
Babies and children welcome: children's menu; high chairs; nappy-changing facilities. Disabled: toilet. Tables outdoors (15, courtyard). Takeaway service. **Map 24 C4**.

Shoreditch

Frizzante@City Farm

Hackney City Farm, E2 8QA (7739 2266, www.frizzanteltd.co.uk). *Liverpool Street tube/rail then 26, 48 bus/Old Street tube/rail then 55 bus.* **Open** 10am-5.30pm Tue, Wed, Fri-Sun; 10am-5.30pm, 7-10pm Thur. **Main courses** £5.45-£10.40. **Credit** DC, MC, V.
Frizzante is like an outsize farmhouse kitchen with its colourful oilcloth-covered tables, make-and-mend style, and noisy hubbub. Visitors tend to opt for the exciting daily specials (usually including a soup, a risotto, a couple of pastas and a few meat and fish dishes), if they're not tucking into one of the legendary breakfasts. It's worth arriving early before the blackboard gets wiped clean. Note that the café gets full of families fresh from petting the animals in the farmyard outside, so on both weekdays and weekends, early means 12.30pm at the latest, and before that if you want some peace and quiet. The warm welcome and laid-back air mean you can forgive any blips in service. The only downside is having to order at the till, where there's invariably a queue (the person taking the orders also makes teas and coffees) – and doing it all over again if you want one of the incredibly good own-made ice-creams and cakes for pudding. Still, it would be churlish to complain: Frizzante has so much to offer, including plenty of outside seating.
Available for hire (autumn and winter only).
Babies and children welcome: children's menu; high chairs; nappy-changing facilities. Booking advisable. Disabled: toilet. Tables outdoors (40, park). **Map 6 S3**.

Jones Dairy Café

23 Ezra Street, E2 7RH (7739 5372, www.jones dairy.co.uk). Liverpool Street tube/rail then 26, 48 bus/Old Street tube/rail then 55 bus. **Meals served** 9am-3pm Fri, Sat; 8am-3pm Sun. **Main courses** £3-£8. **No credit cards.**

When nearby Columbia Road's Sunday morning flower market is in full bloom, this little old Ezra Street café is sometimes overwhelmed. Market-goers park themselves on bench seating at the trestle tables within, or at a couple of outdoor tables (on sunnier days), to wolf down bagels with organic smoked salmon and cream cheese (optional gherkins, tomatoes), mugs of Nicaraguan coffee and yummy own-made cakes. If you're after something more substantial, say Welsh dry-cured bacon, egg, own-made baked beans and all the trimmings (or the fish breakfast with a Norfolk-caught kipper), you're better off visiting on a Friday or Saturday, when the kitchen is quieter. On our visit service was so slow that our exasperated neighbouring diners simply left. The quality however is not in question. Ingredients are either locally sourced or the best available, and prices are extremely reasonable. A delicious caldo verde (cabbage soup with sausage and black pudding) costs only £4, as does fabulous welsh rarebit (two toasts). On a Sunday, if the season is right, settle for half a dozen Colchester rock oysters (£7.50) – they're almost served quickly.
Babies and children welcome: high chairs. Tables outdoors (2, pavement). Takeaway service. **Map 6 S3.**

Taste of Bitter Love NEW

276 Hackney Road, E2 7SJ (07963 564095, www.tasteofbitterlove.com). Old Street tube/rail then 55 bus/Liverpool Street tube/rail then 26, 48 bus/Cambridge Heath rail. **Open** 7.30am-4pm Mon-Fri; 10am-3pm Sun. **Main courses** £2.75-£4. **No credit cards.**

Home to small manufacturers and wholesalers of various kinds, no one could call Hackney Road charming. All the more surprising, then, that it includes this sweet new enterprise, a tiny, glass-fronted café on the busy thoroughfare, opposite a radiator cover showroom. Taste of Bitter Love (remember the old Gladys Knight song?) has just seven seats inside, with more on the pavement in summer months. Inside there's just room for small brown Formica tables, and the few retro items that lend the place its original vibe (a cocktail-cabinet-like display case (showing off the Square Mile coffee and Teapigs tea), a bodybuilding book featuring Arnold Schwarzenegger, some old records. Gorgeously smooth lattes come in tumblers, and chunky sandwiches are served on retro china. Some come in Turkish bread – like a tasty combo of halloumi, asparagus, sweet potato, sundried tomatoes and courgettes, delicious toasted – while others, like an upmarket cheddar cheese and pickle, come on doorsteps of granary. Sweet treats might be pear flan or a fruit crumble. Iced coffees and smoothies are also served.
Babies and children admitted. Tables outdoors (2, pavement). Takeaway service. **Map 6 S3.**

Spitalfields

Nude Espresso NEW

26 Hanbury Street, E1 6QR (07804 223 590, www.nudeespresso.com). Liverpool Street tube/rail. **Open** 7.30am-6pm Mon-Fri. **Main courses** £4. **Credit** MC, V.

This pillar box-red newcomer is certainly a bright spot on Hanbury Street, attracting a talkative crowd of characters and people who wish they were. There's plenty of dark-brown banquette seating and laminate tables to accommodate them. The blackboard lists espresso, latte, flat white, mocha and so on, with soy milk, decaf and extra shots all at 30p. Crafting the drinks is taken very seriously and Monmouth is the choice of coffee. Organic milk is specified for the hot chocolate. Alternatively, you could sip New Zealand sauvignon or pinot noir, or Mac's gold lager. For breakfast there's muesli with or without fruit and yoghurt, and raisin toast. At lunchtime a range of sandwiches (made freshly on the premises each

morning) is displayed on the counter; we enjoyed cumberland sausage with cheese and spinach. The mostly Mediterranean focaccias can be served toasted or untoasted. For a sweet finish, there are berry scones, brownies and pinwheels. Our banana and chocolate muffin was not in itself a reason to return, but in all, Nude Espresso is a useful and likeable place. Staff will also advise on coffees, grinders and espresso machines for home use.
Babies and children admitted. Tables outdoors (2, pavement). Takeaway service. **Map 12 S5.**

Tea Smith

8 Lamb Street, E1 6EA (7247 1333, www.tea smith.co.uk). Liverpool Street tube/rail. **Open** 11am-6pm daily. **Set tea** (Sat, Sun) £18-£25. **Credit** MC, V.

As Teasmith's guide states, there are several categories of tea (white, green, oolong, red and black, aged and puer), all of which are offered here on a regularly changing menu. You'll also leave with information on how to infuse your chosen leaves correctly (just watch the staff). On our visit to the minimalist bar, the atmosphere wasn't quite as calm as a tea ceremony would usually demand. Strange acoustics meant that we learned a lot about a fellow drinker's forthcoming nuptials, and more than we wanted about another's birthing plans. That aside, service is assured, friendly and professional. Having ordered a refreshing Mandarin Oriental oolong, we were treated to a taste of Oriental Beauty, a darker and smokier oolong. An afternoon tasting menu – a selection of teas with pâtisserie and chocolates by William Curley (*see right*) – is priced at £25. You can also buy packets of tea, as well as some beautiful cups, pots and tea paraphernalia.
Babies and children admitted. Takeaway service. **Map 12 R5.**

North East

Clapton

Venetia

55 Chatsworth Road, E5 0LH (8986 1642). Homerton rail/242, 308 bus. **Open** 8am-5pm Mon-Wed; 8am-6pm Thur-Sun. **Main courses** £3-£4.20. **Credit** MC, V.

This small café does a roaring trade; it's full of *Guardian*-reading locals who know a good thing when they see it. Namely, great fresh food at low prices. Venetia is small and narrow, yet makes the most of the space with white wood-panelled walls, a bar with stools down one side, and a few tables at the back. In fine weather, customers take advantage of the large, pretty walled garden with its fresh herbs that are used in a range of sandwiches and salads. Hearty slabs of bread come with imaginative fillings like artichoke hearts and olives, salami and peppers, or brie and tomato. Our lentil salad was full of chopped mint, feta and red onion, with a simple lettuce and tomato side salad that tasted divine, thanks to great raw ingredients and lashings of french dressing. The lentils were soft but still had bite, and the accompanying bread was rustic and tasty. Coffee comes in two sizes and is strong but smooth. Service on our visit was efficient and attentive. Own-made cakes in the front window looked tempting (chocolate brownies and lemon drizzle cake among them), but we plumped for a slightly disappointing carrot cake that was doughy and lacked flavour. Still, we'll return.
Babies and children welcome: high chairs; nappy-changing facilities; toys. Tables outdoors (2, pavement; 8, garden). Takeaway service.

Dalston

Tina, We Salute You NEW

47 King Henry's Walk, N1 4NH (3119 0047, www.tinawesaluteyou.com). Dalston Kingsland rail/bus 38. **Open** 8am-7pm Tue-Fri; 9am-7pm Sat; 10am-7pm Sun. **Main courses** £3.30-£5. **No credit cards.**

Who is Tina? Readers of a certain age will remember this sultry lady with the improbable '60s hairdo from a thousand living room walls as she is

the most well known of the foxy ladies in woodland glades painted by artist J H Lynch. The art theme continues inside this chatty café, with artists painting directly on to the white walls. Tina began life as a cupcake stall at Brick Lane's Sunday Upmarket, before relocating to the Newington Green/Dalston fringes in early 2009. It's a tribute to the likeable chaps behind the counter that it already feels as if it's been here for ages. With most of the seating around a communal table, usually topped with the day's newspapers and a laptop or two (there's free Wi-Fi), it's friendly and space is at a premium, but it doesn't feel squeezed. Coffee is from Square Mile, fed through a covetable La Marzocco espresso machine. The menu is short but includes generously filled bagels (from Brick Lane Beigel Bake), breakfast munchies (granola, thick-sliced toast, lovely preserves made in the neighbourhood, plus pancakes at weekends), crumpets, and splendid own-made cupcakes, supplemented by a variety of other cakes.
Babies and children welcome. Bookings not accepted. Disabled: toilet. Tables outdoors (2, pavement). Takeaway service; delivery service. **Map 25 B4.**

North

Muswell Hill

Feast on the Hill

46 Fortis Green Road, N10 3HN (8444 4957). East Finchley or Highgate tube then 43, 134 bus. **Open** 8am-6pm Mon, Tue; 8am-10pm Wed-Sat; 9am-5pm Sun. **Main courses** £4.95-£12.50. **Credit** MC, V.

This popular establishment was formerly known as Café on the Hill, but having joined forces with the neighbouring Feast Delicatessen, it has adjusted its name accordingly. A transitional phase had visitors that wanted cake having to trot next door to the deli to choose; thankfully, the café now has a small selection of its own on display (although you'll be hard-pressed to fit one in if you're having a main meal). It's the all-day breakfasts that are Feast's main event, with full english, vegetarian and free-range eggs benedict among the many options. A short lunch menu, served from 11am to 4pm, offers paninis, salads and a few heartier platefuls like beef lasagne or steak-frites. Dishes sound simple, but are cooked with loving attention to detail. Lasagne was set deep within a tomato sauce tangy with fresh herbs. With its low-key decor (all dark-wood floors, plain wood furniture and white walls), friendly service and reliably good food, Feast on the Hill is always busy and popular with all age groups. If you love the cooking, head next door for takeaway traiteur-style dishes to enjoy on weary week-nights.
Babies and children welcome: children's menu; high chairs. Disabled: toilet. Tables outdoors (6, pavement). Takeaway service.

Newington Green

That Place on the Corner

1-3 Green Lanes, N16 9BS (7704 0079, www.thatplaceonthecorner.co.uk). Canonbury rail/73, 141, 341 bus. **Open** 9.30am-7pm Mon-Thur; 9.30am-8pm Fri; 10am-6pm Sat, Sun. **Main courses** £4.85-£8.25. **Credit** MC, V.

Adults aren't allowed inside this Newington Green café unless they have a child with them. There's a buggy park at the door, regular activities for the kiddies, and a well-stocked bookshelf and large dressing-up cupboard so that carers can have their coffee in peace while small fry are entertained. Breakfasts are served until noon and feature the full english as well as eggs or mushrooms on toast, bacon or sausage sandwiches, and muesli. Lunches are kept simple, with sandwiches, salads and pasta for the grown-ups and a good variety of kids' classics for their offspring (babies can have freshly prepared organic vegetable mush in varying consistencies). Cakes are bought in and weren't very exciting on our last visit, although at least the kids' cupcakes are a sensible size and the coffee's good. If you're a parent, it's a lovely, light place to sit and take a breather.

North West

Kensal Green

★ Brilliant Kids Café

8 Station Terrace, NW10 5RT (8964 4120, www.brilliantkids.co.uk). Kensal Green tube/ Kensal Rise rail. **Open** 8am-6pm Mon-Fri; 9am-5pm Sat. Closes 2pm Sat during birthday parties. **Main courses** £6.95-£7.50. **Credit** MC, V.

As the name suggests, this café is aimed directly at those with children, but the food is good enough to warrant a journey even if you haven't got any. Customers of all ages can appreciate the abundant all-day breakfasts, which arrive loaded with thick bacon rashers, sausage, perfectly judged eggs, tomatoes and mushrooms. The bread, cakes and muffins have clearly been cooked by someone who loves cooking and wants you to love the food too. Locals make the most of the daily lunch special, which is unfailingly superb (all meat comes from Devon Rose Organics – one of several ethically-based suppliers). Also on the board are salads, bagels and sandwiches, all made with fresh and imaginative ingredients. Everything can be scaled down to children's portions. Owner Arabella Lewis goes out of her way to be welcoming and helpful, and the café's friendly atmosphere makes Brilliant a laid-back place to linger. Children's parties are a speciality, with peanut butter and jelly sandwiches, houmous with raw veg, mini sausages and jam tarts among the catering options. Coffee mornings cover subjects such as reviving intimate relations for new parents.
Available for hire. Babies and children welcome: children's portions; high chairs; play area; supervised activities. Tables outdoors (3, garden).

Gracelands

118 College Road, NW10 5HD (8964 9161, www.gracelandscafe.com). Kensal Green tube. **Open** 8.30am-5pm Mon-Fri; 9am-5pm Sat; 9.30am-3.30pm Sun. **Main courses** £3.95-£11.95. **Credit** MC, V.

Gracelands inhabits three different spaces: a lovely airy room at the front, a generous courtyard full of tables out back, and a large slab of the wide pavement outside. Food is lovingly assembled and full of imaginative touches – when it finally comes. Service was utterly chaotic on our visit, even when there seemed to be one staff member for every customer. Meals were travelling around the café, garden and pavement tables several times before finding the mouths to eat them. We were snapped at for not realising we had to help ourselves to soft drinks from the fridge after paying at the till. Still, when our large mixed salads arrived after a mood-crushing wait, they were full of talking points, including grated beetroot and celeriac in lemon juice, crushed potatoes with fresh herbs, perfectly roasted pepper and butternut squash, and black beans in a zingy dressing. The all-day breakfast menu, lunchtime specials, cakes and pastries looked equally appealing. In all, this is a great local resource (especially for families who make use of the play area inside and the workshops next door), but one that knows it has a captive market.
Babies and children welcome: children's menu; high chairs; nappy-changing facilities; play area; toys. Tables outdoors (4, pavement; 11, garden). Takeaway service.

Outer London

Richmond, Surrey

William Curley

10 Paved Court, Richmond, Surrey TW9 1LZ (8332 3002, www.williamcurley.co.uk). Richmond tube/rail. **Open** 9.30am-6.30pm Mon-Sat; 9am-6.30pm Sun. **Main courses** £4.50-£5.20. **Credit** (over £8) MC, V.

Chocoholics flock to this temple of cocoa nestled near Richmond Green. Winner of many accolades, William Curley enjoys a varied and loyal clientele, all in search of a truly special sweet treat. The melding of classic French techniques and Japanese flavours intrigues even the most experienced palates, and the display of too-pretty-to-eat pastries and chocolate sculptures is mesmerising. Knowledgeable staff provided extensive explanations of their wares, eventually leading us to the award-winning truffles and other couture chocolates. We opted for unusual varieties such as Japanese black vinegar, Japanese saké, and apricot with wasabi. All were technically faultless – a silky smooth ganache enrobed in a thin shiny, snapping coat of chocolate – although we didn't entirely embrace the rather aggressive flavours. We carried some pâtisserie to the nearby green for a posh picnic (the few tables outside were full). Blinged out with gold leaf and chocolate decoration, these pastries unabashedly asked for admiration. Forêt noire (black forest gateau) featured a boozy kirsch crème sharply cutting through layers of bitter Toscano chocolate. Raspberry delice successfully fused chocolate and raspberry with notes of almond, and certainly soothed sugar cravings.
Babies and children admitted. Tables outdoors (2, pavement). Takeaway service.

PARK CAFÉS

Central

Knightsbridge

Serpentine Bar & Kitchen NEW

Serpentine Road, Hyde Park, W2 2UH (7706 8114, www.serpentinebarandkitchen.com). Hyde Park Corner tube. **Open** 8am-9pm. **Main courses** £4.50-£9.50. **Credit** AmEx, MC, V.

A big basket of fresh rhubarb displayed near the entrance tries to hint that this Benugo-run waterside café-restaurant is passionate about food, but it doesn't take long to see past the pretence. Kudos to the management for offering proper beers such as Sharp's Doom Bar and Cornish Coaster among what could have been a clichéd clutch of lagers. Table staff are competent too, but otherwise the vibe seemed slapdash. At the height of spring, soup of the day was leek and potato – or was it celery? Honestly, we couldn't tell from the vapid flavour. Ham hock terrine was better (chunky and spiked with the anise flavour of fresh tarragon), but the heap of coarse piccalilli and thick-sliced granary it came with was rusticity taken too far. The menu does have tempting dishes for all times of day, with an ambitious showing of fish and seafood options, but also some pretty dull pizzas. Argentinian Bianchi brut is the cheapest of four fizzes on the enticing wine list. Would we stop by Sunday afternoon for tea? The view is still gorgeous, but the plastic-wrapped tiles of cake seemed as appealing as something you could pick up at a cheap sandwich bar.
Babies and children welcome: children's menu; colouring books; high chairs; nappy-changing facilities. Bookings not accepted. Disabled: toilet. Tables outdoors (20, pavement; 10 balcony). Takeaway service. **Map 8 E8.**

Marylebone

Garden Café

Inner Circle, Regent's Park, NW1 4NU (7935 5729, www.thegardencafe.co.uk). Baker Street or Regent's Park tube. **Open** 9am-dusk daily. **Breakfast served** 9-11am, **lunch served** noon-4pm, **dinner served** (summer) 5-8pm daily. **Set lunch/dinner** £13.50 2 courses, £17.50 3 courses. **Main courses** £8.50-£12.50. **Credit** MC, V.

Adjacent to Queen Mary's rose garden in Regent's Park, this upmarket eaterie points visitors in one direction or the other depending on whether they want counter or table service. On a sunny day, the outdoor tables are an exquisite place to sit and watch the world go by, although the utilitarian 1960s-retro interior is an acquired taste. Staff will laugh you out of the building if you haven't got a table booked at the weekend, and they don't seem much friendlier if your name is down on their books in indelible black ink. Frankly, Company of Cooks, which runs the place, does a much more impressive job at Kenwood's Brew House (*see p297*). Still, the food here is a cut above what you'd get in the average park hut, with classics like fish pie, chicken and leek risotto and a ploughman's given imaginative and seasonal touches. Food isn't cheap though. We found our sliver of goat's cheese and pine-nut tart with its accompanying (count 'em) two lettuce leaves a trifle expensive at £8.50. You may prefer the simplicity of the Honest Sausage – run by the same company, incidentally – in the middle of the park.

Orange Pekoe. See p291.

Brand values

You've seen them around the capital; you've probably been tempted to lunch at one. But how do London's growing band of café-bakery chains compare?

Baker & Spice

54-56 Elizabeth Street, SW1W 9PB (7730 3033, www.bakerandspice.uk.com). Sloane Square tube. **Open** 7am-7pm Mon-Sat; 8am-5pm Sun. **Main courses** £5-£14. **Credit** MC, V.

An awkward, rather stuffy dining area with communal table and bar stools means the pavement spots are most coveted at this bakery-café. The lunch menu features the likes of organic topside beef marinated in fresh herbs and red wine, and tamarind-marinated chargrilled poussin, but you could opt for a savoury muffin or tart from the shop counter. Bitter Musetti coffee tends to be a style you like or don't, but even so our cappuccino was poor, the foam deflating quickly to a sludge resembling washing-up liquid. *Babies and children admitted. Tables outdoors (5, pavement). Takeaway service.* **Map 15 10G**. **For branches see index.**

Gail's

5 Circus Road, NW8 6NX (7722 0983, www.gailsbread.co.uk). St John's Wood tube. **Open** 7am-8pm Mon-Fri; 8am-8pm Sat, Sun. **Main course** £3.95-£5.95. **Credit** MC, V.

Gail's is a younger cousin of Baker & Spice, but is growing quickly since its Hampstead birth. Staff at the St John's Wood branch, which can squeeze about 16 diners inside, are a hyper-chirpy lot, yet to their credit cope well with the area's high-maintenance customers. Good-looking sandwiches and salads (feta and mango, say, or moroccan chicken with couscous) form the backbone of the lunch menu. We loved the feta, aubergine and egg bureka, a rich layer of undercooked pastry adding to its delectableness. *Babies and children admitted. Tables outdoors (2, pavement). Takeaway service.* **Map 2 E2**. **For branches see index.**

Konditor & Cook

30 St Mary Axe, EC3A 8BF (0845 262 3030, www.konditorandcook.co.uk). Liverpool Street tube/rail. **Meals served** 7.30am-6.30pm Mon-Fri. **Main courses** £4.75-£5.25. **Credit** AmEx, MC, V.

Most customers seem to take their order and head back to the office, but a seat at this pleasant City branch of Konditor & Cook allows a peep at the architectural intricacies of its landmark location. The menu invariably features a hearty salad, a few pizzas and tarts, and jacket potatoes. Inventive soups such as courgette with lime show a foodie sensibility many lunch-spots sadly lack. Risotto is served from hot trays behind the counter; smoked haddock with saffron and serrano ham was very fishy, our server advised, so we opted for a thai veg curry laden with chickpeas for protein. A rhubarb and custard muffin

wrapped in brown paper did not live up to the usual high standard of the cakes. *Babies and children admitted. Tables outdoors (7, patio). Takeaway service.* **For branches see index.**

Ladurée

Harrods, entrance on Hans Road, SW1X 7XL (7893 8293, www.laduree.com). Knightsbridge tube.
Shop **Open** 9am-9pm Mon-Sat; 11.30am-6pm Sun.
Restaurant **Breakfast served** 9-11.30am daily. **Lunch served** 11.30am-3.30pm Mon-Sat; noon-3.30pm Sun. **Tea served** 3.30-6.30pm Mon-Sat; 3.30-6pm Sun. **Dinner served** 6.30-8pm Mon-Sat. **Main courses** £15-£27.50. **Set meal** £32 2 courses, £37.50 3 courses. **Set tea** £21.
Both **Credit** AmEx, DC, MC, V.

The London flagship of this Parisian chain is a collection of individually designed rooms set into a corner of Harrods, yet in good weather the desirable tables are outside. From the low, brick-coloured velvet chairs of the mezzanine, you can catch glimpses of the street or look over the chandelier to the pastel greens and pinks of the shop counter, where all manner of boxes are stacked ready to hold take-home treats. Omelette with fine herb salad was a little overcooked, but the nice mix of leaves included chives and chervil. Ispahan, a lovely rose-flavoured combination of raspberries, cream and meringue, was on the dry side. *Babies and children welcome: high chairs. Bookings not accepted (tea). Disabled: lift; toilet. Separate rooms for parties, seating 20-25. Tables outdoors (20, pavement).* **For branch see index.**

Napket

61 Piccadilly, W1J 0DY (7629 4622, www.napket.com). Green Park tube. **Open** 7am-11pm daily. **Main courses** £4-£5.85. **Credit** AmEx, MC, V.

Now with a flagship branch on Piccadilly, Napket (strapline: 'snob food') seems to have surrounded Mayfair in a carefully planned battle manoeuvre, but it has also launched a sortie in the City. The food, almost traiteur-style when the first branch opened in Chelsea, has been redesigned to suit takeaway-style containers, yet the quality has generally remained high. Tall tubs contain salads based on pasta, quinoa, rice and puy lentils. Indian chicken needed a good stir thanks to all the rocket on top, but the flavour was great and the rice firm. In addition to coffees and teas, a drinks counter offers juice combos with healthy boosters. Napket's cakes and sugary muffins have tended to disappoint us, but the black-and-gold designer bags for take-outs have an undeniable cachet. *Babies and children admitted.* **Map 9 J7**. **For branches see index.**

Le Pain Quotidien

18 Great Marlborough Street, W1F 7HS (7486 6154, www.lepainquotidien.co.uk). Oxford Circus tube. **Open** 7.30am-10pm Mon-Fri; 9am-10pm Sat; 9am-7pm Sun. **Main courses** £3.50-£9.95. **Credit** MC, V.

Part of LPQ's popularity lies in the fact that many people believe eating here is cheaper than going to a restaurant. Yet

it's not cheap, and 12.5% service charge is routinely added to diners' bills. Open sandwiches, the core of the menu, arrive on flat white platters that make it easy for them to go flying across the table when cut. Harissa and ricotta proved a good combination with rocket and tomato on earthy bread, but was hardly sparkling fare. An evening menu proffers the likes of hot lyonnaise salad, confit duck or grilled sirloin. Desserts range from Aussie pavlova to American brownies; a Belgian sugar waffle represents the chain's motherland. *Babies and children welcome: high chairs. Takeaway service.* **Map 17 A3**. **For branches see index.**

Pâtisserie Valerie

44 Old Compton Street, W1D 5JX (7437 3466, www.patisserie-valerie.co.uk). Leicester Square, Piccadilly Circus or Tottenham Court Road tube. **Open** 7.30am-9pm Mon, Tue; 7.30am-11pm Wed-Sat; 9am-9pm Sun. **Main courses** £3.75-£8.25. **Credit** (over £5) AmEx, MC, V.

New branches doff their beret to the vintage interior of the original, but never achieve its quirky, Toulouse-Lautrec warmth. Here you're as likely to find yourself sitting next to Hermès-bedecked ladies as Soho-ites or businessmen killing time between meetings. Cappuccino came with a thick layer of foam as distinct as the layers of the garishly decorated gateaux in the counter display. A big pile of moist tuna and plump white anchovies featured in a generous salade niçoise – though grey rings around the egg yolks are never a pleasant sight. Custard doughnut had a glazed plastic look and bubble-gum flavour, but was made from good light dough and decent crème pâtissière. *Babies and children welcome: high chairs. Tables outdoors (2, pavement). Takeaway service.* **Map 17 C4**. **For branches (incl Chelsea Left Wing Café) see index.**

Paul

29 Bedford Street, WC2E 9ED (7836 5321, www.paul-uk.com). Covent Garden tube. **Meals served** 7.30am-9pm Mon- Fri; 9am-9pm Sat; 9am-8pm Sun. **Main courses** £4-£8. **Credit** MC, V.

Attracting a mix of business-people, shoppers and tourists, Paul's flagship London branch has a large restaurant at the rear with pretty, retro-French decor. Dishes such as paillasson (a giant rösti topped with discs of goat's cheese, served with roast tomatoes and salad) come with a selection of rolls and butter. A quiche, eaten cold, was crisp on the bottom, but still had an uncooked layer of pastry. The chocolate macarons were correctly moist and creamy at centre with a good clean cocoa flavour. The caring, attentive waiters here put many in posh restaurants to shame – pity we can't say the same about staff in the small Paul branches dotted around town. *Babies and children welcome: high chairs. Disabled: toilet. Takeaway service.* **Map 18 D5**. **For branches see index.**

Babies and children welcome: children's menu; high chairs. Booking advisable. Disabled: toilet. Tables outdoors (38, garden). Takeaway service. **Map 3 G3.**

West

Kensington

Kensington Palace Orangery

The Orangery, Kensington Palace, Kensington Gardens, W8 4PX (7376 0239, www.digbytrout. co.uk). High Street Kensington or Queensway tube. **Open** *Mar-Oct* 10am-6pm daily. *Nov-Feb* 10am-5pm daily. **Main courses** £8.75-£12.95. **Set tea** £13.50-£28.50. **Credit** AmEx, MC, V.
Proudly positioned in the midst of meticulously manicured Kensington gardens, the Orangery is the setting for a proper palatial affair. At weekends, prepare to queue among tourists and locals seeking regal refuge and refuelling. Towering piles of scones, pillowy meringues, and a wide assortment of traditional cakes tiered on a grand central table entice everyone who is escorted through from the outdoor terrace to their table by the maître d'. Charming potted miniature orange trees, complete with dangling fruit, provide a splash of colour amid the otherwise bleak stony-white decor. The devourers of afternoon tea and scones populate most of the tables, but we took our friendly server's advice and opted for the Belgium chocolate cake – which turned out to be a dense and stale-tasting disappointment. In contrast, coffee banana cake was a triumph, with its haughty height, moist texture and addictive coffee cream. We relaxed with a glass of prosecco and marvelled at the intricate Corinthian pillars soaring overhead. The best views in summer, however, are from shaded tables outside on the vast veranda overlooking the greenery.
Babies and children welcome: children's menu; high chairs; nappy-changing facilities. Disabled: toilet. Tables outdoors (14, terrace). **Map 7 C8.**

South West

Wandsworth

Common Ground

Wandsworth Common, off Dorlcote Road, SW18 3RT (8874 9386). Wandsworth Common rail. **Open** 9am-5.30pm Mon-Fri; 10am-5.30pm Sat, Sun. **Main courses** £3.50-£9. **Credit** MC, V.
This former lodge building overlooking the cricket pitches and bowling green of Wandsworth Common keeps things simple. There are wooden floors and wooden tables in the conservatory, a generous patio with seating outside, and a cosier room with deep sofas, local notices and buckets of toys where parent-and-toddler groups meet on weekdays. The whole place is crawling with families at the weekend. Nevertheless, there's a general sense of missed opportunity and under-achievement here – a lovely site such as this deserves a slicker operation. The food is tastier than its simple presentation might suggest, with sandwiches deep-filled and wrapped in thick fresh slices of bread, and a range of quiches, baked potatoes and specials offered. Breakfasts are served until 11.30am and feature a wide range of classics, from porridge and own-made granola to french toast and cooked breakfasts, via bacon sandwiches. Cakes too are much better than they seem at first glance. The only thing disturbing the peace are the local dogs, tied up and yapping outside while their owners take their refreshment.
Available for hire. Babies and children welcome: children's menu; high chairs; nappy-changing facilities; play area. Takeaway service. Vegetarian menu.

South East

Dulwich

Pavilion Café

Dulwich Park, SE21 7BQ (8299 1383, www. pavilioncafedulwich.co.uk). West Dulwich rail/ P4 bus. **Open** *Summer* 8.30am-6.30pm daily.

Winter 9am-4pm daily. **Main courses** £3.50-£6.95. **Credit** MC, V.
A benchmark among park cafés, this spot is busy on weekdays, heaving at weekends. Adult daily specials (soups, salads and so on) tend to be overshadowed by the all-day breakfasts of top-quality sausages and bacon, free-range eggs and chunky toast (white or wholemeal). Children are the focus and have a well-considered menu of grilled chicken, penne pasta, 100% Scotch beef burgers, chunky chips, and sandwiches. There's also organic baby food, Innocent smoothies and garishly coloured ice drinks, plus raisins, crisps, fruit, and dairy ice-cream (sold through a side hatch in summer). Various infusions are available, adult and infant, but grown-ups needing an extra kick can indulge in a Baileys latte or rum hot chocolate. Sources are impeccable (Borough Market for veg, William Rose for meat and Moxon's for fish), cakes are own-made, and much of the other food is freshly prepared on site. The café has become a social hub, providing information on local events, a colourful play corner for kids, baby-change and clean toilets, and bird food for feeding ducks. A light, airy space, with floor-to-ceiling windows, it has verdant views in summer. If you have children, it's a life-saver.
Babies and children welcome: children's menu; high chairs; nappy-changing facilities; play area. Parties. Tables outdoors (12, terrace). Takeaway service.

Greenwich

Pavilion Tea House

Greenwich Park, SE10 8QY (8858 9695, www.companyofcooks.com). Blackheath rail/ Greenwich rail/DLR. **Open** 9am-5.30pm Mon-Fri; 9am-6pm Sat, Sun. **Main courses** £4.95-£6.60. **Credit** MC, V.
Diagonally opposite the Royal Observatory, set in its own pretty, fenced-in grounds, the Pavilion Tea House provides a convivial cake-and-a-break for weary parents. Its breakfasts, hot meals, salads, snacks and sandwiches are a notch above average, reflected in the prices on certain items – £6.50 for the pie of the day, £6.60 for smoked salmon and scrambled egg. For a simple snack, Mum or Dad can get away with a slice of chocolate fudge cake or a fresh cream scone for under £3; charges for coffee and Fairtrade tea are set lower than most chain-brand cafés. Soup of the day, served with a hunk of granary bread, is recommended at £3.95. If parents really need a pick-me-up, they'll have to fork out £4.95 for a glass of standard Stellar Organics sauvignon blanc or shiraz. At a serving hatch by the entrance, Roskilly's organic Cornish ice-cream is sold in blackcurrant-cheesecake and mint-chocolate-chip flavours, among others. Topped by a weather vane, the hexagonal building floods with natural light. Entertainment within is provided by invasions of fearless pigeons. Outside, children can chase squirrels and couples can gaze at the panoramic view of London by the landscaped greenery.
Babies and children welcome: children's menu; high chairs; nappy-changing facilities. Disabled: toilet. Tables outdoors (20, terrace).

East

Victoria Park

Pavilion Café

Victoria Park, E9 5DU (8980 0030, www.the-pavilion-cafe.com). Mile End tube then 277 bus. **Meals served** *Summer* 8.30am-5pm Mon-Fri; 8.30am-6pm Sat, Sun. *Winter* 8.30am-4pm daily. **Main courses** £4-£9. **No credit cards.**
After an exhausting stint of feeding the ducks, stroll to Victoria Park's recently refurbished lakeside pavilion for a reviving bacon and egg sandwich and a mug of builder's tea. The lovely glass rotunda houses a mishmash of tables made from old wooden cable drums and Victorian school chairs, but there's nothing random about the food. Delicious dishes are written up on blackboard walls; classier palates will be delighted with the likes of eggs benedict with

spinach, or roast beef with potato salad, watercress and anchovy mayo. The ingredients are all well sourced (Ginger Pig meats, Monmouth coffees) and, where possible, organic. The only downside is the place's popularity. On a sunny day it's invariably overrun with babies, buggies and (outside) bikes. Fortunately, there are more seats next to the lake, so it's worth taking your coffee and cake (moreish brownies, lemon drizzle) and heading for a park bench.
Babies and children welcome: high chairs; nappy-changing facilities. Disabled: toilet. Tables outdoors (25, park). Takeaway service.

North

Highgate

Pavilion Café

Highgate Woods, N10 3JN (8444 4777). Highgate tube. **Open** 9am-1hr before park closing daily. **Main courses** £6-£10. **Credit** AmEx, MC, V.
This charming pavilion with its picket fence and large, sheltered-garden seating area is packed whatever the time of day, week or year. While the main menu is Mediterranean-influenced (meze and flatbreads, heaping bowls of pasta), the breakfast and brunch options come from both sides of the Channel. Plates of full english looked very full indeed, and scrambled eggs on thick slices of granary bread were creamy and delicious. Croissants were buttery and soft in the middle, with the requisite crispy exterior. The chef then came round with samples of a lemon polenta cake, which he'd just taken out of the oven for the lunchtime sitting. It was the perfect consistency, just a little bite, but not off-puttingly crunchy as some polenta cakes can be. There's a good choice of drinks with an eco-bent, including organic beer from Pitfield brewery. Service is presided over by the ever-attentive head waiter, whose charm puts a twinkle in local mums' eyes while their children go ga-ga for the outstanding ice-cream, also served at weekends and holidays, from a hatch at the side of the building.
Babies and children welcome: children's menu; crayons; high chairs; nappy-changing facilities. Disabled: toilet. Tables outdoors (30, garden). Takeaway service.

North West

Hampstead

★ Brew House (100)

Kenwood, Hampstead Lane, NW3 7JR (8341 5384, www.companyofcooks.com). Archway or Golders Green tube then 210 bus. **Open** *Apr-Sept* 9am-6pm daily (7.30pm on concert nights). *Oct-Mar* 9am-dusk daily. **Main courses** £4.25-£8. **Credit** (over £10) MC, V.
Brew House is a self-service café in the gorgeous setting of the Kenwood estate. Inside are stone floors, decorative walls and high ceilings; there's plenty of outdoor seating too. New customers struggle to get to grips with the queueing system, but it's a lot less complicated than it looks. The hot food counter serves generous breakfasts (be here before 10am on dry weekends to secure a table), with huge sausages, scrambled eggs, very good bacon, field mushrooms and tomatoes. At lunch, there's usually a choice of quiche, a hearty meat dish or soup (with or without cheese, bread and an apple). If you're just after coffee and one of the very tempting cakes (spicy carrot cake, hefty bread pudding, and pecan pie are among our favourites), go to the alternative tills, or the adjacent Steward's Room, which offers a pared-back range of goodies. The chiller contains a concise selection of beers and wines, along with farm apple juice and OJ. On sunny days, few London venues could equal the beautiful, sheltered terrace for top outdoor dining. It's impossible to come away and not feel as if you've had lunch in the countryside.
Available for hire. Babies and children welcome: children's menu; high chairs; nappy-changing facilities. Separate room for parties, seats 120. Tables outdoors (400, garden). Takeaway service. Vegetarian menu. **Map 28 C1.**

Fish & Chips

Given that it's seen as one of Britain's national dishes, fish and chips has a remarkably multicultural past and present. Chipped potatoes were probably first created in France, whereas fish fried in batter is likely to have been a borrowing from Jewish cuisine. Chippies are still popular in Jewish districts of London today, especially if they fry the fish in matzo meal. **Sam's** of Golders Green, Finchley's excellent **Two Brothers** and Edgware's **Booba's** are three such venues. Which brings us to another characteristic of the London chippy: they're often owned and run by folk of Greek or Turkish ancestry. Booba's is Turkish-run and Covent Garden's **Rock & Sole Plaice** is under Turkish-Cypriot ownership; **Toff's** of Muswell Hill is Greek-Cypriot run, as are Notting Hill's **Costas** and Marylebone's **Golden Hind**. Doubtless there are more. All this has little importance, of course, when compared to what's on the plate. The most fragile of batters encasing perfectly moist fresh fish; thick, golden-brown chips, crisp outside, soft within; mushy peas not too liquid, not too thick – it's not rocket science, but so few places get it right. This year our favourite chippies are **Fish Club** of Battersea, West Hampstead's **Nautilus**, the aforementioned Two Brothers and, a new entry, **Fisher's** of Fulham. New this year, too, is the **Fishery**, in the Turkish heartland of Stoke Newington. For restaurants specialising in a wide variety of marine life, see **Fish** (pp84-89).

Central

Barbican

Fish Central
149-155 Central Street, EC1V 8AP (7253 4970, www.fishcentral.co.uk). Old Street tube/rail/55 bus. **Lunch served** 11.30am-2.30pm Mon-Sat. **Dinner served** 5-10.30pm Mon-Thur; 5-11pm Fri, Sat. **Main courses** £7.95-£12.95. **Credit** MC, V.
A large colour photograph on the wall shows Fish Central as it was pre-makeover – your common or everyday chippy. Today it's quite a trendy set-up, with moody black-and-white images hinting at a fishing theme, curvy black butterfly chairs, frosted glass pendant lamps and palest green tables. You may be surprised at such smart fittings, given the adjacent council housing, but proximity to the City brings in a well-heeled clientele too. The resultant mix is lively, helped by forthright, jokey international staff. The elongated strip of paper menu doesn't try to offer all sizes in all colours, but for tradition-seekers there's cod, haddock, plaice, rock, skate and scampi deep-fried. The specials board may contain the likes of warm squid salad, queenie scallops with Thai noodles, or roast hake. Our fisherman's platter (piles of bite-sized and crumbed fish and seafood, including juicy chunks of skate) was so huge we asked for the leftovers to be packed up to take away. Good chips and mushy peas, decent wines by the glass and a welcome choice of tap beers make this an enviable local, if not worth a long trip.
Babies and children welcome: children's menu; high chairs. Booking advisable. Separate room for parties, seats 70. Takeaway service. **Map 5 P3**.

Bloomsbury

North Sea Fish Restaurant
7-8 Leigh Street, WC1H 9EW (7387 5892). Russell Square tube/King's Cross tube/rail/ 68, 168 bus. **Lunch served** noon-2.30pm,

dinner served 5.30-10.30pm Mon-Sat. **Main courses** £8.90-£18.95. **Credit** MC, V.
A line of single malt whiskies along the counter, and surprisingly decent wine and beer (bottles of Speckled Hen, a reasonable muscadet) suggest that middle-aged businessmen and old-school hacks become beached in the North Sea. However, a pretty young Spanish couple were also tucking in when we arrived. Behind the unassuming frontage, several wood-trimmed anterooms make the place bigger than it looks. Staff seemed sufficiently nimble and switched-on to police the various corners – even if things were to get much busier than we experienced for a late weekday lunch. The starters list tempts with smoked mackerel and cod's roe, but we reckon it's best to plunge straight into the options served with chips: perhaps a grilled sea bass off the printed specials list, or a battered haddock fillet. Portion sizes are such that it's hard to imagine anyone managing the advertised jumbo versions. Cooking is competent, if more assured at the fryer than at the grill. Puddings are thoroughly geographically confused, perhaps with a view to drawing in tourists and foreign students, but none would be out of place in a public school canteen.
Babies and children welcome: high chairs. Booking advisable Thur-Sat. Separate room for parties, seats 40. Takeaway service. **Map 4 L4**.

Covent Garden

Rock & Sole Plaice
47 Endell Street, WC2H 9AJ (7836 3785). Covent Garden tube. **Meals served** 11.30am-10.30pm Mon-Sat; noon-9.30pm Sun. **Main courses** £9-£12. **Credit** MC, V.
Exactly when Rock & Sole (or its predecessor) first started battering fish is in dispute; some say 1871, others maintain that it opened just after World War II. Today, this small corner chippy near Drury Lane and Covent Garden Piazza has a green and white frontage, a cheery fish logo with jaunty union jack bib, large windows and West End

theatre posters on the walls. During the week, tourists compete with nearby office workers to secure one of the few tables on the ground floor, and to attract the attention of the somewhat impervious staff. A plaice from the hot cabinet was juicy enough, but our less popular rock had been fried to order and was as fantastic as the large-cut chips. A Turkish-Cypriot family now runs the joint, which shows in the small selection of starters that includes calamares and houmous. Desserts, however, are of the English school-dinner variety. Saveloys, chicken nuggets and pies are among the options available for those not in the mood for fish. In the summer, there are several highly popular tables on the wide pavement outside; in winter, the rather dingy basement dining room becomes a little more appealing.
Tables outdoors (7, pavement). Takeaway service. **Map 18 D3**.

Holborn

Fryer's Delight
19 Theobald's Road, WC1X 8SL (7405 4114). Holborn tube/19, 38, 55 bus. **Meals served** noon-11pm Mon-Sat (takeaway only after 10pm). **Main courses** £5.40-£6.70. **Unlicensed. Corkage** no charge. **No credit cards.**
Cross the black-and-white tiled floor of this no-frills cabbies' fave, and plonk yourself at one of the lurid pinky-red Formica tables. The brief menu mysteriously offers 'chop sauce', and a little wooden replica cart informs you that Fryer's Delight serves 'sea-fresh fish and home-grown potatoes'. Faded celebrity photos capture Carol Vorderman, Gary Lineker and Jeff Capes with an unexplained person in rabbit costume. Sadly, the lack of English-speaking staff meant we were unable to discover the nature of the sauce, the identity of the rabbit, or exactly where on the premises the potatoes were grown. However, we did receive a sizeable portion of haddock in crunchy, dark-brown batter, and some cod's roe cooked just long enough to leave it nice and soft inside. Portions of chips were slightly on the small side, and we felt disappointed that mushy peas had been eschewed for the processed variety. It was also a shame that, on our Tuesday evening visit, the place was virtually empty. Is the taxi-driver's love affair with this basic chippy starting to wane?
Babies and children admitted. Takeaway service. **Map 4 M5**.

Marylebone

Golden Hind (100)
73 Marylebone Lane, W1U 2PN (7486 3644). Bond Street tube. **Lunch served** noon-3pm Mon-Fri. **Dinner served** 6-10pm Mon-Sat. **Main courses** £5-£10.70. **Minimum** (dinner) £5. **Unlicensed. Corkage** no charge. **Credit** AmEx, MC, V.
Pride is taken in the Golden Hind's history. Its walls are lined with black-and-white photos of the locality at the turn of the 20th century, and there's a blackboard listing the names of owners dating back to the 1914 opening of this Marylebone chippy, along with their nationalities. The current Hellenic ownership is reflected in a menu that places mixed greek pickles and tart, creamy deep-fried feta alongside a selection of standard starters such as fish cakes (which were overpoweringly peppery). A portion of battered rock salmon had an unpleasant wetness to it, but the kitchen redeemed itself with a crisp serving of cod so big it spilled over the edges of our plate. Certainly, the place seems popular with locals. A Friday night visit saw both floors full of the chatter of after-work groups of suits. Cross your fingers for a seat on the ground floor, so you can gawp at the stunning art-deco fryer, but there's plenty to marvel at, even in the brick-flued basement. The super-jovial staff were almost self-flagellating in their apologies for starters arriving at the same time as main courses.
Babies and children admitted. Takeaway service. **Map 9 G5**.

Sea Shell

49-51 Lisson Grove, NW1 6UH (7224 9000, www.seashellrestaurant.co.uk). Marylebone tube/ rail. **Lunch served** noon-2.30pm Mon-Fri; noon-4pm Sun. **Dinner served** 5-10.30pm Mon-Fri. **Meals served** noon-10.30pm Sat. **Main courses** £12.75-£24.50. **Set meal** (lunch, 5-7pm Mon-Thur) £12.50 2 courses, £14.95 3 courses. **Credit** AmEx, DC, MC, V.

Glass and wood partitions lend a degree of intimacy to this otherwise vast establishment that commands a sizeable corner off Lisson Grove. Draught beers are one of the benefits of choosing the Sea Shell, though the Guinness was off on our visit and we weren't told until well after we'd ordered – a rare slip from the proficient, elegantly white-shirted service team. There's a choice of dry white, medium white and red French house wines and they're perfectly pleasant, but even better is to plump for the £16.95 South African sparkler from Eikendal Estate. Starters range from classics (melon, whitebait, prawn cocktail) to more modish fare (scallops with garlic and chilli oil). Mains are served with a choice of chips, new potatoes, mash or baked potato. Fish cakes with caper, gherkin, anchovy and mustard mayo appealed, but we couldn't resist simple haddock and chips. Grilled fish comes with a choice of sauces; the pot of hollandaise that arrived with our lemon sole was surprisingly cold but tasted fine. Spotted dick with a good cakey texture and plump fruit was let down by a bland mass of goo that the menu called 'custard'. As we went to press, the restaurant had been badly damaged in a fire, but hopes to reopen by Christmas 2009.
Babies and children welcome: children's menu; high chairs. Booking advisable Thur-Sat. Disabled: toilet. Takeaway service. **Map 2 F4**.

Soho

Golden Union Fish Bar NEW

38 Poland Street, W1F 7LY (7434 1933). Oxford Circus tube. **Meals served** noon-9pm Mon-Sat; noon-6pm Sun. **Main courses** £4.50-£7.50. **Credit** AmEx, MC, V.

Tucked off Oxford Street at the top edge of Soho, the canteen formerly known as the Chippy is well-placed to pull in tourists seeking authentic, unfussy British cooking. It's refreshingly no-frills, clean and spacious, with cheery yellow laminated tables and bold black wall tiles spelling out the legend: FISH. You'll find everything that your local chippy has: pickled eggs, mushy peas, tartare

sauce, and battered saveloy. The limited fish menu changes daily and might feature coley, pollock, prawns and plaice, alongside standard fillets of cod and haddock. There are fish cakes and pies too, but otherwise the owners have been shrewd enough to stop at anything fancy. Unfortunately, we can't rate this place as the best showcase of Britain's national cuisine. Chips were pallid, the batter was a touch greasy and the haddock lacked succulence or flakiness. Nevertheless, portions are huge (go for a 'small' unless you're ravenous) and the recession-busting £4.50 lunch is a genuine bargain. Despite the misgivings, this joint is worth remembering as a pit-stop if you're braving the Oxford Street crowds and in need of sustenance.
Babies and children admitted. Bookings not accepted. Disabled: toilet. Takeaway service. **Map 17 A3**.

Victoria

Seafresh Fish Restaurant

80-81 Wilton Road, SW1V 1DL (7828 0747, www.fishandchipsinlondon.com). Victoria tube/ rail/24 bus. **Lunch served** noon-3pm, **dinner served** 5-10.30pm Mon-Fri. **Meals served** noon-10.30pm Sat. **Main courses** £6.25-£22. **Set lunch** £11.50 2 courses incl tea or coffee. **Credit** AmEx, MC, V.

Situated where grimy Victoria gives way to posher Pimlico, the family-run Seafresh tries to bridge the gap between the two areas. Its vast premises look much like a standard café, but are just that bit brighter, cleaner and fresher, with wider spaces between the tables. The same sort of distinctions apply to the food: the standard repertoire of fish and chips is produced with slightly more panache than usual and charged at prices that can't exactly be termed giveaway (£14 for haddock, chips and mushy peas – and that's before you throw in a drink or bread and butter). The cost doesn't seem to bother the regulars at lunchtime, though: a mix of businessmen and elderly locals. Helpings are well proportioned, so you don't feel like too much of a pig after leaving the table. However, the problem with charging higher prices is that punters find themselves getting a little more picky – we felt the batter on our fish was rather too oily. For those who want to steer clear of the fish and chip staples, the menu also does a good line in grilled fish and fisherman's pies.
Available for hire. Babies and children welcome: high chairs. Takeaway service. **Map 15 J10**.

Westminster

Laughing Halibut

38 Strutton Ground, SW1P 2HR (7799 2844). St James's Park tube. **Meals served** 11.15am-8pm Mon-Fri; 11.15am-4pm Sat. **Main courses** £6.75-£7.45. **Unlicensed** no alcohol allowed. **No credit cards.**

'Nice piece of fish – out of the Thames?' quipped a portly gentlemen in this back-to-basics takeaway and caff. 'Yeah, I pulled it out myself this morning' came the deadpan response. We like the Halibut's front and lack of pretension, but our crunchily fried haddock didn't seem as fresh as this gent's; the flesh collapsed out of its snug batter shell rather than waiting to be forked into firm flakes. Service is appealingly cheeky and swift, chips and batter are golden and crisp, but the menu over-extends itself (spring rolls, pies, a terrifying breakfast that lists burger, sausage and bacon before the eggs even get a look in), and tartare sauce comes in a squeezy sachet. Things were far busier at the popular takeaway counter at the front. The rear seated section, with its fixed tables, is certainly no looker; we liked the mosaic fish but have never gone a bundle on plastic sea life and ersatz fishing nets. Proudly advertising itself as selling 'Traditional British Fish & Chips', the Laughing Halibut means what it says: for better and worse.
Babies and children welcome: high chairs. Bookings not accepted lunch. Takeaway service. **Map 16 K10**.

West

Bayswater

Mr Fish

9 Porchester Road, W2 5DP (7229 4161, www.mrfish.uk.com). Bayswater, Queensway or Royal Oak tube. **Meals served** 11am-midnight (takeaway only after 11pm) daily. **Main courses** £6.25-£12.95. **Set lunch** (11am-3pm) £6.75 cod & chips incl soft drink, tea or coffee. **Credit** AmEx, MC, V.

You'd expect oil from a chippy, but Grease? Step past the metal deep-fat fryer at the front of Mr Fish, underneath the yellow neon-lit 'restaurant' sign and you're amid a black-and-white tiled, metallic bar-stooled tribute to 1950s America. Staff clad in baseball caps and polo shirts hurry around the plastic seating and fake plants, serving large parties of French tourists apparently attracted by the restaurant's policy of distributing 10%

Golden Union Fish Bar

CHEAP EATS

discount flyers outside Bayswater station. Ignore the curious stylistic touches and the fried chicken and burgers, because this is a better than average chippy. Fish comes either battered, breadcrumbed, coated in matzo meal, grilled or poached (the latter two cost £1 extra). Steaks of halibut and salmon, plus fillets of sea bass and lemon sole are offered too, with parsley sauce for £1 extra. Yet it's in standard fish and chips that Mr Fish excels. The batter on our cod was a light, crisp casing to a firm, tasty fish, but an overly thick covering of matzo meal meant our sea bass fillet was overcooked and chewy. For afters you can tuck into classic English pre-made desserts including jam sponge, spotted dick, and apple and blackberry crumble.
Babies and children welcome: children's menu; high chair. Takeaway service. Map 7 C5.
For branch see index.

Notting Hill

Costas Fish Restaurant
18 Hillgate Street, W8 7SR (7727 4310). Notting Hill Gate tube. **Lunch served** noon-2.30pm, **dinner served** 5.30-10.30pm Tue-Sat. **Main courses** £5.20-£8. **No credit cards.**
Sure, it's good to know that the gentrification of Notting Hill hasn't swept through every crack and crevice of W8, but Costas looks like it hasn't changed a bit since opening in 1981. Even then its feet were firmly stuck in the 1970s. Walk past the fryers into the restaurant at the back and it's like a set from *Life on Mars*: all maroon leatherette chairs, brown tables and dodgy Greek landscapes on the walls. Although the air smelt musty when we arrived for an early lunch, as soon as the fryers were on, the atmosphere perked up. Service was efficient and friendly – and you can't argue about decor when the fish and chips are this good. Juicy rock salmon was fried to order, and reassuringly irregular chips had soft middles and crisp exteriors. The menu contains Greek touches, such as taramasalata or houmous and pitta as starters (the owner's brother runs the Greek restaurant next door), but frankly, you'll be too full for the main course if you order them. Avoid the uninspiring salads (iceberg lettuce, chunks of cucumber and tomato with barely any dressing) and feast on the main attraction.
Babies and children admitted. Booking advisable dinner. Tables outdoors (2, pavement). Takeaway service. Map 7 A7.

South West
Fulham

★ Fisher's NEW
19 Fulham High Street, SW6 3JH (7610 9808, www.fishersfishandchips.com). Putney Bridge tube. **Lunch served** 11am-3pm, **dinner served** 5.30-11.30pm Mon-Fri. **Meals served** noon-11.30pm Sat; 1-11pm Sun. **Main courses** £5.95-£11.95. **Credit** MC, V.
Fisher's, frying since 1982, certainly seems to have hit its stride. The dining area, decorated with a jumble of car-boot art, is small and rather old-fashioned, so it's no surprise that many customers choose to grab takeaways. Most plates of fish and chips cost around a tenner; the market-fresh fish can be steamed or breaded instead of fried in batter. Add-ons such as golden grease-free chips, proper mushy peas and own-made tartare sauce are exemplary, but with portions so huge, you're unlikely to need side orders – or starters or desserts for that matter. If you do, there's cod's roe, avocado and prawns, and jumbo prawn cocktail for starters. Puds, such as banana fritters or chocolate fudge cake, are equally retro; ice-creams come from Loseley and Rocombe Farm. Kids can have cod, sausage, fish cakes or nuggets, all with chips; vegetarians are offered spicy bean burgers or meat-free sausage with chips, beans or peas. The drinks list has a few decent wines in the £12-£20 range that no doubt appeal to the well-heeled clientele, such as sauvignon blanc from Marlborough, Margaret River chardonnay and prosecco for those wanting bubbly. There's even an English white – plus Leffe and Budvar for the beer lovers.

Babies and children welcome: children's menu; high chairs. Booking advisable dinner. Separate room for parties, seats 20. Takeaway service.

Wandsworth

Brady's
513 Old York Road, SW18 1TF (8877 9599, www.bradysfish.co.uk). Wandsworth Town rail/ 28, 44 bus. **Lunch served** 12.30-2.30pm Tue-Sat. **Dinner served** 6.30-9.45pm Mon; 6.30-10pm Tue-Wed, Sat; 6.30-10.30pm Thur, Fri. **Main courses** £4.95-£7.95. **Credit** MC, V.
Trying to take fish and chips upmarket since way before the gastro-revolution, Brady's has been dishing up affordable seafood suppers to genteel Wandsworth families for 18 years. Decor is a curious hotchpotch of retro aqua and cream wall-mounted menus, and a clean, modern IKEA-like dining room overlooked by a Little Mermaid fresco and massive plastic swordfish. In contrast, the menu's about one thing only: quality produce, simply cooked. There's a punchy selection of starters, including sweetly pickled herring fillets and anchovies with nary a hint of saltiness. Mains consist of an array of battered fish, served with glass jars of dilly aïoli, basil and mint mayonnaises, tartare sauce and ketchup. It's the oft-changing choice of grilled fish that stands out, though, with our oregano-scattered lemon sole fillet cooked to chargrilled perfection. The various own-made desserts cost £3.95, with delicious honeycomb ice-cream a highlight; other puds can verge on the school-dinnerish. Service is jovial and neighbourly (although not all staff understand English). Some customers are such regulars that on our visit fellow diners offered menu suggestions. Excellent value.
Babies and children welcome: high chair. Takeaway service. Map 21 A4.

South
Battersea

★ Fish Club (100)
189 St John's Hill, SW11 1TH (7978 7115, www.thefishclub.com). Clapham Junction rail. **Meals served** 5-10pm Mon; noon-10pm Tue-Sun. **Main courses** £4.95-£10.95. **Credit** AmEx, MC, V.
Past the classy outdoor furniture, over the babbling in-floor water feature, and straight up to a glass

counter gleaming with fresh fish – it's immediately apparent that Fish Club is London's king of the sea. Staff are laid-back, but their knowledge is excellent and they confidently advise on how fish is cooked, which species are a hit with children, and the type and location of bones. Order from the blackboard menu by the counter and your food will be brought to you. Pan-fried cuttlefish with chilli and garlic, royal bream with lemon and rosemary and chargrilled grey mullet are among the tempting alternatives to traditional over-fished species; sustainable coley is offered in lieu of cod. Our battered haddock wasn't the biggest in town, but sensibly portioned and perfectly cooked. Prawn and chorizo kebabs, exuding zingy paprika-flavoured oil, didn't need a rich side sauce of saffron aïoli, but tender mixed-leaf salad was a welcome adjunct. Fish Club's crunchy roughed-up chips are among the capital's best, while its fresh herby tartare sauce beats all rivals. Desserts (crème brûlée, bakewell tart and ice-cream) are superb too, and there's a savvy drinks list. Simple things done really well: trainee chefs could learn more from a stage here than they'd pick up in many posh restaurants.
Babies and children welcome: children's menu; high chairs. Disabled: toilet. Tables outdoors (3, courtyard; 2, pavement). Takeaway service. Map 21 B4.
For branch see index.

Waterloo

Masters Super Fish
191 Waterloo Road, SE1 8UX (7928 6924). Waterloo tube/rail. **Lunch served** noon-3pm Tue-Sat. **Dinner served** 5.30-10.30pm Mon; 4.30-10.30pm Tue-Thur, Sat; 4.30-11pm Fri. **Main courses** £7.25-£12.50. **Set lunch** £7 1 course incl soft drink, tea or coffee. **Credit** MC, V.
Masters is a well-run, no-messing fish and chip shop, from its wipe-clean tables to the functional, well-lit, red-brick interior. A few spider plants, photographs of the founders, a poster of various species of fish, and a signed Arsenal ball for a charity raffle pretty much sum up the decor. The menu is a little more elaborate than you might expect; grilled swordfish and Cromer crab cocktail are offered alongside all the battered fish. Service was more brisk than friendly, yet faultlessly attentive, and we appreciated free extras like the trio of prawns offered as an unannounced appetiser and the buttered slices of baguette

The Fishery Fish Bar. See p302.

(charged for in many places). As we crunched into our haddock (no soggy inner layer to the batter here), the boss came round with big metal bowls of pickled whole onions and sizeable gherkins: typical of Masters' lack of pretension. The clientele is mostly elderly, as at most chippies, but is almost entirely made up of return custom. Skip the puddings; a doughy apple pie with ice-cream looked bought-in, and convinced us it was best to sate our appetites on the generously sized mains.
Babies and children welcome: high chairs. Bookings not accepted Fri. Takeaway service.
Map 11 N9.

South East
Dulwich

Sea Cow
37 Lordship Lane, SE22 8EW (8693 3111, www.theseacow.co.uk). East Dulwich rail/176, 196 bus. **Meals served** noon-11pm Tue-Sat; noon-8.30pm Sun. **Main courses** £5-£9. **Credit** MC, V.
One of the new breed of contemporary fish and chip joints, with its fresh catch displayed appetisingly on ice, the Sea Cow has a modern, pared-down interior and chunky communal wooden tables. Standard cod or haddock and chips are cooked just so: the batter crisp, the fish firm but flaky, the chips fat and fluffy. Portions are generous – a kid's size satisfies most moderately hungry adults. The grilled fish too is splendid, including lemon sole, red snapper, tilapia and sea bass. Most fish arrives straight from the coast or Billingsgate Market, and the sustainability credentials of each species are expounded in literature on every table (monkfish, swordfish and marlin have been removed from the menu, and bluefin tuna substituted with Pacific yellowfin). Anything beyond the fresh and simple is less successful: our crab cakes were bland and lacking in texture; salad amounted to leaves and a single cherry tomato, quartered; lime mayo lacked zing; and the minted mushy peas were too smooth and pretentious (not to mention pricey at £2 a cup). The wine menu, though not extensive, takes itself seriously enough to partner wines with specific fish. Avoid Friday evenings from around 7.30pm when tables and takeaway area are rammed.
Babies and children welcome: children's menu; high chairs. Takeaway service. **Map 23 C4**.

Herne Hill

Olley's
65-69 Norwood Road, SE24 9AA (8671 8259, www.olleys.info). Herne Hill rail/3, 68, 196 bus. **Lunch served** noon-3pm, **dinner served** 5-10.30pm Tue-Sun. **Main courses** £8.45-£18.45. **Set lunch** £7.50 1 course. **Credit** AmEx, MC, V.
Olley's could almost pass for a quaint Mexican or Spanish restaurant. Behind the decorative window panes it's all pine wood, draping leaves and terracotta and blue tones; outside there's a pleasing view over Brockwell Park, plus some heavy traffic. 'The Famous Olley's Fish Experience' can be as cheap as £7, if you eat off-peak between 5pm and 7pm. The menu offers several fish rarely seen in chippies, plus the choice of having them fried, grilled or served in tomato and herb sauce. You can even have battered and deep-fried tuna, which the menu tells us one BBC local radio presenter favours. Our hake was perfection – fresh-tasting, moist and with crisp brown batter. By comparison, the thinner pieces of deep-fried mahi mahi were dry and overcooked. Chips and mushy peas are reliably good. Service, attentive at first, fell off entirely when it came to dessert; the kitchen didn't improve matters, eventually producing a sickly treacle sponge with smooth yellow sauce that lacked the vanilla and egg flavours one hopes to find in custard. Still, the drinks list shows discernment, with Innis & Gunn bottled beer, and a classy Pavilion Boschendal shiraz cabernet sauvignon 2006 that, at just £18.45, is the most expensive wine in the joint, bar champagne.
Babies and children welcome: children's menu; crayons; high chairs; nappy-changing facilities. Booking advisable weekends. Disabled: toilet. Separate room for parties, seats 40. Tables outdoors (12, pavement). Takeaway service. **Map 23 A5**.

Lewisham

Something Fishy
117-119 Lewisham High Street, SE13 6AT (8852 7075). Lewisham rail/DLR. **Meals served** 9am-5.30pm Mon-Sat. **Main courses** £4.95-£6.65. **No credit cards.**
Wedged on Lewisham High Street, this large traditional workers' café is perfectly located for the local street market, whose patrons and vendors make up much of the clientele during the

lunchtime rush. Such folk know their stuff; lunch is when the fish is fresh, the golden batter is super-crispy and the mushy peas are a particularly radioactive shade of green. The bright blue ground-floor canteen is decked out with plastic seating and easy-wipe tables. It's impressive that anybody tucking in here then has the energy to go back and man a stall or continue shopping, because portions are gargantuan. Protein and carbs are piled high on huge plates that overflow with food. As well as fish and chips – reasonably cheap, and you're unlikely to want any dinner that night – Something Fishy also serves up cockney classics such as pie, mash and eels, but even in Lewisham the market for the latter is not what it was. Stolid English desserts (spotted dick and custard, and suchlike) are also available for those looking to move up a belt notch.
Babies and children welcome: children's menu; high chairs. Tables outdoors (5, pavement). Takeaway service.

East
Victoria Park

Fish House
126-128 Lauriston Road, E9 7LH (8533 3327). Mile End tube then 277 bus. **Meals served** noon-10pm Mon-Fri (full menu from 6pm); noon-11pm Sat, Sun. **Main courses** £7.95-£12.95. **Credit** AmEx, MC, V.
You may want to take the weather into account on your visit to this gastro reinterpretation of a chip shop. At 7pm on a sunny Sunday, an attempt to dine at this Livebait-style fish restaurant saw such a queue that Fish House ran out of fish. Takeaways are the biggest draw, with most customers clustering around the metal deep-fat fryers at the front of the shop, while young Topshop-clothed couples and groups of families pore over the extensive menu in the stylish white-tiled dining area at the back. Starters cost £5-£8, with quality varying. A mornay sauce, tangy with wine, on four half-shell scallops was delightful – if bordering on the marinière in its liquidity. Calamares were impressively chunky, yet marred by a floury batter. There was a nice salmony kick to two hollandaise-coated smoked haddock and salmon fish cakes. Cod came clothed in a light batter, but the chips were dry and overcooked. However, we couldn't fault the desserts: a lovely, sloppy eton mess and a delicious rich pistachio ice-cream from Oddono's in South Ken.
Babies and children welcome: children's menu; crayons; high chairs. Booking advisable Fri dinner; Sat, Sun. Takeaway service.

North East
Dalston

Faulkner's
424-426 Kingsland Road, E8 4AA (7254 6152, www.faulkners.uk.com). Dalston Kingsland rail/67, 76, 149, 242, 243 bus. **Lunch served** noon-2.30pm Mon-Fri. **Dinner served** 5-10pm Mon-Thur; 4.30-10pm Fri. **Meals served** 11.30am-10pm Sat; noon-9pm Sun. **Main courses** £10.50-£18. **Set meal** £15.90-£19.90 4 courses (minimum 2). **Credit** MC, V.
With its net curtains, branded milk jugs and napkins fussily tied up with ribbons, Faulkner's feels like an old-fashioned seaside tea room adrift on the Kingsland Road. In addition to fish grilled or battered (including a matzo meal alternative), the menu covers East End classics (jellied eels and oysters among the starters) and the now-familiar Turkish interlopers (calamares, halloumi). Battered options (a firm-fleshed haddock in properly crispy batter) proved a safer bet than grilled (lemon sole was clumsily boned and served barely warm). The chips were disappointingly pale and lacking in crunch. Jam roly-poly (chosen in preference to an advertised 'triffle') was worse: dry, despite a generous helping of custard, and short of jam. The complicated dietary requirements of a querulous group of pensioners were cheerfully dealt with by an on-the-ball and obliging waitress. Nevertheless,

patatas fritas (battered potato pieces) and a frightening 'cocktail' list that included such delights as a BMW (Baileys, Malibu and whisky) reminded us that it is better to do one thing well than to attempt to accommodate all-comers. *Babies and children welcome: children's menu; high chairs. Booking advisable weekends. Disabled: toilet. Separate room for parties, seats 25. Takeaway service.* **Map 6 R1.**

Stoke Newington

Fishery Fish Bar NEW
90 Stoke Newington High Street, N16 7NY (7249 6444, www.the-fishery.net). Stoke Newington rail/73, 149, 243 bus. **Meals served** noon-10pm Mon-Thur; noon-10.30pm Fri, Sat; noon-10pm Sun. **Main courses** £3.95-£10.95. **No credit cards.**

Alongside the grim-faced Beşiktaş FC members' club, surrounded by greasy spoons and Turkish grills, the Fishery welcomes a steady stream of locals who pop in for chips. It's a classy place that cheerfully and efficiently caters for everyone. You'll find battered sausages, 60p pickled eggs and moreish virid mushy peas alongside some highfalutin alternatives – tilapia, monkfish, pollock – to the old staples, sourced from the associated fishmonger down the road. The large, single room is crisp and handsome. A wet counter faces the window; smart white wipe-clean tables and chairs line up opposite the long serving counter; gleaming tiles and moody black-and-white prints provide further interior decoration. We were perhaps wise to avoid the more elaborate dishes (mussels with cider and fennel, griddled swordfish with 'samphia' and cherry tomatoes), as those we have sampled weren't uniformly successful. A ramekin of apple crumble was dry and short of apple; chips were of the old-fashioned, pale and soft variety; and the own-made tartare sauce lacked punch. In contrast, the main event was a great success: fresh, firm-fleshed tilapia, crisply cased. Rather than try the house wine or summer-special strawberry proseccos, we happily glugged bottled Peroni.
Babies and children welcome: children's menu; high chairs. Booking advisable Fri. Disabled: toilet. Takeaway service; delivery service (over £10 within 3-mile radius). **Map 25 C2.**

North
Finchley

★ Two Brothers Fish Resaurant
297-303 Regent's Park Road, N3 1DP (8346 0469, www.twobrothers.co.uk). Finchley Central tube. **Lunch served** noon-2.30pm, **dinner served** 5.30-10.15pm Tue-Sat. **Main courses** £9-£21.50. **Minimum** £10.95. **Credit** AmEx, MC, V.

The line of prestige vehicles parked outside offers a clue to the customer-base of this smart-casual restaurant with popular next-door takeaway. Touchy-feely grey-blue banquettes line the walls, giving a subtle luxury-yacht theme to the decor, but otherwise maritime references have been thrown overboard. Fish cakes with sauce piquante and Tony's arbroath smokies in cream sauce with tomato and cheese are old menu favourites, though we found the brief list of blackboard specials (among them moules marinière, grilled black cod with tomato relish, and tiramisu) disappointingly familiar. Both our generously portioned main courses looked a tad dry on the plate, but grilled halibut and haddock fried in matzo meal proved to be delectably moist and fabulously fresh. Staples such as chips and own-made tartare sauce are of a high standard. Starters – only for those with gargantuan appetites – include jellied eels and deep-fried cod's roe. An enjoyable bottle of house rosé is one option from Wine Share vineyard Domaine du Grand Mayne in the Côtes de Duras (neighbouring Bordeaux). Service was brisk and smiling, befitting a busy restaurant with a high turnover of close-set tables.
Babies and children welcome: high chairs. Bookings not accepted dinner. Takeaway service.

Muswell Hill
Toff's
38 Muswell Hill Broadway, N10 3RT (8883 8656). Highgate tube then 43, 134 bus. **Meals served** 11.30am-10pm Mon-Sat. **Main courses** £7.95-£22.50. **Set meal** £8.95 1 course. **Credit** AmEx, DC, MC, V.

Toff's is so integral to Muswell Hill it's a wonder The Kinks didn't sing about it. Seemingly always full-to-bursting, this convivial wood-panelled canteen attracts the gamut of north London life: from lusty students to widowed pensioners. The unusually high five-star Scores on the Doors (food hygiene) rating is reassuring. The certificate greets diners and takeaway customers, as do various other accolades collected over the past 40-odd years. The house red and white wines are unmemorable; better to opt for a refreshing Keo lager from Cyprus. Whole deep-fried plaice emitted enticing wafts of steam as its crisp batter was cracked open. The fish was delicious, though arguably might have been better grilled (£1 extra; frying in egg and matzo, rather than batter, costs 75p more). Staff didn't hesitate to recommend the dover sole (£22.50) when the chap next-to us hesitated over what to order. Chips, fried in ground-nut oil, were a bit pale and insipid. If you can squeeze in anything else, choose from salads (tomato and red onion, an olive-topped coleslaw, greek), fish cakes, soups, deep-fried camembert and traditional British puds served in veritable ponds of custard.
Babies and children welcome: children's menu; crayons; high chairs. Booking advisable weekends. Disabled: toilet. Separate rooms for parties, seating 20 and 24.

North West
Golders Green

Sam's
68-70 Golders Green Road, NW11 8LN (8455 9898/7171). Golders Green tube. **Meals served** noon-10pm daily. **Main courses** £8.45-£13.75. **Set lunch** (noon-4pm) £7.95 2 courses incl tea or coffee. **Credit** MC, V.

There's no extra charge for matzo at Sam's fish bar, but then this is Golders Green. The thick cream and gold coloured tablecloths look like a Jewish grandmother's bedspread, and the homely vibe (green walls, wood panelling) is enhanced by sweet, warm service. Things move along promptly too; the spacious room is large enough for queuing not to be necessary, at least not in our experience. Takeaways are dealt with next door. In the restaurant, nearly everything comes with chips or jacket potato and a fresh, generous chopped salad with light dressing and a smattering of parsley, which really lifts the meal and underlines the value. Fish (all the regulars: cod, haddock, sea bass, salmon, dover sole) is sourced from Billingsgate Market. Start with spinach and yoghurt dip, or taramasalata if necessary. A fresh grilled halibut steak was deliciously dense; plaice, deep-fried in ground-nut oil, hit all the right minerally notes of this distinctively flavoured fish. Sam's short wine list limits by-the-glass options to house wine, though bottles of Wolf Blass are reliable and the very acceptable Turkish beer Efes is also offered.
Available for hire. Babies and children welcome: children's menu; high chairs. Disabled: toilet. Takeaway service.

Mill Hill
Booba's
151 Hale Lane, HA8 9QW (8959 6002). Edgware tube/Mill Hill Broadway rail. **Meals served** noon-10pm Tue-Sun. **Main courses** £8-£15. **Credit** MC, V.

A takeaway hatch and marble-topped tables is an odd juxtaposition, but so is a Turkish fish and chip joint in the Jewish heartland of Edgware. On this evidence, multiculturalism is a marvellous thing: the menu is simple, the fish fresh and the service kindly. Though the houmous and taramasalata are excellent, don't fill up on them, as this will mean missing first-rate fish and chips. Fish are the usual

species: cod, plaice, haddock, some filleted, some on the bone. They're especially good when breaded with matzo meal (battered is available; the griddled fish is crisp outside and tender inside). The chips have no excess grease, and the bill is fat-free too: even service is left off, despite the fact we were offered tea or coffee on the house, and that staff waited politely for us to leave an empty restaurant late at night. The only cultural misstep (apart from a wine list as plain as the food menu and far less enticing) is the serving of sliced pickles as a palate cleanser. These large, crunchy pickles deserve the company of pitta bread and houmous. But that's not, as they say in these parts, much of a kvetch.
Babies and children welcome: children's menu. Booking advisable Fri, Sat. Takeaway service.

West Hampstead

★ Nautilus
27-29 Fortune Green Road, NW6 1DT (7435 2532). West Hampstead tube/rail then 328 bus. **Lunch served** 11.30am-2.30pm, **dinner served** 4.30-10pm Mon-Sat. **Main courses** £9.50-£19.50. **Credit** MC, V.

Pine wood panelling, a few boat pictures, raffia chairs and condiment trays illustrated with fruit – Nautilus's decor would be wonderfully ironic were it not for the smattering of blue glass bricks that look like a misguided effort to update. The drinks list is unsophisticated too, offering 'bottle of muscadet' and Strongbow cider, but Keo lager is a decent brew. Anyway, you're here for the fish – the freshest and most accurately cooked fish this side of the Thames. Just-done rock salmon had all the omega richness characteristic of this creamy variety of shark, making the huge, steaming portion hard to finish. A fine matzo crust locked the moisture inside a sprawling fillet of delicious haddock. There's houmous to start, chicken if you've brought the wrong companion. Motherly service (would we like some more chips? – yes please) and Judy Tzuke and Chicago ballads on the sound system continue the unpretentious, homely vibe, which consistently draws in locals and connoisseurs from further afield (and given Nautilus's position way up Fortune Green Road, that might include West Hampstead).
Babies and children welcome: high chairs. Booking advisable. Takeaway service. **Map 28 A1.**

Outer London
Kingston, Surrey

fish! kitchen
58 Coombe Road, Kingston, Surrey KT2 7AF (8546 2886, www.fishkitchen.com). Norbiton rail/57, 85, 213 bus. **Meals served** noon-10pm Tue-Sat. **Main courses** £9.95-£24.95. **Credit** AmEx, MC, V.

Smart alfresco decking, shiny stainless-steel surfaces and bistro-style blackboards don't quite disguise the fact that this is a chippy. Better known locally for Jarvis the Fishmonger next door, Fish Kitchen is an annexe-eaterie specialising in lightly battered British favourites: cod, haddock, halibut and plaice, all from sustainable sources. Other fish and seafood choices are on the specials menu, but these were either very expensive (five diver-caught scallops wrapped in bacon, £16.95) or unavailable on the night of our visit (sea bass). Still, the classics come well-prepared. Haddock was clean, white and quite meaty, if lacking salt; fish pie was pink, yummy and filling. The lightly golden chips are very fine indeed, and the mint-tinged mushy peas as good as you'll get in London. A shared fruit crumble with custard filled us to capacity. There are drawbacks, however. The wine list is limited and the reserve vintages have hefty price tags. There's not much ambience either: no music, lots of metallic clatter, and the air quality is improved only when the toilet door is closed. Fish Kitchen could be great, but improvements are needed. Until then it's best used as an above-average takeaway.
Babies and children welcome: children's menu; high chairs. Disabled: toilet. Tables outdoors (20, terrace). Takeaway service. **For branch see index.**

Pizza & Pasta

Easy to do, hard to do well – it's small wonder that the two Italian staples of pizza and pasta attract the attentions of so many chain operators. Yet though the primary ingredients are cheap, they need to be cooked with accuracy. Cardboard pizza bases and congealed spaghetti are the distressing results of ill-timing in the kitchen. We've collected the chain restaurants together in a box for easy comparison, but our aim here is to highlight more singular venues such as our favourite pizza specialists, Brixton's **Franco Manca** and Battersea's **Donna Margherita** and **Pizza Metro**. Praise this year also goes to Hampstead's **Fratelli la Bufala**, with its forte in all things buffalo, and genuinely Italian chain **Rossopomodoro**, which uses the ingredients of various artisan producers belonging to the Slow Food Movement. If more outré pizza toppings appeal, try **Fire & Stone**, which has new branches in Covent Garden and Westfield.

Central

Clerkenwell & Farringdon

Santoré

59-61 Exmouth Market, EC1R 4QL (7812 1488). Farringdon tube/rail/19, 38, 341 bus. **Lunch served** noon-3pm, **dinner served** 5.30-11pm Mon-Sat. **Main courses** £7.95-£15. **Set lunch** £8.95 2 courses. **Set meal** (5.30-7.30pm) £12.95 2 courses. **Credit** AmEx, MC, V.

On busy Exmouth Market, any restaurant has its work cut out to attract customers. Unfortunately, Santoré has all the atmosphere of an airport concourse: bright, clean and soulless. This is in spite of a soundtrack of loud Neapolitan music (a request to turn it down elicited a raised eyebrow from the waiter, but thanks from our neighbouring diners). The two courses for £8.95 lunchtime specials (£12.95 in the evening) are cheap enough, yet not so special. Our starters – tortino of the day (three medallions of layered broccoli and aubergine combined with egg) and a plate of roasted vegetables – were quite pleasant. The chicken with pepper was well-flavoured too. But the real letdown, for a restaurant that prides itself on its Neapolitan roots, was the pizza: sloppy wet tomato sauce topped with almost tasteless cheese and poor-quality pepperoni. Our neighbour's plate of mozzarella balls, tomatoes, salad and bruschetta looked much better, though it was left half-finished. Then the bill: we were charged £5.20 for a glass of Nero d'Avola, and £3.45 for a bottle of sparkling water. Service, which was good, added a further 12.5%.

Babies and children welcome: high chairs. Tables outdoors (10, pavement). Takeaway service; delivery service (over £8 within 3-mile radius). **Map 5 N4**.

Covent Garden

Fire & Stone `NEW`

31-32 Maiden Lane, WC2E 7JS (0844 371 2550, www.fireandstone.com). Covent Garden or Leicester Square tube. **Open** noon-12.15am Mon-Sat; noon-11.15pm Sun. **Main courses** £6.95-£15.95. **Credit** AmEx, DC, MC, V.

Big, bold and bustling, Fire & Stone is a novelty pizza emporium tucked in the Covent Garden backstreets. It's the sort of place that attracts office groups on bonding sessions, stressed parents seeking a child-friendly haven, and the theatre posse looking for somewhere that's still serving after the show. Staff are friendly, in a corporate kind of way, and there are all sorts of special offers: children's deals, Sunday deals, two for £10 pizza deals, theatre ticket deals. The menu has clearly been devised as a talking point, rather than a gastronomic experience. Toppings, named after world cities, eschew the familiar in favour of celebrated regional dishes in pizza form. In our book, there are certain things that simply shouldn't be teamed with a dough base, and on this list we'd include thai green curry (the 'Koh Samui') and hoi sin duck (the 'Peking'). There was much debate at our table over whether said bases (stone-baked in a huge wood-fired oven) were biscuity and low-rent or the best ever tasted. If you're bored with routine margherita-siciliana-fiorentina menus, or are just looking for food and shelter in the West End, you could do worse.

Available for hire. Babies and children welcome: children's menu; high chairs; nappy-changing facilities. Booking advisable weekends. Disabled: toilet. Takeaway service. **Map 18 E5**. **For branch see index.**

Rossopomodoro

50-52 Monmouth Street, WC2H 9EP (7240 9095, www.rossopomodoro.co.uk). Covent Garden tube. **Meals served** noon-11.30pm daily. **Main courses** £6-£19. **Set lunch** (noon-4pm Mon-Fri) £6.99 pizza or pasta incl drink; £7.99 salad or main incl drink. **Credit** AmEx, MC, V.

Part of an Italian chain that's expanding into the UK, this Neapolitan pizzeria nevertheless hasn't lost sight of its roots. 'Prego! Prego!' come the cheery greetings as Italian waiters ferry customers across a dining room lined with floor-to-ceiling windows. To the side, graduates of the restaurant's Naples pizza school slide dough into

Red Pepper. See p304.

a wood-fired oven tiled in gold mosaic. Walls are lined with shelves containing the imported Neapolitan ingredients on which Rossopomodoro prides itself. The generous antipasti platter, including ripe caciocavallo cheese and tangy buffalo bresaola, didn't disappoint, despite the waiter's determination to shift additional mozzarella. A parsley-flecked helping of prawns, mashed chickpeas and durum-wheat tagliatelle was slightly too glutinous, but the pizzas are the main attraction – available rosse (with tomato sauce) or bianche (without). Crusts are dense yet well-aerated. Diners are urged to tuck in with their hands, Italian-style, to the likes of Angrisella: pungent with capers and a thick layer of endive- and olive-topped provola cheese. There are interesting desserts, plus a decent house red. We had a slightly long wait for food, but staff were attentive and apologetic, which may explain the large crowd of office lunchers here.
Babies and children welcome: high chairs. Booking advisable pre-theatre, weekends. Separate room for parties, seats 16. Tables outdoors (4, pavement). Takeaway service. **Map 18 D4. For branches see index.**

Euston

Pasta Plus
62 Eversholt Street, NW1 1DA (7383 4943, www.pastaplus.co.uk). Euston tube/rail. **Lunch served** noon-2.30pm Mon-Fri. **Dinner served** 5.30-10.30pm Mon-Sat. **Main courses** £6.50-£16. **Credit** AmEx, DC, MC, V.
It's pleasant to walk inside this unpretentious pasta café and get off the rather seedy street outside. Unfortunately, the view is of Euston station's side wall, but the interior is likeable enough; walls are painted a neutral cream and decorated with a mix of photos (Italy, Duke Ellington) and a Kandinsky print. A glass roof at the back makes the room airy. Tortellini in brodo – a salty broth containing pasta parcels stuffed with minced pork – is a nice, straightforward starter. The same can be said of the rocket and parmesan salad. To follow, we enjoyed the sauce in a main course of cannelloni, but the dish could have contained better-quality meat. There were no complaints about the pescatore spaghetti, however, which featured many juicy prawns, calamares and mussels. Service was quietly efficient throughout our visit. Pasta Plus serves a range of daily specials, yet these seem geared towards the lunchtime crowd and were finished by the time we arrived early in the evening. Nothing is exceptional here, but this is a pleasingly competent operation.
Available for hire. Babies and children welcome: high chairs. Tables outdoors (26, conservatory). **Map 4 K3.**

Knightsbridge

Frankie's Italian Bar & Grill
3 Yeomans Row, off Brompton Road, SW3 2AL (7590 9999, www.frankiesitalianbarandgrill.com). Knightsbridge or South Kensington tube. **Lunch served** noon-2.30pm Sat, Sun. **Dinner served** 5.30-10.30pm Mon-Fri, 4-11pm Sat, 4-10pm Sun. **Main courses** £7.50-£14.40. **Credit** AmEx, MC, V.
It's hard to imagine either jockey Frankie Dettori or celeb-chef Marco Pierre White eating here, but this chain of New Jersey-style Italian-American restaurants is associated with both men. There are other branches in Selfridges basement, Chelsea FC's Stamford Bridge stadium, and in Dubai. Despite all the glitz, the results are surprisingly pedestrian. This Knightsbridge flagship is a cavernous underground room brightened by wall-to-wall mirrors, red-and-white checked tablecloths, and no fewer than ten oversized disco balls, set to a soundtrack of classic lounge crooners. Succulent pork belly came with a 'glaze' that was more sweet soup than thinly applied basting, and was peculiarly offset with bitter coriander seeds. The accompanying 'Frankie's salad' was little more

than a bowl of watercress. Given the complete lack of vegetarian mains (though a larger starter was offered), we opted for a passable but unambitious spaghettini sorrentina (one of around ten pasta dishes), in which neither the tomatoes nor the mozzarella impressed. A range of burgers, canapés and cocktails is available too – but we're in no hurry to try them after this lacklustre performance.
Available for hire. Babies and children welcome: high chairs. Booking essential weekends. **Map 14 E10. For branches see index.**

Mayfair

Rocket
4-6 Lancashire Court, off New Bond Street, W1S 1EY (7629 2889, www.rocketrestaurants.co.uk). Bond Street or Oxford Circus tube. **Bar Open** noon-11pm, **meals served** noon-6pm Mon-Sat. *Restaurant* **Lunch served** noon-3pm, **dinner served** 6-11pm Mon-Sat. **Main courses** £9-£15. *Both* **Credit** AmEx, MC, V.
This lively bar and restaurant, tucked away in a small network of alleyways in Mayfair, specialises in upmarket exotic pizzas, grills and creative salads. Weekday lunchtimes see the smart but airy first-floor dining room (dominated by a large picture of a black labrador) filled with business lunchers. Evenings bring a more diverse and relaxed clientele. We opted for pizzas: pancetta and goat's cheese with balsamic syrup was bracing; smoked chicken and caramelised baby onion was a little disappointing, with baby onions that tasted as if they'd been pickled in a previous life. Other intriguing pizza toppings include black pudding with prawns, and pumpkin with chorizo. Starters can be equally unusual, such as the excellent salad of crispy pancetta, gorgonzola, candied pecans and poached peas. Those seeking more simple combinations can opt for buffalo mozzarella and peperonata on ciabatta. The wine list offers a good choice by the glass and includes helpful tasting notes. In all, Rocket makes a pleasant bolt-hole whether you're a Mayfair hedge-funder on a budget or taking a break from retail therapy on Oxford Street. It also has a branch in the City.
Babies and children welcome: high chairs. Booking advisable. Separate rooms for parties, seating 10 and 26. **Map 9 H6. For branch see index.**

Soho

Italian Graffiti
163-165 Wardour Street, W1F 8WN (7439 4668, www.italiangraffiti.co.uk). Oxford Circus tube. **Lunch served** noon-3pm, **dinner served** 5.30-11.30pm Mon-Fri. **Meals served** noon-11.30pm Sat. **Main courses** £7-£14. **Credit** AmEx, DC, MC, V.
Once the staple dining experience of Soho, the old-school Italian trattoria is now a lesser-spotted breed – but it can still be spotted from time to time. Italian Graffiti is a classic of the genre: a dark interior, surprisingly spacious and endearingly unpretentious (we can also recommend the Trattoria Da Aldo round the corner on Greek Street). A visit here is like a trip back to the 1970s, with a menu that offers ripe pickings for nostalgics and a wood-heavy decor that's simply waiting for a preservation order. You half expect waiters to have the *Godfather* theme as their ringtone. Cream of asparagus soup made good use of seasonal ingredients, but tricolore salad was unspectacular. A main course of filling, creamy rigatoni with pancetta and peas was comforting, yet clearly designed to appeal to the steady flow of fiftysomething punters. At lunchtime, businessmen on reduced expenses flock here searching for a taste of their youth. Pizzas are more satisfying, but it's the experience you're paying for here – and prices are reasonable. Our only disappointment was that pudding didn't arrive on a dessert trolley.
Babies and children admitted. Booking advisable. Takeaway service. **Map 17 B3.**

West

Maida Vale

Red Pepper
8 Formosa Street, W9 1EE (7266 2708). Warwick Avenue tube. **Dinner served** 6.30-11pm Mon-Fri. **Meals served** 11am-11pm Sat; 11am-10.30pm Sun. **Main courses** £9-£17. **Credit** MC, V.
Spread over ground floor and basement, Red Pepper is busy, modern and functional. During our visit, staff were rushing about, and locals were constantly dropping in for the takeaway pizza service. The interior is brightly lit, with striking red walls. We were shown to a table under a staircase. Our starter of Sardinian carasau bread with misticanza (mixed green leaves), gorgonzola and walnuts was very promising: a salad in a crispy bread 'bowl'. However, this was followed by such a long wait for our main course that the woman in charge came and apologised to us. When the dish finally arrived, the large triangular sea bream ravioli was extremely good, with superb pasta. Nevertheless, Red Pepper's main business is in pizzas, and diavola was spicy and tasty, if less outstanding than the pasta. A side dish of sautéed spinach was simple and excellent. It's a pity the atmosphere here didn't encourage diners to savour their food. The dessert menu looked inviting, but by this time we felt disinclined to linger.
Babies and children admitted. Booking essential. Separate room for parties, seats 25. Tables outdoors (5, pavement). Takeaway service. **Map 1 C4.**

Westbourne Grove

Mulberry Street
84 Westbourne Grove, W2 5RT (7313 6789, www.mulberrystreet.co.uk). Bayswater or Queensway tube. **Breakfast served** 9.30am-1pm Sat, Sun. **Meals served** noon-midnight Mon-Sat; noon-11pm Sun. **Main courses** £7.50-£25. **Credit** AmEx, MC, V.
Named after the main thoroughfare in New York's Little Italy, Mulberry Street promises an authentic Manhattan pizzeria experience, with massive portions, family-sized booths and pizza dough made with water specially filtered to match New York samples. A giant photo-montage of Times Square dominates the back wall, jazzing up the low-lit, open-plan dining area. US sports are shown on big screens behind the bar, making this a popular destination for expats. The main draw is the choice of 20in pizzas (around £17-£25), which are more than big enough for two. If such a vast expanse of one flavour seems monotonous, order by the slice. We tried one colourful wedge with spinach and creamy ricotta, which was dominated by the cheese, and a more well-balanced slice with artichoke and parma ham. Both needed more tomato sauce, but their perfectly executed bases had a crispness that played to the restaurant's Italian rather than American heritage. Pasta was a letdown, with chalky meatballs covered in a very salty tomato sauce. To desalinate, there's a choice of classic American beverages such as root beer, cream soda and Brooklyn lager.
Babies and children welcome: high chairs. Booking advisable. Separate room for parties, seats 30. Takeaway service; delivery service (over £20 within 5-mile radius). **Map 7 B6.**

South West

Fulham

Napulé
585 Fulham Road, SW6 5UA (7381 1122, www.madeinitalygroup.co.uk). Fulham Broadway tube. **Lunch served** noon-3.30pm Sat, Sun. **Dinner served** 6-11.30pm Mon-Sat; 6-10.30pm Sun. **Main courses** £6.95-£14.50. **Credit** MC, V.
Napulé is usually bustling, especially on match days when blue shirts compete for space with a core clientele of young couples and families. Service is friendly, staff weaving through the warren of higgledy-piggledy tables delivering

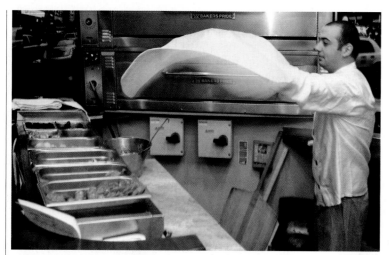

Peroni and smiles. Starters, such as antipasto misto (salami, parma ham, olives), are good for sharing. Excellent bruschettina arrived brimming with flavoursome tomatoes and high-quality oil, sloshed on to buffalo mozzarella. Pizzas by the metre are the speciality. Ordering more than two varieties means they're cooked together on one piece of dough, up to a metre long. All the usual toppings are available, plus a few surprises. The Fra Rosario was a hit: chunks of potato and rosemary nestling among sweet sun-dried tomatoes, caramelised onions, capers and rustic Italian sausage. Our margherita was a bit watery, but the quality and chewiness of the dough was not in doubt. Contorni side dishes are limited; verdure alla griglia offered a pleasing heap of rocket, but the grilled vegetables were curiously dry and featured carrot among the Mediterranean veg. Close with puds in the tiramisu style, or Italian coffee. The wine list is extensive, arranged by region, with 12 wines by the glass.

Available for hire. Babies and children welcome: high chairs. Booking advisable. Separate room for parties, seats 14. Takeaway service. **Map 13 A13**. **For branches (Luna Rossa, Made in Italy, Marechiaro, Regina Margherita, Santa Lucia) see index**.

South
Balham

Ciullo's
31 Balham High Road, SW12 9AL (8675 3072). Clapham South tube/Balham tube/rail. **Dinner served** 6-11pm Mon-Thur; 6-11.30pm Fri, Sat; 5-10.30pm Sun. **Main courses** £5.50-£12.50. **Credit** MC, V.

Anyone straining to imagine how the food might taste at Gene Hunt's favourite haunt in *Ashes to Ashes* should head to Balham, where Ciullo's is stuck in the nicest kind of time warp. The interior is enlivened by risqué Beryl Cook-style holiday scenes on the walls, and a welcome that's authentically Italian. Our amusingly deadpan waiter had the immaculately sculpted grey hair of a Neapolitan barber. A simple spaghetti pomodoro, knocked up for a two-year-old in our party, was easily the best thing we tasted: strongly flavoured with basil and polished off pronto. A starter of deep-fried discs of breaded mozzarella was entertainingly stringy, but bland. Tuna pizza could have benefited from a more punchy tomato sauce, while the calamares in a prawn and squid dish were so uniform that they looked bought-in; a whole squid might have been a better match for the trio of sweet, shell-on prawns. Of the accompanying veg, roast potatoes were hard as bullets and the asparagus mystifyingly battered. In partial compensation, an own-made tiramisu was a memorable final flourish, having just the right consistency and being easily ample for two.
Available for hire. Babies and children welcome: high chairs. Booking advisable. Tables outdoors (3, terrace).

Battersea

★ Donna Margherita
183 Lavender Hill, SW11 5TE (7228 2660, www.donna-margherita.com). Clapham Junction rail. **Dinner served** 6-10.30pm Tue-Fri. **Meals served** noon-11pm Sat; 12.30-10.30pm Sun. **Main courses** £7-£16. **Credit** AmEx, DC, MC, V.

The menu at Donna Margherita runs to two pages of rave notices about its pizzas from the great and not-so-good of London critics (including, erm, Johnny Vaughan). After reading these, we didn't dare deviate, though the next table's gnocchi all sorrentina looked tempting. Fully booked on a Thursday night, this out-of-the-way trattoria is a local gem, with attentive service, gently buzzing atmosphere, and even politically correct pizza (there's a Gay and a Lesbica). Calamares and prawns made a light but plentiful starter and didn't need any adornment. A Donna Margherita pizza was generously dotted with creamy mozzarella and truly tasty cherry tomatoes on a wafer-thin, smoky base. The seafood pizza looked a picture,

Mulberry Street. See p304.

Chain gang

A safe harbour in uncertain economic times, or spreaders of soulless ubiquity? We sent our critics to investigate the pros and cons of London's key pizza and pasta chains.

ASK

216 Haverstock Hill, NW3 2AE (7433 3896, www.askrestaurants.com). Belsize Park tube. **Meals served** noon-11pm Mon-Thur, Sun; noon-11.30pm Fri, Sat. **Main courses** £5.95-£11.95. **Credit** AmEx, MC, V.
There's much to like about ASK, even though the food doesn't have the verve of some of its rivals. Proper chilled glasses for the Peroni makes a good start, and the Ribena-like zinfandel rosé goes down a treat in warm weather. Our chicken and ham calzone arrived looking like a massive pasty, golden and shiny thanks to a sprinkling of grana padano. It was fine, as was the seafood napoletana pizza, though desserts of leathery profiteroles with milk-chocolate sauce, and a special of dark-chocolate pudding, were like supermarket food. Staff at this neighbourhood branch set in a converted house are amiable, yet they turned away many disappointed customers during our weekend lunchtime visit; if they had been more adept at turning tables they could have kept everyone happy and made a healthy profit as well.
Babies and children welcome: high chairs. Booking advisable weekends. Disabled: toilet. Tables outdoors (11, terrace). Takeaway service. **Map 28 B3.**
For branches see index.

Pizza Express

187 Kentish Town Road, NW1 8PD (7267 0101, www.pizzaexpress.com). Kentish Town tube/rail/Kentish Town West rail. **Meals served** 11.30am-11pm Mon-Thur, Sun; 11.30am-11.30pm Fri, Sat. **Main courses** £5.90-£10.95. **Credit** AmEx, MC, V.
The problem with booklets on each table showing lush photography of your fancy chef's new range of pizzas is that it's all too easy to compare them with what arrives on the plate (or in this case, on the black platter). We like what Theo Randall has been doing with this stalwart chain – producing rectangular bubbly-based pizzas of brown shrimp, courgette and garlic, and of santos tomatoes, parma ham and hand-torn fior di latte mozzarella – but getting quality consistent across such a number of pizza chefs and kitchens is the challenge. So whether the new pizzas are an improvement on old-school American hots, fiorentinas and venezianas is something to consider if your budget's tight. We were impressed by the cheerful and considerate staff at this cavernous, under-populated branch.
Babies and children welcome: high chairs; nappy-changing facilities. Booking advisable weekends. Disabled: toilet. Takeaway service. **Map 27 D1.**
For branches see index.

Pizza Paradiso

9 St Christopher's Place, W1U 1NE (7486 3196, www.pizzaparadiso.co.uk). Bond Street tube. **Meals served** noon-midnight daily. **Main courses** £6.60-£12.95. **Set lunch** (noon-5pm Mon-Fri) £12.95 2 courses. **Credit** AmEx, MC, V.
A useful trattoria complete with tiled floors, and tables spilling on to the pavement. The £12.95 two-course set lunch menu seemed a good idea, but on a warm day felt unseasonally wintry with plates of orrecchiette and sausage, and tagliatelle with pan-fried chicken and mushroom sauce. Paradiso's own-made pasta is, however, very good, as shown in a special of tagliatelle with sea bass, tomato and herb sauce. Look to the specials list too for an extended choice of wines (four rosés on our visit, including a dry but brightly coloured nerello mascalese). Generally the Sicilian desserts – again own-made – are of a high standard, but strawberry ice-cream cake suffered from a stale-tasting topping of whipped cream. Finish with an espresso as authentically bitter as you'd find in any coffee bar in Palermo.
Babies and children welcome: high chairs. Booking advisable weekends. Tables outdoors (6, pavement). Takeaway service. **Map 9 H6.**
For branches (Ristorante Olivelli Paradiso, Caffè Paradiso) see index.

La Porchetta

33 Boswell Street, WC1N 3BP (7242 2434, www.laporchettapizzeria.co.uk). Holborn or Russell Square tube. **Lunch served** noon-3pm Mon-Fri. **Dinner served** 5-11pm Mon-Sat. **Main courses** £5.90-£9.90. **Credit** MC, V.
Almost full when we entered and with punters continuing to pile in as we left, La Porchetta is clearly doing something right. We're just not sure what it is. Staff weren't particularly welcoming, despite our booking, and the small, closely packed tables at this Bloomsbury branch don't make for a relaxing evening. Yes the pizzas are huge – they threaten to fall off both plates and tables – and the toppings are OK for the prices charged (£5.20-£9.20), but our Messicana (fresh Italian sausage and chilli) and frutti di mare were soggy at centre. House wines by the litre and half-litre carafe are cheap and taste it too, but the kitchen produces some good-looking plates of pasta.
Babies and children welcome: high chairs. Booking advisable (5 or more people). Takeaway service. **Map 10 L5.**
For branches see index.

Prezzo

161 Euston Road, NW1 2BD (7387 5587, www.prezzoplc.co.uk). Euston tube/rail. **Meals served** noon-11pm daily. **Main courses** £6.25-£9.95. **Credit** AmEx, MC, V.
It's all about comfort at Prezzo – a refuge when you're in an unfamiliar area and want a quick, inexpensive meal of familiar foods. Hence this new branch's popularity with travellers through Euston (it looks something like a modern airport-terminal bistro), and the installation of a rotisserie oven for

chicken. Several of the pasta dishes and salads suffer from the inclusion of too many ingredients; best stick with simple meatballs and penne, or a sauce like arrabbiata. A modest piece of honeycomb cheesecake was low on promised choc-coated honeycomb, yet surprisingly pleasant thanks to a soft, rich and fresh-tasting cheese mix. House red from Montepulciano is better than it need be for £12.65 too: result.
Babies and children welcome: high chairs; children's menu. Disabled: toilet. Takeaway service. **Map 4 K3.**
For branches see index.

Strada

4 South Grove, N6 6BS (8347 8686, www.strada.co.uk). Highgate tube. **Meals served** 11.30am-11pm Mon-Sat; 11.30am-10.30pm Sun. **Main courses** £6.95-£16.50. **Set lunch** (noon-5pm Mon-Fri) £8.50 1 course incl glass of wine, beer or soft drink. **Credit** AmEx, MC, V.
'You don't have a booking?' No mate, it's 8.30pm on a Monday night and this is remotest Highgate. We got the last table – go figure. All around were couples and pairs of couples sharing bottles of rosé and tucking happily into salads, pasta, and risotto, but mainly ordering from the ten-strong list of pizzas. We enjoyed the speck pizza with smoked ham and the light tang of gorgonzola. The rossa (topped with spicy salami, roast peppers, caramelised onion and more) had a very hot kick thanks to more than a smatter of sliced raw chillies. Staff were pretty good, though not always on the ball – we weren't told there was no chocolate fondant until after we'd ordered it. But we found desserts respectable, and the ice-cream excellent.
Babies and children welcome: high chairs; nappy-changing facilities. Booking advisable weekends. Tables outdoors (6, terrace). Takeaway service.
For branches see index.

Zizzi

20 Bow Street, WC2E 7AW (7836 6101, www.zizzi.co.uk). Covent Garden tube. **Meals served** noon-11.30pm Mon-Sat; noon-11pm Sun. **Main courses** £6.50-£11.95. **Credit** AmEx, DC, MC, V.
This grown-up sister of the ASK chain is becoming quite fanciable after a series of makeovers with glamorous new interiors. Like ASK, Zizzi offers calzone as well as pizza, 15 or so plates of pasta and risotto, and salads. The fiorentina pizza is made delicious with creamy buffalo-milk ricotta and a final flourish of grated nutmeg and garlic oil. Wines start at £12.95 a bottle for trebbiano or Montepulciano d'Abruzzo, and all apart from the Chianti and champagnes are under £25. Desserts looked interesting (caramelised bananas with waffles, warm tart of plums), but service was so slow we began to wish we'd never ordered them.
Babies and children welcome: children's menu; high chairs. Booking advisable. Disabled: toilet. Tables outdoors (6, pavement). Takeaway service. **Map 18 E4.**
For branches see index.

yet lacked something to counterpoint its abundant catch (including a squid tentacle and a clam in its shell). Tiramisu was obviously own-made and wickedly creamy. The only low point was a slightly harsh bottle of house white. On leaving, we noted the restaurant has a delivery service; sure enough, two days later we forsook our usual takeaway for another taste of Donna Margherita's Italy.
Available for hire. Babies and children welcome: high chairs. Booking advisable. Tables outdoors (6, terrace). Takeaway service; delivery service (over £10, within 1-mile radius). **Map 21 C3**.

★ Pizza Metro
64 Battersea Rise, SW11 1EQ (7228 3812, www.pizzametropizza.com). Clapham Junction rail. **Dinner served** 6pm-midnight Mon-Fri. **Meals served** noon-midnight Sat, Sun. **Main courses** £8.50-£15. **Set meal** £17 2 courses. **Credit** MC, V.
'Waiter, there's a Lambretta scooter parked next to our table.' Really, this permanently packed Clapham Junction trattoria doesn't need such gimmicks to reassure customers of its credentials. For a start, most ingredients are sourced in Italy. And the pizzas are cooked on the stone floor of what's claimed to be London's first wood-fired oven (dating back to 1979; the wood's delivered daily, with the produce. An eminently shareable starter of calamari fritti came in a perfectly light batter, its black pepper and lemon waking the taste buds in readiness for the mains. Pizzas here are rectangular and arrive on metre-long metal plinths, making for some sociable grazing. The base of our napoli was thin, crisp and winningly scorched, its tomato sauce a zesty cut above your local takeaway. Pasta-wise, an oily fusilli san gennaro seemed to be without its advertised smoked mozzarella; the peanuts were in short supply too, but the clumps of rustic sausage, perfect firm pasta and hint of alcohol more than satisfied. A lively panna cotta with hazelnuts added to the textural delights.
Babies and children welcome: high chairs. Booking advisable. Tables outdoors (10, pavement). Takeaway service; delivery service (over £15 within 2-mile radius). **Map 21 C4**.

Brixton

★ Franco Manca (100)
4 Market Row, SW9 8LD (7738 3021, www.francomanca.com). Brixton tube/rail. **Meals served** noon-5pm Mon-Sat. **Main courses** £4-£5.90. **Credit** MC, V.

Since opening inside one of the arches on Brixton Market, Franco Manca has been showered with acclaim. It won the Best Cheap Eats category of the 2008 Time Out Eating & Drinking Awards; the *Observer* went even further, saying it made 'the best pizzas in Britain'. Run by Giuseppe Mascoli and Bridget Hugo, this is undeniably a terrific venture. The dining area is split across both sides of a corridor in the covered market and has a mix of indoor and outdoor seating, with communal and individual tables. The menu is precise (just six pizzas) and astonishingly cheap; the most expensive pizza, with chorizo and mozzarella, costs less than £6. The key is in the sourdough bases, thin and flavoursome, prepared 20 hours before they're cooked, or rather blasted, at 260°C for 40 seconds. Timing and temperature have been meticulously researched to find the optimum for cooking, yet not drying-out, both base and topping. The quick turnaround also means your wait – and you'll almost certainly have to wait – won't be long, and will be worth it. Extras and drinks stick to the theme, being simple, well sourced and cheap; the organic lemonade is almost as unmissable as the pizza itself. A delight.
Babies and children admitted. Disabled: toilet. Tables outdoors (6, pavement). Takeaway service. Vegan dishes. **Map 22 E2**.

Clapham

Eco
162 Clapham High Street, SW4 7UG (7978 1108, www.ecorestaurants.com). Clapham Common tube. **Lunch served** noon-4pm, **dinner served** 6-11pm Mon-Fri. **Meals served** noon-11.30pm Sat, Sun. **Main courses** £6.95-£13.90. **Credit** AmEx, MC, V.
By 7.30pm on a Thursday evening, this Clapham stalwart was packed. Clearly catering to a young crowd, Eco throbbed with loud house music, its low lighting creating more of a bar than a restaurant feel. The menu is oddly unbalanced. There's a huge assortment of pizzas – 21 by our reckoning, including tempting vegetarian choices such as blue cheese and rocket – plus antipasti, pasta and al forno, but only three desserts. We started with shell-on prawns in a feisty tomato and chilli sauce. Next, calzone came smothered in another lively sauce (all smoky tomato), but the filling of ham, artichokes and mozzarella lacked the punch to compete with such an expanse of base. Speaking of which, Eco is proud of its sourdough bases, which aren't as thin as is fashionable but – on the evidence of our napoletana

– are certainly filling and not as soggy as the dreaded deep pan. Service was brisk yet not unfriendly. We weren't so rushed that we couldn't enjoy a couple of coffees before our table was taken by the next customer from the queuing hordes. If you're looking for somewhere to eat before, during or after a Clapham bar crawl, schedule a pit-stop here.
Babies and children welcome: high chairs. Booking advisable; essential weekends. Tables outdoors (4, pavement). Takeaway service. **Map 22 B2**. **For branch see index.**

South East

Peckham

The Gowlett
62 Gowlett Road, SE15 4HY (7635 7048, www.thegowlett.com). East Dulwich or Peckham Rye rail/12, 37, 40, 63, 176, 185, 484 bus. **Lunch served** 12.30-2.30pm, **dinner served** 6.30-10.30pm Mon-Fri. **Meals served** 12.30-10.30pm Sat; 12.30-9pm Sun. **Main courses** £7.50-£9. **Credit** AmEx, DC, MC, V.
A cosy local boozer in Peckham (albeit the stretch that's spiritually in East Dulwich) is not necessarily where you'd go looking for cracking, stone-baked pizzas, but the Gowlett produces top-notch pub grub. All pizzas are handmade from scratch, which can mean waits of 45 minutes. Though the menu appears limited, quality extras allow you to create your own combinations. The house 'Gowlettini' – mozzarella, goat's cheese, pine nuts, rocket, prosciutto, sun-dried tomatoes – is a lighter option for those stuck for inspiration. Bases are huge and crisp, and toppings overly generous. The garlic pizza starter comes oozing with cheese and could be a meal in itself, but a surfeit of anchovies and capers left the siciliana overpoweringly salty. Above all, though, the Gowlett is a pub, and a darned good one. The interior remains largely unreconstructed (leatherette banquettes, dark wood furniture, scruffy carpet) and the clientele is a cross-section of the local community: from young families (children allowed up to 9pm) to retired couples, hip twentysomethings and bearded men with dogs. There's also a pool table, DJs, art, squishy sofas, a decked beer garden, and serious ales – three guests and the house Adnams.
Babies and children welcome (until 9pm): nappy-changing facilities. Disabled: toilet. Entertainment: quiz 8.30pm Mon; DJs 6.30pm Sun. Tables outdoors (3, heated terrace; 4, pavement).

CHEAP EATS

StringRay Globe Cafe Bar & Pizzeria. See p310.

Donna Margherita. See p306.

CHEAP EATS

East
Bethnal Green

StringRay Globe Café Bar & Pizzeria
109 Columbia Road, E2 7RL (7613 1141, www.stringraycafe.co.uk). Bus 26, 48, 55.
Meals served 11am-11pm daily. **Main courses** £4.95-£9.95. **Credit** AmEx, MC, V.
The decor here hasn't changed much since the premises housed the Globe pub over a decade ago. Chunky wooden tables with garden-style bench seating and wooden chairs fill the space; brightly coloured walls display the odd picture or poster. But you're not here for the interior. StringRay is so popular that you may have to book on a Tuesday night, let alone on Sunday lunchtime when the flower market is in full bloom. That's hardly surprising when meze (marinated organic olives, houmous and own-made bread) costs a mere £3.95 and pizzas start at £4.95 – even though they're heavily topped and falling off your plate. Kids love their special pizza/pasta menu, while the cheerful and patient staff are parent-pleasers. There's even a ludicrously cheap range of cocktails. Standards have slipped a bit, however: the olives tasted little better than tinned, and the bread had been toasted. Still, the enormous artichoke and feta cheese salad contained plenty of leaves and a delicious dressing and, with an enormous quattro stagioni and a bottle of very decent Rioja, we managed to feed two (and tip the lovely staff) for less than £40.
Babies and children welcome: children's menu; high chairs. Booking essential. Tables outdoors (7, pavement). Takeaway service. **Map 6 S3.**

Shoreditch

Furnace
1 Rufus Street, N1 6PE (7613 0598, www.hoxton furnace.com). Old Street tube/rail. **Lunch served** noon-3pm Mon-Fri. **Dinner served** 6-11pm Mon-Sat. **Main courses** £6.85-£13. **Credit** MC, V.
Globalisation, eh? Where are we when the identifying feature of an Italian restaurant is neither its staff nor its gigantic pepper grinders? The interior of Furnace has more of a Swedish aesthetic – brightly lit with beech wood furniture and wooden flooring – but the cooking is strictly Italian and eccellente. This explains why, after ten years, this Hoxton joint survives in an area where little endures. On our visit, a steady stream of youngish folk – mostly couples – drifted in. We began our meal with a super-fresh warm salad of artichokes, peas and broad beans, and prawns in a rich, pepper-studded gravy. Pizzas are key: lovely crispy bases, just as we like 'em. Verdura, topped with pecorino and roast peppers, was particularly good. Daily specials (just one pasta dish) and some main-course salads complete the choices. Tuna topped with tapenade was sushi-standard, though too low on leaves to merit the title 'salad'. Finish with a grappa from the selection of digestivi. Things get going late here, but at 9pm on a weeknight the 'Swedish gym' suddenly began to hop.
Babies and children admitted. Separate room for parties, seats 40. Takeaway service. **Map 6 R4.**

Wapping

Il Bordello
81 Wapping High Street, E1W 2YN (7481 9950). Tower Hill tube/Tower Gateway DLR then 100 bus. **Lunch served** noon-3pm Mon-Fri. **Dinner served** 6-11pm Mon-Sat. **Meals served** 1-10.30pm Sun. **Main courses** £8.95-£28.95. **Credit** AmEx, DC, MC, V.
Set on a corner site, Il Bordello is a relaxed and entertainingly old-fashioned neighbourhood Italian. Step down from the street, past shiny sheets of copper, into a low-ceilinged interior decorated with Tamara de Lempicka prints. A small army of mostly elderly staff, all sporting red bow-ties and waistcoats (even the waitress), dote prodigiously on any accompanying children. The menu of Italian classics (gamberetti, bresaola, all the usual pizzas and pastas) is disconcertingly long, but everything we tried was pretty much up to the mark, despite rough-handed presentation. What was that decorative scattering of roughly chopped parsley doing all over our (huge) veal chop with sage butter? Still, pizza napoletana was a knock-out, the anchovies and capers invigoratingly salty rather than the usual assault on the taste buds – which suggests that it's best to keep your selections simple here. Punters are mostly local and middle-aged, plus a few young families. Grab a window seat for a diverting ankle-height view of the habitués of Wapping, or pretend you're at a continental café from one of the outdoor tables on the cobbles.
Babies and children welcome: high chairs. Booking advisable. Disabled: toilet. Takeaway service. Vegetarian menu.
For branch (La Figa) see index.

North East
Newington Green

Trattoria Sapori [NEW]
Alliance House, 44-45 Newington Green, N16 9QH (7704 0744, www.trattoriasapori.co.uk). Canonbury rail/21, 141 bus. **Open** 8am-11pm Mon-Sat; 9am-11pm Sun. **Main courses** £5.75-£14.50. **Credit** AmEx, MC, V.
The tumultuous southern end of Green Lanes makes a great location for an Italian deli, though the restaurant element to this operation works less well. A picture window and an outside eating area let diners see the delights of the Newington Green gyratory; inside, the long deli counter has pride of place, and the sparse and functional tables allow a widescreen view of blue lino. The menu of basic pasta and pizza choices is similarly uninspired, although every dish we tried did have a mitigating factor: bruschetta with dried basil but cheery cherry tomatoes; overcooked orecchiette with matching broccoli that nevertheless made judicious use of garlic and chilli; and florentine pizza that might have lacked pzazz, but had a nice crispy base. There's no feel of a particular region here, which allows the wine list to prowl across Italy; the selection is better than you might expect, with several choices of each colour by the glass. Staff were under-employed on our visit, and were shielded from diners' demands by the giant deli counter. Nevertheless, service was competent, if less than warm.
Available for hire. Babies and children welcome: children's menu; high chairs; nappy-changing facilities. Booking advisable weekends. Disabled: toilet. Separate room for parties, seats 30. Tables outdoors (10, terrace). Takeaway service. Vegan dishes. **Map 25 A1.**

Stoke Newington

Il Bacio

*61 Stoke Newington Church Street, N16 0AR
(7249 3833). Stoke Newington rail/73, 393, 476
bus.* **Dinner served** 6-11.15pm Mon-Fri. **Meals
served** noon-11.15pm Sat, Sun. **Main courses**
£5.50-£15.95. **Credit** MC, V.

This is the original of a small group of family
restaurants that have recently been joined by the
sleek Bacio Mare fish bar up the road. Il Bacio
departs from trattoria clichés with a variety of
Sardinian specialities (not least a pizza dedicated
to the island's favourite footballer, Gianfranco Zola)
and a dozen Sardinian wines. We particularly
enjoyed the culurgiones in tomato sauce with mint
– described as 'Sardinian ravioli' but, stuffed
fluffily solid with pecorino cheese and potato,
seeming more like gnocchi. Pennette mare e vento
(king prawns in white wine, garlic, chilli and basil,
with ubiquitous cherry tomatoes and pecorini)
didn't pack enough punch, but the insalata
prosciutto pere nicely balanced salty ham against
sweet pear. Sebadas – think Sardinian baklava,
stuffed with sweet cheese – were also a success.
The gratis basket of flatbread and olives, and a
jug of tap water volunteered and regularly topped
up, make this a good place for families. The
surprisingly large rear section (cavernously empty
when we arrived early on a Monday evening)
doubtless does good service for party groups. A
bouncy country soundtrack, winningly cheeky
service and a free stirrup cup of limoncello
certainly indicate an aptitude for fun here.
*Babies and children welcome: high chairs. Booking
advisable. Tables outdoors. Takeaway service;
delivery service (over £10 within 2-mile radius).*
Map 25 B1.
For branches see index.

North West

Hampstead

★ Fratelli la Bufala

*45A South End Road, NW3 2QB (7435 7814,
www.fratellilabufala.com). Belsize Park tube/
Hampstead Heath rail.* **Lunch served** noon-3pm
Fri. **Dinner served** 6-11pm Mon-Fri. **Meals
served** noon-11pm Sat, Sun. **Main courses**
£7.90-£16. **Set lunch** (Fri) £9.50 2 courses.
Credit MC, V.

If you look through the front window at Fratelli la
Bufala, the restaurant appears very small. The
majority of floor space is on a higher level and
consequently not visible. On our visit, the lighting
was low in the spacious interior: a family-friendly
place, with interesting nooks and crannies. A grand
piano dominated proceedings, the pianist playing
lamentably bland cocktail music. A remarkably
wide selection of daily specials is displayed on a
blackboard. There's also a large wood-fired pizza
oven visible to diners. Misto napoletano made an
excellent starter of complementary textures: three
fried parcels stuffed with light mozzarella. As the
restaurant's name suggests, buffalo is a speciality,
and bufala ragù with large pappardelle pasta,
cream and truffle was tremendous. A delicately
flavoured, but filling spinach tagliatelle came with
squash, garlic, parmesan and parsley. Staff were
friendly and attentive. The menu emphasises the
healthiness of the dishes, perhaps to counter a
guilty suspicion that food so delicious must be bad
for you. Though this Hampstead branch is part of
an international franchise, it doesn't give the
impression of being off the shelf.
*Available for hire. Babies and children welcome:
high chairs. Booking advisable dinner. Separate
room for parties, seats 20. Tables outdoors
(3, pavement). Takeaway service.* Map 28 C3.

Kilburn

Osteria del Ponte

*77 Kilburn High Road, NW6 6HY (7624 5793).
Kilburn Park tube.* **Open** 4-11pm Mon-Fri; noon-
11pm Sat, Sun. **Main courses** £6-£13. **Credit**
MC, V.

The Bridge is a big echoey pub at the less
fashionable lower end of Kilburn High Street. It
includes an Italian kitchen, Osteria del Ponte, with
a traditional wood-fired pizza oven. The pub was
very busy on the Friday night of our visit, and the
restaurant suffered because of it – the uncovered
wooden floors and tables making the noise echo
around the space. Staff who wait on tables also
serve at the bar. Our rather harassed waitress didn't
tell us until after we had opened a bottle of wine
that the restaurant was only serving pizzas, and the
main kitchen was closed. Focaccia was the only
starter available. Never mind: the pizzas themselves
were tremendous, with a fine base well-covered. A
quattro stagioni featured artichokes, mushrooms,
parma ham and carpets of black olives; the fantasia
consisted of ham, crisp rocket and fresh cherry
tomatoes. Unfortunately, by the time we finished
our meal, the waitress was serving behind the bar,
leaving us to queue to get our bill.
*Available for hire. Babies and children welcome:
high chairs. Booking advisable. Tables outdoors
(5, pavement).* Map 1 B1.

West Hampstead

La Brocca

*273 West End Lane, NW6 1QS (7433 1989).
West Hampstead tube/rail/139, C11 bus.*
Bar **Open** noon-11pm Mon-Thur; noon-1am Fri;
11am-1am Sat; noon-midnight Sun. **Lunch
served** noon-4pm Mon-Fri; noon-4.30pm Sat.
Meals served noon-midnight Sun. **Main
courses** £6-£14.
Restaurant **Dinner served** 6-11pm daily.
Main courses £10-£16.
Both **Credit** AmEx, MC, V.

There's a popular bar area at street level, but diners
descend into La Brocca's dimly lit basement. We
were seated in the conservatory at the back, where
a glass ceiling, combined with the plants and trees
outside, meant that the interior was filled with a
pleasant greenish hue. Tables are decorated with
old-fashioned red-check tablecloths, lending the feel
of a family-run restaurant. La Brocca is a land of
plenty. Big portions arrived in enormous bowls. A
large focaccia with fresh rosemary made a
satisfying starter, though it would have benefited
from slightly less rock salt. Main courses were rich
and flavoursome; we especially recommend the
saffron risotto with chunky pieces of squash,
taleggio cheese and roasted walnuts. Large parcels
of ravioli with spinach and pine kernels were
equally appealing, if not exceptional. Abstract
paintings adorn the walls of the restaurant,. Staff
were generally attentive, if sometimes distracted by
playing with customers' small children.
*Available for hire. Babies and children welcome:
high chairs. Booking advisable. Tables outdoors
(2, pavement). Takeaway service.* Map 28 A2.

With the most extensive gin collection in the UK, Graphic is the destination of choice for the perfect G&T, Dry Martini or delicious gin-based cocktail punches served in signature oversized paint tins.

Every six months Graphic Bar will be collaborating with a different graphic artist, who will use the bar to showcase their creations.

Now showcasing Ben Allen

Graphic
4 Golden Square
London W1F 9HT
0207 287 9241
info@graphicbar.com
graphicbar.com

Opening hours:
Mon – Fri: 12:00 – 00:00
Saturday: 17:00 – 00:00
Sunday: Available for private hire,
please contact us for details

URBAN
LEISURE
GROUP

Graphic is a part of Urban Leisure Group
urbanleisuregroup.com

Drinking

Bars

North, south, east and west (with a few more in the north than other areas), London's newest independent bars are proof that you don't have to head to the West End, or indeed a glitzy hotel, to enjoy a fabulous cocktail. Great bartenders are coming to an area near you. The standard of nominees, all local set-ups, in the Best New Bar category of the 2009 Time Out Eating & Drinking Awards was particularly high, but Tony Conigliaro's diminutive new Islington venture **69 Colebrooke Row** edged it in the end. All this praise for independent locals does not mean we've fallen out of love with the great hotel bars, however. You'll find several make our Hot 100 list, including the recently revamped **Connaught Bar**, **Blue Bar** at the Berkeley, and the discreetly glitzy **Dukes Hotel**, where making the perfect dry martini is their raison d'être.

Don't forget too that many restaurants have excellent stand-alone bars: we review some special favourites here, but also worthy of note are **Christopher's** (see p33), **Medcalf** (see p52) and **St John** (see p52).

Central

Aldwych

Lobby Bar (100)

One Aldwych, WC2B 4RH (7300 1070, www.onealdwych.com). Covent Garden or Temple tube. **Open** 8am-11.30pm Mon-Sat; 8am-10.30pm Sun. **Food served** noon-5pm, 5.30-11pm Mon-Sat; noon-5pm, 5.30-10.30pm Sun. **Credit** AmEx, DC, MC, V.

This bar at the luxurious One Aldwych hotel proves that lobby bars don't have to resemble airport lounges, although the unflattering flight attendant-style uniforms of the staff might suggest otherwise. Fashion lapses aside, visitors won't fail to be wowed by the soaring space, with its triffid-sized flower arrangements, elegant pillars and ceiling-height windows. Despite the majesty of the room, intimacy is introduced by high-backed armchairs, properly comfortable sofas and candles shimmering in the dusk. The sleek black bar dispenses an expertly mixed selection of cocktails at decent prices – from £10.50, or £12 for champagne varieties – from a list that includes the fragrant Aldwych Sling, with fresh lavender and Beefeater gin, and an unusual goji berry martini. On our visit, we were served house champagne instead of the requested Louis Roederer, but service is otherwise slick and friendly.
Babies and children admitted. Disabled: toilet. Function room (capacity 100). Wireless internet; free. **Map 18 F4.**

City

Hawksmoor (100)

157 Commercial Street, E1 6BJ (7247 7392, www.thehawksmoor.com). Liverpool Street tube/rail. **Open** noon-midnight Mon-Fri; 6pm-midnight Sat. **Food served** noon-3pm, 6-10.30pm Mon-Fri; 6-11pm Sat. **Credit** AmEx, DC, MC, V.

How much of the Hawksmoor is given over to drinkers seems to depend on how busy the restaurant is. On quieter nights, you may be able to snag a table; otherwise, you'll have to hope there's a stool free at the corner bar. If there's so little space for drinkers, why include it here? Simple: the cocktails are among the best in London. The menu is a joy to read, with erudite explanations and elucidations on all the drinks; offerings include a lengthy list of variations on the mint julep, the Prohibition-era Scoff Law (rye whiskey, vermouth, lemon and pomegranate juice), the similar-vintage Bloodhound (gin mixed with dry and sweet vermouths, lent a lovely tang by fresh raspberries) and an assortment of other arcane recipes, some of which date back the better part of 150 years. But while the menu detail is welcome, the drinks pretty much sell themselves, especially given the reasonable prices (£6.50-£7.50, on the whole). Best of all, they're mixed by clubbable, talkative cocktail obsessives, who define the bar as much as the drinks they mix so expertly.
Available for hire. Babies and children admitted. Disabled: toilet. Function room (capacity 30). Wireless internet; free. **Map 6 R5.**

Fitzrovia

Crazy Bear

26-28 Whitfield Street, W1T 2RG (7631 0088, www.crazybeargroup.co.uk). Goode Street tube. **Open/food served** noon-10.45pm Mon-Sat; noon-10pm Sun. **Credit** AmEx, MC, V.

Perfectly groomed hostesses greet arrivals to this chic den of decadence, leading drinkers down to a sunken basement bar with low cowhide seating. While the cocktails are superb and the atmosphere lively, Crazy Bear charges luxury hotel prices but without the complimentary touches such as nuts and other nibbles served in the best hotel bars. Cocktails stretch from £8.50 to £15 – £40 should you want the luxury old-fashioned. Order two rounds and some eats (dim sum, tempura, satay, £3.90-£8 each) and you've had a bigger night out than you might have expected. Still, it's delicious fun – expect lots of lychee, lemongrass and ginger flavours to complement the oriental restaurant menu upstairs. We loved the lychee mojito, fusing havana anejo blanco, lime juice, lychees and mint, and a precision-made dry martini with Hendrick's gin and cucumber garnish. Crazy Bear's loos have acquired a reputation, not just for shimmering decor but for being difficult to find – don't worry too much: male staff and customers are quite used to ladies accidentally opening the wrong door.
Babies and children admitted. **Map 17 B1.**

Hakkasan (100)

8 Hanway Place, W1T 1HD (7907 1888, www.hakkasan.com). Tottenham Court Road tube. **Open** noon-12.30am Mon-Wed; noon-1.30am Thur-Sat; noon-midnight Sun. **Food served** noon-3pm, 6-11.30pm Mon-Wed; noon-3pm, 6-12.30am Sat; noon-4pm, 6-11.30pm Sun. **Credit** AmEx, MC, V.

A long, thin strip of a bar behind the Chinese screens of Hakkasan's exalted dining room gets astonishingly crowded – and with good reason. It hasn't lost an ounce of its glamorous sheen since opening in 2001 and the cocktails are superb. Saketini (£9.50), made with Hendrick's gin and Belvedere vodka as well as Akashi-tai sake, is a thrilling diversion for dry martini connoisseurs. We love the Sushi Bartender's Breakfast, too, a herby riff on the bloody mary theme. Six non-alcoholic cocktails (£5.50) offer all the tropical fruit and spice flavours of the main list without the headache. Japanese beer (Yebisu) and wines by the glass cherry-picked from countries as diverse as Turkey and Uruguay add interest even to the simplest round of after-work drinks. Then there's the bar food (though not much room to eat it): dim sum platters, crispy duck rolls, sesame prawn toast, all cooked to the restaurant's fabulously high standards. Don't be put off by the door staff, dark descent to the basement, or bevy of hostesses asking about your booking: this is worth some perseverance.
Available for hire (capacity 150). Babies and children admitted (until 7.30pm). Disabled: toilet. Entertainment: DJs 9pm nightly; free. Function room (capacity 65). Wireless internet; free. **Map 17 C2.**

Long Bar

The Sanderson, 50 Berners Street, W1T 3NG (7300 1400, www.morganshotelgroup.com). Oxford Circus or Tottenham Court Road tube. **Open/food served** 11.30am-2am Mon-Wed; 11am-3am Thur-Sat; noon-10.30pm Sun. **Credit** AmEx, DC, MC, V.

Empty, this is a prime spot: long and light, with flimsy white curtains and a courtyard that feels a long way further than a block from Oxford Street. There's still something unsettling about it, however: those single eyes on the backs of the chairs, and the glint of steel along the long bar don't make for a cosy drinking experience. And the acoustics mean that every fashionista squawk reverberates. The house vodka is Wyborowa, but it's hard to trust a drinks menu that lists most of its cocktails, including daquiris, under 'martinis'. An oriental daquiri costs £13 plus 10% service and tasted of neither lemongrass nor ginger, although the measure was pleasingly hefty. And olives were dull, overly salty and an outrageous £6 before service and the extra gratuity the bill encourages you to add. Granted, there were a lot of them. But you don't come to an Ian Schrager hotel for quantity over quality.
Babies and children admitted (terrace). Disabled: toilet (in hotel). Entertainment: DJ 10.30pm Fri; free. Function room (capacity 80). Tables outdoors (20, terrace). Wireless internet; free. **Map 17 A2.**

Shochu Lounge

Basement, Roka, 37 Charlotte Street, W1T 1RR (7580 9666, www.shochulounge.com). Goode Street or Tottenham Court Road tube. **Open** 5pm-midnight daily. **Food served** 5.30-11.30pm Mon-Sat; 5.30-10.30pm Sun. **Credit** AmEx, DC, MC, V.

Beneath landmark Noho Japanese restaurant Roka, the similarly chic Shochu Lounge purveys drinks based on the vodka-like distilled spirit of the same name. Shochu is often overlooked for its more widespread counterpart, saké, but here it is used in healthy tonics (75ml measures, £6.90), in cocktails (£8.30) and sold by the 50ml measure, each concocted with varied basic ingredients. Tonics, seven in number, include ki lazubeli shu ('helps improve memory') and jasmine flower shu ('for coughs and sore eyes'). Among the cocktails you'll find the Nightingale (shisho shu, lime, elderflower and orange bitters) as well as the house punch of Hallo Kitty with shochu, raspberry, rose, lemon and sparkling water. Premium shochus, at around £10 a long hit, include the sweet potato (kappa no sasolimizu) and barley-and-date (tempo miyazaki) varieties. Spirit choice is not limited to shochu; some 15 vodkas (Kauffmann, Stolichnaya

Elite, Slwucha, Uluvka, Luksusowa, Potocki) as single measures, or mixed in martinis such as the Rose Petal with rose petal vodka, gin and lychee juice. With the 13.5% service charge, most drinks run to £10 anyway, but they're expertly mixed from the rustic bar counter surrounded by shochu-making implements and storing jars, and served with style. The full Roka menu is available too.
Entertainment: DJ 8.30pm Thur-Sat; free. **Map 17 B1**.

Social

5 Little Portland Street, W1W 7JD (7636 4992, www.thesocial.com). Oxford Circus tube. **Open** noon-midnight Mon-Wed; noon-1am Thur, Fri; 5pm-1am Sat; 6pm-midnight occasional Sun. **Food served** noon-11pm Mon-Fri; 5-11pm Sat. **Credit** AmEx, MC, V.
Neil Thomson's photographs of the Social's tenth birthday celebrations sum up this most successful of music bars. Featured party acts the Doves, Saint Etienne and the Magic Numbers link the Social with Heavenly Recordings, the seminal indie record label with whom its roots lie. A decade in, the mission remains the same: to provide proper cocktails, decent global beers, awesome jukebox tunes and defiantly prole grub to the masses. Five booths, each with a retro round-cornered table centrepieced by Heinz and HP sauce bottles, accommodate music-savvy bohos munching signature square pies and, improbably, fishfinger salads. Cocktails (£6-£7), three dozen in number, are equally inventive. Drambuie, Havana Club Especial, pear purée and coffee comprise I Wish It Could Be Christmas Every Day; Cazadores tequila provides the kick in the sparky Mi Caza Es Su Caza (somebody had to say it) and dovetails nicely with Chambord, peach purée, fresh lime and ginger beer (remember that?) in Sympathy For The Devil. Draught beers include Moretti and San Miguel; the equally Latin Sagres and Estella also provided by the bottle.
Babies and children admitted (until 5pm). Entertainment: DJs/bands 7pm Mon-Sat, occasional Sun; free-£5. **Map 9 J5**.

King's Cross

Big Chill House

257-259 Pentonville Road, N1 9NL (7427 2540, www.bigchill.net). King's Cross tube/rail. **Open** noon-midnight Mon-Thur, Sun; noon-3am Fri, Sat. **Food served** noon-11pm daily. **Admission** £5 after 10pm Fri, Sat. **Credit** MC, V.
The Big Chill Festival may only run for four days in August but the multi-faceted organisation responsible runs this place full-time. The large, funky bar-club is now two years young and still earning acclaim. The festival spirit is continued in the artwork (a large photo mural of a field of dandelions as you enter), the signage ('brothers' and 'sisters' on the toilet doors) and the sharing nature of the food and drink. A Big Chill Punch (Finlandia vodka, Funkin White peach purée) can be ordered by the glass (£7.75) or pitcher (£23.25), while platters include a vegetarian plate and a meaty mix of peri-peri marinated chicken skewers, merguez sausages and lamb meatballs. On our visit, a happy-hour offer involved four beers for £10 (there's Amstel and Heineken, with Hoegaarden and Stowford Press Cider also on tap). Other cocktails include bellinis, mojitos and a bloody mary, quality bar snacks (roast chicken wings, king prawns, vine leaves) abound and DJs spin from Wednesday to Saturday. An upstairs patio comes into its own in summer.
Babies and children admitted (until 6pm). Disabled: toilet. Entertainment: DJs/bands Wed-Sat. Tables outdoors (5, terrace). **Map 4 L3**.

Knightsbridge

Blue Bar (100)

The Berkeley, Wilton Place, SW1X 7RL (7235 6000, www.the-berkeley.co.uk). Hyde Park Corner tube. **Open/food served** 4pm-1am Mon-Sat; 4-11pm Sun. **Credit** AmEx, DC, MC, V.
The name isn't just a caprice – this David Collins-designed bar really is as blue as a Billy Connolly

joke. The sky-blue bespoke armchairs, the deep-blue ornate plasterwork and the navy-blue leather-bound menus combine with discreet lighting to striking effect. It's more a see-and-be-seen place than somewhere to kick back, but don't let the celeb-heavy reputation put you off – staff treat everyone here like royalty, and the cocktails are a masterclass in sophistication. Not everyone can afford to scale the frightening heights of the bar list, which is worth perusing just to confirm that there is such a thing as a £4,200 bottle of champagne or a £925 shot of whisky (Macallan 55-year-old, if you're interested). Leave those to the A-list, and just enjoy the elegance and luxury of one of the finest hotel bars in the city.
Disabled: toilet (in hotel). Dress: smart casual. Wireless internet; free. **Map 9 G9**.

Mandarin Bar

Mandarin Oriental Hyde Park, 66 Knightsbridge, SW1X 7LA (7235 2000, www.mandarin oriental.com). Knightsbridge tube. **Open/food served** 10.30am-1.30am Mon-Sat; 10.30am-11.30pm Sun. **Admission** £5 after 10.30pm Mon-Sat. **Credit** AmEx, DC, MC, V.
Step out of the Knightsbridge chaos into the Mandarin Oriental's cool marble and you might expect a proper British colonial drinking experience, all obsequious waiters and drinks with hints of opium. But this bar smacks more of the 1980s: the staff mix your drinks (about £14 each) behind a glowing frosted glass panel, the floor is as shiny as a banker's pearl cufflink, and the size of the cocktails bespeaks an era that recession forgot. They're not bad, either; a bit sweet (five spoonsfuls is a lot of sugar even for a caipirinha) but well balanced – and they are gargantuan. Obligatory service isn't added which, given that service was splendid and the crisps replenished at five-minute intervals, is impressive. And for eye candy, how about a glass corridor containing the restaurant's fine wines? These are storage conditions to make a sommelier weep, but those of us who can't afford the contents can at least appreciate a good look at we're missing.
Disabled: toilet (in hotel). Entertainment: jazz 9pm Mon-Sat. **Map 8 F9**.

Zuma

5 Raphael Street, SW7 1DL (7584 1010, www.zumarestaurant.co.uk). Knightsbridge tube. **Open** noon-11pm Mon-Fri; 12.30-11pm Sat; noon-10.30pm Sun. **Food served** noon-2.15pm, 6-10.45pm Mon-Thur; noon-2.45pm, 6-10.45pm Fri; 12.30-3.15, 6-10.45pm Sat; 12.30-3.15pm, 6-10.15pm Sun. **Credit** AmEx, MC, V.
Despite its prosaic location on an off-Knightsbridge sidestreet, this contemporary Japanese izakaya attracts a loyal, monied clientele. The 40-deep saké selection is as attractive as any in town – there's even Azure Ginjoshu Tosatsuru, sourced from a spring at the bottom of the North Pacific – but it's the cocktails that keep the chattering shoppers coming back. Three sparkling 'kaze' types include the house Zuma spritzer with Ume-shu plum wine, prosecco, orange and angostura bitters, while four long ('mizu') and six short ('tsuchi') types include Ega-nya, made with Whitley Neill gin, shisho and mint leaves, aloe vera, fresh lemon and lime. The dozen signature drinks include Zumanuka, with fresh basil, fresh pineapple, apple juic and 42 Below Manuka Honey vodka. Martinis and daiquiris show another touch of south-east Asia, with Thai-spiced mango used with abandon. Most mixes carry a £10.50 price tag (and that's before the 'optional' 13.5% service charge is added to the bill). Kirin Ichiban and Asahi Super Dry and Black comprise the beers, while snacks will up your bar bill astronomically – it's £19.50 for jumbo finger prawns with Yuzu pepper.
Babies and children welcome: high chairs. Disabled: toilet. Function room (capacity 14). **Map 8 F9**.

Marylebone

★ Artesian

Langham Hotel, 1C Portland Place, W1B 1JA (7636 1000, www.artesian-bar.co.uk). Oxford Circus tube. **Open/food served** 2pm-1am daily.

Admission (non-guests) £5 after 11pm Mon-Tue, Sun; £7 after 11pm Wed-Sat. **Credit** AmEx, DC, MC, V.
David Collins's recent redesign in the historic Langham hotel has updated the pillars, marble and high ceilings of this classically handsome room with a typically considered yet glamorous touch. The result has unforgettable visual impact: the Artesian artfully blends grand Victorian decadence (a marble bar, soaring inset mirrors, pressed and embroidered napkins) with modern details (faultless service, purple snakeskin-effect leather seats, an imposing, carved pagoda-style back bar). Rum is clearly a passion here – the impressive drinks menu lists over 60 varieties, from a £9 Gosling's Black Seal to a £300 Havana Club Maximo, and this dedication is apparent in the cocktails too. We enjoyed a heady Artesian Punch, made with Poire William, pineapple, citrus and three rums, including Pyrat Pistol. Even more impressive was the sensational Tiny 10 Club – served straight up, it mixed tangy pomelo grapefruit, Tanqueray No.10 and camomile tea and was sipped through a jasmine foam. There's also a clever 'cocktail grazing menu' which allows you to work your way through the extensive selection with less impact on both wallet and sobriety.
Babies and children admitted (until 6pm). Disabled: toilet (in hotel). **Map 9 H5**.

Mayfair

Donovan Bar

Brown's Hotel, 33-34 Albemarle Street, W1S 4BP (7493 6020, www.roccofortecollection.com). Green Park tube. **Open/food served** 11am-1am Mon-Sat; noon-midnight Sun. **Credit** AmEx, DC, MC, V.
Any bar that features something called a Sticky & Sweet-ini needs to be approached with caution, even if it is named after one of the finest photographers ever to snap London's Swinging Sixties. The tartan couches are a nicely dufferish touch, taking the icicle edge off the trendier-than-thou wood and monochrome Terence Donovan pictures, but the gooey cocktails are a step too far: there's nothing cool or ironic about a pineapple daiquiri that costs £13 and tastes like a boiled sweet. The wine list here is decent, but the bar really wins on spirits: 21 rums, 17 single malt whiskies and various blends, eaux-de-vie, brandies and liqueurs. These are people who care about strong drink – perhaps that's why they think anyone who wants to dilute it with juice is actually asking for a lollipop.
Disabled: toilet (in hotel). Entertainment: jazz 9pm Mon-Sat; free. **Map 9 J7**.

Library

The Lanesborough, 1 Lanesborough Place, Hyde Park Corner, SW1X 7TA (7259 5599, www.lanesborough.com). Hyde Park Corner tube. **Open** 11am-1am Mon-Sat; noon-10.30pm Sun. **Food served** noon-midnight Mon-Sat; noon-10.30pm Sun. **Credit** AmEx, DC, MC, V.
Across the road from Hyde Park, and carefully muffled against the noise of Hyde Park Corner, sits the Lanesborough, a former hospital that now offers a rather more luxurious kind of sleepover. The Library Bar no longer boasts master bartender Salvator Calabrese, which may account for a slight slippage in cocktail quality: the Lanesborough (£14.50 plus 12.5% service), a combination of champagne, limoncello, aperol and fresh orange juice, tasted more like a simple Buck's Fizz. But the upholstery is still comfortable, the rosewood and mahogany bookshelves gracious, the service gently attentive and the house gin Tanqueray. And, if you're clever enough to arrive mid-afternoon, you'll be offered proper canapés as well as Bombay mix and olives.
Disabled: toilet. Entertainment: pianist 6.30pm daily; free. Function rooms (capacity 180). Wireless internet; free. **Map 9 G8**.

Mahiki

1 Dover Street, W1S 4LD (7493 9529, www.mahiki.com). Green Park tube. **Open** 5.30pm-3.30am Mon-Fri; 7.30pm-3.30am Sat. **Food served** 5.30-10.30pm Mon-Fri; 7.30-

Lobby Bar. See p314.

10.30pm Sat. **Admission** £10 after 9.30pm Mon-Wed; £15 after 9.30pm Thur-Sat. **Credit** MC, V.
Mahiki, 'tropical cocktails and island grill', cannot be taken seriously. It's silly, tacky, attracts an air-headed, monied custom – and is bags of fun. An international bar staff well versed in the arts of mixing and dealing with way-too-trashed idiocy, make the place. Respect must be given to any barman who can smile while sorting out the perfect pina colada (with Appleton VX and Koko Kanu coconut rum) in a terribly loud shirt for customers he'd probably rather strangle. Given the setting – just off Piccadilly – and the surroundings of candlelit Hawaiiana, prices for early-evening drinks are pretty reasonable. You'll be laying out £8 for a Honolulu Honey (with Chairman's Reserve rum from St Lucia) or a Dark & Stormy (with Gosling's Black Seal Bermudan rum). You'll need to factor in the hefty (up to £15) admission fee if you go later on, however. Shared drinks are the way to go then, with the three-person Bikini Blast (with El Jimador tequila), the four-person Zombie (with various rums and absinthe), or the eight-person Mystery Drink (it's a mystery!).
Available for hire. Entertainment: DJs 10.30pm nightly. Map 9 J7.

Polo Bar

Westbury Hotel, New Bond Street, W1S 2YF (7629 7755, www.westburymayfair.com). Bond Street or Oxford Circus tube. **Open** 9am-1am Mon-Fri; 11am-1am Sat; noon-midnight Sun. **Food served** 9am-10.30pm Mon-Fri; 11am-10.30pm Sat, Sun. **Credit** AmEx, DC, MC, V.
Art deco lite might best describe the look of the Polo Bar: the bar is marble-topped, the tables are inlaid wood, the pillars chunky and square. Yet, perhaps because it's such a long, large room (no eavesdropping here), the place doesn't blare its design at you, and the drinks can take precedence. Or they could, if they weren't a little lacklustre. The Ketel One martini doesn't kick you in the head quite as it should, although it contains a very fine oversize olive. And the bellini lacked the scent of summer and that unctuous mix of peach and alcohol that makes the imbiber feel like a drunken wasp. The location is useful for shoppers on Regent, Oxford or New Bond Streets, but this is not a destination bar.
Available for hire. Babies and children admitted (until 6pm). Disabled: toilet (in hotel).
Map 9 H7.

★ Connaught Bar NEW (100)

The Connaught, Carlos Place, W1K 2AL (7499 7070, www.the-connaught.co.uk). Bond Street tube. **Open/food served** 4pm-1am Mon-Sat. **Credit** AmEx, DC, MC, V.
The Connaught is another top-end bar to have had designer David Collins wave his magic wand over it. It pulls off the trick of being both cosy and elegant, with unobtrusive lighting, pressed-powder pastel walls and a conspiratorial duskiness that settles through the rooms as the evening goes on. It's the only bar we've visited that has offered us a liquid 'amuse bouche' on arrival – a dainty flute of pineapple juice with mint and berry-infused gin. Complimentary nibbles were exemplary – one bowl of perfect Spanish olives and another of honey-roasted nuts. The drinks had a lot to live up to, but exceeded expectations. The Connaught Martini is worth ordering for the tableside theatre alone: a waiter pours gin and vermouth from a crystal tumbler into a frozen glass in front of you, then invites you to select a dash of infused bitters from an apothecary-style array. Service is never less than charming and effortlessly involved. The Connaught's other bar, the Coburg, was runner-up in Time Out's Best Bar award in 2008 – both set the standard in London luxury drinking.
Disabled: toilet (in hotel). Dress: smart casual. Wireless internet; free. **Map 9 H7.**

Piccadilly

Brumus Bar

Haymarket Hotel, 1 Suffolk Place, SW1Y 4BP (7470 4000, www.firmdale.com). Piccadilly Circus tube. **Open/food served** 7am-11.30pm Mon-Sat; 8am-10.30pm Sun. **Credit** AmEx, MC, V.
Say what you like about Brumus, but you couldn't call it shy and retiring. It's a cacophony of colour, an explosion of pink, fuchsia, magenta, red and crimson – everything from the cute furniture to the wallpapered ceiling screams for attention. Set in the exclusive Haymarket Hotel, its upmarket class stands out in touristy Piccadilly Circus and brings in a mixed, relaxed crowd, including a fair sprinkling of hotel guests and elderly theatregoers. The extensive cocktail menu steers through standards and new creations. On our visit a Haymarket Cosmo (£10.50) was made with limoncello and fresh mint and served over crushed ice to add a fresh twist to an old classic. Despite the loud colour scheme, it's surprisingly

unintimidating and welcoming, and the attentive staff hit the perfect balance of friendliness and professionalism.
Babies and children admitted. Disabled: toilet. Function rooms (capacity 30-50). Tables outdoors (6, pavement). **Map 10 K7.**

St James's

★ Dukes Hotel (100)

Dukes Hotel, 35 St James's Place, SW1A 1NY (7491 4840, www.dukeshotel.co.uk). Green Park tube. **Open** noon-11pm Mon-Sat; noon-10.30pm Sun. **Food served** noon-4pm daily. **Credit** AmEx, DC, MC, V.
This titchy, sinfully comfortable bar, with its engravings and fringed chairs, looks like an upper-class Georgian sitting room – but very few butlers could manage martinis of this calibre. They are among the best in London, possibly in the world, although all the quiet waiters do is flick extra dry vermouth in an iced glass, fill it with vodka (there are ten options, all premium) then drop in a sliver of lemon peel. Perhaps it's the wooden tray, or the vermouth flask that so resembles the vinegar bottle on tables in cheap chippies. It's certainly not the prices, which are hefty but worth it (£14.90 plus 12.5% service). Whatever the secret, sipping a drink amid the polite murmur of the very adult clientele, while munching on complimentary nuts and Puglian olives, is one of the most soothing experiences this city offers. And if you don't like martinis, there are plenty of alternatives, including nearly a dozen good wines by the glass.
Dress: smart casual. Tables outdoors (4, garden). **Map 9 J8.**

Soho

Floridita

100 Wardour Street, W1F 0TN (7314 4000, www.floriditalondon.com). Tottenham Court Road tube. **Open** 4.30pm-2am Tue, Wed; (members/ guest list/doorman's discretion) 4.30pm-3am Thur-Sat. **Food served** 4.30pm-1am Tue, Wed; 4.30pm-1.30am Thur-Sat. **Admission** £15 after 9.30pm Thur-Sat. **Credit** AmEx, DC, MC, V.
Now so established it could almost be an authentic Hemingway haunt, perfectly sited at 100 Wardour Street, above the similarly upscale Latin Mesa tapas bar, Floridita is named after its legendary Cuban counterpart, nicknamed 'the Cradle of the Daiquiri'. Thus the 21st-century Soho version has

DRINKING

Lexington. See p323.

a Daiquiri Cradle section on its 75-cocktail drinks menu with, for example, Havana Club Añejo Especial being mixed with Manzana Verde and home-made vanilla sugar syrup, apple and lime juices in the Jenning's Daiquiri. Nearly all cocktails are priced at £8 (plus 12.5% service) and involve Havana Club of some sort. Most typical are the Cuban Cocktail Classics, the Floridita itself being HC Añejo Especial with fresh lime, sugar syrup and a dash of maraschino. Among the New Cuban Cocktails you'll find the an enticing mojito, in which passion-fruit purée and vanilla liqueur mingle with HC Añejo Blanco. International favourites (mai tai, manhattan, cosmpolitan) also feature, but that's not really the point. Cuban bands give regular shows, and Floridita hamburgers, made with Aberdeen Angus minced steak and ground chorizo, provide sustenance.
Booking advisable. Disabled: toilet. Entertainment: DJ & Cuban band 7.30pm Tue-Sat. Function rooms (capacity 40-150). Map 17 B3.

LAB (100)

12 Old Compton Street, W1D 4TQ (7437 7820, www.lab-townhouse.com). Leicester Square or Tottenham Court Road tube. **Open** 4pm-midnight Mon-Sat; 4-10.30pm Sun. **Food served** 6-11pm Mon-Sat; 6-10.30pm Sun. **Credit** MC, V.
Other, newer bars may have overtaken LAB's '70s-meets-'90s decor, but there are few to match the sheer enthusiasm and knowledge of the bartenders. Cocktails are king here, and many original combinations are mixed using LAB's own infusions and syrups (chorizo tequila, anyone?). The daunting 31-page bible of a drinks menu contains more than 120 creations, but pull up a chair at the bar and let one of the ultra-friendly, helpful mixologists guide you through it. We tried a Providores, with pomegranate molasses, whiskey, black pepper and apple, a well-balanced blend of unusual flavours; a Ching was a refreshing mix of Tanqueray, velvet falernum (a spiced syrup), ginger and mint. The unashamed party vibe means this place fills up early, and the exuberant staff, who clearly love their jobs, make sure it stays that way all night.
Available for hire. Dress: no ties. Entertainment: DJs 8pm Mon-Sat. Map 17 C3.

★ Milk & Honey (100)

61 Poland Street, W1F 7NU (7292 9949, www.mlkhny.com). Oxford Circus tube. **Open** *Non-members* 6-11pm Mon-Fri; 7-11pm Sat. *Members* 6pm-3am Mon-Fri; 7pm-3am Sat. **Food served** 6pm-2am Mon-Sat. **Credit** AmEx, DC, MC, V.
You could walk past the inconspicuous door of this semi-mythical Soho speakeasy every day and never know it was here – and that's probably just

how they like it. The Prohibition theme is carried through to the vaguely art deco interior (dimly lit, adding to the air of secrecy), the jazz and ragtime soundtrack and the perfectly executed classic cocktails. It's members-only most of the time, but mere mortals can book a table until 11pm at the beginning of the week. While the place may not be at its best then, what it lacks in atmosphere it more than makes up for with the cocktail list – it's rightly famed for its dedication to the mixed drink. Everywhere you look, the emphasis is on pure quality, from the daily squeezed juices and twice-frozen ice to the stock of premium spirits. It's enough to make you want to join.
Booking essential for non-members. Dress: smart casual; no sportswear. Function rooms (capacity 25). Wireless internet; free. Map 17 A3.

South Kensington

190 Queensgate

The Gore Hotel, 190 Queensgate, SW7 5EX (7584 6601, www.gorehotel.co.uk). Gloucester Road or South Kensington tube. **Open** noon-1am, **food served** noon-11.30pm Mon-Sat. **Credit** AmEx, MC, V.
In a library atmosphere of dark wood and low lighting, the bar of the Gore Hotel goes about its business of providing varied, classy cocktails to a varied, classy clientele. There are 20 flavours of mojito (£9.95) alone, from mandarin to blueberry, and pear to lychee. The dozen-strong house selection includes a Raspberry Mule of Absolut Raspberri, fresh raspberries and ginger beer; the 190 Royale is a variation on the mojito, with fruity sloe berries, gin and champagne. Beaumont des Crayères is the bubbly of choice. Wines and beers display a Spanish touch – Rioja Crianza Solabal is one of eight reds available by the glass or bottle, San Miguel one of four bottled beers, but the Iberian management could do far better than the desultory tapas on offer – the patatas bravas are like nothing seen in Madrid. On a happier note, a quality Chablis (Domaine de la Genillotte 2007) also comes by the glass, and the 30 varieties of vodka include Snow Leopard, Reyka and Grey Goose. And the service is excellent.
Babies and children admitted. Entertainment: DJs 10pm Sat; free. Function room (capacity 100). Wireless internet; free. Map 8 D9.

West

Ladbroke Grove

Montgomery Place

31 Kensington Park Road, W11 2EU (7792 3921, www.montgomeryplace.co.uk). Ladbroke Grove tube. **Open** 5pm-midnight

Mon-Fri, Sun; 2pm-1am Sat. **Food served** 6-11pm daily. **Credit** AmEx, MC, V.
A temple to the cocktail, Montgomery Place keeps a low profile, its dark exterior embellished by a couple of tables outside in summer. Within, the prime table by the window is usually taken, as are the places at the bar – for intimacy, find a seat in the more spacious back area. 'We take our inspiration from the Hemingway and Rebirth of Cool eras,' declares the juicy, thick drinks menu, packed full of top drinks and their histories. Some are not so old – the Old Cuban (£9.75), for example, was created by Audrey Saunders, owner of New York's Pegu Club, in 2004. The half-dozen martinis include the house Montgomery Style, its ice-cold Tanqueray London gin served 15:1 with Noilly Prat French Vermouth, 'the same ratio as Field Marshal Montgomery liked to outnumber his opponents'. Drinks are categorised by spirits, high-end labels all (Santa Teresa Gran Reserva rum, El Jimador tequila, Bombay Sapphire gin); look out for in-house mixes such as the Silver Pine (Havana Club, Campari, fresh grapefruit, agave nectar, passion-fruit syrup), created at (now closed) sister bar Dusk in Battersea.
Babies and children admitted (afternoon Sat). Tables outdoors (2, pavement). Map 19 B3.

★ Portobello Star NEW

2009 RUNNER-UP BEST NEW BAR
171 Portobello Road, W11 2DY (7229 8016). Ladbroke Grove tube. **Open** 11am-11pm Mon-Thur; 11am-12.30am Fri, Sat; 11am-11.30pm Sun. **Credit** MC, V.
Gentrification has at long last sunk its claws into this once-scruffy old boozer, which for years was one of the holdouts against progress along the Portobello Road. Fronted by a couple of pavement tables but no real sign to advertise its existence, Portobello Star version 2.0 is a long, thin room; the only real relief from the plain walls is provided by the sturdy bar along one side, and a lovely radio-themed mural right at the back. It's a handsome little space, certainly more appealing than it seems at first glance, but the real selling points are the likeable bartenders' powerful, convincing renditions of cocktails both traditional (a richly flavourful mint julep made with Woodford Reserve, a margarita modified by agave) and contemporary (the Bramble, invented by Dick Bradsell in the '80s and now a modern classic). You may have to shout to make yourself heard when the DJs crank it up a little – the music policy bounces from generic indie to more danceable tunes – but the kinetic crowd of Notting Hillbillies don't mind a bit.
Available for hire. Babies and children admitted (until 7pm). Entertainment: DJs 9.30pm Fri, Sat. Function room (capacity 20). Tables outdoors (2, pavement). Wireless internet; free. Map 19 B3.

Trailer Happiness

177 Portobello Road, W11 2DY (7727 2700, www.trailerhappiness.com). Ladbroke Grove or Notting Hill Gate tube. **Open** 6-11pm Mon-Sat. **Food served** 5-10.30pm Tue-Sat; 6-10.30pm Sat. **Credit** AmEx, MC, V.
Laudably tongue-in-cheek when the rest of Ladbroke Grove is drowning in chi-chi spots, this retro basement tiki bar has a serious side too – its core drinks are made according to recipes concocted in 1934 at Don the Beachcomber's in Hollywood, and Trader Vic's in Oakland. California, here we come. Sure enough, the mai tai (Appleton V/X rum, orange curaçao, orgeat, bitters, fresh lime, £9) and Blue Hawaiian (Havana Club Añejo Especial, Wray & Nephew Overproof and Sailor Jerry rums, fresh pineapple, Blue Curaçao) do justice to the legend. Zombie, another Don the Beachcomber creation of five rums, absinthe and exotic juices, are limited to two per person. But Trailer Happiness is not a cocktail bar as such – with its tacky decor and DJ hatch, it's far too informal for that. Recommended beer is König Pilsener from Duisberg, food ('TV dinners' such as beef fajitas) is sourced as much as possible from local sources. TH is also a shrine to JH Lynch, the British artist whose mass-market images of sultry women have decorated many a Chinese takeaway.

Entertainment: DJs 8pm Thur-Sat. Tables outdoors (4, pavement). Map 19 B3.

Westbourne Grove

Lonsdale
44-48 Lonsdale Road, W11 2DE (7727 4080, www.thelonsdale.co.uk). Ladbroke Grove or Notting Hill Gate tube. **Open** 6pm-midnight Mon-Thur; 6pm-1am Fri, Sat; 6-11.30pm Sun. **Food served** 6-10.30pm daily. **Credit** AmEx, MC, V.
Although it's been five years or so since London's leading bartender Dick Bradsell was behind the counter here, his legacy lives on in the form of outstanding contemporary cocktails – the Rose Petal Martini (Bombay Sapphire stirred with Lanique rose liqueur, lychee juice and Peychaud bitters, £8) for example, or the Elderflower Fizz (elderflower cordial, lemon juice and champagne). There are 'London contemporary classics' too – the best in British mixes from the last ten years – such as Jason Fendick's Quiet Storm (Ketel One vodka, guava, lychee and pineapple juices, coconut cream and lime) or Giovanni Burdi's Markee (Maker's Mark bourbon, cranberry juice, Chambord, lemon juice). The Lonsdale, comprising a sun-catching front terrace, a long bar counter and wide, candlelit main seating area at the back, also treats cocktail history with due reverence, and drinks invented in London between 1914 and 1934 are a specialist subject: note the Bloodhound, consisting of fresh raspberries, Noilly Prat, Plymouth gin and maraschino, invented by the Duke of Manchester in 1922. Mixing and service are fittingly and reassuringly old school too.
Babies and children admitted (until 8.30pm). Function room (capacity 75). Tables outdoors (4, terrace). Map 19 C3.

Westbourne House
65 Westbourne Grove, W2 4UJ (7229 2233, www.westbournehouse.net). Bayswater or Royal Oak tube. **Open** 11am-11.30pm Mon-Thur; 11am-12.30pm Fri; 10am-midnight Sat; 10am-10.30pm Sun. **Food served** 11am-3pm, 5-11pm Mon-Fri; 11am-4.30pm, 5-11pm Sat; 11am-4.30pm, 5-10.30pm Sun. **Credit** AmEx, DC, MC, V.
On quiet stretch between Bayswater and Notting Hill, Westbourne House provides professional drinks to professional people. Colin Appiah of the London Academy of Bartending is behind some of the original mixes here. Polish U'Luvka vodka was the spirit of the month when we visited. Other ingredients are more recherché, such as the little-seen ratafia in the zingy Scarlet Letter (with U'Luvka and cherry liqueur). Drinks' history is revered here, with 'kangaroo' cocktails (martinis made with vodka rather than gin) a major feature, as in the Adam & Eve, made with Zubrówka, blackberries and Pêche de Vigne. House Millers Westbourne gin is also used with abandon, and contemporary references get a nod in mixes such as the Courtney Love (Plymouth gin, Finlandia vodka, green olives, French dry Vermouth and a splash of olive brine). Cocktail prices are around £8, £9.25 for the (Devaux Grand) champagne variety. Wine, plus bottled Asahi, Peroni and San Miguel, offer alternatives. Mixing and service from the zinc-topped bar counter match the ambition of the menu; candles, and a fire in winter, provide ambience. There are outdoor tables in summer.
Available for hire. Babies and children admitted (until 5pm). Function room (capacity 45). Tables outdoors (7, pavement). Map 7 B6.

South West
Parsons Green

The Establishment
45-47 Parsons Green Lane, SW6 4HH (7384 2418, www.theestablishment.com). Parsons Green tube. **Open** 5pm-midnight Tue-Fri; noon-midnight Sat; noon-10.30pm Sun. **Food served** 5-10.30pm Tue-Thur; noon-4pm, 6-10.30pm Sat; noon-4pm, 6-9.30pm Sun. **Credit** AmEx, DC, MC, V.
A very clever place indeed, this. Continually referencing its British roots, either by dint of decor (grainy images of Michael Caine and classic post-war film villains) or ingredients, this tidy establishment mixes a reverence for heritage with contemporary tastes. Take, for example, Phillips Lovage, an old English cordial distilled from Devon herbs and spices according to a secret recipe, here used in a Love On The Green cocktail (£7); or Malmesbury dry mead, which is stirred with Tanqueray gin in the Old English Martini. Moving north, but keeping tongue in cheek, Cariel premium Swedish vodka comes to the fore in the Porn Star Martini, with fresh passion fruit, champagne and vanilla sugar. Classic mixes are also given an Establishment twist, the muddled Braeburn apples and home-made hibiscus and basil cordial complementing El Jimador tequila in the margarita; the Plymouth sloe gin stirred with cassis and fresh berries in the Devon Spring Punch. Quick mention must be made of the encyclopaedic selection of gins (when did you last see a No.209 from San Francisco?) and 50-strong wine list.
Available for hire (restaurant, capacity 55). Babies and children admitted (until 5pm). Disabled: toilet. Function room (capacity 25). Tables outdoors (6, courtyard). Wireless internet; free.

South
Battersea

Lost Angel [NEW]
2009 RUNNER-UP BEST NEW BAR
339 Battersea Park Road, SW11 4LF (7622 2112, www.lostangel.co.uk). Battersea Park rail. **Open** noon-11pm Tue, Wed; noon-midnight Thur; noon-2am Fri, Sat; noon-11pm Sun. **Food served** noon-10pm Mon-Thur; noon-10.30pm Fri, Sat; noon-9pm Sun. **Credit** AmEx, MC, V.
You don't expect to find a bar like Lost Angel along this sorry-looking stretch of the Battersea Park Road, but there is a precedent: this building was once home to Dusk, a bar-club that brought a little glamour to the street several years ago. Pleasingly, Lost Angel, from the folks behind nearby Lost Society, is an even more likeable place. The frontage reads 'Bar, Restaurant, Boozer', which is more a sign of genuine versatility than a management identity crisis. The range of drinks covers most bases: the three ales may include Wandle from Sambrook's Brewery, while the

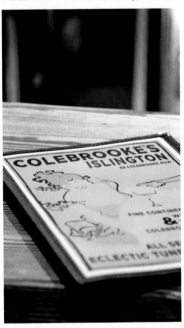

69 Colebrooke Row. See p323.

DRINKING

cocktail list is split between classics, reinventions, and shouldn't-work-but-do corruptions (a mojito made with pomegranate juice and gin, for instance). It's all served within an eye-catching interior that falls pleasingly between corner pub (tiles, dark wood, central bar) and modish bar (trombones on the ceiling, white phone box, mirrors galore); there's also a nice little garden at the back. The kitchen offers poshed-up bar food, and entertainment runs from DJs to quiz nights; service couldn't be friendlier. This will never be a charming street, but it's good to see a little light emanating from it.

Babies and children admitted (until 6pm). Entertainment: DJs 9pm Fri, Sat; live music 5pm alternate Sun. Function room (capacity 80). Tables outdoors (18, garden). Wireless internet; free.

Clapham

The Loft

67 Clapham High Street, SW4 7TG (7627 0792, www.theloft-clapham.co.uk). Clapham North or Clapham South tube. **Open** 6pm-midnight Tue-Thur; 5pm-1.30am Fri, Sat; noon-midnight Sun. **Food served** 6-10pm Tue-Thur; 5-10pm Fri; 5-9pm Sat; noon-7pm Sun. **Credit** AmEx, MC, V.

Despite being an award winner, this first-floor bar, with panoramic picture windows, is still missed by the party-hunting 20-year-olds who trawl Clapham High Street. There's little reason to enter its inconspicuous doorway unless you already know what lies within. A savvy Italian management has sited the best selection of cocktails in SW4 amid spacious, slightly industrial surroundings, nine black swivel bar chairs lining a long slab of bar counter. Of the 30 options (plus sharing jugs and shooters), house specials such as the Blueberry Collins (£7.50) of home-made blueberry gin and grape juice, and the Wonderfizz of Whitley Neill gin, pomegranate juice and home-made grenadine, stand out. Further inventions include Holy Stone Roller, with cranberry-infused bourbon, sarsparilla cordial and Calvados liqueur, and the Pink Swizzle, with Sagatiba Cachaça, home-made spiced Caribbean syrup and home-made citrus and cardamom bitters. Bottled beers include Brahma, Paulaner, Moretti and Negra Modelo. Tables round the corner from the main bar accommodate diners tucking into Loft burgers of Scottish beef.

Available for hire (Restaurant; capacity 50). Babies and children admitted (restaurant). Disabled: toilet. Entertainment: DJs 9.30pm Fri, Sat; 4.30pm Sun; free. **Map 22 B1.**

Lost Society

697 Wandsworth Road, SW8 3JF (7652 6526, www.lostsociety.co.uk). Clapham Common tube/ Wandsworth Road rail/77, 77A bus. **Open** 5pm-1am Tue-Thur; 5pm-2am Fri; noon-2am Sat, Sun. **Food served** 5-10pm Tue-Sun. **Admission** £5 after 9pm Fri, Sat. **Credit** AmEx, MC, V.

Lost Society? You must be joking! They're all here, spunking their bonuses on £6.75-a-pop Bartender's Bad Boy Creation cocktails, gossiping in the small square of courtyard garden while picking at the meagre meat platter (£14) or better-value Oriental plate (£8). For the quality of ingredients and mixing, the 60-long cocktail list is an affordably handsome proposition, the aforementioned Bad Boy Creations including a Basilimo, containing Havana Especial rum and Midori Melon liqueur with basil leaves and pear jam, and an Apple Rubarbski, with Godminster rhubarb-infused vodka, Cherry Marnier, cinnamon syrup and cherry jam. Both are inventions of barman LL Cool Luke. Mr Luke is also responsible for Society's Mac (Maker's Mark infused with goji berries and honeycomb, muddled with ginger wine), one of a dozen in the Twisted Bartender range. Wines too, are at standard prices, from the White Australian Viognier to the Château de Thauvenay Sancerre. Beers are bottled and quite obscure, whether from New Zealand (Monteith's Lager), America (Flying Dog, Old Scratch), Suffolk (St Peter's Honey Porter) or Brighton (Dark Star Espresso Stout).

Available for hire. Entertainment: DJs 7pm Thur; 9pm Fri, Sat. Tables outdoors (20, garden). **Map 22 A1.**

South East
Blackheath

Zerodegrees

29-31 Montpelier Vale, SE3 0TJ (8852 5619, www.zerodegrees.co.uk). Blackheath rail. **Open** noon-midnight Mon-Sat; noon-11.30pm Sun. **Food served** noon-11pm Mon-Sat; noon-10.30pm Sun. **Credit** AmEx, MC, V.

With branches in Bristol, Reading and Cardiff, and a mission 'to create internationally inspiring gourmet dishes and exceptional freshly brewed beers', Zerodegrees brings a mainly young clientele to its sunken restaurant and two-floor bar and pizzeria on the edge of Blackheath village. It's all open plan, the preparing of fire-roasted pizzas providing visual entertainment when the match isn't occupying the four large screen at one end: you may have to wait for a dining table or book the TV sofas on big-game nights. Behind the bar, huge copper vats contain the four house brews, uniformly priced in half-pint (£1.50), pint (£2.80) and four-pint (£10.25) measures. There's Czech-type pilsner, US-style pale ale, a chocolatey black lager, and the Belgian-influenced wheat variety. All are also available in take-home kegs. Special and seasonal ales, and fruit beers are also produced, but the bar area could do with more signposting – non-regulars could do with a little more hand holding. Standard Sicilian D'Istinto from Calatrasi provides the house wine in chardonnay and sangiovese-merlot varieties.

Available for hire (restaurant, capacity 180). Babies and children welcome: high chairs. Tables outdoors (10, terrace). Wireless internet; free.

London Bridge & Borough

Hide Bar

39-45 Bermondsey Street, SE1 3XF (7403 6655, www.thehidebar.com). London Bridge tube/rail. **Open** 10am-midnight Mon, Tue; 10am-1am Wed, Thur; 10am-2am Fri; 5pm-2am Sat. **Food served** noon-4pm, 5.30-10pm Mon-Fri; 5.30-10pm Sat. **Credit** AmEx, MC, V.

A connoisseur's cocktail-and-spirit bar, though you wouldn't know it from the somewhat drab location near the London Bridge railway viaduct. The Hide Bar has ridden out the credit crunch with aplomb, filling to the gills from Thursday nights onwards with nine-to-fivers happy to be sinking quality mixed drinks near a transport hub. There's even a Credit Crunch cocktail (£4) of Beefeater gin, cranberry juice and Triple Sec. Other cocktails are priced at £6.50-£7, including the house specials such as the Passionate Englishman (Hendrick's gin stirred with passion fruit purée), the Bermondsey Martini (Jensen's Bermondsey gin, Noilly Prat vermouth) and the Hide & Seek, of bourbon, maple syrup and grapefruit juice. Thirty-odd other options are available, plus a selection of spirits that would put nearly every other bar in London to shame – all sold by the glass. Vintage armagnacs go back 50 years. Wines are equally well sourced – you won't find Francis Ford Coppola's Director's Cut Zinfandel in too many places. Light lunches involve the likes of minute steak sandwiches, Brazilian seafood chowder and wild boar and Chimay sausages.

Available for hire. Babies and children admitted (until 6pm). Entertainment: drinks tasting alternate Tue; £10. Function room (capacity 50). **Map 12 Q9.**

Rake

14 Winchester Walk, SE1 9AG (7407 0557). London Bridge tube/rail. **Open/snacks served** noon-11pm Mon-Fri; 10am-11pm Sat. **Credit** AmEx, MC, V.

When asked how often his team change the draught options here (seasonally? monthly?), the barman casually replied that it depended on consumption – perhaps every day, perhaps every couple of days. The Veltins lager and Maisels Weiße taps stay in place. Therefore to say this blue-fronted cubicle of a bar has Aechte Schlenkerla Rauchbier (a rare smoked variety from Bamberg), Jenlain, Meteor Pils and Grisette, Fruits Des Bois,

on tap, may not be true tomorrow, or the next day. What is sure is that, as the yellow sign says above the bar, 'No crap on tap'. What is also sure is that they will be replaced by equally recherché global varieties (note the mounted advertising for St Feuillien, Stiegl and Alhambra from Granada); and, furthermore, that they only represent the tip of a beery iceberg, as displayed in two barman-sized fridges behind the two metres of bar counter. Draught beers are offered in third-of-a-pint measures, just in case a perhaps unusual taste isn't to your liking. A slightly larger square of beer garden caters for the regular overflow of customers on busy Borough Market days.

Babies and children admitted (outside decking). Disabled: toilet. Tables outdoors (7, decking). **Map 11 P8.**

East
Bethnal Green

Bistrotheque Napoleon Bar (100)

23-27 Wadeson Street, E2 9DR (8983 7900, www.bistrotheque.com). Bethnal Green tube/ rail/Cambridge Heath rail/55 bus. **Open** 6pm-midnight Tue-Sat; 4-11pm Sun. **Credit** AmEx, MC, V.

What looks like an East End warehouse is actually one of east London's most noteworthy establishments. Don't look for any garish neon signs, though; a few picnic tables – usually full of animated young smokers – is all that marks the entrance. Once inside, stairs lead you to the restaurant on the top floor. The bar runs down the side of the building and, in contrast to the light, white and airy eaterie up top, is all dark wood, plush armchairs and flickering lights. Glasses of wine come in dinky little tumblers, a nice touch. Cocktails include the moreish passionfruit caipirinha – Sagatiba Cachaca rum with fresh passion fruit, lime and passion fruit syrup. On performance nights, the tiny cabaret room next door keeps the bar full to bursting before and after shows. Sound levels vary – sometimes too loud, sometimes too quiet; sit close to the door and you'll hear occasional flushing water from the pipes. But this lo-fi approach is part of what makes Bistrotheque such a wonderfully unpolished and much-loved sort of place.

Babies and children admitted. Disabled: toilet. Entertainment: cabaret (dates vary, ticket only). Function room (capacity 64).

Shoreditch

★ Calloch Callay NEW
2009 RUNNER-UP BEST NEW BAR

65 Rivington Street, EC2A 3AY (7739 4781). Old Street tube/rail. **Open/food served** 5-11pm Mon-Thur, Sun; 4pm-1am Fri; 5pm-1am Sat. **Credit** MC, V.

At first glance, this Rivington Street newcomer looks like just another Shoreditch bar. Storefront location? Check. Hipster staff? Check. Mismatched furniture offset by self-consciously quirky design touches (a wall of cassettes outside the toilets, modified gramophones on the bar, a page of the drinks list devoted to 'Random Shit')? Check and check. However, the most appealing characteristics of this Lewis Carroll-inspired bar aren't immediately apparent from the street. For a start, there's the room at the back, hidden behind a heavy wardrobe door (not a looking glass, but it's a nice touch regardless). It is a very handsome little space, designed in a similar way to the front area but far more atmospheric. And for seconds, there's an inventive cocktail list, heavy on unusual and obscure spirits (and light on actual description; not everyone knows that, for instance, Mozart Black is a chocolate liqueur) but with its fair share of classics. We enjoyed a pungent sazerac along with a floral, gin-based sherbert, though the signature drink is a massive tiki punch served in one of the aforementioned gramophones and designed for sharing. Fun, all told.

Available for hire. Disabled: toilet. Entertainment: DJs 8pm Fri, Sat. Separate room for parties (capacity 40-50). **Map 6 R4.**

Green & Red

51 Bethnal Green Road, E1 6LA (7749 9670, www.greenred.co.uk). Liverpool Street tube/rail/ 8, 26, 48 bus. **Open** 5.30pm-midnight Mon-Thur; 5.30pm-2am Fri, Sat; 5.30-10.30pm Sun. **Food served** 6-11pm Mon-Sat; 6-10pm Sun. **Credit** AmEx, MC, V.

Named after the green and red of the Mexican flag, its large Sol-sponsored mural of a Latin American street scene perfectly suiting the cantina feel, G&R attracts people going to the nearby Rich Mix cinema arts complex and couples happy to pick at plates of meatballs or octopus ceviche. There is also some serious drinking to be done, for which the low-level brown slouchy sofas and Chamucos late-night basement bar may be more suitable. At the end of the working day, young professionals necking bottles of Sol fill the modest front terrace. Tequilas of every shape, size and era occupy the back bar, the standard pour put to best use in the popular Lolita cocktail (£6.90), along with pomegranate juice, lemonade and lime, served long ('sexy, elegant, simply beautiful'). Or there are any number of shot combinations, although the bar counter is a little too small and busy to get a really messy night going on the slammers. There are salsa classes on Mondays, perhaps handy when the occasional DJ spins downstairs.
Babies and children admitted: high chairs. Disabled: toilet. Entertainment: DJs 9pm Fri, Sat; free. Wireless internet; free. **Map 6 S4.**

Loungelover (100)

1 Whitby Street, E1 6JU (7012 1234, www.lounge lover.co.uk). Liverpool Street tube/rail. **Open** 6pm-midnight Mon-Thur, Sun; 5.30pm-1am Fri; 6pm-1am Sat. **Food served** 6-11.30pm Mon-Fri, Sun; 7-11.30pm Sat. **Credit** AmEx, DC, MC, V.

First, the cocktails. Often brilliant, they involve deft mixes such as Citadelle raspberry vodka with white cranberry and grape juice (Love Letter, £7.50); red peppers, passion fruit and Creole Shrubb spiced orange rum served short and frappé (Pepperita, £8.50); and fig liqueur and lemon oil with prosecco (Loungelover, £9). Second, the pricing policy. An initial 'discretionary' 12.5% service charge on drinks is later followed by a Mexican stand-off over the card-swipe as you are invited to negotiate its tricky buttons to either add even more gratuity or stick at 12.5%, all the while under the anticipative glare of your black-uniformed waiter. To be fair, you will have been shown to your table and served during your stay; bar space is at a premium. Food comprises sushi and hot Japanese snacks, teriyaki chicken and the like. The jury is still out on the decor, a jarring mish-mash of baroque, kitsch and exotic, perhaps not the 'seamless marriage of old and new' suggested by the management, which is responsible for nearby Les Trois Garçons.
Booking advisable. Disabled: toilet. **Map 6 S4.**

Sosho

2 Tabernacle Street, EC2A 4LU (7920 0701, www.sosho3am.com). Moorgate or Old Street tube/rail. **Open** noon-1am Wed, Thur; noon-3am Fri; 7pm-4am Sat; 10pm-6am Sun. **Food served** noon-10pm Wed, Thur; noon-11pm Fri, Sat. **Admission** free-£12 after 9pm Fri, Sat **Credit** AmEx, DC, MC, V.

It's a rare club that looks the part in daylight hours, but, perhaps because it was once a photographic studio, Sosho certainly does. Visit when the sun's up and floods of natural light stream into the two-floored space, which has bare brick walls covered in modern – mostly street – art. Sosho's part of the Match Bar empire which, since opening its first branch in 1997, has spread from Clerkenwell to the West End via Old Street and now has outposts in Ibiza and Melbourne. For all its Shoreditch cool, there are no lukewarm drinks halfheartedly served in cracked glasses here – the barfolk take their cocktails very seriously indeed. After a consultation worthy of any West End hairdresser (only with more laughs and flirty banter from the Spanish barman), we were presented with a Match Spring Punch (£7.25) – vodka with lemon juice, raspberries, cassis and framboise, topped with champagne – and a Long Mango, with cranberry, lime juice and passionfruit cutting through the sweet mango purée. There's plenty here, too, for the local party people: club nights take in house and electronic sounds.
Babies and children admitted (until 6pm). Disabled: toilet. Entertainment: DJs 8pm Wed-Fri; 9pm Sat, Sun. Function room (capacity 100). Wireless internet; free. **Map 6 Q4.**

North

Camden Town & Chalk Farm

Gilgamesh

Stables Market, Chalk Farm Road, NW1 8AH (7482 5757, www.gilgameshbar.com). Camden Town tube. **Open** 6pm-2.30am Mon-Thur; noon-2.30am Fri-Sun. **Food served** noon-3pm, 6-11pm daily. **Credit** AmEx, MC, V.

Hidden at the Camden Town end of Stables Market, and reached by escalator between ornate walls carved with Ancient World-style motifs, Gilgamesh feels part Mesopotamian epic, part Cecil B DeMille. Once shown to your seat in the expansive main bar/restaurant (reserve at weekends), you'll still be gawping long after the thick drinks menu has been delicately offered. Drinks are also themed along Babylonian lines: the Sun God Anu is celebrated in martini form with Absolut Peach, Bombay gin, peach and cucumber (£9.50); the Sumerian city of Shuruppak is honoured with 42 Below vodka, apricot, peach, watermelon, berries and pineapple. Even the mocktails are named after the Tigris and Euphrates, and involve a whole mess of cranberry,

lychee, pink grapefruit and rose petal. Fresh juices include guava and passion fruit. The only beer is Tiger, from Singapore – surely somebody could have dug up a bottle of ancient Sumerian Ninkasi? Note that 12.5% is added to your bill – although the many customers ordering prime spirits by the bottle (£110) won't be batting an eyelid at the cost.
Babies and children admitted. Entertainment: DJs 8pm Fri, Sat; free. Function room (capacity 500). **Map 27 C1**.

Islington

Elk in the Woods
39 Camden Passage, N1 8EA (7226 3535, www.the-elk-in-the-woods.co.uk). Angel tube. **Open** 8.30am-11pm daily. **Food served** 8.30am-10.30pm daily. **Credit** MC, V.
Having started out as a bar, the Elk presents more of a gastro face during busy lunchtimes, but regulars aren't discouraged from ordering up a Cucumber Martini (with Hendrick's gin, £8) or Tobia Rioja and occupying a wooden table for a while. Martinis, seven in number (Polish with Zubrówka Bison Grass vodka, Watermelon & Basil with Pinky vodka) dominate the cocktail list, but you'll also find zingy options such as a Grapefruit Mojito (with Matusalem Classico and fresh mint) or the Elderflower Fizz (with Buffalo Trace bourbon). Draught beers include Sagres, Kronenbourg and Theakston's ale, with bottled Moretti, Corona and Asahi alongside, and there are a few non-alcoholic cocktails to choose from: the Orange & Ginger Zing (orange juice, freshly squeezed lemon, ginger ale) hits the spot. The Elk is also a place for a quality breakfast, with the likes of duck egg with asparagus, sausage and toast dippers, and rare-breed lamb burger in torteno roll with grilled courgette and mint jelly.
Babies and children admitted. Booking advisable. Tables outdoors (4, pavement). **Map 5 O2**.

★ Lexington NEW
96 Pentonville Road, N1 9HS (7837 5371, www.thelexington.co.uk). Angel tube. **Open** noon-2am Mon-Thur; noon-4am Fri, Sat; noon-midnight Sun. **Food served** noon-3pm, 5-11pm Mon-Fri; noon-10pm Sat, Sun. **Credit** AmEx, MC, V.
Situated in the building that for a number of years housed La Finca, the Lexington is an unexpectedly handsome place. Many punters head here for the roomy music venue on the first floor, which stages an assortment of indie-ish bands and club nights throughout the week. But the ground-floor bar is open to all (you only need to pay an admission charge if you go upstairs), and is worthy of investigation in its own right. There's little pretence at inatimacy: the decor offers a few swanky touches (plush lampshades, heavy red curtains), but this is basically a big, tall corner room with bells on. The real selling point, though, is the array of American drinks: the list of unusual beers include potent, flavourful brews from the likes of Goose Island in Chicago, and the array of rare American whiskeys is, if anything, even more tempting. Food options include po'boys, hotdogs, burgers and nachos. The clientele seems to be largely made up of people taking a break from the show upstairs, preferring the appetising jukebox to the presumably avoidable support bands.
Babies and children admitted (until 7pm). Entertainment: live music 8pm daily; DJs 10pm Fri-Su; free-£8. Function room (capacity 200). Wireless internet; free. **Map 5 N2**.

★ 69 Colebrooke Row NEW
2009 WINNER BEST NEW BAR
69 Colebrooke Row, N1 8AA (07540 528593, www.69colebrookerow.com). Angel tube. **Open** 5pm-midnight Mon-Wed; 5pm-1am Thur; 5pm-2am Fri, Sat. **Credit** AmEx, MC, V.
Tucked away off the Islington Green end of Essex Road, 69 Colebrooke Row bears an impressive pedigree. Opened in mid 2009, it's the brainchild of Tony Conigliaro, familiar to keen-eyed cocktail hounds for his work at the likes of Isola, Roka and Shochu Lounge, and Camille Hobby-Limon, who runs the much-garlanded Charles Lamb pub a couple of streets away. If the Charles Lamb is

Loungelover

diminutive, then 69 Colebrooke Row is positively microscopic: with just a handful of tables supplemented by a few stools at the bar, it may be smaller than your front room. The understated, intimate space proves a fine environment in which to enjoy the pristine cocktails, made with quiet ceremony by an elegantly bow-tied Conigliaro on our visit (which came a week after he'd won the International Bartender of the Year award at the Tales of the Cocktail wing-ding in New Orleans). We were particularly impressed by a wonderfully smooth liquorice whisky sour. But for all the excellence of the drinks, it's the little touches (impeccably dressed staff, handwritten bills, tall glasses of water poured from a cocktail shaker) that elevate this lovely enterprise from the pack.
Booking advisable. Entertainment: pianist 8pm Tue. **Map 5 O2**.

25 Canonbury Lane
25 Canonbury Lane, N1 2AS (7226 0955). Highbury & Islington tube/rail. **Open** 5pm-midnight Mon-Thur; 4pm-1am Fri; noon-1am Sat; 1pm-12.30am Sun. **Food served** 6-10pm Mon-Thur; 1pm-1am Fri; noon-1am Sat; 1pm-12.30pm Sun. **Credit** AmEx, MC, V.
Regulars enjoy the intimacy of neat, petite 25 Canonbury Lane – the main room is just bigger than the average corner newsagent's – and the fact that the chatty staff can fix a proper cocktail, strong and fruity. As in the name, there are 25 in number (and 25 wines of each colour too). They include a Raspberry Sling (£7.50), with Grey Goose vodka, muddled fresh raspberries and Pimm's; Negronis, with Bombay Sapphire gin, Martini Rosso and Campari, and martinis. Or find your spot on the squishy brown sofa or counter barstool and call up a Belvedere Espresso Martini with Illy coffee, Toussaint dark coffee liqueur, white chocolate cocoa and the eponymous vodka; or a French Martini with Finlandia, Chambord liqueur and pineapple juice. If that sounds a bit girly (and it's fair to tell you that your table will probably be topped by a single rose), then beers include Beck's Vier and Grolsch, or Tiger, Asahi or Sol by the

bottle. A concise menu for lunch, served until 4pm, includes Ginger Pig bangers 'n' mash and hot roast porchetta or lamb rolls.
Babies and children admitted (until 7pm).

North West

Kensal

Paradise by Way of Kensal Green
19 Kilburn Lane, W10 4AE (8969 0098, www.theparadise.co.uk). Kensal Green tube/ Kensal Rise rail. **Open** noon-midnight Mon-Wed; noon-1am Thur; noon-2am Fri, Sat; noon-11.30pm Sun. **Food served** noon-2.30pm, 6.30-10.30pm Mon-Sat; noon-9.30pm Sun. **Credit** MC, V.
Paradise makes decorative use of its name, taken from GK Chesterton's 'The Rolling English Road', by filling its high-ceilinged interior with religious icons, angels, cherubs, flowery chandeliers and so on, extending the allegory to two huge stone vases of flowers on the bar counter. There you'll find prices to be more than reasonable for the quality of mixing (very good) and service (ditto): a mojito will set you back £6.50, a margarita likewise. Wines by the glass, ten in number, include the house Malbec, and Campo Nuevo Viura, an organic Chilean sauvignon blanc from Soleus. By the bottle you'll find an organic Jean-Marc Brocard Chablis (2006) and a Château La Croix de Grezard, Lussac-St-Emilion (2003). Beers include a Shepherd Neame Spitfire, plus the standard lagers at standard prices. With banquet-sized dining hall, courtyard garden and roof terrace, Paradise does a roaring trade in private dining, so bar snacks here are easily a notch above the norm: grilled monkfish and garlic butter, Poole harbour rock oysters and shallot dressing and grilled Goosnargh chicken skewers with coronation sauce.
Babies and children admitted until 8pm. Entertainment: bands/DJs/comedy (check website for details); quiz 7.30pm 1st Thur of mth £2. Function rooms (capacity 40-150). Wireless internet; free.

Pubs

With traditional boozers going out of business at a frightening rate, often to be replaced by outposts of soulless bar chains, the fight is on to save the British pub. The places we list here offer something above the norm, whether it's original Victorian features, a riverside setting, or some of the striking and unusual beers and ciders that can now be found in London: organic bitter and cider from Suffolk, perhaps, extra stout from Yorkshire, or traditional London porter – and that's before you start exploring the Belgian fruit beers, and the German, Californian and Japanese options available on tap. For pubs where food is a large part of the offer, see the **Gastropubs** chapter (pp102-116).

Central

Bloomsbury

Duke
7 Roger Street, WC1N 2PB (7242 7230, www.dukepub.co.uk). Chancery Lane, Holborn or Russell Square tube. **Open** noon-11pm Mon-Sat; noon-10.30pm Sun. **Food served** noon-10pm Mon-Sat; noon-9.30pm Sun. **Credit** MC, V.
Down a mews beside a school is a slice of London from between the wars: heavy-framed mirrors, long-leafed plants, a black bakelite phone and amusing deco details (pale green glass in the shape of a whipped ice-cream, a nymph cavorting under a lamp). The main bar has scuffed lino, wooden booths and, as if a warbly 'When You're Smiling' and Billie Holiday on the stereo weren't front-parlour enough, a red-painted piano. A couple of real ales (Black Sheep Best, Adnams Broadside) are served – our pint topped up without our having to ask, despite there being a rush on at the bar – as well as Staropramen and plenty of whiskies. The secluded location keeps the few street-side tables tranquil, and a tea-candlelit dining room has an unambitious menu (chargrilled sea bass, pork cutlet, sausage of the week) at £12.50 for two courses and a glass of wine. Otherwise, cheap beer fodder sustains a nicely mixed crowd of student girls in vintage garb and well-fed architects tightly belted into their suit trousers.
Babies and children admitted. Tables outdoors (3, pavement). **Map 14 M4.**

★ **Lamb**
94 Lamb's Conduit Street, WC1N 3LZ (7405 0713). Holborn or Russell Square tube. **Open** 11am-midnight Mon-Sat; noon-10.30pm Sun. **Food served** noon-9pm daily. **Credit** AmEx, MC, V.
The venerable Lamb does justice to the term 'historic'. In operation for 280 years, this relaxing Young's pub is characterised by its Victorian period, when stars of the stage and music hall would frequent it. Black and white publicity shots of Lillian Braithwaite, Seymour Hicks and contemporaries form two decorative rows across the walls of a cosy, varnished-wood interior. The standard range of Young's beers, plus Heineken and Guinness, are dispensed from the central horseshoe bar. Around it are ringed original etched-glass snob screens, used to prevent Victorian gentlemen from being seen when liaising with 'women of dubious distinction'. They would have been wooed by tunes from the polyphon, a 19th-century music machine still standing in the corner. A sunken back area known as the Pit gives access to a convenient square of summer patio. Upstairs, the Empire Theatre bar can be hired out. The stand-out dishes are British and well sourced

(Exmouth beefburger, free-range Devonshire chicken breast, Exmoor rump steak) and there's sticky toffee pud or chocolate cheesecake for afters. *Children admitted (until 6pm). No piped music or jukebox. Tables outdoors (3, patio; 3, pavement).* **Map 4 M4.**

City

Castle
26 Furnival Street, EC4A 1JS (7405 5470). Chancery Lane tube. **Open** 11am-11pm Mon-Fri. **Food served** noon-3pm, 6-9pm Mon-Thur; noon-3pm Fri. **Credit** MC, V.
This cosy, black-fronted pie-slice of a pub, set in a quiet corner of the City, is an unlikely place to find such a range of sought-after, quality ales. Redcar Bitter, Redcar Summer Ale, Harvest Moon, That Old Chestnut, Bank Top Bitter, Cavendish Gold and Salopian Oracle all featured on a recent visit, with the upcoming promise of Elgoods Mad Dog, Summer Solstice, Hare's Breadth and Orange Wheat Beer. Large taps of Peroni and Erdinger Weissbier cater for beer drinkers, as do bottled Cobra and Corona. Food is another important feature: doorstep sandwiches of slow-roasted leg of lamb with mint sauce, and rare topside of beef with horseradish, as well as home-made burgers, and bangers and mash. A dozen or so wines of both colours, by glass and bottle, include an Alsace pinot blanc and Gran Reserva Castillo San Carlos. A big fan by the bar counter gives relief in summer; fat candles in glasses provide atmosphere in winter. Hits of the '60s drown out commentary on the BBC News channel, but everything here is commendably low-key.
Children admitted (until 9pm). Function room (capacity 40). **Map 11 N6.**

Clerkenwell & Farringdon

★ **Fox & Anchor**
115 Charterhouse Street, EC1M 6AA (7250 1300, www.foxandanchor.com). Barbican or Farringdon tube/rail. **Open** 7am-11pm Mon-Fri; 8.30am-11pm Sat; 8.30am-7pm Sun. **Food served** 8-11am, noon-10pm Mon-Fri; 8.30-11am, noon-10pm Sat; 8.30-11am, noon-4.30pm Sun. **Credit** AmEx, MC, V.
Pristine mosaic tiling and etched glass scream 'sensitive refurbishment' from the moment you arrive at this Smithfield treasure. Inside, the dark wood bar is lined with pewter tankards (don't expect to be given one if you want to drink outside), while to the back is the Fox's Den – a series of small intimate rooms used for both drinking and dining. Local sourcing is a priority and pleasure: in addition to the own-label ale, cask beers on our last visit included Red Poll and Old Growler from Suffolk's Nethergate brewery, Purity Brewing Company's Mad Goose from Warwickshire and the rarely seen Adnam's Oyster.

Look to the bottles and there are plenty more delights – Harviestoun Schiehallion lager and Samuel Smith's superb organic fruit beers among them. Bar food ranges from pork scratchings, pickled eggs and cockles to generous mains – roasts, pies, steaks and burgers, with excellent chips cooked in goose fat. Even if you don't stay overnight in the seductively masculine bedrooms upstairs, you can drop by for breakfast (full montys, grilled kippers, egg and bacon rolls), accompanied by various hair-of-the-dog libations.
Babies and children admitted (until 7pm). Disabled: toilet. **Map 5 O5.**

Jerusalem Tavern ⑩
55 Britton Street, EC1M 5UQ (7490 4281, www.stpetersbrewery.co.uk). Farringdon tube/rail. **Open** 11am-11pm Mon-Fri. **Food served** noon-3pm Mon, Fri; noon-3pm, 6-9pm Tue-Thur. **Credit** AmEx, MC, V.
In premises that date back to the early 18th century (although the current shopfront wasn't added until 1810 and the place didn't open as a pub until the 1990s), the Jerusalem is wonderfully atmospheric. The wonky, green-painted, scratched-wood interior has two front tables and a fireplace partially screened off from the main room, which has a large fixed table at the back and a sweet little table raised up above the friendly melée of lawyers, media workers and businessmen who like a bit of heritage with their beer. That beer is the full seasonal range from the St Peter's Brewery – including Ruby Red Ale, Mild and Golden Ale – winningly served from a row of small wooden casks lined up behind the counter. Lager and cider are on tap, and there's a wine list, if you're so inclined. Decent food offerings range from lemon and pork sausages with mash and gravy to sourdough sandwiches with potato wedges. The place is small, so avoid the immediate after-work rush if you don't want to share a table.
Available for hire weekends. No piped music or jukebox. Tables outdoors (2, pavement). **Map 5 O4.**

Covent Garden

Lamb & Flag
33 Rose Street, WC2E 9EB (7497 9504). Covent Garden tube. **Open** 11am-11pm Mon-Thur; 11am-11.30pm Fri, Sat; noon-10.30pm Sun. **Food served** noon-3pm Mon-Fri; noon-4.30pm Sat, Sun. **Credit** MC, V.
Rose Street was not always the domain of tourists puzzlingly sipping pints of Bombardier or Harvey's Sussex Best. Squeezed between Garrick Street and the old Covent Garden market, this dog-leg alleyway was a part of prostitution and bare-knuckle bashes, the latter hosted at this historic, low-ceilinged tavern, then called the Bucket of Blood; Dryden was beaten up here in 1679; today's regulars are now more fittingly honoured with a photograph and a plaque – Robert 'Bob' Townley even has his flat cap framed in the back room. Space here is always at a premium – hence the pavement cluster on summer evenings. Along with Foster's and Heineken, Kirin Ichiban makes a welcome if pricy appearance as a draught lager option, although most seem to stick to bottled Corona, Beck's or Peroni. Food comprises ploughman's lunches (with brie, blue shropshire or cambozola) and doorstep sandwiches. Heartier meals (sausages, roasts) can be taken upstairs or in the back room. Two centuries' of mounted cuttings and caricatures amplify the sense of character and continuity.
Babies and children admitted (lunch only). Entertainment: jazz 7.30pm occasional Sun; free. No piped music or jukebox. **Map 18 D4.**

Fitzrovia

Green Man
36 Riding House Street, W1W 7ES (7580 9087, www.thegreenmanw1.co.uk). Goodge Street or Oxford Circus tube. **Open** noon-11pm Mon-Sat; noon-10.30pm Sun. **Food served** noon-10pm Mon-Sat; noon-9.30pm Sun. **Credit** AmEx, MC, V.

Cider may be what marks out the Green Man from the pack, but it's also a decent boozer in its own right. A young loquacious crowd comes to shout over the indie soundtrack and sample London's best choice of ciders and perries (11 on draught when we looked, with 20 more by the bottle). Weston's is well represented, and their Organic Vintage was our favourite draught tipple: a dry, still, smooth drink unsullied by sweeteners. Purists may blanch, but there are also such bottled concoctions as Brothers Pear and Strawberry; our choice for a sweeter drink would be a bottle of demi-sec cider from Normandy. Friendly young staff, regular events (including a monthly meeting of the London Air-Accordion Society) and a menu of superior pub grub (West Country burgers, warm goat's cheese salad) are further attractions. So too is the interior of this largely unspoiled Victorian pub: high plastered ceilings, bare floorboards and a cosy back area with padded leather banquettes and a large painting of London drinkers at play. There's a more mellow bar upstairs. *Entertainment: DJs/bands 7pm Fri; free. Function room (capacity 70). Tables outdoors (2, pavement).* **Map 9 J5.**

Holborn

Princess Louise
208-209 High Holborn, WC1V 7BW (7405 8816). Holborn tube. **Open** 11am-11pm Mon-Fri; noon-11pm Sat; noon-10.30pm Sun. **Food served** noon-2.30pm, 6-8.30pm Mon-Thur; noon-2.30pm Fri, Sat. **Credit** AmEx, MC, V.
With half-a-dozen ornately carved, sumptuously tiled bar areas under one high, stucco ceiling, the Princess Louise, set near the busy junction by Holborn tube, is a classic example of the Victorian public house in which drinking was segregated according to social class. Today, it's an across-the-board Sam Smith's pub, prices starting at an egalitarian £1.88 for a pint of standard bitter. Organic Wheat Beer, Extra Stout, and Pure Brewed and Alpine lagers from this Tadcaster brewery are also on tap; a fuller range is available by the big bottle in the fridges behind the horseshoe island bar. Sandwiches, baguettes and pub grub of jumbo sausages or scampi satisfy hungrier diners, who are also accommodated in the upstairs bar (open mealtimes only). London buses roll past the frosted glass windows as American tourists tentatively sample the strange dark ales at room temperature, while across the bar, regulars pass carefully calculated coinage over the counter without looking up from the racing form.
No piped music or jukebox. **Map 8 E2.**

Seven Stars
53 Carey Street, WC2A 2JB (7242 8521). Chancery Lane or Holborn tube. **Open** 11am-11pm Mon-Fri; noon-11pm Sat; noon-10.30pm Sun. **Food served** noon-10pm Mon-Fri; 1-10pm Sat; 1-9pm Sun. **Credit** AmEx, MC, V.
In the heart of London's legal district, the tiny Seven Stars is the spot where barristers bring their clients for champagne after winning a big case at the Royal Courts of Justice. Walls feature vintage film posters for flicks such as *A Pair of Briefs* and *Action for Slander*. In a glass display case is a copy of *Home From the Inn Contented*, a cookbook by landlady Roxy Beaujolais, and a sign that the simple pub food scrawled on the blackboard (herring with potato salad; bruschetta with piquillo peppers and anchovies; 'luxurious' chicken pie) is going to be a cut above the norm, well conceived and cooked with flair. Real ales are the tipple of choice and on our visit included Dark Star Hogshead and Old Chestnut as well as Adnams Broadside and bitter. The short list of wines by the glass is keenly priced at £3.95-£4.75 for 175ml. Seats at the tables covered with green and white checked oilcloth are hard to come by, but considerate bar staff do their best to alert customers to vacancies.
No piped music or jukebox. **Map 10 M6.**

Marble Arch

Mason's Arms
51 Upper Berkeley Street, W1H 7QW (7723 2131). Marble Arch tube. **Open** noon-11pm Mon-Thur, Sun; noon-11.30pm Fri, Sat. **Food served** noon-2.30pm, 6-9pm daily. **Credit** MC, V.
The Mason's is one of those pubs you're happy to stumble upon – unless you lived in this transitory neighbourhood just east of the Edgware Road, you're hardly likely to make a beeline for it. But, once having found it, you would be equally happy to discover draught options of Badger's Original, Tanglefoot and Hopping Hare, Stingo barley wine, Peroni, HB and HB Extra Cold. The interior couldn't be more publike, all dark wood and scuffed floorboards, the seating areas divided in two by a horseshoe bar counter manned by attentive, smiling young Spanish staff. There's food too: eight types of sandwiches or baguettes (steak and red onion chutney; ham, grain mustard and new potato salad), snacks (messy garlic bread, potato wedges) and mains ('Our Famous' Sussex Smokey with white and smoked fish in crumble, steak and Tanglefoot pie). Outdoor seating is overhung by baskets of greenery, while an upstairs space comes into good use on rare busy

evenings. All in all, the perfect place for a quiet pint or to conduct a discreet lunchtime affair.
Tables outdoors (7, pavement). **Map 8 F6.**

Marylebone

Windsor Castle
27-29 Crawford Place, W1H 4LJ (7723 4371). Edgware Road tube. **Open** 11am-11pm Mon-Thur; 11am-midnight Fri, Sat; noon-10.30pm Sun. **Food served** noon-3pm, 6-10pm Mon-Fri, Sun; 6-10pm Sun. **Credit** MC, V.
If Alf Garnett ever made it to heaven, this might be what it would look like. Royals in plate, porcelain and photographic form grimace for space with regimental crests and sundry souvenirs of National Service. No wonder the Handlebar (Moustache) Club chooses this as its meeting place. Plaques mark every drinking space, each dedicated to a cherished regular whose christian name reflects pre-war fashion, while signed photos of lesser British celebrities (Dennis Waterman, PC Snow from *Softly Softly*) testify to a relaxed bonhomie. Visiting Americans seem to like it, perhaps plumping for draught Guinness over the ale options (Adnams, Wadworth 6X, Bombardier) or choosing from the usual G&T, Blue Max Liebfraumilch by the glass (!) or a half-decent Mâcon Villages Cuvée Henri Bowlay Lugny. George Best in autograph-signing form presides atop a horseshoe bar counter, behind which an adept kitchen turns out Thai curries. Outside, tables clothed in green checks offer respite from the low-ceilinged, somewhat claustrophobic interior.
Babies and children admitted. Function room (capacity 60). Tables outdoors (5, pavement). **Map 8 F5.**

Soho

Crown & Two Chairmen
31-32 Dean Street, W1D 3SB (7437 8192, www.thecrownandtwochairmenw1.co.uk). Tottenham Court Road tube. **Open** noon-11pm Mon-Thur; noon-11.30pm Fri, Sat; noon-10.30pm Sun. **Food served** noon-10pm Mon-Sat; noon-9pm Sun. **Credit** AmEx, MC, V.
The darkly handsome Crown & Two Chairmen is a bit of a crowd-pleaser: there's real ale (of the three on offer, Sharp's Doom Bar – served in a liveried pint glass – was good value for the West End at £2.50), plenty of lager and cider on tap, cocktails long and short, and food that ranges from £3.50 weekday 'sandwich specials' or sharing platters for around a tenner, to more substantial pub grub. Bar stools at the windows allow singletons to entertain themselves with central

Windsor Castle

Old Ship

Soho streetlife, while a low-lit slouchy area of tattered red leather banquettes and red-beaded lampshades at the back gets the vote of courting couples. Quirky details – such as the 'Staff measurements' chalked up on a board (their heights, you may be relieved to learn, rather than anything more private), the 'Beer tastes better in a plastic glass' sign for those wanting to drink outside, and an 'I heart Soho' collage in a picture frame – appeal to the chatty, friendly mix of slumming business types and self-consciously bohemian media workers.
Babies and children admitted (until 6pm).
Map 17 B3.

Dog & Duck
18 Bateman Street, W1D 3AJ (7494 0697).
Tottenham Court Road tube. **Open** 10am-11.30pm Mon-Sat; noon-10.30pm Sun. **Food served** 10am-10pm Mon-Sat; noon-9pm Sun. **Credit** AmEx, MC, V.
A Soho landmark, the Dog & Duck is known for its literary heritage and ever-changing ale selection. A choice of Deuchar's IPA, Greene King IPA, Fuller's London Pride and Timothy Taylor Landlord confronted us on the week of our visit; a few days later and it would have been Sharp's Doom Bar, Brains SA, Cairngorm Nessie's Monster Mash and Newman's Mount Snowdon. Sausages are another feature: the likes of lincolnshire smokey, cumberland, and lamb and mint. Bloody Mary sausage is also one of the salad options. Surroundings are authentically vintage: etched mirrors, carved mahogany and so forth. The George Orwell room upstairs (where the writer celebrated a successful book launch) usually offers more room, while punters spill out on to the pavement below.
Babies and children admitted (dining area only).
Function room (capacity 35). **Map 17 C3**.

South Kensington

Anglesea Arms
15 Selwood Terrace, SW7 3QG (7373 7960,
www.capitalpubcompany.com). South Kensington tube. **Open** 11am-11pm Mon-Sat; noon-10.30pm Sun. **Food served** noon-3pm, 6.30-10pm Mon-Fri; noon-5pm, 6-10pm Sat; noon-5pm, 6-9.30pm Sun. **Credit** AmEx, MC, V.
This splendid pub, which was the local of both Dickens and DH Lawrence, is packed tight on summer evenings, the front terrace and wide main bar area filled with professional blokes chugging Adnams Broadside or Twickenham Naked Ladies, and their female equivalents putting bottles of Sancerre Gérard Flou on expenses. Solicitors may celebrate a successful case with a Châteauneuf-du-Pape Clefs d'Or Jean Deydier et Fils. But the Anglesea has always had more aura than the

average South Ken hostelry – perhaps it's the erotic painting of Fifi, the ghost that roams its cellar; perhaps it's the link with the Great Train Robbery, allegedly planned here. On quieter winter lunchtimes, it's the ideal place for a quality foreign lager (Kirin, Bitburger) and a heart-to-heart over a plate of squid linguine at one of the bottle-green banquettes overlooked by random portraits.
Babies and children admitted. Function room (capacity 70). No piped music or jukebox.
Map 14 D11.

West
Barons Court

Colton Arms
187 Greyhound Road, W14 9SD (7385 6956).
Barons Court tube. **Open** noon-3pm, 5.30-11.30pm Mon-Thur; noon-3pm, 5.30pm-midnight Fri; noon-4pm, 6.30pm-midnight Sat; noon-4pm, 6.30-11pm Sun. **Food served** noon-3pm Mon-Fri; noon-4pm Sat, Sun. **Credit** MC, V.
Far enough from the beaten track to attract only the occasional irregular, the Colton Arms is warming in winter (trusty fireplace) and convivial in summer ('Biergarten' out back). At one point, someone seems to have tried to generate a tourist trade by naming the toilets 'Sires' and 'Wenches' and hanging up all manner of tankards and horse brass – not to mention a royal crest of unknown European heritage – but visits by the Osaka branch of the Sharp's Doom Bar Beer Appreciation Club are few and far between. The Colton Arms serves Fuller's London Pride, Sharp's, standard lagers and basic food. A sturdy cash till, guarded by a portrait of a late-lamented mastiff, registers a pre-decimal ring-up and at one point a clock might chime. If this place were a little more Tardis-shaped (it does its best) you'd swear you were in an episode of *Doctor Who*.
Children admitted (garden). No piped music or jukebox. Tables outdoors (4, garden).

Hammersmith

Dove
19 Upper Mall, W6 9TA (8748 9474).
Hammersmith or Ravenscourt Park tube. **Open** 11am-11pm Mon-Sat; noon-10.30pm Sun. **Food served** noon-3pm, 6-9pm Mon-Fri; noon-4pm, 5-9pm Sat; noon-7pm Sun. **Credit** AmEx, MC, V.
On the Upper Mall embankment upriver from Hammersmith Bridge – amid the rowing clubs, dog-walkers and strategically placed park benches with river views – stand several pubs: the Dove is perhaps the best. Much is made of its history, a handbill detailing the comings and goings here of Charles II and Nell Gwynn as well as its makeover

as the Dove Coffee House in 1796; a photograph dated 1897 is one of the many visual nods to its prime location. As well as providing one of those duck-your-head heritage pub experiences, the Dove does great food, at a price – sandwiches, including rare roast beef, run at £9.50 each; the house burger and the slow-roasted pork belly with celeriac mash cost a fraction more. As Mr Fuller was one of the gentlemen involved in the 1796 takeover, it's no surprise to find the full range of Fuller's ales, Honeydew and Discovery included. Most, though, come here to sit in the vine-entangled conservatory or the riverside terrace overlooking the houseboats.
No piped music or jukebox. Tables outdoors (12, terrace). **Map 20 A4**.

Old Ship
25 Upper Mall, W6 9TD (8748 2593,
www.oldshipw6.com). Ravenscourt Park tube. **Open** 9am-11pm, **meals served** 9am-10pm daily. **Credit** AmEx, MC, V.
It's a long walk from Hammersmith Bridge – along a lazy bend in the Thames, a world away from belching buses and hideous intersections – but once you pass a few pubs to make it as far as this one, you'll be pleased you've made the trek. The boathouse feel of the airy building is continued in the maritime-themed decor of sailing paintings and iconography. Depending on which areas have been hired out, you should have a choice of outdoor seating upstairs or down, or a spot in the classy main bar/restaurant. Bitburger or Beck's by the bottle seem the best choices for lager drinkers, Young's or Well's Bombardier for ale aficionados. A long list of wines features New Zealand Cloudy Bay sauvignon blanc, Henry Bourgeois Sancerre Blanc and New Zealand Churton pinot noir (all in the £35-£45 range), as well as more affordable, standard options. Food is an attraction; try the venison lasagne or lamb shoulder with mash and vegetables. Sandwiches include brie, pear and watercress ciabatta, and ham and gruyère baguette.
Babies and children admitted. Function rooms (capacity 20-30). Tables outdoors (8, terrace; 12, riverside). Wireless internet; free. **Map 20 A4**.

Holland Park

Ladbroke Arms
54 Ladbroke Road, W11 3NW (7727 6648,
www.capitalpubcompany.com). Holland Park tube. **Open** 11am-11pm Mon-Sat; noon-10.30pm Sun. **Food served** noon-2.30pm, 7-9.30pm Mon-Fri; 12.30-2.45pm, 7-9.30pm Sat, Sun. **Credit** AmEx, MC, V.
The prominent, self-standing pub sign outside proudly declares 'Free House' and, indeed, the Ladbroke Arms is a law unto itself. Happy to cater

to monied fortysomethings sinking Sancerre on the sunny front terrace, and ale aficionados after a pint of Sharp's Cornish or Hogs Back Brewery's summer variety, the Ladbroke stands on a quiet, residential street in Holland Park lined with police cars attached to the station opposite. Decor in the light main bar is noteworthy, with an original 1920s poster for Fap'Anis ('celui des connoisseurs' and worth a few bob) on one side, another pre-war French ad for olive oil on the other. A back room fills with middle-aged chatter, while a narrow corridor behind provides peace and quiet for book-readers – every pub should have one. Dining is of the smart, upscale variety.
Babies and children admitted (dining only). No piped music or jukebox. Tables outdoors (12, terrace). **Map 7 A7**.

Kensington

Churchill Arms
119 Kensington Church Street, W8 7LN (7727 4242). High Street Kensington or Notting Hill Gate tube. **Open** 11am-11pm Mon-Wed; 11am-midnight Thur-Sat; noon-10.30pm Sun. **Food served** noon-10pm Mon-Sat; noon-9.30pm Sun. **Credit** AmEx, MC, V.
Not that most American tourists would know, but there seems to be a contradiction here. The Churchill, a celebration of the wartime leader in hostelry form (they even estimate the number of champagne bottles Winnie consumed), is in fact an Irish pub – didn't Ireland remain neutral during World War II? That notwithstanding, this is a fine, fine establishment, part homely tavern (serving Fuller's ESB, Discovery and London Pride, and George Gale Seafarer's Ale) and part Thai restaurant (serving dishes cooked to order in the butterfly-themed conservatory). There's wine too, nine of each colour, two each by the glass, including a Calafate malbec and Coastline chenin blanc. Character is provided by the lived-in feel and mass of junk – portraits of prime ministers and American presidents, the documented triumphs of the Clare GAA hurling team, shiny copper implements. The verdant frontage, embellished by an image of Churchill giving the V, is a regular winner in its category of the London in Bloom competition. Tourists love it, yes, but regulars include locals and not just the posh ones either.
Babies and children admitted (until 10pm). **Map 7 B8**.

Maida Vale

★ Prince Alfred & Formosa Dining Rooms
5A Formosa Street, W9 1EE (7286 3287). Warwick Avenue tube. **Open** noon-11pm Mon-Sat; noon-10.30pm Sun. **Food served** noon-3pm, 6.30-10pm Mon-Thur; noon-3pm, 6.30-10.30pm Fri, Sat; noon-9pm Sun. **Credit** MC, V.
So well preserved an example of Victorian interior design that it could almost be a life-sized model, this pub comprises a maze of partitioned snugs around an ornate main bar, each seemingly smaller than the next (did we miss the bottle saying 'Drink Me'?). In any case, the wow factor for first-time visitors is almost guaranteed, and there'll be more exclamation when the price of their pint becomes apparent – £4.20 for a Peroni, £4.13 for a Pilsner Urquell. There's Erdinger and Leffe at similar prices too. That notwithstanding, the Prince Alfred is an atmospheric spot for an intimate drink, on a quiet junction where Castellain Road, Warrington Crescent and Formosa Street meet. Once you've gawped at the interior, try and get a scuffed wooden table outside on the pretty tiled front patio.
Babies and children admitted. Disabled: toilet. Tables outdoors (2, pavement). **Map 1 C4**.

Warrington
93 Warrington Crescent, W9 1EH (7592 7960, www.gordonramsay.com). Maida Vale tube. **Open** noon-11pm Mon-Thur; noon-midnight Fri, Sat; noon-10.30pm Sun. **Food served** 5.30-10.30pm Mon-Thur; noon-2.30pm, 5.30-10.30pm Fri; noon-3pm, 6-10.30pm Sat; noon-9pm Sun. **Credit** AmEx, MC, V.

First, a word about the Warrington, pre-Gordon Ramsay. Built in 1857, it became – long after its heyday – the haunt of has-been glam-rockers and the Fulham punk fraternity. Sundry lurkers would mingle with members of Mud amid the Victorian frippery. The Boys' 'Ballad of the Warrington' summed up the scene nicely. Fast forward 30 years and it's a £5.2 million Gordon Ramsay gastropub – upstairs, that is. Downstairs has had a spruce-up and considerable improvement to its drink selection, but it's still the same old Warrington, all marble columns and art-nouveau friezes. So, gawp at the cherubs over the bar as you sip your Bonsecours Framboise raspberry ale (£3.95), draught Wells Banana Bread beer (£5) or Greene King Hen's Tooth (£5). The wine list includes many that are rarely available by the glass, including Domaine Colette Gros Chablis (£6.85). A standard Ayala Brut Majeur or Bergerie de la Bastide starts at £3.75. As for the bar menu, you'll pay a bit more for your ploughman's or bangers and mash with onion gravy, but it'll be quality. The black-clad staff may look like restaurant refugees, but they have been well trained in the intricacies of the drinks.
Babies and children admitted. Function room (capacity 14). Tables outdoors (6, pavement). **Map 1 C3**.

South West

Chelsea

King's Arms
190 Fulham Road, SW10 9PN (7351 5043, www.kingsarmschelsea.com). Bus 14, 211, 414. **Open** 11am-midnight Mon-Sat; noon-11pm Sun. **Food served** 11am-10pm Mon-Sat; noon-10pm Sun. **Credit** MC, V.
The former Finch's, once the haunt of thespian hellraisers from the 1960s, is now a high-ceilinged Young's pub. Despite touches of modernisation – arty black and white photos, TV sports on a smallish screen – the newly named King's Arms still has the feel of a classic pub, thanks to the glazed tiling and lived-in feel of its wood interior. Bombardier, Peroni and Leffe are the draught options accompanying the standard Young's range on the long, prominent bar counter. Wine drinkers have not been neglected, with JM Brocard Chablis available by the glass and bottle, as well as a Domaine la Condamine l'Evêque merlot cabernet. Food is an equally important part of the business here, with an express lunch menu for £5.95, which includes a 6oz Exmoor beefburger. More relaxed diners can take their time over a 28-day aged Exmoor rump steak.
Babies and children admitted. Wireless internet; free. **Map 13 C12**.

Colliers Wood

Sultan
78 Norman Road, SW19 1BT (8542 4532). Colliers Wood tube then 200 bus. **Open** noon-11pm Mon-Thur, Sun; noon-midnight Fri, Sat. **Credit** MC, V.
No beturbaned Muslim ruler beams out from the free-standing pub sign here, on a quiet residential road behind All Saints' Church in Mitcham, but an imposing black stallion, the Sultan, who sired many a champion racehorse in the 19th century. Step inside this homely community boozer and you'll find a detailed history of Selim, sire of Sultan – a suitable backdrop for the old geezers who sit around the bar studying the racing form and sipping affordable pints of Summer Lightning and other flagship ales produced by the Hop Back Brewery of Salisbury. (Soon to appear: First Gold at £2.60 a pint!) Also available are Chimera IPA and Honey Blonde from the Downton Brewery, also a Wiltshire concern. The saloon bar is named after Ted Higgins, one of the original cast members of Radio 4's *The Archers*. This is a lovely local, with a leafy beer garden and plenty of parking space, plus a beer club night on Wednesday. Everyone seems to know each other, but strangers can expect a warm welcome too.
Disabled: toilet. Entertainment: beer club 6pm Wed; free. Tables outdoors (8, garden).

Parsons Green

★ White Horse (100)
1-3 Parsons Green, SW6 4UL (7736 2115, www.whitehorsew6.com). Parsons Green tube. **Open** 9.30am-11.30pm Mon-Wed, Sun; 9.30am-midnight Thur-Sat. **Food served** 10am-10.30pm daily. **Credit** AmEx, MC, V.
Only a lack of ceiling fans stop the main bar of this renowed hostelry from feeling like something from the days of the Raj. The Victorian ceilings are airily high and wide windows with wooden venetian blinds let plenty of light into the bar. Chesterfield-style sofas surround huge tables, ideal for families and groups of friends, though the umbrella-covered pavement tables are most coveted. Expect plenty of turned-up collars, rugby shirts and pashminas, but the mix of customers is actually wider than you might imagine. There are usually six to eight handpumped ales served from the mahogany bar – on our visit Old Hooky, Fuller's bitter and Harvey's Best among them. And it doesn't stop there: look for the likes of Sierra Nevada pale ale, Jaipur IPA, Duvel Green, perry and kriek on tap, or choose from the list of 135 bottled beers. On a busy Sunday there were plenty of staff but they were achingly slow.
Babies and children admitted. Disabled: toilet. Function room (capacity 90). No piped music or jukebox. Tables outdoors (30, garden). Wireless internet; free.

Putney

Bricklayer's Arms
32 Waterman Street, SW15 1DD (8789 0222, www.bricklayers-arms.co.uk). Putney Bridge tube/Putney rail. **Open** noon-11pm Mon-Sat; noon-10.30pm Sun. **Food served** 5-10pm Mon-Sat; 1-10pm Sun. **Credit** MC, V.
There's something of a village-pub feel to this hostelry – Putney's first – which started life in 1826. Although it's since been surrounded by a modern housing estate, its historic prints and still-functioning games of nine-pin skittles and shove ha'penny lend a rustic feel, underlined by classic handpumps for such Timothy Taylor ales as Ram Tam, Dark Mild, Landlord, Best and Golden Best. There's Sambrook's Brewery Wandle too. Lager drinkers may opt for Budvar, San Miguel, Pilsner Urquell or Staropramen; Perry's cider is also available. A regular winner of awards in CAMRA's London regional section, the Bricklayer's Arms has had a chequered ownership of late, a family saga outlined on the wall, underscored by a fierce sense of independence and 'holding out against the chains'. 'We have no desire to be themed, modernised, sanitised! There's not a drizzled sun-dried tomato in sight,' it proclaims. Sadly, there's not much passing trade; Putney High Street is close by, but a world away.
Babies and children admitted (until 7pm). Tables outdoors (7, garden).

Wandsworth

Nightingale
97 Nightingale Lane, SW12 8NX (8673 1637). Clapham South tube/Wandsworth Common rail. **Open** 11am-midnight Mon-Sat; noon-midnight Sun. **Food served** noon-10pm daily. **Credit** AmEx, DC, MC, V.
A number of elements lift the Nightingale from its apparent status as just another Young's pub. Built in 1853 by Thomas Wallis, this cosy community local offers a fireplace and blankets in winter, and a back beer garden in summer, accessed through a conservatory decorated with museum artefacts depicting the history of the brewery. This vintage feel is continued with displays of Wills cigarette cards in the main bar, where you can pick up souvenir postcards or badges of the pub. Board games include Scrabble and Taboo, and there's a popular alfresco darts set-up in the beer garden. The standard Young's ale range is complemented by 15 wines, including Chablis Laroche and Château Moulin du Barrail Bordeaux Supérieur by the bottle.
Babies and children admitted (until 9pm). Tables outdoors (14, garden).

South

Clapham

Bread & Roses

68 Clapham Manor Street, SW4 6DZ (7498 1779, www.breadandrosespub.com). Clapham Common or Clapham North tube. **Open** 4-11pm Mon-Thur; 4pm-midnight Fri; noon-midnight Sat; noon-10.30pm Sun. **Food served** 6-9.30pm Mon-Fri; noon-9.30pm Sat; noon-6pm Sun. **Credit** MC, V.

A collaboration between the Battersea and Wandsworth Trades Union Council and the Workers Beer Company, Bread & Roses (named after the James Oppenheim poem inspired by an early industrial textile strike, the lines of which are written over the bar) is about far more than just fundraising or class struggle – it's a very good bar. Taps of Mad Goose pale ale, Sharp's Doom Bar, little-seen Stiegl, Budvar, Erdinger and Beck's Vier line the bar counter, behind which a fridge contains bottles of Vedett, Sierra Nevada, Pacifico Claro, Anchor Steam and Brooklyn Chocolate Stout. A better-stocked bar you'd be hard pressed to find. Wines start with a £3.50 South African shiraz and Chilean sauvignon blanc, rising to £27 for a New Zealand Matahiwi pinot noir. Entertainment is provided by a DJ in one corner, and a large screen for TV sports in the conservatory at the back, which gives access to the beer garden. There are terrace tables at the front too.
Babies and children admitted (until 9.30pm). Disabled: toilet. Entertainment: DJs/bands 9pm Thur-Sat; quiz 7.30pm 1st Wed of mth £2. Function room (capacity 100). Tables outdoors (15, garden; 8, patio). **Map 22 B1**.

South East

Greenwich

Greenwich Union

56 Royal Hill, SE10 8RT (8692 6258, www.greenwichunion.com). Greenwich rail/DLR. **Open** noon-11pm Mon-Fri; 11am-11pm Sat; 11.30am-10.30pm Sun. **Food served** noon-10pm Mon-Fri, Sun; 11am-10pm Sat. **Credit** MC, V.

The GU is not just a damn fine pub – it's the headquarters of Alistair Hook's successful mission to bring beers brewed according to true German tradition to the British public. Having learned his trade at the Weihenstephan School of Brewing in Munich, Hook set up his Meantime Brewery just west of the Greenwich Meridian, on the gentle slope of Royal Hill beside the Young's pub, Richard I. Six house draught options – Pale Ale, Single London Stout, Helles, Kölner, Wheat and Raspberry – complement two dozen or more international labels by the bottle, including the little-seen Schneider Aventinus, Aecht Schlenkerla Marzen (a smoked beer otherwise only available in its native Bamberg) and Cantillon Gueuze. Food runs from a humble bacon butty to chargrilled, aged rib eye Angus steak, and you'll also find wines (Spy Valley sauvignon blanc, Punto Alto pinot noir), fairtrade coffee and several types of tea. Throw in signature imagery by Hook's schoolmate Ray Richardson, some framed front covers from *Picture Post* and a small front terrace, and you have a very tidy operation indeed.
Babies and children admitted (until 9pm). Tables outdoors (12, garden). Wireless internet; free.

Herne Hill

Commercial

212 Railton Road, SE24 0JT (7733 8783, www.thecommercialhotelhernehill.co.uk). Brixton tube/rail then 3, 196 bus/Herne Hill rail. **Open** noon-midnight Mon-Thur; noon-1am Fri; 11am-1am Sat; 11am-midnight Sun. **Food served** noon-10pm Mon-Fri; 11am-11pm Sat; 11am-9pm Sun. **Credit** MC, V.

On a narrow bend opposite Herne Hill station, and a short bus hop from Brixton, the Commercial is a pleasurable pub to spend time in. A board in the trendified main bar proclaims 21 draught beers (including Red Stripe, Paulaner, Franziskaner,

Peroni and Beck's Vier), not to mention three ciders (Aspall's, Addlestones and Bulmers) and four ales (Fuller's London Pride, Marston's Pedigree, Bombardier and the little-known Morrissey Fox from York). There are two dozen snacks to choose from (including lamb kofta and duck quesadilla), sharing platters, sandwiches (fish finger, sirloin steak), burgers (topped with chorizo, emmenthal and so on), chunky chilli and other mains. Sundays feature several types of roast. You can opt for a single dessert (chocolate brownie, baked vanilla cheesecake or pavlova) or, for a real pig-out, a selection of all three for £4.95. Two expansive rooms of stripy furniture and contemporary colours, with Wi-Fi and board games, accommodate drinkers and diners. A pie-slice of back garden houses a handful of tables and umbrella heaters.
Babies and children admitted (until 6pm). Disabled: toilet. Tables outdoors (5, garden). Wireless internet; free. **Map 23 A5**.

London Bridge & Borough

Gladstone Arms

64 Lant Street, SE1 1QN (7407 3962). Borough tube. **Open** noon-11pm Mon-Fri; noon-midnight Sat; noon-10.30pm Sun. **Food served** noon-3pm daily. **Credit** MC, V.

Now the wing of libertine live-music den Filthy McNasty's, 'the Glad' is no longer a staid, empty corner pub in a forgotten backstreet of Borough. While the Victorian prime minister still glares from the massive mural on the outer wall, inside is now funky, freaky and candlelit. Gigs (blues, folk, acoustic) take place at one end of a cosy one-room space; opposite, a friendly bar dispenses pints of Red Stripe, Beck's Vier, Austell Tribute and Deuchar's IPA. Pies (conveniently from 'Pieminister') provide sustenance. A crammed back bar embellished by a retro 'On Air' studio sign manages to find space for bottles of Moretti, Früli, Corona, Peroni and Budvar. The retro feel is completed by the kind of clock you still might see on the platform of a provincial railway station in Slovakia. Live music is performed five nights a week, the programme chalked up on the wall. Lovers of board games should choose a Monday or Tuesday for that slow, strategic game of Risk.
Babies and children admitted (until 7pm). Entertainment: bands 8pm Sat, Sun. **Map 11 P9**.

Lord Clyde

27 Clennam Street, SE1 1ER (7407 3397, www.lordclyde.com). Borough tube. **Open** 11am-11pm Mon-Fri; noon-11pm Sat; noon-6pm Sun. **Food served** 11am-2.30pm, 5.30-11pm Mon-Fri; noon-5.30pm Sun. **Credit** AmEx, MC, V.

A haven of tranquillity in a Borough sidestreet bookended by Peabody Trust residences, the Lord Clyde is a lived-in home from home for middle-aged regulars and penny-conscious students. A Truman's landmark – note the pub sign outside and etched mirror within ('Unrivalled Mild Ales & Double Stout') – the Clyde now offers a multitude of brewery flagship ales: Young's, John Smith's Smooth, Fuller's London Pride, Greene King IPA, Adnams Bitter and Shepherd Neame Spitfire. Prices are more than reasonable but perhaps not as affordable as the 1/-6d pale ale on offer when England last won the World Cup, as revealed by a July 1966 price list mounted under a large TV linked up to Sky Sports. Draught lagers comprise Stella and San Miguel, glugged by regulars playing darts in a back room otherwise decorated by a print depicting the Battle of Balaclava, Lord Clyde's heroic stand of the Crimean War. Pictures of ships and Spitfires, and an old Player's cigarette ad, continue the armed forces theme.
No piped music or jukebox. Tables outdoors (2, pavement). **Map 11 P8**.

East

Brick Lane

Carpenter's Arms

73 Cheshire Street, E2 6EG (7739 6342, www.carpentersarmsfreehouse.com). Liverpool Street tube/rail. **Open** 4-11.30pm Mon; noon-

11.30pm Tue-Thur, Sun; noon-12.30am Fri, Sat. **Meals served** 4-10pm Mon; 1-10pm Tue-Sun. **Credit** MC, V.

On an undistinguished corner beyond Cheshire Street's illustrious boutiques, the buzzy Carpenter's looks tiny from the outside, but wasn't overwhelmed on the Sunday market afternoon of our most recent visit. The handsome wood decor and old black-and-whites of Brick Lane in the barroom are glammed up with chandeliers, mirrors and an appropriately expressionless painting of the Kray brothers (who bought a previous incarnation of this place for their dear old ma). There's a second cosy room that opens on to a neat, heated deck that combines hanging ivy and a neoclassical statuette. The drinks selection is great, including three beers on hand pump (among them a nice pint of Adnams) and separate blackboards listing wines and bottled beers (the latter, pleasingly, has a British section alongside the Belgians). The cut-above food (boards of cheese or charcuterie, home-made chips, Sunday roasts) isn't sold at stupid prices, and the clientele is fashionably Hoxditch without making a song and dance about it.
Babies and children admitted (until 5pm). Tables outdoors (6, garden). Wireless internet; free.

Pride of Spitalfields

3 Heneage Street, E1 5LJ (7247 8933). Aldgate East tube. **Open** 11am-11pm Mon-Sat; noon-10.30pm Sun. **Food served** noon-2.30pm Mon-Fri; 1-4.30pm Sun. **Credit** MC, V.

This is such a straightforward operation, it's a blessing and surprise it has survived the fate of most pubs hereabouts. Not yet either a gastropub or a chicken shop, the Pride is a place for beer (three from Fuller's and two guests on handpump), with pint glasses stored above the counter in the old style, and decoration that's largely a matter of pinned-up beer mats from previous visiting ales and a multitude of empty international beer bottles on a high shelf. Still, the location preserves it from becoming too much of an old-man's pub, with slumming hipsters, male and female, a sizeable minority here. In addition to the beerabilia, you'll find those deep red plush fabrics that used to be pub uniform everywhere and heritage London black and white photos, but there's also space for a pull-down screen for big games. Two tables out front on a scrubby pavement are soothed a little in summer by the tree next door, while a stove in the fireplace provides cosiness on rainy winter nights.
Babies and children admitted. Tables outdoors (2, pavement). **Map 12 S5**.

Limehouse

Grapes

76 Narrow Street, E14 8BP (7987 4396). Westferry DLR. **Open** noon-3pm, 5.30-11pm Mon-Wed; noon-11pm Thur-Sat; noon-10.30pm Sun. **Food served** noon-2.30pm, 7-9.30pm Mon-Sat; noon-3.30pm Sun. **Credit** AmEx, MC, V.

If you're trying to evoke the feel of the Thames docks before their Disneyfication into Docklands, these narrow, ivy and etched-glass riverside premises aren't a bad place to start your ruminations. Decent age? 1720. Dickens connection? Check. The downstairs is all wood panels and nautical jetsam (and mercifully devoid of mobile ringtones and music), while a tight stairway leads up to a plainer restaurant room that accommodates the Sunday roast overspill. The pub is a fairly blokey place, so expect good ales (Timothy Taylor Landlord, Adnams Broadside, Marston Pedigree and a guest, on our visit a delicious Hopback Summer Lightning), but a half-dozen wines of each colour by glass and bottle – plus jugs of kir royale or strawberry fizz for summer and port for winter – should keep everyone happy. The new staff seems especially accommodating, but the clientele remains a cheerful mix of well-heeled locals and grown-up heritage junkies. Watch out for your shoes if you step up out of the main bar room on to the tiny outside deck at high tide.
No piped music or jukebox.

White Horse

Mile End

Palm Tree
127 Grove Road, E3 5BH (8980 2918). Mile End tube/8, 25 bus. **Open** noon-midnight Mon-Thur; noon-2am Fri, Sat; noon-1am Sun (last admission 11pm). **No credit cards**.
This is a real East End boozer, albeit one cast adrift in the green acres of Mile End Park, nestled up against the Regent's Canal. You can run through a checklist of trad features – shelf of china plates, dried hops hung in a corner, London Fives dartboard, signed pictures of 'celebrity' drinkers (Jim Bowen being one of the few you might recognise) above the oval central bar – but that doesn't do it justice. Yes, the shiny copper-coloured metallic wallpaper provides a wonderful light, but the place also has a great mix of punters: the more enterprising students from the university across the canal and sundry lunatics from the nearby climbing wall brush shoulders with the suit-and-sovereign old blokes and their wives, who breeze in from the estate for the weekend trad jazz sessions. For liquor, the choice isn't huge: beer-lovers do best, with a couple of interesting guests always on tap (Marston's seasonal Ashes and one from Maldon's Mighty Oak on our last visit), whereas wine comes from a Stowells dispenser behind the bar.
Entertainment: jazz 9.40pm Fri, Sat, 9pm Sun; free. Tables outdoors (4, park).

Shoreditch

Wenlock Arms
26 Wenlock Road, N1 7TA (7608 3406, www.wenlock-arms.co.uk). Old Street tube/rail. **Open** noon-midnight Mon-Thur, Sun; noon-1am Fri, Sat. **Food served** noon-9pm daily. **No credit cards**.
Peek through the door of this friendly, single-room, traditional boozer and you'll immediately see its raison d'être: almost a dozen handpumps await the beer-head's considered attention along the cramped central bar counter, with a mild and something from the local Pitfield brewery always among the enticing options. Opened as a pub in 1836, it somehow survived the Blitz to be reopened in 1994, and doesn't look like it's been touched since. The decor is a perfect match for the location – both its down-at-heel – and the clientele has for the most part seen better days as well, but there's a real community feel to the place. How many Islington pubs have cricket and football teams? Or let you help yourself to free white-bread, triangular sandwiches on a Sunday evening as an

excellent impromptu jazz session unfolds in the corner beside you? More formal jazz and blues gigs take place on Friday and Saturday nights, and the Fat Controller runs a quiz each Thursday, but the regulars are on hand to provide slice-of-life entertainment all week.
Babies and children admitted (until 9pm). Entertainment: jazz/blues 9pm Fri, Sat, 4pm Sun; quiz 9pm Thur; all free. Function room (capacity 25). Map 5 P3.

Stratford

King Edward VII
47 Broadway, E15 4BQ (8534 2313, www.kingeddie.co.uk). Stratford tube/rail/DLR. **Open** noon-11pm Mon-Wed; noon-midnight Thur-Sat; noon-11.30pm Sun. **Food served** noon-3pm, 5-10pm Mon-Fri; noon-10pm Sat, Sun. **Credit** MC, V.
On the other side of the Stratford Centre from the ever expanding transport hub stands a sea-green front topped by a somewhat hungover image of sleep-around monarch King Edward VII. He may have approved of what lies within, for even today his namesake pub is divided by ornately tiled walls and frosted glass dividers. The sunken front bar fills with the loud banter of builders from the Olympics site, while the more comfortable dark-wood saloon bar, and certainly the back room and verdant rear patio, hum with the chatter of young professionals whose property is increasing in value thanks to the Olympics. Catering to them means that the pub now lays on pumpkin, carrot and kidney bean curry and couscous, a wine of the week and the reassuring strum of an acoustic guitar on open-mic Thursdays. Regulars can still look forward to a pint of Sharp's Doom Bar, Bombardier or Nethergate Eddie's Best, with whiskies such as Laphroaig, Lagavulin and the Glenlivet providing a late-night chaser. Draught lagers include San Miguel and Grolsch.
Babies and children admitted (upstairs only). Entertainment: acoustic/open mic 9pm Thur; quiz 8.30pm Sun; both free. Function room (capacity 100). Tables outdoors (5, yard).

North East

Dalston

Prince George
40 Parkholme Road, E8 3AG (7254 6060). Dalston Kingsland rail/30, 38, 56, 242, 277 bus. **Open** 5pm-midnight Mon-Thur; 5pm-1am Fri; 2pm-1am Sat; 2-10.30pm Sun. **Credit** MC, V.

Tucked down a residential street in Dalston and heralded by a faded sign over the front-terrace beer garden, the Prince George is an accomplished all-rounder. The main room wraps in a U-shape around a central bar, at which – under busts of dignitaries and a number of stuffed animals – you'll find nearly half a dozen handpumps (two from Fuller's plus three changing guests), plus Czech lagers and cider on tap; otherwise, choose from the blackboard list of wines. There's been a shift in clientele over the last few years – prices have risen to greet those Hoxditch pubbers who managed to make the scary jump to the north-east – but the George remains accommodating to all comers: the Monday-night quiz, jukebox (still excellent but now, sadly, a pound for five plays), pool table and Wi-Fi are all attractions, and a telly high up on one wall screens big sporting matches.
Babies and children admitted (until 8.30pm). Entertainment: quiz 9pm Mon £1. Tables outdoors (8, heated forecourt). Wireless internet; free. **Map 25 C5**.

North

Archway

Swimmer at the Grafton Arms
13 Eburne Road, N7 6AR (7281 4632). Holloway Road tube/Finsbury Park tube/rail then bus 29 or 253.. **Open** 5-11pm Mon-Thur; noon-11pm Fri, Sat; noon-10.30pm Sun. **Food served** 6-9pm Mon-Thur; noon-3pm, 6-9pm Fri-Sun. **Credit** MC, V.
A large front terrace enveloped by Litovel-branded umbrellas gives way to a classic, high-ceilinged pub, one end dedicated to an open kitchen manned by a commendably grisly southern Italian. Rump steak with chips is all well and good, but most customers are here for the 'handpumped cellar-cooled real ales' as promised on the sign above the bar counter. Traditional Butcombe Bitter, Fuller's Honey Dew, London Pride and Summer Ale are complemented by Litovel Premium and Classic, Erdinger Weissbier, Leffe and Früli, with bottles of Duvel, Pilsner Urquell and Corona chilling in the fridge behind. Comfortably sparse, the interior also features a fireplace surrounded by gilt-framed mirrors, plus memorabilia relating to the history of swimming: photographs of Buster Crabbe, Johnny Weissmuller and the White City pool of 1908 (the first time the Olympic sport wasn't held in open waters).
Entertainment: quiz 8.30pm Mon £1. Tables outdoors (15, garden). Wireless internet; free.

Camden Town & Chalk Farm

Quinn's
65 Kentish Town Road, NW1 8NY (7267 8240). Camden Town tube. **Open/food served** 11am-midnight Mon-Wed, Sun; 11am-2am Thur-Sat. **Credit** AmEx, MC, V.
There aren't many pubs named after the landlord, but old Mr Quinn can still be seen working around the bar at this conspicuous yellow and blue establishment on the corner of Kentish Town Road. It's in dire need of some refurbishment, but the inside is spacious, there's an appealing little garden with mural out back, and the selection of beers is excellent. Greene King takes the lead on the handpumps; Guinness is a point of pride (it's an Irish pub after all) and tap beers on our visit included Mort Subite kriek lambic. There are more Belgian fruit beers in the fridge, including mango, myrtle and raspberry flavours, plus a range of first-class German varieties rarely seen in London. These alone make this family-run spot worth a visit, though football, rugby and cricket screenings on the couple of unobtrusive flatscreens keep locals coming back too, and food from the wide-ranging menu is decent. We'd hate to see it fitted out with glittery floral wallpaper and fringed lampshades, but the brightly coloured bench seats are downright shabby.
Babies and children admitted (until 7pm). Tables outdoors (7, garden). **Map 27 D1**.

DRINKING

Harringay

Salisbury Hotel

1 Grand Parade, Green Lanes, N4 1JX (8800 9617). Manor House tube then 29, 141 bus. **Open** 5pm-midnight Mon-Wed; 5pm-1am Thur; 5pm-2am Fri; noon-2am Sat; noon-11pm Sun. **Food served** 6-10.30pm Mon-Fri; 1-10pm Sat; 1-7pm Sun. **Credit** MC, V.

A wonderful, wonderful pub, well worth a bus journey to the junction with St Ann's Road in the heart of Harringay. The draught beers alone would justify the trek: George Gale HSB, Fuller's London Pride, Discovery and Honey Dew, Belgian Palm, Paulaner, Leffe, and Litovel, both Premium and Classic. Bottled, the world's your oyster: Chimays of all colours, Erdingers of all shades, St Helier pear cider. Then again, there's room to stack a warehouse-load behind the oval bar counter, with efficient continental bar girls panting as they rush all the way along it to serve another customer. This place is so bloody enormous, it feels like Ally Pally, just to the north of here. The trouble is, once you get stuck into the jukebox ('Pet Sounds', 'Sticky Fingers', 'The Gram Parsons Anthology') or the regular live music in another barn-like side room, leaving becomes a problem. There's food too: thin-crust pizzas (such as the vegetarian Salisbury with rocket, spinach and oven-dried tomatoes), salads and home-made burgers. Monday is quiz night, so the jukebox is out of operation then.
Babies and children admitted. Disabled: toilet. Entertainment: bands/DJs 9pm Fri, Sat; poker Wed 8pm; quiz 8.45pm Mon £1. Function room (capacity 120).

Islington

Island Queen

87 Noel Road, N1 8HD (7354 8741, www.theislandqueenislington.co.uk). Angel tube. **Open** noon-11pm Mon, Sun; noon-11.30pm Tue, Wed; noon-midnight Thur-Sat. **Food served** noon-3pm, 6-10pm Mon-Thur; noon-4pm, 6-10pm Fri; noon-10pm Sat, Sun. **Credit** MC, V.

No question, this Islington landmark is a notch above most pubs. First, the beers – a truly superb selection: Peroni, Sierra Nevada, Leffe, Früli, Schneider Weisse, Küppers Kölsch, Paulaner, Pilsner Urquell and Staropramen, all on draught, complemented by tap ales Timothy Taylor Landlord, Deuchar's IPA and Fuller's London Pride. Second, the wines – some 20 in number, all but a couple available by bottle and glass, including Madfish pinot noir and Spy Valley riesling. There's also the food, not only affordable (weekday specials at £5, for instance) but well sourced, like the burgers of Casterbridge beef, and substantial, like the toulouse sausages in a sandwich with rocket and red-onion chutney. Inside, high ceilings tower over etched mirrors and abundant greenery; there are a couple of outdoor tables too. But the Island Queen's main asset is that it has personality in spades: it's a proper pub for people who want a proper drink. And if the staff feel the need to place a collection plate on the bar under a sign saying 'Keep Newcastle United Afloat Fund', so be it.
Babies and children admitted (until 7pm). Entertainment: quiz 8pm Tue £2. Function room (capacity 60). Tables outdoors (4, pavement). **Map 5 O2.**

North West

Hampstead

Holly Bush

22 Holly Mount, NW3 6SG (7435 2892, www.hollybushpub.com). Hampstead tube/ Hampstead Heath rail. **Open** noon-11pm Mon-Sat; noon-10.30pm Sun. **Food served** noon-10pm daily. **Credit** (over £10) MC, V.

Negotiate the steep steps from Heath Street up to isolated, cobbled Holly Mount and a sign will appear: 'Benskins Holly Bush'. It stands over the house that portrait painter George Romney built in the 1790s; used as the Assembly Rooms in the 1800s, it was taken over by Benskins, a Watford

brewery, in 1928 (later bought out by Ind Coope) but an independent, higgledy-piggledy air remains. Three low-ceilinged bar areas exude a lived-in feel, the one bar counter purveying pints of Brakspear Bitter, Fuller's London Pride, Harvey's Sussex Best, Adnams Broadside, Leffe, Beck's, Löwenbräu and Hoegaarden. Pimm's and lemonade is a summer treat, as is a spot out front; tomorrow's weather forecast is chalked up should you be contemplating another steep climb the next day – perhaps to work off the Colchester rock oysters, smoked mackerel salad, sausage rolls, pies or roast beef sandwiches on offer. Wines, four each by the glass, 20 each by the bottle, run from the house Italian red from Puglia (£1.90/£14) to a Châteauneuf-du-Pape Domaine Grand Veneur Rhône and a Hubert Lamy Chassagne Montrachet (£38).
Babies and children admitted. Function room (capacity 50). Wireless internet; free. **Map 28 B2.**

Roebuck

15 Pond Street, NW3 2PN (7435 7354, www.roebuckhampstead.com). Belsize Park tube. **Open** noon-11pm Mon-Thur; noon-midnight Fri, Sat; noon-10.30pm Sun. **Food served** noon-10pm Mon, Sat; noon-9.30pm Sun. **Credit** AmEx, DC, MC, V.

Now under the Young's banner, this favourite escape for staff from the nearby Royal Free Hospital has been given a colourful facelift: purply floral wallpaper, mirrors and '70s swivel chairs are matched with a grandly tiled fireplace and old piano – though don't expect anyone to knock out 'Knees Up Mother Brown'. The high arched windows offer a surprisingly leafy view of the hospital, or head out to the spacious paved garden where there's a barbecue in summer. Emphasis has been taken off the cocktails (there were just seven available on a recent visit) and placed firmly on the four handpumps, with Waggle Dance, Bombardier, and Young's Special and Bitter now typical. Alternatively there is draught Peroni, Kirin Ichinar and Addlestone's cider. Wines start at £3.50 a glass for Old Vines grenache or carignan from Le Sanglier de la Montagne. The Tuesday quiz nights are still in place, and Sunday lunches are accompanied by a film. Express lunches are offered during the week: soup and half a sandwich, sausage and mash, or fish cakes, for £5.95.
Babies and children admitted (until 7pm). Entertainment: quiz Tue; film Sun. Function room (capacity 50). Tables outdoors (15, garden). **Map 28 C3.**

Spaniards Inn

Spaniards Road, NW3 7JJ (8731 8406). Hampstead tube then 210 bus. **Open** noon-11pm Mon-Fri; 11am-11pm Sat, Sun. **Food served** noon-10pm Mon-Fri; 11am-10pm Sat, Sun. **Credit** AmEx, MC, V.

On a narrow bend on the north-west corner of Hampstead Heath, angry one-way traffic is funnelled past two roadside huts; the danger from being knocked down by a school-run mum with personalised licence plates is as real to today's visitor as was being accosted here back in Dick Turpin's day. Signs on either side proclaim 'Spaniards Inn 1565 AD', referring to the Elizabethan tavern, which now stands beside a large car park. They say Turpin was born here in 1705, a century before Keats wrote 'Ode to a Nightingale' in the beer garden. The range of beers (Sierra Nevada, St Austell Tribute, Adnams Broadside, Fuller's London Pride, Franziskaner, Leffe, Hoegaarden) are as big an attraction as any historic tie-in, as is the huge outdoor eating area. Seasonally changing food, prepared until 10pm, might include barnsley lamb chop with greek salad, Rhug estate organic meat pie, mash and gravy, or poached chicken caesar salad with sunblushed tomatoes; the cheese plate features Cropwell Bishop stilton and Cornish yarg. In summer, you can treat the children to a 'posh squash' (£1) of pomegranate and raspberry, or ginger and lemon, and have Fido or Hercules pampered at the doggie wash. Expect long queues and a tussle for tables on bank holiday weekends.
Babies and children admitted. Function room (capacity 40). Tables outdoors (80, garden).

St John's Wood

Clifton

96 Clifton Hill, NW8 0JT (7372 3427). St John's Wood tube. **Open** noon-11pm Mon-Sat; noon-10.30pm Sun. **Food served** noon-2.30pm, 6-9.30pm Mon-Fri; noon-3pm, 6-9.30pm Sat; noon-4pm, 6.30-9pm Sun. **Credit** MC, V.

This former hunting lodge is a pub in disguise. Edward VII had the Clifton declared a hotel so that he could pursue his human prey without being accused of doing so in a pub, while a large etched mirror ('Assirati's Temperance Bar') is probably another Edwardian ruse. Today it's a relaxing spot for enjoying a pint. Adnams likes it, anyway, holding its beer festival here and selling its brew in four-pint jugs; Sharp's Cornish Coaster and Hogs Back Brewery Hop are the ale alternatives. The large front terrace (warmed in winter by gas heaters) fills with paint-splattered workmen and couples, while inside, the dormouse quiet is only broken by the clack of Othello counters or Sky Sports on Sunday afternoons. Diners may retire to the conservatory or secluded back garden to tuck into the Clifton platter of mature cheddar, Milano salami, chicken terrine and hot mini chorizo; children can take a break from the many board games with lunch (£6.50).
Babies and children admitted (until 7pm, later if dining). Entertainment: quiz 8.30pm Wed £2. Tables outdoors (12, garden). **Map 2 D1.**

Outer London

Richmond, Surrey

Cricketers

The Green, Richmond, Surrey TW9 1LX (8940 4372). Richmond tube/rail. **Open** 11am-11pm Mon-Sat; noon-10.30pm Sun. **Food served** noon-9pm daily. **Credit** AmEx, MC, V.

Cut down Golden Court from Richmond High Street and, with Richmond Green spread out before you, you'll see touches of Old England: a couple of Macmillan-era phone boxes and this pub among them. The current premises were rebuilt on a previous pub site in 1834 after a fire. The undated photograph of the Surrey XI by the main door was taken perhaps 50 years later. In any case, the Cricketers exudes a bucolic timelessness; you can sip your Greene King IPA or Guinness on the Green (albeit in a plastic mug). Lager drinkers can choose between Staropramen, Grolsch, Stella, Kronenbourg and Foster's; better wines (Chablis, Châteauneuf-du-Pape) also come by the glass (around £4). The 15 main dishes are of the British beef-and-ale pie variety, but smaller appetites can be satisfied with the £1.95 tapas-style nibbles served on a long board, with plenty of Indian selections among the choices.
Babies and children admitted. Function room (capacity 60). Tables outdoors (3, pavement).

Twickenham, Middlesex

Eel Pie

9-11 Church Street, Twickenham, Middx TW1 3NJ (8891 1717). Twickenham rail. **Open** 11am-11pm Mon-Wed; 11am-midnight Thur-Sat; noon-10.30pm Sun. **Food served** noon-3pm daily. **Credit** MC, V.

Halfway down medievally narrow Church Street, parallel to the Thames and Eel Pie Island (of early 1960s music lore), and past the 17th-century Fox Inn, this Hall and Woodhouse pub is a real rugby haunt. Walls of framed tickets, colour caricatures and signed shirts line the far end of the two-space interior, historic prints of this sleepy area the other. The bar features taps of HB Export and Premium, Badger's Gold, Hopping Hare, Tanglefoot and Lemony Cricket, as well as Harvey's Sussex Best and Peroni. Prices are so reasonable it's a wonder the place stays in business when there is no Six Nations game or big-name concert going up the road. On summer weekends you can sit outside when the street is closed off to traffic.
Babies and children admitted (until 7pm). Disabled: toilet. Entertainment: quiz 9pm Thur £1. Tables outdoors (4, pavement).

Wine Bars

The past year has been a period of retrenchment for London's wine bars. Previous over-expansion has resulted in some closures, but the most successful venues have been those offering their customers transparent value. Most notably, the enoteca model has been triumphant; the best wine bars offer the choice of drinking-in or buying a bottle to take away. Outstanding examples include the trail-blazing **Green & Blue** and **Vinoteca**, the new **Kensington Wine Rooms**, and London's two excellent department-store wine bars **1707** and the **Wonder Bar**. The blurring of distinctions between on and off sales is reflected in the wine-retailing operations at restaurants such as the Argentinian Gaucho Piccadilly (*see p37*), the Spanish Ibérica Food & Culture (*see p240*), French RSJ (*see p98*) and British St John (*see p52*). In the case of Gaucho (Argentina) and RSJ (the Loire) their wine-merchant arms offer significant regional specialities. Likewise, a wine merchant, the Sampler in Islington (266 Upper Street, N1 2UQ, 7226 9500, www.thesampler.co.uk) is offering a selection of 80 wines to taste, available in small measures (the same format that trading standards officials banned at the Wonder Bar). The place gets packed with people eager to learn, who are suddenly able to try expensive wines for little outlay. Rigid enforcement of the minimum 125ml pour has done much to hinder the development of London wine bars; a tasting flight of three of the smallest legal glasses adds up to a half bottle, which hardly encourages sensible experimentation. The government is looking into the matter, but it's unclear when (or if) any changes will be implemented.

Despite all this, the biggest new story this year has been the growth of the 'natural' wine bar. The natural wine movement can be broadly defined as a commitment to non-interventionist vinification, with sulphur dioxide as the only permitted additive and then only at bottling and in small amounts; the growers work sustainably in the vineyards and many produce organic or biodynamic wines. 'Natural' wine makers are hugely fashionable in France; Paris teems with bars dedicated to their wines. London now has two such venues: **Terroirs** and **Artisan & Vine**.

Central

Belgravia

Ebury Wine Bar & Restaurant
139 Ebury Street, SW1W 9QU (7730 5447, www.eburywinebar.co.uk). Sloane Square tube/Victoria tube/rail.
Bar **Open** 11am-11pm Mon-Sat; 6-10.30pm Sun.
Restaurant **Lunch served** noon-2.45pm Mon-Sat. **Dinner served** 6-10.15pm daily. **Main courses** £10-£19.50. **Set meal** (noon-2.45pm, 6-8pm) £15.50 2 courses, £18.50 3 courses.
Both **House wine** £13.50 bottle, £3.60 glass.
Credit AmEx, MC, V.
A Belgravia fixture for over 40 years, the Ebury is an appealing synthesis of new and old. Yes, there's the dark wood panelling, and a garish trompe l'oeil fresco in the rear dining room, but don't be deceived into thinking this is a mere refuge for aging Sloanes. The menu is happy to nod to grand French tradition, with dishes such as pork fillet with prunes and brandy, but the kitchen is also at ease with more Mediterranean flavours: the likes of roasted aubergine and chickpea compote, garnishing a fillet of sea bass. Simple grills are also available. A small front bar caters to those who just want to pop in for a quick drink from the eclectic wine list, which offers a good 30 choices by the glass. New and Old Worlds receive roughly equal billing. From the Rheingau region of Germany, Johannisberger Erntebringer riesling kabinett 2004 was packed with unpretentious charm.
Available for hire. Booking advisable. Dress: smart casual. **Map 15 H10**.

City

Dion St Paul's
Paternoster House, 65 St Paul's Churchyard, EC4M 8AB (0871 223 6186, www.dionlondon.co.uk). St Paul's tube. **Open** noon-midnight Mon-Fri. **Meals served** 5-10.30pm Mon-Fri. **Main courses** £4.95-£17.95. **House wine** £16 bottle, £4.75-£8.50 glass. **Credit** AmEx, MC, V.
The bankers' champagne bar has had as difficult a year as the rest of the City, leading to the closure of the Canary Wharf branch. Just off the Paternoster Square developments, Dion St Paul's inhabits a long, low-ceilinged room with the choice between banquettes and high wooden tables. Beige is the colour and City professionals the game; the drinks list is geared towards groups buying bottles (only three champagnes are sold by the glass). The likes of 2000 Cristal (£350) and 1999 Dom Pérignon (£160) on a Grand Marque-dominated list provide ample opportunity to flash the cash, and this is the only bar in London with a room officially sponsored by Krug. Jacquart Brut Mosaique (£9.50 a glass) or Louis Roederer Brut (£9.95 a glass – ours was served far too cold) provide some slightly more accessible options. The menu wanders through the usual wine-bar clichés, from chicken caesar salad to a range of sandwiches and wraps. Salmon fish cakes and cottage pie are typical main courses. *Booking advisable. Entertainment: jazz 8pm Wed. Separate rooms for parties, seating 40-60. Tables outdoors (8, patio).* **Map 11 O6**.
For branch see index.

Clerkenwell & Farringdon

Bleeding Heart Tavern
Bleeding Heart Yard, 19 Greville Street, EC1N 8SJ (7404 0333, www.bleedingheart.co.uk). Farringdon tube/rail.
Tavern **Open** 7am-11pm Mon-Fri. **Lunch served** noon-3pm, **snacks served** 3-6pm, **dinner served** 6-10.30pm Mon-Fri. **Main courses** £8.45-£14.45.
Bistro **Lunch served** noon-3pm, **dinner served** 6-10.30pm Mon-Fri. **Main courses** £8.45-£15.50.
Restaurant **Lunch served** noon-2.30pm, dinner served 6-10.30pm Mon-Fri. **Main courses** £12.95-£24.50.
All **House wine** £16.95 bottle, £4.50 glass.
Credit AmEx, DC, MC, V.
The current incarnation of this historic site might be somewhat more refined than its 18th-century forebears (you're unlikely to get 'drunk for a penny, dead drunk for two pence'), but the Bleeding Heart is well aware of its heritage as a tavern; there's ale from Adnams on draught and the relaxed atmosphere is more pub than wine bar. However, owner Robert Wilson (who also runs the restaurant next door) has a real wine geek's enthusiasm, and the extensive list covers every major wine-producing area in some depth. Wilson also has a stake in Trinity Hill in New Zealand's Hawke's Bay and his own wines feature prominently; the 2006 sauvignon blanc (served far too cold on this occasion) leans towards fresh, bright precision. However, the real strength lies in the (far more expensive) red wines – the Homage syrah is one of New Zealand's greatest reds. In the basement, the Tavern Dining Room offers a choice of straightforward roasts and grills, together with comfort food, such as fish pie or deep-fried haddock. *Booking advisable. Dress: smart; no shorts, jeans or trainers (restaurant). Separate rooms for parties, seating 12-125. Tables outdoors (10, terrace).* **Map 11 N5**.

★ Cellar Gascon
59 West Smithfield, EC1A 9DS (7600 7561, 7796 0600, www.cellargascon.com). Barbican tube/Farringdon tube/rail. **Open** noon-midnight Mon-Fri. **Tapas served** noon-11.30pm Mon-Fri. **Tapas** £3.50-£8. **House wine** £18 bottle, £5 glass. **Credit** AmEx, MC, V.
The wine-bar arm of Vincent Labeyrie and Pascal Aussignac's Smithfield temple to the gastronomy of their native Gascony has a distinctly clubby feel. Certainly, the well-dressed City workers who come here to enjoy the excellent selection of wines from south-west France should feel right at home amid the leather banquettes and subdued lighting. Food comes in tapas-sized portions and, as at next-door French restaurant Club Gascon, foie gras is king. Presentation is striking: we adored the foie gras carpaccio, the thinly sliced liver presented as a delicately coiled rosette. The region's reds are dark and brooding, but with all of the rich foie gras there's an admirable selection of sweet wines to match; Monbazillac from Domaine de l'Ancienne Curé combines limpid sweetness with beautiful refreshing acidity. Service is skilled. We'd prefer a little more choice by the glass, but overall this is an outstanding operation.
Available for hire. Babies and children admitted. Tables outdoors (3, pavement). **Map 11 O5**.

DRINKING

Cellar Gascon. See p331.

★ Vinoteca (100)

7 St John Street, EC1M 4AA (7253 8786, www.vinoteca.co.uk). Farringdon tube/rail. **Open** noon-11pm Mon-Sat; noon-5pm Sun. **Lunch served** noon-2.45pm Mon-Fri; noon-3pm Sat; noon-4pm Sun. **Dinner served** 6.30-10pm Mon-Fri; 6-10pm Sat. **Main courses** £8.50-£14. **House wine** £12.95 bottle, £3.20 glass. **Credit** MC, V.

It seems unfair to compare the food at Vinoteca with that served at other wine bars. The crowds happily tucking into the well-priced Modern European menu know that this is a serious restaurant, and a good one at that. Dishes vary from well-sourced assemblages (of the likes of Spanish charcuterie and cheese) to more ambitious technical exercises like our oxtail crepinette accompanied by a cool scoop of horseradish cream. The exceptional succulence of a breast of guinea fowl (a difficult bird to cook well) with asparagus and a coarse, herby salsa verde indicated real skill in the kitchen. Owners Brett Woonton and Charlie Young met while working for Italian specialists Liberty Wines – hence the scope of the wine list, which holds plenty of top names. Australia is another strength. Each dish has a suggested wine pairing, and with a weekly changing selection of 25 wines by the glass it's possible to sample some lesser-known bottles; Denbies Surrey Gold 2007 from the UK, an off-dry aromatic white, is a particular favourite. All wines are available to take home at retail price.
Babies and children admitted. Bookings not accepted for dinner. Separate room for parties, seats 30. Tables outdoors (3, pavement). **Map 5 O5.**

Covent Garden

Bedford & Strand

1A Bedford Street, WC2E 9HH (7836 3033, www.bedford-strand.com). Covent Garden tube/Charing Cross tube/rail. **Open** noon-midnight Mon-Fri. **Lunch served** noon-3pm, **dinner served** 5.30-10pm Mon-Fri. **Main courses** £11-£18.75. **House wine** £13.50 bottle, £3.50 glass. **Credit** AmEx, MC, V.

In an area otherwise dominated by cynical tourist traps, Bedford & Strand is popular with local office workers who stream to the basement bar for after-work drinks. Named American-style after its two cross streets, the bar also has a New York feel to its wine list. Four sections, 'Honest', 'Decent', 'Good', and 'Staff Picks' are all available by the glass, carafe, or bottle. Pricing is not aggressive and the list balances New and Old Worlds, along with some curiosities for the adventurous (Brazilian wine anyone?). It pays to trade up. From the 'Staff Picks',

the 2007 Domaine Lafage Cuvée Centenaire makes a good introduction to the nutty, oaked whites being made around Perpignan. A windowed partition separates off the white table-clothed dining area, where bistro staples like shepherd's pie and ribeye béarnaise are served. A separate deli counter offers finger food, cheese and charcuterie.
Available for hire. Babies and children admitted restaurant only. Booking advisable. **Map 18 E5.**

Café des Amis

11-14 Hanover Place, WC2E 9JP (7379 3444, www.cafedesamis.co.uk). Covent Garden tube. **Bar Open** 11.30am-1am Mon-Sat. **Meals served** 11.30am-11.30pm Mon-Sat. *Restaurant* **Meals served** noon-11.30pm Mon-Sat. *Both* **Set meal** (noon-7pm, 10-11.30pm) £14.50 2 courses, £16.50 3 courses. **Main courses** £12.50-£21.50. **House wine** £15.90 bottle, £4.45 glass. **Credit** AmEx, DC, MC, V.

A useful bolt-hole if you don't fancy the Opera House bars, this Covent Garden veteran is determinedly French in outlook. With mini-chandeliers, dark alcoves and prints of ballet divas, the basement bar is studiously inoffensive and fills up quickly at peak times; a 1am licence allows for more protracted post-theatre drinking. Wines are split between France and 'vins étrangers' with the emphasis on the former. Although the list gives descriptions that are an exercise in risible pseudo-winespeak, the quality is sound and there's an emphasis on reliable producers. Louis Jadot is one of the best Burgundian négotiant houses and is featured heavily (the 2003 Morgan is a food wine par excellence). The Springfield Whole Berry cabernet sauvignon 2005 is a fine choice for a velvety South African red. Bar food is standard brasserie fare (steak tartare, terrine, omelettes), along with some large salads and sandwiches made with Poilâne bread. Desserts such as chocolate mousse and crème brûlée continue the theme.
Available for hire. Babies and children admitted. Booking advisable. Entertainment: pianist 7pm Tue. Separate rooms for parties, seating 20-70. Tables outdoors (10, terrace). **Map 18 E4.**

King's Cross

Champagne Bar at St Pancras

St Pancras International Station, Pancras Road, NW1 2QP (7870 9900, www.searcystpancras.co.uk). King's Cross tube/rail. **Open** 7am-11.30pm daily. **Meals served** 7am-10pm daily. **Main courses** £6-£16.95. **Champagne** from £42 bottle, £7.50 glass. **Credit** AmEx, DC, MC, V.

The Eurostar station's Champagne Bar lies beneath William Henry Barlow's magnificent Victorian roof

(the largest single-span structure ever built when it was completed in 1868). Drinking here is rather like sipping champagne in a vast secular cathedral. The muted dark wood and leather banquettes of the bar make appropriate pews, and if you look in the right direction you can see the statue of Sir John Betjeman gazing on in wonder. Behind the bar, catering group Searcy's has installed a professional operation with witty references to Anglo-French endeavour. Gallic bar staff pour champagne into English-made Dartington flutes. The champagne list is comprehensive, with every significant Grand Marque featured in depth. It's possible to spend £880 on a bottle of 1996 Krug Clos de Mesnil, but tempting choices start at around £50 a bottle (Philipponnat Royale Réserve NV for £54). Fifteen champagnes are offered by the glass, so there's ample opportunity to try something new; the house De Nauroy Brut NV is £7.50 a glass. The short menu focuses on British ingredients, so you might see asparagus in season, or dressed Cornish crab.
Available for hire. Babies and children admitted. Bookings not accepted. Disabled: lift; toilet. **Map 4 L3.**

Leicester Square

Cork & Bottle

44-46 Cranbourn Street, WC2H 7AN (7734 7807, www.corkandbottle.net). Leicester Square tube. **Open/meals served** 11am-11.30pm Mon-Sat; noon-10.30pm Sun. **Main courses** £10.95-£15.95. **House wine** £15.95 bottle, £4 glass. **Credit** AmEx, MC, V.

Surrounded by grim pizza joints and the Leicester Square chains, the Cork & Bottle is a bit of a haven. Mumm Champagne is on display as you head down to the basement bar, which gets packed with pre-theatre diners munching burgers and escaping the tourist traps above. Don Hewitson, a New Zealander, founded the bar in 1971, and he pairs a simple menu with a diverse global wine list. Names to watch out for might include Yves Cheron of the Rhône, or Peter Barry from South Australia's Clare Valley. The advantage of such a long-standing venue is that interesting older bottles are also available; fans of mature Aussie shiraz might relish the 1992 Grant Burge Meshach (£55). The Verre de Vin wine preservation system helps keep the 30-odd wines by the glass in good condition; a glass of Cline zinfandel from California displayed lovely depth of fruit, but was ruined by being served in a tiny pub-style glass. Better stemware would do justice to this attractive list.
Babies and children admitted. Bookings not accepted after 6.30pm. Tables outdoors (2, pavement). **Map 18 C5.**

The big four

There are four main wine bar chains in London, together responsible for more than 60 outlets, many in the City. For venue details, check each chain's website; we also list all branches in the indexes at the back of this guide.

Balls Brothers

www.ballsbrothers.co.uk
Founded by Henry Balls in the mid 19th century, Balls Brothers is still run by the family. Venues range from traditional drinking dens populated by claret-swilling gents to the minimalist banquettes of the self-styled gastro-bars of the Lewis + Clark chain (in all there are 15 bars, plus the seven branded under the Lewis + Clark name). Balls Brothers also owns Gow's, a restaurant near Liverpool Street station, and Mulligans, an Irish-themed bar in Mayfair. Across the group, sandwiches dominate the menu, but there might also be main-course options like battered haddock or ribeye steak.
Pick of the bunch Balls Brothers Victoria is one of the branches with a more modern feel. The corner site has attractive outdoor seating for warmer weather, and a generously proportioned back bar. It's a useful after-work venue in an otherwise poorly served area.
Best flavours Wine lists are admirably free from big brands, but the same list is replicated at every bar. The Old World dominates, although the selection of claret keeps things youthful and avoids the classic British taste for past-their-best vintages. Spanish reds are well featured and the Chablis Premier Cru Vaillon 2000 from Daniel-Etienne Defaix at £35 is very well priced for a mature wine from a great vintage. The Lewis + Clark bars have more enterprising global lists, although their reluctance to list vintages for all the wines is frustrating.
Buy the case All wines in the bars can be ordered by the case, but Balls Brothers has considerable heritage as a wine merchant and it's worth exploring the choice of more than 400 wines. France is the strength, and there's useful material on the producers and vintage notes. Best of all is the selection of older vintages, many at prices below those of current releases. Nicolas Potel's Gevrey-Chambertin Premier Cru 'la Perrière' 2002 is just one such example.

Corney & Barrow

www.corney-barrow.co.uk
The wine bar arm of this distinguished wine merchant was launched in the 1990s. Many of the sites retain a whiff of that era of self-conscious style bars; with their big windows they are the antithesis of the dark, masculine, City wine bar. After an abortive attempt at West End expansion, the 13 Corney & Barrow venues are now entirely confined to the City and Canary Wharf. Many are open for breakfast, and then serve classic dishes (caesar salad, bangers

and mash, fish cakes) at lunch before shifting to an evening menu of bar bites and canapés.
Pick of the bunch The Paternoster Square, EC4, branch has a slick nightclub feel, with a mix of dark booths for parties and well-spaced tables. The highlight is the outdoor seating on the square itself; in the shadow of St Paul's cathedral, it could almost be on a continental piazza.
Best flavours With over 70 wines available by the glass, it's possible to dip in and out of the slickly put-together list. Unlike other chains, Corney & Barrow covers the Old and New Worlds in equal depth, so you might choose between a glass of Olivier Leflaive Bourgogne Blanc or chardonnay from La Crema in California. A reserve section of fine wines gives a glimpse of the strengths of the merchant branch of the business, with the likes of Corton-Charlemagne from Bonneau du Martray or Californian Bordeaux blend Napanook.
Buy the case This is the real strength. Complete with a separate web address (corneyandbarrow.com) and a dazzling array of prestige agencies (including both the Domaine de la Romanée Conti in Burgundy and Château Pétrus in Bordeaux), Corney & Barrow has easily the best selection of the competition. A serious brokerage arm also allows you to buy mature wines that have been traded on the secondary market. However, compared to its wine merchant peers, Corney & Barrow's website has poor navigability and lacks in-depth information on the wines.

Davy's

www.davy.co.uk
With names like the Mug House, and the City Flogger, Davy's branches might have been named by a second-string Victorian novelist. They look the part too: many basement venues have dark alcoves filled by men in suits, old prints on the wall and sawdust on the floor. Most of the 35 outlets are in central London. Under James Davy, the fifth generation of the vintner family, there's an effort to shift towards something lighter and more contemporary in feel; the estate has even elevated itself, and is now 40% above ground level. Food is by and large solid and traditional.
Pick of the bunch Davy's at Plantation Place (off Mincing Lane, EC3) is one of the new generation of bar-restaurants, with no sawdust in sight. Catering to the demands of the City trade, this branch is also open for breakfast. The menu nods towards Mediterranean flavours; you can eat bangers and mash, but there's also the likes of pesto lamb brochette served with wild rice.
Best flavours The same basic list is available at all Davy's outlets, with most wines also sold by the glass. As you'd expect, classic regions of the Old World predominate. Pricing is keen, especially

towards the high end (at £65 Jean-Noël Gagnard's Chassagne-Montrachet Premier Cru 'Caillerets' 2003 is barely above retail), but we tend to gravitate towards something fortified. Davy's Finest Manzanilla is delicious and a snip at £1.85 for a 50ml glass.
Buy the case Bordeaux is the strongest suit of Davy's retail arm (davywine.co.uk), with the opportunity to pick up some well-priced older vintages from the mid 1990s. Château Phélan Ségur 1996 at £34.95 is a real bargain. Burgundy is covered in almost as great a depth, with wines from top names like Pierre Morey and William Fèvre. The Davy's website is easy to use, but is let down by the lack of useful information about the wines and growers.

Jamies

www.jamiesbars.co.uk
New owner the Kornicis Group has kept just four branches in London under the Jamies brand. In style they lean more towards the sleek corporatism of Corney & Barrow than the old-fashioned charm of traditional Davy's. The surviving bars are straightforward watering holes for City workers in search of a drink in unfussy environs. Menus are similarly unchallenging, with the typical wine bar selection of nibbles, sandwiches, salads and the odd simple grill.
Pick of the bunch Jamies Fleet Place, EC4, is next door to the City Thameslink station. Outside seating on the terrace is the key attraction, but the main room is perfectly functional and attractive.
Best flavours The recently revamped list is New World-dominated and kicks off with 28 wines available by the glass. It reads like the product of some careful market research and keenly reflects mainstream trends. Reds lean towards richer, more readily accessible styles (with some nice Spanish choices), while chardonnay and sauvignon blanc are the most heavily represented white grapes. More interest is to be found in the 'Off Piste' section, where the 2007 Madfish riesling from Western Australia offers generous limey fruit. A separate section of 'Fine & Classic' wines adds a little Old World glitz, but this is not the place for wine geeks chasing the latest obscure cult bottling.
Buy the case Wines can be bought through an affiliate scheme with merchant Bibendum Wine, although the link to Jamies is unclear; clicking through on the website simply brings up the main Bibendum site. The Bibendum list vastly exceeds anything at Jamies in scope and ambition, although it is geared towards wholesale purchases of un-spilt cases. The broking arm of the business lists some seriously fine wines at commensurately high prices. Bruno Paillard is one of the newest and most interesting houses in Champagne and its non-vintage Brut Premier Cuvée is a perennially good buy.

DRINKING

Vivat Bacchus. See p336.

Marble Arch

Wonder Bar

Selfridges, 400 Oxford Street, W1A 2LR (0800 123400, www.selfridges.com). Bond Street or Marble Arch tube. **Open/meals served** 11am-9pm Mon-Sat; noon-6pm Sun. **Main courses** £7.50-£15. **House wine** £23.99 bottle, £4.25 glass. **Credit** AmEx, DC, MC, V.

When the Wonder Bar opened a couple of years ago, occupying a red and blond wood space on a mezzanine above Selfridges' wine department, the concept seemed so attractive. The new Enomatic machines would serve as 'wine jukeboxes' and customers would be able to help themselves to small measures from up to 52 different wines. With a tiny 25ml pour, it would be possible to taste extremely expensive wines without spending a vast fortune. Then came trading-standards officials, and now the same hardware is restricted to standard 125ml and 175ml servings. It makes it all rather detached; you place your order, then the waitress uses her card to operate the machines, although pre-paid cards are available for something more self-directed. The choice of wines is good, with a nice mix of favourites and new, challenging flavours (we were intrigued by Abbazia di Novacella's 2007 Kerner, a lovely floral aromatic white from the Italian Alps). *Available for hire. Babies and children admitted. Booking advisable. Disabled: lift; toilet.* **Map 9 G6**.

Piccadilly

★ 1707

Lower ground floor, Fortnum & Mason, 181 Piccadilly, W1A 1ER (7734 8040, www.fortnum andmason.com). Piccadilly Circus tube. **Open/ meals served** noon-9pm Mon-Sat. **Main courses** £8-£32. **House wine** from £18.90 bottle, from £5 glass. **Credit** AmEx, MC, V.

Named after the foundation year of the Piccadilly store, 1707 nevertheless looks firmly towards the future. Unpolished wooden slats line the walls, and the lines are clean and modern, but the star is the wine list. The choice is good, and Fortnum's has collaborated with some top-flight producers for its own-label wines (the likes of Verget, Torbreck, and István Szepsy), but the real fun comes if you're willing to pay £10 corkage on the retail price of any of the wines within the wine department. There's predictable (if pricey) strength in traditional areas of France, but also a fine selection of Austrian and Hungarian wines. Best of all, the champagne list is superior to that of any self-styled champagne bar and includes the full range from cult producer Jacques Selosse. Flights are available, but are rather spoiled by the legal requirement that each pour be a full 125ml. Food highlights produce available in the adjacent food hall, but tends to be average (bread and houmous were disappointingly dull), yet with such drinking options we're not complaining.

Available for hire. Babies and children admitted. Booking advisable. Disabled: lift; toilet (ground floor). **Map 9 J7**.

Strand

Gordon's

47 Villiers Street, WC2N 6NE (7930 1408, www.gordonswinebar.com). Embankment tube/ Charing Cross tube/rail. **Open** 11am-11pm Mon-Sat; noon-10pm Sun. **Meals served** noon-10pm Mon-Sat; noon-9pm Sun. **Main courses** £7.95-£10.95. **House wine** £13.95 bottle, £3.85 glass. **Credit** AmEx, MC, V.

Gordon's has been established in its present form since 1890, but with the atmospheric exposed brickwork and flickering candlelight in the low basement vaults, it feels older still. Although this is the definitive old-school wine bar, it gets packed with a young and lively crowd. The wine list is also surprisingly modern, and hops readily from the classic regions of France to South America and beyond. But in such surroundings it seems a shame not to drink the fortified wines that are drawn directly from casks behind the bar. A schooner (120ml) of amontillado sherry was satisfyingly woody, although served alarmingly warm. There's a pleasing selection of Madeira too. Food is presented buffet-style and ranges from traditional pies through to salads and cheese. When the subterranean rooms are crammed it can get

distinctly warm in the semi-darkness, but Gordon's remains a wonderful London experience.
Babies and children admitted. Bookings not accepted. Tables outdoors (30, terrace). **Map 10 L7.**

★ Terroirs NEW

5 William IV Street, WC2N 4DW (7036 0660, www.terroirswinebar.com). Charing Cross tube/ rail. **Open** noon-11pm Mon-Sat. **Lunch served** noon-3pm, **dinner served** 5.45-11pm Mon-Sat. **Main courses** £12-£14. **House wine** £14.50 bottle, £3.50 glass. **Credit** AmEx, MC, V.
Despite old French adverts and posters on its white walls, Terroirs is no Gallic parody. Rather, this bright, split-level venue (ground and lower ground) is a confidently modern bar where food and drink are taken seriously but without pretension. Office-workers and red-nosed connoisseurs swarm here. 'Natural' wines are the speciality, which means those made with organic and biodynamically grown grape varieties, or without added sulphur, sugar or acid. The unstuffy list is dominated by French regions, augmented by a short Italian section plus a 'token Spanish' red and white. We sat at the metal bar, facing an impressive line-up of Calvados and Armagnac bottles. The young barman earned points by tasting the opened bottle of white Château Clément-Termes Gaillac (a tangy counterpoint to rich dishes), before pouring us a glass with practised accuracy. Food is terrific: a tapas-style selection of French bar snacks, charcuterie and seafood, plus plats du jour of the pot-roasted quail or brandade de morue variety. Our salad of lardons and frisée featured high-quality bacon, well-dressed salad and perfect poached egg. We also sampled cervelle de canut – not brains of a weaver, but a yoghurty cheese dip topped with tarragon. Our only caveat: bread is charged for. There are plans to open a basement restaurant: hurrah!
Babies and children admitted. Booking advisable. **Map 18 D5.**

West
Notting Hill

★ Kensington Wine Rooms NEW

127-129 Kensington Church Street, W8 7LP (7727 8142, www.greatwinesbytheglass.com). Notting Hill Gate tube. **Open/meals served** noon-11pm Mon-Sat; noon-10.30pm Sun. **Main courses** £11.95-£19.95. **House wine** £14.50 bottle, £2.70 glass. **Credit** MC, V.
Thor Gudmunsson and Richard Okroj have put together a delightful and stylish wine bar where around 100 well-chosen bottles are offered, together with five Enomatic wine machines serving 40 varieties by the glass. There are many bargains to be had, such as Tin Pot syrah from Hawkes Bay (£6.45) – and glasses start at well under £3 each – but if you want to splash out £63.65 on 125ml of 1999 Bordeaux from Château Margaux, here's your chance. Superior hams hang over the sleek metal bar; burgundy colours and dark wood add warmth to the seating area. Through the arches is a spacious, relaxing dining room with open brickwork and a friendly French waiter. Here you can choose from a short menu of mostly Mediterranean dishes, though there's also the likes of tempura-style fish with skin-on, hand-cut chips and minted mushy peas, steaks and, at weekends, brunch food such as eggs benedict. Each dish has a compatible wine recommendation listed, naturally.
Babies and children welcome: high chairs. Booking advisable evenings. **Map 7 B7.**

Shepherd's Bush

Albertine

1 Wood Lane, W12 7DP (8743 9593). Shepherd's Bush Market tube. **Open** 11am-11pm Mon-Thur; 11am-midnight Fri; 6.30pm-midnight Sat. **Meals served** noon-10.30pm Mon-Fri; 6.30-10.30pm Sat. **Main courses** £6.10-£10.30. **House wine** £12.20 bottle, £3.10 glass. **Credit** MC, V.
Just down the road from Television Centre, it's no surprise that Albertine is popular with BBC types. The small bar has something of the student union about it, with close-packed battered wooden

furniture and a blackboard for wine and food specials. Bottles are displayed on shelves for off-sales at lower prices, or you can drink here from a global list of over 130 wines, with plenty of options by the glass. There are some real gems: champagne from top-flight grower Larmandier-Bernier (the Premier Cru Tradition NV – all floral minerality), or sophisticated cool-climate Australian whites such as the Shaw & Smith M3 Vineyard chardonnay. Food ranges from bar nibbles (olives, charcuterie) through to homely mains like fish pie or sausages with mash. A better alternative might be to pair a glass of the sumptuously sweet and complex Yalumba Antique Tawny with something from the extensive cheeseboard.
Babies and children admitted. Separate room for parties, seats 28. **Map 20 B2.**

Westbourne Grove

Negozio Classica

283 Westbourne Grove, W11 2QA (7034 0005, www.negozioclassica.co.uk). Ladbroke Grove or Notting Hill Gate tube. **Open/meals served** 3.30pm-midnight Mon-Thur; 11am-midnight Fri, Sun; 9am-midnight Sat. **Main courses** £7.95-£17.95. **House wine** £6.99 bottle (retail), £3.25 glass. **Corkage** £6.50. **Credit** AmEx, MC, V.
On a Saturday, with Portobello Market in full swing, there can be few better places than Negozio Classica for people watching. Bohemian locals perch next to the occasional tourist, to be served by flamboyant Italian waiters in the tiny dining room. Wine can be purchased to take home or be consumed on the premises, where it might accompany a menu of cheeses, cured meats and classic antipasti. A glass of San Romano Dolcetto di Dogliani 2006 was a delightful wine for quaffing with food. The bar's interior display could have been arranged by the Italian Tourist Board (regional specialities and dry goods are none too subtly interspersed amid the shelves of wine), but the quality of stock is excellent. Tuscany and Piedmont are the mainstays of the wine list, alongside interesting selections from Sicily and Slovenia. Most producers are stocked in multiple bottlings, so it's possible to sample relatively inexpensive wines from iconic names; Dolcetto and Barbera from the leading Barolo wine-makers are among the great bargains to be enjoyed here.
Babies and children admitted. Separate room for parties, seats 13. Tables outdoors (3, pavement). **Map 7 A6.**

South West
Parsons Green

Amuse Bouche

51 Parsons Green Lane, SW6 4JA (7371 8517, www.abcb.co.uk). Parsons Green tube. **Open** 4-11pm Mon; 4pm-midnight Tue-Thur; 4pm-12.30am Fri, Sat; 4-10.30pm Sun. **Dinner served** 4-10pm daily. **Main courses** £5-£8.50. **House wine** £17.50 bottle, £4.50 glass. **Credit** AmEx, MC, V.
Dedicated to the democratisation of champagne (although the bright young things of Parsons Green could hardly be described as the unwashed masses), Amuse Bouche has hit on a winning formula: relaxed, modern surroundings and a list of 40 or so champagnes, with more than ten also offered by the glass. Bubbles are the thing here, with only a token offering of still wines. Food is restricted to tapas-style nibbles on a global theme (wun tuns, mini fish and chips, plates of cured meats). Prices are admirably restrained, but with such specialisation it would be good to see some of the exciting champagnes being produced by the new wave of growers, rather than the big brands to which Amuse Bouche sticks so resolutely. Still, a glass of Charles Heidsieck 2002 Vintage (a very reasonable £7) had a lovely creamy texture and nutty aromatics. On a warm weekend evening, the windows opened on to the street and the champagne cocktails flowed happily.
Babies and children admitted until 8pm. Booking advisable Thur-Sat. Separate room for parties, seats 40. Tables outdoors (3, courtyard). **For branch see index.**

Interview
ED WILSON

Who are you?
Chef-partner at **Terroirs** (*see left*).
How did you start in the catering business?
My first job in a kitchen was washing up at age 15 and I haven't looked back.
What's the best thing about running a restaurant in London?
Making our customers happy with good food, great wine and offering great value in a relaxed, informal and fun environment.
What's the worst thing?
Not having enough space! And we've found that not installing air-conditioning at the beginning means we're suffering the consequences now.
Which are your favourite London restaurants?
It is worth going to **Tayyabs** (*see p150*) in Aldgate just for the dry meat and lamb chops. It's always packed but worth queuing. **Barrafina** (*see p242*) in Soho still has the best tapas in town, and **Galvin Bistrot de Luxe** (*p95*) has great French cooking, a great atmosphere, and is great value.
What's the best bargain in the capital?
The set lunch at **Le Gavroche** (*see p129*) is pretty hard to beat.
What's your favourite treat?
A box of macaroons from **Ladurée** (*see p296*), especially the pistachio ones.
What is missing from London's restaurant scene?
A late-night eating culture. We are so far behind cities like Paris and New York when it comes to eating after midnight and our attitude and approach needs to change. Eating after midnight shouldn't be restricted to kebabs and Chinese food.
What does the next year hold?
A greater focus on quality and value for the customer as everyone will be having to tighten their belts. In these circumstances people take much greater consideration of where they choose to spend their money, but I believe quality and good value will always prevail.

DRINKING

BEST WINE BARS

Your place or mine?
Imbibe in a bar or buy bottles to take home at London's enotecas: **1707** (*see p334*), **Albertine** (*see p335*), **Artisan & Vine** (*see p335*), **Green & Blue** (*see p336*), **Kensington Wine Rooms** (*see p335*), **Negozio Classica** (*see p335*), **Vinoteca** (*see p332*) and **Wonder Bar** (*see p334*).

Whizzo fizzo
Great champagne lists at **1707** (*see p334*), **Amuse Bouche** (*see p335*), the **Champagne Bar at St Pancras** (*see p332*) and **Dion St Paul's** (*see p331*).

Au naturel
Experience biodynamic wines, organics and the natural wine movement at **Artisan & Vine** (*see below*), **Green & Blue** (*see p336*) and **Terroirs** (*see p335*).

Matchmaker, matchmaker...
Pair great wine and food at **Cellar Gascon** (*see p331*), **Kensington Wine Rooms** (*see p335*), **Negozio Classica** (*see p335*), **Terroirs** (*see p335*) and **Vinoteca** (*see p332*).

Lap it up
Book for tastings at **Artisan & Vine** (*see below*), **Green & Blue** (*see p336*), **Vinoteca** (*see p332*), **Vivat Bacchus** (*see p336*), and **Wine Wharf** (*see p336*).

Old school
Soak in the surroundings of old London at **Albertine** (*see p335*), **Bleeding Heart Tavern** (*see p331*) and **Gordon's** (*see p334*).

Putney

Putney Station
94-98 Upper Richmond Road, SW15 2SP (8780 0242, www.brinkleys.com). East Putney tube. **Bar Open** 11am-11pm Mon, Sun; 11.30am-midnight Tue-Sat. *Restaurant* **Meals served** noon-10.30pm Mon, Sun; noon-11.30pm Tue-Sat. **Main courses** £5-£17. *Both* **House wine** £7.50 bottle, £3 glass. **Credit** AmEx, MC, V.
This outpost of the Brinkley's restaurant group is a vision of 1980s styling – all big plate-glass windows, venetian blinds and pot plants. It's very much a

neighbourhood joint, and food consists of a populist collection of pizzas, burgers and salads with the odd modern Euro classic thrown in. The real attraction is the well-constructed wine list, which has a revolutionary pricing policy that does away with the conventional restaurant mark-ups. No one country or region dominates the 60-bottle list, but the Hamilton Russell chardonnay 2007, one of South Africa's greatest whites, is a bargain at £21. And at a level-headed £40, Domaine de l'Arlot's Nuits-St-Georges Premier Cru 2003 makes for some toothsome drinking. With prices like these, it's easy to forgive the limited choice of wine by the glass. *Babies and children welcome: high chairs; nappy-changing facilities. Booking advisable weekends. Disabled: toilet. Separate room for parties, seats 40. Tables outdoors (3, pavement; 12, garden).*

Wandsworth

Artisan & Vine NEW
126 St John's Hill, SW11 1SL (7228 4997, www.artisanandvine.com). Clapham Junction or Wandsworth Town rail. **Open** 5pm-midnight Mon-Thur; 5pm-2am Fri; 10am-2am Sat; 10am-midnight Sun. **Meals served** 6-10pm Mon-Fri; 10am-10pm Sat, Sun. **Main courses** £8-£9. **House wine** £14.50 bottle, £2.90 glass. **Credit** MC, V.
Artisan & Vine doesn't look like a wine bar dedicated to minimal-interventionist organic and biodynamic wines. With its comfy sofas and wooden tables this could be any other bar for Battersea thirtysomethings. The difference is in the genuinely interesting drinks list, with 120 or so wines organised by style. Big names and brands are blessedly avoided in favour of a quirky selection of wines of real character. Roughly five per cent (including the majority of the sparkling wines) are English, and there's a fixed cash mark-up, rather than a percentage, on all wines over £26 – good for the adventurous. A glass of Macatela Roble 2006, Tierra de Castilla, brimmed with juicy fruit. Food is inexpensive and leans towards the homely, but the salad garnish on our mozzarella and bacon crostini was wilted and sad. Wine-tasting sessions are held at the bar every Wednesday night. *Babies and children welcome: high chairs. Booking advisable Fri, Sat. Disabled: toilet. Tables outdoors (6, pavement).* **Map 21 B4**.

South East

East Dulwich

★ Green & Blue
36-38 Lordship Lane, SE22 8HJ (8693 9250). East Dulwich rail. **Open/meals served** 9am-11pm Mon-Wed; 9am-midnight Thur-Sat; 11am-10pm Sun. **Main courses** £5-£10. **House wine** from £10 bottle, £2.75 glass. **Credit** MC, V.

With an understated, slightly shabby charm, Green & Blue is perhaps the purest example of the new generation of wine shop/bar/cafés. One room has a small deli counter, together with the shelves of wine for retail, while the other has the equally small bar and the majority of the seating. The wine list isn't huge, but there's a lot to love. Owner Kate Thal has done an excellent job in making her selections, which combine big-name superstars with some oddities and new discoveries. Emile Heredia's Domaine de Montrieux, Pétillant Naturel 'Boisson Rouge' falls squarely in the latter category; a joyously sparkling Loire red, it's a wine that defies classification but bursts with exuberant summer fruit. The food is an exercise in good sourcing, with paninis, salads, and some platters of cheese and cured meats. In a neat inversion of the usual corkage fee, for £3 you can bring your own food, and staff will provide plates and cutlery. We wish every high street had a place like this. *Babies and children welcome: high chairs; nappy-changing facilities. Booking advisable weekends. Disabled: toilet.* **Map 23 C4**.

London Bridge & Borough

Vivat Bacchus
4 Hays Lane, SE1 2HB (7234 0891, www.vivatbacchus.co.uk). London Bridge tube/rail. *Bar* **Open** noon-midnight Mon-Sat. *Restaurant* **Lunch served** noon-2.30pm Mon-Fri. **Dinner served** 6-9.30pm Mon-Sat. **Main courses** £14.95-£22.95. *Both* **House wine** £15.50 bottle, £3.90 glass. **Credit** AmEx, MC, V.
In a bland modern development just off Tooley Street, this branch of the South African-owned mini-group sticks to a winning formula, with a restaurant in the basement complementing the deli counters upstairs. Much use is made of South African meats; it's possible to eat springbok, blesbok and biltong here, alongside European dishes. Although there's wine-themed decoration in the form of posters and crates, the climate-controlled cheese and wine rooms provide the most attractive element of the design. The wine list pays attention to all of the classic French regions (Champagne is particularly well represented, though mark-ups are brutal), but we always find ourselves drifting back to the outstanding selection of South African wines. From a good choice by the glass, Ken Forrester's FMC 2007 chenin blanc from Stellenbosch is one of South Africa's best whites, matching clever use of oak with lovely ripeness. *Babies and children admitted. Booking advisable Wed-Sat. Disabled: lift, toilet. Tables outdoors (16, terrace).* **Map 12 Q8**. **For branch see index.**

Wine Wharf
Stoney Street, SE1 9AD (7940 8335, www.winewharf.co.uk). London Bridge tube/rail. **Open** noon-11pm Mon-Sat. **Meals served** noon-10pm Mon-Sat. **Main courses** £4.50-£9. **House wine** £17 bottle, £4 glass. **Credit** AmEx, DC, MC, V.
Part of the Vinopolis complex, Wine Wharf inhabits a reclaimed Victorian warehouse – all exposed brickwork and high-ceilinged industrial chic. Set over two storeys, there are plenty of leather sofas to accommodate the after-work throng. You could drink very well indeed here (the 250-bin list stretches to 1953 d'Yquem and some very serious prestige cuvée champagnes), but with nearly half the wines available by the glass, there's a great opportunity to experiment. The wine list is organised by country and price rather than region or style, which can make navigation difficult. Tasting flights are also available, daringly poured as five 50ml glasses. From an introductory mixed flight (£10), the highlight was the soft cassis fruit of a 2005 Chocálan syrah Reserva from the Maipo Valley in Chile; in contrast, Loimer's 2007 LOIS grüner veltliner had sacrificed typical grüner veltliner taste to get a lower price. Bar bites and sharing platters are available, together with more substantial dishes. Sadly on our visit the smell of the deep-fryer hung in the air of the dining room. *Available for hire. Babies and children welcome (before 8pm): high chairs. Booking advisable. Disabled: toilet.* **Map 11 P8**.

Kensington Wine Rooms. See p335.

Eating & Entertainment

Burlesque

Brickhouse

*152C Brick Lane, E1 6RU (7247 0005,
www.thebrickhouse.co.uk). Liverpool Street
tube/rail.* **Open** 6pm-2am, **dinner served**
6.30-10.30pm Tue-Sun. **Set dinner** £25-£35
3 courses. **Credit** AmEx, MC, V.
This converted warehouse tries to bring something
of an 1930s speakeasy atmosphere to Brick Lane.
The place is a modern take on traditional cabaret:
it's whitewashed, with wooden floors, plus red
velvet curtains. Two mezzanine levels rise above a
small stage on the ground floor, where you can
catch performances from tassel-twirling burlesque
dancers, cabaret acts, magicians and DJs. There's
a £5-£10 cover charge for dinner during shows,
which goes to the performers. Food is Modern
European, featuring dishes such as rump of lamb,
fish or ricotta and basil ravioli. The space is also
available for hire for exclusive use, or floor by floor.
*Available for hire. Booking advisable. Disabled:
toilet. Entertainment: live acts, DJs 9pm nightly.
Separate rooms for parties, seating 10-50.*
Map 6 S5.

Volupté

*7-9 Norwich Street, EC4A 1EJ (7831 1622,
www.volupte-lounge.com). Chancery Lane tube.*
Open 5pm-1am Tue-Wed; 5pm-3am Thur, Fri;
2pm-3am Sat. **Tea served** 2.30-5pm Sat. **Dinner
served** 6.30-10pm Tue-Sat. **Main courses** £12-
£22. **Set dinner** £25 2 courses, £30 3 courses.
Credit MC, V.
Elegant, retro supper club Volupté hosts a wide
variety of performers and eccentric entertainment
in its cosy Moulin Rouge-style basement, with ivy
hanging from the ceiling and candlelit tables
arranged around a small stage area and piano.
There are cabaret shows from Wednesday to
Saturday. Afternoon Tease takes place on selected
Saturdays, with burlesque entertainment and a
gracious afternoon tea of champagne, finger
sandwiches, own-made scones and mini pastries.
Evenings might feature Ivy Paige's Scandalous –
an '18th-century romp', or the Marquis of Gray's
Great Exhibition: cabaret with acrobats, sword
dancing and a bevy of burlesque beauties. The
dinner menu has a Modern European bent, with
dishes such as vodka-marinated salmon steak with
new potatoes and beetroot purée or duck leg confit
with lentils. Decently priced retro cocktails are
served in an upstairs bar.
*Available for hire. Booking essential. Dress: smart
casual. Entertainment: cabaret 8pm Wed-Fri;
2.30pm, 7pm, 10pm Sat.* **Map 11 N5.**

Comedy

It's difficult to find a comedy venue that
serves food and laughs of equal standard.
There are, however, a few places in the
capital that offer dishes of a higher quality
than standard old-style pub grub. In south-
east London, **Up the Creek** (302 Creek
Road, SE10 9SW, 8858 4581, www.up-the-
creek.com) is well worth a visit. Over in
Maida Vale there's the **Canal Café Theatre**
(first floor, the Bridge House, on the corner
of Westbourne Terrace Road and Delamere
Terrace, W2 6ND, 7289 6056, www.canal
cafetheatre.com; map 1 C5), while in

Shoreditch there's the **Comedy Café** (66-
68 Rivington Street, EC2A 3AY, 7739 5706,
www.comedycafe.co.uk; map 6 R4).
   The best-known comedy club in London
is probably Leicester Square's **Comedy
Store** (1A Oxendon Street, SW1 4EE,
bookings Ticketmaster 0870 060 2340,
www.thecomedystore.co.uk; map 17 B5).
Another favourite is **Jongleurs Camden
Lock** (11 East Yard, Camden Lock, Chalk
Farm Road, NW1 8AB, 0844 499 4064,
www.jongleurs.com; map 27 C1) – which
has two other London branches, in
Battersea and Bow.
   For up-to-date information on the capital's
comedy clubs, see the Comedy section in
the weekly *Time Out* magazine.

Dining afloat

Vessels for hire include canal cruisers from
the **Floating Boater** (Waterside, Little
Venice, Warwick Crescent, W2 6NE, 7266
1066, www.floatingboater.co.uk; map 1
C5); the **Leven is Strijd** (West India Quay,
Hertsmere Road, West India Docks, E14
4AE, 7987 4002, www.theleven.co.uk), a
classic Dutch barge, for views of Canary
Wharf; and the **Elizabethan** (8780 1562,
www.thamesluxurycharters.co.uk), which is
a replica of a 19th-century Mississippi
paddle steamer that cruises from Putney
eastwards to beyond the Thames Barrier.
   The **RS Hispaniola** next to Hungerford
Bridge (Victoria Embankment, WC2N 5DJ,
7839 3011, www.hispaniola.co.uk; map 10
L8) is a popular party venue with tapas bar,
cocktail lounge and a large restaurant.

Dogs' dinners

Wimbledon Stadium

*Plough Lane, SW17 0BL (8946 8000, www.love
thedogs.co.uk). Tooting Broadway tube/Earlsfield
rail/44, 270, 272 bus.* **Dinner served** 7-9.30pm
Tue, Fri, Sat. **Set meal** £24.95-£27.95 3 courses.
Admission £5 grandstand. **Credit** MC, V.
A night at the dogs entails an awful lot of whiling
away time in between very brief races, so a sit-down
dinner instead of hotdogs and tea out of plastic
cups makes good sense. Star Attraction is the main
restaurant here. Seating is tiered, overlooking the
racetrack, and once booked, the table is yours for
the evening. The three-course set meal is good value,
and even includes lobster (£5 supplement). There's
a fast-food takeaway stand too, and another
restaurant, the Bistro, used for private parties.
Various corporate packages and executive suites are
available; see the website for details.
*Babies and children welcome: high chairs; nappy-
changing facilities. Booking advisable. Disabled: lift;
toilet. Separate rooms for parties, seating 28-120.*

Jazz & soul

Green Note

*106 Parkway, NW1 7AN (7485 9899,
www.greennote.co.uk). Camden Town tube.*
Dinner served 7-10pm Wed, Thur, Sun;

7-10.30pm Fri, Sat. **Music** 9-11pm daily. **Main
courses** £7.95-£9.95. **Tapas** £2.95-£4.95.
Admission £4-£15. **Credit** MC, V.
An international line-up of acts at this relaxed
Greenwich Village-style hangout has included the
Coal Porters (the 'world's first alt-bluegrass
band') and in summer 2009 the venue staged its
third annual Festival of Latin Music – follow on
Twitter for updates. Paintings of folk icons
including Joni Mitchell and Bob Dylan line the
walls. Food is vegetarian and organic; daily
specials, salads and tapas can be eaten in the café/
restaurant area out front, or in the music venue
at the back.
*Babies and children admitted: high chair. Booking
advisable. Vegan dishes. Vegetarian menu.*
Map 27 C3.

Jazz After Dark

*9 Greek Street, W1D 4DQ (7734 0545,
www.jazzafterdark.co.uk). Leicester Square or
Tottenham Court Road tube.* **Open** 2pm-2am
Mon-Thur; 2pm-3am Fri, Sat. **Meals served**
2pm-midnight Mon-Sat. **Music** 9pm Mon-Thur;
10.30pm Fri, Sat. **Main courses** £8.50-£10.95.
Set meal £10.95 3 courses. **Admission** £5
Mon-Thur; £10 diners, £15 non-diners Fri, Sat.
Credit AmEx, DC, MC, V.
A jazz club of the old school with few pretensions.
It's a low-lit and laid-back spot, where a young,
after-work crowd enjoys a mixture of jazz, blues,
funk and soul. The party menu is good value for
money, or choose from the burgers, burritos, pasta
or steak dishes. A tacky cocktail list (anyone for a
Kick in the Balls, or Slippery Nipple?) is clearly
aimed at hen and stag groups. Much is made of
impromptu appearances by the likes of Pete
Doherty and Amy Winehouse (that's unless they're
otherwise engaged).
*Booking essential Fri, Sat. Dress: smart casual.
Tables outdoors (2, pavement).* **Map 17 C3.**

Jazz Café

*5-7 Parkway, NW1 7PG (7485 6834, www.jazz
cafelive.com). Camden Town tube.* **Open** 7pm-2am
Mon-Thur, Sun; 7pm-3am Fri, Sat. **Meals served**
7-10.30pm daily. **Music** daily; call for times.
Main courses £16.50. **Set meal** £26.50
3 courses. **Admission** varies; call for details.
Credit AmEx, MC, V.
A recent spruce-up (new seat covers, lick of paint)
has given this venue, formerly a Barclays bank, a
fresh face without changing its layout, or informal
atmosphere. A balcony restaurant overlooks the
stage, where a variety of jazz, soul, funk and world
music acts appear. Weekend club nights, such as
cheesy 'I love the '80s' on Saturdays, attract the
students, but the place remains best known for
proper music, with a line in soon-to-be-huge US
acts: Mary J Blige and John Legend played their
first European dates here. The menu offers crowd-
pleasing dishes such as caribbean chicken with
rice and peas, roasted butternut squash risotto,
and lime mousse with a passion-fruit coulis.
Booking advisable. Disabled: toilet. **Map 27 D2.**

Pizza Express Jazz Club

*10 Dean Street, W1D 3RW (7439 8722,
www.pizzaexpresslive.com). Tottenham Court
Road tube.*
Restaurant **Meals served** 11.30am-midnight
Mon-Sat; 11.30am-11.30pm Sun.
Club **Meals served** 7.30-11pm daily. **Music**
9-11pm daily. **Admission** £15-£25.
Both **Main courses** £5.90-£10.95. **Credit**
AmEx, DC, MC, V.
There's music every night of the week at this long-
standing basement club, showcasing anything
from fresh new talent, to successful singers like
Norah Jones or old stager of the British jazz scene
John Dankworth. The atmosphere is relaxed and
friendly, and the advantage of it being a Pizza
Express is that you know what you're getting
when it comes to the food – and that it won't be
too pricey. Check the website for upcoming acts
and to book tickets.
*Babies and children welcome (restaurant): high
chairs. Booking advisable. Takeaway service.*
Map 17 B3.

Le Quecum Bar

42-44 Battersea High Street, SW11 3HX (7787 2227, www.quecumbar.co.uk). Clapham Junction rail. **Open** 7pm-midnight Mon-Thur; 6pm-1am Fri, Sat; 6pm-midnight Sun. **Meals served** 7-10pm Mon-Thur; 6-10pm Fri-Sun. **Music** varies Mon, Sun; 8pm Tue-Sat. **Main courses** £8-£14. **Admission** varies Mon, Sun; free Tue; £5 after 8pm Wed-Sat. **Membership** £65/yr. **Credit** AmEx, MC, V.

Pre-war France meets Django Reinhart-style gypsy jazz at this wine bar with music. French bistro food is on the menu, including frogs' legs, mussels in wine and cream, escargots, and daily specials. To drink, there's Kronenberg and Amstell on tap and reasonably priced wine (from £13 a bottle). Regular nights include the free Gypsy Swing Jam on Tuesdays (bring your own instrument). Sunday and Monday nights are often ticketed affairs, a recent highlight being the 1930s Soirée Fleur de Paris, with Edith Piaf sound-a-like Lo Polidoro.

Booking advisable Fri, Sat. Dress: smart casual. **Map 21 B2**.

Ronnie Scott's

47 Frith Street, W1D 4HT (7439 0747, www.ronniescotts.co.uk). Leicester Square or Tottenham Court Road tube. **Open** 6pm-late Mon-Sat; 6.30pm-late Sun. **Meals served** 6pm-1am Mon-Sat; 6-11pm Sun. **Main courses** £11.50-£14.50. **Music** 7pm-12.30am Mon-Thur; 7pm-1.30am Fri, Sat; 8-10.30pm Sun. **Admission** (non-members) £20-£36. **Membership** £165/yr. **Credit** AmEx, DC, MC, V.

Ronnie Scott's celebrated its golden anniversary in 2009, with special performances throughout the year, and a film and TV season at the BFI on the South Bank. It remains one of the oldest and best-known jazz venues, possibly in the world. Acts on the bill often have a long pedigree, with links to some of the greats. The grub is none too shabby either; butternut squash risotto and pan-fried sea bream sit on the menu alongside the usual burgers and steaks. There's also a separate bar menu. If you've never been, then now's the time to step into a slice of jazz history.

Available for hire. Booking advisable. Disabled: toilet. Dress: smart casual. **Map 17 C3**.

606 Club

90 Lots Road, SW10 0QD (7352 5953, www.60 6club.co.uk). Earl's Court tube then C3 bus/Sloane Square tube then 22 bus. **Open/meals served** 7.30-11.45pm Mon; 7pm-12.30am Tue, Wed; 7pm-midnight Thur; 8pm-1.30am Fri, Sat; 12.30-11.15pm Sun. **Music** 9pm Mon; 7.30pm Tue, Wed; 8pm Thur; 9.30pm Fri, Sat; 1.30pm, 8.30pm Sun. **Main courses** £8.95-£18.45. **Admission** (non-members) £8-£12. **Membership** £95 first yr; £60 subsequent yrs. **Credit** AmEx, MC, V.

Low-ceilinged and candle-lit, this basement club serves as a relaxed hang-out for south-west London's cool, finger-snapping set. Run by musician Steve Rubie, it's known for attracting a knowledgeable crowd. There's music every night; check the website for line-ups. Diners can choose from a regularly changing menu, but steak, pasta and fish are always available. Licensing regulations mean that non-members can only drink alcohol with meals, and at the weekend are only admitted if dining. The 606 is now also open for Sunday lunch, and there are bands playing on some Sundays (check before you go).

Available for hire. Babies and children admitted. Booking advisable Fri, Sat. **Map 13 C13**.

Latin

Nueva Costa Dorada

47-55 Hanway Street, W1T 1UX (7631 5117, www.costadoradarestaurant.co.uk). Tottenham Court Road tube. **Open/meals served** noon-3am Mon-Sat. **Main courses** £11.95-£16.50. **Credit** AmEx, DC, MC, V.

Nightly flamenco shows are the draw at this Spanish stalwart. There's a warm, cosy bar feel to the place, with tables arranged around the stage for an informal, easy-to-mingle atmosphere – no surprise that it's popular with office parties and birthday bashes. Food comes in the form of tapas,

Wimbledon Stadium. See p337.

such as tortilla and calamares, as well as a solid à la carte menu, with the likes of paella and swordfish. An all-Spanish wine list complements the menu, and there are bar nibbles and a small cocktail selection too.

Available for hire. Entertainment: flamenco shows 9.30pm Tue-Thur, 10pm Fri, Sat; DJ 11pm Thur-Sat. **Map 17 B2**.

Salsa!

96 Charing Cross Road, WC2H 0JG (7379 3277, www.barsalsa.info). Leicester Square or Tottenham Court Road tube. **Bar Open** 5.30pm-2am Mon-Sat; 6pm-1am Sun. *Café* **Open** 9am-5.30pm Mon-Sat. **Snacks served** noon-5.30pm Mon-Sat. **Set buffet** (noon-6pm Mon-Sat) 99p/100g. *Restaurant* **Meals served** 5.30-11pm daily. **Main courses** £4.75-£11.50. *Bar & restaurant* **Admission** £4 after 9pm Mon-Thur; £2 after 7pm, £4 after 8pm, £8 after 9pm, £10 after 11pm Fri, Sat; £3 after 7pm, £4 after 8pm Sun. *All* **Credit** All AmEx, MC, V.

Salsa! is a restaurant, café, bar and dance club all rolled in to one. There are dance classes in the bar every night of the week, suitable for everyone from complete beginners to salsa pros (from £5, £3 for diners), as well as a free two-hour introduction to Latin dance, including salsa, merengue and lambada, on Friday nights. Latin-themed drinks promotions (such as two-for-one mojitos on Thursdays) help lubricate your dancefloor performance. Food is a traditionally Latin mixture of tapas and larger dishes such as chargrilled steaks and fajitas. There is also a Brazilian buffet in the café, costing 99p per kilo.

Booking advisable; essential weekends. Dress: smart casual. Entertainment: DJs 9.30pm daily; dance classes 7pm daily. Tables outdoors (10, pavement). **Map 17 C3**.

Music & dancing

Dover Street

8-10 Dover Street, W1S 4LQ (7629 9813, www.doverstreet.co.uk). Green Park or Piccadilly Circus tube. **Open** 5pm-3am Mon-Sat. **Dinner served** 6pm-2am Mon-Thur; 7pm-2am Fri, Sat. **Music** Bands 9.30pm Mon; 10pm Tue-Sat. *DJs* until 3am Mon-Sat. **Main courses** £13.95-£21.95. **Set dinner** £24.95-£45 3 courses. **Admission** £6 after 10pm Mon; £7 after 10pm Tue; £8 after 10pm Wed; £12 after 10pm Thur; diners only until 10pm, then £15 Fri, Sat. **Credit** AmEx, DC, MC, V.

A recent refurb has changed little at this cool jazz and dining venue. Enjoy early evening cocktails at one of the two elegant bars, admiring the black-and-white fashion prints that adorn the walls, then dine from a Modern European menu, with last orders for food now extended until 2am. After dinner, guests are invited on to the dancefloor to boogie to the sounds of bands such as the Jazz Dynamos, Funkification and the Blues Engineers. Check the website for a diary of events.

Booking advisable; essential weekends. Dress: smart casual. Separate rooms for parties, seating 20-100. **Map 9 J7**.

ZIGFRID *Von* UNDERBELLY

of
Hoxton

* bar *
* restaurant *
* music *
* sofas *
* world cup *
* terrace *
* talk *
* listen *
* drink *
* eat *
* live music *

11 Hoxton Square
London
T : +44(0)207 613 1988
www.zigfrid.com
E : office@zigfrid.com

MISS Q's
Pool Bar, Diner & Live Music Saloon

www.missQs.com
info@missQs.com
Tel : +44 (0)20 7370 5358

180 - 184
Earls Court Rd
London

ROADTRIP LIVE BAR & DJ DELI

243 OLD STREET, LONDON, EC1V 9EY
T : +44(0)20 7253 6787
OFFICE@ROADTRIPBAR.COM
WWW.ROADTRIPBAR.COM

RELAXED ROCK 'N ROLL COCKTAIL FEEL GIVES IT A GREAT VIBE TO WATCH SOME LIVE MUSIC, CATCH YOUR FAVOURITE DJ, PICK A TUNE FROM OUR KILLER JUKE BOX OR JUST CHILL ON OUR SOUTH FACING TERRACE. PIG OUT ON ONE OF OUR DELI PIZZAS & WATCH THE WORLD CUP... BABY!

Pigalle Club

215-217 Piccadilly, W1J 9HN (7734 8142, www.thepigalleclub.com). Piccadilly Circus tube. **Open** 7pm-2am Mon-Wed; 7pm-3am Thur-Sat. **Dinner served** 7-11.30pm Mon-Sat. **Set dinner** £45 3 courses. **Admission** £10 after 10pm Mon-Thur; £10 after 7pm, £15 after 10.30pm Fri, Sat. **Credit** AmEx, DC, MC, V.

This basement supper club aims to bring 1940s swing, and the glamour of that era, back to the West End. The mezzanine-level restaurant overlooks the stage: booths, antique fittings, and diamond shaped mirrors contribute to a glitzy, retro feel. Food from the £45 three-course menu (show included) covers such standards as warm summer chicken salad and chargrilled strip loin of beef; service, by waiting staff in period uniform, is efficient. Non-diners are welcome to perch at the bar. Big band jive music, and torch-song crooners keep the small dancefloor packed with hen and stag dos, as well as couples; '40s aficionados often dress up for the occasion.

Available for hire. Booking essential (if dining). Entertainment: music 9pm. **Map 17 B5**.

Roadhouse

35 The Piazza, WC2E 8BE (7240 6001, www.roadhouse.co.uk). Covent Garden tube. **Open** 5.30pm-3am Mon-Sat; 5.30pm-midnight Sun. **Meals served** 5.30pm-1.30am Mon-Sat; 5.30pm-midnight Sun. **Main courses** £8.25-£17. **Admission** £5 after 10.30pm Mon-Wed; £7 after 10pm Thur; £10 after 9pm Fri; £5 after 7pm, £12 after 9pm Sat; £5 after 9pm Sun. **Credit** AmEx, MC, V.

Roadhouse is more than just a prime target for beer-loving lads and riotous hen bashes (stag parties are limited to one a night) attracted by the drinks promotions and diner-style comfort food. It also hosts the World Flair Championships – a competition to find who's best at the bartender's art of spinning bottles while mixing a pina colada: think Tom Cruise in *Cocktail* but much, much more serious (there's a top prize of £10,000). There's music every night, while Rocky-oke on Sundays gives punters a chance to sing with a real backing band.

Booking advisable. Dress: smart casual. Entertainment: bands/DJs daily. **Map 18 E4**.

Tiroler Hut (100)

27 Westbourne Grove, W2 4UA (7727 3981, www.tirolerhut.co.uk). Bayswater or Queensway tube. **Open** 6.30pm-1am Tue-Sat; 6.30pm-midnight Sun. **Dinner served** 6.30pm-12.30am Tue-Sat; 6.30-11.30pm Sun. **Main courses** £12.90-£25. **Set meal** (Tue-Thur, Sun) £23 3 courses; (Fri, Sat) £26 3 courses. **Credit** AmEx, DC, MC, V.

'Nothing changes here, except the colour of my hair,' says Joseph, the accordion-playing proprietor of this super-kitsch Austrian restaurant, done out to resemble an Alpine ski chalet. Joseph also takes charge for the nightly cowbell performance, which gets diners on their feet for the occasional sing-a-long. More serious is the good selection of German and Austrian beers (served in steins) and wines, while the dinner menu includes plenty of authentic Austrian fare: schnitzel, sauerkraut, stuffed cabbage and goulash. Best to go in a group for a bit of raucous communal thigh-slapping.

Available for hire. Babies and children admitted. Booking essential. Entertainment: cowbell show times vary Tue-Sun. **Map 7 B6**.

One-offs

Dans Le Noir

30-31 Clerkenwell Green, EC1R 0DU (7253 1100, www.danslenoir.com/london). Farringdon tube/rail. **Lunch served** by appointment. **Dinner served** (fixed sittings) 7-7.30pm, 9-9.30pm Mon-Thur; 7-7.30pm, 9.15-9.45pm Fri, Sat. **Set dinner** £32 2 courses, £38 3 courses. **Credit** AmEx, MC, V.

The USP of this restaurant and bar is that you eat your meal in complete darkness, enabling you to focus only on taste and smell. Diners start in the (well-lit) bar, and can choose from four secret, colour-coded menus: blue for fish lovers, green for vegetarians, red for meat lovers, and white for 'chef's surprise'. Food is served in a pitch-black dining room, where you are guided and served by blind staff. The experience is intended to be an emotional, as well as culinary, experience, encouraging diners to empathise with their waiter/guide. A dark bar also operates on Fridays (5.30-6.30pm) in the lounge area. To answer two frequently asked questions: Are the chefs blind? No, they're not. And are the toilets in the dark? Also, thankfully, no.

Booking essential. Children admitted. Disabled: toilet. Separate room for parties, seats 60. **Map 5 N4**.

Lucky Voice

52 Poland Street, W1F 7LR (7439 3660, www.luckyvoice.co.uk). Oxford Circus tube. **Open/food served** 5.30pm-1am Mon-Thur; 3pm-1am Fri, Sat; 3-10.30pm Sun. **Main courses** £8. **Credit** AmEx, MC, V.

Those too shy, or too sober, to get up and sing in front of a large audience will appreciate these Japanese-style private karaoke booths. There are nine rooms, or pods, at this Soho venue, each with space for four to 12 singers; larger rooms also come with props such as hats and wigs. An extensive drinks menu includes cocktails (£7), saké, spirits by the bottle, and plenty of wine and beer. All are brought to your pod when you press the 'thirsty' button. Food is limited to pizzas and snacks. You can create a playlist before visiting using the song database on the website (and yes, they do have 'How Do You Want Me to Love You' by 911). The perfect place to discover your inner Susan Boyle.

Booking essential. Entertainment: karaoke pods for hire, £5-£10.80/hr per person. Over-21s only. **Map 17 A3**.

For branch see index.

Rainforest Café

20 Shaftesbury Avenue, W1D 7EU (7434 3111, www.therainforestcafe.co.uk). Leicester Square or Piccadilly Circus tube. **Meals served** noon-10pm Mon-Thur; noon-8pm Fri; 11.30am-8pm Sat; 11.30am-10pm Sun. **Main courses** £12.95-£18.90. **Credit** AmEx, MC, V.

This jungle-themed restaurant, populated by animatronic wildlife, is the closest thing to Disneyland in London. Very popular for children's parties, the emphasis is on family fun. Score a table upstairs to sit amid the fish, elephants and gorillas, and choose from a global menu offering meze, pasta, seafood, ribs, steaks and burgers. It's worth paying £3 extra for the children's Adventure meal: it comes with a mask, purse, stationery and sticker book gift pack. If that doesn't keep them quiet, and if your wallet can take it, there's also a shop stocked with soft toys and T-shirts on the way in. You can't book a table, but there is a priority seating system online.

Babies and children welcome: children's menu; crayons; high chairs; nappy-changing facilities. Bookings not accepted. Entertainment: face painting weekends & school hols. Separate rooms for parties, seating 11-100. **Map 17 B5**.

Troubadour

263-267 Old Brompton Road, SW5 9JA (7370 1434, www.troubadour.co.uk). West Brompton tube/rail. *Café* **Open** 9am-midnight, **meals served** 9am-11pm daily. *Wine bar/shop* **Open** noon-10pm daily. *Club* **Open** 8pm-midnight Mon-Wed, Sun; 8pm-2am Thur-Sat. **Meals served** 8-11pm daily. **Admission** £6-£10. *All* **Main courses** £8.25-£13.50. **Credit** AmEx, MC, V.

A key player in London's 1950s bohemian folk movement, the Troubadour has seen a lot of history. Bob Dylan played his first London gig here; it was also incubator for *Private Eye*, as well as the friendship between Ken Russell and Oliver Reed. With a collection of coffee pots in the windows, pots and pans hanging from the ceiling, stained-glass windows and wood-panelled walls, the ground-floor café area certainly looks the part.

DRINKING

Bel Canto. See p342.

Food is bistro-style, with the likes of omelettes, burgers, salads and sandwiches. The basement club hosts events from poetry readings and open-mic nights to gigs from local musicians and even big names, such as the Chemical Brothers. The deli next door is now a wine bar and shop, holding regular wine-tasting evenings. You can even stay the night in the Arts and Craft-style apartment on the top floor.
Available for hire. Babies and children welcome (café): high chair. Booking advisable. Separate rooms for parties, seating 15-32. Tables outdoors (8, garden; 6, pavement). **Map 13 B11**.

Twelfth House

35 Pembridge Road, W11 3HG (7727 9620, www.twelfth-house.co.uk). Notting Hill Gate tube. **Open/meals served** 11.30am-11pm Thur, Fri; 9am-11pm Sat, Sun. **Main courses** £6.50-£13. **Credit** MC, V.
A place of astrological myth and mystery, Twelfth House draws on the 18th-century tradition of coffee shop fortune telling. You can have your chart read by owner Priscilla or fellow stargazer Elise for £30, or select a 'tarot card of the day' for £3. There are also cocktails for each sign of the zodiac and some seriously good coffee, along with light snacks, cakes and brunch at weekends. A real curio on this parade of retro clothes shops and designer boutiques.
Babies and children admitted. Booking advisable. Separate room for parties, seats 25. Tables outdoors (4, garden). **Map 7 A7**.

Opera

Bel Canto

4 Minster Court, EC3R 7AA (7444 0004, www.lebelcanto.com). Monument or Tower Hill tube/Fenchurch Street rail. **Dinner served** 7-11pm Tue-Sat. **Set dinner** £55 3 courses. **Credit** AmEx, MC, V.
Bel Canto offers classic French cuisine (there's a sister restaurant in Paris) with a musical twist – the waiting staff are also classically trained opera singers and burst into song every 15 minutes. Dishes are selected from the three-course Lyric Menu (£55), with trad dishes such as pan-fried foie gras and prime beef fillet. Decor is suitably theatrical; the place looks like a cross between an auditorium and a luxury cruise ship, complete with velvet curtains and a red carpet. The musical menu is based around mainstream opera favourites such as *Carmen* and *The Marriage of Figaro*; audience participation is also encouraged, with diners invited to join in with the famous toast – 'Brindisi' from *La Traviata*.
Available for hire. Booking essential. Children admitted. Disabled: lift; toilet. Dress: smart casual. Entertainment: opera 7.30pm (every 15mins until 11pm). **Map 12 R7**.

Sarastro

126 Drury Lane, WC2B 5QG (7836 0101, www.sarastro-restaurant.com). Covent Garden or Holborn tube. **Meals served** noon-11.30pm daily. **Main courses** £7.50-£15.50. **Set lunch** (noon-6.30pm Mon-Sat) £14.50 2 courses. **Set meal** £26.50 3 courses incl coffee. **Credit** AmEx, DC, MC, V.
Named after a character from Mozart's *The Magic Flute*, this flamboyant restaurant continues their operatic theme with ten individually styled opera boxes, velvet drapes, theatrical props and other colourful frippery. Food is Mediterranean-Turkish, but the big draw here are the opera and string quartet performances on Monday and Sunday evenings and Sunday lunchtimes, featuring singers and musicians from the nearby ENO and Royal Opera House, along with students and rising stars. The three-course Opera Menu (£26.50) offers the likes of boreks for starters, followed by roast duck with plum sauce, slow-cooked shank of lamb or vegetarian crêpes, then baked pumpkin in spicy syrup or fresh fruit. There's also an à la carte menu.
Babies and children welcome: high chairs. Booking advisable. Disabled: toilet. Entertainment: opera, string quartet 8.30pm Mon; 2.30pm, 8.30pm Sun. **Map 18 F3**.

Sports bars

All Star Lanes

Victoria House, Bloomsbury Place, WC1B 4DA (7025 2676, www.allstarlanes.co.uk). Holborn tube. **Open/meals served** 5-11.30pm Mon-Wed; 5pm-midnight Thur; noon-2am Fri, Sat; noon-11pm Sun. **Main courses** £9.50-£14.50.
Bowling (per person per game) £7.50 before 5pm, £8.50 after 5pm. **Credit** AmEx, MC, V.
Styling itself on stateside 'boutique' bowling alleys, this retro-themed venue is the more upmarket of Bloomsbury's two bowling dens). There are four lanes (plus two private lanes upstairs), diner-style booths and a glamorous side bar with red leather banquettes, subdued lighting, an extensive cocktail menu and DJs at the weekends. Food is good ol' American diner fare – think ribs, steaks, Texas chilli con carne – or you can just have a peanut butter and banana shake, which constitutes a meal in itself. Be sure to save room for dessert, though; it's difficult to turn down Momma's sweet potato pie, or a mississippi mud cake.
Available for hire. Babies and children admitted (until 6pm). Booking essential. Disabled: toilet. Entertainment: DJs 10pm Fri, Sat. Separate room for parties, seats 30. **Map 18 E1**.
For branches see index.

Bloomsbury Bowling Lanes

Basement, Tavistock Hotel, Bedford Way, WC1H 9EU (7691 2610, www.bloomsburylanes.com). Russell Square tube. **Open** noon-midnight Mon-Thur; noon-3am Fri, Sat; 1pm-midnight Sun. **Meals served** noon-10pm daily. **Main courses** £6.95-£7.95. **Bowling** (per person per game) £3 before 4pm Mon-Wed, all day Sun; £4.50 before 4pm Thur, Fri; £5.50 after 4pm Mon-Fri, all day Sat; (lanes) from £36/hr (maximum 6 people). **Credit** AmEx, MC, V.
Simply throwing down a few strikes can take second preference at this multi-purpose big kids' playground. Take your pick from the pool tables, table football, private karaoke booths, occasional cinema screenings, club nights or time in the Las Vegas-style Kingpin Suite, complete with four private lanes, games room and a hot tub. Lucky's Diner serves up burgers, burritos and chilli dogs, with laneside snacks also available. There's always something on at the weekend, when DJs, bands, and novelty theme nights entertain a young crowd, many of them students from nearby UCL. The regular Shake Rattle & Bowl event has been running since 2006.
Booking essential. Children admitted before 4pm Mon-Fri, Sun. Disabled: toilet. Entertainment: DJs, bands, karaoke; times/days vary. Separate room for parties, seats 50. **Map 4 K4**.

Elbowroom

89-91 Chapel Market, N1 9EX (7278 3244, www.theelbowroom.co.uk). Angel tube. **Open** 1pm-2am Mon; noon-2am Tue-Thur; noon-3am Fri, Sat; noon-1am Sun. **Meals served** 1-10pm Mon, noon-10pm Tue-Sun. **Main courses** £5-£8. **Pool** £6-£10/hr. **Credit** MC, V.
This Islington branch of the bar-cum-pool hall chain is well designed and welcoming. At the time of writing a refit was in progess, with an overhaul of the private party room and leather upholstery being installed throughout the premises. The front third of the L-shaped space is taken up by the bar, with private booths and high tables. The pool area is bookable, and free on Mondays. Lighting and music are set to just the right levels; you should feel at home as you sink some balls, and a few drinks too. Wines start at £13 a bottle, cocktails at £5.95 (and there's a two-for-one offer between 5pm and 8pm). A basic menu includes burgers, wraps and salads.
Booking advisable weekends. Disabled: toilet. Entertainment: DJs 9pm Thur-Sun. Separate room for parties, seats 30. **Map 5 N2**.
For branches see index.

Sports Bar & Grill

Marylebone Station, Melcombe Place, NW1 6JJ (7723 8890, www.sportsbarandgrill.co.uk). Marylebone tube/rail. **Open** 7.30am-midnight

Mon-Fri; 10.30am-midnight Sat, Sun. **Meals served** 7.30am-11pm Mon-Fri; 10.30am-11pm Sat, Sun. **Main courses** £4.95-£18.95. **Pool** £1/game. **Credit** AmEx, DC, MC, V.
This upmarket sports bar comprises a brasserie-style restaurant on the ground floor – decorated with distinctly unsporty chandeliers – and a basement lounge complete with five American pool tables and a darts room. The restaurant menu is made up of brasserie classics such as burgers, sandwiches and grills. Portions are large and well presented, and good value for money. A bar snacks menu also serves up fun finger food such as platters of mini burgers and nachos.
Available for hire. Babies and children admitted restaurant until 9pm. Booking advisable. Disabled: toilet. Separate room for parties, seats 50. Tables outdoors (4, pavement). **Map 2 F4**.

Sports Café

80 Haymarket, SW1Y 4TE (7839 8300, www.thesportscafe.com). Piccadilly Circus tube/Charing Cross tube/rail. **Open/meals served** noon-3am daily; noon-10.30pm Sun. **Main courses** £7.95-£16.95. **Admission** £5 after 10pm Mon, Tue, Fri, Sat. **Credit** AmEx, MC, V.
Grab a beer and relish the opportunity to soak in the sport from 100 screens beaming out an eclectic range from football and Rugby League to Formula One and tennis. Key American sports are also shown, and are popular with the sizeable expat and tourist crew who love this place. The Sports Café is also popular with the England cricket team's Barmy Army, so expect big turnouts and lots of noise for major fixtures. There are also six pool tables, free wi-fi access and a Nintendo Wii console if you feel the need for a diversion from on-screen sports. Buffalo wings, nachos, wraps, burgers, ribs and steaks are served in the dining area, and DJs play chart hits from 10pm on most nights.
Available for hire. Children admitted (until 9pm, dining only). Disabled: toilet. Entertainment: DJs 10pm Mon, Tue, Fri, Sat. **Map 10 K7**.

24-hour eats

Vingt-Quatre

325 Fulham Road, SW10 9QL (7376 7224, www.vingtquatre.co.uk). South Kensington tube then 414 bus. **Meals served** 24hrs daily. **Main courses** £7.25-£14.75. **Credit** AmEx, MC, V.
Vingt-Quatre caters for a posh after-club Kensington and Chelsea crowd, fresh out of the high-class hotspots nearby, and thirsty for more champers. A half-bottle of Krug will set you back £75 after 10pm – in fact, all prices, particularly those of drink, shoot up after this hour. Alternatively wind down with a cup of tea; a range starts at £3. The menu features a small full english breakfast (with organic, free-range eggs) that starts at £7.50 (£8.50 at night). Other dishes include fish and chips, club sandwiches, steak, lasagne, omelettes and – for those feeling a little adventurous in those early hours – kimchee dumplings.
Babies and children admitted. Tables outdoors (2, pavement). **Map 14 D12**.

Views & victuals

Vertigo 42 Champagne Bar

Tower 42, 25 Old Broad Street, EC2N 1HQ (7877 7842, www.vertigo42.co.uk). Bank tube/ DLR/Liverpool Street tube/rail. **Open/lunch served** noon-3pm Mon-Fri. **Open/dinner served** 5.30-11pm Mon-Fri. **Main courses** £11.50-£22.50. **Credit** AmEx, DC, MC, V.
Drink prices may be as breathtaking as the views (white wine from £7.50 a glass, up to £795.50 for a magnum of Krug champagne), suggesting the economic downturn hasn't hit every banker's bonus. Food, though, is more down to earth. Options include wild mushroom tart with artichoke salad, and seared peppered tuna steak, each coming with a recommended tipple. A more complete menu is available at Rhodes 24 (*see p51*), some 18 floors below. Seating is arranged so that everyone can enjoy the panorama.
Available for hire. Booking essential. Disabled: lift; toilet. **Map 12 Q6**.

Maps

The following maps highlight London's key restaurant areas: the districts with the highest density of good places to eat and drink. They show precisely where each restaurant is located, as well as major landmarks and tube stations.

Key to Maps

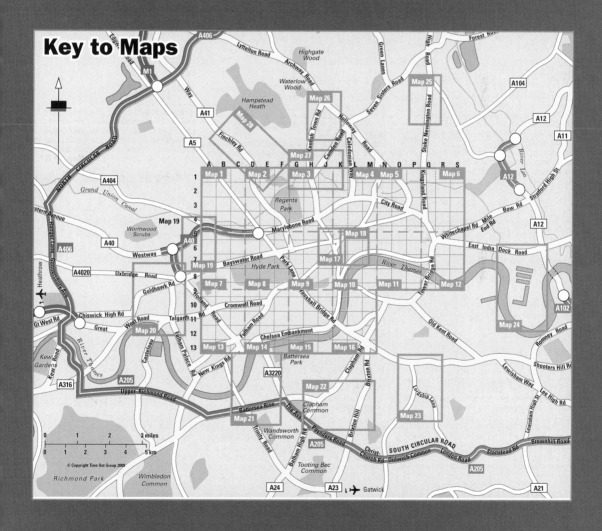

Queen's Park & Maida Vale

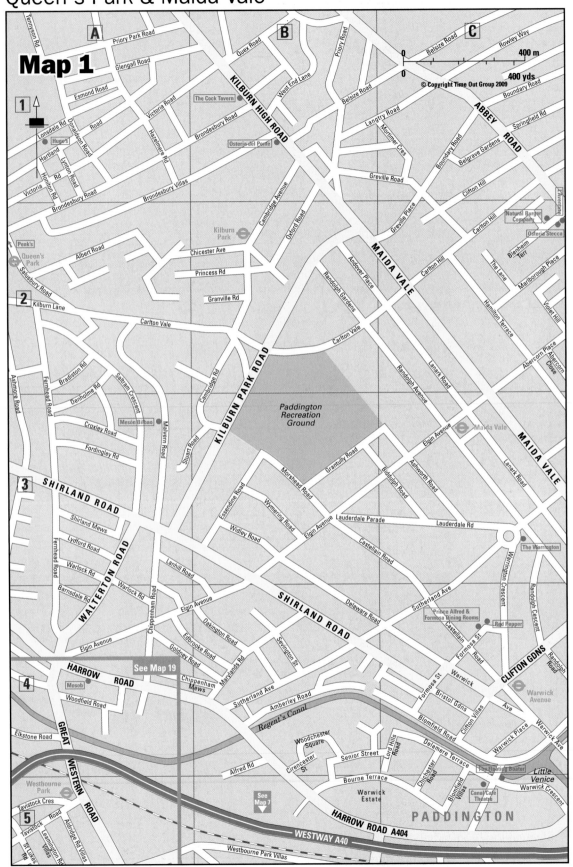

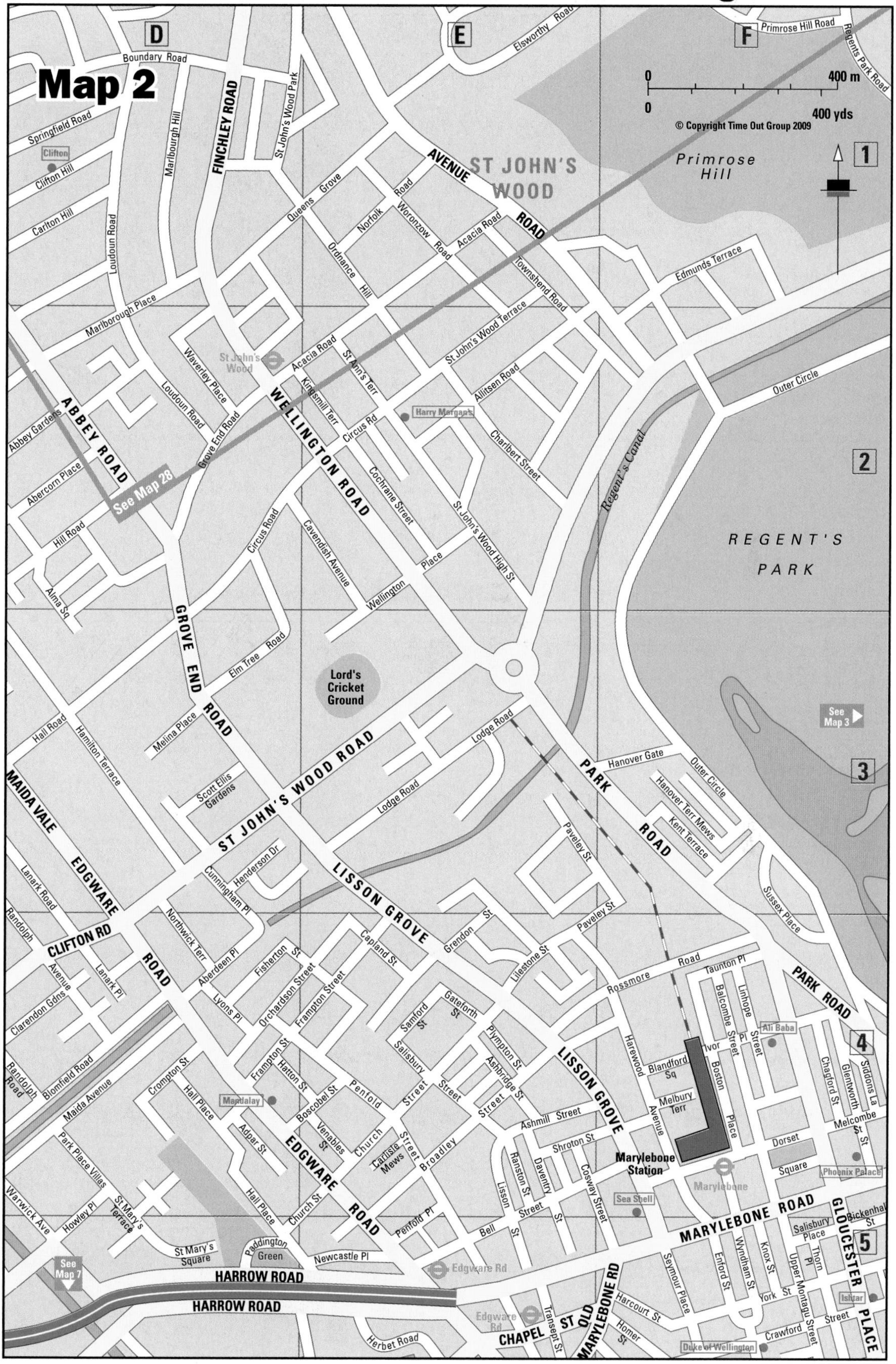

Map 2

D   E   F

Boundary Road

Springfield Road

Clifton

Clifton Hill

Carlton Hill

Marlborough Hill

Marlborough Place

Loudoun Road

Waverley Place

FINCHLEY ROAD

St John's Wood Park

AVENUE

ST JOHN'S WOOD

ROAD

Queens Grove

Norfolk Road

Woronzow Road

Acacia Road

Townshend Road

Elsworthy Road

Primrose Hill Road

Regents Park Road

0   400 m
0   400 yds
© Copyright Time Out Group 2009

Primrose Hill

1

Ordnance Hill

Acacia Road

St Ann's Terr

Kingsmill Terr

Circus Rd

Harry Morgan's

St John's Wood Terrace

Allitsen Road

Charlbert Street

Edmunds Terrace

Outer Circle

2

Abbey Gardens

Abercorn Place

ABBEY ROAD

See Map 28

Hill Road

Alma Sq

WELLINGTON ROAD

GROVE END ROAD

Loudoun Road

Grove End Road

Circus Road

Cochrane Street

Cavendish Avenue

Wellington Place

St John's Wood High St

St John's Wood

REGENT'S PARK

Regent's Canal

Hall Road

Hamilton Terrace

Melina Place

Scott Ellis Gardens

Elm Tree Road

Lord's Cricket Ground

ST JOHN'S WOOD ROAD

Lodge Road

Lodge Road

Hanover Gate

Outer Circle

Hanover Terr Mews

Kent Terrace

See Map 3

3

MAIDA VALE

EDGWARE ROAD

CLIFTON RD

Lanark Road

Lanark Pl

Randolph Avenue

Clarendon Gdns

Blomfield Road

Maida Avenue

Park Place Villas

Warwick Ave

Howley St

St Mary's Terrace

Cunningham Pl

Henderson Dr

Northwick Terr

Aberdeen Pl

Lyons Pl

Fisherton St

Orchardson Street

Frampton Street

Frampton St

Hatton St

Crompton St

Boscobel Street

Venables St

Adpar St

Hall Place

Church St

LISSON GROVE

Capland St

Lilestone St

Samford St

Salisbury Street

Penfold Street

Church Street

Broadley Street

Carlisle Mews

Grendon St

Gateforth St

Plympton St

Ashbridge St

Ashmill Street

Shroton St

Daventry St

Ranston St

Lisson Street

Bell Street

LISSON GROVE

Rossmore Road

Harewood Avenue

Cosway Street

Penfold Street

Taunton Pl

Linhope Street

Balcombe Street

Ivor Pl

Boston Place

Melbury Terr

Blandford Sq

Marylebone Station

Marylebone

Sea Shell

Ali Baba

Dorset Square

Phoenix Palace

PARK ROAD

Sussex Place

4

Salisbury Place

Wyndham St

Knox St

Thorn

Upper Montagu Street

Siddons La

Glenworth St

Chagford St

Melcombe St

Dorset St

Bickenhall St

GLOUCESTER PLACE

Ishtar

5

See Map 7

St Mary's Square

Paddington Green

Newcastle Pl

HARROW ROAD

HARROW ROAD

Herbet Road

Edgware Rd

CHAPEL ST

MARYLEBONE RD

Harcourt St

Transept St

Homer St

Seymour Place

Enford St

York St

Crawford Street

MARYLEBONE ROAD

Duke of Wellington

MAPS

Camden Town & Marylebone

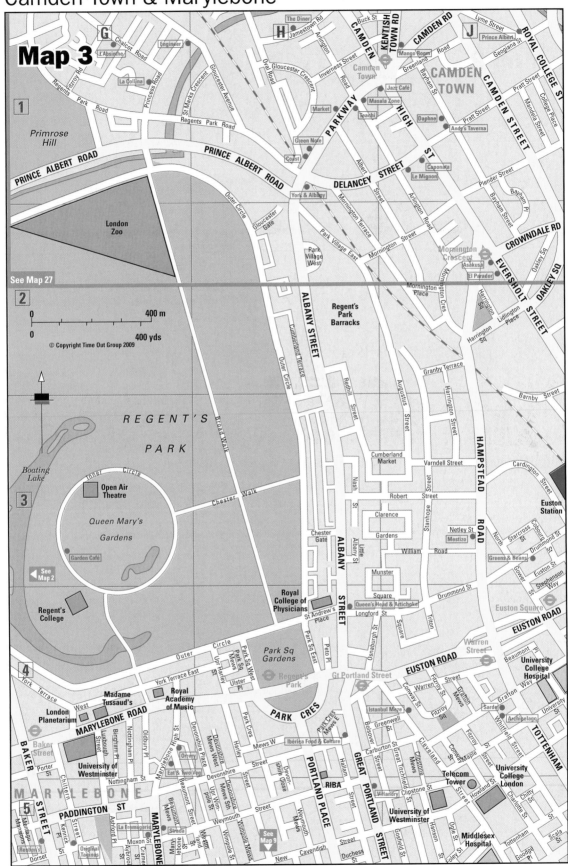

Map 3

G L'Absinthe Chalcot Road Engineer
La Collina

Primrose Hill

PRINCE ALBERT ROAD
Regents Park Road
Fitzroy Rd
Gloucester Avenue
St Marks Crescent
Princess Road

PRINCE ALBERT ROAD

London Zoo

Outer Circle
Gloucester Gate

The Diner Jamestown Rd Buck St CAMDEN
H Arlington Camden Town
Oval Road Gloucester Crescent Inverness Street
Mango Room J Lyme Street Prince Albert
Greenland Road Georgiana St
KENTISH TOWN RD CAMDEN RD ROYAL COLLEGE ST

Market PARKWAY Jazz Café Masala Zone Teachi Bayham St CAMDEN TOWN
Green Note Daphne HIGH Pratt Street Pratt Street Andy's Taverna Mandela Street
Coast DELANCEY STREET ST Caponata Plender Street College Place
York & Albany Le Mignon Arlington Road Bayham St CAMDEN STREET

See Map 27

CROWNDALE RD
Mornington Terrace Mornington Crescent Asakusa EVERSHOLT OAKLEY SQ
Park Village East El Parador STREET
Park Village West Mornington Street Mornington Place Harrington Sq Lidlington Place
Regent's Park Barracks ALBANY STREET Augustus Street Harrington Street Granby Terrace Barnby Street

REGENT'S PARK

Cumberland Terrace Outer Circle Redhill Street Nash Street Cardington Street

Boating Lake
Inner Circle
Open Air Theatre
Queen Mary's Gardens
Garden Café

MAPS

Chester Walk

Cumberland Market Varndell Street HAMPSTEAD ROAD Euston Station
Robert Street Clarence Gardens Netley St Mestize Starcross St Cobourg St Drummond St
Chester Gate Little Albany St William Road Greens & Beans North Gower Euston St Stephenson Way
Munster Square Drummond Street Euston Square
Royal College of Physicians St Andrew's Place Queen's Head & Artichoke Longford St Triton Warren Street

Regent's College
Circle Park Sq West Park Sq Gardens Peto Pl Gt Portland Street EUSTON ROAD University College Hospital
Outer York Terrace East Ulster Pl Regent's Park Beaumont Warren St Gratton Mews Gratton University
Madame Tussaud's Royal Academy of Music Istanbul Maze Conway St Fitzroy Sardo University
London Planetarium MARYLEBONE ROAD PARK CRES Park Cres Mews E Greenwell Fitzroy Sq Whitfield Street Archipelago TOTTENHAM
Bingham Pl Nottingham Pl Devonshire Iberica Food & Culture Carburton St Cleveland Telecom Tower University College London
BAKER Luxborough Street Oldbury Pl Mews West Great Portland Villandry University of Westminster Middlesex Hospital
Baker Street Porter St Orrery Devonshire Street Hallam RIBA Great Portland Street Charlotte St Scala
University of Westminster Eat & Two Veg Devonshire Weymouth PORTLAND PLACE Goodge
MARYLEBONE La Fromagerie Strada Weymouth Mews Weymouth PORTLAND STREET
PADDINGTON ST Original Tagines Moxon St New Cavendish Duchess Street See Map 9

0 ——— 400 m
0 ——— 400 yds
© Copyright Time Out Group 2009

See Map 2

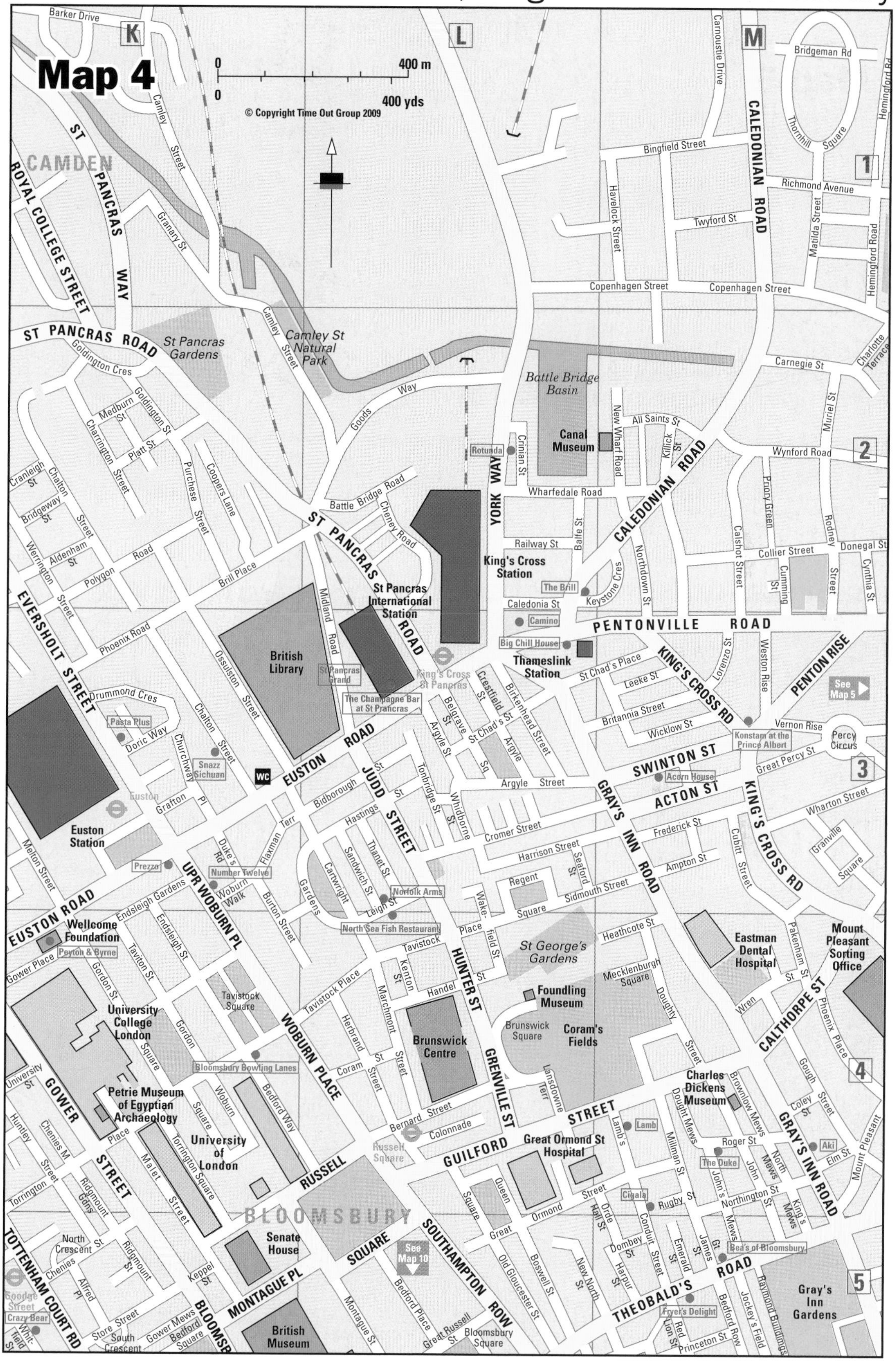

Map 4

Barker Drive

K

L

M

0 400 m
0 400 yds

© Copyright Time Out Group 2009

Bridgeman Rd

Carnoustie Drive

Thornhill Square

Hemingford Rd

Bridgeman Rd

1

CAMDEN

ST PANCRAS WAY

ROYAL COLLEGE STREET

Camley Street

Granary St

CALEDONIAN ROAD

Bingfield Street

Richmond Avenue

Matilda St

Hemingford Road

Charlotte Terrace

ST PANCRAS ROAD

St Pancras Gardens

Camley St Natural Park

Copenhagen Street

Copenhagen Street

Twyford St

Havelock Street

Carnegie St

2

Goldington Cres

Goldington St

Camley St

Way

Battle Bridge Basin

New Wharf Road

All Saints St

Muriel St

Wynford Road

Medburn St

Charrington St

Platt St

Purchase St

Cooper's Lane

Goods

Rotunda

Canal Museum

Killick St

Priory Green

Rodney St

Donegal St

Cranleigh St

Chalton St

Road

Brill Place

Battle Bridge Road

Cheney Road

Wharfedale Road

CALEDONIAN ROAD

Calshot Street

Cynthia St

Bridgeway St

Aldenham St

Polygon

Railway St

Balfe St

Northdown St

Collier Street

Werrington St

Phoenix Road

ST PANCRAS ROAD

King's Cross Station

The Brill

Cumming St

PENTON RISE

Drummond Cres

British Library

St Pancras International Station

MIDLAND ROAD

St Pancras Grand

Caledonia St

Camino

PENTONVILLE ROAD

Weston Rise

Vernon Rise

See Map 5

EVERSHOLT STREET

Ossulston Street

Chalton Street

The Champagne Bar at St Pancras

King's Cross St Pancras

Keystone Cres

Big Chill House

Thameslink Station

St Chad's Place

Leeke St

KING'S CROSS RD

Britannia Street

Percy Circus

Konstam at the Prince Albert

3

Pasta Plus

Doric Way

Churchway

EUSTON ROAD

JUDD STREET

Belgrave St

Argyle St

St Chad's

Argyle St

Crestfield St

Birkenhead Street

Wicklow St

Argyle Square

SWINTON ST

ACTON ST

Great Percy St

Wharton Street

Granville Square

Snazz Sichuan

WC

Grafton Pl

Bidborough

Hastings St

Tonbridge St

Windmore

Argyle Street

Cromer Street

GRAY'S INN ROAD

Frederick St

KING'S CROSS RD

Cubitt St

Euston

Euston Station

Melton Street

Prezzo

UPR WOBURN PL

Duke's Rd

Flaxman Terr

Burton Street

Number Twelve

Woburn Walk

Cartwright Gardens

Thanet St

Sandwich St

Leigh St

Norfolk Arms

Wake-field St

Regent Square

Harrison Street

Seaford St

Sidmouth Street

Ampton St

4

Wellcome Foundation

Peyton & Byrne

Endsleigh Gardens

Taviton St

Gordon St

Endsleigh St

Gordon St

Tavistock Place

Marchmont

Kenton St

Handel St

North Sea Fish Restaurant

Tavistock Place

Place

Field St

St George's Gardens

Heathcote St

Mecklenburgh Square

Doughty

Pakenham St

Wren

Eastman Dental Hospital

Mount Pleasant Sorting Office

EUSTON ROAD

Gower Place

University College London

Tavistock Square

Hartland

Coram

Bernard Street

Foundling Museum

Brunswick Square

Coram's Fields

Lansdowne Terr

CALTHORPE ST

Phoenix Place

Mount Pleasant

GRAY'S INN ROAD

University Street

GOWER STREET

Chenies M

Huntley Street

Malet Street

Torrington Square

Bloomsbury Bowling Lanes

Petrie Museum of Egyptian Archaeology

University of London

WOBURN PLACE

Woburn Sq

Bedford Way

Brunswick Centre

GRENVILLE STREET

Great Ormond Street Hospital

Lamb

Charles Dickens Museum

Roger St

Doughty Mews

Brownlow Mews

The Duke

Coley St

Gough Street

Aki

GRAY'S INN ROAD

4

Torrington

Ridgmount Gdns

Ridgmount

Gordon Square

Russell Square

STREET

Colonnade

GUILFORD STREET

Millman St

Cigala

John's Mews

Northington St

King's Mews

Elm St

North Crescent

Chenies St

Alfred Pl

Keppel St

Senate House

RUSSELL SQUARE

MONTAGUE PL

Montague St

Queen Square

Ormond Street

Great

Ord's Hall St

Dombey St

Emerald St

Gt James St

Conduit Street

Rugby Street

Bea's of Bloomsbury

Gough Square

THEOBALD'S

ROAD

Bedford Row

5

TOTTENHAM COURT RD

Crazy Bear

Goodge Street

Whit-field St

Store Street

South Crescent

Gower Mews

Bedford Ave

BLOOMSBURY SQUARE

British Museum

Bedford Square

Great Russell Street

Bloomsbury Square

See Map 10

Bedford Place

SOUTHAMPTON ROW

Boswell Street

New North St

Old Gloucester St

Harpur St

Dombey St

Conduit Street

Princeton St

Cosmo St

Fryer's Delight

Bedford Row

Jockey's Field

Gray's Inn Gardens

Raymond Buildings

BLOOMSBURY

York Way

MAPS

Islington, Clerkenwell & Farringdon

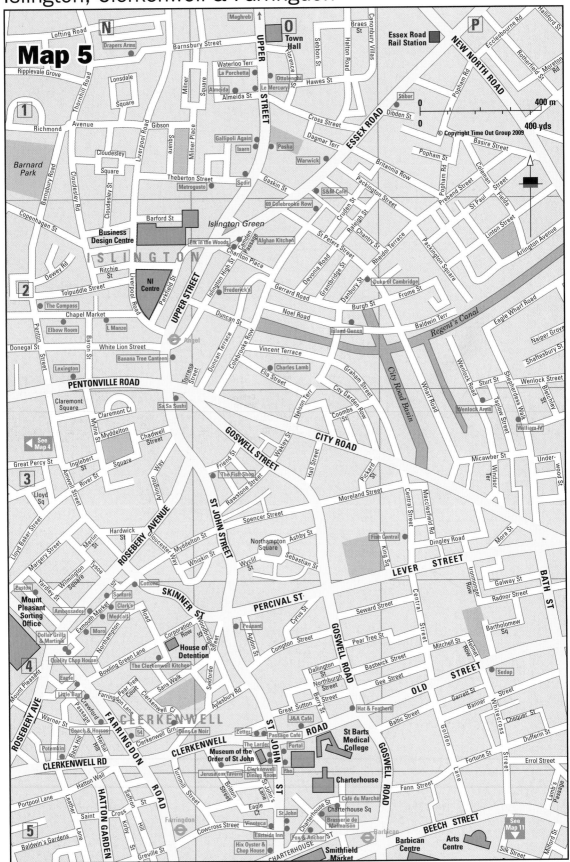

Map 5

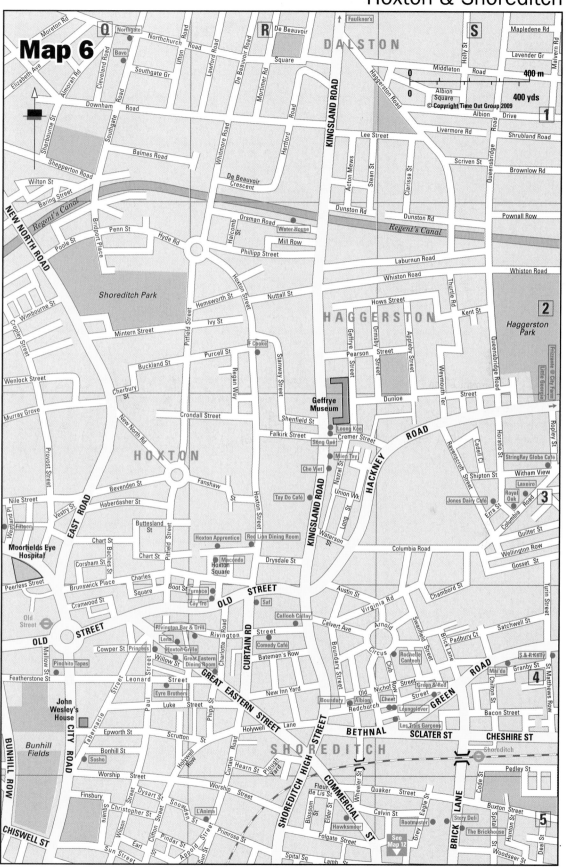

Notting Hill, Bayswater & Kensington

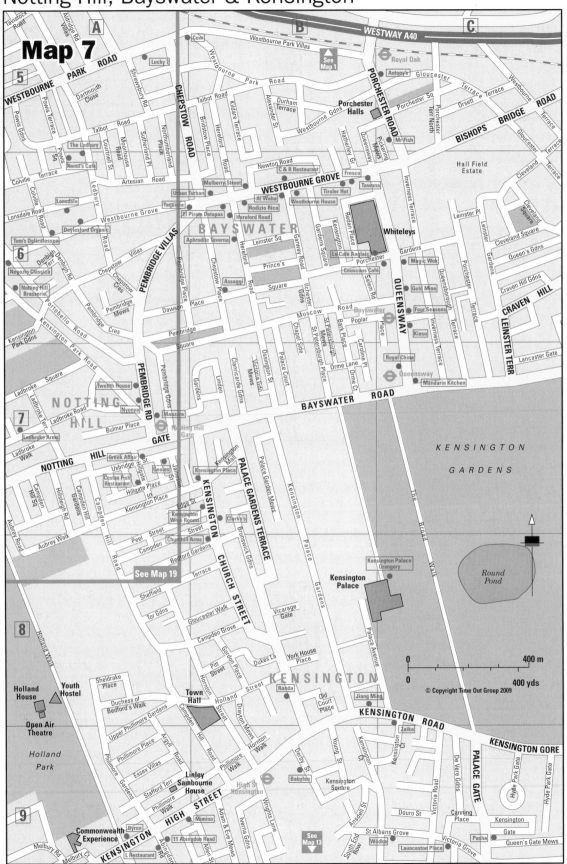

Map 7

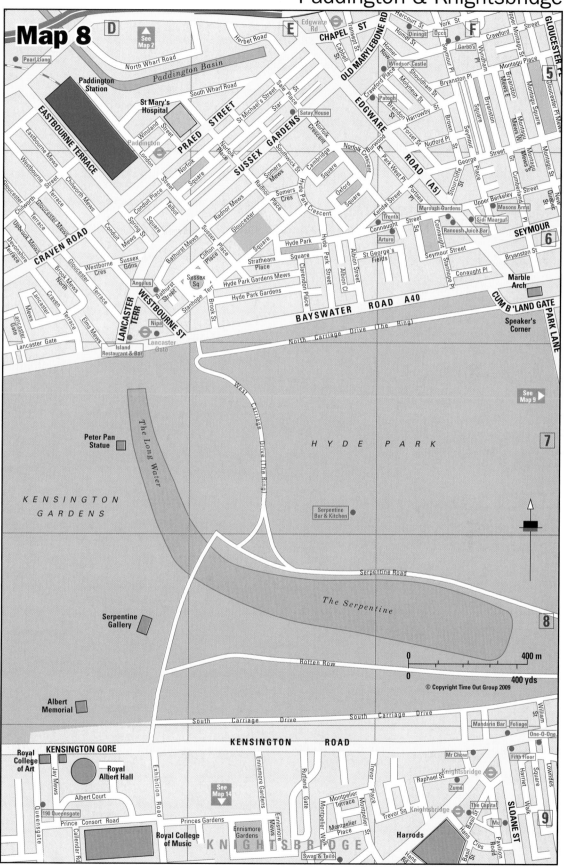

Map 8

Marylebone, Fitzrovia, Mayfair & St James's

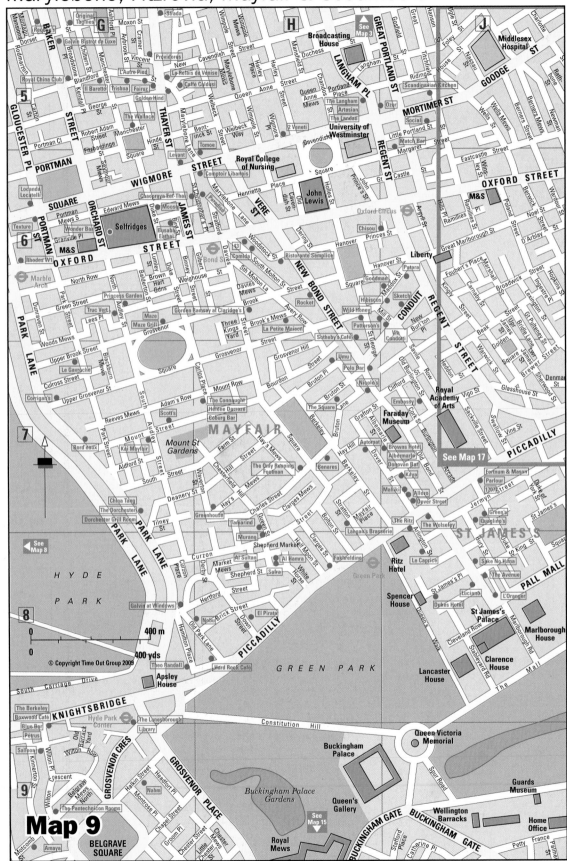

MAPS

Map 9

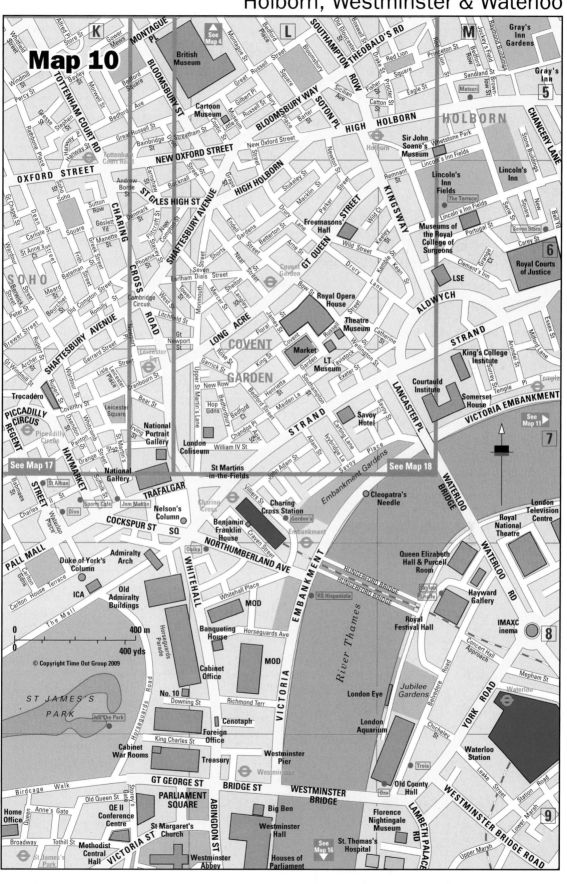

Map 10

City, Waterloo & Borough

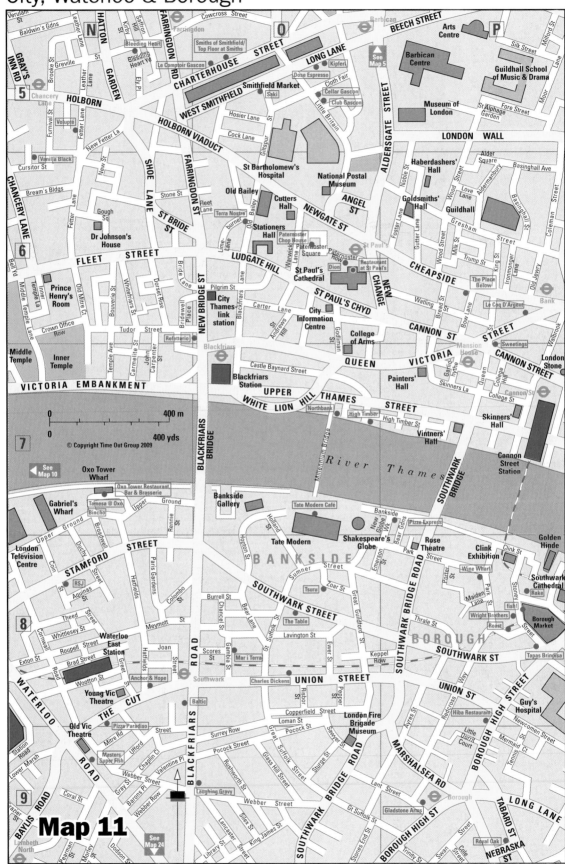

Map 11

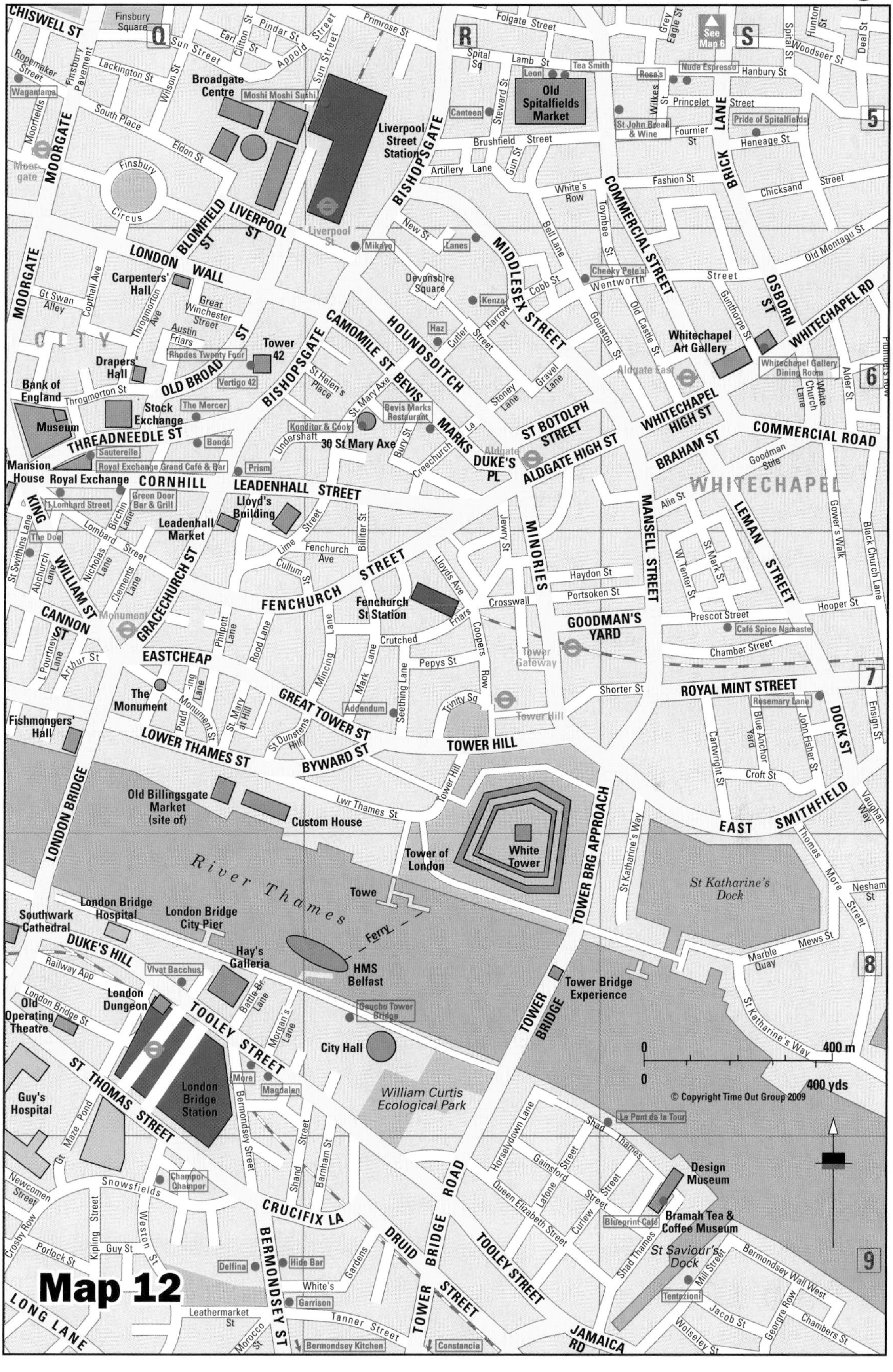

Q R See Map 6 S

5

CHISWELL ST
Finsbury Square
Ropemaker Street
Wagamama
Moorfields
Moor gate
MOORGATE
Finsbury Pavement
Lackington St
Wilson St
South Place
Earl St
Clifton St
Pindar St
Sun Street
Appold St
Broadgate Centre
Moshi Moshi Sushi
Primrose St
Folgate Street
Spital Sq
Lamb St
Tea Smith
Leon
Canteen
Old Spitalfields Market
Brushfield St
Artillery Lane
Grey Eagle St
Nude Espresso
Rosa's
Wilkes St
Princelet Street
Pride of Spitalfields
St John Bread & Wine
Fournier St
Heneage St
Chicksand Street
Hanbury St
Woodseer St
Hunton St
Deal St
BRICK LANE
Old Montagu St

MOORGATE
South Place
Eldon St
Liverpool Street Station
BLOMFIELD ST
LIVERPOOL ST
LONDON WALL
Mikayo
Liverpool St
New St
Lanes
White's Row
Toynbee St
Bell Lane
COMMERCIAL STREET
Wentworth Street
Cheeky Pete's
Old Castle St
Gunthorpe St
Whitechapel Art Gallery
WHITECHAPEL RD
Whitechapel Gallery Dining Room
Alder St
OSBORN ST

6

CITY
Gt Swan Alley
Copthall Ave
Carpenters' Hall
Great Winchester Street
Austin Friars
Rhodes Twenty Four
Tower 42
Vertigo 42
BISHOPSGATE
CAMOMILE ST
BEVIS MARKS
HOUNDSDITCH
Devonshire Square
Haz
Cutler Street
MIDDLESEX STREET
Harrow Pl
Cobb St
Stoney Lane
Gravel Lane
St Botolph Street
Aldgate East
WHITECHAPEL HIGH ST
Whitechapel High St
White Church Lane
COMMERCIAL ROAD
Goodman Stile

Drapers' Hall
Throgmorton St
OLD BROAD ST
St Helen's Place
St Mary Axe
Bevis Marks Restaurant
Kenza
Bank of England
Stock Exchange
Museum
The Mercer
THREADNEEDLE ST
Bonds
Sauterelle
Royal Exchange
Grand Café & Bar
Prism
Undershaft
Konditor & Cook
30 St Mary Axe
Creechurch Lane
Bury St
Aldgate
DUKE'S PL
ALDGATE HIGH ST
BRAHAM ST
MANSELL STREET
WHITECHAPEL
Alie St
W Tenter St
St Mark St
LEMAN STREET
Gower's Walk
Black Church Lane

Mansion House
Royal Exchange
CORNHILL
Green Door Bar & Grill
LEADENHALL STREET
Lloyd's Building
Leadenhall Market
Lime Street
Fenchurch Ave
Billiter St
ST BOTOLPH STREET
MINORIES
Jewry St
Haydon St
Portsoken St
GOODMAN'S YARD
Prescot Street
Café Spice Namaste
Chamber Street
W Tenter St
ROYAL MINT STREET
Rosemary Lane
Blue Anchor Yard
John Fisher St
DOCK ST
Ensign St

7

KING WILLIAM ST
Lombard Street
Nicholas Lane
Clements Lane
Abchurch Lane
St Swithins Lane
The Dog
Birchin Lane
GRACECHURCH ST
Cullum St
FENCHURCH STREET
Fenchurch St Station
Lloyds Ave
Crosswall
Crutched Friars
Coopers Row
Tower Gateway
Shorter St
Cartwright St
Croft St
EAST SMITHFIELD
Vaughan Way

CANNON ST
Arthur St
L Pountney Hill
Monument St
EASTCHEAP
St Mary at Hill
Monument
GREAT TOWER ST
Mincing Lane
Mark Lane
Seething Lane
Pepys St
Addendum
Trinity Sq
Tower Hill
TOWER HILL
Shad Thames

Fishmongers' Hall
The Monument
LOWER THAMES ST
St Dunstan's Hill
BYWARD ST
Tower Hill
Lwr Thames St
TOWER HILL
TOWER BRG APPROACH
St Katharine's Way
Thomas More St
Marble Quay
Mews St
Nesham St

8

LONDON BRIDGE
Old Billingsgate Market (site of)
Custom House
Tower of London
White Tower
St Katharine's Dock
TOWER BRIDGE

River Thames

Southwark Cathedral
London Bridge Hospital
London Bridge City Pier
Towe
Ferry
HMS Belfast
Tower Bridge Experience

DUKE'S HILL
Railway App
Vivat Bacchus
Hay's Galleria
London Bridge Hospital
London Dungeon
Old Operating Theatre
TOOLEY STREET
Banca Bar Lane
Morgan's Lane
Gaucho Tower Bridge
City Hall
St Katharine's Way

Guy's Hospital
ST THOMAS STREET
Gt Maze Pond
London Bridge Station
More
Magdalen
William Curtis Ecological Park
Shad Thames
Le Pont de la Tour

Newcomen Street
Snowsfields
Champor-Champor
Crosby Row
Porlock St
Kipling St
Guy St
Weston St
CRUCIFIX LA
BERMONDSEY ST
Shand St
Barnham St
DRUID STREET
TOWER BRIDGE ROAD
Horselydown Lane
Gainsford Street
Queen Elizabeth Street
Lafone Street
Curlew St
Blueprint Café
St Thomas St
Design Museum
Bramah Tea & Coffee Museum
St Saviour's Dock
Bermondsey Wall West

9

Delfina
Hide Bar
White's
Garrison
Gardens
Leathermarket
Morocco St
TOOLEY STREET
Bermondsey Kitchen
Constancia
JAMAICA RD
Tentazioni
Mill St
George Row
Jacob St
Chambers St
Wolseley St

LONG LANE

Map 12

400 m
400 yds
© Copyright Time Out Group 2009

MAPS

MAPS

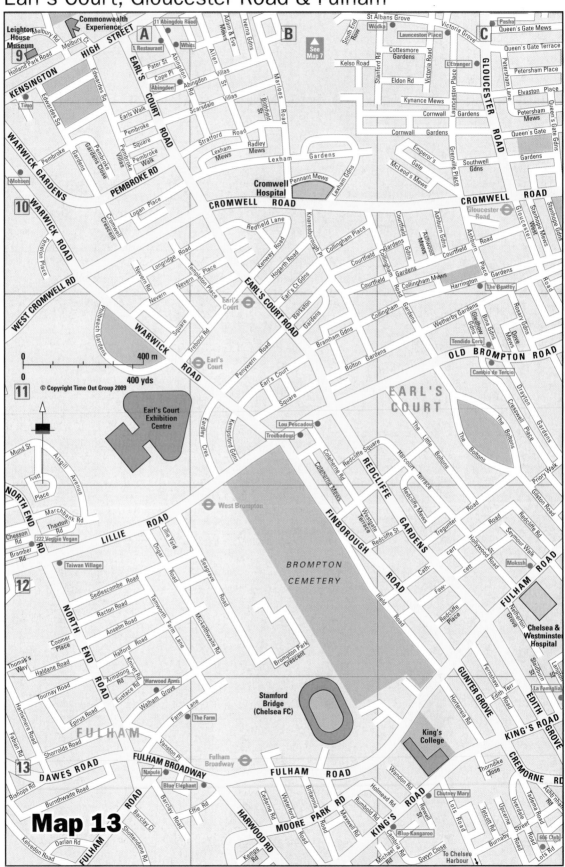

Map 13

Knightsbridge, South Kensington & Chelsea

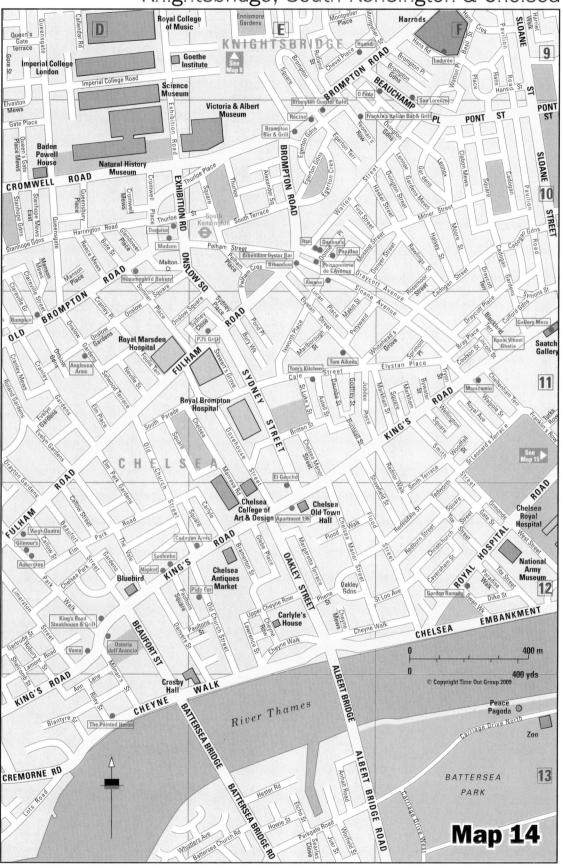

MAPS

Map 14

Belgravia, Victoria & Pimlico

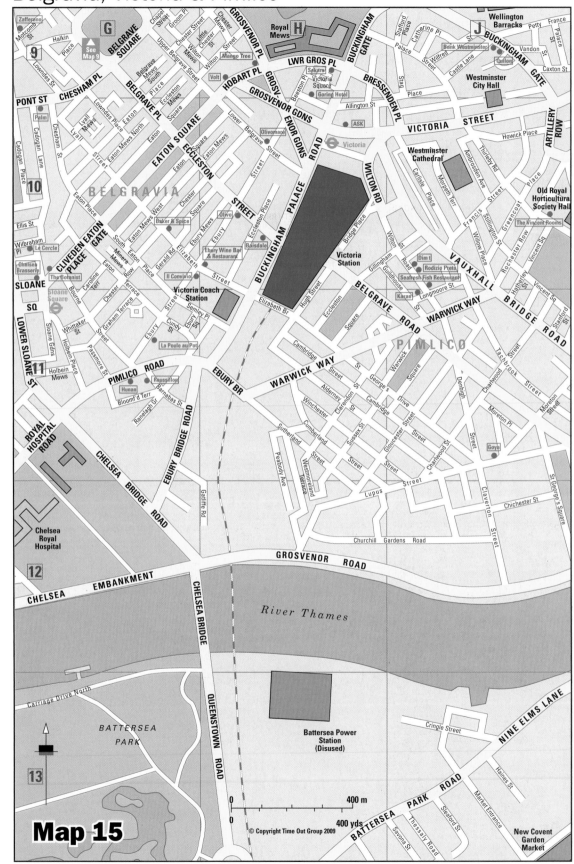

Map 15

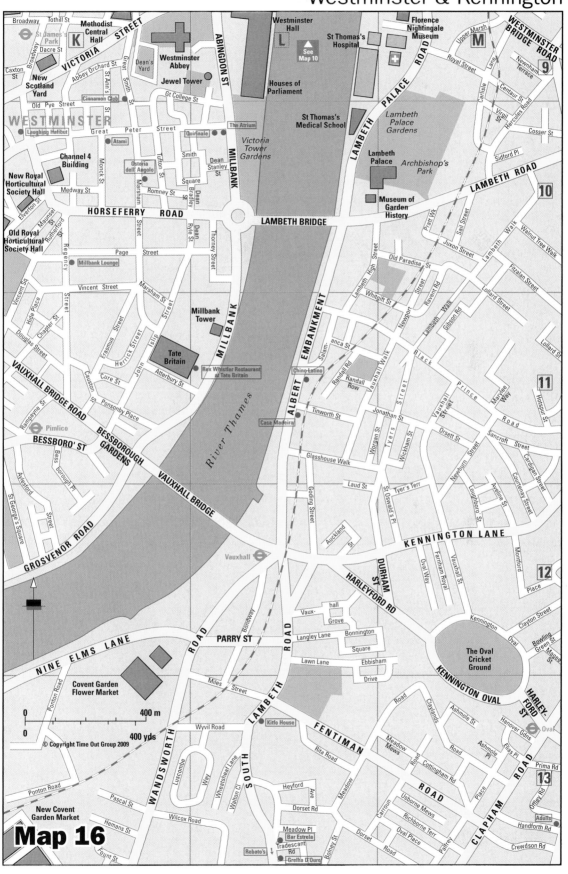

Map 16

© Copyright Time Out Group 2009

Fitzrovia, Soho & Chinatown

MAPS

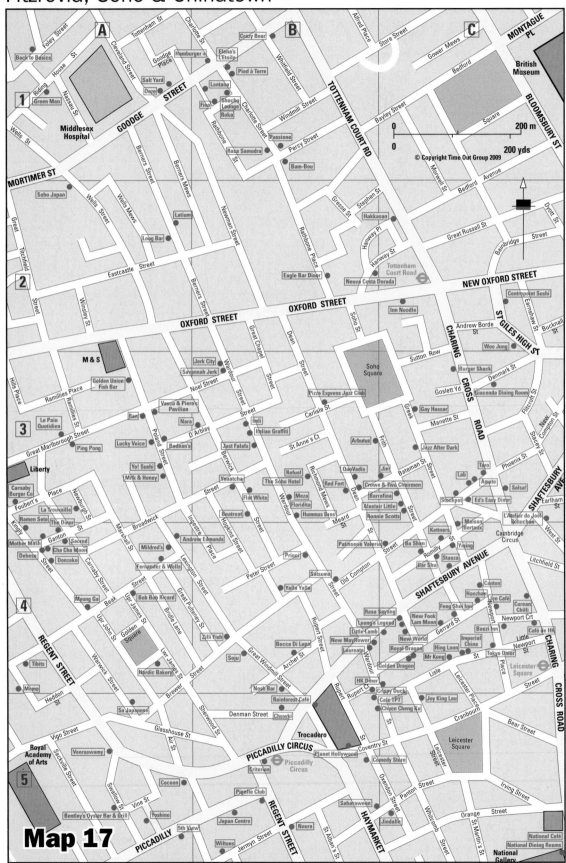

Back to Basics
Foley Street
Tottenham St
Charlotte St
Crazy Bear
A
B
Alfred Place
Store Street
Gower Mews
C
MONTAGUE PL
Goodge St
Goodge Place
Hamburger +
Elena's L'Etoile
Pied à Terre
Bedford
British Museum
BLOOMSBURY ST
House St
Cleveland Street
Whitfield Street
Salt Yard
Ooze
Lantana
Square
200 m
Riding
Nassau St
Fino
Shochu Lounge
Roka
Charlotte Street
Windmill Street
Bayley Street
0
200 yds
Green Man
1
GOODGE STREET
Rathbone
Passione
Percy Street
0
© Copyright Time Out Group 2009
Dyott St
Wells St
Middlesex Hospital
Berners Street
Berners Mews
St
Raza Samudra
Bam-Bou
TOTTENHAM COURT RD
Gresse St
Stephen St
Morwell St
Bedford Avenue
Street
MORTIMER ST
Soho Japan
Wells Street
Wells Mews
Newman Street
Latium
Hakkasan
Great Russell Street
Bainbridge Street
Great Titchfield Street
Long Bar
Berners Mews
Hanway Pl
Hanway St
NEW OXFORD STREET
Eastcastle Street
Eagle Bar Diner
Tottenham Court Road
Centrepoint Sushi
2
Neuva Costa Dorada
Winsley St
Berners Street
OXFORD STREET
OXFORD STREET
Soho St
Inn Noodle
Andrew Borde St
St GILES HIGH ST
Earnshaw St
Bucknall St
Street
OXFORD STREET
Dean
CHARING
Woo Jung
M & S
Jerk City
Wardour Street
Great Chapel Street
Sutton Row
Burger Shack
Denmark St
Hills Place
Savannah Jerk
Noel Street
Soho Square
CROSS
Giaconda Dining Room
Golden Union Fish Bar
Ramillies Place
Vasco & Piero's Pavilion
Pizza Express Jazz Club
Greek
Goslett Yd
Fitzcroft St
Ramillies St
Ban
Nara
Imli
Carlisle St
Gay Hussar
Manette St
ROAD
New Compton St
3
Le Pain Quotidien
D'Arblay
Italian Graffiti
Frith
Phoenix St
Great Marlborough Street
Lucky Voice
Poland Street
Bodean's
Just Falafs
St Anne's Ct
Arbutus
Jazz After Dark
Stacey St
Ping Pong
Berwick
Street
Dean
Jin
Bateman Street
Lab
Taro
Liberty
Yo! Sushi
Milk & Honey
Yauatcha
Refuel
Richmond Mews
QuoVadis
Crown & Two Chairmen
Ameto
Salsa!
SHAFTESBURY AVE
Carnaby Burger Co
Place
The Soho Hotel
Red Fort
Barrafina
Stockpot
Ed's Easy Diner
Earlham
Foubert's
Newburgh St
Flat White
Meza
Floridita
Alastair Little
Ronnie Scotts
Maison Bertaux
L'Atelier de Joël Robuchon
West St
La Trouvaille
Beatroot
Wardour
Hummus Bros
Meard St
Kettners
Cambridge Circus
Ramen Seto
The Diner
Broadwick
Ingestre Place
Hopkins Street
Patisserie Valerie
Ba Shan
Romilly
Yming
Litchfield St
Mother Mash
Ganton
Sacred
Andrew Edmunds
Prince
Bär Shu
Stanza
Dehesa
Donzoko
Street
Mildred's
Fernandez & Wells
Old Compton
Street
SHAFTESBURY AVENUE
Canton
Myung Ga
Beak
Lexington Street
Peter Street
Satsuma
Haozhan
Jen Café
Corean Chilli
Bob Bob Ricard
Great Pulteney St
Yalla Yalla
Feng Shui Inn
Newport
Newport Crt
4
Upr James St
Bridle Lane
Zilli Fish
Rupert Street
Rasa Sayang
New Fook Lam Moon
Gerrard St
Baozi Inn
Café de HK
Golden Square
Upr John St
Bocca Di Lupo
Leong's Legend
Little Lamb
New World
Imperial China
Little Newport St
REGENT STREET
Warwick Street
Lwr James St
Soju
Archer St
New Mayflower
Royal Dragon
Hing Loon
Tokyo Diner
CHARING
Tibits
Nordic Bakery
Great Windmill Street
Laureate
Mr Kong
St
Place
Leicester Square
Momo
Brewer
HK Diner
Golden Dragon
Lisle
Leicester Place
CROSS
Heddon St
Rainforest Café
Café TPT
Crispy Duck
Joy King Lau
ROAD
So Japanese
Sherwood St
Nosh Bar
Chuen Cheng Ku
Cranbourn
Bear Street
Vigo Street
Glasshouse St
Denman Street
Chowki
Coventry St
Leicester Square
Royal Academy of Arts
Sackville Street
Veeraswamy
Air St
Trocadero
PICCADILLY CIRCUS
Planet Hollywood
Comedy Store
Irving Street
5
Piccadilly Circus
Criterion
Oxenden Street
Panton Street
Whitcomb Street
Cocoon
Pigalle Club
Sahataween
St Martin's
Swallow St
Vine St
PICCADILLY
Bentley's Oyster Bar & Grill
Yoshino
Japan Centre
Jermyn Street
5th View
Wiltons
Noura
REGENT STREET
St Alban's St
Jindalle
HAYMARKET
Orange Street
National Café
National Dining Rooms
Map 17
National Gallery

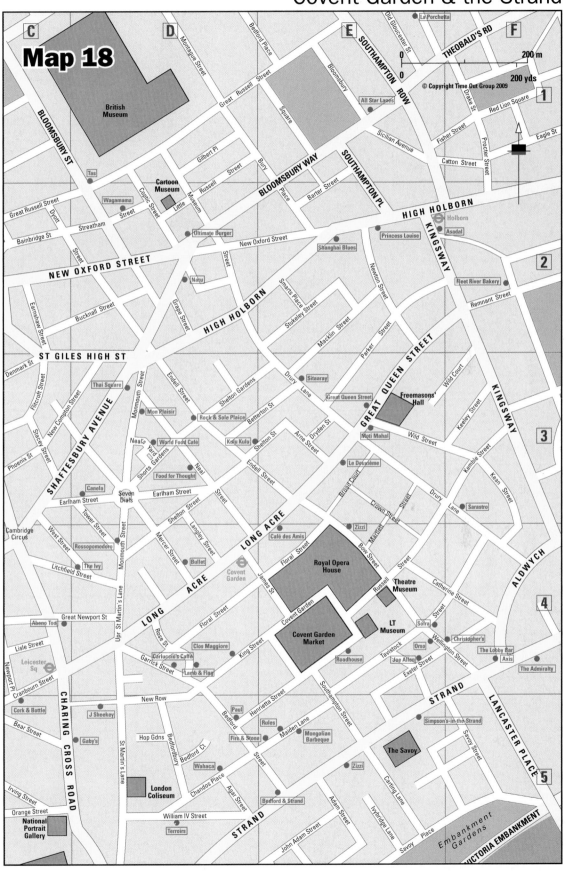

Hammersmith & Shepherd's Bush

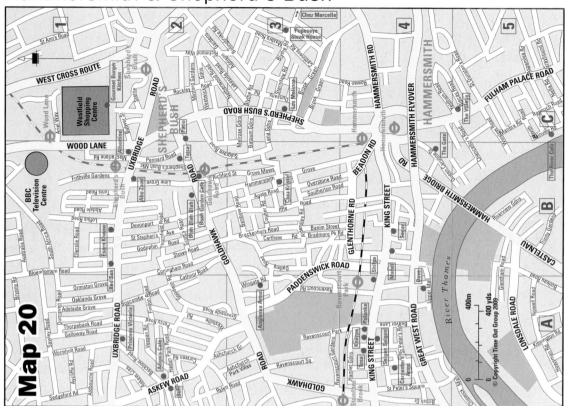

Notting Hill & Ladbroke Grove

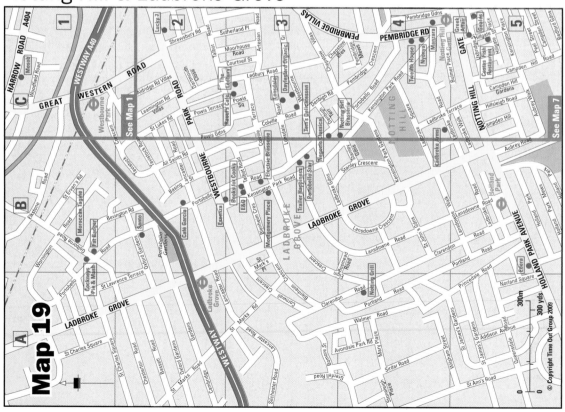

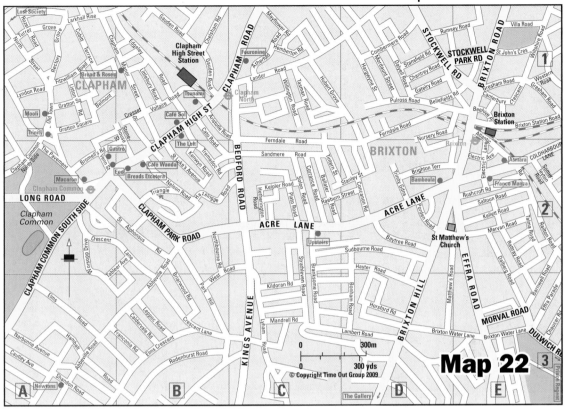

Map 22

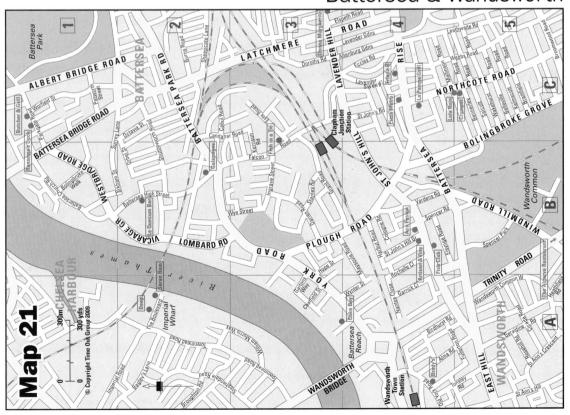

Map 21

Docklands

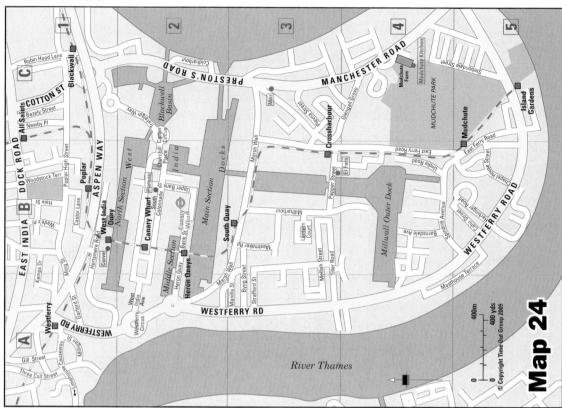

Map 24

Camberwell & Dulwich

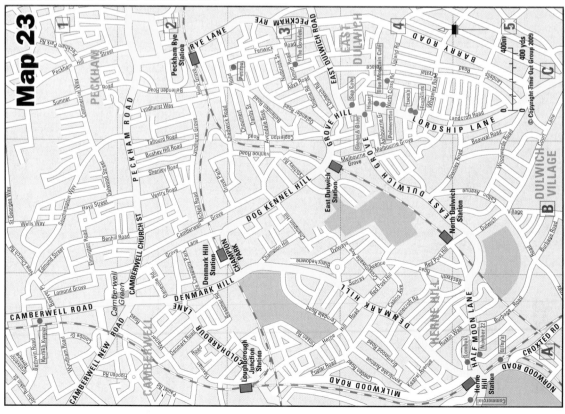

Map 23

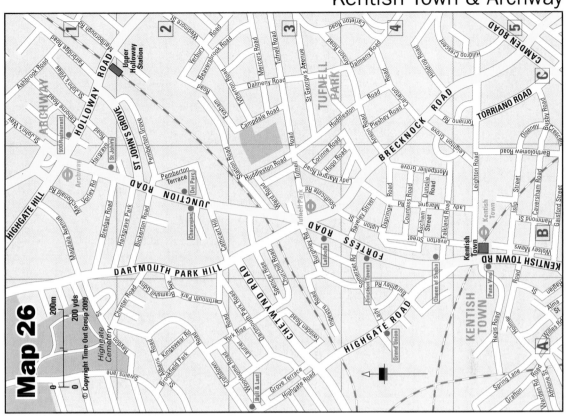

Map 26

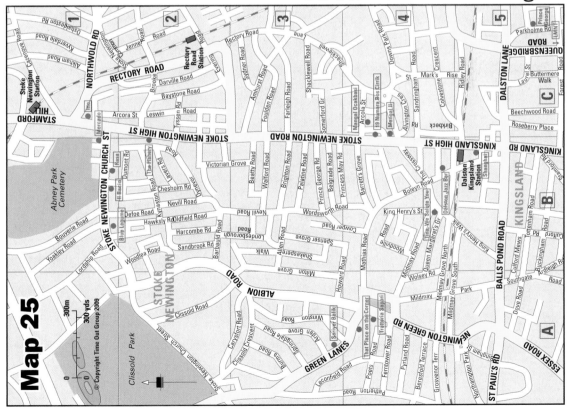

Map 25

MAPS

Hampstead & St John's Wood

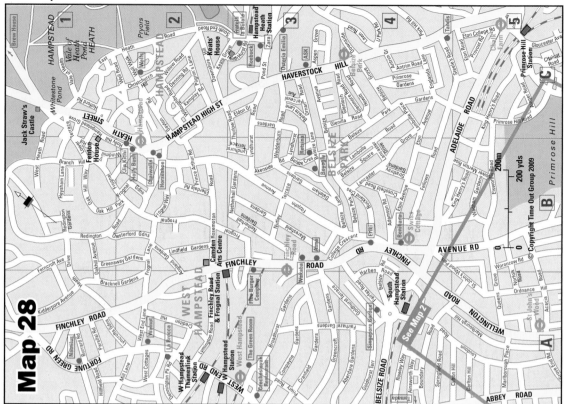

Camden Town & Chalk Farm

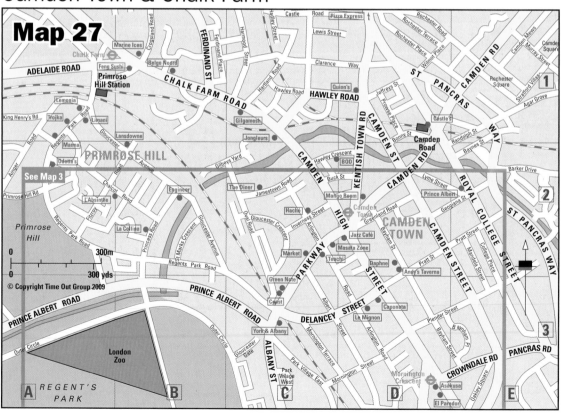

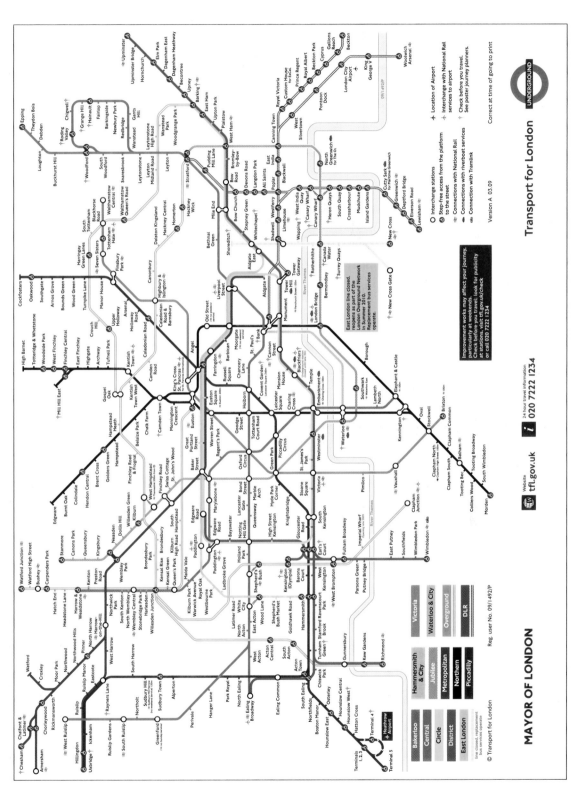

MAPS

MAYOR OF LONDON

Transport for London

UNDERGROUND

Website
tfl.gov.uk

24 hour travel information
020 7222 1234

© Transport for London
Reg. user No. 09/1492/P

Bakerloo
Central
Circle
District
East London
line closed, replacement
bus services operate.

Hammersmith & City
Jubilee
Metropolitan
Northern
Piccadilly

Victoria
Waterloo & City
Overground
DLR

Improvement works may affect your journey,
particularly at weekends.
Check before you travel, look for publicity
at stations, visit tfl.gov.uk/Check
or call 020 7222 1234

East London line closed,
reopens as part of the
London Overground Network
in Summer 2010.
Replacement bus services
operate.

+ Location of Airport
+ Interchange with National Rail
  services to airport
+ Check before you travel.
  See poster journey planners.

Correct at time of going to print

Version A 03.09

○ Interchange stations
◐ Step-free access from the platform
  to the street
≈ Connections with National Rail
⛴ Connections with riverboat services
↺ Connection with Tramlink

Street Index

Grid references not allocated to a specific map can be found on Maps 1-16, which are contiguous and cover central London. Maps 17-28 cover individual areas, most of them outside the centre. The areas covered by all the maps are shown on p343.

A

Abbeville Road - Map 22 A3/B2/3
Abbey Gardens - C2/D2
Abbey Orchard Street - K9
Abbey Road - B1/C1/D2; Map 28 A5
Abbey Street - R10/S10
Abchurch Lane - Q7
Abdale Road - Map 20 B1
Abercorn Close - C2/D2
Abercorn Place - C2/D2
Aberdare Gardens - Map 28 A3/4
Aberdeen Place - D4
Abingdon Road - A9/B10
Abingdon Street - L9
Abingdon Villas - A9/B9
Acacia Road - D2/E1/2; Map 28 A5/B5
Acre Lane - Map 22 C2/D2
Acton Mews - R1
Acton Street - M3
Adam & Eve Mews - B9
Adam Street - L7; Map 18 E5
Adam's Row - G7
Adamson Road - Map 28 B4
Addison Avenue - Map 19 A5
Addison Gardens - Map 20 C2/3
Adelaide Grove - Map 20 A1
Adelaide Road - Map 27 A1; Map 28 B4/5/C5
Adpar Street - D4
Adys Road - Map 23 C3
Agar Grove - Map 27 E1
Agar Street - L7; Map 18 D5
Agate Road - Map 20 B3
Agdon Street - O4
Ainger Road - Map 27 A1/2; Map 28 C5
Ainsworth Way - C1; Map 28 A4
Air Street - J7; Map 17 A5
Aisgill Avenue - A11/12
Akenside Road - Map 28 B3
Albany Street - H2/3; Map 27 C3
Albemarle Street - H7/J7
Albert Bridge - E12/13
Albert Bridge Road - E13; Map 21 C1/2
Albert Court - D9
Albert Embankment - L10/11
Albert Road - A2
Albert Street - H1/J2; Map 27 C3/D3
Albion Close - E6
Albion Drive - S1
Albion Road - Map 25 A2/3/B2
Albion Square - S1
Albion Street - E6
Aldbourne Road - Map 20 A1
Aldenham Street - K2
Aldensley Road - Map 20 B3
Alder Square - P6
Alder Street - S6
Aldermanb'y - P6
Alderney Street - H11
Aldersgate Street - O6/P5/6
Aldford Street - G7
Aldgate High Street - R6
Aldridge Road Villas - Map 19 C2: A5
Aldwych - M6; Map 18 F4
Alexander Square - E10
Alexander Street - B5
Alfred Place - K5; Map 17 B1
Alfred Road - B4

Alice Street - Q10
Alie Street - S6
Alkham Road - Map 25 C1
All Saints Road - Map 19 B2
All Saints Street - M2
Allen Road - Map 25 B3
Allen Street - B9/10
Allington Street - H10
Alma Road - Map 21 A4/5
Alma Square - D2/3
Alma Street - Map 26 A5
Almeide Street - O1
Almorah Road - Q1
Alscot Road - R10/S10
Altenburg Gardens - Map 21 C4
Alvington Crescent - Map 25 C4
Amberley Road - B4
Ambrosden Avenue - J10
Amhurst Road - Map 25 C3
Amott Road - Map 23 C3
Ampton Street - M3
Amwell Street - N3
Andover Place - B2
Andrew Borde Street - K6; Map 17 C2
Angel Street - O6
Angland Gardens - Map 28 B2
Anhalt Road - E13
Ann Lane - D13
Ansdell Street - B9
Anselm Road - A12
Anson Road - Map 26 C3/4
Antrim Grove - Map 28 C4
Antrim Road - Map 28 C4
Appleby Street - S2
Appold Street - Q5/R5
Aquinas Street - N8
Archer Street - K7; Map 17 B4
Arcola Street - Map 25 A4
Arcora St - Map 25 C1/2
Arden Grove - Map 25 A3
Ardleigh Road - Map 25 A5/B5
Argyle Square - L3
Argyle Street - L3
Argyll Road - A9/3 A9/B9
Ariel Way - Map 20 C1
Aristotle Road - Map 22 B1
Arlington Avenue - P2
Arlington Road - H1/ J1/2; Map 27 C2/D3
Arlington Street - J8
Arlington Way - N3
Armstong Road - A12
Arne Street - L6; Map 18 E3
Arnold Circus - R4/S4
Artesian Road - Map 19 C3; A6
Arthur Street - Q7
Artillery Lane - R5
Artington Way - N3
Arundel Street - M6/7
Aryll Street - J6
Ascham Street - Map 26 B4
Ashbourne Grove - Map 23 C4
Ashbridge Street - E4
Ashbrook Road - Map 26 C1
Ashburn Gardens - C10
Ashburn Place - C10
Ashburnham Road - C13/14; D13
Ashby Street - O3
Aschurch Grove - Map 20 A2/3
Ashchurch Park Villas - Map 20 A2/3
Ashmill Street - E4
Ashmole Place - M13
Ashmole Street - M13
Ashmore Road - A2/3
Ashwood Mews - C10
Ashworth Road - C2
Askew Crescent - Map 20 A1
Askew Road - Map 20 A2
Aspemlea Road - Map 20 C5
Aspen Grove - Map 28 C3

Aspen Way - Map 24 A1/B1/C1
Astell Street - E11
Atherfold Road - Map 22 C1
Athlone Street - Map 26 A5
Atlantic Road - Map 22 E1/2
Atterbury Street - K11
Aubrey Road - Map 19 B5/C5; A7/8
Aubrey Walk - Map 19 C5; A7/8
Auckland Street - L12
Augustus Street - J2/3
Austin Friars - Q6
Australia Road - Map 20 B1
Aveline Street - M11/12
Avenue Road - E1; Map 28 B5
Avery Row - H6
Avondale Park Road - Map 19 A3
Avondale Rise; Map 23 B3/C3
Aybrook Street - G5
Aycliffe Road; Map 20 A1
Ayers Street - P8/9
Aylesbury Road - O4
Aylesford Street - K11/12

B

Babmaes Street - K7
Baches Street - Q3
Back Church Lane - S6/7
Back Hill - N4
Bacon Street - S4
Bagley's Lane - Map 21 A2
Bainbridge Street - K5; Map 17 C2; Map 18 C2
Baker Street - G4/5
Balcombe Street - F4
Balderton Street - G6
Baldwin Terrace - P2
Baldwin's Gardens - N5
Balfe Street - L2
Ballater Road - Map 22 C2
Balls Pond Road - Map 25 A5/B5
Balmes Road - Q1
Baltic Street - P4
Banim Street - Map 20 B3
Bank Street - Map 24 B2
Bankside - P7
Banner Street - P4
Barbauld Road - Map 25 B2
Barclay Close - A13
Barclay Road - A13
Barford Street - N2
Baring Street - Q1/2
Bark Place - B6/7
Barker Drive - K1; Map 27 E2
Barkston Gardens - B11
Barnabas Street - G11
Barnby Street - J3
Barnham Street - Q9
Barnsbury Road - N1/2
Barnsbury Street - N1/O1
Barnsdale Avenue - Map 24 B4
Barnsdale Road - A3/4
Barnwell Road - Map 22 E2/3
Baron Street - N2
Barons Place - N9
Barrett's Grove - Map 25 B4
Barry Road - Map 23 C4/5
Barter Street - L5; Map 18 E1/2
Bartholomew Square - P4
Barttholomew Road - Map 26 B5
Basil Street - F9
Basing Street - Map 19 B2
Basinghall Avenue - P6
Basinghall Street - P6
Basire Street - P1
Bassett Road - Map 19 A2
Bastwick Street - O4/P4
Bateman Street - K6; Map 17 C3
Bateman's Row - R4

Bath Street - P3/4
Bathurst Mews - D6
Bathurst Street - D6
Batoum Gardens - Map 20 B3/C3
Battersea Bridge - E13
Battersea Bridge Road - E13; Map 21 B1/C1/2
Battersea Church Road - E13; Map 21 B1
Battersea High Street - Map 21 B2
Battersea Park Road - H13/J13; Map 21 C2
Battersea Rise - Map 21 B4/C4
Battle Bridge Lane - Q8
Battle Bridge Road - L2
Bayham Street - J1/2; Map 27 D3/E3
Bayley Street - K5; Map 17 C1
Baylis Road- N9
Baynes Street - Map 27 E1/2
Baynham Place - J1/2; Map 27 E3
Baystone Road - Map 25 C2
Bayswater Road - B7/C7/D7/E6/F6
Baytree Road - Map 22 D2
Bazely Street - Map 24 C1
Beadon Road - Map 20 B4
Beak Street - J6; Map 17 A4
Bear Gardens - P7/8
Bear Lane - O8
Bear Street - K7; Map 17 C5; Map 18 C5
Beatty Road - Map 25 B3
Beauchamp Place - F9/10
Beaufort Street - D12
Beaumont Mews - G5
Beaumont Place - J4
Beaumont Street - G5
Beauval Road - Map 23 B5/C5
Beaversbrook Road - Map 26 C2/3
Beavor Lane - Map 20 A4
Becklow Road - Map 20 A2
Beckwith Road - Map 23 A4/5/B4
Bedford Avenue - K5; Map 17 C1/2
Bedford Court - L7; Map 18 D5
Bedford Gardens - Map 19 C5; A8/B8
Bedford Place - L5; Map 18 D1/E1
Bedford Road - Map 22 C1/2
Bedford Row - M5
Bedford Square - K5; Map 17 C1
Bedford Street - L7; Map 18 D5/E5
Bedford Way - K4
Bedfordbury - L7; Map 18 D5
Beech Street - P5
Beechwood Road - Map 25 C5
Beehive Place - Map 22 E1
Beeston Place - H9
Belgrade Road - Map 25 B3
Belgrave Gardens - C1
Belgrave Mews North - G9
Belgrave Mews South - G9
Belgrave Place - G10
Belgrave Road - H10/J11
Belgrave Square - G9
Belgrave Street - L3
Bell Lane - R6
Bell Yard - M6
Bellefields Road - Map 22 D1
Bellenden Road - Map 23 C2
Belleville Road - Map 21 C5
Belmont Close - Map 22 A1
Belsize Avenue - Map 28 C3
Belsize Crescent - Map 28 B3
Belsize Grove - Map 28 C4
Belsize Lane - Map 28 B3/4/C3
Belsize Park - Map 28 B4
Belsize Park Gardens - Map 28 C4
Belsize Road - B1/C1; Map 28 A4/B4
Belsize Square - Map 28 B4
Belvedere Road - M8/9
Benbow Road - Map 20 B3

Benhill Road - Map 23 B1/2
Bennerley Road - Map 21 C5
Bentinck Street - H5
Beresfold Terrace - Map 25 A4
Berkeley Square - H7
Berkeley Street - H7
Bermondsey Street - Q8/9/10
Bermondsey Wall West - S9
Bernard Street - L4
Berners Mews - J5; Map 17 A1/2/B2
Berners Street - J5/6; Map 17 A1/2
Berry Street - O4
Berwick Street - J6/6 K6; Map 17 B3/4
Bessborough Gardens - K11
Bessborough Place - K11/12
Bessborough Street - K11
Bessmer Road - Map 23 A2/3
Bethnal Green Road - R4/S4
Bethwin Road - Map 23 A1
Betterton Street - L6; Map 18 D3/E3
Bevenden Street - Q3
Bevington Road - Map 19 B1/2
Bevis Marks - R6
Bickenhall Street - F5
Bickerton Road - Map 26 B2
Bidborough Street - L3
Biddulph Road - B3/C3
Bina Gardens - C11
Bingfield Street - M1
Bingham Place - G4
Bingham Street - Map 25 A5
Binney Street - G6
Birchin Lane - Q6
Bird Street - G6
Birdcage Walk - K9
Birdhurst Road - Map 21 A4
Birkbeck Road - Map 25 C4/5
Birkenhead Street - L3
Biscay Road - Map 20 C4/5
Bishops Bridge Road - C5/D5
Bishops Road - A13
Bishopsgate - Q6/R5/6
Black Prince Street - L11/M11
Blackfriars Bridge - O7
Blackfriars Lane - O6
Blackfriars Road - N8/O8
Blackland Terrace - F11
Blanchedowne - Map 23 B3
Blandford Square - F4
Blandford Street - G5
Blantyre Street - D13
Bleeding Heart Yd - N5
Blenheim Crescent - Map 19 A3/B3
Blenheim Terrace - C2
Bletchley Street - P3
Blithfield Street - B10
Blkbrne's Mews - G7
Bloemfontein Road - Map 20 B1
Blomfield Road - C4/D4
Blomfield Street - Q5/6
Blomfield Villas - C5
Bloomfield Terrace - G11
Bloomsbury Square - L5; Map 18 E1
Bloomsbury Street - K5; Map 17 C1; Map 18 C1/D1/2
Bloomsbury Way - L5; Map 18 D2/E1/2
Blossom Street - R5
Blue Anchor Yard - S7
Blythe Road - Map 20 C3
Boileau Road - Map 20 A5/B5
Boleyn Road - Map 25 B4/5
Bolingbroke Grove - Map 21 B5/C5
Bolingbroke Road - Map 20 C2/3
Bolingbroke Walk - Map 21 B1
Bolney Street - L13
Bolsover Street - H4/J5
Bolton Gardens - B11/C11
Bolton Street - H7/8
Boltons, The - C11
Bomore Street - Map 19 A3
Bondway - L12

STREET INDEX

Advertisers' Index

Please refer to relevant sections for addresses/telephone numbers

Subject Index

SUBJECT INDEX

SUBJECT INDEX

SUBJECT INDEX

SUBJECT INDEX

Area Index

AREA INDEX

AREA INDEX

Camberwell

Branches
Nando's
88 Denmark Hill, SE5 8RX
(7738 3808)
Global
Kazakh Kyrgyz Restaurant
p119
Pasha Hotel, 158 Camberwell
Road, SE5 0EE (7277 2228)

Camden

The Americas
The Diner   p37
2 Jamestown Road,
NW1 7BY (7485 5223,
www.goodlifediner.com)
Guanabana   p43
85 Kentish Town Road,
NW1 8NY (7485 1166,
www.guanabanarestaurant.com)
Bars
Gilgamesh   p322
Stables Market, Chalk Farm
Road, NW1 8AH (7482 5757,
www.gilgameshbar.com)
Branches
Grand Union
102-104 Camden Road,
NW1 9EA (7485 4530)
Lisboa Pâtisserie
4 Plender Street, NW1 0JP
(7387 1782)
Pizza Express
85 Parkway, NW1 7PP
(7267 2600)
Strada
40-42 Parkway, NW1 7AH
(7428 9653)
Wagamama
11 Jamestown Road,
NW1 7BW (7428 0800)
British
Market   p60
43 Parkway, NW1 7PN
(7267 9700, www.market
restaurant.co.uk)
Budget
Castle's   p283
229 Royal College Street,
NW1 9LT (7485 2196)
Burger Bars
Haché   p286
24 Inverness Street,
NW1 7HJ (7485 9100,
www.hacheburgers.com)
Caribbean
Mango Room   p63
10-12 Kentish Town Road,
NW1 8NH (7482 5065,
www.mangoroom.co.uk)
Chinese
Teachi   p79
29-31 Parkway, NW1 7PN
(7485 9933)
Eating & Entertainment
Green Note   p337
106 Parkway, NW1 7AN (7485
9899, www.greennote.co.uk)
Jazz Café   p337
5-7 Parkway, NW1 7PG (7485
6834, www.jazzcafelive.com)
Fish
Coast Dining   p89
108 Parkway, NW1 7AN (7267
9555, www.coastdining.co.uk)
Gastropubs
Prince Albert   p114
163 Royal College Street,
NW1 0SG (7485 0270,
www.princealbertcamden.com)
Greek
Andy's Taverna   p122
81-81A Bayham Street,
NW1 0AG (7485 9718,
www.andystaverna.com)
Daphne   p122
83 Bayham Street, NW1 0AG
(7267 7322)
Indian
Masala Zone   p152
25 Parkway, NW1 7PG (7267
4422, www.masalazone.com)
Italian
Caponata   p175
3-7 Delancey Street,
NW1 7NL (7383 7808,
www.caponatacamden.co.uk)
Japanese
Asakusa   p187
265 Eversholt Street, NW1
1BA (7388 8533/8399)

Middle Eastern

Le Mignon   p209
98 Arlington Road, NW1 7HD
(7387 0600)
Modern European
York & Albany   p228
127-129 Parkway,
NW1 7PS (7388 3344,
www.gordonramsay.com)
Pubs
Quinn's   p329
65 Kentish Town Road,
NW1 8NY (7267 8240)
Spanish
El Parador   p248
245 Eversholt Street,
NW1 1BA (7387 2789,
www.elparadorlondon.com)

Catford

Branches
Nando's
74-76 Rushey Green,
SE6 4HW (8314 0122)
Gastropubs
Perry Hill   p109
78-80 Perry Hill,
SE6 4EY (8699 5076,
www.theperryhill.co.uk)

Chalk Farm

Branches
Cottons
55 Chalk Farm Road,
NW1 8AN (7485 8388)
Nando's
57-58 Chalk Farm Road,
NW1 8AN (7424 9040)
La Porchetta
74-77 Chalk Farm Road,
NW1 8AN (7267 6822)
Sardo Canale
42 Gloucester Avenue,
NW1 8JD (7722 2800)
Budget
Marine Ices   p284
8 Haverstock Hill,
NW3 2BL (7482 9003,
www.marineices.co.uk)
Chinese
Yum Cha   p79
27-28 Chalk Farm Road,
NW1 8AG (7482 2228,
www.silks-nspiceyumcha.co.uk)
East European
Trojka   p83
101 Regents Park Road,
NW1 8UR (7483 3765,
www.troykarestaurant.co.uk)
French
L'Absinthe   p100
40 Chalcot Road, NW1 8LS
(7483 4848)
Gastropubs
Engineer   p113
65 Gloucester Avenue,
NW1 8JH (7722 0950,
www.the-engineer.com)
Lansdowne   p114
90 Gloucester Avenue,
NW1 8HX (7483 0409,
www.thelansdownepub.co.uk)
Global
Belgo Noord   p118
72 Chalk Farm Road,
NW1 8AN (7267 0718,
www.belgo-restaurants.com)
Greek
Lemonia   p122
89 Regent's Park Road,
NW1 8UY (7586 7454)
Limani   p122
154 Regent's Park Road,
NW1 8XN (7483 4492)
Italian
La Collina   p175
17 Princess Road,
NW1 8JR (7483 0192)
Japanese
Feng Sushi   p182
1 Adelaide Road,
NW3 3QE (7483 2929,
www.fengsushi.co.uk)
Middle Eastern
Tandis   p210
73 Haverstock Hill, NW3 4SL
(7586 8079)
Modern European
Odette's   p228
130 Regent's Park Road,
NW1 8XL (7586 8569,
www.odettesprimrosehill.com)

Oriental

Gilgamesh   p236
Stables Market, Chalk Farm
Road, NW1 8AH (7482 5757,
www.gilgameshbar.com)
Vegetarian
Manna   p273
4 Erskine Road, NW3 3AJ
(7722 8028, www.manna-
veg.com)

Chancery Lane

Branches
Gaucho Chancery
125-126 Chancery Lane,
WC2A 1PU (7242 7727)
Konditor & Cook
46 Gray's Inn Road, WC1X 8LR
(7404 6300)
Paul
147 Fleet Street, EC4A 2BU
(7353 5874)
Eating & Entertainment
Volupté   p337
7-9 Norwich Street,
EC4A 1EJ (7831 1622,
www.volupte-lounge.com)
Pubs
Seven Stars   p325
53 Carey Street, WC2A 2JB
(7242 8521)

Cheam, Surrey

Branches
Pizza Express
4-6 Ewell Road, Cheam,
Surrey, SM3 8BU (8770 0082)
Prezzo
26 Station Way, Cheam,
Surrey, SM3 8SQ (8643 7490)

Chelsea

The Americas
El Gaucho   p37
Chelsea Farmers' Market,
125 Sydney Street,
SW3 6NR (7376 8514,
www.elgaucho.co.uk)
Branches
Apartment 195
(branch of Jamies)
195 King's Road, SW3 5ED
(7351 5195)
Baker & Spice
47 Denyer Street, SW3 2LX
(7589 4734)
Benihana
77 King's Road, SW3 4NX
(7376 7799)
Chelsea Left Wing Café
(branch of Pâtisserie Valerie)
Duke of York Square, SW3 4LY
(7730 7094)
Daylesford Organic
31 Sloane Square, SW1W 8AG
(7881 8020)
Gaucho Sloane
89 Sloane Avenue, SW3 3DX
(7584 9901)
Haché
329-331 Fulham Road, SW10
9QL (7823 3515)
Le Pain Quotidien
201-203 King's Road,
SW3 5ED (7486 6154)
Lisboa Pâtisserie
6 World's End Place, off King's
Road, SW10 0HE (7376 3639)
Made In Italy
(branch of Napulé)
249 King's Road, SW3 5EL
(7352 1880)
Marechiaro (branch of Napulé)
257 King's Road, SW3 5EL
(7351 2417)
Napket
342 King's Road, SW3 5UR
(7352 9832, www.napket.com)
Paul
134 King's Road, SW3 4XB
(7581 9611)
Paul
166 Fulham Road, SW10 9PR
(7373 0429)
Pizza Express
363 Fulham Road, SW10 9TN
(7352 5300)
Pizza Express
The Pheasantry, 152-154
King's Road, SW3 4UT
(7351 5031)
Ranoush Juice
338 King's Road, SW3 5UR
(7352 0044)

Santa Lucia

(branch of Napulé)
2 Hollywood Road, SW10 9HY
(7352 8484)
Sophie's Steakhouse & Bar
311-313 Fulham Road,
SW10 9QH (7352 0088,
www.sophiessteakhouse.com)
Stockpot
273 King's Road, SW3 5EN
(7823 3175)
Brasseries
Gallery Mess   p47
Saatchi Gallery, Duke of York's
HQ, King's Road, SW3 4LY
(7730 8135)
Tom's Kitchen   p47
27 Cale Street,
SW3 3QP (7349 0202,
www.tomskitchen.co.uk)
British
Gilmour's   p59
9 Park Walk, SW10 0AJ
(7349 6800,
www.gilmoursparkwalk.com)
Kings Road Steakhouse
& Grill   p59
386 King's Road, SW3 5UZ
(7351 9997, www.kingsroad
steakhouseandgrill.com)
Eating & Entertainment
606 Club   p339
90 Lots Road, SW10 0QD
(7352 5953, www.606club.
co.uk)
Gastropubs
Cadogan Arms   p107
298 King's Road,
SW3 5UG (7352 6500,
www.thecadoganarms
chelsea.com)
Pig's Ear   p107
35 Old Church Street,
SW3 5BS (7352 2908)
Hotels & Haute Cuisine
Aubergine   p132
11 Park Walk, SW10 0AJ
(7352 3449, www.aubergine
restaurant.co.uk)
Gordon Ramsay   p133
68 Royal Hospital Road,
SW3 4HP (7352 4441,
www.gordonramsay.com)
Indian
Chutney Mary   p144
535 King's Road, SW10 0SZ
(7351 3113,
www.chutneymary.com)
Painted Heron   p144
112 Cheyne Walk, SW10 0DJ
(7351 5232,
www.thepaintedheron.com)
Rasoi Vineet Bhatia   p144
10 Lincoln Street, SW3 2TS
(7225 1881,
www.rasoirestaurant.co.uk)
Italian
Manicomio   p172
85 Duke of York Square,
SW3 4LY (7730 3366,
www.manicomio.co.uk)
Osteria dell'Arancio   p172
383 King's Road, SW10 0LP
(7349 8111,
www.osteriadellarancio.co.uk)
Modern European
Bluebird   p223
350 King's Road,
SW3 5UU (7559 1000,
www.bluebirdchelsea.com)
The Botanist   p224
7 Sloane Square, SW1W 8EE
(7730 0077, www.thebotanist
onsloanesquare.com)
Oriental
Itsu   p234
118 Draycott Avenue, SW3 3AE
(7590 2400, www.itsu.com)
Sushinho   p234
312-314 King's Road,
SW3 5UH (7349 7496,
www.sushinho.com)
Pubs
King's Arms   p327
190 Fulham Road,
SW10 9PN (7351 5043,
www.kingsarmschelsea.com)

Chinatown

Chinese
Baozi Inn   p64
25 Newport Court,
WC2H 7JS (7287 6877)

Café de Hong Kong   p72

47-49 Charing Cross Road,
WC2H 0AN (7534 9898)
Canton   p72
11 Newport Place, WC2H 7JR
(7437 6220)
Feng Shui Inn   p64
4-6 Gerrard Street, W1D 5PG
(7734 6778,
www.fengshuiinn.co.uk)
Golden Dragon   p64
28-29 Gerrard Street,
W1D 6JW (7734 2763)
Haozhan   p64
8 Gerrard Street, W1D 5PJ
(7434 3838,
www.haozhan.co.uk)
Hing Loon   p72
25 Lisle Street, WC2H 7BA
(7437 3602)
Imperial China   p66
White Bear Yard, 25A Lisle
Street, WC2H 7BA (7734
3388, www.imperial-china.
co.uk)
Jen Café   p73
4-8 Newport Place, WC2H 7JP
(no phone)
Joy King Lau   p66
3 Leicester Street, WC2H 7BL
(7437 1132)
Leong's Legends   p66
4 Macclesfield Street,
W1D 6AX (7287 0288)
Little Lamb   p66
72 Shaftesbury Avenue,
W1D 6NA (7287 8078)
Mr Kong   p66
21 Lisle Street, WC2H 7BA
(7437 7341, www.mrkong
restaurant.com)
New Mayflower   p67
68-70 Shaftesbury Avenue,
W1D 6LY (7734 9207)
New World   p67
1 Gerrard Place, W1D 5PA
(7734 0396)
Royal Dragon   p67
30 Gerrard Street, W1D 6JS
(7734 1388)
Japanese
Tokyo Diner   p183
2 Newport Place,
WC2H 7JP (7287 8777,
www.tokyodiner.com)
Korean
Corean Chilli   p195
51 Charing Cross Road,
WC2H 0NE (7734 6737)
**Malaysian, Indonesian &
Singaporean**
Rasa Sayang   p200
5 Macclesfield Street, W1D
6AY (7734 1382)

Chingford

Branches
Pizza Express
45-47 Old Church Road,
E4 6SJ (8529 7866)

Chiswick

Branches
Carluccio's Caffè
324-344 Chiswick High Road,
W4 5TA (8995 8073)
Chakalaka
1-4 Barley Mow Passage,
W4 4PH (8995 4725)
The Devonshire
(branch of Narrow)
126 Devonshire Road,
W4 2JJ (7592 7962,
www.gordonramsay.com)
Eco
144 Chiswick High Road,
W4 1PU (8747 4822)
Frankie's Italian Bar & Grill
68 Chiswick High Road,
W4 1SY (8987 9988)
Giraffe
270 Chiswick High Road,
W4 1PD (8995 2100)
Gourmet Burger Kitchen
131 Chiswick High Road,
W4 2ED (8995 4548)
Nando's
187-189 Chiswick High Road,
W4 2DR (8995 7533)
Pâtisserie Valerie
319 Chiswick High Road,
W4 5TA (8995 0234)
Pizza Express
252 High Road, W4 1PD
(8747 0193)

AREA INDEX

Saran Rom p253
Waterside Tower, The
Boulevard, Imperial Wharf,
Townmead Road, SW6 2UB
(7751 3111, www.saran
rom.com)

Gipsy Hill
Global
Numidie p119
48 Westow Hill, SE19 1RX
(8766 6166, www.numidie.
co.uk)
Oriental
Mangosteen p235
246 Gipsy Road, SE27 9RB
(8670 0333)

Gloucester Road
Branches
ASK
23-24 Gloucester Arcade,
Gloucester Road, SW7 4SF
(7835 0840)
Byron
75 Gloucester Road, SW7 4SS
(7244 0700)
dim t
154-156 Gloucester Road,
SW7 4TD (7370 0070,
www.dimt.co.uk)
Green Door Steakhouse
152 Gloucester Road,
SW7 4QH (7373 2010)
Nando's
117 Gloucester Road,
SW7 4ST (7373 4446)
Paul
73 Gloucester Road, SW7 4SS
(7373 1232)
Hotels & Haute Cuisine
The Bentley p128
27-33 Harrington Gardens,
SW7 4JX (7244 5555,
www.thebentley-hotel.com)
Modern European
L'Etranger p214
36 Gloucester Road,
SW7 4QT (7584 1118,
www.etranger.co.uk)
North African
Pasha p230
1 Gloucester Road,
SW7 4PP (7589 7969,
www.pasha-restaurant.
co.uk)

Golders Green
Branches
Pizza Express
94 Golders Green Road,
NW11 8HB (8455 9556)
Fish & Chips
Sam's p302
68-70 Golders Green Road,
NW11 8LN (8455 9898/
7171)
Italian
Philpott's Mezzaluna p176
424 Finchley Road, NW2 2HY
(7794 0452)
Japanese
Café Japan p190
626 Finchley Road, NW11 7RR
(8455 6854)
Eat Tokyo p190
14 North End Road, NW11 7PH
(8209 0079)
Jewish
Bloom's p192
130 Golders Green Road,
NW11 8HB (8455 1338)
Dizengoff p192
118 Golders Green Road,
NW11 8HB (8458 7003,
www.dizengoffkosher
restaurant.co.uk)
La Fiesta p192
235 Golders Green Road,
NW11 9ES (8458 0444,
www.lafiestauk.com)
Met Su Yan p192
134 Golders Green Road,
NW11 8HB (8458 8088,
www.metsuyan.co.uk)
Novellino p192
103 Golders Green Road,
NW11 8EN (8458 7273)
Solly's p192
146-150 Golders Green Road,
NW11 8HE (ground floor &
takeaway 8455 2121/
first floor 8455 0004)

Korean
Kimchee p198
887 Finchley Road, NW11 8RR
(8455 1035)

Greenwich
Branches
**Buenos Aires Café
& Delicatessen**
86 Royal Hill, SE10 8RT
(8488 6764)
Davy's Wine Vaults
161 Greenwich High Road,
SE10 8JA (8858 7204)
Gaucho O2
The O2, Peninsula Square,
SE10 0DX (8858 7711)
Gourmet Burger Kitchen
45 Greenwich Church Street,
SE10 9BL (8858 3920)
Nando's
The O2, Millennium Way,
SE10 0AX (8269 2401)
Nando's
UCI Cinema Complex, Bugsby's
Way, SE10 0QJ (8293 3025)
Pizza Express
4 Church Street, SE10 9BG
(8853 2770)
Pizza Express
Unit 8, Entertainment Avenue,
The O2, SE10 0DY
(8293 5071)
Prezzo
35 Bugsby's Way, Millennium
Park, SE10 0QJ (8858 2760)
Rivington Greenwich
178 Greenwich High Road,
SE10 8NN (8293 9270)
Rodizio Rico
O2 Arena, SE10 0AX
(8858 6333)
S&M Café
O2 Arena, Peninsula Square,
SE10 0DX (8305 1940)
Zizzi
The O2, Millennium Way,
SE10 0UZ (8858 9097)
Cafés
Pavilion Tea House p297
Greenwich Park, Blackheath
Gate, SE10 8QY (8858 9695,
www.companyofcooks.com)
Chinese
Peninsula p78
Holiday Inn Express, Bugsby's
Way, SE10 0GD (8858 2028,
www.mychinesefood.com)
Modern European
Inside p226
19 Greenwich South Street,
SE10 8NW (8265 5060,
www.insiderestaurant.co.uk)
Pubs
Greenwich Union p328
56 Royal Hill, SE10 8RT
(8692 6258, www.greenwich
union.com)

Hackney
The Americas
Buen Ayre p39
50 Broadway Market,
E8 4QJ (7275 9900,
www.buenayre.co.uk)
Branches
**Lang Nuong
(branch of Tre Viet)**
249 Mare Street, E8 3NS
(8986 8885)
19 Numara Bos Cirrik III
1-3 Amhurst Road, E8 1LL
(8985 2879)
**Prince Arthur
(branch of Cadogan Arms)**
95 Forest Road, E8 3BH
(7249 9996, www.theprince
arthurlondonfields.com)
Budget
F Cooke p283
9 Broadway Market, E8 4PH
(7254 6458)
LMNT p284
316 Queensbridge Road,
E8 3NH (7249 6727,
www.lmnt.co.uk)
Vietnamese
Green Papaya p277
191 Mare Street, E8 3QE
(8985 5486)
Tre Viet p278
251 Mare Street, E8 3NS
(8533 7390)

Hammersmith
African
The Village p30
95 Fulham Palace Road,
W6 8JA (8741 7453)
Branches
Grand Union
243 Goldhawk Road, W12 8EU
(8741 2312)
Pizza Express
158 Fulham Palace Road,
W6 9ER (8563 2064)
East European
Knaypa p82
268 King Street, W6 0SP
(8563 2887, www.theknaypa.
co.uk)
Polanka p82
258 King Street, W6 0SP
(8741 8268, www.polanka-
rest.com)
French
Chez Kristof p97
111 Hammersmith Grove,
W6 0NQ (8741 1177,
www.chezkristof.co.uk)
Gastropubs
Carpenter's Arms p104
91 Black Lion Lane, W6 9BG
(8741 8386)
Indian
Sagar p143
157 King Street, W6 9JT
(8741 8563)
Shilpa p143
206 King Street, W6 0RA
(8741 3127, www.shilpa
restaurant.co.uk)
Italian
The River Café p171
Thames Wharf, Rainville Road,
W6 9HA (7386 4200,
www.rivercafe.co.uk)
Japanese
Tosa p185
332 King Street, W6 0RR
(8748 0002)
Middle Eastern
Mahdi p208
217 King Street, W6 9JT
(8563 7007)
Pubs
Dove p326
19 Upper Mall, W6 9TA
(8748 9474)
Old Ship p326
25 Upper Mall, W6 9TD (8748
2593, www.oldshipw6.com)
Spanish
Los Molinos p245
127 Shepherd's Bush Road,
W6 7LP (7603 2229,
www.losmolinosuk.com)
Vegetarian
The Gate p270
51 Queen Caroline Street,
W6 9QL (8748 6932,
www.thegate.tv)
Vietnamese
Saigon Saigon p274
313-317 King Street,
W6 9NH (0870 220 1398,
www.saigon-saigon.co.uk)

Hampstead
Branches
Banana Tree Canteen
237-239 West End Lane,
NW6 1QH (7431 7808)
Carluccio's Caffè
32 Rosslyn Hill, NW3 1NH
(7794 2184)
dim t
3 Heath Street, NW3 6TP
(7435 0024)
Gail's
64 Hampstead High Street,
NW3 1QH (7794 5700)
Gaucho Hampstead
64 Heath Street, NW3 1DN
(8731 8222)
Giraffe
46 Rosslyn Hill, NW3 1NH
(7435 0343)
Le Pain Quotidien
1 South End Road, NW3 2PT
(7486 6154)
Paul
43 Hampstead High Street,
NW3 1QG (7794 8657)
Ping Pong
83-84 Hampstead High Street,
NW3 1RE (7433 0930)

Pizza Express
70 Heath Street, NW3 1DN
(7433 1600)
Cafés
Brew House p297
Kenwood, Hampstead Lane,
NW3 7JR (8341 5384,
www.companyofcooks.com)
Gastropubs
Horseshoe p116
28 Heath Street, NW3 6TE
(7431 7206)
Wells p116
30 Well Walk, NW3 1BX
(7794 3785, www.thewells
hampstead.co.uk)
Japanese
Jin Kichi p190
73 Heath Street, NW3 6UG
(7794 6158, www.jinkichi.com)
Pizza & Pasta
La Brocca p311
273 West End Lane, NW6 1QS
(7433 1989)
Fratelli la Bufala p311
45A South End Road,
NW3 2QB (7435 7814,
www.fratellilabufala.com)
Pubs
Holly Bush p330
22 Holly Mount,
NW3 6SG (7435 2892,
www.hollybushpub.com)
Roebuck p330
15 Pond Street,
NW3 2PN (7435 7354,
www.roebuckhampstead.com)
Spaniards Inn p330
Spaniards Road, NW3 7JJ
(8731 8406)

Harringay
Pubs
Salisbury Hotel p330
1 Grand Parade, Green Lanes,
N4 1JX (8800 9617)
Turkish
Antepliler p265
46 Grand Parade, Green
Lanes, N4 1AG (8802 5588)
Selale p265
2 Salisbury Promenade, Green
Lanes, N8 0RX (8800 1636)

Harrow, Middx
Branches
Nando's
300-302 Station Road, Harrow,
Middx, HA1 2DX (8427 5581)
Nando's
309 Northolt Road, Harrow,
Middx, HA2 8JA (8423 1516)
Pizza Express
2 College Road, Harrow, Middx,
HA1 1BE (8427 9195)
Prezzo
St George's Shopping Centre,
St Ann's Road, Harrow, Middx,
HA1 1HS (8427 9588)
Sakonis
5-8 Dominion Parade, Harrow,
Middx, HA1 2TR (8863 3399)
Chinese
Golden Palace p79
146-150 Station Road, Harrow,
Middx, HA1 2RH (8863 2333)
Global
Masa p117
24-26 Headstone Drive,
Harrow, Middx, HA3 5QH
(8861 6213)
Indian
Mumbai Junction p153
231 Watford Road, Harrow,
Middx, HA1 3TU (8904 2255,
www.mumbaijunction.co.uk)
Ram's p155
203 Kenton Road, Harrow,
Middx, HA3 0HD (8907 2022)

Hayes, Middx
Indian
Desi Tadka p155
148 Uxbridge Road, Hayes,
Middx, UB4 0JH (8569 0202,
www.desitadka.co.uk)

Hendon
Jewish
Adam's p193
2 Sentinel Square, NW4 2EL
(8202 2327)

Eighty-Six Bistro Bar p193
86 Brent Street, NW4 2ES
(8202 5575)
Kavanna p193
60 Vivian Avenue,
NW4 3XH (8202 9449,
www.kavanna.co.uk)

Herne Hill
Fish & Chips
Olley's p301
65-69 Norwood Road,
SE24 9AA (8671 8259,
www.olleys.info)
Gastropubs
Prince Regent p111
69 Dulwich Road,
SE24 0NJ (7274 1567,
www.theprinceregent.co.uk)
Oriental
Lombok p235
17 Half Moon Lane, SE24 9JU
(7733 7131)
Pubs
Commercial p328
212 Railton Road,
SE24 0JT (7733 8783,
www.thecommercialhotel
hernehill.co.uk)
Spanish
Number 22 p246
22 Half Moon Lane,
SE24 9HU (7095 9922,
www.number-22.com)

Highbury
The Americas
Garufa p41
104 Highbury Park,
N5 2XE (7226 0070,
www.garufa.co.uk)
Branches
La Fromagerie
30 Highbury Park, N5 2AA
(7359 7440)
Turkish
Iznik p265
19 Highbury Park, N5 1QJ
(7354 5697, www.iznik.co.uk)

Highgate
Branches
**Bull (branch of Only
Running Footman)**
13 North Hill, N6 4AB (0845
456 5033, www.inthebull.biz)
dim t
1 Hampstead Lane, N6 4RS
(8340 8800)
Pizza Express
30 High Street, N6 5JG
(8341 3434)
Zizzi
1 Hampstead Lane, N6 4RS
(8347 0090)
Cafés
Pavilion Café p297
Highgate Woods, Muswell Hill
Road, N10 3JN (8444 4777)
Greek
Carob Tree p123
15 Highgate Road, NW5 1QX
(7267 9880)
Pizza & Pasta
Strada p307
4 South Grove, N6 6BS (8347
8686, www.strada.co.uk)

Holborn
Branches
ASK
74 Southampton Row,
WC1B 4AR (7405 2876)
**Bierodrome
(branch of Belgo Noord)**
67 Kingsway, WC2B 6TD
(7242 7469)
Bunghole (branch of Davy's)
57 High Holborn, WC1V 6DT
(7831 8365)
Hummus Bros
Victoria House, 37-63
Southampton Row, WC1B 4DA
(7404 7079)
Kipferl
Coram's Fields, WC1N 1DN
(07966 524 174)
Le Pain Quotidien
174 High Holborn, WC1V 7AA
(7486 6154)
Paul
296-298 High Holborn, WC1V
7JH (7430 0639)

AREA INDEX

Pizza Express
114 Southampton Row, WC1B 5AA (7430 1011)
Pizza Express
99 High Holborn, WC1V 6LF (7831 5305)
Villandry Kitchen
95-97 High Holborn, WC1V 6LF (7242 4580)
White Swan Pub & Dining Room (branch of Cadogan Arms)
108 Fetter Lane, EC4A 1ES (7242 9696, www.thewhiteswanlondon.com)

British
Great Queen Street p54
32 Great Queen Street, WC2B 5AA (7242 0622)

Cafés
Fleet River Bakery p289
71 Lincoln's Inn Fields, WC2A 3JF (7691 1457, www.fleetriverbakery.com)

Chinese
Shanghai Blues p69
193-197 High Holborn, WC1V 7BD (7404 1668, www.shanghaiblues.co.uk)

Eating & Entertainment
All Star Lanes p342
Victoria House, Bloomsbury Place, WC1B 4DA (7025 2676, www.allstarlanes.co.uk)

Fish & Chips
Fryer's Delight p298
19 Theobald's Road, WC1X 8SL (7405 4114)

Hotels & Haute Cuisine
Pearl Bar & Restaurant p125
Chancery Court Hotel, 252 High Holborn, WC1V 7EN (7829 7000, www.pearl-restaurant.com)

Japanese
Aki p178
182 Gray's Inn Road, WC1X 8EW (7837 9281, www.akidemae.com)
Matsuri p178
71 High Holborn, WC1V 6EA (7430 1970, www.matsuri-restaurant.com)

Korean
Asadal p195
227 High Holborn, WC1V 7DA (7430 9006, www.asadal.co.uk)

Modern European
The Terrace p214
Lincoln's Inn Fields, WC2A 3LJ (7430 1234, www.theterrace.info)

Pubs
Princess Louise p325
208-209 High Holborn, WC1V 7BW (7405 8816)

Holland Park

Branches
Pâtisserie Valerie
94 Holland Park Avenue, W11 3RB (7985 0890)
Paul
82A Holland Park Avenue, W11 3RB (7727 3797)

Cafés
Gelato Mio p292
138 Holland Park Avenue, W11 4UE (7727 4117, www.gelatomio.co.uk)

French
The Belvedere p97
Holland House, off Abbotsbury Road, in Holland Park, W8 6LU (7602 1238, www.whitestarline.org.uk)

Italian
Edera p171
148 Holland Park Avenue, W11 4UE (7221 6090)

Pubs
Ladbroke Arms p326
54 Ladbroke Road, W11 3NW (7727 6648, www.capitalpubcompany.com)

Holloway

Branches
Sacred
Highbury Studios, 8 Hornsey Street, N7 8EG (7700 1628)

East European
Tbilisi p80
91 Holloway Road, N7 8LT (7607 2536)

Hornchurch, Essex

Branches
Mandarin Palace
197-201 High Street, Hornchurch, Essex, RM11 3XT (01708 437 951)
Nando's
111-113A High Street, Hornchurch, Essex, RM11 1TX (01708 449537)
Zizzi
41-43 Station Lane, Hornchurch, Essex, RM12 6JT (444 740)

Hornsey

Branches
Queens Pub & Dining Room (branch of Roebuck)
26 Broadway Parade, N8 9DE (8340 2031)

French
Le Bistro p100
36 High Street, N8 7NX (8340 2116)

Japanese
Sushi Café Maco p188
50 Topsfield Parade, N8 8PT (8340 7773)

Hounslow, Middx

Branches
Nando's
1-1A High Street, Hounslow, Middx, TW3 1RH (8570 5881)
Pizza Express
41-43 High Street, Hounslow, Middx, TW3 1RH (8577 8522)

Ilford, Essex

Branches
Nando's
I-Scene, Clements Road, Ilford, Essex, IG1 1BP (8514 6012)

Chinese
Mandarin Palace p79
559-561 Cranbrook Road, Ilford, Essex, IG2 6JZ (8550 7661)

Islington

The Americas
Sabor p43
108 Essex Road, N1 8LX (7226 5551, www.sabor.co.uk)

Bars
Elk in the Woods p323
39 Camden Passage, N1 8EA (7226 3535, www.the-elk-in-the-woods.co.uk)
Lexington p323
96 Pentonville Road, N1 9HS (7837 5371, www.thelexington.co.uk)
69 Colebrooke Row p323
69 Colebrooke Row, N1 8AA (07540 528593, www.69colebrookerow.com)
25 Canonbury Lane p323
25 Canonbury Lane, N1 2AS (7226 0955)

Branches
ASK
Business Design Centre, 52 Upper Street, N1 0PN (7226 8728)
Carluccio's Caffè
305-307 Upper Street, N1 2TU (7359 8167)
Duchess of Kent (branch of Morgan Arms)
441 Liverpool Road, N7 8PR (7609 7104)
Fine Burger Company
330 Upper Street, N1 2XQ (7359 3026)
Gallipoli Bazaar
107 Upper Street, N1 1QN (7226 5333)
Gallipoli Café Bistro
102 Upper Street, N1 1QN (7359 0630)
Giraffe
29-31 Essex Road, N1 2SA (7359 5999)
Grand Union
153 Upper Street, N1 1RA (7226 1375)
Hamburger+
341 Upper Street, N1 0PB (7359 4436)
House (branch of Only Running Footman)
63-69 Canonbury Road, N1 2DG (7704 7410, www.inthehouse.biz)
Lucky Voice
173-174 Upper Street, N1 1RG (7354 6280)
Masala Zone
80 Upper Street, N1 0NU (7359 3399)
Nando's
324 Upper Street, N1 2XQ (7288 0254)
Pizza Express
335 Upper Street, N1 0PB (7226 9542)
La Porchetta
141 Upper Street, N1 1QY (7288 2488)
Regina Margherita (branch of Napulé)
57 Upper Street, N1 0NY (7704 8882)
Strada
105-106 Upper Street, N1 1QN (7226 9742)
Thai Square
347-349 Upper Street, N1 0PD (7704 2000)
Wagamama
N1 Centre, 39 Parkfield Street, N1 0PS (7226 2664)
Yo! Sushi
N1 Centre, 39 Parkfield Street, N1 0PS (7359 3502)

Budget
L Manze p283
74 Chapel Market, N1 9ER (7837 5270)
Le Mercury p284
140A Upper Street, N1 1QY (7354 4088, www.lemercury.co.uk)
S&M Café p284
4-6 Essex Road, N1 8LN (7359 5361, www.sandmcafe.co.uk)

Eating & Entertainment
Elbowroom p342
89-91 Chapel Market, N1 9EX (7278 3244, www.theelbowroom.co.uk)

Fish
The Fish Shop p89
360-362 St John Street, EC1V 4NR (7837 1199, www.thefishshop.net)

French
Almeida p100
30 Almeida Street, N1 1AD (7354 4777, www.danddlondon.com)
Morgan M p100
489 Liverpool Road, N7 8NS (7609 3560, www.morganm.com)

Gastropubs
Charles Lamb p114
16 Elia Street, N1 8DE (7837 5040, www.thecharleslambpub.com)
Compass p114
58 Penton Street, N1 9PZ (7837 3891, www.thecompassn1.co.uk)
Drapers Arms p114
44 Barnsbury Street, N1 1ER (7619 0348, www.thedrapersarms.com)
Duke of Cambridge p115
30 St Peter's Street, N1 8JT (7359 3066, www.dukeorganic.co.uk)
Marquess Tavern p115
32 Canonbury Street, N1 2TB (7354 2975, www.themarquesstavern.co.uk)
Northgate p116
113 Southgate Road, N1 3JS (7359 7392)

Global
Afghan Kitchen p117
35 Islington Green, N1 8DU (7359 8019)

International
Ottolenghi p161
287 Upper Street, N1 2TZ (7288 1454, www.ottolenghi.co.uk)

Italian
Metrogusto p176
13 Theberton Street, N1 0QY (7226 9400, www.metrogusto.co.uk)

Japanese
Sa Sa Sushi p188
422 St John Street, EC1V 4NJ (7837 1155, www.sasasushi.co.uk)

Malaysian, Indonesian & Singaporean
Puji Puji p201
122 Balls Pond Road, N1 4AE (7923 2112, www.pujipujirestaurant.com)

Modern European
Frederick's p228
Camden Passage, N1 8EG (7359 2888, www.fredericks.co.uk)

North African
Maghreb p232
189 Upper Street, N1 1RQ (7226 2305, www.maghrebrestaurant.co.uk)

Oriental
Banana Tree Canteen p236
412-416 St John Street, EC1V 4NJ (7278 7565)

Pubs
Island Queen p330
87 Noel Road, N1 8HD (7354 8741, www.theislandqueenislington.co.uk)

Thai
Isarn p257
119 Upper Street, N1 1QP (7424 5153)

Turkish
Bavo p265
105-107 Southgate Road, N1 3JS (7226 0334, www.bavo-restaurant.co.uk)
Gallipoli Again p265
120 Upper Street, N1 1QP (7226 8099, www.cafegallipoli.com)
Pasha p265
301 Upper Street, N1 2TU (7226 1454, www.pasharestaurant.co.uk)
Sedir p266
4 Theberton Street, N1 0QX (7226 5489, www.sedirrestaurant.co.uk)

Kennington

African
Adulis p31
44-46 Brixton Road, SW9 6BT (7587 0055, www.adulis.co.uk)

Branches
Grand Union
111 Kennington Road, SE11 6SF (7582 6685)
Pizza Express
316 Kennington Road, SE11 4LD (7820 3877)

Budget
WJ Arment p283
7 & 9 Westmoreland Road, SE17 2AX (7703 4974)

Kensal

Thai
Tong Kanom Thai p257
833 Harrow Road, NW10 5NH (8964 5373)

Kensal Green

Bars
Paradise by Way of Kensal Green p323
19 Kilburn Lane, W10 4AE (8969 0098, www.theparadise.co.uk)

Cafés
Brilliant Kids Café p295
8 Station Terrace, NW10 5RT (8964 4120, www.brilliantkids.co.uk)
Gracelands p295
118 College Road, NW10 5HD (8964 9161, www.gracelandscafe.com)

Kensington

Branches
Côte
47 Kensington Court, W8 5DA (7938 4147)
Feng Sushi
24 Kensington Church Street, W8 4EP (7937 7927)
Giraffe
7 Kensington High Street, W8 5NP (7938 1221)
Le Pain Quotidien
9 Young Street, W8 5EH (7486 6154)
Ottolenghi
1 Holland Street, W8 4NA (7937 0003)
Pâtisserie Valerie
27 Kensington Church Street, W8 4LL (7937 9574)
Prezzo
35A Kensington High Street, W8 5BA (7937 2800)
Ranoush Juice
86 Kensington High Street, W8 4SG (7938 2234)
Strada
29 Kensington High Street, W8 5NP (7938 4648)
Wagamama
26 Kensington High Street, W8 4PF (7376 1717)

Burger Bars
Byron p286
222 Kensington High Street, W8 7RG (7361 1717, www.byronhamburgers.com)

Cafés
Kensington Palace Orangery p297
The Orangery, Kensington Palace, Kensington Gardens, W8 4PX (7376 0239, www.digbytrout.co.uk)

Chinese
Min Jiang p78
10th floor, Royal Garden Hotel, 2-4 Kensington High Street, W8 4PT (7361 1988, www.minjiang.co.uk)

East European
Mimino p80
197C Kensington High Street, W8 6BA (7937 1551, www.mimino.co.uk)
Wódka p81
12 St Alban's Grove, W8 5PN (7937 6513, www.wodka.co.uk)

Indian
Zaika p143
1 Kensington High Street, W8 5NP (7795 6533, www.zaika-restaurant.co.uk)

International
Abingdon p159
54 Abingdon Road, W8 6AP (7937 3339, www.theabingdonrestaurant.com)

Italian
Timo p171
343 Kensington High Street, W8 6NW (7603 3888, www.timorestaurant.net)

Middle Eastern
Randa p208
23 Kensington Church Street, W8 4LF (7937 5363, www.maroush.com)

Modern European
Babylon p222
7th floor, The Roof Gardens, 99 Kensington High Street, W8 5SA (7368 3993, www.roofgardens.com)
Clarke's p222
124 Kensington Church Street, W8 4BH (7221 9225, www.sallyclarke.com)
Kensington Place p222
201-209 Kensington Church Street, W8 7LX (7727 3184, www.kensingtonplace-restaurant.co.uk)
Launceston Place p222
1A Launceston Place, W8 5RL (7937 6912, www.danddlondon.com)

Pubs
Churchill Arms p327
119 Kensington Church Street, W8 7LN (7727 4242)

Spanish
L Restaurant & Bar p245
2 Abingdon Road, W8 6AF (7795 6969, www.l-restaurant.co.uk)

AREA INDEX

A-Z Index

A-Z INDEX

A-Z INDEX

Zizzi
11-13 Widmore Road, Bromley, Kent, BR1 1RL (8464 6663). Branch
Zizzi
157 High Street, Beckenham, Kent, BR3 1AE (8658 2050). Branch
Zizzi
19 High Street, Chislehurst, Bromley, Kent, BR7 5AE (8467 8302). Branch
Zizzi
57-59 Southend, Croydon, Surrey, CR0 1BF (8649 8403). Branch
Zizzi
33 Westferry Circus, E14 8RR (7512 9257). Branch
Zizzi
198 George Lane, E18 2QL (8989 1001). Branch
Zizzi
12 Ivory House, St Katherine's Docks, E1W 1AT (7488 0130). Branch
Zizzi
2 Church Hill, Loughton, Essex, IG10 1LA (8418 9489). Branch
Zizzi
43 Market Place, Kingston, Surrey, KT1 1ET (8546 0717). Branch
Zizzi
38 Victoria Road, Surbiton, Surrey, KT6 4JL (8399 4160). Branch
Zizzi
1 Bridge Road, East Molesey, Surbiton, Surrey, KT8 9EU (8941 7478). Branch
Zizzi
202-208 Regent's Park Road, N3 3HP (8371 6777). Branch
Zizzi
1 Hampstead Lane, N6 4RS (8347 0090). Branch
Zizzi
O2 Centre, Finchley High Road, NW3 6LU (7433 8259). Branch
Zizzi
41-43 Station Lane, Hornchurch, Essex, RM12 6JT (444 740). Branch
Zizzi
The Cardamon Building, 31 Shad Thames, SE1 2YR (7367 6100). Branch
Zizzi
The O2, Millennium Way, SE10 0UZ (8858 9097). Branch
Zizzi
13-15 High Street, Sutton, Surrey, SM1 1DF (8661 8778). Branch
Zizzi
15 Cardinal Walk, Cardinal Place, SW1E 5JE (7821 0402). Branch
Zizzi
194-196 Earl's Court Road, SW5 9QF (7370 1999). Branch
Zizzi
36-38 York Street, Twickenham, Middx, TW1 3LJ (8538 9024). Branch
Zizzi
4-5 King Street, Richmond, Surrey, TW9 1ND (8332 2809). Branch
Zizzi
2-6 Notting Hill Gate, W11 3JE (7243 2888). Branch
Zizzi
33-41 Charlotte Street, W1T 1RR (7436 9440). Branch
Zizzi
110-116 Wigmore Street, W1U 3RS (7935 2336). Branch
Zizzi
35-38 Paddington Street, W1U 4HQ (7224 1450). Branch
Zizzi
17 Sheldon Square, W2 6EP (7286 4770). Branch
Zizzi
231 Chiswick High Road, W4 4PU (8747 9400). Branch
Zizzi
73-75 The Strand, WC2R 0DE (7240 1717). Branch
Zuma   p180, p316
5 Raphael Street, SW7 1DL (7584 1010, www.zuma restaurant.co.uk). Japanese, Bars

Published by
Time Out Guides Limited
Universal House
251 Tottenham Court Road
London W1T 7AB
Tel +44 (0)20 7813 3000
Fax +44 (0)20 7813 6001
email guides@timeout.com
www.timeout.com

Editorial
Editor Jenni Muir
Deputy Editor Phil Harriss
Group Food & Drink Editor Guy Dimond
Listings Editors Alex Brown, William Crow, Gemma Pritchard
Proofreader John Pym
Indexer Jacqueline Brind

Managing Director Peter Fiennes
Editorial Director Sarah Guy
Series Editor Cath Phillips
Business Manager Daniel Allen
Editorial Manager Holly Pick
Assistant Management Accountant Ija Krasnikova

Design
Art Director Scott Moore
Art Editor Pinelope Kourmouzoglou
Senior Designer Henry Elphick
Graphic Designers Kei Ishimaru, Nicola Wilson
Advertising Designer Jodi Sher

Picture Desk
Picture Editor Jael Marschner
Deputy Picture Editor Lynn Chambers
Picture Researcher Gemma Walters
Picture Desk Assistant Ben Rowe

Advertising
Commercial Director Mark Phillips
Sales Manager Alison Wallen
Advertising Sales Ben Holt, Jason Trotman
Copy Controller Alison Bourke

Marketing
Marketing Manager Yvonne Poon
Sales & Marketing Director, North America & Latin America Lisa Levinson
Art Director Anthony Huggins
Circulation & Distribution Manager Dan Collins

Production
Group Production Director Mark Lamond
Production Manager Brendan McKeown
Production Controller Damian Bennett

Time Out Group
Chairman Tony Elliott
Chief Executive Officer David King
Group General Manager/Director Nichola Coulthard
Time Out Communications Ltd MD David Pepper
Time Out International Ltd MD Cathy Runciman
Time Out Magazine Ltd Publisher/MD Mark Elliott
Group IT Director Simon Chappell
Marketing & Circulation Director Catherine Demajo

Sections in this guide were written by

African Tamara Gausi. **The Americas** (North American) Will Fulford-Jones; (Latin American) Ramona Andrews, Chris Moss, Patrick Welch. **Brasseries** Martin Horsfield, Ruth Jarvis, Jenni Muir, Anna Norman, Holly Pick, Ros Sales. **British** Richard Ehrlich, Sarah Guy. **Caribbean** Chris Moss. **Chinese** Antonia Bruce, Terry Durack, Phil Harriss, Tim Luard, Charmaine Mok, Jenni Muir, Sally Peck. **East European** Jenni Muir, Sally Peck, Janet Zmroczek. **Fish** Jenni Muir, Francis Percival. **French** Richard Ehrlich, Peter Fiennes, Ruth Jarvis, Anna Norman, Cath Phillips, Nick Rider, Ethel Rimmer, Caroline Stacey, Simon Tillotson, Elizabeth Winding. **Gastropubs** Guy Dimond, Lewis Esson, Sarah Guy, Ruth Jarvis, Andrea McGinniss, Neil McQuillian, Jenni Muir, Cath Phillips, Holly Pick, Nick Rider, Ethel Rimmer. **Global** Phil Harriss, Charmaine Mok, Jenni Muir, Holly Pick. **Greek** Alexi Duggins, Lewis Esson, Natasha Polyviou. **Hotels & Haute Cuisine** Richard Ehrlich, Roopa Gulati, Judy Joo, Jenni Muir, Jeff Ng. **Indian** Guy Dimond, Roopa Gulati, Phil Harriss, Amy Sohanpaul. **International** Claire Fogg, Richard Ehrlich. **Italian** Elena Berton, Richard Ehrlich, Lewis Esson, Ronnie Haydon, Susan Low, Jenni Muir, Natasha Polyviou, Ros Sales, Caroline Stacey, Yolanda Zappaterra. **Japanese** Tim Jackson, Kei Kikuchi, Jennifer Lee, Susan Low, Charmaine Mok, Jenni Muir. **Jewish** Judy Jackson. **Korean** Judy Joo, Charmaine Mok, Jenni Muir. **Malaysian, Indonesian & Singaporean** Kerry Cheah, Jeff Ng. **Middle Eastern** Neil McQuillian, Natasha Polyviou, Ros Sales, Cyrus Shahrad. **Modern European** Antonia Bruce, Fuchsia Dunlop, Terry Durack, Richard Ehrlich, Sarah Guy, Ruth Jarvis, Emily Kerrigan, Susan Low, Patrick Marmion, Jenni Muir, Nick Rider, Ethel Rimmer, Ros Sales, Caroline Stacey. **North African** Jenni Muir, Janet Zmroczek. **Oriental** Simone Baird, Lewis Esson, Jennifer Lee, Jenni Muir, Veronica Simpson. **Portuguese** Amanda Smith. **Spanish** Tom de Castella, Caroline Hire, Susan Low, Chris Moss, Jenni Muir, Elizabeth Winding. **Thai** Elena Berton, Jenni Muir, Sally Peck. **Turkish** Will Fulford-Jones. **Vegetarian** Simone Baird, Jenni Muir, Natasha Polyviou. **Vietnamese** Kerry Cheah, Judy Joo, Charmaine Mok. **Budget** Alex Brown, Martin Horsfield, Jenni Muir, Anna Norman, Holly Pick, Patrick Welch. **Burgers** Alexi Duggins, Jenni Muir, Peter Watts. **Cafés** Jessica Cargill-Thompson, Jan Fuscoe, Judy Joo, Charmaine Mok, Jenni Muir, Emma Perry. **Fish & Chips** Simon Coppock, Alexi Duggins, Jenni Muir. **Pizza & Pasta** Jan Fuscoe, Martin Horsfield, Jenni Muir, Ken Olende, Peter Watts. **Bars** Simone Baird, Nina Caplan, Peterjon Cresswell, Euan Ferguson. **Pubs** Simon Coppock, Peterjon Cresswell, Jenni Muir. **Wine Bars** Francis Percival. **Eating & Entertainment** Alex Brown, Gemma Pritchard.

Additional reviews by Simone Baird, Alex Brown, Antonia Bruce, Nina Caplan, Jessica Cargill-Thompson, Tom de Castella, Simon Coppock, Silvija Davidson, Guy Dimond, Fuchsia Dunlop, Euan Ferguson, Claire Fogg, Peter Fiennes, Will Fulford-Jones, Jan Fuscoe, Tamara Gausi, Roopa Gulati, Sarah Guy, Phil Harriss, Michael Hodges, Ruth Jarvis, Emily Kerrigan, Tom Lamont, Jennifer Lee, Andrea McGinniss, Patrick Marmion, Charmaine Mok, Chris Moss, Jenni Muir, Anna Norman, Ken Olende, Emma Perry, Cath Phillips, Holly Pick, Natasha Polyviou, Ros Sales, Cyrus Shahrad, Veronica Simpson, Amanda Smith, Caroline Stacey, Daniel Starza Smith, Simon Tillotson, Peter Watts, Patrick Welch, Elizabeth Winding, Yolanda Zappaterra.

Interviews Jenni Muir. **Shelf Life boxes** Jenni Muir. **The Dish boxes** Jenni Muir, except p139 Roopa Gulati.

The Editors would like to thank Alex Brown, Jessica Cargill-Thompson, Guy Dimond, Alexi Duggins, Will Fulford-Jones, Susan Low, Charmaine Mok, Ros Sales and our sponsor, Wines from Spain.

Maps JS Graphics (john@jsgraphics.co.uk). Maps 1-18 & 24 are based on material supplied by Alan Collinson and Julie Snook through Copyright Exchange. London Underground map supplied by Transport for London.

Cover photography Liquid image by Emil Larsson, www.adamsky.se; knife and fork by Rob Greig. Retouching by They Did It (020 7928 9008).

Contents photography (clockwise from top left) Craig Deane, Tricia de Courcy Ling, Ming Tang-Evans, Alys Tomlinson, Britta Jaschinski, Ming Tang-Evans, Michael Franke, Alys Tomlinson, Britta Jaschinski, Olivia Rutherford, Michelle Grant.

Photography page 1 (left) Joana Henderson; pages 1 (middle), 27 (bottom), 40, 79, 85, 87, 96, 97, 103, 112, 182, 188, 207, 329, 334 Michelle Grant; pages 1 (right), 54, 165, 215, 271, 273, 275, 306, 309, 325, 341 Tom Baker; pages 12, 127, 128, 174, 313 (middle top), 335 Rob Greig; pages 22, 25 (bottom), 28 (right), 41, 115, 166 Alys Tomlinson; pages 19 (left), 48, 55, 101, 111, 169, 224, 295 Michael Franke; pages 19 (top right), 30, 34, 147, 152, 208, 209, 247, 266, 300, 301 Jitka Hynkova; pages 19 (bottom right), 28 (left), 29 (middle), 42, 51, 61, 73, 74, 89, 91, 92, 125, 130, 132, 133, 138, 139, 143, 180, 184, 218, 219, 230, 234, 236, 263, 277, 313 (middle bottom), 319, 332 Ming Tang-Evans; pages 23 (top), 223 (top), 279 (bottom) Heloise Bergman; pages 27 (top), 106, 107, 117, 122, 170, 193, 248, 268, 313 (bottom), 317, 323 Jonathan Perugia; pages 28 (middle), 45, 65, 76, 159, 223 (bottom), 279 (middle top), 281 Britta Jaschinski; page 29 (top), 67, 204, 285, 326 Ed Marshall; page 29 (bottom) Matthew Booth; page 39 Yusuf Ozkizil; pages 58, 80, 135, 153, 251, 259, 279 (top & middle bottom), 288, 291, 303, 310, 311, 339 Michelle Grant; pages 108, 195, 299 Tricia de Courcy Ling; pages 109, 205 Ben Rowe; pages 118, 178, 212, 217, 221, 227, 232, 240, 242, 262 Olivia Rutherford; pages 201, 289 Christina Theisen; page 231 Neil Setchfield; page 243 Marzena Zoladz; page 253 Steven Atkinson; pages 313 (top), 318 Craig Deane.

The following images were provided by the featured establishments: pages 47, 57, 71, 95, 235, 229.

Printer Polestar – Colchester, 2 Wyncolls Road, Severalls Industrial Park, Colchester, Essex CO4 4HT.
Time Out Group uses paper products that are environmentally friendly, from well managed forests and mills that use certified (PEFC) Chain of Custody pulp in their production.

ISBN 978-1-905042-38-8
ISSN 1750-4643
Distribution by Comag Specialist (01895 433 800).
For further distribution details, see www.timeout.com.